MW01613822

Annotated Teacher's Edition

Prentice Hall

WRITING and GRAMMAR

Communication in Action

Put Students' Words Into Action!

A new approach to language learning designed to produce competent, confident communicators.

- Active learning for today's high school students.
- Systematic Learning Strategies.
- Easy-to-use handbook style saves time.
- Teacher's Edition provides all the support.

3-Part Organization

Prentice Hall Writing and Grammar: Communication in Action is conveniently divided into the following three sections for ease of use:

- **Writing:** Guides students through each step of the writing process with an emphasis on revision.
- **Grammar:** Provides more grammar practice than any other program, including unique hands-on grammar activities.
- **Academic and Workplace Skills:** Focuses on practical, real-world skills for today's multimedia generation.

Grade 9-Gold   ISBN: 0-13-043350-0
Grade 10-Platinum   ISBN: 0-13-043351-9
Grade 11-Ruby   ISBN: 0-13-043352-7
Grade 12-Diamond   ISBN: 0-13-043353-5

3 4 5 6 7 8 9 10
05 04 03 02 01

Only Prentice Hall Writing and Grammar: Communication in Action...

- Engages today's students with active, hands-on learning.

- Provides extensive practice opportunities and strategies for all stages of the writing process.

- Saves time with its easy-to-use handbook style.

Engage Today's Students

Relevant instruction for today's student

7.1 Model From Literature

Nevada Barr, a writer of mystery novels, uses the national parks as the setting of many of her stories. Drawing on the writer's experiences as a park ranger, this essay asserts the benefits of the national park system for all citizens.

Reading Writing Connection
Reading Strategy:
Interpret Connotation Be alert to a word's **connotation**—the way a specific word can make you feel. As you read, take special notice of the emotional power of the words Barr chooses. You'll see that effective per-

25.1 GRAMMAR IN LITERATURE

from **Glory and Hope**
Nelson Mandela

In the following passage, the indefinite pronoun all refers to a group acting as individuals. Therefore, it takes the plural verb do.

Your majesties, your royal highnesses, distinguished guests, comrades and friends: Today, *all* of us *do,* by our presence here, and by our celebrations in other parts of our country and the world, confer glory and hope to newborn liberty.

Our daily deeds as ordinary South Africans must produce an actual South African reality that will reinforce humanity's belief in justice, strengthen its confidence in the nobility of the human soul and sustain all our hopes for a glorious life for all.

Indefinite Pronouns Some indefinite pronouns are always

Connect to the Language Arts

Connection to literature, writing, and grammar show students the relevance of what they learn.

Grammar in Your Writing
Using the Conventions for Writing Titles

As you proofread, make sure you have used the conventions for writing titles. Long works are set off by underlining or italics. In addition to the titles of novels and plays, other titles that are italicized include the names of newspapers, magazines, movies, paintings, and sculptures.

Enclose short works in quotation marks. In addition to the titles of poems and short stories, other titles that are enclosed in quotation marks are essays, articles, and songs.

Titles of books:	*West With the Night* by Beryl Markham
Titles of short stories:	"A Day's Wait" by Ernest Hemingway
Titles of long poems:	*Paradise Lost* by John Milton
Titles of short poems:	"The Bells" by Edgar Allan Poe

Find It in Your Reading Find three titles in the completed student essay on pp. 130–133. Explain the conventions used for writing the titles.

Find It in Your Writing As you proofread your persuasive essay, check that you have written all titles correctly.

For more on writing titles co

Hands-on Grammar

Subject-Verb Agreement Color Match

Cut three strips of paper of equal length. Draw a blue line across the center of one. Draw a red line across the center of the other. Fold the strip into thirds, as shown in the illustration. Then, write a sentence with a singular subject, a singular verb form, and a phrase across the blue line. Write the subject in the first fold, the verb in the second, and the remaining words in the third fold. Write the same sentence on the strip with the red line, but use a plural subject and plural verb form. Next, cut each strip on the folds. Finally, try to line up the parts of the sentence. You will find that you can't create a color match between a singular subject and a plural verb form.

The Minister	attends	every session

The Ministers	attend	every session

The Ministers	attends	every session

Find It in Your Reading Do this activity with a sentence from the Grammar in Literature passage from "Glory and Hope," on page 578. If the sentence has too many phrases, just use the subject and verb.

Find It in Your Writing Review a recent piece of writing in your portfolio. Use this activity with several sentences from the piece.

Engage Students

Address varied learning styles by actively involving students with Hands-on Grammar activities.

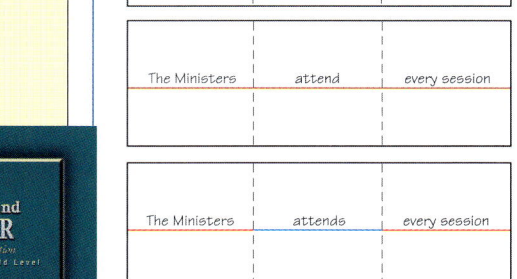

Prentice Hall
WRITING and GRAMMAR
Communication in Action
Gold Level

Grammar Exercise Workbook

•Two practice pages for each grammar concept

Prentice Hall

Connect to Students' Lives

An authentic student model in every writing chapter tracks the development of one student's writing through a particular writing mode.

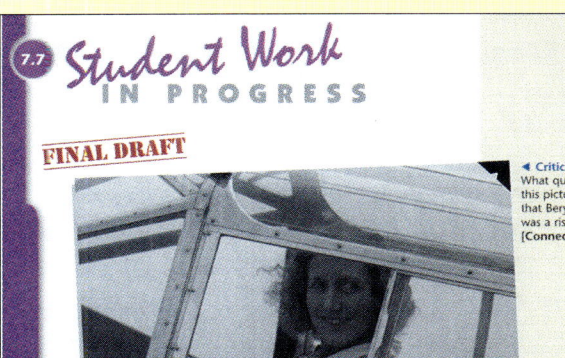

7.7 Student Work IN PROGRESS

FINAL DRAFT

◄ **Critical Viewing**
What qualities in this picture suggest that Beryl Markham was a risk-taker? [Connect]

Who Wrote West With the Night?

Janaki Spickard-Keeler
Clark High School
San Antonio, Texas

For years, no one even knew the question existed. For years, too, no one even knew that the book existed. After a brief period of success, reaching *The New York Times* bestseller list, the book faded into obscurity with the onset of World War II. It was rediscovered in the 1980's by George Gutekunst while he read through some of Ernest Hemingway's letters. In a letter to Maxwell Perkins, Hemingway wrote: "Did you read Beryl Markham's book, *West With the Night?* I knew her fairly well in Africa and never

Janaki's research provided a compelling quotation to invite readers' interest.

148 • Persuasive Essay

Persuasion in Everyday Life

Whenever you argue with a friend over which movie to see or debate the merits of one musical group over another, you're using persuasive skills. **Persuasion** is writing or speaking that attempts to convince others to accept a position or take a desired action. Effective persuasion can decide a defendant's fate in a trial, lead to a change in government leadership, or even end a war.

Engage Today's Multimedia Generation

Media and Technology Skills workshops teach students relevant, real-world skills and offer a full array of online and multimedia resources.

Media and Technology Skills

Recognizing Persuasive Techniques

Activity: Find Persuasion in Television Programs

Television entertains and informs, but often it also persuades. Even programs that seem to be simply entertainment carry subtle messages that influence the way you look at the world. Learn to view television programs critically, and evaluate what you see and hear

Think About It News shows, documentaries, sportscasts, sitcoms, weekly dramas, talk shows, and awards programs are just some of the types of programs offered on television. News programs and documentaries may influence you by lingering on one image or by using words with strong connotations, such as *generous* and *risky*. Sports announcers interject their opinions as they narrate the action of a game. The way the plot of a sitcom turns out carries a message. Talk-show hosts share their opinions, and awards programs place a value on performance. Think about other ways that television programs persuade or influence your perceptions.

Watch It Choose a television program that you enjoy watching. Watch an episode with a notebook and pencil nearby, taking notes on a chart like the one below:

What Is Shown	What I Think
1.	
2.	
3.	

Analyze It Review your notes, and read the boxed side column on this page. Identify the techniques used in the program to influence your perceptions and responses.

Techniques Used to Influence Viewer Response

In a News Program or Documentary
- Focusing on an image
- Comments by the newscaster
- Using words with connotations

In a Sportscast
- Comments by the announcer
- Shots of crowd reaction
- Close-ups on the winning or losing team

In Sitcoms and Dramas
- Plot events in which characters are rewarded or punished
- Portraying certain types of characters as cool or popular
- Music and lighting

In Talk Shows
- Choice of guests
- Host reactions and comments

In Award Shows
- Who wins
- Shots of crowd reaction and candid "behind the scenes" shots

Media and Technology Skills • 153

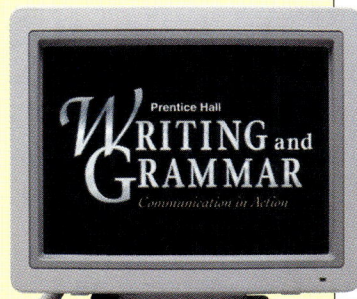

Prentice Hall
WRITING and GRAMMAR
Communication in Action

More Practice and Revision Support

Section 26.2 Review Exercises

GRAMMAR EXERCISES 23–28

EXERCISE 23: Correcting Errors in Pronoun and Antecedent Agreement
In the following sentences, most of the pronouns do not agree with their antecedents. If a pronoun does not agree, write the correct form. If agreement in the sentence is correct, write *C*.

1. Anyone who has e-mail probably corresponds with their best friends often.
2. Both Marissa and Tashina check their mailboxes every day.
3. Neither likes to open their mailbox to find that no one has written to them.
4. However, each of the girls always has messages waiting for them.
5. One of the interesting things about an e-mail program is their ability to store messages.
6. Tashina stored a message from Tim Ring, who had attached a photograph of their dog, Molly.
7. In the picture, Molly is sitting next to Tim with a ball in its mouth.
8. Neither Marissa nor Tashina has ever tried to attach a photo of themselves to an e-mail message.
9. Have any of these correspondents ever had an "instant conversation" through their e-mail programs?
10. No doubt, each of them has had an "instant conversation" going with a few of their friends at the same time.

EXERCISE 24: Correcting Special Problems in Pronoun and Antecedent Agreement Rewrite the paragraph, correcting the errors in pronoun and antecedent agreement. Not all sentences have errors.

(1) There is a little gray thing attached to every computer. (2) It is a device that is needed to operate it. (3) They call it a mouse. (4) A mouse is a small gray object that you roll along a hard, flat surface. (5) The connecting wire looks like its tail.

(6) You use a mouse to control the movement of the pointer on the screen. (7) As it moves, the pointer on the screen moves in the same direction. (8) Mice have at least one button and sometimes three. (9) They have different uses, depending on which program is running. (10) Some newer ones include a scroll wheel for scrolling through long documents quickly and easily.

EXERCISE 25: Revision Practice Revise the paragraph, correcting errors in pronoun and antecedent agreement.

(1) There are homes in America in which they don't watch much TV. (2) Instead, each family member spends their time on other activities. (3) This is much better for you. (4) One health expert reports that when someone stares at TV, they don't use their imagination. (5) National TV-Turnoff Week is sponsored by TV-Free America, and millions of Americans participate in it.

EXERCISE 26: Find It in Your Reading Reread the excerpt from Bill Gates's *The Road Ahead* on page 55. Find at least three personal pronouns, and write them down along with their antecedents.

EXERCISE 27: Find it in Your Writing Select a writing sample from your portfolio. On your draft, draw a circle around each pronoun, and underline its antecedent. Finally, check to be sure that the pronouns and the antecedents agree.

EXERCISE 28: Writing Application Write five sentences in the form of an e-mail message in which you describe an event you attended with a friend. Make sure that each pronoun has a clear antecedent and that the pronouns and antecedents agree.

Chapter 26 Review Exercises

GRAMMAR EXERCISES 29–37

EXERCISE 29: Making Subjects and Verbs Agree Choose the verb that agrees with the subject in each sentence.

1. (Do, Does) your group of friends enjoy movies?
2. One of my favorite old films (is, are) *The Wizard of Oz.*
3. *The Wizard of Oz,* as well as *Return to Oz,* (was, were) based on a novel by Frank Baum.
4. Very popular today (is, are) action films.
5. Almost every one of them (features, feature) dazzling special effects.
6. Sophisticated electronics (has, have) made the visual effects possible.
7. Acoustics (is, are) the science that has given us the frighteningly realistic sound effects.
8. *Tarzan and the Amazons* (was, were) made with simple special effects in 1945.
9. Back then, only a small percentage of films (was, were) shot in color.
10. Black and white (was, were) more common.

EXERCISE 30: Using the Rules of Subject and Verb Agreement Rewrite each sentence, revising it according to the instructions given in brackets. Change the verb form as needed. Not all verbs will change.

1. After the regular baseball season comes the long-awaited event. [Change *event* to *championship games.*]
2. The World Series contests bring baseball fever to its highest pitch. [Delete *contests.*]
3. The cheering crowd is a thrilling sight. [Change *crowd* to *fans.*]
4. Excited indeed is every baseball lover across the country. [Change *every baseball lover* to *all baseball lovers.*]
5. The early part of the series starts the buildup to the final game. [Change *part* to *games.*]
6. The maximum number of series games is seven. [Change the word order, making *seven* the subject of the sentence.]
7. However, there (has, have) been series won in only four or five games. [Insert *some* before *series.*]
8. Both teams try hard to come out on top. [Change *Both teams* to *Each team.*]
9. Donald Honig's book <u>The October Heroes</u> describes great World Series games. [Delete *Donald Honig's book.*]
10. A Web site giving baseball statistics is located at www.baseballstats.com. [Delete *A Web site giving.*]

EXERCISE 31: Correcting Errors in Pronoun and Antecedent Agreement Revise the paragraph, correcting all errors in pronoun and antecedent agreement.

(1) In the Hawaiian Islands, they have some of the best scuba diving in the world. (2) If yourself and your friends want a truly exciting experience, you should try it. (3) Each of the diving sites around the island of Oahu has their own special attractions. (4) The guides always take the divers to the places they like best. (5) A person diving in Maunalua Bay, for example, will see exotic fish that they won't see anywhere else. (6) A reef on the south shore contains a shipwreck, but a diver must be experienced to explore it. (7) Anyone who sees the orange cup corals at Ulua Cave won't believe their eyes. (8) Some divers might think that an occasional shark or octopus is dangerous, but usually they're not. (9) All the instructional manuals say that you must be physically fit to scuba dive. (10) If my sister and myself were invited to go scuba diving in the Hawaiian Islands, we'd jump at the chance.

Section 26.1 Review Exercises

GRAMMAR EXERCISES 8–17

EXERCISE 8: Singular and Plural Subjects and Compound Subjects Choose the verb in parentheses that agrees with the subject of each sentence.

1. Democracy (exists, exist) when the people direct the nation's activities.
2. Free systems of government (is, are) common in Western nations.
3. Concepts of democracy (includes, include) the election of representatives.
4. An individual in a free system (possesses, possess) many basic rights.
5. Freedom of speech and freedom of the press (is, are) protected.
6. Unreasonable search and seizure (is, are) forbidden under the law.
7. Neither Congress nor the President (has, have) absolute authority.
8. The President and each elected member of Congress (swears, swear) to uphold the Constitution.
9. Either the citizens or the press (monitors, monitor) the government.
10. ...ers (rules, rule).

EXERCISE 9: ...ed Sentences
...renthenses that ...each sentence.

...olitical conven-
... nominations.
...e campaign.
...] each candi-
...] swing?
...merous personal
...ndidates.
...ds on television?
...p in the ads.
...ing and the
...ome) the vote.
...ons of the win-
...he polls close.
...several hours (is,
...unt.

EXERCISE 10: Linking Verbs and Collective Nouns Choose the verb in parentheses that agrees with the subject of each sentence.

1. Our courts (is, are) a large system.
2. The ninety-one district courts (is, are) one level of the system.
3. A higher level of courts (is, are) the Federal Courts of Appeals.
4. This group of courts (hears, hear) appeals from lower court decisions.
5. Usually, a panel of three judges (sits, sit) to hear a case.
6. The district courts (is, are) the source of most cases in the appeals courts.
7. Criminal and civil cases (is, are) the responsibility of the district courts.
8. The responsibility of the Supreme Court (is, are) appeals from the district courts.
9. The Court (has, have) nine justices.
10. In the Supreme Court, the majority (determines, determine) the decision.

EXERCISE 11: Plural-Looking Verbs and Indefinite Pronouns Choose the verb in parentheses that agrees with the subject of each sentence.

1. Not everybody (knows, know) how laws are established.
2. However, each of us (realizes, realize) the importance of laws.
3. Usually, someone in the House or Senate (introduces, introduce) a bill.
4. Everything in the bill (is, are) weighed by a committee.
5. The committee then (votes, vote) on whether to send the bill further.
6. In the House or Senate, many (debates, debate) aspects of the bill.
7. Politics always (plays, play) a role.
8. Economics (is, are) also considered.
9. Some of the bill (is, are) amended.
10. Any representative or senator (is, are) entitled to speak for or against the bill.

Practice, Practice, and More Practice

More grammar exercises than any other program provide the practice your students need to improve their grammar skills and apply them in writing and speaking.

More Strategic Revision

More Systematic, hands-on revision strategies help students examine what they write and how to improve it.

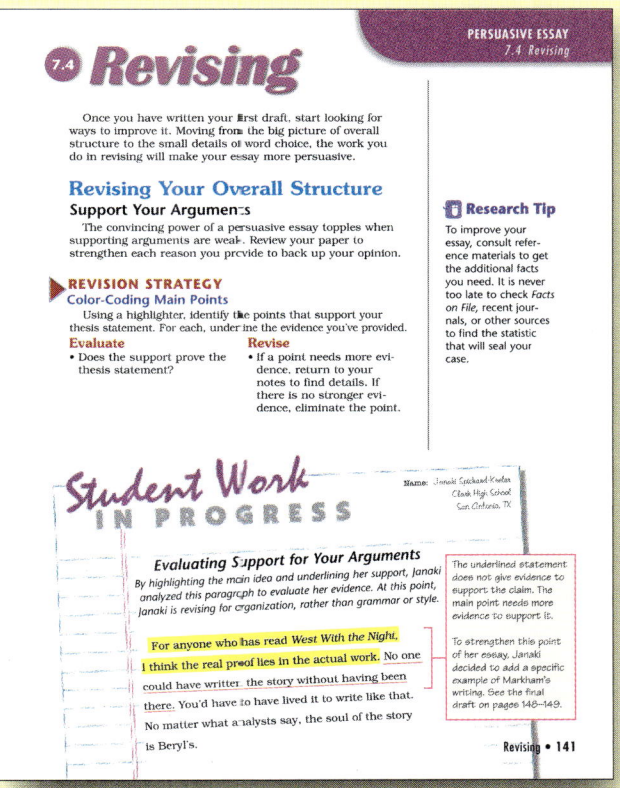

7.4 Revising

Once you have written your first draft, start looking for ways to improve it. Moving from the big picture of overall structure to the small details of word choice, the work you do in revising will make your essay more persuasive.

Revising Your Overall Structure

Support Your Arguments

The convincing power of a persuasive essay topples when supporting arguments are weak. Review your paper to strengthen each reason you provide to back up your opinion.

▶ **REVISION STRATEGY**
Color-Coding Main Points

Using a highlighter, identify the points that support your thesis statement. For each, underline the evidence you've provided.

Evaluate
• Does the support prove the thesis statement?

Revise
• If a point needs more evidence, return to your notes to find details. If there is no stronger evidence, eliminate the point.

📘 **Research Tip**

To improve your essay, consult reference materials to get the additional facts you need. It is never too late to check *Facts on File*, recent journals, or other sources to find the statistic that will seal your case.

Student Work
IN PROGRESS

Name: Janaki Spickard-Keeler
Clark High School
San Antonio, TX

Evaluating Support for Your Arguments
By highlighting the main idea and underlining her support, Janaki analyzed this paragraph to evaluate her evidence. At this point, Janaki is revising for organization, rather than grammar or style.

For anyone who has read *West With the Night*, I think the real proof lies in the actual work. No one could have written the story without having been there. You'd have to have lived it to write like that. No matter what analysts say, the soul of the story is Beryl's.

The underlined statement does not give evidence to support the claim. The main point needs more evidence to support it.

To strengthen this point of her essay, Janaki decided to add a specific example of Markham's writing. See the final draft on pages 148–149.

Revising • 141

7.4

Revising Your Sentences

Use Transitions

Minor revisions to sentences can make a big difference. Look at each sentence to see whether rearranging or adding words will make your meaning more clear to your readers. Use transitions to clarify or reinforce the connections between ideas.

▶ **REVISION STRATEGY**
Using Transition Boxes

You may want to try this strategy with one paragraph:

1. Draw a box between the end punctuation of one sentence and the first word of the next sentence.
2. Identify the relationship that connects the sentences on either side of the box.
3. Evaluate your writing as it exists. Place a check in the box if the relationship between the sentences it connects is clear.
4. If the relationship is not clear, add a transition. (Use the chart on the next page as a reference.) Place the new word or phrase at the point where the box is located. As an alternative, you might draw a line from the box to a space where the transition makes the most sense.

Challenge yourself to apply this strategy to other paragraphs in your essay.

🖥 **Writing Lab CD-ROM**

Use the Transition Word Bin in the Persuasion lesson to help improve your sentences.

Student Work
IN PROGRESS

Name: Janaki Spickard-Keeler
Clark High School
San Antonio, TX

Using Transition Boxes to Smooth Writing
In the paragraph that argued that Beryl Markham was not illiterate, Janaki saw that readers might not see the connections she wanted them to see. She added several transitions to make the connections more clear.

Beryl practically worshiped her father. □ So naturally, She would do as he wished and read the classics. □ She had quite a library, and Denys Finch-Hatton encouraged her to educate herself. □ Furthermore, She wrote diligently with a practiced hand in her logbook. ☑ She also had to write a lengthy theory paper to pass her flying exam.

The first sentence gives a reason for the second sentence. The transition "so naturally" clarifies the relationship.

TRANSITIONS THAT INDICATE LOGICAL RELATIONSHIPS

Point to a Reason	Identify a Single Conclusion	Show a Contrast	Signal a Sequence
since, because, if	therefore, consequently, as a result, thus, hence, accordingly, so, then, in conclusion	although, even though, however, despite, yet, but, on the other hand, in contrast, except for	first, second, then, next, finally, before, after, later, soon, daily, recently, when

Revising Your Word Choice

Use Persuasive Language

The words you choose can influence the readers' reactions to your argument. If you maintain a polite tone, you can use language that points readers in the direction you want them to go.

When you want to sharpen criticism: Use words like *unfounded, shameful,* and *implausible.*

When you want to polish a recommendation: Add words like *superior* and *wise.*

When you want to defend your ideas: Include words like *obvious, clear,* and *evident.*

▶ **REVISION STRATEGY**
Reading Aloud

Read your draft aloud, as if it were a speech. Mark the ideas or sentences that you would want to stress to a crowd. Then, go back into your draft, adding the forceful words you need.

Peer Review

Say Back

In a small group, share your revised draft. Read your persuasive essay twice, asking readers to listen the first time and respond the second time. Use these questions as a starting point for group discussion:

1. What is the most persuasive point?
2. About which point would a reader want to know more?

After you've heard from your classmates, consider using their suggestions to improve your draft.

▲ **Critical Viewing**
In what ways might a peer conference like the one shown here help you fine-tune your persuasive essay? [Hypothesize]

144 • Persuasive Essay

Revising • 145

Assessment resources to help your students need to succeed

Standardized Test Preparation Workshops

Standardized Test Preparation Workshops after each chapter provide unmatched preparation for PSAT, SAT, ACT, AP, state, and local standardized tests.

Success for all Students

Accommodate your students' diverse needs by customizing instruction with assignments that address different ability levels and learning styles.

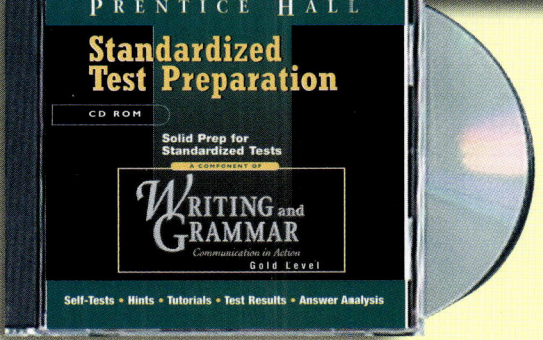

Diagnostic Tests

Begin each Grammar Chapter to help you assess students' skill levels and identify areas for improvement.

Flexible Assessment Options

Develop confident and successful test-takers with a variety of test-taking opportunities.

Time-Saving Options!

Save time with an easy-to-use handbook style and a variety of integrated ancillary support options.

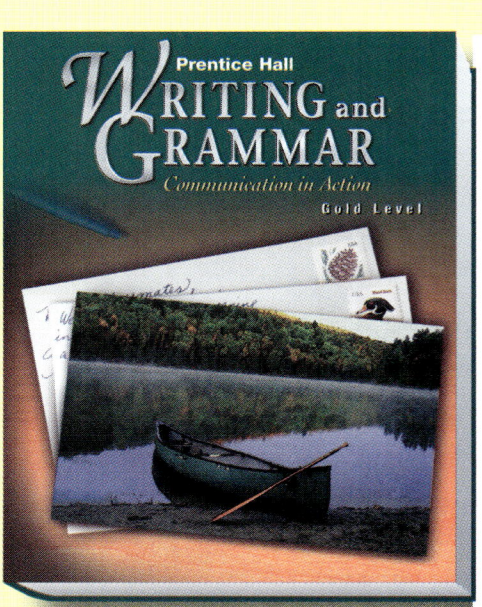

Easy-to-use

Handbook style gives you and your students immediate access to review sections when necessary.

Save time

with point of use support.

Choose from

in-depth, accelerated, or block-scheduling lesson plans to best meet your needs and the needs of your students.

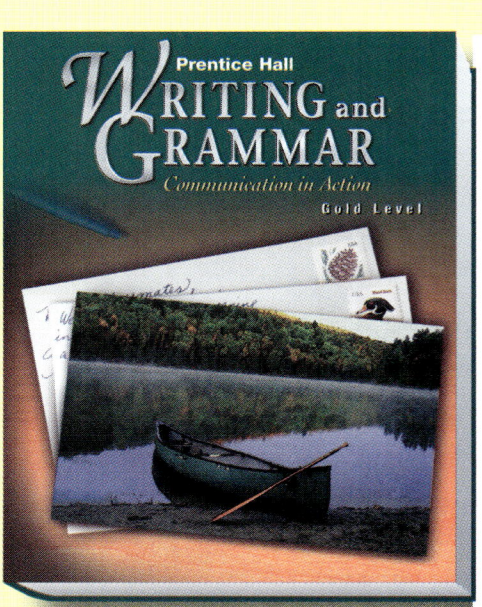

20.3 COMPLEMENTS

Indirect Objects

In addition to a verb and direct object, the complete predicate of a sentence may contain an *indirect object*.

KEY CONCEPT An **indirect object** is a noun or pronoun that appears with a direct object and names the person or thing that something is given to or done for.

A sentence cannot have an indirect object unless it has a direct object. You can tell whether a word is an indirect object by finding the direct object and asking *To* or *for whom?* or *To or for what?* after the action verb.

EXAMPLE: I bought my brother a new pair of skis.
Bought *for whom?* Answer: brother

Like subjects, verbs, and direct objects, indirect objects can be compound.

EXAMPLE: We wrote Sue and Al letters about our trip.
Wrote *to whom?* Answer: Sue and Al

Exercise 22 Recognizing Indirect Objects Write the indirect object in each sentence.

EXAMPLE: He brought me his old bowling shoes.
ANSWER: me

1. Many colleges offer students bowling as an elective course.
2. The instructor teaches each class basic rules.
3. My father lent John and me his bowling balls.
4. My friend gave me a wrist brace to help keep my wrist straight as I bowled.
5. Mr. Neil taught us the history of bowling.

More Practice
On-line
Exercise Bank
• Section 20.2
Grammar Exercise
Workbook
• pp. 53–58

Exercise 23 Supplying Indirect Objects Supply an indirect object that logically completes each sentence.

EXAMPLE: I lent ___?___ my new racquet.

Chapter 7 Time and Resource Manager

7 PERSUASION

7.2 Prewriting

Choosing Your Topic

TOPIC BANK

Make planning easier

with a variety of suggested lesson plans and a wealth of integrated ancillary support.

Prentice Hall
WRITING and GRAMMAR
Communication in Action
Gold Level
Grammar Exercise Answers on Transparencies

- Answers to all grammar exercises in the student textbook
- Facilitates self- and peer-correction

Prentice Hall

Prentice Hall
WRITING and GRAMMAR
Communication in Action
Gold Level
Teaching Resources
Scoring Rubrics on Transparencies

- Scoring rubrics for each writing chapter

Prentice Hall

Prentice Hall
WRITING and GRAMMAR
Communication in Action
Gold Level
Prentice Hall LITERATURE
Timeless Voices, Timeless Themes
Teaching Resources
Daily Language Practice Transparencies

- Brief daily activities to build skills in grammar, usage, and mechanics

Prentice Hall

PRENTICE HALL
Standardized Test Preparation
CD ROM
Solid Prep for Standardized Tests
A COMPONENT OF
WRITING and GRAMMAR
Communication in Action
Gold Level
Self-Tests • Hints • Tutorials • Test Results • Answer Analysis

PRENTICE HALL
Test Bank CD-ROM
Solid Prep for Tests
A COMPONENT OF
WRITING and GRAMMAR
Communication in Action
Gold Level
Self-Tests • Hints • Tutorials • Test Results • Answer Analysis

PRENTICE HALL
RESOURCE PRO
with Literature Database
teaching resources & classroom management at your fingertips
WRITING and GRAMMAR
Communication in Action
GOLD

PRENTICE HALL
Interactive Student CD ROM
A COMPONENT OF
WRITING and GRAMMAR
Communication in Action
Gold Level

Multimedia Instruction for the Future!

Connect to today's multimedia generation with a variety of fully-integrated technology practice and support options.

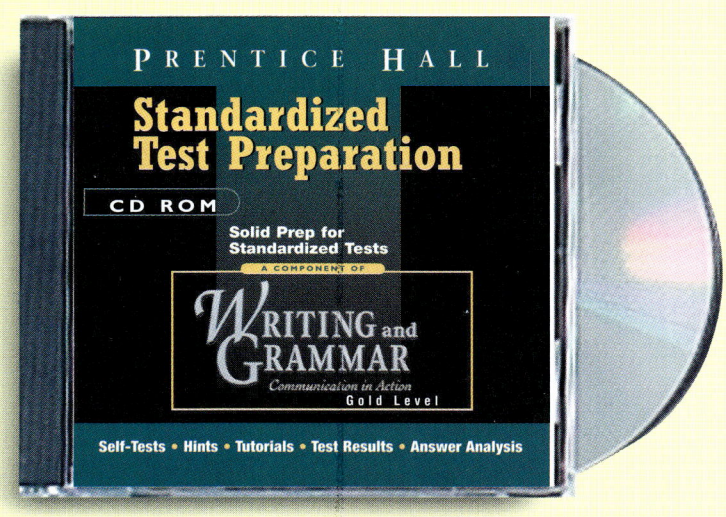

Prentice Hall's Internet Homepage

brings the world of writing to your students through support and extension activities and related links.

Resource Pro

helps you manage your lesson planning and resources with a simple click of a mouse.

ormal Assessment CD-Rom

lows you to gauge your students' ility levels and establish your own ills objectives.

TEACHING RESOURCES

Writing

Writing Support Activity Book
Topic Bank for Heterogeneous Classes
Multigenre Research Project

Grammar, Usage, and Mechanics

Grammar Exercise Workbook, Teacher's Edition
Daily Language Practice
Hands-on Grammar Activity Book
Extra Grammar and Writing Exercises

Academic and Workplace Skills

Academic and Workplace Skills Activity Book, Teacher's Edition
Vocabulary and Spelling Practice Book, Teacher's Edition
Reading Support Practice Book, Teacher's Edition

Assessment

Standardized Test Preparation Workbook, Teacher's Edition
Writing Assessment and Portfolio Management
Formal Assessment/Assessment Resources Software CD-ROM

Professional Resources

How to Manage Instruction in the Block
How to Assess Student Work
Putting Patterns to Work
Kick Off for Success: Organizing for School
Hearing All Sides: Resolving Conflict

ADDITIONAL ANCILLARIES

Workbooks

Hands-on Grammar Activity Book
Writing Support Activity Book
Grammar Exercise Workbook
Reading Support Practice Book
Vocabulary and Spelling Workbook
Academic and Workplace Skills Workbook
Standardized Test Preparation Workbook

Transparencies

Writing Support Transparencies
Daily Language Practice Transparencies
Grammar Exercises Answers on Transparencies
Scoring Rubrics on Transparencies

Technology

Writing and Grammar Interactive CD-ROM
   Writing Lab CD-ROM
   Language Lab CD-ROM
Interactive Writing and Grammar Web site
Resource Pro CD-ROM (including Test Bank)
Writers at Work Videotape

Spanish Support
Extra Grammar and Writing Exercises
Multigenre Research Writing

Correlation to the Six Traits Analytic Model

Chapter	Ideas	Organization	Voice	Word Choice	Sentence Fluency	Conventions
1 The Writer in You			p. 3			
2 A Walk Through the Writing Process						
2.1	pp. 16–20	p. 21	p. 18			
2.2	p. 22					
2.3	p. 24			p. 25	p. 24	
2.4						p. 26
Spot/Hum.	p. 28					
3 Paragraphs and Compositions						
3.1	pp. 33–5					
3.2	p. 37	p. 37, p. 39				
3.3			pp. 42	p. 42	p. 42	p. 43
Spot/Hum.	p. 44					
4 Narration: Autobiography						
4.1	p. 50					
4.2	pp. 52–5		p. 55			
4.3		p. 56				
4.4	p. 58	p. 58		p. 62	p. 60	p. 61
4.5						p. 63
4.7	pp. 65–6	pp. 65–6		pp. 65–6		
Spot/Hum.	p. 68					
5 Narration: Short Story						
5.1		pp. 74–5				
5.2	pp. 76–8		p. 78			
5.3	pp. 81	p. 80				
5.4	pp. 82–3			pp. 83–4	p. 84	p. 85
5.5						p. 86
5.7	pp. 89–90	pp. 89–90				
Spot/Hum.	p. 92					
6 Description						
6.1	pp. 98–9			pp. 98–9		
6.2	pp. 100–03					
6.3	p. 104	p. 104				
6.4	p. 106	p. 105		p. 105, p. 108	p. 107	
6.5						p. 109
6.7	pp. 111–13	pp. 111–13		pp. 111–13		
Spot/Hum.	p. 114					
7 Persuasion: Persuasive Essay						
7.1	pp. 120–1			p. 122		
7.2	pp. 124–6, p. 128		p. 127			
7.3	p. 130	pp. 129				
7.4	pp. 131–2			p. 134	p. 133	p. 133
7.5						p. 136
7.7	p. 138	p. 138	p. 138	p. 138		
Spot/Hum.	p. 142					
8. Persuasion: Advertisement						
8.1				p. 148		
8.2	pp. 149–50, p. 152		p. 151			
8.3	p. 155			p. 153		
8.4				p. 156	p. 155	
8.5						p. 157
Spot/Hum.	p. 162					
9 Exposition: Comparison and Contrast						
9.1	pp. 168–71	pp. 168–71				
9.2	pp. 172–4, p. 176		p. 175			
9.3	p. 178	p. 177				
9.4	p. 179	pp. 180		p. 183		pp. 181–2
9.7	pp. 187–8	pp. 187–8		p. 187		p. 185
Spot/Hum.	p. 190					

Chapter	Ideas	Organization	Voice	Word Choice	Sentence Fluency	Conventions
10 Exposition: Comparison and Contrast						
10.1	pp. 196–7					
10.2	pp. 198–201					
10.3	p. 203	p. 202				
10.4	p. 205	p. 205		p. 214, p. 207	p. 206	
10.5					p. 208	
10.7	pp. 210–12	pp. 210–12				
Spot/Hum.	p. 214					
11 Exposition: Problem and Solution						
11.1	p. 220		p. 221	p. 221		
11.2	pp. 222–5		p. 225			
11.3	p. 227	p. 226				
11.4	p. 229	p. 228		p. 231	p. 230	p. 233
11.5						
11.7	pp. 235–7	pp. 235–7				
Spot/Hum.	p. 238					
12 Research: Documented Essay						
12.1	pp. 244–5					
12.2	pp. 246–8, p. 249		p. 248			
12.3	p. 251	p. 250				
12.4	p. 252	p. 253		p. 256	p. 254, p. 255	p. 257
12.5	pp. 259–60	pp. 259–60				
12.7	p. 262					
Spot/Hum.						
13 Research: Research Paper						
13.1	pp. 268–71	p. 269, p. 271				
13.2	pp. 273–4, p. 276	p. 277	p. 275			
13.3	p. 278, p. 280	p. 279				
13.4	p. 281	p. 281–2		p. 284	p. 283	p. 286
13.5	pp. 289–91	p. 291				
13.7						
Spot/Hum.	p. 294					
14 Response to Literature						
14.1	pp. 300–03			p. 301		
14.2	p. 304–08		p. 307			
14.3	p. 310	p. 309				
14.4	p. 311–12	p. 312		p. 314		p. 313
14.5	pp. 318–20					p. 316
14.7						p. 316
Spot/Hum.	p. 322					
15 Writing for Assessment						
15.1	pp. 328–9			p. 329		
15.2	pp. 330–1	pp. 330–1				
15.3	p. 333	p. 332		p. 333		
15.4						p. 334
Spot/Hum.	p. 340					
16 Workplace Writing						
16.1	p. 347	pp. 346–7		pp. 346–7		p. 347
16.2	pp. 348–9	pp. 348–9		pp. 348–9		
16.3	p. 351	p. 351		p. 351		
Spot/Hum.	p. 356					
17 Nouns and Pronouns						
17.1						pp. 364–73
17.2						pp. 374–9
17.3						pp. 380–7
17.4						pp. 388–95
17.5						pp. 396–403
18 Basic Sentence Parts						
18.1						pp. 406–13
18.2						pp. 414–19
18.3						pp. 420–9

Correlation to the Six Traits Analytic Model

Chapter	Ideas	Organization	Voice	Word Choice	Sentence Fluency	Conventions
19 Phrases and Clauses 19.1 19.2 19.3 19.4						pp. 434–41 pp. 442–53 pp. 454–65 pp. 466–71
20 Effective Sentences 20.1 20.2 20.3 20.4 20.5 20.6 20.7					pp. 481–6 pp. 487–91 pp. 500–03 pp. 504–08 pp. 509–15	pp. 478–80 pp. 481–6 pp. 487–91 pp. 492–9 pp. 500–03 pp. 504–08 pp. 509–15
21 Verb Usage 21.1 21.2 21.3 21.4						pp. 520–31 pp. 532–47 pp. 548–51 pp. 552–7
22 Pronoun Usage 22.1 22.2						pp. 562–71 pp. 572–9
23 Agreement 23.1 23.2 23.3						pp. 584–95 pp. 596–603 pp. 604–15
24 Using Modifiers 24.1 24.2						pp. 620–7 pp. 628–37
25 Miscellaneous Problems in Usage 25.1 25.2						pp. 642–7 pp. 648–63
26 Capitalization						pp. 670–87
27 Punctuation 27.1 27.2 27.3 27.4 27.5 27.6						pp. 692–5 pp. 696–715 pp. 716–23 pp. 724–41 pp. 742–55 pp. 756–67
Sentence Diagraming Workshop						pp. 772–83
28 Speaking Listening, Viewing and Representing 28.1	pp. 788–90	pp. 788–90	pp. 788–90	pp. 788–90	pp. 788–90	
29 Vocabulary and Spelling 29.1 29.2 29.3 29.4	p. 804			pp. 809–13 pp. 814–15 pp. 816–19		pp. 820–9
30 Reading Skills 30.2 30.3	pp. 840–1 pp. 846–8	p. 840 pp. 847–9	p. 840 p. 846	pp. 844–5 pp. 846–9	p. 846, p. 849	
31 Study, Reference, and Test-Taking Skills						
34 Workplace Skills and Competencies						

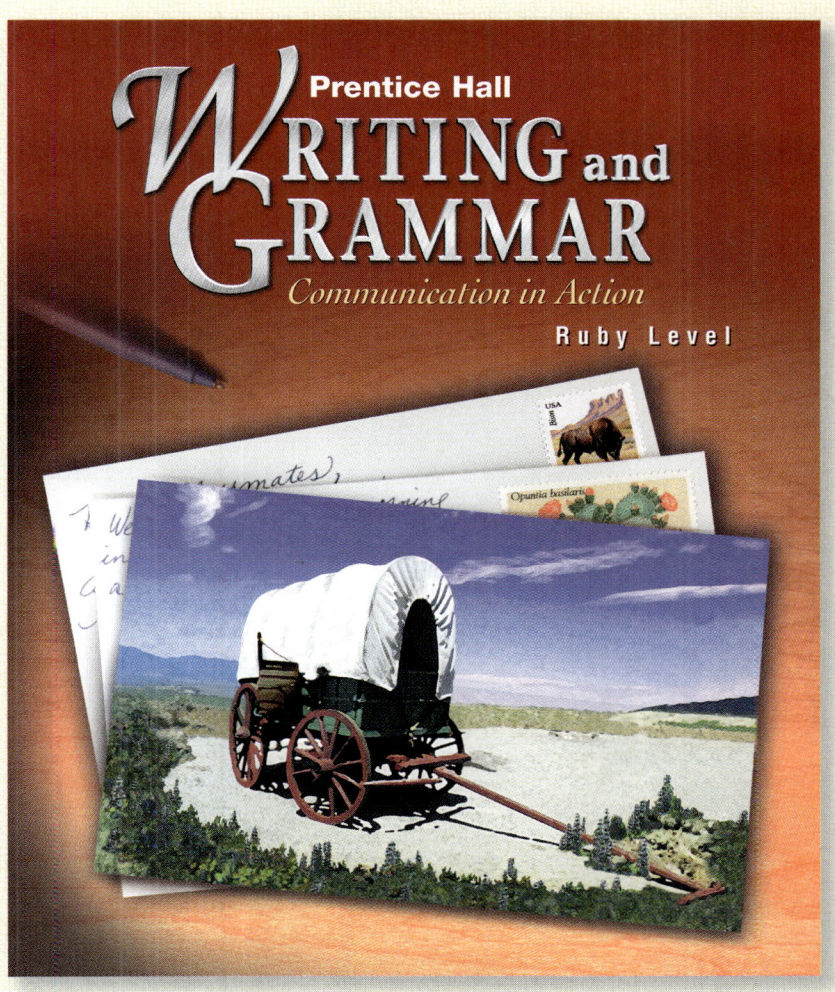

Prentice Hall

WRITING and GRAMMAR
Communication in Action

Ruby Level

Ruby Level

Prentice Hall

Upper Saddle River, New Jersey
Needham, Massachusetts
Glenview, Illinois

ISBN 0-13-436969-6

5 6 7 8 9 10   05 04 03 02 01

WRITING and GRAMMAR

Communication in Action

Copper
Bronze
Silver
Gold
Platinum
Ruby
Diamond

Program Authors

The program authors guided the direction and philosophy of *Prentice Hall Writing and Grammar: Communication in Action.* Working with the development team, they contributed to the pedagogical integrity of the program and to its relevance to today's teachers and students.

Joyce Armstrong Carroll

In her forty-year career, Joyce Armstrong Carroll, Ed.D., has taught on every grade level from primary to graduate school. In the past twenty years, she has trained teachers in the teaching of writing. A nationally known consultant, she has served as president of TCTE and on NCTE's Commission on Composition. More than fifty of her articles have appeared in journals such as *Curriculum Review, English Journal, Media & Methods, Southwest Philosophical Studies, Ohio English Journal, English in Texas,* and the *Florida English Journal.* With Edward E. Wilson, Dr. Carroll co-authored *Acts of Teaching: How to Teach Writing* and co-edited *Poetry After Lunch: Poems to Read Aloud.* Beyond her direct involvement with the writing pedagogy presented in this series, Dr. Carroll guided the development of the Hands-on Grammar feature. She co-directs the New Jersey Writing Project in Texas.

Edward E. Wilson

A former editor of *English in Texas,* Edward E. Wilson has served as a high-school English teacher and a writing consultant in school districts nationwide. Wilson has served on the Texas Teacher Professional Practices Commission and on NCTE's Commission on Composition. With Dr. Carroll, he co-wrote *Acts of Teaching: How to Teach Writing* and co-edited the award-winning *Poetry After Lunch: Poems to Read Aloud.* In addition to his direct involvement with the writing pedagogy presented in this series, Wilson provided inspiration for the Spotlight on Humanities feature. Wilson's poetry appears in Paul Janeczko's anthology *The Music of What Happens.* Wilson co-directs the New Jersey Writing Project in Texas.

Gary Forlini

Gary Forlini, a nationally known education consultant, developed the grammar, usage, and mechanics instruction and exercises in this series. After teaching in the Pelham, New York, schools for many years, he established Research in Media, an educational research agency that provides information for product developers, school staff developers, media companies, and arts organizations, as well as private-sector corporations and foundations. Mr. Forlini was co-author of the *S.A.T. Home Study* program and has written numerous industry reports on elementary, secondary, and post-secondary education markets.

National Advisory Panel

The teachers and administrators serving on the National Advisory Panel provided ongoing input into the development of *Prentice Hall Writing and Grammar: Communication in Action.* Their valuable insights ensure that the perspectives of teachers and students throughout the country are represented within the instruction in this series.

Dr. Pauline Bigby-Jenkins
Coordinator for Secondary English
 Language Arts
Ann Arbor Public Schools
Ann Arbor, Michigan

Lee Bromberger
English Department Chairperson
Mukwonago High School
Mukwonago, Wisconsin

Mary Chapman
Teacher of English
Free State High School
Lawrence, Kansas

Jim Deatherage
Language Arts Department
 Chairperson
Richland High School
Richland, Washington

Luis Dovalina
Teacher of English
La Joya High School
La Joya, Texas

JoAnn Giardino
Teacher of English
Centennial High School
Columbus, Ohio

Susan Goldberg
Teacher of English
Westlake Middle School
Thornwood, New York

Jean Hicks
Director, Louisville Writing Project
University of Louisville
Louisville, Kentucky

Karen Hurley
Teacher of Language Arts
Perry Meridian Middle School
Indianapolis, Indiana

Karen Lopez
Teacher of English
Hart High School
Newhall, California

Marianne Minshall
Teacher of Reading and Language Arts
Westmore Middle School
Columbus, Ohio

Nancy Monroe
English Department Chairperson
Bolton High School
Alexandria, Louisiana

Ken Spurlock
Assistant Principal
Boone County High School
Florence, Kentucky

Cynthia Katz Tyroff
Staff Development Specialist
 and Teacher of English
Northside Independent School District
San Antonio, Texas

Holly Ward
Teacher of Language Arts
Campbell Middle School
Daytona Beach, Florida

Grammar Review Team

The following teachers reviewed the grammar instruction in this series to ensure accuracy, clarity, and pedagogy.

Kathy Hamilton
Paul Hertzog
Daren Hoisington
Beverly Ladd

Karen Lopez
Dianna Louise Lund
Sean O'Brien

CONTENTS IN BRIEF

Chapters 1–16

Part 1: Writing 1

Chapters 17–27

Part 2: Grammar, Usage, and Mechanics 360

Chapters 28–32

Part 3: Academic and Workplace Skills . . 784

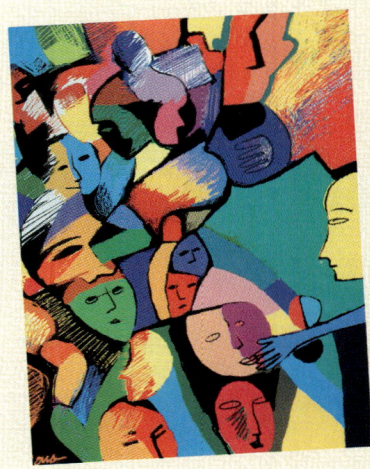

Resources

CONTENTS
PART 1: WRITING

INTEGRATED SKILLS

INTEGRATED SKILLS

INTEGRATED SKILLS

Chapter 4

Narration
Autobiographical Writing 48

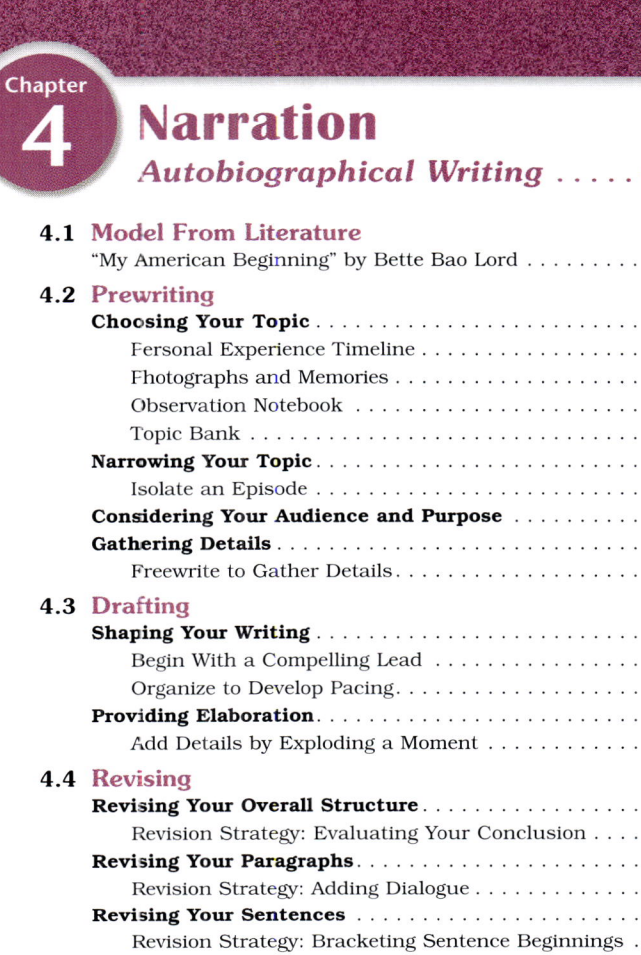

Student Work
IN PROGRESS

Featured Work:
"Train Tracks"
by Lauren Mizock
Whitney Young Magnet School
Chicago, Illinois

INTEGRATED SKILLS

Chapter 5 — Narration

Short Story 72

Student Work IN PROGRESS

Featured Work:
"Too Much Information"
by Ben Spoer
Santa Monica High School
Santa Monica, California

INTEGRATED SKILLS

Description 96

INTEGRATED SKILLS

Contents • **xi**

Student Work
IN PROGRESS

INTEGRATED SKILLS

Contents • **xiii**

Chapter 9

Exposition: *Comparison-and-Contrast Essay* 166

INTEGRATED SKILLS

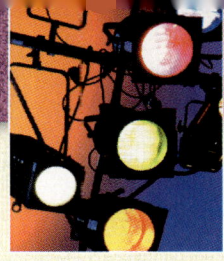

Chapter 10

Exposition
Cause-and-Effect Essay 194

Student Work
IN PROGRESS

Featured Work:
"Notes From the Footlights"
by Hilary Odom
Athens High School
Athens, Texas

INTEGRATED SKILLS

Chapter 11

Exposition

Problem-and-Solution Essay . . 218

Student Work
IN PROGRESS

Featured Work:
"Zap the Zombie Syndrome"
by Jennifer Tufts
Broken Arrow High School
Broken Arrow, Oklahoma

INTEGRATED SKILLS

12 Research

Documented Essay 242

Student Work
IN PROGRESS

Featured Work:
"The Armed Forces: The Right
Choice for Some Seniors"
by Shira Pinsker
Miami Palmetto High School
Pinecrest, Florida

INTEGRATED SKILLS

Contents • **xvii**

Student Work
IN PROGRESS

Featured Work:
"Sandra Cisneros: Modern-Day Heroine" by J. B. Nelson
Hart High School
Newhall, California

INTEGRATED SKILLS

Contents • xix

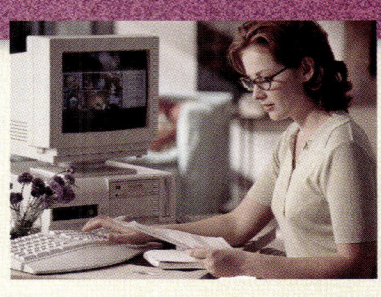

Chapter 16 Workplace Writing 344

INTEGRATED SKILLS

Contents • **xxiii**

Contents • **xxv**

Chapter 28

Speaking, Listening, Viewing, and Representing 786

Chapter 29

Vocabulary and Spelling 808

Objectives

1. To understand writing as a recursive process and to develop ownership of one's own writing process

2. To write in a variety of forms, including narrative, descriptive, persuasive, expository, and literary texts, and to develop skills in writing for assessment

3. To analyze works of literature and student drafts as models and examples of specific writing strategies

4. To develop voice and adjust one's writing to various audiences and purposes

5. To develop research skills and to use writing as a tool for learning

6. To apply specific prewriting strategies for generating and narrowing writing topics

7. To use graphic organizers and other methods for organizing and supporting ideas in drafting

8. To approach revision in a systematic way in terms of overall structure, paragraphs, sentences, and word choice

9. To edit and proofread drafts to ensure appropriate usage and accuracy in spelling and the conventions and mechanics of written English

10. To understand rubrics and to use them to evaluate one's own writing and the writing of others

Writing

Responding to Fine Art

Harry Cohen, Builder by Jack Beal

Use this artwork to start a discussion about the process of writing.

1. Have students examine the painting on page 1. You might use the following questions to prompt discussion:

   What are some of the objects in the room? What do they suggest about the man's experiences? Which of them might make an intriguing writing topic, and why?

   What is the man preparing to read? How does he seem to feel about this document? Anxious? Calm? Which details reveal his mood?

2. Point out the mirror behind the man. What ideas does it suggest? How can the process of writing resemble looking in a mirror?

3. The man seems to be alone in the room. Ask students to explain how writing is simultaneously a private exercise and a public one. How does writing affect our relationship with the world?

About the Artist

Jack Beal was born in Richmond, Virginia, in 1931. Around 1960 he rejected his abstractionist style and adopted a more traditional style of painting called contemporary realism, termed by many the New Realism. Beal is always conscious of the viewer. "I'm trying to paint people and things the way I think most people see people and things," Beal has written. Beal's canvasses are often dramatically lighted, and his scenes are typically filled with various items chosen to display shapes and textures—"to convey some mysterious message."

Time and Resource Manager

In-Depth Lesson Plan

	LESSON FOCUS	PRINT AND MEDIA RESOURCES
DAY 1	**Introduction to Writing** Students discuss the value of writing in everyday life and the qualities of good writing. (pp. 2–3)	*Writers at Work* **Videotape**, selected segments *Writing Lab* **CD-ROM**, selected segments
DAY 2	**Developing Your Writing Life** Students identify strategies for generating and organizing ideas for writing. Coverage of organizing includes notebooks, clipping files journals, portfolios, and journals. (pp. 4–7)	**Teaching Resources** *Writing Support Transparencies,* 1-A; *Writing Support Activity Book,* 1-1
DAY 3	**Reflecting on Writing** Students review careers in writing and write a reflective response on their own writing practices. (pp. 8–9)	**Teaching Resources** *Formal Assessment,* Ch. 1

Accelerated Lesson Plan

	LESSON FOCUS	PRINT AND MEDIA RESOURCES
DAY 1	**Introduction; Developing Your Writing Life** Students identify qualities of good writing and learn strategies for generating and organizing ideas. (pp. 2–7)	**Teaching Resources** *Writing Support Transparencies,* 1-A; *Writing Support Activity Book,* 1-1
DAY 2	**Reflecting on Writing** Students review careers in writing and write a reflective response on their own writing practices. (pp. 8–9)	**Teaching Resources** *Formal Assessment,* Ch. 1

Options for Adapting Lesson Plans

HOMEWORK

Have students read the chapter as homework before discussing it in class.

FEATURES

Extend coverage with Spotlight on the Humanities (p. 10), Media and Technology Skills (p. 11), and the Standardized Test Preparation Workshop (p. 12).

INTEGRATED SKILLS COVERAGE

Viewing and Representing
Critical Viewing, SE pp. 2, 4, 7, 8, 10
Analyzing How Meaning Is Communicated Through the Arts, SE p. 10

Real-World Connection
ATE p. 4

ASSESSMENT SUPPORT

Standardized Test Preparation Workshop, SE p. 12
Standardized Test Preparation Workbook, pp. 1–2
Formal Assessment, Ch. 1

MEETING INDIVIDUAL NEEDS

Less Advanced Students ATE p. 5, 13. See also Ongoing Assessment ATE p. 5.
AP Students ATE p. 13
ESL Students ATE p. 9

BLOCK SCHEDULING

Pacing Suggestions
For 90-minute Blocks
• Cover the content of Chapter 1 in a single period.
• You may wish to use part of a second period to administer the sample prompt from the Standardized Test Preparation Workshop and the assessment for Chapter 1 from *Formal Assessment.*

Resources for Varying Instruction
• *Writing Lab* CD-ROM If your students have access to hardware, a 90-minute block provides an ideal opportunity for students to work on computer.
• *Writers at Work* Videotape Show selected segments in class to introduce several professional writers.

Professional Development Support
• *How to Manage Instruction in the Block* This Teaching Resource provides management and activity suggestions.

MEDIA AND TECHNOLOGY

For the Teacher
• *Writers at Work* Videotape, selected segments
• *Resource Pro* CD-ROM

WRITING AND GRAMMAR WEB SITE

The Interactive Writing and Grammar Web Site provides a wide array of support for students, teachers, and parents. Writing support includes:

• Interactive revision checkers
• Scoring rubrics with complete models

www.phschool.com

LITERATURE CONNECTIONS

Relevant selections from *Prentice Hall Literature: Timeless Voices, Timeless Themes,* The American Experience:

"The Writer in the Family," E. L. Doctorow, ATE p. 3
from *Pilgrim at Tinker Creek,* Annie Dillard, ATE p. 6
"The Far and the Near," by Thomas Wolfe, ATE p. 7
"For the Love of Books," Rita Dove, ATE p. 9
from *The Names,* N. Scott Momaday, ATE p. 9
"Who Burns for the Perfection of Paper," Martín Espada, ATE p. 9

Lesson Objectives

1. To understand the purposes and significance of writing in everyday life
2. To identify the qualities of good writing, including organization, voice, word choice, sentence fluency, and appropriate usage
3. To compile and represent information in a variety of ways
4. To use writing as a study tool to clarify and remember information
5. To analyze the strategies that writers in different fields use to compose
6. To explore options for working together, including group brainstorming and peer reviews
7. To examine possible outlets for publishing written material

Critical Viewing

Speculate Students should note the open books and notebooks on the desk. The posters and charts on the wall suggest the room is some sort of science classroom. Therefore, one would assume that the girl is taking notes from a textbook or is completing an assignment for science class.

Chapter 1 The Writer in You
Your Writing Life

Writing in Everyday Life

You may not be aware of how heavily you rely on writing every day. At home, you might jot down a "To Do" list, take a phone message, send a letter or an e-mail, or fill out an application or order form. At school, you might write to answer a test question, produce a research report, take notes during a lecture, or generate ideas for a new project. Every time you pick up a pen or pencil or use a keyboard, you are writing.

▲ **Critical Viewing**
What kind of writing do you think the students in this photograph might be doing? **[Speculate]**

2 • The Writer in You

⏱ TIME AND RESOURCE MANAGER

Resources
Print: *Writing Support Transparencies*, 1-A; *Writing Support Activity Book*, 1-1; *Formal Assessment*, Ch. 1
Technology: *Writers at Work* Videotape, selected segments

In-Depth Coverage	Accelerated Pace
• Cover pp. 2–9 in class. • Bring in samples of a clipping file or reader's journal for students to review. • Assign the creation of files, notebooks, and journals as you require. • Preview segments of the *Writers at Work* Videotape.	• Have students read pp. 2–9 independently. • Discuss in class students' ideas about writing and the writing process. • Review materials students have prepared for class, such as files, journals, and notebooks.

Why Write?

Writing is one of the most powerful communication tools you will use today and for the rest of your life. You will use it to share your thoughts and ideas with others and even to communicate with yourself. Journals, class notes, and shopping lists are just a few of the ways you can use writing to help you remember facts and details. Even after you have finished your last school assignment, writing will still be part of your daily business and personal life.

What Are the Qualities of Good Writing?

Ideas Your ideas are the heart of your writing. Ordinary ideas turn into ordinary writing. Intriguing ideas turn into intriguing writing. Whatever you write, give it a fresh perspective. Use details to help readers see your topic in a new way.

Organization For writing to be effective, it must be presented in a way that readers can follow and understand. Every kind of writing should have a basic structure—a pattern or an organization. Choose a structure, and use it consistently throughout a piece of writing. Make sure readers have the information they need to understand each new piece of information or each new idea you introduce. Conclude your writing by wrapping up any loose ends and leaving the reader with something to think about.

Voice When you call a friend on the telephone, your friend can probably recognize your voice, even though he or she can't see your face. Make your writing voice as distinctive as your speaking voice. Observe the conventions of written English, but give your writing a personal touch that makes it your own.

Word Choice The words you choose influence the effectiveness of your writing. Choose vivid, precise words to communicate your experiences. Use words with powerful connotations to communicate feelings and reactions. Word choice involves more than learning a lot of new words. It involves learning to use the words you already know.

Sentence Fluency Effective writing has a rhythm—a flow. Write sentences that can be read aloud without difficulty or awkwardness.

Conventions Conventions refer to the grammatical correctness of a piece of writing. Don't let errors in grammar, usage, mechanics, and spelling interfere with your message. Carefully proofread all your writing.

Writers in ACTION

Novelist E.L. Doctorow is known for writing in a variety of genres, sometimes combining elements of several genres in one novel. He once commented:

"Writing is an exploration. You start from nothing and learn as you go."

Keep Track of Your Ideas

1. If possible, bring to class models of a writer's notebook, a clipping file, and a journal.

2. Ask students to begin keeping a clipping file and either a writer's notebook or a journal for the next week or two.

3. Have students make a class list of places they might get ideas for writing (classes, a movie, friends or family, at work, old stories).

Critical Viewing

Speculate Students may suggest that the students in the photograph might record ideas about experiments, descriptions of chemical processes, or plots for science-fiction stories.

Real-World Connection

Scientists record many aspects of their experiments. In addition to writing up experiments, scientists also publish their research in professional journals. The articles must be carefully written, revised, edited, and proofread. Ask students to find in the library, or on the Internet, an article from a scholarly, scientific, or medical journal and take a look at the format and style. Compare the scientific article to an article in a magazine aimed at the general public, for example, *National Geographic*. Discuss the differences. Which do they think is more difficult to write?

Developing Your Writing Life

Keep Track of Your Ideas

Writers can get ideas from hundreds of different sources. Anything from an overheard conversation to a fascinating Internet page might trigger a new project. It's important to keep track of ideas that might lead you down new writing paths.

Writer's Notebook You never know when a great idea will land in your lap. You might see an ad in a bus or subway that demands a response. Maybe you want to jot down a line of dialogue during a movie. An activity in science or math may raise questions you want to explore. Be prepared by carrying a small writer's notebook. Jot down anything you hear or see that interests you. Later, if you're stuck for a writing idea, browse through your notebook, and you'll find a collection of thoughts that could help you launch your writing.

Clipping File You can create a clipping file to store materials that are too large to carry around in your writer's notebook. Simply label one or more file folders, and store anything that might inspire you: newspaper or magazine articles, printed pages from the World Wide Web, travel brochures, letters, or postcards. Add your own annotations, or highlight interesting passages with a marker.

Writer's Journal
Many professional writers suggest that the best way to improve writing is to write often. By writing regularly in a journal, you can build your writing skills and become more comfortable with putting your thoughts in writing. Because your journal is written for yourself, not everything needs to be polished into a finished product. Jot down your thoughts and feelings about current events, subjects you've studied, books you've read, or ordinary daily events.

▼ **Critical Viewing**
What questions might these students write in their writer's notebooks or journals to be used as ideas for future writing projects? **[Speculate]**

Keep Track of Your Writing and Reading

Writing Portfolio Maintaining an up-to-date writing portfolio can help you reflect on your progress as a writer. A portfolio can include your most successful writing, as well as early drafts that illustrate revision strategies. If you work on a computer, you might keep a portfolio disk instead of— or as well as—a paper portfolio. Remember that a portfolio is only effective if you use it. Review and update your portfolio regularly.

Reader's Journal Writing and reading are linked activities. The more you read, the more you will grow as a writer. Keeping a reader's journal will help you remember and learn from what you have read. You might list your reading selections and include sample quotations that capture the writer's style.

What Works Best for You?

Freewriting Many writers get started by freewriting—writing as the thoughts pour in. Would this strategy work for you? It might make you feel like novelist Edna O'Brien, who said, "My hand does the work and I don't have to think; in fact, were I to think, it would stop the flow."

Collecting Ideas Effective writers don't wait for inspiration—they find it themselves. You may find inspiration for your writing in a clipping file or writer's journal (see previous page). You might also look to the media as a source for writing topics.

Drafting Some writers like to use an outline to create a complete draft. Others prefer to work on one section at a time. Of course, you don't need to begin at the beginning. You might want to start by writing a dramatic conclusion, and then work backward.

Improving Your Work How do you like to revise? Do you cross out and add words as you go? Do you like to get everything down on paper first, and then go back and review it? Do you prefer to work with a partner or alone? Your choices might depend on what you are writing. For example, you might want to revise a poem by yourself but ask a peer reviewer for help in revising a research report.

Experiment

Try to keep a flexible attitude toward writing. When you try a new approach or strategy, give it your full attention and energy. Then, take time to evaluate the results. This type of experimentation will help you develop an effective personal writing process.

Writing Lab CD-ROM

Use the multimedia inspirations in the writing lessons to spark ideas on a wide variety of topics.

The Writer in You • 5

Organize Your Environment

Teaching Resources: Writing Support Transparencies, 1-A; Writing Support Activity Book, 1-1

1. Ask volunteers to explain what they think Annie Dillard means by "imagination can meet memory in the dark." (As writers we take details, facts, and feelings from our memories and use our imaginations to shape them into something new. This new story is believable because it has the stamp of reality supplied by our memories of other, real events.)

2. Ask students to share their feelings about the writing tools that work best for them.

3. Have students discuss realistic time frames for completing various types of writing. Use these questions to prompt discussion:

    How long would you expect to spend on a short story? On a research paper?

4. Display Transparency 1-A and walk students through a plan for budgeting time. Emphasize the importance of allowing time for each stage, from finding ideas and planning to proofreading the final draft.

More About the Writer

Annie Dillard was twenty-nine when she won the Pulitzer Prize for general nonfiction for her book *Pilgrim at Tinker Creek.* She spent part of her life living closely with nature and studying the natural world around her. Students will find an excerpt from *Pilgrim at Tinker Creek* in *Prentice Hall Literature: Timeless Voices, Timeless Themes,* The American Experience.

1

Organize Your Environment

In any activity, your surroundings greatly influence your productivity. Writing is no exception. Organize your time and surroundings to create an efficient and inspiring writing environment.

Choose Your Surroundings Write in a place where you can focus your attention and will not be distracted. Author Annie Dillard offers this advice: "Appealing workplaces are to be avoided. One wants a room with no view, so imagination can meet memory in the dark."

Be Prepared Before you begin to write, double-check that you have everything you will need: pens, paper, your notes, a dictionary, and other reference sources. You don't want to waste time searching for materials once your writing is flowing.

Budget Your Time A firm schedule can help you make the most of your writing time. Dillard points out that "a schedule defends from chaos and whim. It is a net for catching days. It is a scaffolding on which a worker can stand and labor with both hands at sections of time." Give yourself a series of deadlines for any complex writing project. Break down a long-term goal into a series of short-term deadlines. Use a calendar to mark each goal. Once a project is underway, you may need to adjust your schedule to accommodate stages that take more or less time than you expected.

SEPTEMBER						
1	2	3	4	5	6	7
8 Review Writing Notebook	9 Brainstorm With Group	10 Choose Topic	11 Write Questions	12 Gather Details →	13	14
15 Gather Details	16	17 Outline Organization	18	19 Drafting	20	21
22 Draft / 29	23 Draft / 30	24 Revise	25	26 Peer Editing	27 Complete Final Draft	28

Work With Others

You may find that you want feedback from others in developing your personal writing style. Outside input can be valuable at every stage in the process.

Group Brainstorming Open and free discussion is a terrific way to generate a lot of ideas quickly. Group brainstorming is the spoken equivalent of freewriting. As ideas flow freely, make sure everyone in the group has a chance to respond. Some groups like to use a tape recorder to capture a rapid brainstorming session.

Collaborative and Cooperative Writing Writers can collaborate throughout the writing process. For example, a team might outline a social studies report and then divide the writing duties according to the outline sections. Partners might even take turns adding lines to a poem. When group members divide writing responsibilities for one project, they are engaging in a kind of collaborative writing called cooperative writing.

Peer Reviewers Even when you draft by yourself, peer reviewers can help you revise your work effectively. Ask reviewers to point out unclear or confusing passages and ideas that need support.

Writers in ACTION

Editors often help writers focus their work. Thomas Wolfe's original manuscript for **Look Homeward, Angel** *was an unwieldy 1,113 pages. Editor Maxwell Perkins spent months working with Wolfe to shape the book into 626 moving pages.*

◄ **Critical Viewing**
Identify an experience you've had with a friend or classmate who has given you insight into your writing. **[Connect]**

The Writer in You • 7

Step-by-Step Teaching Guide

Work With Others

1. Explain that publishing a book requires the efforts and expertise of many people besides the author. Literary agents discuss ideas. The editor suggests and makes changes to an author's work. Proofreaders catch mistakes and inaccuracies. Designers decide how the book will look.

2. Point out that group brainstorming can help develop ideas, much as the agent does. Peer reviewers can take the place of editors, proofreaders, and designers.

3. Divide students into groups, or allow them to select their own groups. Ask them to write a "short story" by passing around a piece of paper, with each student adding another line. (You may want to suggest the same first line to all groups in order to demonstrate how different people develop even the same initial idea differently.)

4. Ask volunteers to share some of their "stories."

More About the Writer

Thomas Wolfe's novel tracks the life of a young man from his childhood in the rural South to his career as a teacher and writer in New York City—a plot that mirrors Wolfe's own life. Students will find Wolfe's story "The Far and the Near" in *Prentice Hall Literature: Timeless Voices, Timeless Themes,* The American Experience.

Critical Viewing

Connect Students may pinpoint experiences with peers or teachers that helped them see their work from the reader's point of view, or that gave them new ideas for writing.

Publish

The final satisfaction for many writers is reaching and connecting with an audience. You can find many opportunities to publish your writing—from student Web sites to magazine contests. Here are a few places that publish student work:

Periodicals

- *The McGuffey Writer and Illustrator,* McGuffey Foundation School, 5128 Westgate Drive, Oxford, OH 45056

- *Merlyn's Pen: Fiction, Essays, and Poems by American Teens,* P.O. Box 910, East Greenwich, RI 02818

- *Skipping Stones,* P.O. Box 3939, Eugene, OR 97403

On-line Publications

- *MidLink Magazine* **http://longwood.cs.ucf.edu:80/~MidLink/**

- *Wild Guess Magazine* **http://members.tripod.com/~WildGuess/**

▲ Critical Viewing
How might writing for publication in a national magazine affect your approach to a subject? **[Connect]**

Contests

- Annual Poetry Contest, National Federation of State Poetry Societies, 3520 State Route 56, Mechanicsburg, OH 43044

- *Seventeen* Magazine Fiction Contest, *Seventeen* Magazine, 850 Third Avenue, New York, NY 10022

- Paul A. Witty Outstanding Literature Award, International Reading Association, Special Interest Group for Reading for Gifted and Creative Students

Reflecting on Your Writing

Writing involves asking yourself questions and then making the answers real. Here are some questions that can lead you to discover more about the writer in you:

- What kind of writing do you like best? Least?
- What kind of writing would you like to try?
- Where is your favorite place to write?
- At what time of day do you get your best writing ideas?
- What book would you most like to have written?

Writers in Action

Careers in Writing, Writing in Careers

Many professionals earn a living by writing words. You know, of course, that poets, novelists, and playwrights are writers. You may not have considered that writing is an essential part of many other jobs as well.

Depending on the job, a worker may need to write a well-organized letter, a persuasive proposal, or a clear, concise summary. Strong writing skills will help you stand out in an overcrowded applicant pool. Even the way you write your résumé can influence a manager making hiring decisions.

Meet the Professionals

In the writing chapters of this book, you'll meet eight professionals who use different types of writing on the job. These writers at work include:

Rita Dove, poet, novelist, and playwright
Inspired by details collected in her writing notebooks, Dove creates vivid and evocative descriptions.

N. Scott Momaday, novelist, poet, and essayist
Momaday uses narrative writing to tell legends and modern tales that reflect his Native American heritage.

Thom Harrington, curator, New York Transit Museum
Museum visitors read Harrington's expository labels to find out more about the art and artifacts on display.

M. Gasby Greely, vice-president of communications for the National Urban League
In powerful public-service announcements and press releases, Greely uses persuasive writing to increase public awareness of vital civil rights issues.

Gillian Gaar, music writer and editor
Gaar conducts extensive research to fuel her many writing projects on a variety of musical topics.

Martin Espada, Latino poet
Using images that appeal to the senses, Espada creates narrative poems that evoke strong reactions.

Theresa Park, literary agent
Reading unpublished manuscripts challenges Park to respond to the writing itself rather than its presentation.

David Herring, technical writer for NASA
Clarity and accuracy are crucial when Herring writes bulletins and articles about NASA's programs and initiatives.

Reading how these professionals apply their own writing skills may help to nourish the growing writer in you.

Writers at Work Videotape

You can view these Writers at Work demonstrating their writing process in the *Writers at Work* videos.

Rita Dove

N. Scott Momaday

Martin Espada

Step-by-Step Teaching Guide

Writers in Action

Teaching Resources: Writers at Work Videotape, selected segments

1. Tell students that in the writing lessons of this book they will be reading works by a variety of writers. In addition, Writers in Action notes are included to share how these writers approach different aspects of the writing process.

2. To give the students an introduction to some of these writers, preview segments from the *Writers at Work* Videotape. You may wish to show initial segments by Rita Dove (Description), N. Scott Momaday (Narration), and Martín Espada (Creative Writing).

Responding to Literature

The works of several writers cited on page 9 may be found in *Prentice Hall Literature: Timeless Voices, Timeless Themes,* The American Experience. You may wish to refer students to "For the Love of Books" by Rita Dove, from *The Names* by N. Scott Momaday, and "Who Burns for the Perfection of Paper" by Martín Espada.

ASSESS and CLOSE

Step-by-Step Teaching Guide

Assessment

Teaching Resources: Formal Assessment, Ch. 1

1. Ask students to write a response to one of the reflecting questions on page 8 for inclusion in their portfolios. This reflection will serve as a benchmark of their current abilities and their perspectives on writing.

2. Review the Standardized Test Preparation Workshop on pages 12–13 and have students respond to the writing prompt.

3. Administer the Chapter 1 assessment from *Formal Assessment* in Teaching Resources to establish students' mastery of concepts.

Customize for
ESL Students

Have students talk or write about a favorite writer in their native language. Encourage them to learn whether this writer ever writes in English. Discuss the differences between writing in their language and English.

Spotlight on the Humanities

Analyzing How Meaning Is Communicated Through the Arts

Introducing the Spotlight on the Humanities

Writing allows you to express yourself in words. Other art forms employ different methods for expression. In the Spotlight on the Humanities feature, you will learn about the connections among various forms of artistic expression. As artists experiment and challenge boundaries, definitions of various art forms grow and change. However, most forms of expression fall into one of the following broad categories:

▲ **Critical Viewing** What words would you use to capture the feelings expressed by the dancers' expressions and gestures? **[Analyze]**

- **Fine art** creates meaning through color, line, texture, and subject. Paintings, sketches, sculpture, and collage can convey literal or abstract ideas.

- **Photography** uses still images to create meaning. While a photograph captures still images on film, photographers express ideas through subject, composition, and lighting.

- **Theater** is designed to be performed by actors on a stage. Using props, scenery, sound effects, and lighting, drama brings a story to life. In some cases, music, lyrics, and dance are incorporated into the story line. For example, in an opera, the story is told completely through singing.

- **Film** captures sound and motion to convey an idea. Like dramatic theater, most films are narratives. Setting, costumes, and characterization are used to develop a story. A filmmaker can create a unique point of view using camera angles, lighting, and sound techniques.

- **Music** uses sound to create meaning. Whether presented as an oboe solo, an operatic aria, or a jazz jam session, music can create moods or present variations on a theme.

- **Dance** creates meaning through organized movement. It can be performed by a single person, a pair, or large groups.

Writing Activity

Devise a Venn diagram that shows the similarities and differences between writing and one of the art forms described above. Save your diagram in your writing portfolio.

Media and Technology Skills

Using a Variety of Technologies

Activity: Introduction to Technology

Computers can change the way you write by speeding up and enhancing many parts of the process. Explore a computer's features, and you'll find new ways to research, to publish your work, to exchange ideas, and to express your creativity.

Learn About It Electronic tools change daily, but the basics discussed here will get you off to a good start:

- The **Internet** offers powerful research resources. Get to know search engines, and choose your favorite. Then, search books, magazines, and databases by subject, title, author, or key word.

- **Word processors** let you write electronically, editing easily and quickly. Revise neatly with *move, copy,* and *paste* functions. Save time with built-in tools such as a dictionary.

- **E-mail** helps you write inquiries to distant research sources and consumer outlets or job and school applications. In addition, you can write to a friend or share ideas electronically. Choose New Message in an e-mail program to compose a letter. Add an e-mail address and message, and then send it.

- **Desktop publishing** can help you design and illustrate books, miniposters, ads, articles, and more. Incorporate materials from word-processor or graphics programs. Publish electronically, and you can include Web hyperlinks.

Explore It Prepare a survey to study ways that you and others communicate using technology. Use the questionnaire shown here as a guide. With your teacher's permission, conduct a survey of your classmates' technology use.

How often do you use:	Never	Sometimes	Often	What do you use it for?
Internet	○	○	○	_____
Word processor	○	○	○	_____
E-mail	○	○	○	_____
Desktop publishing	○	○	○	_____

Ways to Use Technology

Internet
- Look for current news and statistics, visual images, and audio clips.
- Try mega-search engines that show top hits from several search engines.
- Import images from on-line encyclopedias.

Word Processor
- Organize documents in a logical structure for easy access.
- Explore fonts, clip art, and formatting for unique visual appeal.
- Fine-tune your writing with the word count, grammar, spell-check, and thesaurus tools.

E-mail
- Send to multiple recipients with cc: functions.
- Work on group projects without travel.

Media and Technology Skills • 11

Using a Variety of Technologies

Teaching Resources: Writing Support Transparencies, 1-C; Writing Support Activity Book, 1-3

1. Review the list of electronic tools with students and ask which ones they are familiar with. Discuss how they are currently using technology and ask whether there are any experiences or recommendations they would like to share.

2. Go over the sidebar text and ask students which search engines they have used. Have they developed any preferences? Why?

3. Display the transparency and point out the important areas of a survey or questionnaire (specify desired information, allow room for responses, etc.). Give students a blank copy of the form (1-3) for their own use.

4. Ask students what other questions might be added to a questionnaire about communicating with technology.

5. Have students create their own surveys and question classmates about their uses of technology.

6. Alternatively, you may wish to conduct the survey as a class, filling in spaces by show of hands or with student comments.

Lesson Objectives

1. To write a response to a prompt
2. To organize ideas in writing to ensure coherence, logical progression, and support for ideas
3. To use prewriting strategies to generate ideas, develop voice, and plan
4. To develop drafts by organizing and reorganizing content and by refining style to suit purpose
5. To proofread writing for appropriateness of organization, content, style, and conventions

Step-by-Step Teaching Guide

Responding to Writing Prompts

Teaching Resources: Standardized Test Preparation Workbook, pp. 1–2

1. Tell students that they will be learning how to respond to various types of standardized tests in this text and that this first lesson is about responding in writing.
2. Go over the bulleted items, and if necessary, define the term *writing prompt*.
3. Ask a student to read the sample prompt aloud.
4. Emphasize that about a quarter of one's time should be used for prewriting, and go over the prewriting steps for this prompt.
5. Give students time to read about drafting, revising and proofreading.
6. Assign this writing prompt for completion during a class period. You may want to place a large clock at the front of the class, so they can see the time passing. Alternatively, you could announce the time every fifteen minutes, so they can judge their progress.

Standardized Test Preparation Workshop

Responding to Writing Prompts on Standardized Tests

As shown in this chapter, writing is an integral part of your everyday life. Because writing is one of the most powerful communication tools you will ever use, it is important that you express your ideas clearly. Your ability to communicate through writing is often measured when you respond to a writing prompt on a standardized test. When scorers evaluate your writing, they will look for evidence that you can do the following:

- Respond directly to the prompt.
- Make your writing thoughtful and interesting.
- Organize your ideas so that they are clear and essay to follow.
- Develop your ideas thoroughly by using appropriate details and precise language.
- Stay focused on your purpose for writing by making sure that each sentence you write contributes to your composition as a whole.
- Communicate effectively by using correct spelling, capitalization, punctuation, grammar, usage, and sentence structure.

The process of writing for a test, or any kind of writing, can be divided into stages. Plan to use a specific amount of time for prewriting, drafting, revising, and proofreading.

Following is an example of one type of writing prompt you might find on a standardized test. Use the suggestions on the following page to help you respond. The clocks next to each stage show a suggested plan for organizing your time.

Sample Writing Situation

Writer E. L. Doctorow has said, "Writing is an exploration. You start from nothing and learn as you go."

Write an essay in which you describe an experience in which you began a writing assignment or a piece of personal writing with a blank page and found that you learned a great deal as you explored your topic. Use specific examples from your experience, such as researching or interviewing, to support your thesis.

12 • The Writer in You

Test Tip

Before beginning your prewriting, mentally map out your plan for writing. Then, implement it when you start prewriting.

✏️ TEST-TAKING TIP

Since this is a practice test, tell students that they should not worry about getting everything right this first time. Suggest that students allow a few minutes to think about their writing plan before they set down a timeline or a K-W-L chart.

Explain to students that, because tests are timed, it is important to organize their points during the prewriting stage since there will not be time to go back and reorganize what they want to say.

Reassure students that, though they should try to be as neat as possible, examiners understand that tests will probably contain crossed-out lines and insertions.

Prewriting

Allow close to one fourth of your time for prewriting.

Focus on a Writing Experience Think about the many papers that reside in your past writing portfolios. List as many topics of papers you have written as you can. Then, choose from your list the piece of writing from which you learned the most.

Writing Timeline Place the details of your writing exploration on a timeline. Plot each event in the composition of your piece in sequential order, beginning with how you got the assignment, how you choose your topic, gathered information, what you learned, how you drafted, and how you polished your composition.

Use a K-W-L Chart To help you gather details about what you learned from your writing use a K-W-L Chart. Under *K*, list what you knew about your topic before you began your paper. Then, list details under *W* that explain what you wanted to learn or explore. Under *L*, list what you learned from your writing.

Drafting

Allow almost half of your time for drafting.

Organize details in a logical and coherent manner.

Write an Introduction In your introduction, include the quotation in its exact words as well as your restatement of it. Then, write a brief statement that previews for readers the experience you will use as an example.

Develop Supporting Paragraphs Each of your supporting paragraphs should begin with a topic sentence that supports your main idea statement. The details in the paragraph should support your topic sentence and fully develop one idea.

Conclude Effectively In your concluding paragraph, summarize the points of your essay. Reinforce how this particular writing experience helped you explore a topic and learn more about it.

Revising and Proofreading

Allow almost one fourth of your time for revising and proofreading.

Revise Details and Language Review your draft for details that do not directly support the main idea of your essay, and remove them. Make sure that you use language that is precise and appropriate for a test response. For example, avoid the use of slang or clichés and, instead, use formal, precise language.

Make Corrections When making changes, place a line through text that you want eliminated, and place it in brackets. Use a caret [^] to indicate places where words should be added.

In-Depth Lesson Plan

	LESSON FOCUS	PRINT AND MEDIA RESOURCES
DAY 1	**Introduction to the Writing Process** Students become familiar with the modes of writing and the five stages of the writing process. (pp. 14–15)	**Teaching Resources** *Writing Support Transparencies, 2-A*
DAY 2	**Prewriting** Students learn strategies for choosing and narrowing a topic, considering audience and purpose, and gathering details. (pp. 16–20)	**Teaching Resources** *Writing Support Transparencies, 2-B–G; Writing Support Activity Book, 2-1–3*
DAY 3	**Drafting** Students learn strategies for shaping their writing and providing elaboration. (pp. 21–22)	**Teaching Resources** *Writing Support Transparencies, 2-H–I*
DAY 4	**Revising** Students learn strategies for revising sentences, paragraphs, and overall structure. (pp. 23–25)	**Teaching Resources** *Writing Support Transparencies, 2-J–K*
DAY 5	**Editing and Proofreading; Publishing and Presenting** Students learn strategies for checking their work and presenting their final drafts. (pp. 26–27)	*Writing Lab* **CD-ROM**, Writer's Toolkit **Teaching Resources** *Writing Support Transparencies, 2-L; Formal Assessment, Ch. 2; Writing Lab* CD-ROM, Writer's Toolkit

Accelerated Lesson Plan

	LESSON FOCUS	PRINT AND MEDIA RESOURCES
DAY 1	**Introduction to the Writing Process and Prewriting** Students become familiar with the five steps of the writing process and learn strategies for prewriting. (pp. 14–20)	**Teaching Resources** *Writing Support Transparencies, 2-A–G; Writing Support Activity Book, 2-1–4*
DAY 2	**Drafting to Presenting** Students learn strategies for drafting, revising, editing, and presenting their writing. (pp. 21–27)	**Teaching Resources** *Writing Support Transparencies, 2-H–L; Formal Assessment, Ch. 2*

Options for Adapting Lesson Plans

HOMEWORK
Have students complete any stage of the lesson for homework.

FEATURES
Extend coverage with Spotlight on the Humanities (p. 28), Media and Technology Skills (p. 29), and the Standardized Test Preparation Workshop (p. 30).

TECHNOLOGY
Students can complete any stage of the lesson on computer. Have them print out their completed work.

INTEGRATED SKILLS COVERAGE

Viewing and Representing
Critical Viewing, SE pp. 14, 28
Examining Ideas Represented in Various Cultures, SE p. 28
Integrating Viewing and Representing, ATE pp. 20, 22, 28

Speaking and Listening
ATE p. 25

Technology
ATE p. 29

Real-World Connection
ATE p. 25

Research Skills
SE p. 25

ASSESSMENT SUPPORT

Standardized Test Preparation Workshop, SE p. 30; ATE pp. 25, 30
Standardized Test Preparation Workbook, pp. 3–4
Formal Assessment, Ch. 2
Writing Assessment and Portfolio Management

MEETING INDIVIDUAL NEEDS

Less Advanced Students ATE pp. 16, 17, 18, 31. See also
Ongoing Assessments ATE pp. 18, 24.
AP Students ATE p. 31
ESL Students ATE pp. 22, 23, 24
Gifted and Talented Students ATE p. 21
Logical/Mathematical Learners ATE p. 26

BLOCK SCHEDULING

Pacing Suggestions
For 90-minute Blocks
- Have students complete the Introduction and the Prewriting and Drafting strategies in a single period.
- Focus one class period on Revising, Editing and Proofreading, and Presenting strategies.

Resources for Varying Instruction
- *Writing Lab* CD-ROM If your students have access to hardware, a 90-minute block provides an ideal opportunity for students to work on computer.

Professional Development Support
- *How to Manage Instruction in the Block* This Teaching Resource provides management and activity suggestions.

MEDIA AND TECHNOLOGY

For the Student
- *Writing Lab* CD-ROM, Writer's Toolkit

For the Teacher
- *Resource Pro* CD-ROM

WRITING AND GRAMMAR WEB SITE

The Interactive Writing and Grammar Web Site provides a wide array of support for students, teachers, and parents. Writing support includes:

- Interactive revision checkers
- Scoring rubrics with complete models

www.phschool.com

Lesson Objectives

1. To write in a variety of forms for various audiences and purposes
2. To analyze strategies that writers in different fields use to compose
3. To use prewriting strategies to generate ideas, develop voice, and plan
4. To use writing to formulate questions, refine topics, and clarify ideas
5. To represent information in a variety of ways such as graphics, conceptual maps, and learning logs
6. To develop and revise drafts in terms of structure, paragraphs, sentences, and word choice
7. To edit and proofread to ensure standard English usage and grammar
8. To respond productively to peer review of one's own work
9. To frequently refine selected work for publication

Critical Viewing

Analyze Students might say a thoughtful approach makes for a logical, organized, and detailed final product.

Chapter 2

A Walk Through the Writing Process

Writing can take many forms: It can be a note to a friend, a movie review, an employment application, or a formal college essay. Whatever your final product, the writing process—a systematic approach to writing that includes prewriting, drafting, revising, and editing—can help you write anything better.

▲ **Critical Viewing**
How can a thoughtful approach to the process of writing help improve your final product? **[Analyze]**

Types of Writing

One way to analyze types of writing is by **modes**—the forms that writing takes. The list on this page shows the modes of writing that you'll encounter in this book.

Another way to think about the writing that you do is to analyze its audience and purpose. Some writing is **reflexive;** it is from yourself and for yourself. Poems and journals are often reflexive. Because it is self-sponsored, reflexive writing is more thoughtful and exploratory and allows you to learn as you write. In contrast, some writing is **extensive;** it is for others based on assignments from others. Extensive writing is frequently school-sponsored and includes short stories, research papers, and other class-based writing. When you write extensively, you adopt a more authoritative tone.

The Modes of Writing

Narration
Description
Persuasion
Exposition
Research
Response to Literature
Poems and Plays
Writing for Assessment
Workplace Writing

⏱ TIME AND RESOURCE MANAGER

Resources
Print: *Writing Support Transparencies*, 2-A

In-Depth Coverage	Accelerated Pace
• Cover pp. 14–15 in class. • Ask students to make a list of examples of each of the modes of writing (example: Narration may include short story, anecdote, autobiography, and novel). • Use the graphic on p. 15 to give an overview of the writing process.	• Assign these two pages as independent reading. • Ask students to write in their own words a half-page description of the writing process. • Discuss their descriptions and make sure students understand the purpose of each step in the writing process.

The Process of Writing

These are the stages of the writing process:

- **Prewriting** is freely exploring topics, choosing a topic, and beginning to gather and organize details before you write.
- **Drafting** is getting your ideas down on paper in roughly the format you intend.
- **Revising** is correcting any major errors and improving the writing's form and content.
- **Editing and proofreading** is polishing the writing and fixing errors in grammar, spelling, and mechanics.
- **Publishing and presenting** is sharing your writing.

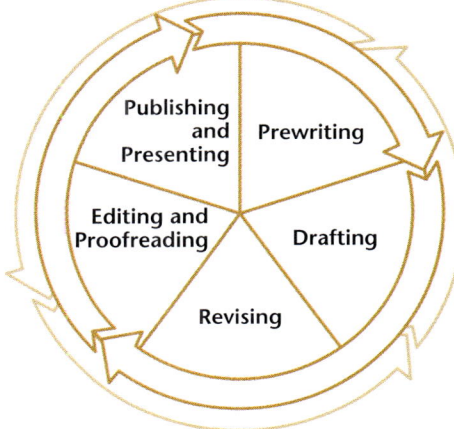

These steps may seem sequential, but writers often jump back to earlier stages as they work. For example, during the drafting stage, you may discover that a topic needs further research, or during revision, you may want to include more of your prewriting work. You may even put down a piece of writing in the prewriting stage, save it in your portfolio, and come back to it several weeks later.

A Guided Tour

Use the information in this chapter to take a guided tour of the writing process. As you read, you'll get to know some of the parts of the process and consider the strategies that effective writers use. Think about how you can apply these techniques when you take a piece of writing from start to finish.

PREPARE and ENGAGE

Interest GRABBER Ask students to predict what the term *writing process* means. What is a *process*? (Students may define *process* as a method of doing something, generally involving many steps.) Do they participate in any other activities that take the form of a process? (Students may suggest such activities as learning to play an instrument, cooking dinner, or preparing for the SAT.) What is the benefit of using a process as opposed to a single step?

Activate Prior Knowledge

Ask students about their own experiences with writing. Have them make a list of the types of writing they have done in the last week. Do they just sit down and write, or do they engage in some type of planning? What types, if any, of revising strategies do they use?

TEACH

Step-by-Step Teaching Guide

The Process of Writing

Teaching Resources: Writing Support Transparencies, 2-A

1. Display Transparency 2-A and make sure students understand each step of the writing process. For example, can they explain the difference between revising and proofreading?

2. Ask students to point to the beginning and end of the process. (Point out that according to the diagram, there is no fixed beginning or end.)

3. Explain that while there is a general order to the process, a writer often revisits many of the steps as he or she writes. For example, a writer might need to return to the list of prewriting ideas after running into difficulties while drafting.

Use one of the following options to diagnose students' current level of proficiency in using the writing process.

Option 1 Write the following terms on the board, and have students explain in writing what they know about each one: Prewriting, Drafting, Revising, Editing and Proofreading, and Publishing and Presenting. Review each student's answers and determine which stages will need the most work.

Option 2 Ask students to make a list of their strengths and weaknesses when it comes to writing. Read over their lists. If you determine that most of their weaknesses can be grouped under a specific step, you will need to devote more time to explaining that step.

1. Be sure students understand the quicklist procedure. You may want to model one on the board with the class. Or, you can show Transparency 2-B as a model.

2. Give students time in class to make their own quicklists. When they finish, have them meet in small groups and discuss some of their topic ideas.

3. Have groups discuss what makes a good writing topic. Tell them to consider characteristics such as whether the topic is broad or narrow, vague or specific, original or overused, and whether or not the writer shows genuine interest in it.

Customize for
Less Advanced Students

Make this activity more structured by giving students a way to focus their quicklists. For example, instead of asking them to simply list people, places, and things, ask them to list people, places, and things related to a specific topic, such as their favorite sport or hobby.

2.1 What Is Prewriting?

When you face a blank page, you may be intimidated by its emptiness. Just as athletes "warm up" before running a marathon, writers use certain techniques to loosen their creative muscles. Many of these mental stretches are performed in the prewriting stage. Each writing chapter will offer you several strategies for getting started.

Choosing Your Topic

You'll find that your writing is usually more successful when you write about a subject that is meaningful to you. Prewriting strategies allow you to consider several ideas before choosing a topic to develop into a full piece of writing. The sample strategies here offer you suggestions for generating writing topics.

SAMPLE STRATEGY

Jotting a Quicklist Fold a piece of paper into three columns. Down the length of the first column, list people, places, and things that come to mind. List for several minutes. When you are finished, unfold the second column. In this column, list descriptive words for each of the people, places, and things in your first column. Finally, open the last third of the paper. Use this column to jot down examples or incidents related to your first two columns. When you are finished, choose one set of the items, descriptions, and examples as a topic.

MAKING A QUICKLIST

Noun	Adjective	Example
Terry	funny	His impressions of famous people
Janet	loyal	She kept in touch after I moved
the track	grueling	Last week's championship meet

Learn More

For additional prewriting strategies suited to specific writing tasks, see chapters 4–16.

⏱ TIME AND RESOURCE MANAGER

Resources
Print: *Writing Support Transparencies,* 2-B–G: *Writing Support Activity Book,* 2-1–3

In-Depth Coverage	Accelerated Pace
• Read and discuss pp. 16–20 in class. • Work through the five sample strategies in class. • Have students complete the Apply the Strategies assignments.	• Have students read pp. 16–20 independently. • Assign students to complete the Apply the Strategies activities for homework.

Narrowing Your Topic

Artists and photographers do more than just reflect what is seen. They focus on a particular aspect to give a unique viewpoint. Similarly, you as a writer will narrow your topic so that you can bring you own unique viewpoint into focus. You will find a topic-narrowing activity in each lesson. Use it to bring your broad topic into focus.

SAMPLE STRATEGY

Applying the Questions of Classical Invention Classical invention is a strategy used by the ancient Greeks to explore a topic. They created categories of questions and found that the answers to those questions helped them understand a subject more fully.

To apply their technique to your writing, take a closer look at your topic and all the specific ideas it may include. Jot down your broad topic at the top of a list. Then, use the questions associated with classical invention to examine the different facets of your topic.

Review your response to each of these questions, looking for links among the details. Draw arrows between connected ideas, and jot down notes that explain the connection you see. Use one of these connections as your narrowed topic.

CLASSICAL INVENTION

TESTIMONY
What do credible sources say about the topic?

CIRCUMSTANCE
What makes it possible?
What makes it impossible?

RELATIONSHIP
What are the causes and effects?
What is its opposite?

COMPARISON
How is the topic similar to or different from connected topics?

DEFINITION
Define and divide it into parts.

Prewriting: Classical Invention

Teaching Resources: Writing Support Transparencies, 2-C; Writing Support Activity Book, 2-1

1. Discuss the method of classical invention with the class. Display Transparency 2-C.

2. On the board, write a list of topics that are too broad. Next to each one, have students think of two or three related topics that are more narrow. You may use the ideas that follow.

   Too broad: *The Revolutionary War, Geography, Movies, Rock-and-Roll, Ernest Hemingway*

   Narrow: *Private Deborah Sampson Gannet of the Continental Army, Careers in Cartography, James Dean: a Filmography, History of the Motown Label: The First Five Years, A Comparison of Two Leading Female Characters in Hemingway's Books.*

3. Have the class choose one of the narrow topics on the board and apply classical invention to it.

Customize for
Less Advanced Students

If students are having difficulty narrowing a broad topic, show them how to use a word web. Write the topic on the board and circle it. Have students offer information or ideas related to it. Then, write this information and these ideas on lines that connect to the circled topic. Explain that these ideas would make more focused writing topics than the original idea at the center of the web.

Prewriting: Considering Your Audience and Purpose

Teaching Resources: Writing Support Transparencies, 2-D; Writing Support Activity Book, 2-2

1. Review page 18 with students and discuss how miscommunication can occur between writers and their audiences. (If the writer chooses language that is too complex or too simple, or examples that readers cannot identify with, then the writer will not connect with his or her audience.)

2. Have students choose a topic and fill in the chart for three different audiences (examples: a group of third-grade students, a town meeting, a group of close friends, their parents). Students should consider the particular characteristics of each audience.

Customize for
Less Advanced Students

To emphasize the importance of using words with a tone and a connotation appropriate for the audience, have students write out instructions for a simple concept such as folding a paper airplane or tying shoelaces. Have them write one version for small children and another for adults. Then, have them examine their work. How do their tone and word choice change? What elements do not change?

2.1

Considering Your Audience and Purpose

To be sure your writing is effective, consider two key elements: your **audience,** or the people you expect to reach; and your **purpose**, the reason you are writing.

Considering Your Audience Before you write, imagine the people you expect will read your work. Think about what your readers know and feel about your topic. Then, try to connect on your audience's level. Include language and details that will appeal to your readers. In the following examples, notice how a specific target audience influences the writer's approach to a topic:

TOPIC: Photography
AUDIENCE: Class of beginners
DETAILS: Define all terms; provide broad introduction

TOPIC: Photography
AUDIENCE: Professional photographers
DETAILS: Assume a basic knowledge of terms; provide information about advanced techniques

Use an audience profile like the one below to analyze your audience. Keep your responses in mind as you draft.

AUDIENCE PROFILE	
What does my audience already know?	
What do they need to know?	
What details will interest or influence my audience?	

Considering Your Purpose Just as a knowledge of your audience will direct the language and details you include, your purpose should factor into the planning of your writing. Following are some common purposes for writing, along with suggestions for achieving these specific goals:

- **Writing to inform:** Include facts and examples that teach your readers. Write objectively; avoid including your opinion.

- **Writing to persuade:** Include reasons and arguments to convince readers to adopt your position.

- **Writing to entertain:** Include humorous situations, anecdotes, or exaggerations that your audience will enjoy.

 Writing Support Transparencies
Use the transparencies for Chapter 2 to facilitate the teaching of strategies.

📖 **Writing Support Activity Book**
Use the graphic organizers for Chapter 2 to facilitate student writing activities.

✓ **ONGOING ASSESSMENT: Monitor and Reinforce**

If you observe that students are having difficulty considering their audience, try one of the following options.

| **Option 1** Students frequently feel they need to write for their teacher. Instead, have them choose a different person on which to focus their writing. | **Option 2** If possible, have students speak with an actual member of their intended audience. This way, they can determine what the audience knows about the topic. |

Gathering Details

Before an artist paints a picture, he or she might sketch the scene to identify the details to be included. As a writer, spend time gathering details that you will use in your work. Once you begin drafting, you can draw upon as many or as few of the details as you need when you write, but the time you spend gathering them gives you the opportunity to make that decision. Each writing chapter offers a strategy for gathering details for specific modes of writing.

SAMPLE STRATEGY

Using the Reporter's Formula

Whether you are writing fiction or non-fiction, include enough details to make your subject clear. For example, if you are writing a short story, gather information about characters, setting, and plot events. If you are writing a factual report, gather clear, detailed information about your subject. Take a tip from professional journalists: Use the Reporter's Formula to gather details about different aspects of your topic. To do this, address the 5 W's: *who, what, when, where,* and *why*.

Reporter's Formula

Who	are the people involved or affected?
What	were the specific reasons it happened? What evidence is there to support this conclusion?
When	did the events take place or the situation develop? When did it start, and when did it end?
Where	did the events take place? Where was the impact greatest?
Why	did it happen?

SAMPLE STRATEGY

Completing a Hexagonal When writing about literature, use a hexagonal like the one shown here to gather details about different aspects of the literature. Using this organizer will help you write a thoughtful, thorough analysis rather than a superficial summary.

For each segment of the hexagonal, follow the directions in the chart. When possible, include references to the work to support your ideas.

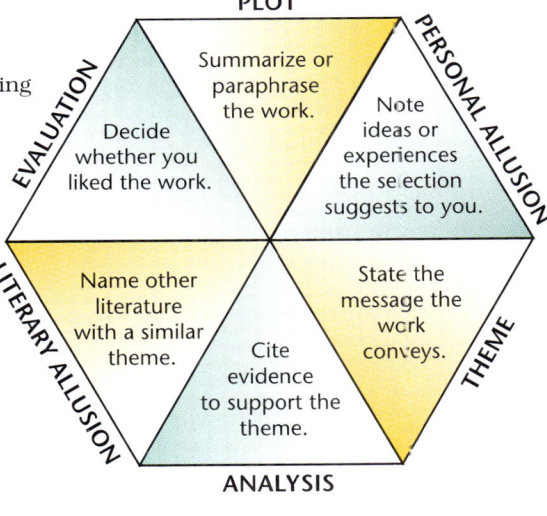

PLOT — Summarize or paraphrase the work.
PERSONAL ALLUSION — Note ideas or experiences the selection suggests to you.
EVALUATION — Decide whether you liked the work.
THEME — State the message the work conveys.
LITERARY ALLUSION — Name other literature with a similar theme.
ANALYSIS — Cite evidence to support the theme.

Step-by-Step Teaching Guide

Prewriting: The Reporter's Formula

Teaching Resources: Writing Support Transparencies, 2-E

1. Read aloud, or have a prepared student read aloud, the explanation of the reporter's formula. Display Transparency 2-E.

2. Divide students into pairs and have each pair choose a topic. They should then write on six separate slips of paper the answers to *who, what, when, where, why,* and *how* about the topic.

3. Have the pairs evaluate their answers and decide whether their topic is feasible (for example, do they know enough about it, or is it narrow enough). If not, have them alter it and then answer the six questions once again.

4. Show students some effective lead paragraphs from stories in your local newspaper.

5. Using those paragraphs as models, have students write lead paragraphs for their own topics. When they finish, have them share their work with the class.

Step-by-Step Teaching Guide

Prewriting: Use a Hexagonal

Teaching Resources: Writing Support Transparencies, 2-F; Writing Support Activity Book, 2-3

1. Brainstorm with the class for a list of some of the selections you have read so far this year. Divide students into groups based on which selection they'd like to focus on.

2. Distribute copies of the hexagonal (2-3) and encourage students to use this organizer whenever they write about literature.

Prewriting: Making an Outline

Teaching Resources: Writing Support Transparencies, 2-G

1. Discuss with students how making an outline helps the writer organize his or her thoughts, write clearly, and get the message across to the reader.

2. Have one or two volunteers share topic ideas and work with the class to make an outline for each.

3. Give students a short piece of nonfiction writing such as a magazine article or a short chapter from a history textbook. Ask students to make an outline for this selection.

4. Show students how to make note cards and how to number or label them to match the sections of their outlines. Explain that the purpose of the note cards is to expand upon each section of the outline by adding details, examples, and explanations.

Integrating Viewing and Representing Skills

Show the class alternatives to traditional outlines. Some students might feel more comfortable with other graphic organizers such as cluster maps, webs, or funnel charts. Remind them that whichever graphic they choose, the goal is to create a clear and sensible way to organize their information.

2.1

SAMPLE STRATEGY

Making a Outline To identify the details that you need to include in an essay that informs, persuades, or analyzes, build an outline that organizes your prewriting work. Sketch out the main ideas you'll want to address, and then jot down several facts or details to support these ideas. Look at this example:

OUTLINE FORM
Topic: Planning a surprise party

1. Practical Information
   -number of guests
   -location
   -food/entertainment
2. Theme and decorations based on purpose of party
   -birthdays: tropical, western, costume party
   -showers: wedding, baby, new house
3. Inventing a surprise
   -get others involved
   -don't tell the guest of honor too early

▶ **APPLYING THE PREWRITING STRATEGIES**

1. Make a quicklist. Identify the topic you would choose based on this exercise.
2. Choose a topic such as loyalty or courage. Use classical invention to narrow your topic to one with a specific focus.
3. Create two different audience profiles for an essay you might write about learning to drive. Identify two unique audiences.
4. For each purpose listed below, identify three details you might include in a paper about student government:
   a. to reflect on your own experiences
   b. to inform
   c. to argue for change
5. Use the reporter's formula to gather details about a current event.
6. Complete a hexagonal for a short story you have recently read.
7. Make an outline to identify details you would include in a pamphlet about weekend vacations.

🟢 Learn More

To see an example of a more formal outline, see Chapter 13.

2.2 *What Is Drafting?*

Shaping Your Writing

Focus on the Form Each form of writing has a specific set of goals or purposes—persuasion convinces, exposition explains, and narrative tells a story. Whatever your final product, keep the focus of your specific form in mind as you draft.

Grab Your Readers' Interest With a Powerful Lead Choose a powerful or intriguing opening statement or question to grab your readers' interest from the very start. This "lead" will introduce your writing style to your readers and set the tone for the rest of your writing.

WRITING MODELS

The great Pullman was whirling onward with such dignity of motion that a glance from the window seemed simply to prove that the plains of Texas were pouring eastward.

—Stephen Crane, "The Bride Comes to Yellow Sky"

> The writer captures the readers' interest by leading with the excitement of a physically risky situation.

It's embarrassing but true: I'm a disposable camera junkie.

—Anita Hamilton, "Flawed Gems"

> An unexplained situation sparks the readers' curiosity.

The phone receiver settled down, cradled uncomfortably in its holder. "Nanie will be here on December 18 at 5:00," my mother announced curtly.

—Denise Palazzo, "Anticipated Arrival"

> The writer starts off with an intriguing statement that makes the readers curious.

The ghost that got into our house on the night of November 17, 1915, raised such a hullaballo of misunderstanding that I am sorry I didn't just let it keep on walking, and go to bed.

—James Thurber, "The Night the Bed Fell"

> Thurber's language and attitude set the stage for comedy.

Have you ever considered asking your doctor about getting a second opinion, then decided not to risk it?

—Christine Gorman, "Second Opinions"

> A question personalizes a subject for readers.

What Is Drafting? • 21

Step-by-Step Teaching Guide

Drafting: Shaping Your Writing

Teaching Resources: Writing Support Transparencies, 2-H

1. Have students read the sample leads and discuss the annotations in the margin. You might use questions such as these to prompt discussion:

   Which lead do students find most enticing?

   What in particular is effective about each one?

2. Have students look in their portfolios for examples of strong lead sentences. Have some volunteers share their leads. Let the class try to predict what the rest of each selection would be about based on the information provided in the lead.

3. Challenge students to rewrite the lead sentence for one of the selections in their portfolios. Have them exchange papers with partners and discuss whether their revised leads are intriguing and clear.

Customize for *Gifted and Talented Students*

Ask students to write two or three engaging leads for stories or articles on any topic, fiction or nonfiction. Each lead should be written on a card. Collect all the cards and shuffle them. Have each student draw a card from the stack and compose an outline for a story based on that lead. If possible, have students write the stories and share them with the student who wrote the lead.

⏱ TIME AND RESOURCE MANAGER

Resources
Print: *Writing Support Transparencies,* 2-H–I

In-Depth Coverage	Accelerated Pace
• Cover pp. 21–22 in class. • Using the board or an overhead projector, demonstrate the SEE method. • Assign the Apply the Strategy activities to be completed in class.	• Assign students to read pp. 21–22 independently. • Assign Apply the Strategy activities. Have students discuss their answers in class.

Step-by-Step Teaching Guide

Drafting: Use the SEE Method

Teaching Resources: Writing Support Transparencies, 2-I

1. Display Transparency 2-I to demonstrate the SEE strategy: make a statement, extend the statement, then elaborate with additional details.

2. Explain to students the difference between elaborating and simply digressing. When they elaborate, they should do so on a key word or idea. They should not add details and sentences about a part of the essay that is of secondary importance.

Integrating Viewing and Representing Skills

Ask students to find examples of magazines and newspaper articles that use photographs and illustrations effectively. Discuss the ways in which the pictures add depth and dimension to the writing.

Customize for
ESL Students

Since elaborating often requires that a student take a broad concept and explore it in detail, it can require precise or customized language. When elaborating, encourage students to write in their native language the specialized words they don't know in English. They can go back later and translate the words.

Providing Elaboration

The difference between writing with elaboration and writing without elaboration is like the difference between watching an old black-and-white film and watching a 3-D movie. As you add details to your draft, your writing will become vivid and textured for your readers. Elaboration can help you explain complex ideas, provide support for a persuasive position, or set a rich stage for a narration. Try the SEE method to add dimension and depth to your writing.

SAMPLE STRATEGY

Use the SEE Method

The SEE method of Statement, Extension, and Elaboration allows you to shed light on a subject by providing a more complete analysis or description. First, start with a statement, or main idea. Then, write an extension by restating or explaining the first sentence. Elaborate further by providing even more detail about the main idea. Look at this example:

STATEMENT: Rosalie and Joe are truly world travelers.

EXTENSION: They have visited cities on six continents.

ELABORATION: From hiking in the Andes and then visiting the museums of Paris to traveling through the jungles of Africa and then enjoying the lights of Broadway, this couple has taken more trips than you can imagine.

Statement   Extension   Elaboration

▶ **APPLYING THE DRAFTING STRATEGIES**

1. Write an exciting or interest-grabbing lead for an account of an event at your school.

2. Complete each of the sentences below. Then, use the depth-charging technique to elaborate on each one.
   a. If I had an extra hour every day, I would ___?___.
   b. Something I'm really happy about is ___?___.

2.3 What Is Revising?

Color-Coding Clues for Revision

When you see writing as a process, you give the revision stage the attention it deserves. Review your writing by asking focused questions. The word **ratiocination** (rash´ ē äs ə nā´ shən) means "to think logically." Color-coding your draft with a system of color-coded clues, will help you logically identify specific issues in your writing. Look at these sample revision strategies suited to color-coding:

- circling "to be" verbs
- bracketing sentence beginnings
- underlining vague words

Once you have isolated these elements, you can make decisions about revising your writing. As you work through the revision sections of the chapters 4–17, you will find strategies to revising structure, paragraphs, sentences, and word choice.

Revising Your Overall Structure

Like the beams and supports that provide the structure for a house, the organization of your writing provides its framework. If the structure is sound or logical, the rest will stand strong. As you revise, you may decide to strengthen the structure of your writing by reordering or adding paragraphs.

SAMPLE STRATEGY

▶ **REVISION STRATEGY**
Cut and Paste

Whether or not you are working on a word processor, you can use the cut-and-paste technique to evaluate the organization of your draft. By experimenting with different paragraph organizations, you may discover a better order for your ideas. You may realize you have missed a key point, or you may choose to eliminate an entire paragraph. Follow these steps:

For electronic editing: Make a copy of your file by using the Save As feature of your word-processing program. Insert double returns between paragraphs, and then cut, copy, and paste until you find the best presentation for your ideas.

For manual editing: Make a photocopy of your essay. Cut paragraphs out of the photocopied draft and rearrange them to discover which sequence is most effective.

Writers in **ACTION**

F. Scott Fitzgerald once said about writing and revising, "To have something to say is a question of sleepless nights and worry and endless ratiocination of a subject—of endlessly trying to dig out the endless truth, the essential justice. . . .

Revising: Color-Coding Clues for Revision

1. Remind students that each time they revise a piece of writing, they should read through the piece several times, looking for ways to employ one or two of these strategies on each reading.

2. Ask students to suggest other revision strategies they know, and add them to the list (rewording to remove excessive prepositional phrases, replacing passive verbs with active verbs, substituting exact and concrete nouns and verbs for adjectives and adverbs, including transitions to guide the reader).

More About the Writer

F. Scott Fitzgerald was regarded in his lifetime as a chronicler of the excesses of the 1920's. It was not until after his death that the complex moral world of his novels *The Great Gatsby, Tender is the Night,* and *The Last Tycoon* was fully appreciated.

Revising: Cut and Paste

1. Discuss the cut and paste strategy in class. Remind students that rearranging paragraphs sometimes requires adding new paragraphs or eliminating existing ones.

2. Ask students to look in their portfolios for a piece of writing on which to apply the cut and paste strategy.

3. If students rearrange paragraphs, remind them to check that the transitions are still clear. Have students brainstorm for a list of transitional words and phrases.

Customize for
ESL Students

When revising, students might notice certain words they've overused. If so, have them consult the thesaurus and other students for appropriate substitutions. Encourage them to make word webs in their notebooks to help them remember words with similar meanings.

⏱ **TIME AND RESOURCE MANAGER**	
Resources **Print:** *Writing Support Transparencies,* 2-J–K	
In-Depth Coverage	**Accelerated Pace**
• Using the board or an overhead projector, demonstrate the color-coding procedures used throughout this chapter. • In class, work through each of the three sample strategies using the transparencies or the examples in the student text.	• Assign students to independently read pp. 23–27 and complete the Apply the Strategy activities on their own or with partners. • Discuss students' results on these activities and respond to individual needs.

Step-by-Step Teaching Guide

Revising: Color-Coding Clues to Evaluate Coherence

Teaching Resources: Writing Support Transparencies, 2-J

1. Explain to students that in the next chapter, they will learn specific ways to improve topic sentences and paragraph structure. For now, they are to make sure paragraphs contain no extraneous elements.

2. Explain to students the importance of a clear topic and effective support. On the overhead projector, use the color-coding activity to evaluate with the class the coherence of a paragraph in a local newspaper.

3. Have students use the color-coding strategy on paragraphs from their own portfolios. After they complete the strategy and revise their paragraphs, have them exchange papers with a partner to make sure they have deleted all extraneous details.

Step-by-Step Teaching Guide

Revising: Track Sentence Lengths

1. Review with students the definition of a simple sentence.

2. Work through a few examples in class to model how to vary sentence lengths.

3. Show students how to combine sentences by using dependent clauses or by beginning sentences with prepositional or other phrases.

4. Discuss how to combine sentences by joining them to make compound or compound-complex sentences to avoid choppy, rapid-fire text.

Customize for
ESL Students

Students will benefit from reading their work aloud to determine whether it has an interesting, varying rhythm. Have them work with more-fluent English speakers to answer any pronunciation questions, including sounds, accented syllables, and other issues that affect the rhythm of a sentence.

Revising Your Paragraphs

After reviewing the structure of your writing, take a closer look at the paragraphs that elaborate your ideas. Each paragraph in your writing should present a specific idea.

SAMPLE STRATEGY

▶ **REVISION STRATEGY**
Color-Coding Clues to Evaluate Coherence

For each topical paragraph in a draft, highlight the topic sentence in yellow. Underline in blue the sentences that restate the idea. Underline in red the sentences that support or illustrate the statement. Then, review your work. Decide whether sentences that are not underlined can be revised to create a stronger connection to the topic sentence or whether they should be eliminated. In the example shown here, the writer deleted a sentence that strayed from the paragraph's main idea.

Revising Your Sentences

Sometimes, perception is everything. When writing is presented in short sentences, ideas seem choppy. In contrast, readers may judge writing that includes long, complex sentences to be equally convoluted. Strive to mix short sentences with longer ones.

SAMPLE STRATEGY

▶ **REVISION STRATEGY**
Tracking Sentence Lengths

To evaluate the variety of sentence lengths in your writing, note the number of words in a representative paragraph. Count the words in each sentence and note the number in the side margin. Use these tips for revision:

Evaluate
- Do you notice a pattern of short or long sentences?

Revise
- Break a sequence of short sentences by combining a few. To make a series of long sentences less weighty, introduce a short sentence.

24 • A Walk Through the Writing Process

⟲ Learn More

To see more strategies for revision, see the writing chapters in this textbook.

EVALUATING COHERENCE

The Thanksgiving Day parade was exciting. We arrived at 6 A.M. to get good spots along the parade route. We found a terrific location near the bleachers. Standing in the cold, we passed the time by meeting other spectators who had come to see the parade. Finally, the parade began to march past us. Bands blared, cymbals crashed, and dancers twirled batons high in the air. We cheered for almost two hours. When it was all over, the street was covered with confetti, and we were thrilled to have been part of the experience.

✓ **ONGOING ASSESSMENT: Prerequisite Skills**

If students have trouble recognizing simple sentences, you may find it helpful to refer them to the following materials to assure coverage of prerequisite knowledge.

In the Textbook	Print Resources	Technology
Complete Subjects and Predicates, pp. 406–412	*Grammar Exercise Workbook,* pp. 23–24	*On-Line Exercise Bank,* Section 18.1

Revising Your Word Choice

Choosing the most precise and powerful words will make your writing clean and direct. As you revise each piece of writing you do, check to see whether each word is the best one for your purpose. In the writing chapters, you will learn specific strategies for revising word choice.

SAMPLE STRATEGY

▶ REVISION STRATEGY
Color-Coding to Strengthen the Use of Nouns

When you use a noun, use the most precise noun, rather than trying to describe a vague noun with a string of adjectives. To evaluate your use of nouns, go through a draft, circling adjectives in blue and underlining the nouns they modify in red. Then, determine whether replacing the noun is in order.

Vague Noun Supported by Adjectives	Precise Noun
mixed breed dog	mutt
lazy person	loafer

Peer Revision

Even professional writers ask for the opinions of others as they revise a work. Each writing lesson offers specific suggestions for having a peer or several peers review your work.

Provide a Specific Task Focus your peer reviewers' comments to get the most specific feedback possible. Look at these suggested discussion starters:

Focusing the Peer Review	
Purpose	**Ask**
Evaluate an introduction	What is memorable about the opening paragraph?
Analyze word choice	Which words are most descriptive?

▶ APPLYING THE REVISION STRATEGIES

Apply each of the revision strategies to the first draft of an essay you've recently written. After you've revised, point out to a partner the techniques that worked well for you.

🔲 Research Tip

Get in the habit of consulting a thesaurus to find the precise words to strengthen your writing.

Revising: Color-Coding to Strengthen the Use of Nouns

1. Read the page aloud in class or have a student read it. Discuss why using a precise noun is usually a better idea than adding a string of adjectives to an unclear noun (the writing can become very wordy and hard to follow).

2. On the board, write a list of vague nouns. Challenge students to offer at least two or three more precise choices for each.

3. Encourage students to choose a selection from their portfolios and revise at least two vague nouns.

Revising: Peer Revision

Teaching Resources: Writing Support Transparencies, 2-K

1. Have students choose a selection from their portfolios and make a list of five specific questions to ask a peer reviewer.

2. Have students trade papers and question lists. When they finish reading the papers and answering the questions, have them return the papers to their owners.

Integrating Speaking and Listening Skills

Students will need to see modeled peer conferences so they know how to word their suggestions for revisions. Role-play a peer revision conference with another teacher or with a student familiar with editorial group procedures.

Real-World Connection

In publishing companies, editors help to revise manuscripts submitted by writers. At times, editors compile revision strategies to assist writers during the revision process. Challenge students to compile five revision strategies they think editors would use when editing either children's picture books or high school biology texts.

✏ STANDARDIZED TEST PREPARATION WORKSHOP

The Four Structures of Sentences
Standardized tests may require students to identify the structure of a sentence.

Read the following sentences.

A We worked all day at the car wash.

B I washed the cars, and she rinsed them.

C When it rains, we postpone the car wash for a week.

D After the car wash, we were exhausted, but we decided to stay and clean up.

Which sentence above is a compound sentence?

A   C

B   D

Students should recognize that **B** is a compound sentence because it consists of two independent clauses joined by a comma and a coordinating conjunction. Sentence A is simple, C is complex, and D is compound-complex.

Editing and Proofreading

Teaching Resources: Writing Support Transparencies, 2-L

1. Review with students various options for dealing with spelling errors. (Examples: ask someone, look in a book, use a dictionary.)

2. Ask pairs of students to write down some tips for proofreading (examples: read for a different type of error on each reading, have each member of the editorial group specialize in a particular type of error, use checklists of frequent errors either from the grammar chapters or compiled by the editorial group).

Customize for
Logical/Mathematical Learners

Ask students to find in the library three or four books published in the last few years. Invariably they will have been published using word processors. Then ask students to find several books published before 1980. Ask them to work out a chart to compare numbers of errors found in the recent, computer-age books vs. the pre-computer books. They can classify the errors as spelling errors, typographical errors, punctuation errors, capitalization errors, and so on. Discuss any patterns they see and why they might occur.

2.4 What Are Editing and Proofreading?

Whether you are writing a note to a friend or a research paper, you want to convey your ideas clearly to your readers. Mistakes in spelling, grammar, usage, or mechanics can distract from this goal. Once you are satisfied with the content of your writing, proofread to make your final draft error-free.

Focusing on Proofreading

To help you develop good proofreading skills, each writing chapter offers a specific focus. Look at your draft with this suggested topic in mind. However, always review your work to correct all errors you see. These are the broad categories for proofreading:

Take a Close Look at Your Spelling Use a dictionary to check the spelling of any word about which you are in doubt. If a dictionary is not available, consider replacing the word in question with a word you know is spelled correctly.

Follow the Conventions of Grammar Look for common grammar errors in your writing. For example, check subject-verb agreement, look to see that each sentence expresses a complete thought, and confirm that you have used pronouns correctly.

Check the Facts If your writing includes details you have incorporated from outside sources, be sure you have included the information correctly. Use the checklist at the right to focus your fact-checking work.

Confirm Legibility If you have written your final draft by hand, make sure that each word is legible. When making corrections or insertions, do so neatly.

▶ **APPLYING THE EDITING AND PROOFREADING STRATEGIES**

1. Using a draft of a paper you've recently written, use the proofreading suggestions on this page.
2. Jot down two errors you frequently make in your writing. With a partner, discuss strategies you could use to recognize these errors during the proofreading stage.

Accuracy Checklist

✓ Names
✓ Dates and titles
✓ Statistics
✓ Exact wording of quotations
✓ Ideas that are not your own

Learn More

For extensive coverage of grammar, usage, and mechanics conventions, see Part 2.

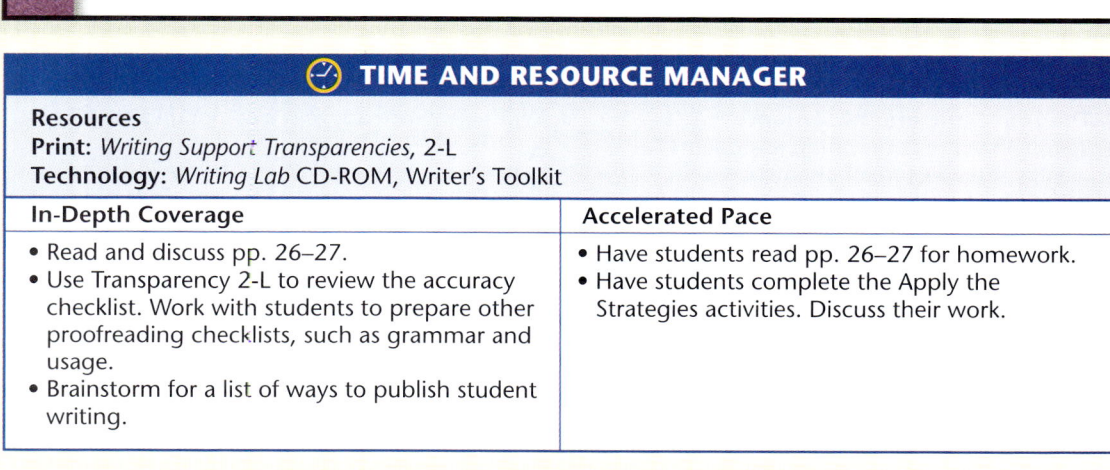

⏱ TIME AND RESOURCE MANAGER

Resources
Print: *Writing Support Transparencies*, 2-L
Technology: *Writing Lab* CD-ROM, Writer's Toolkit

In-Depth Coverage	Accelerated Pace
• Read and discuss pp. 26–27. • Use Transparency 2-L to review the accuracy checklist. Work with students to prepare other proofreading checklists, such as grammar and usage. • Brainstorm for a list of ways to publish student writing.	• Have students read pp. 26–27 for homework. • Have students complete the Apply the Strategies activities. Discuss their work.

2.5 What Are Publishing and Presenting?

Moving Forward

This walk through the writing process gives you an overview of the strategies and techniques that are available to you as part of the writing process. Each of the chapters in the writing section will teach you strategies suited to specific forms of writing.

Building Your Portfolio To track your own progress, keep your finished writing products in a folder, box, or other organized container. In addition to providing a record of your writing growth, your portfolio can also serve as a place where you keep unfinished writing, thought-provoking ideas, clippings, or photographs that may inspire future writing projects.

PORTFOLIO

Reflecting on Your Writing Each piece of writing you complete will teach you something about yourself, your topic, and your own unique writing process. Questions at the end of each chapter will prompt you to reflect on your writing by considering what you have learned and how you have learned it.

Assessing Your Writing At the end of each chapter, you will find a rubric, or set of criteria, on which you can evaluate your own work. Refer to the rubric throughout the writing process to make sure you are addressing the main points of the specific mode. Then, use the rubric to assess your final draft.

▶ APPLYING THE PUBLISHING AND PRESENTING STRATEGIES

1. Choose one of the prewriting activities you developed during this introductory walk-through. Put it in your portfolio to build into a fully developed piece of writing at a later time. Discuss with a partner why you chose the activity you did.
2. To begin reflecting on your writing process, jot down your response to one of these questions. Add your reflection to your portfolio:

   • Which of the strategies or activities did you find most useful or usable? Explain.

   • What are your strengths as a writer?

What Are Publishing and Presenting? • **27**

Publishing and Presenting

1. Read aloud to the class, or have prepared students read aloud, the first four paragraphs on page 27.
2. Ask students to brainstorm for a list of things they might learn by reflecting on their writing over a period of a month or an entire school year. Why is reflecting an important part of the writing process? Do students participate in any other activities in which reflecting is an important part?
3. Give students time to complete Activity 1 on this page. If they have ideas about how they might develop the piece, make sure they write them down and place these notes in their portfolio.

ASSESS and CLOSE

Assessment

Teaching Resources: Formal Assessment, Ch. 2

1. Have students answer the questions in Activity 2 in Apply the Strategies on this page.
2. Discuss their answers. Which strategies did they find most useful, and why? Do students have any additional strategies they'd like to suggest?
3. You may wish to assign one of the assessment options in the Ongoing Assessment chart on this page. You may also consider the following:

   • review the Standardized Test Preparation Workshop on pages 30–31, and have students respond to the writing prompt within a set time limit.

   • administer the Chapter 2 assessment from *Formal Assessment* in the Teaching Resources to measure students' grasp of the concepts presented.

✓ ONGOING ASSESSMENT: Assess Mastery

Use one of the following options to assess students' understanding of the writing process.

| **Option 1** Ask students to describe in their own words each step in the writing process and explain why each one is important. Also, have them name the most important writing tip or strategy they learned in this chapter. | **Option 2** Have students choose one of the steps in the writing process and make a list of three to five helpful strategies for this step. Combine some of the best strategies into a class reference booklet for the writing process. |

Step-by-Step Teaching Guide

Examining Ideas Represented in Various Cultures

1. Review page 28 with the class. If possible, make copies of the myth of Orpheus and have the class read and discuss that, too.

2. If you wish to continue to focus on this myth, you might assign some students to listen to parts of Gluck's opera *Orpheus and Eurydice* or to find fine art depicting Orpheus. In addition, Jean Cocteau made two films based on the myth.

3. Alternately, have students explore bossa nova music. They might be interested to know that bossa nova comes from the Portuguese *bossa* meaning "trend" and *nova* meaning "new."

4. If you want students to research other myths, have the class brainstorm for a list of myths and mythological characters. Students can choose a research topic from this list.

Viewing and Representing

Activity Before students work on updating their myths, you might want to show them a short clip of a film version that has updated or modernized an older work of literature, such as director Baz Luhrmann's *William Shakespeare's Romeo + Juliet*, which takes place in Florida in the present day.

Spotlight on the Humanities

Examining Ideas Represented in Various Cultures

Focus on Myth: *Orpheus*

Just as writers use a specific set of processes to move from inspiration to final draft, artists and filmmakers use similar techniques when they plan, create, and polish their art. The legendary character of Orpheus, featured in both Greek and Roman mythology, has inspired many retellings through the ages. In the original story, Orpheus was a musician with incredible talent. When his wife Eurydice died, he traveled to the underworld to save her. Through his musical gifts, he was able to regain his wife, but he lost her again when he disobeyed Hades and Persephone, the rulers of the underworld.

Orpheus and Eurydice ©1659, Nicolas Poussin

Film Connection In 1958, French film director Marcel Camus produced *Black Orpheus*. In Camus's film, Orpheus plays his music in the streets of Rio de Janiero, Brazil. Winner of the 1959 Cannes Film Festival Grand Prize and the Academy Award for Best Foreign Film, the film used a vibrant Latin setting and bossa nova music to re-create this mythological legend in a modern setting.

Music Connection *Black Orpheus* featured a new type of music that became known as Brazilian bossa nova. This style, first introduced by Antonio Carlos Jobim, integrated harmony, melody, and rhythm and de-emphasized vocals. Throughout the 1960's, bossa nova's popularity grew in the United States and soon moved into Europe. One of the most popular songs in this genre was "The Girl from Ipanema," released in 1963.

Writing Process Activity: Generating Topic Ideas

Camus was inspired by the Greek myth of Orpheus when he wrote his film version. With a partner, jot down several myths, fairy tales, or folk tales you know. For each, list a few ideas for updating the story and presenting it on the silver screen. As a group, present your ideas to the class. Add this prewriting work to your portfolio; it may inspire a full writing project later in the year.

28 • A Walk Through the Writing Process

▲ Critical Viewing
Which figure in this painting represents Orpheus? How do you know?
[Connect]

Critical Viewing

Connect Since they know Orpheus was a musician, students may identify the figure holding the lyre as Orpheus.

Media and Technology Skills

Lesson Objectives
1. Use technology for aspects of creating, revising, editing, and publishing texts
2. To compile information in systematic ways using available technology

Using Technology for Writing

Activity: Building an Electronic Portfolio

You can jump-start the writing process by organizing your files logically on the computer. If you learn to structure a portfolio and manipulate files within it, you can keep your work available to you for ready reference or revision.

Learn About It To build an electronic portfolio, start with the largest categories—consider school subjects or each unique writing project you undertake. Use the New Folder function of your system's software to create folders for each category. Then, break down each into smaller categories and again into smaller subcategories, creating folders as you go. The graphic below suggests a format that allows you to keep copies of your draft through each stage of the writing process.

Name	Date Modified
▽ 📁 09/15 --camping essay	Sep 15
📄 a-prewriting notes	Sep 5
📄 b-first draft	Sep 8
📄 c-revision	Sep 9
📄 d-final draft	Sep 14
📄 e-reflection	Sep 15
▷ 📁 10/11--college search letter	Oct 11
▷ 📁 12/02--comparing candidates	Dec 2

Techniques for Organizing Files
- Create subfolders when several files relate to one topic.
- Store assignments by writing process stage—notes, draft, revision, reflection.
- If several people use one hard drive, assign folders to each computer user.

Techniques for Accessing and Moving Files
- Copy files from a hard-drive folder to a floppy disk or zip drive by dragging the file icon to the drive icon.
- Use the Find function in your system's software to locate a file by name.

Practice It Choose a recent school assignment or other document you've created. Think about how you would store it in a traditional file folder or school binder. Then, with a partner, discuss the pros and cons of having the draft in an electronic version.

Apply It Use the suggested organizing process for several new documents, or analyze the way your existing electronic documents are stored. After a few weeks, reflect on your electronic portfolio by deciding which features are essential and whether the system helps you structure your writing process.

Step-by-Step Teaching Guide

Using Technology for Writing

Teaching Resources: Writing Support Transparencies, 2-M

1. Read this page and discuss the benefits of maintaining an electronic portfolio. Review the techniques in the sidebar for organizing, accessing, and moving files.
2. Ask students to mention any particular techniques they use to organize files.
3. If possible, bring students to the computer lab and have them set up portfolios to use for the year.
4. If students encounter difficulties, ask them to explain their problems in class so that you or other class members can help to solve them.

Integrating Technology Skills

Remind students to keep hard copies of all important documents. This way, they will have insurance against possible computer glitches.

Lesson Objectives

1. To write a speech appropriate to audience and purpose
2. To organize ideas in writing to ensure coherence, logical progression, and support for ideas
3. To present and advance a clear thesis and logical points, claims, or arguments to support messages
4. Use appropriate appeals to support claims and arguments

Step-by-Step Teaching Guide

Responding to Test Prompts

Teaching Resources: Standardized Test Preparation Workbook, pp. 3–4

1. Students might not be accustomed to using prewriting strategies when taking standardized tests. They might be hesitant to take time away from drafting. Explain that their drafts will be much more thorough and clear if they take the time to organize their thoughts before beginning to write.

2. Have students read the sample writing prompt, and ask them to restate the question in their own words.

3. Be sure that students focus on their audience, the town council, which will affect the tone of their speech.

4. Remind students to state their position clearly in their opening sentence. They can think of this as a topic sentence; it should introduce the main idea of the speech.

Standardized Test Preparation Workshop

Using the Writing Process to Respond to Test Prompts

Using the writing process helps writers create interesting, well-organized, and coherent works. When responding to a test prompt for a standardized test, use the writing process to construct an effective response. You will be evaluated on your ability to do the following:

- Choose a logical, consistent organization.
- Elaborate with the appropriate amount of detail for your specific audience and purpose.
- Use appropriate transitions to present ideas coherently.
- Use complete sentences, and follow the rules of grammar.
- Use correct spelling and grammar.

Plan to use a specific amount of time for prewriting, drafting, revising, and proofreading.

Following is an example of one type of writing prompt that you might find on a standardized test. Use the suggestions on the following page to help you respond. The clocks next to each stage show a suggested plan for organizing your time.

Sample Writing Situation

Your town is voting on whether a proposition to develop vacant land by building affordable new homes would help the community grow and increase home values. Those who oppose this proposition want to preserve the land and wildlife by making it a park. Choose a position, and prepare a speech to be presented to the town council. Support your argument with convincing reasons.

Test Tips

- When writing for a test, focus on prewriting or preparing to write. Once you complete the groundwork, you will be able to draft your response quickly and correctly .
- Keep word choice in mind as you write. You won't be able to make major revisions, so try to avoid repeating the same word too often.

TEST-TAKING TIP

The tone of a speech is conveyed in part by word choice. Students should consider which words are appropriate for a certain audience. Remind students that slang is inappropriate in a formal written speech.

Explain that a persuasive speech should be sensitive to those listeners who hold opposing views. Rather than ignoring these views, the speaker should acknowledge them and then use evidence to soundly refute them.

Prewriting

Allow about one quarter of your time for prewriting.

Pro-and-Con Chart After choosing your position on the town land, gather details using a pro-and-con chart. On the Pro side, list details that support your position; and on the Con side, list all the details against your position. While you may be tempted to ignore the negative aspects of your position, your writing will be stronger if you address and refute them.

Consider Your Audience and Purpose As you gather details for your response, remember the audience indicated in the prompt. Since you will be addressing members of the town council, you should use formal and polite language. Because your purpose is to persuade your audience, gather details and information that will appeal to their interests and concerns.

Drafting

Allow almost half of your time for drafting.

Using your prewriting work, draft your response. The following tips will help you:

Write a Powerful Lead Your purpose is to convince your audience to adopt your position on a critical issue; you need to grab their attention from the very beginning. Choose a powerful or intriguing opening statement, question, or prediction to introduce your ideas.

Provide Elaboration The most important part of your persuasive speech will be the details that you include to convince your audience. Include information to support your cause. Wherever possible, use personal experience, anecdote, or description to persuade your readers to take your side.

Revising, Editing, and Proofreading

Allow about one quarter of your time for revising, editing, and proofreading.

Check Against the Prompt Before you put the final touches on your paper, review the prompt once again. Then, read your draft to be sure you have answered the question exactly. If necessary, add words or phrases to make the connection between the prompt and your answer more clear.

Make Proofreading Corrections Reread your paper, focusing on grammar, spelling, and punctuation errors. When you find errors, neatly cross out any words you'd like to delete.

Time and Resource Manager

In-Depth Lesson Plan

	LESSON FOCUS	PRINT AND MEDIA RESOURCES
DAY 1	**Introduction; Main Idea and Topic Sentence** Students are introduced to paragraphs and compositions, review samples from literature, and learn how to identify and write topic sentences. (pp. 32–34)	*Language Lab* CD-ROM, Composing
DAY 2	**Support Sentences and Paragraph Organization** Students examine strategies for supporting the main idea of a paragraph and learn a basic pattern of organization. (pp. 35–36)	**Teaching Resources** *Writing Support Transparencies,* 3-A; *Writing Support Activity Book,* 3-1
DAY 3	**Unity and Coherence in Compositions** Students learn the importance of unity in a composition and study organizational strategies and transitions that create coherence. (pp. 37–38)	**Teaching Resources** *Writing Support Transparencies,* 3-B
DAY 4	**Parts of a Composition and Types of Paragraphs** Students plan a composition, examine functional and block paragraphs, and review an example of functional paragraphs in literature. (pp. 39–41)	*Writers at Work* **Videotape,** Description **Teaching Resources** *Writing Support Transparencies,* 3-C
DAY 5	**Writing Style** Students discover how sentence variety, diction, and tone contribute to style, and when to use formal and informal English. (pp. 42–43)	*Language Lab* CD-ROM, Writing Style **Teaching Resources** *Writing Support Transparencies,* 3-D; *Formal Assessment,* Ch. 3

Accelerated Lesson Plan

	LESSON FOCUS	PRINT AND MEDIA RESOURCES
DAY 1	**Main Idea and Paragraph Organization** Students review paragraph purpose and structure, and utilize the TRI pattern. (pp. 32–36)	*Language Lab* CD-ROM, Composing **Teaching Resources** *Writing Support Transparencies,* 3-A; *Writing Support Activity Book,* 3-1
DAY 2	**Unity and Coherence and Types of Paragraphs** Students review unity and coherence and paragraph types. (pp. 37–41)	**Teaching Resources** *Writing Support Transparencies,* 3-B–C
DAY 3	**Writing Style** Students review diction, tone, and appropriate use of formal and informal English. (pp. 42–43)	*Language Lab* CD-ROM, Writing Style **Teaching Resources** *Writing Support Transparencies,* 3-D; *Formal Assessment,* Ch. 3

Options for Adapting Lesson Plans

FEATURES

Extend coverage with Spotlight on the Humanities (p. 44), Media and Technology Skills (p. 45), and the Standardized Test Preparation Workshop (p. 46).

TECHNOLOGY

Students can complete any stage of the lesson on computer. Have them print out their completed work.

INTEGRATED SKILLS COVERAGE

Integrating Grammar
Formal and Informal English, SE p. 43
ATE p. 47

Viewing and Representing
Critical Viewing, SE pp. 32, 33, 34, 37, 39, 44
Exploring Cultural History Through the Arts, SE p. 44
Analyzing the Role of Technology, SE p. 45
ATE p. 38

Vocabulary
ATE p. 40

Real-World Connection
ATE p. 41

Workplace Skills
ATE p. 36

BLOCK SCHEDULING

Pacing Suggestions
For 90-minute Blocks
• Follow the Accelerated Lesson Plan and cover topic and support sentences and paragraph organization in one class period, and compositions and writing style in a second class period.
• Allow class time for students to complete and discuss exercises in lesson.

Resources for Varying Instruction
• *Language Lab* **CD-ROM** If your students have access to hardware, a 90-minute block provides an ideal opportunity for students to work on computer.
• *Writers at Work* **Videotape** Show the Description segment in class.

Professional Development Support
• *How to Manage Instruction in the Block* This Teaching Resource provides management and activity suggestions.

ASSESSMENT SUPPORT

Standardized Test Preparation Workshop, SE p. 46; ATE p. 34
Standarized Test Preparation Workbook, pp. 5–6
Formal Assessment, Ch. 3

MEDIA AND TECHNOLOGY

For the Student
• *Language Lab* **CD-ROM,** Composing, Writing Style

For the Teacher
• *Writers at Work* **Videotape,** Description
• *Resource Pro* **CD-ROM**

MEETING INDIVIDUAL NEEDS

Less Advanced Students ATE pp. 35, 47. See also Ongoing Assessments ATE pp. 35, 38, 43.
AP Students ATE p. 47
Gifted and Talented Students ATE p. 42
ESL Students ATE pp. 34, 42
Logical/Mathematical Learners ATE p. 36
Bodily/Kinesthetic Learners ATE p. 37

WRITING AND GRAMMAR WEB SITE

The Interactive Writing and Grammar Web Site provides a wide array of support for students, teachers, and parents. Writing support includes:
• Interactive revision checkers
• Scoring rubrics with complete models

www.phschool.com

LITERATURE CONNECTIONS

Related selections from *Prentice Hall Literature: Timeless Voices, Timeless Themes,* The American Experience:
"Gardening," by Bailey White, SE p. 33
from *My Bondage and My Freedom,* by Frederick Douglass, SE p. 33

Lesson Objectives

1. To write in various forms in a voice and style appropriate to audience and purpose
2. To use prewriting strategies to generate ideas and plan
3. To organize ideas in writing to ensure coherence, logical progression, and support for ideas
4. To use writing to discover, organize, and support what is known and what needs to be learned about a topic
5. To analyze strategies that writers in different fields use
6. To evaluate writing for both mechanics and content

Critical Viewing

Connect Students should recognize that, like a puzzle, the pieces in writing (paragraphs) need to be put together correctly to work as a whole.

PREPARE and ENGAGE

Interest GRABBER Tell students that the ancient Roman army was divided into legions. These large units were divided into groups of one hundred men, led by a centurion. Discuss how refining the smaller groups would strengthen the whole legion. How might this strategy apply to paragraphs?

Activate Prior Knowledge

Ask students to think of situations in which parts made a difference in how the whole turned out. Ideas could range from recipes to model building to team sports. Point out that effective paragraphs contribute similarly.

Paragraphs and Compositions
Structure and Style

What Is a Paragraph?

A **paragraph** is a group of sentences that shares a common topic or purpose. Each paragraph is a logical unit of expression focused on a single main idea or thought. Where you divide your ideas into paragraphs depends on the content of your writing and the way in which you choose to organize it.

In the same way that sentences in a paragraph share a common topic or purpose, so, too, do paragraphs within a composition share a topic or purpose. A **composition** is a group of related paragraphs that develops a main idea. The paragraphs fit together like the pieces of a puzzle to present a complete picture. There are many types of compositions, including essays, reports, and autobiographical narratives. Although short stories are not usually referred to as compositions, they, too, are composed of paragraphs with a shared focus, presented in an organized way.

▲ **Critical Viewing**
In what way can this picture represent the way sentences and paragraphs are used in writing? **[Connect]**

32 • Paragraphs and Compositions

⏱ TIME AND RESOURCE MANAGER

Resources
Print: *Writing Support Transparencies,* 3-A; *Writing Support Activity Book,* 3-1
Technology: *Language Lab* CD-ROM, Composing

In-Depth Coverage	Accelerated Pace
• Cover pp. 32–36 in class.	• Assign pp. 32–36 as independent reading.
• Have prepared students read the two Writing Models.	• Review topic sentences and supporting sentences in class.
• Work through pp. 34–36 in class, and have students complete exercises in class.	• Have students complete exercises as homework.

3.1 Writing Effective Paragraphs

Main Idea and Topic Sentence

The main idea of many paragraphs is stated in a **topic sentence.** This topic sentence is supported or explained by the other sentences in the paragraph. Facts, details, restatements, and explanations are used to develop the paragraph's main idea.

When the main idea is suggested but not directly stated, then the paragraph has an **implied main idea.** In a paragraph with an implied main idea, the facts and details provide the information that allows a reader to infer the point of the paragraph.

WRITING MODELS

from **Gardening**
Bailey White

The first winter, I could relax only a little. Bermuda grass can establish itself during a winter and get away from you the following spring. So every evening at dusk, I would stalk up and down my garden like a demented wraith, peering at the ground for each loathed blue-green blade, my cloak billowing in the wind and my scarf snagging on the bare gray branches of last summer's sunflowers.

In this paragraph, the stated topic sentence is shown in blue italics.

from **My Bondage and My Freedom**
Frederick Douglass

When I was about thirteen years old, and had succeeded in learning to read, every increase of knowledge, especially respecting the free states, added something to the almost intolerable burden of the thought—"I am a slave for life." To my bondage I saw no end. It was a terrible reality, and I shall never be able to tell how sadly that thought chafed my young spirit.

In this paragraph, all the sentences work together to develop the unstated main idea of the paragraph: The more the author learned, the more he realized the injustice of his situation.

▲ **Critical Viewing**
What statement can you make that pulls together the details in this picture? [Synthesize]

Critical Viewing

Synthesize Answers will vary, but will likely focus on spring, gardening, flowers, or similar details.

Teaching From the Model

You can use these models to illustrate how paragraphs focus on a key idea. Point out that both paragraphs focus on a single idea. Ask students what they think each paragraph accomplishes.

TEACH

Step-by-Step Teaching Guide

Writing Models

1. Point out that the paragraph by Bailey White uses cause and effect to link the topic sentence with its supporting statements.

2. Ask students to identify the cause-and-effect relationship. *(The effect is the topic sentence and the supporting statements show the cause—she had to be vigilant to keep the Bermuda grass controlled.)*

3. Explain that, in the paragraph by Frederick Douglass, the first sentence might appear to be a topic sentence. However, the other sentences do not relate to it as supporting statements. They do not explain it; they work with it to reinforce the horror of being a slave.

More About the Writer

Born in Thomasville, Georgia, in 1950, Bailey White still lives in the house where she grew up. She is a first-grade teacher who now writes full time. She is also a commentator for the NPR news program "All Things Considered."

More About the Writer

Frederick Douglass escaped from slavery at the age of twenty-one. Seven years later, in 1845, he wrote and published an autobiography. He later founded a newspaper and became an important figure in the abolition movement.

☑ **ONGOING ASSESSMENT: Diagnose**

Use one of the following options to diagnose students' current level of proficiency in writing effective paragraphs.

Option 1 Ask students to select two examples of strong paragraphs they have written recently. They might choose from reports or essays prepared for a class, or from personal writing. Ask them to be prepared to describe, in a conference setting, how their paragraphs are organized and why they are effective. Use the conference to determine which students will need extra help in developing their ability to write effective paragraphs.

Option 2 Ask students to write an informational paragraph about a favorite period or event in history with which they are familiar. Have them include a topic sentence and at least three supporting sentences in their paragraphs. Plan extra help for those students who have difficulty completing this assignment.

Step-by-Step Teaching Guide

Writing a Topic Sentence

1. Ask students to suggest a familiar topic. Brainstorm for a few details on the topic, writing them on the board. Have students suggest a topic sentence that unites the details.

2. Explain that, since all the sentences in a paragraph are supposed to share a common topic, it should be possible to sum up what the topic or main idea of a paragraph is. This summary is the topic sentence, stated or implied.

3. Suggest two or three simple, familiar topics from which students can choose. Give them about ten minutes to create a topic sentence for one of the topics, with a few notes about the kinds of details they might want to gather to support the topic.

Customize for
ESL Students

For step three, above, either make certain that one of the topics you suggest is one that students will know, or ask students to suggest a topic with which they are familiar.

Critical Viewing

Connect Students will probably respond that the construction worker's life depends on a solid framework. You may wish to point out that, while no one will die from bad paragraph construction, communication can be weakened or lost if the framework of a paragraph is not good.

34

3.1

▶ **Exercise 1** **Identifying a Stated Topic Sentence** Identify the stated topic sentence of the paragraph.

The devastation of World War I left many people with a feeling of uncertainty and disillusionment. They no longer trusted the ideas and values of the world out of which the war had developed. Artistic traditions were abandoned in favor of experimentation. Social values were questioned and challenged. In a variety of ways, people sought to find new ideas that better suited twentieth-century life.

▶ **Exercise 2** **Identifying an Implied Topic Sentence** Identify the implied topic sentence of the following paragraph.

Although William Faulkner never finished high school, he read a great deal and developed an interest in writing from an early age. In 1918, he enlisted in the British Royal Flying Corps and was sent to Canada for training. However, World War I ended before he had a chance to see combat, and he returned to Mississippi. A few years later, longing for a change of scene, Faulkner moved to New Orleans. There, he became a friend of Sherwood Anderson. In 1926, Faulkner returned to Oxford, Mississippi, to devote himself to his writing.

Writing a Topic Sentence

Many of the paragraphs you write will be organized around a topic sentence. In a **topic sentence,** you state the main idea that will be developed in a paragraph. Although the details and explanations that you provide in the rest of the sentences of the paragraph are what give your composition depth and form, the topic sentences are the framework on which the composition is built.

To write a topic sentence, review the details you will use. Group related details. For each group, make a single statement that expresses what they mean all together. Polish this statement into a topic sentence.

◀ **Critical Viewing** What do you think this construction worker would say about the importance of a solid framework? **[Connect]**

34 • Paragraphs and Compositions

Writing Supporting Sentences

Use **supporting sentences** to develop, support, or explain the key idea expressed in a topic sentence. You can support or develop the idea using one or more of the following strategies:

Use Facts Facts are statements that can be proved. They support your key idea by providing proof.

FACT: Our school building is open from 7:00 A.M. to 5:00 P.M.

Use Statistics A statistic is a fact, usually stated in numbers.

STATISTIC: At least 60 percent of the students use the building after regular classroom hours.

Use Examples, Illustrations, or Instances An example, illustration, or instance is a specific thing, person, or event that demonstrates a point.

ILLUSTRATION: Last week, three clubs had meetings in the cafeteria at four o'clock.

Use Details Details are the specifics—the parts of the whole. They make your point or main idea clear by showing how all the pieces fit together.

DETAIL: Each club has a specific amount of time to meet but would like more.

▶ **Exercise 3** **Writing a Topic Sentence** Write a topic sentence for the following paragraph.

People used to describe the United States as a "melting pot" to suggest that individuals of different ethnic backgrounds came to the United States and blended into a single American culture. Today, many Americans argue that the "melting pot" metaphor is no longer accurate. They say that the United States is a society in which many cultures exist side by side, retaining their individual identities. New images that are used to represent the country's diversity include a *tapestry*, a *mosaic*, and a *quilt*.

▶ **Exercise 4** **Writing Supporting Sentences**

1. Write two more supporting sentences to add to the above paragraph.
2. Write four sentences that support the following statement after you complete it:
   ___?___ is the most interesting sport to watch.

✓ ONGOING ASSESSMENT: Monitor and Reinforce

If students are having trouble differentiating topic and supporting sentences, try the following strategy.

Have students work in pairs to find examples of effective paragraphs in a textbook they use in another class. Have them identify topic and supporting sentences in these paragraphs. Ask students to note whether topic sentences are stated or implied. You may also want to ask students where in the paragraph the topic sentence is found (some are at the end of the paragraph).

Writing Supporting Sentences

1. Explain that when a writer uses a topic sentence (stated or implied) and supports that topic or main idea with several supporting sentences, the paragraph is said to be a *topical paragraph*. (Two other types of paragraphs, functional and block, will be covered later in the chapter.)

2. After reviewing the support strategies, ask volunteers to suggest facts, details, examples, or statistics that they know and a topic that each might support.

3. Point out that personal experience would also be a useful support strategy. If students visit, see, create, or do something, that experience can be used to support some topics.

Answer Key

▶ **Exercise 3**

Sample topic sentence: In the U.S., people's attitudes toward assimilation have changed.

▶ **Exercise 4**

1. Support may include information about increased immigration, increase in non-European immigration, growth of ethnic neighborhoods, and increased awareness of world cultures.
2. Answers will vary, depending on the sport selected, but sentences should support the topic. You may want to ask volunteers to share their favorite sport and sentences they used to support their interest.

Customize for
Less Advanced Students

For Exercise 4, vote on a sport to complete the sentence, then create the four sentences as a class. Students may suggest details and examples; volunteers then can turn these elements into complete sentences. Write sentences on the board as the exercise progresses. Edit for clarity once four sentences have been suggested.

Placing Your Topic Sentence

Teaching Resources: Writing Support Transparencies, 3-A; Writing Support Activity Book, 3-1

1. Explain that patterns in which topic sentences are at the beginning or end are sometimes called (respectively) *pyramid* and *inverted-pyramid* paragraphs. Ask students to speculate why that might be. (In a pyramid the "point" is at the top with support beneath. In an inverted pyramid the "point" is on the bottom with support above.)

2. Using Transparency 3-A, demonstrate how the TRI pattern has been used to identify the parts of the paragraph about the parking lot.

3. Explain that this pattern can be used for building paragraphs, as well as for analyzing them. Have students brainstorm for a question or topic, then "build" a paragraph as a class using the TRI pattern.

Customize for
Logical/Mathematical Learners

Point out that the TRI pattern is not unlike a well-prepared chart or graph. A chart or graph is only meaningful with a title (topic sentence) and supporting information (appropriate labels and data). Good writing is a matter of logic and discipline.

Answer Key

▶ **Exercise 5**

Tell students that they may modify sentences when trying variations of the TRI pattern. After they have completed the exercise, discuss how the TRI pattern worked for them.

Integrating Workplace Skills

Write on the board a topic sentence that might be used in a business report (We must improve sales or The market is ready for this product). Ask students to suggest supporting statements to develop the paragraph (sales statistics, facts about competitors, market research).

3.1

Placing Your Topic Sentence

Evaluate each paragraph to determine whether to place your topic sentence at the beginning, in the middle, at the end, or to leave it unstated. Placing your topic sentence at the beginning of the paragraph focuses your readers' attention before you present your details. You may choose to place it in the middle when you need to lead into it with background information. Placing your topic sentence at the end of the paragraph summarizes the details you have supplied. Leaving it unstated allows readers to synthesize the information you have presented; this is often a more sophisticated approach.

Paragraph Patterns Sentences in a paragraph can be arranged in a variety of patterns. One of these patterns is the TRI pattern.

TOPIC SENTENCE:	You state your key idea.
RESTATEMENT:	You interpret your key idea—put it into other words.
ILLUSTRATION:	You support your key idea with an illustration or an example.

T	**Our town doesn't need a new parking lot.**
R	**We have enough parking to meet everyone's needs.**
I	**On any weekday, the municipal lot is only half full. On Saturdays, the busiest day, the longest wait for a parking spot is ten minutes.**

Once you have identified the basic elements of your paragraph, experiment with variations of the TRI pattern, such as TIR, TII, or ITR, until you are satisfied with the effect.

▶ **Exercise 5** Placing a Topic Sentence Use the TRI pattern, or a variation, to arrange the sentences below in a paragraph. Then, revise the paragraph, using another variation of TRI. You may add transitions and additional sentences as needed.

Many of the merchants in town are willing to hire teens for part-time work after school.

The local day-care center is always looking for volunteers.

After-school clubs provide a forum for students to meet others with similar interests.

No teen in our town can honestly say he or she has nothing worthwhile to do after school.

36 • Paragraphs and Compositions

3.2 *Paragraphs in Essays and Other Compositions*

Unity and Coherence

In a paragraph or composition that has **unity,** all the parts are clearly connected to a single main idea. In a unified composition, the topic sentence of each paragraph connects to the main idea, or **thesis statement,** of the composition. Within a unified paragraph, each sentence connects to the topic sentence or implied main idea of the paragraph.

In a **coherent** composition, ideas follow a logical order and the connections between ideas are clear. Paragraphs are arranged so that one leads logically to the next. Sentences within paragraphs are ordered so that readers can easily follow the flow of ideas.

Unity

When you plan a composition, identify your main points—the topic sentences you will use for your paragraphs. Read each one, and make sure it is relevant to the main idea of your composition. As you draft, be cautious that you do not begin to insert ideas that occur to you but that are unrelated to the main idea. As you revise your composition, evaluate the topic of each paragraph and how relevant it is to the main idea of the composition. As you revise each paragraph, delete any sentences that do not clearly connect to the topic sentence of the paragraph.

▲ **Critical Viewing**
Why do the members of a team need to focus on a common purpose?
[Draw Conclusions]

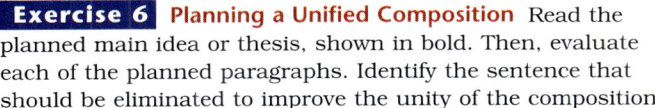

▶ **Exercise 6 Planning a Unified Composition** Read the planned main idea or thesis, shown in bold. Then, evaluate each of the planned paragraphs. Identify the sentence that should be eliminated to improve the unity of the composition.

Equal funding should be provided for girls' and boys' sports.

- Many girls participate in sports.
- Individual sports have more long-term benefits than team sports.
- Participation in sports benefits girls as well as boys.
- Federal law prohibits gender discrimination in educational programs, including athletics.

Paragraphs in Essays and Other Compositions • **37**

Step-by-Step Teaching Guide

Unity

1. Have students read the first two paragraphs in the text.
2. Tell students that the word *unity* comes from a Latin word meaning "one." Ask students to explain how this might be used to explain the idea of unity. (*Unity* in reference to writing means one main idea, one theme that runs through the paragraph.)
3. Ask students how they think unity could be maintained in a paragraph and in a composition. (Students may mention being aware of main points, making sure all sentences support a topic, having an outline so paragraphs support the main idea of the composition.)

Answer Key

▶ **Exercise 6**

"Individual sports have more long-term benefits . . . " is the sentence that should be deleted.

Customize for
Bodily/Kinesthetic Learners

Some students may benefit from physical examples of unity. Examples might include a selection of objects that are similar with one dissimilar item (an assignment book, a notebook, a textbook, and a pen) or something with parts that can be combined into a whole (perhaps a simple children's puzzle with one extra piece that doesn't belong).

Critical Viewing

Draw Conclusions Teammates must work together to successfully create and execute plays.

⏱ **TIME AND RESOURCE MANAGER**

Resources
Print: *Writing Support Transparencies,* 3-B–C
Technology: *Writers at Work* Videotape, Description

In-Depth Coverage	Accelerated Pace
• Go over pp. 37–41 in class.	• Have students read pp. 37–41 independently.
• Discuss unity and coherence in class.	• Discuss unity and coherence in class.
• Assign the Exercises 6–10 to be completed in class.	• Assign Exercises 6–10 to be completed independently.

Answer Key

"Other common injuries . . . " is the sentence that does not belong.

Step-by-Step Teaching Guide

Coherence

Teaching Resources: Writing Support Transparencies, 3-B

1. Explain to students that a laser beam is a form of light that is powerful because it is coherent. In this case, *coherence* means "holding together, with consistent qualities and direction." (Regular light bounces all over.)

2. Explain that writing, like light, gains strength from being coherent, that is, holding together, being consistent, and going in the same logical direction.

3. Point out that different purposes utilize different organizational strategies. Whichever strategy is used, a writer should continue to move in the same direction after he or she starts—for example, for chronology, from past to present; for spatial, from left to right, near to far.

4. Review the chart with students, focusing on the *transitions*, words used to make connections clear or to establish the direction in which topics flow, shown on the right in the chart.

Answer Key

This exercise can be completed individually or in groups. Ask volunteers to share examples of how they improved the paragraph.

Integrating Representing Skills

Have students create images (graphs, charts, drawings) that illustrate one or more of the organizational strategies. Ask volunteers to share their images.

▶ Exercise 7 **Revising a Paragraph for Unity** Identify which sentence should be eliminated to improve the unity of the following paragraph.

Wearing a bike helmet is just good sense. Studies show that bike helmets reduce the risk of head injury by 85 percent! Other common injuries from bike accidents include broken wrists and lacerations. States with helmet laws have reported a reduction in head injuries from bike accidents, ranging between 20 and 40 percent. Although inconvenient, or perhaps even uncomfortable, bike helmets are worth the trouble.

Coherence

Organize and Show Connections The key to coherence is organization. Order your ideas logically, and use transitional words and phrases to keep connections clear as you move from one idea or detail to the next. The type of organization you choose when you write depends on your topic and purpose.

Types of Organization	Possible Reasons to Use	Words That Show Connections
Chronological	to narrate; to explain a process	before, after, during, meanwhile, first, next, finally
Spatial	to describe	above, below, behind, next to, near, within, outside
Comparison and Contrast	to show similarities and differences; to evaluate	however, in contrast, similarly, conversely
Cause and Effect	to analyze; to explain reasons and results	accordingly, as a result, consequently, therefore
Order of Importance	to persuade; to describe; to evaluate	furthermore, significantly, moreover, most of all

▶ Exercise 8 **Revising for Coherence** Revise this paragraph to create coherence. Reorganize sentences, add transitions, and make other minor changes as needed.

Americans called the purchase of the land that is now Alaska "Seward's Folly." Today, Alaska enjoys a vital tourist industry and is an important source of oil. The land was not expensive. William Seward purchased the land from Russia in 1867 for two cents an acre. Many Americans believed the area to be nothing but a barren wasteland.

38 • Paragraphs and Compositions

✓ ONGOING ASSESSMENT: Monitor and Reinforce

If students are having difficulty with the concepts of organization or transition, try one of the following strategies.

Option 1 Give students examples of things that might be described by a writer, and ask which organizational strategy works best for each. For example: a person's life *(chronological)*, a room *(spatial)*, two different brands of cereal *(comparison and contrast)*, and a person who studied hard and improved his or her grades *(cause and effect)*.

Option 2 Discuss the meaning and function of transitions in writing (to act as a bridge, to connect). Have students write one or two sentences for each organizational strategy, utilizing one or more of the appropriate transition words. This may be done individually or as a class, with students suggesting sentences out loud.

The Parts of a Composition

A composition is a group of paragraphs that all work together to develop a single focus. In most compositions, this single focus is expressed in a thesis statement. The rest of the paragraphs in the composition are organized to develop that thesis statement. Whatever organizational strategy you choose, it will have a beginning, a middle, and an end. In writing, these parts are called the *introduction*, the *body*, and the *conclusion*.

Introduction

The **introduction** serves two purposes: It captures readers' attention with a strong lead, and it introduces the focus of the composition in a thesis statement. The **lead** is the first sentence. It can be a startling observation, an intriguing statement, or a quotation. The **thesis statement** declares what you intend to show or prove in your composition. Frequently, the thesis statement is followed by another sentence or two that extend the thesis statement by indicating how it will be shown or proved.

Body

The **body** of a composition is the part that develops, explains, and supports the key idea expressed in the thesis statement. Organize the body paragraphs in a logical order, and make sure that each paragraph is related to your thesis.

Conclusion

The **conclusion** is the final paragraph of the essay. Like the introduction, it serves two purposes. First, it should restate the thesis and sum up the support. Second, it should leave readers with a memorable statement, a call to action, or a thought.

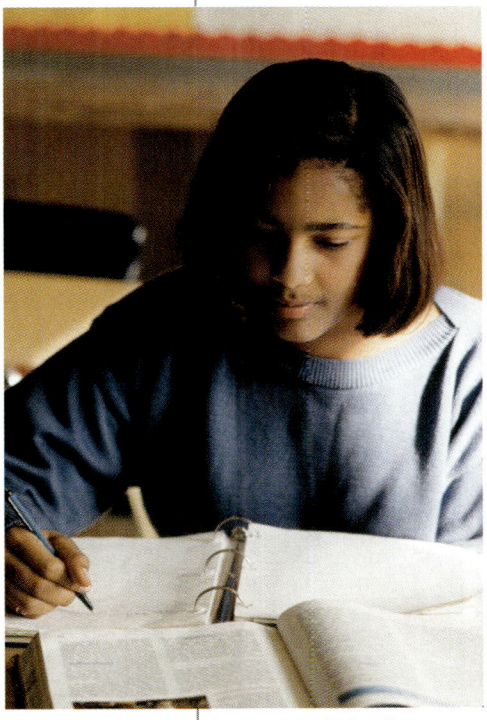

▲ **Critical Viewing**
How can a knowledge of the parts of a composition make you a more effective writer? **[Connect]**

▶ **Exercise 9** **Planning a Composition** On a separate sheet of paper, outline the parts of a composition on a topic related to a subject you are studying in science or social studies. Write a thesis statement and a possible lead for the introduction. Write a topic sentence for each of several paragraphs.

Paragraphs in Essays and Other Compositions • 39

Step-by-Step Teaching Guide

The Parts of a Composition

1. After students have read the text, ask them how the organization of a composition is similar to that of a paragraph. How is it different? (Like a paragraph, it starts with a topic and adds support. Unlike a paragraph, it is longer and has a conclusion.)

2. Point out that an outline can often help make these parts clearer. Tell students that, once they decide on an organizational strategy, they can create a simple outline.

3. Suggest that students work first on the thesis statement, then outline the points they need to support the thesis statement. After some research is done, it will be easier to go back and create an introduction and conclusion that tie all the points together. The thesis statement should be woven into the introduction, but it may not be the first sentence. It may be implied, just as the topic of a paragraph sometimes is.

Answer Key

▶ **Exercise 9**

This exercise may be done in class or as homework. Have students trade papers with partners and check each other's outlines. You may want to find out which students picked science and which picked social studies for their topics, and pair students with someone who picked a similar subject. This may help partners identify logical inconsistencies, if they are reviewing a paper in a subject with which they are comfortable.

Critical Viewing

Connect Students should note that compositions written according to accepted standards generally convey information and ideas more successfully.

Functional Paragraphs

1. Point out that writers often make use of paragraphs that are functional, rather than topical.

2. Ask students which of the three purposes of functional paragraphs they see most often.

3. Ask students why they think a new paragraph is needed each time a speaker changes (to help the reader keep track of who is speaking).

Writing Model

1. Explain that creating transitions between paragraphs when topics in a composition change, as in this excerpt by Barbara Kimenye, is an important use of functional paragraphs.

2. Have a prepared student read the excerpt, or have the class read it silently.

3. Ask students to discuss the effect of the transition Barbara Kimenye makes in this excerpt. Why does it work so well?

More About the Writer

Ugandan writer Barbara Kimenye discovered when her sons were small that few children's books tell of African life. She decided to fill this void by writing stories that have meaning for African children.

Integrating Vocabulary Skills

The word *paragraph* comes from the Greek *paragraphos*. Literally, this word means "beside writing," and originally referred to a line or mark made in the margin to indicate a change of topic or break in the sense of what was being said. In days when paper or other writing media were scarce and expensive, writers would fill every inch of the page, and only a mark in the margin would show where ideas changed.

Types of Paragraphs

Functional Paragraphs

Functional paragraphs, as their name suggests, perform specific functions. They may not have a topic sentence, but they are unified and coherent because the sentences (if there is more than one sentence) are clearly connected and follow a logical order. Functional paragraphs can be used for the following purposes:

To arouse or sustain interest A few vivid sentences can work together to capture a reader's attention.

To indicate dialogue One of the conventions of dialogue is that a new paragraph begins each time the speaker changes.

To make a transition A short paragraph can help readers move between the main ideas in two topical paragraphs.

WRITING MODEL

from **The Pig**
Barbara Kimenye

. . . He was still worried about the state his filing system must be in today, for having once called in at the Headquarters, merely to see if the youngster who had replaced him needed any advice or help, he had been appalled at the lack of order. Papers were scattered everywhere, confidential folders were open for all the world to read, and his successor was flirting madly with some pin-brained girl at the other end of the newly installed telephone.

The visit had not been anything near a success, for not even his former colleagues showed anything but superficial interest in what Kubka had to say.

So there he was, destined to waste the remainder of his life in the little cottage beside the Kalasanda stream, with plenty indeed to look back on, but not very much to look forward to, and his greatest friend, Yosdfu Mudkasa, was away in Buddu County on business.

> This paragraph makes a transition from the paragraph that looks back on the character's former place of employment to the paragraph that tells about his present situation.

40 • Paragraphs and Compositions

Paragraph Blocks

Sometimes, you may develop a single idea over several paragraphs. The paragraphs in this "block" all support the same key idea or topic sentence but contain too much information to include in one paragraph because that paragraph would become long and unmanageable. By breaking the development of the idea into separate paragraphs, you make your ideas clearer.

USING PARAGRAPH BLOCKS

Topic of Composition
Many students have difficulty fitting required classes into their schedules.

Supporting Topic Sentence: Required classes should be offered more frequently.

> **Paragraph 1** – Statistics of how frequently offered and how many students
> **Paragraph 2** – Suggestion of how frequently should be offered and how many students could be accommodated
> **Paragraph 3** – Summary of impact on school budget

PARAGRAPH BLOCK

Supporting Sentence 2: Students should be allowed more scheduling flexibility.

▶ **Exercise 10** **Analyzing Functional Paragraphs** Look through essays and speeches in your literature book and in other sources to find examples of each type of functional paragraph. Make a photocopy of each example. Mark the functional paragraph with a brace, and label it by the function it performs.

41

Developing Style

Teaching Resources: Writing Support Transparencies, 3-D

1. Remind students that sentences can also vary in word order and function (questions, commands, statements). Varying sentences not only expresses style, it also keeps the writing interesting.

2. Explain that connotation is an important part of determining diction. For example, *thoroughbred* and *nag* both refer to horses, but do not have the same connotation.

3. Point out that tone can be subtle or obvious, depending on the author's purpose.

Answer Key

▶ **Exercise 11**

Discuss the style of the excerpt in class. You may want to have a volunteer read the excerpt aloud, using the tone he or she feels the writing projects.

Customize for
Gifted and Talented Students

Ask students to look at Edgar Allan Poe's short story "The Fall of the House of Usher" and read aloud the first paragraph. Then ask them to note which vowel sounds dominate in the passage. Explain that certain sounds evoke certain feelings and are used as an element of style. The *o*'s and *u*'s establish a gloomy, ghostly mood and tone for Poe's story about the rotting, doomed house of Usher.

Customize for
ESL Students

Students learning English may be surprised to see the word *diction* in a context related to writing, since it usually refers to enunciation. Ask them to consult a dictionary to learn how these uses of *diction* are related. *Tone* may also be a difficult concept. It is probably most easily modeled with speech: demonstrate by saying something somberly, happily, and excitedly. Explain that in writing, word choice replaces tone of voice.

3.3 Writing Style

Developing Style

Your personal style is the way you present yourself to the world. Writing style is the way you express yourself in writing. Just as you might choose different styles of clothing for different occasions, you can use different writing styles for different purposes The qualities that contribute to writing style are diction, tone, and sentence variety.

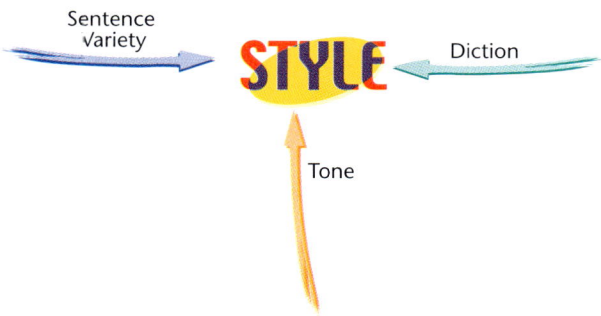

Sentence Variety The lengths and structures of the sentences you use contribute to the effect of your writing. Longer, more complex sentences create a sophisticated, mature style. Shorter, more direct sentences create emphasis and vary the rhythm of your writing. In most types of writing, use a variety of lengths and structures to keep the writing from becoming monotonous.

Diction Diction refers to word choice. The words you choose contribute to the overall effect, or style of a paragraph. You can use words with positive connotations or associations for an upbeat style, or you can use words with negative connotations if you are trying to make a point about a problem or situation. The sounds of words can also contribute to the style of a paragraph.

Tone Tone is the attitude you take when you write about your subject. You may write about your topic with objectivity, with dismay, or with humor. If you are writing an explanation of a process, your paragraphs will have a serious, formal tone. If you are writing a letter to a friend, your paragraphs will have a casual, friendly tone.

▶ **Exercise 11** Analyzing Styles Read the excerpt from "The Pig" on page 40. Describe the style of the writing, using specific examples of sentence variety, diction, and tone.

42 • Paragraphs and Compositions

⏱ TIME AND RESOURCE MANAGER

Resources
Print: *Writing Support Transparencies*, 3-D; *Formal Assessment*, Ch. 3
Technology: *Language Lab* CD-ROM, Writing Style

In-Depth Coverage	Accelerated Pace
• Cover pp. 42–43 in class. • Do Exercise 11 in class. • Exercise 12 may be assigned as homework. Review in class.	• Assign students to cover pp. 42–43 independently. • Ask students to do Exercise 11, but focus on a selection from their literature anthologies. • Assign Exercise 12 as homework.

Formal and Informal English

Different types of writing require different levels of formality. When writing a letter or note to a friend, you might use language in a casual way—similar to the way you use everyday speech. When writing a report or a business letter, you would use formal English—following all the conventions of correct grammar and usage.

Using the Conventions of Formal English

You should use formal English for most of your school assignments, such as reports, persuasive essays, and test responses. When writing in formal English, observe the following conventions:

- Do not use contractions.
- Do not use slang.
- Use standard English usage and grammar.

Using Informal English

Informal English is the everyday speech that people use in conversation. Often, informal English is used in dialogue to express certain patterns of speech. You might also use informal English when writing friendly letters, humorous anecdotes, or journal entries. When writing in informal English, you can

- use contractions
- use popular expressions and slang

FORMAL ENGLISH: I am writing to request information about the current status.

INFORMAL ENGLISH: What's new? Drop me a line and let me know.

Exercise 12 **Using Formal and Informal English** On a separate sheet of paper, rewrite the following sentences. Use formal English for those written in informal English. Use informal English for those written in formal English.
1. So, what's your reaction to the flick?
2. I can't stand the food that place dishes up.
3. I am writing to suggest an alternative to your plan.
4. Those who shared the experience agreed that it was exhilarating.
5. I'm boggled by how tricky this problem is!

Formal and Informal English

1. Explain to students that purpose and audience must always be considered in writing, but especially when it comes to deciding whether to use formal or informal English.

2. Suggest that, whenever students are unsure of an audience, they always err on the side of formality.

3. Make certain students know your expectations for any assignments. Identify when informal English is acceptable. Otherwise, emphasize the need to use formal English in all classroom writing.

Answer Key

▶ **Exercise 12**

Answers will vary. Possible rewrites are given. Have volunteers share what they wrote.

1. What is your opinion of the film?
2. I dislike the food they serve in that establishment.
3. Here's another option to think about.
4. We all loved it.
5. I am overwhelmed by the difficulty of this problem!

ASSESS and CLOSE

Assessment

Teaching Resources: Formal Assessment, Chapter 3

1. Review the chapter by asking students to state the key points of the chapter.

2. You may wish to use the following assessment options:

   - review the Standardized Test Preparation Workshop on pages 46–47 and have students complete the practice items.

   - administer the Chapter 3 assessment from *Formal Assessment* in the Teaching Resources to measure students' grasp of the concepts presented.

☑ ONGOING ASSESSMENT: Monitor and Reinforce

If students are having difficulty understanding diction, as well as when it is appropriate to use formal English, try one of the following strategies.

Option 1 Identify three potential audiences for students: a close friend, a parent, a college board member. Have them write three short paragraphs stating why they want to go to a specific college, changing the language for the three different audiences.

Option 2 Since it is likely that formal English will be more difficult than informal, ask students to write a paragraph in formal English. Then have students exchange papers and assess the level of formality in the writing, noting any contractions or slang. Review in class how slang terms can be "translated" into formal language, since some students may not know the appropriate parallels.

Step-by-Step Teaching Guide

Exploring Cultural History

1. Focus on one of the Spotlight features for discussion, or have students research a feature.
2. Students will find that, in Hopi culture, a Kachina is an ancestral spirit, and the dolls represent these spirits. Encourage students to find photographs of Kachina dolls.
3. Native American music varies widely, depending on the area of North America from which it arose. Recordings of flutist Nakai are widely available.
4. Wright first visited Arizona in 1927. One of the structures he built there, Taliesin West, was both a home and an art school. Wright was famous for suiting his buildings to their environments, picking up elements from each region to help buildings fit their surroundings. So while his hotel in Tokyo fits with its Japanese surroundings, his Taliesin West fits beautifully amid the desert's rocks.

Viewing and Representing

Activity Give students an opportunity to display their art "histories" in class and explain the meaning of their symbols.

Exploring Cultural History Through the Arts

Focus on Art: Native American Sculpture

In a composition, each sentence contributes to the strength of the whole paragraph, and each paragraph contributes to the strength of the overall composition. The same is true with sculptures and carvings—each piece of material that you add or take away enhances the strength and beauty of the finished work of art. Since A.D. 400, the people of the Anasazi and Conchiti Pueblos have created storyteller dolls that are usually small animals, birds, or frogs, which are central to the oral tradition of storytelling in Native American culture. Helen Cordero became a contemporary creator of these dolls, which can take the form of mothers, grandmothers, cowboys, or even dancing bears. The Hopi Indians carved Kachina dolls that were either full-figure dolls with all body parts included or sculptures that consisted of several dolls from one piece of wood.

Music Connection Native American flutist R. Carlos Nakai of Navajo-Ute heritage plays the music of the plains and woodlands Indian tribes. In the late 1960's, Nakai began to research Native American music and became interested in the wooden flute. He now has twenty-seven albums and tours the world, bringing Native American music to people of other cultures.

Architecture Connection Architect Frank Lloyd Wright (1867–1959) designed some of the most important homes and buildings that the world has seen. Wright founded the "prairie school" of architecture, and many of his creations were influenced by the art of the Native Americans in the southwestern United States. Wright's architecture also includes the Guggenheim Museum in New York City, the Dallas Theater Center, and the Imperial Hotel in Tokyo.

Writing Activity: Creating Symbols

Create a piece of art that represents your own "history." Fold a piece of paper in quarters. In each quarter, sketch something that represents a part of the whole you. You can use symbols of your cultural heritage, hobbies, or sports—whatever makes you *you*. Choose different parts of your personality to represent the whole picture. Write a brief explanation of how each part contributes to your personality.

▲ **Critical Viewing**
How do the parts of this sculpture contribute to an overall effect? [**Analyze**]

Critical Viewing

Analyze Students may observe that the multiple small figures and the look on the face of the figure make this look like it tells a story.

Media and Technology Skills

Analyzing the Role of Technology

Activity: Keep a Media Log

You are watching a baseball game on television, and the fans sitting behind first base notice the red "on" light has flashed on the camera pointed toward them. Forgetting about the game, they leap to their feet and begin waving their arms as though signaling for rescue from drowning. They have achieved the peak American experience: They have appeared, however fleetingly, on television.

Think About It Among the first technologies was the printing press, which published books, newspapers, and magazines. Then, sound made information more available: The phonograph, telephone, and radio pushed the information explosion along. Next, television, movies, and computers have pushed at the communications boundaries between nations and people to form what philosopher Marshall McLuhan called a "global village." So many moments of our lives are influenced by one of these forms of communication technology that we may even take the technology for granted.

Analyze It To see just how large a role these communication technologies play in your everyday life, keep a daily log for a week. Track your use of a medium of communications technology. Include the newspaper, telephone, books, radio, stereo, film, television, computer, or Internet. For each use, record the amount of time spent and indicate your purpose. For example, you may need to gather information, share news, or just spend some time relaxing or being entertained.

Evaluate It Review your media log to see how much of a role technology plays in your life. Compare your results with a classmate's. Together, draw a conclusion about the role of technology in today's world.

Varieties of Communication Technology

Print
- books
- magazines
- newspapers
- paper mail
- fax
- word-processing software
- e-mail
- computer instant messaging

Audio
- radio
- CDs
- tapes
- records
- telephone

Audiovisual
- movies
- television
- computer
- Internet

MONDAY			
Type of Technology	Time Spent Using	Purpose	Comments
Internet			
Television			
Radio			
Movies			

Media and Technology Skills • 45

Lesson Objectives

1. To evaluate writing for content
2. To analyze text structures for how they influence understanding
3. To analyze the characteristics of written texts, including the patterns of organization, syntax, and word choice

1. Tell students that in this practice test, which is multiple choice, they will be analyzing part of a report on American literature.

2. Discuss the sample question. Ask students why they knew the sentence needed to be fixed (obviously, Whitman is not America). Why is A the best answer? (B and D can be eliminated, because they don't make sense; C might be true but doesn't reflect the ideas in the paragraph.)

3. Administer the practice test during class. You may wish to time it, so that students learn to pace themselves during tests of this nature. Then, review the answers in class, discussing why each selection is best.

Standardized Test Preparation Workshop

Revising and Editing

Your knowledge of writing and revising effective paragraphs and compositions may be tested on standardized tests through sample situations in which you are asked to identify the best revision of a sentence or paragraph. On some tests, these types of items are set up with a hypothetical peer-conferencing session.

The sample test items that follow will give you practice in responding to standardized test preparation questions that are set up in this way.

Test Tip

Before reading the questions, read the paragraph, noting any places where the text does not flow or seems incorrect. Refer back to this as you answer the questions.

Sample Test Item

Directions: This paragraph is part of a report that Alison has written for her American literature course. As part of a peer conference, you are asked to read the report and think about suggestions you might make. Then, choose the letter of the best answer.

1 Walt Whitman is often considered America. In 1855, New Yorker
2 Walt Whitman publishing his groundbreaking series of poems, *Leaves of Grass*.
3 Proudly, he broadcasted his "barbaric yawp" from Brooklyn to the universe.
4 Most American readers didn't pay any attention to the irregular forms and frank language
5 of this revolutionary poet, but Emerson knew an American original when he saw one.
6 He told everyone about Whitman's work. Of all them of the period between
7 1800 and 1870, Whitman has had the most lasting effect on American
8 literature—the first edition of *Leaves* sold fewer than twenty copies.

1 What is the **BEST** way to rewrite the sentence in line 1? ("Walt Whitman . . . America.")
   A Walt Whitman is often considered the voice of America.
   B Walt Whitman is often considered like America.
   C Walt Whitman knows America.
   D Make no change

Answer and Explanation

The correct answer is *A.* The passage focuses on how Whitman's poetry affected American literature. Adding the words "the voice of" to line 1 creates the best sentence to express this idea.

✏️ TEST-TAKING TIP

Tell students to jot down the numbers of sentences that seem incorrect or confusing as they read the test paragraph. This will give them a head start on answering questions about how to improve it.

Students should note that on a test of this type, they are asked to analyze the best choices for combining sentences, rewriting sentences, changing individual words, inserting additional information, removing extraneous information,

and adding or improving transitional words and phrases. At times, choosing which choice is best may require an analysis of the topic or purpose of the entire paragraph. For example, for the sample question about line 1, the sentence could not be revised without determining the topic of the paragraph.

Caution students to read the paragraph carefully and judge the multiple-choice items thoughtfully.

Answer Key
1. C
2. D
3. A
4. C
5. A
6. B
7. B

▶ **Practice**   **Directions:** Using the passage shown on the previous page, choose the letter of the best answer for the following questions.

1 What is the **BEST** way to combine the two sentences in lines 2–3? (In 1855 . . . universe.)

A In 1855, New Yorker, Walt Whitman published his groundbreaking series of poems, *Leaves of Grass*; proudly he broadcasted his "barbaric yawp" from Brooklyn to the universe.

B Walt Whitman published his groundbreaking series of poems, *Leaves of Grass*, and proudly he broadcasted his "barbaric yawp" from Brooklyn to the universe.

C In 1855, New Yorker Walt Whitman published his groundbreaking series of poems, *Leaves of Grass*, proudly broadcasting his "barbaric yawp" from Brooklyn to the universe.

D Walt Whitman published his groundbreaking series of poems, *Leaves of Grass*, proudly broadcasting his "barbaric yawp" from Brooklyn to the universe in 1855, New York.

2 What is the **BEST** way to write the introductory clause in lines 4–5? (Most . . . poet,)

A American readers didn't pay any attention to the poetry of this poet,

B Most American readers didn't pay any attention to the weird forms and straight language of this poet,

C Most American readers ignored the irregular forms and frank language of this revolutionary poet,

D Make no change.

3 Which sentence would **BEST** add information about Whitman and Emerson to the passage?

A Emerson and Whitman both had a lasting effect on American poetry.

B Emerson and Whitman came from different states.

C Emerson and Whitman greatly admired nature.

D Both writers lived in America.

4. What is the **BEST** way for the sentences in lines 5–6 to make the language more appropriate for a formal piece of writing. (Emerson . . . work)

A Change *American* to *poetic*

B Place a comma after *original*

C Change *told everyone about* to *praised*

D Make no change.

5 The meaning of the introductory phrase "Of all them of the period between 1800 and 1870 " in lines 6–7, can **BEST** be improved by changing *them* to—

A the poets

B the Americans

C the writers

D the critics

6 Which of the following sentences, if any, would be **BEST** inserted between the sentences in line 6 (He . . . Of all them)?

A Whitman remained unknown until after his death.

B Whitman's work then gained the attention of many.

C Shortly after, Whitman stopped producing poems and began writing novels.

D Make no change.

7 Which transition should be added after the dash in line 8 to make the meaning clearer?

A according to

B despite the fact that

C regardless of

D for example,

Customize for
Less Advanced Students

If students had difficulty in deciding on the best choice for combining sentences, review with them the several strategies for this technique.

Customize for
AP Students

Ask students what questions the paragraph raises. (Possibilities: what is a "barbaric yawp," and to what does it refer—Whitman or the poems? Who are "all of them?" Why were the poems "groundbreaking?") Ask students where they think this paragraph should be placed within the report, and why. (Students may suggest that this should be the opening paragraph, since it raises so many questions.) Have students create a rough outline of the report based on the information in the first paragraph.

Integrating Grammar Skills

Ask students what other corrections they would make to the sample paragraph. Encourage them to consider word choice, grammar, punctuation, and style. You may want to have them rewrite the paragraph in their own words.

In-Depth Lesson Plan

	LESSON FOCUS	PRINT AND MEDIA RESOURCES
DAY 1	**Introduction to Autobiographical Writing** Students learn key elements of autobiographical writing and analyze the Model From Literature. (pp. 48–51)	*Writers at Work* **Videotape**, Narration *Writing Lab* **CD-ROM**, Narration
DAY 2	**Prewriting** Students choose and narrow a topic, consider their audience and purpose, and gather information. (pp. 52–55)	**Teaching Resources:** *Writing Support Transparencies,* 4-A–C; *Topic Bank for Heterogeneous Classes,* Ch. 4
DAY 3	**Drafting** Students organize their ideas and write their first drafts. (pp. 56–57)	**Teaching Resources:** *Writing Support Transparencies,* 4-D–E; *Writing Support Activity Book,* 4-1
DAY 4	**Revising** Students revise their drafts in terms of overall structure, paragraphs, sentences, and word choice. (pp. 58–62)	**Teaching Resources:** *Writing Support Transparencies,* 4-F–G
DAY 5	**Editing and Proofreading; Publishing and Presenting** Students check their work for accuracy and correctness and present their final drafts. (pp. 63–64)	**Teaching Resources:** *Scoring Rubrics on Transparency,* Ch. 4; *Writing Assessment and Portfolio Management; Formal Assessment,* Ch. 4

Accelerated Lesson Plan

	LESSON FOCUS	PRINT AND MEDIA RESOURCES
DAY 1	**Drafting** Students review characteristics of autobiographical writing, select topics, and write drafts. (pp. 48–57)	*Writing Lab* **CD-ROM**, Narration **Teaching Resources:** *Writing Support Transparencies,* 4-A–E; *Writing Support Activity Book,* 4-1
DAY 2	**Revising to Presenting** Students work individually or with peers to revise, edit, and proofread their work for presentation. (pp. 58–64)	**Teaching Resources:** *Writing Support Transparencies,* 4-F–G; *Scoring Rubrics on Transparency,* Ch. 4; *Writing Assessment and Portfolio Management; Formal Assessment,* Ch. 4

Options for Adapting Lesson Plans

HOMEWORK

Have students complete any stage of the lesson for homework.

FEATURES

Extend coverage with Connected Assignment (p. 67), Spotlight on the Humanities (p. 68), Media and Technology Skills (p. 69), and the Standardized Test Preparation Workshop (p. 70).

TECHNOLOGY

Students can complete any stage of the lesson on computer. Have them print out their completed work.

INTEGRATED SKILLS COVERAGE

Integrating Grammar
Three Cases of Personal Pronouns, SE p. 61
Avoiding Usage Errors With *It's* and *Its*, SE p. 63

Reading/Writing Connection
Identify Main Points, SE p. 50
Writing Application, SE p. 51

Viewing and Representing
Critical Viewing, SE pp. 48, 50, 58, 62, 65, 67, 68
Deconstructing Media to Get the Main Idea of the Message's Content, SE p. 68
Using Video to Convey Ideas, SE p. 69

Speaking and Listening
ATE pp. 57, 66

BLOCK SCHEDULING

Pacing Suggestions
For 90-minute Blocks
- Have students complete the Prewriting and Drafting stages in a single period.
- Focus one class period on Revising and Editing and Publishing and Presenting. Allow at least 30 minutes for peer revision.

Resources for Varying Instruction
- *Writing Lab* **CD-ROM** If your students have access to hardware, a 90-minute block provides an ideal opportunity for students to work on computer.
- *Writers at Work* **Videotape** Show the Narration segment in class.

Professional Development Support
- *How to Manage Instruction in the Block* This Teaching Resource provides management and activity suggestions.

ASSESSMENT SUPPORT

Standardized Test Preparation Workshop SE p. 70; ATE p. 60

Standardized Test Preparation Workbook, pp. 7–8

Scoring Rubrics on Transparency, Ch. 4

Formal Assessment, Ch. 4

Writing Assessment and Portfolio Management

MEDIA AND TECHNOLOGY

For the Student
- *Writing Lab* **CD-ROM,** Narration
- *On-Line Exercise Bank,* Section 22.1

For the Teacher
- *Writers at Work* **Videotape,** Narration
- *Resource Pro* **CD-ROM**

MEETING INDIVIDUAL NEEDS

Less Advanced Students ATE pp. 54, 60. See also Ongoing Assessments ATE pp. 51, 53, 57, 61.

Gifted and Talented Students ATE pp. 59, 65

ESL Students ATE pp. 54, 71

Visual/Spatial Learners ATE pp. 55, 56

WRITING AND GRAMMAR WEB SITE

The Interactive Writing and Grammar Web Site provides a wide array of support for students, teachers, and parents. Writing support includes:

- Interactive revision checkers
- Scoring rubrics with complete models

www.phschool.com

LITERATURE CONNECTIONS

Related selections from *Prentice Hall Literature: Timeless Voices, Timeless Themes,* The American Experience:

"For the Love of Books," Rita Dove, SE p. 51

"Song of Myself," Walt Whitman, SE p. 53

Lesson Objectives

1. To write an autobiographical narrative appropriate to audience and purpose

2. To read to appreciate a writer's craft and to discover models for writing

3. To use prewriting strategies to generate ideas and plan

4. To use writing to refine an autobiographical topic and clarify ideas

5. To represent information in a variety of ways, including graphics

6. To develop and revise drafts in terms of structure, paragraphs, sentences, and word choice

7. To edit and proofread to ensure standard English usage and grammar

8. To evaluate writing for both mechanics and content

9. To refine selected work for publication

Critical Viewing

Analyze Students might suggest that an autobiographical narrative might include details about training and preparing for adventure, and the responses of friends and family.

Chapter

4 Narration
Autobiographical Writing

▲ **Critical Viewing**
What details of this water adventure might you expect to read in an autobiographical narrative? **[Analyze]**

Autobiography in Everyday Life

You flick on the television to see your favorite rock musician being interviewed about the evolution of his band. You are riveted to the set as the story of his success unfolds. Learning the truth about an event from an eyewitness or reading a book whose events actually happened grabs our interest because we are invited to share part of someone's life.

Every day, you share bits and pieces of your life. Whether you spin the story of your game-winning soccer goal or explain what occurred during a school trip to the nation's capital, you are telling bits and pieces of the story of your life. When you retell a part of your life story, you are sharing an autobiographical narrative.

48 • Narration

⏱ **TIME AND RESOURCE MANAGER**

Resources
Technology: *Writing Lab* CD-ROM, Narration; *Writers at Work* Videotape, Narration

In-Depth Coverage	Accelerated Pace
• Cover pp. 48–49 in class. • Show Narration section of the *Writers at Work* Videotape. • Read the Model From Literature (pp. 50–51) in class and discuss key features of autobiographical writing.	• Discuss the definitions and types of autobiographical writing in class. • Assign the Model From Literature for independent reading.

What Is Autobiographical Writing?

Autobiographical writing tells a true story about an important period, experience, or relationship in the writer's life. Effective autobiographical writing includes

- a series of events that involve the writer as the main character.
- details, thoughts, feelings, and insights from the writer's perspective.
- a conflict or an event that affects the writer.
- a logical organization that tells the story clearly.

To preview the criteria upon which your autobiographical writing may be evaluated, see the Rubric for Self-Assessment on page 64.

Types of Autobiographical Writing

You can choose from one of the following forms of autobiographical writing to share your personal experience:

- **Autobiographical sketches** often include information about a writer's early life and personal qualities or achievements.
- **Memoirs** are accounts of a writer's relationship with a person, place, or animal.
- **Reflective essays, personal narratives**, or **autobiographical incidents** share a writer's personal experience and provide the writer's reactions to the experience.
- **Anecdotes** are brief and usually humorous accounts of single events that provide some insight into life in general.

PREVIEW
Student Work
IN PROGRESS

Lauren Mizock, a high-school student at Whitney Young Magnet School in Chicago, Illinois, wrote an autobiographical narrative about the experience of riding a commuter train. In this chapter, you will see how Lauren used prewriting, drafting, and revising strategies to write her narrative "Train Tracks." You can read Lauren's completed narrative at the end of this lesson.

Writers in ACTION

While much of her writing is fiction inspired by the events of her life, Julia Alvarez's book Something to Declare *tells the actual stories and conflicts that have framed her life. In this quotation, she explains how the events of her own autobiography influence her approach to writing:*

"I came into English as a ten-year-old from the Dominican Republic. . . . My own island background was steeped in a tradition of storytelling that I wanted to explore in prose."

Autobiographical Writing • 49

PREPARE and ENGAGE

Interest GRABBER Ask students to think of the most interesting thing that has happened to them at school this week. After they jot down their experiences, ask for volunteers to share their stories. Tell them that these brief stories are a type of autobiographical narrative.

Activate Prior Knowledge

Ask students to recall the last time they read or heard a person tell an interesting autobiographical story. The story may have been told by a relative or friend, read in a magazine, or heard on television. What made the story captivating? Would it have been as captivating if it were told by someone other than the subject? Why or why not?

More About the Writer

Julia Alvarez was ten years old when her family fled a dictatorship in the Dominican Republic to live in the United States. Here she learned to speak English and to love books. In fact, she says that writing helped her to adjust to her new life. Alvarez is the acclaimed author of novels, poetry, essays, and many stories and articles. Much of her writing focuses in some way on her Caribbean heritage. Her work has been translated into nine languages.

✓ ONGOING ASSESSMENT: Diagnose

Use one of the following options to diagnose students' current level of proficiency in autobiographical writing.

Option 1 Have students bring in an autobiographical selection or journal entry from their previous year's writing portfolio. Hold conferences with students in order to assess which of them may need extra help.	**Option 2** Ask students to write a short personal anecdote. Even if the story is brief, the structure of their accounts should include some suggestion of exposition, rising action, climax, and resolution. If it does not, students may need more help.

Reading\Writing Connection

Reading: Identify Main Points

In order to understand what is happening in a piece of literature, it is essential to identify main points. Let students read aloud some of the writer's thoughts and reactions. Discuss how these reactions express the main points of the narrative. For example, when the narrator thinks of the bridge as "the portals to heaven," she reveals the wonder with which she sees the United States. This is one of the essay's main points.

Step-by-Step Teaching Guide

Engage Students Through Literature

1. Read "My American Beginning" aloud, or have a prepared student read it.

2. Use questions such as these to discuss the essay with students:

    What are some of the struggles the narrator experiences?

    What insights has she gained from this experience?

3. Ask students to brainstorm for other autobiographical topics for the author. Here are some possibilities:

    The author's life in China

    How the author's family reacted to America

    How the author learned English

    The author's view of how Chinese and American customs compare

4. Students may add similar autobiographical ideas to their topic banks.

Critical Viewing

Hypothesize Students may say boarding the ship, exploring it, meeting others on board, or being homesick.

4.1 Model From Literature

In her reflective essay "My American Beginning," Bette Bao Lord shares her thoughts and feelings about her childhood move to a new country. By reflecting on her experiences in the United States, she gains insight into how being an American has affected her life.

Reading → **Writing Connection**

Reading Strategy: Identify Main Points As you read, identify the **main points,** or most important ideas, in the work. Look for places where the writer has included her thoughts and reactions to events. These reactions often directly express the writer's main points.

▲ **Critical Viewing**
What memories might this photograph bring back to the writer? **[Hypothesize]**

My American Beginning

Bette Bao Lord

My voyage to America began in the autumn of 1946. I was eight years old, sporting pigtails—an innocent, not even armed with a passing acquaintance of A, B, or C. To my chagrin, the ocean was not the vast jade lagoon that I had always envisioned but about as pacific as a fierce dragon with chilies up its snout. And so I bravely cowered in my bunk battling to keep down what I assumed was an authentic American delicacy—spaghetti with meatballs.

Only yesterday, resting my chin on the rails of the S.S. *Marylinx,* I peered into the mist for *Mei Guo,* beautiful country. It refused to appear. Then, within a blink, there was the golden gate, more like the portals to heaven than the arches of a man-made bridge.

I arrived in Brooklyn, New York, on a Sunday. On Monday I was enrolled at P.S. 8. By putting up 10 fingers, I found myself sentenced to the fifth grade. It was a terrible mistake. By American reckoning, I had just turned eight. And so I was the

The writer begins by establishing herself as the main character in this narrative.

Contrasting images of China and the United States helps the writer introduce the conflict. By comparing San Francisco's Golden Gate Bridge to the entry to heaven, the writer shows the awe she feels about entering the United States.

shortest student by a head or two in class. In retrospect, I suppose that everyone just supposed that Chinese were supposed to be small.

Only yesterday, holding my hand over my heart, I joined schoolmates to stare at the Stars and Stripes and say along: "I pledge a lesson to the frog of the United States of America. And to the wee puppet for witches' hands. One Asian, in the vestibule, with little tea and just rice for all."

Only yesterday, rounding third base in galoshes, I swallowed a barrelful of tears wondering what wrong I had committed to anger my teammates so. Why were they all madly screaming at me to go home, go home?

Only yesterday, parroting the patter on our Philco radio, I mastered a few mouthfuls of syllables and immediately my teacher began eliciting my opinions. . . . I was amazed by the fact that an exalted teacher would solicit the opinion of a lowly student. Teachers in China never did that.

Eventually, I came to realize that the merits of one's opinions were not the determining goal of the exercise. The goal was to nurture a civil society where everyone is free to speak. Today, when political correctness threatens the rigor of our intellectual debates, how I value this aspect of my early education! To me, the cacophony of puddingheads spewing their views is preferable to the clarion call of even the greatest emperor.

Only yesterday, standing still a head or two short at graduation, I felt as tall as the Statue of Liberty as I recited Walt Whitman: "I hear America singing, the varied carols I hear. . . . Each singing what belongs to him or her and to none else."

Thus I have never forgotten that one need not lose one's native culture in order to become an American. On the contrary, this individual feels doubly blessed. For to me, Americans—though as different as sisters and brothers are—belong to the same family. For to me, America is a road cleared by the footfalls of millions of immigrants and paved with something far more precious than gold—grit and hope.

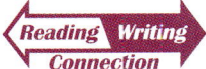 **Reading Writing Connection**

Writing Application: Help Readers Identify the Main Idea As you draft your own autobiographical narrative, use details of your thoughts, feelings, and reactions to emphasize your main ideas.

By including her misinterpretation of both the Pledge of Allegiance and the rules of baseball, the writer provides insight into specific childhood experiences.

Lord organizes memories and experiences in three separate paragraphs. She links the paragraphs by repeating the phrase "only yesterday" at the beginning of each one.

Here, Lord elaborates on how her childhood experience has influenced her adult attitudes.

The writer concludes with an insight about the perspective she has gained from her experiences.

LITERATURE

To read another autobiographical essay about a treasured childhood memory, see Rita Dove's essay, "For the Love of Books." You can find Dove's essay in *Prentice Hall Literature. Timeless Voices, Timeless Themes, The American Experience.*

Teaching From the Model

You can use this model from literature to show students one way to find a relevant topic for an autobiographical narrative. The author, Bette Bao Lord, relates her early experiences as an immigrant in the United States. Have students remember a time they faced something unfamiliar, such as a new school or a new neighborhood. How did they react to this situation? How did it make them feel?

More About the Writer

Bette Bao Lord was born in Shanghai, China, and she became a naturalized U.S. citizen in 1964. The author draws upon her life and the lives of her family members in China and America for much of her writing.

Integrating Vocabulary Skills

The author states, "To me, the *cacophony* of puddingheads *spewing* their views is preferable to the *clarion call* of even the greatest emperor." Have students guess at the meanings of the words in italics based on the context clues. Then, have them look up the words in the dictionary to determine whether their guesses were accurate.

Reading\Writing Connection

Writing Connection: Help Readers Identify Main Ideas

Review the main points that Lord makes. (A new culture is confusing to a young immigrant. In America, everyone is free to speak. One need not lose one's native culture in order to become an American.) Note that Lord describes events, feelings, and reactions to support these points. Tell students as they draft to maintain a connection between their main points and the autobiographical details they include.

✔ **ONGOING ASSESSMENT: Monitor and Reinforce**

If some students have difficulty understanding the implied reality behind the childhood scenes that Lord describes, try the following option.

Have students compose a list of questions they would like to ask the author, for example, "Why was putting up ten fingers a terrible mistake?"	or "Why did you call the teacher 'exalted'"? Have students brainstorm for possible answers to these questions.

Step-by-Step Teaching Guide

Prewriting: Personal Experience Timeline

1. Have students tear a sheet of paper in half vertically and use one of the resulting strips to make their timelines. Tell them to save the other half of the piece of paper.

2. As students list important events in their lives, encourage them to include items without worrying about finding the perfect topic.

3. As students review their timelines, have them circle any events they may want to consider further for narrative writing.

4. Have students list vertically on the other piece of paper the topics they circled. Under each topic have them list events and people they associate with the topic.

Step-by-Step Teaching Guide

Prewriting: Photographs and Memories

1. Suggest that students put their photographs in chronological order as they look through them.

2. On a piece of paper, have students list a topic for each photo and write down any incident related to the photo that occurs to them.

3. Have students select the topic they would most like to write about.

Step-by-Step Teaching Guide

Prewriting: Observation Notebook

Teaching Resources: Writing Support Transparencies, 4-A

1. Display Transparency 4-A to show the student writer's observations.

2. Encourage students to allow their ideas to flow freely as they jot down information.

3. Ask students to review their observations and circle the ideas they find the most interesting.

4.2 Prewriting

Choosing Your Topic

Autobiographical writing draws on specific events or incidents that have significance to you. To help you choose a memorable experience for your writing, use these strategies:

Strategies for Generating a Topic

1. **Personal Experience Timeline** On a timeline, plot dates and descriptions of memorable experiences or events. After you complete the timeline, review your experiences and choose one of special significance as your topic.

2. **Photographs and Memories** Look through a family album or a personal photo collection you have kept. Jot down notes about the experiences in your life that the photographs depict. Choose one, and expand upon it.

3. **Observation Notebook** For the next few days, keep a journal of what you see and observe wherever your life takes you—at school, at home, at work, at the mall. Choose one incident or event to describe in a piece of autobiographical writing. The sample below shows how Lauren Mizock used an observation notebook.

Writing Lab CD-ROM

For more help finding a topic, explore the activities and suggestions in the Choosing a Topic section of the Narration lesson.

Student Work IN PROGRESS

Name: Lauren Mizock
Whitney Young Magnet School
Chicago, IL

Using an Observation Notebook

Lauren Mizock, a high-school student from Chicago, Illinois, used an observation notebook to find a topic for her autobiographical sketch "Train Tracks." She decided to write about her job.

...I've just learned to stir-fry vegetables. This new skill makes me feel independent. . . .

...The argument in social studies class made me wonder: What do I really think about students being denied the right to work after school?

...At night, I really like time to devote to winding down from the events of the day.

52 • Autobiographical Writing

⏱ TIME AND RESOURCE MANAGER

Resources
Print: *Writing Support Transparencies,* 4-A–C
Technology: *Writing Lab* CD-ROM, Narration; *Writers at Work* Videotape, Narration

In-Depth Coverage	Accelerated Pace
• Work through the prewriting strategies with the class. • Use the Responding to Fine Art transparency (4-B) to generate additional topics. • Demonstrate the Isolating an Episode technique (p. 54) for narrowing a topic.	• Discuss strategies for generating topics. • Have students work independently to choose and narrow their topics. • Have students work with partners to focus on audience, purpose, and gathering details.

TOPIC BANK

If you are having trouble finding a topic, consider these possibilities:

1. **Narrative About an Achievement** Focus on a specific goal that you have worked hard to achieve. In a narrative, tell how you set your sights and met a difficult challenge.

2. **True-Friends Narrative** Tell the true story of how you met a friend who has had an influence on your life. Include your experiences, thoughts, and feelings to show how your friend has affected you.

Responding to Fine Art

3. Sports often provide a good framework for autobiographical writing. Let *Out at Third* spark your own writing ideas. Consider professional sports events you have attended, or choose an incident from your own athletic experience to describe in an autobiographical essay.

Out at Third, Nelson Rosenberg, The Phillips Collection, Washington, DC.

Responding to Literature

4. Read the opening lines of Walt Whitman's "Song of Myself." Use Whitman's inspirational poetry to reflect on your life. Write a narrative about a life experience that illustrates the line "I celebrate myself, and sing myself." You can find more of the poem in *Prentice Hall Literature: Timeless Voices, Timeless Themes*, The American Experience.

📝 Cooperative Writing Opportunity

5. **Class Autobiography** With a group, divide the task of creating a class autobiography. Some group members can collect or take photographs of class events and activities; some can write narrative sections to describe class milestones; and others can conduct interviews to collect personal reactions and thoughts from classmates and teachers. Make copies of your work to share with the class.

Prewriting • 53

Step-by-Step Teaching Guide

Responding to Fine Art

Out at Third by Nelson Rosenberg
Teaching Resources: Writing Support Transparencies, 4-B

1. Display the transparency and use questions such as the following to engage students in discussion about it. *What is happening in this picture? How do you think these players are feeling?*

2. Ask students to brainstorm for autobiographical narrative ideas suggested by this piece of art.

    Here are some possibilities:

    "My Greatest Triumph/Disaster"
    "My Trip to the Ballpark"

3. Tell students they may include any of these topic ideas, along with their own suggestions, in their topic banks.

Responding to Literature

You can find Walt Whitman's "Song of Myself" on page 408 of *Prentice Hall Literature: Timeless Voices, Timeless Themes,* The American Experience. Students might use these lines as a jumping-off point for an essay about a time they learned something by "walking a mile in someone else's shoes."

"I celebrate myself,
And what I assume you shall assume,
For every atom belonging to me as good belongs to you."

✅ **ONGOING ASSESSMENT: Monitor and Reinforce**

If you observe that some students are having difficulty choosing a topic, try one of the following strategies.

Option 1 Have students consult with family and friends. Do others remember incidents that might make an interesting autobiographical narrative? People who have known them may well remember significant incidents that students themselves have forgotten.

Option 2 Suggest that students review old letters or diaries for inspiration. In addition, students might review their writing portfolios from previous years to help jog their memories.

Prewriting: Isolate an Episode

Teaching Resources: Writing Support Transparencies, 4-C

1. Assure students that even if their ideas about an autobiographical topic are unformed, they can find an aspect to write about.

2. Display Transparency 4-C to show students how Lauren generated a list and selected one idea.

3. Tell students to write their lists quickly, without pausing to consider any individual item. They should evaluate their ideas only when the lists are as complete as possible.

4. Suggest that students jot down sublists of events associated with each episode in their lists in the left margin. This will help them see which of the events contain the most detail and are thus most promising to write about.

Customize for
Less Advanced Students

Some students may benefit by having their lists reviewed by another person. Have students trade their lists with a partner. What item in the list does the reviewer find most interesting? What questions does he or she want to have answered about that topic? The lists are returned and the writers can consider the suggestions.

Customize for
ESL Students

Encourage students to talk with a more-fluent English speaker about their topics before they begin to write. Some students may choose to write about a topic that is not familiar to many of their classmates, such as a particular aspect of their native culture. If so, have them work with their partners to determine which details need to be explained and which they may assume their classmates will already understand.

4.2

Narrowing Your Topic

The more focused your topic is, the sharper the image you can create for your readers. Before you begin drafting, focus your topic by making a list to isolate an episode.

Isolate an Episode

Take the time to list all of the events related to your topic. Review the list, and choose a significant event that you could develop into an effective piece of autobiographical writing. For example, if you are writing a reflective essay, choose an episode that shows how your experience provided you with an insight. Note how Lauren Mizock narrowed her topic by isolating an episode.

Student Work IN PROGRESS

Name: Lauren Mizock
Whitney Young Magnet School
Chicago, IL

Isolating an Episode

Lauren generated a list of all the events surrounding her after-school job. She narrowed her topic by choosing to develop one idea—waiting for the train.

- Getting ready to go to work.
- Walk across town.
- ✓ Wait for train.
- Ride train.
- Get to work.
- Begin to paint.

54 • Autobiographical Writing

Considering Your Audience and Purpose

Your audience is your readers—the people with whom you intend to share your narrative. Keep their experiences in mind as you write. You may need to include characterizations of the people you describe or explanations of the places you include. For example, if you describe a speech that you gave at a local library, you may need to tell your readers how and why you were invited to speak.

Your purpose—your reasons for writing a narrative—will also guide the types of details you choose to include. If you want to entertain, include humorous elements. In contrast, if you want to share a serious insight, replace humor with an analysis of your experiences.

Gathering Details

You are the best source of information for your autobiographical writing. Begin by gathering details from your own recollections. Use freewriting as a way to get started.

Freewrite to Gather Details

Freewriting is one way to gather details from memory. Give yourself a time limit of ten or fifteen minutes. As you write, let the memory of one detail lead to the next. At this stage, do not worry about organization or sentence structure. Concentrate on remembering everything you can. Later, you'll be able to shape your writing correctly.

When you finish freewriting, review what you've written to identify other information you'll want to collect. Use these ideas:

Using the Power of Observation Review your freewriting to identify people and places that you can observe. Study the real-life characters and settings further by looking at photographs, visiting settings, or interviewing people who played a part in your experience. Jot down additional details that can be used in your narrative.

Adding Factual Information Some autobiographical incidents may require research beyond your memory or power of observation. For example, if you are describing your trip to a city in another state, you may need to incorporate facts like climate or tourist spots so your readers will understand the incident you describe. Do not assume that your experience has provided you with this knowledge; a reference book can give you the details you need to make your writing accurate.

Writing Lab CD-ROM

To help you identify your audience and shape your writing appropriately, use the Audience Profile activity.

Prewriting: Freewrite to Gather Details

1. Before students begin to freewrite, ask them to identify their audience. They may find it helpful to imagine a specific individual who will eventually read the essay.

2. Remind students that, as in the preceding listing activity, they are to write as quickly as they can, without pausing to worry about spelling, punctuation, or the quality of details. The point is to get ideas from brain to paper with as little interference as possible.

3. Once their ideas are on paper, students can begin to focus and extend particular ideas.

4. Tell students that after using the freewriting strategy to gather details, they may find it necessary to research some details to add clarity and assure accuracy for their audience.

Customize for
Spatial Learners

Once students have focused on a particular incident (a vacation trip, a family celebration, a first-time experience) they may wish to retrieve available snapshots from family albums or collections. The photographs may help add details and could become part of their final presentation.

Drafting: Begin with a Compelling Lead

1. You may wish to refer students to their literature anthologies to find first lines of essays and stories that they find compelling.

2. Have students share and discuss strong examples of first lines that they have encountered.

3. Suggest that students scan their freewriting for any sentences or phrases that might hook readers.

Drafting: Organize to Develop Pacing

Teaching Resources: Writing Support Transparencies, 4-D; Writing Support Activity Book, 4-1

1. Display Transparency 4-D and use it to show how Lauren organized her narrative.

2. If the class has recently read a short story, you may wish to use the transparency to show how the story's plot could be diagrammed.

3. As students plan their own work, suggest that they first determine the climax, the highest point of conflict or reader interest. Then, work in the details that lead up to and follow the climax.

4. Give students copies of the blank organizer (4-1) to use as they structure and pace their narratives.

Customize for
Visual/Spatial Learners

Suggest that students sketch quick "storyboards" that include the beginning, middle, and end of their narratives. Then, have them make notes under each scene and compare these notes with their drafts to identify any missing information or gaps.

4.3 Drafting

Shaping Your Writing

Like all narratives, an autobiographical narrative tells a story that has a beginning, a middle, and an end. To maintain your readers' interest, establish the proper pacing for each of these parts.

Begin With a Compelling Lead

Sometimes, a simple but poignant sentence can provide just the right amount of information to build the reader's curiosity. Look at these opening sentences:

EXAMPLES: My grandfather handed me a silver box, and suddenly the room became silent.

I think my dog would write me a good recommendation.

Devise a simple sentence to hook your reader. Then, let the rest of your essay develop the point you've introduced.

Organize to Develop Pacing

To keep up the pace of your writing, balance descriptions with events that move the plot along. In the diagram shown here, notice how plot events leading up to the climax add to the conflict and raise interest in the character's success. Be sure your narrative includes a conflict, and keep these tips for each stage of the plot in mind as you draft.

- In the *exposition*, provide background to help your readers understand the narrative to follow.

- Develop the *rising action* by identifying the problem and building toward the *climax* of the narrative.

- In the *falling action*, tie up any loose ends that remain by describing events that follow the climax.

- Use the *resolution* to show the insight you gained from your experience.

Writing Lab CD-ROM

Use the Outline tool to help you organize your narrative.

Did well until the last ten minutes of taping; lost in final rounds

Practiced, studied, prepped for audition

Invited to try out for game show

Climax

Rising Action

Falling Action

Came home disappointed but excited about my experience

Exposition

I was living a quiet life, happily enjoying high school.

Resolution

Looking forward to the next big challenge

56 • Autobiographical Writing

⏱ TIME AND RESOURCE MANAGER

Resources
Print: *Writing Support Transparencies,* 4-D–E; *Writing Support Activity Book,* 4-1
Technology: *Writing Lab* CD-ROM, Narration

In-Depth Coverage	Accelerated Pace
• Work through the Shaping Your Writing strategies with the class. • Have students prepare plot diagrams. • Have students write their first drafts in class.	• Have students review pp. 56–57 independently, and then write their drafts. • Respond to individual drafting issues as needed.

Providing Elaboration

As you write your draft, look for places to develop your narrative by adding details that bring your experience to life for your readers. Include details that reveal your thoughts and feelings, as well as details about people and places. One way to add such elaboration is to "explode a moment."

Add Details by Exploding a Moment

When you "explode a moment," you expand a description by telling more about what happened, what it looked like, or how the people involved reacted. Cut several "explosion" shapes from construction paper. Your shapes, like those shown in the student model, should be large enough to write on. After you draft a paragraph or two, pause and look for places where you can "explode a moment" by using elaboration. Write the details you want to add on the colored-paper explosions, and paste them lightly on your draft. You can incorporate these details when you revise.

Student Work
IN PROGRESS

Name: *Lauren Mizock*
Whitney Young Magnet School
Chicago, IL

Exploding a Moment

Lauren pasted explosions into the second paragraph of her draft where she wanted to add details about her thoughts and reactions.

I sit down between a homeless man and a young professional man. The homeless man is in layers of gray, tattered clothes. **Once, his clothes were new.** The urban commuter is wearing a bright white shirt and a silk tie. It is a cleanliness that is as important an element of his daily uniform as his silk tie. **it gleams in the sunlight** As a teenage painter, decked in red, **and splattered with paint** my presence completes a Chicago social rainbow on that bench.

Drafting: Add Details by Exploding a Moment

Teaching Resources: Writing Support Transparencies, 4-E

1. Use the transparency to show students how "Exploding the Moment" looks in practice. Point out that the author added the "explosions" to add details about her thoughts and reactions.

2. Explain that using "explosions" makes writing much more interesting because it gives vivid insights into the thoughts and feelings of the author. This is especially important in autobiographical narratives, because understanding the perspective of the author is integral to understanding the story.

3. Suggest that students "explode" verbs and nouns. In other words, have them examine the verbs and nouns they've used and determine whether any of them are unclear or vague. If they are, students might replace the words or they might add some explanation to them.

Integrating Speaking and Listening Skills

After students have written their drafts, let them choose one paragraph that has been troublesome and read it to a partner. After listening carefully to the paragraph, let the partner make suggestions about wording and about adding details. Remind students that sometimes they will achieve clarity by removing details rather than by adding them.

ONGOING ASSESSMENT: Monitor and Reinforce

If you observe that students are having difficulty completing their elaboration charts, try one of the following strategies.

Option 1 Suggest that students exchange drafts and note where they feel more information or more detail is called for. Each student might prepare a short list of suggestions for elaboration.

Option 2 Model the process of "Exploding the Moment" for students, using a passage of your own writing.

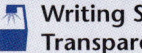

TIME SAVERS!

Writing Support Transparencies
Use the transparencies for Chapter 4 to facilitate the teaching of strategies.

Writing Support Activity Book
Use the graphic organizers for Chapter 4 to facilitate student planning.

Revising: Write a Strong Conclusion

1. Have your students review the endings of their essays. Do they end on a strong note? Have students review the list of techniques for writing conclusions on this page. Invite them to describe which technique, if any, they used. Have them explain why they picked a certain technique.

2. Have students rewrite their conclusions using a different technique. Then, have them read both versions aloud to partners and discuss which one is more effective.

3. Ask whether any students devised new techniques for ending their essays. If they have, ask them to share these ideas with the class.

Critical Viewing

Hypothesize Students may suggest that *road, path,* and the other words suggest direction, change, progress, and transition. Many autobiographies focus on changes or transitions in life.

Revising

Revision is your chance to polish your writing. Add details that make people and settings more vivid, make dialogue more realistic, and improve the flow of your writing. Begin your revision by evaluating the overall structure of your narrative.

Revising Your Overall Structure

Write a Strong Conclusion

The conclusion of your narrative is your opportunity to sum up main points and leave your readers with a strong final impression. An especially appropriate way to end a piece of autobiographical writing is to step back from the experiences you've described and take a moment to explain the significance of the ideas, event, or situation that is central to your essay.

▶ REVISION STRATEGY
Evaluating Your Conclusion

Review your conclusion to identify what it accomplishes. It may end with a thought-provoking question, it may provide an insight you've gained from the experience, or it may do little more than indicate the end of the essay. Take this opportunity to improve your conclusion. Consider these solutions:

- **Make a Bridge to the Present** If you wrote about a memory, conclude your narrative with an observation from your current point of view. By showing a contrast or a connection between the past and the present, you can emphasize the influence that the experience has had.

- **Provide an Insight** Review your prewriting notes to recall your purpose for writing and your reasons for choosing a writing topic. Consider how the event was significant, how it affected or changed your life, or how it let you see others differently. Finish your paper by addressing these issues in the closing paragraphs.

🔲 Research Tip

To see how others have concluded their autobiographies, browse through the library to research the work of professional writers.

▼ Critical Viewing

Why do you think the words *bridge, road, path,* and *journey* frequently appear in titles of autobiographies? **[Hypothesize]**

58 • Autobiographical Writing

⏱ TIME AND RESOURCE MANAGER	
Resources **Print:** *Writing Support Transparencies,* 4-F–G **Technology:** *Writing Lab* CD-ROM, Narration	
In-Depth Coverage	**Accelerated Pace**
• Work through the revision strategies in class. • Have students begin to revise their paragraphs in class. Encourage them to use the strategies they have been learning. Address individual revision concerns as they arise.	• Assign students to review pp. 58–62 independently. • Have students revise their drafts in response to peer review.

Revising Your Paragraphs

Use Dialogue to Give Information

Once you have revised the overall structure of your paper, focus on improving each paragraph. One way to revise lengthy paragraphs in your writing is to break them up with dialogue. Consider using dialogue instead of narration to convey plot events, to introduce further conflict, or to reveal the thoughts, feelings, and reactions of the people in your narrative.

REVISION STRATEGY
Adding Dialogue

As you read each paragraph of your narrative, mark places where you have described a plot event or a character's thoughts or feelings. When you mark a long block of narration or description, draw a dialogue bubble near the text. Jot down ideas for revising by turning description into dialogue, inserting conversations to show new information or revealing a character's thoughts in his or her own words. Then, build the content of your dialogue bubbles into your draft.

 Speaking and Listening Tip

The next time you're involved in a class discussion, notice the way natural dialogue sounds. Incorporate your observations into your draft to make the dialogue sound more realistic.

Student Work IN PROGRESS

Name: *Lauren Mizock*
Whitney Young Magnet School
Chicago, IL

Adding Dialogue

Instead of using a description to convey how her fellow passenger feels, Lauren adds dialogue that moves the narrative along and provides additional information.

"I'm not gonna even bother to get up when the next train decides to pass us by," he says. Surprised and pleased by his friendliness, I laugh, "Seriously."

I look at the commuter sitting next to me. His hands are pressed to his temples as if to calm his impatience. He gets up with each ~~passing~~ *approaching* train, and sits down in frustration as each one passes.

Revising: Adding Dialogue

Teaching Resources: Writing Support Transparencies, 4-F

1. Display Transparency 4-F to show how Lauren uses dialogue to give the reader information and add interest to the story.

2. Then, have students reread the dialogue they have added to their narratives and make any additions or corrections.

3. If necessary, review the rules for punctuating dialogue. Remind students that when writing dialogue, they should begin a new paragraph with each change of speaker.

Customize for
Gifted and Talented Students

Challenge students to rewrite all or part of their narratives in dialogue form. Encourage them to have classmates perform their work as a play. Discuss how using only dialogue changes the narrative. Ask them what other tools can help communicate meaning in a dialogue. (Students should mention facial expressions, body language, scenery, and props.)

 TIME SAVERS!

 Writing Support Transparencies
Use the transparencies for Chapter 4 to facilitate the teaching of strategies.

Step-by-Step Teaching Guide

Revising: Check Sentence Beginnings

Teaching Resources: Writing Support Transparencies, 4-G

1. Allow students time to list their sentence beginnings on paper.

2. Use the transparency (4-G) to show how Lauren used listing to identify the overuse of the pronoun *I* and to revise sentence beginnings. Discuss the way each of the revisions was made.

3. Let students rewrite or combine their sentences to vary their sentence beginnings.

4. When they finish, have them repeat the bracketing exercise. Do they now have more variety in their sentence beginnings?

5. After the revisions, have students reread their sentences in the context of the paragraphs they have written to check the flow of their writing.

Customize for
Less Advanced Students

To give students more practice in sentence beginnings, have them list the first words in the first three paragraphs of the Model From Literature on page 50.

Revising Your Sentences
Check Sentence Beginnings

Look closely at each sentence in your draft. Although your autobiographical narrative focuses on your experiences and insights, don't fall into the habit of starting each sentence with *I*. If you vary the way you begin your sentences, you can improve the flow of your writing and make it more interesting to your readers.

▶ **REVISION STRATEGY**
Bracketing Sentence Beginnings

Take an objective look at your sentence beginnings by bracketing the first word of each sentence. Then, make a list of the words you've bracketed. You will probably find that a number of sentences begin with *I*. Challenge yourself to break this pattern by combining sentences, adding introductory phrases, or inverting the normal subject-verb order to achieve variety in your sentence beginnings.

Student Work
IN PROGRESS

Name: *Lauren Mizock*
Whitney Young Magnet School
Chicago, IL

Bracketing Sentence Beginnings

Lauren listed the first words of her sentences and identified the overuse of the pronoun I. By eliminating one case, she broke the pattern and created a stronger, simpler sentence in the process.

I
Four
I
There

[I] lean my head over the train tracks and look for an oncoming flutter of headlights. [Four thirty-seven] P.M. [I] have less than a half hour to get to the other side of town. [I realize]There is no train in sight.

60 • Autobiographical Writing

✦ STANDARDIZED TEST PREPARATION WORKSHOP

Personal Pronouns Standardized test questions may require students to choose the correct personal pronoun to replace a noun or group of nouns. Provide students with opportunities to practice identifying the correct personal pronouns in writing.

Which personal pronoun below completes the sentence?

Alex and Mark cried because ___ both skinned their knees on the driveway.

A I
B he
C they
D we

Students should recognize that **C** is the correct answer because it is a third-person, plural pronoun that refers to the two boys. A and B are incorrect because they are singular pronouns. D is incorrect because it is a first-person pronoun.

Grammar in Your Writing
Using the Three Cases of Personal Pronouns

To avoid unnecessary repetition in your narrative, use pronouns to replace repeated nouns. There are three cases of personal pronouns: **nominative, objective,** and **possessive.**

Nominative Pronouns	**Objective Pronouns**	**Possessive Pronouns**
I, you, he, she, it, we, you, they	*me, you, him, her, it, us, you, them*	*my, mine, your, yours, his, her, hers, its, our, ours, their, theirs*

Nominative case pronouns are used as subjects or predicate nominatives.

Subject: **She** traveled all over Europe.

Predicate nominative: The president of the ski club is **he.**

Objective case pronouns are used as indirect objects, direct objects, or objects of prepositions.

Indirect object: Mary gave **him** the book.

Direct object: Rick moved **it** across the room.

Object of a preposition: Why can't you share the news with **me**?

Possessive pronouns show possession or ownership. Some possessive pronouns can serve as subjects or predicate nominatives. Others can function as direct objects or objects of prepositions.

Subject: **Ours** is the most creative solution.

Predicate nominative: The essay the group listened to was **mine.**

Direct object: Jonah put **yours** and **theirs** on the table.

Object of a preposition: Put your photographs in the album near **his.**

Some possessive pronouns can serve as adjectives.

Adjective: Let's discuss **my** report, **your** questions about the author, and then look for more information about **his** life.

Find It in Your Reading Read "My American Beginning" by Bette Bao Lord. List examples of each of the three cases of pronouns in the narrative.

Find It in Your Writing As you proofread your autobiographical narrative, underline the pronouns you have used. Make sure that you have used the correct case.

For more on pronoun usage, see Chapter 22.

Revising • 61

Using the Three Cases of Personal Pronouns

1. Give students a copy of an article written in the first person from a magazine or newspaper. Have them underline the personal pronouns, classify them according to case, and then share their answers with the class.

2. Then, have students cross out the pronouns and substitute each pronoun with its antecedent. Discuss with students how the omission of pronouns affects the reading of the narrative. (The continual use of nouns in place of pronouns makes the writing repetitive and cluttered.) This will emphasize to students the importance of pronouns.

3. Ask students to reread their own essays to determine whether any nouns should be replaced by pronouns. Remind them also to make sure that each pronoun has a clear antecedent.

Find It in Your Reading

Students may find the following personal pronouns in Lord's essay:

Nominative: *I, it, they*
Objective: *me, him, her*
Possessive: *my, its, our, their*

Ask students why they think *I* and *my* come up so frequently. (Students should realize it is because the author is writing in the first person.)

Find It in Your Writing

Have students exchange papers with partners to check pronoun usage. If students find sentences that require correction, let them write the suggested pronoun corrections on separate paper so that the authors may consider the changes.

✓ **ONGOING ASSESSMENT: Prerequisite Skills**

If students have difficulty with correct usage of the three cases of personal pronouns, you may wish to refer them to the following material to ensure coverage of prerequisite skills.

In the Textbook	Print Resources	Technology
Pronoun Usage, Section 22.1, pp. 562–568	*Grammar Exercise Workbook,* pp. 103–108	*On-Line Exercise Bank,* Section 22.1

Revising Your Word Choice

Replace Colorless Words

Although several words may convey the same general idea, some words are so vague that they do not contribute to a mental picture of a scene or character. Review the chart below, and then revise your writing to replace vague, colorless words with precise ones.

These sentences are colorless.	These sentences paint a clear contrast.
The youth wore casual clothes.	The young man was dressed in baggy jeans and a tie-dyed T-shirt.
The older man wore a shirt and a tie.	The middle-aged man wore a dark, pinstriped, double-breasted suit.

▶ **REVISION STRATEGY**
Using a Thesaurus to Find Colorful Synonyms

One way to generate precise words is to create a word list. Choose a word to revise. Brainstorm for a list of synonyms or phrases that convey similar ideas. Add to your list by consulting a thesaurus. After you have gathered several different options, consider the shades of meaning each choice conveys. Then, decide on the word that best suits your narrative.

Peer Review

Process Share

Get together with a group to discuss the experience of writing your autobiographical essay. As a group, consider these focus points:

- **Discuss Difficulties** Ask members of your group to identify the problems they faced and the solutions they tried. Group members may trade solutions and insights.

- **Find Similarities** As you listen to your peers discuss concerns about their writing, look for common problems or successes that each writer in the group encountered.

By discussing the process of writing and the issues that each member of your group has addressed, you may improve your approach to future writing projects.

4.5 Editing and Proofreading

Before you finalize your autobiographical writing, proofread it to correct errors. Mistakes in grammar, spelling, or mechanics in your writing may distract your readers from the ideas you want to convey. Proofread your draft to make your final copy error-free.

Focusing on Your Spelling

As you proofread your essay, double-check to make sure that you have spelled words correctly. Use the following methods to catch misspellings:

- Reread your paper, and circle any words that you are unsure how to spell. Don't leave accuracy to chance; find the correct spelling in a dictionary.
- If you worked on a computer, run your paper through the spell-check function. Don't rely solely on the software, however. Reread your paper to find words that are not identified by a spell checker.
- Review the spelling of proper nouns, including the names of people and places.

Grammar in Your Writing
Avoiding Usage Errors With *It's* and *Its*

It's and *its* look similar and sound the same, but the two different spellings indicate different meanings. Review the following examples to become familiar with the rules of usage for them.

It's is a contraction that stands for the words "it is."

> EXAMPLE   It's time to hand in your papers. (It is time to hand in your papers.)

Its is a possessive pronoun. Like *his* or *hers*, *its* shows ownership.

> EXAMPLE: The dog wagged its tail. (The dog wagged his tail.)

Find It in Your Writing As you proofread your autobiographical narrative, check to make sure that you have used *it's* and *its* correctly.

For more on miscellaneous problems in usage, see Chapter 25.

Editing and Proofreading • 63

Step-by-Step Teaching Guide

Proofreading: Spelling

1. Inform students that editing and proofreading may be viewed as extensions of the paragraphing process. Suggest that students check punctuation and spelling paragraph by paragraph.

2. Check that students reread carefully to proofread for spelling errors. Have all questionable spellings been checked with a dictionary or computer spell checker? Are commonly used homonyms misspelled?

Step-by-Step Teaching Guide

Avoiding Usage Errors With *It's* and *Its*

1. Remind students that errors involving *it's* and *its* must be spotted in proofreading. These words cannot be picked up when a work is read aloud because they sound the same.

2. Write the following sentence on the board.

   Its important for America to live up to it's potential.

3. Then, challenge students to correct the sentence. Have someone write it correctly on the board. (**It's** important for America to live up to **its** potential.) Ask students to name which form is the pronoun and which is the contraction.

Find It in Your Writing

Have students circle each use of *it's* and *its* in their writing. Have them reread the sentences in which the words are used to be sure that they are spelled correctly.

⏱ TIME AND RESOURCE MANAGER

Resources
Print: *Scoring Rubrics on Transparency*, Ch. 4; *Writing Assessment and Portfolio Management*; *Formal Assessment*, Ch. 4
Technology: *Writing Lab* CD-ROM, Narration

In-Depth Coverage	Accelerated Pace
• Review p. 63 in class, including Grammar in Your Writing. • Have students edit and proofread their narratives in class. • Give step-by-step coverage of Publishing and Presenting (p. 64).	• Assign pp. 63–64 for independent review. • Have students independently edit and proofread their narratives. • Respond to individual editing issues as needed.

1. Encourage students to brainstorm for other ideas for publishing their writing.

2. Tell students that as they prepare their narratives for publication, they might add illustrations or photos to their work. Remind them that visual components can help to convey meaning. Ask them to consider what type of illustration would be most helpful to a reader.

ASSESS and CLOSE

Step-by-Step Teaching Guide

Assessment

Teaching Resources: Scoring Rubrics on Transparency, Ch. 4; Writing Assessment and Portfolio Management; Formal Assessment, Ch. 4

1. Display the Scoring Rubric transparency and review the criteria in class.

2. Before students proceed with self-assessment, you may wish to review Lauren's final draft on pages 65–66. Have students score the final draft in one or more of the rubric categories.

3. In addition to student self-assessment, you may wish to:

   • score student essays yourself using the rubric and scoring models from *Writing Assessment and Portfolio Management*.

   • review the Standardized Test Preparation Workshop on pages 70–71 and have students respond to a narrative writing prompt within a set time limit.

   • administer the Chapter 4 assessment from *Formal Assessment* in the Teaching Resources to assess students' grasp of concepts presented.

4.6 Publishing and Presenting

Building Your Portfolio

Sharing your essay is an effective way to provide insights into your personal history, your beliefs, and your unique point of view. Consider these ideas for sharing your work:

1. **Create an Illustrated Edition** Present your final draft in an illustrated version. Use photographs or illustrations to enhance the ideas in your writing.

2. **Post Your Essay** Create a bulletin board display of your essay and those of your classmates. Have each writer supply a short commentary about the event or idea that inspired the writing.

Reflecting on Your Writing

Take a few minutes to write about the process of writing an autobiographical essay. Use these suggestions to spark your reflection. Then, add your comments to your portfolio.

• Identify an insight that you gained as a result of writing this essay.

• Explain the strategies you used to make changes between your first and final draft.

Internet Tip

To see model essays scored with this rubric, go to **www.phschool.com**

Rubric for Self-Assessment

Use these criteria to evaluate your autobiographical writing:

	Score 4	Score 3	Score 2	Score 1
Audience and Purpose	Contains details that engage the audience; provides a clear insight about an experience	Contains details appropriate for an audience; addresses a clear reason for writing	Contains few details that appeal to an audience; gives a reason for writing	Is not written for a specific audience or purpose
Organization	Organizes events to create an interesting narrative	Presents a clear sequence of events	Presents a confusing sequence of events	Presents no logical order of events
Elaboration	Contains rich details that create vivid characters; uses dialogue that develops characters and plot	Contains details that develop character and describe setting; uses dialogue	Contains characters and setting; uses some dialogue	Contains few or no details to develop characters or setting; uses no dialogue
Use of Language	Uses an excellent variety of sentence beginnings; contains no errors in grammar, punctuation, or spelling	Uses a good variety of sentence beginnings; contains few errors in grammar, punctuation, and spelling	Introduces some variety in sentence beginnings; contains some errors in grammar, punctuation, and spelling	Uses monotonous pattern of sentence beginnings; has many errors in grammar, punctuation, and spelling

64 • Autobiographical Writing

☑ ONGOING ASSESSMENT: Assess Mastery

Use one of the following options to assess final drafts of students' autobiographical narratives.

Self-Assessment Ask students to score their narratives using the rubric provided. Then, have students write a paragraph discussing how, or whether, writing about the topic experience changed their point of view about it.

Teacher Assessment Use the rubric and the scoring models provided in *Writing Assessment and Portfolio Management* to score students' work.

FINAL DRAFT

◀ **Critical Viewing**
Why do train stations and airports provide good settings for reflection?
[Hypothesize]

Train Tracks

Lauren Mizock
Whitney Young Magnet School
Chicago, Illinois

I lean my head over the train tracks and look for an oncoming flutter of headlights. Four thirty-seven P.M. I have less than a half hour to get to the other side of town, and there is no train in sight. I'm so nervous about being late for my mural job that I imagine the train pulling in just to make myself feel better. The platform fills with other impatient people. Maybe our collective mind power could will the train to arrive faster. It's an inspiring thought.

I sit down between a homeless man and a young professional man. The homeless man is in layers of gray, tattered clothes. I think of how, at one point, his clothes were neither gray nor tattered. The urban commuter is wearing a bright white shirt and a silk tie that gleams in the sunlight. It is a cleanliness that is as

A startling opening sentence draws readers into Lauren's narrative.

Details of the writer's thoughts and feelings show events from her perspective.

Step-by-Step Teaching Guide

Final Draft

1. Have students read Lauren's final draft, or read it aloud yourself.

2. Point out that "Train Tracks" incorporates key elements of the autobiographical narrative.

   • The topic has been well chosen and the audience and purpose have been carefully considered.

   • The introduction establishes the identity of the author and engages the reader with what is happening.

   • The body of the narrative contains colorful details, enlivened with dialogue.

   • Word choice is vivid and sentences are varied.

   • The writing has been edited and proofread to avoid errors.

Critical Viewing

Hypothesize Students may say that train stations and airports prompt reflection because people are often forced to wait for trains or planes, allowing time to reflect.

Customize for
Gifted and Talented Students

Encourage students to write short poems that capture the spirit of this autobiographical narrative. Prompt them to include descriptions and details that convey personality and the overall mood of the experience. Have students share their poems when they finish. Did they all get the same impression of the author and her experience on the train?

Teaching From the Final Draft

Note that the body of the narrative describes what it is like waiting for and traveling on the train. Details of the train ride are presented in chronological order, and dialogue is used to reveal characters' feelings.

Point out how the conclusion shows how riding the commuter train influences the author's thinking and helps her focus on what she has in common with the other passengers. Suggest that students focus on the conclusions to their own autobiographical narratives. Can they see changes they might make to connect their conclusions to the larger world around them?

Integrating Speaking and Listening Skills

Explain to students that it is not only in writing that we communicate autobiographical information. When students talk to good friends, to people they have recently met, or to small groups of people, they are conveying information about themselves. Challenge students to list some of the autobiographical information they convey every day through their tone of voice, word choice, body language, and clothing.

important an element of his daily uniform as his silk tie. As a teenage painter, decked in red and splattered with paint, my presence completes a Chicago social rainbow on that bench.

"I'm not gonna even bother to get up when the next train decides to pass us by." I look at the commuter sitting next to me, surprised and pleased by his friendliness.

"Seriously," I laugh. His hands are pressed to his temples as if to calm his impatience.

"This is a train-servicing station and we have to wait for a train." He shakes his head.

I smile. "It'd be nice if we could get one."

Another train approaches, and I'm hopeful it will open its doors to us. It slows down and allows the crowd to board. Shuffling along with the boarding crowd, I spy a single seat and weasel my way over to it.

I try to read, but the inner-city commuters are so wonderfully distracting. Older women protect themselves from germs by holding on to the metal posts with handkerchiefs. Toddlers in neon jumpers bounce up and down the aisles. There are punks with plumes of purple ponytails, chains, and leather. Hip-hop kids sport baggy clothes and huge disks of headphones over their ears. It's as if the string of train cars is pierced with creativity.

The train submerges into the subway tunnel, trading the sun for dim rays of fluorescence emanating from the concave walls. I amuse myself by watching the tourists get jumpy and disoriented. They seem helpless, their sense of direction meaningless in the endless black tunnels. I remember the time I was turned around on the west branch of the train, and I feel a twinge of sympathy. My passenger status had surrendered me to the strange lands of warehouses, factories, and industrial neighborhoods. Nervous energy spilled through my blood. The sight of the familiar Chicago skyline, when we reached downtown at last, was a complete relief. I wanted to hug those buildings like long-lost relatives.

I look through the crowd for my commuter friend. The steady rumble of the train wheels has lulled him and several other seated people to sleep. They share their slumber, the train turning them into the narcoleptic infants they once were. I feel warm and fuzzy, a part of some collective spirit of the train. Whether we know where we're going or are lost, whether we're yuppie, teenager, working class, or retired, we have put our trust in the rusty steel girders and jumping blue sparks of metal on metal. Whether the iron wheels lull us, jar us, or carry us to our day, inside these compartments of life, we are all passengers.

Lauren uses dialogue to move the plot along.

Details of the event are narrated in chronological order.

A higher level vocabulary indicated by words such as "submerges," "emanating," and "disoriented" makes the writing style more sophisticated.

Lauren began her trip by citing a conflict: the differences between herself and others. After her experience, a conclusion focuses on the resolution of this conflict. Now, she sees the qualities shared among herself and the other riders.

66 • Autobiographical Writing

Connected Assignment Firsthand Biography

Somewhere between telling your life story in an autobiography and researching the biography of a total stranger is the hybrid called a **firsthand biography.** In this type of narrative writing, you record the life of someone you know—a parent, community member, or local celebrity. You may still research for information that falls outside your observation, but you give the biography a personal flavor by including your personal insights.

Use the following writing-process steps to write a firsthand biography:

Prewriting To choose a subject, spend a few minutes making a list of people you know well enough to address in an essay. Review your list to choose a person whose story you think readers should learn. Use a chart like this one to gather information from your own experience, jotting down key events, personality traits, and appearance details. When you complete the chart, narrow your topic to one incident or idea.

▲ **Critical Viewing**
What words might the child in this photograph use to describe the older man? **[Describe]**

☑ engineered popular youth service program

☑ local resident since my earliest childhood

☑ leads healthy lifestyle, exercising daily—I see her jogging

Topic: Town Mayor

☑ studied political science at community college where my dad now teaches

Drafting As you draft, refer to your diagram to recall the sequence of events and to highlight interesting details. Include incidents that show your relationship to your subject or that provide insights to make your firsthand biography worthwhile. If you write in the first person—using the pronoun *I*—you can emphasize the personal nature of the biography.

Revising and Editing Have someone who knows the biography subject read your draft. Ask your reviewer to identify characteristics, words, or events that don't seem appropriate to his or her perception of the person. Revise your text or add details to make your subject more believable.

Publishing and Presenting Add photographs to illustrate your firsthand biography. Then, create a booklet to copy and share as a gift with people who know your subject.

Lesson Objectives

1. To deconstruct media to get the main idea
2. To analyze ideas as presented in various media
3. To recognize how visual and sound techniques convey messages in media

Step-by-Step Teaching Guide

Deconstructing Media to Get the Main Idea

1. Focus on one of the spotlight elements for class discussion, or allow students to work in small groups or individually on the elements of their choice.
2. Encourage students to research the works of Man Ray, Marcel Duchamp, and James Joyce. Assign interested students to present their research findings to the class, using visuals and short readings.
3. Then, have students compare and contrast the works of these artists. What similarities and differences do students find in these artists' main ideas?

Viewing and Representing

Activity Ask students to transfer their anecdotes to a transparency and have them display their unconventional punctuation to the class.

Critical Viewing

Compare and Contrast Students should point out that like a traditional portrait, this photograph focuses on a person's face. However, the photograph emphasizes a detail (an eye) and is not intended to show a realistic likeness of the model.

Spotlight on the Humanities

Deconstructing Media to Get the Main Idea of the Message

Focus on Photography: Man Ray

A biographer of the American photographer Man Ray (1890–1976) might have difficulty trying to summarize this artist's life. Always challenging the expectations of the art world—even challenging the name he was given—Emmanuel Radnitsky waited until his early twenties to change his name to Man Ray. At twenty-five, he had his first one-man painting exhibition. When he moved to Paris in 1921, he photographed such literary luminaries as James Joyce and Gertrude Stein, becoming a major figure in the city's community of artists. He later developed "Rayographs"—abstract images of objects with light-sensitive surfaces. With painter Marcel Duchamp, he founded the Dada group in New York City and became a champion of an innovative style of art known as Surrealism.

Art Connection Marcel Duchamp (1887–1968) was an experimental painter in the style known as Dadaism. As a response to the destruction caused by World War I, artists of the Dadaist movement challenged the existing art forms and structures. For example, one of Duchamp's most famous works is *Bicycle Wheel*, which consists of a bicycle wheel connected to a kitchen stool.

Literature Connection In the 1920's, Ray photographed the Irish writer James Joyce (1882–1941). Just as Ray stretched the boundaries of photography and Duchamp questioned the accepted materials of sculpture, Joyce experimented with language and the stream-of-consciousness method, which had a profound effect on literature. His major works include *A Portrait of the Artist as a Young Man* (1916) and *Ulysses* (1922).

Narrative Writing Activity: Challenge the Conventions

To see how style can affect meaning, write an anecdote in which you use capitalization and punctuation in unconventional ways. For example, you might capitalize the most important words or use only exclamation points. With a group, discuss how your own conventions convey content.

▲ **Critical Viewing** How is this photograph similar to and different from a traditional portrait? **[Compare and Contrast]**

Media and Technology Skills

Using Video to Convey Ideas

Activity: Video Slide Show

In an autobiographical essay, you use written language to tell a story. You can also visually reveal your life story to others by creating a video slide show that includes photographs, illustrations, and other images.

Learn About It Whether your family owns a camcorder or you borrow one from your school technology department, learn everything you can about how to use it. Explore the camera by reading the manual from cover to cover and then creating a practice tape. Practice filming still images, and try special techniques like fading in and out between images.

Focus It Pictures can communicate a world of ideas. To make a video slide show convey what you want it to convey, choose a main impression to develop. List characteristics, places, information, or emotions that you want to illustrate. Alternatively, you might choose a specific incident or experience to document. Once you choose an angle, select images that suit your needs.

Storyboard It Before you videotape, use a storyboard like the one shown here to map out your video. Note the narration you might use, the order you'll show the images, and the music that can help set the mood. Use the tips on this page to help you create your storyboard.

Video Slide Show: Amy's surprise party

Type of Treatment: _music_ / _narration_ / _music_

Tape It Make sure your camera is working, and use your storyboard to make your video slide show. Consider making a practice video to test the equipment and identify any trouble spots. Shoot a final slide show, and share it with friends and family—you might even want to mail it to friends in other cities.

Techniques for Creating a Video Slide Show

- Choose appropriate music or prepare narration of your slide show. Practice coordinating the video and audio aspects before your final filming.
- Be creative. If your camcorder has options, such as fade and subtitles, explore how you can incorporate their use.
- Avoid overnarrating; let the images tell the story.

▶ **Lesson Objectives**

1. To use a variety of forms and technology, including videotape and photographs, to communicate a specific message

2. To recognize how visual and sound techniques convey messages in media

3. To use a range of techniques to plan and create a media text and reflect critically on the work produced

Step-by-Step Teaching Guide

Using Video to Convey Ideas

Teaching Resources: Writing Support Transparencies, 4-I; Writing Support Activity Book, 4-3

1. Display Transparency 4-I to illustrate the storyboarding process. Supply students with copies of the storyboard chart (4-3) from the *Writing Support Activity Book*.

2. As an alternative to a chart, students might write their video ideas on note cards. This will give students greater flexibility to shift the cards around to try different sequences of images.

3. Assign students to complete their storyboards before they begin filming. Ask volunteers to post their storyboards as models for other students.

4. Give interested students the opportunity to make class presentations of their video slide shows.

Responding to Narrative Writing Prompts

Teaching Resources: Standardized Test Preparation Workbook, pp. 7–8

1. Remind students that the key to writing for standardized tests is preparation. Discourage the impulse to begin writing immediately. Urge students to use these first impulses for note-taking and outlining. Students will then have writing guides, rather than having to pause during writing time to generate or recall ideas. You might provide students with note paper for the purpose.

2. Remind students that different tests may require different things from them. Some tests require a clean, rewritten draft; others do not. Encourage them to read instructions carefully before they begin to write, and to budget their time accordingly. Suggest that students estimate how long they will spend on each step and time themselves as they proceed.

3. During a class period, have students respond to the narrative writing prompt on this page. Set a time limit so students can become familiar with writing short narratives in a set time.

Standardized Test Preparation Workshop

Responding to Narrative Writing Prompts

Standardized tests often measure your ability to write an autobiographical narrative for a specific audience and purpose. For example, prompts may ask you to describe a memorable moment or summarize an important experience. These are the criteria upon which your writing will be evaluated:

- Respond directly to the prompt, varying your word choice for the specific audience and purpose.
- Organize the details in a meaningful way.
- Elaborate your experience through the effective use of description, characterization, and other details.
- Use correct grammar, spelling, and punctuation.

When writing for a timed test, divide your time among prewriting, drafting, revising, and proofreading.

Use the suggestions on the following page to help you respond to this sample writing situation. The clocks show a suggested percentage of time to devote to each stage.

Test Tip

Before drafting your narrative, make sure that the details you have gathered support your response to the prompt. If not, eliminate them.

Sample Writing Situation

Choosing a college that is right for you can be a challenge. A university in a major city may be right for some, while a small college on a wooded campus may be better for others. Think about the qualities of the school that would best suit your academic and personal needs, and then respond to one of the following prompts:

Prepare a letter to your parents in which you explain to them why you have chosen a certain college setting, and ask for their help in your school search. To convince them, describe an experience that illustrates how your personality is compatible with the school setting of your choice.

In applying to the college of your choice, you must complete an essay that describes why you might thrive in a specific school environment. In an admissions essay to the college of your choice, describe an incident in your life that shows how your personality is compatible with the setting of the school of your choice.

70 • Autobiographical Writing

🔧 TEST-TAKING TIP

A clear understanding of the writing prompt is the first step to success on a written test. Tell students to make sure to identify the exact words in the prompt that specify audience, purpose, topic, and form. They might find it useful to mark these words in the prompt before they begin to plan their responses.

Ask students to pick out the key words in the sample prompts on this page.

Prompt 1: letter, parents, explain, ask, describe an experience

Prompt 2: admissions essay, college, describe an incident

Prewriting

Allow about one fourth of your time for prewriting.

Gather Details Begin to gather information from your personal experiences that illustrates how your personality would fit with the college setting of your choice. Consider freewriting to gather the people, places, and events in your life that could support your essay or letter. To review the freewriting technique, see page 55.

Consider Your Audience and Purpose As you begin to gather details for your narrative, keep in mind the audience indicated in the prompt you have chosen. For example, if you are writing a letter to the college admission board, you would use formal language and longer sentence construction. On the other hand, if you were writing to your parents, you might use less formal language and a more conversational tone. In either case, be sure to state your purpose for sharing your experiences.

Drafting

Allow almost half of your time for drafting.

Organize Begin your paper with an introduction that states your reasons for telling your narrative. The body paragraphs should develop the narrative, providing details that explain why your experience is important, how it shows your personality, and how it influences your college choice. Finally, sum up your narrative by restating your purpose.

Elaborate To effectively demonstrate how your personality is compatible with the environment of the college of your choice, include details that elaborate on your experience. For example, if you organized a group of students and led them on a tour of major museums in your area, this would illustrate that you might enjoy the challenges of a large university in a city.

Revising, Editing, and Proofreading

Allow almost one fourth of your time to revise and edit. Use the last few minutes to proofread your work.

Make Corrections Review your narrative response for errors. Neatly cross out any details that do not support your purpose. Change language that is inappropriate for your audience, and make sure transitions keep the ideas flowing smoothly. Check for errors in spelling, grammar, and punctuation. When making changes, place one line through text that you want to eliminate, and use a caret [^] to indicate the places you want to add words.

Time and Resource Manager

In-Depth Lesson Plan

	LESSON FOCUS	PRINT AND MEDIA RESOURCES
DAY 1	**Introduction to the Short Story** Students learn key elements of narrative writing and analyze the Model From Literature. (pp. 72–75)	*Writers at Work* **Videotape**, Narration *Writing Lab* **CD-ROM**, Narration
DAY 2	**Prewriting** Students choose and narrow a topic, consider their audience and purpose, and gather details. (pp. 76–79)	**Teaching Resources:** *Writing Support Transparencies*, 5-A–E; *Writing Support Activity Book*, 5-1–2; *Topic Bank for Heterogeneous Classes*, Ch. 5
DAY 3	**Drafting** Students develop their plots and write first drafts. (pp. 80–81)	**Teaching Resources:** *Writing Support Transparencies*, 5-F–G; *Writing Support Activity Book*, 5-3–4
DAY 4	**Revising** Students revise their drafts in terms of overall structure, paragraphs, sentences, and word choice. (pp. 82–85)	**Teaching Resources:** *Writing Support Transparencies*, 5-H–I
DAY 5	**Editing and Proofreading; Publishing and Presenting** Students check their work for accuracy and correctness and present their final drafts. (pp. 86–87)	**Teaching Resources:** *Scoring Rubrics on Transparency*, Ch. 5; *Writing Assessment and Portfolio Management; Formal Assessment*, Ch. 5

Accelerated Lesson Plan

	LESSON FOCUS	PRINT AND MEDIA RESOURCES
DAY 1	**Drafting** Students review characteristics of narrative writing, select topics and write drafts. (pp. 72–81)	*Writing Lab* **CD-ROM**, Narration **Teaching Resources:** *Writing Support Transparencies*, 5-A–G; *Writing Support Activity Book*, 5-1–4
DAY 2	**Revising to Presenting** Students work individually or with peers to revise, edit, and proofread their work for presentation. (pp. 82–87)	**Teaching Resources:** *Writing Support Transparencies*, 5-H–I; *Scoring Rubrics on Transparency*, Ch. 5; *Writing Assessment and Portfolio Management; Formal Assessment*, Ch. 5

Options for Adapting Lesson Plans

HOMEWORK

Have students complete any stage of the lesson for homework.

FEATURES

Extend coverage with Connected Assignment (p. 91), Spotlight on the Humanities (p. 92), Media and Technology Skills (p. 93), and the Standardized Test Preparation Workshop (p. 94).

TECHNOLOGY

Students can complete any stage of the lesson on computer. Have them print out their completed work.

INTEGRATED SKILLS COVERAGE

Integrating Grammar
Action vs. Linking Verbs, SE p. 85
Punctuating Dialogue, SE p. 86

Reading/Writing Connection
Identify Chronological Order, SE p. 74
Writing Application, SE p. 75

Viewing and Representing
Critical Viewing, SE pp. 72, 74, 85, 88, 91, 92
Analyzing a Composer's Influence on Art and Popular Culture, SE p. 92
Analyzing Media Content, SE p. 93

Speaking and Listening
ATE p. 78

Real-World Connection
ATE p. 82

Workplace Skills
ATE pp. 85, 90

ASSESSMENT SUPPORT

Standardized Test Preparation Workshop SE p. 94; ATE p. 84
Standardized Test Preparation Workbook, pp. 9–10
Scoring Rubrics on Transparency, Ch. 5
Formal Assessment, Ch. 5
Writing Assessment and Portfolio Management

MEETING INDIVIDUAL NEEDS

Less Advanced Students ATE pp. 77, 81, 84, 95. See also Ongoing Assessments ATE pp. 77, 81, 85.
AP Students ATE pp. 89, 95
ESL Students ATE pp. 78, 84
Linguistic Learners ATE p. 80
Spatial Learners ATE p. 80

BLOCK SCHEDULING

Pacing Suggestions
For 90-minute Blocks
• Have students complete the Prewriting and Drafting stages in a single period.
• Focus one class period on Revising and Editing and Publishing and Presenting. Allow at least 30 minutes for peer revision.

Resources for Varying Instruction
• *Writing Lab* **CD-ROM** If your students have access to hardware, a 90-minute block provides an ideal opportunity for students to work on computer.
• *Writers at Work* **Videotape** Show the narration segment in class.

Professional Development Support
• *How to Manage Instruction in the Block* This Teaching Resource provides management and activity suggestions.

MEDIA AND TECHNOLOGY

For the Student
• *Writing Lab* **CD-ROM,** Narration
• *On-Line Exercise Bank,* Section 17.2

For the Teacher
• *Writers at Work* **Videotape,** Narration
• *Resource Pro* **CD-ROM**

WRITING AND GRAMMAR WEB SITE

The Interactive Writing and Grammar Website provides a wide array of support for students, teachers, and parents. Writing support includes:

• Interactive revision checkers
• Scoring rubrics with complete models

www.phschool.com

LITERATURE CONNECTIONS

Related selections from *Prentice Hall Literature: Timeless Voices, Timeless Themes,* The American Experience:

"To Build a Fire," Jack London, SE p. 75

"The Notorious Jumping Frog of Calaveras County," Mark Twain, SE p. 77

"A Worn Path," Eudora Welty, SE p. 78

Lesson Objectives

1. To write a short story appropriate to audience and purpose

2. To read to appreciate a writer's craft and to discover models for writing

3. To use prewriting strategies to generate ideas and plan

4. To develop and revise drafts in terms of structure, paragraphs, sentences, and word choice

5. To edit and proofread to ensure standard English usage and grammar

6. To evaluate writing for both mechanics and content

7. To refine a short story for publication

Critical Viewing

Hypothesize Students may suggest a story with an unhappy ending, a story about hard work and dashed hopes.

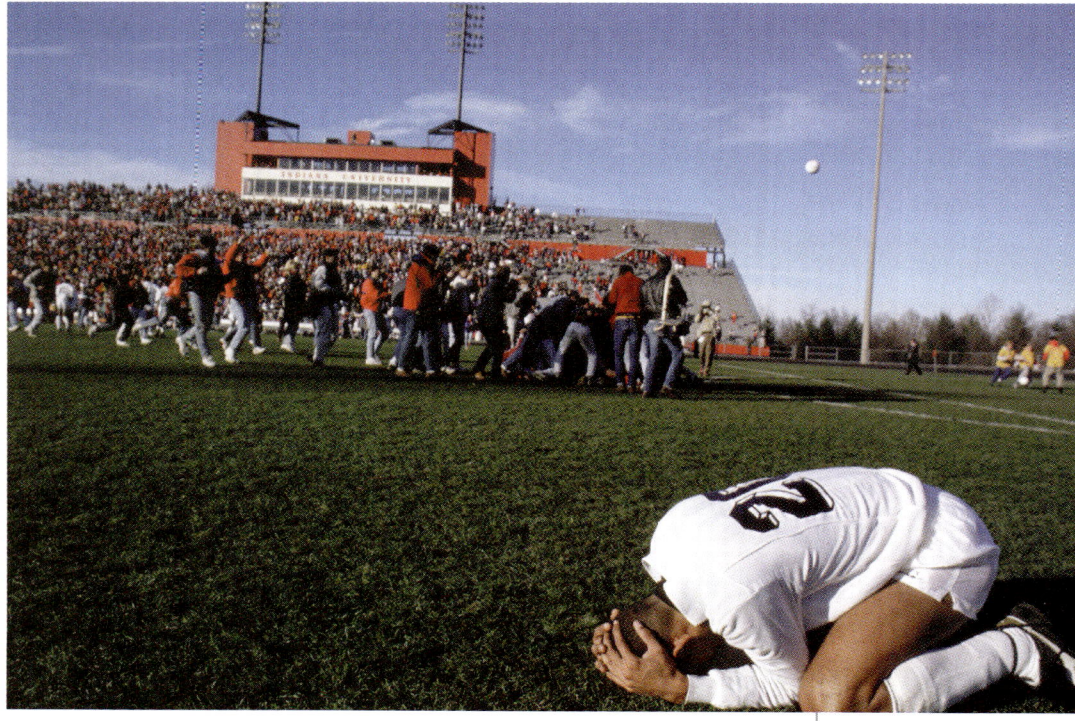

Chapter 5 Narration
Short Story

Short Stories in Everyday Life

You tell stories, or narratives, just about every day. For instance, you might tell friends or family about a big soccer game, recounting how a critical play dashed your team's chances at victory. If you were to use your imagination to alter some of the events in the game, you would be creating a short story—a fictional account of a series of events. At times, you have probably entertained friends by creating stories that stray even further from real events. For example, when you were younger, you may have told scary stories at a sleepover party. Whether you knew it or not, you were using elements of storytelling to entertain your friends.

▲ **Critical Viewing**
What kind of story would you expect this soccer player to tell? **[Hypothesize]**

72 • Narration

⏱ TIME AND RESOURCE MANAGER

Resources
Technology: *Writers at Work* Videotape, Narration; *Writing Lab* CD-ROM, Narration

In-Depth Coverage	Accelerated Pace
• Cover pp. 72–73 in class. • Show Narration section of the *Writers at Work* Videotape. • Read the Model From Literature (pp. 74–75) with students and use it to discuss elements of the short story.	• Discuss the characteristics and types of short stories in class. • Assign the Model From Literature for independent reading.

What Is a Short Story?

As the name suggests, a **short story** is a brief fictional narrative. The American writer Edgar Allan Poe celebrated the unique qualities of short stories and helped to define the genre. He felt that a short story should be brief enough to be read in one sitting. An effective short story

- establishes the setting in time and place.
- presents a main character who takes part in the action as the problem is resolved.
- introduces and develops a conflict, a problem to be resolved.
- weaves a plot, the series of events that make up the action of the story.
- suggests a theme or generalization about life.

To see the criteria against which your short story may be judged, preview the Rubric for Self-Assessment on page 87.

Types of Short Stories

There are as many types of short stories as there are writers and times. Here are a few examples of types of short stories you may encounter as both a reader and a writer:

- **Historical narratives** illuminate some historic event or moment in time using fictionalized elements, such as dialogue.
- **Mysteries** present a riddle to be solved. These suspenseful pieces often feature a detective who puts clues together to solve a crime.
- **Thrillers** arouse a high level of tension by introducing danger in the conflict they present.
- **Science-fiction stories** are usually based in futuristic settings but address issues of value to today's society.

PREVIEW
Student Work
IN PROGRESS

In this chapter, you will find the work of Ben Spoer, a student at Santa Monica High School in Santa Monica, California. As you will see, Ben used prewriting, drafting, and revising techniques to develop his short story "Too Much Information."

Writers in ACTION

Native American storyteller N. Scott Momaday finds sources for his writing in his cultural heritage. He taps his own work experience to inspire his writing, as he explains in this quotation:

"When I turn my mind to my early life, it is the imaginative part of it that comes first and irresistibly into reach, and of that part I take hold. This is one way to tell a story."

Short Story • 73

PREPARE and ENGAGE

 Interest GRABBER Ask students to imagine they have just been awarded a prize for short-story writing and they are being interviewed. Ask volunteers to respond to the question, "How do you come up with ideas for your wonderful short stories?"

Activate Prior Knowledge

Ask students to recall the last short story they read. Who was the main character and what was his or her role in the plot? After discussing these issues, refer students to the characteristics of the short story listed in the text.

More About the Writer

Navarre Scott Momaday's work has been critically acclaimed for its focus on Kiowa tradition, custom, and belief, and on the role of Native Americans in contemporary society. All of his writings have been greatly influenced by oral tradition, and frequently address the nature and origin of Native American myths. Momaday is featured in the Narration section of the *Writers at Work* Videotape.

☑ ONGOING ASSESSMENT: Diagnose

Use one of the following options to diagnose students' current level of proficiency in short-story writing.

Option 1 Ask students to bring in a short story from their writing portfolio from the previous year. Confer with students individually to pinpoint which students may need extra help with constructing a narrative.	**Option 2** Ask students to write a short-story synopsis. Use the synopses to assess whether students' story ideas include a strong main character or characters, a central plot conflict, and an identifiable resolution.

Reading: Chronological Order

Using transitional words, writers indicate a sequence of events. In the story, "Crossing Spider Creek," Dan O'Brien uses flashbacks to fill in the full picture of his dilemma. Ask students to identify some transitional words and phrases that O'Brien uses to clarify for the reader the order of events that led to Tom's predicament, and to suggest events that are to come. (Students might suggest *here is, has tried twice before, both times, will try, will take.*)

Step-by-Step Teaching Guide

Engage Students Through Literature

1. Read the excerpt aloud, or have students read it. Use questions like these to prompt discussion:

   How do you think you would handle yourself if you were in Tom's situation?

   Have you ever been in danger?

   Can Tom ensure a successful third try?

2. Ask students to brainstorm for short-story ideas suggested by the passage. Some possibilities are:

   A man and his horse

   Sudden disaster

   Fighting for survival

3. Let students know that they may add these ideas to their topic banks.

Critical Viewing

Connect Students will point out that an injury in such unyielding terrain would dictate a story conflict dealing with a character's survival in the wild.

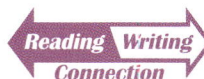

5.1 Model From Literature

The action of "Crossing Spider Creek" spans only minutes. In his short story, Dan O'Brien uses a strategy called flashback to share information about earlier events that have led to the conflict.

Reading → **Writing** **Connection**

Reading Strategy: Identify Chronological Order

Look for transitional words the writer uses to indicate the sequence of events, or chronological order.

Crossing Spider Creek

Dan O'Brien

Here is a seriously injured man on a frightened horse.

They are high in the Rocky Mountains at the junction of the Roosevelt Trail and Spider Creek. Tom has tried to coax the horse into the freezing water twice before. Both times the horse started to cross then lost its nerve, swung around violently, and lunged back up the bank. The pivot and surge of power had been nearly too much for Tom. Both times he almost lost his grip on the saddlehorn and fell into the boulders of the creek bank. Both times, when it seemed his hold would fail, he had thought of his wife, Carol. He will try the crossing once more. It will take all the strength he has left.

This is not the Old West. It is nineteen eighty-seven, autumn, a nice day near the beginning of elk season. Two days ago Tom had led the horse, his camp packed in panniers hung over the saddle, up this same trail. He had some trouble getting the horse to cross the creek but it hadn't been bad. This was a colt, Carol's colt and well broke to lead. It had come across without much fuss. But that was before the nice weather had swelled Spider Creek with runoff, and of course the colt had not had the smell of blood in his nostrils.

Tom's injury is a compound fracture of the right femur. He has wrapped it tightly with an extra cotton shirt but he cannot stop

74 • Short Story

▲ **Critical Viewing**
How would an injury, like the one described in the story, present a conflict in an environment like the one shown here? **[Connect]**

The first sentence presents the story's conflict.

Details as specific as freezing water, autumn, and elk season establish the Rocky Mountain setting.

the bleeding. The blood covers the right shoulder of the horse, the rifle scabbard, and the saddle from the seat to the stirrup. Tom knows that it is the loss of blood that is making him so weak. He wonders if that is why his thoughts keep wandering from what he is trying to do here, with the horse, to Carol. She has never understood his desire to be alone. From time to time, over the years, she has complained that he cares less for her than for solitude. He has always known that is not true. But still it seems vaguely funny to him that now she is all he wants to think about. He wishes she could know that, hopes he will have a chance to tell her.

Perhaps it is being on this particular horse, he thinks, the one Carol likes better than any of the others. Maybe Carol has spent enough time with this horse to have become part of it.

The horse moves nervously under him as he reins it around to face the water again. Tom wishes there were a way to ease the animal through this. But there is not, and there is clearly little time. There is just this one last chance.

They begin to move slowly down the bank again. It will be all or nothing. If the horse makes it across Spider Creek they will simply ride down the trail, be at a campground in twenty minutes. There are other hunters there. They will get him to a hospital. If the horse refuses and spins in fear, Tom will fall. The horse will clamber up the bank and stand aloof, quaking with terror and forever out of reach. Tom sees himself bleeding to death, alone, by the cascading icy water.

As the horse stretches out its nose to sniff at the water, Tom thinks that there might be time, if he falls, to grab at the rifle and drag it from the scabbard as he goes down. He clucks to the horse and it moves forward. Though he would hate to, it might be possible to shoot the horse from where he would fall. With luck he would have the strength to crawl to it and hold its warm head for a few moments before they died. It would be best for Carol if they were found like that.

Here is a seriously injured man on a frightened horse. They are standing at the edge of Spider Creek, the horse's trembling front feet in the water and the man's spurs held an inch from the horse's flanks.

Reading\Writing Connection

Writing Application: **Clarify Order of Events**
O'Brien expands one moment into a story by using flashback to describe the events that led up to it. He keeps the order of plot events clear by using phrases like "two days ago" and "but that was before." Make your story clear by including transitions like these that identify the order of events.

LITERATURE

For another example of a short story featuring a man in a potentially fatal conflict, see "To Build a Fire," by Jack London, in *Prentice Hall Literature: Timeless Voices, Timeless Themes,* The American Experience.

The writer includes Tom's thoughts about his desperate situation. These thoughts increase the tension of the conflict.

This paragraph develops one possible resolution.

By not revealing the final outcome, the writer leaves the reader to imagine the resolution. This uncertainty suggests a theme: Life can be unpredictable and fragile.

The writer repeats the story's first sentence, finishing the flashback by bringing the action back to the same moment that the story began.

Model From Literature • 75

Teaching From the Model

Use this model from literature as a way to show students how to build a story around a compelling conflict. Tom has not been able to coax his horse to make the crossing and, in his weakened condition, he believes he has only one more chance. Ask students what they believe the outcome will be and why.

Connections With Literature

Ask students to think about how momentum is built into the plot of "To Build a Fire" by Jack London. Does the author introduce his potentially fatal conflict early in the story or later? What devices does he use to introduce and resolve the conflict? Encourage students to investigate the steps used to build momentum in the plots of other short stories and apply them to their own work.

More About the Writer

Dan O'Brien was born and raised in South Dakota. Other short stories he has written include "Cowboy on the Concord Bridge," "Final Touches," "The Georgia Breeze," "The Inheritance," "Seals," "Strand of Wire," "Weightless," "The Wild Geese," and "Winter Cat."

Reading\Writing Connection

Writing Application: Clarify Order of Events

Tell students that using chronological order can help them draw a more detailed picture of events for their readers. Have students carefully reread "Crossing Spider Creek," taking notes on all the events mentioned in the text. Have students place these events on a time line that shows the sequence of events in the story. (Time lines might show Carol and Tom discussing his need to be alone, Carol training the colt, Tom crossing Spider Creek the first time, Tom breaking his femur, the two attempts to recross the creek, Tom's present dilemma.)

Step-by-Step Teaching Guide

Prewriting: Blueprint

1. If you wish to have students do the blueprinting activity in class, you might supply drawing paper and pencils.

2. Ask volunteers to share the ideas generated by their sketches.

Step-by-Step Teaching Guide

Prewriting: Song List

1. Students might use the Internet to find any of several sites that list popular songs and lyrics.

2. As a group, students can brainstorm for song titles and possible associated topics.

3. Encourage students to select a song as a springboard for writing.

Step-by-Step Teaching Guide

Prewriting: Character Sound Off

Teaching Resources: Writing Support Transparencies, 5-A

1. Use familiar stories or other narratives to model the character sound-off process for your students:

   I want to tell the story of a young girl and her wicked stepmother. What kind of conversation might they have?

   Stepmother: So you're the fairest of them all, eh? We'll see about that.

   Young girl: What can I do to please you, Stepmother?

2. Draw students' attention to the student model. Discuss which characters from student lists might be suitable for a character sound off.

5.2 Prewriting

Choosing Your Topic

You can build a story around one strong element. Start with a compelling conflict, an interesting character, or an unusual setting. Use these strategies to help you choose a topic:

Strategies for Generating Topics

1. **Blueprint** Sketch out the setting of a place. This might be a familiar neighborhood, a football stadium, or a completely fictional world. As you draw, consider events that might unfold in the setting you have created. List three or four ideas, and then choose one you'd like to develop.

2. **Song List** Music often sparks memories of people or places. To recall a memory you would like to use as the basis of a short story, list several songs you enjoy. Jot down the ideas the song brings to mind. Then, review your list, and choose a springboard for your own writing.

3. **Character Sound Off** To generate characters for your story, consider the people you have encountered recently. Make a list of these people, and include a description of each one. Circle the ones who might create an interesting pair. Then, write the dialogue they might have together. Use this dialogue to generate an idea for your story.

Writing Lab CD-ROM

For more help finding a topic, explore the activities and topic suggestions in the Choosing a Topic section of the Narration lesson.

Student Work **IN PROGRESS**

Name: Ben Spoer
Santa Monica High School
Santa Monica, CA

Creating a Character Sound Off
Ben prepared to write by making a character list. He circled people he'd like to use in a story, and then he created a dialogue between them.

cheerful lunch aide

efficient nurse in doctor's office

confused patient — *What happened to me?*

friendly physics teacher

busy doctor — *You've had an accident!*

mellow bus driver

76 • Short Story

⏱ TIME AND RESOURCE MANAGER

Resources
Print: *Writing Support Transparencies,* 5-A–E; *Writing Support Activity Book,* 5-1–2
Technology: *Writing Lab* CD-ROM, Narration

In-Depth Coverage	Accelerated Pace
• Work through one of the strategies for generating topics: blueprint, song list, or character sound off. • Use the Responding to Fine Art transparency to generate additional interest.	• Have students work independently to choose and narrow their topics. • Have students work with partners to focus on audience, purpose, and gathering details.

TOPIC BANK

If you are having difficulty coming up with a topic, consider these possibilities:

1. **"What-If" Story** Choose a recent challenge you have faced, and rewrite it with a different outcome. You could write a story surmising what might have happened if you had lost a key game or had taken a risk you've been afraid to confront.

2. **Story About a Conflict Between Friends** Friendships can be rewarding, harmonious, or tension-filled. In a story, create a conflict between friends who find a way to save their friendship—or decide to call it quits.

Responding to Fine Art

3. The painting *Beach Scene ca. 1935*, at right, might inspire you to imagine an enjoyable day at the beach. Perhaps it suggests a survival story beginning on an ordinary day at the shore. Use one of these suggestions to write a story about a day at the beach.

Responding to Literature

4. Read "The Notorious Jumping Frog of Calaveras County" by Mark Twain. Using the story's exaggerated style as a model, write your own humorous tale. You can find the story in *Prentice Hall Literature: Timeless Voices, Timeless Themes*, The American Experience.

Beach Scene ca. 1935, Jane Peterson, The National Museum of Women in the Arts

Cooperative Writing Opportunity

5. **"Many-Sided" Story** With a group, plan a story together. Meet to map out the plot, characters, conflict, and setting. Then, assign each person in the group a specific character. Each group member will then write the story from his or her character's perspective. Collect the stories, and let your readers compare the versions.

Step-by-Step Teaching Guide

Responding to Fine Art

Beach Scene by Jane Peterson

Teaching Resources: Writing Support Transparencies, 5-B

1. Engage students in discussion about *Beach Scene*. Use questions like these to prompt discussion:

   Where in the world do you think this scene takes place?

   Which of these people is different from all the others? Why?

2. Ask students to brainstorm for short-story ideas suggested by this piece of art. Here are some possibilities:

   A mysterious stranger sits among the happy, chatting bathers.

   The figures on the beach are actually all movie actors.

3. Students may include these topic ideas along with their own suggestions in their topic banks.

Responding to Literature

Students might use Mark Twain's "The Notorious Jumping Frog of Calaveras County" as a starting point for a short story. Ask students to name ten seemingly impossible events, and then list those events on the board. Ask students whether any ideas suggest a possible story topic.

Customize for
Less Advanced Students

Students might work as a class to select and develop a single topic, choosing from the topic bank or from ideas generated by students. This will enable you to focus effectively on students' particular learning issues, apply strategies more easily, and allow for more effective collaborative learning situations during Prewriting.

✓ ONGOING ASSESSMENT: Monitor and Reinforce

If you observe that some students are having difficulty generating or selecting a topic, use one of the following strategies.

Option 1 Students having difficulty choosing a topic might select one from the *Topic Bank for Heterogeneous Classes* in the Teaching Resources.	**Option 2** Have students choose an idea from the Topic Bank on this page. You might assign all students to write either a "What-If" story or a story about conflict between friends. When students turn in their work, the class can compare and contrast the stories that result.

Prewriting: Narrowing Your Topic

Teaching Resources: Writing Support Transparencies, 5-C; Writing Support Activity Book, 5-1

1. To help students narrow their topics, you might give an example:

   Too broad: *cooking*

   Narrow enough: *cooking dinner for four guests*

2. If topics are too broad, list smaller elements of the topics on the board, and invite students to suggest which of these offers the more-focused topic.

3. Use Transparency 5-C to demonstrate the CASPAR method.

Prewriting: Considering Your Audience and Purpose

Teaching Resources: Writing Support Transparencies, 5-D; Writing Support Activity Book, 5-2

1. Remind students that analyzing the intended audience helps writers choose characters, action, and details that connect with their readers.

2. Display the purpose transparency (5-D) and use it to point out that by listing details to support their ideas, writers can begin to clarify their purposes.

Integrating Speaking and Listening Skills

Writing is not the only place where it is important to keep topics sufficiently narrow. A speaker who has twenty minutes to give a speech needs to narrow his or her topic. Suggest that students think about the length of the narrative they will write. Which of the details they have gathered are crucial to their stories, and which might be omitted?

Customize for
ESL Students

Taking notes can be a time-consuming task for students learning English as a second language. You might allow them to tape their notes, and then have them incorporate those notes into their drafts.

Narrowing Your Topic

To avoid writing a story that goes in all directions, narrow your focus by identifying the major elements of your story. Use the letters in the acronym CASPAR to organize these key items. Following is an example based on Eudora Welty's story "A Worn Path."

Characters	Phoenix Jackson and people she encounters
Adjectives	Old, fragile, determined, weak
Setting	Rural South, bumpy forest path, small town
Problem	Phoenix needs to travel into town to get medicine for her grandson.
Action	hike, struggle, survive, fight
Resolution	Phoenix gets to town and gets medicine.

Considering Your Audience and Purpose

Before you begin your draft, identify your audience—the people you expect to read your short story. Knowing the age of your intended audience will help you choose the vocabulary and sentence complexity that is appropriate for your readers.

In addition, consider your purpose in writing your story. You may want to amuse your readers, to frighten them, or to create a character who will confide in them. This chart shows the kinds of details you might use to achieve a specific purpose:

If Your PURPOSE Is	INCLUDE
to frighten	• gloomy setting • description of silences
to amuse	• exaggerated characters • funny situations
to inspire reflection	• unexpected event • thoughtful narrator

LITERATURE

To read Eudora Welty's short story "A Worn Path," see *Prentice Hall Literature: Timeless Voices, Timeless Themes,* The American Experience.

Gathering Details

As a last step before drafting, take some time to expand your own knowledge of the story you will tell. Gather details on these key elements of narration:

Identify the Conflict Clarify the problem your story will develop. Make notes about the ways the problem will reveal itself and intensify, the ways different characters will react to the problem, and the results of the resolution.

Picture Your Setting Decide on the specific time and place of your story. Then, list details that identify this exact location. Using details of the setting in your narrative will enrich your writing. For example, showing your narrator sitting in rush-hour traffic will convey the setting and possibly raise the conflict level.

Interview Your Character To gather details about the people in your story, devise a questionnaire. Create questions about their personalities, experiences, and the conflict that they face. Then, answer the questions from each character's perspective.

Student Work
IN PROGRESS

Name: Ben Sooer
Santa Monica High School
Santa Monica, CA

Gathering Details Through Character Interviews
Here is part of the interview Ben created to develop his main character.

How do you like to spend your free time? I enjoy talking to my friends. We go to coffee bars and people-watch. I like to see the way people interact. I think there are a lot of people who talk one way and think another.

How would you describe yourself? I'm very introspective. I think I am an honest person who wants to trust the things people tell me. I want to be liked. I don't think I am part of the "in" crowd.

How would you describe the weeks following your accident? For a brief period, I had the ability to hear people's thoughts. It was interesting but frightening. I wouldn't wish that on anyone.

Prewriting • 79

Step-by-Step Teaching Guide

Prewriting: Identify the Conflict

1. Have students list details about the story's conflict. Which characters are affected? How do they respond?

2. Then encourage students to ask themselves questions such as: What caused the problem? What effect does the problem have on the plot? How is the problem resolved?

Step-by-Step Teaching Guide

Prewriting: Picturing the Setting

1. Have volunteers read aloud their lists of details about their story settings without giving away the actual locations.

2. Invite the class to make guesses about the setting from the details they are given.

Step-by-Step Teaching Guide

Prewriting: Character Interviews

Teaching Resources: Writing Support Transparencies, 5-E

1. To start this activity, have students make a list of questions they have about their characters. Suggest that they leave space between questions.

2. Students should then answer the questions from the character's perspective. In this way, they are gathering specific details about the people in the stories.

3. Draw students' attention to the Student Work in Progress on this page, or display Transparency 5-E to model gathering details.

☑ **ONGOING ASSESSMENT: Monitor and Reinforce**

Students often lapse into writing for the same audience: a teacher. To help break this pattern, try the following strategy.

Tell students to write for a very specific individual (a relative or friend) or for a much younger person. Have students draw up and complete charts that list what their reader will need to know. Students may find that this will affect not only the level of detail and vocabulary in their writing, but also the level of formality or informality.

Drafting: Review the Elements of Plot

1. Remind students that when they have gathered details about events in their stories, they will order them logically. Ordering events creates plot.

2. Point out to students that a well-constructed plot is a strong narrative element that will help the reader understand the story's main theme. Suggest that students think about how they may best order the events in their stories.

Drafting: Build Toward a Climax

Teaching Resources: Writing Support Transparencies, 5-F; Writing Support Activity Book, 5-3

1. Suggest that students diagram the stages of plot development. Display Transparency 5-F to show plot details. Give students a blank copy of the diagram (5-3) to apply to their own work.

2. Challenge students to experiment to see how early they can introduce the plot conflict. Have students review the Model From Literature on page 74, where the conflict is introduced in the story's first line.

Customize for
Linguistic Learners

Some students may find they can more readily talk about their topics than write about them. If that is the case, suggest that students discuss their plans in small groups. Students might also use a tape recorder to draft their stories orally.

Customize for
Spatial Learners

Suggest that students sketch quick storyboards of the stages of plot development in their stories. Have them jot down notes under each scene and compare these notes with their drafts to identify any spots in the narrative where more information might help a reader.

Shaping Your Writing

As you prepare to write, gather all the prewriting you have done. Review your ideas, and sketch out a plan for telling your story.

Review the Elements of Plot

The plot, or sequence of events, in your narrative will probably center on a conflict. Begin with an exposition that establishes the conflict and introduces the setting and characters. In the next part of your draft, called the rising action, build the conflict until it reaches its high point—the story's climax. Next, describe the resolution of the conflict, where the problem is solved. In the falling action of your story, tie up any loose ends of the plot.

Build Toward a Climax Use a plot diagram like the one below to help you plan your plot. To keep the story moving, introduce the problem as soon as you can. Then, add events and details that intensify the problem. Once you know how the climax of your story will play out, add details and events to the rising action to intensify the conflict.

⚑ Challenge

Tell your story as a flashback by starting the action after events have already taken place. The narrator can jump back in time to share the events that have occurred previously.

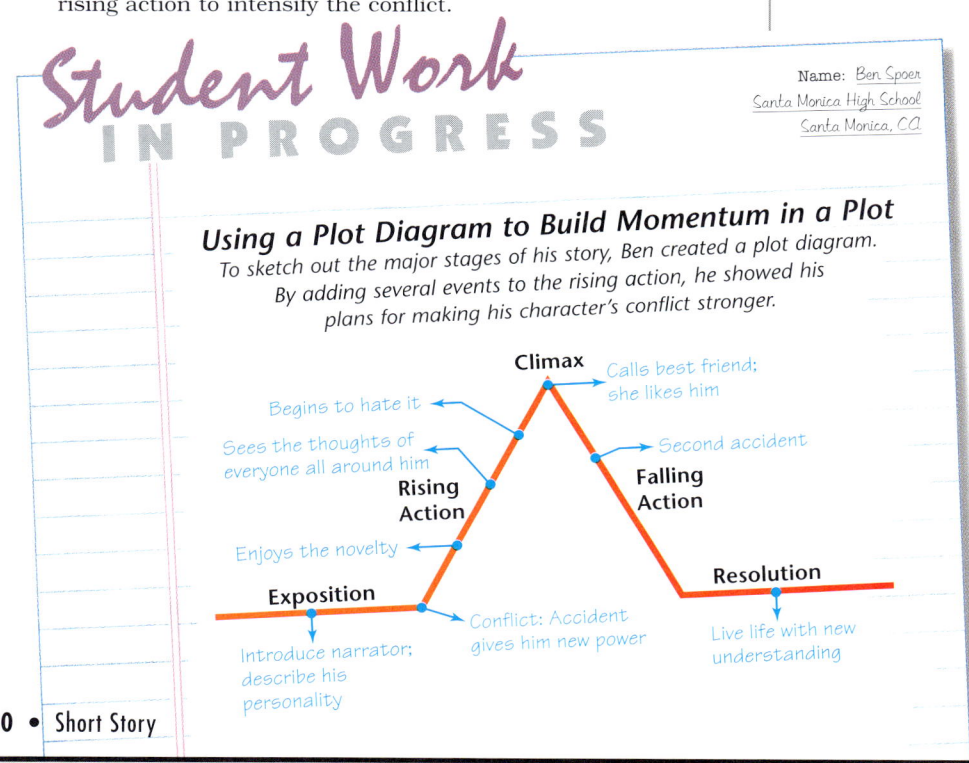

Student Work IN PROGRESS

Name: *Ben Spoer*
Santa Monica High School
Santa Monica, CA

Using a Plot Diagram to Build Momentum in a Plot
To sketch out the major stages of his story, Ben created a plot diagram. By adding several events to the rising action, he showed his plans for making his character's conflict stronger.

80 • Short Story

🕐 TIME AND RESOURCE MANAGER

Resources
Print: *Writing Support Transparencies, 5-F–G; Writing Support Activity Book, 5-3–4*
Technology: *Writing Lab* CD-ROM, Narration

In-Depth Coverage	Accelerated Pace
• Work through the plot diagram strategy with the entire class using the transparency. • Demonstrate how to build momentum in the plot using the transparency.	• Have students review pp. 80–81 independently; then have them write their first short-story draft. • Respond to individual drafting issues as needed.

Providing Elaboration

Once you have developed the frame for your story, fill in the details to create a complete picture for your readers. Remember that you are constructing your story to achieve a specific effect; choose only information that suits your purpose. Knowing what to tell and what to leave out is an important skill of good storytelling.

Show, Don't Tell

To bring a scene to life for readers without dictating what they should think about every character and action, challenge yourself to show more and tell less. Whenever possible, use action to move the story along, use repetition to stress an emotion, and include dialogue to illustrate the characters' personalities. Look at these examples:

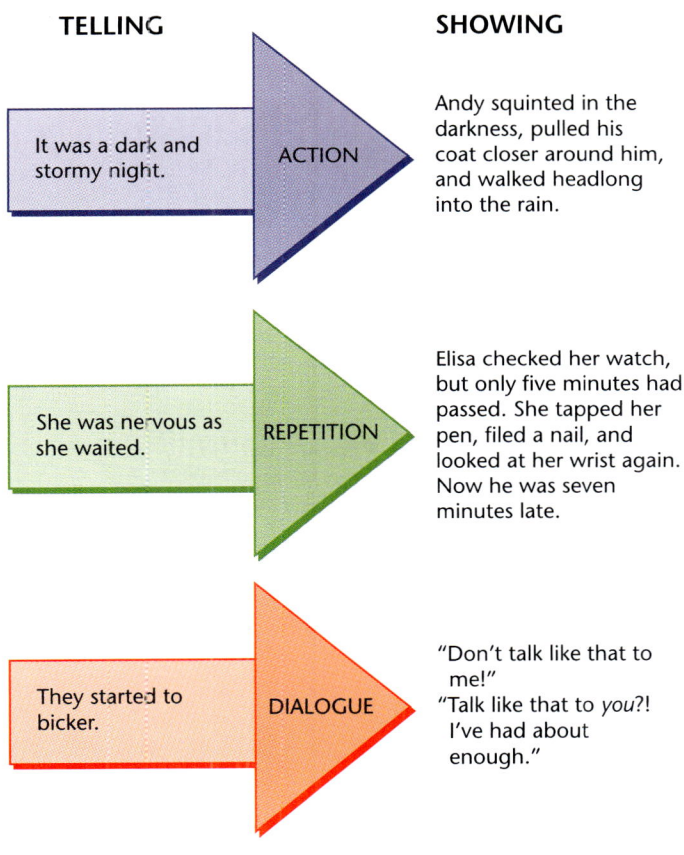

TELLING		SHOWING
It was a dark and stormy night.	ACTION	Andy squinted in the darkness, pulled his coat closer around him, and walked headlong into the rain.
She was nervous as she waited.	REPETITION	Elisa checked her watch, but only five minutes had passed. She tapped her pen, filed a nail, and looked at her wrist again. Now he was seven minutes late.
They started to bicker.	DIALOGUE	"Don't talk like that to me!" "Talk like that to *you*?! I've had about enough."

Step-by-Step Teaching Guide

Drafting: Show, Don't Tell

Teaching Resources: Writing Support Transparencies, 5-G; Writing Support Activity Book, 5-4

1. Suggest that students consult their lists of details, and draft a passage of dialogue for each that shows rather than tells a part of the story.

2. Use the transparency (5-G) to show students how "show, don't tell" might look in practice. Give students copies of the blank form (5-4) to apply the strategy.

3. Ask volunteers to use excerpts from other stories in *Prentice Hall Literature: Timeless Voices, Timeless Themes*, The American Experience, to show where dialogue, repetition, or action is used to make a point.

Customize for
Less Advanced Students

Point out to students that stories in movies and on television make a point of showing rather than telling about events. Suggest that students try to see their stories in the mind's eye as films. What scenes could they add to the story to increase the suspense?

✓ ONGOING ASSESSMENT: Monitor and Reinforce

If you observe that students are having difficulty completing their plot diagrams, try the following strategy.

Have students list, in no particular order, the major events in their stories. Have them identify which event is the climax of their story, and enter it at the top of the diagram. Then ask them to divide the remaining events into two sub-lists, events that occur before the climax and those that come after. Breaking down events in the plot into smaller groups should make it easier for students to decide where they might place events in their diagrams.

⏲ TIME SAVERS!

 Writing Support Transparencies
Use the transparencies for Chapter 5 to facilitate teaching of strategies.

 Writing Support Activity Book
Use the graphic organizers for Chapter 5 to facilitate student planning.

Revising: Get the Reader Involved Early

1. Review exposition with students. Remind them that a good introduction grabs readers' attention, introduces a character or characters, sets the scene, and introduces or hints at the conflict. Make sure students review their introductions for these elements.

2. Have students consider ways to make their writing more compelling. Suggest that they add surprising details to their introductions to draw the reader into reading further.

Revising: Using Snapshots

Teaching Resources: Writing Support Transparencies, 5-H

1. Explain to students that creating "snapshots" helps set the mood of the story by adding details to the introduction, and thus heightens reader interest. Display the transparency (5-H) to show how Ben applied the strategy.

2. Ask students to close their eyes for a moment and visualize themselves in the opening scene in their stories. Where are they? What does it look like there? What is happening around them?

3. Have students open their eyes and jot down any new details they can use to revise their story expositions.

Real-World Connection

When pulling together a yearly budget for office supplies, an office manager writes a funding request for expense approval. Along with an itemized list of supplies, the request must include a narrative detailing the business impact of not having the needed supplies. Ask students what might happen if the narrative detailing the business impact is not complete. (The funding for the supplies might not be approved.)

5.4 Revising

Once you have written your first draft, take the time to improve the story. Starting with the big picture and moving in to focus on the smaller details will help you build up your short story.

Revising Your Overall Structure

Get the Reader Involved Early

The first paragraphs of your story should set the mood of your writing, pulling your readers in from the start. Review the exposition of your draft, and consider making the writing more compelling by offering vivid details that make the reader feel part of the scene. Snapshots may help you do this.

▶ **REVISION STRATEGY**
Using Snapshots

Think of each episode in your story as a photograph or a snapshot of a moment in time. Review your exposition, or the beginning of your story, to identify places where the view could be made clearer. Then, add details to make the picture more vivid.

Writing Lab CD-ROM

To clarify the relationships among events in your narrative, use the transitions checker in the Narration lesson.

Student Work IN PROGRESS

Name: *Ben Spoer*
Santa Monica High School
Santa Monica, CA

Using Snapshots to Grab the Reader's Attention

When Ben looked at his exposition, he asked questions to bring out more description in his writing. The answers helped him provide a clearer snapshot of the scene.

"I wish I could be normal again. I really do," *begin as I stare at the full glass of root beer in front of me.* I̶ ̶s̶a̶y̶ ̶t̶o̶ ̶m̶y̶ ̶f̶r̶i̶e̶n̶d̶. "But I guess that's impossible since I discovered my power." *In the shadows of the dimly lit booth,* My listener nods his head silently.

What is the speaker doing? Where is he?

What does the place look like?

82 • Short Story

⏱ TIME AND RESOURCE MANAGER

Resources
Print: *Writing Support Transparencies,* 5-H–I
Technology: *Writing Lab* CD-ROM, Narration; *Writers at Work* Videotape, Narration

In-Depth Coverage	Accelerated Pace
• Work through the revising strategy with the entire class. • Use the relevant transparencies to demonstrate strategies for analyzing overall structure, sentence beginnings, and word choice. • Divide the class into groups for peer review activity.	• Assign independent review of pp. 82–85. • Have students revise their short stories independently.

Revising Your Paragraphs

Create Stronger Characterization

While characterization can be directly revealed by the narrator of a story, a character's own words and actions reveal a voice and a personality. Look for places where you can develop characters through dialogue and action.

▶ REVISION STRATEGY
Adding Dialogue to Reveal Your Characters

Reread your paragraphs one by one. Find places where you can add dialogue to reveal more about your characters. These might be events that you simply described or emotions and attitudes that you explained. In the instances you have found, let the characters speak for themselves.

While a writer may have described the end of an interview with a few brief sentences of narration, notice how the example below shows the character Jeanne to be professional and calm, despite an awkward interview situation.

EVENT NARRATED WITH DIALOGUE:

"So," Jeanne began, wondering how to leave gracefully. "I guess you'll call me when you know who you've chosen."

"Yes, that's right." The manager had already turned her attention to other things.

"Well," again Jeanne kept friendly optimism in her voice, "I enjoyed our meeting, and I look forward to hearing from you soon."

Silence.

"Thanks so much for your time. . . . I'll find my way out." She gathered her things, smiled weakly, and left.

Use Structure to Make Dialogue Realistic To get the feel of the natural way that people talk, listen to a few conversations. Note the rhythms and pacing of conversations and the way the subject affects the way people converse. Then, to achieve that natural effect in your writing, add pauses, use sentence fragments, or let your characters interrupt each other.

Choose the Right Words Just as you use your own diction as you speak, let your characters use the language that is right for them. In your draft, use words that suit the character and the situation. For example, use slang if the character is talking with friends, but use more formal language if the character is talking to someone unfamiliar.

⚙ Grammar and Style Tip

Instead of repeating "said" over and over, choose tag words that show your characters' attitudes. For example, to convey someone's anger, you could write, "'No, I will not!' Amy retorted." To convey her excitement, write "'Yes!' Amy responded enthusiastically."

Revising: Adding Dialogue to Reveal Your Characters

1. Review with students how dialogue often shows more about a character than narration can tell.

2. Suggest that students reread their stories paragraph by paragraph. Have them identify paragraphs that contain information that could be shown more compellingly with dialogue.

3. Ask students to place a bracket in the margin next to each such paragraph. Have students write a few lines of dialogue for each bracketed paragraph.

4. Ask for volunteers to write their lines of dialogue on the board. Have them read the dialogue aloud with a classmate.

5. Ask the class whether they have suggestions for making the dialogue more realistic or more dramatic. Be sure students record these suggestions for consideration as they revise.

Step-by-Step Teaching Guide

Revising: Vary Sentence Beginnings

Teaching Resources: Writing Support Transparencies, 5-I

1. Ask students to quickly scan their drafts looking only at sentence beginnings. Do they seem repetitive?

2. Display Transparency 5-I to discuss the changes Ben made to improve his sentence beginnings.

3. Do students agree with Ben's changes, or would they have made different choices?

Customize for
Less Advanced Students

Ask students to circle the action verbs in their stories, and underline linking verbs. Suggest that they evaluate which weaker verbs or verb phrases could be profitably revised. Ask volunteers to read both the old and revised paragraphs. Invite students to use these as models when making further changes.

Customize for
ESL Students

Students learning English as a second language may use some words repetitively because they are sure of the meanings of these words. Students with a more limited English vocabulary may wish to use their word lists to help them brainstorm for synonyms in their first language, which they can then translate into English with the help of a dictionary.

Revising Your Sentences
Vary Sentence Beginnings

Don't fall into the habit of beginning several sentences the same way. To revise this dull pattern in your writing, look at your sentence beginnings and introduce variety where you can.

▶ REVISION STRATEGY
Listing Sentence Starters

Make a list of the first words in each sentence of your draft. Challenge yourself to break any pattern that presents itself.

Writing Lab CD-ROM

Use the Sentence Openers Variety Checker tool to evaluate your sentence beginnings. You can find it in the Revising and Editing section of the Narration lesson.

Student Work
IN PROGRESS

Name: Ben Spoer
Santa Monica High School
Santa Monica, CA

Using a Word List to Vary Sentence Beginnings
When Ben looked at the first words in his draft, he noticed that he started several sentences with "I." He made corrections to vary his writing style.

+ Because
~~People~~ There
It
I

Because of those experiences,
I believed acting one way and thinking another was just an adult thing until I got into middle school. *There,* People spoke nicely to . . .

Revising Your Word Choice
Use Specific Verbs

Action verbs can provide description without adding too many modifiers. Be sure you have chosen the most efficient verbs.

▶ REVISION STRATEGY
Circling Action Verbs

Choose one paragraph, and circle the action verbs it contains. List other verbs that might fit the sentence. Evaluate the meaning each one conveys, and then choose the best verb.

EXAMPLE: The batter *hit* the ball into right field.
             The batter *looped* the ball into right field.

✎ STANDARDIZED TEST PREPARATION WORKSHOP

Vocabulary Standardized test questions may require students to recognize homonyms. Write these sentences and word choices on the board. Ask students to find the word that fits in both of the sentences.

1. Do you know that story about the three ___?

2. The bottle ___ the label "poisonous."

A   animals   C   nations
B   bears   D   carries

Students should recognize that **B** is the only word that fits both sentences. A, B, and C fit the first sentence but not the second, and D fits the second sentence but not the first. In the first sentence, the word *bears* means "animals." In the second sentence it means "carries."

Grammar in Your Writing
Action vs. Linking Verbs

Action verbs tell what action someone or something is performing. Action verbs can show both physical and mental action.

Physical action: The bear **swats** the branches away.

Mental action: I **agree** with you.

Linking verbs help one word in a sentence to name or describe the condition of another word in a sentence. The most common linking verb is some form of *be.*

Linking in order to name: The lion **is** the king of the forest.

Linking in order to describe: The argument **was** exhausting.

Find It in Your Reading Reread "Crossing Spider Creek," by Dan O'Brien, on pages 74–75. Identify five action verbs and five linking verbs the writer uses.

Find It in Your Writing Look through your story draft, and find five action verbs and five linking verbs you have used. Challenge yourself to revise sentences that would be improved by a more precise action verb.

For more on action and linking verbs, see Chapter 17.

Peer Review
Group Feedback

Before you make final changes to your draft, get together with a small group of classmates. As writers, share your work, and give each other suggestions for making your short stories better. Listen and participate in the review of each story; you may hear an idea that you can apply to your work.

Read your story aloud to the group twice. The first reading will give your peers a chance to hear the story, meet the characters, and understand the plot. You may ask for initial reactions, but after a second reading, your peers will be more prepared to give you supported responses. Use these questions to guide your peer review:

1. What scene was most vivid?
2. What would you like to know more about?

▲ **Critical Viewing** How might hearing another student's writing in a group like the one shown here actually improve your writing? **[Support]**

Revising • 85

Step-by-Step Teaching Guide

Editing and Proofreading

1. Suggest that students check their stories for spelling, punctuation, and grammar one paragraph at a time.

2. Have students look carefully at their choices of action and linking verbs. If they find sentences in which they have not chosen the most effective verbs, urge them to consult a thesaurus and replace those verbs.

Step-by-Step Teaching Guide

Punctuating Dialogue Correctly

1. Review with students how commas and quotation marks are used to punctuate dialogue.

2. Ask for two volunteers to have a short conversation on a topic of their choice. Have them stand in the front of the classroom and record what they say on a tape recorder.

3. Replay their conversation, writing it on the board without any punctuation. Ask students where commas and punctuation marks should be added.

Find It in Your Writing

Using student narratives that contain dialogue is a beneficial exercise. Ask students to choose a short story containing dialogue from their portfolios. Ask students to circle each piece of dialogue. Then have students review their punctuation using the punctuation conventions for dialogue on page 86.

5.5 Editing and Proofreading

Once you have finalized your draft, review it for errors in spelling, punctuation, and grammar. Mechanical mistakes like these pull attention away from the story you have written. Strive to make your final draft error-free.

Focusing on Punctuation

Be sure you have used punctuation correctly.

End marks Check that each sentence has an end mark, such as a period(.), an exclamation point(!), or a question mark(?).

Commas Commas are used to prevent misreading. They can set up relationships among parts of a sentence and make long sentences easier to read. Commas are also critical to punctuating dialogue correctly. Be sure you have not included commas too generously or too sparingly.

💡 Spelling Tip

If you are using a computer word-processing program, use the Spelling and Grammar tool. Then, confirm your draft by asking a classmate to help you identify mis-spelled words.

Grammar in Your Writing
Punctuating Dialogue Correctly

Punctuate dialogue within quotation marks. Use these conventions to punctuate the exact words of conversation correctly:

- Begin a new paragraph each time the speaker changes.

- Use a comma inside the closing quotation mark when a remark comes before the speaker tag, the narrative identifying the speaker:

"It looks as if it will be a gorgeous day," he said.

- Use a comma after the speaker tag when the speaker tag precedes a quoted statement:

She smiled and replied, "I had hoped it would be."

- When a speaker tag interrupts a direct quotation, use commas to set off the two parts of the quotation:

"Come on," he shouted to the people upstairs, "let's get going!"

Find It in Your Writing As you proofread your short story, check the punctuation of any dialogue you have used.

For more on the conventions of punctuating dialogue, see Chapter 27.

86 • Short Story

⏱ TIME SAVERS!

 Writing Support Transparencies
Use the transparencies for Chapter 5 to facilitate teaching of strategies.

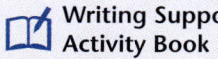 **Writing Support Activity Book**
Use the graphic organizers for Chapter 5 to facilitate student planning.

⏱ TIME AND RESOURCE MANAGER

Resources
Print: *Scoring Rubrics on Transparency,* Ch. 5; *Writing Assessment and Portfolio Management; Formal Assessment,* Ch. 5
Technology: *Writing Lab* CD-ROM, Narration

In-Depth Coverage	Accelerated Pace
• Review p. 86 in class, including Grammar in Your Writing. • Give step-by-step coverage to Publishing and Presenting (p. 87). • Analyze the Final Draft (pp. 88–90). • Have students edit and proofread their stories in class.	• Assign independent review of pp. 86–90. • Have students edit and revise their short stories independently. • Respond to individual editing needs as needed.

5.6 Publishing and Presenting

Building Your Portfolio

Use these suggestions to share your short story with others:

1. **Submit Your Story to a Literary Magazine** Many schools publish student works in a newspaper or magazine. Submit your story to your school's literary magazine. To reach a wider audience, contact a national magazine.

2. **Make a Class Anthology** Form an editorial committee, and ask classmates to submit their papers for a collection of short stories. Add photographs or illustrations to enhance the writing. Design a cover, compose a table of contents, and include an "About the Authors" section, if you like. Then, make copies for your classmates.

Reflecting on Your Writing

Once you've finished your story, use these questions to reflect on the process. Add your response to your portfolio.

- What did you learn about the techniques of professional fiction writers?
- Which strategy worked best for you? How did it help you improve your writing?

 Internet Tip

To see model essays scored with this rubric, go to
www.phschool.com

Rubric for Self-Assessment

Use the following criteria to assess your short story:

	Score 4	Score 3	Score 2	Score 1
Audience and Purpose	Presents an unusual perspective on a conflict	Presents a series of events leading to a clear conflict	Presents little conflict or narrative	Contains no conflict or narrative
Organization	Presents a clear sequence of events in a logical order	Presents a clear sequence of events with some inconsistencies in organization	Presents a weak or unclear connection between ideas or events	Presents no connections between ideas or events
Elaboration	Provides rich details and/or illuminating illustrations; incorporates apt, striking word choice; makes effective use of dialogue	Provides many details but some vague words; includes good use of dialogue	Provides some details through limited word choice; includes some use of dialogue	Provides no details; includes limited dialogue
Use of Language	Demonstrates overall clarity and fluency; presents very few errors in spelling, capitalization, punctuation, and/or usage	Demonstrates good sentence variety; presents some errors in spelling, capitalization, punctuation, and/or usage	Uses awkward or overly simple sentence structures; presents many errors in spelling, usage, and punctuation	Includes incomplete thoughts; creates confusion through errors in spelling, usage, and punctuation

Publishing and Presenting • **87**

Step-by-Step Teaching Guide

Publishing and Presenting

1. In preparing their stories for publication, students may wish to add artwork or photographs. Ask them whether pictures would enhance the story for the reader.

2. Suggest that students submit their stories to a literary magazine, post them on the Internet, or start their own literary publication.

ASSESS and CLOSE

Step-by-Step Teaching Guide

Assessment

Teaching Resources: Scoring Rubrics on Transparency, Ch. 5; Writing Assessment and Portfolio Management; Formal Assessment, Ch. 5

1. Display the Scoring Rubric transparency and review the criteria in class.

2. Before students proceed with self-assessment, you may wish to review the Final Draft of the Student Work in Progress on pages 88–90.

3. In addition to student self-assessment, you may wish to use the following options:

- score student essays yourself, using the rubric and scoring models in *Writing Assessment and Portfolio Management*.

- review the Standardized Test Preparation Workshop on pages 94–95 and administer a timed writing assessment.

- administer the Chapter 5 assessment in *Formal Assessment* to measure students' grasp of the concepts presented.

✓ **ONGOING ASSESSMENT: Assess Mastery**

Use one of the following options to assess drafts of students' short stories.

Self-Assessment Ask students to score their stories using the rubric provided. Then have students write a paragraph that discusses the strategy they found most helpful in composing their stories.

Teacher Assessment Use the rubric and the scoring models provided in *Writing Assessment and Portfolio Management* to score students' work.

Final Draft

1. Help students see that "Too Much Information" incorporates key elements of the short story:

   - The topic is well chosen. The story is built around an interesting character with an unusual power.

   - Audience and purpose have been carefully considered; the story is clearly addressed to young people familiar with the world of high school.

   - The plot unfolds early, as the narrator's power to hear what people are thinking becomes a conflict.

   - Momentum builds as the narrator describes its painful consequences.

2. Ask students which details establish the conflict, and how the use of dialogue helps set the scene. What does the dialogue reveal about the narrator?

3. Ask students if they have any recommendations for improving the flow of this story. How might they apply their suggestions to their own writing?

Critical Viewing

Hypothesize Students may say that such a seemingly wholesome and innocent scene of laughing, chatting students was only a cover for darker, more painful thoughts.

5.7 *Student Work* IN PROGRESS

FINAL DRAFT

▲ **Critical Viewing**
What would the narrator of "Too Much Information" say about the group interaction shown here? **[Hypothesize]**

Too Much Information

Ben Spoer
Santa Monica High School
Santa Monica, California

"I wished I could be normal again. I really did," I begin as I stare at the full glass of root beer in front of me. "But I thought that was impossible since I discovered my power."

In the shadows of the dimly lit booth, my listener nods his head silently.

"No, it wasn't a power. Actually, it was more of a jinx," I say, as I go off in a reverie. "Being able to hear what people are really thinking is one of those things you think would be great until you can do it. Then, you understand that some knowledge has a sting."

Ever since I was a little kid, I've wondered what people really felt

The use of dialogue and description sets the scene, mood, and situation.

88 • Short Story

inside, compared to how they seemed on the outside. I recall from my childhood those nice moms who would volunteer at school. They acted so sweet and full of praise in the classroom, but once they hit the street, they'd complain about how hard it was to volunteer.

Until I reached middle school, I believed acting one way and thinking another was just an adult thing. There, people spoke nicely to each other but really didn't seem nice at all. It struck me as surreal while others accepted it as normal. I would sit in the cafeteria daydreaming and observing others. The girls would tell each other 'I love you" and "we'll be best friends forever." But forever was a short time. It ended when they saw one of the girls wearing something unfashionable. The guys were just as bad. They pretended that nothing ever bothered them, saying, "Forget it! It was nothing," but they kept score and never let you forget when you blew it. Of course, I seemed to be one of those who were blowing it a lot.

There were rules for things I had never even dreamed had rules. No one had bothered to tell me. The summer before high school started, I had one simple wish—to know what the popular people really thought, because then I might understand them better.

That first Wednesday in the science room something happened to grant my wish. I mixed the chemicals wrong, and the experiment exploded in my face. All I know for sure is that I woke up in the hospital with bandages covering my head and a loud ringing in my ears. When the doctor removed the bandages, the change began.

I asked the doctor, "Well, doc, how do I look?"

Reading the chart at the end of my bed, he replied, "Fine, son." But in a low whisper, barely audible, I heard, "Look at that poor kid's ears!"

When I asked him what was wrong with my ears, he reeled back as if I had slapped him. "Nothing, they're fine," he insisted.

When I looked into the mirror, I saw that they were not fine. Now they stuck out from my head like two satellite dishes, and I was receiving more signals than ever. "Why me?" I moaned as I fell back into bed.

At first, I didn't realize how much this changed my looks. But then I heard, "Get a load of those ears!" and "Hey, Dumbo, want a peanut?" as I walked down the halls at school. I ducked my head and kept going.

"Who was saying that?" my listener asked.

"Good question," I replied. "And one I needed to know how to answer."

In the exposition, the narrator provides information to explain his personality. This sets up the conflict.

A meeting with the doctor after the accident reveals the conflict. Because the narrator can hear people's thoughts, he must decide what is real and what is not real.

Integrating Grammar Skills

Ask students to evaluate the use of quotation marks in the model. Explain to students that direct quotations are surrounded by double quotation marks ("), while quotes within quotes use single quotation marks ('). (Example: "You call that a 'dog'?") Direct students to review their use of quotation marks in their stories.

Customize for
AP Students

Ask students to research the genre of speculative fiction for examples of stories about people who can read minds. Have them pool their lists and post them in the classroom for other students who may be interested in reading more such fiction.

Teaching From the Final Draft

Point out the many details that Ben includes about the thoughts of others that the narrator hears. Point out that such details help clarify why having the ability to hear the thoughts of others creates a conflict for the narrator, and thus a conflict for the story. Remind students that changing the details of a story can dramatically change the story as a whole. How might the story have been different if the narrator had been unable to rid himself of his ability? (Students may suggest that the story might take a negative turn as the narrator is oppressed by painful information. On the other hand, the narrator might find a lucrative career as a mind reader.)

Integrating Workplace Skills

Tell students that most workplaces have internal, or in-house, publishing facilities. Discuss with students how their own classroom works like a publishing house. (Students write a manuscript, edit and proofread, then they type it or write it neatly to produce a final product.)

I was stunned by the fact that besides these horrific jabs, the hall was calm. It was then that I realized no one's lips were moving.

By lunch, I wanted it to stop. Knowing what everyone was really thinking was giving me a pounding headache. I heard one girl say to another, "Oh, what a beautiful dress," and then in a whispery low voice, "Doesn't she ever look in the mirror?"

Then, I heard another voice. "She looks adorable. I wonder where she got it."

I heard everything—the pain of people pining away, the anticipation of others waiting for football practice, happiness, fear, jealousy, boredom. The whispering dinned into my head like the world's loudest hammer. It wasn't just the sound, but the agony of all the unmet desires that made me want to flee. Finally, I had my lunch on the lawn, alone—more isolated than ever before.

"You mean you could hear people's thoughts?" my listener asked, totally perplexed by the story I was telling.

"Yes, and I was beginning to feel desperate."

That night sitting at home, I searched my mind to find one true friend, someone I could trust. "Lisa," I thought. She was a girl that I had known before the accident. She'd even come to the hospital to visit me. Jumping up, I called her and asked her out. I heard two responses—"Oh, I would love to, but I'm going out of town this weekend," and then, in that faint whisper, "I can't believe this! I've been waiting forever for him to ask me!"

At least it was nice to hear that secret admiration. Still, it was not worth living with all this mess just for a few silent secrets. For about an hour, I just sat in my room wishing I could go back to the superficial but normal world of pleasantries and appearances. There, the only insecurities I could hear in my head were my own.

My listener leaned forward, "Well, what did you do?"

"Well, call me Mr. Lucky," I said, laughing at the strangeness of it all. A week after my accident, I was at football practice. I did not have my helmet on, and Barry, the center, decided it was time for some tackling practice. All I remember was the ground coming at me fast. I woke up in the hospital again. However, this time, I could only hear the doctor remarking on how I would not really notice the stitches, not how horrible my ears looked.

I could no longer read minds! The power was gone! What a relief it is to be back to my old self. I'll never wish to get into other people's minds again. The memory of this experience, and the workings of my own mind, make life interesting enough as it is.

To intensify the conflict by showing the narrator becoming aware, the writer shows how painful the power to hear people's thoughts can be.

The narrator elaborates on the kinds of thoughts he can hear.

In the last moment of rising action, the narrator calls a good friend.

By using a listener within the story, the writer can include his audience's anticipated question.

Life returns to normal, but the narrator and the reader have learned a lesson about life.

Connected Assignment Drama

Drama is a story conveyed through performance instead of written narration. In drama, the audience learns about the characters and conflict by watching and listening to events. An effective drama tells a story and

- uses the conventions of a script, indicating dialogue and stage directions.
- makes use of lighting, props, and staging.

MODEL

from **The Glass Menagerie**
by Tennessee Williams

LAURA: Hello, Mother, I was—[*She makes a nervous gesture toward the chart on the wall.* AMANDA *leans against the shut door and stares at* LAURA *with a martyred look.*]

AMANDA: Deception? Deception? [*She slowly removes her hat and gloves, continuing the sweet suffering stare. She lets the hat and gloves fall on the floor—a bit of acting.*]

LAURA [*shakily*]: How was the D.A.R. meeting? [AMANDA *slowly opens her purse and removes a dainty white handkerchief which she shakes out delicately and delicately touches to her lips and nostrils.*]

▲ Critical Viewing
How can an actor's portrayal change your interpretation of a literary character? [Contrast]

Prewriting Identify characters, choose a conflict, and plan the setting in which your drama will take place. Sketch a plan for the set that identifies the names of rooms and the placement of furniture.

Drafting Unfold the plot through the characters' dialogue. Include details of setting and emotions in the stage directions to help the actors and other readers envision your scenes.

Revising and Editing Ask a group to read your script aloud. Use this opportunity to listen for authenticity in the dialogue. You may also want to review your stage directions to add or change wording until you are sure that the information is clear. Make revisions as necessary.

Publishing and Presenting When you've finalized your work, consider staging a live performance.

Connected Assignment • 91

Lesson Objectives

1. To write a dramatic scene
2. To use prewriting strategies to generate ideas
3. To use writing processes to develop and revise drafts
4. To respond productively to peer review
5. To present a live performance of a dramatic scene

Step-by-Step Teaching Guide

Drama

Teaching Resource: Writing Support Transparencies, 5-J

1. Display Transparency 5-J to point out details: the use of boldface and colons for speakers; italic type and brackets for stage directions.
2. Use the model to show how Williams combines dialogue and stage directions to reveal character and conflict.
3. Refer students to Chapter 5 for resources as needed. See the chart below for suggestions.
4. After scripts have been revised in response to group readings, encourage interested students to stage a performance for the class.

Critical Viewing

Contrast Students may note that an actor's portrayal can elicit either sympathy for or antagonism toward a character.

☑ ONGOING ASSESSMENT: Prerequisite Skills

Students may find the following resources from Chapter 5 particularly helpful in completing their scripts.

In the Textbook	Print Resources	Technology
Character Sound Off, p. 76 Drafting, pp. 80–81	*Writing Support Transparencies,* 5-A, F *Writing Support Activity Book,* 5-2	*Writing Lab* CD-ROM, Narration

Lesson Objectives

1. To analyze relationships and ideas represented in various media

2. To recognize how visual and sound techniques convey messages in media

3. To present an interpretation of a short story

Analyzing a Composer's Influence

1. Choose one of the Spotlight elements for class discussion, or have students work individually or in groups on the elements of their choice. Give students the initiative to find the necessary music, videotapes, or art.

2. Interested students might research additional information about the leitmotifs in Richard Wagner's operas.

3. If you obtain a videotape of *The Wizard of Oz,* play a well-known scene with the screen darkened so students can concentrate on the music. How does the soundtrack alone suggest what might be happening in the scene? (You can achieve a similar effect by playing a movie soundtrack.)

4. Ask students to work in pairs to analyze the soundtrack of a recent film in order to identify leitmotifs.

Viewing and Representing

Activity Give students the opportunity to share their story soundtracks with the class. They might ask a friend to play a musical instrument as the story is read.

Critical Viewing

Analyze Students will see that the cartoon characters appear to be costumed and onstage, with one of them singing.

Spotlight on the Humanities

Analyzing a Composer's Influence on Art and Popular Culture

Focus on Music: Leitmotif

Like short stories, art forms like operas, ballets, cartoons, and movies often weave characters, plot, and conflict to tell a story. German composer Richard Wagner (1813–1883) greatly influenced nineteenth-century music. He even had an effect on music of the twentieth century—especially film scores. Wagner is known for evolving the technique of "leitmotif," in which a specific melody is associated with a character or situation.

▲ Critical Viewing
What elements of this cartoon image suggest opera to viewers? **[Analyze]**

Film Connection You may know an example of leitmotif without even knowing the term. In the classic film *The Wizard of Oz*, whenever the Wicked Witch of the West appears, a threatening melody plays—a leitmotif.

Animation Connection Wagner's operatic style is also apparent in the soundtrack of cartoons. For example, in the 1930's, classic cartoons included such characters as Bugs Bunny, Daffy Duck, and Elmer Fudd. Unique soundtrack elements often connected with the specific characters on screen. In addition, Elmer Fudd, Bugs Bunny's arch enemy, took the opera connection even further in one cartoon when he appeared in an opera and sang "Kill the Wabbit" in the comical lisp that is forever linked to Fudd.

Art Connection The success of Wagner's music made his operas a popular subject for art. German artist Ferdinand Leeke (1859–1925) was commissioned by Richard Wagner's son, Siegfried, to paint ten scenes from Wagner's operas. Leeke, one of the most famous painters to illustrate Wagner's work, completed the series in 1898.

Narrative Writing Activity: Short-Story Soundtrack

Apply Wagner's leitmotif technique to create a soundtrack that accompanies a reading of a story. Using a short story you wrote or one you know very well, identify the main characters and choose a melody appropriate to each one's personality. Record a reading of the story, and share it with an audience.

Media and Technology Skills

Lesson Objectives

1. To analyze relationships, ideas, and cultures as represented in various media
2. To recognize how visual and sound techniques convey messages in media
3. To draw conclusions from information gathered

Analyzing Media Content

Activity: Review Plot in a Television Drama

Like short stories that are meant to be read, the episodes of a dramatic television series also contain the elements of narration: plot, character, setting, and theme. Knowing the techniques the professionals use to turn television into a storytelling medium can improve your ability to view the programs critically.

Think About It The setting of a drama provides you with a general expectation of how the story will unfold. For example, if a show is set in a hospital, you can expect that the plot will revolve around patients and the stories behind their injuries. Keeping your expectation in mind helps you actively follow the story line.

One-hour dramas often consist of several distinct story lines whose relationship becomes clear at the climax of the show. For instance, a family drama may weave the experiences of each family member into one episode. Viewers jump between story lines but can expect that in the end, the subplots will be brought together.

Watch It Using a chart like the one below, track the separate story lines in a television drama of your choice. Note which characters are involved in each story line, and then summarize the way all the story lines are brought together.

Techniques for Weaving Multiple Story Lines Together

- The most important story lines are introduced at the start of the program.
- As different story lines are reintroduced, key details are restated in dialogue between the characters.
- One character serves as a link between the different story lines.
- Music signals transitions between the story lines.
- Outdoor setting shots also signal transitions.

Drama: Setting: Main Characters: Conflict:		
Story Line A Conflict: Characters: Resolution:	**Story Line B** Conflict: Characters: Resolution:	**Story Line C** Conflict: Characters: Resolution:
Story Lines Merge When:		

Evaluate It After you've seen the drama, use your chart to write an evaluation. Explain whether you felt the episode told each story effectively.

Step-by-Step Teaching Guide

Analyzing Media Content

Teaching Resources: Writing Support Transparencies, 5-K; Writing Support Activity Book, 5-5

1. Go over the techniques of multiple story lines in television drama (see box on page 93). For each technique, ask students to give an example from a program they have seen recently.
2. Ask students to give examples of how the setting of a program determines viewer expectations. What do viewers expect will happen in a program set in a police station? Family home? Space ship?
3. Display Transparency 5-K and show students how the chart may be used to track story lines. Give students copies of the blank organizer (5-5) to use to prepare their evaluations.

Lesson Objectives

1. To analyze literary elements in a short story
2. To use prewriting strategies to plan
3. To organize ideas to ensure coherence, logical progression, and support for ideas
4. To edit and proofread to ensure standard English usage and grammar

Step-by-Step Teaching Guide

Questions About Short Stories

Teaching Resources: Standardized Test Preparation Workbook, pp. 9–10

1. Emphasize the importance of keeping the main elements of a short story in mind when responding to an essay test about a short story.

2. Remind students to identify key words in the test question, such as *describe* and *compare*.

3. Suggest that creating an outline or a list of points they want to address will make the best use of the time students have for drafting.

4. Tell students that when they revise, they should make sure they have enough examples to support their thesis statement.

5. Administer the sample prompt during class time. You may wish to use a different prompt based on another story the class has read recently.

Standardized Test Preparation Workshop

Responding to Questions About Short Stories

Some standardized tests require you to write a short response to a story that is printed in the test booklet. Use the knowledge you gain from the process of writing a short story to help you complete this task. Before responding to a test prompt on a short story, read the story and keep these short-story elements in mind:

- Plot is the sequence of events that catches your interest and takes you through the story.
- Characters are the people, animals, or other beings that take part in the story's action.
- Setting is the time and place in which the story occurs.
- Theme is the message about life that the story conveys.

As you read the story, think about how the writer uses each narrative device to create an effective short story. Then, read the prompt, and analyze the question you must answer. As you write, concentrate on using details from the story to create a unified response.

Read "Crossing Spider Creek" on pages 74–75, and then write an essay to respond to the following sample prompt.

Sample Prompt

Characters in literature often make important realizations at critical moments. In a short response, describe the realization Tom makes about his wife. Then, compare his experience with that of a person you know or another literary character who has made a similar realization.

Test Tip

- If time permits, read the story twice. The first time, read to get the general plot of the story. The second time, read with a directed purpose: to gather details for your writing.

TEST-TAKING TIP

A clear understanding of the story is the first step to success when responding to questions about short stories. Tell students to focus on the plot of the story first and then, if they have time, to reread the story and jot down ideas that can support the specifications in the writing prompt.

Ask students to pick out the key words in the Sample Prompt on this page, noting that they will need to compare Tom's experience with that of someone they know or with another literary character. Remind them that a comparison requires noting similarities.

Prewriting

Allow about one quarter of your time for prewriting.

Identify the Key Words in the Question Read the test prompt to analyze your assignment. Note words like *compare, describe, explain,* or *predict,* and use your prewriting time to collect information that will help you complete the task. For example, the sample test prompt on page 94 asks you to discuss two realizations that are made at critical moments. To prepare to write, identify the second person you will discuss.

Gather Details From the Selection Scan the story for details that will help you answer the question. Look for information that will show the realization Tom made.

Drafting

Allow approximately half of your time for drafting.

Organize Your Essay Create an outline or a list of points you want to include. In this situation, it is probably best to address Tom's situation first, provide a second example next, and briefly compare the two. Use the outline as a starting point, and jot down ideas for each point. Although your time is limited, don't rush through this part of the job. Write down as many ideas as you can.

Put It on Paper Address the question in an introduction, and then write your response. Use your outline and notes as a guide. Provide the details to make your examples clear, but try not to give more background information than is necessary. Write neatly, since you may not have time to recopy your essay.

Revising, Editing, and Proofreading

Allow about one quarter of your time to revise, edit, and proofread your paper.

Check Against the Prompt After you have written your essay, review the test prompt to be sure the question and your answer have the same focus. If necessary, add details or examples to make your thesis clear, and draw a single line through material that seems unrelated. You may want to revise the wording of your thesis statement or review the conclusion to give your writing a stronger focus.

Clean It Up When you are satisfied with your answer, read the draft one last time for accuracy. If you are unsure about a grammar or mechanics problem, consider rewriting a sentence to eliminate the need to correct it. Make all corrections neatly so that the test reviewer can read your work.

Customize for
Less Advanced Students

Students who have difficulty comparing Tom's experience with that of another literary character should focus on the experience of someone they know.

Customize for
AP Students

Ask students to focus on writing and revising clear and concise thesis statements for their essays, ensuring that they can relate the conclusion to this statement.

In-Depth Lesson Plan

	LESSON FOCUS	PRINT AND MEDIA RESOURCES
DAY 1	**Introduction to Description** Students learn key elements of descriptions and analyze the Model From Literature (pp. 96–99)	*Writers at Work* **Videotape,** Description *Writing Lab* **CD-ROM,** Description
DAY 2	**Prewriting** Students choose and narrow a topic, consider their audience and purpose, and gather information. (pp. 100–103)	**Teaching Resources** *Writing Support Transparencies,* 6-A–D; *Writing Support Activity Book,* 6-1–2; *Topic Bank for Heterogeneous Classes,* Ch. 6
DAY 3	**Drafting** Students organize their ideas and write their first drafts. (p. 104)	**Teaching Resources** *Writing Support Transparencies,* 6-E
DAY 4	**Revising** Students organize their ideas and write their first drafts. (pp. 105–108)	**Teaching Resources** *Writing Support Transparencies,* 6-F–G
DAY 5	**Editing and Proofreading; Publishing and Presenting** Students check their work for accuracy and correctness and present their final drafts. (pp. 109–112)	**Teaching Resources** *Scoring Rubrics on Transparency,* Ch. 6; *Writing Assessment and Portfolio Management; Formal Assessment,* Ch. 6

Accelerated Lesson Plan

	LESSON FOCUS	PRINT AND MEDIA RESOURCES
DAY 1	**Drafting** Students review characteristics of description, select topics, and write drafts. (pp. 96–104)	*Writing Lab* **CD-ROM,** Description **Teaching Resources** *Writing Support Transparencies,* 6-A–E; *Writing Support Activity Book,* 6-1–2
DAY 2	**Revising to Presenting** Students work individually or with peers to revise, edit, and proofread their work for presentation. (pp. 105–112)	**Teaching Resources** *Writing Support Transparencies,* 6-F–G; *Scoring Rubrics on Transparency,* Ch. 6; *Writing Assessment and Portfolio Management; Formal Assessment,* Ch. 6

Options for Adapting Lesson Plans

HOMEWORK

Have students complete any stage of the lesson for homework.

FEATURES

Extend coverage with Connected Assignment (p. 113), Spotlight on the Humanities (p. 114), Media and Technology Skills (p. 115), and the Standardized Test Preparation Workshop (p. 116).

TECHNOLOGY

Students can complete any stage of the lesson on computer. Have them print out their completed work.

INTEGRATED SKILLS COVERAGE

Integrating Grammar
Combining Sentences, SE p. 107
Avoiding Fragments, SE p. 109

Reading/Writing Connection
Make Inferences, SE p. 98
Writing Application, SE p. 99

Viewing and Representing
Critical Viewing, SE pp. 96, 98, 105, 111, 112, 113, 114
Analyzing How Meaning Is Communicated in the Arts, SE p. 114
Examining Media's Power to Construct a Perception of Reality, SE p. 115

Speaking and Listening
ATE p. 112

Vocabulary
ATE pp. 102, 103

Real-World Connection
ATE p. 99

Workplace Skills
ATE p. 111

ASSESSMENT SUPPORT

Standardized Test Preparation Workshop SE p. 116; ATE p. 106
Standardized Test Preparation Workbook, pp. 11–12
Scoring Rubrics on Transparency, Ch. 6
Formal Assessment, Ch. 6
Writing Assessment and Portfolio Management

MEETING INDIVIDUAL NEEDS

Less Advanced Students ATE pp. 101, 106, 117. See also Ongoing Assessment, ATE pp. 98, 101, 103, 105, 107.
ESL Students ATE p. 107
Visual/Spatial Learners ATE pp. 103, 104
Interpersonal Learners ATE p. 104

BLOCK SCHEDULING

Pacing Suggestions
For 90-minute Blocks
- Have students complete the Prewriting and Drafting stages in a single period.
- Focus one class period on Revising and Editing and Publishing and Presenting. Allow at least 30 minutes for peer revision.

Resources for Varying Instruction
- *Writing Lab* **CD-ROM** If your students have access to hardware, a 90-minute block provides an ideal opportunity for students to work on computer.
- *Writers at Work* **Videotape** Show the Description segment in class.

Professional Development Support
- *How to Manage Instruction in the Block* This Teaching Resource provides management and activity suggestions.

MEDIA AND TECHNOLOGY

For the Student
- *Writing Lab* **CD-ROM,** Description
- *On-Line Exercise Bank,* Section 20.2

For the Teacher
- *Writers at Work* **Videotape,** Description
- *Resource Pro* **CD-ROM**

WRITING AND GRAMMAR WEB SITE

The Interactive Writing and Grammar Web Site provides a wide array of support for students, teachers, and parents. Writing support includes:

- Interactive revision checkers
- Scoring rubrics with complete models

www.phschool.com

LITERATURE CONNECTIONS

Related selections from *Prentice Hall Literature: Timeless Voices, Timeless Themes,* The American Experience:

"For the Love of Books," Rita Dove, SE p. 99
from *The Right Stuff,* Tom Wolfe, SE p. 101

Lesson Objectives

1. Write a description appropriate to audience and purpose

2. To read to appreciate the writer's craft and to discover models for writing

3. To use prewriting strategies to generate ideas, develop voice, and plan

4. To use writing to refine topics and clarify ideas

5. To develop and revise drafts in terms of structure, paragraphs, sentences, and word choice

6. To use sentence combining to compose increasingly more involved sentences

7. To edit and proofread to ensure standard English usage and grammar

8. To evaluate writing for both mechanics and content

9. To refine a description for publication

Critical Viewing

Describe Students may mention the silvery sounds of cool water, rustling green leaves, a bright blue sky.

Chapter 6 Description

▲ **Critical Viewing**
What words would you use to convey the sights and sounds suggested by this photograph? **[Describe]**

Description in Everyday Life

Imagine returning from a vacation without a single photograph or postcard. Try making a story scary without adding details to bring a scene to life. Challenge yourself to provide a radio-style play-by-play account to audiences who can't see the game. In each case, descriptive language that communicates sights, sounds, and other sensory details can enrich the way you communicate. We give and receive descriptive messages all day long. Advertisements describe products, your social studies text describes places and people, you and your friends describe favorite songs or movies. On the pages that follow, you'll learn how to improve your descriptive writing skills to use description for a variety of purposes.

96 • Description

⏱ **TIME AND RESOURCE MANAGER**

Resources
Technology: *Writers at Work* Videotape, Description; *Writing Lab* CD-ROM, Description

In-Depth Coverage	Accelerated Pace
• Cover pp. 96–97 in class. • Show Description section of the *Writers at Work* Videotape. • Read the Model From Literature (pp. 98–99) in class and use it to discuss key elements of descriptive writing.	• Share examples of descriptive writing and hold critical discussions on them. • Assign the Model From Literature for independent reading.

What Is Description?

Description is writing that uses vivid details to capture a scene, setting, person, or moment. Effective descriptive writing includes

- sensory details—sights, sounds, smells, tastes, and physical sensations.
- vivid, precise language.
- figurative language or comparisons.
- adjectives and adverbs that paint a word picture.
- an organization suited to the subject.

To see the criteria on which your descriptive writing may be evaluated, preview the Rubric for Self-Assessment on page 110.

Types of Description

Description can be useful in other forms of writing, but it can also stand alone. Here are some examples of descriptive writing:

- **Physical descriptions** may focus on the appearance of a person, place, or thing, as well as on its significance.
- **Descriptions of ideas** use concrete images or analogies to help readers understand abstract or complicated concepts.
- **Functional descriptions** describe the component parts of a whole for a practical purpose, such as fixing a bicycle.
- **Remembrances** illustrate memorable parts of the writer's past by describing a person, place, thing, or event.
- **Character sketches** illustrate the appearance and personality of a real or fictional character.

PREVIEW
Student Work
IN PROGRESS

Cheryl Boudreau, a student at Boone County High School in Florence, Kentucky, wrote a description entitled "An Autumn Memory." In the following pages, you'll see how Cheryl used the stages of the writing process to plan and write her essay. You can see her final draft at the end of the chapter.

Writers in
ACTION

Rita Dove uses vivid language to add life to her writing. Here's the challenge she sets for herself and others:

"When we can feel the breeze that sweeps through a valley—that's the kind of descriptive writing that comes alive."

Description • 97

PREPARE and ENGAGE

PREPARE and ENGAGE

Interest GRABBER Invite students to write a classified advertisement that would make their classmates interested in an ordinary household item. Students might use vivid words to describe a light bulb, fly swatter, or used baseball glove. After they share examples, have students underline or list the descriptive words they used to make their advertisements effective.

Activate Prior Knowledge

Bring a stack of used newspapers and magazines to school. Invite students to scan these and consider how descriptions make what is advertised more appealing. Then have students compare these with the characteristics of effective description listed in the text.

More About the Writer

Rita Dove (b. 1952), the youngest poet ever to receive the honor, served as United States Poet Laureate from 1993–1995. She once said that her appreciation of poetry and literature came from her parents, who encouraged her to read anything she chose during her childhood. Rita Dove is featured in the Description section of the *Writers at Work* Videotape.

☑ **ONGOING ASSESSMENT: Diagnose**

Use one of the following options to diagnose students' current level of proficiency in descriptive writing.

Option 1 Ask students to provide you with a sample of descriptive writing from their previous year's writing portfolio. Individual conferences with students can help you to pinpoint which of them may need extra help.	**Option 2** Ask students to write a short descriptive poem on a topic you suggest for them. Poems should contain descriptive and/or figurative language and detail. If they do not, students may need more help.

Reading: Make Inferences

Point out to students that writers don't always tell readers everything directly. For example, a writer can suggest a character's mood by describing slouched posture, a frown, a curt manner of speaking. Tell students that in the description they are about to read, the writer never directly states Virginia's feelings. As students read the description of the concert, ask them to identify details that help them infer Virginia's mood.

Step-by-Step Teaching Guide

Engage Students Through Literature

1. Invite students to discuss the excerpt. Here are some questions to stimulate discussion:

   How does the writer immediately bring readers into the conservatory?

   Was Virginia impressed with the singer? How do you know?

2. Invite students to share details that intrigued them.

3. Have students consider some of the details Virginia might notice if she were to visit your classroom. Point out some details to get them started such as:

   the colors and condition of the paint, ceiling, or floors

   any words written on the board

   how the light in the room appears

4. Record students' suggestions on the board.

Critical Viewing

Describe Students may mention adjectives such as *stark, graphic, brief,* or *melodic.*

6.1 Model From Literature

In this excerpt from a novel, Pulitzer Prize-winning writer Rita Dove describes an unforgettable concert. As you read, notice how Dove uses vivid details and figurative language to capture a memorable event.

▲ **Critical Viewing**
What words would you use to describe the musical notation shown here? **[Describe]**

Reading Writing Connection

Reading Strategy: Make Inferences As you read this passage, you will notice that the author never states directly how the character feels about the music. Instead, the descriptive details help readers **make inferences** about the character's feelings. Look for the details in the description that help you determine her feelings about her experience.

from
Through the Ivory Gate
Rita Dove

The interior of the conservatory was a network of light and air, blond wood and white linoleum hallways. At the end of each corridor

The writer organizes the beginning of the description spatially.

98 • Description

✔ ONGOING ASSESSMENT: Monitor and Reinforce

After previewing the Model From Literature, you may anticipate that some students may have difficulty with the selection's vocabulary. Use one of the following options.

Option 1 Ask students to help you compile a class list of unfamiliar terms such as *upholstered, labyrinth, luminosity, microcosm,* or *versatility.* Then have students look the words up in a dictionary and record their definitions in their reader's journals.

Option 2 Have students list any words with which they are unfamiliar and meet in small groups to try to determine their meanings using context clues. Have one student in the group record students' speculative definitions and confirm or refute them with a dictionary.

was a little seating area of upholstered chairs and low tables tucked into the alcove, potted ficus and hanging ferns dripping their spidery green down the windows that peered out into a windblown courtyard, so that the boundaries between outside and inside seemed to evaporate. At every turn in the labyrinth more light poured in golden shafts from the little square windows in studio doors, and interlaced with this luminosity strains of music—a clarinet afloat on the comic-sad suspensions of Mozart, the thunk of a double bass, a sprinkle of piano, even a harpsichord— how intimate a microcosm, how familiar this profusion of sounds! Virginia found herself humming along with scraps of melody until she passed another door and a new motif sprang up to supersede it.

On the bulletin board she read that there was a recital going on that very minute, a mezzo-soprano performing the usual student program designed to show range and versatility: assorted French and Italian arias, a few Schubert Lieder,[1] wrapping up with a spattering of modern selections: Charles Ives, Gershwin, a young American composer Virginia didn't recognize. The concert hall wasn't hard to find; she waited outside until she heard the applause between pieces, then slipped in, taking a seat in the last row.

The amphitheater rose gently away from the stage, where a robust young woman stood resplendent, her caramel-colored skin glowing against the emerald green of her dress.

Virginia caught her breath. The singer held her pose until the rustling in the audience subsided, then, with a barely perceptible nod, signaled the pianist that she was ready for the Schubert, seven chords and a pause, then twelve, each measured cluster of notes a leaf shaken of the last rain before the voice unscrolled like a sheath of dark silk: *Ihr lieben Mauern hold und traut,/Die ihr mich kühl umschließt.*[2]

Writing Application: Help Your Readers Make Inferences As you write your description, leave clues for your readers about your attitude toward your subject. Instead of including stark declarative sentences that announce your attitudes, challenge yourself to make deliberate word choices that develop the main impression you want to convey.

---

1. **Lieder** (le´der): German lyrical songs.
2. Lines from a song by Austrian composer Franz Schubert (1797–1828). They may be translated, "You dear walls, so sweet and true, / You pleasantly enclose me."

Sensory details such as "golden shafts" appeal to sight and help to capture the setting.

Vivid, precise language such as "thunk of a double bass" provides details that help readers imagine the environment.

As the main character walks through the conservatory, the writer adds details to convey the musical atmosphere.

Dove uses adjectives such as "robust" and "resplendent" to add detail to her description.

Figurative language such as "unscrolled like a sheath of dark silk" communicates the smooth and elegant quality of the singer's voice.

For another example of descriptive writing by Rita Dove, see "For the Love of Books" in *Prentice Hall Literature: Timeless Voices, Timeless Themes,* The American Experience.

Teaching From the Model

Ask students to discuss how Dove uses descriptive words in the excerpt from her 1992 novel *Through the Ivory Gate.* Have students identify the various kinds of details Dove provides. Remind them that such details can appeal to the senses, but they can also refer to common experiences with which readers may be familiar. Encourage students to consider referring to details such as music, movies, art, clothes, and other aspects of their own experience in their writing.

Real-World Connection

The ability to describe a problem or situation in detail is crucial to problem-solving. People who master this skill are often best able to resolve problems. Suggest that students name occupations in which people must describe problems in detail (lawyers, business executives, teachers).

Reading\Writing Connection

Writing Application: Help Your Readers Make Inferences

Successfully using inference requires that the writer leave some ideas or impressions unstated but implied for the reader. Encourage students to focus on making their descriptions so vivid that they evoke the emotions they wish the reader to feel, rather than stating them outright.

Prewriting

Prewriting: Blueprint

1. Model the blueprinting process on a transparency or on the board. You might use the school grounds or a well-known common area such as the school library. Make labels descriptive enough so students can see connections among them. You may need to support these connections with questions:

   What associations do students make with the entrance to the school?

   with the auditorium?

   with the playing field?

2. This activity is useful in helping students translate spatial relationships into verbal ones that can help organize their writing.

Prewriting: Personal Experience Timeline

Teaching Resources: Writing Support Transparencies, 6-A; Writing Support Activity Book, 6-1

1. Display the timeline transparency (6-A) and point out that the principle of the timeline will be the same whether the experience students select is an hour long or months in duration.

2. Give students a copy of the blank timeline (6-1). As they begin to list events, have students label the timeline at each end so that they have their beginning and end points firmly in mind at the start.

3. Once the timelines are completed, encourage students to use them as outlines to tell the story of their experience.

4. Suggest that students first tell some or all of their stories out loud as the basis for a written story. This process underscores the idea that telling a story well requires the same elements whether it is written or spoken.

Choosing Your Topic

To choose a subject that you want to describe, begin by looking at your surroundings or looking within yourself. You might describe something in your immediate environment or a person or place from memory. Use one of the following strategies to help you choose a topic:

Strategies for Generating Topics

1. **Blueprint** Draw the floor plan for a place you remember well—such as your home, your school, or a park. Label each part of your blueprint with words that identify each area of the map. Using the labels as column heads, jot down words, phrases, sentences, or names that you associate with each label. Look for connections among your items. Then, choose an idea or a memory that your blueprint inspired.

2. **Magazine Review** Flip through a magazine to find compelling images or articles that inspire ideas for description. As you scan the pages, note ideas that come to mind. Review your list to choose a topic for description.

3. **Personal Experience Timeline** Construct a timeline that highlights important events in your life. Focus your timeline on a specific event; for example, the experience of getting an after-school job or the events leading up to a personal victory. Review your timeline to choose a moment, person, or place as the topic of your description.

Writing Lab CD-ROM

For more help finding a topic, explore the activities and suggestions in the Choosing a Topic section of the Description lesson.

Student Work
IN PROGRESS

Name: Cheryl Boudreau
Boone County High School
Florence, KY

Creating a Personal Experience Timeline

Cheryl analyzed the important events in her high-school career. She decided to focus a descriptive essay on a championship football game.

| My first day of freshman year. | I meet my friend Denise for the first time. | I make the cheerleading team. | I go to my first prom. | I receive my high-school ring. | I cheer for the championship football game. |

⏱ TIME AND RESOURCE MANAGER

Resources
Print: *Writing Support Transparencies*, 6-A–D; *Writing Support Activity Book*, 6-1–2
Technology: *Writing Lab* CD-ROM, Description

In-Depth Coverage	Accelerated Pace
• Cover pp. 100–103 in class. • Demonstrate the timeline strategy. • Have students apply the cubing strategy to gather details.	• Have students work in groups to ask questions that would make the timelines or blueprints more complete. • Have students work independently to choose and focus their topics.

TOPIC BANK

If you are having trouble choosing a topic, consider one of these suggestions:

1. **Description of an Artist at Work** Observe and describe a painter, dancer, singer, or other artist working at his or her craft. Use figurative language and comparisons to create a colorful description.

2. **Time-Lapse Description** Choose one location—such as a supermarket or the main lobby at your school—and visit it at three or four different times of day. Note the mood, people, and activity as you witness the location during each of your visits. Then, write a description showing the changes over time.

Responding to Fine Art

3. *Messenger on 42nd* conveys the fast pace and excitement of a city street. Consider another setting that communicates an emotion. For example, in a description you might show the calm of a beach at sunset or the anxiety of a rush-hour crowd waiting for a train.

Messenger on 42nd, Tom Christopher, Courtesy of The David Findlay Galleries

Responding to Literature

4. Read a descriptive portion of Tom Wolfe's book *The Right Stuff.* Use it as a model to write your own vivid description of a historic or fictional event as a participant would experience it. You can find an excerpt from *The Right Stuff* in *Prentice Hall Literature: Timeless Voices, Timeless Themes,* The American Experience.

☑ Cooperative Writing Opportunity

5. **Descriptive Flyer** With a group, create a flyer to illustrate the features of a city in your state. Divide the writing tasks of describing the geographical layout, the cultural landmarks, and the atmosphere. Include pictures or photographs to accompany the text. Then, share your flyer with classmates.

Prewriting • 101

Prewriting: Narrowing Your Topic

Teaching Resources: Writing Support Transparencies, 6-C

1. To help students narrow their topics, you might give examples such as these.

   Too broad: *My Year in School*

   Narrow enough: *An Average Day*

   Too broad: *Foods I Like*

   Narrow enough: *My Favorite Dinner*

2. Display Transparency 6-C and use it to show how to generate details from a broad topic such as "last winter's blizzard." Ask students what details they find most interesting.

3. Encourage students to recognize how narrowing a topic makes the writer's job easier and the results more interesting to readers.

Prewriting: Audience and Purpose

1. In discussing the "blizzard" example, ask:

   How would a friend react if you sent a postcard containing only scientific data about the blizzard?

   What would a meteorologist want to know from my description?

2. Encourage students to recognize that identifying their audience will help them to plan which details to include and what tone to adopt in their descriptive drafts.

Integrating Vocabulary Skills

Adverbs and Adjectives Review with students the concept that description is conveyed through word choice. Adjectives provide color in descriptions of people, places, and things. Adverbs help describe how an action occurred.

6.2

Narrowing Your Topic

As you plan your description, narrow your topic into one you can cover in the time and space you have. For example, you would not be able to describe the entire state of Washington in a short essay, but you might successfully describe a single natural feature, such as Mount Saint Helens.

Use Categorizing to Narrow a Topic

To narrow your topic, jot down all the ideas that your broad topic suggests to you. Review your list with the goal of making categories to organize your random ideas. Highlight words that seem similar or related. When you reorder your list into the groups you have identified, you can choose one of these focused topics to develop in your descriptive writing. Look at this example:

Broad topic: Last winter's blizzard

3 feet of snow
drifts to 10 feet

kids sled the next day

5 degrees below zero
-25 degrees wind chill

roads closed
people stranded

snowmen appear the next day

temperature
5 degrees below zero
-25 degrees wind chill

snow
3 feet deep
drifts to 10 feet

problems
roads closed
people stranded

fun
kids sled the next day
snowmen appear the next day

Narrowed topic: Kids have fun after a big blizzard.

Considering Your Audience and Purpose

Take a moment to identify the people you hope your writing will reach and the purposes you expect your writing to achieve.

Identify Your Audience Whether they are young children with a limited knowledge or people who share similar experiences with you, knowing your audience will help you choose the level of language and detail to use in your description.

Clarify Your Purpose You may want to describe in order to inspire awe or reflection. In contrast, you may want to describe to amuse or inform. Whatever your purpose, provide details that suit your specific writing goal.

Writing Lab CD-ROM

Use the Considering Audience and Purpose section of the Description lesson to gear your work to a particular group of readers.

Gathering Details

Gathering details before you begin writing will give you the raw materials you need to make your description vivid. Take time to identify details that will help you show your subject.

Use Cubing to Gather Details

Cubing lets you examine a topic from six different angles. Review these instructions for cubing, and then use the strategy to collect information about your topic.

1. **Describe it** by noting its physical characteristics. As you do this, challenge yourself to address all five senses—sight, sound, smell, texture, and taste.
2. **Associate it** by explaining how it reminds you of something else.
3. **Apply it** by considering the ways your topic can be used.
4. **Analyze it** by breaking it into smaller parts.
5. **Compare and contrast it** by showing how your topic is similar to or different from other items.
6. **Argue for or against it** by evaluating your topic's worth.

✔ Collaborative Writing Tip

You may generate more creative ideas when you work with others. If several classmates are writing about the same topic, complete the cubing activity together.

Student Work IN PROGRESS

Name: Cheryl Boudreau
Boone County High School
Florence, KY

Cubing to Gather Details

Cheryl looked at the football game from six different angles. When she was finished, she decided to generate more sensory details to capture the experience.

SUBJECT: Championship Game

Describe:
- a brisk evening
- expectant faces in the crowd

Associate:
- like my family, our school sticks together during the low times, too

Apply:
- generates pride for our team and devoted fans

Analyze:
- even through defeat, school spirit is strengthened

Compare and contrast:
- team losing was like balloons slowly deflating

Argue for or against:
- fan support should be evident in both good and bad times

describe it · *apply it* · *associate it* · *analyze it* · *compare and contrast it* · *argue for or against it*

Prewriting • 103

Drafting: Using the SEE Technique

Teaching Resources: Writing Support Transparencies, 6-E

1. Use the transparency to model how the SEE technique can help to develop descriptive writing. Discuss how particular details might amplify a main idea, using examples from this chapter.

2. Point out that an absence of elaboration can lead to flat, insubstantial writing.

3. Explain that an extension is not just a repetition of the main idea, but a restatement in different, and usually more concise, form.

4. Students can practice the SEE strategy by working with index cards. Deal out these cards to groups or pairs of students. Have students write their main idea statement on the first card, and use subsequent cards to record extension and elaboration ideas.

Customize for
Spatial Learners

Some students may find a visual organizing tool such as an idea web useful for generating and developing a flow of ideas. You might demonstrate this concept by modeling such a map with elements of Dove's *Through the Ivory Gate* for the class. Encourage students to use a cluster map as a brainstorming device before beginning a piece of writing.

Customize for
Interpersonal Learners

Suggest that students work together orally in groups when practicing the SEE technique. Invite one student to state a main idea, a second one to offer a restatement of that idea, and a third to offer an elaboration that illustrates the concept. By sharing and changing roles, students can enlarge their understanding of the process.

6.3 Drafting

Shaping Your Writing

Before you begin drafting, select a method for organizing your description. Consider these two organizational plans:

Plan an Organization

Organizing Details Spatially This organization is useful for physical or functional descriptions. Describe your topic as the eye might see it, moving from top to bottom, left to right, front to back, or outward from the most prominent feature. To make the arrangement of details clear, include directional terms, such as *to the right, on the top,* or *in the center.*

Organizing by Order of Importance This organization is effective in description that conveys an experience, shows a personality, or addresses an idea. Grab your readers' interest with your second most important point. Then, cover your less important points, and build to your strongest one.

Providing Elaboration

To make your description full, include details that build the impression you want to convey.

Use the SEE Technique to Add Details

The step-by-step approach of the SEE method can help you develop your ideas. Here's what the labels mean:

S Statement—Write a sentence to convey a main idea.

E Extension—Restate or develop the main idea.

E Elaboration—Provide further information to amplify or expand on the main idea.

Writing Lab CD-ROM

Use the note-cards activity to rearrange your details until you find an organization that works. You can find this activity in the Toolkit.

Name: Cheryl Boudreau
Boone County High School
Florence, KY

Adding Details With the SEE Technique

Here's how Cheryl used SEE to develop a paragraph.

[Statement] I felt an overwhelming sense of pride as I looked up into the sea of expectant faces. [Extension] I saw cheering teachers, students, parents, and alumni. [Elaboration] Not only had they all come, but they had made banners, painted their faces in our school's colors, and were on their feet.

104 • Description

⏱ TIME AND RESOURCE MANAGER

Resources
Print: *Writing Support Transparencies,* 6-E–G
Technology: *Writers at Work* Videotape, Description; *Writing Lab* CD-ROM, Description

In-Depth Coverage	Accelerated Pace
• Cover pp. 104–108 in class.	• Have students review pp. 104–108 independently, then write their first description draft.
• Guide students through the development of their ideas using the SEE technique.	• Respond to individual drafting and revising issues as needed.
• Have students write their description drafts in class.	

6.4 Revising

Once you've written your first draft, take the time to review your description. First review the structure of the writing, and then move into an analysis of paragraphs, sentences, and word choice.

Revising Your Overall Structure

Focus Your Description

Just as a painting or photograph is enhanced by the right frame, your writing can be enhanced by the right words to begin and end it. Frame your description to help the readers focus on your description.

- Your **introduction** should establish the topic of your writing, give readers the general impression you want to convey, and indicate the purpose of your description.
- **Body paragraphs** describe your topic in depth.
- A **conclusion** should return your discussion back to a general level, adding some insight or leaving readers with a new way to see your topic.

REVISION STRATEGY
Evaluating Your Frame

Review the opening and closing paragraphs of your writing. As you read each section, decide whether it provides context for your readers. Consider the following suggestions for revision:

Lead With a Comparison Revise your introduction by strengthening the opening two sentences. Create a striking comparison or a particularly dramatic image.

EXAMPLE: The Sequoias, as tall as any skyscraper, are majestic examples of nature's architecture.

Conclude With Figurative Language
Strengthen your conclusion by adding a *metaphor* that synthesizes the details you have presented. To write a metaphor, set your topic equal to another whose qualities you want to stress. In the example below, trees are set equal to towering giants.

EXAMPLE: These towering giants continue to impress visitors with the sheer improbability of their size.

▼ Critical Viewing
How does the unusual angle of this photograph change your perspective of the trees it shows? **[Evaluate]**

Revising • 105

Step-by-Step Teaching Guide

Revising: Focus Your Description

1. Point out to students that a strong metaphor, comparison, or image at the beginning of a piece of writing can grab the reader's attention. You may wish to bring examples from a newspaper or magazine.

2. Give students practice in creating striking comparisons by asking them to generate *like* or *as* statements for ideas such as the following:

    The weather was as gloomy as . . .

    The cafeteria food was like . . .

    On the first day of school, students were as nervous as . . .

3. Ask students to review their introductions. Do their first and second paragraphs frame their descriptions with powerful images?

4. Have them consider their concluding paragraphs. Have they summed up their descriptions with a vivid and fitting metaphor or a statement that reflects the spirit of the piece as a whole?

Critical Viewing

Evaluate Students may say that the foreshortened perspective makes viewers feel even smaller in relation to the trees than they would if they were standing beneath them.

✓ ONGOING ASSESSMENT: Monitor and Reinforce

If you observe that students are having difficulty organizing their descriptions, try one of the following options.

Option 1 Suggest that students construct a graphic organizer to help them collect and organize descriptive details spatially. They might also make a simple sketch before they begin to write.

Option 2 Help students organize details in order of their importance by asking them to assign the number 5 to the most crucial details and the number 1 to the least important. This should make it easy for them to assign the numbers 2, 3, and 4 to remaining details. Students should then be able to easily rank details in order of importance.

Step-by-Step Teaching Guide

Revising: Checking Paragraph Unity

Teaching Resources: Writing Support Transparencies, 6-F

1. Display Transparency 6-F and tell students that by highlighting the topic sentences, Cheryl can more easily see the structure of her draft.

2. Remind students that a paragraph's central idea is usually expressed in a single well-focused topic sentence.

3. Suggest that students practice restating central ideas briefly and in their own words.

4. Ask students to read their topic sentences again. Is each supporting detail clearly related to the topic sentence?

Customize for
Less Advanced Students

Provide students with visual metaphors to illustrate the concept of the central idea and supporting details. Images such as a hand and its fingers or a table and its legs can convey the concept.

Revising Your Paragraphs

Focus on Unity in Paragraphs

Body paragraphs focus on a central idea that is usually expressed in a topic sentence. In a unified paragraph, every other sentence supports, illustrates, or develops this idea. Review your body paragraphs to evaluate paragraph unity.

▶ REVISION STRATEGY
Color-Coding to Evaluate Paragraph Unity

Highlight the topic sentence of each topical or body paragraph in your draft. Use another color to underline the supporting details. Then, use these tips to evaluate and revise your writing:

Evaluate

- Does each paragraph have a topic sentence?

- Does each paragraph have enough specific details?

- Is each detail clearly related to the topic sentence?

Revise

- In some cases, your topic may be implied. Consider adding a topic sentence to focus your writing.

- Consider adding elaboration to develop your point.

- Eliminate details that are not related to the topic.

Language Lab CD-ROM

To learn more about revising body paragraphs, use the Unity and Coherence in Paragraphs and Composition lessons in the Composing unit.

Student Work IN PROGRESS

Name: *Cheryl Boudreau*
Boone County High School
Florence, KY

Checking Paragraph Unity

When Cheryl evaluated this body paragraph, she decided to add more elaboration to support the main idea.

First, we were up by a touchdown, but two minutes later, the other team had rallied to tie the score.

The game proved to be a close one. ^

[Topic sentence needs more support.]

Back and forth it went. This exhausting process continued throughout the entire game, but not once did the crowd so much as sit down. They could not stop supporting the team with their enthusiastic spirit.

106 • Description

✎ STANDARDIZED TEST PREPARATION WORKSHOP

Adverbs and Adjectives Standardized tests may require students to distinguish between adverbs and adjectives. Provide students with opportunities to practice distinguishing between adverbs and adjectives in their reading and writing.

Circle the adjectives and underline the adverb in the sentence.

The anxious student nervously tapped his foot on the shiny floor.

Students should recognize that *anxious* and *shiny* are adjectives that describe the *student* and the *floor* respectively. Students should also recognize that *nervously* is an adverb that describes the action *tapped*.

Revising Your Sentences

Eliminate Dull Sentence Patterns

To improve the rhythm of your writing, review the sentences in your first draft, focusing on sentence length. Challenge yourself to make your final draft more sophisticated by including a variety of sentence lengths.

▶ **REVISION STRATEGY**
Combining Short Sentences

As you evaluate sentence lengths in your draft, identify places where you have created a series of short sentences. If you find that you have two or three short sentences in sequence, consider combining some to create longer sentences. When you rewrite two short sentences into one, you can stress the ways the information or ideas are related.

Grammar in Your Writing
Combining Sentences

Short sentences can be combined in a variety of ways.

- Join two independent clauses with a comma and a coordinating conjunction such as *and, but, or, nor,* or *for* to create a compound sentence:

| Simple Sentences: | The canyon colors were beautiful. I was most impressed by the rock formations. |
| Compound Sentence: | The canyon colors were beautiful, **and** I was most impressed by the rock formations. |

- When ideas are very closely related, join two independent clauses with a semicolon to create a compound sentence:

| Simple Sentences: | The sunset was gorgeous. We stood in awe. |
| Compound Sentence: | The sunset was gorgeous; we stood in awe. |

- Create a complex sentence by changing one of the sentences into a subordinate clause:

| Simple Sentences: | We spent all day there. There was so much to see. |
| Complex Sentence: | We spent all day there **because there was so much to see.** |

Find It in Your Reading Review the excerpt from *Through the Ivory Gate* on pages 98–99. Identify examples of compound and complex sentences that Dove uses to combine related ideas.

Find It in Your Writing Identify places in your draft where you have used compound or complex sentences to combine related ideas. Challenge yourself to improve your writing by combining sentences where appropriate.

For more on sentence combining, see Chapter 20.

Step-by-Step Teaching Guide

Combining Sentences

1. Give students a series of short, choppy sentences that you have composed or found in the work of another writer. Have them choose two sentences to combine.

2. Ask students to combine the sentences they chose to make a compound and a complex sentence.

3. Invite students to share the examples they made and extend this activity to combining sentences from their own writing.

Find It in Your Reading

Students will find several examples of compound and complex sentences in the passage on pages 98–99. Choose one intricate sentence (the second or third, for example) to analyze with students.

Find It in Your Writing

Have students review their portfolios to find short sentences used to describe an object. Challenge students to combine this information into one or two sentences without omitting any details. Have volunteers share their revisions in class.

Customize for
ESL Students

Students less fluent in English may benefit from a review of the standard subordinate conjunctions *because, until,* and *although.* You may also wish to review the usage of *and, but, or, for,* and *nor.*

✓ **ONGOING ASSESSMENT: Prerequisite Skills**

If students have difficulty identifying where short, choppy sentences may be combined, you may wish to refer them to the following materials to ensure coverage of prerequisite knowledge.

In the Textbook	Print Resources	Technology
Sentence Combining, pp. 481–485	*Grammar Exercise Workbook,* pp. 63–64	*On-Line Exercise Bank,* Section 20.2

Revising: Circling Vague Words

Teaching Resources: Writing Support Transparencies, 6-G

1. Display the transparency (6-G) and mention some of the specific word changes Cheryl made. Then have students circle vague or abstract words and replace them with more specific language that sharpens the impact of their writing.

2. Have volunteers read several "before" and "after" versions from their essays and ask students to describe how the effect of the writing changed when vague words were replaced.

Revising: Analytical Talk

1. Let students know that all good writers engage in evaluation and revision of their own work. You may wish to bring in essays by or interviews with famous writers in which they discuss the revision process.

2. Divide students into small response groups and have them work together to identify the main idea and the strongest images in each piece.

3. After students have provided each other with feedback, give them time to work on revising their work. Some students may find it easier and more productive to revise another writer's work than their own.

4. Make sure to provide time for writers to share their revised pieces and talk about how the revision process affected their work.

6.4

Revising Your Word Choice

Vague and empty words can make your description longer, but they do not make it more vivid. To make your description powerful and evocative, make every word count.

▶ **REVISION STRATEGY**
Circling Vague Words

Review your draft to circle any vague or empty words in your description that do not add meaning. Then, decide whether to replace or eliminate each one you find.

Student Work
IN PROGRESS

Name: _Cheryl Boudreau_
Boone County High School
Florence, KY

Replacing Vague Words

In this passage, Cheryl replaced several vague words with specific, concrete words.

As I absorbed the ~~many~~ emotions surrounding me, I felt a
wave of pride ~~come~~ _wash_ over me; we had done our best and had
~~really~~ _valiantly_ fought until the end, never once doubting or giving up.
Our fan support had been ~~great~~ _phenomenal_ and although we had lost,
everyone ~~came~~ _filed_ out of the bleachers with their heads held high
and a ~~good~~ _warm_ feeling in their hearts.

Peer Review
Analytic Talk

Read your description to a small group. Focus a discussion around these revision suggestions:

• Ask your reviewers to identify the main impression that your description conveys. If their response does not match your original plan, you may want to extend the conversation. Ask your reviewers to tell you which images and details contributed to the central impression they identified.

• As you read your essay a second time, ask your reviewers to jot down the words that seemed most powerful to them. Your classmates might also note areas of description that could be sharpened. In a discussion, note their ideas and consider making revisions to your draft.

6.5 Editing and Proofreading

When you have revised the content of your description, you are ready to edit it, proofread it, and create a final draft. Review your paper for errors in grammar, usage, mechanics, and spelling. Strive to make your description error-free.

Focusing on Complete Sentences

When you are writing to convey an impression, it may be easy to fall into the trap of adding a detail that is not expressed as a complete thought. Review your paper to check that every group of words that is punctuated as a sentence can stand alone. Use this tip to guide your analysis:

Read each sentence aloud. Listen as you read to be sure that each sentence conveys a complete idea. To focus on this task, pause between sentences to avoid being distracted by the content.

Grammar in Your Writing
Avoiding Fragments

While all clauses contain both a subject and a verb, subordinate clauses do not express a complete thought and therefore cannot be punctuated as sentences. There are two ways to correct fragments that begin with a subordinating conjunction.

1. **Eliminate the subordinating conjunction:**

Fragment: As the final seconds of the game approached.

Sentence: The final seconds of the game approached.

2. **Connect the subordinate clause to a main clause:**

Fragment: As the final seconds of the game approached.

Sentence: As the final seconds of the game approached, our team needed one touchdown to clinch the victory.

Find It in Your Writing Look through your draft to catch fragments that have crept into your writing. Correct any fragments that you find.

For additional instruction on sentence fragments, see Chapter 20.

Editing and Proofreading • 109

Step-by-Step Teaching Guide

Editing and Proofreading

1. Remind students that even a round of revision that improves a piece of writing's content and clarity overall may introduce grammatical errors. Encourage students to be tolerant of their own errors during the extension and elaboration phases.

2. Assure students that writing is a process and that the final stage of the process involves checking their work for correct form.

3. When pieces are nearing completion, encourage students to check for grammatical and mechanical errors.

Step-by-Step Teaching Guide

Avoid Fragments

1. Remind students that in descriptive writing, sentence fragments can easily crop up when phrases that lack a subject or verb are added during elaboration.

2. Write the following sentence on the board:

   The parking lot was empty of cars. Quiet at the end of a long night.

3. Point out that the second sentence is a fragment because it lacks a verb.

4. Ask students to offer a revision that would turn the fragment into a complete sentence. (*It was quiet at the end of a long night. The parking lot was empty of cars, and quiet at the end of a long night.*)

Find It in Your Writing

Ask students to correct each fragment they find in their writing by combining it with the previous or subsequent sentence.

⏱ TIME AND RESOURCE MANAGER

Resources
Print: *Scoring Rubrics on Transparency*, Ch. 6; *Writing Assessment and Portfolio Management; Formal Assessment*, Ch. 6
Technology: *Writing Lab* CD-ROM, Description

In-Depth Coverage	Accelerated Pace
• Cover pp. 109–110 in class. • Have students edit and proofread their descriptions in class. • Students present their final drafts.	• Assign pages 109–110 for independent student review. • Students edit and proofread their descriptions as homework. • Students prepare and present their final drafts.

Publishing and Presenting

1. Encourage students to seek varied audiences for dramatic readings and presentations. Senior centers, hospitals, and elementary and middle school classrooms would welcome visits from young actors and performers.

2. You may want to encourage all students to take on important roles in creating the class magazine.

ASSESS and CLOSE

Assessment

Teaching Resources: Scoring Rubrics on Transparency, Ch. 6; Writing Assessment and Portfolio Management; Formal Assessment, Ch. 6

1. Display the scoring rubric transparency and review the criteria in class.

2. Before students proceed with self-assessment, you may wish to review the Final Draft of the Student Work in Progress on pages 111–112. Have students score the Final Draft in one or more of the rubric categories. For example, how would students score Cheryl's description in terms of its details?

3. In addition to student self-assessment, you may wish to use the following assessment options.

   • score students' descriptions yourself, using the rubric and scoring models from *Writing Assessment and Portfolio Management.*

   • review the Standardized Test Preparation Workshop on pages 116–117 and have students respond within a set time to writing prompts that test for their knowledge of revision strategies, organization, and style.

   • administer the Chapter 6 assessment from *Formal Assessment* in your Teaching Resources to measure students' grasp of the concepts presented.

6.6 Publishing and Presenting

When you finish writing your description, consider these ideas for sharing it with others:

Building Your Portfolio

Present a Dramatic Reading Working with a group of classmates who have written descriptions on a common theme, prepare a presentation. Select music, develop a sequence of readings, and present an introduction that connects the works. Then, share your work with an audience.

Publish a Literary Magazine Collect the finished descriptions, and publish them in a classroom magazine. As a group, split the tasks of designing the magazine's format, creating a cover and illustrations, and typing and proofreading the descriptions. Print copies of the magazine for your classroom library.

Reflecting on Your Writing

Consider the experience of writing your descriptive essay.

• How did your understanding of your subject change as a result of writing about it?

• What did you discover about the power of specific words that you can apply to your next writing assignment?

Internet Tip

To see model essays scored with this rubric, go to **www.phschool.com**

Rubric for Self-Assessment

Use the following criteria to evaluate your description.

	Score 4	Score 3	Score 2	Score 1
Audience and Purpose	Contains details that work together to create a single, dominant impression of the topic	Contains details that create a main impression of the topic	Contains extraneous details that detract from the main impression	Contains details that are unfocused and create no dominant impression
Organization	Consistently presents a logical and effective organization	Presents most details in a suitable organization	Presents some details in an illogical organization	Presents a confusing organization
Elaboration	Contains creative use of figurative language, creating interesting comparisons	Contains figurative language that creates comparisons	Contains figurative language, but the comparisons are not fresh	Contains no figurative language
Use of Language	Contains sensory language that appeals to the five senses; contains no errors in grammar, punctuation, or spelling	Contains some sensory language; contains few errors in grammar, punctuation, and spelling	Contains some sensory language, but it appeals to only one or two of the senses; contains some errors in grammar, punctuation, and spelling	Contains no sensory language; contains many errors in grammar, punctuation, and spelling

110 • Description

☑ ONGOING ASSESSMENT: Assess Mastery

Use one of the following options to assess final drafts of students' descriptive writing

Self-Assessment Ask students to score their writing using the rubric provided. Then have students make an entry in their writer's notebooks describing which strategies and techniques worked best for them in composing their descriptive writing assignment.	**Teacher Assessment** Use the rubric and the scoring models provided in *Writing Assessment and Portfolio Management* to score students' work.

6.7 Student Work IN PROGRESS

FINAL DRAFT

An Autumn Memory

Cheryl Boudreau
Boone County High School
Florence, Kentucky

Family, friends, teachers, AP courses, sporting events, cheer-leading, final exams, dances: As I sit here and reflect on my past experiences, these are the things that immediately come to mind. However, when I'm asked to describe my most memorable high-school experience, I am, needless to say, baffled. Racking my brain to think of something significant, I suddenly notice an old football program lying on my bedroom floor. I pick it up and begin to browse through it. Almost immediately, I think of that brisk, bittersweet evening of the championship football game.

I remember the smell of hot dogs, the anxious crowds milling about, and the teams—tense and ready to pounce—warming up

◄ **Critical Viewing**
What high-school tradition does this illustration suggest? **[Relate]**

Cheryl captures the audience's attention by creating a nostalgic mood. After listing several ideas, she narrows her writing to focus on a specific high-school moment.

Sensory descriptions make the memory come to life. Cheryl includes details that tap the senses of smell, sight, sound, and touch.

Student Work in Progress • 111

Teaching From the Final Draft

Point out to students that the organization of Cheryl's descriptive writing is similar to that of narrative writing. She uses chronological order to describe the course of the fall day that is her topic, and concludes her description at the end of the football game. Suggest to students that they might revise their essays so that details are presented in chronological order.

Integrating Speaking and Listening Skills

Using a tape recorder can help some students capture ideas they expressed to a study partner or group that might not otherwise have reached the written stage. Students' writing often improves dramatically when they see connections between spoken and written speech.

Critical Viewing

Connect Students should mention that the band music that was "belted out" echoed the "wave of pride" that characterized the final mood of the essay.

on the freshly painted football field. As my cheerleading squad and I began to stretch, the pep band started to play one of its familiar, energizing songs. Motivated by the excitement and tension in the air, the crowd grew restless, ready for the game to begin.

I can recall standing down on the track with the rest of my squad as kickoff drew near and feeling the overwhelming sense of pride and ecstasy as I looked up into the sea of expectant faces. Teachers, students, parents, alumni: Not only had they all come, but they had made enormous banners, painted their faces in our school's colors, and were on their feet, proudly singing the school's fight song and yelling the familiar chants and cheers that my squad and I had started. I felt an overwhelming surge of pride and school spirit as I scanned the packed bleachers and realized the tremendous support behind our team.

The game proved to be a close one. First, we were up by a touchdown, but two minutes later, the other team had rallied to tie the score. Back and forth it went. This exhausting process continued throughout the entire game, but not once did the crowd so much as sit down. They could not stop supporting the team with their enthusiastic spirit.

As the final seconds of the game approached, our team needed one touchdown to clinch the victory. One yard that seemed to stretch for miles was all that separated triumph from defeat. One, two, three attempts: Our team's wholehearted efforts were blocked. On the fourth and final down, everything seemed to move in slow motion as we were once again denied. The crowd that had been collectively holding their breath simultaneously exhaled as if they were balloons slowly deflating.

However, as the band belted out the fight song for the final time, hundreds of loyal fans rose, sang, and applauded as our defeated team marched off the field with dignity, knowing that they had given it their all. As I absorbed the many emotions surrounding me, I felt a wave of pride wash over me; we had done our best and had valiantly fought until the end, never once doubting or giving up. Our fan support had been phenomenal, and although we had lost, everyone filed out of the bleachers with their heads held high and a warm feeling in their hearts.

▶ **Critical Viewing** How did band music contribute to the mood Cheryl's essay described? **[Connect]**

112 • Description

Details about the crowd, the team, and the atmosphere help to create an overall impression of pride and excitement.

Cheryl elaborates on her ideas by providing details of the game.

Cheryl's description allows the reader to feel the sense of unity that flowed from the crowd that day.

Cheryl concludes with an insight that pulls together all the details she has included about the game.

Connected Assignment Poem

If you saw a descriptive essay rewritten as a poem, you would notice some similarities and differences between the two pieces. Both descriptive prose and poetry focus on creating mental images for readers. **Poems,** however, express ideas in special formats, focus on how words sound, and may strive more intensely to create a particular mood.

These tips can help you write your own poem:

Prewriting To choose a topic for your poem, consider a natural object, an event, or an abstract idea. Make a few poetic choices: Consider whether you will use rhyme, rhythm, or a set line length. Then, gather words to create images for your writing. As you do this, plan the mood you want to convey.

In this model, the poet uses descriptive language to create an image for her readers.

▲ **Critical Viewing**
Why do you think nature is a common topic for poetry and fine art? [Hypothesize]

MODEL

from **Suppose**
Siv Cedering

It could be
that the place my words are looking for
will turn out to be so small
that there will be room for nothing
but silence
—or an ocean so large
some waves will never reach
the sound of the shore

Drafting With poetry that has a set rhyme, rhythm, or line length, work from form to content. With free verse, you can work from content to form. Either way, keep the mood in mind as you draft and choose words that help you achieve it.

Revising and Editing Read your poem aloud, listening for the flow and sound of the words. Revise your word choice by replacing words that don't support the poem's mood.

Publishing and Presenting Share your poetry with classmates in an organized "poetry reading" day.

✿ **Grammar and Style Tip**

Create alliteration by starting successive words with the same consonant sound. You may also take advantage of onomatopoeia by using words like *crackle* and *buzz* that suggest the sound they name.

Connected Assignment: Poem • 113

113

Spotlight on the Humanities

Analyzing How Meaning Is Communicated in the Arts

Focus on Photography: Edward Steichen

The ability to capture descriptive detail though the eye of a lens is what separates great photographers from amateur ones. Born in Luxembourg, American photographer Edward Steichen (1879–1973) established himself as one of the most important figures in photography in the twentieth century. In 1900, Steichen was in Paris and discovered the work of French sculptor Rodin. Since Steichen had assisted fellow photographer Alfred Stieglitz in opening Gallery 291 in New York City, Steichen referred Rodin's work to the gallery along with the work of painters Matisse, Picasso, and Cezanne. Throughout his career, Steichen photographed famous people, including Carl Sandburg, Greta Garbo, Gloria Swanson, and Charlie Chaplin.

Art Connection Steichen used the work of French sculptor Auguste Rodin (1840–1917) as the subject of many of his photographs. Rodin's sculpture was noted for its wide variety of sizes and finishes. For example, when Rodin worked in bronze, many of his sculptures had the roughness of clay. In contrast, Rodin's marble sculptures often had a smooth finish. A large collection of Rodin's work is on display at the Musée Rodin in Paris.

Film Connection Steichen also photographed Greta Garbo, one of the most fascinating and visually stunning film actresses of the twentieth century. Born in Stockholm, Sweden, Greta Louisa Gustafsson later took the stage name of Greta Garbo. She studied at the Royal Dramatic Theatre in Stockholm before winning a contract for movies with Metro-Goldwyn-Mayer in Hollywood. Steichen photographed Garbo in 1928, after she had completed several silent films.

Descriptive Writing Activity: Descriptive Poem

Write a descriptive poem to accompany Steichen's photograph of Greta Garbo that appears on this page. Include details about the feeling or mood the picture conveys.

▲ **Critical Viewing**
What is the central impression that this photograph of Greta Garbo conveys? **[Distinguish]**

Media and Technology Skills

Examining Media's Power to Construct a Perception of Reality

Activity: Evaluate Images in Magazines

While the words in published descriptive writing are chosen to offer specific information, images that accompany such writing in magazines and newspapers are equally important in conveying a specific idea.

Think About It The pictures that accompany a magazine article are supporting details of the article's topic and must communicate without words. Knowing how to evaluate the images that appear with articles will make you a more critical consumer of magazines. Consider these powerful effects of photographs:

- A photograph of a candidate smiling may convey a different impression from one of the same person scowling or arguing. Generally, a photo editor makes a deliberate choice to include one over the other.
- Models in photographs are often chosen for their attractive looks. While many models are known for beauty, a category of professionals is chosen because they look like "average" people.

Scan It Before you read an article, the first thing you may notice is the picture that appears on the opening page. This image sets the tone for the entire article. Examine the photograph, noting setting, background, facial expressions, and any subtle attitude the image presents. Be aware of the assumptions you make, and note how these assumptions influence your attitude toward the topic. Preview the other images, and draw conclusions about the article.

Evaluate It Using a chart like the one shown here, evaluate the picture choice and layout of a magazine article. List each image, write a summary, and note your initial reactions. Use your notes to make a prediction about the article. After you have read the article, add additional information about what the image may have been chosen to illustrate or convey. Then, write an analysis of the picture choice and arrangement and whether you find it effective.

Techniques for Evaluating Picture Choice

- Preview all images, and read subtitles before reading the article. Determine what information the images silently convey.
- Pay special attention to the first image accompanying the article. What does it tell you about the article? Does it convey any biases of the author or editor?
- After reading the article, evaluate the arrangement of images within the text. Does each image illustrate a point in the text? Does it influence your opinion?

Article Title:
Image 1:
Summary:
Image 2:
Summary:
Image 3
Summary:

▶ Lesson Objectives

1. To examine the effect of media on constructing the student's own perception of reality
2. To evaluate and critique the persuasive techniques of media messages
3. To compare, contrast, and critique media coverage in newspapers and magazines

Step-by-Step Teaching Guide

Examining Media's Power to Construct a Perception of Reality

Teaching Resources: Writing Support Transparencies, 6-H; Writing Support Activity Book, 6-3

1. Review the techniques used by the media in choosing photographs to accompany an article.
2. Ask students to volunteer other striking uses of photography to sway viewers' perception of an event. In which publications did these images appear?
3. Use the transparency to model evaluating an article for students.
4. Give students a copy of the blank organizer (6-3) to use as they evaluate the pictures chosen and the layout of an article.

Lesson Objectives

1. To demonstrate control over grammatical elements
2. To establish purposes for reading such as to find out, to understand, to interpret, and to solve problems
3. To analyze text structures such as compare/contrast, cause/effect, and chronological order for how they influence understanding

Step-by-Step Teaching Guide

Strategy, Organization, and Style Questions

Teaching Resources: Standardized Test Preparation Workbook, pp. 11–12

1. Instruct students to read each test passage carefully. Suggest that students consider taking notes on features of the text.

2. Let students know that the key to answering organization clues is to read carefully for sequence words that indicate the order in which pieces of texts should appear. Encourage students to underline words such as *first, next, then, before, beyond,* and *further.*

3. Point out that answering style questions correctly often requires readers to determine the author's purpose for writing.

4. Assign students to complete the practice on page 117. After they do so, review the correct answers with students.

Standardized Test Preparation Workshop

Analyzing Strategy, Organization, and Style

Using a multiple-choice format, standardized tests often measure your knowledge of writing skills. These types of test items include a passage in which parts of sentences are marked for your analysis. Questions may ask about the writer's strategy, organization, sequence of sentences, diction, or overall style of the passage. The following are three types of questions that you may encounter:

- **Strategy questions** ask whether a given revision is appropriate in the context of the passage.
- **Organization questions** ask you to choose the most logical sequence of ideas or to decide whether a sentence should be added, deleted, or moved.
- **Style questions** focus on your ability to identify the writer's point of view or evaluate the use of language for an intended audience.

The sample test items that follow will give you practice in answering these types of questions.

Sample Test Item	Answer and Explanation

Read the passage, and then answer the questions that follow.
 	
¹ Watch <u>this</u> and check out the special effects of years ago. ² A man looks out his airplane <u>window</u>. ³ He sees a hideous <u>monster</u> on the wing. ⁴ It is a man dressed in a costume of rags being blown by a wind machine!
 	
1 In which part should the underlined word be replaced by a more precise word?
  A. Part 1
  B. Part 2
  C. Part 3
  D. Correct as is.
	The correct answer is A. The pronoun *this* does not refer to anything specific and would be best replaced by a more precise word or phrase.

116 • Description

▶ **Practice 1** **Directions:** Read the passage, and then answer the questions that follow. Choose the letter of the best answer.

[1]Special effects are the creation of the impossible for film viewers. [2]Physical special effects are those in which the action happens in front of the camera, such as creating storms or other weather conditions, explosions, fires. and car crashes. [3]Special props or models are used for the safety of the actors. [4]For instance, a huge boulder might be made of foam.

[5]Beyond movies, optical effects such as the combination of two images are also used in commericals and in television. [6]For example, meteorologists stand in front of weather maps. [7]To film this, the reporter stands before a blue screen and sees the composite image on a monitor. [8]Seeing the image that actually gets broadcast allows the reporter to point accurately at spots on the map.

[9]Physical effects are quite different from optical effects. [10]Optical effects range from simple combinations of film to complicated computer-generated effects. [11]These effects are often the subject of movie reviews. [12]To create optical effects, several things that have been filmed separately are put together in one shot. [13]Rear-screen projection is one of the most basic ways to combine film. [14]An already filmed scene is projected onto a screen as background while actors perform in front of it.

1 Which of the following is the best order of the paragraphs?
A. 1, 2, 3
B. 3, 2, 1
C. 1, 3, 2
D. 2, 1, 3

2 Which of the following changes would be best to make the sequence of ideas in the third paragraph clearer?
A. Delete the sentence about movie reviews.
B. Add the transition "in contrast" to the beginning of Part 10.
C. Add an example of a physical effect.
D. Reverse the order of the first two sentences.

3 If the author wanted to include more information about special effects in movies, which of the following would be an appropriate addition?
A. Stunt actors work according to a set of safety guidelines.
B. Some actors do their own stunts.
C. Special effects make actions look real.
D. Special effects are expensive and cause the price of films to skyrocket.

4 If the writer wanted to add more information about physical effects to the first paragraph, which of the following statements would be suitable?
A. One type of physical prop is a breakaway—props that break easily, such as chairs, tables, bottles.
B. Fires can be difficult to produce.
C. Manipulating old film footage is an optical effect.
D. Physical effects are filmed in front of the camera.

5 Which best identifies the author's purpose?
A. To evaluate
B. To entertain
C. To criticize
D. To inform

6 Which of the following draws attention away from the main focus?
A. Part 7
B. Part 4
C. Part 10
D. Part 1

Time and Resource Manager

In-Depth Lesson Plan

	LESSON FOCUS	PRINT AND MEDIA RESOURCES
DAY 1	**Introduction to Persuasive Essays** Students learn key elements of persuasive writing and analyze the Model From Literature. (pp. 118–123)	*Writers at Work* **Videotape**, Persuasion *Writing Lab* **CD-ROM**, Persuasion
DAY 2	**Prewriting** Students choose and narrow a topic, consider their audience and purpose, and gather information. (pp. 124–128)	**Teaching Resources:** *Writing Support Transparencies, 7-A–E; Writing Support Activity Book, 7-1–3; Topic Bank for Heterogeneous Classes,* Ch. 7
DAY 3	**Drafting** Students organize their ideas and write their first drafts. (pp. 129–130)	**Teaching Resources:** *Writing Support Transparencies, 7-F–G;* Writing Support Activity Book, 7-4–5
DAY 4	**Revising** Students revise their drafts in terms of overall structure, paragraphs, sentences, and word choice. (pp. 131–135)	**Teaching Resources:** *Writing Support Transparencies, 7-H–J;* Writing Support Activity Book, 7-6
DAY 5	**Editing and Proofreading; Publishing and Presenting** Students check their work for accuracy and correctness and present their final drafts. (pp. 136–137)	**Teaching Resources:** *Scoring Rubrics on Transparency,* Ch. 7; *Writing Assessment and Portfolio Management; Formal Assessment,* Ch. 7

Accelerated Lesson Plan

	LESSON FOCUS	PRINT AND MEDIA RESOURCES
DAY 1	**Drafting** Students review characteristics of persuasive writing, select topics, and write drafts. (pp. 118–130)	*Writing Lab* **CD-ROM**, Persuasion **Teaching Resources:** *Writing Support Transparencies, 7-A–F; Writing Support Activity Book, 7-1–4*
DAY 2	**Revising to Presenting** Students work individually or with peers to revise, edit, and proofread their work for presentation. (pp. 131–137)	**Teaching Resources:** *Writing Support Transparencies, 7-G–I; Scoring Rubrics on Transparency,* Ch. 7; *Writing Assessment and Portfolio Management; Formal Assessment,* Ch. 7

Options for Adapting Lesson Plans

HOMEWORK
Have students complete any stage of the lesson for homework.

FEATURES
Extend coverage with Connected Assignment (p. 140), Spotlight on the Humanities (p. 142), Media and Technology Skills (p. 143), and the Standardized Test Preparation Workshop (p. 144).

TECHNOLOGY
Students can complete any stage of the lesson on computer. Have them print out their completed work.

INTEGRATED SKILLS COVERAGE

Integrating Grammar
Adverb Clauses, SE p. 133
Serial Commas, SE p. 136

Reading/Writing Connection
Distinguish Fact from Opinion, SE p. 120
Writing Application, SE p. 123

Viewing and Representing
Critical Viewing, SE pp. 118, 120, 123, 132, 135, 138, 140, 142
Analyzing Cultures Represented in the Arts, SE p. 142
Analyzing Persuasive Messages, SE p. 143

Speaking and Listening
ATE pp. 121, 139

Real-World Connection
ATE p. 121

Workplace Skills
ATE pp. 122, 128

ASSESSMENT SUPPORT

Standardized Test Preparation Workshop SE p. 144; ATE p. 133

Standardized Test Preparation Workbook, pp. 13–14

Scoring Rubrics on Transparency, Ch. 7

Formal Assessment, Ch. 7

Writing Assessment and Portfolio Management

MEETING INDIVIDUAL NEEDS

Less Advanced Students ATE pp. 122, 126, 141, 145. See also Ongoing Assessments ATE pp. 121, 125, 127, 130.

AP Students ATE pp. 130, 141, 145

ESL Students ATE pp. 127, 134

Visual/Spatial Learners ATE p. 124

BLOCK SCHEDULING

Pacing Suggestions
For 90-minute Blocks
- Have students complete the Prewriting and Drafting stages in a single period.
- Focus one class period on Revising and Editing and Publishing and Presenting. Allow at least 30 minutes for peer revision.

Resources for Varying Instruction
- *Writing Lab* **CD-ROM** If your students have access to hardware, a 90-minute block provides an ideal opportunity for students to work on computer.
- *Writers at Work* **Videotape** Show the Persuasion segment in class.

Professional Development Support
- *How to Manage Instruction in the Block* This Teaching Resource provides management and activity suggestions.

MEDIA AND TECHNOLOGY

For the Student
- *Writing Lab* **CD-ROM,** Persuasion
- *On-Line Exercise Bank,* Section 19.3

For the Teacher
- *Writers at Work* **Videotape,** Persuasion
- *Resource Pro* **CD-ROM**

WRITING AND GRAMMAR WEB SITE

The Interactive Writing and Grammar Web Site provides a wide array of support for students, teachers, and parents. Writing support includes:

- Interactive revision checkers
- Scoring rubrics with complete models

www.phschool.com

LITERATURE CONNECTIONS

Related selections from *Prentice Hall Literature: Timeless Voices, Timeless Themes,* The American Experience:

from "The Declaration of Independence," Thomas Jefferson, SE p. 123
"The Life You Save May Be Your Own," Flannery O'Connor, SE p. 125

Lesson Objectives

1. To write a persuasive essay appropriate to audience and purpose

2. To read to appreciate the writer's craft and to discover models for writing

3. To use prewriting strategies to generate ideas and plan

4. To research self-selected topics using texts and technical resources

5. To represent information in a variety of ways, including graphics

6. To develop and revise drafts in terms of structure, paragraphs, sentences, and word choice

7. To edit and proofread to ensure standard English usage and grammar

8. To evaluate writing for both mechanics and content

9. To refine selected work for publication

Critical Viewing

Compare and Contrast Students may find the image of political debates in Lincoln's day similar to those in the present. Two candidates take turns speaking to an audience. Some students may point out that the presence of the news media is not as apparent as it would be today.

Chapter 7 Persuasion
Persuasive Essay

Abraham Lincoln-Stephen Douglas Debate at Charleston, Illinois - September 18, 1858, Robert Marshall Root, Courtesy of the Illinois State Historical Library

Persuasion in Everyday Life

To present your best ideas and defend your unique opinions, you probably use persuasive skills every day. **Persuasion** is writing or speaking that tries to convince others to agree with you or to take an action that they might not take on their own. You use persuasive skills when you convince your friends to read a book you enjoyed, when you argue about whether your school should adopt a controversial new rule, or when you debate an issue in the news. When used effectively, persuasion can be powerful. It can influence election results, gain or lose a job opportunity, even decide whether a great idea is accepted at all.

▲ **Critical Viewing**
This painting depicts a famous debate between Abraham Lincoln and Stephen Douglas. What similarities and differences can you identify between the debate pictured in the painting and today's political debates? **[Compare and Contrast]**

118 • Persuasion

⏱ TIME AND RESOURCE MANAGER

Resources
Technology: *Writers at Work* Videotape, Persuasion; *Writing Lab* CD-ROM, Persuasion

In-Depth Coverage	Accelerated Pace
• Cover pp. 118–119 in class. • Show Persuasion section of the *Writers at Work* Videotape. • Read the Model From Literature (pp. 120–123) in class, and use it to brainstorm for persuasive essay ideas with students. • Discuss examples of persuasive writing that you or your students bring to class.	• Discuss the definitions and types of persuasive essays in class. • Assign the Model From Literature for independent reading.

What Is a Persuasive Essay?

As a student, you will often be asked to write persuasively. A **persuasive essay** presents your position on an issue, urges your readers to accept that position, and may encourage them to take an action. An effective persuasive essay

- explores an issue of importance to the writer.
- addresses an issue that is arguable.
- uses facts, examples, statistics, or personal experiences to support a position.
- tries to influence its audience through appeals to the readers' knowledge, experiences, or emotions.
- uses clear organization to present a logical argument.

To see the criteria on which your final persuasive essay may be judged, preview the Rubric for Self-Assessment on page 137 of this lesson.

Types of Persuasion

Persuasion can take many forms, ranging from the notes you write to friends asking them to join you in a difficult project to the President's formalized, scripted State of the Union address. Following is a list of a few forms of persuasion accompanied by explanations of the unique purpose of each form:

- **Editorials** are published by the editors of newspapers to share their opinions of events in the news.
- **Position papers** are written to influence policy decisions or to present a stand on a current issue.
- **Persuasive speeches** are presented aloud to an audience.
- **Debates** pit speakers against each other to present opposing sides of controversial issues.

Writers in

ACTION

Persuasion played a pivotal role in America's struggle for independence. In a memorable persuasive speech, Patrick Henry said:

"I know not what course others may take; but as for me, give me liberty or give me death."

PREVIEW

Student Work

IN PROGRESS

In this chapter, you will follow the work of Joseph Dangelmaier, a student at Archbishop Ryan High School in Philadelphia, Pennsylvania. Notice how he uses prewriting, drafting, and revising techniques to develop his essay "Life in the Fast Lane Just Got Faster."

Persuasive Essay • 119

PREPARE and ENGAGE

Interest GRABBER Ask students to consider arguments for or against awarding all college financial aid on the basis of need only. Have them jot down brief statements of their initial arguments. Then, ask volunteers to read their statements aloud. Have students identify which statements present facts and which contain opinions.

Activate Prior Knowledge

Ask students to recall a time when they tried to persuade someone to change his or her mind—to convince a parent to take them to a concert, or persuade a friend to see a particular movie. What do they think made them succeed or fail? After discussing these events, refer students to the characteristics of the persuasive essay listed in the text.

More About the Writer

Patrick Henry was an early practitioner of the fine art of persuasion. A contemporary said, "He is by far the most powerful speaker I ever heard. Every word he says not only engages but commands the attention." In order to sway others to his point of view, he became the first American politician to call voters his "fellow citizens."

☑ ONGOING ASSESSMENT: Diagnose

Use one of the following options to diagnose students' current level of proficiency in persuasive writing.

Option 1 Suggest that each student select the strongest example of his or her persuasive writing from the previous year's writing portfolio. You may wish to hold brief conferences with each student to review and assess these samples.

Option 2 Ask students to write a paragraph persuading a friend to vote for an imaginary candidate in a presidential election. Students who fail to write a concise topic sentence or include sufficient supporting evidence for their persuasive writing may need extra help.

Reading\Writing Connection

Reading: Distinguish Fact from Opinion

Remind students that factual statements express reality; they can be checked and proved to be true or false. (*The room temperature is eighty-four degrees.*) Opinions are statements of judgment or belief. (*This room is too warm.*) Opinions can't be proved true, but they can be supported by facts and the opinions of others, especially those of experts or authorities. Stating opinions effectively and supporting them with facts and other details is an essential skill of persuasive writing.

As students read the testimony by Michael J. Fox, ask them to identify three opinions and to observe how Fox supports each one.

Step-by-Step Teaching Guide

Engage Students Through Literature

1. Use questions such as these to prompt discussion:

   Why does Fox feel it is important to search for the cause of Parkinson's disease? (Finding the cause may lead to a cure and/or better treatments for the symptoms of Parkinson's disease.)

   Why did Fox testify before Congress? (Fox hoped to persuade Congress to grant more funds for research.)

2. Allow students to make other observations and comments about the essay. Ask students to brainstorm for other persuasive essay topics. Some possibilities:

   Government involvement in curing disease

   The role of celebrities as spokespeople for a cause

   The effect of a positive outlook on the course of a disease

3. Let students know that they may add these ideas to their topic banks.

7.1 Model From Literature

Michael J. Fox is a popular actor who has achieved success in both film and television roles. In 1998, Fox disclosed that he suffers from Parkinson's disease. In his testimony before a Senate subcommittee, Fox argues persuasively that federal funding is critical to finding a cure for Parkinson's disease.

Reading **Writing** **Connection**

Reading Strategy:
Distinguish Fact From Opinion As you read, look to see how Fox has supported his opinions—beliefs that may not necessarily be proved—with facts that can be supported by proof.

▲ **Critical Viewing**
How might Michael J. Fox (pictured here) use body language and tone of voice to strengthen his connection with his audience and convince them of the need to take action? **[Speculate]**

By praising the past efforts of the legislators, Fox makes immediate, positive contact with his audience.

The Balancing Act
Testimony Before the Senate Subcommittee on Labor, Health, and Human Services and Education Committee on Appropriations

September 28, 1999
Michael J. Fox

Mr. Chairman, Senator Harkin, and members of the Subcommittee—thank you for inviting me to testify today about the need for a greater federal investment in Parkinson's research. I would like to thank you, in particular, for your tremendous leadership in the fight to double funding for the National Institutes of Health.

Some or perhaps most of you are familiar with me from twenty years of work in film and television. What I wish to speak to you about today has little or nothing to do with celebrity—save for this brief reference.

120 • Persuasive Essay

Critical Viewing

Speculate Students may suggest that the speaker make direct eye contact with members of the subcommittee and use hand and body gestures to emphasize various points. They might also suggest that he speak clearly, raising his voice for emphasis and speaking more softly when sharing personal information.

When I first spoke publicly about my eight years of experience as a person with Parkinson's, many were surprised, in part because of my age—although 30 percent of all Parkinson's patients are under fifty, and 20 percent are under forty, and that number is growing. I had hidden my symptoms and struggles very well, through increasing amounts of medication, through surgery, and by employing the hundreds of little tricks and techniques a person with Parkinson's learns, to mask his or her condition for as long as possible.

While the changes in my life were profound and progressive, I kept them to myself for a number of reasons: fear, denial for sure, but I also felt that it was important for me to just quietly "soldier on."

When I did share my story, the response was overwhelming, humbling, and deeply inspiring. I heard from thousands of Americans affected by Parkinson's, writing and calling to offer encouragement and to tell me of their experience. They spoke of pain, frustration, fear, and hope. Always hope.

What I understood very clearly is that the time for quietly "soldiering on" is through. The war against Parkinson's is a winnable war, and I am resolved to play a role in that victory.

What celebrity has given me is the opportunity to raise the visibility of Parkinson's disease and focus more attention on the desperate need for more research dollars. While I am able, for the time being, to continue to do what I love best, others are not so fortunate. There are doctors, teachers, policemen, nurses, and parents who are no longer able to work, to provide for their families, and live out their dreams.

The one million Americans living with Parkinson's want to beat this disease. So do the millions more Americans who have family members suffering from Parkinson's. But it won't happen until Congress adequately funds Parkinson's research.

For many people with Parkinson's, managing their disease is a full-time job. It is a constant balancing act. Too little medicine causes tremors and stiffness. Too much medicine produces uncontrollable movement and slurring. And far too often, Parkinson's patients wait and wait for the medicines to "kick in." New investigational therapies have helped some people like me control my symptoms, but in the end, we all face the same reality: The medicines stop working.

For people living with Parkinson's, the status quo isn't good enough.

In this paragraph, Fox includes his personal experience of Parkinson's, facts and statistics about the people the disease has targeted, and strategies people use to combat the disease.

In the four paragraphs following "When I first spoke," Fox uses a chronological organization to explain how his own attitude toward his illness has changed over time.

With a reference to "thousands of Americans," Fox appeals to the concerns of his audience again.

Fox includes facts by naming the range of professionals whose lives are touched by Parkinson's disease. He also includes opinions by citing his belief that there is a need for more research funding.

Fox succinctly introduces his thesis: Finding a cure for Parkinson's disease hinges on Congress's increasing research funds.

Model From Literature • **121**

Teaching From the Model

Michael J. Fox feels strongly about the need for more research funding for Parkinson's disease, from which he himself suffers. Have students consider how personal experience can shape a person's opinions. Can students think of other problems that they believe the government should help to resolve? (Students may mention unemployment or the trade in illegal drugs.) What methods other than testifying before Congress would students use to try to convince government agencies to provide funds?

More About the Writer

Michael J. Fox was born in Alberta, Canada, on June 9, 1961. He arrived in Hollywood at the age of eighteen, determined to become an actor. Though he had a difficult start to his career, he won the part of a teenager named Alex in the hit television comedy *Family Ties* at the age of twenty-one, the role that launched his career. In addition to his television work, Michael J. Fox has starred in more than a dozen feature films, including *Back to the Future*, directed by Steven Spielberg.

Real-World Connection

Parkinson's disease was named for James Parkinson, a British physician, who first described its symptoms in 1817. Ask students whether they know how scientists find funds to conduct research into the cause and cure of disease. (Scientists must write persuasive grant proposals.)

Integrating Speaking and Listening Skills

Remind students that Fox's audience listened to, rather than read, his testimony. Read Fox's address aloud, and ask students whether they think delivering the message orally had a greater impact on the subcommittee than if Fox had submitted his remarks in written form. Why or why not?

☑ **ONGOING ASSESSMENT: Monitor and Reinforce**

You may feel that some students will need extra help with some technical terms that appear in the excerpt. Consider one of the following options.

Option 1 Students who are reading the Model From Literature on their own should list any unfamiliar words they encounter. Suggest that students then look up the words on their lists in a dictionary or encyclopedia.

Option 2 If the model is being read during class time, you can gloss unfamiliar or troublesome vocabulary words as they are encountered. Words such as *appropriations, investigational, meager, neurological,* and *dyskinesia* may need definition.

Teaching From the Model

Have students briefly scan the page to find examples of varied sentence lengths. Ask them to consider the effect on listeners of Fox's two brief sentences: "The medicines stop working" and "I know I didn't." Ask students to consider why Fox used these brief statements at the ends of paragraphs. (Here he uses brief sentences to state a personal response. It gives us an insight into his fears.)

Customize for
Less Advanced Students

Students are unlikely to know the meaning of the word *dyskinesia,* which Fox uses in a list of symptoms on page 123. Ask students how they might find the meaning of this word without using a dictionary. (An Internet site or a medical dictionary would provide the definition: "an abnormal, involuntary movement, a frequent side effect of L-dopa, a drug used to treat Parkinson's.")

Integrating Workplace Skills

In speaking to the Senate, Fox is acting as an advocate for people with Parkinson's disease. An advocate is a person who publicly supports and works to promote a cause or group. Ask students to identify personal attributes and skills that are needed to be an advocate. (Students may mention attributes such as compassion, logical thinking, and organizational ability. Personal skills may include talents for speaking, listening, and persuasive writing.)

As I began to understand what research might promise for the future, I became hopeful I would not face the terrible suffering so many with Parkinson's endure. But I was shocked and frustrated to learn that the amount of funding for Parkinson's research is so meager. Compared with the amount of federal funding going to other diseases, research funding for Parkinson's lags far behind.

In a country with a $15 billion investment in medical research we can and we must do better.

At present, Parkinson's is inadequately funded, no matter how one cares to spin it. Meager funding means a continued lack of effective treatments, slow progress in understanding the cause of the disease, and little chance that a cure will come in time. I applaud the steps we are taking to fulfill the promise of the Udall Parkinson's Research Act, but we must be clear—we aren't there yet.

If, however, an adequate investment is made, there is much to be hopeful for. We have a tremendous opportunity to close the gap for Parkinson's. We are learning more and more about this disease. The scientific community believes that with a significant investment in Parkinson's research, new discoveries and improved treatment strategies are close at hand. Many have called Parkinson's the most curable neurological disorder and the one expected to produce a breakthrough first. Scientists tell me that a cure is possible, some say even by the end of the next decade—if the research dollars match the research opportunity.

Mr. Chairman, you and the members of the Subcommittee have done so much to increase the investment in medical research in this country. I thank you for your vision. Most people don't know just how important this research is until they or someone in their family faces a serious illness. I know I didn't.

The Parkinson's community strongly supports your efforts to double medical research funding. At the same time, I implore you to do more for people with Parkinson's. Take up Parkinson's as if your life depended on it. Increase funding for Parkinson's research by $75 million over current levels for the coming fiscal year. Make this a down payment for a fully funded Parkinson's research agenda that will make Parkinson's nothing more than a footnote in medical textbooks.

I would like to close on a personal note. Today you will hear from, or have already heard from, more than a few experts, in the fields of science, bookkeeping, and other areas. I am an expert in only one—what it is like to be a young man, husband, and father with Parkinson's disease. With the help of daily medication and

In the body of his speech, Fox uses powerful words like "hopeful," "suffering," and "meager" to convey his feelings about his future and those of others living with this illness.

Fox bolsters his argument by citing scientific support for his point of view.

Fox urges the committee to action by imploring members to act as if the disease affected each of them personally.

selective exertion, I can still perform my job, in my case in a very public arena. I can still help out with the daily tasks and rituals involved in home life. But I don't kid myself . . . that will change. Physical and mental exhaustion will become more and more of a factor, as will increased rigidity, tremor, and dyskinesia. I can expect in my forties to face challenges most wouldn't expect until their seventies or eighties—if ever. But with your help, if we all do everything we can to eradicate this disease, in my fifties I'll be dancing at my children's weddings. And mine will be just one of millions of happy stories.

Thank you again for your time and attention.

Reading Writing Connection

Writing Application: Help Your Reader Distinguish Fact From Opinion By providing both opinions and the facts to back them up, Fox crafts a strong persuasive argument. As you write your persuasive essay, be sure to include enough facts to support your opinions and to make your case.

▶ **Critical Viewing**
What link does Fox make between scientific research, the future for persons living with Parkinson's, and the action that he asks his audience to take? **[Connect]**

Fox ends his persuasive speech with a personal reflection on what the foreseeable future holds for him. This final point is a potent appeal to the minds and emotions of the members of his audience and may convince them to act on his position.

LITERATURE

For another example of a persuasive essay delivered in a political forum, see Thomas Jefferson's "The Declaration of Independence," in *Prentice Hall Literature: Timeless Voices, Timeless Themes*, The American Experience.

Connections With Literature

Persuasive essays need not be about an issue that affects you personally, such as an illness. Persuasive essays can be written about any issue that is of interest to you and others. Ask students to review the persuasive techniques used by Thomas Jefferson in "The Declaration of Independence" in *Prentice Hall Literature: Timeless Voices, Timeless Themes:* The American Experience.

Reading\Writing Connection

Writing Application: Help Your Reader Distinguish Fact From Opinion

Ask students to cite specific statements of opinion they found in Fox's testimony. Discuss the details Fox uses to support his opinions. For example, Fox supports his belief that "We have a tremendous opportunity to close the gap" (p. 122) by citing research progress, scientists' expectations of new discoveries and treatments, and the possibility of a cure. Remind students that, while they may choose topics based on their opinions about a subject, they will convince their readers most by supplying supporting facts.

Critical Viewing

Connect Student responses should indicate that Fox believes an increase in research funding from Congress will lead to improved treatments and a cure for Parkinson's disease.

Step-by-Step Teaching Guide

Prewriting: "News" Notebook

1. Supply small groups of students with recent copies of newspapers and magazines.

2. Have students look for articles that suggest a need for action. (Examples: stories about school funding or foreign policy, which invite more than one possible opinion.)

3. Have each group formulate a list of three or more topics that provoke strong feeling.

4. Collect and present topic lists from each group on the board.

5. Encourage groups to discuss and share their topics with the class.

Step-by-Step Teaching Guide

Prewriting: Round-Table Discussion

Teaching Resources: Writing Support Transparencies, 7-A; Writing Support Activity Book, 7-1

1. Organize students into groups of four to six. Display Transparency 7-A to show how Joseph's group organized their pro and con statements.

2. Give a student recorder in each group a blank copy of the organizer (7-1) to keep notes on ideas.

3. Encourage groups to select and discuss two or three topics, noting possible positions on each topic and preliminary arguments for or against each.

Customize for
Visual/Spatial Learners

Suggest that students create posters to illustrate a stand they might take on an issue generated from either the News Notebook or Round-Table Discussion. Ask each student to be aware of whether his or her statements are opinions or facts.

7.2 Prewriting

Choosing Your Topic

To write a persuasive essay that convinces others to accept your views, select a topic that affects you personally. To be sure the issue you select could provoke argument, check that the subject has at least two sides. Consider these strategies:

Strategies for Generating Topics

1. **"News" Notebook** You can find many topics for a persuasive argument in the daily news. Watch television, scan newspapers, and listen to the issues that your friends are discussing now. Record the topics in a news notebook. Circle those that provoke strong feelings in you. Then, select one that you'd like to develop into a persuasive essay.

2. **Round-Table Discussion** Meet with a group of classmates to discuss issues that you consider important. Generate a list of topics, and for each idea, develop opposing statements. Star the ones that create the sharpest controversy or disagreement. On your own, choose a subject and a position that you could defend in a persuasive essay.

Writing Lab CD-ROM

For more help finding a topic, explore the activities and suggestions in the Choosing a Topic section of the Persuasion lesson.

Name: *Joseph Dangelmaier*
Archbishop Ryan High School
Philadelphia, PA

Collaborating in a Round-Table Discussion

When Joseph met with a group, he and his classmates outlined these general categories and created "pro" and "con" statements for each. Joseph decided to write a persuasive essay on technology's benefits.

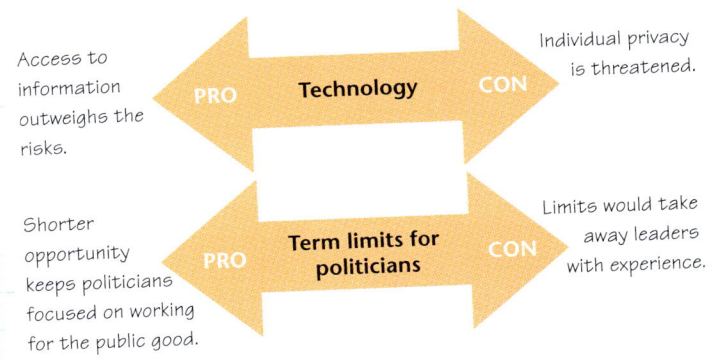

Access to information outweighs the risks.

PRO **Technology** **CON**

Individual privacy is threatened.

Shorter opportunity keeps politicians focused on working for the public good.

PRO **Term limits for politicians** **CON**

Limits would take away leaders with experience.

124 • Persuasive Essay

⏱ **TIME AND RESOURCE MANAGER**

Resources
Print: *Writing Support Transparencies, 7-A–E; Writing Support Activity Book, 7-1–3; Topic Bank for Heterogeneous Classes,* Ch. 7
Technology: *Writing Lab* CD-ROM, Persuasion

In-Depth Coverage	Accelerated Pace
• Cover pp. 124–128 in class. • Guide students as necessary as they narrow topics, analyze audience, and gather details. • Conduct the Round-Table Discussion in class.	• In class, discuss strategies for generating topics. • Have students work with partners to focus on audience, purpose, and gathering details.

TOPIC BANK

If you haven't found a topic that inspires you, consider these possibilities:

1. **A Letter to the Editor About Resource Use** The struggle between land developers and environmentalists pits the two sides against each other. Find out about such a controversy in your area. Write a letter to the editor of your local paper to express your position on the conflict.

2. **Persuasive Essay on Dress Codes** High schools often have rules that prohibit short skirts, torn jeans, or T-shirts with slogans. In a persuasive essay, argue the benefits or disadvantages of a school dress code.

Responding to Fine Art

3. This painting of people joining hands might prompt you to think of issues that bring people together. For example, an election can inspire a grass-roots effort to influence voting, or a flood might bring neighbors together to help those in need. Write a persuasive essay about such an occurrence. In your essay, convince others to contribute time, money, or energy to the issue.

Repeat Again, I Do Believe, Phoebe Beasley, Courtesy of the artist

Responding to Literature

4. Read "The Life You Save May Be Your Own," by Flannery O'Connor. In that story, a drifter takes advantage of a family. In a persuasive essay, argue for or against punishing him. You can find the story in *Prentice Hall Literature: Timeless Voices, Timeless Themes,* The American Experience.

☑ Cooperative Writing Opportunity

5. **Persuasive Flyer to Promote Literacy** With a group, research the issue of adult literacy. Some students can report on the programs in your community, and others can investigate the problems that arise from an inability to read. Then, create a flyer on the values of teaching everyone to read.

Prewriting • 125

Prewriting: Looping to Narrow a Topic

Teaching Resources: Writing Support Transparencies, 7-C

1. Display the transparency of the Student Work in Progress. Ask students to state the result of the looping process shown. (Joseph starts with a broad idea, "technology is both good and bad." He then moves to the more focused idea, "powerful benefits of technology." And finally, he narrows his topic to "people should embrace technology.")

2. Model a broad topic and the looping process on the board.

3. Allow students class time to use the looping process on their topics. Encourage them to write freely at each stage, and review their ideas at the end of each five-minute period.

4. Ask volunteers to read their broad and narrowed statements to the class.

Customize for
Less Advanced Students

As a variation of the looping strategy, have students work with partners. After students write freely, have them exchange papers. Each partner circles the most important idea and writes freely. The papers are then returned to the original writers. This cross-pollination of ideas may help both students narrow their topics.

⏱ TIME SAVERS!

📄 Writing Support Transparencies
Use the transparencies for Chapter 7 to facilitate the teaching of the strategies.

📖 Writing Support Activity Book
Use the graphic organizers for Chapter 7 to facilitate student planning.

Narrowing Your Topic

After you have decided on a topic, consider the arguments that you will need to make in order to convince your audience. For example, if you plan to argue that people should eat nutritious foods, you will have to discuss many kinds of diets and explain why each one is beneficial or harmful. That is probably too broad a topic for the length of your essay. In contrast, a narrower topic such as "Improve Your Health: Eat More Vegetables" can be covered in the space you have. Looping is one strategy for narrowing a topic.

Use Looping to Narrow a Topic

To help you focus on a topic, use these steps in the process of looping: Write freely on your topic for about five minutes. Read what you have written. Circle the most important idea. Write for five minutes on the idea that you circled. Repeat the process until you reveal a topic that is narrow enough to cover well in a persuasive essay.

Student Work IN PROGRESS

Name: Joseph Dangelmaier
Archbishop Ryan High School
Philadelphia, PA

Looping

Here is how Joseph used looping to narrow his topic:

Broad topic: Technology is both good and bad.

Technology is a mixed bag. On the one hand, technology has always been around. Humans wouldn't have gotten anywhere without it. This goes for everything from making fire to transplanting organs. There are so many powerful benefits of technology, in medicine, education, and communication. Naturally, there are drawbacks, too.

Powerful benefits of technology:
The powerful benefits of technology far outweigh the challenges and risks involved in adopting new things. Improvements in medicine, education, and especially communication make the point convincingly that people should embrace new technologies.

Narrow topic: People should embrace new technologies.

Considering Your Audience and Purpose

While the purpose of all persuasive writing is to sway readers, the specific audience you expect to address will affect the way you persuade them. Therefore, the first step in convincing your audience is knowing your audience.

Analyze Your Audience

Knowing such characteristics as the age, occupation, values, and prior knowledge of your readers will help you appeal to them effectively. For example, if you were writing to promote research into blue-laser DVDs, which have a higher storage capacity than conventional CDs, you could use a variety of details to support your position. The graph below shows the different appeals that you might make to specific groups of people.

TARGET YOUR APPEAL TO DIFFERENT AUDIENCES

Business executives
wish to broaden the audience for their work.

Artists and filmmakers
look for innovative ways to create products.

Students
want to have greater convenience while having fun.

Writers in
ACTION

As vice president of communications for the National Urban League, M. Gasby Greely creates letters, essays, and speeches to persuade. She sees each specific audience as an engine that directs her power to persuade. Here she explains how an analysis of each audience can drive her writing:

"The best way I can focus my writing is to keep the audience in mind . . . what is going to get them to understand my point of view?"

Writing Lab CD-ROM

Use the Audience Profile activity to help you identify your audience so that you can shape your argument to persuade them.

☑ ONGOING ASSESSMENT: Monitor and Reinforce

If students have trouble identifying their audience, suggest that they try one of the following strategies.

Option 1 Encourage students to narrow their proposed audience much as they narrowed their topics. Assure students that it is perfectly acceptable to write for a very small audience, even an audience of one, such as a friend or family member.

Option 2 Have students examine their topics carefully and compose a profile of their ideal reader. Have them imagine a reader who would be sympathetic to their point of view, and jot down notes about this person's occupation, interests, and beliefs. Students can then address their writings to this person.

Prewriting: Analyze Your Audience

Teaching Resources: Writing Support Transparencies, 7-D; Writing Support Activity Book, 7-2

1. Display the Audience Appeal transparency. Ask students to imagine how different readers might respond to their arguments. Students should ask themselves "Would students, sports fans, or medical professionals be more likely to share my point of view?" "Would my topic appeal more to certain groups than to others?"

2. Have students imagine that their ideal reader holds an opposite opinion from their own. Suggest that such a reader may be swayed more readily by facts than by statements of opinion.

3. Give students blank copies of the Audience Appeal diagram (7-2). Have students complete the diagram on their topic for three different audiences: their friends, their parents, a group of visiting teachers. Provide markers and tabloid-sized paper so students have adequate room to write.

More About the Writer

M. Gasby Greely, as vice-president of communications for the National Urban League, aims to assist African Americans in the achievement of social and economic equality. Writing persuasive essays is part of the Urban League's advocacy mission.

Customize for
ESL Students

After reviewing the Audience Appeal diagram, organize students into small groups. Ask groups to each complete an Audience Appeal diagram on a topic for three different audiences: their younger friends, their parents, their grandparents. Provide a model on the board. Encourage groups to talk about which parts of the topic are the most important and least important to each audience.

Step-by-Step Teaching Guide

Prewriting: Make a T-Chart

Teaching Resources: Writing Support Transparencies, 7-E; Writing Support Activity Book, 7-3

1. Display the transparency to show students how to organize information with a T-chart. Then give them blank copies (7-3) and have them write their own proposed topic at the top. Students should brainstorm for arguments for and against their positions.

2. Ask students to consider how they can support their opinions with facts, and how they can support their statements of fact with statistics or other evidence.

3. Remind students that research will be necessary to complete their persuasive writing. (Example: To support the statement in favor of lowering the driving age, students can research to find whether students aged fifteen have adult responsibilities, and what those responsibilities are.)

Step-by-Step Teaching Guide

Prewriting: Conduct Interviews

1. Have students work in groups of four or five. Each student then presents his or her position to the group and records the group's feedback.

2. After students have presented their positions and recorded the group's response, they should each create a T-Chart that shows the pro and con responses to their position statements.

3. Suggest that students contact a person with expertise in the area related to their topics. Students should add these responses to their T-Charts.

Integrating Workplace Skills

A job interview may be framed as persuasive speech. Prospective employees offer statements of fact about their education and job experience (*I received a B.A. degree*

Gathering Evidence

To write a strong persuasive essay, support your position with convincing examples. One of the most effective ways to make your examples convincing is to address both sides of your topic.

Get Information on Both Sides of the Issue

In addition to providing arguments and examples that support your position, you should know and address arguments that can be used to attack your ideas. Use the strategies below to marshal the arguments for and against your position. Then, collect the evidence that will lead readers to accept your ideas or to take the action that you recommend.

Make a T-Chart Write your position at the top of a sheet of paper. Then, draw a line down the middle of the page to create two columns. In one column, jot down facts and ideas that support your position. In the other, note arguments and evidence that might be used to attack your position. Use your T-chart to guide further collection of evidence.

SAMPLE T-CHART

The Driving Age Should Be Lowered to Fifteen

Pro	Con
Many teens at 15 have adult responsibilities, so they should have adult privileges like driving.	Many speeding tickets and car accidents involve teenagers.

Conduct Interviews You can gather valuable information by asking the right questions. Consider setting up the following data-collection interviews:

- **Survey Your Audience** To tailor your appeal to your intended readers, find out what they believe about your topic. Talk to classmates, family, or friends and take notes about people's concerns relative to your position.

- **Question the Experts** To strengthen your argument, find out what the experts say. Interview people who study or work in an area related to your topic. Jot down evidence that supports your position and that your readers may not typically know.

128 • Persuasive Essay

📶 **Internet Tip**

The Internet often has the most up-to-date information on many subjects. As you research your topic, consider going on-line to find arguments for and against your position.

from the University of Richmond in 2002), as well as opinion (*I think I work well with others*).

Ask students to create a T-Chart with the head, "I Am a Good Candidate for this Position." On the left, they may note any concerns the employer may have that might prompt them to hire someone else. On the right, they should note rebutting evidence in their favor.

7.3 Drafting

Shaping Your Writing

Develop a Thesis Statement

An effective persuasive essay is built around a clearly worded **thesis statement,** a statement of the position you will prove.

SAMPLE THESIS STATEMENTS

- Televised trials often weaken the defendants' ability to gain a fair hearing because lawyers and judges play to the camera.
- Broadcasting trials improves our legal system by exposing general audiences to the everyday workings of the court system.

Organize to Emphasize the Strongest Support

In your draft, introduce your topic and state your thesis. In the body of your essay, make the arguments that support and prove your thesis statement. Follow the organization below:

- Use your second-best argument for a good start.
- Show and argue against the opposing views.
- Organize your details to lead up to your conclusion.
- Save your best argument for a strong finish.

Writing Lab CD-ROM

Use the Outline Tool in the *Writing Lab CD-ROM* for help in organizing your persuasive essay.

Student Work
IN PROGRESS

Name: *Joseph Dangelmaier*
Archbishop Ryan High School
Philadelphia, PA

Organizing an Essay Diagram

Joseph made a diagram to show the order in which he planned to present his ideas for maximum effect.

INTRODUCTION → THESIS STATEMENT → BENEFITS OF TECHNOLOGY

ACKNOWLEDGE OPPOSITION

BEST BENEFIT OF TECHNOLOGY

REFUTE OPPOSITION

CONCLUSION

Drafting • 129

Step-by-Step Teaching Guide

Drafting: Develop a Thesis Statement

1. Help students determine whether a clear thesis statement emerged from their exercises in brainstorming, looping, making T-charts, and interviewing.

2. Remind students that a thesis is best stated in a single, strongly worded sentence. The thesis statement is always presented as a fact, even when it states an opinion. ("Television is an underrated educational tool" is more effective than "I think that television is educational and has been underrated.")

3. Have students work in teams to review one another's thesis statements, editing and revising in response to feedback.

Step-by-Step Teaching Guide

Drafting: Organizing to Emphasize Strongest Support

Teaching Resources: Writing Support Transparencies, 7-F; Writing Support Activity Book, 7-4

1. Display Transparency 7-F. Ask students to state what they think Joseph's strongest statement is.

2. Lead students in a discussion that helps them see the merit in saving their best argument for their conclusion. Show students that beginning a persuasive essay with their strongest argument would not allow facts and other supporting material to lead to a strong conclusion.

3. Give students blank copies of the chart (7-4) to organize their statements for the strongest support.

⏱ **TIME AND RESOURCE MANAGER**

Resources
Print: *Writing Support Transparencies, 7-F–G; Writing Support Activity Book, 7-4–5*
Technology: *Writing Lab CD-ROM, Persuasion*

In-Depth Coverage	Accelerated Pace
• Cover pp. 129–130 in class. • Have students write their thesis statements and flowcharts in class. • Have students write their persuasive drafts in class or as a homework assignment.	• Have students review pp. 129–130 independently and write their first persuasive essay drafts. • Respond to individual drafting issues as needed.

Providing Elaboration
Consider a Variety of Points for Illumination

Build a strong case for your position by choosing the best methods of elaboration. Consider these strategies to support your position:

- **Give the Facts** Include information that is objective and that can be proved. Insert names, dates, and other data that provide background for your topic.

- **Provide Statistics** Strengthen your argument by citing numbers that prove your position. Give information that shows *how many* or *what percentage.*

- **Make a Comparison** Show your readers how your topic matches others they may already know.

- **Share a Personal Experience** Explain how the topic you are addressing has personal meaning for you.

- **Include Details to Fill Out Your Ideas** Details are the specifics that clarify the points you are making. Show the pieces of the larger position you are arguing.

As the chart below indicates, you can elaborate using each of these techniques:

Thesis: The admission price at sporting events should be lowered.

Details:
Admission is expensive. Add it to the cost of programs, souvenirs, and food, and the cost skyrockets.

Comparisons:
Game tickets are more expensive than museum and movie admissions.

Thesis:
The admission price of professional sporting events should be lowered.

Facts:
Most league stadiums can hold more than 50,000 people per game. Teams make money on television rights and advertising revenue, too.

Personal Experience:
I am a die-hard fan, but my family can't afford to go to all the games I want to see.

Statistics:
The price of these tickets has more than tripled in fifteen years. In 1980, a box seat was $8; now, it is $25.

130 • Persuasive Essay

7.4 *Revising*

After you have drafted your persuasive essay, look for ways to make it better. Check to make sure that your argument is clear and your essay well organized. Then, review the details, such as the types of sentences you have used and your choice of words. Revisions that come from such analysis will make your essay more persuasive.

Revising Your Overall Structure

Strengthen Your Introduction

In addition to presenting your thesis statement, the introduction is your first and greatest chance to grab the reader's interest in your topic. The first few sentences of your draft are your lead; they are your chance to build interest in your topic. Review and revise your introduction to take full advantage of this once-in-an-essay opportunity.

▶ **REVISION STRATEGY**
Adding Information to Build Interest

Evaluate your lead to see whether added details might help to generate more interest in your topic. Make notes to suggest areas for further development, and jot down ideas that will make the introduction more appealing.

🔲 Research Tip

Consult reference materials to obtain additional information that you need to strengthen your introduction. You can find facts, statistics, and useful details in sources like *InfoTrac* and *Facts on File.*

Student Work
IN PROGRESS

Name: Joseph Dangelmaier
Archbishop Ryan High School
Philadelphia, PA

Adding Information to Build Interest

Here is Joseph's first version of the lead in his introduction. When he looked at it again, he decided to perk it up by adding information to it. Look at the final draft on page 138 to see Joseph's revision.

Technology, like life, evolves to meet new challenges. People wanted a faster tool for making mathematical calculations, so they developed the processor—then the microprocessor. The need for a more efficient way to transport data inspired the networking technology that we know as the Internet.

> What other example of technology can I show? Fire. Ships. Airplanes.

Revising • 131

Step-by-Step Teaching Guide

Revising: Strengthen Your Introduction

1. Let students know that readers often hope to have their own opinions confirmed by persuasive essays. Strong writing helps readers consider having their opinions changed or challenged.

2. A strong and engaging introduction can counter reader resistance to reading further. Ask students to review their introductory statements. Does the introduction "hook" the reader? Have students evaluate their introductory statements for their "hooks."

3. Have students evaluate their language. Are the words strong and direct? Are the sentences well written and of varying lengths?

Step-by-Step Teaching Guide

Revising: Adding Information to Build Interest

Teaching Resources: Writing Support Transparencies, 7-H

1. Display Transparency 7-H and use it to show how Joseph improved his introduction.

2. Ask students to review the details that they have included in their introductions. Are any pertinent details missing? Are more details given than are needed?

3. Have students analyze the details they have included. Are they sufficiently varied? Do they appeal to both the reader's logic and emotions?

4. Have students review their introductions and evaluate their language and details. Are they using strong and precise words?

🕐 TIME AND RESOURCE MANAGER

Resources
Print: *Writing Support Transparencies, 7-H–J; Writing Support Activity Book, 7-6*
Technology: *Writing Lab* CD-ROM, Persuasion

In-Depth Coverage	Accelerated Pace
• Work through the Revision Strategies with the class (pp. 131–135). • Demonstrate strategies for analyzing overall structure, sentence beginnings, and word choice. • Divide the class into groups for peer review activity.	• Have students review pp. 131–135 independently, and then revise their persuasive essays. • Respond to individual revising issues as needed.

Step-by-Step Teaching Guide

Revising: Circular Reasoning

1. Write the following sentences on the chalkboard.

   A persuasive essay needs to be logical so it makes sense.

   A persuasive essay should be logical or readers might dismiss any arguments it makes.

2. Ask students which statement is an example of circular reasoning. Ask why the second statement presents a better argument. (It explains the results of a failure in logic rather than simply restating the need for logic.)

Step-by-Step Teaching Guide

Revising: Either/Or Argument

1. After reviewing the example and revision in the textbook, ask students to think of other examples of either/or arguments that they have read or heard.

2. Have students reread their drafts, including their revised introductions, for any examples of faulty logic.

Step-by-Step Teaching Guide

Revising: Look for Logic

1. Have students review their drafts, highlighting any sentences that appeal to the reader's logic.

2. Ask students to list their logic-driven sentences on a separate sheet of paper and to exchange their papers with a classmate. Have students respond to one another's arguments.

3. Based on their classmate's suggestions and their own editing skills, have students revise any faulty arguments.

Critical Viewing

Hypothesize Students may suggest that the advertisement should stress shopping convenience and the open, attractive design of the mall.

Revising Your Paragraphs
Eliminate Faulty Logic

The more critical your audience, the more important it is for you to draw reasonable conclusions based on adequate evidence that supports your position. A discerning audience will quickly see through errors in logic. Review your draft to eliminate the following patterns of weak arguments:

Circular Reasoning A writer thinks he or she is advancing an argument but is simply restating ideas instead of defending them.

EXAMPLE: The mall is losing business because nobody shops there.

REVISION: The mall is losing business because people are shopping on-line.

Either/Or Argument A writer oversimplifies the issue by offering only two extremes, when in fact there are other possibilities.

EXAMPLE: If store owners don't have more sales, the mall will go out of business.

REVISION: If store owners don't have more sales, provide more conveniences, and improve security, shopping revenue will continue to drop.

▲ Critical Viewing
If you were developing an advertisement for the mall pictured here, how might you attract customers? **[Hypothesize]**

▶ **REVISION STRATEGY**
Looking for Logic

You can avoid exasperating your readers by finding and eliminating faulty logic. Review your draft, evaluating each sentence. Bracket any sentences that make logical appeals to your readers, and revise any that contain faulty logic or unreasonable appeals.

Revising Your Sentences

Use Transitions

Adding words that make your reasoning more obvious to your readers can enhance the power of your writing. Consider adding these transitions to improve your sentence clarity.

- **To show a contrast:** however, although, despite
- **To point to a reason:** since, because, if
- **To signal a conclusion:** therefore, consequently, so, then

▶ **REVISION STRATEGY**
Color-Coding to Check Connections

Circle any transitions in your paper. Then, read each paragraph of your essay. Underline in green the places where you set up contrasts, underline in blue where you provide reasons, and underline in red where you have drawn conclusions. In each case, decide whether the transition you have used is a strong one. Revise or add transitions as needed.

Grammar in Your Writing
Adverb Clauses

Adverb clauses are groups of words that show the relationship between ideas by telling more about the action of a sentence. Although they contain both a subject and a verb, adverb clauses cannot stand alone. Instead, they can tell *where, when, how, why, to what extent,* or *under what condition* the action of the rest of the sentence occurred.

- Time relationship (when): After the hurricane touched down
- Cause-and-effect relationship (why): Because the university has such a wonderful library
- Opposing relationship (under what condition): Although the deputy said that the evidence was insufficient

When an adverb clause introduces a sentence, use a comma to separate it from the rest of the sentence. Note, however, that it is usually not necessary to use a comma before an adverb clause at the end of a sentence.

Find It in Your Reading Review Michael J. Fox's congressional testimony on pages 120–123 of this chapter. Identify two adverb clauses.

Find It in Your Writing Circle all of the adverb clauses in your draft. Check that you have punctuated them correctly. If you discover you haven't used at least two adverb clauses, challenge yourself to add one.

For more on adverb clauses, see Chapter 19.

Step-by-Step Teaching Guide

Revising: Consider the Power of Words

Teaching Resources: Writing Support Transparencies, 7-I; Writing Support Activity Book, 7-6

1. Remind students that words can have more than one denotation. Refer students to the dictionary to find the denotation of the following words on the board.

   present (now or a gift)

   kind (nice or type of)

   function (operate or an event)

2. Display Transparency 7-I to remind students that certain words they use in their writing may have different connotations for their intended audience.

3. Give students blank copies of the connotation chart (7-6). Read the following pairs of words and ask students to place each word on either the positive or negative side of the chart.

sunny	*scorching*
exciting	*tense*
skinny	*slender*

Step-by-Step Teaching Guide

Revising: Using a Thesaurus

1. Remind students that a thesaurus can help them find synonyms, or words that share a similar meaning. Have students use a thesaurus to find synonyms for these words.

   send (catapult, transmit, convey, expedite, etc.)

   save (rescue, deliver, preserve, liberate, etc.)

   anger (wrath, rage, fury, etc.)

2. Direct students to highlight the verbs and nouns in their drafts. Encourage students to use a thesaurus to replace weaker words with stronger ones.

Customize for
ESL Students

Have students keep lists of English words that have strong connotations or that have both a formal and a more casual meaning. As an aid to memory, students might create word

---

Revising Your Word Choice
Consider the Power of Words

The words that you choose can strongly influence your readers' responses to your argument. In making word choices, distinguish between a word's denotations and its connotations.

Check the Denotation The **denotation** of a word is its direct, explicit meaning. By referring to a dictionary, you can see a word's denotation. For example, when you compare the words *mandatory* and *optional*, you will see that they have contrasting denotations.

Measure the Connotation A word's **connotation** is the informal meaning a reader or listener attaches to a word. Each time you choose a word, make sure you know how its connotation will affect your audience. The chart below illustrates how words with similar denotations can have opposite connotations.

Words With Strong Connotations

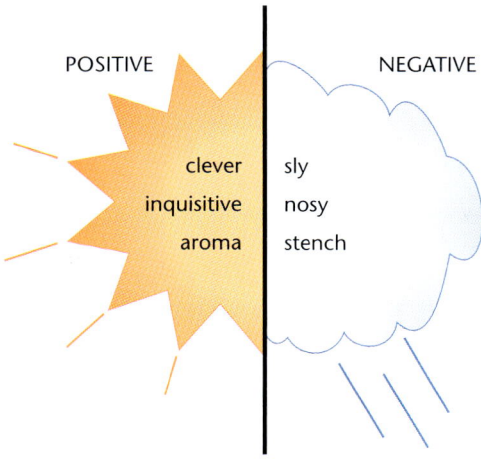

POSITIVE	NEGATIVE
clever	sly
inquisitive	nosy
aroma	stench

▶ REVISION STRATEGY
Using a Thesaurus

Look for places in your draft where you criticize your opposition, defend your ideas, or appeal to your readers' emotions. In each case, circle key nouns or verbs. Consult a thesaurus to find synonyms. Then, decide whether words with stronger connotations might sway your readers even more. Revise to achieve this goal.

134 • Persuasive Essay

drawings that visually demonstrate the denotations and connotations of words.

Peer Review

Analytic Flags

Share your revised draft with a partner. Ask your reviewer to use self-sticking flags or paper clips and small squares of colored paper. Your reviewer can jot down suggestions, comments, or questions for improving your draft and attach each idea to appropriate places in your essay. Ask your partner to consider questions like these:

- Do I create enough interest in my topic?
- Is there any more background information a reader would need to know?
- Do you notice any errors in logic?
- Where can I add more persuasive language?

◀ **Critical Viewing**
What are some good ways to evaluate the feedback you receive in a peer conference like the one shown here? [Speculate]

Writing Lab CD-ROM

The Revising and Editing section of the Persuasive Writing tutorial offers some helpful strategies for peer revision.

Student Work IN PROGRESS

Name: *Joseph Dangelmaier*
Archbishop Ryan High School
Philadelphia, PA

Using Analytic Flags for Peer Review

Notice the suggestions that Joseph's partner made on his flags. Joseph evaluated each idea and then accepted one and rejected the other.

Students respond more enthusiastically to the colors, *interesting* sounds, and *entertaining* animation of a computer program than to a static chalkboard.

> Use adjectives to increase appeal.

> Add info about computer labels.

> Joseph felt this suggestion would pull readers away from the point he was making. He chose not to make the change.

Revising • 135

Step-by-Step Teaching Guide

Revising: Peer Review

Teaching Resources: Writing Support Transparencies, 7-J

1. Urge students to be encouraging about a draft's strengths rather than focusing exclusively on its drawbacks.

2. Remind students that some errors will be corrected at the proofreading stage, and that the focus here should be on content, logic, and language. Use Transparency 7-J to review the Student Work in Progress on this page.

3. Be sure that students have supplied their reviewers with sticking flags or small colored paper and paper clips.

4. After students review the four questions on page 135, suggest that they prepare questions for their peer reviewers that address the particular concerns they have about their drafts.

Critical Viewing

Speculate Good ways to evaluate the feedback one receives in a peer conference include being open to suggestions, not being defensive, and being willing to reconsider one's work objectively.

135

Proofreading: Commas

1. Suggest that students check their persuasive essays paragraph by paragraph, looking for prepositional phrases, participial phrases, and infinitive phrases. Have them determine whether they have used commas correctly. Students should also check that their opinions are supported by facts.

2. Ask students to review their use of commas in their introductory material. Do they show the reader when to pause?

Serial Commas

1. Explain that serial commas have that name because they separate items in a series, or list. Further explain that without commas, several items could be viewed as one and create confusion.

2. Write the following sentence on the board.

   John jotted down his ideas wrote an outline and began his draft.

3. Ask students to correctly punctuate the sentence, and have a volunteer write it on the board.

   John jotted down his ideas, wrote an outline, and began his draft.

Find It in Your Reading

Fox's speech includes many examples of serial commas, beginning with his very first sentence.

Find It in Your Writing

Students may find it helpful to use a highlighter to mark all commas in a draft. Later, they can check to make sure they've used serial commas correctly.

7.5 Editing and Proofreading

Errors in writing can confuse your audience and weaken your credibility as an author. To eliminate errors in your writing, double-check spelling, punctuation, and grammar before writing your final draft.

Focusing on Commas

Commas can make your persuasive essay easier to understand by showing the reader when to pause. However, when commas are used incorrectly, your writing can be confusing. One of the most common uses of commas is to set off the following introductory material:

- **Prepositional phrases:** After the coming attractions, the feature will start.
- **Participial phrases:** Packed to the doors, the theater could hold no more patrons.
- **Infinitive phrases:** To be sure we got a seat, we arrived at the theater an hour early.

Review your draft, and add commas where necessary.

Learn More

For more on commas separating introductory elements, see Chapter 27.

Grammar in Your Writing
Serial Commas

In addition to their function of separating introductory elements of a sentence, commas are also used to separate items in a series. Use commas to separate three or more words, phrases, or clauses in a list.

- **Separating words:** Maria paints, sings, and dances.
- **Separating phrases:** Maria paints in art class, sings in the choir, and dances after school.
- **Separating clauses:** Maria learned that painting is challenging, that singing provides an outlet for tension, and that dancing develops coordination.

Find It in Your Reading Find one example of serial commas in Michael J. Fox's speech on pages 120–123.

Find It in Your Writing As you proofread your persuasive essay, check to make sure that you have used serial commas correctly.

For more information on serial commas, see Chapter 27.

⏱ TIME AND RESOURCE MANAGER

Resources
Print: *Scoring Rubrics on Transparency*, Ch. 7; *Writing Assessment and Portfolio Management*, Persuasive Essay; *Formal Assessment*, Ch. 7
Technology: *Writing Lab* CD-ROM, Persuasion

In-Depth Coverage	Accelerated Pace
• Cover pp.136–139 in class. • Read and discuss the Final Draft on pp. 138–139. • Have students edit and proofread their essays in class.	• Assign pp. 136–139 for independent student review. • Have students edit and proofread their essays as homework. • Students present their final drafts.

7.6 Publishing and Presenting

Building Your Portfolio

Sharing your persuasive essay might just achieve results—your ideas could inspire a positive change in behavior, open minds to a fresh perspective, or help to change an unfair policy. Consider these ideas for publishing and presenting your work:

1. **Send Class Letters** Ask your classmates to join you in writing persuasive letters on your topic, if it is appropriate to the purpose, and mail them to a state or federal congressional representative.

2. **Publish in a Newspaper** Send your essay as an opinion piece, or condense it into a letter to the editor of your school or community newspaper.

Reflecting on Your Writing

Take a moment to learn from your writing experience. In a journal, jot down your reflections on the persuasive writing process. Use these questions to get you started:

- What techniques of persuasion can you apply in future writing situations?

- How might persuasive writing affect the way you are influenced?

 Internet Tip

To see model essays scored with this rubric, go to
www.phschool.com

Rubric for Self-Assessment

Use this rubric to evaluate your persuasive essay.

	Score 4	Score 3	Score 2	Score 1
Audience and Purpose	Demonstrates highly effective word choice; clearly states focus on persuasive task	Demonstrates good word choice; states focus on persuasive task	Shows some good word choices; minimally states focus on persuasive task	Shows lack of attention to persuasive task
Organization	Uses clear, consistent organizational strategy	Uses clear organizational strategy with occasional inconsistencies	Uses inconsistent organizational strategy; presentation is not logical	Demonstrates lack of organizational strategy
Elaboration	Provides convincing, well-elaborated reasons to support the writer's position; includes no examples of faulty logic	Provides two or more moderately elaborated reasons to support the writer's position; includes few examples of faulty logic	Provides several reasons but only one is elaborated; includes several examples of faulty logic	Provides no specific reasons or does not elaborate most ideas indicate faulty logic
Use of Language	Incorporates many transitions to create clarity of expression; includes very few mechanical errors	Incorporates some transitions to help flow of ideas; includes few mechanical errors	Incorporates few transitions; does not connect ideas well; includes many mechanical errors	Does not connect ideas; includes many mechanical errors

Publishing and Presenting • 137

Final Draft

1. Have students read Joseph's final draft as if they were doing a peer review.

2. Make the following points.

   • The topic has been well chosen. Students are surrounded by technology at school and at home, and this essay clearly is pitched at young people whose futures will be greatly affected by technology.

   • The introduction engages the reader and provides a historical context for the debate.

   • The issue Joseph addresses has two sides, and he provides a rounded argument by discussing both sides.

   • The body of the persuasive essay addresses advances in technology that his readers would know about or have experienced.

   • In a strong conclusion, Joseph returns to the original opposing argument and refutes it.

3. Ask students whether they agree or disagree with the argument. Does Joseph allay or increase their fears of technology?

4. What, if any, changes would students recommend to strengthen Joseph's argument or fine-tune the language? How might these suggestions apply to their own writing?

Critical Viewing

Analyze Students may note that the photograph implies a contrast between the convenience of a computer search and the task of looking through a number of books in a library.

7.7 Student Work
IN PROGRESS

FINAL DRAFT

◀ **Critical Viewing**
How does this photograph illustrate the benefits of technology to students conducting research? **[Analyze]**

Life in the Fast Lane Just Got Faster

Joseph Dangelmaier
Archbishop Ryan High School
Philadelphia, Pennsylvania

Technology, like all other inventions, grows and changes to meet new challenges. When ancient humans were cold, they learned how to build fires. When people discovered lakes and oceans, they built boats and ships to cross them. Hundreds or thousands of years after people first dreamed of traveling free from the constraints of land, they developed the airplane. People wanted a faster tool than the abacus for making mathematical calculations, so they developed the processor—then the micro-processor. The need for a more efficient way to transport data inspired the networking technology that we know as the Internet.

There are always ramifications of integrating new technologies into our lives. For example, profound social changes accompanied the first use of fire, the building of ships, and the dawn of aviation. The dangers inherent in cooking on a gas range, riding on a

In his introduction, Joseph provides historical context for his argument as well as details that match the knowledge level of his intended audience of high-school students.

The issue Joseph addresses has two sides. In the second paragraph, he addresses and refutes his opposition.

138 • Persuasive Essay

Students should consider how they might need to change their persuasive essays when reading them aloud to a small group or to the whole class. What changes might they make to sentence length or to the supporting evidence they select? What elements of their writing might they keep to grab the listener's attention, hold interest, or change points of view?

passenger ship, or traveling in an airplane are at least as great as those involved in computer technologies. Yet cooking fires, ocean-borne ships, and aircraft propelled humankind into a new era. The same process occurred again more recently when we entered the computer age.

What benefits has the development of "cutting-edge" technologies already given humankind? Modern technology has improved medicine and health care. Some people who, in an earlier era, would almost certainly be blind can opt for laser surgery to restore their vision. Modern surgical techniques have also made possible the transplant of organs, such as the heart and kidneys, to persons whose lives would, in an earlier era, have ended prematurely.

In this paragraph and the two that follow, Joseph gives three examples of how new technology benefits people.

Technology has also improved education, notably through the use of computers. Students respond more enthusiastically to the colors, interesting sounds, and entertaining animation of a computer program than to a static chalkboard. Computer programs can correct errors in grammar and spelling and can make suggestions for improving writing. It's almost like having a personal tutor close at hand.

The connotations of words like "entertaining," and "static" add an extra push to the job of persuasion.

Enhanced communication is perhaps the greatest benefit of computer technology. Today, communication is faster, easier, and wider reaching than ever before. Students can do research all over the world using the Internet, instead of being restricted to their local library. Writers and painters can present their work in a "virtual" venue where it can be viewed and critiqued by readers and collectors everywhere. Family members can communicate across oceans with something as simple as a plain text e-mail or as elaborate as a two-way, audiovisual, real-time conversation.

Joseph saves the greatest benefit for last, to finish his argument with power.

Consider this hypothetical situation: A fan of a television show wants to remember a quotation from a recent episode. In the past, he would have had to telephone friends and hope that they remembered the quotation—or wait indefinitely for the episode to be aired again. Today, that fan could use a single message—created and sent with a few simple keystrokes—to jog the memories of everyone he knows. Alternatively, he could visit Web sites created by other fans to find the quotation and a whole lot more.

This hypothetical situation will appeal to his audience's interests.

Today, as in every age, some people argue that the risks outweigh the benefits of the new technology. Some of their arguments are compelling. Clearly, we should not leap blindly into a new frontier, such as biotechnology, which could prove not only disappointing but dangerous. Nor should we allow fear to constrain us. Think of the humans who devised the first free-standing shelter. Do we wish that they had clung to the relative safety of a cave?

For a strong conclusion, Joseph returns to the opposing argument, refuting it with a rhetorical question.

Lesson Objectives

► *Lesson Objectives*
1. To write an editorial
2. To organize material to ensure support for idea
3. To use writing processes to develop and revise drafts
4. To publish an editorial for a specific audience

Editorial

Teaching Resources: Writing Support Transparencies, 7-K; Writing Support Activity Book, 7-7

1. Encourage students to peruse television news shows and newspaper op-ed pages for editorials about current events. In this way, students can become familiar with editorial style and inform themselves about events that might make good topics.

2. Suggest that students quickly review their prewriting notes from pages 124–126. Did students generate any ideas that they did not choose to write a persuasive essay about that would offer a good topic for an editorial?

3. Display Transparency 7-K and show students how a chart can help them organize supporting facts and reasons. Give students a copy of the blank form (7-7) for their own use.

4. As they draft their editorials, remind students that the newspaper editorial is typically quite short. Urge students to pay special attention to their introductions and make sure that they both set out their arguments in pithy terms and quickly arrest the reader's attention.

Critical Viewing

Analyze Students may note that most newspapers and news programs have credibility as sources of information and reach large audiences.

Connected Assignment
Editorial

Like other forms of persuasive writing, editorials convey a writer's opinion. **Editorials** usually appear in printed or spoken news media and are the network producers' and newspaper editors' way of expressing their views about a particular issue. As with all persuasion, the views in an editorial must be backed up with reasons and supporting facts or details.

Use the writing process skills outlined in this chapter to generate an editorial on an issue that interests you.

Prewriting To choose a topic, talk with a small group of classmates about the headlines in today's newspaper or about other issues that interest and concern any of you. Add your own ideas to the following list, and then choose a topic:

- television, movie, or music content ratings

- a new law that affects your life

- potential spending of community funds

- the candidates in the next election

- college admission practices

- prices of specific products or services

Once you have chosen a topic, start by developing your point of view. Write it in a single sentence for clarity. Then, in a chart like the one shown on the next page, identify the facts and reasons you already know that support your position. Gather evidence and expand your knowledge at the library, on the Internet, or through personal research. Add additional reasons and facts to your chart.

▲ **Critical Viewing**
Why is a newspaper or a news program an effective forum for presenting an opinion? **[Analyze]**

☑ **ONGOING ASSESSMENT: Prerequisite Skills**

Students may find the following resources from Chapter 7 particularly helpful in completing their editorials.

In the Textbook	Print Resources	Technology
Choosing Your Topic, p.124 Gathering Evidence, p. 128 Drafting, pp. 129–130	*Writing Support Transparencies,* 7-A, 7-D–G *Writing Support Activity Book,* 7-4–5	*Writing Lab* CD-ROM, Persuasion

Support

Thesis: A highway should not be built along the beach.	Increased traffic will affect the coastal wildlife.
	It will interfere with the area's natural beauty.
	More cars will mean more pollution.

Drafting Grab the reader's attention by opening with an anecdote or a vivid example, and convincingly state your view in the first paragraph. Then, proceed through your reasons, saving your most persuasive point for last. As you draft, use effective persuasive language, choosing precise and forceful verbs to convey your commitment to the position.

Although you will address the opposition, stay positive by focusing on selling your view more than on attacking people who disagree with you. End your editorial with a strong conclusion that restates your views and inspires readers to action.

Revising and Editing Return to your brainstorming group, and read your editorial aloud. Ask peers to restate your position in one sentence. Use their comments to revise the structure of your paper. If they disagreed with your views at the outset, ask whether your words changed their views. Most of all, find out whether your readers feel moved to action by your editorial. If not, add persuasive reasons, strengthen your vivid details, and replace flat verbs with more powerful words.

Publishing and Presenting Submit your editorial to your school newspaper. Check future issues of the newspaper to read any letters that respond to your editorial.

Writing Lab CD-ROM

To find the language that will emphasize your position, use the Word Bin activity in the Revising and Editing section of the Persuasive Writing lesson.

Customize for
AP Students

Do students know whether newspaper editorials have ever prompted the reading public to take action about something? Assign students to research this question and report on it to the class.

Customize for
Less Advanced Students

You may wish to have students work in groups to create word banks of forceful verbs. If you have newspapers in class, have the groups scan headlines and editorials to highlight forceful verbs to add to their word banks.

Spotlight on the Humanities

Analyzing Cultures Represented in the Arts

Focus on Theater: The Kabuki Tradition

Because an artist or writer can address a variety of issues in the medium of his choice, the arts are a powerful medium of persuasion. For example, a playwright can make audiences look at situations in a new light and, through the work, inspire change. Kabuki plays, introduced in seventeenth-century Japan, were frequently persuasive. As the theater of the working class, townspeople, and farmers, these plays often centered on conflicts between humanity and the feudal system.

With colorful schemes and spectacular beauty of sets, costumes, and choreography, Kabuki programs ran from morning until evening. Audience interaction with the performers was part of the experience. Chikamatsu Monzaemon is considered the greatest Kabuki playwright and is often referred to as "the Japanese Shakespeare." Developed between the late sixteenth and early eighteenth century, the Kabuki style of Japanese theater is still performed today.

▲ Critical Viewing
What inferences can you draw about Kabuki theater from this painting by Sharaku? [Infer]

Art Connection Eighteenth-century Japanese painter Toshusai Sharaku was known for his famous portraits of Kabuki actors. In fact, 136 out of 146 of his paintings are portraits of actors who were involved in Kabuki drama. His first series of portraits appeared in May 1794. Sharaku once created 140 pieces of art in ten months.

Music Connection In 1976, American composer Stephen Sondheim wrote the book and music to the Broadway show *Pacific Overtures.* The musical reflected the style of Japanese Kabuki theater. *Pacific Overtures* won Tony Awards for Best Costume Design and Best Scenery Design.

Persuasive Writing Activity: Persuasive Essay

Learn more about Kabuki theater, the works of Sharaku, or Sondheim's *Pacific Overtures.* In an essay, write to convince a friend that the art form is worth studying.

Media and Technology Skills

Analyzing Persuasive Messages

Activity: Keep a Product-Placement Log

Advertising was once limited to clearly defined areas. We could see ads in magazines or newspapers or watch commercials on television. However, over the past twenty-five years, marketers have been inserting advertisements into the main action of movies and television shows. These programs now contain subtle advertisements for nearly everything from candy bars, hotels, and restaurants to cell phones, watches, computers, and cars.

Think About It The practice of "product placement" blurs the line between entertainment and advertising. Entertainment is increasingly evolving into a form of advertising. When you think you're just enjoying your favorite show, you might still be a target for advertisers. How can you tell? One good method is by training yourself to detect even the most subtle forms of product placement.

Learn About It Be on the lookout for product placements in three categories. First, logos and brand names often appear on clothing, on posters or banners, or in the background of a fictional setting. Second, characters or announcers often mention a product by name, as in a company-sponsored half-time report. Third, the product serves a function on screen; for example, an action hero might drink a particular brand of orange juice or drive a specific type of sports car.

Watch It With a friend, evaluate the effects of product placement. Watch a big-budget Hollywood movie, noting the products and brand names you see. As you watch, use a chart like this one to note each product placement and its type.

Analyze It With your partner, use your findings as a basis for discussing whether the product placements added to your enjoyment or detracted from the film's overall realism and message. Together, decide whether you would be more or less likely to purchase the products you identified because of their placement on the big screen.

Product	Visual Reference	Spoken Reference	Functional Reference

Sample Product Placement

- Television shows: A character eats a specific breakfast cereal or mentions an Internet site by name.
- Movies: Scenes are set in familiar restaurants, coffee shops, or bookstores
- Sporting events: Athletes wear logos on their uniforms or a specific brand of shoes.

Lesson Objectives

1. To write a persuasive essay in response to a prompt
2. To write appropriately to the audience and purpose of a topic
3. To organize ideas to ensure logical progression and support for ideas
4. To edit and proofread to ensure standard English usage and grammar

Step-by-Step Teaching Guide

Responding to Persuasive Writing Prompts

Teaching Resources: Standardized Test Preparation Workbook, pp. 13–14

1. Urge students to use prewriting time to compose a simple outline to which they can refer during the drafting phase.

2. Remind students that persuasive essay prompts in standardized tests have been written to ensure that the writer has at least two positions to choose from on the topic.

3. Assure students that test examiners are interested only in competent argumentation, not in which point of view they adopt in writing the essay.

4. Caution students to budget time to reread their essays. In the haste to finish work, it is easy to blur connections, introduce faulty logic, or write so quickly that parts of sentences, or even whole sentences, are omitted.

Standardized Test Preparation Workshop

Responding to Persuasive Writing Prompts

The writing prompts on standardized tests often measure your ability to use the elements of persuasive writing. The following are the criteria upon which your writing will be evaluated:

- varied word and sentence choice for the purpose and audience named in the response
- a method of organization that allows you to organize details in a meaningful and coherent sequence, such as pro-and-con or cause-and-effect organization
- appropriate transitions that help ideas flow and create unity and coherence in your persuasive writing
- effective use of description, facts, and other details
- correct grammar, spelling, and punctuation

When writing for a timed test, plan to devote a specified amount of time to prewriting, drafting, revising, and proofreading.

Following is an example of a persuasive writing prompt. Use the suggestions on the following page to help you respond. The clock next to each stage shows a suggested percentage of time to devote to that stage.

Test Tip

- When writing a persuasive essay, always address opposing arguments. By addressing these points and refuting them, you will strengthen your own position.

Sample Writing Prompt

> The only opportunity many people have to see exotic or rare animals is in zoos or other places where animals are held in captivity. While many believe that these animals are protected during their stay in the zoo, others feel that they should be in their natural environment.
>
> Write a persuasive essay for your school newspaper in which you either support or refute the idea of keeping animals in captivity. Be sure to state your position clearly and to support it with reasons and facts.

✏️ TEST-TAKING TIP

Under the pressure of a time limit, student writers often work quickly through the prewriting stage and begin writing too soon. Tell students that the time invested in carefully reading the prompt, developing a strong thesis statement, and organizing supporting ideas will make the actual writing go more smoothly.

Suggest that students use a T-chart or other simple graphic organizer to list the arguments for and against their position. They might also jot down words with strong connections that would make their essay more emphatic.

Prewriting

Allow close to one fourth of your time for prewriting.

Focus Your Purpose The general purpose of persuasive writing is, obviously, to persuade. Before you begin writing, however, you should have a more specific purpose in mind. For example, if you do not support keeping animals in captivity, you may want your audience to sign a petition or join a peaceful gathering against it.

Consider Your Audience As you begin to gather details for your persuasive speech, keep in mind the audience indicated in the prompt. For example, because you are writing for students and teachers, you would use language that consists of formal words, longer sentences, and no slang.

Drafting

Allow almost half of your time for drafting.

Use the Essay Form When drafting your persuasive essay, start with information that states your position. In the body of your essay, identify the main reasons that support and clarify your position. Finally, write a concluding paragraph that sums up the main points of your essay and reinforces your position.

Avoid Faulty Logic As you write, make sure your evidence accurately supports your position. Avoid generalizations that are too broad to be backed up; steer clear of circular reasoning that attempts to support an argument by simply restating it; and don't introduce cause-and-effect statements that are not necessarily true.

Revising, Editing, and Proofreading

Allow almost one fourth of your time to revise and edit. Use the last few minutes to proofread your work.

Make Clear Connections In order for your audience to follow your ideas, use transitional words that indicate the logical connections between ideas. For example, *as a result of, because,* and *caused by* indicate a cause-and-effect relationship, while *most importantly* and *less importantly* indicate the significance you place on ideas.

Make Corrections Review your response for errors. Neatly cross out any details that do not support your purpose, and look for factual mistakes. Change language that is inappropriate for your audience. Check for errors in spelling, grammar, and punctuation. When making changes, draw a line through text that you are deleting, and place it in brackets. Use a caret [^] to indicate the places you would like to add words.

Customize for
Less Advanced Students

If you plan to administer this assessment prompt in class, spend some time the day before reviewing with students some of the key strategies of persuasive writing that they learned in this chapter. You will also want to give suggestions about how much time they should spend on each step of the process when writing with a time limit.

Customize for
AP Students

Suggest that students give themselves more practice in working with time limits by imposing time limits on themselves when writing independently.

Chapter 8

Time and Resource Manager

In-Depth Lesson Plan

	LESSON FOCUS	PRINT AND MEDIA RESOURCES
DAY 1	**Introduction to Advertisements** Students learn key elements of an advertisement and analyze the Model From Literature. (pp. 146–148)	*Writers at Work* **Videotape,** Persuasion *Writing Lab* **CD-ROM,** Persuasion
DAY 2	**Prewriting** Students choose and narrow a topic, consider their audience and purpose, and gather information. (pp. 149–152)	**Teaching Resources** *Writing Support Transparencies,* 8-A–C; *Writing Support Activity Book,* 8-1–3; *Topic Bank for Heterogeneous Classes,* Ch. 8
DAY 3	**Drafting** Students organize their ideas and write their first drafts. (p. 153)	**Teaching Resources** *Writing Support Transparencies,* 8-D; *Writing Support Activity Book,* 8-4
DAY 4	**Revising** Students revise their drafts in terms of overall structure, paragraphs, sentences, and word choice. (pp. 154–156)	**Teaching Resources** *Writing Support Transparencies,* 8-E–F
DAY 5	**Editing and Proofreading; Publishing and Presenting** Students check their work for accuracy and correctness and present their final drafts. (pp. 157–159)	**Teaching Resources** *Scoring Rubrics on Transparency,* Ch. 8; *Writing Assessment and Portfolio Management; Formal Assessment,* Ch. 8

Accelerated Lesson Plan

	LESSON FOCUS	PRINT AND MEDIA RESOURCES
DAY 1	**Drafting** Students review characteristics of an advertisement, select topics, and write drafts. (pp. 146–153)	*Writing Lab* **CD-ROM,** Persuasion **Teaching Resources** *Writing Support Transparencies,* 8-A–D; *Writing Support Activity Book,* 8-1–4
DAY 2	**Revising to Presenting** Students work individually or with peers to revise, edit, and proofread their work for presentation. (pp. 154–159)	**Teaching Resources** *Writing Support Transparencies,* 8-E–F; *Scoring Rubrics on Transparency,* Ch. 8; *Writing Assessment and Portfolio Management; Formal Assessment,* Ch. 8

Options for Adapting Lesson Plans

HOMEWORK

Have students complete any stage of the lesson for homework.

FEATURES

Extend coverage with Connected Assignment (p. 160), Spotlight on the Humanities (p. 162), Media and Technology Skills (p. 163), and the Standardized Test Preparation Workshop (p. 164).

TECHNOLOGY

Students can complete any stage of the lesson on computer. Have them print out their completed work.

INTEGRATED SKILLS COVERAGE

Integrating Grammar
Conventions for Providing Practical Information, SE p. 157

Reading/Writing Connection
Writing Application: Evaluate Word Choice, SE p. 148

Viewing and Representing
Critical Viewing, SE pp. 146, 155, 159, 160, 162
Examining Historical Context in the Arts, SE p. 162
Using Video Technology to Extend Meaning, SE p. 163
ATE p. 161

Workplace Skills
ATE p. 150

BLOCK SCHEDULING

Pacing Suggestions
For 90-minute Blocks
• Have students complete the Prewriting and Drafting stages in a single period.
• Focus one class period on Revising and Editing and Publishing and Presenting. Allow at least 30 minutes for peer revision.

Resources for Varying Instruction
• *Writing Lab* **CD-ROM** If your students have access to hardware, a 90-minute block provides an ideal opportunity for students to work on computer.
• *Writers at Work* **Videotape** Show the Persuasion segment in class.

Professional Development Support
• *How to Manage Instruction in the Block* This Teaching Resource provides management and activity suggestions.

ASSESSMENT SUPPORT

Standardized Test Preparation Workshop, SE p. 164; ATE p. 155
Standardized Test Preparation Workbook, pp. 15–16
Scoring Rubrics on Transparency, Ch. 8
Formal Assessment, Ch. 8
Writing Assessment and Portfolio Management

MEDIA AND TECHNOLOGY

For the Student
• *Writing Lab* **CD-ROM**, Composing, Writing Style

For the Teacher
• *Writers at Work* **Videotape**, Persuasion
• *Resource Pro* **CD-ROM**

MEETING INDIVIDUAL NEEDS

Less Advanced Students ATE pp. 149, 152, 161, 165. See also Ongoing Assessments ATE pp. 151, 152, 156.

AP Students ATE pp. 152, 165

ESL Students ATE p. 149

Gifted and Talented Students ATE p. 147

WRITING AND GRAMMAR WEB SITE

The Interactive Writing and Grammar Web Site provides a wide array of support for students, teachers, and parents. Writing support includes:

• Interactive revision checkers
• Scoring rubrics with complete models

www.phschool.com

LITERATURE CONNECTIONS

Related selection from *Prentice Hall Literature: Timeless Voices, Timeless Themes,* The American Experience:
"The Rockpile," James Baldwin, SE p. 149

Lesson Objectives

1. To write a persuasive advertisement appropriate to audience and purpose
2. To read to appreciate the writer's craft and to discover models for writing
3. To use prewriting strategies to generate ideas and to plan
4. To test and revise a project using questionnaires, group discussions, and feedback forms
5. To use writing to formulate questions, refine topics, and clarify ideas
6. To develop and revise drafts in terms of structure, paragraphs, sentences, and word choice
7. To edit and proofread to ensure standard English usage and grammar
8. To evaluate writing for both mechanics and content
9. To refine selected work for publication

Critical Viewing

Hypothesize Students may think of an upcoming jazz concert or anything related to music.

Chapter

8 Persuasion
Advertisement

Battle of Big Horns, 1988, Phoebe Beasley, Courtesy of the artist

Advertisements in Everyday Life

Newspapers and magazines boast page after page of sales announcements. During most half-hour television programs, eight minutes are devoted to commercials touting new products or services. Imprints on the walls of big-league stadiums—and even the names of many of these arenas—are linked to products. In addition, the layout of many Internet pages makes room for catchy ads to distract Web surfers. In today's commercial environment, you can't go far without seeing an advertisement. As a category of persuasion, advertising seeks to convince an audience to accept a point of view. However, advertising usually has a more focused purpose—to influence what and how much consumers buy.

▲ **Critical Viewing**
In your opinion, what product or service is this artwork suited to advertise? **[Hypothesize]**

146 • Persuasion

⏱ TIME AND RESOURCE MANAGER

Resources
Technology: *Writers at Work* Videotape, Persuasion; *Writing Lab* CD-ROM, Persuasion

In-Depth Coverage	Accelerated Pace
• Cover pp. 146–147 in class. • Analyze the Model From Literature (p. 148) with students, and use it to discuss elements of advertising.	• Students review pp. 146–148 independently. • Discuss elements and types of advertisements.

What Is an Advertisement?

An **advertisement** is a planned communication meant to be seen, heard, or read. It attempts to persuade an audience to buy a product or service, accept an idea, or support a cause. Advertisements may appear in printed form—in newspapers and magazines, on billboards, or as posters or flyers. They may appear on radio or television, as either commercials or public-service announcements. An effective advertisement includes

- a memorable slogan to grab the audience's attention.
- a call to action, which tries to rally the audience to do something.
- details that provide such information as price, location, date, and time.

To see the criteria by which your final advertisement may be judged, preview the Rubric for Self-Assessment on page 158.

Types of Advertisements

From public-service announcements to billboards to product packing, written advertisements come in a variety of types and styles. Several common types of advertisements are described below:

- **Public-service announcements** provide persuasive information to educate audiences about issues of social concern.
- **Billboards** are posted on highways and in train stations where people have limited time to see the ad.
- **Product packaging** involves the use of an item's container to persuade consumers to buy the product.
- **Political campaign literature** presents a candidate and his or her record to educate and persuade voters.

REVIEW
Student Work
IN PROGRESS

In this chapter, you'll see how Catherine Johns, a student at Bel Air High School in El Paso, Texas, used the stages of the writing process to create an advertisement for a fictional business.

Writers in ACTION

Entrepreneur and author David Ogilvy founded one of the world's largest advertising agencies, known today as Ogilvy and Mather. His firm creates ads for a wide range of products and services, including airlines, credit cards, and luxury cars. Ogilvy sounds a cautionary note to the aspiring copywriter:

"You cannot bore people into buying your product, you can only interest them in buying it."

Advertisement • 147

Reading: Evaluate Word Choice

The careful choice of words is of primary concern in ad copywriting. Ask students how the ad on page 148 would change if the copy read "Enjoy Basketball." Discuss the following questions:

What does it mean to "stand up" for someone?

Why is this word choice particularly significant here?

Step-by-Step Teaching Guide

Engage Students Through Literature

1. Explain to students that all forms of writing contain specific elements. Essays have introductions, letters have salutations, and stories have resolutions. Advertisements have specific elements as well.

2. Using the model or an example from a magazine or newspaper, review the following elements that are found in most ads:

   • A slogan or trademarked statement about the product

   • A call to action

   • Specific features of the product that make it appealing

Reading\Writing Connection

Writing Application: Evaluate Word Choice

Remind students that certain words have the power to anger or soothe, inspire or amuse. Careful word choice will be essential in students' persuasive writing.

8.1 Model From Literature

This magazine advertisement introduces audiences to a new Web site called **Wemedia.com**

Wemedia.com is a web site mobilizing the collective voice of the 54 million Americans with disabilities and over $1 trillion in buying power. The bottom line is access. Access to education, healthcare, financial services and employment. Access to the ear of corporate America and Washington D.C. Access to quality of life. Nothing more, nothing less.

Cary Fields, President/CEO

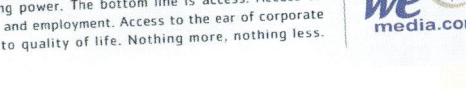

Reading Writing Connection

Writing Application: Evaluate Word Choice
Like the creators of this ad, choose your words carefully to convey a specific impression.

148 • Advertisement

LITERATURE

To see an advertisement the U.S. Navy used to attract recruits during World War I, see "A Graphic Look at the Period," Unit 5.

Set in the largest type size on the page, a compelling slogan, "I'm standing up for you," sets up a contradiction with the photograph.

Copy in a smaller size beneath the slogan provides details to introduce the purpose and content of the new Web site.

The Web address at the end of the ad gives readers the practical information they need to visit the Web site.

8.2 *Prewriting*

Choosing Your Topic

Good advertising conveys enthusiasm. To write a persuasive ad, choose a product, service, or political campaign that excites you. The strategies that follow can help.

Strategies for Generating Topics

1. **Product Survey** With a group, identify the products and services that people in your school enjoy. Develop a questionnaire to identify specific product categories and the most popular brand names. Review the survey results, and choose a product or service to promote in an ad.

2. **Twenty-four Hour List** Pay attention to the products and services you use in a typical day. In a list that breaks the time into hour-long blocks, jot down two or three items you use regularly during each interval. Look over your chart to choose a topic for your advertisement.

Writing Lab CD-ROM

For more help finding a topic, explore the activities and suggestions in the Choosing a Topic section of the Persuasion lesson.

TOPIC BANK

If you're having trouble coming up with your own topic, consider these possibilities:

1. **Advertisement for a Wilderness Adventure** For a print media ad, develop a catchy slogan and text that includes specific details about a trip with an adventure travel company. For example, consider writing an ad to promote backpacking, canoeing, or kayaking trips.

Responding to Literature

2. Read "The Rockpile," by James Baldwin. Create a flyer announcing the start-up of a block association for Roy's block. You can find the story in *Prentice Hall Literature: Timeless Voices, Timeless Themes*, The American Experience.

☑ Cooperative Writing Opportunity

3. **Political Campaign Literature** With a group, choose a real or fictional personality to transform into a candidate for political office. Divide the task of generating or collecting information about the candidate into different areas: experience, background, and contributions to the community. Create a series of print ads to generate support.

Prewriting • 149

⏱ TIME AND RESOURCE MANAGER

Resources
Print: Writing *Support Transparencies*, 8-A–C; *Writing Support Activity Book*, 8-1–3
Technology: *Writing Lab* CD-ROM, Persuasion

In-Depth Coverage	Accelerated Pace
• Work through all prewriting activities in class.	• Discuss prewriting strategies with students. • Allow students to choose and narrow topics independently. • Have students work with partners to focus on audience and gathering details.

Prewriting: Use Cubing to Narrow a Topic

Teaching Resources: Writing Support Transparencies, 8-A; Writing Support Activity Book, 8-1

1. Explain to students that when they have selected a product or service to advertise, they must identify how it will appeal to an audience.

2. Display Transparency 8-A to demonstrate that cubing works by making writers consider a subject in six different ways.

3. Give students copies of the cubing activity page (8-1) for their own use and allow class time for them to complete the activity.

4. Once they have filled in each side of the cube, give students time to share ideas and get responses from one another.

5. Ask students why each of the six cubing questions is important. (Combined, they help the students examine an object from all sides. This will give them an in-depth understanding of it.)

Integrating Workplace Skills

Explain that collaborative brainstorming is used not only in advertising but in many other fields. Any time a new idea or a solution to a problem is needed, brainstorming may be the optimal method for coming up with a solution. The more people involved in the process, the more opportunities there are to come up with creative ideas.

8.2

Narrowing Your Topic

The real work of advertising is not in choosing a topic, but in deciding which part of the product will appeal to an audience. After you have decided on a topic, identify what your ad will convey about it. The cubing strategy allows you to examine a topic from several angles.

Use Cubing to Narrow a Topic

Study your topic using these six methods:

1. **Describe It** Explain the physical attributes of your topic to an audience who has never seen it.
2. **Associate It** Show how your topic relates to something else or how it reminds you of something else.
3. **Apply It** Tell how your topic can be used.
4. **Analyze It** Separate your topic into smaller parts.
5. **Compare and Contrast It** Explain how other items are similar and different from yours.
6. **Argue for It** While traditional cubing lets you provide reasons to promote or reject an idea, narrow this cubing angle to collect only positive reasons to sell your product or service.

Student Work
IN PROGRESS

Name: *Catherine Johns*
Bel Air High School
El Paso, TX

Cubing to Narrow a Topic

Catherine chose to promote a company that offers classes in foreign language instruction. When she addressed the "Apply" angle of cubing, she narrowed her topic to focus on this service's usefulness to business professionals.

Describe:

Associate:

Apply: You can do many things with a foreign language, including travel more easily and communicate with people in different cultures. The latter is very important in today's global economy. International business is expanding at a rapid pace. To succeed in the international arena, corporate executives need to know the language spoken in countries where they do business.

150 • Advertisement

Considering Your Audience and Purpose

Remember that the purpose of advertising is to convince people to buy a product or service or to support a candidate for office. The content and appearance of your advertisement must be directed to convince a specific audience.

Identify the Target Audience

There are many ways to sell a product. To be most effective, take the time to figure out whom your advertisement will reach. For example, you may want to reach classmates, parents, or a group of experts. The chart below shows how knowing your target audience will allow you to include details and use language that will appeal to them.

Audience	Appeal	Details to Emphasize
Classmates	Show them it's FUN	exciting, cool, relaxing, interesting
Parents	Show them it has VALUE	money-saving, time-saving, safe, educational
Experts	Show them it has QUALITY	tested, well-built, top-of-the-line

Writing Lab CD-ROM

Use the Audience Profile activity to help you identify your audience and target your advertisement effectively.

Step-by-Step Teaching Guide

Prewriting: Identify Target Audience

Teaching Resources: Writing Support Transparencies, 8-B; Writing Support Activity Book, 8-2

1. Ask students to name the ultimate purpose of any ad (to convince readers, viewers, or listeners to take some action).

2. Display Transparency 8-B. Explain that they must first specify their audience, the people they expect to use their product or service (teenagers, adults, children, experts).

3. Next, explain that students need to identify the single greatest appeal of their product. Is it fun? Is it delicious? Is it valuable? Is it educational? Would it appeal to their intended audience? If not, perhaps they should target a different audience.

4. Give students copies of the graphic organizer (8-2) and have them list information about audience, appeal, and details to emphasize.

✓ **ONGOING ASSESSMENT: Monitor and Reinforce**

If students have difficulty with subject-verb agreement, you may find it necessary to review the following to assure coverage of prerequisite knowledge.

Once students determine their target audience, have them make a list of five to ten questions about what that group values. (Sample questions: How do they spend most of their time? What are their major responsibilities? What do they care about most in life? What are

their goals?) Then, have them answer the questions and tailor the words in their ads to match their answers. (For example, if the audience values safety and responsibility, use words that convey these qualities.)

⏱ **TIME SAVERS!**

 Writing Support Transparencies
Use the transparencies for Chapter 8 to facilitate teaching of strategies.

 Writing Support Activity Book
Use the graphic organizers for Chapter 8 to facilitate student planning.

Teaching Resources: Writing Support Transparencies, 8-C; Writing Support Activity Book, 8-3

1. Explain to students that word choice is important in all kinds of writing, but it is especially important in advertisements, which have limited space. In ads, every word stands out and every word counts.

2. Display the Word Web transparency (8-C) to show how to generate words for an ad. Ask students which words in the example seem most important.

3. Give students a copy of the graphic organizer (8-3) to help them generate words for their ads. After students complete Word Webs for their products, direct them to choose the words on the web that will best promote their products. Have them circle or underline these words.

4. Remind students that in persuasive communication, it is essential to support claims with proof. Allow students time to focus on the features of their products that support the claims they intend to make.

Customize for
Less Advanced Students

Have students highlight words from car advertisements in newspapers and magazines. Do any words in the ads also appear in the example Word Web on page 152?

Customize for
AP Students

Suggest that students create word webs based on the emotional connotations of words. Ask them to monitor radio, television, and print ads for words that evoke confidence, pride, safety and reassurance, worry, fear, or anger.

8.2

Gathering Details

Before you begin writing your advertisement, gather lively and powerful words to describe your product. Then, identify the product features that deserve these words in your ad.

Build a Parts-of-Speech Word Web

In a Word Web like the one shown here, gather details about your topic. Write your main idea or topic in the center of it. Then, identify the nouns, verbs, adverbs, adjectives, and interjections you might use to describe your subject. To make your Word Web even more useful, use a thesaurus to find exactly the right words for each category.

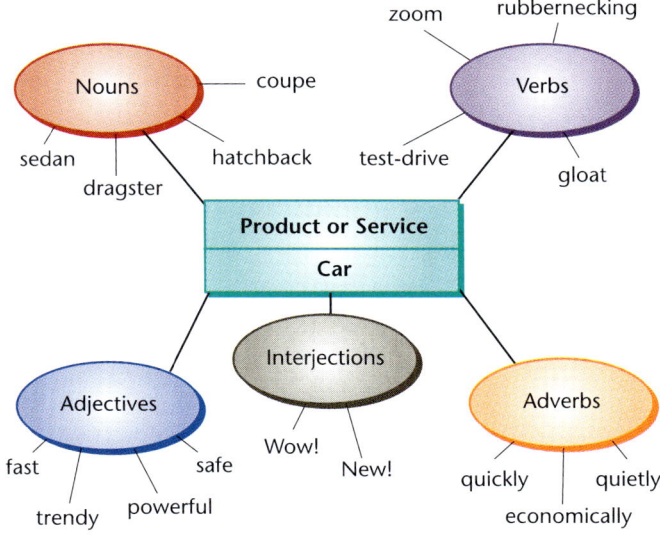

Identify the Features to Promote

Whether you've decided to announce that your topic is sporty or practical, high-fashion or high-tech, you need to back up that assertion with specific references. For each concept you want to convey, jot down the features of your topic that support your idea. Use these suggestions to guide your prewriting:

- **To show a product is practical:** Gather details that address cost and ease of use. Show that the product is necessary, not frivolous.

- **To show a product is fun:** Collect the specific information to show what makes the product exciting or enjoyable.

152 • Advertisement

Writing Lab CD-ROM

To find persuasive words to help you emphasize the main features of your topic, use the Word Bins in the Persuasion lesson.

 ONGOING ASSESSMENT: Monitor and Reinforce

If students are having difficulty gathering details about their topics, try using the following strategy.

Have students write a short description of their topic and give it to a partner. Then, have the partner read it and write down five questions he or she has about the topic. These questions should elicit important information about the topic that they could not glean from reading the description. By answering these questions, students will be forced to identify details about their topics that are of interest to readers.

8.3 Drafting

Shaping Your Writing

Create a Slogan

Draft a slogan to shape the details you'll include in your advertisement. Your slogan should grab the audience's attention and make them want to learn more about the product.

SAMPLE SLOGANS

"There are a zillion things to do at the Seattle Street Fair."

"All Over the Map Bookstore—your first stop in travel."

Providing Elaboration

Once you have created an attention-grabbing slogan, it is time to select points to illuminate in your advertisement.

Use a Pentad to Identify Key Points

Because every word in an advertisement counts, you must identify the essential points to illuminate in a limited space. Use a pentad like the one below to develop your elaboration.

Collaborative Writing Tip

Share your lists of slogans with a group. In exchange for a quick first response to your ideas, help the others in your group decide what slogan strategies are most successful and which need more refining.

Student Work IN PROGRESS

Name: *Catherine Johns*
Bel Air High School
El Paso, TX

Using a Pentad

Catherine used a pentad to identify the information she will use to elaborate her slogan: "Everyone can learn another language."

Actors:
Who does the action?
business owners, executives

Purposes:
Why is it done?
ensure success in foreign markets

Acts:
What is done?
learn languages through intensive training

Agencies:
How is it done?
training in five sessions

Scenes:
When or where is it done?
on site, anywhere in the United States

Drafting • 153

Step-by-Step Teaching Guide

Drafting: Use a Pentad to Identify Key Points

Teaching Resources: Writing Support Transparencies 8-D; Writing Support Activity Book 8-4

1. Allow students to brainstorm for slogans individually or in groups. Remind them that the point is to grab the audience's attention.

2. Bring in sample slogans from magazines and newspapers and discuss them with students. Have them point out some strategies that make a slogan successful (vivid adjectives, a clever title or pun, rhyming words, brevity, etc.).

3. Next, have students create a pentad to help elaborate on the ideas for the ads. Display Transparency 8-D to show that each arm of the pentad addresses a question about the product: who, what, when or where, why, and how.

4. Give students a blank copy of the pentad (8-4), or have students create their own. When the pentads are complete, direct students to review all of their prewriting materials and then draft an advertisement. At this time you may wish to discuss your criteria for assessment (examples: catchy slogan, correct target audience, genuine appeal, support of claims, good word choice, visual elements). Refer students to the evaluation rubric on page 158.

TIME AND RESOURCE MANAGER

Resources
Print: *Writing Support Transparencies*, 8-D; *Writing Support Activity Book*, 8-4
Technology: *Writing Lab* CD-ROM, Persuasion

In-Depth Coverage	Accelerated Pace
• Allow students time to develop slogans and get feedback from classmates. • Demonstrate and work through the Pentad Elaboration activity. • Have students write their drafts in class.	• Have students independently review p. 153. • Have students write their drafts as homework. • Respond to individual drafting questions as needed.

TIME SAVERS!

 Writing Support Transparencies
Use the transparencies for Chapter 8 to facilitate teaching of strategies.

 Writing Support Activity Book
Use the graphic organizers for Chapter 8 to facilitate student planning.

Step-by-Step Teaching Guide

Revising: Color-Coding to Improve Layout

Teaching Resources: Writing Support Transparencies, 8-E

1. Have students evaluate their drafts for layout and visual impact. Ask students the following questions.

   Is the layout interesting? Does it direct attention to the most important words?

2. Remind them that consumers will not read the fine print if the ad does not capture their attention in the first place.

3. Display Transparency 8-E. In the model, the writer highlights her strongest points with a marker. She then reviews the highlighted points to make sure they stand out visually. Ask students to name ways they can draw attention to the main points of their ad (use of color, bullets, font size, placement).

8.4 Revising

After drafting your advertisement, begin looking for ways to improve it. In the revising stage, check to make sure that your slogan is catchy and your information persuasive. From the big picture of an overall concept, move toward the small details, such as sentence structure and word choice. Your reward will be an ad that prompts your audience to answer your call to action with a resounding "Yes!"

Revising Your Overall Structure

Review Visual Layout

Before you polish the copy in your ad, devote attention to its visual layout. Remember that visual appeal and persuasive copy work together to create a positive audience response.

▶ **REVISION STRATEGY**
Color-Coding to Improve Layout

Review the text of your advertisement. Use a highlighter to mark the strongest points you want to convey. Make sure that the reader notices these points by making them stand out in some way. Consider placement or font size. Alternatively, use color or bullets to call readers' attention to these key points.

⊙ Technology Tip

Explore the wide range of fonts, point sizes, and design styles available in your word-processing program. Select those that will increase the persuasive power of your ad.

Student Work IN PROGRESS

Name: Catherine Johns
Bel Air High School
El Paso, TX

Improving Layout Through Color-Coding
Catherine color-coded her main ideas to evaluate the layout of her ad.

I can make this a leaner bulleted list.

ILTC benefits include a ==teacher-student ratio== of one to five; that's three language and culture experts for every 15 students; 30 instructional days of intensive language and cultural awareness training; and ==on-site instruction,== anywhere in the United States.

When she saw key ideas buried in a paragraph, Catherine decided to try another approach.

⏱ TIME AND RESOURCE MANAGER

Resources
Print: *Writing Support Transparencies*, 8-E–F
Technology: *Writing Lab* CD-ROM, Persuasion

In-Depth Coverage	Accelerated Pace
• Work through Color-Coding and Parallel Structure activities in class. • Have students do the Focus Group activity on p. 156 in class.	• Have students independently review and apply the strategies on pp. 154–156. • Respond to individual revising issues as needed.

Revising Your Paragraphs and Sentences

Use Parallel Structure

Once you are satisfied with the layout of your ad, return to the copy. Check it for clarity and ease of reading. Consider using parallel structures—expressing similar details using similar grammatical structures—to make the information you have presented easier for your readers to absorb.

PARALLEL ADJECTIVES: This drink is *nutritious*, *refreshing*, and *economical*.

PARALLEL VERBS: Enjoy it while you are *relaxing*, *talking*, and *laughing*.

PARALLEL PHRASES: Take it with you *to the gym*, *to the park*, *on the go*!

▶ REVISION STRATEGY
Identifying Sentence Types to Create Parallelism

Identify the sentence types you have used in your advertisement. In a list, indicate the function of each sentence—declarative, imperative, interrogative, or exclamatory. Evaluate this list to see whether you have used parallel structure. Make corrections if necessary. In this example, highlighted material shows a problem in parallelism and its solution.

EXAMPLE: Cool off with Freddie's Fruit Smoothie. Choose black raspberry, strawberry, or lemon-lime. You may wish to add a dollop of whipped cream for even more enjoyment.

ANALYSIS: The first two sentences in this paragraph are imperatives. As a declarative, the last sentence is not parallel with the others. Revising it strengthens the impact of the ad.

REVISION: Cool off with Freddie's Fruit Smoothie. Choose black raspberry, strawberry, or lemon-lime. Add a dollop of whipped cream for even more enjoyment.

 Learn More

For more on the four functions of sentences, see Chapter 20.

▶ **Critical Viewing** What features of these fruitful concoctions would you emphasize in an advertisement? [Synthesize]

Revising • 155

Step-by-Step Teaching Guide

Revising: Use Parallel Structure

1. Explain that parallelism requires the repetition of a grammatical form within or among sentences. One can repeat word types, phrases, or clauses. Review the examples on page 155.

2. Write the following example on the board.

   It's great at work. It's great when you play. It's great for the end of the day!

   Then, have them revise the sentences using parallelism:

   It's great at work, at play, or at the end of the day!

   Ask students why the long sentence is easier to read than three short sentences.

3. Tell students to consider the function of their sentences and stick to a single function in a paragraph. Whether they use imperatives, declaratives, interrogatives, or exclamations, they should keep to one functional mode.

4. Allow students time to revise their drafts using this method.

Critical Viewing

Synthesize Students may choose the natural fruit ingredients that provide both a tangy taste and a healthful energy boost.

155

Revising Your Word Choice

Add Modifiers to Sell

You've probably realized by now that using vivid modifiers is the key to writing a persuasive advertisement. Lively adjectives, in particular, can make your ad more successful.

▶ **REVISION STRATEGY**
Underlining Nouns to Assess Adjectives

Underline all the nouns in your draft. Check each noun to see if it is modified by an adjective or adjective phrase. Then, add modifiers where you think they will increase the power of your advertisement. Alternatively, consider choosing a stronger noun to convey your idea.

Language Lab CD-ROM

For more on using modifiers, see Identifying Adjectives and Adverbs in the Handbook.

Student Work
IN PROGRESS

Name: Catherine Johns
Bel Air High School
El Paso, TX

Adding Modifiers to Strengthen Audience Appeal
Catherine added modifiers to strengthen the appeal of her advertisement. Notice that she used adverbs as well as adjectives.

of the fastest growing and most profitable
ILTC clients include many companies in North America.

Peer Review

Focus Groups

When people in the advertising industry create product campaigns, they often test their concepts before launching the ads. Try one of their techniques: the focus group. Show your revised ad to a group of classmates, and listen as they comment on its effects. To get feedback on specific points of concern, formalize the review with these discussion questions:

- What do you think the product is?
- Would you buy the product based on this advertisement?
- What aspect of the advertisement stands out most?

156 • Advertisement

8.5 Editing and Proofreading

Errors in grammar, usage, or mechanics can undermine your audience's trust in the product or service your advertisement promotes. To make your advertisement error-free, check your work carefully before creating a final draft.

Focusing on Spelling

Check that each word in your advertisement is spelled correctly. To be sure that you read each word, check the advertisement from the last word to the first. Be especially careful with the spelling of names and addresses.

✔ Spelling Tip

Beware of errors that a spell-check function will not catch, such as homophones like *their* and *there* and proper nouns.

Grammar in Your Writing
Conventions for Providing Practical Information

As you proofread, make sure you have used commonly accepted conventions for writing addresses, telephone numbers, dates, and times.

Addresses Use one line for the street address and another one for city and state. Use a comma to separate the city and state, but do not use one to separate the state from the ZIP Code.

Example: 1000 Maple Avenue
Dallas, Texas 75205

Web addresses Write the exact wording of the address, showing the specific punctuation and spacing of the domain name.

Examples: www.phschool.com   www.senate.gov

Telephone numbers Use parentheses, a hyphen, or a slash to separate the area code from the main number. Use a hyphen before the last four digits.

Examples: (847) 555-4704 or 847-555-4704 or 847/555-4704

Dates Capitalize the month. Place a comma between the day of the month and the year.

Example: January 30, 2003

Find It in Your Reading Review the ad for **Wemedia.com** on page 148. Identify the conventions used in the ad for providing practical information.

Find It in Your Writing Proofread your advertisement to make sure that you have correctly written addresses, telephone numbers, dates, and times.

For more on postal abbreviations to be used in addresses, see the Abbreviations Guide.

• 157

Publishing and Presenting

1. Select a presentation option from page 158 or ask students to brainstorm for other means of publishing their advertisements.

2. Tell students that the ads must be accompanied by a note indicating the names of the writer or writers and a brief description of how they chose the product.

ASSESS and CLOSE

Assessment

Teaching Resources: Scoring Rubrics on Transparency, Ch. 8; Writing Assessment and Portfolio Management; Formal Assessment, Ch. 8

1. Display the Scoring Rubric transparency and review the criteria in class.

2. Before students proceed with self-assessment, you may wish to review Catherine's final draft on page 159. Have students score the final draft in one or more of the rubric categories.

3. In addition to student self-assessment, you may wish to:

   • score student essays yourself using the rubric and scoring models from *Writing Assessment and Portfolio Management*.

   • review the Standardized Test Preparation Workshop on pages 164–165 and have students complete the practice items.

   • administer the Chapter 8 assessment from *Formal Assessment* in the Teaching Resources to measure students' grasp of the concepts presented.

8.6 Publishing and Presenting

Building Your Portfolio

Advertisements are meant to be shared. Consider these ideas for publishing and presenting your ad:

1. **Create a Newsletter** Prepare a newsletter that reports issues and activities in your class or school. Incorporate the advertisements that you and your classmates have prepared. To avoid confusion, include an article or note informing readers that the ads promote fictional products and services.

2. **Design a Display** Post your advertisements on a bulletin board entitled "Copywriters in Our Class." Add a note to each ad that explains how the writer developed the ad.

Reflecting on Your Writing

Write a reflection on your writing process. Use these questions to get your ideas started:

• How did your understanding of persuasive writing change or develop as a result of writing an advertisement?

• Having written an ad yourself, what strategies for evaluating claims in advertisements would you recommend to a friend?

 Internet Tip

To see model ads scored according to this rubric, go to **www.phschool.com**

Rubric for Self-Assessment

Use the following criteria to evaluate your persuasive advertisement.

	Score 4	Score 3	Score 2	Score 1
Audience and Purpose	Presents effective slogan; clearly addresses persuasive task	Presents good slogan; addresses persuasive task	Presents slogan; minimally addresses persuasive task	Does not present slogan; shows lack of attention to persuasive task
Organization	Uses layout and design to show clear, consistent organizational strategy	Uses layout and design to show clear organizational strategy with few inconsistencies	Uses inconsistent organizational strategy; creates illogical presentation	Demonstrates lack of organizational strategy; creates confusing presentation
Elaboration	Successfully combines words and images to provide convincing, unified support for a position	Combines words and images to provide unified support for a position	Includes some words or images that detract from a position	Uses words and images that do not support a position
Use of Language	Successfully communicates an idea through clever use of language and parallelism; includes very few mechanical errors	Conveys an idea through adequate use of language and parallelism; includes few mechanical errors	Misuses language and lessens impact of ideas; includes many mechanical errors	Demonstrates poor use of language and confuses meaning; includes many mechanical errors

158 • Advertisement

☑ ONGOING ASSESSMENT: Assess Mastery

Use one of the following options to assess final drafts of students' advertisements.

Self-Assessment Ask students to score their advertisements using the rubric provided. Then, have students write a single paragraph reflecting on the most valuable thing they learned in completing this project.

Teacher Assessment You may wish to use the rubric and the scoring models provided in *Writing Assessment and Portfolio Management* to score the advertisements.

8.7 Student Work IN PROGRESS

FINAL DRAFT

Catherine Johns
Bel Air High School
El Paso, Texas

"Todos son capaces de aprender otro idioma."
"Everyone can learn another language."

The International Language Training Center (ILTC)

ILTC offers innovative and individualized programs for business owners and corporate executives. In just five sessions of intensive language and cultural awareness training, we can teach you—and your team—the basic skills that you need to succeed in your designated foreign market.

ILTC benefits include:
- a teacher-student ratio of one to five
- on-site instruction, anywhere in the United States

ILTC clients are among the fastest growing and most profitable companies in North America. Become one of them. Call today.

The International Language Training Center (ILTC)
2344 Palomino Drive, Suite 214
El Paso, Texas 79336
915-555-1805
ILTC@address.org

Catherine begins her ad with a slogan in Spanish; by translating it, she introduces the service ILTC provides.

◀ **Critical Viewing**
How does this image suit Catherine's advertisement? **[Analyze]**

Varied font sizes and styles strengthen the visual appeal.

Information selected for its persuasive power tells what makes ILTC unique.

The ad ends with a call to join the winners by becoming an ILTC client—today.

Practical details give readers the information they need to sign up.

159

Connected Assignment
Ad Campaign

In an **ad campaign**, advertisers coordinate their persuasive advertising messages in an organized plan of radio, television, print, Internet, billboard, and other media ads. Often, the pieces of an ad campaign will share a particular focus, such as the introduction of a new product, the participation of a celebrity spokesperson, or a sale.

Use the writing process guidelines suggested below to create your own advertising campaign for a product you enjoy.

Prewriting Choose a product that you believe is suited to a media blitz. For example, advertisements for products like food, restaurants, cars, and movies can translate well into many forms. However, some specialized products, such as filing cabinets and silver polish, may not be appropriate for ads in a variety of media. Consider the following topic suggestions:

- **Entertainment** offers a variety of potential topics. Consider a television show, concert, or a new movie to promote.
- **Health and beauty products** are the frequent subject of competitive advertising campaigns because they are a common purchase. List the shampoo, toothpaste, or vitamins you use, and consider one to feature in your campaign.
- **Web sites** provide a wealth of opportunities for persuasive ads. Consider search engines, shopping sites, or home pages for communities and agencies. Identify your favorite Web site, and consider it as the focus of your ad campaign.
- **Big-ticket items**—such as cars, computers, vacations, or stereo equipment—provide another opportunity for your creative ideas. Choose an item you'd buy if you suddenly won the lottery, and design an ad campaign.

Once you choose a product for your campaign, plan the appeal that might be most effective. You might provide information to show the product is economical, popular, or exciting. Then, focus on the product itself. Pinpoint a feature or an angle to highlight in the campaign. Record it in the main idea section of a chart like the one shown on the next page. Below the main idea, list media outlets in which you'd want to advertise.

▲ **Critical Viewing**
What products or services are well suited to newspaper advertisements? [Analyze]

🔲 **Research Tip**

Make an effort to locate elements of the same advertising campaign in different media. Note the similarities and differences you see, and apply your findings to the advertising campaign you develop.

160 • Advertisement

```
┌──────────────────────────────┐
│        PRODUCT:              │
│    NEW TEEN MAGAZINE         │
├──────────────────────────────┤
│         MAIN IDEA            │
│  New magazine understands teens │
│  and has the articles and info they want. │
└──────────────────────────────┘
```

Internet	Electronic	Print
Web page	Radio	Billboards
Ads on booksellers' sites	TV	Newspapers
	Preview of spot before teen movie or video	

Drafting Before planning individual advertisements for each medium, identify the common information each advertisement will include. Experiment with slogans that communicate your main idea. Use punchy language that quickly and vividly communicates your message.

Once you have the main ideas down, create advertisements for at least three media from your plan. To plan and create the campaign, write detailed scripts or produce print advertisements. Use the following tips to make the best use of each medium you address:

- **Newspaper or Magazine Ads** Limit the amount of text you use, and find interesting images to help convey your message.
- **Radio Spots** While you might plan to use sound effects, the words you use must communicate your ideas. Keep the advertisement interesting and short.
- **Television Commercials** Use live action to tap television's strengths. For example, you might include a video of a car driving down a country road and use a voice-over to provide product information. Alternatively, you could script a short scene with actors in a supermarket.

Revising and Editing Present your advertising campaign to a peer group. Ask them to role-play a client meeting in which you act as the creative director of an advertising agency and your peers play the part of the client. Present your media choices, explain your slogan, and show your three sample ads. Incorporate the group's comments as you tighten up any wordiness or add more information.

Publishing and Presenting Before creating your final product, check facts, such as phone numbers and prices, for accuracy. Share your work with classmates. Then, include copies of the print ads and scripts for the radio and television ads in your portfolio.

4. After students have planned their overall campaign, they should create a slogan and three ads. Each ad should be for a different medium.

5. Allow adequate time for students to develop and revise their campaigns and set aside class time for presentations.

Integrating Viewing and Representing Skills

Media Students may wish to publish their campaigns in one of the following ways: on posterboard (students display print ads, radio scripts, and TV storyboards), orally (students perform their broadcast ads in front of the class, using props to illustrate the ads), or on printed matter (students design flyers using a word processing package and distribute their print ads). Ask students to brainstorm for ways to represent ideas. Remind them that the focus of their ad campaign might influence how they publish it.

Customize for
Less Advanced Students

Students will benefit from utilizing models of ads and creating word maps and storyboards to represent them. Help students address the layout of print ads for visual impact. What catches their eye first in an ad? How will their ads capture attention?

Lesson Objectives

1. To learn about the source of a media production
2. To analyze relationships and ideas represented in various media
3. To recognize how visual and sound techniques convey messages in media
4. To write an advertisement for a musical

Step-by-Step Teaching Guide

Examining Historical Context in the Arts

1. Choose one of the Spotlight elements for class discussion, or have students work in groups on the element of their choice. They can find the Gershwins' music on audiotape or compact disk.

2. Students who play instruments or sing might find the score of the opera and perform one of the songs for the class.

3. Interested students might research the lives of DuBose Heyward, Dorothy Dandridge, and the Gershwin brothers, and present their findings to the class.

4. If students want to view and write an ad for another film musical, they might consider *An American in Paris* (1951), which features many Gershwin songs.

Viewing and Representing

Activity Give students the opportunity to make class presentations of their ads, explaining why they decided on a particular angle to appeal to present-day audiences. Encourage them to use audio and visual media as appropriate.

Critical Viewing

Contrast Students might suggest that the greatest difference between a movie production and a stage version of an opera is the set.

Spotlight on the Humanities

Examining Historical Context in the Arts

Focus on Opera: *Porgy and Bess*

Before an opera, play, or film opens, it is usually promoted by an ad campaign to attract audiences. In all its versions, the opera *Porgy and Bess* has been no different. Based upon DuBose Heyward's 1925 novel *Porgy*, the classic American opera was written by Heyward (1885–1940) and the musical team of George Gershwin (1898–1937) and Ira Gershwin (1896–1983). *Porgy and Bess* premiered in New York in 1935. The opera is still performed today all over the world. Set on the waterfront in Charleston, South Carolina, the opera captures the lives and loves of the African American community on "Catfish Row." The Gershwin score contains such memorable songs as "I Got Plenty o' Nothin'" and "Summertime."

Music Connection In addition to their work on *Porgy and Bess*, George and Ira Gershwin composed many songs that are part of the canon of American show tunes. They co-wrote "Someone to Watch Over Me," for the musical *Oh, Kay!* (1926), and the title song for *Strike Up the Band* (1927). George Gershwin moved beyond musical theater to write *Rhapsody in Blue* (1924), an orchestral composition that played a role in the growing popularity of jazz.

Film Connection Dorothy Dandridge (1922–1965) portrayed the role of Bess in the 1959 screen version of *Porgy and Bess*. Dandridge was the first African American woman to sing at the Waldorf Astoria hotel in New York. However, she dreamed of becoming a film star. After playing several smaller roles, she landed the title role in the film *Carmen Jones* (1954). The film was a great success, and Dandridge was nominated for an Academy Award in 1954. Achieving her dream, she commanded a salary equal to the most popular stars in Hollywood at that time.

Persuasive Writing Activity: Advertisement for a Musical

Locate and watch a copy of the 1959 film *Porgy and Bess* or another popular film musical produced before 1980. After you watch it, write an advertisement for the film to attract a wide audience. Include information to explain the historical context of the film, and decide on an angle that will appeal to today's audiences.

162 • Advertisement

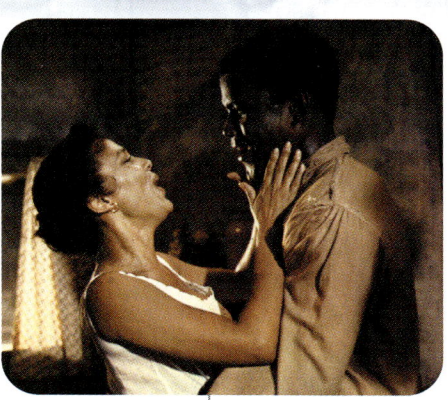

▲ **Critical Viewing**
This still from the movie version of *Porgy and Bess* shows the lead artists, Dorothy Dandridge and Sidney Poitier. In what ways would a movie production of an opera be different from a stage version? **[Contrast]**

Media and Technology Skills

Using Video Technology to Extend Meaning

Activity: Creating a Video Advertisement

Advertising professionals spend thousands of dollars on spots that air for thirty seconds! As they would quickly tell you, technology has changed the face of advertisements. While you don't need to spend nearly so much money to produce a video ad, learning the bells and whistles of your video camera can help you develop an advertisement with graphics, sound, and other special effects. These features of the video camera can turn your ad into a professional-quality product that grabs viewer's attention.

Learn About It Read the directions to your video camera to find out just what it can do. If you are a complete novice, limit your study to the most common features: the fade, pause, and zoom options. Each lets you control the images viewers see. Explore ways to use sound for special effect, too. You can add familiar music to create a mood or experiment with different voice-over styles to lend authority or emotion to your ad.

Plan It Choose an ad you've created for school. Plan to make it into a video by drawing or describing a potential scene. Then, work with a partner to brainstorm for different possible special effects. Discuss the impact each would have on viewers. List your ideas in an organizer like the one shown here:

Scene:	
Special Effects Desired:	**Video Techniques:**

Shoot It Consider the video techniques listed in the sidebar. Then, record your ad several times, experimenting with different special effects until you're pleased.

Video Techniques in Ads

- Fade to black, and then show a single word or image for impact.
- Show user reactions, highlighted with voice-overs.
- Zoom in on the product at work.
- Change focus to show a positive or negative impact on the user.
- Overlay text or graphics on your images by shooting against a backdrop.

1. To recognize how visual techniques and design convey messages in media
2. To use video technology to communicate a message
3. To create a video advertisement

Step-by-Step Teaching Guide

Using Video Technology to Extend Meaning

Teaching Resources: Writing Support Transparencies, 8-H, Writing Support Activity Book, 8-6

1. Have students form groups to complete this project. Each group will need to assign roles for writing the script, directing, operating the camera, creating necessary props, and acting.

2. You might ask students to briefly discuss the techniques of television ads they have recently seen and to comment on their effectiveness. If your library or media center has a videotape collection of award-winning commercials, you may wish to show several to the class.

3. Review with students the video ad techniques shown in the box.

4. Display Transparency 8-H and give students copies of the blank organizer to use in planning their video advertisements.

5. Allow class time for presentation of their finished projects.

Lesson Objectives

1. To distinguish the purposes of an advertisement
2. To get the main idea of a persuasive text
3. To evaluate the persuasive techniques of media messages such as glittering generalities, logical fallacies, and symbols

---

Step-by-Step Teaching Guide

Analyzing Persuasive Texts

Teaching Resources: Standardized Test Preparation Workbook, pp. 15–16

1. Review the four evaluation methods with students.

2. Have students review the two sample test items and discuss the answers and explanations.

3. Students may need a review of the following terms:

   - *Loaded language* (words or phrases that have strong emotional connotations, either positive or negative)

   - *Circular reasoning* (an argument that attempts to prove its point by restating it in other words)

   - *Bandwagon appeal* (a statement based on the desire of people to conform or be part of a group)

   - *Overgeneralization* (an inference too broad or sweeping for its limited supporting evidence)

   - *Questionable cause-and-effect reasoning* (statements that mistake a time-order relationship for a cause-and-effect relationship)

4. Tell students that the key to success in analyzing a persuasive text is careful reading. Suggest that students mark questionable statements in the text as they read.

Standardized Test Preparation Workshop

Analyzing Persuasive Texts

Standardized test questions often measure your ability to evaluate an advertisement objectively. As a reader, you must discern what information is valid by seeing past the attempts to persuade you. The following are methods that will help you evaluate an advertisement:

- Decide whether the argument or claim is supported.

- Search for facts.

- Check for missing information, vague statements, or partial truths.

- Recognize examples of faulty logic that cause you to draw false conclusions.

The following sample test items will give you practice with questions that present you with advertisements for analysis.

Test Tip

When evaluating it is just as important to question what has been left out of a persuasive text, as it is to examine what is there.

Sample Test Items	Answers and Explanations

Directions: Read the passage, and then choose the letter of the best answer to each question.
 	
Join Healthwise Gym for $15 a month!!! A lifetime membership includes use of exercise equipment, aerobic classes, and facilities. Beat the crowds. Call and join today.
 	
1 What important information has been left out of this advertisement?
  A The requirements of a lifetime membership
  B The privileges a membership includes
  C The price to be paid per month
  D The name of the gym
	The correct answer is *A.* The requirements of a lifetime membership are not described. The privileges described in the passage are those of any membership and not necessarily those of a lifetime membership that costs $15 per month.

2 What type of unreasonable appeal does "Beat the crowds" exemplify?
  F Loaded language
  G Circular reasoning
  H Bandwagon appeal
  J Questionable cause-and-effect reasoning
	The correct answer is *H.* The statement implies that everyone is going to join and that people who do not act quickly will be left out.

164 • Advertisement

✦ TEST-TAKING TIP

Tell students to ask questions as they read the persuasive text of a test item. Questions such as, "Does this make sense?" "What is the writer trying to get me to do?" "What information has been left out?" and "Is this a fact or an opinion?" will help students analyze the text. Students should also note missing or weak support for a statement.

Students should also analyze texts for the following information:

What are the benefits of following the course of action the writer urges?

Are any possible drawbacks to the proposed course of action clearly explained?

Is the writer trying to appeal more to my fears than to my common sense?

▶ **Practice 1** **Directions:** Read the passage, and then choose the letter of the best answer to each question.

How can anyone resist the building of a cellular phone tower in our town? The tower, which will be located on the land of the Volunteer Ambulance Corps, will only benefit the town. The volunteers, who give all of their free time to ensure the safety of the citizens of this town, will use the revenue from the tower to buy new ambulances and update equipment. Because many citizens have not donated funds and the town gives only a small amount of money toward the emergency squad's operation, the ambulance corps is left with no other alternative. Wouldn't you want the fastest response and best equipment if you or someone you loved needed an ambulance? For the safety of all town members, please vote *Yes* on Tuesday.

1 You can tell from this political advertisement that the writer intends to—
  A vote against the building of the tower
  B vote for the building of the tower
  C join the volunteer ambulance corps
  D donate money to the volunteer ambulance corps

2 Which of the following is an example of an overgeneralization—a statement too broad to be backed up by evidence?
  F "The volunteers, who give all of their free time to ensure the safety of the citizens of this town, . . ."
  G "How can anyone resist the building of a cellular phone tower . . ."
  H ". . . please vote *Yes* on Tuesday."
  J None of the above

3 The statement "How can anyone resist the building of a cellular phone tower in our town?" is an example of which of the following types of faulty logic?
  A Circular reasoning
  B Bandwagon appeal
  C Loaded language
  D Overgeneralization

4 You can tell the speaker is—
  F indifferent to the building of the tower
  G trying to discredit town officials
  H attempting to win readers' votes
  J including information that doesn't apply to the situation

5 The author indicates that the ambulance corps—
  A receives a portion of its money from donations
  B does not receive any financial support from the community
  C is given ample support by the town council
  D needs more media coverage

6 Which of the following statements is an example of an either/or argument that does not provide all the potential outcomes of a decision?
  F "How can anyone resist the building of a cellular phone tower in our town?"
  G "Wouldn't you want the fastest response and best equipment if you or someone you loved needed an ambulance?"
  H "Because many citizens have not donated funds and the town gives only a small amount of money toward the emergency squad's operation, the ambulance corps is left with no other alternative."
  J "The volunteers, who give all of their free time to ensure the safety of the citizens of this town, will use the revenue from the tower to buy new ambulances and update equipment."

7 Which of the following uses words that appeal to the fears of citizens?
  A "Wouldn't you want the fastest response and best equipment if you or someone you loved needed an ambulance?"
  B "How can anyone resist the building of a cellular phone tower in our town?"
  C ". . . please vote *Yes* on Tuesday."
  D None of the above

Customize for
Less Advanced Students

Go over with students the definitions of circular reasoning, bandwagon appeal, loaded language, and glittering generalizations, and explain why the writer's first statement is an example of bandwagon appeal.

Customize for
AP Students

Ask students what questions they would have for the writer of the political advertisement. They might want to ask, for example, how the writer knows that volunteers give all their free time, whether new ambulances and equipment are really needed, and how much money is the "small amount" donated by the town.

Time and Resource Manager

In-Depth Lesson Plan

	LESSON FOCUS	PRINT AND MEDIA RESOURCES
DAY 1	**Introduction to Comparison-and-Contrast Essays** Students learn key elements of a comparison-and-contrast essay and analyze the Model From Literature. (pp. 166–171)	*Writers at Work* **Videotape**, Exposition *Writing Lab* **CD-ROM**, Exposition
DAY 2	**Prewriting** Students choose and narrow a topic, consider their audience and purpose, and gather information. (pp. 172–176)	**Teaching Resources** *Writing Support Transparencies, 9-A–E; Writing Support Activity Book, 9-1–2; Topic Bank for Heterogeneous Classes,* Ch. 9
DAY 3	**Drafting** Students organize their ideas and write their first drafts. (pp. 177–178)	**Teaching Resources** *Writing Support Transparencies, 9-F; Writing Support Activity Book, 9-3*
DAY 4	**Revising** Students revise their drafts in terms of overall structure, paragraphs, sentences, and word choice. (pp. 179–184)	**Teaching Resources** *Writing Support Transparencies, 9-G–J; Writing Support Activity Book, 9-4*
DAY 5	**Editing and Proofreading; Publishing and Presenting** Students check their work for accuracy and correctness and present their final drafts. (pp. 185–186)	**Teaching Resources** *Scoring Rubrics on Transparency,* Ch. 9; *Writing Assessment and Portfolio Management; Formal Assessment,* Ch. 9

Accelerated Lesson Plan

	LESSON FOCUS	PRINT AND MEDIA RESOURCES
DAY 1	**Drafting** Students review characteristics of comparison-and-contrast writing, select topics, and write drafts. (pp. 166–178)	*Writing Lab* **CD-ROM**, Exposition **Teaching Resources** *Writing Support Transparencies, 9-A–F; Writing Support Activity Book, 9-1–3*
DAY 2	**Revising to Presenting** Students work individually or with peers to revise, edit, and proofread their work for presentation. (pp. 179–186)	**Teaching Resources** *Writing Support Transparencies, 9-G–J; Writing Support Activity Book, 9-4; Scoring Rubrics on Transparency,* Ch. 9; *Writing Assessment and Portfolio Management; Formal Assessment,* Ch. 9

Options for Adapting Lesson Plans

HOMEWORK
Have students complete any stage of the lesson for homework.

FEATURES
Extend coverage with Connected Assignment (p. 189), Spotlight on the Humanities (p. 190), Media and Technology Skills (p. 191), and the Standardized Test Preparation Workshop (p. 192).

TECHNOLOGY
Students can complete any stage of the lesson on computer. Have them print out their completed work.

INTEGRATED SKILLS COVERAGE

Integrating Grammar
Informal Language, ATE p. 170
The Six Verb Tenses, SE p. 182
Comma Splices, SE p. 185
Verb Tenses, ATE p. 188
Transitions, ATE p. 189

Reading/Writing Connection
Set a Purpose for Reading, SE p. 168
Writing Application, SE p. 171

Viewing and Representing
Critical Viewing, SE pp. 166, 169, 170, 171, 178, 181, 184, 187, 188, 189, 190
Engaging in Critical Listening, SE p. 190
Comparing Media Coverage, SE p. 191

Speaking and Listening
ATE p. 180

Real-World Connection   ATE p. 169

Workplace Skills   ATE p. 170

ASSESSMENT SUPPORT

Standardized Test Preparation Workshop SE p. 192; ATE p. 181

Standardized Test Preparation Workbook, pp. 17–18

Scoring Rubrics on Transparency, Ch. 9

Formal Assessment, Ch. 9

Writing Assessment and Portfolio Management

MEETING INDIVIDUAL NEEDS

Less Advanced Students ATE pp. 172, 176, 178, 179, 193. See also Ongoing Assessments ATE pp. 173, 175, 176, 183.

AP Students ATE pp. 169, 188, 193

ESL Students ATE pp. 178, 183, 188

Bodily/Kinesthetic Learners ATE p. 171

Verbal/Linguistic Learners ATE p. 174

BLOCK SCHEDULING

Pacing Suggestions
For 90-minute Blocks
- Have students complete the Prewriting and Drafting stages in a single period.
- Focus one class period on Revising and Editing and Publishing and Presenting. Allow at least 30 minutes for peer revision.

Resources for Varying Instruction
- *Writing Lab* CD-ROM If your students have access to hardware, a 90-minute block provides an ideal opportunity for students to work on computer.
- *Writers at Work* Videotape Show the Exposition segment in class.

Professional Development Support
- *How to Manage Instruction in the Block* This Teaching Resource provides management and activity suggestions.

MEDIA AND TECHNOLOGY

For the Student
- *Writing Lab* CD-ROM, Exposition
- *On-Line Exercise Bank,* Section 21.1

For the Teacher
- *Writers at Work* Videotape, Exposition
- *Resource Pro* CD-ROM

WRITING AND GRAMMAR WEB SITE

The Interactive Writing and Grammar Web Site provides a wide array of support for students, teachers, and parents. Writing support includes:

- Interactive revision checkers
- Scoring rubrics with complete models

www.phschool.com

LITERATURE CONNECTIONS

Related selections from *Prentice Hall Literature: Timeless Voices, Timeless Themes,* The American Experience:

"The Far and the Near," Thomas Wolfe, SE p.171

"Stopping by Woods on a Snowy Evening," Robert Frost, SE p. 173

"Acquainted With the Night," Robert Frost, SE p. 173

Exposition
Comparison-and-Contrast Essay

Lesson Objectives

1. To write a comparison-and-contrast essay appropriate to audience and purpose
2. To analyze text structures such as compare/contrast for how they influence understanding
3. To read to appreciate a writer's craft and to discover models for writing
4. To use prewriting strategies to generate ideas, develop voice, and plan
5. To develop and revise drafts in terms of structure, paragraphs, sentences, and word choice
6. To edit and proofread to ensure standard English usage and grammar
7. To evaluate writing for both mechanics and content
8. To refine a comparison-and-contrast essay for publication

Critical Viewing

Analyze Students may suggest that the varieties of fishes and birds invite a natural comparison and contrast.

Moons and Crows on Fish, Marilee Whitehouse-Holm

Comparison and Contrast in Everyday Life

Whenever you consider whether to go out and see a movie or watch one at home, whether to order pizza or a sub, or whether to vote for one candidate over another, you use **comparison-and-contrast** skills to make a decision. Faced with two choices, you decide between them by considering their similarities and differences. You also use these critical thinking skills in a variety of subject areas—in science to describe different types of cells, in language arts to compare characters in a novel, and in social studies to discuss different periods in a country's history. To write about these topics successfully, you examine the characteristics of one subject by observing how it is like and unlike others of a similar kind.

▲ **Critical Viewing**
How does the artist demonstrate comparison-and-contrast skills in this painting? **[Analyze]**

166 • Comparison-and-Contrast Essay

⏱ **TIME AND RESOURCE MANAGER**	
Resources **Technology:** *Writers at Work* Videotape, Exposition; *Writing Lab* CD-ROM, Exposition	
In-Depth Coverage	**Accelerated Pace**
• Cover pp. 166–167 in class. • Show Exposition section of the *Writers at Work* Videotape. • Read Model From Literature (pp. 168–171) with students and use it to brainstorm with students for ideas that they might compare and contrast.	• Discuss in class the definitions and types of comparison-and-contrast essays. • Assign the Model From Literature for independent reading.

What Is a Comparison-and-Contrast Essay?

A **comparison-and-contrast essay** is a short piece of expository writing that describes the similarities and differences between two or more subjects. An effective comparison-and-contrast essay

- identifies a purpose for comparison and contrast.
- identifies similarities and differences between two or more things, people, places, or ideas.
- gives factual details about the subjects being compared.
- uses an organizational plan suited to its topic and purpose.

To see the criteria on which the final draft of your comparison-and-contrast essay may be evaluated, preview the Rubric for Self-Assessment on page 186.

Types of Comparison-and-Contrast Essays

Explaining similarities and differences can provide a wealth of information. Following are some common types of comparison-and-contrast essays:

- Report about consumer goods ("Which Is Better? Brand A or Brand B?")
- Essay on economic or historical developments ("How Was Japan's Postwar Economic Development Different From Germany's?")
- Comparison and contrast of literary works ("A Comparison and Contrast of the Styles of Charlotte and Emily Brontë")

PREVIEW

Student Work
IN PROGRESS

In this chapter, you'll follow the writing process of Vanessa Serna, a student at Bel Air High School in El Paso, Texas. In her essay, Vanessa used the writing process strategies of prewriting, drafting, and revising to compare and contrast authentic Mexican food and Americanized Mexican food.

Writers in
ACTION

The playwright Edward Albee is known for creating stark contrasts and striking similarities between the worlds he presents on stage and the worlds his audience inhabits. While some of his plays are disturbing, Albee feels his observations are vital. He explains his writing in this way:

"The act of writing is an act of optimism. You would not take the trouble to do it if you felt that it didn't matter."

Comparison-and-Contrast Essay • 167

PREPARE and ENGAGE

 Interest GRABBER Ask students to consider which local pizza shop (convenience store, movie theater, etc.) is the best and why. After they jot down notes about their preferences, invite them to share their opinions. Point out that the students are comparing and contrasting the pizza shops.

Activate Prior Knowledge

Ask students to list examples of things they often compare and contrast in everyday life. They might mention activities such as deciding which pair of jeans to buy, figuring out what to make for dinner, or choosing one after-school activity over another. Choose one of these examples and discuss which specific qualities they focus on when comparing and contrasting these items.

More About the Writer

Pulitzer Prize–winning playwright Edward Albee was adopted at two weeks of age by a family who owned a chain of vaudeville theaters. He was exposed from a very early age to theater. Albee dropped out of college to pursue a career in writing poetry and fiction, but eventually found success in playwriting. Many of his plays, such as *Who's Afraid of Virginia Woolf, A Delicate Balance,* and *Three Tall Women,* examine and critique social values. He is widely credited with bringing challenging, substantive work back to American theater.

✓ ONGOING ASSESSMENT: Diagnose

Use one of the following options to diagnose students' current level of proficiency in writing comparison-and-contrast essays.

Option 1 Ask each student to select the strongest example of his or her comparison-and-contrast writing from last year. Conference with students individually to pinpoint which students may need extra help with forming a comparison-and-contrast essay.

Option 2 Ask students to compare and contrast situations in their environments, such as freeways and turnpikes, two school sports, or types of exercise programs. If students have difficulty in expressing similarities and differences, you will need to devote more time to explaining the idea behind comparison and contrast.

Technological advances have changed people's lives in many ways. In this essay, author Stephen Kuusisto uses comparison and contrast to evaluate whether new technology for people who are visually impaired is better than the old technology—or just different. The writer, who has published a memoir entitled Planet of the Blind, *uses his experiences to explain the comparisons and contrasts between reading with a hi-tech solution and using the time-tested system of Braille.*

Reading Strategy: **Set a Purpose for Reading** Before you begin reading, **set a purpose,** such as learning about a specific item, event, or person; challenging a writer's ideas; or getting involved in a wonderful narrative. Keeping a focus in mind as you read will help you identify the significant details that are related to your purpose. In this case, you'll probably read to learn more about the similarities and differences between two reading systems for the blind.

In the Dark

Stephen Kuusisto

If you're like most folks with good eyes, you've probably examined the Braille in hotel elevators. You may even have touched the raised dots signifying your floor and marveled at the capacity of the blind to travel and read in the dark. Who would imagine that Braille would be supplanted by machines? Who would guess that Braille is even now nearly extinct?

Approximately 10 percent of the blind read Braille today, a fact that has many blind advocates worried. Computerized reading machines are taking the place of Louis Braille's tactile reading system. Braille will soon be as foreign to the blind as hieroglyphs are to us.

I have on my desk a machine called "The Reading Edge." It resembles a desktop copier, and it translates printed pages into synthetic speech. I need this gadget because I'm a blind man who can't read Braille. Its voice is pure sci-fi, but I've grown immensely fond of its

The introduction immediately connects the writer to his audience.

Statistics and information about reading systems for the blind offer context for the comparison and contrast to come.

Use this Model From Literature to help students find an effective topic for a comparison-and-contrast essay. In the model, Stephen Kuusisto compares reading Braille to "reading" by listening to a machine. His personal experience makes him an authority. Have students think about topics in which they have some expertise. They might write down a list of talents or subjects they know a lot about as the first step in choosing a topic for this essay.

▼ **Critical Viewing** How might learning Braille change your perception of people who use this system exclusively? **[Hypothesize]**

intonation. It reads robotically. It sweats through the prosody of George Herbert. Sometimes it spells words aloud if the software can't identify them.

The truth is, synthetic reading is a trial. I must wait for the scanner to decode each page. This gives me time to wonder if I'm really reading at all. Many blind people argue that machine reading is really illiteracy: by relying on microchips or audiotape, the blind become dependent. According to them, I'm illiterate. It makes no difference that my own written work has been translated into a dozen languages. Because my words are mediated, I'm nothing more than a helpless listener. Braille, on the other hand, gives the blind instant contact with language. No batteries are required.

"Yes," says the machine man, "but Braille is manufactured by paid Braillists, and this takes time. I've already devoured this week's *New Yorker.* Did you see that piece by Calvin Trillin on fat-free truffles?"

"You're a slave," says the Braille man.

"Yes, I am," the machine man answers, "but I'm a slave on his way to Balducci's for fat-free truffles. Come on, Fido."

The writer uses a point-by-point organization. In his first comparison-and-contrast paragraph, the writer focuses on the experience of reading.

This fictional dialogue reveals two points of comparison that favor the technology: time and speed.

More About the Writer

Stephen Kuusisto was born with a condition of the retinas that left him legally blind at birth. As a result of his parents' attitude and an ignorant society, Kuusisto spent much of his early life trying to hide his blindness. This dangerous pretense caused him many problems. When he received his guide dog, Corky, he felt as if life had begun anew. Critics say that Kuusisto's writing has all the clarity that his vision lacks. His warm and humorous poems and essays allow readers to learn what life is like for those who cannot see.

Real-World Connection

"The Reading Edge" is a machine that uses a scanner, a speech synthesizer, a speaker, a keypad, and word recognition software to read books, magazines, and other printed material to people with vision problems. It can read in nine different voices and seven languages. The listener can also adjust the reading rate. Encourage students to use the Internet to gather information about products and services designed to help those with vision problems. Provide time for them to share what they learn.

Customize for
AP Students

Encourage students to read Kuusisto's memoir, *Planet of the Blind*, and share what they learn with the class. How was Kuusisto able to hide his blindness for so long? How was he finally able to reveal it?

Critical Viewing

Hypothesize Students may suggest that appreciating the skill required to read Braille gives them the realization that sightless people make up for their deficiency in one of the senses by becoming highly proficient in one or more of the other senses, such as touch.

Integrating Workplace Skills

Encourage students to consider what it might be like to have a co-worker or a supervisor with limited vision. Have them focus on various work situations, such as an office, a manufacturing plant, a store, and a restaurant. What might they do differently in each setting to make sure this person does not miss important information?

Integrating Grammar Skills

Informal Language Remind students that dialogue may include sentence fragments and even grammatical errors in order to sound realistic. For example, the author responds to his reading machine by saying, "Me too, Pablo." Ask students to convert this phrase into a complete sentence. (I also spend too much time inside, Pablo.) Discuss how this change affects the tone and feeling of Kuusisto's words.

Critical Viewing

Analyze Students may feel that the size of the reading machine requires that the blind be indoors, sitting near a table at all times, in order to effectively use it. It does not seem readily mobile.

If I really think about it, between bites of my truffle, I must admit that I have great sympathy for the Braille man's view. As a poet, I admire location and pressure in language. I love Kenneth Rexroth's translation of the ancient Chinese poet Tu Fu that reads in part:

> Soon now
> In the winter dawn I will face
> My 40th year. Borne headlong
> Towards the long shadows of sunset
> By the headstrong, stubborn moments,
> Life whirls past like drunken wildfire.

Given a choice, I would prefer to feel these words under my fingers. Without sight, only the flesh can assimilate the torque of Tu Fu's line, "Life whirls past like drunken wildfire."

Unfortunately, I have to listen to poetry by means of silicon. And more and more blind people are just like me. Nowadays most blind children go to public schools and don't learn Braille. In a digital age, why waste resources teaching something so outdated? Besides, Braille is cumbersome. An average Braille edition of a book looks like a sofa cushion. Compare that to a 3-1/2-inch floppy disk.

Meanwhile, I switch the "Reading Edge" from English to Spanish and scan a poem by Pablo Neruda. The machine pinches its nose and reads: "¿Por qué yo vivo desterrado/del esplendor de las naranjas?" "Why," asks Neruda, "do I live in exile/from the shine of the oranges?"

"The Reading Edge" sounds like a tourist in Santiago. It pronounces the question with too much display. In the poem Neruda feels vaguely sorry for himself. Like most writers he has spent too much time sitting indoors.

◄ **Critical Viewing** How does the "desk-top copier" size of a reading machine like the one shown influence its convenience? **[Analyze]**

170 • Comparison-and-Contrast Essay

The writer states his own preference, clarifying his purpose in comparing and contrasting the two systems.

A poem shows the writer to be well-versed in literature; this demonstrates his interest in the comparison and contrast he develops.

This paragraph points out the difficulty of learning the Braille system.

The poems quoted here are artfully linked to the essay's subject.

"Me too, Pablo," I say half aloud, and the sound of my voice—a human voice—brings my Guiding Eyes dog, Corky, to my side. Together we go outside and stand under a poplar. Corky explores the grass. I lean against the tree. Until I have a command of Braille, I'm an eavesdropper, not a reader.

I sit in the garden and finger a sleeve of fallen birch bark. Can I distinguish it from the bark of a holly tree? Can I distinguish one orange from another through acquisitive touching? To learn Braille in your 40's you must refresh the very infancy of touching and recharge your hands. Braille can't be learned like Berlitz Spanish. You have to think with your skin.

The poet Charles Olson imagined that our tissues and organs can think. Sitting beneath the trees I'll settle for one thinking index finger. I'm going to read Walt Whitman in the dark, without batteries.

Writing Application: **Set a Purpose for Writing** Help your readers see the purpose of your comparison-and-contrast essay by including information that shows why a study of the similarities and differences between your subjects is important to you.

LITERATURE

To see how one short-story writer used comparison and contrast to create a conflict, read Thomas Wolfe's "The Far and the Near." You can find the story in *Prentice Hall Literature: Timeless Voices, Timeless Themes,* The American Experience.

◄ **Critical Viewing**
How do the printed words included in this sculpture contribute to its meaning? **[Analyze]**

After stating the comparison and contrast he draws between his subjects, the writer stresses his own choice. He would prefer Braille over the technology-based reading machine.

Customize for
Bodily/Kinesthetic Learners

In your school or local library, locate materials translated into Braille and let students try to distinguish among some of the letter patterns with their fingertips. What does Kuusisto mean when he says that to learn Braille, "You have to think with your skin"?

Reading\Writing Connection

Writing Application: Set a Purpose for Writing

Tell students that readers respond more to reading something if they get a feeling that the subject matter is important to the writer. Have students reread "In the Dark," taking notes on the places where they detect Kuusisto's deep involvement with his subject. Have them imagine how much less interesting this essay would have been if it were a description of how a reading machine works by someone whose connection to such a machine is not established.

Critical Viewing

Analyze The printed words add a textural, rather than an informational, element to the sculpture.

Prewriting: Categories

1. Explain to the class that this activity is a form of brainstorming. That means they should accept each other's suggestions without questioning them. The goal of the activity is to generate ideas.

2. Explain to students that choosing two things from the same category to compare and contrast ensures that they will have at least some similarities in addition to their differences.

3. Ask students why it's important that the things they choose contain at least some similarities. (They should realize that a comparison of two completely different things, like a grape and a motorcycle, would not be very informative.)

Prewriting: Magazine Review

Teaching Resources: Writing Support Transparencies, 9-A

1. Display Transparency 9-A and have students review the Student Work in Progress feature. Ask why Vanessa's ideas for comparing and contrasting are better than the magazine pictures she found. (Her ideas are very specific.)

2. If you wish, provide sticky notes that students can use to mark pictures that interest them.

3. Encourage students to use the pictures and articles they marked as springboards for their ideas, as Vanessa did.

Customize for
Less Advanced Students

To get their ideas flowing, invite students to think of things they really enjoy. Encourage them to compare and contrast these things with other things they enjoy less. (Example: They might compare the music of their favorite rock group with that of another popular group.)

9.2 Prewriting

Choosing Your Topic

To write an effective comparison-and-contrast essay, choose a topic that has enough similarities between parts to make a comparison logical and enough differences to make a contrast meaningful. The specific subjects that you choose might be two related items, like hiking and rock-climbing. Alternatively, you might address two aspects of a single topic, like starting a project and finishing it. Use these strategies to choose a topic:

Strategies for Generating Topics

1. **Categories** With a group, make a list of categories like the ones often used on game shows. Your categories might include winter sports, animals of Africa, or historic battles. List several items, and choose two or three items in one of the categories as the basis for a comparison-and-contrast essay.

2. **Magazine Review** Look through several magazines, and scan the articles and images. Use bookmarks to write notes about what you found and how you could use the idea for a comparison-and-contrast essay. Review the pages that you marked, and choose a topic to develop into an essay.

Writing Lab CD-ROM

For more help finding a topic, explore the activities and suggestions in the Choosing a Topic section of the Exposition lesson.

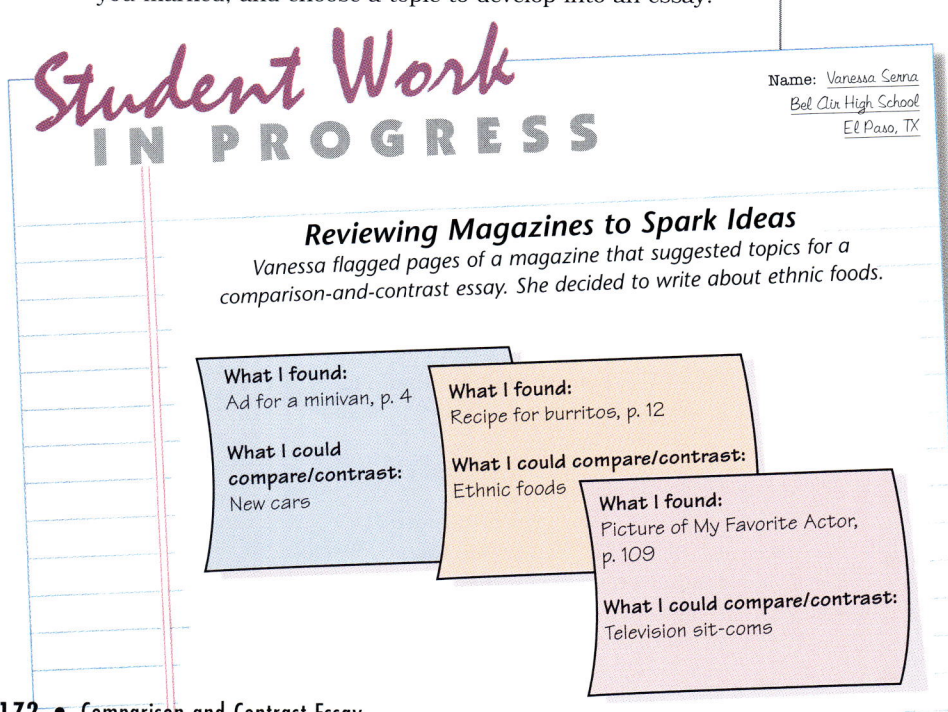

Student Work IN PROGRESS

Name: *Vanessa Serna*
Bel Air High School
El Paso, TX

Reviewing Magazines to Spark Ideas
Vanessa flagged pages of a magazine that suggested topics for a comparison-and-contrast essay. She decided to write about ethnic foods.

What I found:
Ad for a minivan, p. 4

What I could compare/contrast:
New cars

What I found:
Recipe for burritos, p. 12

What I could compare/contrast:
Ethnic foods

What I found:
Picture of My Favorite Actor, p. 109

What I could compare/contrast:
Television sit-coms

172 • Comparison-and-Contrast Essay

⏱ TIME AND RESOURCE MANAGER

Resources
Print: *Writing Support Transparencies*, 9-A–E; *Writing Support Activity Book*, 9-1–2
Technology: *Writing Lab* CD-ROM, Exposition

In-Depth Coverage	Accelerated Pace
• Work through the Choosing Your Topic strategies with the class. • Use the Responding to Fine Art transparency to generate additional topics.	• Discuss strategies for generating topics. • Have students work independently to choose and narrow their topics. • Have students work with partners to focus on audience, purpose, and gathering details.

TOPIC BANK

If you are having trouble choosing a topic, consider the following possibilities:

1. **Essay About Two Possessions** Think of a possession that you treasured at some time in your life and another one that took its place or was similar in some way. Write an essay in which you compare and contrast the two.

2. **Essay About Colleges** Use college admissions brochures, Web site information, or your own knowledge to write a comparison-and-contrast essay about two colleges.

Responding to Fine Art

3. Andy Warhol's paintings provide a new way of looking at everyday objects, which is just what a good comparison-and-contrast essay should do. Use your response to *Diamond Dust Shoes*, at right, to write an essay that compares and contrasts items of clothing that seem similar at first glance.

Responding to Literature

4. Read "Stopping by Woods on a Snowy Evening" and "Acquainted With the Night," by Robert Frost. In a comparison-and-contrast essay, show how the writer addresses night in two separate works. You can find the poetry in *Prentice Hall Literature: Timeless Voices, Timeless Themes*, The American Experience.

✓ Cooperative Writing Opportunity

5. **Report on Celebrities Then and Now** With a group, collect information comparing the celebrities of an earlier generation with those who are popular today. After creating and using a questionnaire to identify the people to include in the report, group members can split the task of researching and writing about the celebrities chosen.

Diamond Dust Shoes, Andy Warhol, ©Copyright The Andy Warhol Foundation for the Visual Arts

---

Responding to Fine Art

Diamond Dust Shoes by Andy Warhol

Teaching Resources: Writing Support Transparencies, 9-B

1. Display the transparency and engage students in a discussion about *Diamond Dust Shoes*. Use questions like these to prompt discussion:

   What do you think attracted the artist to this subject?

   What do you think Warhol's attitude toward these shoes is?

2. Ask students to brainstorm for further possible comparison-and-contrast essay topics suggested by this piece of art. Some other possibilities are shoes for use in different activities and footwear in the nineteenth and twentieth centuries.

Responding to Literature

If students have read the poems, discuss the similarities in Robert Frost's portrayal of night in both poems. (Night is a time for thinking.) Then, discuss what is different about Frost's references to night in each poem. (Night plays a smaller role in "Stopping by Woods on a Snowy Evening." Readers do not realize it is night until halfway through the poem. However, Frost stresses the nighttime setting in the other poem, mentioning the city lights, the watchman, and the clock glowing against the sky.)

✓ ONGOING ASSESSMENT: Monitor and Reinforce

If you observe that some students are having difficulty generating or selecting a topic, use one of the following strategies.

Option 1 Suggest that students choose an idea from the Topic Bank. If many students have difficulty, work with the whole class on one idea selected from the Topic Bank or from ideas suggested by students.

Option 2 If Topic Bank ideas seem too difficult, suggest that students try one of the assignments from the *Topic Bank for Heterogeneous Classes* in the Teaching Resources.

 TIME SAVERS!

 Writing Support Transparencies
Use the transparencies for Chapter 9 to facilitate teaching of responses to fine art and other strategies.

Prewriting: Looping to Narrow a Topic

Teaching Resources: Writing Support Transparencies, 9-C

1. To help students narrow their topics, give examples such as the following:

   Too broad: *Comparing and contrasting part-time jobs*

   Narrow enough: *Comparing and contrasting part-time jobs at local fast-food restaurants*

   Too broad: *Comparing and contrasting brands of clothing*

   Narrow enough: *Comparing and contrasting two brands of jeans*

2. Have students come up with some examples of their own to make sure they understand the idea.

3. Display Transparency 9-C. To emphasize why Vanessa's first topic is too broad, have students name all the different subjects that could be discussed under the heading "The variety of ethnic foods."

Customize for
Verbal/Linguistic Learners

Encourage students to try the looping activity orally with a partner. Students can talk about their topics for a few minutes while their partners listen and jot down interesting ideas in what they hear. Then the speakers will read the list, select one of the ideas, and talk about that one, narrowing it further. After the first student selects a topic, the partners can switch roles.

9.2

Narrowing Your Topic

Once you've chosen a topic, consider whether you can effectively cover the topic in an essay. If your topic is too broad, you won't be able to provide enough details to make it worthwhile. If you focus on a specific idea, you can make your writing more insightful and valuable. Looping can help you narrow your topic.

Looping to Narrow a Topic

Looping is a way of discovering the features of a topic that are most interesting to you. Begin by freewriting about the subjects that you have chosen. Review your writing, and circle the idea that you think is most important. Freewrite about that idea, review it, and again circle the most important idea. Continue looping until you've narrowed your topic to an idea that you can cover well in an essay.

Student Work
IN PROGRESS

Name: *Vanessa Serna*
Bel Air High School
El Paso, TX

Looping

Vanessa used looping to narrow the broad topic of ethnic food to one she could use to write a good comparison-and-contrast essay.

Broad Topic: The variety of ethnic foods

I like a lot of different ethnic foods. There are many different kinds of ethnic restaurants in the United States. It seems like everywhere I go, I see restaurants that serve Chinese, Italian, and Mexican food along with restaurants that serve American food. These ethnic foods are so popular that they are served in fast-food restaurants as well as in more traditional restaurants.

Mexican food is my favorite ethnic food. I especially like gorditas and chili with everything, but Mexican restaurants in the United States usually don't have real chili. Actually, most TexMex food is a lot different from the real Mexican food.

Narrowed Topic: Authentic Mexican food is different from TexMex food.

174 • Comparison-and-Contrast Essay

Considering Your Audience and Purpose

Identify Your Audience

To best communicate your ideas to your readers, take a moment to identify the people you expect to read your writing. A knowledge of your audience will help you decide what level of language, formality, and detail to include in your writing.

Focus Your Purpose

While you will set out to compare and contrast two items, you should have an even more focused purpose in mind. Consider why such an analysis is valuable or necessary, and then include details to help you achieve your goal. You may write to advocate one idea over the other, to reveal connections that may not be obvious, or to show the causes of similarities and differences you describe. The following examples may help you to focus your purpose.

Writing Lab CD-ROM

If you need help identifying your audience, see the Audio-Annotated Writing Models in the Exposition lesson.

Sample Purposes

Purpose	Examples
To advocate one over the other.	☐ home-cooked food vs. restaurant cuisine ☐ living in the city vs. the country ☐ soccer vs. football
To reveal connections that might not be obvious.	☐ having a pet and having a friend ☐ math and music ☐ soccer and tennis
To show what causes similarities or differences.	☐ Sahara vs. Death Valley ☐ the Internet vs. a library ☐ jazz vs. blues

Prewriting • 175

Prewriting: Identify Your Audience

1. To help students recognize the importance of their audience, have them pretend they are writing a letter describing their weekend. Would they send the same letter to their grandmother and to a friend from school? Why or why not?

2. Have students suggest the kinds of details they would include in letters to a grandparent and a friend from school.

3. Discuss how language and formality might vary for each letter. Remind them that details and tone will also vary depending on the intended audience for their essays.

Prewriting: Focus Your Purpose

Teaching Resources: Writing Support Transparencies, 9-D; Writing Support Activity Book, 9-1

1. Explain to students that a comparison-and-contrast essay often has a persuasive element because the writer usually prefers one of the items being compared to the other.

2. Display Transparency 9-D. Be sure students see that purpose precedes examples.

3. Give students a blank copy of the Purposes organizer (9-1). Ask them to fill it in for a sample topic, such as comparing and contrasting different models of cars. Ask them to brainstorm for possible purposes for writing about this topic (to show that one model is more accident-prone than another, to compare features, or to compare prices or resale values).

☑ **ONGOING ASSESSMENT: Monitor and Reinforce**

Often, students will lapse into writing only for the teacher as an audience. To help break this pattern, try one of the following strategies.

Option 1 Suggest that students write for a very specific audience of one—a relative, a friend, or a much younger person.

Option 2 Have students write a brief profile of their intended audience, including their level of education, skills, and background knowledge of the topic.

Prewriting: Identifying Points of Comparison and Contrast

Teaching Resources: Writing Support Transparencies, 9-E; Writing Support Activity Book, 9-2

1. Start this activity by having students write each item they are going to compare and contrast as a heading on a separate sheet of paper. Then, have them try to fill each page with details about the items.

2. Have students read the Student Work in Progress. Point out the way Vanessa organizes the details according to category by labeling the middle column of her chart "Points of Comparison and Contrast."

3. Display Transparency 9-E to show students how to organize their elements to be considered. Then give them a blank copy of the details chart (9-2). In order to determine what to write in the middle column, they should read over the details they listed in step 1 and try to classify them into categories.

4. Explain to students that each completed row in the column could be expanded to form a paragraph in their comparison-and-contrast essays.

Customize for
Less Advanced Students

After students complete their charts, ask them to mark each topic they listed in column two as either a point of comparison or a point of contrast. If most or all the points involve contrasts, ask them to add several points that show similarities.

9.2

Gathering Details

Once you have identified your purpose, begin to focus on gathering details that develop the comparisons you want to draw. You may need to conduct research or use your own knowledge and experience to identify the key elements you'll describe. As you gather details, focus on points of comparison and contrast between your subjects.

Identify Points of Comparison and Contrast

Charting the elements to be considered in a comparison-and-contrast essay will help you note the details to include in your writing. Using a chart like the one shown on this page, identify the points you'll address in your writing. As you fill in the chart with facts, details, or examples, you'll see which points reveal similarities and which points show the differences between your subjects. At this point, you might start considering which details you will want to emphasize in your draft.

Student Work IN PROGRESS

Name: Vanessa Serna
Bel Air High School
El Paso, TX

Gathering Details Using a Chart

After deciding on the elements she would include in her essay, Vanessa listed the ideas that would help her support her position.

Details for Each Type of Food

Mexican Food	Points of Comparison and Contrast	Americanized Mexican Food
Grown on farms, much time is spent preparing them	Ingredients	Canned or frozen, prepared quickly
Real chili	Spices	Mild, tomatolike mixture
Fresh guacamole and bean dip	Side Dishes	Dip that is ready-made
Colorful	Appearance	Colorless

176 • Comparison-and-Contrast Essay

9.3 Drafting

Shaping Your Writing

When you are ready to start writing, gather your prewriting notes together. As you begin to draft, you'll need to make choices about how to group the details of comparison and contrast into a logical organization.

Organize to Show Comparison and Contrast

To avoid confusing your readers, choose an organizational strategy that will make your writing clear. There are two basic ways to organize a comparison-and-contrast essay: subject by subject or point by point.

Subject-by-Subject Organization Using this type of organizational plan, you compare and contrast the subjects as wholes: First, you discuss all the features of one subject; then, you discuss all the features of the other subject. While this format allows you to focus your full attention on one subject at a time, be sure that you address the same features and devote equal time to each subject.

Point-by-Point Organization This plan of organization allows you to move back and forth between your subjects as you discuss each point of comparison and contrast. First, you develop one point by showing how it applies to both subjects. Then, you move on to your next point, shifting back and forth between subjects until you have addressed each point of comparison. The advantage of this method is that it allows you to sharpen your points of comparison and contrast. It also makes it easy for you to make sure that you address each feature for both subjects.

Two Basic Organizational Plans

Subject by Subject
I. Introduction
II. Mountain bikes
Frames; tires
III. Touring bikes
Frames; tires
IV. Conclusion
Uses of both bikes

Point by Point
I. Introduction
II. Frames
Mountain bikes
Touring bikes
III. Tires
Mountain bikes
Touring bikes
IV. Conclusion
Uses of both bikes

Writing Lab CD-ROM

If you need help organizing your essay, see the Audio-Annotated Writing Models in the *Writing Lab CD-ROM.*

Drafting • 177

Step-by-Step Teaching Guide

Drafting: Organizing to Show Comparison and Contrast

Teaching Resources: Writing Support Transparencies, 9-F; Writing Support Activity Book, 9-3

1. Suggest to students that outlining will help them take control of details. Display Transparency 9-F to show the two organizational strategies. Give students a blank copy of the two organizers (9-3) to apply to their own work.

2. Write the examples (below) of subject-by-subject and point-by-point comparisons on the board. Ask students to consider which method of organization is better for this topic. (Answers may vary.)

Subject by Subject

I. Introduction

II. Tony's Pizza Shop
    taste
    selection
    cost

III. Four Corners Pizza Shop
    taste
    selection
    cost

IV. Conclusion
    better pizza

Point by Point

I. Introduction

II. Taste
    Tony's Pizza Shop
    Four Corners Pizza Shop

III. Selection
    Tony's Pizza Shop
    Four Corners Pizza Shop

IV. Cost
    Tony's Pizza Shop
    Four Corners Pizza Shop

V. Conclusion
    better pizza

⏱ TIME AND RESOURCE MANAGER

Resources
Print: *Writing Support Transparencies, 9-F; Writing Support Activity Book, 9-3*
Technology: *Writing Lab* CD-ROM, Exposition

In-Depth Coverage	Accelerated Pace
• Work through the Subject-by-Subject and Point-by-Point Organization with the class. • Demonstrate the SEE method of Statement, Extension, and Elaboration. • Have students draft their comparison-and-contrast essays in class.	• Have students review pp. 177–178 independently and choose how to organize their comparison-and-contrast essays. • Respond to individual drafting issues as needed.

Drafting: Elaborating Using the SEE Method

1. Provide other examples, such as the one below, of the SEE method on the board.

   Statement: *Trying out for the band is a lot like trying out for the football team.*

   Extension: *When you try out for the band at our school, you have as much competition as those who try out for the football team.*

   Elaboration: *This year forty-three students tried out for twenty-one openings in the band. Only thirty-eight students tried out for the thirty-three openings on the football team.*

2. Write the following statement on the board. Ask students to extend and elaborate upon it.

   Statement: *Drivers education programs offered by the school are more efficient than programs offered by private companies.*

Customize for
ESL Students

Make sure that students understand the meaning of the three terms represented by *SEE*. You might use a visual demonstration to explain the term *extension*, such as extending a line on a chalkboard. Have students think of simple English synonyms for *extend* and *elaborate* (add to, make bigger) to make sure they understand the words.

Customize for
Less Advanced Students

If students are confused by the SEE approach, explain that the process is a continuum, from a "bare-bones" statement to one supported with facts and details. You might have students work in small groups to choose a topic and use the SEE method to elaborate on it.

Critical Viewing

Respond Students may suggest comparisons of types of music, costs of products, or quality of packaging.

Providing Elaboration

Whether your purpose in comparing your two subjects is to describe, persuade, or explain, you should provide enough details to allow your readers to fully understand the similarities and differences. To elaborate on the points that you make as you draft, extend your points of comparison and contrast using the SEE method.

Use the SEE Method

For each main topic of comparison in your draft, develop support using the SEE method of *Statement, Extension,* and *Elaboration.*

- **Statement:** State the main idea in a topic sentence.
- **Extension:** Extend the idea of the topic statement by restatement.
- **Elaboration:** Provide examples, details, or facts to further prove the point.

Look at this example of the SEE method in action:

STATEMENT: CDs are more visually appealing than audio-cassettes.

EXTENSION While cassettes are stacked in shelves without calling attention to their cover art, CD cases are used to present walls of display.

ELABORATION: At just less than 6 square inches, the art on the CD case is visible from a short distance. When customers enter a music store, the faces of popular artists smile out at them from these miniature frames.

◀ **Critical Viewing**
What subjects for a comparison-and-contrast essay does this photograph suggest to you? **[Respond]**

178 • Comparison-and-Contrast Essay

9.4 Revising

Revising Your Overall Structure

Once your first draft is complete, review it by checking the structure, paragraphs, sentences, and word choice. The changes you make can make your essay more effective.

Be Sure Your Draft Reflects Your Purpose

Make sure that your essay does what you set out to do. Check that the points of comparison and contrast that you present and the elaboration you provide reflect your original purpose in writing. To verify this, identify sentences that connect to your purpose.

▶ **REVISION STRATEGY**
Bracketing Sentences That Address Your Purpose

Write your specific purpose on a self-sticking note, and attach it to your draft for easy reference. Then, go through your draft to bracket sentences that address your purpose. If you can't identify at least one sentence in each paragraph, consider adding or revising a sentence to clarify how the details in the paragraph support your purpose.

Student Work
IN PROGRESS

Name: Vanessa Serna
Bel Air High School
El Paso, TX

Bracketing Sentences That Address Your Purpose

To review her essay's ability to achieve her writing purpose, Vanessa bracketed sentences that helped her prove her point.

One of the major differences between the two forms of Mexican food is in its preparation. Because many Mexican families work on farms, they grow most of their own ingredients. [As a result, authentic Mexican food is juicier and tastier.] . . . Because there is not a vegetable garden outside of every Mexican restaurant . . . most restaurants' ingredients are canned or frozen. *TexMex food lacks the freshness of authentic Mexican food.*

> Purpose: To show that authentic Mexican food is better than TexMex food.

> Vanessa found one sentence in her paragraph that addressed her purpose. She decided to add another sentence to connect the points in this paragraph more strongly with her writing goal.

Revising • 179

Revising: Bracketing Sentences That Address Your Purpose

Teaching Resources: Writing Support Transparencies, 9-G

1. Remind students that it is easy to get distracted while writing. We might think of an interesting fact to add or get bogged down in details. This can make us forget our reason for writing.

2. Have students focus on the Student Work in Progress. Help them recognize that the sentence Vanessa bracketed clearly states a reason authentic Mexican food is better than Mexican food served in fast-food restaurants in the United States. The rest of the sentences in this paragraph lead up to her bracketed sentence.

3. If you wish, provide sticky notes so students can post their purpose in writing on their handwritten draft or beside their computer screen.

4. Have students evaluate their drafts to be sure they reflect their original purpose in writing. Ask them to bracket the sentences that help prove their point. If there are none, urge them to revise their drafts so they more closely reflect their purpose.

Customize for
Less Advanced Students

Point out that the first step in revising is for writers to step back and take a look at the "big picture." It is the time for them to question whether their work accomplishes its intended purpose. After they are sure their work is on target, they are ready to review individual sentences and words.

⏱ TIME AND RESOURCE MANAGER

Resources
Print: *Writing Support Transparencies, 9-G–J; Writing Support Activity Book, 9-4*
Technology: *Writing Lab* CD-ROM, Exposition

In-Depth Coverage	Accelerated Pace
• Work through the revising strategies with the class. • Use the relevant transparencies to demonstrate these strategies. • Organize the class into groups for the Peer Review activity.	• Ask students to review pp. 179–184 independently. • Have students apply the revision strategies to their essays independently.

Revising: Color-Coding to Evaluate Transitions

Teaching Resources: Writing Support Transparencies, 9-H

1. Remind students that paragraphs without transitions sound choppy and awkward. Transitions help to make writing flow smoothly. In addition, they clarify the relationships between sentences and ideas.

2. Write the following sentence pairs on the board and ask students to suggest transitions to logically link the two pairs of sentences.

   Home-cooked meals are the best. Going to a restaurant is fun for a change.

   (Add a transition that shows differences or contrasting ideas, such as *but, however,* or *still.*)

   Some Mexican food is too spicy for me. Enchiladas give me heartburn.

   (Add a transition that indicates that the second sentence is an example, such as *for example* or *for instance.*)

3. Display Transparency 9-H. Provide time for students to color code their drafts, following the directions on page 180. Have students add any missing transitions to their drafts. Then, ask them to read their drafts aloud to a partner, who will listen for appropriate transitions.

Integrating Speaking and Listening Skills

Remind students that we need to use transitions when we speak, too. Discuss times when they have had trouble understanding a speaker who jumped from topic to topic without explaining the connection. Ask how it feels to listen to such a speaker.

Revising Your Paragraphs

After you have reviewed the structure of your draft, take a look at each paragraph of your draft. Make sure that the sentences within each paragraph work together to call attention to the points of comparison and contrast between your subjects. Transitions can help you stress the points you want to make.

▶ **REVISION STRATEGY**
Color-Coding to Evaluate Transitions

Read your draft, and identify the places where you address each subject. Use one color to underline every instance in which you refer to one subject, and use a second color to underline every reference to the other subject. To evaluate your writing in places where the colors meet, judge the connection between the two subjects. Add transitions like the ones below to make the shift clearer.

- **Transitions that show similarities:** *all, similarly, both, in the same way, closely related, equally.*
- **Transitions that show differences:** *on the other hand, in contrast, however, instead, yet.*

Writing Lab CD-ROM

Use the Transition Words Revision Checker in the Exposition lesson to help you make strong connections between your ideas.

Student Work IN PROGRESS

Name: *Vanessa Serna*
Bel Air High School
El Paso, TX

Evaluating Transitions

When she color-coded her paper, Vanessa realized that most of her points of comparison and contrast might not be obvious to readers. She added transitions to make the relationships clear.

Another difference between the two cuisines is in the use of spices and side dishes. For example, chili has an important role in almost every Mexican meal, including breakfast. *Chili is not included in most TexMex meals* In most of the United States, the term "chili" refers to a mild mixture. In Mexican culture, "chile" refers to a wide variety of peppers, sauces, and mixtures.

180 • Comparison-and-Contrast Essay

Revising Your Sentences

Once you have added transitions to sharpen your points of comparison and contrast within paragraphs, examine your essay on the sentence level. Check that you have used the correct verb tense in each sentence to indicate the time that an action occurred.

Make Verb Tense Work for You

The tenses of verbs allow you to express time by showing when events occurred in a sequence. Unless you want to show action in the past, present, or future, you should be sure that the verb tense of your writing is consistent. For example, if you're writing about two subjects that still exist, use the present tense consistently. However, if you are comparing items in different time periods, you may need to make use of the past tense. Evaluating the verbs in each sentence can help you to avoid unnecessary shifts in verb tense.

▶ **REVISION STRATEGY**
Identifying the Verb Tense of Each Paragraph

Circle all the verbs in your draft; then, analyze your use of verbs. For each paragraph, confirm that all the verbs fit the same general tense. If they do not, make sure that the verb shift is necessary to indicate a time shift. Look at this example:

EXAMPLE:	The drivers *became* tired after the long interstate trip. They *are driving* for days!
ANALYSIS:	*Became* expresses action that happened in the past. *Are driving* expresses action that is still happening.
EVALUATION:	This unnecessary shift in tense causes confusion. Change the verb to indicate that the second action happened before the first action and does not continue into the present.
REVISION:	The drivers *became* tired after the long interstate trip. They *had been driving* for days!

▲ **Critical Viewing**
What comparison and contrast can you draw between this truck and a family station wagon? **[Compare and Contrast]**

181

Six Tenses of Verbs

1. Guide students to recognize that the six tenses of verbs allow them to explain complex time relationships in their writing. To communicate exact meanings, they need to use these tenses correctly.

2. Give students copies of an article from an encyclopedia or a magazine. Ask them to underline the verbs and mark the tense of each one.

3. Then, have a volunteer read the article aloud, changing the tense of each verb. For example, *discovered* might become *will discover* or *had discovered*.

4. Discuss how these changes in verb tense affect the clarity of the article.

Find It in Your Reading

Examples of present tense verbs in the third paragraph: *have, resembles, translates*, etc.
Example of present perfect tense verbs in the third paragraph: *I've (I have) grown*
Ask students to consider why most of Kuusisto's verbs are in the present tense. (He is comparing the efficiency of two reading methods that are currently being used.)

Find It in Your Writing

If students are confused about whether their shifts in verb tense are necessary, have them read the sentence to the class and discuss whether the verbs need to be changed.

9.4

Grammar in Your Writing
Six Tenses of Verbs

By expressing time through tense, **verbs** can clarify the sequence of events in your writing. The basic forms of the six tenses show the time of an action or condition in the present, past, or future. Each verb form shows the time of an action and whether it is still happening. Use the following as a guide to the correct use of six tenses of verbs.

- **Present** indicates an action that happens regularly or a general truth:
  My family **visits** Chicago every year.
- **Past** indicates an action that has already happened:
  We **visited** Chicago last year.
- **Future** indicates an action will happen:
  We **will visit** Chicago again next year.
- **Present perfect** indicates an action that happened at some indefinite time in the past or an action that happened in the past and is still happening now:
  We **have visited** Chicago every year for the last three years.
- **Past perfect** indicates an action that has happened before another action in the past:
  We **had visited** Chicago before we heard about the art exhibit.
- **Future perfect** indicates an action that will have been completed by a specified time in the future:
  We **will have visited** eight museums by the time we get home.

Use the six tenses of verbs to show a sequence of events. However, be careful not to shift verb tenses unnecessarily within a sentence or as you move from one sentence or paragraph to another.

INCORRECT: We **speed** into the house and **grabbed** a drink in the kitchen.

CORRECT: We **sped** into the house and **grabbed** a drink in the kitchen.

Find It in Your Reading Read Stephen Kuusisto's essay "In the Dark" on pages 168–171 to see the variety of verb tenses he uses. In the third paragraph, find three examples of the present tense and one example of the present perfect tense. Explain your choices.

Find It in Your Writing Identify any shifts in verb tense in your draft. Make sure that each one is necessary to indicate correctly the time when an action happened.

For more on verb tenses, see Chapter 21.

182 • Comparison-and-Contrast Essay

✓ ONGOING ASSESSMENT: Prerequisite Skills

If students have difficulty with verb tense, you may find it helpful to refer them to the following material to ensure coverage of requisite skills.

In the Textbook	Print Resources	Technology
The Six Verb Tenses, pp. 520–521	*Grammar Exercise Workbook,* pp. 87–88	*On-Line Exercise Bank,* Section 21.1

Revising Your Word Choice

Stress the Opposites

The words that you use to describe your subjects can sharpen points of comparison and contrast just as much as transitions can. As you evaluate your word choice, you may find that you can strengthen your points of contrast by adding opposite or nearly opposite words to describe differences. Use a T-chart to examine your word choice for points of contrast.

▶ ### REVISION STRATEGY
Charting Opposites

In a T-chart like the one shown below, identify the words you've used to create contrast in describing your subjects. In one column, write the strongest words you've used to describe one topic. In the other, jot down the words that describe the other topic. Review your chart to see whether opposites are strongly expressed. Revise some of these words in your draft to make your comparison and contrast stronger.

🗋 Research Tip

Use a thesaurus to find the most precise words to convey the contrasts you make.

Student Work
IN PROGRESS

Name: Vanessa Serna
Bel Air High School
El Paso, TX

Charting to Stress Opposites

Vanessa charted opposite points to improve her word choice and describe the features of both authentic Mexican and Americanized Mexican food more vividly. See her final draft to see how she used opposite words to describe the features of the two types of food.

Mexican Food	TexMex Food
Ripe, fresh	Canned, frozen, processed
From mild to burning hot, spicy	Mildly hot, tomatolike mixture
Fresh avocados and slow-cooked beans	Ready-made from a container
Colorful, bright colors	Colorless

Vanessa decided to use the words "processed" and "spicy" to make her contrasts more clear.

Revising • 183

Step-by-Step Teaching Guide

Revising: Charting Opposites

Teaching Resources: Writing Support Transparencies, 9-I; Writing Support Activity Book, 9-4

1. Display Transparency 9-I and draw students' attention to the Student Work in Progress and ask them to point out the two words Vanessa added (processed, spicy). Discuss why she made these revisions. (They contrast with words on the other side of the chart.)

2. Have students name the opposite of *processed* (fresh) and *spicy* (mild). Invite them to think of other pairs of opposite words that Vanessa might use in her essay.

3. Give students a blank copy of the T-chart (9-4) and ask them to create their own T-charts and record the words they used to compare and contrast the items.

4. Have students add more descriptive words where they are needed. Provide thesauruses for reference if possible.

5. Encourage students to use pairs of opposite words wherever they are appropriate. Urge them to consider the context and the meanings of the words before automatically using opposite words.

Customize for
ESL Students

Choosing stronger words may be a challenge for English learners. Invite them to brainstorm for stronger words in their native languages. Then, they can translate the words into English with the help of a dictionary or a more-fluent English speaker.

✓ ONGOING ASSESSMENT: Monitor and Reinforce

If you find that students are having difficulty spotting problems in verb tense from their own reading of their drafts, use the following strategy.

Students should listen to someone reading his or her draft aloud. This "hearing" of verbs can often make illogical verb-tense shifts more apparent, something that sometimes doesn't come through during the writer's silent rereading of his or her own draft.

1. Display Transparency 9-J. Ask students whether they agree with the suggestions on the notes. What other suggestions would they make?

2. Begin the peer review process by inviting students to identify a draft's strengths before focusing on its weaknesses.

3. In addition to the two questions listed on this page, have students list several questions, specific to their own essays, that they want to ask. Give students some examples of specific questions and vague questions, and tell them to make sure their questions are clear and specific. For example:

   Specific: *Did I use any verbs that should be more vivid?*

   Vague: *How is my word choice?*

4. Remind students that some errors will be corrected at the proofreading stage and that the focus here should be on content and clarity.

Critical Viewing

Relate Students may feel that a classmate can be a good sounding board by being attentive and honest in his or her reactions.

Peer Review

Sharing your revised draft with a small group can help you to look more objectively at your work. Peer reviewers can help you see whether your points of comparison are well developed, clear, and purposeful.

Ask Reviewers to Offer Suggestions

Give a copy of your essay to each member of a group of classmates. Ask each reviewer to read your essay and consider the following questions:

- Is the purpose of comparing and contrasting the two subjects clearly addressed?
- Are both subjects covered equally well?

Your reviewers can attach self-sticking notes with their comments to any areas of your essay that they think could be improved.

▲ **Critical Viewing** In what ways can a classmate be a good sounding board for your writing? **[Relate]**

Student Work
IN PROGRESS

Name: *Vanessa Serna*
Bel Air High School
El Paso, TX

Asking Reviewers to Respond to Questions

Vanessa asked her peer reviewers to respond to her essay in specific ways. She used her reviewers' comments about this paragraph to develop it more fully. You can see her final draft on pages 187–188.

The look of authentic Mexican food as opposed to TexMex food is also very different. Authentic corn and flour tortillas, for example, look much different from those served at American restaurants. Authentic corn and flour tortillas are a shade of creamy white and have a much softer texture than those served in American restaurants. Another difference in the appearance of the two types of Mexican food is color. Combinations of different fresh ingredients make Mexican food very colorful.

> Add a sentence telling how American tortillas look.

> You could give some concrete examples of the ingredients that make Mexican food colorful.

9.5 Editing and Proofreading

Errors in grammar or mechanics can distract readers from seeing your ideas. Proofread to make your writing error-free.

Focusing on Sentences

Sentences should express a complete thought. Use these tips to review the mechanics of each sentence in your draft:

Avoid Fragments Be sure that each sentence contains a subject and a verb. Revise fragments—those that don't meet these criteria—to create complete sentences.

Avoid Run-on Sentences Run-on sentences are two or more complete sentences written as if they were a single sentence. Revise them to create separate sentences.

Learn More

To study the criteria for effective sentences, see Chapter 20.

Grammar in Your Writing
Comma Splices

A **comma splice** is an error in which a comma by itself joins two independent clauses.

COMMA SPLICE: He loves math, he wants to learn more.

To revise a comma splice, use one of these strategies:

Add a coordinating conjunction such as *and, but, or, nor, for, so,* or *yet*: He loves math, and he wants to learn more.

Use a period or a semicolon between the clauses: He loves math; he wants to learn more. [or] He loves math. He wants to learn more.

Revise one independent clause into a dependent clause: *Because* he loves math, he wants to learn more.

Find It in Your Reading Review Stephen Kuusisto's essay on pages 168–171. Find two sentences in which the writer uses a semicolon or a coordinating conjunction to combine independent clauses.

Find It in Your Writing Read your draft to find and revise any comma splices you have included.

For more on comma splices, see Chapter 20.

Editing and Proofreading • 185

Publishing and Presenting

1. Remind students that the publishing phase is their chance to share their thoughts and ideas with the world. Have students name some additional ways of sharing their work. Before choosing a way to publish their work, remind them to consider the type of audience they are hoping to attract.

2. If students wish to add visual information, ask them to extend the writing process by considering which type of visual aid would help readers better understand their comparison-and-contrast essays.

3. Gather copies of the students' essays in one location and allow time for them to read each other's work.

ASSESS and CLOSE

Assessment

Teaching Resources: Scoring Rubrics on Transparency, Ch. 9; Writing Assessment and Portfolio Management; Formal Assessment, Ch. 9

1. Display the Scoring Rubric transparency and review the criteria in class.

2. Before students proceed with self-assessment, you may wish to review the Final Draft of the Student Work in Progress on pages 187–188.

3. In addition to student self-assessment, you may wish to use the following options:

   • score student essays yourself, using the rubric and scoring models in *Writing Assessment and Portfolio Management*.

   • review the Standardized Test Preparation Workshop on pages 192–193 and administer a timed writing assessment.

   • administer the Chapter 9 assessment in *Formal Assessment* to measure students' grasp of the concepts presented.

9.6 Publishing and Presenting

Building Your Portfolio

Consider the following ways to publish or present your final comparison-and-contrast essay for an audience:

1. **Give a Presentation to the Class** Collect photos, maps, or other visuals to enhance your writing. Use the information in your essay along with visual support to make a formal presentation to the class.

2. **Publish Your Essay On-line** Share your essay with others who are interested in your subject by posting it on an Internet site that offers student writing. If you're not sure of the procedures for publishing on-line, ask an experienced Internet user for help.

Reflecting on Your Writing

When your comparison-and-contrast essay is complete, jot down your ideas about the writing process. Use these questions to get started. Add your comments to your writing portfolio.

• What new insight into your subjects did you gain?

• Which strategy for prewriting, drafting, revising, or editing will be most useful to you in future writing projects?

🖥 Internet Tip

To see model essays scored with this rubric, go to www.phschool.com

Rubric for Self-Assessment

Use these criteria to evaluate your comparison-and-contrast essay.

	Score 4	Score 3	Score 2	Score 1
Audience and Purpose	Clearly provides a reason for a comparison-contrast analysis	Adequately provides a reason for a comparison-contrast analysis	Provides a reason for a comparison-contrast analysis	Does not provide a reason for a comparison-contrast analysis
Organization	Clearly presents information in a consistent organization best suited to the topic	Presents information using an organization suited to the topic	Chooses an organization not suited to comparison and contrast	Shows a lack of organizational strategy
Elaboration	Elaborates most ideas with facts, details, or examples; links all information to comparison and contrast	Elaborates many ideas with facts, details, or examples; links most information to comparison and contrast	Does not elaborate all ideas; does not link some details to comparison and contrast	Does not provide facts or examples to support a comparison and contrast
Use of Language	Demonstrates excellent sentence and vocabulary variety; includes very few mechanical errors	Demonstrates adequate sentence and vocabulary variety; includes few mechanical errors	Demonstrates repetitive use of sentence structure and vocabulary; includes many mechanical errors	Demonstrates poor use of language; generates confusion; includes many mechanical errors

186 • Comparison-and-Contrast Essay

✓ ONGOING ASSESSMENT: Assess Mastery

Use one of the following options to assess final drafts of students' essays.

Self-Assessment Ask students to score their essays using the rubric provided. Then, have students write a paragraph that discusses the strategy they found most helpful in composing their essays.

Teacher Assessment Use the rubric and the scoring models provided in *Writing Assessment and Portfolio Management* to score students' work.

9.7 Student Work IN PROGRESS

FINAL DRAFT

The Real Deal With Mexican Food

Vanessa Serna
Bel Air High School,
El Paso, Texas

Imagine yourself enjoying a vacation in Mexico. You take advantage of the warm weather, sightseeing, and the beaches. If you are lucky enough to be invited to a Mexican home, you jump at the chance to have a home-cooked Mexican meal. But wait! If you are expecting the same burritos and tacos you're used to eating stateside, you may not be prepared for the surprisingly different meal you'll be enjoying.

Anyone who has ever paid a visit to Mexico will agree that there are many differences between authentic Mexican food and the Americanized version. Although many in the United States have tried to replicate popular dishes such as tacos and gorditas, most have failed to accurately re-create the originals. From the ingredients used in the preparation of the food to its appearance, smell, and taste, most stateside attempts are not like real Mexican food.

To get a better idea of this contrast, imagine that you are back in that Mexican home. Your hosts might prepare a dish called *carne asada*. This is a grilled flank steak prepared with local spices. In the United States, chefs have transformed that dish into *fajitas* by char-grilling the steak and cutting it into strips, making it more palatable for the tastes of customers.

One of the major differences between the two forms of Mexican food is in its preparation. Because many Mexican families have access to farm-fresh vegetables, they include this garden produce in their cooking. The corn, tomatoes, onions, peppers, and other vegetables that are used are ripe and fresh. In addition, many hours are devoted to the preparation and cooking time of some essential ingredients, such as pinto beans. As a result, authentic Mexican food is much juicier and tastier than American Mexican

▲ **Critical Viewing**
What adjectives would you use to describe this meal? **[Respond]**

Vanessa's opening paragraph addresses the reader directly and uses descriptive details that create interest in the topic.

Vanessa identifies her purpose. Instead of simply setting out to contrast two cuisines, the writer will advocate her preference for one over the other.

Vanessa organizes her essay using a point-by-point strategy. First, she discusses a feature of Mexican food. Then, she also discusses the same feature of Mexican food served in the United States.

Step-by-Step Teaching Guide

Final Draft

1. Ask students whether Vanessa's essay convinces them that authentic Mexican food is preferable to that served in "Mexican" restaurants in the United States. Why or why not? Which are her most convincing and least convincing points? What might she have added to make her argument stronger?

2. Invite students to explain any changes they would make to this essay.

3. Then, have students annotate their own essays in the way Vanessa's work is annotated. Make sure they call attention to the following characteristics: the items to be compared are clearly named; the purpose of the essay is clear; the preference, if any, is clear; both similarities and differences have been identified; word choice is appropriate for the audience; organization is clear.

4. If students cannot find a place to call attention to one or more of these characteristics, their essays might need to be revised.

Critical Viewing

Respond Students may suggest *spicy, tangy, delicious, festive, bountiful, mouth-watering,* and *tempting.*

Integrating Viewing and Representing Skills

Invite students to discuss the effect of television advertisements on our concept of "good" Mexican food. What qualities do they encourage us to value? (low prices, large portions, quick service, etc.) These qualities of Mexican food are very different from those that Vanessa deems important. How do students explain this difference?

Customize for
AP Students

Point out that many words used to describe Mexican food and its ingredients are now part of our vocabulary in the United States. For example, *avocado* is from the Spanish word *aguacate*, which in turn is based on *áhuacatl*. This is the Aztec word for *avocado*, used in Central America centuries ago. Ask students to research the origins of other names for Mexican food that are now familiar to most people in the United States (chili, tortilla, guacamole, taco, etc.).

Integrating Grammar Skills

Verb Tenses After students read Vanessa's essay, have them identify the different verb tenses she uses. Are any of them used incorrectly? Do any sentences combine two tenses? If so, why?

Customize for
ESL Students

Invite students who have lived in other nations to compare the food prepared there to "imitations" they have tasted in the United States. Have they come to the same conclusion as Vanessa—that the "real thing" is better? If so, what are their reasons?

Critical Viewing

Compare and Contrast Students should realize that what are presented are photographs of authentic Mexican food (p. 187) and Americanized Mexican food (p. 188). After reading the essay, they should be able to make several points of comparison.

◀ **Critical Viewing** Using Vanessa's essay as a starting point, compare this dish with the one that appears on page 187. **[Compare and Contrast]**

food. Because there is not a vegetable garden growing outside every fast-food restaurant that sells Mexican food and because most companies cannot afford to pay their employees to slow-cook ingredients such as pinto beans for six hours, many restaurants use ingredients that are canned or frozen. This isn't to say that Americanized Mexican food doesn't taste good; it just lacks some of the freshness and the homemade touch of authentic Mexican food.

Another difference between the two cuisines is in the use of spices and side dishes. For example, chile has an important role in almost every Mexican meal, including breakfast. In most of the United States, the term *chili* refers to a mildly hot tomatolike mixture, whereas in Mexican culture, *chile* refers to a wide variety of peppers, sauces, and mixtures: red peppers, green peppers, and jalapeños—from mild to burning hot! Chile goes anywhere and everywhere and is essential to an authentic Mexican meal. In contrast, chile is not included in many Mexican meals served in the United States.

Another popular side dish served at both real Mexican and Americanized Mexican meals is guacamole. In Mexico, classic guacamole is created by mashing an avocado and letting the flavor come directly from the creamy green produce. Stateside, guacamole is doctored with onions, lemon juice, and tomatoes to create a clear variation of the Mexican style.

The look of authentic Mexican food as opposed to American Mexican food is also very different. Authentic corn and flour tortillas, for example, look much different from those served at American restaurants. In Mexico, tortilla shells do not come in lovely shades of bright yellow like those used for "taco supremes." Authentic corn and flour tortillas are a shade of creamy white and have a much softer texture. This is because of the contrast in ingredients. Mexican tortillas are made from an ingredient called *maiza*, which makes them light. The tortillas made in United States restaurants are created from flour and cornmeal, so they are thicker and not as light.

The United States is a long way from mastering the art of creating authentic Mexican food. Perhaps one day Americans will be able to duplicate the fresh ingredients, the combination of spices, the colorful look, and the delicious taste of the real thing. When that day comes, viva Mexican food made by American chefs!

188 • Comparison-and-Contrast Essay

Concrete details like ingredients and cooking methods provide elaboration on Vanessa's ideas.

Transitions such as "whereas," and "in contrast," show the connections between points of contrast.

This paragraph addresses the difference in the look of the two foods and gives reasons for the differences.

Vanessa closes her essay with a restatement of her purpose. She extends her conclusion by making a hopeful prediction about the future of Americanized Mexican food.

Connected Assignment

Consumer Report

One of the most practical applications of comparison-and-contrast writing is the report that compares similar products or services to help shoppers make informed decisions. A **consumer report,** filled with facts, examples, and evaluations of several different brands, shows readers how one item stacks up against the competition.

Consumer report writers use comparison-and-contrast to explore similarities and differences among brands, usually by rating them against several criteria.

Challenge yourself to write a consumer report. The writing process steps below offer some starting points.

Prewriting Review the products and services you use regularly. Once you've chosen a product, identify several examples and develop criteria for comparison and contrast. Gather details about several examples of your topic either by personal experience or through telephone and library research. For each brand you address, list your findings on index cards, as shown here:

Exercise Facility #1

- 80% membership renewal each year
- Up-to-date equipment
- Variety of classes

Exercise Facility #2

- 50% membership renewal each year
- Old equipment
- Small selection of classes

Drafting Consider creating a chart to show your findings at a glance. For each category, provide a plus or a minus sign or assign a grade. Then, in your writing, support your evaluations. Define your standard, and then rate each example against it. Provide specific supporting details. In a conclusion, offer readers your best advice.

Revising and Editing Read your draft to be sure you have identified each product by name, model number, and specific cost. Add comparative or superlative modifiers, such as *more dependable* or *most reliable,* to emphasize your evaluation.

Publishing and Presenting Share your findings in a presentation. To make your speech more lively, consider demonstrating the items you included in your report.

▲ **Critical Viewing**
What items in this photograph might be appropriate subjects for a consumer report? **[Identify]**

⚙ **Grammar and Style Tip**

Use comparative modifiers such as *faster* and *more economical* to compare two items. Use superlative modifiers such as *fastest* and *most economical* to compare three or more items.

▶ Lesson Objectives

1. To write a consumer report
2. To compile information from primary sources
3. To use prewriting strategies to plan the report
4. To develop a draft by organizing content and refining style to suit the purpose
5. To proofread the report for appropriateness of content and conventions

Step-by-Step Teaching Guide

Consumer Report

1. If possible, bring some sample consumer reports to class, or suggest that students find some on their own.
2. Refer students to Chapter 9 resources as needed. To help students find a topic, suggest that they refer to the Prewriting section on pages 172–176. (For other helpful resources from Chapter 9, see the chart below.)
3. Emphasize that students need to choose something to research that has substantial competition, not a product or service that seems unique.

Critical Viewing

Identify Students may point out the barbeque kettle, charcoal briquets, and athletic shoes as subjects.

Integrating Grammar Skills

Transitions Point out that comparison-and-contrast order requires frequent use of transitions to keep readers clear on similarities or differences. Remind students that words such as *but, likewise, whereas,* and *similarly* and phrases such as "another difference," "on the other hand," "in contrast," and "similar to" will help unify the essay.

☑ **ONGOING ASSESSMENT: Prerequisite Skills**

Students may find the following resources from Chapter 9 particularly helpful in completing their essays.

In the Textbook	Print Resources	Technology
Identifying Points of Comparison and Contrast, p. 176 Drafting, pp. 177–178	*Writing Support Transparencies,* 9-D, 9-F, 9-I *Writing Support Activity Book,* 9-1, 9-3–4	*Writing Lab* CD-ROM, Exposition

Lesson Objectives

1. To learn about the source of a media production

2. To analyze relationships, ideas, and cultures represented in various media

3. To recognize how visual and sound techniques convey messages in media

4. To compare and contrast two musical performances

Step-by-Step Teaching Guide

Engaging in Critical Listening

1. Choose one of the Spotlight elements for class discussion, or have students work individually or in groups on one of the elements. Ives's and Joplin's music is readily available on compact disc. "Concord" is the subtitle for Ives's Sonata No. 2 for Piano (1909–1915), a work with dissonant harmonies quite ahead of their time.

2. Some students may be interested in researching additional information about Charles Ives or Scott Joplin (1868–1917).

3. "Maple Leaf Rag" is one of the most famous of Joplin's rags, and you might want to play a recording of it for the class.

4. Since the four Transcendentalist authors are all represented in this text, ask students to make some guesses as to why they would have inspired Ives.

5. If students view *The Sting,* ask whether they think the music is or is not appropriate to the action in the film.

Viewing and Representing

Activity Give students the opportunity to make class presentations of their essays. Encourage students to play excerpts of the recordings to illustrate their points.

Spotlight on the Humanities

Engaging in Critical Listening

Focus on Music: Charles Ives

Like most of the humanities, music creates ample opportunity for comparison and contrast as artists draw inspiration from other works and make them their own. Considered one of the most original American composers of the late nineteenth and early twentieth centuries, Charles Ives (1874–1954) composed music inspired by the period of literary experimentation known as Transcendentalism. His "Concord Sonata" is a tribute to four Transcendentalist authors who lived in Concord, Massachusetts, in the middle of the nineteenth century: Ralph Waldo Emerson, Nathaniel Hawthorne, Louisa May Alcott, and Henry David Thoreau. The sonata contains elements of ragtime, brass band, hymn writing, and the sounds of trains. Ives was awarded the Pulitzer Prize in 1947.

Literature Connection Just as Ives's music incorporated elements of several musical forms, Transcendentalist writing incorporated human experience and intuition into a philosophy for living. Transcendentalism was a nineteenth-century American literary movement that produced philosophical writings by its two major authors: Ralph Waldo Emerson and Henry David Thoreau. Thoreau's *Walden* and Emerson's essay "Self-Reliance" are two outstanding and important pieces of Transcendentalist literature.

Film Connection One of the musical elements Ives used in the "Concord Sonata" was ragtime, the syncopated and melodically complex style of music made famous by composer Scott Joplin. Ragtime made a comeback when it formed the soundtrack of the 1973 film *The Sting,* starring Paul Newman and Robert Redford.

Comparison-and-Contrast Writing Activity: Comparing "Covers"

In musical jargon, a "cover" is an artist's interpretation of another's composition. Locate an original and its cover, or find one song performed by two different artists. In a brief essay, compare and contrast the two performances.

190 • Comparison-and-Contrast Essay

▲ **Critical Viewing** What details of costume help to create the setting for *The Sting,* shown here? **[Respond]**

Critical Viewing

Respond Help students identify elements of Robert Redford's clothing, such as his hat, that define the setting as the 1920's, the time period of the movie.

Media and Technology Skills

Comparing Media Coverage

Activity: Track the Stories

Thanks to the Internet and television news, it takes just a click of a TV remote or a mouse to keep us in touch with what's happening in almost any part of the world. However, even though information now spans the continents in an instant, it's difficult to be sure you're getting the straight story about what is going on across town or across the ocean. As you make a plan to stay informed, it's important to know whom you can trust.

Think About It Even with so many sources, we can find conflicting perspectives on major issues. We get news quickly from the Internet and television, but it may not provide depth. We read newspapers and magazines, but the stories there may not include the latest events. The best way to stay informed may be to find a mix of many media. To figure out the best news combination for you, track a specific story, reviewing coverage from a variety of sources. Then, consider what the comparison tells you.

Evaluate It Pick a currently hot story in an area that interests you—politics, the economy, health care, the environment—and follow the coverage of it in several media sources for a few days. Summarize each of the accounts, taking special notice of any differences in emphasis, approach, or opinion that you find.

Analyze It Use a chart like the one here to summarize the coverage you observed. When you complete the chart, rate each source, using a score of 1–10. Then, explain which of these sources you think is the most informative and reliable, and why you think so. Share your findings in a class discussion.

Checklist for Comparing News Sources

	Internet	Local TV	National TV	All-News Radio	Daily Newspaper	Weekly News-magazine
Basic Facts:						
Analysis:						
Updates:						
Extended Coverage:						
Objectivity:						

News Sources

Television
- Nightly network news
- Weeknight public television network news
- Sunday morning network news commentary programs
- Twenty-four-hour cable news networks
- Local nightly newscasts

Radio
- Local, all-news commercial radio stations
- Public radio network news shows
- Hourly local and/or network newscasts on music or talk stations

Internet
- Web pages
- Newsgroups

Print
- Local daily newspapers
- National daily newspapers (e.g., *USA Today, The New York Times* [national edition], *The Christian Science Monitor*)
- National weekly newsmagazines

Lesson Objectives

1. To write an editorial
2. To organize ideas to ensure coherence, logical progression, and support for ideas
3. To use prewriting strategies to develop voice and plan
4. To develop a draft by refining style to suit audience and purpose
5. To produce error-free writing in the final draft

Step-by-Step Teaching Guide

Responding to Expository Writing Prompts

Teaching Resources: Standardized Test Preparation Workbook, pp. 17–18

1. Review the five bulleted items with students.
2. Ask students to read the sample test item, and have them note the audience for their editorial.
3. Review the point-by-point method and the subject-by-subject method with students.
4. Assign this writing prompt for completion within a class period.

Standardized Test Preparation Workshop

Responding to Expository Writing Prompts

The writing prompts on standardized tests often measure your knowledge of expository writing, including comparison-and-contrast writing. When you write a comparison-and-contrast response for a standardized test, your writing will be evaluated on the following criteria:

- Varying word and sentence choice for the purpose and audience named in the response
- Choosing a method of organization that allows you to present details in a logical sequence, such as the subject-by-subject plan or the point-by-point plan
- Using appropriate transitions to support the flow of ideas
- Elaborating through effective use of detail
- Following the conventions of grammar, spelling, and punctuation

Following is an example of an expository writing prompt that addresses the skills of comparison and contrast. Use the suggestions on the following page to help you respond. The clocks next to each stage show a suggested percentage of time to devote to each stage.

Test Tip

When writing your comparison-and-contrast response, clearly state the two subjects you are comparing and their relationship to each other in the introduction.

Sample Prompt

> The Internet has taken a prominent role in everyday shopping, basic research, and even schoolwork. Teachers may even give assignments that require Internet research. Although there is a great deal of information available on the Web, it is often difficult to discern whether or not the information is factual and valid or whether a provider is reputable.
>
> Write an editorial for your school paper stating your position on whether library or Internet research is best for school assignments. For support, use details from your own researching experiences to describe the differences and similarities between library and Internet research.

192 • Comparison-and-Contrast Essay

✎ TEST-TAKING TIP

Students should make sure that they know exactly what a writing prompt asks for. After reading a prompt that asks for similarities and differences, they should quickly jot down in two columns the ideas that immediately occur to them. Also, they should look for the exact words that specify audience and purpose.

Tell students that the number of paragraphs in their editorial may depend on how many categories or key points they are contrasting and comparing. They should recall that they have about thirty minutes for drafting.

Prewriting

Allow close to one fourth of your time for prewriting.

Consider Your Audience and Purpose Because your audience may not have experience with these types of research, list specialized terms concerning both library and Internet research. When you explain these terms, you guarantee your audience will understand your ideas.

Gather and Organize Information As you gather information for your response, identify the points of comparison you might use. For example, to compare library and Internet research, you may want to consider convenience, availability, and reliability, or other categories that suit your position.

Drafting

Allow almost half of your time for drafting.

Organize Details There are two ways to organize details effectively for a comparison-and-contrast essay—the point-by-point method and the subject-by-subject method. Refer to page 177 to review these two options. Then, review your prewriting notes, and draft according to the most appropriate organization.

Construct Paragraphs Begin your response with an introduction that states your position. Use body paragraphs to elaborate on the subjects of your comparison and support your position. Finally, write a conclusion that sums up the main points of your response and restates your position.

Focus on Persuasive Diction Since you want to convince readers that one type of research is better than the other, emphasize your main points with persuasive language—use forceful words that will strengthen your writing and make your argument more effective. Consider using some of the following terms:

Positive: *superior, best, leading, incredible, incomparable*
Negative: *awful, insubstantial, inadequate, insignificant*

Revising, Editing, and Proofreading

Allow almost one fourth of your time to revise and edit. Use the last few minutes to proofread your work.

Make Corrections Review your response. Decide whether some terms need definition. Neatly cross out any details that do not support your purpose. Check for errors in spelling, grammar, and punctuation. When making changes, place one line through text that you want eliminated. Use a caret [^] to indicate the placement of added words.

Time and Resource Manager

In-Depth Lesson Plan

	LESSON FOCUS	PRINT AND MEDIA RESOURCES
DAY 1	**Introduction to the Cause-and-Effect Essay** Students learn key elements of cause-and-effect essays and analyze the Model From Literature (pp. 194–197)	*Writers at Work* **Videotape**, Exposition *Writing Lab* **CD-ROM**, Exposition
DAY 2	**Prewriting** Students choose and narrow a topic, consider their audience and purpose, and gather information. (pp. 198–201)	**Teaching Resources** *Writing Support Transparencies*, 10-A–D; *Writing Support Activity Book*, 10-1–2; *Topic Bank for Heterogeneous Classes*, Ch. 10
DAY 3	**Drafting** Students organize their ideas and write their first drafts. (pp. 202–203)	**Teaching Resources** *Writing Support Transparencies*, 10-E
DAY 4	**Revising** Students revise their drafts in terms of overall structure, paragraphs, sentences, and word choice. (pp. 204–207)	**Teaching Resources** *Writing Support Transparencies*, 10-F–H
DAY 5	**Editing and Proofreading; Publishing and Presenting** Students check their work for accuracy and correctness and present their final drafts. (pp. 208–212)	**Teaching Resources** *Scoring Rubrics on Transparency*, Ch. 10; *Writing Assessment and Portfolio Management; Formal Assessment*, Ch. 10

Accelerated Lesson Plan

	LESSON FOCUS	PRINT AND MEDIA RESOURCES
DAY 1	**Drafting** Students review characteristics of cause-and-effect essays, select topics, and write drafts. (pp. 194–203)	*Writing Lab* **CD-ROM**, Exposition **Teaching Resources** *Writing Support Transparencies*, 10-A–E; *Writing Support Activity Book*, 10-1–2
DAY 2	**Revising to Presenting** Students work individually or with peers to revise, edit, and proofread their work for presentation. (pp. 204–212)	**Teaching Resources** *Writing Support Transparencies*, 10-F–H; *Scoring Rubrics on Transparency*, Ch. 10; *Writing Assessment and Portfolio Management; Formal Assessment*, Ch. 10

Options for Adapting Lesson Plans

HOMEWORK

Have students complete any stage of the lesson for homework.

FEATURES

Extend coverage with Connected Assignment (p. 213), Spotlight on the Humanities (p. 214), Media and Technology Skills (p. 215), and the Standardized Test Preparation Workshop (p. 216).

TECHNOLOGY

Students can complete any stage of the lesson on computer. Have them print out their completed work.

INTEGRATED SKILLS COVERAGE

Integrating Grammar
Using Gerunds to Combine Sentences, SE p. 206
Placement of Adverbs, SE p. 208
Prepositions, ATE p. 205

Reading/Writing Connection
Connect to Your Experience, SE p. 196
Writing Application, SE p. 197

Viewing and Representing
Critical Viewing, SE pp. 194, 196, 203, 210, 212, 213, 214
Responding to Fine Art, SE p. 199
Examining How Meaning Is Communicated Through Elements of Design and Texture, SE p. 214
Recognizing Visual and Sound Techniques in the Media, SE p. 215

Vocabulary   ATE p. 207

Technology   SE pp. 200, 206, 209

Real-World Connection   ATE p. 204

Workplace Skills   ATE p. 200

ASSESSMENT SUPPORT

Standardized Test Preparation Workshop SE p. 216; ATE p. 207

Standardized Test Preparation Workbook, pp. 19–20

Scoring Rubrics on Transparency, Ch. 10

Formal Assessment, Ch. 10

Writing Assessment and Portfolio Management

MEETING INDIVIDUAL NEEDS

Less Advanced Students ATE pp. 211, 217. See also Ongoing Assessments ATE pp. 199, 203, 205.

AP Students ATE p. 203, 217

ESL Students ATE p. 197, 201

Visual/Spatial Learners ATE p. 202

Verbal/Linguistic Learners ATE p. 211

BLOCK SCHEDULING

Pacing Suggestions
For 90-minute Blocks
- Have students complete the Prewriting and Drafting stages in a single period.
- Focus one class period on Revising and Editing and Publishing and Presenting. Allow at least 30 minutes for peer revision.

Resources for Varying Instruction
- *Writing Lab* **CD-ROM** If your students have access to hardware, a 90-minute block provides an ideal opportunity for students to work on computer.
- *Writers at Work* **Videotape** Show Exposition segment in class.

Professional Development Support
- *How to Manage Instruction in the Block* This Teaching Resource provides management and activity suggestions.

MEDIA AND TECHNOLOGY

For the Student
- *Writing Lab* **CD-ROM**, Exposition
- *On-Line Exercise Bank,* Section 19.2

For the Teacher
- *Writers at Work* **Videotape**, Exposition
- *Resource Pro* **CD-ROM**

WRITING AND GRAMMAR WEB SITE

The Interactive Writing and Grammar Web Site provides a wide array of support for students, teachers, and parents. Writing support includes:

- Interactive revision checkers
- Scoring rubrics with complete models

www.phschool.com

LITERATURE CONNECTIONS

Related selections from *Prentice Hall Literature: Timeless Voices, Timeless Themes,* The American Experience:

"The Night the Ghost Got In," James Thurber, SE p. 197
John F. Kennedy's inaugural speech, SE p. 199

Lesson Objectives

1. To write a cause-and-effect essay appropriate to audience and purpose

2. To read to appreciate the writer's craft and to discover models for writing

3. To use prewriting strategies to generate ideas and plan

4. To use texts and technical resources to research self-selected topics

5. To represent information in a variety of ways, including using graphics

6. To develop and revise drafts in terms of structure, paragraphs, sentences, and word choice

7. To edit and proofread to ensure standard English usage and grammar

8. To evaluate writing for both mechanics and content

9. To refine selected work for publication

Critical Viewing

Analyze Students may mention the possibility of people being struck by lightning, as well as fires started by lightning strikes.

Chapter 10 Exposition
Cause-and-Effect Essay

▲ **Critical Viewing**
What are some of the dangerous effects of lightning? **[Analyze]**

Cause-and-Effect Analysis in Everyday Life

It is usually not enough to know that airplanes fly, that exercise can extend your life, or that a television show is generating especially high ratings; we want to know *why*. Understanding how and why things happen is a central part of human curiosity. When you begin to look for relationships to enrich your understanding of how things happen, you are investigating causes and effects.

Understanding cause-and-effect relationships can help you predict future events, plan for goals, and avoid problems.

194 • Exposition

⏱ TIME AND RESOURCE MANAGER

Resources
Technology: *Writers at Work* Videotape, Exposition; *Writing Lab* CD-ROM, Exposition

In-Depth Coverage	Accelerated Pace
• Cover pp. 194–197 in class. • Review pp. 194–195, and provide additional examples of cause-and-effect writing. • Have students discuss their own thoughts on aging as a class or in small groups. • Ask students to read the essay and be prepared to summarize its most important information.	• Assign pp. 194–197 as independent reading.

What Is a Cause-and-Effect Essay?

A **cause-and-effect essay** examines the relationship between events, explaining how one event or situation causes another. A successful cause-and-effect essay includes

- a discussion of a cause, the event or condition that produces a specific result.
- an explanation of an effect, the outcome or result.
- evidence and examples to support the relationship between cause and effect.
- a logical organization that makes the explanation clear.

To see the criteria upon which your final cause-and-effect essay may be evaluated, preview the Rubric for Self-Assessment on page 209.

Types of Cause-and-Effect Essays

Cause-and-effect essays can address subjects in a variety of fields. In addition to the standard cause-and-effect essay, cause-and-effect writing may take one of the following forms:

- **Scientific reports** ("The Causes and Effects of Pollution in the Atmosphere")
- **Current events articles** ("How Megamalls Influence Main Street, U.S.A.")
- **Health studies** ("The Effects of a High-Protein Diet")

PREVIEW
Student Work
IN PROGRESS

This chapter includes the work of Hilary Odom, a student at Athens High School in Athens, Texas. In her writing, she describes the effects of her involvement in her school's drama program. You will see how she used the techniques of prewriting, drafting, and revising to write her essay "Notes From the Footlights." Her final draft appears at the end of the chapter.

Writers in ACTION

Thom Harrington, the curator of the New York Transit Museum, often uses cause-and-effect writing to describe the development of the subway system and the transit system's ability to influence city life. He explains his angle on cause-and-effect writing this way:

"When I think about expository writing, I think about telling my reader what I want to say as concisely as possible...."

PREPARE and ENGAGE

Interest GRABBER Ask students to consider the effects that standardized testing might have on their school day. How does the need to prepare for such tests influence what is taught and how? Ask students to draw connections between what they have studied thus far this year and how their learning might or might not have been influenced by test preparation.

Activate Prior Knowledge

How do students respond to headline events of the day? Invite students to discuss what skills or techniques they use to understand and explain current events. Discuss some examples and then invite students to consider how journalists use the same skills to draw cause-and-effect connections among events.

More About the Writer

Thom Harrington, curator of the New York Transit Museum, helps organize and display the museum's collection of signs, posters, and historic objects from the New York City public transportation system. New York City has one of the oldest and most extensive subway systems in the world. New York's transit system has been central to its growth and emergence as one of largest and most prosperous cities in the world.

☑ **ONGOING ASSESSMENT: Diagnose**

Use one of the following options to diagnose students' current level of proficiency in cause-and-effect writing.

Option 1 Ask each student to select the best example of cause-and-effect writing from last year's writing portfolio. Hold conferences to review each student's sample and to determine which students may need extra help in developing a cause-and-effect essay.

Option 2 Students may write a short paragraph detailing their choices for elective courses during this school year, and list three reasons they used to make their decisions. If students have difficulty completing this exercise, they may need in-depth coverage of the cause-and-effect essay.

Reading\Writing Connection

Reading: Connect to Your Experience

Readers who relate personally to the main idea can more readily understand and evaluate the essay's cause-and-effect reasoning. Have students discuss their experiences with exercise in their own words. Do students derive benefits from exercise? Do they have older friends and relatives who pursue a program of regular exercise?

Step-by-Step Teaching Guide

Engage Students Through Literature

1. Use the following questions to prompt discussion.

   Why would a 51-year-old continue to run?

   What are some of the effects of growing old without exercise?

   What might improve the body's ability to consume and circulate oxygen?

2. Ask students to brainstorm for cause-and-effect ideas suggested by the excerpt. Possibilities:

   Making time for relaxation helps students get more work done.

   Drinking eight glasses of water per day promotes health.

3. Students might add these to their own cause-and-effect ideas in their topic banks.

Critical Viewing

Evaluate Students might or might not view marathon running as a greater accomplishment for older people. However, they should be able to acknowledge that undertaking and meeting physical challenges is especially valuable as a response to medical problems presented by aging.

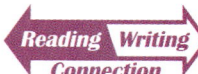 **Model From Literature**

In this article, Marlene Cimons, a writer for Runner's World *magazine, discusses the physical effects caused by aging and the beneficial effects caused by exercise.*

Reading Writing Connection

Reading Strategy: Connect to Your Experience As you read this article, look for ways to relate the topic to your life. For example, while you are certainly not the target audience for this piece, you can probably relate to the attitudes about exercise that the writer reports.

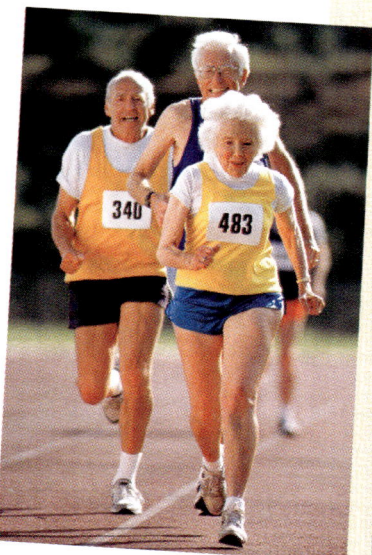

◀ **Critical Viewing** Do you think finishing a marathon should be considered a greater accomplishment for people who are older? Why? **[Evaluate]**

Healthy Aging
Marlene Cimons

Don't call 51-year-old Sam Underwood an "old" runner. "When I turn 70, you can call me an *older* runner, but not an old runner," he says. "I'm running more miles this year than any other year. I love to run. I hate *not* to run."

Underwood, who works in the technical support department of an East Lansing, Mich., bank, acknowledges some of the changes that have occurred with age. "My times are getting slower, my energy level is lower, I take naps after my long runs, and my expectations exceed my results," he admits. "But I don't care. Running is an important part of growing old. And it slows the aging process."

Within the next three decades, more than 70 million Americans will be older than 65, and the 85-and-older group will be the fastest growing segment.

Although aging causes inevitable physical challenges, it is during these later years that exercise becomes even more important, regardless of performance. . . .

By quoting an athlete at the start of the essay, Cimons personalizes her topic.

The writer introduces a cause-and-effect relationship: Exercise can be beneficial to the aging process.

196 • Cause-and-Effect Essay

Over time, a sedentary lifestyle can lead to obesity, diabetes, heart disease, hypertension, depression, insomnia, fatigue, loss of muscle mass, loss of mobility and balance and, ultimately, loss of independence.

However, exercising can prevent or reduce most of these health problems. Several studies show the benefits of exercise on aging, documenting that lifestyle choices are vastly more important than genetics. Moreover, a paper released by the American College of Sports Medicine in July 1998 confirmed that consistent exercise reduces the risks of cardiovascular disease and other age-related diseases.

"The rewards of exercising as we age are enormous," says Robert S. Mazzeo, Ph.D., who wrote the paper. "Regular physical activity contributes to the physical and psychological well-being that defines healthy aging."

In general, the body's ability to consume and circulate oxygen decreases 5 to 15 percent per decade in adults older than 25. But if older adults are involved in some type of endurance training, Mazzeo says, there is less of a decline. And the amount of change in oxygen consumption also depends on the intensity of training; the harder you train, the less you lose.

Another health benefit is that older hypertensive adults who exercise regularly can lower their blood pressure to the same extent as younger adults. Some data indicate that exercising also reduces cholesterol levels in the bloodstream.

"When I talk about people being young or old, I'm thinking of physically active compared to physically inactive," says Chhanda Dutta, Ph.D., director of musculoskeletal research within the geriatrics program at the National Institute of Aging of the National Institutes of Health. "There are people younger than I am who are 'old,' who can't walk a mile to the grocery store. But I've met people at the gym in their seventies and eighties who still work out and do strength training."

Case in point: Lindsay Russell, a 72-year-old living in Boston, still runs a "peppy" 4 miles every day, enters races, and thinks there should be a special designation for older runners beyond masters and veterans. "We need a name," he says "Methuselahs? Fossils? Elders? Ancients? Actually, the only name I like at all is Sunset Kids. But suggestions are welcome."

Reading Writing Connection

Writing Application: Help Readers Connect With Their Experience As you draft your essay, include information and examples that help your readers identify with your subject.

To set up a contrast, this paragraph outlines the effects of a sedentary, or nonactive lifestyle.

The writer cites specific studies that show the link between exercise and healthy aging.

To elaborate the effects of exercise, including physical and mental well-being, the essay explains how activity can increase oxygen circulation and lower blood pressure.

The writer concludes and frames her thesis by describing the experiences of another athlete.

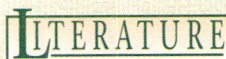

For a humorous example of cause-and-effect writing, read "The Night the Ghost Got In," by James Thurber. You can find the essay in *Prentice Hall Literature: Timeless Voices, Timeless Themes,* The American Experience.

Model From Literature • 197

Teaching From the Model

You can use this Model From Literature as a way of introducing or illustrating the elements of a cause-and-effect essay. In the model, Marlene Cimons points out that a growing number of older Americans are using regular exercise to help them avoid problems associated with aging. How does Cimons educate and persuade readers to see the connections between exercise and healthful aging?

More About the Writer

Marlene Cimons is a National Correspondent for the *Los Angeles Times* based in Washington, D.C. She has had a special interest in writing articles about public health policies and personal health choices.

Connections With Literature

If students have read Thurber's essay, have them discuss whether the plot structure in "The Night the Ghost Got In" is in any way similar to Cimons's cause-and-effect patterns in "Healthy Aging."

Customize for
ESL Students

To support students' comprehension of this selection, preview key vocabulary and concepts such as *aging, exercise, sedentary lifestyle, obesity, oxygen consumption,* and *cholesterol.* You might want to supplement written or spoken definitions of these words with illustrations or photos.

Reading\Writing Connection

Writing Application: Help Readers Connect With Their Experience

Have students speculate about how the writer's essay might relate to her own personal experience. Might she know an older person who enjoys exercise? Suggest that students list friends and family members who might spur ideas for an essay topic.

Step-by-Step Teaching Guide

Prewriting: News Analysis

1. Most newspapers and weekly news magazines publish a year-end wrap-up that surveys the year's important stories. Provide students with copies of one such article to stimulate discussion.

2. As students identify topics of interest, list them on the chalkboard. Lead students to see connections among the events, their causes, and their effects on society. (Example: Increased Internet use changes the ways that people work and shop.) Encourage students to speculate about the consequences of these changes.

Step-by-Step Teaching Guide

Prewriting: Discussion Group

1. Have students generate a list of health issues that they are interested in exploring. Conduct a survey to determine the most popular of these topics. Assign each topic a number and then write these numbers on slips of paper for students to draw at random. Students with matching numbers may be assigned to the same discussion groups.

2. Have each group appoint a recorder to write down the cause-and-effect connections identified by the group. Once each group has generated their lists, have them decide which narrowed topic would make the most interesting essay.

Step-by-Step Teaching Guide

Prewriting: Roster of Memorable Events

Teaching Resources: Writing Support Transparencies, 10-A

1. Display Transparency 10-A to show students how Hilary created a list of memorable events in her life.

2. Record students' topic ideas on the board and model some of your own ideas as well.

10.2 Prewriting

Choosing Your Topic

In order to write an effective essay on a cause and its effect, you must choose two subjects that are clearly linked. Here are some possible strategies for generating topics:

1. **News Analysis** Skim magazines, newspapers, or history books for recent or past events that have had significant effects. When you find one that moves you or quickens your interest, write a cause-and-effect essay about it.

2. **Discussion Group** Meet with a group of friends to discuss health issues, such as the link between diet and exercise or the connection between genetics and disease. As a group, list as many of these connections as you can uncover. Later, review the list to choose a topic.

3. **Roster of Memorable Events** Develop a list of events that have influenced your life in positive ways. Select one event, and write a cause-and-effect essay that explains how the event affected you.

Writing Lab CD-ROM

For more help finding a topic, explore the activities and suggestions in the Choosing a Topic section of the Exposition lesson.

Student Work IN PROGRESS

Name: Hilary Odom
Athens High School
Athens, TX

Listing Memorable Events to Find a Topic

In looking for a topic for her essay, Hilary created this roster of memorable events from her life. Hilary selected the standing ovation and saw a cause-and-effect link to develop into an essay.

- My first day of school
- The birth of my little brother
- The standing ovation I got when I sang a solo in <u>Fiddler on the Roof</u>
- The family trip last summer to the Grand Canyon

I could write about the causes and effects of being in the drama club.

198 • Cause-and-Effect Essay

⏱ TIME AND RESOURCE MANAGER

Resources
Print: *Writing Support Transparencies*, 10-A–D; *Writing Support Activity Book*, 10-1–2; *Topic Bank for Heterogeneous Classes*, Ch. 10
Technology: *Writing Lab* CD-ROM, Exposition

In-Depth Coverage	Accelerated Pace
• Work through the News Analysis, Discussion Group, or Roster of Memorable Events strategies with the class (p. 198). • Use the Responding to Fine Art transparency to explore the relationship between phenomena and their causes.	• Discuss strategies for generating topics for cause-and-effect essays. • Have students work independently to select and develop a topic. • Have students work independently to focus on audience, purpose, and gathering details.

TOPIC BANK

If you are having trouble choosing a topic, consider one of the following ideas:

1. **Report on Effects of the Internet** Surfing the Web has helped people to learn more about their favorite actors, to understand health issues, and to meet new people in discussion groups. In an essay, show how the Internet has changed the way people find up-to-date information on almost any subject.

2. **Essay About Causes and Effects in History** Choose a historical event, such as a declaration of war, the signing of a treaty, or the election of a leader. In an essay, analyze the causes and effects of the topic you've chosen.

Responding to Fine Art

3. *The Dow Is Up!* shows the stock market in action. While you may not follow the ups and downs of the stock market, you probably see the effects of increased or decreased prices of gas, clothing, or the food you buy. In a cause-and-effect essay, analyze the causes and effects of economic changes like these.

The Dow Is Up!, Jane Wooster Scott, Private Collection

Responding to Literature

4. Read John F. Kennedy's inaugural speech. Use his comments as a springboard for a cause-and-effect essay discussing the legacy of Kennedy's presidency on volunteer programs such as the Peace Corps. You can find the speech in *Prentice Hall Literature: Timeless Voices, Timeless Themes*, The American Experience.

☑ Cooperative Writing Opportunity

5. **Analysis of the Effects of Temperature** With classmates, conduct an experiment to record the effects of extreme temperatures on various liquids. Each student can develop one part of the lab report: the background, the explanation of the experiment, the presentation of the results, and the discussion of your group's findings.

Prewriting • 199

Step-by-Step Teaching Guide

Responding to Fine Art

The Dow Is Up! by Jane Wooster Scott
Teaching Resources: Writing Support Transparencies, 10-B

1. Display the transparency of *The Dow Is Up!* and tell students that the painting depicts a scene from the floor of a stock exchange. You may need to explain that stocks are bought and sold on the exchange. *Dow* refers to the Dow Jones Industrial Index, an indicator of the increase or decrease in the overall value of the market.

2. Use questions like these to prompt discussion:

   What details in the painting suggest business and excitement?

   What seems to be the cause of these emotions?

3. Let students know that art has often illustrated the connections between political decisions and the effects they cause. Invite students to name other examples of visual art, entertainment, or information that show connections between causes and effects.

4. Students might include these topic ideas along with their own suggestions in their topic banks.

Responding to Literature

Discuss with students how speeches can motivate and inspire people to take action. Invite them to reflect on times that a public figure, teacher, friend, or other leader motivated them to do something through their words. Have them discuss which elements of John F. Kennedy's message persuaded people to take action.

☑ ONGOING ASSESSMENT: Monitor and Reinforce

If students are having difficulty coming up with a topic, try one of the following strategies:

Option 1 Pair up students to share ideas, or to be advisors or sounding boards for one another. In some cases, you might suggest that students assign topics for each other.

Option 2 If Topic Bank ideas seem too difficult, suggest that students try one of the assignments from the *Topic Bank for Heterogeneous Classes* in the Teaching Resources.

Narrowing Your Topic

When you have selected a topic, consider its scope. To limit your topic to a subject you can address effectively in your essay, consider all the connections your subject suggests. For example, if you have chosen the effects of the NASA space program on science, you might find this topic too broad. NASA professionals are involved in research, publicity, and space launches, so writing a paper on all of the effects of their work would be too involved for your purposes. You can narrow a topic by pinpointing your interests.

Pinpoint to Narrow Your Topic

Begin by writing your topic at the top of a triangle like the one shown here. To focus your subject, use this first idea to generate a more specific subtopic. Continue this process until you arrive at a cause-and-effect relationship narrow enough to address in your essay.

NARROWING A TOPIC

NASA's Research and Development

Satellite technology

Benefits to average citizen

Improvements in long-distance telephone service

Considering Your Audience and Purpose

Identify an Audience Before you begin to draft, spend a moment identifying your audience. When you know your intended audience, you can tailor the information you include to reach them. For example, you may need to define more terms for a younger audience.

Clarify a Purpose When you write to explain something, your purpose should be to make the information clear to readers. However, you may also want to show your readers how the topic affects them, why they should be interested in it, or how they can create change. Clarify your reason for writing, and choose language and details to suit this refined purpose.

☑ ONGOING ASSESSMENT: Prerequisite Skills

In order to pinpoint and develop a topic, students must be able to summarize and identify main ideas in an extended text or discussion. To help them do this, try the following strategy.

Ask a student to choose a topic and give a short oral report on it to the class. Select another student to summarize the main ideas of the speaker. Emphasize to students that a summary is not the same as a reconstruction, but should be a concise identification of the most important points.

Gathering Details

When you are satisfied that your topic is appropriate for your audience, begin to assemble the details to create your draft. In order to establish a sound cause-and-effect relationship, find evidence to prove your point.

Use a Cause-and-Effect Organizer

To find the links you'll describe, use a cause-and-effect organizer like the one below. Above your topic, identify the causes; below it, identify the effects. List as many as you find through research or experience. You can weed out the weaker details as you prepare to draft.

Consider Causes Identify the reasons that produced the topic you will address, and don't limit your information gathering to just one cause. For example, if you are analyzing a flood, heavy rains might be the obvious cause, but don't rule out poor drainage as you list ideas.

List Effects While you look for the effects your topic has produced, consider changes both large and small. When you think small, you might cite a minor inconvenience a flood can cause, but when you look for bigger issues, you may discover that a flood ruined a farmer's entire crop.

Student Work **IN PROGRESS**

Name: Hilary Odom
Athens High School
Athens, TX

Completing an Organizer to Gather Details

Here is the bottom half of the cause-and-effect organizer that Hilary constructed to show the effects she wanted to include in her essay.

MY PARTICIPATION IN HIGH-SCHOOL DRAMA

- Recognition I've Received
  - Parents
  - Fans
- Friendships I've Made
  - Cast and Crew
- Personal Growth
  - Commitment
  - Cooperation
  - Responsibility

Prewriting • 201

Step-by-Step Teaching Guide

Prewriting: Completing an Organizer to Gather Details

Teaching Resources: Writing Support Transparencies, 10-D; Writing Support Activity Book, 10-2

1. Begin this activity by displaying Transparency 10-D. Help students recognize how the outcomes are caused by Hilary's decision to participate in dramatic activities in high school.

2. Invite students to discuss or freewrite about ideas related to their topics. Then, ask students to generate a list of effects associated with their topics.

3. Give students copies of the blank organizer (10-2) to use as they organize their own details.

Customize for
ESL Students

Cause-and-effect relationships might be difficult for students to articulate. You might want to provide them with the option of making notes and an organizer using their first languages and then translating key terms into their first languages for later consultation. Refer students to the key terms shown on the Cause-and-Effect Transitions chart on page 205.

⏱ **TIME SAVERS!**

 Writing Support Transparencies
Use the transparencies for Chapter 10 to facilitate teaching of strategies.

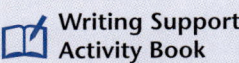 **Writing Support Activity Book**
Use the graphic organizers for Chapter 10 to facilitate student planning.

Step-by-Step Teaching Guide

Drafting: Chronological Order

1. Ask students to identify some advantages of using chronological order to present details. (It is natural to recall an event and note the effects of it that followed.)

2. Caution students that simply because one event follows another, it does not necessarily mean that one event caused the other. (Photography was invented before the Civil War, but photography did not *cause* the Civil War.)

Customize for
Visual/Spatial Learners

Suggest that students write historical events on individual cards and their effects on separate cards. Have them place these cards on a two-column chart in such a way that the primary events are on the left-hand column and the events that followed from them are on the right. This will help students see a visual link between cause and effect.

Step-by-Step Teaching Guide

Drafting: Order of Importance

Teaching Resources: Writing Support Transparencies, 10-E

1. Use Transparency 10-E to show students how organizing effects according to the order of importance might look in practice. Point out that "My personal growth" is more important than "People's reaction to my performance," because it has more long-term significance.

2. Students might wish to write their details on self-sticking notes so that they can be arranged or replaced as they develop their thoughts.

10.3 Drafting

Shaping Your Writing

Choose an Organization

Once you have gathered enough details to establish a clear cause-and-effect link, select an organization that suits your needs. Here are two strategies for presenting information:

Chronological Order This organizational strategy presents events as they occurred. For example, you could use this plan to explain how one historic event had an impact on a subsequent event. You might indicate the order by indicating the time of day, the day of the week, or the month of the year. Transitional words like *first* or *second* can also help establish sequence.

Order of Importance This organizational strategy presents events in a sequence based on the relative importance of each idea to the purpose of the essay. For example, if you are arguing that there are several effects of a stressful environment, you might organize your paper by starting with the annoying nuisances stress generates and building up to the most important effects—the damage stress inflicts on a healthy heart.

Student Work IN PROGRESS

Name: Hilary Odom
Athens High School
Athens, TX

Organizing According to Order of Importance

Hilary identified three main effects, wrote them on self-sticking notes, and tried several different orders. She finally arrived at this sequence—and decided to present her ideas from least to most important.

LEAST IMPORTANT
1. The friendships I've made
2. People's reactions to my performances

MOST IMPORTANT
3. My personal growth

202 • Cause-and-Effect Essay

⏱ TIME AND RESOURCE MANAGER

Resources
Print: *Writing Support Transparencies,* 10-E
Technology: *Writing Lab* CD-ROM, Exposition

In-Depth Coverage	Accelerated Pace
• Work through the Chronological Order and Order of Importance strategies with the class (p. 202). • Read aloud the Providing Elaboration strategy (p. 203). Discuss how providing specific facts and personal testimonies can enhance the power of a cause-and-effect essay.	• Have students review pp. 202–203 independently and then write their first cause-and-effect draft. • Respond to individual drafting issues as needed.

Providing Elaboration

As you draft your cause-and-effect essay, provide details that show a strong relationship between effects and their causes.

Prove the Connection

To convince your audience that the topics you connect are not just mere coincidence, elaborate the link you are showing.

WEAK CONNECTION:	Many college graduates earn higher salaries than those who are not college graduates.
ANALYSIS:	Without an explanation that proves a cause and an effect, the relationship may just be a coincidence.
CAUSE-AND-EFFECT CONNECTION:	Because their education provides them with marketable skills, many college graduates earn higher salaries than those who are not college graduates.

Specific Facts To prove that the cause-and-effect relationship you describe actually exists, provide supporting evidence that backs up your claim. For example, to prove your belief that a college education translates to higher salaries in the work force, provide the facts that make the connection. You can include facts that show how a college graduate brings specific problem-solving skills, planning abilities, and a focused, professional attitude to a job based on years of academic training.

Personal Testimonies Interview your classmates or other people who have experience related to your subject. Use their comments to help illustrate your ideas. Their stories can provide an interesting human slant to statistics or scientific studies you may cite from other sources. For example, to elaborate the connection between a college education and a future salary, use quotations from an interview with a recent college graduate, a guidance counselor, or a human resources representative.

Writers in
ACTION

In addition to his work as an inventor and statesman, Benjamin Franklin wrote many aphorisms that provided his readers with practical wisdom. Notice how he elaborates one such idea through a cause-and-effect chain:

"A little neglect may breed mischief: for want of a nail the shoe was lost; for want of a shoe the horse was lost; and for want of a horse the rider was lost."

▼ **Critical Viewing**
What do you think is the most important effect of a college education? **[Evaluate]**

Drafting • 203

Step-by-Step Teaching Guide

Drafting: Prove the Connection

1. Provide a supplementary example of a weak connection.

   Weak connection: *Although seatbelts have been added to cars made in the U.S. since 1965, the number of deaths and injuries has increased.*

   Analysis: *Because the cause-and-effect connection is not explained, readers might be led to think that seatbelts have made the cars less safe.*

   Cause-and-effect connection: *Deaths and injuries increased because of the huge increase in the number of cars on the road.*

2. Help students illustrate the cause-and-effect relationship in a persuasive or attention-getting way. One such method is through the use of personal testimony or quotations.

Customize for
AP Students

Encourage students to write a cause-and-effect essay that points out the benefits or drawbacks of a school, state, or national policy. Remind students that letters to the editor often address pertinent or timely issues and are useful models.

More About the Writer

Benjamin Franklin's education as a young boy consisted largely of his own reading as a printer's apprentice. His writing was first published in his brother James's newspaper. Later, he became a publisher himself for the *Pennsylvania Gazette* and a popular annual called *Poor Richard's Almanac*.

Critical Viewing

Evaluate Students may cite the possibility of better employment, higher salaries, and more complete use of talents and abilities.

✓ **ONGOING ASSESSMENT: Monitor and Reinforce**

Students sometimes have problems recognizing the causes and effects in their topics. If this is the case with your students, try the following strategy.

Write the following questions on the board. *What made something happen?* [cause] *What happened?* [effect]	Have students work in pairs and apply these questions to their topics. Students can also write up this information in a chart before continuing to draft.

Revising: Clarify the Cause-and-Effect Relationship

Teaching Resources: Writing Support Transparencies, 10-F

1. Have students review their prewriting notes to make sure that their opening and closing paragraphs concisely state a cause-and-effect relationship.

2. Remind students that some subjects use specialized vocabulary that may not be familiar to general readers. Display Transparency 10-F, and discuss how the writer might define or find other words to describe "audition" and "cast list." Ask students for words they might use instead ("try-outs" and "a list of people chosen for the play").

3. Remind students that they will need to use commas, dashes, or parentheses to separate their definitions from the terms they describe. Provide a model on the board.

Real-World Connection

The ability to analyze cause-and-effect relationships is an important skill that helps citizens make decisions in a democracy. During political campaigns, voters need to understand and evaluate not only the effects of actions already taken by government officials, but the possible effects of policies proposed by those running for office. A good grasp of cause-and-effect relationships can help students make informed choices about policies and candidates.

10.4 Revising

When your first draft is finished, take the time to review your cause-and-effect essay. The time you spend polishing your writing will strengthen your ability to convey your ideas.

Revising Your Overall Structure

Clarify the Cause-and-Effect Relationship

Review your introduction and conclusion to check that these paragraphs identify the cause-and-effect relationship you are addressing. Then, to make sure your readers can understand the cause-and-effect relationship you describe throughout your paper, provide more background or definition where necessary. Since a cause-and-effect essay may contain many new terms, make sure that your audience understands all of them.

▶ **REVISION STRATEGY**
Circling Unfamiliar Terms

Reread your essay, circling any terms that may not be familiar to your audience. Challenge yourself to include the definition of these terms in your essay.

Writing Lab CD-ROM

To use a self-evaluation checklist for your cause-and-effect essay, see the Revising and Editing section of the Exposition lesson.

Student Work IN PROGRESS

Name: Hilary Odom
Athens High School
Athens, TX

Defining Unfamiliar Terms

When Hilary reviewed her draft, she realized that anyone who had not participated in a drama production might not know what an audition is and how it proceeds. Therefore, she added the following text to her second paragraph.

The first day of auditions lasted four-and-a-half hours. This was nearly half a day of hopeful actors rereading their audition scenes in successive waves, trying to prove themselves completely worthy.

The theatrical experience begins with a nerve-racking (audition). . . . After that obstacle, we were forced home to wait until the posting of the cast list. Some people would shriek with joy; others would weep with disappointment. . . .

⏱ TIME AND RESOURCE MANAGER

Resources
Print: *Writing Support Transparencies,* 10-F–H
Technology: *Writing Lab* CD-ROM, Exposition

In-Depth Coverage	Accelerated Pace
• Work through revising strategies with the entire class. • Use the relevant transparencies to demonstrate strategies for Defining Unfamiliar Terms (p. 204), Cause-and-Effect Transitions (p. 205), and Identifying Empty and Vague Words (p. 207).	• Have students review pp. 204–207 independently. • Have students revise their cause-and-effect essays as homework.

Revising Your Paragraphs

Review Body Paragraphs

To support the cause-and-effect relationship you are addressing, review each body paragraph of your essay. Be sure the main idea of each paragraph explains, develops, or supports the cause-and-effect relationship you identify. Review your writing to determine whether you have provided enough support for your ideas, and add transitions to clarify connections.

Adding Additional Support Review each body paragraph to identify the main idea you want to develop. Then, evaluate whether you need to add more support for your ideas. If so, return to your prewriting notes or conduct further research to support the cause-and-effect relationship you describe.

Using Transitions to Show Connections Transition words can help you to make sure the relationship between cause and effect is obvious to your readers. Transition words and phrases signal a connection between ideas and assist the reader in following your line of thinking. Use transitional words and phrases to clarify connections.

Cause-and-Effect Transitions

Introducing Causes	Introducing Effects
Since	Therefore
If	Consequently
Because	As a result
As soon as	Subsequently
Until	Then

▶ REVISION STRATEGY
Color-Coding to Identify Transitions

Use two different colors to identify places in your draft in which transitions could strengthen the writing. Underline any discussion of cause in one color; underline any discussion of effect in another. Look for areas where the two colors meet, and evaluate your writing.

Evaluate
- Are there places in your draft in which the connections from cause to effect might not be clear to the reader?

Revise
- Add transition words in your draft where they are needed.

🌪 Challenge

Read your paper with a skeptical eye. If you imagine the doubtful attitude your audience may have, you can anticipate their hesitancy and make your argument more convincing.

Revising: Review Body Paragraphs

Teaching Resources: Writing Support Transparencies, 10-G

1. A common challenge for student writers is providing clear and fully-explained support throughout their essays. Make sure students can explain the central cause-and-effect relationship for their drafts in a phrase or sentence.

2. Suggest that students exchange papers with a classmate when evaluating whether or not their body paragraphs offer sufficient support for their ideas.

3. Point out the Cause-and-Effect Transitions chart on page 205 or display Transparency 10-G. Point out that the words that introduce causes will tend to come earlier in a piece of writing than those introducing effects.

4. Remind students that cause-and-effect transition words need not be limited to those shown in the table on page 205 and that they might include phrases as well as words. Ask students to think of additional words (causes: *whenever,* and *depending on;* effects: *so* and *for this reason.*)

Integrating Grammar Skills

Prepositions Point out that prepositions identify relationships and provide information about relative positions in space or time. (Examples: *under, above, before, behind, after,* and *since.*) Prepositions often occur in phrases that provide the same kind of information but are not limited to one word. (Example: *under the table, above the ceiling,* or *behind the refrigerator.*) Ask students to identify prepositions and prepositional phrases in their drafts.

✓ ONGOING ASSESSMENT: Monitor and Reinforce

Try the following strategy with students who have difficulty identifying cause-and-effect transitions.

Challenge students to make up paired sentences in which of both types of transitions appear. Here is an example you can use as a model.

Because the fire department was so near, the fire trucks arrived almost immediately. As a result, the house was saved.

("Because," introduces the cause of the fire trucks arriving so quickly. "As a result," introduces the effect of the trucks' rapid arrival, the effect of the first sentence having now become the cause of the second.)

Step-by-Step Teaching Guide

Revising: Combine Short Sentences

1. Use the following passage to illustrate short, choppy sentences:

   Look out for short sentences. Short sentences sound odd. They're like red lights. Drivers hate stopping so often. So do readers. They don't like it. They want information to flow. Short sentences stop readers. They make them do extra work. They're stopped in the middle of an idea.

2. Ask students to consider why they might include a few shorter sentences in their drafts (to provide contrast and variety and to help make an important point stand out).

Step-by-Step Teaching Guide

Using Gerunds to Combine Sentences

1. Discuss examples of gerunds.
2. Discuss the techniques for combining short sentences using gerunds. Work through some examples on the board.

Find It in Your Reading

Possible answers:
Paragraph 2: running—subject.
Paragraph 4: aging—subject.
Paragraph 6: exercising—subject; aging—object of preposition.
Paragraph 7: exercising—object of preposition; aging—direct object.

Find It in Your Writing

When students use short sentences without gerunds, it may be because they lack confidence as writers and want each sentence to be correct. Students may need direct support and assurance from you in order to begin to try sentence combining.

Revising Your Sentences

Combine Short Sentences

Short, choppy sentences interrupt the flow of your writing. Read your draft to see where you can combine short sentences into longer ones that smooth the flow of ideas.

EXAMPLE: Satellites are useful because they relay television signals. We use satellites to communicate by telephone as well. Satellites also help us to study weather conditions.

REVISED: Satellites allow us to relay telephone messages, communicate by telephone, and study weather conditions.

▶ REVISION STRATEGY
Tracking Sentence Length

To determine whether too many of your sentences are short and choppy, count the words in each sentence and note the results in the margin. If a majority of your sentences are ten words or less, consider combining some short sentences.

◉ Technology Tip

The word-processing software you use probably has a word-count tool that can be used to count the words in a sentence.

Grammar in Your Writing
Using Gerunds to Combine Sentences

When a verb ending in *-ing* functions as a noun, it is called a **gerund.**

Direct Object: I like skiing.

Subject: Skiing has captured the hearts of many.

Object of a Preposition: I have read several books about skiing.

By transforming the action of a short sentence into a gerund, this verb form can be used to combine sentences.

Verbs: Some people swim to exercise. Others run. Some also dance.

Gerunds: Popular forms of exercise are swimming, running, and dancing.

Find It in Your Reading Look for three gerunds in "Healthy Aging," by Marlene Cimons on pages 196–197. For each, identify the function it serves.

Find It in Your Writing Review your draft to see whether you have used any gerunds. If not, combine sentences to include at least one gerund in your writing.

For more information on gerunds, see Chapter 19.

206 • Cause-and-Effect Essay

✓ ONGOING ASSESSMENT: Prerequisite Skills

If students have difficulty with using gerunds to combine sentences you might find it helpful to review the following to assure coverage of prerequisite knowledge.

In the Textbook	Print Resources	Technology
Gerunds and Gerund Phrases, pp. 446–447	*Grammar Exercise Workbook,* pp. 49–50	*On-Line Exercise Bank,* Section 19.2

Revising Your Word Choice

Delete Empty and Vague Words

An effective writer is careful to make every word count. To tighten your essay, review it for empty words—such as *really* and *very*—that do not add to your writing. Also, look for vague words that can be replaced with more precise language.

▶ **REVISION STRATEGY**
Color-Coding Empty and Vague Words

Draw a red deletion line through all of the empty words you find. Draw a red circle around vague words, such as *good*, *nice*, *weird*, or *thing*. Replace the words you've circled with others that convey exactly what you mean.

Student Work
IN PROGRESS

Name: Hilary Odom
Athens High School
Athens, TX

Identifying Empty and Vague Words

In this section of her draft, Hilary found several empty words to delete. She also revised some vague words to make her writing more accurate.

One ~~really~~ positive effect of being involved in the productions
is the (wonderful) [familial] bond that is created between the cast and
crew members. . . . I have also found a (nice friend) [confidante] in my
director. . . . I find it ~~very~~ reassuring that age does not ~~really~~
seem to matter to any of us. Each year, there is ~~always~~ another
group of freshmen. They are ~~easily~~ recognizable by their (weird) [wide-eyed]
expressions and timid whispers.

Peer Review

Pointing

Read your essay twice to a small group of classmates. Ask them to listen the first time. The second time, ask them to point out the strengths of your paper.

To get more critical feedback, ask your peers to jot down places in which they did not clearly perceive the cause-and-effect connections you intended to make. Consider using their suggestions to clarify your writing.

Revising: Color-Coding Empty and Vague Words

Teaching Resources: Writing Support Transparencies, 10-H

1. Compare words such as *nice* and *bad* to junk mail. They are not personal or specific and reveal little about the author's perspective or feelings. Can students identify other such words?

2. Review Transparency 10-H. Discuss with students how the circled words are "junk mail" words. Encourage them to explain how the revisions and deletions improve the draft.

3. Ask students to quickly scan their drafts looking for empty or vague words. Invite them to volunteer examples for you to put on the board.

Revising: Peer Review

1. Begin the peer review process by pointing out that feedback is offered as a service to fellow writers. For this reason, you might want to offer discussion time for group members to reach an understanding about the form of feedback that is most helpful to them.

2. Encourage students to point out what was most vivid or memorable in a draft before they offer criticism.

3. Suggest that listeners ask questions about things they did not understand or were confusing to them. This is a good way to prompt practical improvements in a draft.

Integrating Vocabulary Skills

The original meaning of *nice* comes from a Middle English word meaning "simple" or "shallow." You might suggest to students that overuse of the word *nice* could create a similar impression of your writing on the reader.

STANDARDIZED TEST PREPARATION WORKSHOP

Vocabulary Standardized tests require students to identify what part of speech a particular word plays in a sentence. Students should draw on their knowledge of parts of speech to answer the question below.

When I buy new track shoes, I like running even more than I usually do.

What part of speech is the word running *in this sentence?*

A adverb   **B** verb   **C** noun   **D** preposition

Students should recognize that the correct answer is **C**. A and D cannot function as direct objects, and B is incorrect because the main verb of the sentence is *like*.

10.5 Editing and Proofreading

Make corrections in grammar, usage, and mechanics to ensure that your final draft is error-free.

Focusing on Sentence Clarity

Read each sentence in your draft to make sure it communicates effectively. Be especially careful of the placement of modifiers, those words or phrases that provide more information about another word in a sentence. Misplaced modifiers may cause confusion. In the example below, a misplaced phrase suggests a famous painting was created by a student. Notice how the revision clarifies the writer's meaning.

EXAMPLE: The essay describes a famous painting *by Steven*.
REVISION: The essay *by Steven* describes a famous painting.

Grammar in Your Writing
Placement of Adverbs

For clarity, an adverb should be placed near the verb it modifies. On occasion, it may be placed elsewhere in the sentence to emphasize a point, create a dramatic effect, or vary a sentence. Here are examples:

Conventional placement before verb: I **usually** drive down Main Street.

Placement for emphasis: **Suddenly,** a boy ran in front of my car.

Sometimes, the placement of an adverb changes the meaning of a sentence. Be sure that the placement of adverbs accurately reflects your meaning.

I **only** hope Beth skates. (Writer worries whether Beth skates.)

I hope **only** Beth skates. (Writer hopes Beth—and no one else—skates.)

Find It in Your Reading In "Healthy Aging" on pages 196–197, the writer uses adverbs sparingly. Find three adverbs, and note where they appear in relation to the verbs they modify.

Find It in Your Writing Circle all the adverbs in your essay. Check that each one is placed where it is most effective. If your essay includes no adverbs, add at least two.

For more about adverbs, see Chapter 17.

208 • Cause-and-Effect Essay

10.6 Publishing and Presenting

Building Your Portfolio

By sharing your cause-and-effect essay, you may help your readers plan for the future or understand the past. Following are some ideas for presenting your work:

1. **Present a Speech** If your essay addresses a situation that other people in your school face, you might offer to speak to classes or clubs that can benefit from your work.
2. **Publish a Feature Article** Submit your essay to your local or high-school newspaper. In a letter accompanying your essay, explain to the editor why the issue you address is important to the newspaper's readership.

Reflecting on Your Writing

After you have completed your essay, use the following questions to begin reflecting on your writing experience. Include your comments, along with the essay, in your portfolio.

- Did learning about the causes and effects of your topic motivate you to take any action?
- What strategy included in this lesson will help you improve your writing in other assignments?

 Internet Tip

To see model essays scored with this rubric, go to **www.phschool.com**

Rubric for Self-Assessment

Use these criteria to assess your cause-and-effect essay:

	Score 4	Score 3	Score 2	Score 1
Audience and Purpose	Consistently targets an audience; clearly identifies purpose in thesis statement	Targets an audience; identifies purpose in thesis statement	Misses a target audience by including a wide range of word choice and details; presents no clear purpose	Addresses no specific audience or purpose
Organization	Presents a clear, consistent organizational strategy to show cause and effect	Presents a clear organizational strategy with occasional inconsistencies; shows cause and effect	Presents an inconsistent organizational strategy; creates illogical presentation of causes and effects	Demonstrates a lack of organizational strategy; creates a confusing presentation
Elaboration	Successfully links causes with effects; fully elaborates connections among ideas	Links causes with effects; elaborates connections among most ideas	Links some causes with some effects; elaborates connections among most ideas	Develops and elaborates no links between causes and effects
Use of Language	Frequently combines sentences to show relationships and ideas; presents very few mechanical errors	Combines sentences to show relationships and ideas; presents few mechanical errors	Misses some opportunities to combine sentences; presents many mechanical errors	Demonstrates poor use of language; presents many mechanical errors

---

✓ ONGOING ASSESSMENT: Assess Mastery

Use one of the following options to assess final drafts of students' cause-and-effect essays.

Self-Assessment Ask students to score their essays using the rubric provided. Then have students write a single paragraph reflecting on the most valuable thing they learned in completing this assignment.

Teacher Assessment You may wish to use the rubric and the scoring models provided in *Writing Assessment and Portfolio Management* to score students' cause-and-effect essays.

Step-by-Step Teaching Guide

Publishing and Presenting

1. In preparing their speeches or feature articles, students might wish to add illustrations, diagrams, or photos. Ask them to extend the process of composition by considering which of these items would help a reader most.
2. Allow class time for students who wish to present their work as a speech.

ASSESS and CLOSE

Step-by-Step Teaching Guide

Assessment

Teaching Resources: Scoring Rubrics on Transparency, Ch. 10; Writing Assessment and Portfolio Management; Formal Assessment, Ch. 10

1. Display the Scoring Rubric transparency and review the criteria in class.
2. Before students proceed with self-assessment, you may wish to review Hilary's Final Draft on pages 210–212. Have students score the essay in one or more of the rubric categories.
3. In addition to student self-assessment, you may wish to:
   - score student essays yourself using the rubric and scoring models from *Writing Assessment and Portfolio Management.*
   - review the Standardized Test Preparation Workshop on pages 216–217 and have students respond to a cause-and-effect writing prompt within a set time limit.
   - administer the Chapter 10 assessment from *Formal Assessment* in the Teaching Resources to measure students' grasp of the concepts presented.

Final Draft

1. Help students see how "Notes From the Footlights" incorporates key elements of the cause-and-effect essay.

   • Hilary shows clearly how her involvement in theater led to a number of specific results, which are elaborated in detail.

   • She connects her discussion of effects to the cause throughout.

   • She employs transitional devices to signal changes of subtopics.

   • Her final paragraph offers a brief restatement and summary of her themes along with a more general conclusion.

2. Ask students which aspects of this essay were most memorable or enjoyable to them. How did the writer make this interesting and informative to read? How might they adopt these same strategies for their own writing?

Critical Viewing

Analyze Students will observe that an audition might provoke anxiety about one's performance.

10.7 *Student Work*
IN PROGRESS

FINAL DRAFT

◄ **Critical Viewing**
How can the competition of an audition like the one shown here challenge a young person's confidence? **[Analyze]**

Notes From the Footlights

Hilary Odom
Athens High School
Athens, Texas

"All the world's a stage,/And all the men and women merely players." Shakespeare never penned truer words, especially when they are applied to the stage that is high school. Therefore, I naturally felt inclined to become involved in drama during my high-school years. Little did I know the far-ranging effects this choice would have on my life: four years of friends, fame, and personal growth that I'll carry with me into my life after high school.

The theatrical experience begins with a nerve-racking audition. For example, the first day of auditions for my school's production of *Fiddler on the Roof* lasted four-and-a-half hours. This was nearly half a day of hopeful actors rereading their audition scenes in

With a quotation from one of the world's most famous dramatists, Hilary sets the scene for her audience.

The introduction cites the three main effects of Hilary's involvement in high-school drama.

210 • Cause-and-Effect Essay

successive waves, trying to prove themselves completely worthy. On the second day—singing auditions—people fled from the building in tears because they were so uncomfortable singing for the director.

After that obstacle, we were forced home to wait in sleepless agony until the early morning posting of the cast list. Some people would shriek with joy; others would weep with disappointment, but as rehearsals began, we all found that there truly are no small parts. Then, the true work began. Night after night of two- to three-hour practices finally started to pay off, and we saw our show transformed into an awesome work of art. On opening night, as we took our places and began singing the first chorus of "Tradition," no words could describe the feeling of satisfaction we shared.

One positive effect of being involved in the productions is the familial bond that is created between the cast and crew members. Upon agreeing to be in a show, I also agree to immediate acceptance into a group of more than fifty friends who will make me smile, push me to do my best, and sometimes even annoy me to the point of madness! However, they have a way of always making me laugh, even when I think I have forgotten how. Not only have I formed lasting relationships with my peers, I have also found a confidante in my director. "Mama Lowe" earned her nickname because even though she can be strict at times, she exhibits the same respect and affection for us that she displays for her own children. Finally, I find it reassuring that age does not seem to matter to any of us. Each year, there is another group of freshmen who are easily recognizable by their wide-eyed expressions and timid whispers. I can remember feeling the same way myself not too long ago. Yet, each year on closing night, everyone is crying, hugging, and counting down the days until auditions for the next show.

Another beneficial effect of being a part of the school play is that everyone gets to experience his or her fifteen minutes of fame. During the run of one show, there are usually about 150 people at each of the seven performances. This means that we get to entertain more than 1,000 audience members, commonly referred to as adoring fans. With so many people coming to see us, it is impossible to finish a show without feeling special. Each cast member has his or her own story and will undoubtedly recount it on request. One might describe her first piece of fan mail that was shyly delivered by a small, awestruck child. Another may never forget the tears in his parents' eyes after they watched his very first performance. A third person would tell about being

Hilary draws on her experience to provide details that help define the activities of the drama club. Later, she will describe the effects of these activities.

Beginning with this paragraph, Hilary presents three of the main effects of her involvement with the drama club. She gives examples to support them.

The transitional words "another beneficial effect" reinforce the order-of-importance organization of the essay.

Customize for
Verbal/Linguistic Learners

Challenge students to jot down a list of the main points, summarizing the cause-and-effect theme and details of the model. Ask each student to use these notes to prepare for an oral report. Ask volunteers to give their oral reports to the class.

Customize for
Less Advanced Students

Students may benefit from hearing the essay read aloud. Have a prepared student read the essay, or read it yourself. Emphasize the words and phrases that indicate causes and effects.

Student Work in Progress • 211

Teaching From the Final Draft

Point out to students that Hilary has organized details by order of importance and has reserved the most important effects for her last two paragraphs. Ask students to note the transition words Hilary uses in the second to last paragraph (*Finally, Most importantly, Second, Lastly*).

Critical Viewing

Analyze Students may say that stage lights might cause performers to feel too conspicuous and thus self-conscious and uneasy.

recognized in the grocery store months after the show had ended. My personal moment of glory occurred when I received my first standing ovation after singing a solo. Similar experiences are inevitable for anyone who becomes involved in his or her school play.

Finally, my participation in high-school theater has taught me several skills that will benefit me throughout my life. Most importantly, I learned the meaning of commitment. This means that once I have committed to a show, it must be among my top priorities, and I have to be willing to sacrifice other things in order to devote enough time and energy to the play. Second, theater has instilled in me a sense of responsibility. My personal struggle was punctuality—I found it extremely difficult to arrive at rehearsals on time. However, this also includes other duties, such as learning lines, songs, and dances by the appointed dates; not doing anything that could seriously jeopardize my safety, since we have no understudies; and always obeying the director. Lastly, I became more able to work with a large group of people. I discovered that diplomacy and cool-headedness are absolutely required and that nothing is impossible when you are willing to cooperate. For these lessons, I am extremely grateful.

I became part of the play because I thought it would be fun, but having been in it has given me and the other student actors so much more. Because of the long-term effects of the love, attention, and wisdom I gained, becoming involved in theater was the best high-school career decision I ever made. It will be the one thing I will miss the most after graduation.

Hilary elaborates on fame by describing the variety of experiences cast members have had with their community celebrity.

Hilary saves the most important effects for the last two paragraphs. Here, she describes the lessons the drama club has taught her about life.

By placing her drama experiences in the larger context of her high-school career, Hilary shows how strongly she values her life in the footlights.

◄ **Critical Viewing**
How can stage lights cause stage fright? **[Analyze]**

212 • Cause-and-Effect Essay

Connected Assignment *Documentary*

Just like a cause-and-effect essay, **documentaries** can explore the relationship between an event and the reasons or causes leading to it. Whether a full-length film or a twenty-minute segment on a television newsmagazine, documentaries report real-life events by presenting factual information. To take advantage of their audio/visual format, these reports often include interviews, historical film footage, and dramatic images of events.

Use the writing process tips below to write your own documentary script on a topic that interests you.

Prewriting Focus on a cause-and-effect story you'd like to tell. You might identify a local injustice or bring a favorite place to viewers' attention. As you research your topic, look for engaging primary source materials. Letters, live interviews, and news headlines can add visual appeal, emotional impact, and authenticity to your documentary.

Remember the cause-and-effect link you're documenting as you review research findings. Use a cause-and-effect organizer to help you see the connections to address.

CAUSE		EFFECT		EFFECT
IF Young people exercise regularly	THEN	They will be healthier and more physically fit.	AND	They will feel more optimistic.

Drafting As you draft your script, include camera directions in brackets. Indicate the visuals you'll use at each point. To stress the causes and effects, use the narration of your script to link visuals that vividly illustrate the ideas you are presenting.

Revising and Editing Read your script aloud, checking the suitability of each film image. Make sure the pieces fit together coherently and that the sequence of information emphasizes the cause and effect.

Publishing and Presenting Videotape your documentary, enlisting the aid of others, if necessary. Follow your script, using the appropriate visuals you have chosen. Share the video with your classmates.

▲ **Critical Viewing** Why do you think twenty-minute documentaries are a popular form of television news? **[Hypothesize]**

▶ *Lesson Objectives*

1. To create a short documentary to engage a specific audience
2. To organize ideas in writing to ensure coherence, logical progression, and support for ideas
3. To use a variety of forms and technologies such as videos, photographs, and web pages to communicate specific messages
4. To recognize genres such as documentaries and television nightly news and identify the unique properties of each

Step-by-Step Teaching Guide

Documentary

Teaching Resources: Writing Support Transparencies, 10-I; Writing Support Activity Book, 10-3

1. To help students identify a topic, encourage them to brainstorm alone or in small groups for a list of topics that seem interesting.
2. Display Transparency 10-I to help students see how to narrow their topics. Give students copies of the blank organizer (10-3) to use to finalize their topics. See the chart below for other useful resources from Chapter 10.
3. Provide some examples of script format which students can use as models. Remind them that unless they are working with others who require a particular format, they should feel free to modify this form to suit their own purposes.
4. Suggest that as students read their scripts they use a watch or timer and note how long each segment will last. This will give them a more precise sense of how much to add or delete from the script to control the tempo and duration of the documentary.

Critical Viewing

Hypothesize Students may suggest that it requires time to sketch out causes and effects and draw connections between them.

✓ ONGOING ASSESSMENT: Prerequisite Skills

Students may find the following resources from Chapter 10 particularly helpful in completing their documentary.

In the Textbook	Print Resources	Technology
Choosing Your Topic, p. 198 Pinpoint to Narrow Your Topic, p. 200 Use a Cause-and-Effect Organizer, p. 201	*Writing Support Transparencies,* 10-C–D *Writing Support Activity Book,* 10-1–2	*Writing Lab* CD-ROM, Exposition

Spotlight on the Humanities

Examining How Meaning Is Communicated Through Elements of Design and Texture

Focus on Art: Georges Seurat

Inspired by the experimentation of Impressionism, French painter Georges Seurat (1859–1891) created a form of artistic cause and effect known as pointillism. At a certain distance, pointillistic images become clear; however, as a viewer approaches the painting, the unity of the image often breaks into a series of contrasting dots or points of color. From 1884 to 1886, Seurat completed his most famous painting, *Sunday Afternoon on the Isle of la Grande Jatte.*

Sunday Afternoon on the Isle of la Grande Jatte, Georges-Pierre Seurat

▲ **Critical Viewing**
How would you describe the texture of this painting by Georges Seurat? **[Describe]**

Theater Connection Steven Sondheim's musical *Sunday in the Park With George* opened on Broadway in 1984. The musical was based on the life of Georges Seurat and, in particular, his painting *Sunday Afternoon on the Isle of la Grande Jatte.* In fact, as the curtain opens on this musical, the actors strike the poses of the painting, re-creating the work in silent tableau. The musical won Tony Awards for Best Scenic Design and Best Lighting Design.

Music Connection Just as pointillism relies on a series of small dots applied individually to the canvas, the musical tempo of staccato creates a similar texture in music. Staccato is a series of individual notes with distinct breaks between successive tones. Aram Khachaturian's "Sabre Dance" (1942), featured in countless commercials and films, is a prime example of the staccato technique.

Cause-and-Effect Writing Activity: Report on Pointillism

Conduct research to learn more about Seurat's scientific approach to painting. Investigate how pointillism is used to create a textured, multicolored image. In a cause-and-effect essay, report on the technique and how it differs from more realistic styles of painting.

214 • Cause-and-Effect Essay

Media and Technology Skills

Recognizing Visual and Sound Techniques in the Media

Activity: Identify Special Effects on the TV News

Special effects is a term we associate mostly with the movies: It suggests exotic space creatures and bioengineered dinosaurs. However, special-effects technology looms large in your local news as well. To become a more informed viewer, watch news programs critically, and notice how visual and sound techniques can influence your reactions to the news.

Learn About It In the 1950's, a television news anchor sat at a desk and read news copy from sheets in his hand. His head bobbed up and down while he maintained some eye contact with the camera and read the news. Television news has changed, incorporating technology to create a smoother product. Consider these advances:

- **Teleprompters** allow the anchor to appear to be looking straight at the viewer—perhaps even speaking spontaneously—while they are actually reading a script from a lighted electronic scroll right next to the camera lens.

- **On-the-spot coverage** lends authenticity and drama to a story by presenting reporters outside the studio, perhaps in a hurricane or standing in front of the Supreme Court Building.

- **Editing, camera angles,** and **reaction shots** allow news producers to present a specific slant on their stories. Interviews generally take longer than the thirty seconds shown on the air; however, postinterview editing allows reporters to get the sentence or two they want to air.

- **Music** adds to a newscast's tone. For example, the national news may have more dramatic theme music than the breezier local news does.

Watch It and Analyze It Pick a thirty-to-sixty-minute stretch of your local evening newscast, and keep a record of how many of these visual and sound techniques are used. For each one, judge whether it helps to convey information or to provide a form of entertainment. Explain how the techniques influenced your reaction to the information presented.

Special Effects	News or Entertainment?

Special Techniques Used to Create Newscasts

- Teleprompter
- Theme music
- Stand-up reports from scenic locations
- Elaborate, space-age sets
- Virtual weather maps
- Superimposed weather maps

▶ *Lesson Objectives*

1. To investigate the source of a media presentation or production such as who made it and why it was made

2. To recognize how visual and sound techniques or design convey messages in media such as special effects, editing, camera angles, reaction shots, sequencing, and music

3. To distinguish between the purposes of media forms such as informative and entertaining texts

---

Step-by-Step Teaching Guide

Recognizing Visual and Sound Techniques in the Media

Teaching Resources: Writing Support Transparencies, 10-J; Writing Support Activity Book, 10-4

1. Review the Special Techniques of news broadcasts found in the sidebar box on page 215.

2. Ask students to supply other special techniques used in news broadcasts. They might suggest film footage of a past political or sports event, use of city maps to pinpoint specific locations of traffic bottlenecks or accidents, and use of maps showing a location in a foreign country.

3. Display Transparency 10-J to show students how to record visual and sound techniques. Give them a copy of the blank organizer (10-4) to record their own information. Ask them to tell which techniques were most effective and whether they helped to provide news or entertainment. Did students see any techniques that were not listed in the textbook?

Lesson Objectives

1. To write in a style appropriate to audience and purpose

2. To organize ideas to ensure coherence and support for ideas

3. To develop a draft by organizing and reorganizing content and by refining style to suit audience and purpose

4. To proofread for appropriateness of organization, content, style, and conventions.

Step-by-Step Teaching Guide

Cause-and-Effect Writing Prompts

Teaching Resources: Standardized Test Preparation Workbook, pp. 19–20

1. To get students thinking about newspapers, ask them to name the various sections and regular features of a daily newspaper.

2. Have students review the cause-and-effect organizer on page 201.

3. Tell students that for this prompt, "Reading a Daily Newspaper" is the cause, and the benefits of such reading are the effects.

4. Assign the writing prompt for completion within a class period.

Standardized Test Preparation Workshop

Responding to Cause-and-Effect Writing Prompts

Questions on standardized tests often measure your ability to use different forms of exposition. In some cases, you will encounter writing prompts that require you to show the relationships between causes and their effects. The following are the criteria upon which your writing will be evaluated:

- responding directly to the prompt
- organizing ideas to be logical, clear, and easy to follow
- elaborating ideas thoroughly by using appropriate details and precise language
- using correct spelling, capitalization, punctuation, grammar, usage, and a variety of sentence structures

When writing for a timed test, plan to devote a specified amount of time to prewriting, drafting, revising, and proofreading.

Following is an example of a writing prompt that you might find on a standardized test. Use the suggestions on the following page to help you respond. The clocks next to each stage show a suggested percentage of time to devote to each stage.

Test Tip

Underline words that indicate your purpose for writing and any specific instructions for developing your answer. Make sure your response is consistent with these directions.

Sample Writing Situation

Many adults read at least one newspaper a day. However, some young people may not see the benefit of developing this habit. In an essay to include in a study-skills packet for students entering your school for the first time, identify the positive effects of reading a newspaper on a daily basis.

✎ TEST-TAKING TIP

Students should always note whether an audience is specified in a writing prompt, since audience affects the tone of the essay. Tell students that in a cause-and-effect essay, they should remember to back up their general statements with specific examples.

Ask students to pick out the key words in the sample prompt (*benefit, students entering school for the first time, identify, positive effects,* and *daily*). Then, let students know that for a cause-and-effect essay, the length of the paper will depend on how many points they feel they can name and support in the time allotted.

Prewriting

Allow close to one fourth of your time for prewriting.

Use a Cause-and-Effect Organizer To help you generate details for your response, sketch a cause-and-effect organizer. For your causes, write *READING A DAILY NEWSPAPER*; then, generate a list of the positive outcomes such a habit could generate. To review the structure of this type of organizer, see page 201.

Address Your Audience Review your organizer to decide which effects would appeal to an audience of students. Choose those ideas that might encourage them to read a newspaper, and plan a strategy for including ideas that will benefit your audience but that may not initially interest them.

Drafting

Allow almost half of your time for drafting.

Strike a Friendly Tone Because you are writing for students your age, use language and details that make your subject accessible. Consider an introduction that welcomes new students, state the main idea of your essay, and develop each effect you have identified.

Elaborate With Examples For each effect you attribute to reading a newspaper daily, support your ideas with specific examples. If you claim that reading can increase vocabulary, offer a few specific examples that might back up your idea. In contrast, if you want to prove that students who read the paper increase their understanding of politics, give examples of the kinds of political activities that appear in print each day.

Revising, Editing, and Proofreading

Allow almost one fourth of your time to revise and edit. Use the last few minutes to proofread your work.

Review the Prompt Before you begin to revise your response, take another look at the writing prompt. With the directions clearly in mind, you may find ways to target your essay more precisely to the question.

Use Precise Language As you revise, look for places in which your language is vague. Neatly replace vague words, such as *good*, with precise words, such as *effective* or *beneficial*.

Make Corrections While you revise, make an effort to keep your essay legible. Cross out details that do not support your purpose. Check for errors in spelling, grammar, and punctuation. When making changes, place one line through text you delete and use a caret [^] to indicate insertions.

Customize for
Less Advanced Students

Have copies of a daily newspaper in the classroom for those students who may not have access to or read a daily paper. Allow time for them to scan the various sections of the paper before you assign this lesson.

Customize for
AP Students

Ask students to suggest some ways they would vary their tone if they were writing this essay for an adult audience. Would they vary the vocabulary? Would they alter the sentence structure? If so, how? Would they list a different set of advantages to reading a daily paper?

In-Depth Lesson Plan

	LESSON FOCUS	PRINT AND MEDIA RESOURCES
DAY 1	**Introduction to Exposition: Problem-and-Solution Essay** Students learn key elements of problem-and-solution essays and analyze the Model From Literature (pp. 218–221)	*Writers at Work* **Videotape,** Exposition *Writing Lab* **CD-ROM,** Exposition
DAY 2	**Prewriting** Students choose and narrow a topic, consider their audience and purpose, and gather information. (pp. 222–225)	**Teaching Resources** *Writing Support Transparencies,* 11-A–D; *Writing Support Activity Book,* 11-1–2; *Topic Bank for Heterogeneous Classes,* Ch. 11
DAY 3	**Drafting** Students organize their ideas and write their first drafts. (pp. 226–227)	**Teaching Resources** *Writing Support Transparencies,* 11-E–F; *Writing Support Activity Book,* 11-3
DAY 4	**Revising** Students revise their drafts in terms of overall structure, paragraphs, sentences, and word choice. (pp. 228–232)	**Teaching Resources** *Writing Support Transparencies,* 11-G–I; *Writing Support Activity Book,* 11-4
DAY 5	**Editing and Proofreading; Publishing and Presenting** Students check their work for accuracy and correctness and present their final drafts. (pp. 233–236)	**Teaching Resources** *Scoring Rubrics on Transparency,* Ch. 11; *Writing Assessment and Portfolio Management; Formal Assessment,* Ch. 11

Accelerated Lesson Plan

	LESSON FOCUS	PRINT AND MEDIA RESOURCES
DAY 1	**Drafting** Students review characteristics of problem-and-solution essays, select topics, and write drafts. (pp. 218–227)	*Writing Lab* **CD-ROM,** Exposition **Teaching Resources** *Writing Support Transparencies,* 11-A–F; *Writing Support Activity Book,* 11-1–3
DAY 2	**Revising to Presenting** Students work individually or with peers to revise, edit, and proofread their work for presentation. (pp. 228–236)	**Teaching Resources:** *Writing Support Transparencies,* 11-G–I; *Writing Support Activity Book,* 11-4; *Scoring Rubrics on Transparency,* Ch. 11; *Writing Assessment and Portfolio Management; Formal Assessment,* Ch. 11

Options for Adapting Lesson Plans

HOMEWORK

Have students complete any stage of the lesson for homework.

FEATURES

Extend coverage with Connected Assignment (p. 237), Spotlight on the Humanities (p. 238), Media and Technology Skills (p. 239), and the Standardized Test Preparation Workshop (p. 240).

TECHNOLOGY

Students can complete any stage of the lesson on computer. Have them print out their completed work.

INTEGRATED SKILLS COVERAGE

Integrating Grammar
Using Infinitives to Combine Sentences, SE p. 230
Avoiding Subordinate Clauses as Sentence Fragments, SE p. 233
Active/Passive Voice, ATE p. 228
Appositives, ATE p. 231

Reading/Writing Connection
Identify Background Information, SE p. 220
Writing Application, SE p. 221

Viewing and Representing
Critical Viewing, SE pp. 218, 220, 226, 232, 235, 237, 238
Analyzing Ideas Represented in Various Art Forms, SE p. 238
Using a Variety of Technologies to Enhance the Writing Process, SE p. 239

Speaking and Listening
ATE pp. 224, 227

Real-World Connection
ATE p. 221

ASSESSMENT SUPPORT

Standardized Test Preparation Workshop SE p. 240; ATE p. 231
Standardized Test Preparation Workbook, pp. 21–22
Scoring Rubrics on Transparency, Ch. 11
Formal Assessment, Ch. 11
Writing Assessment and Portfolio Management

MEETING INDIVIDUAL NEEDS

Less Advanced Students ATE p. 241. See also Ongoing Assessments ATE pp. 220, 223, 225, 227.
AP Students ATE pp. 225, 241
ESL Students ATE pp. 222, 226, 236
Logical/Mathematical Learners ATE pp. 229, 239
Musical/Rhythmic Learners ATE p. 238

BLOCK SCHEDULING

Pacing Suggestions
For 90-minute Blocks
- Have students complete the Prewriting and Drafting stages in a single period.
- Focus one class period on Revising and Editing and Publishing and Presenting. Allow at least 30 minutes for peer revision.

Resources for Varying Instruction
- *Writing Lab* **CD-ROM** If your students have access to hardware, a 90-minute block provides an ideal opportunity for students to work on computer.
- *Writers at Work* **Videotape** Show Exposition segment in class.

Professional Development Support
- *How to Manage Instruction in the Block* This Teaching Resource provides management and activity suggestions.

MEDIA AND TECHNOLOGY

For the Student
- *Writing Lab* **CD-ROM,** Exposition
- *On-Line Exercise Bank,* Section 19.2

For the Teacher
- *Writers at Work* **Videotape,** Exposition
- *Resource Pro* **CD-ROM**

WRITING AND GRAMMAR WEB SITE

The Interactive Writing and Grammar Web Site provides a wide array of support for students, teachers, and parents. Writing support includes:

- Interactive revision checkers
- Scoring rubrics with complete models

www.phschool.com

LITERATURE CONNECTIONS

Related selections from *Prentice Hall Literature: Timeless Voices, Timeless Themes,* The American Experience:

"Chicago," Carl Sandburg, SE p. 221
"A Wagner Matinée," Willa Cather, SE p. 223

Lesson Objectives

1. To write a problem-and solution essay appropriate to audience and purpose
2. To read to appreciate the writer's craft and to discover models for writing
3. To use prewriting strategies to generate ideas and plan
4. To research self-selected topics using texts and technical resources
5. To represent information in a variety of ways, including graphics
6. To develop and revise drafts in terms of structure, paragraphs, sentences, and word choice
7. To edit and proofread to ensure standard English usage and grammar
8. To evaluate writing for both mechanics and content
9. To refine selected work for publication

Critical Viewing

Analyze The young people have coordinated their efforts to solve the problem of getting heavy bags from one place to another.

Chapter
11 Exposition
Problem-and-Solution Essay

▲ Critical Viewing
How do the activities shown in this photograph demonstrate effective problem-and-solution skills? [Analyze]

Problems and Solutions in Everyday Life

When you live in a world as fast-paced as ours, you confront problems every day. You may hear your parents complain about traffic or taxes; you may hear your classmates gripe over new school rules. Even celebrities can find some issue that riles them. Everyone can find something to protest. The challenge is to get beyond the complaining stage and make a difference. For example, people who want to find solutions might insist that a new traffic light be installed, that the way a tax is computed be changed, or that students be invited to join a committee to review new policies. By offering practical solutions to the problems they face, people can call attention to the matters that concern them and may even change a process.

218 • Exposition

⏱ TIME AND RESOURCE MANAGER	
Resources **Technology:** *Writers at Work* Videotape; *Writing Lab* CD-ROM, Exposition	
In-Depth Coverage	**Accelerated Pace**
• Cover pp. 218–219 in class. • Show the Exposition section of the *Writers at Work* Videotape. • Read the Model From Literature (pp. 220–221) with students and use it to discuss elements of a problem-and-solution essay.	• Discuss the characteristics and types of problem-and-solution essays in class. • Assign the Model From Literature for independent reading.

What Is a Problem-and-Solution Essay?

Since problem-and-solution essays are generally meant to explain a subject, they are part of the larger category of expository writing. However, a **problem-and-solution essay** goes further than just identifying an issue: It offers an idea for changing it. An effective problem-and-solution essay includes

- a clear statement of the problem, with its causes and effects summarized for the reader.
- a proposal of at least one realistic solution.
- facts, statistics, data, or expert testimony to support the solution.
- language appropriate to the audience's knowledge and ability levels.
- a clear organization that makes the relationship between problem and solution obvious.

To preview the criteria upon which your final problem-and-solution essay may be evaluated, see the Self-Assessment Rubric on page 234.

Types of Problem-and-Solution Essays

Following are some of the types of issues you might address in a problem-and-solution essay:

- **Consumer issues:** quality control and price control
- **Time-management issues:** finding a balance between work, school, and leisure time
- **Local issues:** neighborhood and community concerns

In this chapter, you'll see how Jennifer Tufts, a student at Broken Arrow High School in Broken Arrow, Oklahoma, used writing process techniques to develop an essay that addresses a problem affecting many students. You can see her final draft of "Zap the Zombie Syndrome" at the end of the chapter.

Writers in ACTION

Bob Vila, the old-house renovation expert, has solved more than his share of problems. In this quotation, he explains how careful observation along with firsthand experience have helped him analyze problems and find workable solutions:

"I had been lucky in that my father was a carpenter. . . . After all those years of asking questions, at last I was in the position of passing along the information to others."

PREPARE and ENGAGE

Interest GRABBER Ask students to brainstorm for responses to the question, "What problems have you seen in the world that you would like to see solved?" After they jot down their responses, ask students to share their ideas, and write any frequently mentioned topics on the chalkboard. Encourage students to speculate about how these problems might be solved.

Activate Prior Knowledge

Ask students to recall the last time they were confronted with a planning problem. (Example: getting their homework done and still finding time for extracurricular activities.) What steps were involved in resolving the conflict? After discussing what steps students took, refer students to the characteristics of the problem-and-solution essay.

More About the Writer

Bob Vila (b. 1946) is best known for the nationally syndicated TV shows *This Old House* and *Bob Vila's Home Again.* Another program, *Restore America,* showcases the most beautifully restored buildings, neighborhoods, and gardens across the country. Bob Vila is also involved with a number of public service organizations, including Habitat for Humanity and Make-A-Wish Foundation. Encourage students to look for more information about Vila on the Internet.

✓ ONGOING ASSESSMENT: Diagnose

Use one of the following options to diagnose students' current level of proficiency in problem-and-solution writing.

Option 1 Ask students to select a piece of writing from the previous year that demonstrates the student's ability to write a problem-and-solution essay. Hold conferences and review each student's work to determine who may need extra assistance.

Option 2 Ask students to write a sentence that addresses the disadvantages of dropping out of school. Then, have them list three reasons or items of evidence that support that sentence. If students have difficulty completing this exercise, you may wish to devote additional time to the gathering evidence and elaboration phases of the process.

Reading\Writing Connection

Reading: Identify Background Information

In this selection the author prepares readers to view the bicycle as a legitimate mode of transportation rather than as a recreational vehicle. This preparation takes the form of background information. Challenge students to find at least three pieces of background information that help to establish the essay's purpose.

Step-by-Step Teaching Guide

Engage Students Through Literature

1. Ask students to discuss the excerpt. Use the following questions to prompt discussion.

   What benefits does the author foresee if bicycles become the vehicles of choice?

   How does the author say that these benefits can be achieved?

2. Ask students to brainstorm for other problem-and-solution topics that this passage suggests, such as:

   How to reduce stress

   How to reduce urban overcrowding

   How to reduce air pollution

Teaching From the Model

You can use this Model From Literature to show students how to find a relevant topic for a problem-and-solution essay. In the model, Benoît Lambert is concerned with the excessive number of automobiles in our cities and on our highways. Ask students to consider how Benoît Lambert substantiates his concern. What solution does he propose? How does he validate this solution? Ask students to think about an issue that concerns them. What solution would they propose and how would they substantiate it?

Critical Viewing

Speculate Students should feel that Lambert would approve of this use of bicycles as an obvious alternative to motorized transportation.

 11.1 Model From Literature

Automobile traffic is not only a threat to pedestrian safety, but also a potential danger to the quality of life in cities as more cars than ever hit the road. In this essay, Benoît Lambert shows how bicycles can help solve the problem.

Reading Writing Connection

Reading Strategy: Identify Background Information As you read, notice the background information the writer provides to help readers new to the concept of bicycles as a mode of transportation understand the ideas he presents.

▲ **Critical Viewing** What would Lambert say about the use of bicycles as shown in this photograph? **[Speculate]**

Pedal Power

Benoît Lambert

Doubts are now being raised about the aura—almost of majesty—that surrounds motor vehicles, which, despite being too noisy and too big and guzzling too much energy, have long been regarded as symbols of national economic success and individual status. Since the 1992 Rio Conference and the cries of alarm that went up from the scientific community about threats to the stability of the Earth's ecosystem, transport policies and especially policies in regard to the car have been under fire from all sides.

Bicycles have seized this opportunity to go on to the offensive. Fifty times lighter than cars, they have plenty going for them. They are nonpolluting, nifty, silent and healthy. The number of cars in circulation worldwide will reach the billion mark in twenty-five years or even less, and this at a time of climate change. A certain measure of self-restraint in terms of individual mobility is thus an essential precaution to be taken to preserve the environment, and in fact more and more city-dwellers want to live in conditions of less pollution and stress. Cycles, especially when taken in conjunction with public transport, seem to provide an answer to this newfound aspiration to win back the streets and public places from colonization by the car.

In Amsterdam in March 1994, the European Union set up a network of car-free cities, to which sixty towns, including Aosta,

The author states the problem by explaining how some scientists are becoming concerned about the overuse of cars.

The author introduces the proposed solution: the increased use of bicycles.

220 • Problem-and-Solution Essay

☑ **ONGOING ASSESSMENT: Monitor and Reinforce**

After previewing the Model From Literature, you may anticipate that some students will have difficulty with some vocabulary.

Option 1 Have students use context clues to decode unfamiliar words. Have them list those words, the presumed definition, and the clues they used to unlock the meaning. As a class, refine the definitions.

Option 2 Have students create a list of unfamiliar words. If no one in the class can provide a definition, have two or three students ready with dictionaries to look up words. Have students write down definitions in their writer's notebooks. Challenge students to use these words in their writing.

Athens, Barcelona, Bremen, Granada, Groningen, Lisbon, Nantes, Reykjavik and Strasbourg, now belong.

The best results achieved so far have been in Copenhagen, where bicycles are regarded as a means of transport in the full sense of the term, and account for 33 percent of journeys—a share equal to that of public transport and private motor vehicles. Since 1962, the policy has been to reduce the number of parking spaces for cars, often to make way for cycle lanes, with the result that motor traffic has gone down by 10 percent since 1970.

For use in town, cycles compare very favorably in many respects with other means of transport.

Efficiency: the modern bike has the highest ratio of distance covered to energy input of any means of transport; at an average speed of 17 km an hour, a cyclist uses between three and four times less energy per kilometer than a pedestrian.

Health: a British Medical Association report published in 1992 pointed out that cycling is one of the simplest and most effective ways of keeping fit.

Cost: the cost of creating a cycle track in Britain is anything from 67 to 230 times less per mile than that of building a road, and even the most expensive bike will always be far more affordable than a car.

Some commentators state categorically that sustainable development is not feasible without multimodal mobility combining public transportation and two-wheelers. The irony is that just when the industrialized countries are starting to realize the virtues of the velocipede, some of the developing countries are trying to clear them off the streets, believing motorized vehicles to be the outward and visible sign of modernization.

This begs the question as to what "modernity" means today. Shouldn't we be standing up for the idea of "cyclomodernity," using the bicycle to treat the planet's ills? By the year 2005, more than half the world's population will be living in towns and cities, and by 2025 the number of city-dwellers will have doubled to five billion. At the same time, the worldwide proliferation of cars has resulted in the "automobile phenomenon." In these circumstances, bikes come to symbolize a simple life attuned to the limitations of our biosphere and responding to the new demands from a growing number of city-dwellers for a less motorized environment.

Writing Application: Provide Background Information In your problem-and-solution essay, give your readers the context to understand the situation you describe.

Lambert provides a list of cities which have adopted pro-bicycle policies. The specific results reported in Copenhagen suggest the solution is workable.

The writer uses a list to point out the strongest reasons for promoting bicycles over cars: efficiency, health, and cost.

High-level vocabulary—such as "sustainable development," "feasible," and "multimodal mobility"—addresses an educated audience.

By explaining the conflict between industrialization and the lower-tech bicycle, the writer points out the difficulty in implementing a worldwide cycling solution.

The writer uses this conflict to urge even stronger consideration of his ideas.

To see another writer's response to conflicts created by modern life, see Carl Sandburg's "Chicago." You can find it in *Prentice Hall Literature: Timeless Voices, Timeless Themes,* The American Experience.

More About the Writer

Swiss environmentalist Benoît Lambert advocates public planning for the development and implementation of carless cities. He has also been active in encouraging the restriction of new road construction. In a personal communication published in 1998 in *Carfree Times,* an on-line newsletter, Lambert revealed that "for about $1,500 you can buy a one-year ticket good on all public transport in Switzerland, including intercity trains." He noted that 200,000 Swiss buy such tickets annually.

Real-World Connection

Many careers require the ability to solve problems. Point out that any occupation requiring contact with people has a problem-solving component. Teachers, lawyers, customer service representatives, and restaurant managers all have to analyze problems and offer solutions. Encourage students to brainstorm for personal attributes and skills needed to be a successful problem solver. (Examples: creativity, curiosity, patience, and good communication skills)

Connections With Literature

Remind students that Lambert focused on the conflict between industrialization and the bicycle. Ask students to identify the contrasting elements in Carl Sandburg's poem "Chicago." (He identifies Chicago as corrupt and brutal, on the one hand, and proud, energetic, strong, and fierce on the other.)

Reading\Writing Connection

Writing Application: Provide Background Information

Tell students that providing background information for readers of problem-and-solution essays is crucial, especially if the students are writing on a subject about which the average person has no knowledge or preconceived concern. Have students reread "Pedal Power," paying particular attention to the way Lambert establishes the relative benefits of bicycle use right from the beginning.

Step-by-Step Teaching Guide

Prewriting: News Journal

1. Have students make a list of at least three problems they identify on the nightly local or national news. Three nights of viewing should offer adequate material. Offer students the option of going on-line to a news source for topics.

2. Have students suggest headlines or photos that might accompany the topics from the television news medium. The discussion of headlines might yield additional topics for essays.

Step-by-Step Teaching Guide

Prewriting: Blueprint

Teaching Resources: Writing Support Transparencies, 11-A

1. Display Transparency 11-A and have students review the Student Work in Progress. Have them trace Jennifer's trail of problem identification in classes. What is surprising about the topic she chose? (Dealing with individual class problems did not involve her in compelling problems, but her lunchtime exhaustion was a problem that did interest her enough to want to write about it.)

2. You may wish to provide unlined paper for this activity. Suggest that students limit the stops on their maps to five or six to leave space to identify the problem associated with that location.

3. Encourage students to share their problems and select one that would make an effective problem-and-solution essay.

Customize for
ESL Students

Pair up students with more-fluent English speakers to review one another's prewriting assignments. Ask ESL students to explain any differences in approaches to problem solving between their countries of origin and those commonly practiced in the United States. Can students give each other new ideas?

11.2 **Prewriting**

Choosing Your Topic

If you have a personal interest in a problem and its solution, your essay will be easier to develop. Think of a problem you'd like to solve. Alternatively, you can use these strategies to help you find a problem that needs a solution:

Strategies for Generating Topics

1. **News Journal** Watch the nightly news, and jot down the problems reported. After a few evenings, review your list to choose a problem for which you can offer a solution.

2. **Blueprint** Draw a simple map of a familiar place. Consider blueprinting your neighborhood, your house, or your school. As you sketch, label points of interest or importance and add the names of people where appropriate. As you "travel" along the map, identify problems that may need attention. When you have a good number of problems on your blueprint, review them to see which one grabs your attention. Then, use it as a basis for your writing.

Writing Lab CD-ROM

For more help finding a topic, explore the activities and suggestions in the Choosing a Topic section of the Exposition lesson.

Name: *Jennifer Tufts*
Broken Arrow High School
Broken Arrow, OK

Blueprinting to Choose a Topic

Jennifer drew a map of her high school. She labeled the classes that she took and identified problems related to each class. When she wrote "I feel like a zombie by lunch time," she knew she had found a problem she wanted to solve.

CAFETERIA
I feel like a zombie by lunch time.
Why am I so tired?

History
How can I study better?

Biology
Are rain forests something I can save?

Math
Why don't we have any group projects?

Literature
Why don't we read more poetry?

222 • Problem-and-Solution Essay

⏱ TIME AND RESOURCE MANAGER

Resources
Print: *Writing Support Transparencies,* 11-A–D; *Writing Support Activity Book,* 11-1–2
Technology: *Writing Lab* CD-ROM, Exposition

In-Depth Coverage	Accelerated Pace
• Work through the news journal or blueprint strategy with the class. • Use the Responding to Fine Art transparency to generate additional topics.	• Discuss strategies for generating topics. • Have students work independently to choose and narrow their topics. • Have students work with partners to focus on audience, purpose, and gathering details.

TOPIC BANK

If you're having trouble choosing a topic, consider the following possibilities:

1. **Report on Preventing Storm Damage** Each year, hurricanes, tornadoes, and floods destroy people's homes and lives. In an essay, offer tips on how to prepare for such violent weather and prevent the most severe damage.

2. **Problem-and-Solution Essay on Pet Ownership** While cats and dogs are often revered members of a family, some family pets can create trouble. Write an essay explaining how to address a pet's disobedience, hyperactivity, or other unwanted behavior.

Responding to Fine Art

3. *Road of Steel*, showing the installation of railroad track, brings to mind several problems that are suitable for a problem-and-solution essay. Consider the ways a railroad can influence communication or transportation needs, or consider the difficulties of completing such a strenuous job. Alternatively, use your response to this painting to address other problems technology poses. Identify one problem to develop into an essay.

Road of Steel, 1944, Carlos Anderson, Courtesy of Springfield Museum of Art, Springfield, Utah

Responding to Literature

4. Read "A Wagner Matinée," by Willa Cather. In the story, a woman who has moved to the frontier realizes how much she misses the culture of the city. In an essay, offer solutions to this problem. You can find the story in *Prentice Hall Literature: Timeless Voices, Timeless Themes,* The American Experience.

☑ Cooperative Writing Opportunity

5. **Welcome-to-School Pamphlet** With a group of classmates, plan and create a pamphlet to help your school's newest students adjust to their surroundings. Together, identify the most common problems these students face. Then, divide the task of researching and writing about these issues.

Step-by-Step Teaching Guide

Responding to Fine Art
Road of Steel by Carlos Anderson
Teaching Resources: Writing Support Transparencies, 11-B

1. Display the transparency (11-B). Prompt discussion with the following questions.

   What problems did the developers have to face when beginning this task? (buying land, finding workers, providing housing and basic needs for them, getting supplies to the site)

   What problems did the workers probably have to face when building the railroad? (difficult working conditions, long hours, little pay)

2. As students generate ideas, have them jot down ideas for possible essays. List their suggestions on the board. Then, ask students to think of a present-day project that might have the same problem-solution impact that building the railroad had in its time. (constructing a highway or building public housing)

Responding to Literature

Ask students to consider what motivated Aunt Georgiana to move to Red Willow County (love). Discuss the challenges people face when emotional needs conflict with practical considerations. Challenge students to find solutions to problems brought about by such conflicts. Could Aunt Georgiana have resolved her problem?

☑ ONGOING ASSESSMENT: Monitor and Reinforce

If you observe that some students are having difficulty generating or selecting a topic, use one of the following strategies.

Option 1 Students having difficulty choosing a topic might select one from the *Topic Bank for Heterogeneous Classes* in the Teaching Resources.

Option 2 Have students choose an idea from the Topic Bank on this page. You might assign all students to write an essay on the social implications of the U.S. becoming bipolar when it comes to computer literacy.

Prewriting: Use Focus Points

Teaching Resources: Writing Support Transparencies, 11-C; Writing Support Activity Book, 11-1

1. Display the transparency (11-C). Show how the items circled in each oval are key words that helped Jennifer generate more-detailed ideas.

2. Model the use of focus points by using a general topic such as choosing a career. Have students help you brainstorm for a sentence on that topic.

3. Then, have students identify key words in the sentence on the board to generate a narrower topic idea.

4. Encourage students to expand upon new details that help limit and focus the topic.

5. Have students practice using focus points independently. Give students copies of the blank form (11-1) to apply the strategy. Consider providing highlighters so that students may highlight the key words in each oval.

Integrating Speaking and Listening Skills

When generating problem-and-solution topics, have students work in groups of three to four. Each student in the group can benefit from listening to the problem-solving experiences of his or her peers.

11.2

Narrowing Your Topic

Complex problems often require a whole network of solutions to remedy them—if the solution were easy, the problem might not exist. Narrow your topic to a problem you can address effectively in an essay. To help you do this, use the focus point strategy.

Use Focus Points

After drawing an oval large enough in which to write only one sentence, summarize the problem you want to develop. Circle the most important word or phrase in that sentence. In a second oval, use the key word you've circled to generate a more narrowed topic. Challenge yourself to continue this process until you have identified a topic narrow enough to develop in your essay.

Student Work IN PROGRESS

Name: *Jennifer Tufts*
Broken Arrow High School
Broken Arrow, OK

Narrowing a Topic With Focus Points
Jennifer started with a topic that was too broad to manage. She used focus points to narrow her topic into one that was more appropriate for a school newspaper article.

High-school students often (fall behind) in school.

To keep up, students need to (stay awake) during the day.

To stay awake, students need more (energy.)

Considering Your Audience and Purpose

Most commonly, your purpose will be to persuade readers. However, knowing your audience is crucial to writing a strong problem-and-solution essay that will get results. Use the following chart to help you customize your essay to your audience's needs:

ANALYZE YOUR AUDIENCE

Questions	Answers
Who is my audience?	
What does my audience already know about my topic? What information do I need to give them?	
How can I make my audience care about the problem?	
Is my solution one that my audience will be able to implement?	

Gathering Details

To best present your ideas, give your readers a definition of the problem and clarify the specifics of your solution. Take time to gather details that will make your ideas clear to your readers.

Define the Problem Make a list of details, facts, and examples that prove there is a problem. To gather further information, conduct interviews with people who have been frustrated by the situation you'll address.

Clarify Your Solution Conduct research to learn about previously failed solutions. Then, identify the specific parts of your solution. Consider cost, implementation, and the potential new problems your solution might cause. Before you begin to draft, list several reasons to confirm that your solution is valuable.

🔋 Research Tip

To gather more concrete information, conduct interviews, consult media coverage, and go on-line.

Prewriting: Considering Your Audience and Purpose

Teaching Resources: Writing Support Transparencies, 11-D; Writing Support Activity Book, 11-2

1. Have students understand how to view one's audience by displaying the transparency (11-D). Then, give students a blank copy of the chart (11-2) to apply to their own analysis.

2. When students have identified the characteristics of their audience, they should bullet their ideas about purpose and audience at the top of the "Focus Points" sheet so that they can keep this focus in mind.

Step-by-Step Teaching Guide

Prewriting: Gathering Details

1. Have students list the specifics of their topic problem.

2. As students examine the problem more closely, have them brainstorm for details, facts, or examples that will prove the validity of the problem.

Customize for
AP Students

Encourage students to interview someone who is affected by the problem they want to write about. They should compose questions beforehand and follow these tips:

- *Introduce yourself and explain your interest.*
- *Establish a convenient time.*
- *Record the interview, if possible, but always verify all direct quotes.*
- *Ask questions that do not require merely a yes or no response.*
- *Always offer thanks.*

Integrating Vocabulary Skills

When writing an essay that relies on a logical presentation of details and facts, students should be aware of the connotations and denotations of their words. Students should understand that connotations might taint an argument. (Example: *immature* has a negative connotation; *youthful* does not.)

☑ ONGOING ASSESSMENT: Monitor and Reinforce

Students will frequently lapse into the habit of writing for the same audience—you. To break this pattern, try one of the following options.

Option 1 Have students write to a specific audience—a close relative or friend, a specific classmate, an elementary-school student.	**Option 2** Have students profile their intended audience. As a class, develop a list of profile questions that can be used for any writing. Ask about the audience's age, skill level, and background knowledge.

1. Display the transparency (11-E) and point out that the transitional sentence is placed at the beginning of the second paragraph. Emphasize that an interesting opening is vital to attracting reader attention.

2. Suggest that students begin with a striking fact or statistic, a direct quote, or an interesting anecdote.

3. Have students prepare the first two or three sentences of their opening paragraph and share these with the class.

4. Students should conclude their introductions with a direct statement of the problem.

5. For the remaining paragraphs of the essay, have students first create a topic outline with the ideas to be supported and the details for each point.

6. Have students create a transition sentence to cue the reader to each successive paragraph.

Customize for
ESL Students

Students tend to use words repetitively because of their limited vocabulary. Suggest that after completing the first draft, students should highlight repeated words. Encourage students to use a dictionary, thesaurus, or word processor to find synonyms to replace the repeated words. A peer tutor can ensure that denotative and connotative meanings fit the topic.

Critical Viewing

Analyze Students should mention that the problems of learning to play an instrument involve the expense of lessons, the sacrificing of time normally spent doing other activities, and the dedication to the often lonely act of practicing the instrument.

11.3 Drafting

Shaping Your Writing

In some of the writing you do, you have probably found that it takes more than one paragraph to explain and support an idea you want to develop. In that case, you use *paragraph blocks*, two or more paragraphs that explain and develop a complex key idea.

Organize in Paragraph Blocks

Paragraph blocks are especially useful in problem-and-solution essays because they allow a writer to explain a problem at great length and then identify the many components of a solution. As you plan your draft, identify the ideas that may be best served by a paragraph block plan. Then, use transitional sentences to keep the connections between your ideas clear. Look at this example:

▲ **Critical Viewing**
What are some of the problems young people face as they learn to play a musical instrument? **[Analyze]**

SAMPLE PARAGRAPH BLOCK

Practicing a musical instrument can sometimes be frustrating, but many consider the rewards to be well worth it. *(Topic Sentence)* At the beginning of my cello lessons, I felt angry when I couldn't play a piece well. However, through weeks of practice, I found my self-confidence and patience level increasing. *(First Subtopic)* I knew that I could eventually master those passages. I also knew the pride I felt when I finally did hit those notes right.

(Transitional Sentence) My personal reward was not limited to a sense of self-confidence. I also began to hear the complexity in other music I enjoyed. *(Second Subtopic)* Since the cello often provides the bass notes to balance out the melodies played by other instruments, I looked for this balance in the popular music I heard on the radio.

Use paragraph blocks to keep your paragraphs focused, so that your writing will not be too cumbersome for the reader to understand.

226 • Problem-and-Solution Essay

⏱ TIME AND RESOURCE MANAGER

Resources
Print: *Writing Support Transparencies,* 11-E–F; *Writing Support Activity Book,* 11-3
Technology: *Writing Lab* CD-ROM, Exposition

In-Depth Coverage	Accelerated Pace
• Work through the paragraph-blocks strategy with the class, using the transparency. • Have students write their opening sentences in class. • Demonstrate the technique of Depth-Charging to gather evidence.	• Have students review pp. 226–227 independently and then write their first drafts. • Respond to individual drafting issues as needed.

Providing Elaboration

Just presenting your opinion of a problem or solution is not sufficient to convince readers. You must support your statements with facts, statistics, personal experiences, expert testimonies, and other documentation that will sway your audience to accept your position.

Extend Your Argument by Depth-Charging

An effective strategy for providing elaboration is *depth-charging*. Using this strategy, begin by making a statement. To elaborate the idea, challenge yourself to provide a fact, statistic, or personal testimony that proves the statement. Then, challenge yourself to provide another type of evidence. Because this strategy encourages you to cite more evidence than you might include otherwise, depth-charging will strengthen your position.

📻 Research Tip

Professional journals are good sources of expert testimony. Law, psychology, and most other fields publish journals from which you can quote material reliably in your essays. Visit a college library or search on-line to get the information you need.

Name: Jennifer Tufts
Broken Arrow High School
Broken Arrow, OK

Using Depth-Charging to Provide Elaboration

Jennifer used the depth-charging strategy convincingly in her essay. As she identified the statements to develop, she jotted down notes to herself about how to include facts, testimony, and personal experience to support the ideas.

Topic sentence: One way to fight fatigue is exercise.

Scientific facts: Prove the energizing effect of exercise on the body.

Peer testimonial: Ask Danny how he feels after his daily workouts.

Personal experience: Share benefits of my daily walks.

Drafting • 227

Step-by-Step Teaching Guide

Drafting: Depth-Charging

Teaching Resources: Writing Support Transparencies, 11-F; Writing Support Activity Book, 11-3

1. Use the transparency (11-F) to focus attention on the types of support students can use to elaborate on an idea. Give students copies of the blank form (11-3) to apply the strategy.

2. Ask students to look at the framework they created for the paragraph blocks. For each topic sentence, have them name the type of support that they intend to use.

Integrating Speaking and Listening Skills

Oral Presentation Ask students to prepare a sixty-second announcement detailing their problem and solution. Have listeners chart the types of support offered and rate the effectiveness of the announcement. Encourage the presenters to spend five minutes jotting down feedback after their presentations.

☑️ **ONGOING ASSESSMENT: Monitor and Reinforce**

If students are having difficulty recognizing the strengths and weaknesses of their arguments, have them try the following strategy.

With students working in pairs, have each one write down the supporting points of his or her solution. Ask the other student to place them in order from strongest to weakest. Students can then discuss the effectiveness of their arrangement of supporting points and determine whether they need to develop further support.

⏱️ **TIME SAVERS!**

 Writing Support Transparencies
Use the transparencies for Chapter 11 to facilitate the teaching of strategies.

 Writing Support Activity Book
Use the graphic organizers for Chapter 11 to facilitate student planning.

Revising: Using Note Cards to Reorder Paragraphs

Teaching Resources: Writing Support Transparencies, 11-G

1. Using the transparency, explain "order of importance" to the class.

2. Make copies of the first drafts. Have students cut apart their body paragraphs and paste them on note cards. Leave the opening paragraph intact.

3. Have peers arrange the paragraphs in the order they believe to be most effective. Encourage students to discuss the results of this activity.

Integrating Grammar Skills

Active/Passive Voice In order to argue more effectively, students should use the active voice. (Example: Lunch was eaten by students on the terrace. [passive] Students ate lunch on the terrace. [active]) Remind students that the active voice is clearer, more direct, less wordy, and more powerful. Have students look for forms of the verb "to be," which signal passive voice in their essays, and rewrite sentences that use the passive voice.

11.4 Revising

Revise your first draft by reviewing the overall structure, paragraphs, sentences, and word choice. The goal of revising is to make your essay as convincing as possible; every sentence and every word must be powerful.

Revising Your Overall Structure

The organization of paragraphs in an effective problem-and-solution essay should proceed in a logical order so that readers can understand the solution you propose.

▶ **REVISION STRATEGY**
Using Note Cards to Reorder Paragraphs

To be sure you have presented your ideas in the clearest way possible, jot down the subject of each supporting paragraph on a separate note card. Then, rearrange the cards to see which order serves your essay best. Choose the sequence you believe will be most convincing, and make revisions to your draft as necessary.

Student Work IN PROGRESS

Name: Jennifer Tufts
Broken Arrow High School
Broken Arrow, OK

Ordering Paragraphs With Note Cards
Jennifer used note cards to arrive at the paragraph order she wanted.

Healthy diet

Water

Exercise (paragraph block)

Natural supplements

Unique solutions

Jennifer's sequence worked best when the cards were arranged in order from most important to least important.

To end with an interesting idea, Jennifer moved "unique solutions" to the end of her paper.

228 • Problem-and-Solution Essay

⏱ TIME AND RESOURCE MANAGER

Resources
Print: *Writing Support Transparencies,* 11-G–I
Technology: *Writing Lab* CD-ROM, Exposition

In-Depth Coverage	Accelerated Pace
• Work through revision strategies with the entire class. • Use the relevant transparencies to demonstrate strategies for analyzing overall structure, taking the opposing view, and revising word choice (p. 231).	• Assign students to independently review pages 228–232. • Have students revise their problem-and-solution essays.

Revising Your Paragraphs

Evaluate Body Paragraphs

Each topical paragraph in your essay should support your proposal by providing enough information to prove that your problem is serious or by elaborating to show that your solution is valid. Check the content of your body paragraphs by reading your essay as if you were opposed to its ideas.

People who oppose new processes often argue that a change will be difficult, too costly, too hard to learn, or just not necessary. Adopt this viewpoint as you review the body paragraphs of your essay.

▶ **REVISION STRATEGY**
Strengthening Content by Taking the Opposing View

As you read your essay, look for places where someone might disagree with your ideas. For each paragraph, generate a question that such a critic might ask you. Use this chart to add new information to paragraphs that exist. Alternatively, you might want to add a single paragraph dedicated to anticipating the negative reactions an audience might have to your ideas. Look at these common points for skepticism:

Opposing View	Strategies for Revision
Why should I care?	Include information to show how the problem affects your audience.
Won't this be too difficult?	Show how the solution can be completed easily, or stress that a difficult solution is necessary because of the severity of the problem.
Why can't someone else do it?	Use language to make your audience see that their participation is a critical part of the solution.

Writing Lab CD-ROM

To see how one student revised her problem-and-solution essay, see the audio-annotated revision models in the Exposition lesson.

Revising • **229**

Step-by-Step Teaching Guide

Revising: Taking the Opposing View

Teaching Resources: Writing Support Transparencies, 11-H

1. Using the transparency (11-H) as a model, have students create an opposing question for each reason they supplied in support of their solution.

2. Ask students to create paragraphs that respond to these questions.

3. Encourage volunteers to read their reasons and opposing questions to the class.

Customize for
Logical/Mathematical Learners

Explain to students that money is often a big factor in the decision to endorse a proposal. Have students prepare charts that enumerate the costs of implementing their solutions and make a presentation to the class. Will funds come from government sources or from the private sector? Have students explain how they arrived at the cost estimates.

 TIME SAVERS!

 Writing Support Transparencies
Use the transparencies for Chapter 11 to facilitate the teaching of strategies.

 Writing Support Activity Book
Use the graphic organizers for Chapter 11 to facilitate student writing.

Step-by-Step Teaching Guide

Revising: Combining Sentences

1. Review the use of coordinating conjunctions with students, especially those other than *and*. Remind students that coordinators are used to link two sentences of equal importance.

2. Review subordinating conjunctions with students. Suggest that they use subordinating conjunctions to join sentences that are unequally related.

3. Remind students that if a subordinating conjunction begins a sentence, a comma must follow the subordinate clause.

4. Have students identify the simple sentences in their essays.

5. Have students look for sentences that can be joined by a coordinating or a subordinating conjunction.

Step-by-Step Teaching Guide

Using Infinitives to Combine Sentences

1. Remind students of the difference between an infinitive phrase and a prepositional phrase. (In an infinitive phrase, *to* is followed by a verb form, while in a prepositional phrase, *to* is followed by a noun or a pronoun.)

2. Create a list on the board of those verbs that are often followed by infinitives. (*Examples: decide, need, try,* or *want*) Have students select a newspaper article and find infinitive phrases. Tell them that journalists use infinitives because they are succinct and powerful.

Find It in Your Reading

Possible answers: *to go* (adjective), *to be taken* (adjective), *to preserve* (adjective), *to live* (noun), *to provide* (adjective), *to win* (adjective).

Find It in Your Writing

Have students read their essay drafts to see whether they have used any infinitives. Ask students to locate sentences that can be improved by changing the structure to include an infinitive.

Revising Your Sentences
Reduce the Frequency of Simple Sentences

The repeated use of simple sentences will make your writing style dull. Use sentence-combining techniques to add variety, sophistication, and vitality to your written work.

▶ **REVISION STRATEGY**
Combining Sentences

Simple sentences contain a single main clause consisting of a subject, a verb, and their modifiers. To make your writing more sophisticated, look for ways to combine simple sentences. First, identify the simple sentences in your essay. When possible, introduce coordinating conjunctions to combine two or more sentences or use a subordinating conjunction to show the relationship between two ideas.

EXAMPLE:	They prepared the document. They stand by its accuracy.
COORDINATING CONJUNCTION:	They prepared the document, *and* they stand by its accuracy.
SUBORDINATING CONJUNCTION:	*Because* they prepared the document, they stand by its accuracy.

Learn More

For more on sentence combining, see Chapter 20.

Grammar in Your Writing
Using Infinitives to Combine Sentences

An **infinitive** is a form of a verb that generally appears with the word *to* and acts as a noun, an adjective, or an adverb.

Noun: The juniors were asked to participate.

Adjective: They showed an eagerness to help.

Adverb: They were sorry to leave.

By turning the content of one simple sentence into an infinitive phrase, you can use this grammatical structure to combine simple sentences.

Simple Sentences: He researched the debate. He learned about the issues.

Combined Sentence: He researched the debate to learn about the issues.

Find It in Your Reading Find infinitive phrases in the second paragraph of "Pedal Power" on page 220. (Don't confuse them with prepositional phrases beginning with *to*.)

Find It in Your Writing As you revise your draft, use infinitives to combine simple sentences.

For more on infinitives and infinitive phrases, see Chapter 19.

230 • Problem-and-Solution Essay

☑ ONGOING ASSESSMENT: Prerequisite Skills

If students have difficulty with infinitives, they might benefit from a review of the following to ensure coverage of prerequisite knowledge.

In the Textbook	Print Resources	Technology
Infinitives, pp. 448–450	*Grammar Exercise Workbook,* pp. 51–52	*On-Line Exercise Bank,* Section 19.2

Revising Your Word Choice

Evaluate Technical Language

Your choice of words should match the knowledge and expectations of your audience. However, when you are providing an educated discussion of a topic, you may have to include technical words that your audience might not know. Review your draft to identify the words that may need definition or further explanation.

▶ REVISION STRATEGY
Color-Coding Technical Language

Review your essay, and highlight words and phrases that your audience might not know. For each, decide whether you should replace a word with a simpler term or provide a definition to make the writing more accessible.

Collaborative Writing Tip

If your classmates represent the type of audience you want to address, share your work with a partner. Ask your reader to identify language that needs definition.

Student Work
IN PROGRESS

Name: Jennifer Tufts
Broken Arrow High School
Broken Arrow, OK

Highlighting Technical Words

When Jennifer identified scientific and technical language in her original draft, she revised to make the writing more clear for her audience—the classmates who would be reading her article in Tiger Eye, *the high-school newspaper.*

First draft: "Another way to ==raise low levels of blood sugar== is to get more exercise. Exercise increases ==venous and arterial circulation,== releases hormones, and stimulates the nervous system to produce ==endorphins.=="

Revised draft: "Another way to fight fatigue is, simply, exercise. Exercise increases blood flow to the muscles and the brain, releases energizing hormones, and stimulates the nervous system to produce chemicals, called endorphins, that elevate mood and produce feelings of well-being."

> Since she could convey information without the high-level language, Jennifer deleted references to blood-sugar levels and the types of circulation.
>
> Jennifer added a definition of "endorphin."

Step-by-Step Teaching Guide

Revising: Color-Coding Technical Language

Teaching Resources: Writing Support Transparencies, 11–I

1. Show the transparency and discuss how Jennifer identified terms that might need clarification for her audience to understand her article.
2. Have students scan their drafts looking for similar terms.
3. Ask students to determine whether they wish to define the word or use a simpler word.
4. Have students revise sentences containing technical words to add appropriate clarification.

Integrating Grammar Skills

Appositives One way for students to incorporate an explanation of a term is to use an appositive or appositive phrase. Remind students that commas usually set off appositives and appositive phrases. Provide students with phrases that could function as appositives.

a cartoon character

a famous explorer

a delicious breakfast food

Have the students individually create sentences using these phrases as appositives.

Infinitives Standardized test questions may require students to identify the function of an infinitive in a sentence. Provide opportunities for students to practice writing sentences using infinitives as nouns, adjectives, or adverbs.

Name the function of the infinitive in the sentence below.

With summer vacation coming up, Nina planned to relax.

A noun   **C** adjective
B verb   **D** adverb

Students should recognize that **A** is the correct answer because "to relax" is the direct object of the verb *planned*. Infinitives never function as a verb in a sentence, so answer B is incorrect. C is incorrect because the infinitive does not modify or describe a noun. D is incorrect because the infinitive does not modify or describe a verb, adjective, or another adverb.

Revising: Peer Review

1. Invite students to identify a draft's strongest arguments, and use these as a measure of what further edits a student author might make.

2. Remind students that mechanical errors will be corrected at the proofreading stage and that the focus here should be on content and support.

3. Provide the reviewer with a copy of the outline prepared in the "Focus Points" section of the chapter. Have the reviewer comment not only about the problem and the solution but also about the validity and quality of the support.

4. Point out that many comments made during peer review will be helpful to all students. Have students make note of important ideas raised in class discussion so that these notes can be consulted later.

Customize for
Interpersonal Learners

You might arrange for students to exchange essays with students in another class. A new perspective on the essay can assist the revision process.

Critical Viewing

Evaluate Students should feel that peers, going through the same stages in writing an essay, can help spot weaknesses in fellow students' essays.

11.4

Peer Review
Group Feedback

Before you finalize your essay, get the feedback of your peers. As a sneak-preview audience, these readers can tell you what works in your essay and what may need further attention. Read your essay aloud, and ask reviewers to offer concrete responses to help you address any difficulties they perceive.

▲ Critical Viewing
How can a peer's opinions help you fine-tune your essay? [Evaluate]

Set a Task Provide an outline of your essay for each member of the group. Ask reviewers to write one question, comment, or statement next to each idea you present. Reviewers can also place a check next to the points they feel have been addressed effectively. Once reviewers have completed this task, ask them to share their ideas.

Get Specific As you discuss your essay, get the most useful information from your reviewers. If necessary, ask follow-up questions to make vague comments more specific. Look at this sample conference prompted by a problem-and-solution paper about museum funding:

VAGUE RESPONSE:	I liked the paragraph that showed the history of the transit museum.
FOLLOW-UP QUESTION:	What exactly did you like about it?
SPECIFIC RESPONSE:	I didn't know that the museum was created by former conductors and rail-car engineers.
FOLLOW-UP QUESTION:	What else might you want to know?
SPECIFIC RESPONSE:	I'd want to know why the city doesn't offer funding to help the museum develop exhibits.

11.5 Editing and Proofreading

Errors in spelling, punctuation, and grammar may not destroy your essay's ability to convince, but they will distract your audience from your message and cast doubt on your credibility. Always check spelling, punctuation, and grammar to ensure that your final draft is error-free.

Focusing on Complete Sentences

Review your writing to be sure that you have left no fragments in the essay. A fragment is an incomplete thought punctuated as a sentence. If you should find any fragments, revise each one by supplying information to complete the idea. Then, review your essay once more to be certain that all sentences are complete.

Language Lab CD-ROM

For more practice with sentence fragments, see the Sentence Errors unit.

Grammar in Your Writing

Avoiding Subordinate Clauses as Sentence Fragments

Although a **subordinate clause** contains both a subject and a verb, it does not express a complete thought. The subordinating conjunction sets up a dependent relationship; without more information, the subordinate clause is incomplete. Look at these examples:

Incorrect: After we spoke to the doctor.

Incorrect: Although we understood the diagnosis.

To correct the sentence fragments created by punctuating subordinate clauses as sentences, add information that completes each idea.

Revised: After we spoke to the doctor, we wanted more information.

Revised: Although we understood the diagnosis, we needed more advice.

Find It in Your Reading Read "Pedal Power" on pages 220–221. Identify two sentences that include subordinating clauses as part of complete sentences.

Find It in Your Writing Review your essay to be certain you have completed all sentences that include subordinate clauses.

For more on sentence fragments, see Chapter 20.

Editing and Proofreading • **233**

TIME AND RESOURCE MANAGER

Resources
Print: *Scoring Rubrics on Transparency*, Ch. 11; *Writing Assessment and Portfolio Management; Formal Assessment,* Ch. 11
Technology: *Writing Lab* CD-ROM, Exposition

In-Depth Coverage	Accelerated Pace
• Review p. 233 in class, including Grammar in Your Writing. • Analyze the Final Draft (pp. 235–236). • Students edit and proofread their essays in class.	• Assign pp. 233–236 for independent review. • Students independently edit, proofread, and publish their essays. • Respond to individual editing needs as needed.

Publishing and Presenting

1. Encourage students to seek audiences in their family, community, or even on the Internet. Depending upon the topic, potential readers might be other students via the school newspaper, your school board, the town or city council, or even an elected official.

2. In preparing their essays for publication, students may wish to add illustrations, diagrams, charts, or photos. Ask them to extend the process of composition by determining which of these items would help a reader most.

ASSESS and CLOSE

Assessment

Teaching Resources: Scoring Rubrics on Transparency, Ch. 11; Writing Assessment and Portfolio Management; Formal Assessment, Ch. 11

1. Display the Scoring Rubric transparency and review the criteria in class.

2. Before students proceed with self-assessment, you may wish to review the Final Draft of the Student Work in Progress on pages 235–236.

3. In addition to student self-assessment, you may wish to use the following options:

   • score student essays yourself, using the rubric and scoring models in *Writing Assessment and Portfolio Management.*

   • review the Standardized Test Preparation Workshop on pages 240–241 and administer a timed writing assessment.

   • administer the Chapter 11 assessment in *Formal Assessment* to measure students' grasp of the concepts presented.

11.6 Publishing and Presenting

Building Your Portfolio

Consider submitting your problem-and-solution essay to a person or group that could benefit from your suggestions. You might try the following options:

1. **Send Your Essay to a Newspaper** By publishing your idea locally, you may win supporters who have the power to implement it. Even if your solution is not adopted, your essay may convince others to tackle the problem.

2. **Mail Your Essay to an Elected Official** Government leaders usually welcome input from the people they represent. Determine whether a local, state, or national leader has the authority to turn your idea into reality, and send a copy of your final draft to the official you identify.

Reflecting on Your Writing

Consider what you have learned from your writing experience. Use these questions to spark your reflection:

• What insight did you gain about the problem you addressed by writing a problem-and-solution essay?

• Which writing process strategy would you use again? Why?

 Internet Ti

To see model essays scored with this rubric, go to **www.phschool.com**

Rubric for Self-Assessment

Use the following criteria to evaluate your problem-and-solution essay.

	Score 4	Score 3	Score 2	Score 1
Audience and Purpose	Contains language and details to engage audience and accomplish purpose	Contains language and details appropriate for audience and that help contribute to overall effect	Contains some language and details not suited for audience; contains some details that detract from purpose	Contains language and details that are not geared for a particular audience; has an unclear purpose
Organization	Consistently presents information in a plan suited to problem and solution	Presents information in a plan suited to problem and solution	Introduces some inconsistencies into organizational plan	Presents no clear organization
Elaboration	Clearly defines problem and solution; elaborates all key points	Defines problem and solution; elaborates many points	States problem and solution with little elaboration	Presents no clear problem or solution; provides no elaboration
Use of Language	Demonstrates excellent word choice; contains no errors in grammar, punctuation, or mechanics	Demonstrates good word choice; contains few errors in grammar, punctuation, or mechanics	Demonstrates fair word choice; contains some errors in grammar, punctuation, or mechanics	Demonstrates poor word choice; contains many errors in grammar, punctuation, or mechanics

234 • Problem-and-Solution Essay

✓ ONGOING ASSESSMENT: Assess Mastery

Use one of the following options to assess student mastery of the problem-and-solution essay.

Self-Assessment Ask students to score their essays using the rubric provided. In a single paragraph, have students reflect on the most valuable thing they learned in completing this essay.

Teacher Assessment You may use the rubric and scoring models provided in *Writing Assessment and Portfolio Management* to score students' work.

11.7 Student Work IN PROGRESS

FINAL DRAFT

Zap the Zombie Syndrome

**Jennifer Tufts
Broken Arrow High
School
Broken Arrow,
Oklahoma**

"Early to bed, early to rise; makes a man healthy, wealthy, and wise." According to recent studies at the University of California's Department of Psychiatry, this is not true for teenagers. The study suggests that most teens have some form of Delayed Sleep Syndrome, which means REM (Rapid Eye Movement) takes longer to set in. Since it is during a series of five to eight REMs, or dream sleep, that the body is truly relaxed, students today feel most rested if they go to sleep late at night and don't get up until late morning the next day. Unfortunately, nowhere in the foreseeable future are schools going to change the long-treasured 8:00 A.M. tardy time to around noon. For now, students are forced to seek other ways to overcome the mid-morning nap in government and the afternoon slump in pre-calculus.

A healthy diet can be the first way to fight energy lows. Students should start the day with a light breakfast that combines low-sugar cereals and low-fat milk or yogurts. Junior Beau Mitchell gets his pick-me-up in the morning with a steaming cup of coffee. "It wakes me up and gives me energy all day," said Beau. Preferably, students should choose juice or milk over coffee in the morning because

▲ **Critical Viewing**
How can exhaustion impair your ability to succeed in school? **[Analyze]**

Jennifer opens with a quotation that gets the reader's attention. Next, she states the problem and includes facts from a research study. Finally, she presents her thesis statement: Students need to find ways to overcome sleepiness.

Jennifer presents her first solution. To elaborate on the value of a healthy diet, she provides suggested foods and includes a quotation from a student.

Student Work in Progress • 235

235

Integrating Grammar Skills

As students read through Jennifer's final draft, ask them to identify sentences written using the passive voice by scanning for forms of the verb "to be." Advise students that there are times when the passive voice is permissible, but generally the active voice is preferred. Have students individually, or in groups, suggest revisions that would eliminate the passive voice.

caffeine, found in coffee, is a serious drug that brings exhausting roller coaster energy highs and lows. It is also essential to combine carbohydrates and proteins for a light lunch, to ensure long-lasting, sleep-fighting energy. After school, the best things to munch on are fruits, pretzels, fresh vegetables, or granola instead of sugar-rich candies and sweets. Snacks that are healthy help provide a steady supply of energy for the rest of the day.

It is also important to pump water into the system even when one is not thirsty. Dehydration is common in teens and can cause crankiness and fatigue. At least six cups of water a day, when combined with at least two of the above tips, is sure to produce rising energy levels.

Another way to fight fatigue is, simply, exercise. Exercise increases blood flow to the muscles and the brain, releases energizing hormones, and stimulates the nervous system to produce chemicals, called endorphins, that elevate mood and produce feelings of well-being. Senior Danny Holland recognizes the importance of daily exercise. He said, "I work out daily; it gives me energy."

Any exercise is better than no exercise. Even just going for an evening walk at the neighborhood park increases energy levels and lowers tension, while eating a sugary snack increases feelings of stress and only temporarily raises energy levels, followed by an increase in fatigue and reduced energy.

According to Dr. C. W. Smith at the University of Arkansas for Medical Sciences in Little Rock, "Exercise should be part of everyone's lifestyle. . . it will reliably and consistently decrease feelings of tiredness and despondency."

If natural changes in diet and exercise habit aren't enough to beat energy slumps, then natural supplements might be the answer. Junior James Camper uses ginseng to "get him out the door in the morning." Sometimes, tiredness is simply a sign of too little sleep. If so, a good night's rest is the cure, yet many know the cure and still fall victim to restless nights.

A healthy balance between a good diet and some form of aerobic exercise will get rid of those sleepless nights; but some students have discovered unique ways to get rid of insomnia. "I put stress-relieving cucumber gel on my eyes and face when I can't sleep," said Junior Shiloh Gentry. "I always wake up refreshed."

The age-old saying should read, "A balanced day of a healthy diet, regular exercise, and a restful sleep makes a man healthy, wealthy, and wise."

Jennifer uses a two-paragraph block to address the issues associated with diet.

A second solution to the problem of student sleepiness is exercise. Jennifer devotes three paragraphs to this concept.

Before her conclusion, Jennifer introduces one last problem-solving suggestion: Tired students should get more sleep.

To frame her essay, Jennifer revisits and revises the quotation that introduced her writing.

Connected Assignment

Question-and-Answer Column

In a problem-and-solution essay, you address both a problem and a solution. In real life, however, you might provide only half of the equation. For example, in a **question-and-answer column** such as those published in a magazine or on an on-line source, people send in questions and an expert provides an answer. The question includes a clearly presented request for information or advice along with background information. The answer proposes solutions and explains how they might help.

Using the letter format, present a frequently asked question about a subject you know well. Then, create a responding letter to propose solutions. The writing process skills discussed below will help you develop your letter.

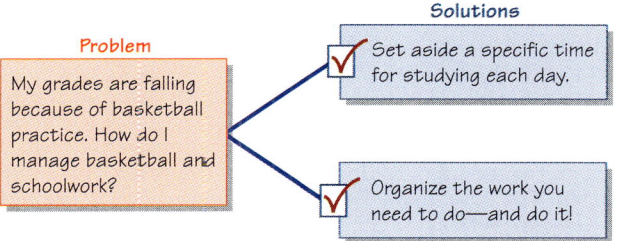

Problem

My grades are falling because of basketball practice. How do I manage basketball and schoolwork?

Solutions

✓ Set aside a specific time for studying each day.

✓ Organize the work you need to do—and do it!

▲ **Critical Viewing**
How might talking with someone else help you overcome some problems?
[Relate]

Prewriting Consider the areas you know especially well. For example, you might be a computer whiz, a pro at dealing with younger siblings, or a cooking expert. Devise a common question or an unusual problem related to the area you've chosen. Then, use a chart like the one above to gather possible solutions.

Drafting Follow an informal format as you draft your letter. In your question, present the problem and provide background to explain the situation. Then, write the answer letter, adjusting the tone to reflect your expertise. Propose at least one solution and explain how it will solve or at least minimize the problem. When appropriate, cite your own experience.

Revising and Editing Ask a peer to read your solution letter to identify the question. If he or she cannot determine what the question was based on your response, rework your letter to more clearly address the problem.

Publishing and Presenting Use your writing as a model for a question-and-answer column for your school newspaper.

Connected Assignment: Question-and-Answer Column • **237**

Lesson Objectives

1. To learn about the source of a media production
2. To analyze relationships, ideas, and cultures represented in various media
3. To recognize how visual and sound techniques convey messages in media
4. To present an interpretation of a story or drama as a blues song

Analyzing Ideas Represented in Various Art Forms

1. Choose one of the Spotlight elements for class discussion, or have students work individually or in groups on the elements of their choice. Give students the initiative to find the necessary videotapes or music.

2. Interested students may research additional information about Carson McCullers and the themes that dominated her work.

3. Show a scene from either *The Ballad of the Sad Cafe* or *The Member of the Wedding*. What ideas are suggested by the words? What relationships are suggested by the camera?

4. Have students listen to songs that Ethel Waters recorded. Ask them which contemporary singer most closely matches her power and versatility.

Viewing and Representing

Activity Give students the opportunity to perform their songs in class, either through live or taped performance. They might ask a classmate to play a musical instrument as the song lyrics are presented.

Critical Viewing

Respond Students may sense concern in the older woman's facial expression and her hands on the young girl's shoulders; they may also sense sorrow or bewilderment on the part of the girl.

Spotlight on the Humanities

Analyzing Ideas Represented in Various Art Forms

Focus on Literature: *The Member of the Wedding*

Sometimes, problems in our lives can inspire us to make major changes; this idea is at the heart of Carson McCullers's 1946 novel *The Member of the Wedding*. On the advice of American playwright Tennessee Williams, McCullers (1917–1967) adapted the novel into a play. On January 5, 1950, the play premiered on Broadway to great acclaim. The story presents a twelve-year-old girl named Frankie, whose tomboyish ways alienate her from other neighborhood girls. When her older brother announces he's going to be married, the impending wedding forces Frankie to face her immaturity and initiates her growth into a young woman. The novel moved from the stage into film. In 1952, the story became a Hollywood film starring blues singer Ethel Waters and actress Julie Harris.

▲ **Critical Viewing** What emotion does this scene from *The Member of the Wedding* convey to you? **[Respond]**

Theater Connection Carson McCullers is no stranger to adaptations of her work. She wrote a novella entitled *The Ballad of the Sad Cafe*. American playwright Edward Albee adapted the story into a play that premiered in New York in 1963. Set in the South, *The Ballad of the Sad Cafe* tells the story of three eccentric characters during the Depression.

Music Connection In addition to acting, Ethel Waters (1900–1977) was one of America's great blues singers. She made the song "Dinah" a hit, and by 1933, she was recording with Duke Ellington and Benny Goodman. Waters was the first woman to sing W. C. Handy's famous "St. Louis Blues." She may be best known for the dramatic intensity she brought to her songs.

Problem-and-Solution Writing Activity: Singing the Blues Many great blues songs were inspired by problems or troubles in the singer's life. Their creative solution was to put their pain into their music, and the result was often a blues classic. Research and listen to several blues songs to take note of the format and common topics. Then, using a story or drama that presents a situation appropriate to the blues, write your own song. Add music to enrich the activity. Then, share the finished product with peers.

238 • Problem-and-Solution Essay

Customize for
Musical/Rhythmic Students

Have students listen to and analyze blues sung by Billie Holiday, Bessie Smith, or Muddy Waters. Have them describe the tone and content of the lyrics, the instrumental and vocal techniques, or the influence of blues on Elvis Presley, the Rolling Stones, or Eric Clapton.

Media and Technology Skills

Using a Variety of Technologies to Enhance the Writing Process

Activity: Getting Help On-line

Don't be surprised if your computer or its software presents you with unexpected troubles. If you encounter computer problems, help is seldom far away. You can get guided assistance from built-in Help programs. Use them as you work to answer questions and master new strategies.

Learn About It Computer programs offer several different kinds of help. These are the most common:

- **Pop-up Labels** To see if your software has this Help feature, slowly roll the cursor over a function icon such as "double-space." Often, a small label will appear identifying the icon's function.

- **Balloon Help** Activate balloon help under the Help menu. Then, when you point your mouse at a function icon, you'll get an explanation of how to use that function.

- **On-screen Assistant** Some programs have an animated guide that offers suggestions and fields questions. Click on its icon or activate it under the Help menu to ask questions or access the index of topics.

- **"Read-Me" Files** Instead of printed manuals, many programs now provide help only on the screen. Find these in the software folder, but access them through text reader programs such as Simple Text.

Apply It Work with a partner to explore Help options on your computer. Identify specific problems you've faced. Then, use two or more Help methods to find solutions, listing results in a chart like the one shown here. Discuss and rate the Help options.

> **Help Techniques**
> - Print out "Read-Me" files and consult them as you work.
> - If you use an on-screen assistant, configure help questions carefully to get results. Reword if necessary.
> - Study any printed manuals supplied with your programs.
> - Visit software makers' Web sites for answers to common questions and software updates.

> **Problem or Question** _____
> _____
>
> **Help Methods**
>   1. _____
>   2. _____
>   3. _____
>
> **Best Method** _____

Media and Technology Skills • 239

► **Lesson Objectives**
1. To learn to use guided assistance Help programs on computers.
2. To compare the relative values of different Help options.

Step-by-Step Teaching Guide

Using a Variety of Technologies to Enhance the Writing Process

Teaching Resources: Writing Support Transparencies 11-K; Writing Support Activity Book, 11-5

1. Identify students with advanced computer skills and ask them to assist students with less advanced skills.

2. As you review the four kinds of "help" described, have students identify the available "helps" in their software.

3. Make certain that each student understands how to access and interpret these "helps."

4. Display Transparency 11-K and have students ask and, if needed, refine their problem or question.

5. Give partners a copy of the blank chart (11-5). Have them investigate methods to resolve their problem or answer their question. Which method was the most helpful? On a scale of 1 (least) to 5 (best), how helpful was it?

Customize for
Logical/Mathematical Learners

Have students evaluate the quality of two or three software makers' Web sites. Prepare a chart for students unfamiliar with the software that answers the following questions:

How do I access the web site?

What kind of information is available?

Does the site have a link to FAQ's (frequently asked questions)?

Lesson Objectives

1. To write a problem-and-solution essay
2. To use prewriting strategies to plan
3. To develop a draft by refining style to suit audience and purpose
4. To organize ideas to ensure coherence, logical progression, and support for ideas
5. To edit and proofread to ensure standard English usage and grammar

Step-by-Step Teaching Guide

Using Problem-and-Solution Skills to Respond to Writing Prompts

Teaching Resources: Standardized Test Preparation Workbook, pp. 21–22

1. Emphasize to students that the key to success on most standardized essay tests is to address the question being asked. Students should read the prompt carefully and confine their answers to the topic area and the format indicated.

2. Have students remind themselves of their intended audience by writing "Parents" at the top of their separate outline page.

3. Tell students that creating an extensive, formal outline would waste their limited time. Suggest they jot down key words or brief phrases.

4. Define each of the three possible methods of organization and discuss the advantages and disadvantages of using each for this prompt.

5. Emphasize that since time limitations make recopying impractical, students' drafts should be neat and readable.

Standardized Test Preparation Workshop

Using Problem-and-Solution Skills to Respond to Writing Prompts

Standardized test prompts often measure your ability to use the different forms of expository writing. For example, a writing prompt may elicit a response that requires you to clearly state a problem and explain a strategy for solving it. Your problem-and-solution response will be evaluated on the following criteria:

- clearly stating a problem and suggesting a realistic solution
- choosing a method of organization that allows you to present your solution in a meaningful and coherent sequence, such as order-of-importance, chronological order, or pro-and-con organization
- elaborating your solution by anticipating readers' questions with clear descriptions, facts, and other details
- using correct grammar, spelling, and punctuation

When writing for a timed test, plan to devote a specific amount of time to prewriting, drafting, revising, editing, and proofreading.

Following is an example of an expository writing prompt that requires a problem-and-solution analysis. Use the strategies that follow to help you respond. The clocks next to each stage show a suggested amount of time to devote to each stage.

Sample Writing Situation

Your school is sponsoring a trip to visit different colleges in your state. The trip includes transportation, meals, and three nights' accommodations at various state universities. Since you are now preparing to choose a college, the information you could gain about the different schools might influence your choice. Unfortunately, the trip is quite costly. You would need to work extra hours after school to save for it while maintaining good grades and completing your responsibilities at home. In order to gain the support of your parents, write them a letter in which you clearly state your problem and propose a solution. Be sure to use convincing details to support your solution.

240 • Problem-and-Solution Essay

Test Tips

- When writing a response that draws on a problem-and-solution format, clearly state the problem in your introduction.
- Review the audience provided in the test prompt. As you draft, suggest solutions that this specific audience could implement.

✎ TEST-TAKING TIP

Many students may have difficulty deciding what sentence should follow the opening salutation, "Dear Mom and Dad." Remind students that in any expository essay, the opening paragraph often contains relevant background information. Students could begin by summarizing details their parents need to know: Who is sponsoring the trip? What colleges will be visited? When will the trip occur? Where will students be staying? Who are the chaperones? How much will the trip cost?

Note that ending with cost information provides a natural transition into the student's financial solution.

Prewriting

Allow close to one quarter of your time for prewriting.

Record Details Record details using a T-chart. Write the problem across the top of the chart. In the left column, list solutions to your problem. For each solution you propose, list in the right column the details that explain how you will achieve it.

Consider Your Audience Remember that in order to save enough money for your trip, you need the support of your parents as well as their permission. When writing your letter, include details that will persuade them to help you implement your plan.

Drafting

Allow almost half of your time for drafting.

Organize Details One way to organize your response is to use a step-by-step organization. Clearly state the problem in the first paragraph, and then summarize your solutions in the next paragraph. In the body of the letter, list and elaborate the point-by-point action plan that will help you achieve your goal.

Elaborate Wherever possible, clarify your plan with examples, facts, or details to show that you have analyzed the problem and its solution. For example, if you propose that your parents lend you money for the trip, show them how you intend to repay the loan.

Finish Strongly In your concluding paragraph, summarize ideas and show how all the action statements contribute to the solution.

Revising, Editing, and Proofreading

Allow almost one quarter of your time to revise and edit. Use the remaining few minutes for proofreading.

Make Connections Because they show the links between ideas, transitional words are especially useful in problem-and-solution writing. Revise your response to insert words, phrases, and sentences that indicate logical connections between the problem and your proposed solution. Transitions such as *because, as a result, therefore, first, then, besides,* and *in addition* may help strengthen your writing.

Clean It Up Use the last few minutes to check your writing for errors in spelling, grammar, and punctuation. Delete words or sentences by drawing a single line through them. Add words or phrases neatly in the margin or the space above the text, using a caret [^] to indicate the exact placement.

Customize for
Less Advanced Students

Students who have limited experience writing letters may need to be reminded of the format of a personal letter. Review the following: form and placement of the date, salutation, complimentary close, and signature.

Customize for
AP Students

Point out to students that one effective technique is to use negative solutions. Begin by discussing one or more solutions that are clearly inadequate for solving the problem. Then move into more logical solutions.

Time and Resource Manager

In-Depth Lesson Plan

	LESSON FOCUS	PRINT AND MEDIA RESOURCES
DAY 1	**Introduction to Documented Essays** Students learn key elements of documented essays and analyze the Model From Literature (pp. 242–245)	*Writers at Work* **Videotape,** Research Writing *Writing Lab* **CD-ROM,** Research
DAY 2	**Prewriting** Students choose and narrow a topic, consider their audience and purpose, and gather information. (pp. 246–249)	**Teaching Resources** *Writing Support Transparencies,* 12-A–C; *Writing Support Activity Book,* 12-1; *Topic Bank for Heterogeneous Classes,* Ch. 12
DAY 3	**Drafting** Students organize their ideas and write their first drafts. (pp. 250–251)	**Teaching Resources** *Writing Support Transparencies,* 12-D
DAY 4	**Revising** Students revise their drafts in terms of overall structure, paragraphs, sentences, and word choice. (pp. 252–256)	**Teaching Resources** *Writing Support Transparencies,* 12-E–F
DAY 5	**Editing and Proofreading; Publishing and Presenting** Students check their work for accuracy and correctness and present their final drafts. (pp. 257–260)	**Teaching Resources** *Scoring Rubrics on Transparency,* Ch. 12; *Writing Assessment and Portfolio Management; Formal Assessment,* Ch. 12

Accelerated Lesson Plan

	LESSON FOCUS	PRINT AND MEDIA RESOURCES
DAY 1	**Drafting** Students review characteristics of documented essays; select topics and write drafts. (pp. 242–251)	*Writing Lab* **CD-ROM,** Research **Teaching Resources** *Writing Support Transparencies,* 12-A–D; *Writing Support Activity Book,* 12-1
DAY 2	**Revising to Presenting** Students work individually or with peers to revise, edit, and proofread their work for presentation. (pp. 252–257)	**Teaching Resources** *Writing Support Transparencies,* 12-E–F; *Scoring Rubrics on Transparency,* Ch. 12; *Writing Assessment and Portfolio Management; Formal Assessment,* Ch. 12

Options for Adapting Lesson Plans

HOMEWORK

Have students complete any stage of the lesson for homework.

FEATURES

Extend coverage with Connected Assignment (p. 261), Spotlight on the Humanities (p. 262), Media and Technology Skills (p. 263), and the Standardized Test Preparation Workshop (p. 264).

TECHNOLOGY

Students can complete any stage of the lesson on computer. Have them print out their completed work.

INTEGRATED SKILLS COVERAGE

Integrating Grammar
Direct Quotations and Paraphrasing, ATE p. 253
Prepositional Phrases, SE p. 255
Providing Internal Documentation, SE p. 257

Technology Skills
Narrowing a Topic Through an Internet Search, ATE p. 248

Vocabulary Skills
Thesaurus and Dictionary Use, ATE p. 256

Reading/Writing Connection
Evaluate Sources of Information, SE p. 244
Writing Application, SE p. 245

Viewing and Representing
Critical Viewing, SE pp. 242, 244, 249, 251, 256, 259, 262
Examining Culture Represented in Art, SE p. 262
Compiling Information Using Available Technology, SE p. 263

Speaking and Listening
ATE p. 260

Real-World Connection ATE p. 247

ASSESSMENT SUPPORT

Standardized Test Preparation Workshop SE p. 264; ATE p. 253
Standardized Test Preparation Workbook, pp. 23–24
Scoring Rubrics on Transparency, Ch. 12
Formal Assessment, Ch. 12
Writing Assessment and Portfolio Management

MEETING INDIVIDUAL NEEDS

Less Advanced Students ATE p. 265. See also Ongoing
Assessments ATE pp. 245, 247, 251, 254.
AP Students ATE pp. 249, 265
ESL Students ATE pp. 248, 254
Gifted and Talented Students ATE pp. 251, 260
Logical/Mathematical Learners ATE p. 254

BLOCK SCHEDULING

Pacing Suggestions
For 90-minute Blocks
- Have students complete the Prewriting and Drafting stages in a single period.
- Focus one class period on Revising and Editing and Publishing and Presenting. Allow at least 30 minutes for peer revision.

Resources for Varying Instruction
- *Writing Lab* **CD-ROM** If your students have access to hardware, a 90-minute block provides an ideal opportunity for students to work on computer.
- *Writers at Work* **Videotape** Show the Persuasion segment in class.

Professional Development Support
- *How to Manage Instruction in the Block* This Teaching Resource provides management and activity suggestions.

MEDIA AND TECHNOLOGY

For the Student
- *Writing Lab* **CD-ROM**, Research
- *On-Line Exercise Bank,* Section 19.1

For the Teacher
- *Writers at Work* **Videotape**, Research Writing
- *Resource Pro* **CD-ROM**

WRITING AND GRAMMAR WEB SITE

The Interactive Writing and Grammar Web Site provides a wide array of support for students, teachers, and parents. Writing support includes:

- Interactive revision checkers
- Scoring rubrics with complete models

www.phschool.com

LITERATURE CONNECTIONS

Related selections from *Prentice Hall Literature: Timeless Voices, Timeless Themes,* The American Experience:

"The Brown Chest," John Updike, SE p. 245
"The First Seven Years," Bernard Malamud, SE p. 247

Lesson Objectives

1. To write a documented essay appropriate to audience and purpose

2. To organize ideas in writing to ensure coherence, logical progression, and support for ideas

3. To read to appreciate a writer's craft and to discover models for writing

4. To use prewriting strategies to generate ideas and plan

5. To use writing to formulate questions, compile information, and support what is known about a topic

6. To develop and revise drafts in terms of structure, paragraphs, sentences, and word choice

7. To edit and proofread to ensure standard English usage and grammar

8. To refine a documented essay for publication

Critical Viewing

Support Students' responses should include such details as smiles, open arms, looks of joy, butterflies that seem to indicate beauty and fun, etc.

Chapter
12 Research
Documented Essay

Miracle of Life, 1996, Christian Pierre, Private Collection

Documentation in Everyday Life

We live in an age of information explosion. Journalists, business people, scientists, and other professional analysts spend an increasing part of their time identifying, categorizing, predicting, and reporting new trends. For example, magazine articles quote experts, news programs use interviews to elaborate the stories they cover, and commentators in round-table discussions provide support for their opinions. In these cases, professionals use documentation—proof gathered from other sources—to back up the analyses they provide.

▲ **Critical Viewing**
How do the details of this painting suggest the joy of research? **[Support]**

⏱ **TIME AND RESOURCE MANAGER**

Resources
Technology: *Writers at Work* Videotape, Research Writing; *Writing Lab* CD-ROM, Research

In-Depth Coverage	Accelerated Pace
• Read and discuss pages 242–243 in class. • Show Research Writing section of *Writers at Work* Videotape. • Read the Model From Literature (pp. 244–245) with students, and use it to discuss elements of the documented essay.	• Discuss definition and cite examples of documented essays. • Assign the Model From Literature for independent reading.

What Is a Documented Essay?

A **documented essay** uses research gathered from outside sources to support an idea. What distinguishes this essay from other categories of research is the level and intensity of the research. In a documented essay, the writer consults a limited number of sources to elaborate an idea. In contrast, a formal research paper may include many more research sources. An effective documented essay includes

- a well-defined thesis that can be fully discussed in a brief essay.
- facts and details to support each main point.
- expert or informed ideas gathered from interviews and other sources.
- a clear, coherent method of organization.
- full internal documentation to show sources of information.

To see the criteria on which your final documented essay may be judged, preview the Rubric for Self-Assessment on page 258.

Types of Documented Essays

Documentation can strengthen the body of most writing. Subjects especially well suited to the documented essay format include the following:

- **Health issues:** The benefits of exercise can be documented.
- **Current events:** The effects of a law on a community can be collected.
- **Cultural trends:** A rising interest in animated films can be shown.

PREVIEW
Student Work IN PROGRESS

Shira Pinsker, a student at Miami Palmetto High School in Pinecrest, Florida, wrote a documented essay about high-school graduates joining the armed forces. In this chapter, you will see Shira's work in progress, including the strategies she used to choose a topic, conduct interviews, develop a thesis statement, and present information clearly. At the end of the chapter, you can read Shira's completed essay.

Writers in ACTION

Annie Dillard's insights into human nature and the writing process have made her a "writer's writer." Here, she tells how research influences the work of writing:

"Your freedom as a writer is not freedom of expression in the sense of wild blurting; you may not let rip. It is life at its most free, if you are fortunate enough to be able to try it, because you select your materials, invent your task, and pace yourself."

Documented Essay • 243

PREPARE and ENGAGE

 Interest GRABBER Ask students to volunteer suggestions about what an "outside source" means (someone other than oneself; someone outside an organization; someone with expert knowledge, authority, or objectivity). How are outside sources used in research? Elicit ideas about how students can identify reliable sources. Encourage students to speculate about the effect of unreliable sources on research.

Activate Prior Knowledge

Initiate discussion about reports students have read in a magazine or newspaper, seen on television, or heard on the radio. What sources were used to document the research? How were the sources revealed to the reader or listener? Tell students that this chapter will help them learn to recognize and use outside sources as effective and creative research tools.

More About the Writer

Annie Dillard is a writer and poet born in Pittsburgh in 1945. She has written several books and many magazine features, including a column for the Wilderness Society. An environmentalist, Dillard has a passion for nature that is evident in her writings.

✓ **ONGOING ASSESSMENT: Diagnose**

Use one of the following options to diagnose students' current level of proficiency in writing documented essays.

Option 1 You may wish to review students' strongest work from their previous year's writing portfolio in order to assess their skills. This will allow you to target those students who may need extra help.

Option 2 Have students write two or three paragraphs on a current event of their choosing. Students who fail to write a concise topic sentence or include sufficient supporting evidence for their writing may need extra help.

Reading: Evaluate Sources

Tell students that when reading factual material, they need to "consider the source." Does the writer have firsthand experience or expert training in the topic being covered? Does the writer use reliable sources, such as quotations from experts and reference works? Is the information current? Tell students to consider Dickinson's sources as they read "Reunion Rules." You may also wish to have them note the methods she uses to identify or cite her sources.

Step-by-Step Teaching Guide

Engage Students Through Literature

1. Elicit discussion about the essay with questions such as the following: What is the effect of linking personal anecdote to documented research? What kinds of sources does Dickinson use? (She cites a research firm report, two Web sites, unidentified "specialized books," interviews, and personal experience.)

2. Help students perceive how Dickinson's techniques connect a humorous personal occasion to a universal human situation.

3. Have students review the text and identify the words and phrases the author uses to informally cite her sources. (". . . according to Reunion Research," "Two useful sources are . . . ," "Specialized reunion source books available in the public library . . . ," "'Remember,' reunion professional Edith Wagner counseled me . . .")

4. Encourage students to think about the research resources that are available to them as they choose a topic for their own documented essay.

Critical Viewing

Hypothesize Students' responses will probably include such ideas as different perspectives for different generations, insight into family history, anecdotes, etc.

12.1 Model From Literature

This documented essay by magazine writer Amy Dickinson takes the form of a feature article to blend three purposes: to describe, to entertain, and to inform.

Reading ◄ Writing Connection

Reading Strategy: Evaluate Sources of Information Dickinson supports her ideas with quotations and information from experts. As you read, notice whom she quotes and determine whether her expert sources seem reliable.

▲ **Critical Viewing**
What can you gain from visiting with the members of an extended family? [Hypothesize]

Reunion Rules

Amy Dickinson

I have been to only one family reunion, a weekend affair on the beautiful farm of one of my favorite aunties. The setting was perfect, with plenty of games, food and swimming. I was primed for a fabulous party, and then I noticed that my relatives were showing up. I remember pulling up to the reunion in a rental car, looking at the gathering clan and thinking, "What are *they* doing here?" So first a warning: if you attend a family reunion, there is every likelihood that you will see your family there.

That includes wacky Uncle "Pull my finger" Bud. "You've gained weight!" he'll say by way of greeting. You will engage in long conversations with people you've never met, about people you'll never meet.

You will be asked repeatedly about your so-called career. You will spend hours trying to figure out the difference between a first cousin once removed and a second cousin. You will pretend to be interested in opera, NASCAR, and fly-fishing. You will, in all probability, have a wonderful time.

Some 200,000 extended families are clogging state parks and V.F.W. halls this summer, according to Reunion Research, a San Francisco–based resource [http://www.reuniontips.com, August

The opening paragraphs present the thesis: A reunion can provide a great opportunity to meet extended family if you approach it the right way.

These examples establish the humor of the situation and set a forgiving tone.

244 • Documented Essay

1999]. Because of the competition for venues and to give participants time to schedule their vacations, you should get started now if you're planning a reunion for next summer. Two useful resources are *Reuniontips.com* and *Reunionsmag.com.* Specialized reunion source books available in the public library provide tips on getting started, including help in finding distant relatives.

While my aunt's farm provided a lovely backdrop for our family's reunion, many planners suggest that sticky problems over "ownership" of the reunion can be averted if you choose a site on neutral ground—an attractive location equally convenient to most of the clan. As many relatives as possible should be enlisted in putting on the show, whether to cook or deliver a toast.

Children should be entertained with plenty of softball games, relay races and water-balloon tosses. Older kids can be recruited to help. "Remember," reunion professional Edith Wagner counseled me, "happy kids make for happy parents and grandparents." (Edith Wagner, personal interview with author, 12 August 1999.) Children should be prepared to have their cheeks pinched repeatedly and to be told that they look exactly like ancestors who died decades ago.

My family reunion actually went very well, although at times it seemed more like a Shriners' convention. I especially remember getting to know an elderly woman who was so fabulous, I couldn't believe we were related. (Later I learned we weren't.) Best of all, I found that some of my most obvious flaws, like my Groucho Marx eyebrows and perennial bad attitude, clearly are genetic. I shared this observation with a similarly afflicted cousin, and we both admitted that we felt relieved.

Tim Ninkovich, founder of Reunion Research, reminded me that at a reunion, we are participating in the ongoing story of our family. (Tim Ninkovich, personal interview with author, 12 August 1999.) Bring scrapbooks, letters and photo albums to share, as well as old uniforms or artifacts used by ancestors. Take lots of pictures, and talk to everyone you can, especially those distant relations on the shady side of the family tree. At a minimum, you'll have something to gossip about later. But be on your best behavior, because they're sure to gossip about you too.

Reading Writing Connection

Writing Application: Quote Reliable Sources
To support your ideas, include references from dependable outside sources. Be sure the people and text that you quote provide accurate information.

The factual information and practical advice in this article come from a variety of sources: an agency in San Francisco, two Web sites, and personal interviews.

The writer offers practical suggestions for structuring a reunion and organizing activities. Dickinson provides documentation for this direct quotation.

Personal experiences support the view that attending a family reunion can be worthwhile.

In keeping with the light tone of the essay as a whole, she closes with an amusing tip, admonishing readers to be on their best behavior.

LITERATURE

For a fiction writer's version of the importance of family history, see John Updike's story, "The Brown Chest" in *Prentice Hall Literature: Timeless Voices, Timeless Themes,* The American Experience.

Model From Literature • 245

Teaching From the Model

Tell students to watch for the author's transitions in this excerpt. How does she move from witty observation to stating facts and citing resources? Lead students to discover how Dickinson moves back and forth between documented research resources and personal anecdotes.

More About the Writer

Amy Dickinson's writing about families in *Time* magazine has addressed topics as diverse as the incidence of depression among young people, young people's role in helping to care for older family members, and "respect" laws that require young people to address adults formally at all times.

Connections With Literature

Ask students to predict some differences between a fictional account of a family history, as in Updike's "The Brown Chest," and a non-fictional account like Dickinson's "Reunion Rules." After reading both accounts, ask students to describe how the writing differs. (A fictional account of a personal occasion might not have as strong a link to the universality of the situation. The non-fictional account draws on real-life sources.)

Reading\Writing Connection

Writing Application: Quote Reliable Sources

Tell students that using reliable sources not only strengthens their writing, it offers the twin advantages of increasing the writer's knowledge and of making it harder for readers to dismiss or disprove the essay. When possible, students should double-check facts and should always consult sources that are likely to be accurate.

✓ ONGOING ASSESSMENT: Monitor and Reinforce

If students need additional help to understand the concept of documentation, use the following option.

Using local magazines or newspapers, show students other examples of researched essays. Point out, or help students locate, examples of people, books, and organizations that served as documented sources of information. Make sure students take note of the language used in referring to these examples.

Step-by-Step Teaching Guide

Prewriting: Brainstorm for Trends

1. Have students work in small groups to generate ideas for trends. Each group should nominate a "scribe" to list its ideas.

2. Ask groups to share their lists, and compare and contrast them for similarities and differences.

3. Permit students to select the same or similar topics for their documented essays. Explain that a similar topic may be handled differently by different writers.

Step-by-Step Teaching Guide

Prewriting: Portfolio Review

Teaching Resources: Writing Support Transparencies, 12-A

1. Display Transparency 12-A and refer students to the Student Work in Progress on this page. Discuss Shira's method of scanning her portfolio for topics.

2. Tell students to list the topics in their portfolios that they might like to learn more about, expand upon, or rewrite. For example, they might want to write a documented essay based on a fictional account.

3. Remind students to consider the available research resources as they select their topics.

⏱ TIME SAVERS!

📋 **Writing Support Transparencies**
Use the transparencies for Chapter 12 to facilitate the teaching of Portfolio Review and other strategies.

12.2 Prewriting

Choosing Your Topic

When you choose a topic for a documented essay, keep two guidelines in mind: Your topic should interest you, and the sources to support your main idea should be readily available. Consider selecting topics that are more contemporary than the ones you might pursue in a formal research paper. The following strategies will help you find a topic:

Strategies for Generating a Topic

1. **Brainstorm for Trends** In a group, identify the new trends you spot in music, clothes, food, and the media. After you generate several ideas, review the list and choose a topic you'd like to develop into a documented essay.

2. **Portfolio Review** Scan the items in your writing portfolio—perhaps a piece of expository or descriptive writing might be strengthened by further research. For example, you might be able to expand a sports article into a documented essay by interviewing the players, the coaches, or some fans. Choose one piece of writing from your portfolio, and develop it into a documented essay.

Writing Lab CD-ROM

For more help finding a topic, explore the activities and suggestions in the Choosing a Topic sections of the Research and Exposition lessons.

Student Work IN PROGRESS

Name: *Shira Pinsker*
Miami Palmetto High School
Pinecrest, FL

Scanning a Portfolio to Choose a Topic

Shira reviewed the work in her writing portfolio to look for topics that might be well suited to a documented-essay format. She decided to build on an interview she'd had with a classmate about joining the armed forces.

Oct 10	Narration	Short story about a race
Oct 18	Persuasion	School should offer a course in visual culture/critical viewing
Nov 1	News Article	Interview with student about joining the army

---

⏱ TIME AND RESOURCE MANAGER

Resources
Print: *Writing Support Transparencies,* 12-A–C; *Writing Support Activity Book,* 12-1
Technology: *Writing Lab* CD-ROM, Research

In-Depth Coverage	Accelerated Pace
• Work through one of the strategies on p. 246. • Demonstrate topic development with an item from the Topic Bank. • Use the Responding to Fine Art transparency to generate additional interest.	• Have students independently read pp. 246–247 and then list suggestions of some topics for their essays. • Have students read pp. 248–249 on their own and make their own lists of possible resources.

TOPIC BANK

If you're having trouble finding a topic, consider the following ideas:

1. **Performing Arts Essay** Many people celebrate the challenges and rewards they experience through participating in theater, dance, or music. Make a list of people you know who are active in the arts. Use the sources to develop a documented essay on the benefits of such participation.

2. **Technology Update** Creative computer engineers often tackle new problems with each software advance. Write a documented essay about the problems they encounter, the methods they use to solve them, and the practical applications of their work for the average computer user.

Responding to Fine Art

3. *Les Coureurs* (*The Runners*) at right, may inspire you to wonder about the effects of competition or the value of exercising with a group. Use one of these suggestions—or another idea the image suggests—to develop into a documented essay.

Les Coureurs (The Runners), Robert Delaunay, Museum of Modern Art, Troyes, France/Lauros-Giraudon, Paris

Responding to Literature

4. Read "The First Seven Years" by Bernard Malamud. Using the story as a springboard, learn more about career development opportunities such as internships or mentoring. You can find the story in *Prentice Hall Literature: Timeless Voices, Timeless Themes*, The American Experience.

☑ Cooperative Writing Opportunity

5. **Sports Recruiting Survey** In a group, split the task of studying athletic recruitment at the college level. Survey several colleges to learn about their practices. Find out what the opportunities and pitfalls for students can be, and identify areas for process improvement. Use charts, graphics, or other visual aids where appropriate. Combine group members' work into a documented essay.

Prewriting • 247

Narrowing Your Topic

Some topics are too broad to be handled in a few pages. Review your topic to decide whether you can split the subject into specific aspects. If so, you may need to narrow your topic. Another way to sharpen the focus of your topic is to conduct some preliminary research. The expertise you accumulate may help you identify subtopics. Use the listing and itemizing strategy to record what you learn and to focus your topic.

Listing and Itemizing to Narrow a Topic

As you become more familiar with your subject, list each main idea or issue you discover. Then, itemize each entry on your list, generating specific details about it. Consider using one of these narrowed lists to develop your writing. If you find your itemized lists are becoming too lengthy or unmanageable, evaluate whether your topic is still too broad or whether you are including more details than your audience needs.

Writing Lab CD-ROM

Use the suggestions for narrowing a topic by employing such strategies as a topic web and a questionnaire. You can find these activities in the Research lesson.

Considering Your Audience and Purpose

If your **audience** for an essay is a group of younger students, you will shape your writing differently from the way you would write for an audience of adult readers. Before you draft your essay, identify the specific audience you will address. Then, include the language and details they will need to understand your topic.

Your **purpose** in a documented essay is generally to inform, to describe, or to persuade. Some essays combine two or three purposes. Considering your exact goal before you write will help you to choose the information that supports your purpose.

248 • Documented Essay

Gathering Details

Write What You Already Know

Because you have chosen a topic in which you have a lively interest, you may already know more about it than you realize. Jot down what you already know, adding as many details as you can. Then, collect documentation to fill in any holes you can detect, gathering details that support the main idea of your essay.

Identify Sources of Further Information

Review your notes to identify who and what might help you get more information about the topic. Make a list of questions you'd like to answer, and then find the facts you need. You can refer to magazine articles, television news shows, and Web sites. For more customized information, consider interviewing classmates, friends, relatives, or local experts.

Review Library Sources Depending on your topic, you may be able to find the concrete facts you need at the library. Consider using the following sources:

- **Public records** for population growth or decline rates
- **Almanacs** for statistics
- ***Current Biography*** for information about professional entertainers or athletes

Use the **card catalog**, **on-line catalog,** available **databases**, Internet **search engines,** as well as such reference tools as the *Readers' Guide to Periodical Literature.*

Take notes, recording any relevant information from the sources you find, just as you would for a research report. In all cases, note the titles and authors of sources as well as publication information such as city, publisher, publication date, and the numbers of the pages you referenced.

Conduct Interviews In some cases, you may be able to contact an expert to explain your topic. In others, an average person's experience may support your main idea best. If you want to show how art students can improve their skill through workshop-based courses, interview a teacher or a student who has been involved in such classes.

To make the most of an interview, make sure you have a goal in mind. Develop focused questions in advance, and be sure to record the responses accurately. You may want to bring a tape recorder to make the job easier. For documentation purposes, note the date of all interviews you conduct.

Learn More

For more on conducting library research, see Chapter 13 and Chapter 31.

▼ **Critical Viewing**
For the topic you are pursuing, identify two facts you could develop through library research. **[Apply]**

Prewriting: Write What You Already Know

1. As students begin to jot notes on what they already know, write the following questions on the board for them to consider:

   How do you know this information?

   Is it from personal experience? Have you read about this topic? If so, where?

   Do you know others who share this knowledge?

2. Encourage students to expand upon their existing resources as they gather new information for their essays.

Prewriting: Identify Sources of Further Information

1. Have students evaluate the flow of information in their notes. Ask them to consider whether there are any gaps in information. Can they back up each point with a documented source?

2. As students identify gaps in their notes, help them identify research sources. Whom might they interview? Where might they read interviews or articles on their topics?

Customize for
AP Students

Encourage students to investigate a newspaper or news group on the Internet. Have them see how many different sources they can find for their topic. Tell them to evaluate the information they gather. Ask students to consider what they would do if they found conflicting research.

Critical Viewing

Apply Students should identify two elements of their essays that they could realistically research at the library.

Drafting: Write a Thesis Statement

1. Explain to students that it is possible, and even common, for a thesis statement to change as research turns up new facts. However, it is difficult to get started at all if they don't have a starting point and direction to go.

2. Ask these questions as students shape their thesis statements. You might also write them on the board.

   Does your statement reflect your opinion?

   What is your purpose?

   Do you have the documentation to back up your thesis?

   Does the information you include provide full support of your thesis statement?

   Who is your audience?

Drafting: Organize to Suit Your Topic

Teaching Resources: Writing Support Transparencies, 12-D

1. Discuss the different types of organization with students. Display the transparency (12-D) and discuss how Shira used subheads in her part-to-whole organization.

2. Illustrate that some topics require specific organizational techniques. Use the example of an autobiography, which often follows a chronological ordering technique.

3. Have students evaluate their information to determine the most suitable organization technique. Have students jot down some notes and then tell the group how and why they made their organizational choices.

12.3 # Drafting

Shaping Your Writing

After you have gathered details for your essay, you need to organize your information effectively. Before you draft, write a thesis statement and plan an organization for your writing.

Write a Thesis Statement

In a single sentence, write the main idea of your essay.

EXAMPLE: Green is making a fashion comeback.

Organize to Suit Your Topic

Choose an organization that will help you communicate your ideas to your audience. Consider these organizational strategies:

- **Chronological order** presents events in time order. Start at the earliest event and move toward the latest.
- **Cause-and-effect order** shows the relationships between events or trends and their causes or results. Start with a cause, and then investigate the effects it has produced. Alternatively, explain the causes behind a particular effect.
- **Part-to-whole organization** presents information in logical categories that make up the whole topic. Use this method to explain the individual elements of a broad topic.

Student Work IN PROGRESS

Name: *Shira Pinsker*
Miami Palmetto High School
Pinecrest, FL

Using a Part-to-Whole Organization

Shira grouped details using a part-to-whole organization. She decided to include subheads for each major section in her essay.

Requirements
- diploma
- testing
- English/math

Rewards
- learn skills
- earn money for college
- grow in pride and discipline

Personal Choices
- examine hopes and dreams
- get more information

250 • Documented Essay

⏱ TIME AND RESOURCE MANAGER

Resources
Print: *Writing Support Transparencies,* 12-D
Technology: *Writing Lab* CD-ROM, Research

In-Depth Coverage	Accelerated Pace
• Read and discuss pp. 250–251 with the group. • Work through the various organizational strategies with the class. Use the transparency to reinforce the part-to-whole organization. Then, have students select organizations suited to their topics. • Demonstrate patterns of attributing information.	• Have students read pp. 250–251 on their own. • Have them form groups for discussion of thesis statement, organizing information, and elaborating on the thesis with quotations and sources.

Providing Elaboration

Let Quotations Tell the Story

Support your thesis with information from your research. Use statistics, facts, examples, details, and expert opinions to support the ideas in your essay. For example, if you want to say that neighborhood safety is a key factor in a family's decision to purchase a home, include a quotation that backs up that claim.

Attribute Information

When you use a quotation to back up an idea, you should provide formal citations that indicate author and page number. Challenge yourself to incorporate references smoothly into your draft. Follow these suggestions for building attribution into your writing:

Name Your Source When providing information gathered through research, introduce your sources in your essay. Use phrases like "according to . . . ," "in an interview," or "on the Web site" to prepare readers for the information you will quote next. Then, include full documentation in parentheses.

EXAMPLE: *According to Elaine Rothman,* director of the Realtors for Community Action, prospective home buyers frequently ask about crime rates in the communities where they plan to live. [Elaine Rothman, personal interview with the author, 10 January 2000]

Build the Source's Authority Whatever phrase you use to attribute the ideas, be sure to provide the background to explain why the person or source quoted can provide useful input. Give the person's title, explain his or her experiences, or show how your source is an authority on your subject.

EXAMPLE: Amy Adler, *a first-time buyer,* explained her decision to live in Rockville: "I want to be able to walk my dogs at night without fear." [Amy Adler, personal interview with the author, 1 May 2000]

EXAMPLE: In last year's annual summary *published by town officials,* Rockville reported increased home sales. [Rockville. *Year in Review.* Rockville, Tennessee: Office of Public Information, 1999.]

▲ **Critical Viewing**
How might a real estate agent use the documented essay format to attract clients? **[Hypothesize]**

Drafting • 251

Step-by-Step Teaching Guide

Drafting: Providing Elaboration

1. Discuss the use of quotations and attributed information with students. Refer students to the examples on this page.

2. Have students look back at "Reunion Rules" on pages 244–245. Help them recall the writing devices that Amy Dickinson uses to cite her sources.

3. Ask a volunteer to retell an example of one of Dickinson's sources in a formal way instead of her informal style.

4. Ask the other students what changes would occur if the author had been more formal. Would it add to or take away from the "feel" of this essay? (The writing might lose some of its warmth if it became formal. It might also become more authoritative and persuasive.)

Customize for
Gifted and Talented Students

Have students write short essays on one thesis statement for two different audiences. (Example: Students might write one essay on their topic for inclusion in a national newspaper and another for an audience of third graders.) Ask students to consider in what ways their writing differed for the two audiences. How was it similar?

Critical Viewing

Hypothesize Students' responses should include house-and-neighborhood-related items, such as local history, owner anecdotes, crime rate, schools, and cost-of-living.

☑ **ONGOING ASSESSMENT: Monitor and Reinforce**

If students seem confused about how to organize their drafts, you might try the following strategies.

Suggest that students try using an outline, diagram, chart, or graph to organize details. Students who find that their material will fit in a timeline, for example, may see that their drafts should follow chronological order. Other students might construct a two-column chart headed "Events" and "Effects," which may help them see how to use a cause-and-effect organization for their drafts. A web diagram labeled in the center with the name of a broad topic can help students organize and order the many details surrounding it. It can encourage them to consider a part-to-whole structure for their essays.

1. Now that students have mapped out their theses and supporting documentation, have them review their structure for coherence.

2. As students answer each question in the evaluation process, encourage them to bracket key words and make the necessary revisions for more coherent structure.

3. Then, have students identify their primary and secondary documentation sources. Students should consider whether their sources are organized appropriately. Does the essay need all the sources listed? Do the sources repeat information? If so, should some be omitted, or do the sources substantiate and reinforce one another?

More About the Writer

Born in Exeter, New Hampshire, John Irving became a wrestler, a wrestling coach, and a best-selling novelist despite his dyslexia. Irving uses a wrestling metaphor when he says, ". . . If I couldn't learn to spell, I would keep a list of my frequently misspelled words . . . Most of all, I rewrote everything; first drafts were like the first time you tried a new takedown—you needed to drill it, over and over again, before you even dreamed of trying it in a match."

12.4 Revising

After you have completed a first draft, analyze your essay to see whether you have achieved the best possible results. Evaluate the content and style of the essay, and make revisions to improve your work.

Revising Your Overall Structure

Confirm Coherence

To be sure your essay presents information clearly, make sure every main idea supports your thesis statement. Then, decide whether a reader who is unfamiliar with your topic would have trouble following your treatment of it in the essay.

▶ REVISION STRATEGY
Bracketing to Identify Paragraph Topics

As you review your draft, identify the focus of each paragraph by bracketing a key word or sentence and numbering each body paragraph. To evaluate the flow of your essay, review the order of ideas you have marked. Consider changing the order of paragraphs or making other revisions to make the progression more logical.

Evaluate	Revise
• Does the order make sense?	• Group closely related paragraphs together. Insert subheads to make these blocks, or sections, of your essay more obvious to readers.
• Does every paragraph contribute to the thesis statement?	• Cut paragraphs that don't support the thesis statement. If you want to keep the information in your draft, revise to make the connection clear.
• Does the information flow smoothly?	• Add transitional paragraphs to connect ideas smoothly. Use brief paragraphs to summarize the previous information or to prepare readers for what will follow.

252 • Documented Essay

Writers in ACTION

Revision can be a tricky part of the writing process, especially when a writer knows what's wrong but not how to fix it. While revising his novel The World According to Garp, *John Irving tried the final paragraph several times before an interruption gave him the ideas he needed. In a letter, he wrote:*

"Of course, all the time I was losing the Monopoly game, I was thinking of the last paragraph, and I believe that the time away from my desk was a valuable part of that last paragraph, which I might have written too quickly without the sizeable interruption."

⏱ TIME AND RESOURCE MANAGER

Resources
Print: *Writing Support Transparencies,* 12-E–F
Technology: *Writing Lab* CD-ROM, Research

In-Depth Coverage	Accelerated Pace
• Read pp. 252–254 in class. • Have students evaluate their drafts based on the questions on p. 252. • Allow class time for Peer Review.	• Have students read pp. 252–256 independently. • Form small groups of students to do the Peer Review. Have groups share the results with the rest of the group.

Revising Your Paragraphs

Smooth Transitions to Quotations

When you quote an interviewee, an expert's ideas, or a research source, you need to ensure that your text is both informative and clear.

▶ REVISION STRATEGY
Color-Coding to Evaluate Links to Quoted Material

Review the first draft of your essay, and highlight direct quotations that provide a speaker's exact words. Also, underline passages where you have paraphrased, or quoted a source indirectly. Examine the way in which you have introduced this material and identified its source. Consider adding phrases such as "he/she said" or "according to." During this evaluation, double-check that you introduce the speaker's authority or the background of the source when you are referring to this source for the first time.

🔦 Challenge

To improve the content of your paragraph, return to your prewriting notes and add more information to support your ideas.

Student Work IN PROGRESS

Name: _Shira Pinsker_
Miami Palmetto High School
Pinecrest, FL

Polishing Transitions

When she reviewed her essay, Shira found that she could improve the integration of quoted material into the text: She added words to attribute the information.

Raoul Fuentes , guidance counselor at Palmetto High School, discussed these requirements in an interview. He says He is happy with the diploma requirements and believes many students will benefit from service in the military. "You must have a high-school diploma to be in the military. "according to Fuentes, " It didn't used to be like that, but it's all technical now." (Raoul Fuentes, personal interview with author, 29 November 1999.)

Step-by-Step Teaching Guide

Revising: Color-Coding to Evaluate Links to Quoted Material

Teaching Resources: Writing Support Transparencies, 12-E

1. Display the transparency of the Student Work in Progress. Discuss how Shira improved the integration of quotes in her text.

2. Write the following questions on the board, and have students consider them as they evaluate and highlight their quoted materials.

   Does this quotation provide the appropriate documentation to support my information?

   Is the quotation recorded accurately?

   Have I clearly identified the source?

   Do I have too many quotations? Too few?

3. Encourage students to read their essays aloud to themselves to help them determine whether the quotes add to the thesis or interrupt the flow of information.

4. If students find that their quotes interrupt their writing, have them re-evaluate their transitions.

Integrating Grammar Skills

Point out the difference between using direct quotations and paraphrasing. Remind students that they may paraphrase in their writing as long as they cite their sources with the same accuracy as they would for a direct quotation.

✏️ STANDARDIZED TEST PREPARATION WORKSHOP

Main Idea Many standardized tests require students to identify a paragraph's main idea. The thesis statement of a documented essay tells the main idea of the essay. Have students read the paragraph and tell which sentence states the main idea.

To a surfer, the weather is not important. It might be a cold, windy, or rainy day. Or it might be sunny and warm. Although the weather affects the ocean tide, it is the tide that a surfer watches.

The main idea is stated in which sentence?

A first   **C** third
B second   **D** fourth

Students should recognize the main idea is stated in sentence 4, choice **D**. The other sentences lead up to the concluding sentence 4. As the conclusion of the opening paragraph of an essay, this statement tells readers what is ahead.

Revising: Identifying Sentence Patterns

Teaching Resources: Writing Support Transparencies, 12-F

1. Display the transparency and review the changes Shira made to vary her sentences.

2. Ask students to identify each of the changes and discuss which parts of speech they are.

3. Model this sentence-revising technique. Ask a volunteer to suggest a sentence and write the sentence on the board.

4. Then, ask volunteers to suggest revisions for the sentence. Write each revision on the board so students can see their own creativity in writing.

Customize for
Logical/Mathematical Learners

Have students evaluate their writing by diagramming their sentences by parts of speech. Then, ask them to look at any patterns in their sentence diagrams. Finally, have them revise their sentences by changing the patterns.

Customize for
ESL Students

Students who are learning English may find it difficult to modify sentence patterns, since they will want to work with patterns that are familiar. In order to familiarize them with different patterns, have them pick a sentence and then work through it with them to show them several possible modifications of the one sentence. Explain how the sentence is still similar to the original and how it is different as well. Create another sentence that is as close in form to the first one as possible and then rework it in the same ways, to demonstrate that the rules are consistent. Then, encourage the students to create another sentence and modify it similarly.

12.4

Revising Your Sentences
Evaluate Sentence Patterns

For your reader, seeing the same type of sentence over and over can be monotonous. Boring writing may not be effective in its aim to persuade, inform, or entertain. To make your writing lively, use a variety of patterns in your sentences.

▶ **REVISION STRATEGY**
Identifying Sentence Patterns

In the example *Penguins eat a diet of crustaceans, fish, and squid*, the subject is the first word of the sentence. Beginning a sentence in this way is one of the most common habits of writers. When you identify your sentence habits, you may see a monotonous pattern that you can revise.

In a list, analyze the beginning words of the sentences in your draft. You may find subjects, verbs, phrases, or clauses. To create variety, add introductory material. Use these tips:

- Start with a prepositional phrase:
  In the Antarctic environment, penguins eat a varied diet.

- Start with an adverb:
  Surprisingly, penguins eat a varied diet.

- Start with a subordinate clause:
  Unless food is scarce, penguins eat a varied diet.

Language Lab CD-ROM

Use the lesson on Varying Sentence Structure in the unit on Writing Style.

Student Work IN PROGRESS

Name: Shira Pinsker
Miami Palmetto High School
Pinecrest, FL

Breaking Up Sentence Patterns

Shira's list showed she began many of her sentences with subjects. To vary her sentences, she added phrases to some of them.

Prepositional phrase — subject
subject
Infinitive phrase — subject
subject

For high-school students like Booker,
The armed forces are an alternative ~~for the high school students like Booker.~~ The requirements are rigorous. To join the armed forces, One must have a high-school diploma, a clean police record, and passing scores on a variety of mental and physical tests. Potential recruits must also take the ASVAB, . . .

254 • Documented Essay

✓ **ONGOING ASSESSMENT: Monitor and Reinforce**

If students are having difficulty incorporating supporting quotations into their drafts, consider using the following strategy.

Stage a classroom mini-debate on a topic of the students' choosing. Conduct a brief review of debating format, including proposition, argument, and rebuttal. For the purpose of this short activity, students need not have authoritative evidence on hand. However, emphasize that each point in an argument must be supported by evidence. As students debate, point out to them how each piece of supporting evidence is used to good effect in the spoken argument, and draw the parallel for them to the use of quotations as supporting evidence in a documented essay.

Grammar in Your Writing
Prepositional Phrases

Prepositions such as *at, over,* and *without* can help you add information to your writing without adding more sentences.

COMMON PREPOSITIONS

about	behind	during	of	through
above	beneath	from	off	under
after	between	in	on	up
before	down	near	over	with

Most **prepositional phrases** include two or three words, but some can be much longer. No matter how long, a prepositional phrase never includes a verb. Prepositional phrases include a preposition and its object, the noun or pronoun that completes the information the preposition provides. In these sample prepositional phrases, the prepositions are indicated in italics and objects are indicated in blue.

SAMPLE PREPOSITIONAL PHRASES

under investigation   *after* further review
in the manila folder   *up* the long and winding staircase

Prepositional phrases can serve as adjectives or adverbs, depending on the words they modify.

Adjective phrases describe nouns. In this example, the prepositional phrase modifies the noun *mammal:*

We noticed a sea mammal with a long tusk.

Adverb phrases describe verbs. In this example, the first prepositional phrase tells *when* the action of the verb took place:

During the cool morning hours, we took a mountain hike.

Find It in Your Reading The first sentence of Amy Dickinson's essay "Reunion Rules" contains four prepositional phrases. Analyze the sentence to identify which phrases serve as adjectives and which serve as adverbs. Find the essay on pages 244–245.

Find It in Your Writing Identify prepositional phrases in your documented essay. If you can't find an example of both a prepositional phrase serving as an adjective and one acting as an adverb, consider revising your sentences to get more informational mileage from them. Challenge yourself to sophisticate your writing by adding two of each type of prepositional phrase.

To learn more about prepositional phrases, see Chapter 19.

Prepositional Phrases

1. Discuss each of the prepositional phrases in Grammar in Your Writing. Discuss with students the differences between adjectival and adverbial phrases.

2. Ask students to select a paragraph from their drafts, highlight all the adjectival and adverbial phrases, and rewrite the paragraph without the prepositional phrases. Ask students to evaluate the paragraph with and without the prepositional phrases. Which is better? Why? Lead students to see that prepositions add more information or detail.

3. Ask volunteers to provide examples of adverbial and adjectival phrases. If necessary, get them started by writing a simple sentence and asking them to add prepositional phrases.

Find It in Your Reading

Ask students to name the phrases and write them on the board.

to only one family reunion (adv.)
on the beautiful farm (adj.)
of one (adj.)
of my favorite aunties (adj.)

Find It in Your Writing

As students review their own documented essays, have them jot down the prepositional phrases they have used. Then, have them use this information as they consider revising their writing to include more prepositional phrases. Can they use prepositional phrases to add information to their essay? To make their writing more vivid? To vary their sentence patterns?

✓ ONGOING ASSESSMENT: Prerequisite Skills

If students are having difficulty using prepositional phrases correctly, you may find it helpful to refer them to the following materials to ensure coverage of requisite skills.

In the Textbook	Print Resources	Technology
Prepositional Phrases, pp. 434–440	*Grammar Exercise Workbook,* pp. 43–44	*On-Line Exercise Bank,* Section 19.1

Revising Your Word Choice

Evaluate "to Be" Verbs

Just as varied sentence patterns make your writing more lively, vivid verbs can add impact to an essay. While it may be convenient to use forms of the verb *be*, that choice may make your writing dull. The verb *be* and its forms usually link the subject of a sentence with a word that renames or describes it. Replace *be* verbs—including *is, am, are, was, were, be, being,* and *been*—with action verbs that communicate ideas with more power.

▶ **REVISION STRATEGY**
Circling Forms of the Verb *Be*

Circle "to be" verbs in your writing. Challenge yourself to make your writing more powerful by replacing these verbs with action verbs wherever you can. Your verb changes may require further revision of the sentence.

"TO BE" VERB:	Jean *was* serious about gardening.
ACTION VERB:	Jean *gardened* with flair and commitment.
"TO BE" VERB:	The garden *is* beautiful.
ACTION VERB:	The flowers in the garden *bloom* beautifully.
ACTION VERB:	The flowers in the garden *burst* with color.

▲ **Critical Viewing** What action verbs could you use to describe this photograph? **[Connect]**

Peer Review

Summarizing

To find the strengths in your writing, ask a group of your classmates to respond to your essay by summarizing its main points.

Read your draft to the group, and then pause. Before you read it a second time, give your listeners a focus: Ask them to tell you what they remember best. Their responses will reveal the ideas you have conveyed most clearly. As you listen to what they tell you, compare their feedback with your intentions. If what you think you communicated doesn't match what they heard, ask your peers for advice on making your thesis and development clearer.

Use the summaries and comments of the group to guide you in making a final revision of your essay.

12.5 Editing and Proofreading

Once you are satisfied with the content of your draft, review it for mistakes in spelling, mechanics, and usage. You should strive to produce a final draft that is error-free.

Focusing on Accuracy

Proofread to confirm that your essay is factually correct.

Check the Titles Review your notes or other information you have gathered to confirm the correct names of sources.

Review the Facts Review your notes to see that dates and statistics are correct. To be certain, find a second source to back up your report.

Grammar in Your Writing
Providing Internal Documentation

When you cite sources without providing a full reference list at the end of your writing, include all the source information parenthetically. The following models demonstrate conventions set by *The Chicago Manual of Style*.

For a book:
(W.P. Kinsella, *Shoeless Joe* [New York: Ballantine Books, 1982] 103.)

For a magazine article:
(Philip Weiss, "Off the Grid, " *The New York Times Magazine*, 14 April 1996, 159.)

For an interview:
(Samuel Lawrence, personal interview with author, 19 October 1998.)

When you cite a source for the second time, provide a shorter reference. Note these examples:

(Kinsella, *Shoeless*, 167.) (Weiss, "Grid," 159.) (Lawrence, 19 October 1998.)

Find It in Your Reading Review the internal documentation style in Amy Dickinson's essay on pages 244–245.

Find It in Your Writing As you prepare your final draft, check that you followed the conventions of internal citation accurately.

For further instruction, see *Citing Sources and Preparing Manuscript* on pages 894–900.

Step-by-Step Teaching Guide

Publishing and Presenting

1. Discuss each presentation strategy with the class. The Class Magazine strategy could build to the Presentation Day strategy.

2. Suggest that students make a group decision on how to present their documented essays.

3. Ask students to consider the use of illustrations, diagrams, pictures, or graphs in their essays.

ASSESS and CLOSE

Assessment

Teaching Resources: Scoring Rubrics on Transparency, Ch. 12; Writing Assessment and Portfolio Management; Formal Assessment, Ch. 12

1. Display the Scoring Rubric transparency and review the criteria in class.

2. Before students proceed with self-assessment, you may wish to review the Final Draft of the Student Work in Progress on pages 259–260. Have students score the Final Draft in one or more of the rubric categories. For example, how would students score the essay in terms of audience and purpose?

3. In addition to student self-assessment, you may wish to use the following assessment options:

   • score student essays yourself, using the rubric and scoring models from *Writing Assessment and Portfolio Management*.

   • review the Standardized Test Preparation Workshop on pages 264–265, and administer a timed writing assessment.

   • administer the Chapter 12 assessment from *Formal Assessment* to measure students' grasp of concepts presented.

12.6 Publishing and Presenting

Building Your Portfolio

The purpose of your documented essay may be to inform, describe, or persuade. Decide how you want to publish your essay and present it to your audience. Consider these ideas:

1. **Develop a Class Magazine** With classmates, use your writing to create a magazine. Organize essays into categories, prepare a table of contents, and choose illustrations. Share the magazine with the school community.

2. **Organize a Presentation Day** Invite members of the community to hear you and your classmates present your research. To avoid reading your paper word for word, prepare note cards and highlight your key points. Use visual aids such as charts or photographs where appropriate.

Internet Tip

To see model essays scored according to this rubric, go to **www.phschool.com**

Reflecting on Your Writing

Consider your experiences in writing your essay. In a note to include in your portfolio, address questions such as these:

• In the process of writing, what did you learn about the topic you chose?

• In what ways did attributing your sources change the way you felt about your writing?

Rubric for Self-Assessment

Use these criteria to evaluate your documented essay:

	Score 4	Score 3	Score 2	Score 1
Audience and Purpose	Consistently targets a unique audience; clearly identifies purpose in thesis statement	Targets a specific audience; identifies purpose in thesis statement	Misses target audience by including too many details; presents no clear thesis	Addresses no specific audience or purpose
Organization	Presents a clear, consistent organizational strategy	Presents a clear organizational strategy with few inconsistencies	Presents an inconsistent organizational strategy; creates illogical presentation	Demonstrates a lack of organization; creates confusing presentation
Elaboration	Supports thesis statement with several documented sources; elaborates all main points	Supports thesis statement with some documented sources; elaborates most points	Supports the thesis statement with one documented source; elaborates some points	Provides no documented sources; does not provide thesis
Use of Language	Clearly integrates researched information into the writing; presents very few mechanical errors	Integrates most researched information into the writing; presents very few mechanical errors	Does not integrate researched information into the writing; presents many mechanical errors	Demonstrates poor use of language; presents many mechanical errors

258 • Documented Essay

✓ ONGOING ASSESSMENT: Assess Mastery

Use one of the following options to assess drafts of students' essays.

Self-Assessment Ask students to score their essays using the rubric provided. Then, have students write a paragraph that discusses the strategy they found most helpful in composing their essays.

Teacher Assessment Use the rubric and the scoring models provided in *Writing Assessment and Portfolio Management* to score students' work.

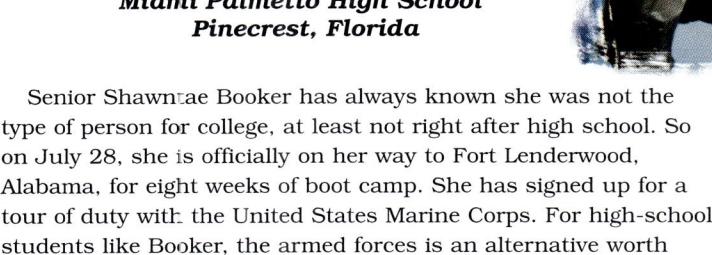

12.7 Student Work IN PROGRESS

FINAL DRAFT

The Armed Forces: The Right Choice for Some Seniors

Shira Pinsker
Miami Palmetto High School
Pinecrest, Florida

Senior Shawntae Booker has always known she was not the type of person for college, at least not right after high school. So on July 28, she is officially on her way to Fort Lenderwood, Alabama, for eight weeks of boot camp. She has signed up for a tour of duty with the United States Marine Corps. For high-school students like Booker, the armed forces is an alternative worth learning more about.

Requirements

The requirements for admission to the military are rigorous. To join the armed forces, one must have a high-school diploma, a clean police record, and passing scores on a variety of tests. Potential recruits must also take the ASVAB, the Armed Forces Vocational Aptitude Battery, a qualifying test for the military. Recruits need an adequate understanding of English and math. In fact, recruits are expected to have completed high-school math through algebra.

Raoul Fuentes, guidance counselor at Miami Palmetto High School, discussed these requirements in an interview. He says he likes the diploma requirement and believes many students benefit from service in the military. "You must have a high-school diploma to be in the military," according to Fuentes. "It didn't used to be like that, but it's all technical now. If people are using all of this million-dollar equipment, they should have a high-school diploma." (Raoul Fuentes, personal interview with author, 29 November 1999.)

▲ **Critical Viewing**
What emotions do the men shown here convey? **[Infer]**

The opening paragraph shows the experience of one student, making the topic more accessible to her readers. In the last sentence of the paragraph, Shira presents her thesis statement.

Subheads make a part-to-whole organization clear.

Final Draft

1. As students read "The Armed Forces: The Right Choice for Some Seniors," encourage them to discuss whether or not it incorporates the elements of a well-documented essay.

2. Point out the personal anecdote that leads up to the thesis statement in the first paragraph.

3. Ask students when the first cited source appears in this essay (in the third paragraph).

4. Ask students to describe how Raoul Fuentes is quoted (both informally and formally).

5. Have students note the sources used by the writer (Raoul Fuentes, Army recruitment spokesman Douglas Smith, Marine Corps Web site, Army Web site, Shawntae Booker).

6. Ask students to identify the type of organization used in this essay (part-to-whole organization).

7. Point out the subheads in the essay, and discuss how they are used as transitions.

8. Have students cite some of the prepositional phrases used in the essay ("of person," "for college," "for a tour," "of duty," "with the United States Marine Corps").

Critical Viewing

Infer Students may observe that the men look determined, and may be feeling eagerness to help, confident in their skills, or concerned about their performance.

259

Integrating Speaking and Listening Skills

Encourage students to deliver their documented essays as speeches, putting particular emphasis on quoted sources. Presentations can come to life when the audience gets a sense of the mood of the essay.

Teaching From the Final Draft

Due to space constraints in this textbook, the Final Draft of this documented essay may not be as long as you will require of your students. As you review the Final Draft, be sure to clarify to students your particular requirements regarding length, quantity of quotations and sources, methods of citation, and other details.

Customize for
Gifted and Talented Students

Ask students if Shira's essay were to be published in a general-interest magazine, what photographs and other visual aids might be added? (Students may mention photographs of Shawntae Booker or Raoul Fuentes, a graph showing the increase in Army recruitment, etc.) Students may wish to sketch a magazine layout for this essay.

The armed forces are seeing a steady flow of high-school graduates signing up for service. For example, United States Army recruitment spokesperson Douglas Smith reports that about 61,000 high-school graduates enter that branch every year. (Douglas Smith, personal interview with author, 18 November 1999.)

Shira uses direct quotations and full internal citation to support her ideas.

The Rewards of Enlisting

The United States military offers recruits the opportunity to learn new skills, meet new challenges, and master both teamwork and emergency management. After completing the famously difficult time at boot camp, which is required regardless of the field a new recruit chooses, the next step is to begin training in that chosen field. According to the Marine Corps site on the Web, educational opportunities in the Marines include communications, radar repair, aviation specialties, and language training. (http://www.Marines.com, 20 November 1999) The Army Web site shows that educational fields available to those who choose that branch of the service include satellite maintenance, food service, and hi-tech aviation repair, to name a few. (http:www.goarmy.com, 20 November 1999.)

In this paragraph, Shira refers to her sources—two Web sites—and the information they provided.

In addition to the opportunities for personal growth and skills training, recruits can earn money toward college. For example, students who score in the top half of the ASVAB can earn scholarships. Colleges in many states offer benefits to people who have served in the Army. (www.Marines.com)

Shira signals the transition to a different but related point with the phrase "in addition to."

Shawntae Booker herself is counting on this added incentive. "I get $36,000 for college when I get out after five years," said Booker, adding, "and serving looks good for colleges because they'll know you're trained and disciplined." (Shawntae Booker, personal interview with author, 28 October 1999.)

Here, Shira smoothly integrates general information about the armed forces with one recruit's specific experiences.

Is It the Choice for You?

Shawntae Booker and the others in her high school who have signed up for the service look forward to the discipline, training, and pride that come from being in the armed forces. That sounds promising to many young people willing to devote time to protecting the country that will provide lifelong security for them. However, the choice doesn't appeal to everyone. Each student must think about his or her own dreams and whether a career in the military—or even a five-year tour of duty—sounds good. Ways to learn more include visiting a Web site or a recruiting office.

Shawntae Booker encourages people to follow her path but warns that they must be ready to take direction. Summing up her decision, Booker says, "I'm doing this for myself. It might be difficult, but you've got to take what comes with every situation." (Booker, 28 October 1999.)

In the conclusion, Shira offers readers directions for learning more. She also gives her main interview subject the last word.

Connected Assignment

Statistical Report

When you rely heavily on numbers, percentages, and ratios to support a thesis, you are creating a **statistical report.** The paper's topic need not be related to numbers—it could be the history of westward expansion—but by citing data such as percentages and sheer quantity, statistics tell the story.

Use the writing process steps below to write your own statistical report:

Prewriting Choose a topic that can be developed through references to statistics. For example, sports lend themselves to numerical analyses, as do surveys on any topic. Explore your topic by listing what you know and need to learn about it—a K-W-L chart like the one shown below might help.

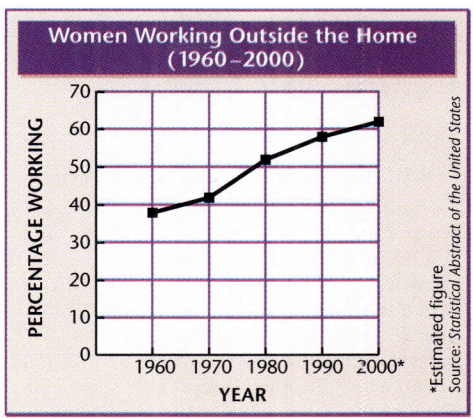

Women Working Outside the Home (1960–2000)

*Estimated figure
Source: Statistical Abstract of the United States*

K - Know	W - Want to Know	L - Learned
Career opportunities have opened up for women over the last 40 years.	What has been the progression, in numbers, of women working outside the home since the 1960's?	In the last decade, we have seen the largest number of women working outside the home.

Use specialized encyclopedias, almanacs, and on-line research to gather your statistics. Then, generate a thesis or main idea from the information you've found.

Drafting Follow these suggestions for drafting:
1. State your thesis in the opening paragraph.
2. Present supporting evidence in a series of paragraphs, incorporating statistics as appropriate.
3. Interpret any charts, tables, or graphs that you include.
4. Finish with a strong conclusion.

Revising and Editing Reread your report, and revise language that is overly opinionated or emotional. Let the facts speak for themselves. Make sure to include only pertinent statistics, and double-check that your statistics are accurately typed.

Publishing and Presenting Share your report with classmates.

Connected Assignment: Statistical Report • 261

Lesson Objectives

1. To learn about the source of a media production
2. To analyze relationships, ideas, and cultures represented in various media
3. To write a documented essay on an artist

Step-by-Step Teaching Guide

Examining Culture Represented in Art

1. Establish the geographic location of Appalachia, and choose one of the Spotlight elements for class discussion.

2. Interested students might research the artistic term "primitive" and look for examples of American primitive style.

3. Some students might like to look for pictures of a dulcimer or bring to class recordings of a folk singer accompanied by a dulcimer.

4. Before deciding on a topic for their documented essay, have students research artists in their community. Mention that *artist* can refer to a painter, writer, sculptor, or musician.

Viewing and Representing

Activity Students' essays might be published in a school literary magazine or newspaper, along with photos of the artists or their work. Alternatively, students might compile and make copies of an anthology of their essays.

Critical Viewing

Analyze Students may observe that antiques or the type of chair may suggest a particular region to students. The clothing of the man in the room may contribute to portrayal, too.

Spotlight on the Humanities

Examining Culture Represented in Art

Focus on Art: Queena Stovall

Just as documented essays address contemporary issues, artwork can also reflect issues, trends, and everyday life. One of the most unique and prolific artists of the Appalachian region was folk artist Queena Stovall (1887–1980). Named Queena by her paternal grandmother, Emma Serena Dillard began studying painting at the age of 63. She documented the country life of Appalachia, capturing the baptisms, auctions, and prayer meetings that were a part of the mountain landscape. Her style was labeled American Primitive, and her work was exhibited at Colonial Williamsburg and the New York State Historical Association. In twenty-five years, Queena created forty-seven major paintings.

Fireside in Virginia (detail), 1950, Queena Stovall, New York State Historical Association, Cooperstown, New York

Literature Connection Stovall captured the Appalachian region in art; George Ella Lyon captured it in poetry and prose. An award-winning author and poet, Lyon was born and raised in the mountains of Kentucky, and her literary work is infused with her Appalachian roots. Her book *Where I'm From* chronicles moments in her life and shows Lyon's gift for preserving moments in words. Lyon's humor, poignancy, and unique perspective of Appalachia have brought national acclaim for her work.

Music Connection Derived from a German instrument called a *scheitholt*, the Appalachian dulcimer can be played with a bow, picked, or strummed. The *scheitholt* made its way into Appalachia near the end of the eighteenth century. These mountain dulcimers are made from regional hardwoods such as maple, pecan, and walnut. The Appalachian dulcimer has become a solo instrument in the region and is also used to accompany singing.

Documented Essay Writing Activity: Artist Biography

Write a documented essay on an artist in your community. Use personal interviews, local newspaper reports, and other sources to enhance your own observations.

▲ **Critical Viewing** What details of this painting help portray a specific region? **[Analyze]**

Media and Technology Skills

Compiling Information Using Available Technology

Activity: Finding and Evaluating Sources On-line

If you turn to on-line resources to conduct research, you'll find a range of valuable research tools. While you will want to tap the ease and convenience of researching on the Web, do so with a critical eye: Not everything you find on-line is accurate.

Learn About It Approach on-line research with a focused topic. Harness the efforts of your favorite search engine or database with subject, title, or author prompts. Scan the listed sites to determine the best choices, choosing sites compiled by recognizable institutions or companies.

- **Moving From Search Engines to Site Content** Click on hyperlinks to select sites you wish to see. You can bookmark sites for future reference and print pages as you gather information.
- **Evaluating a Site** To decide whether the content is reliable, consider who created the site and look for evidence of the content provider's credentials. For example, when researching a celebrity, you may find more reliable information on a Web site posted by a reputable magazine than you might find on a site maintained by a single fan. Read any home page information carefully or e-mail inquiries to answer your questions.

Find It Find at least three on-line information sources for a topic of your choice. Take notes in a chart like the one below. Then, rank your sources in order of usefulness and credibility.

Source Title: _____

How You Found Source: _____
_____

Web Address: _____

Content Provider: _____

Date: ☐ Current (within 1 year)
      ☐ Recent (within 5 years)
      ☐ Older (more than 5 years old)

Credentials: 1   2   3   4   5
      (inadequate ——→ outstanding)

Search Tips

- See on-line vendors (books, equipment, travel) for product information linked to your topic, but check their facts carefully.
- Scan printed directories of Web sites by topic.
- Obtain lists of educational Web sites from local libraries.
- Use Forward and Back buttons to navigate a series of Web sites.

Analyze Tips

- Check the date on Web sites. Current is better unless the topic is not time-relevant.
- Read the author info and bibliography attached to sites.

Media and Technology Skills • 263

► **Lesson Objectives**

1. To use technology as a source of information
2. To evaluate an on-line content site
3. To compile information from primary and secondary sources using available technology

Step-by-Step Teaching Guide

Compiling Information Using Available Technology

Teaching Resources: Writing Support Transparencies, 12-H; Writing Support Activity Book, 12-3

1. Emphasize that narrowing a topic for on-line research is just as important as narrowing a topic before one begins to write.
2. Tell students that they can check the accuracy of facts by comparing information on the same topic from more than one site.
3. Display the transparency, and walk students through filling in information for a sample source.
4. Distribute copies of the blank organizer for students to use in their research.
5. When students have taken notes on at least three information sources, ask them how they determined the ranking they gave each source.

Lesson Objectives

1. To respond to document-based writing prompts
2. To organize ideas to ensure coherence, logical progression, and support for ideas
3. To use prewriting strategies to gather details and plan
4. To organize details and incorporate quotations to support analysis
5. To revise, edit, and proofread for coherence, style, and conventions

Step-by-Step Teaching Guide

Responding to Document–Based Writing Prompts

Teaching Resources: Standardized Test Preparation Workbook, pp. 23–24

1. Go over the first paragraph on this page, clarifying if necessary the terms *analyze, evaluate, synthesize,* and *draw conclusions*.

2. Remind students that they should be sure they understand the prompt.

3. Tell students that they will need to organize their time, just as they do on other essay tests.

4. After students have reread "Reunion Rules," assign the writing prompt for completion within the class period.

Standardized Test Preparation Workshop

Responding to Document-Based Writing Prompts

Standardized test questions often test your ability to use evidence from an article to support a response. For example, this type of prompt may require you to analyze an issue, evaluate the writer's position, or draw a conclusion. In some cases, you may be required to synthesize information from several documents provided. Your response will be evaluated on your ability to do the following:

- Respond directly to the prompt.
- Show a clear comprehension of the text included.
- Elaborate using details from the text to support your response.
- Organize details in a logical manner.
- Use conventions of correct grammar, usage, spelling, and punctuation.
- Compare and contrast several documents, when available.

The process of writing for a test, or any kind of writing, can be divided into stages. Plan to use a specific amount of time for prewriting, drafting, revising, and proofreading.

Use the suggestions on the following page to help you respond to a document-based writing prompt. The clocks next to each stage show a suggested plan for organizing your time.

Reread Amy Dickinson's "Reunion Rules" on pages 244–245. Then, respond to the following sample prompt.

Sample Prompt

In her article "Reunion Rules," does Amy Dickinson effectively accomplish her purposes for writing—describing, entertaining, and informing? Use details and information from the article in your response.

Test Tip

When analyzing a document provided in a test, don't overuse direct quotations. The basis of the response is your interpretation.

✦ TEST-TAKING TIP

Tell students that when a writing prompt asks for opinions or interpretation, they need to decide immediately what their opinions are before beginning to write. Making notes as they read a document-based writing prompt should help them focus their writing and decide on organization before they begin to draft. Quotations should be used sparingly since evaluators are interested in a student's interpretation.

Ask students to pick out the key words in the sample prompt and underline them.

They should underline *describing, entertaining, informing, details,* and *information*.

Prewriting

Allow close to one fourth of your time for prewriting.

Gather Details Before you write, use listing to gather details for your response. As you review the article, list details that will help you analyze how the writer accomplishes each of the purposes identified in the prompt. Note which details are informative, which entertain, and which are descriptive. Then, refer to this list when you are drafting.

Use Subheads to Organize To organize the details in your draft, use subheads. Using the details from your list, organize the information into major sections—describe, entertain, and inform.

Drafting

Allow almost half of your time for drafting.

Organize Details One way to organize this response would be to use a part-to-whole organization. Using the subheads you devised in prewriting, present information in logical categories that make up the whole. For example, you could separate your response by addressing each purpose in the prompt separately.

Incorporate Quotations To support your analysis, quote lines or words from Dickinson's article. Introduce them by using transitions, such as *according to Dickinson*, or *she states in her paper*, to show the connection between the quotation and your interpretation.

Revising, Editing, and Proofreading

Allow almost one fourth of your time to revise and edit. Use the last few minutes to proofread your work.

Confirm Essay Coherence Check that your essay has a clear thesis statement and that each paragraph supports your main idea. If you find words, sentences, or paragraphs that distract from your thesis statement, delete or revise them to make them relevant to your work.

Make Corrections Review your response for errors. Neatly cross out any details that do not support your purpose. Change language that is completely inappropriate for your audience, and make sure transitions keep ideas flowing smoothly. Check for errors in spelling, grammar, and punctuation. When making changes, place one line through text that you want eliminated and place in brackets. use a caret [^] to indicate the places you would like to add words.

In-Depth Lesson Plan

	LESSON FOCUS	PRINT AND MEDIA RESOURCES
DAY 1	**Introduction to Research Papers** Students learn key elements of a research paper and analyze the Model From Literature. (pp. 266–271)	*Writers at Work* **Videotape,** Research Writing *Writing Lab* **CD-ROM,** Research Writing
DAY 2	**Prewriting** Students choose and narrow a topic, consider their audience and purpose, and gather information. (pp. 272–277)	**Teaching Resources** *Writing Support Transparencies,* 13-A–E; *Writing Support Activity Book,* 13-1–2; *Topic Bank for Heterogeneous Classes,* Ch. 13
DAY 3	**Drafting** Students organize their ideas and write their first drafts. (pp. 278–280)	**Teaching Resources** *Writing Support Transparencies,* 13-F
DAY 4	**Revising** Students revise their drafts in terms of overall structure, paragraphs, sentences, and word choice. (pp. 281–285)	**Teaching Resources** *Writing Support Transparencies,* 13-G–I
DAY 5	**Editing and Proofreading; Publishing and Presenting** Students check their work for accuracy and correctness and present their final drafts. (pp. 286–291)	**Teaching Resources** *Scoring Rubrics on Transparency,* Ch. 13; *Writing Assessment and Portfolio Management; Formal Assessment,* Ch. 13

Accelerated Lesson Plan

	LESSON FOCUS	PRINT AND MEDIA RESOURCES
DAY 1	**Drafting** Students review characteristics of a research paper, select topics, and write drafts. (pp. 266–280)	*Writers at Work* **Videotape,** Research Writing *Writing Lab* **CD-ROM,** Research Writing **Teaching Resources** *Writing Support Transparencies,* 13-A–F; *Writing Support Activity Book,* 13-1–2
DAY 2	**Revising to Presenting** Students work individually or with peers to revise, edit, and proofread their work for presentation. (pp. 281–291)	**Teaching Resources** *Writing Support Transparencies,* 13-G–I; *Scoring Rubrics on Transparency,* Ch. 13; *Writing Assessment and Portfolio Management; Formal Assessment,* Ch. 13

Options for Adapting Lesson Plans

HOMEWORK

Have students complete any stage of the lesson for homework.

FEATURES

Extend coverage with Connected Assignment (p. 292), Spotlight on the Humanities (p. 294), Media and Technology Skills (p. 295), and the Standardized Test Preparation Workshop (p. 296).

TECHNOLOGY

Students can complete any stage of the lesson on computer. Have them print out their completed work.

INTEGRATED SKILLS COVERAGE

Integrating Grammar
Active vs. Passive Voice, SE p. 283
Conventions for Citing Sources, SE p. 287
ATE pp. 269, 291

Reading/Writing Connection
Evaluate the Writer's Ideas, SE p. 268
Writing Application, SE p. 271

Viewing and Representing
Critical Viewing, SE pp. 266, 268, 276, 280, 285, 286, 289, 292, 294
Analyzing Relationships as Represented in Various Media, SE p. 294
Creating Media Products, SE p. 295

Integrating Vocabulary Skills   ATE pp. 270, 277

Technology Skills   SE pp. 276, 288; ATE p. 272

Real-World Connection   ATE p. 270

Workplace Skills   ATE p. 284

ASSESSMENT SUPPORT

Standardized Test Preparation Workshop SE p. 296;
ATE pp. 275, 282
Standardized Test Preparation Workbook, pp. 25–26
Scoring Rubrics on Transparency, Ch. 13
Formal Assessment, Ch. 13
Writing Assessment and Portfolio Management

MEETING INDIVIDUAL NEEDS

Less Advanced Students ATE pp. 269, 278, 285, 287, 293, 297.
See also Ongoing Assessments ATE pp. 268, 271, 273, 277, 279.
AP Students ATE pp. 287, 291, 297
ESL Students ATE pp. 270, 273
Visual/Spatial Learners ATE pp. 274, 290
Verbal Linguistic Learners ATE p. 271
Logical/Mathematical Learners ATE p. 271

BLOCK SCHEDULING

Pacing Suggestions
For 90-minute Blocks
- Have students complete the Prewriting and Drafting stages in a single period.
- Focus one class period on Revising and Editing and Publishing and Presenting. Allow at least 30 minutes for peer revision.

Resources for Varying Instruction
- *Writing Lab* **CD-ROM** If your students have access to hardware, a 90-minute block provides an ideal opportunity for students to work on computer.
- *Writers at Work* **Videotape** Show the Research segment in class.

Professional Development Support
- *How to Manage Instruction in the Block* This Teaching Resource provides management and activity suggestions.

MEDIA AND TECHNOLOGY

For the Student
- *Writing Lab* **CD-ROM**, Research Writing
- *On-Line Exercise Bank,* Section 21.4

For the Teacher
- *Writers at Work* **Videotape**, Research Writing
- *Resource Pro* **CD-ROM**

WRITING AND GRAMMAR WEB SITE

The Interactive Writing and Grammar Web Site provides a wide array of support for students, teachers, and parents. Writing support includes:

- Interactive revision checkers
- Scoring rubrics with complete models

www.phschool.com

LITERATURE CONNECTIONS

Related selections from *Prentice Hall Literature: Timeless Voices, Timeless Themes,* The American Experience:

from *Hiroshima,* John Hersey, SE p. 269

"Nobel Prize Acceptance Speech," William Faulkner, SE p. 273

Lesson Objectives

1. To write a research paper appropriate to audience and purpose
2. To read to appreciate the writer's craft and to discover models for writing
3. To use prewriting strategies to generate ideas and to plan
4. To use writing to formulate questions, refine topics, and clarify ideas
5. To represent information in a variety of ways such as graphics and conceptual maps
6. To develop drafts by organizing content to suit purpose
7. To edit and proofread to ensure standard English usage and grammar
8. To evaluate writing for both mechanics and content
9. To refine selected work for publication

Critical Viewing

Analyze Students may say the painting suggests that people may find themselves reflected in the research they do—that the research process can teach you about yourself.

Chapter 13 Research
Research Paper

Untitled, John Martin

Research Writing in Everyday Life

Whenever you want to learn more about a person, an issue, a product, or an event, you use research skills. Whenever you turn on a television news program, read an article in the newspaper, or type in a key word on an Internet search engine, you are conducting informal research and accessing the results of someone's investigation. You may have already used more formal research skills for a writing assignment in school. As you move into adulthood, research writing skills can serve you well in the workplace, in the marketplace, and in your intellectual life.

▲ **Critical Viewing**
What does this painting suggest about the nature of research? **[Analyze]**

266 • Research

⏱ TIME AND RESOURCE MANAGER

Resources
Technology: *Writers at Work* Videotape, Research Writing; *Writing Lab* CD-ROM, Research

In-Depth Coverage	Accelerated Pace
• Discuss pp. 266–267 in class. • Read the Model From Literature (pp. 268–271) in class. Encourage students to point out places where Richard Lederer may have used research skills to support his statements.	• Discuss the definitions and different types of research papers in class. • Have students read pp. 268–271 independently. Tell them to note different research sources as they read.

What Is a Research Paper?

A **research paper** presents and interprets information gathered through an extensive study of a subject. An effective research paper has

- a clearly stated thesis statement.
- convincing factual support from a variety of outside sources, including direct quotations whose sources are credited.
- a clear organization that includes an introduction, body, and conclusion.
- a bibliography, or works-cited list, that provides a complete listing of research sources.

To preview the criteria on which your research may be judged, see the Rubric for Self-Assessment on page 288.

Types of Research Papers

There are as many types of research papers as purposes for research. Here are some of the research formats you may encounter:

- **Lab reports** present the purposes, processes, and results of an experiment.
- **Annotated bibliographies** provide a list of materials about a specific topic. In addition to source information, such as titles and authors, these bibliographies summarize and evaluate each entry.
- **Multigenre research papers** present research using a variety of genres. For example, a multigenre approach might include an essay, a short story, poetry, letters, and new articles to convey the information gathered through research.

Writers in ACTION

Music writer and editor Gillian Gaar incorporates research into many of the projects she undertakes. While she reviews bands and live concerts, she also uses the material she finds through library research and interviews:

"Research is really the backbone of my writing because it gives me access to information I wouldn't have otherwise. You probably wouldn't put everything you learned about your subject in one article—or even one book. But it gives you an overall familiarity with the subject. . . . [I]f I'm interested in a subject, I like to learn . . . as much as I can about it."

PREVIEW Student Work IN PROGRESS

In her research paper, Rebecca Potter, a student at Central High School, Omaha, Nebraska, examines the legacy and influence of an African American sculptor. As you will see, Rebecca used prewriting, drafting, and revising techniques to develop her essay "Augusta Savage: Artist of the Harlem Renaissance." Her final draft appears at the end of the chapter.

Research Paper • 267

PREPARE and ENGAGE

Interest GRABBER Ask students to name some things about which they know only a little but would like to learn more. Let students share their topics with the group for discussion and further topic suggestions. Encourage students to suggest sources that others could use to research their topics.

Activate Prior Knowledge

Ask students to think about articles or books they have read recently, either in or outside the classroom. Tell them to think about how much research the writer must have done before writing about the topic. Elicit discussion about different ways of conducting research.

More About the Writer

Gillian Gaar writes and edits stories, feature articles, and reviews about music and film. She is the author of *She's a Rebel: The History of Women In Rock and Roll.* Articles by or about Gillian Gaar can be found on the Internet. Gaar is featured in the Research Writing section of the *Writers at Work* Videotape.

✓ ONGOING ASSESSMENT: Diagnose

Use one of the following options to diagnose students' current level of proficiency in research writing.

Option 1 Ask each student to select the strongest example of his or her research writing from last year. Hold conferences in which you review each student's example. Use the conferences to determine which students need extra support in researching an essay topic.

Option 2 Ask students to develop a list of sources they could use to research a report on dinosaurs. Students should list at least three different types of sources. If students have difficulty completing this exercise, you will need to devote more time to explaining where and how to research a topic.

Reading: Evaluate the Writer's Ideas

As students read the Model From Literature, tell them to jot down the main idea or thesis and then make notes about ways the writer uses research to support his main idea.

Step-by-Step Teaching Guide

Engage Students Through Literature

1. After they have read the essay, ask students to identify the thesis statement or main idea. (English is a global language.)

2. Then, ask volunteers to name some of the ways Lederer uses research to support his thesis. (He uses historical facts to illustrate how the language spread from one part of the world to another. He makes a chart to illustrate word changes. He uses comments made by other writers.)

3. Ask students, "Does Lederer conclude the essay with research?" (No, the essay ends with a hypothetical conclusion.)

4. Ask students to identify some of the strategies Lederer uses to cite his research (dates, transition words, summarization).

Critical Viewing

Support Students should recognize that the image of people exchanging written texts suggests the linguistic borrowing between cultures that is Lederer's topic.

13.1 Model From Literature

From studying the history of the English language to delving into the origins of new words, Richard Lederer uses research to support his ideas.

Reading Writing Connection

Reading Strategy: Evaluate the Writer's Ideas Facts can often be interpreted in more than one way. For example, a writer may claim that one event caused another or that one detail proves a theory. As you read this essay, evaluate whether the writer has correctly interpreted the information his research provides.

Hamburger Ms. GKS4, fol. Royal Library, Copenhagen

▲ **Critical Viewing** How does this image from an illustrated manuscript suit Lederer's topic? **[Support]**

from
Our English Language: One From All

Richard Lederer

All around the globe, the English language is spoken by people of all races and nearly all religions and cultures. With 700 million speakers worldwide, more than one out of every eight of us riding this planet can be reached by English in some form.

The rise of English as a planetary language begins long ago, in the middle of the fifth century A.D. At the onset of the Middle Ages, several large tribes of sea rovers—the Angles, the Saxons, and the Jutes—lived along the continental North Sea coast, from Denmark to Holland. Around A.D. 449, these fierce warrior people sailed their beaked ships across the North Sea and came to the islands then known as Britannia. They found the land pleasant and the people, who were fighting among themselves, very easy to conquer, and so they remained there.

You may be surprised to learn that the speech of these North German sea rovers and plunderers, whom we call the Anglo-Saxons, became the parent of our English language. They would have been surprised to know it too!

The low Germanic tongue that the invaders brought with them to

Lederer uses an interesting opening to present his thesis.

Lederer states his thesis: English is a planetary language that includes parts of many languages.

By presenting information from the earliest points of the development of the English language, Lederer organizes his research chronologically.

✓ **ONGOING ASSESSMENT: Monitor and Reinforce**

After previewing the Model From Literature, you may anticipate that some students will have difficulty with some Anglo-Saxon words and other words. Use one of the following options.

Option 1 If students read the model independently have them list any unfamiliar words they encounter. If the new words are Anglo-Saxon, discuss how the words have changed. If the unfamiliar terms are related to the historical elements, encourage students to consider these items as potential topics for research.

Option 2 If you or a prepared student reads the model aloud in class, take time to identify the words that evolved from *bedd, candel, eorth, faeder, freondscipe, healf, healp, mann, moder, waeter,* and so on.

Britannia became, in its new setting, Anglo-Saxon, or Old English, the ancestor of the English we use today. In A.D. 827, King Egbert first named Britannia Englaland, "land of the Angles" (McCrum, Cran, and MacNeil 61), because the Angles were at that time the chief people there. The language came to be called Englisc. Old Englisc differs so much from modern English that it is harder for us to learn it than German or Latin. Still, we can recognize a number of Anglo-Saxon words: *bedd, candel, eorth, faeder, freondscipe, healf, healp, mann, moder,* and *waeter* (Bryson 54–57).

From its earliest beginnings, English was a diverse and multicultural tongue. During the reign of the Danish King Alfred (A.D. 849–901) and thereafter, many Danish words entered our language, including the pronouns *they, them,* and *their* and other important words such as *anger, get, ill, odd, scare, skill, skin, sky, want,* and *window* (Pei 27–28).

A dramatic evolution in the language came after yet another conquest of England—the last—this one by the Norman French two centuries after the rule of Egbert. In 1066, under William, Duke of Normandy, the Normans invaded England. In the bloody Battle of Hastings, they conquered the Saxons and the Danes who resisted them and forced the nobles to choose William the Conqueror as king of England. One result was that Old English changed rapidly as many of the French words used by the Normans flooded the vocabulary of their adopted tongue. Examples include *sir* and *madam; courtesy, honor,* and *chivalry; dine, table,* and *roast;* and *court* and *royal.* From this infusion of French words emerged a tongue that we today call Middle English.

These French borrowings were so extensive that they changed the balance in our language and prepared the way for the unparalleled hospitality to words from other tongues that has marked English ever since. In the Middle Ages, then, English was already a multicultural language consisting of Celtic, Anglo-Saxon, Danish, Latin, and Norman French.

Latin had been creeping into English for many centuries. But the mightiest infusion of Latin words into the great river of English came after the Norman Conquest, either through Norman French or directly through Latin.

The European Renaissance, from the fourteenth into the seventeenth century, began as educated men and women rediscovered the world of ancient Greece and Rome. The Renaissance was a love affair with all things classical, including all manner of Greek and Latin words. Because these classical words entered the language primarily through writing, often scholarly writing, they are the kind that we use formally rather than in everyday conversation. Almost

LITERATURE

John Hersey's book *Hiroshima* s a narrative based on research. You can find an excerpt of *Hiroshima* in *Prentice Hall Literature: Timeless Voices, Timeless Themes,* The American Experience.

Lederer uses dates as well as transitions such as "after" and "one result" to help his thoughts and paragraphs flow.

Lederer summarizes the information he has presented so far, listing several languages that play a part in the development of English.

More About the Writer

Linguist and humorist Richard Lederer has been characterized by William F. Buckley, Jr., as being one of the "guardians of American English." His witty approach to teaching the English language has made him a highly successful author, with more than a million copies of his books in print. Lederer has published thirteen books and writes a nationally syndicated column, "Looking at Language."

Connections With Literature

Encourage students to read the excerpt from *Hiroshima* by John Hersey. Ask students to identify the main idea of the excerpt, implied in the long opening paragraph (people survived the bomb for different reasons). What kind of research does it appear that Hersey used? How is research used to support Hersey's main idea?

Customize for
Less Advanced Students

As they read the Model From Literature, have students jot down ideas for research topics of their own. (Examples: from this page they might list King Egbert, Old English, King Alfred, William the Conqueror, and the Norman Conquest.)

Integrating Grammar Skills

Transitions Have students point out some of the transitional words and phrases that connect Lederer's ideas and information *(still, from, during, thereafter).* Encourage students to view transitions as devices for "smoothing out" their writing styles.

Integrating Vocabulary Skills

Use the informal word chart in the excerpt on this page to reinforce dictionary skills. Have students look up the words and point out where they can find the language origin. Have them note the differences between the related words (for example, *ask* versus *interrogate*). Ask volunteers to use the words in sentences that show their specific meanings.

Customize for
ESL Students

Discuss the words in students' first languages that they have found being used (or that have close relatives) in English. If the words are simply derivatives, and not pure adoptions, have students give both the original (from their own languages) and the English alternatives of words that are familiar to them.

Real-World Connection

Ask students whether they have ever noticed the announcements during the Olympic Games. They are made in English and French. For a long time, French was considered the language of diplomats. However, English is now the most widely spoken language in the world. Discuss the advantages of speaking a language that is widely understood.

Integrating Language Skills

Summaries and Transitions Ask students to point out where the writer summarizes in this essay. Lead students to understand how a summation of one part of a thesis is used to make a transition to the next part.

all the useful terms in the study of literature, for example, are of Greek origin: *poetry, drama, comedy, tragedy, metaphor, simile,* and so on. For another example, all the parts of speech in the study of grammar are of Latin origin: *noun, verb, adjective, adverb,* and so on.

The result of this diverse history is a rich mix of Anglo-Saxon, French, and Latin synonyms that offer us at least three choices for conveying somewhat the same meaning. A sampling of word triplets reveals how we can play the music of English with considerably more than one string at just the register we decide is appropriate. Note how the synonyms become more formal-sounding as they move from Anglo-Saxon to Latin:

Anglo-Saxon	French	Latin
ask	question	interrogate
end	finish	conclude
fair	beautiful	attractive

At the center of our language are the Anglo-Saxon words of everyday life—*sun* and *moon, home, eat, sleep, read, love* and *hate, hot* and *cold.* In contrast to the popular Anglo-Saxon, but equally important, is the Latin portion of our vocabulary, usually the more learned part. The difference between these two great classes of words is that Anglo-Saxon English makes us feel more deeply and see things about us more truly, while Latin English arouses our minds to more exact and complex thinking.

English is the most democratic and hospitable language that has ever existed. It has welcomed into its vocabulary words from other countries far and near, ancient and modern. Although Anglo-Saxon is the foundation of the English language, more than seventy percent of our words have been imported from other lands. Quite simply, there is no other language so packed with words from so many faraway sources.

Joseph Bellafiore described English as "the lagoon of nations" because "in it there are hundreds of miscellaneous words floating like ships from foreign ports freighted with messages for us." (Bellafiore 77). The three largest word-bearing galleons are Latin, Greek, and French, but just about every country seems to have given some words to English. And, over the centuries, the multicultural heritage of our language has increased in power. When you speak English, you speak a hundred languages. Among them:

Algonquian: raccoon	Russian: mammoth	Irish: banshee
Spanish: rodeo	Italian: opera	Dutch: boss
German: kindergarten	West African: banana	Chinese: tea
Yiddish: kibitzer	Czech: polka	(Hook 52–53)

270 • Research Paper

By providing specific words and their origins, Lederer supports his ideas that English includes words from many languages.

A chart helps the writer make many examples accessible to his readers.

After a treatment of his study of the history of English, the writer summarizes what he has learned about the language's continued growth. Before moving to his next subtopic, he restates his thesis.

No wonder that Sir Philip Sidney called English "a mingle tongue" (Barnett 156). No wonder that Ralph Waldo Emerson called English speech "the sea which receives tributaries from every region under heaven" (Barnett 23). No wonder that Dorothy Thompson referred to "that glorious and imperial mongrel, the English language" (Bellafiore 70). No wonder that the poet Carl Sandburg once said, "The English language hasn't got where it is by being pure" (Pyles 339).

English continues to be one of the world's great growth industries, adding to its word store more than a thousand new words a year. A little more than 1,500 years ago, it was the simple tongue of a few isolated Germanic tribes. Today it is an international medium of exchange in air traffic control, science, commerce, politics, diplomacy, tourism, the arts, and pop culture.

Because our English language has welcomed into its vocabulary so many languages of the world, it has become something very close to a global language. Because of its liberal borrowings from Latin and French, English has a familiar look to speakers of those languages. Because of its Anglo-Saxon origins, English is strongly connected with the Germanic languages as well. If ever our descendants make verbal contact with beings from other planets and solar systems, English will doubtless start adding and adapting words from Martian, Saturnian, and Alpha Centaurian and beaming its expanded vocabulary across outer space. Then English will become a truly universal language.

Works Cited

Barnett, Lincoln. *The Treasure of Our Tongue.* New York: Alfred A. Knopf, 1964.
Bellafiore, Joseph. *Words at Work.* New York: Amsco School Publications, Inc., 1968.
Bryson, Bill. *The Mother Tongue: English & How It Got That Way.* New York: William Morrow and Company, Inc., 1990.
Hook, J. N. *The Story of British English.* Glenview, IL: Scott, Foresman and Company, 1974.
McCrum, Robert, William Cran, and Robert MacNeil. *The Story of English.* New York: Penguin Books, 1987.
Pei, Mario. *The Story of the English Language.* New York: Touchstone, 1967.
Pyles, Thomas. *The Origins and Development of the English Language, Second Edition.* New York: Harcourt Brace Jovanovich, Inc., 1971.

Writing Application: Support Your Main Ideas As you write your research paper, be sure to show logical connections to accurately interpret the facts you report.

Lederer employs several paragraphs to conclude his research. The first one quotes a variety of well-known writers. With each quotation, he indicates the source of the information.

A second paragraph of Lederer's conclusion summarizes the growth his paper has addressed.

The final paragraph moves the thesis into the future. The writer whimsically suggests future languages that could influence English.

A works-cited list provides bibliographic information for each source referenced in the text. This list uses the format suggested by the Modern Language Association.

Teaching From the Model

This Model From Literature offers an example of a thesis statement and facts to back up that thesis. Richard Lederer begins the essay by saying that the use of the English language is global. He provides language history, quotes other writers, and concludes with a bit of theoretical whimsy. Ask students to note examples of how Lederer's facts back up his opinions.

Customize for
Verbal/Linguistic Learners

Encourage students who have a special interest in language to do further research on word origins and connections. One possibility is to check words beginning with "al" to see how many are Arabic in origin. You might wish also to direct them to the section of the dictionary that identifies the abbreviations for some languages (OE is Old English, and so on).

Customize for
Logical/Mathematical Learners

Let students use the information provided in this excerpt to create a language timeline, tracing the movement of the English language from the mid-fifth century A.D.

Integrating Language Skills

Bibliography Have a volunteer explain the elements of the bibliography to the group (author, book title, city of publisher and publisher, year published).

Reading\Writing Connection

Writing Application: Support Your Main Idea

As a reminder to students about using facts to support the main idea, review the writer's main idea in the Model From Literature. Then, let students identify facts discussed in the excerpt and explain how they support the main idea or thesis.

✓ ONGOING ASSESSMENT: Monitor and Reinforce

If students have trouble understanding the concept of main idea and supporting details, try the following strategies.

Option 1 Provide in-class practice by reading short paragraphs and having students identify the main idea. Then, have them cite the details that supports each idea.	**Option 2** For homework, ask students to read three newspaper articles that appeal to them. Have them write down the main idea and at least two supporting details from each.

Prewriting: Choosing a Topic

Teaching Resources: Writing Support Transparencies, 13-A

1. Display Transparency 13-A. Have students suggest sources in which they might find information on Rebecca's topic: the Harlem Renaissance.

2. Name, or have a student name, a broad topic and write it on the board. Then, have students brainstorm for similar or narrower ideas. Explain that this kind of process helps to focus on a topic that is both interesting and manageable.

3. Tell students to follow the same procedure in beginning their own topic search. Suggest that they list, diagram, or make a chart of their ideas.

4. Suggest that students check their resources (school and public libraries, Internet, encyclopedias, etc.) to determine whether there is enough information available to make research possible on their area of interest.

Integrating Technology Skills

Show students how to use the Internet to find a topic for a research paper. One possible way is to click on a category list on a search engine (for example, sports or world geography) and see what subcategories the search engine identifies for the topic. Alternatively, tell students to begin with one or two key words representing broad categories and do a search. Search results may help them define and narrow their topics.

Choosing Your Topic

Because your study will be extensive, two key issues should drive your choice of a research topic. First, you should have a commitment to the topic and an interest in learning more. Second, your topic should be one for which you can find enough information to present it well.

Strategies for Generating Topics

1. **Dewey Decimal Brainstorm** The Dewey Decimal System is a classification system used by some libraries to organize books by topic. You can find a chart of the major categories in Chapter 31, "Study, Reference, and Test-Taking Skills." Refer to this chart, and use the general categories to spark ideas for topics. Jot down one idea or question per category. Select one on which to write a research paper.

2. **Reviewing Notebooks, Journals, and Textbooks** As you flip through school notebooks, textbooks, and your writing journal, make a list of topics you may be able to pursue in a research paper. Consider the development of the theorems you've studied in math, a specific event in history that interests you, or a writer whose work you enjoy. Review your list, and choose a topic for research.

Writing Lab CD-ROM

For more help finding a topic, explore the activities and topic suggestions in the Choosing a Topic section of the Research lesson.

Student Work
IN PROGRESS

Name: Rebecca Potter
Central High School
Omaha, NE

Reviewing Notebooks, Journals, and Textbooks

In looking for a topic, Rebecca began with the table of contents of her literature textbook. By listing the main periods of American literature, she identified a period she wanted to research.

- Beginnings to 1750
- A Nation Is Born (1750–1800)
- A Growing Nation (1800–1870)
- Division, Reconciliation, and Expansion (1850–1914)
- Disillusion, Defiance, and Discontent (1914–1946) — *Harlem Renaissance*
- Prosperity and Protest (1946–Present)

⏱ TIME AND RESOURCE MANAGER

Resources
Print: *Writing Support Transparencies*, 13-A–E; *Writing Support Activity Book*, 13-1–2
Technology: *Writing Lab* CD-ROM, Research

In-Depth Coverage	Accelerated Pace
• Read and discuss pp. 272–277 in class. • Brainstorm with students for effective ways of eliciting ideas: charts, lists, graphs, word webs, and diagrams.	• Have students bring a list of possible topics to class. • Let students share their lists with the group and use the peer feedback to help them choose a research topic.

TOPIC BANK

1. **Report on the Uses of Music** From formal symphonic concerts to pervasive elevator melodies, some form of music can be found in most aspects of modern life. Research the power of music to fulfill a specific function, and present your findings in a research paper.

2. **Analysis of the Origins of Basketball** Dr. James Naismith has traditionally been credited as the inventor of basketball. More recently, some claim that the game originated elsewhere. Research this question, and write a research paper to report your conclusions.

Responding to Fine Art

3. The painting *Tourists,* at right, might inspire you to ask several questions about tourism. You might wonder about the history of the national parks, the geological causes of the Grand Canyon, or the ways in which such natural wonders have inspired writers and artists. Use one of these issues as the basis of a research paper.

Tourists, Woody Gwyn, Courtesy of the artist

Responding to Literature

4. Use William Faulkner's "Nobel Prize Acceptance Speech" as a springboard for your research topic. You might explore the work of other winners or categorize the themes that prize-winning authors have addressed. You can find the speech in *Prentice Hall Literature: Timeless Voices, Timeless Themes,* The American Experience.

☑ Cooperative Writing Opportunity

5. **Brochure on Health Issues Affecting Teens** Work with a group to research the health concerns of people your age. Together, brainstorm for a list of topics to include; for example, you might address nutrition, exercise, and sleep needs. Assign each member an area to study. Then, publish your findings in a documented brochure.

Prewriting • **273**

Prewriting: Narrowing Your Topic

Teaching Resources: Writing Support Transparencies, 13-C; Writing Support Activity Book, 13-1

1. After students have had a chance to follow some of the tips in the text, discuss which strategies they found to be most effective. How did they use the Internet or the library to help them narrow their topics?

2. Display Transparency 13-C. Discuss how Rebecca used webbing to narrow her topic. Point out that Rebecca might also have started with Harlem itself and identified its effect on the artists. The way the web grows depends on what is turned up during preliminary research.

3. Give students a blank organizer (13-1) or allow students time in class to create their own topic webs. Then, discuss what students discovered about their topics by using this strategy.

Customize for
Visual/Spatial Learners

Have students use different colors to connect related items in their webs and then use another color to highlight items that are of greatest personal interest. This will give them a way of assessing their topic ideas visually.

274

13.2

Narrowing Your Topic

Browse through the library's reference section, and surf the Internet to see what has been written on your general topic. Make sure there are solid references to support your topic. Once you have determined that there is enough information available, narrow your subject into a suitably focused topic.

To make your research project manageable, be sure your topic is narrow enough to be presented thoroughly. For example, the Civil War is too broad to address effectively in a short research paper. To focus that subject, you might research only the role of women in the war or the effects of Sherman's march through Atlanta. Use webbing to narrow your topic.

Complete a Topic Web to Narrow Your Topic

As you begin your preliminary research, complete a topic web to help you narrow the subject of your research paper. Write your broad subject in the middle of a circle. Identify subtopics by writing them in circles radiating off the main topic. For each of these categories, identify the ideas that you have found. Use these categories to generate even more specific ideas until you find a topic that is narrow enough to cover in a research paper.

Student Work **IN PROGRESS**

Name: Rebecca Potter
Central High School
Omaha, NE

Webbing to Narrow a Topic

Rebecca used webbing to narrow her topic. Her preliminary research provided her with several artists and writers to pursue. She chose to focus on one: Augusta Savage.

Considering Your Audience and Purpose

When you research, you'll probably find more information than you can use in your report. A knowledge of your audience and purpose will help you clarify which information to include and how to present it.

Analyze Your Audience

How much your audience knows about your subject will influence the amount of detail you include. If your audience has little knowledge of your topic, you should provide background, context, and a definition of each unfamiliar term you use. As the chart below suggests, identifying a specific audience can help you determine the degree of detail to include.

BUILDING AN INFORMATION BASE

Statement: One major reason for the rise in baseball's popularity is the introduction of inter-league play.

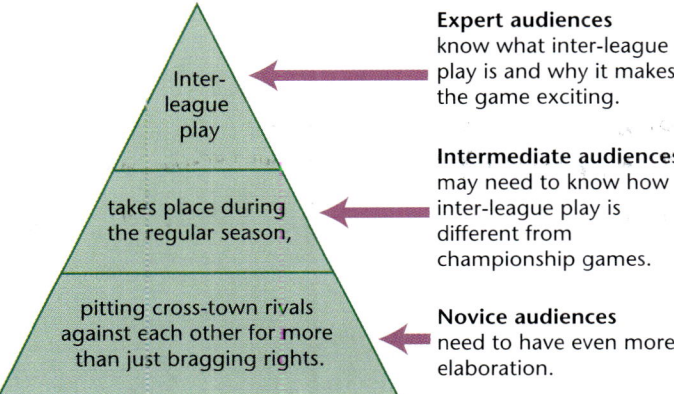

Expert audiences know what inter-league play is and why it makes the game exciting.

Intermediate audiences may need to know how inter-league play is different from championship games.

Novice audiences need to have even more elaboration.

Refine Your Purpose

You can use the results of research to achieve a variety of purposes. You might want to describe, explain, or persuade. Refine your purpose, and then use language and details that support it. Following are three common research purposes:

- **To praise your subject:** Include words and details that show your subject's positive qualities.

- **To persuade your readers to adopt your position:** Include facts and examples that support your ideas.

- **To explain a complex cause-and-effect relationship:** Include facts and details that show the connection.

🔲 **Research Tip**

To understand the knowledge level of your audience, interview the people you think will read your paper. Take notes about ideas and questions they may have about your subject.

Step-by-Step Teaching Guide

Prewriting: Analyze Your Audience

Teaching Resources: Writing Support Transparencies, 13-D; Writing Support Activity Book, 13-2

1. To illustrate why a writer needs to analyze an audience, have students think about interests they share with peers with which their parents might be unfamiliar (books, games, music, movies). With friends, a quote or tune may be all that is needed for them to understand the context. However, it might take a great deal of explanation to inform a parent of the significance of a comment or the punchline of a joke.

2. Point out that most papers will be written to a middle ground. Using the example in the chart, you can guess that an American audience will know what you mean by baseball, so you will not need to write to an audience with no knowledge. But you can also assume that not all of your readers will be experts.

3. Note that the research tip suggests interviewing your audience. Explain that one needs only to interview a sample of the types of people that will comprise the audience, if a broad audience is intended.

4. Suggest that students can, as an alternative, select their peer group as their audience and then write to clarify what *they* did not know about the topic before doing research.

Step-by-Step Teaching Guide

Prewriting: Refine Your Purpose

1. Explain that there can be some overlap between the purposes listed here. A writer may want to praise someone in order to support a position, or a cause-and-effect relationship may lead to a conclusion about which the writer wants to persuade the reader. The key is to know the purpose, not to limit it.

2. Have each student write a sentence telling the purpose of his or her research paper. Remind students that the purpose contains the thesis statement or main idea.

✏️ STANDARDIZED TEST PREPARATION WORKSHOP

Sentence Structure Standardized tests may require students to choose the best way to correct the structure of a sentence. Use the sample test item below to demonstrate.

Scientists were certainly surprised when monotremes were discovered. Monotremes are rare egg-laying mammals. Only two monotremes exist, the platypus and the echidna, both live in Australia.

Choose the best way to rewrite the underlined section of the passage.

A Only two monotremes exist, the platypus and the echidna, living in Australia.

B Only two monotremes exist, the platypus and the echidna, and they both live in Australia.

C Only two monotremes the platypus and the echidna exist, in Australia.

D Correct as is.

The correct answer is **B**; it is the only sentence that is correctly structured and punctuated.

Gathering Details

Your sources give you the data you need to write an effective research piece. Begin with the goal of learning as much as possible about your topic. Then, explore a wide range of sources. Knowing where to look for facts about a specific topic will save a lot of time and energy. Use these tips to make your research more effective:

Use Library Resources

Reference Books You might begin with a good general reference article in an encyclopedia to give you introductory information and to suggest subtopics. Other reference books—such as collections of biographies, atlases, and almanacs—might provide additional information.

Nonfiction Books Locate good nonfiction books about your topic to give you necessary background information and general knowledge. Books with bibliographies are particularly useful because these can lead you to further sources of information.

Newspaper and Magazine Articles Use these to focus on specific aspects of the topic. You can locate articles by using an index called *Readers' Guide to Periodical Literature*.

Databases A library reference section may have databases, or on-line reference lists, for larger topics such as language. For example, the Modern Language Association has articles about different aspects of the English language and humanities. Educational Resources Information Center (ERIC) has an extensive list of sources relating to anything about education.

Internet Using the Web, you can access the holdings of most major libraries to find sources. Once located, you can request these through an interlibrary loan. While there is much information directly available on the Internet, choose Web sites wisely. Internet sources should not represent the bulk of your research because they are not always reliable.

Interviews If you cannot find printed matter to cover an aspect of your topic, consider interviewing people with expert knowledge. Professionals become an important source of information when you are researching new areas or when you wish to provide interpretation of a survey you have conducted.

▲ **Critical Viewing**
How can investigation lead you to refine your research topic? [Hypothesize]

🖥 **Internet Tip**

Some browsers have a tab called "What's Related." If you have found a site that provides useful information, click on this link to view other sites related to your subject.

Take Notes

Make your work efficient by establishing a system for collecting information as you conduct your research. Creating both source cards and note cards will save you time later when you'll need to reference this information.

Source Cards On a separate card for each source, include all the information that you'll need in order to reference the material you use; note title, author, publisher, and the city and date of publication. Jot down information that would help you find the source if you need to locate it again. Assign a number to each source. Write this number on the card and on any note card you create using this source.

Note Cards Use note cards to record specific information. Place only one item on a card, and include a categorizing label to identify the contents. When copying a direct quotation, record the words accurately. In addition to any notes, indicate the source number you assigned, and note the exact page numbers to indicate where you found the information.

High-Tech Options Print out information you find on-line, or photocopy articles that address your topic. Copy the publishing information found on the copyright page; you will need it when you reference the material. Then, circle or highlight the key facts or details you find.

Research Tip

Avoid plagiarism, the dangerous practice of presenting someone else's work as your own. When using another writer's words, quote your source directly. If you summarize or rephrase, be sure the words are your own and be sure you give credit.

Student Work IN PROGRESS

Name: Rebecca Potter
Central High School
Omaha, NE

Creating Source Cards and Note Cards

Here is an example of the notes that Rebecca prepared while she was researching her paper. Note that she assigned this source the number 2 and used the categorizing word TEACHING on the note card to make her note-taking system more efficient.

> 2
> Anderson, Jervis. This Was
> Harlem. New York:
> Farrar Straus Giroux, 1982.
>
> Central High School library

> 2
> TEACHING
> Savage felt her teaching was
> an important part of
> her legacy.

Prewriting • 277

Step-by-Step Teaching Guide

Prewriting: Taking Notes

Teaching Resources: Writing Support Transparencies, 13-E

1. Review the elements students will need to include in a bibliography (title, author, date, publisher, location of publication, and so on). Explain that this is the information they should record on their source cards.

2. Suggest that in addition to listing the library at which the source was found, students might want to include such items as the library reference number or department so they can go straight to the book. For nonlibrary items, URLs (Web addresses) or other information that helps locate the reference would be useful.

3. Display the transparency and point out how, in the Student Work in Progress, Rebecca's source card includes the needed information. In addition, her note card includes one item and has the reference number (2) which identifies the source of the item.

4. Explain that having the note card refer to a source offers two advantages: When writing their papers, students will know where to go for more details; and when creating their bibliographies, they will know which sources supplied information they used.

Integrating Vocabulary Skills

Tell students that the word *plagiary* originally meant "kidnapping," but evolved to mean "plagiarism." The word *plagiary* is not used often today, but *plagiarism* is—and it is still a common problem. Ask a student to find out more about plagiarism and its meaning. You might suggest "plagiarism" as a topic for research.

Drafting: Propose a Thesis Statement

Teaching Resources: Writing Support Transparencies, 13-F

1. Display the transparency (13-F). Ask students to identify how the elements in the key notes Rebecca selected as her focus evolved into her thesis statement. (The background card reveals the period—the Harlem Renaissance—and the teaching and sculpture cards identify the dual roles.)

2. Point out that though three note cards are shown in the example, it might take more, or just one note card, to provide the focus of the research. At this point, some of the note cards may even be eliminated, as the focus of the paper narrows.

3. Tell students that the purpose of the thesis is to give direction to the research. Explain that, as research progresses, it is common for writers to change their original theses. Sometimes, new evidence shows that the original statement was incorrect, or a fascinating fact leads the writer in a different direction.

4. Ask students to write their thesis statements. Remind them that their statements may change.

Customize for
Less Advanced Students

If possible, pair less advanced students with more advanced students. Have the more advanced students show how they arrived at their thesis statements. Encourage students to talk about their notes, their ideas, and possible thesis topics as they work together, forming statements for the less advanced students.

13.3 Drafting

Shaping Your Writing

How you shape your writing depends on your audience, your purpose, and the data you have researched. Begin the drafting process with a thesis statement.

Propose a Thesis Statement

Whether you developed a thesis statement before you began your research or you are proposing one now, review your research to formalize your idea. Your thesis statement summarizes the main idea of your paper. It should express an idea that can be defended or refuted.

One way to write a thesis statement is to look for one idea that can be supported by a majority of the information you have found in your research. To do this

- Put your notes in front of you, and read through them.
- Find the relationships, and decide on the idea that best summarizes your research notes. Write a sentence that sums up the main idea.
- Confirm that your thesis is narrow enough to be addressed clearly in your writing.

Research Tip

In drafting your paper, you may notice your ideas shifting or the focus of your paper changing. Be open to the idea that your thesis statement may need to be revised later.

Student Work
IN PROGRESS

Name: Rebecca Potter
Central High School
Omaha, NE

Writing a Thesis Statement
Rebecca defined her thesis by organizing the main ideas in her notes.

3 SCULPTURES
Key works were Gamin and bust of W.E.B. Du Bois

2 TEACHING
Savage felt her teaching was an important part of her legacy.

1 BACKGROUND
She lived and worked during the Harlem Renaissance, an important time in art history.

Thesis Statement: As both an artist and a mentor, Augusta Savage held an influential position in the Harlem Renaissance.

278 • Research Paper

⏱ TIME AND RESOURCE MANAGER

Resources
Print: *Writing Support Transparencies*, 13-F
Technology: *Writing Lab* CD-ROM, Research

In-Depth Coverage	Accelerated Pace
• Read and discuss pp. 278–280 in class. • Have students bring their notes to class and use them to begin their outlines.	• Have students read the text independently. • Have students use their notes to write an outline and bring it to class.

Develop an Organizational Plan

After you have decided on your thesis statement, choose an organizational plan for your paper. Consider the strategies in the chart below, and identify one that suits your topic.

Types of Organization	Examples
Chronological Order • Presents events in order in which they occurred • Ideal for reporting the history of a subject	Explaining the events leading up to the launch of the space shuttle
Order of Importance • Presents details in order of increasing or decreasing importance • Ideal for writing persuasively or for building an argument	Defending or opposing an amendment to the Constitution
Comparison and Contrast • Presents similarities and differences • Ideal for addressing two or more subjects	Discussing the writing style of two best-selling authors
Parts to Whole • Presents information in categories that make up a whole • Ideal for analyzing elements of a large topic	Categorizing the instruments in a symphony

Writing a Formal Outline An outline will help you to implement the organizational plan you've chosen. Next to each Roman numeral, list the main points you'll cover. Next to the capital letters, write the topics that fall under the main points. Finally, next to the numbers, list details about each topic.

OUTLINE FOR A PART-TO-WHOLE ORGANIZATION

```
I.  Edgar Allan Poe's Fiction
    A. Horror Stories
       (1) "The Cask of Amontillado"
       (2) "The Fall of the House of Usher"
    B. Detective Stories
       (1) "The Murders in the Rue Morgue"
       (2) "The Purloined Letter"
II. Edgar Allan Poe's Poetry
    A. Love poem
    B. Narrative poem
```

Writing a Sentence Outline To expand your ideas before writing the final draft, use a sentence outline. For each part of your essay, identify a topic sentence you'll develop.

⚡ Challenge

Consider organizing your paper using inductive reasoning. Using this strategy, cite specific examples and build to a general conclusion. In contrast, an argument based on deductive reasoning starts with a general claim and concludes with a specific statement.

Drafting: Develop an Organizational Plan

1. Write on the board the following topics:
   • *The rise of Napoleon Bonaparte*
   • *Useful herbs*
   • *Walking versus running*
   • *Making voting mandatory*

   Ask students which organizational type might work best for each topic (in descending order: chronological, part to whole, comparison and contrast, order of importance).

2. Explain that these organizational plans can be applied to many different topics. For example, chronological order can chronicle the age of dinosaurs, or it can track one hour in the life of a police dispatcher. Part-to-whole order can focus on entire star systems or on a single cell.

Drafting: Write an Outline

1. Explain that when they outline, students will appreciate having written information on different note cards. They can move the cards around as much as necessary to determine the best order for the outline.

2. Refer students to the part-to-whole outline. Ask them to think of other topics that might fit into this part-to-whole pattern.

3. Ask students how the outline would differ if the subject were Poe's life, instead of his work (chronological: early years, education, beginning writing, and so on).

4. Remind students that the outline does not need a lot of detail, but it does need enough information to make it helpful when it is time to write their papers.

✓ ONGOING ASSESSMENT: Monitor and Reinforce

If you observe that students are having difficulty differentiating main ideas from supporting facts and details, try the following strategy.

Have students work in pairs. Have partners exchange note cards and then ask questions about their topics to help focus on the main idea. Ask the pairs to come to a decision about which organizational plan each should use and then help each other develop an outline from their information. Students can then discuss their outlines with you and explain how they organized their information.

Providing Elaboration

Include a Variety of Outside Sources

As you draft, make use of the information you've collected. Review all your research notes, and choose the quotations or visuals that best prove your point.

Choosing Material to Support Your Thesis Your research has provided information that you may want to include in your draft as elaboration. Consider these options:

- **Direct Quotations and Paraphrases** When you refer to another writer's work, you have two options: You can either include direct quotations or paraphrase by restating another writer's ideas in your own words. In either case, you need to cite your source and make the relationship between your thesis and the researched information clear.

- **Visuals** If a visual will make your topic more accessible, take the opportunity to include one. For example, when appropriate consider these formats for conveying information visually:

  Charts can provide information concisely.

  Graphs can show a growth or decline over time.

  Maps can illustrate geography, climate, or population.

Rural and Urban Population in the United States, 1890–1920

Year	Rural Population	Urban Population
1890	65%	35%
1900	60%	40%
1910	54%	46%
1920	49%	51%

Integrating References by Framing Just as you write an introduction and conclusion to frame the body of your draft, you need to provide context for the quotations or visuals that you include in your research paper. For each quotation, follow a simple strategy. First, introduce the quotation by naming the writer or linking the quotation to the material it follows. Then, give the quoted material. Finally, explain the quotation by showing how it supports the point you are presenting.

Prepare to Credit Your Sources

When you include a direct quotation, present an original idea that is not your own, or report a fact that is available from only one source, you must include documentation. In writing your first draft, circle all ideas and words that are not your own. At this stage, for each circled item, use parentheses to note the author's last name and the page numbers of the material used. Later, you can use this record to create the necessary formal citations your research paper requires.

▲ **Critical Viewing**
How could this chart support a research paper on the growth of cities in the United States? **[Support]**

13.4 Revising

Your research paper reflects an extensive amount of time, commitment, and effort. To polish your draft, read it over several times, each time focusing on a different aspect of the writing.

Revising Your Overall Structure

Check Coherence

You want your readers to be able to identify your thesis statement and to follow your organizational plan. To achieve this level of coherence, be sure that each paragraph has a manageable topic sentence that is covered by the content of the paragraph. When you track coherence, you may find that some paragraphs actually comprise several topic sentences.

▶ **REVISION STRATEGY**
Bracketing to Track Coherence

Use a separate color to bracket sentences that introduce your discussion of each main idea in your outline. Review the marked items to see whether the ideas support the thesis statement and connect logically. If you have two or more colors in the same paragraph, break the paragraph into separate ones. Create appropriate topic sentences, and then decide whether you provide enough support for each idea.

Language Lab CD-ROM

For examples of effective introductions, body paragraphs, and conclusions, see the audio-annotated models in the Drafting section of the Research lesson.

Student Work IN PROGRESS

Name: Rebecca Potter
Central High School
Omaha, NE

Improving Coherence by Restructuring Paragraphs
Rebecca had written one long paragraph about Augusta Savage's background. When she listed the points she had included, she saw that she was trying to cover too much in a single paragraph.

- born in Florida in 1892
- traveled to Harlem
- attended Cooper Union

- life-changing opportunity - bust of W.E.B. Du Bois
- busts of other prominent people

- recognition grew
- sculpts Gamin

- leading artist
- teaching art to children most important achievement

By bracketing ideas that she could group into single paragraphs, she created a plan for revision.

Revising • 281

Step-by-Step Teaching Guide

Revising: Check Coherence

Teaching Resources: Writing Support Transparencies, 13-G

1. Display the transparency. Point out that each idea listed was once part of a single, long paragraph.

2. Ask students which organizational plan Rebecca has selected (chronological).

3. Discuss how Rebecca grouped related ideas together to help her develop paragraphs that would be manageable.

4. Have students bracket their drafts to identify each item of their original outlines. If they find that too many ideas are covered in one paragraph, suggest that they use Rebecca's strategy for breaking up and reorganizing the paragraph.

5. Ask students to notice, too, whether there is enough support for each main idea within the thesis. Is the support logical, and does it contribute in some way to the overall thesis?

⏱ TIME AND RESOURCE MANAGER

Resources
Print: *Writing Support Transparencies,* 13-G–I
Technology: *Writing Lab* CD-ROM, Research

In-Depth Coverage	Accelerated Pace
• Read and discuss pp. 281–285 in class. • Have students work in pairs or individually on the revising strategies. • Make sure students can differentiate between active and passive voice.	• Have students read pp. 281–285 and revise their work on their own. • Make sure students can differentiate between active and passive voice.

Revising: Using Transition Boxes

Teaching Resources: Writing Support Transparencies, 13-H

1. Remind students that transitions helped the paragraphs flow in the Model From Literature.

2. Use Transparency 13-H to show how Rebecca used the revision strategy in two of her paragraphs. Emphasize that not every sentence will need a transition, but encourage students to search for places where a transition would enhance clarity.

3. Point out that a transition may need to be more than just a word. A phrase or, if the transition is between paragraphs, an entire sentence may be needed to create a smooth bridge.

4. Have students use transition boxes to determine whether and where they might need to add transitions.

5. Explain that if making a good transition does not clarify a connection, then students should consider revising or rearranging paragraphs.

13.4

Revising Your Paragraphs
Add Transitions to Improve the Flow of Ideas

Review your paragraphs to be sure that the connection you make between ideas is clear. Transitional words and phrases like *because*, *as a result*, *if*, *therefore*, *in addition*, *despite*, and *recently* can clarify the connections you want to stress.

▶ **REVISION STRATEGY**
Transition Boxes

To evaluate your use of transitions, use this strategy in several paragraphs of your research paper:
1. Draw a box between the end punctuation of each sentence and the first word of the next sentence.
2. Identify the relationship that connects the sentences on either side of the box.
3. Evaluate the writing as it exists. Place a check in a box if the relationship between the sentences it connects is clear.
4. If the relationship is not clear, add a transition. Place the new word or phrase at the point where the box is located. As an alternative, you might draw a line from the box to a space where the transition makes the most sense.

Challenge yourself to apply this strategy to other paragraphs in your essay.

Writing Lab CD-ROM

Use the revision checkers for unity and coherence, sentence length, and transitions in the Revising section of the Research lesson.

Student Work **IN PROGRESS**

Name: Rebecca Potter
Central High School
Omaha, NE

Using Transition Boxes
Rebecca added transitions to make her ideas flow more smoothly.

Savage showed talent at the school and a special interest in African art.☐ She received what would be a life-changing opportunity... *While at the school*

A transition is needed to clarify the life-changing opportunity occurring while at the school.

The NAACP believed the bust of Du Bois that Savage created to be one of the finest of him ever made.☐ Savage was asked to make busts of other prominent people. . . . *Consequently,*

"Consequently" needs to be added to show that the second sentence is a result of the first.

✎ STANDARDIZED TEST PREPARATION WORKSHOP

Transitions Standardized tests may require students to identify whether a transition is needed in a sentence. Provide students with practice in inserting transitions.

Determine whether a transition is needed and where it might be added to these sentences.

When I was young, I loved to climb trees. I stopped climbing them.

A When I was young, I loved to climb trees. However, when I got older, I stopped climbing them.

B When I was young, I loved to climb trees. But I stopped climbing them.

C When I was young, however, I loved to climb trees. Now, I have stopped climbing them.

D Correct as is.

Students should recognize that **A** is the correct answer because it inserts a transitional phrase that connects the two sentences in a logical way. Neither B nor C improves the flow.

Revising Your Sentences

Change Passive to Active Voice

Voice is the form of a verb that shows whether the subject is performing or receiving the action. Review your sentences to see whether the subject completes or receives the action of a sentence. Lively and direct writing usually employs the active voice and shows the subject completing the action.

▶ **REVISION STRATEGY**
Bracketing to Identify Passive Voice

Use red to bracket sentences in which the subjects receive the action. These are written in the passive voice. For each one you've marked, decide whether recasting to use the active voice will improve the writing. If so, revise these sentences.

Grammar in Your Writing
Active vs. Passive Voice

A verb is in the **active voice** when the subject performs the action named by the verb. A verb is in the **passive voice** when the subject undergoes the action named by the verb. Here are some examples:

Passive Voice	Active Voice
The barn was struck by lightning.	Lightning struck the barn.
The house is being painted by my sister and me.	My sister and I are painting the house.

While active voice is preferred in most cases, the passive voice is used to stress the action, not the performer. It is also used when the performer of the action is unspecified or unknown.

To indicate an unknown performer: The door was closed.
To stress action: The goal was exceeded.

Find It in Your Reading Review "Our English Language: One From All" on pages 268–271. As you read, identify one sentence written in the passive voice and one written using the active voice.

Find It in Your Writing Review your draft to identify sentences using the passive voice. When appropriate, rewrite the sentences in the active voice.

For more on active and passive voice, see Chapter 21.

Revising: Define Specialized Vocabulary

Teaching Resources: Writing Support Transparencies, 13-I

1. Suggest that students think about how much or how little they knew about their topic before they started doing research. If it was already a favorite subject, suggest they think of terms or ideas that raise questions in conversations with peers.

2. After having students use the Revision Strategy to highlight words or terms that a reader might not understand, discuss ways of incorporating definitions. Point out the example in Rebecca's Student Work in Progress (on Transparency 13-I). Other possibilities include simply stating the word and giving a definition, or having an introductory paragraph introduce terms as well as the main idea.

3. Tell students that another way to evaluate whether language is appropriate for the audience is to read the paper aloud to a partner.

Integrating Workplace Skills

Explain to students that most jobs have specialized words and phrases that relate to that career or job. Writers, for example, use the word *proof* to mean "proofread," *delete* to mean "take something out," and *stet* to mean "leave it as it is." While it is important to learn and use the vocabulary of one's job, it is also important to remember that "outsiders" may not understand the "lingo."

13.4

Revising Your Word Choice
Define Specialized Vocabulary

Keeping your audience's level of knowledge in mind is a critical part of helping your readers understand your research paper. For example, you might not need to identify Harry S. Truman as the thirty-third president of the United States, but if you consistently refer to the Truman Doctrine, you should be sure your audience knows this important Cold-War policy. When in doubt, define terms that are central to your research. Look out for these categories of specialized vocabulary:

- **Technical Terms and Jargon** Words that are particular to a specific field may present difficulty to a general audience. For example, common legal terms like *prosecutor*, *defendant*, *indictment*, and *acquittal* may be unfamiliar to a general audience.

- **Historical References** Without some background, specific people, places, or events in history may challenge a general audience.

▶ REVISION STRATEGY
Highlighting to Identify Specialized Vocabulary

Review your draft to identify specific words that your audience might not know. Highlight words in your research paper that your audience may not be able to define themselves. To revise, work a definition of these terms into your writing.

✦ Spelling Tip

If you are using a word-processing program, rerun the spell-checking program each time you have made changes. Do a visual check for misplaced words correctly spelled, however, such as *ant* for *and* or *it* for *in*.

Student Work
IN PROGRESS

Name: *Rebecca Potter*
Central High School
Omaha, NE

Identifying Words to Define for an Audience

In the first paragraph, Rebecca underlined words that might be unknown to her audience. As she revised, she included a definition of each.

Huggins's *Harlem Renaissance* identifies an American renaissance occurring roughly in the 1920's and ending in the first years of the Great Depression (Huggins 1). This centered in Harlem, .

rebirth of creativity and arts

the main African American neighborhood of New York City

Revising: Peer Review

1. As they prepare for their "editor's conferences," encourage students to identify a draft's strengths before its weaknesses.

2. Remind students that some errors will be corrected at the proofreading stage and that the focus here should be on supporting facts and details, active voice, and transitions.

3. Suggest that writers consider the questions modeled on the page and decide whether there is anything else they would like to ask their "editor" about their paper.

4. Have students use what they learned in the peer reviews to evaluate and revise their research papers.

◄ **Critical Viewing**
What qualities of a research paper make it especially suited to peer review?
[Evaluate]

Peer Review
Editor's Conference

When professional writers submit manuscripts for publication, their writing is reviewed by editors who often suggest changes. Choose an in-class editor, submit your draft, and meet to discuss your paper.

Pre-conference In advance of a conference with your class editor, take a moment to jot down a list of questions to focus the review. If you point out your specific concerns, you may get more out of the conference. Consider asking questions like these:

- After reading my introduction, could you summarize the paper's focus?
- Which quotation was the strongest support of my thesis?
- Were there parts of the paper that were confusing? How could I improve them?

Post-conference After you've met with your editor, return to your draft to make the changes you feel would improve your paper.

Critical Viewing

Evaluate Research papers often investigate new or unfamiliar topics. Peer reviewers can make sure this new information is clearly explained.

Customize for
Less Advanced Students

Remind students of the author's use of summarizing in the Model From Literature, pages 268–271. Encourage students to incorporate summaries as a transition between parts of their essays.

1. Tell students that going straight from writing to proofreading makes proofreading difficult, since they will know what is supposed to be there and are less likely to notice errors. If the proofreading stage comes after a break from the work, errors become more obvious.

2. Point out that this break from writing is the perfect time to create a reference list.

3. Specify whether you want students to provide a works-cited page or a complete bibliography.

4. Explain to students the format in which you want the bibliographic material recorded, and refer them to the style manual that reflects your preferences.

5. Once reference lists are completed, have students return to their writing. Ask them to read their papers carefully and correct errors in capitalization, punctuation, abbreviation, spelling, and usage.

6. Point out that the Learn More note shows students where to get help if they need additional information for correcting their work.

Critical Viewing

Support Students should note that the library houses reference works and is therefore the perfect site for generating reference lists.

13.5 Editing and Proofreading

Perhaps the hardest work of your research paper is over—researching, organizing, and drafting—but you should attend to the final touches so that your paper shows the pride you take in your work. Write a reference list, a title page, and then proofread the entire document to catch and correct any errors in spelling, usage, and mechanics.

Creating a Reference List

Your research writing should document your sources of information. A works-cited page provides your readers with full bibliographic information on each source you cite in your paper. In contrast, a bibliography is a complete list of the sources you used to research your topic. Confirm the type of reference list that your teacher requires. In either case, arrange your sources alphabetically by author or by title for works with no known author.

Use Style Manuals

Standards for documentation are set by several organizations. Most writers use the style set by the Modern Language Association (MLA), the American Psychological Association (APA), or *The Chicago Manual of Style* (CMS).

Identify the format that your teacher prefers. Following that format, check that each entry is complete and properly punctuated.

Focusing on Mechanics

Carefully review your research paper for errors in capitalization, punctuation, and abbreviation. Pay special attention to these conventions for including quoted material:

- Introduce all quotations in order to explain how they support your thesis statement.

- When quoting a few words or part of a sentence, make sure the quoted material fits grammatically with the rest of the sentence.

- When you provide a quotation of five lines or more, indent the material ten spaces. In this case, no quotation marks are necessary.

▲ **Critical Viewing**
Why is a library a good setting for generating your reference list? **[Support]**

 Learn More

To double-check your knowledge of mechanics issues, see Chapter 26, "Capitalization," and Chapter 27, "Punctuation."

⏱ TIME AND RESOURCE MANAGER

Resources
Technology: *Writing Lab* CD-ROM, Research

In-Depth Coverage	Accelerated Pace
• Read and discuss pp. 286–287 in class. • Have students bring their final drafts to class to proofread and edit.	• Have students read the text independently. • Have students edit and proofread their papers as homework. Allow time for one more editorial "pass" in class if applicable.

Grammar in Your Writing
Conventions for Citing Sources

To credit the sources in a research paper, include direct documentation—in the form of footnotes, endnotes, or internal citations—within your text and provide a bibliography or a works-cited list at the end of your paper.

Bibliographic Form Present your sources in a standardized format based on the type of resource referenced. Include authors' names, source titles, places, publishers, and dates of publication. For electronic sources, note the date you accessed the information. These examples are in MLA format.

For a book with one author:
Bryson, Bill. *Made in America.* New York: Morrow, 1994.

For a book with more than one author:
Jaffe, Nina, and Steve Zeitlin. *While Standing on One Foot.* New York: Henry Holt, 1993.

For an article:
Chan, Vincent W.S. "All-Optical Networks." *Scientific American.* Sept. 1995: 72–76.

For an encyclopedia entry:
"Energy Conversion." *Encyclopaedia Britannica.* 1999 ed.

For an on-line source:
The History Channel On-line. 1998. History Channel. 19 June 1998 <http://historychannel.com/>

Footnotes and Endnotes When using footnotes or endnotes to provide internal documentation, include full details about the source and cite the page number. Indicate a footnote or an endnote by placing a number at the end of a cited passage. For a footnote, place the documentation at the bottom of the page on which the information cited appears; for an endnote, place the documentation in numerical order on a page preceding the reference list.

First footnote or endnote for a book:

1. Bill Bryson, *Made in America* (New York: Morrow, 1994) 20.

Subsequent footnotes or endnotes citing same source:

2. Bryson 50.

Parenthetical Citations When using parenthetical documentation, include source information in parentheses after the quoted material. This information can direct readers to the full information in your reference list.

The bird called a robin is actually a thrush (Bryson 20).

Find It in Your Reading and Writing As you finalize your paper, choose a system of documentation. Proofread to make your citations and reference list error-free.

For more on documenting, see *Citing Sources and Manuscript Preparation* on pages 894–900.

Step-by-Step Teaching Guide

Conventions for Citing Sources

1. Review the conventions for citing sources. If the style book you prefer is *not* the MLA, point out how the forms given differ from your preferences so that students know what to expect. Refer students to the pages on *Citing Sources,* 894–900.

2. Discuss the differences among footnotes and endnotes, parenthetical citations, and bibliographic form with students. Model each form on the board and discuss each element within the citations.

3. If you have specific source requirements, make sure students understand how to cite those kinds of sources. To help them determine how to cite their sources, make sure they understand the conventions.

Find It in Your Reading and Writing

Encourage students to have a model of their chosen citation method available when proofreading their writing. Doing so will ensure that all citations follow the same form.

Customize for
Less Advanced Students

If students are having trouble gathering reference information, walk them through a selection of copyright and title pages to show them how to locate the information they need.

Customize for
AP Students

Explain to students the use of the term *ibid.* in footnotes. *Ibid.* is an abbreviation of the Latin *ibidem,* which means "in the same place." *Ibid.* is used in a footnote to mean "in the same book or article as the immediately preceding footnote." Show that to use *ibid.,* a writer lists the footnote number followed by *ibid.* and the page number. For example:

1 Smith, John, Jamestown, (etc.)

2 ibid., p. 119.

Step-by-Step Teaching Guide

Publishing and Presenting

1. As students try to decide on a way to present their ideas, suggest that they think about the intended audience. Encourage them to think about how to reach this audience.

2. Explain that many fields of work require the writing of research papers, but even if students don't go into one of these fields, research skills are valuable in most areas of life.

3. As students consider the reflection questions, suggest that they think about what was easiest and hardest to do and whether they would do anything differently on their next research paper.

ASSESS and CLOSE

Step-by-Step Teaching Guide

Assessment

Teaching Resources: Scoring Rubrics on Transparency, Ch. 13; Writing Assessment and Portfolio Management; Formal Assessment, Ch. 13

1. Display the Scoring Rubric transparency and review the criteria in class.

2. Before students proceed with self-assessment, you may wish to review the Final Draft of the Student Work in Progress on pages 289–291. Have students score the Final Draft in one or more of the rubric categories. For example, how would students score the essay in terms of audience and purpose?

3. In addition to student self-assessment, you may wish to use the following assessment options:

   • score student essays yourself, using the rubric and scoring models from *Writing Assessment and Portfolio Management.*

   • administer the Chapter 13 assessment from *Formal Assessment* in the Teaching Resources to measure students' grasp of concepts presented.

13.6 Publishing and Presenting

Building Your Portfolio

Share your research with others by publishing or presenting your ideas. You might want to try one of these suggestions:

1. **Organize a Conference** Plan a conference for students to present their findings. Researchers on similar topics may want to share their reports in panel discussions, explaining their research and offering comments on each other's work.

2. **Create an Annotated Bibliography** As an extension of your research, create an annotated bibliography to help others learn about your topic. Collect similar bibliographies from classmates, and post them in the school library.

Reflecting on Your Writing

Take a moment to think about the experience of writing your research paper. Write responses to questions like the ones below, and add your ideas to your portfolio.

• What did you learn about the topic of your research writing? What else might you want to learn about this topic?

• If you were to start your research over again, what would you do differently? Why?

 Internet Tip

To review model essays scored with this rubric, go to www.phschool.com

Rubric for Self-Assessment

Use these criteria to assess your research paper.

	Score 4	Score 3	Score 2	Score 1
Audience and Purpose	Focuses on a clearly stated thesis, starting from a well-framed question; gives complete citations	Focuses on a clearly stated thesis; gives citations	Focuses mainly on the chosen topic; gives some citations	Presents information without a clear focus; few or no citations
Organization	Presents information in logical order, emphasizing details of central importance	Presents information in logical order	Presents information logically, but organization is poor in places	Presents information in a scattered, disorganized manner
Elaboration	Draws clear conclusions from information gathered from multiple sources	Draws conclusions from information gathered from multiple sources	Explains and interprets some information	Presents information with little or no interpretation or synthesis
Use of Language	Shows overall clarity and fluency; uses predominantly active voice; contains few mechanical errors	Shows good sentence variety; frequently uses active voice; contains some errors in spelling, punctuation, or usage	Uses awkward or overly simple sentence structures; uses mostly passive voice; contains many mechanical errors	Contains incomplete thoughts and mechanical errors that make the writing confusing

288 • Research Paper

⏱ TIME AND RESOURCE MANAGER

Resources
Print: *Scoring Rubrics on Transparency,* Ch. 13; *Writing Assessment and Portfolio Management; Formal Assessment,* Ch. 13
Technology: *Writing Lab* CD-ROM, Research

In-Depth Coverage	Accelerated Pace
• Read and discuss p. 288 in class. • Have students assess their work using the Rubric for Self-Assessment (p. 288). • Point out the introduction, thesis statement sources, and summaries as students read the Final Draft (pp. 289–291).	• Have students review pp. 288–291 independently. • Discuss the Final Draft in class, having students point out Rebecca's use of conventions discussed in this chapter.

13.7 Student Work IN PROGRESS

FINAL DRAFT

▶ **Critical Viewing**
What do you think is the most notable feature of *Gamin,* this sculpture by Augusta Savage? **[Respond]**

Augusta Savage: Artist of the Harlem Renaissance

Rebecca Potter
Central High School
Omaha, Nebraska

Without careful study, many might imagine the creation of culture in the United States to have been most critical as the country's founders were setting out the Constitution and trying to break free of European influence. In fact, the development of art

In her introduction, Rebecca provides a context for her subject by explaining how the Harlem Renaissance was part of a larger move to create American culture.

Step-by-Step Teaching Guide

Final Draft

1. Have students read Rebecca's final draft.

2. Ask a student volunteer to identify Rebecca's thesis statement. *(As both an artist and a mentor, Augusta Savage held a dual position in the Harlem Renaissance and left a double legacy.)* Discuss how the student concluded that this was the thesis statement.

3. Ask students to look back through Rebecca's writing process and find where she determined her thesis statement (page 278, Drafting). Ask questions such as the following to stimulate discussion.

   • Where is Rebecca's thesis statement? (It is located at the end of the second paragraph.)

   • How does Rebecca use her introduction? (She sets a historical background of the Harlem Renaissance.)

4. Have students point out places where the writer cites sources. What method does she use?

5. Ask students to tell how the writer summarizes in her research paper. (She summarizes Augusta Savage's career to reiterate her thesis point. She summarizes near the end as a transition to her concluding statement, a confirmation of her thesis.)

6. Ask students to tell how the writer provides background and definitions for her readers. (Rebecca provides information about W.E.B. Du Bois and the NAACP as background for her readers.)

7. Point out how the writer uses direct quotations to further elaborate on her main point.

Critical Viewing

Respond Students might say that the boy's gentle, inquisitive expression is his most notable feature.

Teaching From the Final Draft

Tell students that Rebecca mentions the names of other Harlem Renaissance figures to provide a context for her discussion of Augusta Savage. Wisely, she does not do much more than mention their names. If she did, she would have diverted her readers' attention from her main point.

and culture has been ongoing ever since, in a cycle of advances and plateaus. Huggins's *Harlem Renaissance* identifies an American renaissance occurring roughly in the 1920's and ending in the first years of the Great Depression (Huggins 1). This rebirth of creativity and arts centered in Harlem, the main African American neighborhood of New York City. The period was a time in which African Americans celebrated their heritage in an outpouring of creative endeavors, such as music, literature, theater, and art (Huggins 4–5, 9–11). This artistic explosion came to be known as the Harlem Renaissance.

Any scholar of American humanities knows well the names of key figures: Langston Hughes, Zora Neale Hurston, Countee Cullen, Duke Ellington, and Aaron Douglas. Though many distinguished figures were involved in this movement, the lesser-known Augusta Savage played a role worth celebrating. As both an artist and a mentor, Augusta Savage held an influential position in the Harlem Renaissance.

Augusta Savage, the creator of sculptures focusing on African themes and an art teacher to African American children, was an eminent artist of the Harlem Renaissance. Born in Florida in 1892, she traveled to Harlem where, in time, her artistic career flourished (Huggins 153). In Harlem, the novice sculptress enhanced her artistic ability with an education at Cooper Union, a fine art school that charged no tuition (Bearden and Henderson 82). Savage showed talent at the school and a special interest in African art. While at the school, she received what would be a life-changing opportunity from the 135th Street branch of the New York Public Library. She was asked to create work to be displayed in this neighborhood institution.

The library asked her to make a bust of W.E.B. Du Bois, the African American leader who founded the National Association for the Advancement of Colored People, a political association better known as the NAACP (Bearden and Henderson 83). As a result of this opportunity, sculpture would become Savage's key to artistic success. The NAACP believed the bust of Du Bois that Savage created was one of the finest of him ever made. Consequently, the organization asked Savage to make busts of other prominent people, including Marcus Garvey, the leader of the United Negro Improvement Association, an organization that, like the NAACP, was dedicated "to awakening America's Black people to take pride in their African heritage" (Bearden and Henderson 83). Through her work making busts of these leaders, Augusta Savage gained fame.

Parenthetical citations show readers where Rebecca found her information.

The writer narrows her focus to one subject, Augusta Savage, and presents the paper's thesis: Augusta Savage held an influential role in the Harlem Renaissance.

This paragraph begins the body of the research paper, offering a chronological account of the artist's early life.

By providing brief explanations of both W.E.B. Du Bois and the NAACP, Rebecca helps build a background for her audience.

A summary of Savage's career and her art helps Rebecca show why and how the artist was successful and influential.

290 • Research Paper

Savage's recognition grew throughout her career. She continued making other sculptures of African Americans, *Gamin* being one of the most famous. This statue of an African American youth attracted large crowds when displayed at City University of New York. According to one writer, it "caught the humanity, the tenderness, and the wisdom of a boy child who has lived in the streets" (Bearden and Henderson 90–91).

Not only did Savage prove herself to be a leading artist through her sculptures of African American subjects, including W.E.B. Du Bois, Marcus Garvey, and the anonymous *Gamin*, but she also proved herself to be an influential artist by teaching art to African American children. Some scholars cite this instruction and encouragement of children as Savage's most important achievement (Anderson 273). As the first director of the Harlem Community Art Center, she inspired such children as Jacob Lawrence, now one of the most famous artists of our century (Anderson 274). Though her work was respected, Savage spent nearly all of her time helping the children, causing her own artwork to suffer in quality (Bearden and Henderson 96). When Savage was confronted with this criticism, she ignored it, saying:

> I have created nothing really beautiful, really lasting. But if I can inspire one of these youngsters to develop the talent I know they possess, then my monument will be their work. No one could ask more than that (Anderson 159).

These comments show how Savage valued her teaching over her own creativity.

Augusta Savage died in 1962, leaving a legacy of art and inspiration. She, like the other figures of the Harlem Renaissance, not only encouraged African American pride but also added to it through her accomplishments. With her famous sculptures, and especially with her passion for teaching art to African American youth, Augusta Savage was clearly one of the most influential and prominent artists of the Harlem Renaissance.

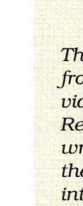

Works Cited
Anderson, Jervis. *This Was Harlem*. New York: Farrar Straus Giroux, 1982.

Bearden, Romare, and Harry Henderson. *Six Black Masters of American Art*. New York: Zenith Books, 1972.

Huggins, Nathan Irvin. *Harlem Renaissance*. New York: Oxford University Press, 1971.

This paragraph supports Rebecca's claim for the importance of Savage's teaching.

This direct quotation from the artist provides elaboration of Rebecca's point. The writer incorporates the quotation by introducing it before giving it. A sentence following explains the quotation.

The writer summarizes the main points of her essay and restates her position: Augusta Savage was an important figure in the Harlem Renaissance.

A works-cited list provides full bibliographic information for the sources Rebecca quoted in her paper.

Integrating Grammar Skills

Ask students to explain how Rebecca uses the quoted passage on this page. If necessary, have them refer to Focusing on Mechanics on page 286 for an explanation about quoting five lines or more.

Customize for
AP Students

Ask students to write a short statement describing Rebecca's opinion of her subject (Augusta Savage). Have them list some examples from the Final Draft that help readers understand the author's opinion.

Teaching From the Final Draft

Due to space constraints in this textbook, the Final Draft may not be as long as you will require of your students. As you review the Final Draft, be sure to clarify to students your particular requirements regarding length, quantity of quotations and sources, methods of citation, and other details.

> **Lesson Objectives**

1. To create a multimedia report appropriate to audience and purpose
2. To use prewriting strategies to generate ideas
3. To use a variety of forms and technologies to communicate specific messages
4. To use effective verbal and nonverbal strategies in presenting oral messages

---

Step-by-Step Teaching Guide

Multimedia Report

Teaching Resources: Writing Support Transparencies, 13-J; Writing Support Activity Book, 13-3

1. After reading the introduction, discuss the types of topics that would be suitable for a multimedia presentation. (Possible responses: topics that include demonstrations of processes or actions; topics that depend on images, from art lessons to travelogues.)

2. Have students brainstorm for places they could gather images for a multimedia report (for example, the library, Internet, CDs, or videos).

3. Display Transparency 13-J. Point out that this chart is similar to creating an outline and some of the same ideas apply. Just as with an outline, students need to decide the organizational type, such as chronological or parts to whole.

4. Explain that a well-crafted chart or outline should contain or feature all of the relevant materials in the appropriate order. Give students a copy of the blank organizer (13-3) for their own planning.

5. When students have revised and rehearsed their multimedia reports, allow time for class presentations. Make a schedule and give students set appointments so they will know the day they will present.

Connected Assignment
Multimedia Report

When you present your research report using writing and nonprint media, it becomes a **multimedia report.** The additional media can include video images, audiotape recordings, slide shows, or even fine art. Multimedia reporting provides you with opportunities to present information in innovative and engaging forms that can make information clearer and more understandable.

You research a multimedia report just as you would a traditional written research report. However, in a multimedia report, you identify audio and visual information to support your thesis statement in addition to the books and journals you investigate.

Plan and develop your own multimedia report using the writing process strategies discussed below.

Prewriting Choose a subject for which multimedia material will be available. The more you can show instead of tell, the more compelling and successful your multimedia report will be. Research within the following categories can provide you with many strong opportunities:

- **Entertainment** List the celebrities whose work you enjoy, the films you know well, even professional sports teams you want to study. Make sure you can imagine the audio or visual material that would support your ideas, and choose a topic.

- **Contemporary Politics** Review the issues that concern you, brainstorming to list new federal legislation, Supreme Court rulings, elections, and local policies that affect you and your classmates. Imagine the types of audio or visual material you might include in your report, and then choose a topic.

- **Consumer Issues** Scan news programs and newspapers, identifying practical issues that affect you and your family. Consider a multimedia report that explains how to create a budget, how to bring a new product to market, or how to choose a family vacation spot. Review your ideas to choose a topic for your multimedia report.

As you research your topic, look for creative ways to involve viewers. Gather audio or video clips of interviews, performances, or television or film documentaries. Consult traditional sources to get the body of your research.

292 • Research Paper

▲ **Critical Viewing**
Why do you think multimedia reports are so common in business?
[Hypothesize]

Critical Viewing

Hypothesize Multimedia reports are effective tools for informing and persuading in part because audiences are already sophisticated consumers of media and will respond well to these types of reports.

Drafting Once you have gathered sufficient information, propose a thesis statement that will summarize the ideas you want to present. Then, use these tips to help draft your work:

- Sketch an outline to show the sequence of ideas you'll develop. Include main headings for an introduction, a body that provides in-depth coverage of your topic, and a conclusion that sums up your research.

- Plan possible media paths under each main heading. Jot down your ideas for incorporating photographs, music, interviews, charts, and graphs to help convey your ideas. Use a sequence chart like the one shown here to plot your presentation.

My Introduction	Competitive tennis is hard	Tennis requires intensive training
- Slide on screen of tennis player winning award - Upbeat music	- Audio-taped interview with player about victory	- Still photo of the player's training equipment

- Strive to strike a balance between the narrative and the audio and visual elements you'll use. As in all other research writing, be sure to weave your ideas and that of others smoothly. To do this effectively, draft a script from the sequence chart and outline. Use stage direction format to indicate where you will be standing throughout the presentation.

Revising and Editing Before you present your report to an audience, do a test run, reading the script and pointing to the media elements you'll use. As you do this, consider the following issues:

- Be sure all the information in your report—whether narrative or audiovisual—supports the main idea.

- Evaluate the sequence of the material, and consider whether adding more to your narrative will improve the flow of ideas.

- If necessary, revise the sequence, define terms, and clarify connections between ideas.

Publishing and Presenting Because you present a multimedia presentation orally, it's important to practice it as you would a speech. Get to know your material so you can speak without a script. Give a practice performance to a peer or family member. In addition, check any equipment for problems, and make sure you know how everything works. Once you've presented your work to an audience, invite questions and comments from the group.

Connected Assignment: Multimedia Report • **293**

Lesson Objectives

1. To analyze relationships and ideas as presented in various media
2. To investigate the source of a media presentation or production
3. To describe how meanings are communicated through elements of design

Step-by-Step Teaching Guide

Analyzing Relationships in Media

1. Students might focus on one of the Spotlight features. Give them the time to find necessary books and photographs.

2. Some students might like to research why the work of Martha Graham and her collaborators was considered so innovative. Other students might try to determine how a ballet could focus on the life of a reclusive poet.

3. Students might read some of Dickinson's poems and compare them in tone and content to specific parts of Graham's *Letter to the World*. (Suggest that they watch it on videotape in the school or local library.) Or, they might read parts of a Dickinson biography and compare the two interpretations (text and dance) of her life.

Viewing and Representing

Activity Give students the opportunity to present their multimedia research reports, either in class or in the school media center.

Critical Viewing

Respond Students might note that a dancer in a rocking chair is probably still moving, whether or not she is on her feet. Modern dance does not require that dancers remain upright.

Spotlight on the Humanities

Analyzing Relationships as Represented in Various Media

Focus on Dance: Martha Graham

Research allows you to study the past and present, finding connections among items you may not have known before. For example, through research you might discover how dancer Martha Graham can be linked to poet Emily Dickinson and to and sculptor Isamu Noguchi.

Considered a prominent performer and choreographer, Martha Graham (1894–1991) led the way in the development of the modern dance form in the twentieth century. Graham joined Charles Weidman and Doris Humphrey to create the first generation of American modern dancers and choreographers. Breaking from classical ballet of the nineteenth century, Graham did not wear ballet slippers. Her movements were angular, austere, and precise yet full of motion.

Literature Connection In 1940, Graham invoked the memory of one of the country's most original writers. Graham's ballet called *Letter to the World* was based on the life of the American poet Emily Dickinson (1830–1886). The poet's life story was well suited to Graham's attention. Although Dickinson was physically isolated, she was a prolific writer and kept most of her work private. When her work was finally discovered and published, Dickinson's writing had a strong influence on American poetry. Just as Graham had set a new standard for modern dance, Dickinson had broken away from traditional styles to create a new standard for American poetry.

Sculpture Connection Working with natural elements of stone, wood, and clay, the American sculptor Isamu Noguchi (1904–1988) designed close to twenty sets for choreographer Martha Graham. After living both in Japan and in the United States, he established a studio in New York City, where he met and collaborated with Martha Graham.

Research Writing Activity: Multimedia Report on the Collaboration Among Artists

At first glance, a sculptor may not seem to be well suited to the task of set design. Conduct research to learn more about Noguchi's sculpture and his collaboration with Martha Graham. Identify the sculpture skills that complement set design and the challenges such a background might present. Present your findings in a multimedia research report.

▲ **Critical Viewing** How does the prop used in the dance scene shown here affect your expectation or definition of modern dance? **[Respond]**

Media and Technology Skills

▶ **Lesson Objectives**

1. To use a variety of forms and technologies to communicate specific messages
2. To use a range of techniques to plan and create a media text
3. To produce a documentary
4. To present the documentary to an audience of peers and invite comments

Creating Media Products

Activity: Producing a Documentary

Professionals who produce celebrity biographies or television newsmagazine segments combine research with audiovisual footage to bring nonfiction writing to life. To film your own documentary using the same techniques, use this multi-step process:

Think About It Start with a well-written script. Review your research materials, organizing subtopics on index cards. To plan your film using the storyboard technique, reorganize the sequence of the cards until you find a suitable order.

Make It Visual For each scene or segment, brainstorm for visual or audio materials to bring the narrative to life for viewers. Show the problem you're highlighting, or interview the film's main subject. Film large-scale charts, graphs, or hands-on demonstrations to present information, and use voice-overs to bridge transitions. When possible, incorporate existing film footage from on-line or library film sources, but check with the rights holder to make sure you may use the material.

Plan It To turn each subtopic index card into a film scene, use a form like the one shown here to plan your video. Note what viewers will see and hear. Summarize dialogue and stage directions, and jot down plans for camera angles. Estimate the scene's length. Then, use these scene plans to direct your filming.

Scene #	
Visuals:	
Narration:	
Music/Sound Effects:	
Actors:	
Stage Directions:	
Time:	

Film It Capture your documentary on film. Use the technical tips in the sidebar to guide your efforts. Share your film with an audience of peers, and invite their comments.

Filming Tips

- Rehearse your actors, finalize props, and preview locations.
- To create a voice-over, read your script off-screen. Use the time to show interesting visuals.
- Use the video camera's portability to film on location for added interest.
- Apply special filming effects, such as zoom and fade, to achieve professional results.
- Create or borrow sound effects (from taped collections) to enliven images.
- Import audio clips as part of your narration.
- Check the function of your recorder, obtain sufficient tape, and carry a backup battery.

Step-by-Step Teaching Guide

Creating Media Products

Teaching Resources: Writing Support Transparencies, 13-K; Writing Support Activity Book, 13-4

1. If you want to limit the length of students' documentaries, tell them their work should be from five to seven minutes long.
2. Students may work more efficiently in small groups. Give them ample time to settle on a subject and choose a director.
3. Display Transparency 13-K and give students copies of the blank organizer 13-4 to help them plan their filming.
4. If students work in groups, suggest that each person in a group be responsible for one aspect of the documentary, including the script.
5. Go over the filming tips in the sidebar. If students do not have access to the technologies suggested, encourage them to come up with creative solutions.

Step-by-Step Teaching Guide

Revising and Editing

Teaching Resources: Standardized Test Preparation Workbook, pp. 25–26

1. Review the bulleted items with students. These clarify which abilities are measured on the test items they will be practicing.

2. Have students read the sample test item, answer the question, and review the correct answer and explanation.

3. Assign the practice test, and go over the answers with students when they have finished.

4. Ask students to tell which item or items caused problems for them.

Standardized Test Preparation Workshop

Revising and Editing

When editing and revising your own writing, you consider how you can summarize complicated information, reword confusing sentences, and add clarifying information. Standardized test questions often measure your ability to apply these skills to given passages, using a multiple-choice format to measure your response. These questions measure your ability to

- evaluate a writer's word choice and indicate where to insert more information.
- decide which information does not contribute to the rest of the passage.
- choose transitions to improve the flow of ideas.
- correct errors in mechanics, grammar, and spelling.

Test Tip

When reading a passage, note your initial reaction. Any questions or confusion you have may indicate the flaw in the passage.

Sample Test Item	Answer and Explanation
Directions: Read the passage, and then answer the questions that follow.	The answer is **A.** Since the sentence refers to the settler's experience in the past, *provided* is the correct verb to use.
[1] In the early 1800's, Americans began to hear about the area of land known as Oregon Country. [2] Within Oregon Country, the Willamette River valley and the land around Puget Sound provide good farming conditions for the early settlers. [3] In addition, fur-bearing animals like beaver could be found in the dense forest along the mountain range in the region. [4] With its varied geography, trappers and farmers were attracted to Oregon Country, which today includes Oregon, Washington, Idaho, and parts of Wyoming, Montana, and Canada.	
Which of the following changes is needed in the above passage?	
A. Part 2: change provide to provided	
B. Part 4: change includes to include	
C. Part 4: change attracted to attract	
D. Part 3: change like to as	

296 • Research Paper

✦ TEST-TAKING TIP

Tell students to make a note of any questions they have or any errors they find as they read through a passage. Students should be alert for information that seems extraneous to a passage and sentences that lack parallelism.

Emphasize that students should look for punctuation errors of all types. Sometimes punctuation will be needed; at other times, a passage may be wrongly punctuated. Capitalization errors can include words that are capitalized but shouldn't be as well as words that should be but aren't.

▶ **Practice 1** **Directions:** Read the passage, and then answer the questions that follow. Choose the letter of the best answer.

[1] The Great Depression, a time of major suffering, was also a turning point in American history. [2] With the Great Depression came the presidential election of Franklin Delano Roosevelt, known as FDR. [3] Roosevelt's place in History is unmatched since he is recognized for creating the New Deal. [4] The New Deal, Roosevelt's series of bills sent to Congress that covered various programs, had a long-lasting effect on our society. [5] The main goals for the New Deal were to plan for economic recovery, find relief for the impoverished and unemployed, and created reforms that would prevent another depression. [6] One of the first bills sent to Congress under the New Deal was the bank bill. [7] Under the bank bill, Roosevelt declared a "bank holiday" for eight days, and only the strongest banks could reopen, after the holiday. [8] Over the radio, Roosevelt gave "fireside chats," in which he explained his programs to Americans. [9] His wife, Eleanor, helped him in many ways. [10] _____ his chats worked. [11] People started depositing money back into banks, and slowly banks grew stronger. [12] Roosevelt deserves recognition for his efforts to end poverty and positively affect the lives of the American people. [13] Since those twelve long years, our country has not suffered through another time as desperate as the Great Depression.

1 What is the best change, if any, to make in Part 3?
A. Change History to history.
B. Change creating to created.
C. Change Roosevelt's to Roosevelt.
D. Make no change.

2 Which of these sentences would best fit after Part 5?
A. Roosevelt was well liked by the American people.
B. Roosevelt worked diligently to create programs to accomplish these goals.
C. Roosevelt was a very intelligent man.
D. The New Deal was a challenging endeavor for the President.

3 Which of the following draws attention away from the main idea?
A. Part 5
B. Part 8
C. Part 9
D. Part 10

4 At the end of which part would you add the words "a plan Roosevelt created to help restore confidence in U.S. banks"?
A. Part 5
B. Part 6
C. Part 7
D. Part 10

5 Which of the following, if inserted into the blank, would best fit the sentence in Part 10?
A. Fortunately,
B. Unfortunately,
C. Nevertheless,
D. However,

6 Which of the following should have a comma deleted?
A. Part 5
B. Part 1
C. Part 7
D. Part 9

7 Which of the following changes is needed in the above passage?
A. Part 5: change created to create
B. Part 5: change find to found
C. Part 7: change declared to declare
D. Part 11: change depositing to deposited

Answer Key

1. A
2. B
3. C
4. B
5. A
6. C
7. A

Customize for
Less Advanced Students

Explain that a test that measures revising and editing skills will probably not require that students look for factual details in a passage. For example, this practice test does not ask students to answer a question about how long FDR's "bank holiday" was. Students will, however, be expected to comprehend the main idea of a passage.

Customize for
AP Students

Tell students that carelessness is often a cause of a poor grade on a test. They should always focus on test directions, noting whether they are to choose a letter, underline, write out an answer, circle an item, and so on.

In-Depth Lesson Plan

	LESSON FOCUS	PRINT AND MEDIA RESOURCES
DAY 1	**Introduction to Response to Literature** Students learn key elements of writing responses to literature and analyze the Model From Literature. (pp. 298–303)	*Writers at Work* **Videotape**, Response to Literature *Writing Lab* **CD-ROM**, Response to Literature
DAY 2	**Prewriting** Students choose and narrow a topic, consider their audience and purpose, and gather information. (pp. 304–308)	**Teaching Resources** *Writing Support Transparencies*, 14-A–E; *Writing Support Activity Book*, 14-1–3 ; *Topic Bank for Heterogeneous Classes*, Ch. 14
DAY 3	**Drafting** Students organize their ideas and write their first drafts. (pp. 309–310)	**Teaching Resources** *Writing Support Transparencies*, 14-F–G
DAY 4	**Revising** Students revise their drafts in terms of overall structure, paragraphs, sentences, and word choice. (pp. 311–315)	**Teaching Resources** *Writing Support Transparencies*, 14-H–J; *Writing Support Activity Book*, 14-4
DAY 5	**Editing and Proofreading; Publishing and Presenting** Students check their work for accuracy and correctness and present their final drafts. (pp. 316–317)	**Teaching Resources** *Scoring Rubrics on Transparency*, Ch. 14; *Writing Assessment and Portfolio Management; Formal Assessment*, Ch. 14

Accelerated Lesson Plan

	LESSON FOCUS	PRINT AND MEDIA RESOURCES
DAY 1	**Drafting** Students review characteristics of writing a response to literature, select topics, and write drafts. (pp. 298–310)	*Writing Lab* **CD-ROM**, Response to Literature **Teaching Resources** *Writing Support Transparencies*, 14-A–G; *Writing Support Activity Book*, 14-1–3
DAY 2	**Revising to Presenting** Students work individually or with peers to revise, edit, and proofread their work for presentation. (pp. 311–317)	**Teaching Resources** *Writing Support Transparencies*, 14-H–J; *Writing Support Activity Book*, 14-4; *Scoring Rubrics on Transparency*, Ch. 14; *Writing Assessment and Portfolio Management; Formal Assessment*, Ch. 14

Options for Adapting Lesson Plans

HOMEWORK
Have students complete any stage of the lesson for homework.

FEATURES
Extend coverage with Connected Assignment (p. 321), Spotlight on the Humanities (p. 322), Media and Technology Skills (p. 323), and the Standardized Test Preparation Workshop (p. 324).

TECHNOLOGY
Students can complete any stage of the lesson on computer. Have them print out their completed work.

INTEGRATED SKILLS COVERAGE

Integrating Grammar
Parallelism, ATE p. 302

Reading/Writing Connection
Evaluate an Opinion, SE p. 300
Writing Application, SE p. 303

Viewing and Representing
Critical Viewing, SE pp. 298, 300, 315, 318, 319, 320, 321, 322
Responding to Fine Art, SE p. 305
Movie Review, SE p. 321
Analyzing Relationships Among Various Arts, SE p. 322

Punctuation
ATE p. 308

Spelling
ATE p. 314

Real-World Connection
ATE p. 302

ASSESSMENT SUPPORT

Standardized Test Preparation Workshop SE p. 324; ATE p. 312
Standardized Test Preparation Workbook, pp. 27–28
Scoring Rubrics on Transparency, Ch. 14
Formal Assessment, Ch. 14
Writing Assessment and Portfolio Management

MEETING INDIVIDUAL NEEDS

Less Advanced Students ATE pp. 306, 321, 325. See also Ongoing Assessments ATE pp. 300, 305, 307, 310, 314.
AP Students ATE pp. 303, 325
ESL Students ATE pp. 301, 307, 309
Visual/Spatial Learners ATE p. 308
Verbal/Linguistic Learners ATE p. 317
Bodily/Kinesthetic Learners ATE p. 305

BLOCK SCHEDULING

Pacing Suggestions
For 90-minute Blocks
• Have students complete the Prewriting and Drafting stages in a single period.
• Focus one class period on Revising and Editing and Publishing and Presenting. Allow at least 30 minutes for peer revision.

Resources for Varying Instruction
• *Writing Lab* **CD-ROM** If your students have access to hardware, a 90-minute block provides an ideal opportunity for students to work on computer.
• *Writers at Work* **Videotape** Show the Response to Literature segment in class.

Professional Development Support
• *How to Manage Instruction in the Block* This Teaching Resource provides management and activity suggestions.

MEDIA AND TECHNOLOGY

For the Student
• *Writing Lab* **CD-ROM,** Response to Literature
• *On-Line Exercise Bank,* Section 20.4

For the Teacher
• *Writers at Work* **Videotape,** Response to Literature
• *Resource Pro* **CD-ROM**

WRITING AND GRAMMAR WEB SITE

The Interactive Writing and Grammar Web Site provides a wide array of support for students, teachers, and parents. Writing support includes:

• Interactive revision checkers
• Scoring rubrics with complete models

www.phschool.com

LITERATURE CONNECTIONS

Related selections from *Prentice Hall Literature: Timeless Voices, Timeless Themes,* The American Experience:

"For the Love of Books," Rita Dove, SE p. 303
"Out, Out—," Robert Frost, SE p. 305

Lesson Objectives

1. To write a response to literature appropriate to audience and purpose

2. To read and appreciate a writer's craft and to discover models for writing

3. To analyze literary elements for their contributions to meaning in literary texts

4. To use prewriting strategies to generate ideas and plan

5. To develop and revise drafts in terms of structure, paragraphs, sentences, and word choice

6. To edit and proofread to ensure standard English usage and grammar

7. To evaluate writing for both mechanics and content

8. To refine selected work for publication

Critical Viewing

Apply Students should remark that a successful communication between an interactive reader and an author requires both sides to "speak" the same language.

Chapter 14 Response to Literature

The human side of technology, James Yang, Courtesy of the Artist

Response to Literature in Everyday Life

When a novel stays at the top of the bestseller list for months, people in the book business can assume only one thing—it is selling more copies than any other. Publishing professionals cannot assume much beyond that. While some readers rave about the book, others may find themselves putting it down long before the final chapter. Some may find the setting interesting but the characters flat. Some may love the characters but dislike another element of the writing. Because readers bring their own unique tastes to a work of literature, each person has an individual response to the works he or she reads.

Whenever you put your thoughts about literature into writing, you use the specific characteristics of response writing.

▲ **Critical Viewing**
How can you apply the ideas expressed in this painting to the interactive nature of reading? **[Apply]**

298 • Response to Literature

⏱ TIME AND RESOURCE MANAGER

Resources
Technology: *Writers at Work* Videotape, Response to Literature; *Writing Lab* CD-ROM, Response to Literature

In-Depth Coverage	Accelerated Pace
• Cover pp. 298–299 in class. • Show the Response to Literature section of *Writers at Work* Videotape. • Read the Model From Literature (pp. 300–303) with students, paying attention to the writer's use of opinions.	• Discuss pp. 298–299 with the class. • Assign the Model From Literature for independent reading.

What Is a Response-to-Literature Essay?

When you write a **response-to-literature essay,** you give yourself the opportunity to discover what, how, and why a piece of writing communicated to you. An effective response

- analyzes the content of a literary work, its related ideas, or the work's effect on the reader.
- presents a thesis statement to identify the nature of the response.
- focuses on a single aspect of the work or gives a general overview.
- supports opinion with evidence from the work addressed.

To see the criteria against which your response to literature may be judged, preview the Rubric for Self-Assessment on page 317.

Types of Responses to Literature

The following are just a few of the ways you might respond in writing to a literary work:

- **Reader's response journals** are informal records of readers' thoughts or feelings about a literary work.
- **Character analyses** use evidence from the text to support a conclusion about a main character in a work of literature.
- **Literary letters** are formal letters written either to the author or for academic audiences such as those of a literary journal or newspaper.
- **Literary analyses** show how the different literary elements of a work—such as theme, character, or plot—work together to create an overall effect or meaning.

PREVIEW

Student Work

IN PROGRESS

In this chapter, you'll see the work of J. B. Nelson, a student at Hart High School in Newhall, California. J. B. used writing process strategies to respond to the writings of Sandra Cisneros. His final draft appears at the end of this chapter.

Writers in
ACTION

As a literary agent, Theresa Park has made a career of responding to literature. In this quotation, she discusses why she enjoys her work:

"I think the most profound way in which literature can really enrich your life is to open the door to worlds that you'll never experience personally. . . . I think that's the wonderful thing about picking up a book. You don't know where it is going to take you."

PREPARE and ENGAGE

Interest GRABBER Have students read a brief newspaper article. On the board, draw a two-column chart labeled "What I Think" and "What I Feel." Ask students to copy it into their notebooks and fill it in based on the article they just read. Have them share their answers. Explain that in this chapter, they will learn how to craft personal responses to literature.

Activate Prior Knowledge

Ask students to list their three favorite books. Call on volunteers to share their lists and explain briefly why those books appealed to them. Emphasize that response to literature is based on individual taste, and any response is valid as long as it is supported by specific evidence. Explain that the class will learn how to respond effectively to literature in this chapter.

Writers in Action

Theresa Park is featured in the Response to Literature section of the *Writers at Work* Videotape.

✓ ONGOING ASSESSMENT: Diagnose

Use one of the following options to diagnose students' current level of experience with responses to literature.

Option 1 Have students select their strongest examples of a response to literature essay from last year. Read their samples to determine which students will need extra support in developing a response essay.

Option 2 Ask students to list one or two of the most challenging aspects they encounter when writing response essays. (Examples: being able to provide sufficient evidence to support a main point) Use their responses to assess which part of the writing process you will want to emphasize.

Reading\Writing Connection

Reading: Evaluate an Opinion

To evaluate an opinion involves distinguishing between facts (information that can be proven) and opinions (statements of belief or judgment). As students read, ask them to note Amy Tan's beliefs or opinions on Belle Yang's work. What facts or other evidence does Tan use to support her opinions?

Step-by-Step Teaching Guide

Engage Students Through Literature

1. Discuss the correct definitions of the vocabulary words introduced in the Ongoing Assessment below.

2. Some of the following questions may be used to encourage discussion of the essay:

   Why did Tan feel guilty after receiving Yang's manuscript and paintings?

   Why did Tan suspect that her angels were Chinese?

   What did she admire about Yang's paintings?

   What are the main points Tan makes in praise of Yang's writing?

   How does she use specific evidence to support her points?

Critical Viewing

Respond Students might notice Yang's ability to depict contrasting ideas, such as fantasy and reality or peacefulness and fear.

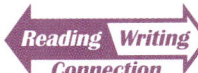

Model From Literature

14.1

Amy Tan is an award-winning, best-selling writer whose novel The Joy Luck Club *was made into a feature film. As the response of a respected author, her positive comments about a work by a new writer can build interest. The essay that follows was published as an introduction to Belle Yang's first published book.*

Reading Strategy:
Evaluate an Opinion
As you read Amy Tan's essay, identify the opinion she presents. Then, in order to evaluate whether you agree with her, look for the evidence she cites to support her ideas. This way, you'll know whether her positive review is valuable to you.

Copyright © 1994 by Belle Yang. Designed by Lisa Peters

▲ **Critical Viewing**
In her essay, Amy Tan describes the watercolors of Belle Yang. Study Yang's cover illustration and compare Tan's evaluation to your own response. **[Respond]**

Preface

Amy Tan

An introduction to Belle Yang's BABA: A Return to China Upon My Father's Shoulders

In March of 1991, a friend of mine in San Francisco, Sue Yung Li, sent me a package with a scribbled note: "Thought you might enjoy reading this." Inside, she said, were photographed illustrations painted by a writer-artist named Belle Yang. Also included: a dozen pages of Belle's prose—something to read in my spare time.

I found myself in a guilt-inducing predicament, for there I was, involuntarily holding in my hands another writer's passion and dreams, a life's work that was either about to blossom or wither, depending on luck, the presence of angels, and the kindness of strangers.

Unfortunately, my reserves of kindness had long been depleted; I didn't have time to write my own work, let alone extra time to read that of a stranger. With much guilt weighing on my heart I sadly placed the young writer's unopened packet in the pile

Tan begins her response informally, sharing a personal experience with readers. However, she names her subject, writer-artist Belle Yang, in the first paragraph.

By explaining how often she is asked to review the work of new writers, Tan sets up a conflict to frame this response to literature.

☑ ONGOING ASSESSMENT: Monitor and Reinforce

After previewing the Model From Literature, you may anticipate that some students will have difficulty with some of the vocabulary. Use the following option.

Give students the following vocabulary words from the essay: *predicament, vignettes, reminiscences, ennui, cynicism, feats, recipient, onomatopoeia, judicious,* and *resonant.* Ask students to define the words using a dictionary. Do this before students read the selection so these words won't impede their reading.

destined for The Junkmail Graveyard, otherwise known as my recycling bin.

Though I lacked kindness, I have had no lack of angels in my life. I cannot explain or describe who these angels are, only that they have showered me with a considerable amount of kindness and luck. Also, they ceaselessly remind me of this fact, which causes me to suspect they are mostly Chinese. In any case, my angels believed that I'd soon come to my senses and open Belle Yang's packet. Didn't I remember, they asked, that they had helped me in just such a way when I was an unpublished writer not so long ago? Didn't they help guide my early writing into the caring hands of writers like Amy Hempel and Molly Giles, while others might have turned my early efforts into handy strips of firestarter? In due time, the angels assured me, I'd retrieve Belle Yang's packet from the graveyard pile. I just needed to be nudged. Ever so lightly.

Over the next few days, Belle Yang's packet fell out whenever I reshuffled the pile. It surfaced to the top, no matter how many times it was buried beneath multiple copies of catalogs and sweepstakes notices. There were other hints. A cousin named Yang called. An issue of *Belle Lettres* arrived. And then I developed an insatiable desire to hear the sound of bells, not just ordinary bells, but Chinese bells. On my desk was a pair of old copper clappers I had recently found in an antique shop. I clanged them together, and they produced a spectacularly resonant *trrrnnng!* that floated into my chest, flowed into my heart, then stubbornly lodged into that place of memory that nags at you like a universal mother asking you if you've done your homework yet. Not yet, not yet, not yet. *Trrrnnng!* You know you're going to have to do it, the angels told me.

I opened Belle's packet. Glossy photographs fell out, the illustrations Sue Yung Li had mentioned. They are stunning: splashes of watercolor creating deceptively simple images woven into vibrant patterns. The paintings are very much alive, capturing balance and disharmony between this world and the underworld, between heaven and earth, between humans and nature. They are both scary and humorous, personal and, yet, a larger view of the world. Whoever this Belle Yang is, I thought to myself, she paints well, I'll grant her that.

I then picked up the pages and began to read the vignettes of Baba, based on stories and boyhood reminiscences of Belle Yang's father. Soon I was gasping and sighing, hearing the music of Belle Yang's words, seeing and experiencing the fullness of a once-lost world she had re-created with the same vibrancy as her paintings.

Although readers can assume Tan eventually reads Yang's work, this information creates suspense about it.

Tan realizes the importance of helping new writers. She names those who were helpful to her early career. This propels her to read Yang's work.

Tan uses the onomatopoetic word "trrrnnng" to create the sound it describes. This attention to word choice makes her writing more lively.

A review of Yang's illustrations helps readers understand the type of art she creates. Descriptions that identify the conflict between "heaven and earth" and "humans and nature" interpret the watercolors the artist created.

Model From Literature • **301**

More About the Writer

Amy Tan was born to Chinese parents in Oakland, California, in 1952. Her novels depict the conflicts experienced by Chinese immigrants in the United States, and her first novel, *The Joy Luck Club,* focuses on the tensions between Chinese-born women and their American-born daughters. Tan's other works include books for children, and the novels *The Kitchen God's Wife* and *The Hundred Secret Senses.*

Teaching From the Model

You can use this model from literature to show students the effective use of specific details. Ask students to point out examples of Tan's use of specific details in discussing her cat on page 302. Which details do students find most vivid? Where else in the essay do they notice vivid and memorable details?

Customize for
ESL Students

Address all unfamiliar vocabulary in the Model From Literature. One option is to write the new words and their definitions on the board. Then, model the context of these words by using them in sentences. Encourage each student to create a vocabulary list in a reader's journal.

Integrating Grammar Skills

Parallelism Call students' attention to the third sentence in the next-to-last paragraph on page 303. Note the parallel structure Tan uses in the long sequence following the colon. She lists the elements of Yang's father's "lost world" as a series of nouns (*rhythms, imagery, undertones, onomatopoeia, tastes, relationship, ironies,* and *ways*) surrounded only by modifying words and phrases. The sentence after that uses parallelism in a simpler fashion, with a series of three prepositional phrases all starting with *with*. Explain that parallelism means using the same grammatical construction to express similar or equal (parallel) ideas. Use the following example to illustrate the definition:

Not parallel: *Abby and I stopped to ask the way to the post office, for change for a dollar, and because we needed to know what time it was. (an infinitive phrase, a prepositional phrase and a subordinate clause)*

Parallel: *Abby and I stopped to ask the way to the post office, to get change for a dollar, and to find out what time it was. (three infinitive phrases)*

Ask students to make the following sentence parallel:

Mr. Davis told Jim to collect the homework and that he should take attendance. (Mr. Davis told Jim to collect the homework and take attendance.)

Real-World Connection

Explain to students that alliteration is the repetition of initial consonant sounds in two or more neighboring words. Advertising often plays on the similar sounds of alliteration when developing catchy slogans or songs. Ask students to bring in examples of advertisements that use alliteration. Challenge students to identify the alliteration in each advertisement.

In reading those few pages, I sensed the excitement veteran editors must feel when, in discovering a fresh voice, they once again find joy abundant enough to sustain them through next year's tedious editorial meetings. Belle's voice is so true and pure it is capable of washing away the grimy layers of cynicism, the dust of ennui, the greasiness of business. I felt lucky to be the recipient of her work. I called Sue Yung Li and thanked her. I called Belle and congratulated her. I called my agent and said, "I have something very, very special I think you should see."

This is *not* to say I discovered Belle Yang, for others had already discovered her writing and art before I did. But that was how I discovered once again why I love to read stories, why I once wanted to paint stories myself.

Baba is a work of twin arts. It reminds me of the earliest reason I became a writer: As a child, I wanted to be an artist. Using charcoal, pastels, and paints, I sought to capture my perceptions of the world or, rather, a precise and specific moment that conveyed what I saw, what I believed, what I *felt* was true about life that no one else could possibly understand unless I rendered it clearly and well.

I possessed more-than-average abilities in executing reasonable likenesses of still life subjects—for instance, my tabby cat, Fufu, lying on his back in the sun. Adults praised my work: "Why, that looks just like Fufu!" But I could capture none of what was important to me. Not the differences: the intelligence of Fufu's naughtiness, for example. Nor the emotions: the twist in my heart when Fufu, lost for days, wailed to me from within a locked closet. Nor the ephemeral aspects of life's quiet intensity: how my breath on Fufu caused his ears to flutter just like the moths that caressed our porchlight.

I always fell short of drawing what I felt, what I saw in that one magical second. And while there is enormous satisfaction in the physicality of drawing, there is a stone-in-the-throat sort of disappointment in seeing large and pitiful results before one's very eyes. Even though I swept my brush boldly across the page, even though I dabbed at details with blind patience, the right lines, colors, and shapes always eluded me. And so I eventually turned to my tools of second choice: I tried to use words to paint pictures.

Those are the reasons I admire and envy Belle Yang's double talents. She writes what she sees and feels. She draws what she sees and feels. She does so with mastery in both crafts. As Yang points out herself, in Chinese art there is no separation between pictures and words. They come from the same source. She creates

302 • Response to Literature

Tan provides a thesis statement to shape her response: Belle Yang's work is "true and pure." The essay will focus on a general overview of the book.

The review, emphasizing the work's effect on the reader, shows that Yang has talent as both a writer and an artist.

Tan responds to the artwork, explaining that Yang's paintings capture the differences, emotions, and intensities that Tan's own artwork never could.

By providing personal experiences of childhood painting, Tan creates a context for her analysis of the artist's work.

painted stories, as well as story paintings. Through bold strokes of poetry and color, Yang evokes a likeness of a world now gone but retrieved through memory: the redbeard bandits, the son on a rooftop crowing instructions to the dead, the *hwwoolong* sounds of bombs landing in the marsh. She captures her own family folktales and long-standing rumors, as well as our own willingness to believe they must be true: that a prophetic dream from a goddess could foretell both judicious and unfair results, that the origins of one family's wealth came from a glowing three-legged creature that served as a divining rod to buried urns of gold.

What is equally amazing to me is the fact that Belle Yang *sees* transparently between Chinese and English. She's an American writer who writes in English and thinks in Chinese. Her writing feels Chinese to me without the awkwardness of word-for-word transliteration and without the paleness of "something lost in translation" for the sake of accessibility to the Western reader. It is as though we, the readers of English, can now miraculously read Chinese.

As an American writer who understands Chinese but speaks it like a child, I both appreciate and envy Belle Yang's literary feats. It is one thing to write proficiently in two languages, another to *sense* the world in two languages. By that, I mean that Belle Yang *senses* the lost world of her father in Chinese: the brusque and matter-of-fact rhythms of life, the folk imagery, the historical undertones of classical art, the noisy onomatopoeia of country and city life, the sour, appeasing, and deeply satisfying tastes of food, the adverse and harmonious relationship between humans and nature, the bitter and belly-laughing ironies, and the circular ways in which everything makes perfect if not logical sense. Yet she conveys all this with English, with poetry, with the universal power of language. She has created a world we can lose ourselves in, and when we emerge we are all the better for it. For a few lingering moments, we can even see magic in our own world. What a gift.

Baba makes me want to paint again. With watercolors, with words, whatever I can use. I want to paint the angels who urged me to see Belle Yang's work.

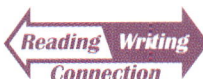 **Writing Application: Support Your Opinion**
As you draft your response to literature, support your ideas and interpretations with evidence from the work you address.

Tan explains the link between Yang's art and prose. She combines her opinion with evidence from the work.

This paragraph points out another strength, adding depth to her thesis statement. Here, Tan addresses Yang's ability to span two cultures and two languages in her writing.

The final paragraph offers a completely personal response to Yang's work, tying Tan's own creative energies to the feelings Yang's work inspired

For another type of response-to-literature essay, read "For the Love of Books," by Rita Dove. You can find it in *Prentice Hall Literature: Timeless Voices, Timeless Themes: The American Experience.*

Customize for
AP Students

Ask students to read Rita Dove's essay "For the Love of Books" in *Prentice Hall Literature: Timeless Voices, Timeless Themes,* The American Experience and write a reader's response in their journals.

Connections With Literature

Ask students to point out the use of sensory details in the essay, "For the Love of Books" ("the warm spot caused by their intimate weight in my lap," "crisp whisper of a page turning"). Further challenge students to point out the use of similes ("it was like contemplating a genie's lamp," "they looked more like over-sided bouillon cubes than books").

Reading\Writing Connection

Writing Application: Support Your Opinion

When they begin to write their response essays, have students write down on note cards or self-sticking notes the supporting points for each idea and interpretation they make. This will serve as a double-check, ensuring that they have adequate backup for their opinions.

Prewriting: Library Walk

1. Stress the importance of choosing a literary work that evokes a clear response. Encourage students to choose genres that appeal to them or are familiar to them.

2. Encourage students to jot down notes during their library visit. These notes can be referred to at a later prewriting session.

3. Ask students to choose one of their topics to develop further.

Prewriting: Discussion Group

1. Remind students of the importance of active listening before beginning the discussion group.

2. Explain to students that topic ideas might include an analysis of a literary element such as imagery or theme; a letter to a character about a decision he or she made; or a journal entry about how the selection relates to students' own lives.

Prewriting: Top-Ten List

Teaching Resources: Writing Support Transparencies, 14-A

1. Display Transparency 14-A. Discuss J.B.'s responses to the literature he read. What criteria did he use to choose his topic?

2. Ask students to create a personal Top-Ten List, following the directions on page 304. Explain that they will add this list to a personal topic bank to be created later.

14.2 Prewriting

Choosing Your Topic

A useful first step in writing a response to literature is to select a passage that moves you to respond—it might be to a character, a conflict in the plot, or the setting of the work. Review the books you've already read, or select a new piece of literature. Consider these strategies for choosing a topic:

Strategies for Generating Topics

1. **Library Walk** Spend some time looking through a variety of literary genres—fiction, biography, poetry, plays—in a library or bookstore. Look for authors, topics, or themes that you have enjoyed in the past. Jot down a few titles you already know, and then choose a topic for your response to literature.

2. **Discussion Group** With classmates, make a list of the literature you have studied in class. For each work you list, generate a few ideas about potential topics for a response to literature. Choose an idea you'd like to develop.

3. **Top-Ten List** Think about the novels, biographies, and other works of literature that are memorable to you. Create a top-ten list by writing down the titles and authors of these works. Next to each, note the ideas you'd want to share about the writing. Review your list, and choose a topic.

Writing Lab CD-ROM

For more help finding a topic, explore the activities and suggestions in the Choosing a Topic section of the Response to Literature lesson.

Student Work IN PROGRESS

Name: J. B. Nelson
Hart High School
Newhall, CA

Creating a Top-Ten List to Find a Topic

Here are a few entries from J. B.'s list of memorable literature. He decided to write an essay prompted by Sandra Cisneros's essay "Straw Into Gold: The Metamorphosis of the Everyday."

4. *Friday Night Lights*   H. G. Bissinger
Football story: I had a similar experience when our team went to the championships and lost.

5. *Frankenstein*   Mary Shelley
This shows how we can misuse technology.

✓ 6. "Straw Into Gold: The Metamorphosis of the Everyday"   *Sandra Cisneros*
The writer helped me see the importance of living for yourself.

⏱ TIME AND RESOURCE MANAGER

Resources
Print: *Writing Support Transparencies*, 14-A–E; *Writing Support Activity Book*, 14-1–3
Technology: *Writing Lab* CD-ROM, Response to Literature

In-Depth Coverage	Accelerated Pace
• Cover pp. 304–308 in class. • Take students through the Strategies for Generating Topics. • Have students use hexagonal writing to narrow their topics. • Work through the Audience Profile and Details list.	• Ask students to read pp. 304–308 for homework. • Have students choose and narrow topics independently. • Have students work with partners to identify their audience and purpose.

TOPIC BANK

If you are having trouble choosing a topic, consider the following suggestions:

1. **Response to a Children's Book** Scan your childhood memories to find a book that was a particular favorite of yours. Visit the public library to find a copy. Then, write a response to the book, explaining why a child might cherish it. In addition, provide your responses to the book from the new perspective you bring to it as a young adult.

2. **Review of a Novel** Whether bestsellers or classics, novels allow readers to meet fascinating characters and embark on adventures they might never experience. In a response to a favorite novel, share your judgment and explain why the book was successful.

Responding to Fine Art

3. *The White Mantel*, right, conveys a wintry scene. Like fine art, literature can give readers a glimpse of a vivid setting. For example, Edgar Allan Poe's writing often creates an eerie setting, and William Faulkner's work reflects a unique image of the rural South. Choose a piece of literature that features a wintry or snowy setting, and write a response to address it.

The White Mantel 1927–1929, Frank Harmon Myers, National Museum of American Art, Washington, DC

Responding to Literature

4. Robert Frost's harrowing poem "Out, Out—" evokes a different response in each reader. In an essay, analyze the poem's effect on you. You can find the poem in *Prentice Hall Literature: Timeless Voices, Timeless Themes*, The American Experience.

☑ Cooperative Writing Opportunity

5. **Author-in-Depth Review** With a group, choose several pieces by an author you'd like to study. Each group member can respond to one selection by the writer the group has chosen. Present your responses together in an anthology of your work.

Responding to Fine Art

The White Mantel **by Frank Harmon Myers**

Teaching Resources: Writing Support Transparencies, 14-B

1. Display Transparency 14-B and ask students to point out the specific details that convey a wintry scene.

2. Ask them to write a paragraph in which they describe the scene, using concrete details and sensory images.

3. Read aloud a few paragraphs from a literary work in which the author creates a memorable setting, such as the opening paragraphs of Poe's "The Fall of the House of Usher." Discuss how the author creates the effect.

4. Ask students to write a journal response about a piece of literature with an especially vivid setting. Tell them this is an option for a final topic.

5. Ask students to create a personal topic bank of the lists generated thus far and keep it in their notebooks or portfolios.

Responding to Literature

Ask students what effect is created by the repeated use of "snarled and rattled." Have them list other specific words or phrases that Frost uses to evoke an emotional response.

Customize for
Bodily/Kinesthetic Learners

Ask these students to choose a poem and create a short presentation. Explain that their responses to the poem should be presented through movement, gestures, and facial expression. Ask students to pair up. One student will read the poem aloud as the other responds physically. The pair will then present the performance to the class.

☑ ONGOING ASSESSMENT: Monitor and Reinforce

If students are having difficulty coming up with a topic, try the following strategy.

Work as a class to generate additions to their topic banks. Ask students to name titles of poems they have enjoyed. What short stories have elicited an emotional response? Have they read essays or dramas that were especially memorable? Encourage students to add to their topic banks during the discussion.

Prewriting: Use Hexagonal Writing to Narrow A Topic

Teaching Resources: Writing Support Transparencies, 14-C; Writing Support Activity Book, 14-1

1. Emphasize the importance of narrowing a topic and developing it through specific support.

2. Display Transparency 14-C. Discuss how the hexagon allows J.B. to explore Cisneros's essay from various angles.

3. Give students a blank copy of the hexagon (14-1). Ask students to choose a topic and narrow it by using hexagonal writing.

4. After completing the hexagons, students should choose one angle as a focus for their literary responses.

5. Ask volunteers to share topics and discuss whether the topics are narrow enough. If not, break the topic into smaller elements and list examples on the board to assist students in selecting a more focused topic.

Customize for
Less Advanced Students

It will be helpful for students to complete a hexagon for more than one work of literature. In this way, they can choose the work about which they have the clearest and most developed thoughts. Monitor and assist students as they work.

14.2

Narrowing Your Topic

Each piece of writing includes so many facets—plot, characters, theme, setting, writing style, elaboration, and evidence—that an essay addressing each of these elements could not discuss any of them well. Instead, a focused response treats one issue thoroughly. Hexagonal writing can help you narrow a topic.

Use Hexagonal Writing to Narrow a Topic

When you use hexagonal writing, you look at a piece of literature from a variety of angles. Complete each angle in a hexagon according to the directions that follow. When you have completed your hexagon, review the notes and narrow your topic.

Plot Summarize or paraphrase the writing you have chosen.

Personal Allusions Jot down people, places, situations, or events from your own life that the selection suggests to you.

Theme Briefly state the generalization or message about life that the selection conveys to you.

Analysis Cite evidence from the text to support the theme you have identified.

Literary Allusions Consider other literature that the selection suggests to you.

Evaluation Decide whether you liked the work.

⚜ Challenge

Find a partner who has chosen the same piece of literature as you have. After you each complete a hexagon, compare your results. It may surprise you, but the finished charts will probably be unexpectedly different!

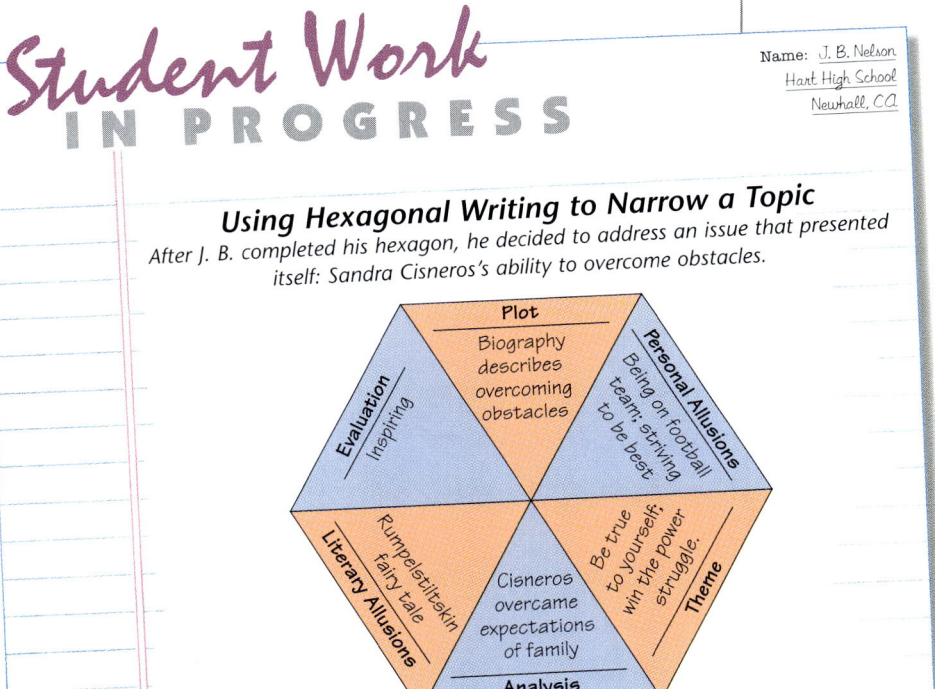

Student Work IN PROGRESS

Name: J. B. Nelson
Hart High School
Newhall, CA

Using Hexagonal Writing to Narrow a Topic

After J. B. completed his hexagon, he decided to address an issue that presented itself: Sandra Cisneros's ability to overcome obstacles.

Plot — Biography describes overcoming obstacles

Personal Allusions — Being on football team; striving to be best

Theme — Be true to yourself; win the power struggle.

Analysis — Cisneros overcame expectations of family

Literary Allusions — Rumpelstiltskin fairy tale

Evaluation — Inspiring

306 • Response to Literature

Considering Your Audience and Purpose

Once you have narrowed your topic, consider the format your response will take. A reader's response to Emily Dickinson's poetry would include personal reactions; a literary analysis of the same work for an audience of classmates who have studied Dickinson would include a more formal examination of her writing. Before you draft, take the time to identify your intended audience and your specific purpose.

Develop an Audience Profile

Your intended audience will affect the length, vocabulary, and level of detail you will use in writing your response to the literature you've chosen. To be sure your draft will address your target audience, complete a profile like the one shown here. Then, use your responses to shape your draft.

AUDIENCE PROFILE	
Age and background	16 and 17 year olds, urban, fairly sophisticated
Interest, biases	Enjoy good stories; are not impressed by especially formal diction
Vocabulary level	average to above average
What they know about the topic	have read several works by this author; know her style and common themes
Literature features of interest	conflict

Writing Lab CD-ROM

To help you identify your audience, use the Audience Profile activity. To help you identify your purpose, use the interactive tips on purpose.

Clarify Your Purpose

Whether you are sharing your enthusiasm for a new writer, expressing your interpretation of a well-known short story, or writing to achieve another purpose, include details that support your writing goal. Consider these tips:

- **To praise,** include concrete details about what you liked.

- **To analyze,** back up your ideas with evidence from the text.

- **To explain a personal response,** show how the writing connects to the experience, ideas, or situation you describe.

Prewriting: Develop an Audience Profile

Teaching Resources: Writing Support Transparencies, 14-D; Writing Support Activity Book, 14-2

1. Read page 307 to students. Display Transparency 14-D and discuss the elements of an audience profile.

2. Ask students to discuss why identifying an audience is important.

3. Explain how analyzing the intended audience can also help them narrow a topic.

4. Hand out a blank copy of the audience-profile chart (14-2). Challenge students to develop an audience profile on a topic in class. Students whose intended audience is the same might want to complete this exercise in pairs.

Customize for ESL Students

Students might respond to a fairy tale written in their first language. Their purpose could be to identify differences between this fairy tale and a similar tale written in English.

☑ ONGOING ASSESSMENT: Monitor and Reinforce

If a number of students are having difficulty defining an audience, try the following strategy.

Students might find it difficult to write an essay for a large group of people, such as academics or peers. It might be easier to aim their essay at one specific person, such as a parent, a mentor, or a classmate. Choosing someone they know will make it easier to fill out the audience profile. This, in turn, will make it easier to use the appropriate diction, tone, and level of detail in their work.

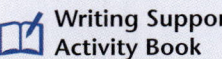

⏱ TIME SAVERS!

📘 Writing Support Transparencies

Use the transparencies for Chapter 14 to facilitate the teaching of strategies.

📖 Writing Support Activity Book

Use the graphic organizers for Chapter 14 to facilitate student planning.

Prewriting: Gathering Details

Teaching Resources: Writing Support Transparencies, 14-E; Writing Support Activity Book, 14-3

1. Display Transparency 14-E and discuss in depth the specific literary elements. Make sure students understand each one.

2. Ask students to follow the example on page 308 and list what they want to show and how they will show it for the topics they have chosen.

3. Encourage students to go back to the text to find details and quotations that support their ideas.

Integrating Punctuation Skills

Quotations Remind students that when they use quotations, they need to make sure that the meaning and significance of the quote is clear.

Not clear: *Ethan Frome is silent and withdrawn. "I simply felt that he lived in a depth of moral isolation too remote for casual access."*

Clear: *Ethan Frome is silent and withdrawn and seems to live "in a depth of moral isolation too remote for casual access."*

Explain that if a word or words within a quote are changed, the word or phrase should be placed in brackets. If a word or words within a quote are omitted, an ellipsis should be used. Challenge students to review their work for their use of quotations.

Customize for
Visual/Spatial Learners

After discussing page 308, ask students to design a chart that illustrates the five literary elements and summarizes information about each. Post this in the classroom as an aid for all students.

Gathering Details

Once you have a clear idea of your audience and purpose, generate a list of the kinds of details you need. To do this, summarize your purpose in one sentence. Then, review the literature to find the details to back it up. Here's a sample:

What I Want to Show:

- James Thurber's "The Night the Ghost Got In"
- Uses exaggeration to create comedy

What Details I Need to Include:

- Characters whose behavior is unusually quirky
- Reactions that are overblown
- Language that creates overstatement

Use these tips to gather details on specific literary elements:

Character If you are planning to discuss a specific character, review the literature to make notes about the character's actions, ideas, appearance, and motivation. Note any changes the character undergoes. Look for any information provided by the narrator, and study the other characters' reactions to the character you'll describe.

Setting To write a response that focuses on setting, clarify the time and place in which the work unfolds. Note the mood or atmosphere that the setting helps to convey, and assemble details that add to it.

Diction When discussing a writer's word choice, back up your ideas with specific examples. Consider the vocabulary level and both the denotations (or dictionary meanings) and the connotations (or emotional meanings) of the words that the writer has used.

Sound Devices If you want to focus on sound devices in poetry, collect examples of rhythm, rhyme, alliteration, or assonance to support your ideas. Look for patterns in rhyme and rhythm, or look for the imagery the poet creates in the writing.

Theme To analyze the message of an author's writing, look at the way a conflict is resolved, examine the attitudes and actions and statements of the characters, and study the expository parts of the writing. Use these details to draw conclusions about the author's generalization about life.

🔲 Research Tip

Treat this stage of the writing process as research. Consider photocopying the selection you'll analyze. Then, use a highlighter or a red pen to identify the elements that support your response.

14.3 Drafting

Shaping Your Writing
Organize to Support a Response

Introduction Start with an interesting lead that connects to the ideas you will present. Consider drafting a description, presenting a problem, or creating context. To keep the momentum going, identify the title and author of the selection, and present the main idea of your essay in a thesis statement.

Summary Before jumping into an analysis of the literature, summarize or paraphrase the work. Limit your summary to a sentence or two, but inform your readers of key elements in the text.

Body Use the body of your essay to develop your thesis statement. Use details, paraphrases, or direct quotations from the work to support the points you make. Strive for analysis; avoid retelling the plot or describing characters in detail.

Conclusion Restate your thesis and summarize your main points, but take your conclusion beyond the basics. Use your conclusion as an opportunity to make a personal recommendation, ask a question, or make a prediction.

Student Work IN PROGRESS

Name: J. E. Nelson
Hart High School
Newhall, CA

Organizing With a Sentence Outline

To organize his essay, J. B. used a sentence outline to present his drafting plan.

Introduction	Describe fairy tale "Rumpelstiltskin" and link to Cisneros's life.
Thesis Statement	The struggle for control over her own future has been a big part of Cisneros's life.
Body Paragraph 1	Analyze "My name." To the narrator, a name represents personality.
Body Paragraph 2	Analyze "A House of My Own." To the narrator, a house represents success.
Summary Paragraph	Connect back to Rumpelstiltskin.
Conclusion	Make a connection to my own experiences

Drafting • 309

Step-by-Step Teaching Guide

Drafting: Organize to Support a Response

Teaching Resources: Writing Support Transparencies, 14-F

1. Define "lead" for the class and give examples of effective leads.

2. Review introductions and conclusions. Show examples from various literary responses if possible. Call attention to the introduction and conclusion in the final draft on page 318. Explain how the introductory statement and the conclusion discuss elements of the thesis statement.

3. Display Transparency 14-F. Tell students that the sentence outline differs from the four organizational steps by not specifically noting the summary step that comes after the thesis statement and by pulling out as a separate step the summary paragraph that is normally part of the conclusion.

4. Ask students to complete a sentence outline on their topics. Confer with individual students to see that they each have a focused thesis and clearly stated main points. Encourage students to use the transparency as a model.

Customize for
ESL Students

When discussing the transparency, make sure students understand the term *thesis statement*. Explain that it is simply a statement of the essay's main idea. Also, clarify that the *body* of an essay is the bulk of it; it is the part that comes between the introduction and the conclusion.

⏱ TIME AND RESOURCE MANAGER

Resources
Print: *Writing Support Transparencies*, 14-F–G
Technology: *Writing Lab* CD-ROM, Response to Literature

In-Depth Coverage	Accelerated Pace
• Discuss the benefits of using a sentence outline to organize an essay. • Emphasize the importance of providing elaboration, and allow time for students to collect specific examples and quotes to support main points. • Have students write the first draft in class.	• Cover pp. 309–310 in class. • Ask students to provide elaboration and write the first draft for homework.

Drafting: Incorporate References From the Text

Teaching Resources: Writing Support Transparencies, 14-G

1. Discuss why providing elaboration is important. Citing details from the text is another way of using "facts" (evidence from the text) to support your opinions.

2. Display Transparency 14-G and discuss how J.B. quotes Cisneros's text to develop or elaborate on his main point.

3. Remind students that they must use quotation marks to enclose words taken directly from the text. Paraphrases do not need quotation marks.

4. Refer students to the *Writing Lab* CD-ROM to learn more about incorporating references. See the Drafting section of the Response to Literature lesson.

Providing Elaboration

For each main idea you develop, include a specific example from the text that illustrates your point.

Incorporate References From the Text

Instead of asking your readers to trust your interpretation, add the proof you need by incorporating references from the text. You can include direct quotations or paraphrases using your own words to summarize the information. In both cases, make sure you incorporate the material by introducing the reference, giving the reference, and then explaining how it supports your ideas.

SAMPLE DIRECT QUOTATION:

In "The Story of an Hour," the reader is presented with an unsettling opening line that sets the stage for a surprising story. The writer begins with this sentence: "Knowing that Mrs. Mallard was afflicted with a heart trouble, great care was taken to break to her as gently as possible the news of her husband's death." From the start, readers can anticipate that Mrs. Mallard's reaction to this news may be dramatic.

Writing Lab CD-ROM

To learn more about incorporating references from a text, use the interactive tips for using quotations. You can find them in the Drafting section of the Response to Literature lesson.

Student Work
IN PROGRESS

Name: J. B. Nelson
Hart High School
Newhall, CA

Incorporating References From the Text

To develop the narrator's desire for a modern name, J. B. quotes Cisneros's text. Showing which names might be considered modern makes the point more clear.

She was given her grandmother's name, Esperanza. That name is Spanish, and the narrator feels it is too traditional. In the story, she says she wants a more modern name, citing the more imaginative "Lisandra or Maritza, or Zeze the X." (Cisneros, *The House on Mango Street*, 13.) Instead of inheriting her grandmother's name, and potentially her life, she wants to live her own life, follow her own rules, and have her own name. To the narrator, a name clearly represents who she is. In her mind, people must earn a name much as they earn respect.

✔ ONGOING ASSESSMENT: Monitor and Reinforce

In order to encourage students to complete their first draft promptly, use the following strategy.

Set a deadline for the draft to be completed and tell students that you will collect and review them. Setting a deadline is an effective way to prevent procrastination. After collecting the drafts, skim each one and mark places that are unorganized or that lack elaboration.

14.4 Revising

Once your draft is written, make the effort to improve your writing. Analyze your response to literature on four levels: overall structure, paragraphs, sentences, and word choice.

Revising Your Overall Structure

Present a United Front

While you may have a mixed response to the literature you've chosen to discuss, avoid confusing your reader. Present a concise, unified opinion, and back it up with support. Unless you can relate the discussion of other elements to the thesis statement, eliminate paragraphs or details that do not support the main impression your response addresses.

▶ REVISION STRATEGY
Identifying Contradictory Information

Write your thesis statement on a small piece of paper to move along the side of your draft. As you read your essay, slide your thesis statement down the page, confirming that each paragraph contains information that supports it. If you notice paragraphs, details, or examples that contradict your main idea, circle them. When you have reviewed your entire draft, evaluate the circled information.

Evaluate	Revise
• Are there several circled items that can be connected in some way?	• If the information is important enough to your analysis, add a single paragraph to address this group of details. Use a transitional sentence to acknowledge this paragraph as a contrast to your thesis.
• Are there some circled items you can delete?	• Eliminate items that seem random or that cannot be connected to your thesis.

Writers in
ACTION

Theresa Park, literary agent, takes as much care analyzing her own writing as she does reviewing that of her clients. Because her response guides their success, she needs to provide concrete details to support her evaluation. She explains here:

"I think it's really important to be as specific about your criticism as possible. It's not enough to say that the writing is bad, or that it's weak. Why is it bad? Why is it weak?"

Step-by-Step Teaching Guide

Revising: Identifying Contradictory Information

1. Write the four areas of revision on the board:

   overall structure

   paragraph

   sentences

   word choice

   Tell students that the class will focus on each area, one at a time.

2. Ask students to use the revision strategy explained on page 311 and eliminate details that do not support the main focus. Explain to students that this will present a united front to their readers.

3. Pair up students. Have them read their essays to their partners and ask for feedback on the overall structure.

4. Partners should point out places where the essay digresses from the main point. They should also point out confusing or distracting passages.

More About the Writer

Students can learn more about literary agent Theresa Park from the *Writers at Work* Videotape, Response to Literature.

⏱ TIME AND RESOURCE MANAGER

Resources
Print: *Writing Support Transparencies,* 14-H–J; *Writing Support Activity Book,* 14-4
Technology: *Writing Lab* CD-ROM, Response to Literature

In-Depth Coverage	Accelerated Pace
• Discuss in class pp. 311–315. Use the relevant transparencies.	• Assign pp. 311–315 as homework.
• Call students' attention to Theresa Park's quote on page 311 and remind them that feedback must be specific.	• Discuss the strategies for revising overall structure and paragraph content in class.
• Have students revise their drafts in class.	• Ask students to revise their drafts for homework.

Revising: Personalizing Your Response

Teaching Resources: Writing Support Transparencies, 14-H

1. Ask a student to read aloud the first few paragraphs of the final draft that begins on page 318.

2. Discuss the organization and support in the body paragraphs.

3. Ask students to read silently the first paragraph in the body of their drafts and ask the following questions:

   Does the paragraph adequately support the main point with specific examples or quotes from the text?

   Does the paragraph flow smoothly, and is its meaning clear?

4. Have students follow the same procedure for each of the body paragraphs of their drafts. Ask volunteers to read some examples of paragraphs in their original and revised forms.

5. Focus on strengthening concluding paragraphs. Ask for volunteers to read some aloud. Display Transparency 14-H and discuss how J.B. strengthened his response to literature by making his conclusion personal.

6. Discuss ways to make the conclusions memorable, personal, or provocative.

14.4

Revising Your Paragraphs

Review each paragraph in your draft to be sure it logically contributes to your thesis statement. Pay special attention to your conclusion; what you include there should leave your reader with something to consider long after reading your essay.

Strengthen Your Conclusion

In revising your conclusion, check that you have restated your thesis and reminded readers of the evidence you used to support it. To take your conclusion beyond the basics, find a way to make your last paragraphs memorable, personal, or provocative. Consider making a recommendation to your readers or linking the literary selection to a larger historical or contemporary context.

▶ **REVISION STRATEGY**
Personalizing Your Response

Review your prewriting work to recall how you found a topic that appealed to you. Review the draft to evaluate whether a personal reflection could improve your conclusion. Make revisions by adding information that links the literature to your life and experiences.

Student Work
IN PROGRESS

Name: *J. B. Nelson*
Hart High School
Newhall, CA

Personalizing the Conclusion

J. B. found a quotation from Cisneros's writing in the body of his essay that he could relate back to his own life.
These are the notes he made to create a more personal conclusion.

J. B. models Cisneros's deliberate use of sentence fragments.

Cisneros's quotation: "Not a man's. Not Daddy's. A house all my own. . . . a space for myself to go, clean as paper before a poem."

Conclusion: To paraphrase the writer, here is the lesson I can take from her: "Not for daddy, not for the coaches, not for your friends, but for yourself. Life, clean as paper before a poem. Don't write what you're told; write what you want."

312 • Response to Literature

✎ STANDARDIZED TEST PREPARATION WORKSHOP

Grammar Standardized tests may require students to know correct use of possessive nouns and pronouns. Provide students with opportunities to practice the correct use of possessives.

Which noun below best completes this sentence?
Three ___ books could not be found.

A girl's
B girls
C girls'
D girl

Students should recognize that **C** is correct. The word is plural, and the apostrophe correctly falls after the "s." B is plural but is not possessive. A is possessive but is not plural, and D is neither plural nor possessive.

Revising Your Sentences

Review Sentence Clarity

As you read your draft, look for sentences that may be incomplete, those that lack a subject or verb, or those that are run-ons. Such sentences can be confusing to your readers.

Language Lab CD-ROM

For more on sentence errors, see the lesson on Fragments and Run-on Sentences.

▶ REVISION STRATEGY
Bracketing Complete Sentences

Bracket each sentence of your draft. Evaluate each group of words you've marked by confirming that it expresses a complete thought. When you come across a fragment or a run-on punctuated as a sentence, revise it to correct the error.

Grammar in Your Writing

Sentence Fragments, Fused Sentences, and Comma Splices

Although they are incorrectly punctuated as sentences, **sentence fragments** do not express complete thoughts. Subordinate clauses beginning with conjunctions such as *after*, *although*, *despite*, *because*, and *since* are common targets for such errors.

Fragment:	When we go to the fiesta in April.
Sentence:	When we go to the fiesta in April, we'll enjoy the food.

One type of run-on sentence, **a fused sentence,** consists of two or more sentences that are neither separated nor joined by any punctuation at all.

Fused Sentence: We love the music we never get to hear it enough.
Correct: We love the music; however, we never get to hear it enough.

A second type of run-on sentence is the **comma splice.** A comma splice is created when two or more main clauses are separated only by commas instead of by commas and conjunctions or by semicolons.

Comma Splice:	They brought plenty of supplies, nothing was left over.
Correct:	They brought plenty of supplies; nothing was left over.

Find It in Your Reading Except for a deliberate use for effect, most professionally published writing does not include errors such as accidental sentence fragments, fused sentences, or comma splices. Review Amy Tan's essay on pages 300–303 to see how she uses punctuation and subordination to generate correct and sophisticated sentences.

Find It in Your Writing Review your draft to find any sentence fragments, fused sentences, and comma splices. Correct fragments by providing what is missing, and punctuate run-on sentences correctly.

For more on sentence fragments, fused sentences, and comma splices, see Chapter 20.

313

Revising: Circling Words of Praise or Criticism

Teaching Resources: Writing Support Transparencies, 14-I

1. Call students' attention to the words listed expressing praise or disapproval on page 314.

2. Display Transparency 14-I and discuss how J.B. strengthened his writing by adding evaluative modifiers.

3. Ask students to read silently their drafts and circle modifiers and other words that could be improved. Tell them to be particularly aware of verbs.

4. Give students time in class to consult a thesaurus or each other to improve word choice.

Integrating Spelling Skills

Proofreading Ask students to examine their personal spelling list or review their portfolios to note past spelling errors. Suggest they skim their current drafts to check for these words.

14.4

Revising Your Word Choice

Review Evaluative Modifiers

The adjectives and adverbs that convey appraisal or judgment in your draft should be words that are precise. These modifiers convey the strength of your response and the depth of your assessment of the literature you address.

▶ REVISION STRATEGY
Circling Words of Praise or Criticism

Review your draft, and circle any words that convey either a positive or negative response. Then, evaluate your draft on three levels. First, decide whether your writing includes enough evaluative modifiers. Second, note whether you repeat the same ones too frequently. Finally, decide whether your evaluative modifiers precisely convey your response. Consider adding words like these to improve your draft:

- **Mild Praise:** *appealing, readable, factual, intelligent, solid, accurate, expressive, comprehensive*
- **High Praise:** *imaginative, refreshing, inspired, lively, brilliant, beautiful, entertaining, honest, original*
- **Mild Disapproval:** *dull, predictable, silly, inaccurate, vague, confusing, repetitious, unfocused*
- **Strong Disapproval:** *insulting, biased, pretentious, trivial, pointless, false, awful*

Writing Lab CD-ROM

To use an Evaluative Modifier Word Bin, see the Response to Literature lesson.

Student Work
IN PROGRESS

Name: J. B. Nelson
Hart High School
Newhall, CA

Revising Evaluative Modifiers
When J. B. circled words that conveyed praise in his draft, he saw the opportunity to make his writing stronger.

These same concerns are (evident) in *The House on Mango Street*, the poetic novel that helped Cisneros break away from *and inspired* other people's plans for her. With this *engaging* novel, she spun straw, the low expectations held for her, into gold, her own success.

☑ ONGOING ASSESSMENT: Monitor and Reinforce

If you find students unsure about the connotative and comparative value of words that reflect praise or criticism, use the following strategy.

Remind students that words of praise or criticism can be subjective. To some, a "mild praise" word such as *intelligent* might seem like "high praise." Or, "mild disapproval" words such as *inaccurate* and *confusing* might be considered by some students an indication of "strong disapproval."

The subjectivity of words can be emphasized by encouraging students, as a class, to try drawing up a lengthy listing of words for each of the four categories. Students should realize that they cannot rely on just a few adjectives to get their opinions across without misunderstanding.

Peer Review

Plus and Minus Scoring

In a small group, share your revised draft. Using the criteria in the chart below, ask your readers to evaluate your work on specific elements. You may want to alter the chart to target your draft more closely.

As you read the criteria in each category, ask your reviewers to give you a plus or minus score. Record their responses, and ask your reviewers to explain their evaluations. Take notes when necessary. Then, use your classmates' responses to revise your draft.

PLUS AND MINUS CHART

| CRITERIA | Group Members | | | COMMENTS |
	1	2	3	
Interesting introduction: first two sentences hook reader				
Identifiable thesis				
Identifiable title and author				
First idea clearly stated and elaborated				
Second idea clearly stated and elaborated				
Successful conclusion				
Overall evaluation				

▲ **Critical Viewing**
How can a peer review discussion spark debate over a literary selection? **[Hypothesize]**

Revising: Peer Review

Teaching Resources: Writing Support Transparencies, 14-J; Writing Support Activity Book, 14-4

1. Divide the class into small groups.
2. Display Transparency 14-J and discuss the elements of the chart. Then hand out blank copies of the chart (14-3).
3. Ask each writer to slowly read his or her essay aloud to the group. Ask the listeners to record their responses on the charts.
4. The members of the group can give feedback by explaining their ratings and responses after each reading.
5. Tell students to use peer feedback to aid them in revision. They should carefully consider all suggestions before deciding which ones to incorporate into their work.

Critical Viewing

Hypothesize Students will observe that the peer review process will prompt discussion about how well the writer has chosen supporting details from literature. This in turn will spur debate about the author's intention.

 TIME SAVERS!

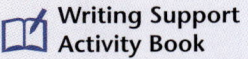 **Writing Support Transparencies**
Use the transparencies for Chapter 14 to facilitate the teaching of strategies.

Writing Support Activity Book
Use the graphic organizers for Chapter 14 to facilitate student planning.

Editing and Proofreading

1. Discuss the importance of proofreading to improve and polish a piece of work.

2. Ask students to follow the suggestion on page 316 and check their spelling by beginning with the last word in each paragraph and moving toward the first.

Common Homophones

1. Ask a prepared student to read the Grammar in Your Writing section to the class. Define homophones to the class, and ask students to think of other examples *(hair/hare, it's/its)*.

2. Review homophones and focus particularly on *allot/a lot, it's/its, principal/principle, their/there/they're,* and *your/you're,* which are often confused in student writing.

3. Consider offering a few points extra credit if a final copy is free of spelling errors.

Find It in Your Writing

Challenge students to develop a list of common homophones and review their drafts with this list in mind. If students find other homophones in their drafts, ask them to add to their lists and later share their additions with the class.

Editing and Proofreading

Errors in spelling, punctuation, and grammar can undermine your credibility or make your draft difficult to read. Proofread your writing several times, looking for different kinds of mistakes with each reading. If you leave a few minutes between each session, your review will be more accurate. When you return to your draft each time with a fresh perspective, you will see errors that you didn't notice before.

Focusing on Spelling

Check the spelling of each word in your draft. To keep your focus on this task, consider looking at each word, starting with the last word in each paragraph and moving toward the first.

Confirm Names If your writing contains many references to literary places or characters, go back to the original works to confirm the correct spelling of the names. Check the spelling of the title and authors of the works you discuss, too.

Collaborative Writing Tip

Trade papers with a classmate. Another editor may find errors you missed.

Grammar in Your Writing
Common Homophones

A common spelling error stems from confusion over homophones. A **homophone** is a word that sounds the same as another word but has a different meaning and a different spelling. Here are some common homophones:

allot/a lot: *Allot* is usually a verb that means "to give out in shares"; *a lot* is an informal expression meaning "a great amount." Although you should avoid using *a lot* in formal writing, note that the phrase is two words and is never spelled *alot.*

principal/principle: *Principal* can be a noun that means "the person who has controlling authority." It is also used an adjective meaning "most important." *Principle* is always used as a noun meaning "a fundamental law."

your/you're: *Your* is generally used as a possessive adjective; *you're* is a contraction of the words *you* and *are.*

Use a dictionary to clarify the meaning and spelling of any homophone pairs that present difficulty.

Find It in Your Writing As you proofread your draft, check that you have not introduced confusion by including a homophone for a word you intended.

For more on common homophones, see Chapter 25.

⏱ TIME AND RESOURCE MANAGER

Resources
Print: *Scoring Rubrics on Transparency,* Ch. 14; *Writing Assessment and Portfolio Management; Formal Assessment,* Ch. 14
Technology: *Writing Lab* CD-ROM, Response to Literature

In-Depth Coverage	Accelerated Pace
• Cover pp. 316–317 in class. • Analyze the Final Draft (pp. 318–320). • Have students edit and proofread their essays in class.	• Assign pp. 316–320 to read for homework. • Have students edit and proofread their essays independently. • Ask for volunteers to read their final essays to the class.

14.6 Publishing and Presenting

Building Your Portfolio

Here are some ways to share your response to literature with a wider audience:

1. **Post an On-line Response** Booksellers on the Web often invite readers to post reviews. In an on-line response, you can share your reactions with potential book buyers. You can also compare ideas with those of other reviewers.

2. **Mail Your Response** You may have a friend or relative who would enjoy the piece of literature you've chosen. You may even want to share your ideas with the author. Send a copy of your essay. Then, keep in your portfolio any responses your mailing generates.

Reflecting on Your Writing

In a brief reflection, jot down your thoughts on the process of writing your response to literature. Use these questions to start your writing:

- In what ways did writing your response to literature deepen your understanding of the work?
- Which prewriting strategy did you find most useful? Explain.

 Internet Tip

To see a model essay scored with this rubric, go to **www.phschool.com**

Rubric for Self-Assessment

Use these criteria to evaluate your response to literature.

	Score 4	Score 3	Score 2	Score 1
Audience and Purpose	Presents sufficient background on the work(s); presents the writer's reactions forcefully	Presents background on the work(s); presents the writer's reactions clearly	Presents some background on the work(s); presents the writer's reactions at points	Presents little or no background on the work(s); presents few of the writer's reactions
Organization	Presents points in logical order, smoothly connecting them to the overall focus	Presents points in logical order and connects them to the overall focus	Organizes points poorly in places; connects some points to an overall focus	Presents information in a scattered, disorganized manner
Elaboration	Supports reactions and evaluations with elaborated reasons and well-chosen examples	Supports reactions and evaluations with specific reasons and examples	Supports some reactions and evaluations with reasons and examples	Offers little support for reactions and evaluations
Use of Language	Shows overall clarity and fluency; uses precise, evaluative words; makes few mechanical errors	Shows good sentence variety; uses some precise evaluative terms; makes some mechanical errors	Uses awkward or overly simple sentence structures and vague evaluative terms; makes many mechanical errors	Presents incomplete thoughts; makes mechanical errors that create confusion

---

✓ ONGOING ASSESSMENT: Assess Mastery

Use one of the following options to assess final drafts of students' essays.

Self-Assessment Ask students to score their work using the rubric provided. Then, have students write a paragraph that discusses the strategy they found most helpful in composing their essays.

Teacher Assessment Use the rubric and the scoring models provided in *Writing Assessment and Portfolio Management* to score students' work.

Step-by-Step Teaching Guide

Publishing and Presenting

1. Remind students that the publishing process is a time to share their work with others.

2. Ask students to consider sharing their responses online or in a written letter to a friend. Ask students to brainstorm for other places to share their writing (school bulletin board, other classes).

ASSESS and CLOSE

Step-by-Step Teaching Guide

Assessment

Teaching Resources: Scoring Rubrics on Transparency, Ch. 14; Writing Assessment and Portfolio Management; Formal Assessment, Ch. 14

1. Display the Scoring Rubric transparency and review the criteria in class.

2. Before students proceed with self-assessment, you may wish to use the rubric to evaluate the Final Draft of the Student Work in Progress on pages 318–320.

3. In addition to student self-assessment, you may wish to use the following options:

- score student essays yourself, using the rubric and scoring models in *Writing Assessment and Portfolio Management*.

- review the Standardized Test Preparation Workshop on pages 324–325 and administer a timed writing assessment.

- administer the Chapter 14 assessment in *Formal Assessment* to measure students' grasp of the concepts presented.

Customize for
Verbal/Linguistic Learners

Make arrangements for the students who wrote a response to a children's story to visit elementary classrooms. They will read the story to the class and then read their response. They can also engage in a dialogue with the younger students, asking for their reactions to the story.

Final Draft

1. Ask students to give specific oral responses to the essay. What did they like? What did they notice about the sentence structure and word choice?

2. Ask students to look closely at the introduction and conclusion and discuss specific strengths of each.

3. Examine each paragraph in the body and ask students to find examples of specific evidence to support each main point.

4. Also ask students to find examples of the following: correct punctuation of appositives and parenthetical expressions, correct use of colons and semicolons, and correct punctuation of possessive nouns.

5. Ask students whether there are any other changes they would recommend for this response. How might they apply these suggestions to their own writing?

Critical Viewing

Hypothesize Students may feel that such photographs help readers identify with the authors by showing that they are people just like anyone else.

14.7 *Student Work*
IN PROGRESS

FINAL DRAFT

▲ **Critical Viewing**
Why do you think publishers include photographs like this shot of Sandra Cisneros on the covers of books? [Hypothesize]

Sandra Cisneros: Modern-Day Heroine

**J. B. Nelson,
Hart High School
Newhall, California**

In the fairy tale entitled "Rumpelstiltskin," a nameless woman is forced by her father to prove to the king that she can spin straw into gold. A strange man by the name of Rumpelstiltskin helps her complete the tasks the king has given her, but as payment she is forced to sacrifice her first-born child unless she is able to guess the man's name and win the power struggle that has been taking place during the story. Sandra Cisneros alludes to this fairy tale in the title of her autobiographical essay

J. B. opens with a summary of the fairy tale that Cisneros references in her own work. By explaining the reference, J. B.'s introduction provides a context for his title and his thesis.

318 • **Response to Literature**

"Spinning Straw Into Gold: The Metamorphosis of the Everyday," explaining how her life has been a similar power struggle.

The struggle for control over her own future has been a big part of Cisneros's life. According to "Spinning Straw Into Gold," the writer's early life was difficult. She fought poverty and the pressures of her family. As the only girl in a family of six children, Cisneros had to overcome her family's expectations. They thought that she would lead a traditional life, leaving her home only when she was married. Much like the heroine of "Rumpelstiltskin," Cisneros struggled against this expectation, not for the respect of her peers or her family, but for herself. She wanted her own name, her own house, and the right to be her own person. These same concerns are evident in *The House on Mango Street*, the poetic and inspired novel that helped Cisneros break away from other people's plans for her. With this engaging novel, she spun straw, the low expectations held for her, into gold, her own success.

In the chapter called "My Name," the narrator candidly expresses the importance of having her own name and not being just another anonymous housewife trapped in the shadows of her husband's life. She was given her grandmother's name, Esperanza. That name is Spanish, and the narrator feels it is too traditional. In the story, she says she wants a more modern name, citing the more imaginative "Lisandra or Maritza, or Zeze the X." (Cisneros, *The House on Mango Street,* 13.) Instead of inheriting her grandmother's name, and potentially her life, she wants to live her own life, follow her own rules, and have her own name. To the narrator, a name clearly represents who she is. In her mind, people must earn a name much as they earn respect.

In the chapter called "A House of My Own," Cisneros again effectively stresses the theme of independence by showing the importance of having a home. This very short chapter reinforces the narrator's idea that success can be measured by the type of home she has. She says it must be special: "Not a flat. Not an apartment in back." (Cisneros, *The House on Mango Street,* 132.) It seems to the narrator that an apartment or one-story house

◀ **Critical Viewing**
What does the web in this painting suggest about the independence J. B. discusses? **[Connect]**

J. B. identifies the title and author of the work he addresses.

A thesis statement indicates that J. B. will analyze the work's content and related ideas. To develop the idea that a struggle for control has been a vital part of Cisneros's life, J. B. will provide details from examples of her writing that support it.

To prove that Cisneros's fiction echoes her own life themes, J. B. cites a second source, the novel The House on Mango Street.

Two body paragraphs develop J. B.'s thesis. In one paragraph, he discusses the importance of a name; in the next, he discusses the importance of a home.

Critical Viewing

Connect Students may feel that the web emphasizes that family members are constantly spreading "nets" of dependence on each other, making breaking away hard to accomplish.

Teaching From the Final Draft

One of J. B.'s main ideas is that a struggle for control has been a major part of Cisneros's life. Have students make a list of the evidence J. B. uses to support this point. Then, have them explain whether they think his evidence is clear and convincing.

Teaching From the Final Draft

Use this essay as an illustration of the power of quotations. Be sure students realize that the effectiveness of the final quote that J. B. used would have been lessened if the essay had been filled with quotations. (There are only three quotations from Cisneros in the essay.) Often, students "discovering" quotations will overuse the device, thinking that the more quotations they use, the better their essays will be. Sometimes quotations can be a crutch that a writer, short of his or her own ideas, will lean on. Help students realize that excessive quotations depersonalize an essay, weakening rather than strengthening it.

Critical Viewing

Connect Most students will probably admit to being drawn to a book by an intriguing or attractive cover.

represents poverty or failure. She needs to prove to herself that she is successful: A house of her own is a symbol that she has made it. Additionally, the house must be hers and hers alone: "Not a man's. Not Daddy's. A house all my own . . . a space for myself to go, clean as paper before the poem." (Cisneros, *The House on Mango Street*, 132.) Once the character has a dream home in mind, she has won the power struggle; she can decide what is best for her and not lead the life someone has picked out for her.

Like the heroine in "Rumpelstiltskin" and the narrator of *The House on Mango Street*, Sandra Cisneros herself has won the power struggle for independence and self-direction. Each of these women has beaten the odds and is happy.

Reading Cisneros's work has given me a new sense of pride in myself. I have realized I need to be doing what is right for me. To Cisneros, a life spent pleasing others and doing everything one is told is not a life; it is more like playing a part in a movie. In that scenario, people read scripts and blindly follow the advice of others. Instead, Cisneros shows how choosing the path is what is important. She believes that in life there is only one person each of us has to impress—oneself. She taught this to me in her work. To paraphrase the writer, here is the lesson I can take from her: "Not for daddy, not for the coaches, not for your friends, but for yourself. Life, clean as paper before a poem. Don't write what you're told; write what you want."

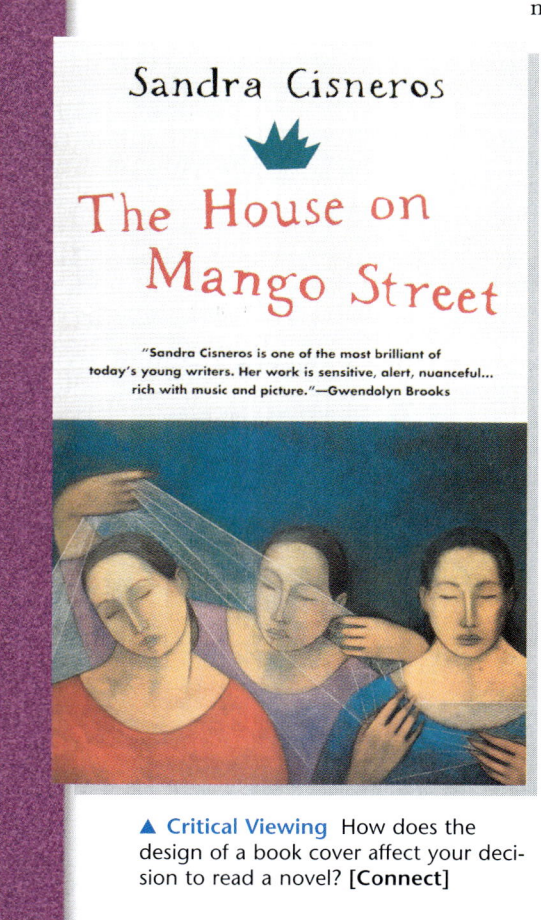

Sandra Cisneros

The House on Mango Street

"Sandra Cisneros is one of the most brilliant of today's young writers. Her work is sensitive, alert, nuanceful... rich with music and picture."—Gwendolyn Brooks

▲ **Critical Viewing** How does the design of a book cover affect your decision to read a novel? **[Connect]**

Before his conclusion, J. B. summarizes the points he has made in his essay.

In his conclusion, J. B. paraphrases a key quote to personalize his response.

Connected Assignment Movie Review

Just like a book review, a **movie review** evaluates its subject in order to identify its strengths and weaknesses. It includes specific examples from the film to support the position it presents. To orient readers to the film's story and support the writer's positions, reviewers provide a skeletal summary of the plot. However, thoughtful writers don't give away the ending for readers who want to enjoy the film for themselves.

Let the writing process strategies offered below guide you in writing your own movie review.

Prewriting Choose a film that evoked a strong reaction in you. If possible, watch the film again with the specific goal of reviewing it. Organize your responses on index cards, color-coded for positive and negative reactions. On each card, describe your ideas and provide a concrete detail for support. When the film is over, review your notes and write a sentence that summarizes your opinion.

Drafting As you draft, refer to your index cards for specific examples that will bolster your opinions. Movie reviews can be written with less formal language than literary responses, so use diction that expresses a more relaxed purpose. Remember that your writing should address and elaborate two questions: First, should your readers see this movie? Second, why?

Revising and Editing As you revise, replace general modifiers with specific evaluative modifiers to convey your reactions. Use comparative words like *better* or superlative words like *best* to compare the film with others you've seen.

Publishing and Presenting If you have a school newspaper or a class newsletter, submit your movie review for others to see. To match your ideas against those of professional movie critics, locate a review and compare and contrast the reviews.

▲ **Critical Viewing**
These viewers seem to be enjoying a film. How can a movie be both a social and an individual experience? **[Compare and Contrast]**

Pro — Special effects were outstanding
- exploding volcano scene was gripping

Con — Plot pacing was uneven
- scene at hospital was too long; could make viewers itchy

Connected Assignment: Movie Review • **321**

Lesson Objectives

1. To analyze relationships, ideas, and cultures as represented in various media

2. To recognize how visual techniques convey messages in media

3. To write a dance review

Step-by-Step Teaching Guide

Analyzing Relationships Among Various Arts

1. Choose one of the Spotlight elements for class discussion, or have students work individually or in groups on the element of their choice.

2. Some students might research additional information about Twyla Tharp. In addition to the works mentioned in the text, she also created *Deuce Coupe* (1973) for the Joffrey Ballet and *Push Comes to Shove* (1976) for Mikhail Baryshnikov at the American Ballet Theatre.

3. Students researching Fats Waller might be able to view him in the 1943 film *Stormy Weather* or listen to some of his many recordings, such as "Honeysuckle Rose."

4. Some students might research the long, illustrious career of Gene Kelly (1912–1996).

Viewing and Representing

Activity Interested students might make a class presentation of their reviews and show sequences from *Singin' in the Rain* to illustrate their points.

Critical Viewing

Contrast Students might note that the movements in the photograph contrast with traditional ballet movements, in which the toes, clad in ballet slippers, are usually pointed and the moves very stylized.

Spotlight on the Humanities

Analyzing Relationships Among Various Arts

Focus on Dance: Twyla Tharp

Just as a great novel, play, or poem causes an emotional response in you, artists often utilize the strengths of their own talent to pay tribute to works that inspire them. American dancer and choreographer Twyla Tharp incorporates music she enjoys into her dances. Born in 1941, Tharp has brought unique innovation to the art of dance in the late twentieth century. She has worked with the American Ballet Theatre, City Center, Joffrey Ballet, Paris Opera Ballet, New York City Ballet, and her own company. In her work, Tharp has used music by contemporary artists and the early jazz of musician Fats Waller. Tharp uses choreographed dance sequences in films such as *Hair*, *Amadeus*, and *White Nights*, as well as for the 1985 Broadway version of *Singin' in the Rain*.

Music Connection Jazz great Thomas "Fats" Waller (1904–1943) earned his living in the early years as an organist in a movie theater and a piano accompanist for vaudeville acts. In 1934, while at a party given by composer George Gershwin, Fats Waller thrilled the crowd with his music and singing. A representative from Victor Records was in the crowd and signed him to a recording contract. In the 1930's, Waller became a radio and nightclub celebrity. One of his most famous songs was "Ain't Misbehavin'."

Film Connection Released in 1952, *Singin' in the Rain*, starring Gene Kelly and Debbie Reynolds, remains one of the most popular musicals in film history. In one of the most famous dance sequences on the silver screen, Gene Kelly sings, dances, and splashes his way into movie-making immortality. In 1985, Twyla Tharp choreographed the Broadway version of this classic musical.

Response to Literature Writing Activity: Dance Review

On your own or with a group of classmates, rent a copy of *Singin' in the Rain* from a video store or borrow it from a local library. Pay particular attention to the dance scenes. After watching it, write a response to the film, describing how the dancing compares with more contemporary dances. Include a vivid description of Gene Kelly's moves to let your readers imagine this famous dance scene.

▲ **Critical Viewing** This photograph shows members of the Twyla Tharp Dance Company in performance. How do the movements contrast with other dance forms you know? **[Contrast]**

Media and Technology Skills

Comparing Your Responses to Others' Responses

Activity: Evaluate Movie Reviews

For every blockbuster movie that comes out, there are movie reviewers who will share their responses within a week of the release. In fact, some critics publish their reviews before the film is even available to the general public. The work of movie critics has the power to influence ticket sales and movie success by building or discouraging interest in a film. As you develop particular tastes in movies, you can use the work of movie critics to inform your decision, but never let a critic think for you.

Think About It As an ancient Latin proverb has it, *de gustibus non est disputandum*—"There is no arguing about taste." If your friend enjoyed *It's a Wonderful Life* but you'd scream if you ever had to see it again, there's no court of taste that will rule that one of you is right. That's why it's a useful exercise to try to find a critic whose tastes reliably, although probably not always, mirror your own.

Try It Choose a film that interests you, and watch it to note the major points you would make in a review. Then, look up reviews of the film by at least two different critics. Use the sidebar column to help you find these reviews. Use a chart like the one below to compare your judgments with those of the two critics. For each category, note specific facts the critics included to support their opinions.

	My Response	Critic A	Critic B
Acting			
Plot			
Cinematography			
Special Effects			
Music Score			

Analyze It Evaluate the ideas of each critic, and use your chart to compare the professionals' ideas with yours. For example, one review may have changed your mind about a specific aspect of the film, while the other may not have been convincing at all. In a brief response, explain what you have learned from this experience.

Sources for Locating Movie Reviews

- newspapers
- magazines
- television and radio news programs
- television movie-review shows
- Web sites about films
- book anthologies
- video movie guidebooks

Step-by-Step Teaching Guide

Comparing Your Responses to Others' Responses

Teaching Resources: Writing Support Transparencies 14-K, Writing Support Activity Book, 14-5

1. Review the sources for movie reviews in the sidebar.

2. Ask students to discuss the ways various film critics describe films. What aspects of a movie do students usually focus on when they discuss it with friends?

3. Display Transparency 14-K to show students how their comparisons might be organized. Give students copies of the blank organizer (14-4) for their own use.

4. Students might expand the organizer by devising their own symbols for rating a movie.

5. Ask students to tell what they learned from this experience. Did they change their mind about a movie? Did they view it more carefully?

Lesson Objectives

1. To use prewriting strategies to generate ideas and plan
2. To develop drafts by organizing and reorganizing content and by refining style to suit purpose
3. To produce legible work that shows accurate spelling and correct use of the conventions of punctuation and capitalization
4. To demonstrate control over grammatical elements

Standardized Test Preparation Workshop

Responding to Literature-Based Writing Prompts

Standardized tests frequently ask you to write essays that provide your response to literature. Whether you are asked to respond to a story or poem included in the test booklet or to use your past reading experiences to support a generalization, the skills you have learned in this chapter will help you in these writing situations. When you write a response-to-literature essay as part of a standardized test, you will be evaluated on your ability to meet the following criteria:

- Develop a thesis that responds directly to the prompt.
- Structure your ideas using a logical and consistent organization.
- Include details from the literature you address to elaborate your ideas.
- Choose language and sentence structure to enhance your ideas.
- Write according to the conventions of correct grammar, usage, and mechanics.

When writing for a timed test, plan to devote a specified amount of time to prewriting, drafting, revising, editing, and proofreading.

Following is an example of a test prompt that requires your response to literature. Use the suggestions on the next page to help you respond. The clock next to each stage shows a suggested percentage of time to devote to that stage.

Sample Writing Situation

> Read the following quotation:
>
> "The only thing necessary for the triumph of evil is for good men to do nothing."—Edmund Burke
>
> The conflict of good against evil is frequently addressed in literature. Choose a short story, poem, or play with which you are familiar. In an essay, show how the literature supports or refutes Edmund Burke's idea.

Customize for
Less Advanced Students

Before assigning this writing prompt, ask the class to brainstorm for a list of short stories, poems, or plays they have read this year that deal with the conflict of good and evil.

Customize for
AP Students

After students have completed the assignment within the allotted time, have them exchange papers with a partner. They can use the scoring rubric on page 317 to evaluate the essays.

Prewriting

Allow about one quarter of your time for prewriting.

Choose an Appropriate Example Read the quote carefully, paraphrasing it to be sure you understand the writer's idea. Then, list several works that deal with the conflict of good and evil. You may think of a selection in which an evil character prevails or one in which a good person prevents that character's success. For each selection you consider, apply the quotation, deciding how the story, poem, or play illustrates or refutes Burke's idea. Then, choose the literature that provides the strongest foundation for your essay.

Gather Details to Prove Your Point To help you build an essay, identify the "good" and "evil" elements in the selection you've chosen. Collect details about the conflict and main characters that will help you link the literature to the quotation.

Drafting

Allow approximately half of your time for drafting.

Focus on Your Thesis Statement Create a compelling introduction to give your topic importance. Provide the title and author of the work you will address, and in a strong thesis statement, tell your reader how the selection supports or disputes Burke's idea.

Organize Details Use your notes to guide your analysis. Write a brief summary of the literature you've selected. Organize the body of your essay in two parts. First, address evil as it is shown in the selection. Next, discuss the reasons for its success or failure. In a conclusion, connect your ideas back to the quotation presented in the prompt.

Name the Specifics Cite specific events or characters to elaborate your point. Link each paragraph to your thesis statement, and explain how specific details prove your analysis.

Revising, Editing, and Proofreading

Allow about one quarter of your time to revise, edit, and proofread your paper.

Check the Connections Review your essay to be sure readers can see the reasons you've developed. Consider including transitional words or phrases to make the links between ideas more obvious. If you choose to insert additional words or delete information, do so neatly.

Correct Errors Before you turn in your paper, check that you have followed the conventions of grammar, usage, and mechanics.

In-Depth Lesson Plan

	LESSON FOCUS	PRINT AND MEDIA RESOURCES
DAY 1	**Introduction to Writing for Assessment** Students learn key elements of writing for assessment. (pp. 326–327)	*Writers at Work* **Videotape,** Practical and Technical Writing *Writing Lab* **CD-ROM,** Practical and Technical Writing
DAY 2	**Prewriting** Students choose and narrow a topic, consider their audience and purpose, and gather information. (pp. 328–329)	**Teaching Resources** *Writing Support Transparencies,* 15-A–B; *Writing Support Activity Book,* 15-1
DAY 3	**Drafting** Students organize their ideas and write their first drafts. (pp. 330–331)	**Teaching Resources** *Writing Support Transparencies,* 15-C
DAY 4	**Revising** Students revise their drafts in terms of overall structure, paragraphs, sentences, and word choice. (pp. 332–333)	*Writing Lab* **CD-ROM,** Practical and Technical Writing
DAY 5	**Editing and Proofreading; Publishing and Presenting** Students check their work for accuracy and correctness and present their final drafts. (pp. 334–337)	**Teaching Resources** *Scoring Rubrics on Transparency,* Ch. 15; *Writing Assessment and Portfolio Management; Formal Assessment,* Ch. 15

Accelerated Lesson Plan

	LESSON FOCUS	PRINT AND MEDIA RESOURCES
DAY 1	**Drafting** Students review characteristics of writing for assessment, select topics, and write drafts. (pp. 326–331)	*Writing Lab* **CD-ROM,** Practical and Technical Writing **Teaching Resources** *Writing Support Transparencies,* 15-A–C; *Writing Support Activity Book,* 15-1
DAY 2	**Revising to Presenting** Students revise, edit, and proofread their work for presentation. (pp. 332–337)	**Teaching Resources** *Scoring Rubrics on Transparency,* Ch. 15; *Writing Assessment and Portfolio Management; Formal Assessment,* Ch. 15

Options for Adapting Lesson Plans

HOMEWORK

Have students complete any stage of the lesson for homework.

FEATURES

Extend coverage with Connected Assignment (p. 338), Spotlight on the Humanities (p. 340), Media and Technology Skills (p. 341), and the Standardized Test Preparation Workshop (p. 342).

TECHNOLOGY

Students can complete any stage of the lesson on computer. Have them print out their completed work.

INTEGRATED SKILLS COVERAGE

Integrating Grammar Skills
Homophones, SE p. 334

Viewing and Representing
Critical Viewing, SE pp. 326, 330, 333, 338, 340
Analyze Ideas Represented in Various Media, SE p. 340
Using Technology to Respond to a Variety of Test Formats, SE p. 341

Spelling
ATE p. 329

Real-World Connection
ATE p. 331

ASSESSMENT SUPPORT

Standardized Test Preparation Workshop SE p. 342; ATE p. 336

Standardized Test Preparation Workbook, pp. 29–30

Scoring Rubrics on Transparency, Ch. 15

Formal Assessment, Ch. 15

Writing Assessment and Portfolio Management

MEETING INDIVIDUAL NEEDS

Less Advanced Students ATE pp. 328, 332, 333, 337, 343. See also Ongoing Assessments ATE pp. 329, 331, 333.

AP Students ATE pp. 330, 339, 343

ESL Students ATE pp. 328, 340

Gifted and Talented Students ATE pp. 331, 337

BLOCK SCHEDULING

Pacing Suggestions
For 90-minute Blocks
• Have students complete the Prewriting and Drafting stages in a single period.
• Focus one class period on Revising and Editing and Publishing and Presenting.

Resources for Varying Instruction
• *Writing Lab* **CD-ROM** If your students have access to hardware, a 90-minute block provides an ideal opportunity for students to work on computer.
• *Writers at Work* **Videotape** Show the Practical and Technical Writing segment in class.

Professional Development Support
• *How to Manage Instruction in the Block* This Teaching Resource provides management and activity suggestions.

MEDIA AND TECHNOLOGY

For the Student
• *Writing Lab* **CD-ROM,** Practical and Technical Writing

For the Teacher
• *Writers at Work* **Videotape,** Practical and Technical Writing
• *Resource Pro* **CD-ROM**

WRITING AND GRAMMAR WEB SITE

The Interactive Writing and Grammar Web Site provides a wide array of support for students, teachers, and parents. Writing support includes:

• Interactive revision checkers
• Scoring rubrics with complete models

www.phschool.com

Lesson Objectives

1. To write for assessment, organizing ideas in writing to ensure coherence, logical progression, and support for ideas

2. To use prewriting strategies to generate ideas and to plan

3. To develop drafts by organizing content to suit purpose

4. To develop and revise drafts in terms of structure, paragraphs, sentences, and word choice

5. To edit and proofread to ensure standard English usage and grammar

6. To evaluate writing for both mechanics and content

Critical Viewing

Contrast Students may say that writing in a test situation does not allow for further research or that time limits add pressure and reduce opportunities to edit and revise.

Chapter 15 Writing for Assessment

Assessment in School

School assessment comes in many forms. Whether it's a lab report, a group discussion, a writing portfolio, or a standardized test, you are often asked to demonstrate your understanding of a topic or your mastery of a body of academic material. This periodic check or assessment helps you and your teachers to identify strengths and weaknesses and to maximize your educational achievement.

When you are prepared, tests are challenges that you can meet with confidence. They offer you the chance to show what you know and to earn good grades. In this chapter, you will sharpen your performance skills for one of the most common types of assessment in school: the essay test.

▲ **Critical Viewing**
How is writing in a test situation different from writing an assigned essay? **[Contrast]**

326 • Writing for Assessment

⏱ TIME AND RESOURCE MANAGER

Resources
Technology: *Writing Lab* CD-ROM, Practical and Technical Writing

In-Depth Coverage	Accelerated Pace
• Cover pp. 326–327 in class. • Discuss the features that should be included in an essay response. • Ask students working in small groups to write two or three examples of essay questions. • Identify the four types of writing tasks usually encountered in an essay question.	• Identify the three features a teacher expects to find in an essay answer. • Discuss the four types of assessment usually found in essay questions.

What Is Assessment?

One of the most common types of school assessment is the written test. Most often, a written test is announced in advance, allowing you time to study and prepare. When a test includes an essay, you are expected to write a response that includes

- a clearly stated and well-supported thesis or main idea.
- specific information about the topic, derived from your reading or from class discussion.
- a clear organization.

To see the criteria on which an essay test may be evaluated, preview the Rubric for Self-Assessment on page 335.

Types of Assessment

While an essay test may be written on any number of topics, the format it takes might be limited to a handful of familiar writing tasks. In your school career, you will probably encounter questions that ask you to address each of the following types of writing:

- **Explain a process** (how a bill becomes a law).
- **Defend a position** (why a character in literature took a certain action).
- **Compare, contrast, or categorize** (the similarities and differences among mammals, reptiles, and amphibians).
- **Show cause and effect** (how the Industrial Revolution changed city life).

Margaret Boehme, a student at Buena High School in Ventura, California, wrote an essay test response about the factors causing the American Revolution. In this chapter, you will see her work in progress, including strategies she used to write and revise the essay. At the end of the chapter, you can see the completed response Margaret wrote.

Writers in ACTION

In the United States, the value of an educated mind has been close to the hearts of teachers and political leaders for centuries. In fact, in a 1936 speech then-candidate Franklin D. Roosevelt extolled the value of learning this way:

"The gains of education are never really lost. Books may be burned and cities sacked, but truth, like the yearning for freedom, lives in the hearts of humble men."

Writing for Assessment • 327

Prewriting: Choosing Your Topic

1. Ask students to pair up and brainstorm for two important points to remember in choosing topics. (Read all questions before choosing one. Choose a topic that can be covered in the designated time.) Encourage students to share their responses.

2. Discuss the three guidelines for choosing a topic. Ask students to consider whether one guideline is more important than another and why. Ask which strategy is the most difficult to complete.

3. Choose one of the questions from the Topic Bank and frame a focused thesis on the board with student input.

Customize for
Less Advanced Students

Encourage students to jot down questions and ideas as they read the essay question. These ideas and questions can be shared with classmates to assist the prewriting process.

Customize for
ESL Students

Choose one of the following questions as a substitute for those given in Topic Bank. Writing about personal experiences can help students to feel more secure about writing.

- Analyze the changes that moving to another town or a foreign country requires. Identify each type, the challenges they present, and what steps can help smooth these changes.

- Compare and contrast education in your country of origin with education in the United States. Discuss school facilities, class schedules, subjects, and textbooks.

15.1 # Prewriting

Choosing Your Topic

In an essay test, the writing topic is generally assigned. Occasionally, however, you will be given a choice of topics. Since an essay test often involves the pressure of time limitations, choosing a suitable topic will help you to make the most of the time available. Read all the prompts or questions before deciding which one to complete. Follow these guidelines:

Match Task With Time Examine each question to determine which will take the least time. Ask yourself how many specific details spring to mind about each one without much effort. As you evaluate the prompts, consider the topics you feel most confident in developing, remember which subjects you have reviewed most recently, and choose a prompt.

Identify Your Strengths Review each prompt to decide whether you can write about the subject in the way the questions require. For example, you may feel comfortable providing the history of an event, but you may not feel as secure in analyzing the aftereffects of the same subject. As you read each prompt, jot down two or three ideas that help you evaluate your potential success. Review your notes to choose a prompt.

Frame a Focus Choose a topic for which you can identify a focus or main idea. With open-ended questions—such as those that ask you to identify and discuss a significant theme, event, or trend—choose a prompt for which you will be able to present a thesis supported by relevant details and examples.

Writing Lab CD-ROM

For more sample test prompts, explore the activities and suggestions in the Choosing a Topic section of the Practical and Technical Writing lesson.

TOPIC BANK

Following are some essay test questions. If you plan to practice writing for assessment, choose one of these or ask your teacher to provide you with one.

1. **Vitamins and Nutrition** Explain how a balanced diet can contribute to a healthy body. Choose three essential vitamins, identify the foods in which they are most commonly found, and explain their influence on the body.

2. **Bravery in the Face of Danger** Characters in literature often display intense courage when they face a difficult or dangerous situation. Choose a character from a work of literature that you have recently read. Summarize the character's situation, and explain how unusual bravery helped resolve the problem.

328 • Writing for Assessment

TIME AND RESOURCE MANAGER

Resources
Print: *Writing Support Transparencies,* 15A–B; *Writing Support Activity Book,* 15-1
Technology: *Writing Lab* CD-ROM, Practical and Technical Writing

In-Depth Coverage	Accelerated Pace
• Discuss the key factors to keep in mind when choosing a topic. • Collect sample essay questions from teachers in other disciplines and provide copies for students. • Ask students to circle key words and identify the type of writing task in each.	• Have students review pp. 328–329 independently. • Give students examples of open-ended questions, and have them circle key words. • Assign an essay question and ask each student to write a clearly focused thesis.

Narrowing Your Response

To answer an essay test question effectively, plan your response by narrowing your focus to provide only what the question requires. Take a moment to analyze the prompt you've chosen. To do this successfully, review the key words and identify your purpose.

Circle Key Words to Identify Your Purpose

Read the prompt and circle verbs, nouns, and other key phrases in the question that provide directions about the type of information the response requires. The chart below shows common key words to expect.

Key Words	Essay Objectives
analyze	examine how elements contribute to the whole
compare/contrast	stress how subjects are alike/different
define	give examples to explain meaning
discuss	support generalizations with facts and examples
evaluate, judge	assign a value or explain an opinion
interpret	support thesis with examples from text

✦ Challenge

While you might feel pressured to start writing right away, take the time to plan your response. Every minute you devote to planning your essay and gathering details will give you a stronger structure and provide you with more content to include in your essay.

Student Work IN PROGRESS

Name: Margaret Boehme
Buena High School
Ventura, CA

Circling Key Words in Test Prompts

Margaret reviewed the prompt she chose, circling the words that would focus her writing. To help shape her answer, she noted her own interpretation of key words.

judgment, opinion   ranked

#1. (Evaluate) the (relative importance) of the following as factors

prompting the Americans to rebel in 1776:

4 factors
- parliamentary taxation
- restriction of civil liberties
- the legacy of colonial religious and political ideas
- British military methods

Prewriting • 329

☑ **ONGOING ASSESSMENT: Monitor and Reinforce**

If you observe that some students are having difficulty choosing a topic, use one of the following options.

Option 1 Suggest that students choose an idea from the Topic Bank. If many students have difficulty, work with the whole class on one idea selected from the Topic Bank or from ideas suggested by students.

Option 2 If Topic Bank ideas seem too difficult, provide one of the assignments from the *Topic Bank for Heterogeneous Classes* in the Teaching Resources.

Drafting: Find a Focus

1. If your class has completed chapters on Exposition (Chapters 9–11), Persuasion (Chapters 7–8), or Response to Literature (Chapter 14), only a brief review is necessary.

2. Emphasize that the purpose of exposition is to explain or clarify, and that the purpose of persuasion is to argue for and support a position.

3. Have students work in pairs to list examples of questions for each type of focus. Share and discuss.

Drafting: Plan a Structure

1. Remind students that in brainstorming for topics or theses they need not evaluate ideas, but should simply jot them down.

2. Ask students to share thesis statements and discuss the effectiveness and clarity of the organization into introduction, body, and conclusion.

Critical Viewing

Relate Students may cite the pressure of working within a time limit, or anxiety over performance.

Customize for
AP Students

Ask students to define each of the words below, and use some or all of them to write two or three paragraphs summarizing the material covered on pages 326–331. Paraphrasing or summarizing helps students to process information into long-term memory. Encourage students to check their spelling carefully.

exposition	conclusion
persuasion	thesis
introduction	elaboration
body	

15.2 Drafting

Shaping Your Writing

Find a Focus

Once you have chosen your topic, identify a focus for your essay. Consider the type of writing you are creating, and draft a simple statement to direct your writing.

- **Exposition** Develop a thesis statement that directly responds to the question presented. For problem-and-solution, cause-and-effect, or comparison-and-contrast essays, follow the expectations of those types of writing.

- **Persuasion** Choose a position to argue, and identify the support you'll use to defend it.

- **Response to Literature** Identify a focus for writing. It might be an analysis of one or more literary elements in a work; for example, conflict in a short story, dialogue in a play, imagery and sound effects in a poem, or theme in a novel.

Plan a Structure

Before you draft your essay, sketch an outline to organize your material. This will keep you on track and help you address all the points you want to discuss in your response. Because your outline is part of your planning and not part of your grade, do not spend time creating an elaborate structure of Roman numerals. For an essay test, strive to get the ideas down and to leave yourself enough time to develop a strong essay.

Introduction, Body, and Conclusion When you sketch an outline for your essay, divide it into three parts: introduction, body, and conclusion. The **introduction** should address the question and state your thesis. The **body** of the essay should present at least two main points to support your thesis. The **conclusion** should restate the answer expressed in the thesis and sum up the main points in the body.

Memory Aids For each section of your outline, note the main ideas you want to convey. If ideas are flowing quickly as you create the outline, jot down key words to remind you of the main points or details you'll want to include as you draft.

▲ **Critical Viewing** What parts of a test-taking situation might challenge a student's ability to concentrate? [Relate

330 • Writing for Assessment

⏱ TIME AND RESOURCE MANAGER

Resources
Print: *Writing Support Transparencies*, 15-C
Technology: *Writing Lab* CD-ROM, Practical and Technical Writing

In-Depth Coverage	Accelerated Pace
• Cover pp. 330–331 in class. • Review expectations for Exposition, Persuasion, and Response to Literature. • Review students' thesis statements before they begin to draft. • Use class time for writing the first draft. Be available for consultations.	• Students review pp. 330–331 independently. • Ask students to write the thesis statement for their chosen essay and discuss with their writing partner. • Students write the first draft of their essay as homework.

Providing Elaboration

A critical part of an essay test response is its level of detail. As you write, include the specific information that supports your main idea or thesis. Whenever you can, refer to ideas that you have learned in class discussions and assigned readings.

Back Up Your Thesis With Support

Whether your purpose in an essay test is to inform, to persuade, to compare and contrast, or to explain cause and effect, you need to include specific evidence supporting your answer. Unless you're taking an "open-book test," these details must come from your memory or personal experience. Here are some types of details you can use in an essay:

- **Facts, Incidents, or Trends** Provide precise information to prove you know your subject. In an essay about a battle during the American Revolution, identify the location, the date, the leaders on both sides, and the outcome.

- **Specific Examples** Often, the best way to prove a point is to include examples that support the point for you. For example, in an essay about the music of Mozart, include specific discussions of at least two of his major works.

- **Descriptive Details** In an essay comparing and contrasting lions and tigers, include specific descriptions of the habitat and social organization of the two species.

Writing Lab CD-ROM

To stress the connection between ideas, review the Transition Word Bins in the Practical and Technical Writing lesson.

Student Work IN PROGRESS

Name: *Margaret Boehme*
Buena High School
Ventura, CA

Including Support

In her essay, Margaret had to evaluate the four factors identified in the prompt. In this passage about taxation, she used insert marks to make her examples and details more specific.

Opposition to the Tea Tax imposed by the British was largely in
—*even with the three-cent tax*—
principle. British tea was often the cheapest tea available, but many
colonists chose to purchase the more expensive (and illegal under the
Navigation Laws) Dutch-imported tea, for it was the notion of being
taxed that they disliked.

Drafting • 331

Revising: Comparing the Question With the Answer

1. Discuss the strategies used for Comparing the Question With the Answer on page 332.

2. Ask students to reread the essay question they chose, circle key words, and reread their drafts, making notes as needed, to ensure compliance with the test prompt.

Revising: Checking the Introduction Against the Conclusion

1. As a class, reread the introduction and conclusion of Margaret's Final Draft, pages 336–337. Have students compare how the question is answered in both introductory and concluding thesis statements.

2. Put a checklist on the board or on a transparency:
   - *clearly stated thesis/topic sentences*
   - *good supporting details and examples*
   - *effective use of transitional/linking expressions*
   - *varied word choice in sentence beginnings, length, and structure*

3. Encourage students to use these criteria for assessing their work.

Customize for
Less Advanced Students

Ultimately students must apply their assessment-writing processes within a time limit (for example, during a test given in class). To give students practice, you may wish to impose time deadlines for students' in-class revising steps.

15.3 Revising

Don't allow the pressure of a test situation to cause you to hand in your essay before you check it for form and content.

Revising Your Overall Structure
Get the Big Picture

Your essay will be judged mainly on how effectively and accurately you answer the test question. Take the time to check your answer against the prompt the test presented.

▶ **REVISION STRATEGY**
Comparing the Question With the Answer

Check to see that you have followed the instructions in the question. Use these tips to guide your evaluation:

- **Check the Numbers** If the question has asked you to provide a specific number of examples, be sure you address the correct number in your response.

- **Review the Tasks** Some questions provide a list of tasks. For example, you might need to summarize an event, critique the people involved, and then make a prediction. Be sure you have completed each segment of the assignment.

Revising Your Paragraphs
Confirm Coherence

Taking a single page from draft to final copy can pose a problem if you change your thesis while you write. To be sure you present one idea coherently without changing direction in the middle, compare your introduction with your conclusion.

▶ **REVISION STRATEGY**
Checking the Introduction Against the Conclusion

The first paragraph of your essay should state your focus or thesis in response to the essay question. Your conclusion should tie the threads of your essay together, explaining how each point you've made supports the thesis.

Evaluate
- Do the main points in the introduction and conclusion match?

Revise
- Revise either paragraph to make your draft more unified. If necessary, revise the body paragraphs or add transitional sentences to bring the essay together.

332 • Writing for Assessment

🌐 Learn More

For specific strategies for taking state and national standardized tests, see the Standardized Test Preparation Workshops at the end of each chapter.

⏱ TIME AND RESOURCE MANAGER

Resources
Technology: *Writing Lab* CD-ROM, Practical and Technical Writing

In-Depth Coverage	Accelerated Pace
• Cover pp. 332–333 in class. • Review the Introduction and Conclusion of the Final Draft (pp. 336–337). • Have students review their essays in class within a specified time limit.	• Have students review pp. 332–333 as homework. • Have students revise their essays in class within a specified time limit.

Revising Your Sentences

Review Paragraph Unity

In an essay test, it is important to show what you know about a subject. However, you need to link every paragraph to your thesis and connect every detail in your body paragraphs to the topic statement. To avoid turning in a paper with paragraphs that ramble, review your support of topic sentences.

▶ REVISION STRATEGY
Reviewing Your Topic Sentences

Use a pencil to place a small check next to the topic sentence of each paragraph. Review each paragraph to see that you have concisely supported the point the topic sentence presents. Insert revisions neatly, and cross out any deletions with a single line.

Revising Your Word Choice

Improve Diction

Examine sentences for word choice, evaluating whether you have used words that express exactly what you mean.

▶ REVISION STRATEGY
Evaluating Vague Words

As you reread your essay, check to see whether there are places in which your language is fuzzy, overly general, or wrong. Without making a mess of your paper, neatly add, substitute, or change the language to make the writing more precise. Look at this revision of a sentence from an essay response on the essay "Cats," by Anna Quindlen:

EXAMPLE:	In Anna Quindlen's *story* "Cats," the narrator describes *a woman's* relationship with her *son*.
ANALYSIS:	• *story* is incorrect; *essay* is more accurate • *neighbor* is more precise than *woman* • *young son* is more precise than *son*
REVISION:	In Anna Quindlen's *essay* "Cats," the narrator describes her *neighbor's* relationship with her *young* son.

**Writing Lab
CD-ROM**

To identify vague words in your essay, use the revision checker in the Practical and Technical Writing lesson.

▼ Critical Viewing
Besides *cat*, what specific words can you list to identify the subject of this photograph? **[Analyze]**

Revising • 333

Step-by-Step Teaching Guide

Revising: Topic Sentences and Vague Words

1. Ask students to make sure that all information in their main paragraphs relates to the topic sentence and that every supporting detail or example is specific and clear.

2. Remind them to check for unsupported generalizations.

3. Ask students to underline or highlight sentences that need revision.

4. Ask for volunteers to read aloud sentences or sections with which they are not satisfied. Encourage the class to provide constructive feedback.

5. Ask students to keep the question, "What else would the reader need to know?" in mind when they read or listen.

6. Remind students to skim their essays and circle vague words.

Customize for
Less Advanced Students

Students may benefit from the chance to practice a new skill. On the board, provide students with models containing vague words, and revise with student input. Or, have students in small groups precisely describe objects you have brought in.

Critical Viewing

Analyze Students may offer nouns such as *feline* or *tabby*, or adjectives such as *whiskered* or *furry*.

✓ **ONGOING ASSESSMENT: Monitor and Reinforce**

It is helpful to allow ample time in class for revision. If you observe that students are having difficulty revising their drafts, use one of the following options.

Option 1 Encourage students to read sections of their drafts to a partner to get peer feedback. Model for the class how to give effective feedback.	**Option 2** Hold individual conferences with students. Begin by asking the student to read aloud his or her writing. It is helpful for the writer to hear his or her work.

Editing: Focusing on Eliminating Errors

1. Review eliminating fragments and run-on sentences with students. Write the following phrase on the board.

   Waving wildly at the crowd.

2. Point out that although the fragment contains a verb, an adverb, and an object, it has no subject. Encourage students to edit their work and remove sentence fragments.

3. Ask students to read their own essays or switch papers and read a partner's essay. Have them check for fragments, run-on sentences, and spelling errors. Discuss errors with the writer.

Homophones

1. Remind students that homophone errors must be spotted by careful proofreading. They cannot be picked up by a computer spellchecking function.

2. Point out that the homophones cited are frequently confused in students' writing. Students should routinely check each of these words when proofreading.

3. Ask students to compile a list of other commonly misused homophones. Students can refer to this list and add to it as they review other pieces of writing.

15.4 Editing and Proofreading

Focusing on Eliminating Errors

In your effort to write an essay with accurate content and correct format, you may have introduced some errors in your writing. Review your essay to identify mistakes in these areas:

- **Sentence Construction** Be sure each sentence has a subject and verb and expresses a complete idea. Be on the lookout for subordinate clauses punctuated as if they were sentences.

- **Spelling** Check the spelling of names, places, and products. Neatly correct the errors you find.

- **Legibility** If you notice some words are not immediately readable, neatly write each word again. If time permits, you may want to recopy your paper so your grader can read your work.

Grammar in Your Writing
Homophones

Homophones are words that sound alike but have different meanings. When you write under a time restriction, you may accidentally substitute one word for another. Take the time to review your paper for such errors. Check your essay for the proper usage of the following commonly confused homophones.

its, it's *Its* is a possessive pronoun showing ownership. *It's* is a contraction standing for "it is" or "it has."

   It's a difficult problem; your agreement is part of its solution.

their, there, they're *Their* is a possessive adjective showing ownership. It always modifies a noun. *There* indicates a location. *They're* is a contraction for "they are."

   Their assignment was to locate the missing piece. They began by looking over there. As usual, they're determined to get it done.

affect, effect *Affect* is almost always a verb meaning "to influence." *Effect* is usually a noun meaning "result."

   Your decision will affect several people. We should consider the effect of the change before we implement it.

To learn more about homophones and other common usage errors, see Chapter 25.

⏰ TIME AND RESOURCE MANAGER

Resources
Print: *Scoring Rubrics on Transparency,* Ch. 15; *Writing Assessment and Portfolio Management; Formal Assessment,* Ch. 15
Technology: *Writing Lab* CD-ROM: Practical and Technical Writing

In-Depth Coverage	Accelerated Pace
• Review p. 334 in class, including Grammar in Your Writing. • Review the Rubric for Self Assessment (p. 335). • Have students edit and proofread their essays in class.	• Assign students pp. 334–337 for independent review. • Have students edit and proofread their essays. • Students present their final drafts.

15.5 Publishing and Presenting

Building Your Portfolio

After your test is graded, place a copy of your essay in your portfolio. Consider these options to make further use of it:

1. **Prepare for Future Exams** As you get ready to take midterms, finals, or standardized tests, use your essay test responses to remind you of the topics and issues you covered in class.
2. **Organize a Class Discussion** Compare your test responses to those of classmates by using your essays as the springboard for a class discussion.

Reflecting on Your Writing

Whether you use the writing prompt you chose to complete this lesson or your memory of a recent essay test situation, take a moment to reflect on your own test-taking experiences. Jot down your thoughts, and include your writing in your portfolio. Use these questions to get you started:

- What are your strengths and weaknesses as a test-taker?
- Which strategy presented in this chapter might help you complete your next essay test?

 Internet Tip

To see model essays scored with this rubric, go to **www.phschool.com**

Rubric for Self-Assessment

Use the following criteria to assess your writing.

	Score 4	Score 3	Score 2	Score 1
Audience and Purpose	Uses appropriately formal diction; clearly addresses writing prompt	Uses mostly formal diction; adequately addresses prompt	Uses some informal diction; addresses writing prompt	Uses inappropriately informal diction; does not address writing prompt
Organization	Presents a clear, consistent organizational strategy	Presents a clear organizational strategy with few inconsistencies	Presents an inconsistent organizational strategy	Shows a lack of organizational strategy
Elaboration	Provides several ideas to support the thesis; elaborates with several references to class notes; links all information to support thesis	Provides several ideas to support the thesis; elaborates with some reference to class notes; links most information to thesis	Provides some ideas to support the thesis; does not elaborate ideas; does not link some details to thesis	Provides no thesis; does not elaborate ideas
Use of Language	Uses excellent sentence and vocabulary variety; includes very few mechanical errors	Uses adequate sentence and vocabulary variety; includes few mechanical errors	Uses repetitive sentence structure and vocabulary; includes many mechanical errors	Demonstrates poor use of language; generates confusion; includes many mechanical errors

Final Draft

1. Point out to students that Margaret focuses on all factors contained in the test question. Note that she clearly states her thesis in the introduction, informing readers of exactly what to expect in the essay, "Relative Causes of the American Revolution." She then expresses her view by clearly ranking the factors in order of their importance.

2. Point out to students how using the topic sentence as the first sentence in each paragraph helps the reader move more easily through the essay. Note also how the writer uses linking expressions to help the essay flow smoothly.

3. Ask students to identify examples of transitional expressions (*most important, in addition, the second factor, for example, in fact, however*).

4. Point out the writer's effective word choice. Ask students to find examples of effective word choice (*foster, abhorrence, catalyst, antagonism, precedent*).

5. Ask students to analyze the supporting evidence in each paragraph of the student model. Which paragraph is the strongest, in their opinion? Why?

15.6 *Student Work*
IN PROGRESS

FINAL DRAFT

Relative Causes of the American Revolution

Margaret Boehme
Buena High School
Ventura, California

Question: Evaluate the relative importance of the following as factors prompting the American colonists to rebel in 1776:

- Parliamentary taxation
- Restriction of civil liberties
- The legacy of colonial religious and political ideas
- British military methods

    The original settlers landed in Jamestown in 1607, and those who followed them to North America in the next century and a half were a rebellious, largely discontented group of people—or else they would not have uprooted themselves from their homelands in search of better lives. So, although some historians would have it that the American Revolution was economic in origin, in fact, it was sparked by the legacy of colonial political and religious ideas. Other causes of the American Revolution—in high to low rank order—include restriction of civil liberties, British military methods, and in a small measure, the taxation imposed by Parliament.

    The most important factor leading to the Revolution was the colonists' political and religious heritage. They possessed an independent spirit. The colonies offered a new sense of independence, and Great Britain's practice of neglecting them allowed the colonists to foster their independence. The English colonists brought with them a rich political inheritance, and, combined with their own notions of self-government, they set up governing bodies for themselves. In addition, the American colonists had a strong religious legacy, with most states offering some measure of religious tolerance. The colonial leaders had recently been exposed to the writings

The writer uses the first paragraph to present an overview of the topic. Margaret states her thesis in the final sentence of this paragraph, acknowledging all the factors identified in the prompt.

Margaret addresses the most important factor first.

✎ STANDARDIZED TEST PREPARATION WORKSHOP

Standardized tests may require students to eliminate incorrect word choice, and revise for clarity. Provide students with practice in such revision.

Supply the best alternative to the underlined word in the sentence.

Presently one may shop for nearly anything on the Internet.

A Correct as is   **C** At the current time

B As of now   **D** Today

Students should recognize that **D** is the best answer. Choice A, "Presently," in this context, means "soon" or "by and by," and B and C are unnecessarily wordy.

of John Locke, who professed that man possessed certain natural rights, and among these was liberty. When Great Britain, under the rule of King George III, tried to restrict these liberties—political and religious—the colonists grew resentful.

The British took measures to limit the colonists' civil rights, and this was a second factor prompting the Revolution. For example, the Intolerable, or "repressive," Acts infringed on the colonists' liberty. The harsh Port Act, passed by Parliament in retaliation for the Boston Tea Party, may have hurt the colonists financially but actually benefited the colonists by serving to spark anger and bring about colonial unity. The colonists viewed the much misunderstood Quebec Act as a British attempt to take away the colonists' hard-won land.

The colonists' abhorrence of British military measures was the third catalyst of the Revolution. The colonists disliked the presence of Redcoats in Boston. The Boston Massacre of 1770 helped to fuel public sentiment and support. The colonists resisted the Quartering Act of 1765, which ordered that colonists must house British soldiers, as well as the writs of assistance, which allowed British officials to obtain almost unrestricted warrants to search the colonists' homes. The antagonism toward these writs set a precedent for the Fourth Amendment to the Constitution, which restricts search warrants.

While many would say that taxation was the greatest cause of the war, I believe that the opposition to the tea tax was largely in principle. In fact, British tea was often the cheapest tea available—even with the three-cent tax—but many colonists chose to purchase the more expensive (and illegal under the Navigation Laws) Dutch-imported tea, for it was the notion of being taxed that they resented. The colonists' resentment at being taxed by Parliament was summed up in their mantra, "No taxation without representation." When the Prime Minister argued that as loyal British subjects the colonists were in fact represented in Parliament, the colonists differentiated between "virtual" and "actual" and demanded actual representation.

Economics, however, played a relatively slight role in the colonists' antagonism. This factor was indeed intertwined with the colonists' resentment of British military measures and of British infringement of civil liberties. In fact, when we evaluate the evidence fairly, we must conclude that the Americans did not fight a Revolutionary War to escape paying taxes; they fought for the principle that "all men are created equal . . . and [have] certain inalienable rights; that among these are life, liberty, and the pursuit of happiness."

By citing the work of John Locke, Margaret elaborates on her idea with specific factual details.

The writer turns to consider the impact of a second factor—limitations on civil liberties. She uses the word "second" to create a smooth transition.

When discussing British military measures, Margaret provides several events by name and date to support her argument.

In discussing the belief that economics was a critical factor in the start of the war, Margaret explains why her essay argues against this idea.

A conclusion restates Margaret's thesis statement and ends with a familiar quotation paraphrased from the Declaration of Independence.

Teaching From the Final Draft

Point out to students that Margaret shaped her conclusion to place her most important point in the final sentence. She does not merely repeat her thesis, but uses a powerful quotation from the Declaration of Independence.

Customize for
Gifted and Talented Students

Ask students to write a song lyric about pre-examination anxiety and how to ease it by using some or all of the key information presented in this chapter. Students might set the words to familiar music and record a performance.

Customize for
Less Advanced Students

Ask students to choose a piece of writing from their portfolio and improve it by adding more supporting details to each paragraph.

Step-by-Step Teaching Guide

Open-Book Test

Teaching Resources: Writing Support Transparencies, 15-D; Writing Support Activity Book, 15-2

1. Review with students the criteria for grading an open-book test on page 338.

2. Emphasize that in an open-book test, students must distinguish between their own ideas and interpretations and those of others.

3. Display Transparency 15-D to show how a simple outline creates structure for the essay and also records reference points to cite.

4. Suggest that, before students begin drafting, they check their outlines against the test question to make sure of accurate and complete coverage.

5. Refer students to Chapter 15 resources as needed. See chart below for suggestions.

6. Give students an assignment from the Topic Bank on page 328, from the *Topic Bank for Heterogeneous Classes* in the Teaching Resources, or one of your own choosing.

7. Grade student responses and have students add them to their portfolios.

Critical Viewing

Contrast Students may note that an open-book essay test will place more emphasis on students' reasoning and organization skills since they need not memorize factual information and will usually have more time.

Connected Assignment
Open-Book Test

Writing for tests can create a lot of anxiety. Time is tight, and you usually have to rely on memory for fact gathering. In an open-book test, however, you have the comfort factor of referring to one of more of your textbooks and possibly class or study notes. You still need to organize your thoughts, plan your essay, and complete the writing process in a short time period. The writing process skills and strategies outlined below can help you excel on open-book tests.

When you write an open-book test essay, your writing will be graded according to your ability to address each of the following criteria:

- Locating facts, including specific names, dates, events, formulas, or theories

- Incorporating these items— not copying complete sentences or paragraphs from sources—in an essay that provides your own ideas, opinions, and interpretations

- Presenting your main idea in a thesis statement that addresses the prompt

- Organizing your writing using a clear and logical organization

- Producing a neat and error-free final draft

Prewriting Essay topics are usually determined by the test developer. You may, however, have the chance to choose from several options. Select the writing prompt you feel most comfortable addressing or the one that interests you most.

With time playing an important role, move directly from choosing a topic to planning your essay. Expand your fact-gathering phase to make use of the open-book format, but leave an adequate amount of time for drafting. As you outline your ideas, take further advantage of your books and notes to locate supporting details. Jot down page numbers for facts or text you may want to cite exactly.

Use an outline like the one shown on the next page to help you get started.

338 • Writing for Assessment

▲ **Critical Viewing**
How is answering an open-book test question different from writing an essay for a traditional in-class exam? [**Contrast**]

✔ ONGOING ASSESSMENT: Prerequisite Skills

Students may find the following resources from Chapter 15 particularly helpful in completing their open-book tests.

In the Textbk	Print Resources	Technology
Circle Key Words, p. 329 Providing Elaboration, p. 331	*Writing Support Transparencies*, 15-A–B *Writing Support Activity Book*, 15-1	*Writing Lab* CD-ROM, Practical and Technical Writing

I. Introduction – How environmental issues affect our community.

II. Trees and their impact on the air
   - use facts about air quality — pp. 192–194
   - cite quotation — p. 193, second paragraph

III. Rivers and their impact on a clean community
   - use facts about marine life — pp. 197–200
   - cite quotation — p. 198, third paragraph

IV. Summary and conclusion

Drafting Before you begin to draft, review the test question one more time. Keep the question in mind, and address it specifically as you write. Follow these tips:

1. Refer to the language of the question, and state your main ideas in a succinct opening paragraph.
2. Allow one body paragraph to elaborate on each key point. If time is limited, don't agonize over wording. Instead, move quickly through your outlined points.
3. You might close by raising a follow-up question that builds on your conclusion.

Revising and Editing Review each part of your essay for clarity. Check your introduction, key points, and conclusion to evaluate each for impact and clarity. Add details—checking with your open-book sources—to bolster any weak points. You may want to add transitional words, phrases, or sentences to make the organization of your writing more clear.

Once you are satisfied with the content of your writing, turn your attention to style and format. Verify that facts and quotations are cited accurately. If time allows, work on style issues such as sentence variety and word choice. Reread your draft, correcting any errors in grammar, usage, or mechanics.

Publishing and Presenting After your open-book test has been graded, add it to your portfolio. This will demonstrate your ability to do research, follow the writing process, and write a strong essay in a short time period.

Lesson Objectives

1. To analyze ideas as represented in various media
2. To investigate the source of a media presentation or production, such as who make it and why it was made
3. To write an evaluation of a film

Analyze Ideas Represented in Various Media

1. Have students work in groups to focus on one of the Spotlight elements.
2. Interested students might research additional information about Mount Rushmore and how Borglum and his assistants created the work.
3. Some student might research Borglum himself. He created many other sculptures, including some the Saint John the Divine Cathedral in New York.
4. Students interested in dance might research the Virginia Reel, which originated in England, where it was called Sir Roger de Coverly and is known as a contra dance.

Viewing and Representing

Activity Give students opportunity for class presentations of their film evaluations. Encourage them to use scenes from *1776* in their presentations.

Critical Viewing

Compare Students might note that the four presidents Borglum depicted governed the country during times of great challenges to the country's unity and well-being. Borglum himself intended the four to represent the nation's founding (Washington), philosophy (Jefferson), unity (Lincoln), and expansion (Roosevelt).

Spotlight on the Humanities

Analyze Ideas Represented in Various Media

Focus on Theater: *1776*

While the American Revolution may seem to you like the perfect subject for an essay test question, artists, dancers, and playwrights have used our nation's history as a springboard for their creative work. In fact, the composer Sherman Edward took nine years to research history and create the Broadway musical *1776.* The show premiered on Broadway in 1969 and won three Tony awards, including Best Musical. Set in Philadelphia, the musical revolves around the lives of Thomas Jefferson and the other statesmen who created the Declaration of Independence.

▲ **Critical Viewing** What might the four presidents whose faces are memorialized on Mount Rushmore have in common? **[Compare]**

Art Connection In addition to providing inspiration for a musical, Thomas Jefferson's image also appears on Mount Rushmore as one of the four faces on one of the greatest mountain sculptures in the world. At a cost of one million dollars and a timeline that spanned fourteen years, sculptor Gutzon Borglum created the sculpture of four presidents on Mount Rushmore in the Black Hills of South Dakota. Beginning in 1927, Borglum sculpted the faces of Presidents George Washington, Thomas Jefferson, Theodore Roosevelt, and Abraham Lincoln. Each face measures sixty feet in height.

Dance Connection Another piece of history that survives to this day is the Virginia Reel—one of the most popular dances in colonial America. Modern filmmakers often use the Virginia Reel in films portraying colonial America. The dance begins with two lines of couples facing each other. As lively music plays, the couple at one end of the line joins hands and slip-slides down the aisle created by the other dancers.

Assessment Writing Activity: Film Evaluation

Watch the film version of *1776* to see how its producers brought history to life. Jot down the major characters and events the film portrays. In an essay, explain whether you would recommend the film to students of American history.

Customize for
ESL Students

Encourage ESL students to listen to the recordings of *1776* at their own pace. As they listen, students should list unfamiliar words, phrases, and concepts for further investigation.

Media and Technology Skills

Using Technology to Respond to a Variety of Test Formats

Activity: Taking Computerized Tests

Computerized tests present many of the same challenges as written tests, but they offer you the advantages of working electronically. Your ability to quickly and easily manipulate text will save you valuable time. Master the electronic tools, and you'll be one step ahead of the pack at test time.

Learn About It As with a traditionally printed test, a critical task for success with a computerized test is to know the rules and understand the directions. Find out what the test covers and, if possible, the types of questions it will contain. For example, you may be asked to write an essay, choose from multiple-choice lists, provide short answers, or complete mathematical computations. Learn about the test-taking program by reading the materials provided and asking questions in advance. If possible, take a trial computerized test to familiarize yourself with the program. For example, practice may show you how to use tab keys to move quickly among answer options. Alternatively, you may learn how to use built-in tools to save time and finalize text.

Practice It The features of test programs will vary; however, you can prepare by studying several test formats. You may be able to locate these programs at school, on CD-ROMs, or at your motor vehicle department's Web site, for example. Locate a few computerized test programs, and explore how each works. For each, concentrate on how the program functions and disregard content. Use a form like this one to note what you learn.

Test Program: _____	
What will you see on the screen?	_____ _____
Can you work at your own pace?	_____ _____
Can you return to the previous questions? How is this done?	_____ _____ _____
How do you review and/or revise answers?	_____ _____

Questions to Ask

- What will you see on the screen? How will questions be presented?
- Can you get larger type or audio questions?
- Can you work at your own pace, or will the test program run on preset timing?
- Can you return to previous questions? How is this done?
- How do you review and/or revise answers?

Tips for Success

- Use built-in tools such as spell and grammar check, word count, and the thesaurus.
- Check answers manually after running built-in checks—look for misused words and other errors that built-in checkers may miss.

▶ **Lesson Objectives**
1. To use technology to respond to test formats
2. To compile information from primary and secondary sources in systematic ways using available technology

Step-by-Step Teaching Guide

Using Technology to Respond to a Variety of Test Formats

Teaching Resources: Writing Support Transparencies 15-E; Writing Support Activity Book, 15-3

1. Focus on the Tips for Success in the sidebar box and emphasize that students must check their work after running a built-in spell check. The program will not recognize that a test-taker has used *pare* instead of *pair* for example, since both words are legitimate spellings.

2. Display Transparency 15-E to show students how to record what they learn about computerized tests. Distribute copies of the blank organizer (15-3) for their own use.

3. If your school has test-taking software available for student practice, arrange for tutorial sessions in the computer lab for the class or groups of students.

Step-by-Step Teaching Guide

Analyzing Mechanical Errors

Teaching Resources: Standardized Test Preparation Workbook, pp. 29–30

1. Go over the two sample test items in class and discuss the answers and explanations.

2. Point out to students that they have already had experience in proofreading their own writing. Most standardized tests offer the additional help of underscoring parts of sentences that may contain errors.

3. Emphasize that some items on a test of this type will not contain errors. Sometimes identifying the "no error" items can be confusing. Tell students to check their "no error" answers carefully.

4. Assign the practice items and have students grade their own work as you give them the answers.

Standardized Test Preparation Workshop

Analyzing Mechanical Errors

When editing your own writing, you pay close attention to the grammar, usage, and mechanics you have used, correcting errors that you have introduced. Standardized tests frequently measure your ability to recognize mechanical errors. In multiple-choice items like the ones you'll see in this workshop, tests ask you to evaluate specific words, phrases, or sentences for errors. The following are some methods that will help you address these types of questions:

- Look closely at the context of an underlined passage to help you decide whether the passage contains a mistake.

- Be aware that some items will not contain mistakes.

The following sample test items will give you practice with errors in writing.

Test Tip

If you think you've spotted a misspelled word, copy the word on a piece of paper. Then, jot down the spelling you think is correct. Compare the two, and make your best choice.

Sample Test Items	Answers and Explanations

Directions: Read the following passages, and decide which type of error, if any, appears in the underlined sections. Choose the letter for your answer.
 	
Angela had a take-home final exam for Social Studies. She <u>prepared by studying researching</u> (1) and reading about her topic.
 	
1   A   Spelling error
     B   Capitalization error
     C   Punctuation error
     D   No error
	The correct answer is *C*. A comma is needed between *studying* and *researching* and between *researching* and *and* in order to separate items in a series.

After participating in sports throughout high school, Joseph was eager to <u>persue a major</u> (2) <u>in sports medicine in college.</u>
 	
2   F   Spelling error
     G   Capitalization error
     H   Punctuation error
     J   No error
	The correct answer is *F*. *Pursue* is spelled incorrectly in the passage.

✏ TEST-TAKING TIP

Go over the following points with students.

- There will be one error only in each underlined or numbered passage on a test of this type.
- Students should look for punctuation errors of all types, not just of internal but of end punctuation as well.
- Students should carefully examine the spelling of any word that is broken at the end of a line

since such errors in spelling are easier to overlook.

- If students anticipate a test on their ability to find mechanical errors, they should review the rules of capitalization.
- Capitalization errors can include words that are capitalized but shouldn't be, as well as words that should be but aren't.

Practice 1 **Directions:** Read the passage, and decide which type of error, if any, appears in each underlined section. Mark the letter for your answer.

Chemistry was the <u>subject that intimadat-</u> <u>ed Anna the most.</u> She was concerned that

$\underset{(1)}{}$ $\underset{(2)}{}$

a poor grade in chemistry would jeopardize

her chances of <u>being in the national honor</u> <u>(3)</u>

society. Therefore, Anna devoted extra time

to her chemistry homework. <u>At the end of</u> <u>(4)</u>

<u>the school year,</u> Anna won an award for

the most outstanding work in Chemistry

for her grade. She becomes <u>a steller exam-</u> <u>(5)</u>

<u>ple; hard work has its rewards.</u>

1 **A** Spelling error
   B Capitalization error
   C Punctuation error
   D No error

2 **F** Spelling error
   G Capitalization error
   H Punctuation error
   J No error

3 **A** Spelling error
   B Capitalization error
   C Punctuation error
   D No error

4 **F** Spelling error
   G Capitalization error
   H Punctuation error
   J No error

5 **A** Spelling error
   B Capitalization error
   C Punctuation error
   D No error

As we publish the literary magazine at

<u>longford high school,</u> we need to address <u>(6)</u>

a few issues. First, to meet our publishing

deadline, <u>we need more student editors, for</u> <u>(7)</u>

<u>the magazine.</u> Current editors can inform

interested students about the require-

ments and <u>responsabilities of being on our</u> <u>(8)</u>

<u>literary magazine</u> team. Second, we need to

invite student submissions. Finally, we

will want to consider <u>collecting more</u> <u>(9)</u>

advertisements instead of sponsoring

fund-raising projects this year. Any stu-

dents who are unable to attend the next

meeting should see Mrs. Harrington in

<u>the main office to find out more details.</u> <u>(10)</u>

6 **A** Spelling error
   B Capitalization error
   C Punctuation error
   D No error

7 **F** Spelling error
   G Capitalization error
   H Punctuation error
   J No error

8 **A** Spelling error
   B Capitalization error
   C Punctuation error
   D No error

9 **F** Spelling error
   G Capitalization error
   H Punctuation error
   J No error

10 **A** Spelling error
    B Capitalization error
    C Punctuation error
    D No error

Answer Key
1. D
2. F
3. B
4. G
5. A
6. B
7. H
8. A
9. J
10. D

Customize for
Less Advanced Students

If students missed items 2, 5, and 8, be sure they know which words were misspelled. Ask for the correct spellings of *intimidated, stellar,* and *responsibilities.*

Customize for
AP Students

Even though students may feel confident in their ability to master a test on mechanical errors, advise them not to go through the items too quickly and to review their answers if there is time.

Time and Resource Manager

In-Depth Lesson Plan

	LESSON FOCUS	PRINT AND MEDIA RESOURCES
DAY 1	**Introduction; Business Letter** Students are introduced to workplace writing. They analyze and then write a business letter. (pp. 344–347)	*Writers at Work* **Videotape**, Practical and Technical Writing **Teaching Resources:** *Writing Support Transparencies,* 16-A
DAY 2	**Memo** Students analyze a model and write a business memo. (pp. 348–349)	**Teaching Resources:** *Writing Support Transparencies,* 16-B
DAY 3	**Résumé** Students analyze a model and write a résumé. (pp. 350–351)	**Teaching Resources:** *Writing Support Transparencies,* 16-C
DAY 4	**Forms and Applications** Students review and complete forms and applications. (pp. 352–354)	**Teaching Resources:** *Writing Support Transparencies,* 16-D–E; *Writing Support Activity Book,* 16-1–2; *Writing Assessment and Portfolio Management; Formal Assessment,* Ch. 16

Accelerated Lesson Plan

	LESSON FOCUS	PRINT AND MEDIA RESOURCES
DAY 1	**Business Letter; Memo** Students review models in class and then draft a business letter and a memo as homework. (pp. 344–349)	*Writing Lab* **CD-ROM**, Practical and Technical Writing **Teaching Resources:** *Writing Support Transparencies,* 16-A–B
DAY 2	**Résumé; Forms and Applications** Students review models in class and then draft a resume and complete an application as homework. (pp. 350–354)	**Teaching Resources:** *Writing Support Transparencies,* 16-C–E; *Writing Support Activity Book,* 16-2; *Writing Assessment and Portfolio Management; Formal Assessment,* Ch. 16

Options for Adapting Lesson Plans

HOMEWORK

Have students complete any stage of the lesson for homework.

FEATURES

Extend coverage with Connected Assignment (p. 355), Spotlight on the Humanities (p. 356), Media and Technology Skills (p. 357), and the Standardized Test Preparation Workshop (p. 358).

TECHNOLOGY

Students can complete any stage of the lesson on computer. Have them print out their completed work.

INTEGRATED SKILLS COVERAGE

Integrating Grammar Skills
Grammar, Spelling, Punctuation in Résumés, ATE p. 351
Abbreviations, ATE p. 353
Helping Verbs, ATE p. 359

Viewing and Representing
Critical Viewing, SE pp. 344, 354, 355, 356
Examining How Meanings Are Communicated Through Design, SE p. 356
Using Technology for Revising and Editing, SE p. 357

Vocabulary Skills
ATE pp. 346, 349, 350, 353

Workplace Skills
ATE pp. 347, 353

Research Skills
ATE p. 356

Real-World Connection
ATE pp. 348, 353

ASSESSMENT SUPPORT

Standardized Test Preparation Workshop SE p. 358; ATE pp. 349, 354

Standardized Test Preparation Workbook, pp. 31–32

Scoring Rubrics on Transparency, Ch. 16

Formal Assessment, Ch. 16

Writing Assessment and Portfolio Management

MEETING INDIVIDUAL NEEDS

Less Advanced Students ATE p. 357. See also Ongoing Assessments ATE pp. 347, 351.

ESL Students ATE p. 349, 353

Gifted and Talented Students ATE p. 351

BLOCK SCHEDULING

Pacing Suggestions
For 90-minute Blocks
- Follow the Accelerated Lesson Plan and cover the business letter and memo in one class period, the résumé and forms and applications in a second class period.
- Allow class time for students to refine one form of workplace writing for inclusion in their portfolios.

Resources for Varying Instruction
- *Writing Lab* **CD-ROM** If your students have access to hardware, a 90-minute block provides an ideal opportunity for students to work on computer.
- *Writers at Work* **Videotape** Show the Practical and Technical Writing segment in class.

Professional Development Support
- *How to Manage Instruction in the Block* This Teaching Resource provides management and activity suggestions.

MEDIA AND TECHNOLOGY

For the Student
- *Writing Lab* **CD-ROM**, Practical and Technical Writing

For the Teacher
- *Writers at Work* **Videotape**, Practical and Technical Writing
- *Resource Pro* **CD-ROM**

WRITING AND GRAMMAR WEB SITE

The Interactive Writing and Grammar Web Site provides a wide array of support for students, teachers, and parents. Writing support includes:
- Interactive revision checkers
- Scoring rubrics with complete models

www.phschool.com

Lesson Objectives

1. To write in various forms with particular emphasis on workplace writing such as a business letter, a memo, and a résumé

2. To write in a voice and style appropriate to audience and purpose

3. To use prewriting strategies to generate ideas, develop voice, and plan

4. To organize ideas in writing to ensure coherence, logical progression, and support for ideas

5. To develop and revise drafts in terms of structure, paragraphs, sentences, and word choice

6. To edit and proofread to ensure standard English usage and grammar

7. To evaluate writing for both mechanics and content

8. To refine selected work for publication

Critical Viewing

Analyze Students may say that technology allows for a rapid exchange of information, and that lap-tops enable people to work at almost any place or time.

▲ **Critical Viewing**
How can technology such as a laptop computer improve communication in the workplace? **[Analyze]**

Chapter 16 Workplace Writing

Workplace Writing in Everyday Life

When you take a phone message while baby-sitting or record the minutes of a debate club meeting, you're using workplace writing skills. *Workplace writing* is the engine that drives smooth communication between team members, co-workers, roommates, and even governments. Effective workplace writing can support successful job hunting, ensure attendance at important events, bring a product defect to a manufacturer's attention, or even address emergencies.

⏱ TIME AND RESOURCE MANAGER

Resources
Print: *Writing Support Transparencies*, 16-A
Technology: *Writers at Work* Videotape, Practical and Technical Writing; *Writing Lab* CD-ROM, Practical and Technical Writing

In-Depth Coverage	Accelerated Pace
• Discuss the picture on p. 344. • Have students read pp. 344–345 and identify types of workplace writing. • Read and identify elements of the business letter on p. 346. • Review the Topic Bank and make sure each student has selected a topic.	• Have students read pp. 344–347 on their own. • Ask them to name the elements of a business letter. • Discuss topics of a business letter and have students select a topic.

What Is Workplace Writing?

Workplace writing is probably the format you'll use most after you finish school. It is used in offices, factories, and by workers on the road. Workplace writing includes a variety of formats that share common features. In general, workplace writing is fact-based writing that communicates specific information to readers in a structured format. Effective workplace writing

- communicates information concisely to make the best use of both the writer's and the reader's time.
- includes a level of detail that provides necessary information and anticipates potential questions.
- reflects the writer's care if it is error-free and neatly presented.

Types of Workplace Writing

From the form you fill out to sign up for computer time at school to a memo to Cabinet members from the President of the United States, workplace writing is something we all do. There are many types of business communication—both electronic and print—and each type addresses a specific purpose:

- **Business letters** are written to formally address and communicate issues of concern to both writers and readers.
- **Memos** are prepared to share information within a company, club, organization, or other group.
- **Résumés** are created by job-seekers to summarize job, educational, and life experiences for potential employers.
- **Forms and applications** are completed to provide specific, factual information necessary for an identified purpose, such as opening a bank account or joining a gym.

PREVIEW

Chapter Contents

In the following pages, you'll see several examples of real-life workplace writing—a letter of complaint about a defective product, a memo welcoming a new employee, the résumé of a student seeking summer employment, an application for a learner's permit, and the forms typically used to cover faxes and transmit phone messages. As you'll see, using the stages of the writing process can make these formal pieces of writing more effective.

Writers in ACTION

Whether or not you have read Lucy Maud Montgomery's popular **Anne of Green Gables** books, you'll probably enjoy her writing advice. Keep it in mind, particularly when writing for the workplace, where people often feel pressed for time:

"The point of good writing is knowing when to stop."

Take her words to heart when you write in a work environment. Strive to limit business writing to one page.

Workplace Writing • 345

ONGOING ASSESSMENT: Diagnose

Use one of the following options to diagnose students' current level of proficiency in workplace writing.

Option 1 Have students select the strongest example of their workplace writing from last year. Review their selections to determine which students will need extra support in the various types of workplace writing.

Option 2 Ask students to write brief definitions that highlight the differences among business letters, memos, and résumés. Students who have difficulty with this exercise will need extra support in workplace writing.

PREPARE and ENGAGE

Interest GRABBER Tell students to imagine that their boss just called and that another family member took the call. Ask students what questions they could ask about the call. (Who called? At what time? Was there a message?) Lead students to conclude that a good way to take a message for someone else is to think about what the recipient of the message would want to know.

Activate Prior Knowledge

Give students two minutes to list all the kinds of writing they do outside the classroom. Then, ask volunteers to share items from their lists. Write them on the board, creating a classroom compilation. Add to it the types of writing studied in this chapter.

More About the Writer

Lucy Maud Montgomery was a Canadian author who wrote stories and poems. She is best known for *Anne of Green Gables*, a novel about an adolescent girl who is adopted by a Canadian family. Anne was such a popular character that Montgomery wrote seven more books in the series.

TEACH

Step-by-Step Teaching Guide

Types of Workplace Writing

1. Explain to students that good communication skills are vital for success in almost every line of work.

2. Point out that written communication is often the only way ideas or information are circulated in business. If the writing is not clear and accurate, people will question the validity of the information and the value of the ideas, often just dismissing them because of the carelessness of the writing.

3. Tell students that the four types of workplace writing covered in this chapter are among the most important and frequently used types.

1. Tell students that workplace writing has a specific audience and purpose, and these must be kept in mind in business writing.

2. Explain that it is wise to always use a formal writing style.

3. Display the transparency (16-A) and tell students that the format is the same in all formal letters. (Even offers for credit cards and magazine subscriptions follow this format.)

4. Have students identify each part of the letter. Which elements are similar to other types of writing they've done and which are different?

5. Point out that in a formal letter, a colon is used in the salutation. In a letter to a friend, a comma is appropriate.

6. Ask students to describe the language used by Jeannette in this letter. Lead them to conclude that the language she uses is polite, yet strong and forceful.

Integrating Vocabulary Skills

Tell students that the word *salutation* comes from the Latin word *salutare*, which means "greet." *Salutare* comes in turn from *salus*, which means "good health." It was common to wish someone good health when greeting him or her. *Salutare* is also the origin of *salute*, which may be most familiar as a formal military greeting, but can also mean "meet with kind words."

16.1

Business Letter

What Is a Business Letter?

Business letters can serve a number of purposes. One letter might request an interview, another might express dissatisfaction with a product, a third might pledge support for an idea. Whatever the subject, an effective business letter

- includes six parts: the heading, the inside address, the salutation or greeting, the body, the closing, and the signature.

- follows one of several acceptable formats—in *block format*, each part of the letter begins at the left margin; in *modified block format*, the heading, the closing, and the signature are indented to the center of the page.

- uses formal language to communicate courteously, regardless of the letter's content.

> A business letter includes two addresses. The **heading** indicates where the letter originates and the date it was written. The **inside address** shows where the letter will be sent.

Model Business Letter

In this letter, the writer used a modified block format to outline the problems she encountered with an audio-cassette.

> A **salutation** allows for a polite greeting and is punctuated by a colon.

> The **body** of the letter identifies the writer's purpose. In this case, the writer politely expresses a complaint.

> Here the writer specifies the actions she wants the company to take in response to her complaint.

> The **closing** *Sincerely* is common, but *Respectfully yours* or *Yours truly* are also acceptable. To end the letter, the writer includes a **signature** and types her name.

200 Oak Street, Apt. G4
Cedar Rapids, IA 52402

March 9th, 20- -

Grant McLaughlin, Manager
Customer Service Department
Audioscope Recordings
4300 Corporate Drive
Herndon, VA 22071

Dear Mr. McLaughlin:

I purchased a tape entitled *The Life and Times of Sherlock Holmes* just two weeks ago at my local bookstore. To my disappointment, the cassette would not play. On closer examination, I noticed that the cassette contained no actual tape—the spools were empty!

I have written to you directly for two reasons. First, the bookstore where I purchased this tape no longer has copies of the audiocassette and, therefore, cannot replace my purchase. Second, I wish to communicate my surprise at this carelessness. Your products always seem produced and packaged with great care. How could a cassette leave your factory without any tape on it?

Please replace the enclosed audiocassette with a functioning copy of *The Life and Times of Sherlock Holmes*. You may send it to me at the address listed above.

Thank you in advance for your prompt attention to this matter.

Sincerely,

Jeannette DuPres

Jeannette DuPres

346 • Workplace Writing

TOPIC BANK

To write a business letter that communicates effectively, choose an issue or problem that matters to you. If you have trouble coming up with a topic, consider these possibilities:

1. **Letter to a Package Delivery Company** People send packages all around the world for many different reasons. What happens when one gets lost? Write a letter of complaint about the loss of an important package.

2. **Letter to a Local Newspaper** The local newspaper is sponsoring a photography contest for high-school students. Write a cover letter to accompany your contest submission.

Prewriting Make every attempt to identify the name and position of the person who can best respond to your letter. Use a phone book or other resource to identify that person and obtain a correct address. Then, jot down the information you'll need to share with the person you've identified. For example, gather the names, dates, or product numbers you'll need to explain your situation clearly.

Drafting Before you write, list the main points that you wish to address. List your central reason for writing, any background or surrounding events, and any response or action you may be seeking. Prioritize your list, and then draft your letter. For ease of reading, allow about one paragraph for each main point.

Revising Review your letter to evaluate whether the format, situation, and purpose are clear. Check that diction or word choice is appropriately respectful. Consider revising words to better convey your feelings. For example, words like *clearly* and *obviously* communicate a different message from *perhaps* and *maybe*.

Editing and Proofreading Once you are satisfied with the content of your letter, focus on the format. Be sure you've used proper punctuation in the salutation and the closing. Confirm the placement of both addresses. Finally, check the spelling of every word—especially names. Nothing undercuts a letter's purpose more than misspelling the recipient's name.

Publishing and Presenting Fold your letter neatly, and enclose it in a properly addressed business envelope. Include your return address and postage before mailing.

Business Letter • 347

Step-by-Step Teaching Guide

Using the Topic Bank

1. Have students brainstorm for ideas about the sort of people to whom they might write business letters. Suggest that they think about local service providers, magazines, stores, or other businesses with which they interact.

2. Discuss the reasons people write business letters (to complain, to ask questions, to get information, to express opinions, and, within the corporate world, to deliver information or tell others what needs to be done).

3. Have students pick one business from the list in step 1 and combine it with one purpose for writing from the list in step 2 for their business letter.

Step-by-Step Teaching Guide

The Writing Process

1. Remind students that each step of the writing process is important with any successful writing.

2. Explain ways to find out whom to address. (For example: call the company and ask to whom you should write, ask your librarian, check the Internet, look on the masthead of magazines or newspapers.)

3. Remind students to keep the language in a business letter polite, formal, and impersonal (that is, never let a business letter be a personal attack).

Integrating Workplace Skills

Demonstrate how to fold a business letter. Write the following instructions on the board.

1. *Fold the bottom third upward.*

2. *Fold the top third downward.*

3. *Hold the letter in this position to insert it into the envelope.*

4. *When the recipient opens and unfolds the letter, it is face up and top to bottom.*

✓ **ONGOING ASSESSMENT: Monitor and Reinforce**

If you observe that some students are having difficulty completing any of the writing assignments in this chapter, try one of the following options.

Option 1 Suggest that students imitate the model fairly closely, changing only the name of the recipient, the name of the company, and perhaps one other item in the piece.	**Option 2** Suggest that students think of any subject or cause that is important to them and freewrite about it. Then have them use the freewriting to help them create a letter to an editor.

Teaching Resources: Writing Support Transparencies, 16-B

1. Ask students to tell about any memos they have received or written. If you have any in-school memos, share those in class.

2. Tell students that one difference between a business letter and a memo is that the memo writer usually knows or has something in common with the audience.

3. Point out that, though the *structure* of a memo is informal (i.e., there is no formal address, salutation, or closing), the language is still generally formal.

4. Have students examine the sample memo and identify parallels to the business letter. For example, the company name identifies the "address," and the "TO" parallels the addressee. (Students should note that *Re* has no clear parallel in the business letter, except that the entire letter conveys what the message is about.)

5. Explain that memos can cover a wide range of business topics, from new employees to rule changes to general information to good news. Audiences will vary, too, from instructions for one person to an announcement for an entire company.

6. Remind students that a memo is not private. While the writer might have a specific audience in mind, many other readers may see the memo as well. Tell students to keep this in mind as they choose the language and content covered in their memos.

Real-World Connection

Point out the company logo on the model memo. Tell students that businesses often have a logo at the top of all business stationery. Ask where else students might see a company logo (advertisements, caps, shirts, pencils, coffee mugs).

16.2 Memo

What Is a Memo?

A memo is a brief, informally structured communication between parties who share an interest in a common issue. It may travel between people who work side by side in an office, or it may reach a more widespread audience, connecting members of a corporate community in several states. An effective memo

- is written in block format, with each new element beginning at the left margin.
- clearly states the sender, audience, date, and topic.
- communicates information briefly, keeping the total memo length under one page whenever possible.
- outlines any actions that the recipient should take.

Model Memo

In this memo, the manager of a key department introduces a new staff member to the rest of the company.

> Capital letters draw readers' attention to the memo topic. The word re: is Latin for "about" and is commonly used in memos.

> The body of the memo elaborates on the topic line, providing information to introduce the new employee.

> The writer assumes her audience shares certain basic knowledge about the subject. For example, she does not elaborate on the function of market research.

> Finally, the memo suggests a course of action: Readers should welcome Perrin.

> The writer includes her title to emphasize her authority in sending the memo.

Memo

TO: All
FROM: Dana Pollero
Vice President, Market Research
DATE: August 26, 20--
RE: WELCOME TO PERRIN SAMUELS

Firefly Multimedia

Please join the Market Research Department in welcoming Perrin Samuels, who is joining our department as Senior Research Consultant, reporting to me.

Perrin has ten years of experience in market research and joins us from Music Markets, a well-known specialty publisher. In her position there as Manager of Market Research, she was involved with secondary research and sales support. She designed and maintained a dozen fact books on the music recording and publication industries for use by fourteen different sales teams.

Prior to Music Markets, Perrin worked for more than six years conducting research for advertisers, publishers, and producers of music-related products and services. She has experience with different information-gathering methods, including questionnaires and focus testing, and has successfully managed several projects. Perrin has directed a wide variety of research projects from start-up to final outcome. She has experience with new-product development, advertising campaigns, and sales analysis.

Perrin holds Bachelor degrees in Business Administration and in Music History from Adelphi University and a Master of Business Administration from the University of Bridgeport.

Please join the Market Research Department in welcoming Perrin to Firefly Multimedia. She will be in office 2K33, opposite Andy Graziano.

348 • Workplace Writing

⏱ TIME AND RESOURCE MANAGER

Resources
Print: *Writing Support Transparencies*, 16-B
Technology: *Writing Lab* CD-ROM, Practical and Technical Writing

In-Depth Coverage	Accelerated Pace
• Read pp. 348–349 and discuss the memo. • Ask students to compare and contrast a memo and a business letter. • Make sure students have selected appropriate topics for writing memos.	• Have students read pp. 348–349. • Ask them to submit their memo topics. • Review using the steps of the writing process in memo writing.

TOPIC BANK

To write a memo that gets the message across quickly and efficiently, choose information that the recipient needs to know. If you're having trouble coming up with your own topic, consider these possibilities:

1. **Memo About a School Dance** Students in many schools are taking charge of planning dances. Write a memo to your classmates or to a faculty advisor in which you outline an idea for a dance at your school.

2. **Memo to Members of a Club** When organized groups, such as the yearbook staff or the computer club, welcome new members, they often provide basic information about schedules, policies, and financial matters. Write a memo to a new club member in which you briefly explain the function of a club that you enjoy.

Prewriting Define your topic narrowly to keep your memo brief. To avoid unnecessary words, remember that the information you and your audience already share does not need to be included. For example, in a memo to teachers about a school dance, you probably won't need to explain the age of students you expect will attend.

Drafting Organize your memo in order of priority, placing the most important information first. Add one or two body paragraphs explaining the issue. Consider using bulleted or numbered lists for your readers' ease.

Revising Compare the language of your memo against your intended audience. For example, if you are enlisting the help of a group, you'll probably want to use *we* more than *I*. In addition, make sure that your language is appropriately formal.

Editing and Proofreading Check content by verifying the accuracy of facts. Then, review mechanics by confirming that sentences are correctly punctuated. Finally, look at the layout and be sure the spacing between paragraphs is consistent.

Publishing and Presenting Photocopy your memo, and deliver it in person, use the e-mail function on your computer to send the memo to interested parties, or deposit it in school or home mailboxes.

Memo • 349

Choosing a Topic

1. Ask students to describe their interests outside the classroom, such as school or community groups, hobbies, or part-time jobs. To help them think about these associations as they select a topic, you might ask the following questions:

   What information is circulated in the group or organization?

   Who receives these memos?

   Have you ever wished more information were offered?

2. Suggest that students think of something one of these groups might want to announce (a special program, for instance), and write this announcement in the form of a memo. (Students' language should be as specific as possible, such as *TO: All Swim Team Members; TO: Fellow Stamp Collectors*, etc.)

3. Once students have selected a memo topic, ask them the following questions:

   Who is your audience?

   What is your purpose?

   How does this affect the language of the memo?

4. Discuss how students will apply the steps of the writing process as they write their memos.

Customize
for ESL Students

Pair students with more fluent English speakers and let them practice writing and reading memos. They might write memos to announce an upcoming event in their neighborhood or to notify relatives of an accomplishment (such as learning how to write memos or improving skills in English). Writing a bilingual memo is also an option.

Integrating Vocabulary Skills

The word *memo* is a shortened form of the word *memorandum*, the Latin word meaning, "to be remembered." Ask students how the definition applies to the way we use the word today.

STANDARDIZED TEST PREPARATION WORKSHOP

Punctuation Standardized tests may require students to know how to punctuate sentences correctly. Use the following example to demonstrate.

"We need to hire someone who writes well, Mr. Sandoz said emphatically. We don't want another employee who doesn't know how to generate good letters and memos."

Which is the correct way to punctuate the underlined part of this sentence?

A . . . writes wel . Mr. Sandoz said emphatically. We don't . . .

B . . . writes wel ," Mr. Sandoz said emphatically. "We don't . . .

C . . . writes well, Mr. Sandoz said emphatically." We don't . . .

D Correct as is

Students should recognize that **B** is punctuated correctly.

Writing a Résumé

Teaching Resources: Writing Support Transparencies, 16-C

1. Ask students if they have ever read or written a résumé or shared in the experience of a friend or relative writing one.

2. Make the connection to the real world by either showing or telling about your own experiences writing or using a résumé.

3. To emphasize the importance of carefully crafting a résumé, bring in either sample books (the library will have many) or a list of titles that shows how many books cover this topic.

4. Review the elements of the model résumé. Encourage students to think about the types of things, other than work experience, that might tell employers what kind of employees they would be (grade point average, scholastic honors, science fairs, outside activities, charity work, tutoring, establishing or running clubs or programs).

5. Point out that this résumé avoids fancy type, italics, and underlining. Today, employers often use scanners to load résumés into computers for sorting, so having a clean, "scannable" résumé is vital.

6. Point out that the writer doesn't write "I worked" but rather "worked." This is standard for résumé writing.

Integrating Vocabulary Skills

Tell students that the word *résumé* comes from the French word *resumer*, meaning "to sum up." Ask them how the original definition applies to the way we use the word *résumé* today.

16.3 Résumé

What Is a Résumé?

One workplace writing form that you will probably use and update frequently as you accumulate skills and experience is the résumé. This document, a written summary of your qualifications, is a key part of most career or job searches. An effective résumé

- includes the writer's name, address, and telephone number.
- briefly presents the writer's educational background, work experience, and other qualifying life experiences.
- organizes information logically and in labeled sections.
- uses visual organization to direct a reader's attention.

> A résumé is almost always typed or printed from a computer or word processor.

Model Résumé

With limited formal work experience, high-school student Rebecca Irizarry expanded her résumé to include life skills and experiences.

REBECCA IRIZARRY
200 Magnolia Street
Garland, TX 75046
(555) 555-1234
E-mail: RI@address.com

WORK EXPERIENCE
Summer 2001: Clerical Assistant   BBS Video Productions
Garland, TX
- Handled general office work: typed manuscripts; entered information into database; checked CD-ROMs for correct content; created and maintained manuscript-tracking charts; prepared packages for large mailings; and conducted Internet searches on behalf of supervisors

Summer 2000: Soccer Trainer   Garland Recreation Department
Garland, TX
- Trained six-to eight-year-olds in soccer techniques and rules; refereed games

August 1999–Present: Staffer   Garland Art Publicity Department
Garland, TX
- Worked on publicity for local cultural organization: put up posters conducted ticket sales; addressed telephone inquiries

SKILLS
- Word processing (Microsoft Word '97), including making charts and graphs; typing; filing; database entry on FileMaker Pro
- Operate latest photocopiers and fax machines

EDUCATION
- Student at Columbia High School, Garland, TX
- College preparatory diploma to be conferred June 2003
- Well-rounded educational experience, including varsity soccer, lacrosse, and tennis; orchestra; science fair projects; yearbook staff; head of holiday spirit committee

AWARDS
- First-prize poster: Foreign Language Week

> The labels Work Experience, Skills, Education, and Awards indicate this résumé is organized by topic.

> Here, the writer focuses information by providing the dates of work experience.

> Résumés should be kept to one page—the goal is to get an interview, not tell an entire life story.

350 • Workplace Writing

⏱ TIME AND RESOURCE MANAGER

Resources
Print: *Writing Support Transparencies*, 16-C
Technology: *Writing Lab* CD-ROM, Practical and Technical Writing

In-Depth Coverage	Accelerated Pace
• Have students read pp. 350–351 in class. • Using the model, point out the elements of a résumé. • Read the Topic Bank and have students list suggestions for writing a sample résumé. • Review the writing process and ways to apply each step to writing a résumé.	• Have students read pp. 350–351 on their own. • Discuss the elements of a résumé. • Have students share their topic choices. • Compare the process of writing a résumé to that of writing a memo.

TOPIC BANK

To write a résumé that propels your application to the top of a pile, create one to fit your job-seeking goals. Include experiences of particular interest to your audience, and highlight the positive. Develop a résumé that conveys your talents and achievements, or practice the format with one of these topics:

1. **Résumé of a Historical Figure** People who have influenced history often have compelling job and life experiences. Consider writers, inventors, government leaders, or professional athletes. Choose a person who interests you, and conduct research in order to write his or her résumé.

2. **Résumé of a Fictional Character** Choose a character who has appeared in literature, film, or television. Use the information you can gather from a close analysis to write a résumé summarizing the character's work and life experiences.

(?) Learn More

To keep your résumé consistent, review the rules of parallelism in Chapter 20.

Prewriting For your own résumé or that of someone else, list highlights from educational and work experiences. Consider life skills that demonstrate responsibility, such as those gained from baby-sitting, extracurricular activities, or community work. Gather key details about dates and locations of these experiences.

Drafting Choose an organization method, and apply it consistently as you draft. Use either sentences or phrases in your experience descriptions, but don't mix the two.

Revising Review the job or experience descriptions you have written. Sharpen the language with action verbs that show what you've done and quantify accomplishments with concrete numbers.

Editing and Proofreading Experiment with layout and typestyles to further highlight important information. Check for mistakes in consistency, and correct any variations in format.

Publishing and Presenting To use the résumé of your talents and skills, print the document on good-quality paper in a neutral color, such as white or ivory. When you hear or read about a job you'd like to pursue, send your résumé along with a cover letter, using standard business-letter format.

Résumé • 351

✓ ONGOING ASSESSMENT: Monitor and Reinforce

If you find that students are having difficulty with ideas for completing a résumé, use one of the following options.

Option 1 Have students work in pairs, asking each other questions about what they've done and what type of work would interest them. Have students jot down résumé items for their partners. Then, have partners show each other the things that might be included in a résumé.	**Option 2** Direct students to one of the many books that cover the topic of résumé writing in detail, and suggest that they use the exercises and suggestions in the book to get comfortable with writing a résumé.

Choosing a Topic

1. After reading the Topic Bank, discuss topics with students. Tell them they may use the suggestions in the Topic Bank or select topics of their own. They might want to write a résumé for a friend, family member, or teacher.

2. Elicit discussion about shaping résumé contents to suit the job. (Example: In the résumé model, if Rebecca wanted to apply for a job as a soccer coach, she might expand on her soccer-playing skills and her interactive skills with children.)

3. Bring in want ads from the newspaper and have students go through to learn the language of job searching. Also, if they find a "dream job" listed, they can think about the sorts of skills and education they would need to get it and write a résumé based on what they want to accomplish in order to reach that goal.

4. Emphasize that the various steps of writing are even more important for a résumé than for a memo. It often takes a good bit of time to think of all the elements that should be included. And proofreading is vital, since this document is the only chance a person may have to make an impression on an employer.

Integrating Grammar Skills

Tell students that grammar, spelling, and punctuation are as important in a résumé as they are in any other writing form. Although résumés are brief and frequently replace full sentences with phrases, résumés still require excellent grammar skills.

Customize for
Gifted and Talented Students

Students with special talents or skills might already have work experience or work goals. Encourage students to write a real résumé.

Filling Out Forms and Applications

Teaching Resources: Writing Support Transparencies, 16-D–E; Writing Support Activity Book, 16-1–2

1. If possible, prepare for this lesson by gathering samples of applications and other forms to bring to class. Display Transparencies D–E, and give student blank copies of the fax cover sheet (16-1) and application (16-2).

2. As students review the bulleted points on this page, ask them to explain further why each point is important. (Example: A person reviewing a job application might get discouraged if the handwriting is illegible. Missing information causes delays and makes a bad impression.)

3. Explain that a fax needs a cover sheet because, unlike e-mail, the systems set up to transmit a fax do not automatically identify the sender, and there is no "reply" button for the recipient to use. If someone doesn't know who sent a fax, it may be impossible for him or her to respond to the message.

4. Point out that, for applications, it is vital that students read directions to determine not only what information is needed, but also what format it should be in (block letters, month or day first for dates, last name first). Applications vary dramatically, depending on the purpose, organization, information needed, and other factors. Also, tell students to be aware of where the information goes—it is not always immediately obvious whether entries should go above or below the direction line, so they should scan the form for clues.

5. Explain that any form that requires a signature is a type of contract. The signer agrees to the rules stated and that all information is true. Depending on the situation, there can be serious consequences if one signs such a form or application without being honest.

16.4 Forms and Applications

What Are Forms and Applications?

At times, it may seem as if all you do is fill out forms and applications—at school, to get a job, even for on-line shopping. These documents are preprinted with spaces provided for specific information. Three common workplace forms are fax cover sheets, applications, and phone message logs. To effectively complete a form:

- Write legibly so that readers can read the information easily.
- Give only pertinent information, and be brief, unless asked for more extensive responses.
- Double-check the headings to be sure you have provided the requested information in the appropriate areas.

Model Fax Cover Sheet

Fax cover sheets accompany faxed documents to provide important identifying information to the recipient. They explain who sent the fax and how to contact the sender. Most fax cover sheets allow space for a brief message. Look at this example:

A company letterhead lets readers quickly recognize the sender of the fax.

TECHNOLOGY and SYSTEMS CONSULTING
67 Camp Street • San Francisco, CA 94110
phone 415.555.7601 • fax 415.555.3355
e-mail: JeffN@address.network

Fax

FACSIMILE COVER SHEET/TRANSMITTAL

The sender completes this information accurately to make sure his fax reaches the intended person.

DATE: 9/14/20- -

TO: Gabriel Saxe – FutureTech Systems

FAX NUMBER: 407/555-1001

FAX SOURCE TRANSMISSION NUMBER: 415/555-3355

FROM: Jeff Nelson

Fax cover sheets typically include a full-page count so recipients can verify successful transmission of all the pages.

TOTAL NUMBER OF PAGES (including this cover sheet): 5

REMARKS:

An explanatory note is optional. The level of formality of this note should be dictated by the writer's knowledge of the receiver.

Gabe - As discussed, here is the information you need to finish the software manual. Please call with any questions.

Thanks, Jeff

⏱ TIME AND RESOURCE MANAGER

Resources
Print: *Writing Support Transparencies*, 16-D–F; *Writing Support Activity Book*, 16-1–3
Technology: *Writing Lab* CD-ROM, Practical and Technical Writing

In-Depth Coverage	Accelerated Pace
• Have students read pp. 352–354 in class. • Using the model, point out the elements of business forms and applications.	• Have students read pp. 352–354 on their own. • Discuss the elements of business forms and applications.

Model Application

In many states, people over a specified age must obtain a learner's permit in order to pursue driving instruction. In the model below, notice how one student completed the application for a learner's permit.

Instructions tell applicants what information will be necessary. Read them carefully, and follow them exactly.

APPLICATION FOR A LEARNER'S PERMIT

DEPARTMENT OF MOTOR VEHICLES

Instructions: Complete 1–17, then present items listed below to Cashier
1. Identifications (evidence of identity and date of birth)
2. Address Verification
3. Certification of Parental Consent (if not properly accompanied by authorized consenter)
4. $6.00 permit fee

1. APPLICANT'S NAME (Last, First, Middle)	2. SEX	3. DATE OF BIRTH
Mulligan, Jack Michael	☑M ☐F	1/15/1982

4. MAILING ADDRESS (No., Street, City or Town, State, Zip Code)	5. RESIDENCE ADDRESS (if different)
605 Alex St. Bridgeport, CT 06607	

6. ARE YOU A CITIZEN OF THE UNITED STATES?	7. ARE YOU A RESIDENT OF THIS STATE?
☑ YES ☐ NO	☑ YES ☐ NO

8. NAME OF DRIVING SCHOOL OR LOCATION OF DMV BRANCH OFFICE	9. SOCIAL SECURITY NUMBER (optional)
Bridgeport	123-45-6789

QUESTIONS	YES (✗)	NO (✗)	
10. Is your right to operate a motor vehicle suspended here or in any other state?		✓	
11. Do you now, or have you ever previously held a license?		✓	

MEDICAL CERTIFICATION	I hereby certify that I meet the vision and health standards contained in Motor Vehicle Regulations 4-45a-1 et seq., as amended, and that I do not have any health or vision problems or conditions that prevent me from driving safely.	SIGNATURE OF APPLICANT *Jack M. Mulligan*

DO NOT WRITE BELOW THIS LINE – OFFICE USE ONLY

PROOF OF IDENTIFICATION	TYPE OF ACCEPTABLE I.D. SHOWN	PREVIOUS LICENSE INFORMATION	DRIVER LICENSE NUMBER
PARENTAL CONSENT	I hereby request that a learner's permit and/or license be issued to the minor (age 16-17) filing this application.	RELATIONSHIP TO MINOR	SIGNED (Authorized Cons...

Here, the applicant had to abbreviate *Street* and *Connecticut* in order to fit the required information into the provided space. If you think you won't be able to fit your facts, try to write smaller or create a second line within the allotted space.

A signature confirms the applicant's agreement to the rules stated in the contract. Read everything on an application before signing your name—especially the fine print.

Integrating Grammar Skills

Abbreviations Point out places in the application where words are abbreviated to save space. Remind students to abbreviate properly. If necessary, review some words commonly abbreviated, such as *Street* (St.), *Boulevard* (Blvd.), *Avenue* (Ave.), *Post Office Box* (P.O. Box), and *Rural Route* (RR.). For state names, students need to know the correct two-letter abbreviation.

Integrating Vocabulary Skills

Use the model on page 352 to point out that *fax* is shortened from the word *facsimile*, which means "an exact copy or likeness" (from the Latin word *facsimilis*, "make similar"). Explain that, when sending a fax, we are not sending the actual paper. Instead, the fax machine makes a copy and sends it to another fax machine. The sender still has the original paper after sending the fax.

Customize for
ESL Students

Students acquiring English might have difficulty with the brief, tiny directions on many applications. If possible, bring in some applications from local organizations, make copies for the class, and let students practice filling them in. If necessary, go through an application line by line with a small group. Help students understand where to print their names and that *signature* means to write their names in their handwriting.

Integrating Workplace Skills

Remind students that any form or application they turn over or send to someone becomes the property of the recipient. Tell them they must always be accurate and truthful when filling out forms.

Real-World Connection

Some of your students may be preparing for or getting their driver's licenses this year. Ask students with experience to tell about the kinds of forms they have to fill out at the Department of Motor Vehicles (DMV).

Step-by-Step Teaching Guide

Phone Messages

Teaching Resources: Writing Support Transparencies, 16-F; Writing Support Activity Book, 16-3

1. Explain that in business, much communication is over the phone, and staying in touch is vitally important. Hence, a phone message can become an important link in the communication process.

2. Display Transparency 16-F and point out the characteristics of the phone message, noting that most phone-message forms are similar to this one.

3. Ask students why it is important for the person who took the message to sign it (in case the recipient has questions). Why didn't the writer put a period after the written message? (It isn't a complete sentence.)

Critical Viewing

Hypothesize Many businesses, from insurance agencies to home repair services, rely on communicating promptly and clearly with customers over the phone.

Model Phone Message

In busy offices, workers often use a standardized format to be sure that important messages are recorded accurately. Pads or booklets of these forms have spaces for all the key facts. When a message is completed, it can be detached and given to the phone-call recipient. Look at this example of a phone message:

PHONE CALL
FOR *Lee Paul Clark* DATE *4/5* TIME *11:05* (AM) PM
M *s. Marcella Ruiz*
OF *FutureTech Systems*
PHONE (*407*) *555-1800* EXT. *45*
MESSAGE *Still needs some input on the budget*
Signed: *Sheila Warner*
☐ Returned Your Call   ☒ Please Call   ☐ Will Call Again

Phrases quickly summarize the purpose of the call as explained by the caller.

A signature tells the recipient who spoke to the caller and where to get more information about the exchange.

Tips for Taking and Leaving Phone Messages

While it is always better to speak directly to the person you want to reach, a phone message that communicates information clearly is the next best thing. To make phone messages most effective, follow these tips:

When taking a message: Get key information, such as a name and a phone number. Ask the caller to repeat any information that is unclear. To be sure of the accuracy of your message, read the message back to the caller.

When leaving a message: Speak clearly and slowly, spelling your name for clarity. State your purpose for calling, and provide your phone number. It may be helpful to indicate the best times you can be reached.

▶ **Critical Viewing**
Why are phone messages critical to the success of some businesses? [**Hypothesize**]

354 • Workplace Writing

✏ STANDARDIZED TEST PREPARATION WORKSHOP

Grammar and Usage Standardized tests often require students to choose the correct word or group of words to complete a sentence. Use the following sample item to demonstrate.

> Choose the form of the verb *blow* that best completes the sentence.
>
> *The wind had ___ all day and most of the night.*

A blew	**C** blown
B blowed	**D** blow

Students should recognize that **C**, the past participle of *blow*, is the correct answer. A is the past form and is not used with the helping verb *have/had*. B is not a form of the verb. D is the present form.

Connected Assignment *E-mail*

In today's workplace, professionals send documents electronically across state and national borders via computers. At the same time, workers communicate with colleagues in the same building with quick notes and updates sent across computer lines. In both cases, people in the workplace may use **e-mail** (letters sent electronically via computer) to share information. E-mail letters, notes, or memos are composed within the format of software programs, but writers can raise or lower the text's formality to suit their level of familiarity with the recipient.

The tips below can help you compose effective e-mail messages.

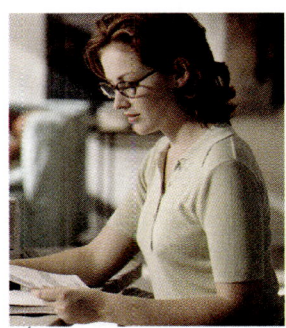

▲ **Critical Viewing**
Identify two industries that rely on e-mail or the World Wide Web to generate business. **[Connect]**

To: Jack_Riley@address.com
Subject: Schedule of meeting

Geneva ▼ | 12 ▼ | B | *I* | U | ☰ ☰ ☰ | A | A | | | | | | ABC ✔

Hello Jack,
Thanks for the update to the schedule. Please keep me posted if there are any changes.
Regards,
Michael

Prewriting Think about the purpose of your letter. You might need to cancel an order through an on-line shopping service, request information from a government agency, or check in with a friend. Before you begin to draft, be sure you have the address you'll need to send the message.

Drafting Draft the body of your e-mail much as you would a conventional letter. Your greeting and closing can be less formal if you know the recipient well. Avoid complicated formatting, such as boldfacing or underlining, that may be garbled by any translations in operation at the receiving computer.

Revising and Editing A single-character error in an e-mail address will result in misdirected mail. Review the body of your e-mail to make sure you've used complete sentences and organized information clearly. Then, attach the necessary files.

Publishing and Presenting When you are satisfied with your e-mail, review the recipient's information and send your message with the touch of a button.

Connected Assignment: E-mail • **355**

Lesson Objectives

1. To describe how meanings are communicated through elements of design
2. To analyze how ideas are represented in various media
3. To write a memo

Examining How Meanings Are Communicated Through Design

1. Look in your local library or on the Internet for photographs of I. M. Pei's buildings. Give students time to peruse the photos, but do not reveal the names or functions of the buildings.

2. Have students try to guess the function of each building based on the mood created by its architectural features. Discuss the way certain shapes, materials, and styles suggest certain moods and ideas.

3. Reveal the correct answers. Then, direct students to the writing assignment. Have them choose a function for the building they will design, such as a new school, a recreation center for teens, or a local history museum.

4. Then, have them design their buildings, making sure the design in some way communicates the building's function.

Viewing and Representing

Activity Encourage interested students to make class presentations of their memos, using models or drawings of their designs to illustrate their proposals.

Critical Viewing

Analyze The wide variety of shapes and forms suggests that the building celebrates the wide variety of sounds and styles that have shaped rock and roll.

Spotlight on the Humanities

Examining How Meanings Are Communicated Through Design

Focus on: I. M. Pei

While many workplaces are standard office buildings, the designs of top architects have made others into works of art. One of the most influential contributors to the art of modern architecture is a native of China and is now a naturalized citizen of the United States. Ieoh Ming Pei (1917–) left China at age 17 to study architecture at MIT and Harvard's Graduate School of Design. Among his creations are the Miho Museum of Shiga, Japan, the Rock and Roll Hall of Fame in Cleveland, the Pyramid of the Louvre Museum in Paris, and the Four Seasons Hotel in midtown Manhattan.

Music Connection After I. M. Pei created the design for the Rock and Roll Hall of Fame in Cleveland, the museum established a system for filling the structure with information and artifacts to honor musicians. One of the museum's first inductees was legendary rhythm-and-blues singer Fats Domino. Born in 1928, Domino sold more records during the 1950's than any of his contemporaries except for Elvis Presley. His recordings and live performances gave him a continuing presence in rock-and-roll music into the early 1960's.

Ancient Art Connection Pei's works, which dot the cities of the modern world, are examples of today's architectural art, but Chinese art dates back to some of the earliest civilizations. Archaeological digs confirm that farming societies had arisen by 5000 B.C. Ancient Chinese pottery has been located at more than 6,000 of these sites. For example, the Yangshao culture that thrived between 5000–3000 B.C. embellished pottery with basket impressions. Higher quality pieces in the form of bowls and cups were painted with glistening colors.

Workplace Writing Activity: Memo About New Design

Imagine that you have been asked to create an innovative design for a new building in your town or city. Write a memo to the building's financiers to propose your ideas. Use proper memo format.

▲ **Critical Viewing**
What does the structure of the Rock and Roll Hall of Fame suggest to you about the contents of the building? **[Analyze]**

Integrating Research Skills

Have students choose an interesting building in the community. Encourage them to research its history, including its architect, its original function, and its current use.

Media and Technology Skills

Using Technology for Revising and Editing

Activity: Evaluating a Word-Processing Program

Error-free writing is essential in the workplace. You can use your computer's tools to identify and eliminate errors quickly and easily. These tools add a second reader's eye to your own as you review and revise documents.

Learn About It Most word processors contain the following essential editing and proofreading tools:

- **Spell Check** Activate this feature under the Tools menu. You can use it to check specific words or paragraphs or to review the entire document. Your computer may cite people's names as incorrect spellings, but you can reject corrections when necessary.

- **Grammar Check** Watch for automatic signals (such as underlined text) that suggest grammatical errors. Run the complete grammar-check function just as you do the spell-check function. As with any computerized check, apply your own knowledge and make final decisions yourself.

- **Thesaurus** If you find you have used one word too frequently, consult the built-in thesaurus to vary your language. Find it under Tools, and then select from the suggested synonyms.

Apply It Choose a recent workplace writing product that you prepared with a word processor. Check it for errors using the techniques discussed above. Take notes on your progress in a form like the one shown here. Then, design a reminder card for computer error checking, and post it near your computer.

Name of file: _____
Tools used: 1. _____
2. _____
3. _____
Errors _____ Tool used: _____
corrected: _____ (enter number)
Check your document visually. Were all errors caught? If not, why not? _____

Tips for Generating Error-Free Writing

- Set tabs or use multi-column formats to keep chart information correctly aligned.
- Activate Undo functions in the Edit menu when necessary.
- Set the Autocorrect function to specific style demands; for example, abbreviation, symbols, and optional spellings.
- Print out a proofreading copy of your document, and correct it by hand before finalizing your work.

1. To use technology for aspects of revising and editing texts
2. To evaluate writing for both mechanics and content
3. To produce error-free writing in the final draft

Step-by-Step Teaching Guide

Using Technology for Revising and Editing

Teaching Resources: Writing Support Transparencies, 16-H; Writing Support Activity Book, 16-4

1. Discuss the reasons that error-free writing is so important in workplace writing. What might an employer think of a job applicant whose résumé is riddled with errors? (He or she might think the applicant would be a careless, lazy employee.)

2. Remind students that spell check should supplement their own proofreading; it should not replace it. Spell check will not pick up misused homonyms, such as *their* and *there*, as long as they are spelled correctly.

3. Grammar checks often consider long sentences to be run-ons even when they are not. In this case as in others, students should be judicious in following the suggestions of the grammar check.

Customize for
Less Advanced Students

Just as the computer has separate features for checking grammar and spelling, encourage students to proof their work twice, once for grammar and once for spelling.

Applying Usage Rules to Writing

Teaching Resources: Standardized Test Preparation Workbook, pp. 31–32

1. Review subject-verb agreement with students. Remind them that singular subjects take singular verbs and plural subjects take plural verbs. Compound subjects joined by *and* generally take plural verbs.

2. Review pronoun case with students. Remind them that *who* can be the subject of a verb or a predicate nominative. *Whom* can be a direct object or the object of a preposition.

3. When answering fill-in questions such as those on this page, suggest that students read the filled-in sentences aloud. Often, they will be able to eliminate answer choices because they sound wrong.

Standardized Test Preparation Workshop

Applying Usage Rules to Writing

Writing in the workplace should be error-free and should follow the rules of grammar, usage, and mechanics. These workplace criteria frequently appear on standardized tests that measure your ability to recognize errors in grammar, spelling, or punctuation. The following methods will help you address some commonly tested verb usage problems:

- Check verbs to make sure they agree with their subjects.

- Make sure the verb tense is consistent throughout a piece of writing.

- Consider the sequence of events in the passage. Identify events that happened before or after others. Use this information to justify a shift in tense.

The following sample test items will give you practice with questions that challenge you to identify usage problems.

Test Tip

When evaluating verb tense in a sentence, reread the passage at least twice, looking closely at the verb tenses the paragraph uses. Unless a time shift makes sense, choose the verb tense that matches the rest of the passage.

Sample Test Item	Answer and Explanation
Directions: Read the passage, and choose the word or group of words that belongs in each space. Choose the appropriate letter for your answer. The office manager __(1)__ from lunch when he discovered the computers were not working because the system was down. **1 A** was returning **B** were returning **C** will return **D** have been returning	The correct answer is *A. Was returning* correctly indicates a continuing action in the past. This action, *returning,* began before the action of *discovering.* Both verbs are in forms of the past tense.

✏ TEST-TAKING TIP

Encourage students to answer fill-in questions on their own before looking at the answer choices. If necessary, they can write the answer on the blank line in the test booklet. Then, they should check to see whether that answer is one of the choices. If so, it is probably correct.

Have students cover the answer choices in the sample question on this page. They should realize that the missing verb should be in the past progressive tense because the manager made the discovery in the past while doing some other continuous action (returning).

Practice 1 Read each passage and choose the word or group of words that belongs in each space.

After the interview, John felt excited about the prospect of __(1)__ for the job. He created a strong résumé, and he __(2)__ that his previous experience would make him a strong candidate for the position. As a follow-up, he wrote a note thanking the interviewer for meeting with him. He hoped that all of his efforts __(3)__ him a new job.

1 **A** hired
  B hiring
  C being hired
  D having hired

2 **F** believes
  G would believe
  H believed
  J could believe

3 **A** will earn
  B would earn
  C could earn
  D have earned

Since my freshman year, I __(4)__ in the campus library. It's a work-study program, so I'm earning money to help pay my tuition. I'm also learning more about library science and finding great literature in the process. During my breaks, I __(5)__ some of my paper topics for class, which helps me get a head start. When I first started, I had no idea that this position __(6)__ me in so many ways.

4 **A** had worked
  B am working
  C will work
  D have worked

5 **F** researched
  G research
  H am researching
  J will research

6 **A** would benefit
  B will benefit
  C had benefited
  D is benefiting

Kate said goodbye to her family. She was on her way to Spain for a semester abroad, a trip she __(7)__ for almost a year. She did not like feeling uneasy, nervous, and sad. She had promised herself that this __(8)__ the experience of a lifetime. She noticed other people who looked like college students. She wondered if they were going to the same university in Spain. She took a deep breath, wiped away her tears, and __(9)__ the plane. Once on board, she __(10)__ better.

7 **A** will be anticipating
  B is anticipating
  C had anticipated
  D anticipated

8 **F** is
  G would be
  H was
  J will be

9 **A** boarded
  B will board
  C had boarded
  D would board

10 **F** feels
   G was feeling
   H felt
   J will have felt

Integrating Grammar Skills

Helping Verbs Remind students that helping verbs are verbs that can be added to another verb to make a verb phrase. For example, in the previous sentence, the verb phrase *can be added* is made of the helping verbs *can be* and the main verb *added*. Reading a sentence aloud will usually make a missing helping verb quite obvious.

Answer Key

Practice 1

1. C
2. H
3. B
4. D
5. H
6. A
7. C
8. G
9. A
10. H

▶ *Objectives*

1. To understand parts of speech and basic sentence patterns and to apply relevant concepts to one's own writing

2. To learn and apply key concepts governing usage of verbs

3. To understand concepts of agreement relating to subjects and verbs and pronouns and antecedents, and to apply this understanding to one's own writing

4. To compose sentences of increasing sophistication and appropriateness

5. To analyze works of literature as models of appropriate and effective English usage

6. To recognize appropriate English usage in one's own reading and writing

7. To use "hands-on" strategies to reinforce understanding of grammar and usage concepts

8. To master the conventions of capitalization, punctuation, and spelling, and to apply them accurately to one's own writing

Grammar, Usage, and Mechanics

Step-by-Step Teaching Guide

Responding to Fine Art

Design drawing for intarsia wood panel with fish by M. C. Escher

Use this work of art to start a discussion about the functions of grammar, usage, and mechanics.

1. Have students examine the image on pages 360–361. You might use the following questions to prompt discussion:

   How many different types of fish can students see? What markings do they use to distinguish one type from another? Which fish are the easiest to spot? Which are the most difficult?

   Do students notice patterns in the painting or are the fish arranged arbitrarily? In what ways do the fish look realistic? In what ways do they look fantastical?

2. Many of the fish seem to blend into one another. How does the viewer know where one fish ends and the next begins? Ask students to relate this idea to the topics covered in this part on the structure of English. For example, how does punctuation show connections and separations among thoughts? How can proper grammar make ideas more distinct and clear?

About the Artist

Born in Holland, M. C. Escher (1898–1972) became one of the world's foremost graphic artists. He produced mostly woodcuts and lithographs, often in black-and-white. His typical style of playful, repetitive, interlocking patterns of animals and other figures is instantly recognizable even to people with little exposure to art. Escher was also adept at "bending" reality. Students may be familiar with his fantastic images of gravity-defying waterfalls and endless staircases.

361

In-Depth Lesson Plan

	LESSON FOCUS	PRINT AND MEDIA RESOURCES
DAY 1	**Nouns and Pronouns** Students learn to identify nouns and pronouns and to recognize antecedents. (pp. 364–373)	*Language Lab* **CD-ROM,** Nouns and Pronouns *On-Line Exercise Bank,* Section 17.1 **Teaching Resources** *Grammar Exercise Workbook,* pp. 1–4; *Grammar Exercises Answers on Transparencies,* Ch. 17
DAY 2	**Verbs** Students identify and understand verb types and verb phrases. (pp. 374–379)	*Language Lab* **CD-ROM,** Using Verbs *On-Line Exercise Bank,* Section 17.2 **Teaching Resources** *Grammar Exercise Workbook,* pp. 5–10
DAY 3	**Adjectives and Adverbs** Students identify and understand the functions of adjectives and adverbs. (pp. 380–387)	*Language Lab* **CD-ROM,** Using Modifiers *On-Line Exercise Bank,* Section 17.3 **Teaching Resources** *Grammar Exercise Workbook,* pp. 11–14
DAY 4	**Prepositions, Conjunctions, and Interjections** Students learn the functions of prepositions, conjunctions, and interjections. (pp. 388–395)	*On-Line Exercise Bank,* Section 17.4 **Teaching Resources** *Grammar Exercise Workbook,* pp. 15–20
DAY 5	**Words as Different Parts of Speech; Review and Assess** Students review word functions in sentences and demonstrate mastery of parts of speech. (pp. 396–401)	*On-Line Exercise Bank,* Section 17.5 **Teaching Resources** *Grammar Exercise Workbook,* pp. 21–22; *Hands-on Grammar Activity Book,* Ch. 17; *Formal Assessment,* Ch. 17

Accelerated Lesson Plan

	LESSON FOCUS	PRINT AND MEDIA RESOURCES
DAY 1	**Nouns, Pronouns, and Verbs** Students identify and understand nouns, pronouns, antecedents, verbs, and verb phrases. (pp. 364–379)	*Language Lab* **CD-ROM,** Nouns and Pronouns, Using Verbs *On-Line Exercise Bank,* Sections 17.1–2 **Teaching Resources** *Grammar Exercise Workbook,* pp. 1–10; *Grammar Exercises Answers on Transparencies,* Ch. 17
DAY 2	**Adjectives to Interjections** Students identify and understand the functions of adjectives, adverbs, prepositions, conjunctions, and interjections. (pp. 380–395)	*Language Lab* **CD-ROM,** Using Modifiers *On-Line Exercise Bank,* Sections 17.3–4 **Teaching Resources** *Grammar Exercise Workbook,* pp. 11–20
DAY 3	**Words as Different Parts of Speech; Review and Assess** Students review word functions in sentences and demonstrate mastery of parts of speech. (pp. 396–401)	*On-Line Exercise Bank,* Section 17.5 **Teaching Resources** *Grammar Exercise Workbook,* pp. 21–22; *Formal Assessment,* Ch. 17

Options for Adapting Lesson Plans

FEATURES

Extend coverage with the Grammar in Literature features (pp. 368, 377, 385), the Hands-on Grammar activity (p. 398), and the Standardized Test Preparation Workshop (p. 402).

TECHNOLOGY

Students can use the *On-Line Exercise Bank* to complete the exercises on computer. The Auto Check feature will grade their work.

INTEGRATED SKILLS COVERAGE

Grammar in Literature
pp. 368, 377, 385

Writing
Find It in Your Writing SE pp. 373, 379, 387, 395, 398, 399
Writing Application SE pp. 373, 379, 387, 395, 399, 401
Grammar and Style SE pp. 368, 376, 381, 384

Spelling Skills   SE p. 365

Vocabulary Skills   ATE p. 384

Viewing and Representing
Critical Viewing, SE pp. 362, 364, 366, 371, 375, 377, 381, 383, 385, 386, 390, 392, 394, 397.

Real-World Connection   ATE p. 370

Technology Skills   SE pp. 370, 393

Research Skills   SE p. 382

ASSESSMENT SUPPORT

Standardized Test Preparation Workshop   SE p. 402; ATE pp. 382, 402

Standardized Test Preparation Workbook, pp. 33–34

Formal Assessment, Ch. 17

MEETING INDIVIDUAL NEEDS

Less Advanced Students   ATE p. 375, 403. See also Ongoing Assessments, ATE pp. 367, 372, 376, 378, 383, 390, 392, 397.
ESL Students   ATE pp. 369, 381
AP Students   ATE p. 403
Visual/Spatial Learners   ATE p. 365

BLOCK SCHEDULING

Pacing Suggestions
For 90-minute Blocks
• Administer the Diagnostic Test to students to determine instructional coverage.
• Have students complete the necessary exercises in class. Use the Hands-on Grammar activity to provide a change of pace.

Resources for Varying Instruction
• *Language Lab* CD-ROM If your students have access to hardware, a 90-minute block provides an ideal opportunity for students to work on computer.

Professional Development Support
• *How to Manage Instruction in the Block* This Teaching Resource provides management and activity suggestions.

MEDIA AND TECHNOLOGY

For the Student
• *Language Lab* CD-ROM, Nouns and Pronouns, Using Verbs, Using Modifiers
• *On-Line Exercise Bank,* Sections 17.1–5

For the Teacher
• *Resource Pro* CD-ROM

WRITING AND GRAMMAR WEB SITE

The Interactive Writing and Grammar Web Site provides a wide array of support for students, teachers, and parents. Grammar support includes:

• *On-Line Exercise Bank* with Auto Check Scoring
• Diagnostic and assessment support

www.phschool.com

LITERATURE CONNECTIONS

Related selections from *Prentice Hall Literature: Timeless Voices, Timeless Themes,* The American Experience:

from *The General History of Virginia,* John Smith, SE p. 368
from "Stopping by Woods on a Snowy Evening," Robert Frost, SE p. 377
from "The Raven," Edgar Allan Poe, SE p. 385

Lesson Objectives

1. To identify the various types of nouns and pronouns and to understand how they are used in sentences

2. To identify the various types of verbs and to understand how they are used in sentences

3. To identify, understand, and use adjectives and adverbs in sentences

4. To recognize and use prepositions, conjunctions, and interjections in sentences

5. To understand that words act as different parts of speech depending on how they are used in a sentence

6. To demonstrate control over grammatical elements such as parts of speech

7. To evaluate writing for both mechanics and content

Critical Viewing

Relate Students may include such nouns as *building, tower, bricks, clock, window.* They may include such adjectives as *red, tall, colonial, dark.*

Chapter 17 The Parts of Speech

City Hall, Alexandria, Virginia

Every English word, depending on its meaning and its use in a sentence, can be identified as one of the eight parts of speech.

THE PARTS OF SPEECH		
nouns	adjectives	prepositions
pronouns	adverbs	conjunctions
verbs		interjections

This chapter provides explanations of, and practice with, the eight parts of speech.

▲ **Critical Viewing**
What nouns can be used to identify details you see in this picture? What adjectives might describe them? [**Relate**]

362 • The Parts of Speech

✓ ONGOING ASSESSMENT: Diagnose

If students miss more than one item in any category, direct them to the relevant pages of the textbook and assign exercises for practice and review.

The Parts of Speech	Diagnostic Test Items	Teach	Practice	Section Review	Chapter Review
Skill Check A, B, and C					
Nouns and Pronouns	A1–5, B6–15, C1–15	pp. 364–370	Ex. 1–6	Ex. 7–9	Ex. 51–52
Skill Check D					
Verbs and Verb Phrases	D 16–20	pp. 374–378	Ex.13–15	Ex.16–19	Ex. 53

Diagnostic Test

Directions: Write all answers on a separate sheet of paper.

Skill Check A. Match each noun with its description.

1. Alexandria Town Hall
2. legislature
3. townhouse
4. self-improvements
5. Europeans

a. concrete, compound, and singular
b. common, compound, and abstract
c. common, singular, and collective
d. proper and plural
e. proper, concrete, and compound

Skill Check B. Identify the pronoun or pronouns in each numbered section of the following paragraph. Then, identify each pronoun's antecedent. Antecedents may appear in previous sentences. The pronoun *I* refers to the person telling the story.

[6] Alexandria, Virginia, was an early colonial settlement. It was founded in 1749. [7] George Washington was one of its trustees and a part-time resident of the town, where he drew early maps of it in 1748 and 1749. [8] I visited Alexandria last year. [9] That was an interesting trip. [10] My brother and I drove to Cameron Street in Old Alexandria. [11] Washington himself had a home there. [12] Residents are proud of their connection to Washington. [13] This is evident in the many buildings named for him. [14] One place you should visit is the Carlyle House. [15] What is a better way to learn about history?

Skill Check C. On your paper, list the pronouns you found in each numbered section in Skill Check B. Then, identify the type of each pronoun. There are fifteen pronouns.

Skill Check D. List the verbs and verb phrases in each sentence. Then, label each *transitive, intransitive,* or *linking.*

16. Nomadic hunters probably first entered what would become Virginia about 10,000 to 12,000 years ago.
17. Native American communities later developed in the East.
18. Almost 20,000 Native Americans were living in Virginia when European explorers and settlers first arrived.
19. Powhatan was the chief of the Powhatan Confederacy of Algonquin tribes when English settlers first built Jamestown.
20. Warfare erupted after colonists had taken lands that belonged to the Powhatan Confederacy.

Skill Check E. Identify the part of speech of each underlined word.

[21] In 1606, King James I granted <u>two</u> <u>companies</u> the right to colonize Virginia. [22] The <u>following</u> year, the <u>Virginia Company of London</u> established a colony called Jamestown. [23] <u>This</u> was the first permanent English settlement <u>in</u> America. [24] The first years <u>of</u> the colony were <u>extremely</u> difficult, as settlers faced an array of problems that included famine, disease, and hostile <u>Native American</u> tribes. [25] Despite these <u>trying</u> times, new settlers moved in <u>almost</u> continually.

The Parts of Speech • 363

Diagnostic Test

Each item in the Diagnostic Test corresponds to a specific section in this chapter. This allows you to tailor instruction to the particular needs of your students. See "Ongoing Assessment: Diagnose" below for further details.

Skill Check A

1. e
2. c
3. a
4. b
5. d

Skill Check B

6. It, Alexandria, VA
7. one, trustees; its, Alexandria; he, George Washington; it, Alexandria
8. I, the speaker
9. That, the visit to Alexandria
10. My, the speaker; I, the speaker
11. himself, George Washington
12. their, residents
13. this, residents' pride; him, Washington
14. you, the reader
15. What, way

Skill Check C

6. It: personal, singular
7. one: indefinite; its: personal, singular; he: personal, singular; it: personal, singular
8. I: personal, singular
9. that: demonstrative
10. my: personal, singular; I: personal, singular
11. himself: intensive
12. their: personal, plural
13. this: demonstrative; him: personal, singular
14. you: personal
15. what: interrogative

Skill Check D

16. entered, T; would become, L
17. developed, I
18. were living, I; arrived, I
19. was, L; built, T
20. erupted, I; had taken, T; belonged, I

Skill Check E

21. adjective, noun
22. adjective, noun
23. pronoun, preposition
24. preposition, adverb, adjective
25. adjective, adverb

✓ ONGOING ASSESSMENT: Diagnose *continued*

Agreement	Diagnostic Test Items	Teach	Practice	Section Review	Chapter Review
Skill Check E					
Adjectives and Adverbs	E 21–22, 24–25	pp. 380–385	Ex. 23–25	Ex. 26–28	Ex. 54
Prepositions, Conjunctions, and Interjections	E 23–24	pp. 388–394	Ex. 32–37	Ex. 38–40	
Words as Different Parts of Speech	E 21–25	pp. 396–397	Ex. 44	Ex. 45–47	Ex. 55–56
Cumulative Reviews and Applications				Ex. 10–12, 20–22, 29–31, 41–43, 48–50	Ex. 55

Have students list five of their favorite things on a sheet of paper. These things may be concrete, such as a bike, a pet, or a person. Or they may be abstract, such as *joy, freedom,* or *compassion.* Explain these ideas to students before they write. Afterward, have a few students share their responses. Explain that their answers are nouns.

Activate Prior Knowledge

Ask a student to give a brief oral narrative of his or her day so far. As the student talks, record on the board or overhead each pronoun that he or she uses. When you have recorded five or more pronouns, stop the student and ask the class what type of words you have recorded. (pronouns)

TEACH

Step-by-Step Teaching Guide

Concrete, Abstract, Singular, and Plural Nouns

1. Point out that we all use nouns and pronouns continually in our daily communication.

2. Explain that while many nouns fall under the well-known person, place, or thing definition, many nouns, such as ideas and qualities, are abstract.

3. Have a student read the five subcategories listed on this page to the class. Ask for examples of other abstract nouns. (*commitment, anger, beauty*)

4. Remind students that *singular* means "one" and that *plural* means "more than one." Ask them to turn these singular nouns into plural ones: *boy* (boys), *university* (universities), *woman* (women).

Critical Viewing

Analyze Students may include such nouns as *window, woman, signs, cellar, trees, shops, footsteps, leaves,* and *shadow.*

Section 17.1

Nouns and Pronouns

Nouns and pronouns are an essential part of language. Together, these two parts of speech make it possible for people to label and refer to everything around them. First, you will examine nouns.

Nouns

You probably recall this common definition of a noun:

▶ **KEY CONCEPT** A **noun** is the part of speech that names a person, place, or thing. ■

The categories of *person* or *place* are self-evident:

PERSON: Bob, colonist, swimmer, Ms. Yang, Captain Smith

PLACE: kitchen, James River, canyon, Oklahoma

The category *thing,* on the other hand, contains several subcategories: visible things, ideas, actions, conditions, and qualities.

VISIBLE THINGS: duck, daffodil, fort
IDEAS: capitalism, recession, freedom
ACTIONS: competition, exercise, labor
CONDITIONS: joy, health, happiness
QUALITIES: compassion, intelligence, drive

Concrete and Abstract Nouns Nouns can be grouped not only as people, places, or things, but also as concrete or abstract. A **concrete noun** names something you can see, touch, taste, hear, or smell. An **abstract noun** names something you cannot perceive through any of your five senses.

CONCRETE NOUNS: person, cannon, road, city, music
ABSTRACT NOUNS: hope, improvement, independence, desperation, cooperation

Theme: American Colonial History

In this section, you will learn about nouns and pronouns. All the examples and exercises are about historic Virginia.

Cross-Curricular Connection: Social Studies

▲ **Critical Viewing** What concrete nouns name things you migh[t] see or experience on [a] cobblestone street in [?] Alexandria, Virginia? **[Analyze]**

⏱ TIME AND RESOURCE MANAGER

Resources
Print: *Grammar Exercise Workbook,* pp. 1–4; *Grammar Exercises Answers on Transparencies,* Ch. 17
Technology: *Language Lab* CD-ROM, Nouns and Pronouns; *On-Line Exercise Bank,* Section 17.1

In-Depth Coverage	Accelerated Pace
• Work through all key concepts, pp. 364–370. • Assign and review Exercises 1–6. • Do the Grammar in Literature activity, p. 368.	• Assign pp. 364–370 for independent student review. • Assign Section Review Exercises 7–9.

Singular and Plural Nouns A noun can also indicate *number*. A **singular noun** names one person, place, or thing. **Plural nouns** name more than one person, place, or thing. Most plural nouns are formed by adding -*s* or -*es* to their singular forms. The plurals of some nouns, however, are formed in other ways and must be memorized. Notice in the examples below that the plural forms of the last two are both formed in unusual ways.

SINGULAR NOUNS: meal, sickness, knife, alumnus
PLURAL NOUNS: meals, sicknesses, knives, alumni

Collective Nouns A **collective noun** names a *group* of people or things.

COLLECTIVE NOUNS			
army	choir	troop	faculty
cast	class	crew	legislature

Compound Nouns A **compound noun** is a noun made up of two or more words functioning as a single unit. Compound nouns may be written as separate words, hyphenated words, or combined words.

COMPOUND NOUNS	
Separated	life preserver, coffee table, bird dog
Hyphenated	sergeant-at-arms, self-rule, daughter-in-law
Combined	battlefield, dreamland, porthole

Check a dictionary if you are not sure when to write a compound noun as two separate words, a hyphenated word, or as a single combined word.

Common and Proper Nouns Any noun may be categorized as either *common* or *proper*. A **common noun** names any one of a class of people, places, or things. A **proper noun** names a specific person, place, or thing. Proper nouns are capitalized while common nouns are not. (See Chapter 26 for specific rules of capitalization.)

COMMON NOUNS: leader, place, book, war
PROPER NOUNS: Jefferson, Virginia, *Leaves of Grass*, Revolutionary War

Spelling Tip

To form the plural for most singular nouns ending with *f* or *fe*, change the *f* to *v* and add -*s* or -*es* (*wife, wives; leaf, leaves*).

Step-by-Step Teaching Guide

Collective, Compound, Common, and Proper Nouns

1. Explain that a collective noun names a group or "collection" of people or things. Ask students to identify a group at school (for example, a team, class, committee, or club). These are collective nouns. Students may also identify groups of individuals (teachers, athletes, women); however, these are plural nouns.

2. Explain that a compound noun is made of two or more words that function as a single unit. Have students try to identify which of the following words are compound nouns. Write the following words on the board: *police department* (yes), *bathtub* (yes), *high school* (yes), *son-in-law* (yes), *history* (no), *mistake* (no).

3. Point out that all nouns are either common or proper. Common nouns identify any nonspecific person, place, or thing (*teenager, city, lake*). Proper nouns name a specific person, place, or thing (*Jonathan, Dublin, Lake Louise*). Because proper nouns name specific people, places, and things, they are capitalized.

Customize for
Visual/Spatial Learners

Using a sheet of standard graph paper, have students create a noun-search puzzle. They must incorporate at least two examples of each type of noun addressed in this section. To begin, have them fill in the squares (approximately 35X35 1/4" squares or 15X15 1/2" squares) with their examples, which can go vertically, horizontally, or diagonally. Then, have them fill in the blank squares with random letters. When they finish, they may trade with a partner and solve one another's puzzles.

366

17.1

◄ **Critical Viewing**
What nouns name things about this picture of rural Virginia that would probably surprise a Jamestown settler? **[Connect]**

> **Exercise 1** **Identifying Types of Nouns** Write the numbered nouns on your paper. Next to each noun, write the correct description from each of these lettered pairs: (A) *concrete* or *abstract*, (B) *singular* or *plural*, (C) *collective* or *not collective*, (D) *compound* or *not compound*, (E) *common* or *proper*.

EXAMPLE: freedom

ANSWER: (A) abstract, (B) singular, (C) not collective, (D) not compound, (E) common

1. colony
2. Jamestown
3. leadership
4. farmer
5. Captain John Smith
6. self-government
7. Pocahontas
8. peace
9. farmland
10. history

> **Exercise 2** **Recognizing and Classifying Nouns** Identify the nouns in the following excerpt from *The General History of Virginia*. Label each as *concrete* or *abstract*, *singular* or *plural*, *common* or *proper*. Then, indicate whether any of the nouns are collective or compound.

He demanding for their captain, they showed him Opechancanough, King of Pamunkee, to whom he gave a round ivory double compass dial. Much they marveled at the playing of the fly and needle, which they could see so plainly and yet not touch it because of the glass that covered them. But when he demonstrated by that globe-like jewel the roundness of the earth and skies, the sphere of the sun, moon, and stars, and how the sun did chase the night round about the world continually, . . . they all stood as amazed with admiration.

366 • **The Parts of Speech**

Pronouns

To avoid the awkward repetition of a noun, speakers and writers use another part of speech—*pronouns*.

> ▶ **KEY CONCEPT** A **pronoun** is a word that takes the place of a noun, another pronoun, or a group of words functioning as a noun. ■

> ▶ **KEY CONCEPT** An **antecedent** is the noun, pronoun, or group of words functioning as a noun to which a pronoun refers. ■

EXAMPLES: A crowd quickly gathered. Looking at the sea, *they*

saw a schooner inching *its* way into Jamestown harbor.

Losing the crops was frightening; *it* was an

experience the colonist said *she* would never forget.

Most pronouns have specific antecedents, but some do not. The rest of this section describes the different kinds of pronouns and tells whether or not they have antecedents.

Personal Pronouns   Personal pronouns are the pronouns commonly used to refer to particular people, places, and things.

> ▶ **KEY CONCEPT** A personal pronoun is a pronoun that refers to the person speaking (first person), the person spoken to (second person), or the person, place, or thing spoken about (third person). ■

PERSONAL PRONOUNS		
	Singular	**Plural**
First Person **Second Person** **Third Person**	I, me, my, mine you, your, yours he, him, his, she, her, hers, it, its	we, us, our, ours you, your, yours they, them, their, theirs

---

If students have difficulty with Exercise 1 or 2, refer them to the following for additional practice.

In the Textbook	Print Resources	Technology
Section Review, Ex. 7–8, p. 373	*Grammar Exercise Workbook,* pp. 1–2	*Language Lab* CD-ROM, Nouns and Pronouns *On-Line Exercise Bank,* Section 17.1

Antecedents and Personal Pronouns

1. Explain that a pronoun is a word that takes the place of a noun.

2. Explain that the noun that the pronoun refers to is called its antecedent. Write the following sentence on the board.

   The teacher gave the student his grade.

   Ask the students to whom the pronoun *his* refers. (It refers to *the student,* which is the antecedent noun.)

3. Point out that the antecedent can be a group of words, not just a single noun. Share another example on the board.

   Breaking her arm was painful. It left her in tears.

   Ask students what *it* refers to in this sentence. (The antecedent is *breaking her arm.*)

4. Explain that personal pronouns refer to people, with the exception of the pronouns *it* and *its*. Have students brainstorm as many personal pronouns as possible and record them on the board or overhead. (Examples: *I, you, me, my, they, she, he.*)

Integrating Speaking Skills

Pronoun and Antecedent Agreement Point out that a common problem is the incorrect use of the personal pronouns *I* and *me*. Write these examples on the board:

"My friend and me are going to the store," says the child.

"My friend and I," responds the parent.

A simple rule to review with students is the subtraction rule. Have them subtract from the subject everything but the personal pronoun and then determine whether the sentence still works. *Me are going to the store* does not work, but *I am going to the store* does. Therefore, *I* should be used.

Step-by-Step Teaching Guide

Reflexive and Intensive Pronouns

1. Point out that both reflexive and intensive pronouns end in the suffix *-self* or *-selves*. Though they share the same form, they serve different functions.

2. Explain that a reflexive pronoun points back to, or "reflects," an earlier noun. Write the following sentence on the board:

   The basketball players won the game not only for <u>themselves</u> *but for the entire school.*

   Explain that *themselves* is a reflexive pronoun that refers to the basketball players.

3. Explain that an intensive pronoun is added only for emphasis. Offer this example:

   Harriet Beecher Stowe <u>herself</u> *helped slaves escape.*

   Discuss with students that in this sentence, *herself* adds intensity to the subject of the sentence.

Step-by-Step Teaching Guide

Grammar in Literature

1. Read or have a prepared student read the passage aloud. Encourage students to identify the pronouns to which the reflexive pronouns refer.

2. Encourage students to suggest sentences about this episode that use intensive pronouns. (*Captain Smith* <u>himself</u> *earned his captors' respect.*)

Connections With Literature

A longer excerpt from *The General History of Virginia* can be found in *Prentice Hall Literature: Timeless Voices, Timeless Themes*, The American Experience.

Reflexive and Intensive Pronouns These two types of pronouns look the same, but they function differently in sentences.

▶ **KEY CONCEPTS** A **reflexive pronoun** ends in *-self* or *-selves* and indicates that someone or something in the sentence acts for or on itself. An **intensive pronoun** ends in *-self* or *-selves* and simply adds emphasis to a noun or pronoun in the same sentence. ■

REFLEXIVE AND INTENSIVE PRONOUNS		
	Singular	**Plural**
First Person	myself	ourselves
Second Person	yourself	yourselves
Third Person	himself, herself, itself	themselves

REFLEXIVE: The settlers prepared *themselves* for the approaching winter.

INTENSIVE: John Smith *himself* wrote an account of the meeting.

GRAMMAR IN
LITERATURE

from The General History of Virginia
John Smith

Leading an expedition on the Chikahominy River, Captain John Smith is taken prisoner. In this account of John Smith's imprisonment, notice that the reflexive pronoun himself *points back to the subject* he *used earlier in the sentence.*

Six or seven weeks [they] kept him prisoner, many strange triumphs and conjurations they made of him, yet he so demeaned *himself* amongst them, as he not only diverted them from surprising the fort, but procured his own liberty, and got *himself* and his company such estimation amongst them, that those savages admired him.

Grammar and Style Tip

Don't be tempted to use a reflexive pronoun in place of a personal pronoun. For example, it is not correct to say, "Eric and myself like early American history." You should say, "Eric and I like early American history."

Demonstrative Pronouns Demonstrative pronouns are used to point out one or more nouns.

KEY CONCEPT A **demonstrative pronoun** directs attention to a specific person, place, or thing. ■

There are four demonstrative pronouns:

DEMONSTRATIVE PRONOUNS	
Singular	**Plural**
this, that	these, those

EXAMPLES: *That* is a beautiful city.

This is my report.

Those are the books you need.

These are the books that need to be returned to the library.

Relative Pronouns Relative pronouns are used to relate one idea in a sentence to another.

KEY CONCEPT A **relative pronoun** introduces an adjective clause and connects it to the word that the clause modifies. ■

There are five relative pronouns:

RELATIVE PRONOUNS				
that	which	who	whom	whose

EXAMPLES: We read a book *that* contained an account of the settlers' experiences.
The settlers *who* had written it described their hardships.
The winter, *which* they knew would be harsh, was quickly approaching.

Nouns and Pronouns • 369

More About the Writer

Before the signing of the Declaration of Independence, most published writing in America was limited to practical topics, including spiritual and political matters. Fiction was considered sinful by the Puritans. John Smith's accounts of his life during this time are some of the few surviving personal stories of that time. Although such accounts were intended to be autobiographical, historians question Smith's credibility as an author. This is due to inconsistencies in his retelling of stories, such as the story of how Pocahontas saved his life.

Step-by-Step Teaching Guide

Demonstrative Pronouns

1. Explain to students that a demonstrative pronoun demonstrates or points out a specific thing that is being addressed, such as "*This* is the homework tonight." Some other examples of demonstrative pronouns are *that, these,* and *those.* Have students write four sentences, using each demonstrative pronoun once. (Example: *That was an awful movie. This is your yearbook.*)

2. Help students avoid confusing demonstrative pronouns with adjectives. Show them that the pronoun *this*, for instance, is a demonstrative pronoun when it does not modify another word. (Example: *This is a puzzle.*) It is an adjective in the next example. (Example: *This puzzle is confusing.*)

Customize for
ESL Students

Some students benefit from visual and hands-on approaches. Model the use of demonstrative pronouns by walking around the classroom and identifying objects using demonstrative pronouns. "*This* is my pen." "*That* is Monika's purse." "*These* are our books." Pick up the objects to further ensure understanding. Then, ask students to point out something in the room and use a demonstrative pronoun to identify it.

Relative, Interrogative, and Indefinite Pronouns

1. Write the following sentence on the board or overhead.

   The exam, which was very difficult, ended promptly at 2:00 P.M.

   Ask students which portion of the sentence could be omitted without making the sentence incomplete (*which was very difficult*). Explain that this portion is called the subordinate clause. It does not hold the main idea of the sentence, but a lesser or subordinate one.

2. Point out that when the subordinate clause is removed from the sentence, the independent clause is revealed:

   The exam ended promptly at 2:00 P.M.

   This clause can stand as its own sentence. The original sentence contains more information, which is linked to the independent clause by the relative pronoun *which*. Relative pronouns can begin subordinate clauses and link them to another idea in the sentence.

Real-World Connection

Many business letters and job recommendations begin with the phrase, *To Whom it May Concern*. Do students understand why *whom* is used in place of *who*? Remind students that *whom* is always the object in a statement, and *who* is always the subject or predicate nominative. If something is done to, with, or for the person, he or she is the object. Ask students what a prospective employer might think of an applicant who uses improper grammar or poor spelling.

Interrogative Pronouns These pronouns are used to ask questions.

▶ **KEY CONCEPT** An **interrogative pronoun** is used to begin a question. ■

There are five interrogative pronouns:

INTERROGATIVE PRONOUNS				
what	which	who	whom	whose

Sometimes, the antecedent of an interrogative pronoun is not known. Notice in the first example that follows that there are no antecedents.

EXAMPLES: *Who* surrendered at Yorktown?
What was the name of the British general?

Indefinite Pronouns Indefinite pronouns require no specific antecedents.

▶ **KEY CONCEPT** An **indefinite pronoun** refers to a person, place, or thing that may or may not be specifically named. ■

INDEFINITE PRONOUNS				
Singular			**Plural**	**Both**
another	everyone	nothing	both	all
anybody	everything	one	few	any
anyone	little	other	many	more
anything	much	somebody	others	most
each	neither	someone	several	none
either	nobody	something		some
everybody	no one			

Although indefinite pronouns do not require specific antecedents, they often have them.

NO SPECIFIC ANTECEDENT: *Several* have visited Williamsburg.

SPECIFIC ANTECEDENTS: *One* of the students prepared a report.

Internet Tip

Many states, cities, and towns, especially those of historic interest, have Web pages and Web sites that provide information about the place's points of interest. These sites can usually be found by using the place's name in a key word search.

Revolutionary Cannon at Yorktown

◄ **Critical Viewing**
The colonial forces defeated the British at the Battle of Yorktown. Using interrogative pronouns, what questions could you prepare for a tour of the battlegrounds? **[Connect]**

▶ **Exercise 3** **Recognizing Pronouns** Identify the pronoun or pronouns in each of the sentences below.

EXAMPLE: The candidate for whom I voted lost the election.

ANSWER: whom, I

1. As the farmers exhausted the soil from tobacco farming, they needed to find new land.
2. Horatio made his decision to move westward in order to sustain himself.
3. Neighbors told him to leave with them.
4. They had heard tales that described the lushness of the Shenandoah Valley.
5. Governor Spotswood himself had led an expedition to the Shenandoah Valley.

▶ **Exercise 4** **Classifying Pronouns** Identify the type of each underlined pronoun below.

EXAMPLE: <u>That</u> is an inspiring story of courage.
ANSWER: demonstrative

(1) Horatio packed his belongings and joined <u>them</u> on the trail. (2) He soon found <u>himself</u> crossing the Blue Ridge Mountains *en route* to a new home. (3) <u>This</u> was the start of a new life for Horatio, and he was eager to begin his work. (4) <u>Others</u> would follow the same trail that took Horatio over the mountains and into the valley. (5) <u>Who</u> could have known how long he would be remembered?

▶ **More Practice**
Language Lab CD-ROM
• Pronouns and Antecedents lesson
On-line Exercise Bank
• Section 17.1
Grammar Exercise Workbook
• pp. 3–4

Nouns and Pronouns • **371**

Critical Viewing

Connect Student responses may include the following questions: Whose lives were lost? What was the role of this battle in the Revolutionary War?

Answer Key

🕑 **TIME SAVERS!**

🔲 **Answers on Transparencies**
Use the *Grammar Exercises Answers on Transparencies* for Chapter 17 to facilitate correction by students.

🖥 **On-Line Exercise Bank**
Have students complete the exercises on computer. The Auto Check feature will grade their work for you!

Exercise 5

1. interrogative
2. personal
3. relative
4. personal
5. personal
6. personal
7. reflexive
8. intensive
9. relative
10. indefinite

Exercise 6

1. it
2. that
3. himself
4. that
5. his
6. nothing
7. them
8. himself
9. Who
10. That

17.1

▶ **Exercise 5** **Identifying Types of Pronouns** Write the word *personal, reflexive, intensive, demonstrative, relative, interrogative,* or *indefinite* to indicate the type of each underlined pronoun.

EXAMPLE: Governor Dinwiddie needed a man <u>who</u> was confident and knew the wilderness well.

ANSWER: relative

(1) <u>What</u> occurred on George Washington's first military adventure? (2) <u>It</u> began soon after Virginia governor Dinwiddie heard reports (3) <u>that</u> a French force was establishing outposts on the headwaters of the Ohio River. (4) <u>He</u> had received orders from the Crown to demand (5) <u>their</u> withdrawal, and this task fell to the young adjutant, Major Washington. In late 1753, Washington led (6) <u>his</u> small band of companions north through the wilderness, and they soon found (7) <u>themselves</u> at Fort Le Boeuf, near Lake Erie. Washington (8) <u>himself</u> gave the demands to the French commander, (9) <u>which</u> were promptly dismissed. Although (10) <u>none</u> could foresee it, this adventure would lead directly to the French and Indian War.

▶ **Exercise 6** **Using the Correct Pronoun** In your notebook, write the paragraph, filling in each blank with the kind of pronoun indicated in parentheses.

EXAMPLE: After (<u>personal</u>) return to Virginia, Washington recommended (<u>relative</u>) an English fort be built on the Ohio River to counteract the French.

ANSWER: After his return to Virginia, Washington recommended that an English fort be built on the Ohio River to counteract the French.

To build a fort on the Ohio River, Governor Dinwiddie sent William Trent and some men to begin work on (1) (<u>personal</u>) in 1754. Washington soon followed, with about 200 troops (2) (<u>relative</u>) he (3) (<u>intensive</u>) had raised on a shoestring budget. When they received news (4) (<u>relative</u>) the French and their Iroquois allies had already defeated Trent and (5) (<u>personal</u>) forces, they immediately dug in and began building Fort Necessity. After a minor battle, the French attacked the fort in force, and, with limited supplies and weapons, (6) (<u>indefinite</u>) could be done to hold out against (7) (<u>personal</u>). The French were impressed by the young colonel who, even in defeat, had conducted (8) (<u>reflexive</u>) with bravery and intelligence. (9) "(<u>interrogative</u>) is that man?" asked the French commander. (10) "(<u>demonstrative</u>) is Lieutenant Colonel Washington of Virginia," answered the aide-de-camp.

▶ **More Practice**

Language Lab CD-ROM
• Pronouns lesson
On-line Exercise Bank
• Section 17.1
Grammar Exercise Workbook
• pp. 3–4

⏱ **TIME SAVERS!**

🖨 **Answers on Transparencies** Use the *Grammar Exercises Answers on Transparencies* for Chapter 17 to facilitate correction by students.

💻 **On-Line Exercise Bank** Have students complete the exercises on computer. The Auto Check feature will grade their work for you!

✓ **ONGOING ASSESSMENT: Monitor and Reinforce**

If students have difficulty with Exercise 3, 4, 5, or 6, refer them to the following for additional practice.

In the Textbook	Print Resources	Technology
Section Review, Ex. 7–9, p. 373	*Grammar Exercise Workbook,* pp. 3–4	*Language Lab* CD-ROM, Nouns and Pronouns *On-Line Exercise Bank,* Section 17.1

Section 17.1 Section Review

GRAMMAR EXERCISES 7–12

Exercise 7 Recognizing Nouns and Pronouns List the nouns and pronouns in each sentence.

1. Thomas Jefferson, born in Goochland County, is another famous Virginian.
2. He studied law at the College of William and Mary, but he made most of his money by working his land.
3. Monticello was the name of the estate that Jefferson had designed himself.
4. During the American Revolution, he was an important member of the Continental Congress.
5. He wrote most of the Declaration of Independence, which was adopted by the colonies on July 4, 1776.

Exercise 8 Identifying Types of Nouns and Pronouns In each sentence, identify one or more examples of the kind of noun or pronoun specified in parentheses.

1. Also a Virginian, Robert E. Lee was a military genius who fought against the Union during the American Civil War. (proper, compound noun)
2. He had been born in January 1807 in Stratford, Virginia, into a prominent family. (common, collective noun)
3. His military career began with his education at the United States Military Academy. (abstract, singular noun)
4. President Lincoln had wanted him to command Northern forces, but Lee remained in Virginia. (proper, singular noun)
5. The War Between the States ended when Lee surrendered to General Ulysses S. Grant. (compound, proper noun)
6. Bull Run is the name of a small stream that is located in Virginia, southwest of Washington, D.C. (concrete, singular noun)
7. It was the site of two battles during the Civil War. (personal pronoun)

8. In both, Stonewall Jackson himself commanded armies. (intensive pronoun)
9. In the first battle in 1861, the outnumbered Confederate troops defended themselves vigorously until their reinforcements arrived. (reflexive pronoun)
10. These quickly crushed the Union troops, who, curiously enough, had many spectators. (relative pronoun)

Exercise 9 Using Pronouns Complete the paragraph below using the type of pronoun indicated in parentheses.

Nat Turner was a Virginian slave [1] (relative) became the leader of a slave revolt. [2] (personal) believed that he [3] (intensive) was destined to free [4] (personal) people. On August 22, 1831, Turner and [5] (indefinite) of his followers struck against their masters.

Exercise 10 Find It in Your Reading Reread the Grammar in Literature example on page 368. Find five common nouns and at least one pronoun other than a reflexive pronoun.

Exercise 11 Find It in Your Writing Look through your writing portfolio. Find examples of the different kinds of pronouns. If you cannot find an example of each, challenge yourself to include the types you have not used.

Exercise 12 Writing Application Using a variety of types of nouns and pronouns, write about a person from history. Underline the nouns and pronouns.

Section Review • 373

ASSESS

Section Review

Answer Key

Exercise 7

1. Thomas Jefferson, Goochland County, Virginian
2. He, law, College of William and Mary, he, most, his, money, working, his, land
3. Monticello, name, estate, that, Jefferson, himself
4. American Revolution, he, member, Continental Congress
5. He, most, Declaration of Independence, which, colonies, July 4, 1776

Exercise 8

1. Robert E. Lee, American Civil War
2. family
3. career, education
4. President Lincoln, Lee, Virginia
5. War Between the States, General Ulysses S. Grant
6. stream
7. It
8. himself
9. themselves
10. who

Exercise 9

1. who
2. He
3. himself
4. his
5. some, each, many, several, most

Exercise 10

Find It in Your Reading
Common nouns: weeks, prisoner, triumphs, conjurations, fort, liberty, company, estimation, savages
Personal pronouns: him, they, him, he, them, his, his, them, him
Relative pronoun: that

Exercise 11

Find It in Your Writing
Tell students that a first-person narrative, written in their own voice or in that of another real or fictional narrator, is an ideal selection for identifying pronouns.

Exercise 12

Writing Application
Encourage students to use at least five different types of pronouns in their work. If they are unsure of the function of a certain type of pronoun, have them reread the relevant section in their textbooks.

Interest GRABBER Write the following incomplete sentences on the board.

Frank the cookies.

When you my car, the gas tank.

Janet at her desk.

Have students add words to make these complete sentences. Explain that the added words are all verbs.

Activate Prior Knowledge

Ask students to think about a fast and exciting amusement park ride they've seen or experienced. Have them describe what the ride actually does. Write on the board the verbs they offer. Based on this list, have them try to write a definition of verbs.

TEACH

Step-by-Step Teaching Guide

Action and Linking Verbs

1. In the following examples, have students identify the action verbs and label mental actions *MA*.

   Tom baked the winning apple pie. (baked)

   The judge quickly declared him the winner. (declared)

   Tom thought about sharing his recipe with the others. (thought, MA)

2. Tell students that linking verbs must agree with the subject in a sentence, not with the subject complement. Write these examples on the board:

   My choice is *french fries.*

   French fries are *my choice.*

   Explain that in the first sentence, the subject, *choice,* takes the singular verb *is.* Have students explain why the plural verb *are* is used in the second sentence. (The subject, *french fries,* is plural.)

3. Students might have trouble distinguishing mental action verbs (such as *wonder, think, decide*) from linking verbs (such as *feel, become, stay*). Remind them that an equal sign can replace a linking verb.

   The air felt *warm.* (linking verb)

   She decided *it was warm enough to go swimming.* (mental action verb)

Section 17.2

Verbs

Verbs are used to help make statements, ask questions, or deliver commands. Every complete sentence must have at least one verb, which may have as many as four words.

▶ **KEY CONCEPT** A **verb** is a word or group of words that expresses time while showing an action, a condition, or the fact that something exists. ■

Action Verbs and Linking Verbs

Action verbs, as their name implies, express action. They are used to tell what someone or something does, did, or will do. Linking verbs, on the other hand, express a condition. Certain linking verbs can also be used to show that something exists.

▶ **KEY CONCEPT** An **action verb** is a verb that tells what action someone or something is performing. ■

ACTION VERBS: The students *are learning* about winter sports. The radio *blared* the broadcast of the hockey game.

Notice in the examples that the action expressed by a verb does not have to be visible. Words expressing mental activities —such as *learn, think,* or *decide*—are also considered action verbs.

The person or thing that performs the action is called the *subject* of the verb. In the examples above, *students* and *radio* are the subjects of *are learning* and *blared.*

▶ **KEY CONCEPT** A **linking verb** is a verb that connects its subject with a noun, pronoun, or adjective that identifies or describes the subject. ■

LINKING VERBS: That man *is* a famous hockey player.

The ice surface *seems* smooth.

In the examples, the linking verbs are shown in italics. An arrow shows which word or words are linked to the subject.

The verb *be* is the most common linking verb. All of the forms of this verb are shown in the following chart.

374 • The Parts of Speech

Theme: Winter Sports

In this section, you will learn about verbs. All the examples and exercises are about winter sports.

Cross-Curricular Connection: Physical Education

⏱ TIME AND RESOURCE MANAGER

Resources

Print: *Grammar Exercise Workbook,* pp. 5–10; *Grammar Exercises Answers on Transparencies,* Ch. 17

Technology: *Language Lab* CD-ROM, Using Verbs; *On-Line Exercise Bank,* Section 17.2

In-Depth Coverage	Accelerated Pace
• Work through all key concepts, pp. 374–378. • Assign and review Exercises 13–15. • Do the Grammar in Literature activity, p. 377.	• Assign pp. 374–378 for independent student review. • Assign Section Review Exercises 16–18.

THE FORMS OF *BE*

am	am being	can be	have been
are	are being	could be	has been
is	is being	may be	had been
was	was being	might be	could have been
were	were being	must be	may have been
		shall be	might have been
		should be	shall have been
		will be	should have been
		would be	will have been
			would have been

Most often, the forms of *be* that function as linking verbs express the condition of the subject. Occasionally, however, they may merely express existence, usually by showing, with other words, where the subject is located.

EXAMPLE: The skater *is* on the rink.

A few other verbs can also serve as linking verbs. These are shown in the following chart.

OTHER LINKING VERBS

appear	look	sound
become	remain	stay
feel	seem	taste
grow	smell	turn

Notice in the following examples that the verbs link their subjects to words that identify or describe them.

EXAMPLES: The winter air *smelled* crisp and clean.

The crowd *sounds* excited.

The driver *stayed* alert.

Some of these verbs may also act as action—not linking—verbs. To determine whether the word is functioning as an action verb or as a linking verb, insert *am, are,* or *is* in place of the verb. If the substitute makes sense while connecting two words, then the original verb is a linking verb.

LINKING VERB: The air *felt* cold. (The air *is* cold.)
ACTION VERB: The skiers *felt* a chilly wind.

▲ **Critical Viewing**
What verbs might you use to describe the actions a skier takes down a mountain slope? **[Apply]**

Customize for
Less Advanced Students

Students often have trouble focusing on whether the subject is singular or plural and making it agree with its verb. Determining which form of the verb to use can be complicated by the words that are between the subject and verb in a sentence. Review on the board.

Our principal, as well as the deans, <u>uses</u> the teachers' lounge. (The subject is *principal.*)

Kathy and Sara <u>like</u> to go shopping together. (The subject is *Kathy and Sara.*)

George or Cynthia <u>is going</u> to be fined for the disturbance. (The subject is *George or Cynthia,* but agreement is with the closer subject when the subjects are connected by *or.*)

There <u>are</u> many reasons for eating healthily. (The subject is *reasons.*)

Economics <u>is</u> an interesting class. (The subject is *Economics,* a singular noun.)

The verbs are underlined. Have students find the subject and explain why the verb agrees (singular/plural).

Critical Viewing

Apply Student responses may include *ski, crouch, jump, race, tuck, skid, bend, push off, balance, lean.*

Verbs • 375

▶ **Exercise 13**

1. action
2. action
3. action
4. linking
5. linking

Step-by-Step Teaching Guide

Transitive and Intransitive Verbs

1. Emphasize to students that not all action verbs can simply be labeled *transitive* or *intransitive*. Instead, they change according to their function in a sentence. For example:

   He drove the car around the block.

   He drove wildly.

   In the first sentence, *drove* is transitive because it transfers action to the car, which is the direct object. In the second, *drove* is intransitive because it does not transfer action to anything.

2. Write the following examples on the board and have students determine whether each verb is transitive or intransitive.

   They climbed the mountain that winter. (transitive)

   They climbed very slowly. (intransitive)

   They stopped frequently to drink water and to rest. (intransitive)

   The dangerous storm stopped the trip. (transitive)

17.2

▶ **Exercise 13** **Identifying Action and Linking Verbs** Identify each underlined verb as an action verb or a linking verb.

EXAMPLE: Tell me the history of skiing.

ANSWER: action verb

1. Archaeologists <u>found</u> pieces of skis in Norway and Sweden dating back four thousand years.
2. Skiing's modern form <u>started</u> in the mid-nineteenth century.
3. Norwegian immigrants <u>brought</u> skiing to the United States in the 1850's.
4. It <u>became</u> popular during the 1930's after the first installation of a rope tow in Woodstock, Vermont.
5. The rope tow <u>looks</u> tricky, but it's an easy way to get to the top of a slope.

Transitive and Intransitive Verbs

All verbs are either *transitive* or *intransitive*, depending on whether or not they transfer action to another word in a sentence.

▶ **KEY CONCEPTS** A **transitive** verb directs action toward someone or something named in the same sentence. An **intransitive** verb does not direct action toward anyone or anything named in the same sentence. ■

The word toward which a transitive verb directs its action is called the *object* of the verb. Intransitive verbs never have objects. You can determine whether a verb has an object by asking *whom* or *what* after the verb. If there is someone or something, that word is the object and the verb is a transitive verb.

TRANSITIVE: The player *shot* the puck. (Shot *what? Answer:* puck)
                                 OBJ

We *ate* the cake. (Ate *what? Answer:* cake)
                   OBJ

INTRANSITIVE: The team *practiced* in the old ice arena. (Practiced *what? Answer:* none)
The fan *shouted* loudly. (Shouted *what? Answer:* none)

▶ **More Practice**

Language Lab CD-ROM
• Using Verbs lesson
On-line Exercise Bank
• Section 17.2
Grammar Exercise Workbook
• pp. 5–8

🌸 **Grammar and Style Ti**

When you want to show action in your writing, avoid words like *seem, feel*, and other linking verbs.

⏱ **TIME SAVERS!**

📘 **Answers on Transparencies**
Use the *Grammar Exercises Answers on Transparencies* for Chapter 17 to facilitate correction by students.

💻 **On-Line Exercise Bank**
Have students complete the exercises on computer. The Auto Check feature will grade their work for you!

✅ **ONGOING ASSESSMENT: Monitor and Reinforce**

If students miss more than one item in Exercise 13 or 14, refer them to the following for additional practice.

In the Textbook	Print Resources	Technology
Section Review, Ex. 16–19, p. 379	*Grammar Exercise Workbook,* pp. 5–8	*Language Lab* CD-ROM, Using Verbs *On-Line Exercise Bank,* Section 17.2

▶ **KEY CONCEPT** Since linking verbs do not express action, they are always intransitive. Most action verbs, however, can be either transitive or intransitive, depending on their use in a sentence. ■

▶ **Exercise 14** **Identifying Transitive and Intransitive Verbs**
On your paper, write all verbs in the following sentences. Label each verb *transitive* or *intransitive*.

EXAMPLE: We heard the latest
bobsledding results
this morning.
ANSWER: heard (transitive)

1. People used bobsleds in America as far back as 1839
2. The sleds carried wood from the forests during the winter.
3. Bobsled racing began in Switzerland in the late nine-teenth century.
4. Racers bob back-and-forth, which increases the sled's speed.
5. The sport gets its name from this action.

▲ **Critical Viewing**
What verbs describe the action in bob-sledding? **[Relate]**

GRAMMAR IN
LITERATURE

from **Stopping by Woods on a Snowy Evening**
Robert Frost

Notice that Frost's verb choices (are, think, know, is, see, watch), a mixture of action and linking verbs, do not express any physical movement, as if to emphasize the stillness and serenity of the winter scene.

Whose woods these *are* I *think* I *know*.
His house *is* in the village though:
He will not *see* me stopping here
To *watch* his woods fill up with snow.

Verbs • 377

Verb Phrases

1. Students might have difficulty identifying a verb phrase when it is interrupted by other words in a sentence. Point out that verb phrases are often interrupted by adverbs, as in this example:

   They will soon be going to the arena. (Soon is an adverb that interrupts the verb phrase will be going.)

   Tell students to rewrite the sentence without the adverb to make the verb phrase clearer: *They will be going to the arena.*

2. Point out that in questions, verb phrases are often interrupted by the subject of the sentence, as in this example:

   Will he go to the arena with them? (He, the subject of the sentence, interrupts the verb phrase will go.)

   Tell students to rewrite the question in the form of a statement to make the verb phrase clearer: *He will go to the arena with them.*

3. Have students write two statements and two questions that contain interrupted verb phrases.

Answer Key

▶ **Exercise 15**

Answers may vary; samples are given.

1. has become
2. may be based
3. might be traced
4. was begun
5. has been played

17.2

Verb Phrases

A verb that has more than one word is a *verb phrase.*

▶ **KEY CONCEPT** A **verb phrase** consists of a main verb and one or more helping verbs. ■

Helping verbs are often called *auxiliary verbs.* As many as three helping verbs may precede the main verb in a verb phrase.

VERB PHRASES: I *will be taking* a horse-and-carriage ride through the snow.
I *should have taken* a horse-and-carriage ride through the snow.

All the forms of *be* listed on page 375 can be used as helping verbs. The following verbs can also be helping verbs.

do	have	shall	can
does	has	should	could
did	had	will	may
		would	might
			must

A verb phrase is often interrupted by other words in a sentence. In the following examples, the helping verbs are in italics and the main verb is underlined.

INTERRUPTED VERB PHRASES: I *will* definitely *be* <u>taking</u> a horse-and-carriage ride through the snow.
Should I <u>take</u> a horse-and-carriage ride through the snow?

▶ **Exercise 15** **Using Verb Phrases** Write the sentences below, filling in the blanks with appropriate verb phrases.

EXAMPLE: We __?__ __?__ __?__ at the ice rink.
ANSWER: We have been skating at the ice rink.

1. Hockey __?__ __?__ one of the most popular games in the world.
2. The game __?__ __?__ __?__ on the ancient Greek game hoquet—a field sport played with a ball and a stick.
3. The first game of ice hockey __?__ __?__ __?__ back to 1875.
4. A professional league __?__ not __?__ until 1917.
5. For years, the sport __?__ __?__ __?__ upon a smooth ice surface.

▶ **More Practice**

Language Lab CD-ROM
• Using Verbs lesson
On-line Exercise Bank
• Section 17.2
Grammar Exercise Workbook
• pp. 9–10

⏱ TIME SAVERS!

🖼 **Answers on Transparencies**
Use the *Grammar Exercises Answers on Transparencies* for Chapter 17 to facilitate correction by students.

💻 **On-Line Exercise Bank**
Have students complete the exercises on computer. The Auto Check feature will grade their work for you!

☑ ONGOING ASSESSMENT: Monitor and Reinforce

If students miss more than one item in Exercise 15, refer them to the following for additional practice.

In the Textbook	Print Resources	Technology
Section Review Ex. 18, p. 379	*Grammar Exercise Workbook,* pp. 9–10	*Language Lab* CD-ROM, Using Verbs *On-Line Exercise Bank,* Section 17.2

Section 17.2 Section Review

GRAMMAR EXERCISES 16–22

Exercise 16 **Identifying Action and Linking Verbs** On your paper, write *action verb* or *linking verb* to identify the underlined verb in each sentence.

1. Skiing <u>is</u> the practice of attaching a runner or ski to each foot.
2. Skis <u>enable</u> the skier to glide over snow.
3. In downhill skiing, the skier <u>battles</u> bumpy and steep slopes.
4. Then, the skier <u>takes</u> a lift back up the mountain for another run.
5. Skiers <u>become</u> exhausted by the end of the day.

Exercise 17 **Distinguishing Between Transitive and Intransitive Verbs** On your paper, write *transitive* or *intransitive* to identify the underlined verb in each sentence.

1. Ice and snow competitions <u>occur</u> in many parts of the world.
2. A group in Fairbanks, Alaska, <u>sponsors</u> an ice-sculpting competition.
3. The carnival <u>originated</u> in 1934.
4. Originally, the carnival <u>included</u> only one ice sculpture.
5. This ice castle or throne <u>belonged</u> to the king and queen of the carnival.
6. The simple design of the first ice throne <u>drew</u> attention.
7. Each year following, competitors <u>created</u> a more and more elaborate throne.
8. One year, the throne <u>was illuminated</u> by lights.
9. Another year, a transplanted forest <u>surrounded</u> the throne.
10. These early designers <u>set</u> the stage for future ice sculptors and competitions.

Exercise 18 **Identifying Verb Phrases** Write the verb phrase in each

sentence on your paper. Circle the helping verb. Underline the main verb.

1. Many activities will be happening at the winter carnival.
2. You can always start by viewing the ice and snow sculptures.
3. There have been both amateur and professional sculpting competitions.
4. The snowmobile race has become a popular event.
5. Thrill seekers can try the sledding or tobogganing areas.

Exercise 19 **Revising a Passage by Changing Verbs** Revise the following passage by replacing the underlined words with verbs that express more precise actions. You may make other minor changes.

Leanne <u>put on</u> her boots. She knew that when she <u>went</u> outside, the wind would <u>go through</u> her thin coat. Still, someone had to <u>get</u> the snow off the driveway. She <u>walked</u> to the door and went out.

Exercise 20 **Find It in Your Reading** On your paper, write two transitive verbs from "Stopping by Woods . . ." on p. 377. Explain why they are transitive.

Exercise 21 **Find It in Your Writing** Review a piece of writing from your portfolio. Find two transitive verbs, two intransitive verbs, and a verb phrase.

Exercise 22 **Writing Application** Write a brief account of a winter event. Then, identify your linking verbs and your action verbs.

Section Review • 379

ASSESS

Section Review

Each of these exercises correlates to the instruction on verbs, pages 374–378.

Answer Key

Exercise 16

1. linking
2. action
3. action
4. action
5. linking

Exercise 17

1. intransitive
2. transitive
3. intransitive
4. transitive
5. intransitive
6. transitive
7. transitive
8. intransitive
9. transitive
10. transitive

Exercise 18

Main verbs are underlined; helping verbs are underlined twice.

1. <u>will be</u> <u>happening</u>
2. <u>can</u> <u>start</u>
3. <u>have</u> <u>been</u>
4. <u>has</u> <u>become</u>
5. <u>can</u> <u>try</u>

Exercise 19

Answers may vary. Sample answers:

1. laced
2. stepped
3. pierce
4. shovel
5. trudged

Exercise 20

Find It in Your Reading
See is transitive because it transfers action to *me*. *Watch* is transitive because it transfers action to *woods*.

Exercise 21

Find It in Your Writing
Have students choose either a poem or a paragraph from their portfolios. On the left-hand side of a piece of paper, have them list the verbs and verb phrases from the selection. Then, have them exchange the selection and the list with a partner. Have the partners identify the type of each verb listed. Make sure they explain each answer.

Exercise 22

Writing Application
Point out that adjectives are not the only words that can create a vivid description. Using a wide variety of vivid, specific verbs can also help to make writing come alive.

✓ ONGOING ASSESSMENT: Assess Mastery

Use the following resources to assess student mastery of verbs.

In the Textbook	Technology
Chapter Review, Ex. 53, p. 400	*Language Lab* CD-ROM, Using Verbs *On-Line Exercise Bank,* Section 17.2

Interest GRABBER Show students a very detailed object, such as a model train, a porcelain doll, or a painting. Ask them to study it carefully, noticing as many details as they can. Then remove the object from view. Ask students to write a list of the details they remember. As students share their answers, write them on the board and circle all the adjectives. Remind them that the circled words, which are used to describe nouns and pronouns, are called adjectives.

Activate Prior Knowledge

Ask students to describe the most unusual animal they have ever seen. Have them share their descriptions. Repeat the exercise with a different subject such as the worst thunderstorm or the most interesting painting they have ever seen. Point out that most of the words they used to describe these things are adjectives.

TEACH

Step-by-Step Teaching Guide

Adjectives

1. Using the list of adjectives generated in the Interest Grabber activity or a list that you supply, have students come up with an appropriate noun for each adjective to modify. Then have students write down which question each adjective answers: *What kind? Which one? How much?* or *How many?*

2. Write the following sentences on the board. Ask students to underline the adjectives and to tell what each one modifies.

   The gray, fuzzy pickle was stuck to the bottom of the glass relish jar. (*Gray* and *fuzzy* are adjectives that modify *pickle. Glass* and *relish* are adjectives that modify *jar.*)

   The shiny white baseball soared through the misty air and landed in a muddy hole in the field. (*Shiny* and *white* are adjectives that modify *baseball. Misty* is an adjective that modifies *air. Muddy* is an adjective that modifies *hole.*)

Adjectives and Adverbs

Adjectives and **adverbs** are *modifiers*. In other words, they are the parts of speech that slightly change the meaning of other words by adding description or by making them more specific. Adjectives modify nouns and pronouns; adverbs modify verbs, adjectives, and other adverbs.

Adjectives

Without adjectives, much of the color in written and spoken language would be missing. These words allow people to describe in more detail the nouns and pronouns they use.

▶ **KEY CONCEPT** An **adjective** is a word used to describe a noun or pronoun or to give a noun or pronoun a more specific meaning. ■

Adjectives modify nouns and pronouns by providing information that answers any of the following questions about the noun or pronoun: *What kind? Which one? How many? How much?*

EXAMPLES: *big* nests (*What kind* of nests?)
            that bird (*Which* bird?)
            seventeen flocks (*How many* flocks?)
            more bird seed (*How much* bird seed?)

These examples show the usual location of an adjective—preceding a noun. Sometimes, however, the adjective is located after the noun it modifies.

EXAMPLE: The nest looked *old*.

An adjective that modifies a pronoun usually follows the pronoun, but, on occasion, it can precede the pronoun.

AFTER: He was tired after the long flight.

BEFORE: *Tired* after the flight, he rested.

More than one adjective may modify a noun or pronoun.

EXAMPLE: The quick, darting falcon captured its prey.

In this section, you will learn about adjectives and adverbs. All of the examples and exercises are about birds.

Cross-Curricular Connection: Science

⏱ TIME AND RESOURCE MANAGER

Resources
Print: *Grammar Exercise Workbook,* pp. 11–14; *Grammar Exercises Answers on Transparencies,* Ch. 17
Technology: *Language Lab* CD-ROM, Using Modifiers; *On-Line Exercise Bank,* Section 17.3

In-Depth Coverage	Accelerated Pace
• Work through all key concepts, pp. 380–385. • Assign and review Exercises 23–25. • Read and discuss Grammar in Literature, p. 385.	• Assign pp. 380–385 for independent student review. • Assign Section Review Exercises 26–28, p. 387.

Nouns Used as Adjectives Occasionally, words that are usually nouns will function as adjectives modifying another noun and answering *what kind* or *which one.*

NOUNS: vegetable
                      bird

USED AS ADJECTIVES: vegetable soup

                      bird food

Proper Adjectives Like nouns, some adjectives can be proper. Proper adjectives are proper nouns used as adjectives or adjectives formed from proper nouns. They modify other nouns and begin with a capital letter.

PROPER NOUNS: Audubon
                      Florida
                      North America
                      Spain

PROPER ADJECTIVES: Audubon paintings

                      Florida sunshine

                      North American birds

                      Spanish language

Compound Adjectives Adjectives can also be compound, or made up of more than one word. Some compound adjectives are hyphenated; some are written as combined words. Compound proper adjectives are usually written as two separate words. Check a dictionary when in doubt.

HYPHENATED: long-term mates, oval-shaped nest

COMBINED: warmblooded animals, lifelong partners

SEPARATED: South American birds

Grammar and Style Tip

Numbers can function as adjectives. In formal writing, most numbers should be spelled out, as in *fifty* eagles or *three* French hens.

▼ **Critical Viewing**
What compound adjectives apply to this bird? [**Apply**]

Adjectives and Adverbs • 381

Customize for
ESL Students

Write the following chart on the board. Ask students to convert each country's name to form a proper adjective that modifies the noun with which it is paired. Visual props are especially helpful for students to grasp the concepts. When they finish, have students write an example to add to the chart about an object from their own country or city of origin.

Ireland	( )	dancing
Spain	( )	peanuts
Hungary	( )	goulash
Canada	( )	bacon
America	( )	cuisine
Mexico	( )	jumping beans
France	( )	toast

Step-by-Step Teaching Guide

Nouns Used as Adjectives

1. Write the following nouns on the board and ask students whether they are nouns or adjectives:

    snow, potato, curtain

Then, write the following words on the board and point out that *snow, potato,* and *curtain* are now adjectives.

    snow storm, potato chips, curtain rod

2. Ask students if they can think of other nouns that modify nouns. (*bear hug, dog bite, ocean view, camera bag, coffee mug, computer desk*)

Step-by-Step Teaching Guide

Proper Adjectives

1. Emphasize that the way to determine whether a proper noun is functioning as a noun or as an adjective is to identify its use in the sentence.

2. Read the examples of proper adjectives and ask students to think of others (e.g., Christmas presents, Wisconsin cheese, Irish dancing).

Step-by-Step Teaching Guide

Compound Adjectives

1. Write the following sentences on the board. Ask students to pick out the compound adjectives.

    The Easter-egg roll was held on the White House lawn. (Easter-egg and *White House* are the compound adjectives.*)*

    The racetrack surface was covered in oil after the speedway crash. (Racetrack and *speedway* are the compound adjectives.*)*

2. Remind students that although they look like single words, *racetrack* and *speedway* are compound words because they are made up of more than one word.

Critical Viewing

Apply Possible answers: keen-eyed, high-flying, sharp-taloned, brown-colored, North American

Step-by-Step Teaching Guide

Pronouns Used as Adjectives

1. Point out to students that a pronoun used as an adjective renames a person, place, thing, or idea. It also shows ownership of a person, place, thing, or idea. Write this example on the board:

    Michael left his *book in the car.* (*His* renames *Michael* and shows ownership of the book.)

2. Write the following sentences on the board. Then ask the students to identify the pronouns that serve as adjectives.

    I picked up my suitcase, and its handle broke. (*My* and *its* are pronouns used as adjectives.)

    Her car had smoke coming out of its engine. (*Her* and *its* are pronouns used as adjectives.)

Step-by-Step Teaching Guide

Verb Forms Used as Adjectives

1. Point out to students that although an easy way to recognize a verb acting as an adjective is to look for *–ing* and *–ed* endings, not all verbs with these endings are adjectives.

2. Write the following sentences on the board and have students determine whether or not each verb serves as an adjective.

    I was walking *my dog.* (verb)

    Joe's walking *shoes slipped as he climbed the hill.* (adjective)

    The repaired *bicycle is in the shed.* (adjective)

    She repaired *the bicycle yesterday.* (verb)

Pronouns Used as Adjectives Some pronouns can be used as adjectives, as shown in the chart that follows.

The seven personal pronouns that are listed at the beginning are known either as *possessive adjectives* or as *possessive pronouns.* These words do double duty. They are pronouns because they have antecedents; they are adjectives because they modify nouns by answering *which one.*

The other pronouns in the chart become adjectives instead of pronouns when they stand before a noun and answer *which one.*

PRONOUNS USED AS ADJECTIVES

Possessive Pronouns or Adjectives	
my, your, his, her, its, our, their	ANTECEDENT The bird built *its* nest.
Demonstrative Adjectives	
this, that, these, those	*That* hummingbird flew to the flowers. *Those* roses wilted in the sun.
Interrogative Adjectives	
which, what, whose	*Which* parakeet will you take? *Whose* money is on the table?
Indefinite Adjectives	
Used with singular nouns: another, each, either, little, much, neither, one	Give me *another* chance.
Used with plural nouns: both, few, many, several	*Many* crows raided the garden.
Used with singular or plural nouns: all, any, more, most, other, some	Give me *some* birdseed, please. I received *some* gifts.

Research Tip

Look in a library or bookstore for field guides about birds. These will offer basic information and descriptions of birds, including vivid descriptive adjectives.

STANDARDIZED TEST PREPARATION WORKSHOP

Pronouns and Adjectives Standardized test questions may require students to distinguish between pronouns and adjectives. Provide students with opportunities to distinguish these differences.

Which word acts as both a pronoun and an adjective in the following sentence?

I love it when my dog sits up.

A I
B my
C it
D up

Students should recognize that **B** is the correct answer because *my* is a personal pronoun and an adjective that modifies *dog.* *I* and *it* are personal pronouns, and *up* is an adverb.

Verb Forms Used as Adjectives

Verb Forms Used as Adjectives Verb forms ending in -*ing* or -*ed* can be used as adjectives.

VERBS USED AS ADJECTIVES

The *rippling* water felt refreshing to the herons.

The *washed* clothes were neatly folded.

Remember that nouns, pronouns, and verbs are adjectives only when they modify nouns or pronouns. Notice how their function can change from one sentence to another.

	Regular Function	As an Adjective
Noun	The *blood* coursed through his veins.	His *blood* count was fine.
Pronoun	*That* is my lovebird.	*That* lovebird is beautiful.
Verb	The President *vetoed* the bill.	The *vetoed* bill was reintroduced.

Exercise 23 **Identifying Adjectives** On your paper, write the adjectives you find in each numbered section and tell which words they modify.

[1] Seventeen known species of penguins inhabit the world. [2] They live in coastal areas of the Southern Hemisphere, and they are generally not found north of the equator. [3] The two largest living penguins are the emperor and king penguins, [4] which are found in Antarctic regions. [5] The emperor is the tallest and heaviest of all penguins. [6] While most penguins lay about two eggs, emperor females lay only one egg. [7] Emperor penguins primarily eat squid and fish, as well as occasional small crustaceans.

[8] The king penguin is the second-largest penguin in the world. [9] These birds have more orange coloring, and they have longer bills. [10] Their dietary choices include crustaceans, squid, small fish, and plankton.

[11] Penguins range in height from fifteen inches to four feet. [12] Their thick feathers protect them from the cold. [13] Although they have a wobbling walk, [14] these birds are excellent swimmers. [15] Penguins are a popular attraction at the New England Aquarium.

More Practice

Language Lab CD-ROM
• Adjectives lesson

On-line Exercise Bank
• Section 17.3

Grammar Exercise Workbook
• pp. 11–12

▼ **Critical Viewing**
Describe this penguin with adjectives telling *What kind? Which one? How many?* or *How much?* [**Analyze**]

Adjectives and Adverbs • 383

✓ ONGOING ASSESSMENT: Monitor and Reinforce

If students miss more than two items in Exercise 23, refer them to the following for additional practice.

In the Textbook	Print Resources	Technology
Section Review, Ex. 26, p. 387	*Grammar Exercise Workbook,* pp. 11–12	*Language Lab* CD-ROM, Using Modifiers *On-Line Exercise Bank,* Section 17.3

⏱ TIME SAVERS!

Answers on Transparencies
Use the *Grammar Exercises Answers on Transparencies* for Chapter 17 to facilitate correction by students.

On-Line Exercise Bank
Have students complete the exercises on computer. The Auto Check feature will grade their work for you!

Adverbs

1. Discuss with students the misconception that if a word ends in *-ly*, it is an adverb. Point out that some *-ly* words are adjectives (manly attitude, friendly dog). Have students come up with other *-ly* words that act as adjectives.

2. Tell students that a more dependable way to recognize an adverb is to determine whether it answers one of the following questions about a verb, adjective, or adverb: *Where? When? In what manner?* or *To what extent?* If it does, it is an adverb.

Integrating Vocabulary Skills

Adjectives A common problem for many people is the incorrect use of the words *real* and *really*. An easy way to figure out the correct word to use is to substitute the word *genuine* for *real* and the word *very* for *really*. Write this sentence on the board:

She is really (very) athletic.

Explain to students that you would not say, "She is genuine athletic." Similarly, the following is correct:

The real (genuine) diamond was brilliant.

Explain to students that you would not say, "The very diamond was brilliant."

17.3

Adverbs

Like adjectives, adverbs describe or make other words more specific.

> **KEY CONCEPT** An **adverb** is a word that modifies a verb, an adjective, or another adverb. ■

An adverb that modifies a verb answers any of four questions: *Where? When? In what way? To what extent?* An adverb that modifies an adjective or another adverb answers the question *To what extent?*

ADVERBS MODIFYING VERBS
Where?
The finch flew *up*.　　　　　　　Her eggs lay *here*.
When?
The flock's migration began *today*.
Now they will fly south for the winter.
In what way?
The falcon *quickly* passed over our heads.
I *was eagerly* awaiting the bird-sighting tour.
To what extent?
We have *just* enough time.
She did *not* warn me it was spicy chicken!
ADVERBS MODIFYING ADJECTIVES
To what extent?
The chicks are *extremely* hungry.
The *overly* excited bird-watcher collapsed.
ADVERBS MODIFYING ADVERBS
To what extent?
She cleans her young chicks *rather* carefully.
The chicken coop was *not* completely clean yet.

Grammar and Style Tip

Use adverbs in your writing to make the meanings of your verbs more vivid and precise.

Nouns Functioning as Adverbs A few words that usually act as nouns can function as adverbs that answer *where* and *when.* Some of these words are *home, yesterday, today, tomorrow, mornings, afternoons, evenings, week,* and *year.*

EXAMPLES: We raced *home* to see the news of the eagle sighting. (Raced *where?*)

I saw them *yesterday.* (Saw *when?*)

Adverb or Adjective? You can distinguish between adjectives and adverbs by remembering that adverbs modify verbs, adjectives, and adverbs; adjectives modify nouns and pronouns.

ADVERB: Spring arrived *early.* (*Early* modifies a verb.)

ADJECTIVE: The early bird gets the worm. (*Early* modifies a noun.)

ADJECTIVES: *slow* flight, *hasty* decision

ADVERBS: flew *slowly,* decided *hastily*

ADJECTIVES THAT END IN *-ly*: a *lonely* thrush, a *ghostly* wail

GRAMMAR IN LITERATURE

from The Raven
Edgar Allan Poe

In this poem, the speaker encounters a raven who seems to be more than an ordinary bird. The adjectives (other than articles) are highlighted in red italics; the adverbs, in blue italics.

Once upon a midnight *dreary,* while I pondered, *weak* and *weary,*
Over *many* a *quaint* and *curious* volume of *forgotten* lore—
While I nodded, *nearly napping, suddenly* there came a tapping,
As of someone *gently rapping, rapping* at *my chamber* door.

▲ **Critical Viewing**
What adverbs could you use to describe the way this raven is perched? **[Apply]**

Adjectives and Adverbs • 385

More About the Writer

Edgar Allan Poe is best known for his dark, psychological stories. Though Poe is widely known and respected today, his life was often as dark as his writing. Poe's parents died before he was three years old, and he was frequently thrown out of schools and saddled with gambling debts. He lived much of his life in poverty. At the age of forty, two years after the death of his wife, Poe was found unconscious on a street in Baltimore. He died four days later.

Connections With Literature

"The Raven" by Edgar Allan Poe can be found in *Prentice Hall Literature: Timeless Voices, Timeless Themes,* The American Experience.

385

Answer Key

17.3

Exercise 24 **Identifying Adverbs** Write the sentences, underlining all the adverbs. Then, draw an arrow from each adverb to the word it modifies.

1. Many paleontologists firmly believe that birds are related to dinosaurs.
2. In centuries past, anatomists frequently noted that birds looked very similar to reptiles.
3. Discovered in 1861, *archaeopteryx* remains the oldest known fossil definitely identified as a bird.
4. Although *archaeopteryx* had many reptilelike features, it also had feathers and claws.
5. With its well-developed wings, *archaeopteryx* probably glided easily.

Exercise 25 **Revising Sentences by Adding Adverbs** Read all the sentences before you begin. Then, revise each sentence by adding one or more adverbs to it. You may make other minor changes as needed.

1. Peregrine falcons fly.
2. They can swoop for prey at a speed of 200 miles per hour.
3. They build nests in cliffs near seacoasts, rivers, and lakes.
4. Peregrine falcons live in many places in the world.
5. They can even be found living in cities.
6. They build nests on the ledges of bridges and skyscrapers.
7. To a falcon, a skyscraper looks like a cliff.
8. A bridge is better, because it is by the water.
9. Time will tell if these new nesting habits are successful.
10. Scientists are monitoring to see if these "city nests" work.

386 • The Parts of Speech

Section Review

GRAMMAR EXERCISES 26–31

Exercise 26 **Recognizing Adjectives** On your paper, write the adjectives in these sentences. Then, write the noun that each adjective modifies.

1. Bald eagles, weighing up to fourteen pounds, are very large birds of prey.
2. Female bald eagles are usually larger than male bald eagles.
3. These North American birds have a dark-brown body, white head, white tail, and sharp yellow beak.
4. An eagle's nest is usually hidden.
5. The cliff towers on which eagles build their homes are safe from predators.
6. Eagles are lifelong partners.
7. If something happens to one eagle, the other eagle may pine for months.
8. The male eagle and female eagle share the eaglet-raising responsibilities.
9. While the male hunts, the female will guard the stick-and-twig nest.
10. When the female hunts, the male takes on guard duty.

Exercise 27 **Recognizing Adverbs and Their Uses** On your paper, write the adverbs in these sentences. Next to them, write the word each one modifies.

1. Many types of hawks live freely throughout North America.
2. The Cooper's hawk is also known, somewhat derogatorily, as the "chicken hawk."
3. This very powerful bird kills large prey, such as chickens.
4. In the nineteenth century, hawks were frequently shot.
5. All hawks have become completely protected by federal law.
6. Today, we better understand the role birds of prey play in the natural world.
7. The Harris's hawk behaves very socially, which greatly puzzles scientists.

8. It is very common to find several birds happily sharing a nest.
9. It is not surprising to find two Harris's hawks flying home with one catch; the hawks even hunt in pairs.
10. On an early March morning, thousands of red-tailed hawks rise up and continue the annual migration.

Exercise 28 **Revising a Passage by Adding Adjectives and Adverbs** Look at the picture on the previous page. Then, revise the following passage to describe a peregrine falcon by adding adjectives and adverbs. You may make other minor changes to sentences as needed.

The peregrine falcon is a bird. Feathers cover its body. Eyes fix a stare on anyone who dares to come near. Feathers near the eyes make the eyes seem larger than they are.

Exercise 29 **Find It in Your Reading** Reread the passage from "The Raven" on p. 385. On your paper, identify the words that are modified by *dreary, weak, weary,* and *suddenly.*

Exercise 30 **Find It in Your Writing** Review a piece of descriptive writing from your portfolio. Identify three adjectives and three adverbs that you used. Challenge yourself to add at least two more of each modifier.

Exercise 31 **Writing Application** Write a description of a real or imaginary bird. Use a variety of adjectives and adverbs in your description.

Answer Key

Exercise 26

1. Bald—eagles; fourteen—pounds; large—birds
2. female—bald eagles; larger—female bald eagles; male—bald eagles
3. These, North American—birds; dark-brown—body; white—head; white—tail; sharp, yellow—beak
4. eagle's—nest; hidden—nest
5. cliff—towers; their—homes; safe—towers
6. lifelong—partners
7. one—eagle; other—eagle
8. male—eagle; female—eagle; eaglet-raising—responsibilities
9. stick-and-twig—nest
10. guard—duty

Exercise 27

1. freely—live
2. also—known; somewhat—derogatorily; derogatorily—known
3. very—powerful
4. frequently—shot
5. completely—protected
6. today—understand; better—understand
7. very—socially; socially—behaves; greatly—puzzles
8. very—common; happily—sharing
9. not—is surprising; home—flying; even—hunt
10. up—rise

Exercise 28

Answers will vary. Sample answer:

The peregrine falcon is a beautiful bird. Brown and white feathers thickly cover its sleek body. Solemn eyes impassively fix a hostile stare on anyone who dares to come too near. White feathers near the dark eyes often make the eyes seem even larger than they actually are.

Exercise 29

Find It in Your Reading
The modified words are *midnight, I, I,* and *came.*

continued

Answer Key continued

Exercise 30

Find It in Your Writing
Encourage students to use modifiers in a variety of ways. When they add adverbs, for example, they should not always choose -ly words that modify verbs. Tell them to use adverbs that modify adjectives and other adverbs as well.

Exercise 31

Writing Application
If students need information, have them choose a bird and then conduct research in the school library or on the Internet.

PREPARE and ENGAGE

Interest GRABBER Using a pencil and a mug or some other container, have students name all the ways the pencil can be situated in relation to the mug (inside the mug, behind the mug, beside the mug). Write these phrases on the board and tell students that the first word in each phrase is called a preposition.

Activate Prior Knowledge

On the board, write the definition of preposition (a word that relates the noun or pronoun that appears with it to another word in the sentence). Then have students work with partners to brainstorm for a list of prepositions they remember from previous years. Have them share these answers with the class.

TEACH

Step-by-Step Teaching Guide

Prepositions

1. Point out to students that many common prepositions can be learned by thinking about spatial relationships. Draw a simple house on the board. Label prepositions according to their position in the house. Write the word *under* beneath the house, *over* above the house, and so on.

2. Explain that prepositions are relationship words that connect parts of a sentence. A preposition is always followed by an object—a noun, pronoun, gerund, gerund phrase, or noun clause.

3. Further explain to students that prepositions are not essential elements of the sentence structure. One test to determine whether a word is a preposition is to ask whether the sentence would still make sense if it and the remainder of the phrase were crossed out. Write the following sentence on the board.

   We ate apples under the tree.

   Lead students to discover that the prepositional phrase *under the tree* can be crossed out. The sentence is still complete.

Prepositions, Conjunctions, and Interjections

Prepositions

Prepositions perform the important job of linking words within a sentence. They indicate relationships between separate things. The relationships may involve such things as location, direction, cause, or possession.

▶ **KEY CONCEPT** A **preposition** is a word that relates the noun or pronoun that appears with it to another word in the sentence. ■

Familiarize yourself with the most common prepositions, which are shown in the chart that follows. Notice that some prepositions are composed of more than one word. These are sometimes called *compound prepositions*.

Theme: African American History

In this section, you will learn about prepositions, conjunctions, and interjections. All the examples and exercises are about significant people and events in African American history.

Cross-Curricular Connection: Social Studies

PREPOSITIONS			
aboard	before	in addition to	out
about	behind	in back of	out of
above	below	in front of	over
according to	beneath	in place of	owing to
across	beside	in regard to	past
after	besides	inside	prior to
against	between	in spite of	regarding
ahead of	beyond	instead of	round
along	but	into	through
alongside	by	in view of	throughout
amid	by means of	like	till
among	concerning	near	to
apart from	considering	next to	toward
around	despite	of	under
aside from	down	off	until
as of	during	on	unto
at	except	on account of	up
atop	for	onto	upon
barring	from	on top of	with
because of	in	opposite	within

⏱ TIME AND RESOURCE MANAGER

Resources
Print: *Grammar Exercise Workbook*, pp. 15–20; *Grammar Exercises Answers on Transparencies*, Ch. 17
Technology: *Language Lab* CD-ROM, Writing Style; *On-Line Exercise Bank*, Section 17.4

In-Depth Coverage	Accelerated Pace
• Work through all key concepts, pp. 388–394. • Assign and review Exercises 32–37.	• Assign pp. 388–394 for independent student review. • Assign Section Review Exercises 38–40, p. 395.

Prepositional Phrases

Prepositional Phrases Prepositions are always part of a group of words called a *prepositional phrase*. A prepositional phrase contains a preposition and a noun or pronoun known as the *object of the preposition*.

In the following examples, the prepositional phrase is in italics. The preposition is underlined, the object of the preposition is circled, and an arrow shows to which word or words the object of the preposition relates.

EXAMPLES: Who is the famous actress *in the* (movie)?

Shawn checked *under the* (couch) and (chair).

▶ **Exercise 32** **Identifying Prepositions and Prepositional Phrases** Copy each sentence onto your paper. Then, underline each preposition, circle each object, and draw an arrow to show the word to which the object relates.

EXAMPLE: Sit beside me, and tell me about Crispus Attucks.

ANSWER: Sit *beside* (me,) and tell me *about* (Crispus Attucks.)

1. Crispus Attucks was a former slave of African ancestry, who probably spent much of his later life aboard whaling ships.
2. To this day, little is known of him aside from a fateful event in 1770.
3. On March 5, in Boston, Massachusetts, British soldiers fired upon a crowd of American colonists.
4. The crowd had gathered outside, opposite the soldiers, and had begun to challenge them.
5. Attucks was killed in the conflict on that day.

Preposition or Adverb? Because many words may be used either as prepositions or as adverbs, you may have difficulty telling them apart. *Around, down, in, off, on, out, over,* and *up* are some of the words that can function either as prepositions or as adverbs. Remember that a preposition must appear with an object of the preposition.

PREPOSITION: Joe Louis sidled *around the rink.*
ADVERB: The boxer slowly looked *around.*

Learn More

For more on prepositions and prepositional phrases, see Chapter 19.

More Practice

Language Lab CD-ROM
• Identifying Prepositions lesson
On-line Exercise Bank
• Section 17.4
Grammar Exercise Workbook
• pp. 15–16

Prepositional Phrases

1. Explain to students that a prepositional phrase is a preposition, its object, and any modifiers. Write the following on the board:

   into the house

   Into is the preposition and *house* is the object of the preposition.

2. Explain that it was once considered improper to end a sentence with a preposition. Write the following example on the board.

   What are you laughing at?

   Point out that this sentence is acceptable. To say "At what are you laughing?" sounds too formal.

Preposition or Adverb?

1. Remind students that adverbs answer the questions *Where? When? In what manner?* or *To what extent?* Prepositions must always be followed by objects.

2. Write the following sentences on the board. Have students decide whether each underlined word is an adverb or a preposition and explain why.

   The boy fell over the garbage can. (preposition; *can* is the object)

   The boy fell over and hit his head. (adverb; it answers the question *Where?*)

Answer Key

▶ **Exercise 32**

Prepositions are underlined. Their objects are double underlined.

1. "of African ancestry" relates to *slave*, "of his later life" relates to *much*, "aboard whaling ships" relates to *spent*
2. "To this day," "of him," and "aside from a fateful event" relate to *is known*; "in 1770" relates to *event*
3. "On March 5," "in Boston, Massachusetts," and "upon a crowd" relate to *fired*; "of American colonists" relates to *crowd*

continued

Answer Key continued

▶ **Exercise 32**

4. "opposite the soldiers" relates to *gathered*
5. "among those killed" relates to *Attucks*; "in the conflict" relates to *killed*; and "on that day" relates to *conflict*

▶ **Exercise 33**

1. adverb
2. preposition; object=Maryland
3. adverb
4. preposition; object=time
5. preposition; object=borders

Critical Viewing

Describe Possible answers: with white hair on his head; with a full beard; with a formal coat and vest over a white shirt

---

Step-by-Step Teaching Guide

Conjunctions

1. Help students to process the word *conjunction* by examining its meaning. Relate it to a junction in a road. A conjunction is the word that joins two ideas together in a sentence.

2. Write the following sentences on the board. Ask students to fill in the blanks. The words they choose will be conjunctions if the sentences make sense.

   The girl wanted spaghetti for dinner, ___ there were no noodles left over.

   Potato chips are greasy ___ fattening.

   Would you like yellow ___ green paper?

3. Explain to students that there are different types of conjunctions, depending on their function. A coordinating conjunction connects two words or groups of words. Compare it to a "social coordinator" whose job on a cruise ship is to link people together.

4. Helping students break down the word *correlative* will help them understand these types of conjunctions. Students must understand that a correlation occurs when two things work together. For example, there is a correlation between snowstorms and snow days. Explain to students that correlative conjunctions always come in pairs because one works with, or correlates with, the other.

continued

▶ **Exercise 33** **Distinguishing Between Prepositions and Adverbs** Identify each underlined word as either a *preposition* or an *adverb*. If the word is a preposition, write its object.

EXAMPLE: Frederick Douglass is renowned <u>above</u> almost all other abolitionists.

ANSWER: preposition (abolitionists)

1. He went <u>outside</u> to retrieve from the car all of his articles on Frederick Douglass.
2. Douglass was born the son of a slave <u>in</u> Maryland in 1817.
3. He yearned <u>over</u> and over to become a free man.
4. <u>Around</u> this time, in secret, he learned to read.
5. He soon crossed <u>over</u> the northern borders into freedom.

Conjunctions

Unlike prepositions, which simply relate words, conjunctions join words into a single unit.

▶ **KEY CONCEPT** A **conjunction** is a word used to connect other words or groups of words. ■

There are three kinds of conjunctions: *coordinating*, *correlative*, and *subordinating* conjunctions. A special kind of adverb, called a *conjunctive adverb*, is often considered a conjunction.

Coordinating Conjunctions These conjunctions connect words or groups of words.

In the following examples, the coordinating conjunctions are in italics. The connected words are underlined.

EXAMPLES: <u>She</u> *and* <u>Grandmother</u> once went to see Bessie Smith.
Turning <u>to the left</u> *or* <u>to the right</u>, all Bessie could see was a throng of admiring fans.
<u>They climbed aboard the midnight train</u>, *for* <u>the tour was just beginning</u>.

COORDINATING CONJUNCTIONS			
and	for	or	yet
but	nor	so	

▲ **Critical Viewing** Use prepositional phrases to describe the appearance of Frederick Douglass in this portrait. **[Describe]**

✓ **ONGOING ASSESSMENT: Monitor and Reinforce**

If students miss more than one item in Exercise 32 or 33, refer them to the following for additional practice.

In the Textbook	Print Resources	Technology
Section Review Ex. 40, p. 395	*Grammar Exercise Workbook,* pp. 15–16	*Language Lab* CD-ROM, Writing Style *On-Line Exercise Bank,* Section 17.4

Correlative Conjunctions These conjunctions also join equal elements in sentences, but they always work in pairs.

CORRELATIVE CONJUNCTIONS		
both . . . and	either . . . or	neither . . . nor
not only . . . but also	whether . . . or	

Here are some of the ways these conjunctions may be used. The conjunctions are shown in italics. The words they connect are underlined.

EXAMPLES: *Neither* <u>Lola</u> *nor* <u>he</u> knows about Paul Robeson.

He was *not only* <u>intelligent</u> *but also* <u>charismatic</u>.

He excelled *both* <u>during college</u> *and* <u>in life</u>.

His choice after college was *either* <u>athletics</u> *or* <u>law</u>.

Subordinating Conjunctions Subordinating conjunctions join two complete ideas by making one of the ideas subordinate—that is, dependent—on the other. (See Chapter 19 for more information about subordinate clauses.)

SUBORDINATING CONJUNCTIONS			
after	because	lest	till
although	before	now that	unless
as	even if	provided that	until
as if	even though	since	when
as long as	how	so that	whenever
as much as	if	than	where
as soon as	inasmuch as	that	wherever
as though	in order that	though	while

EXAMPLES:

main idea　　　subordinate idea

I watch Robeson's films *whenever I can.*

subordinate idea

Now that the new video store is open,

main idea

we probably will watch videos more often.

Step-by-Step Teaching Guide continued

5. Point out that the prefix *sub-* means "less" or "lower." A subordinating conjunction takes two complete sentences and hooks them together, making one part dependent on, or "lower than," the other. Write the following sentences on the board and have students point out the subordinate part of each sentence.

You may go to the game if you wash the dishes.

(if you wash the dishes)

There will be homework tonight unless you have finished the assignment in class.

(unless you have finished the assignment in class)

TIME SAVERS!

Answers on Transparencies Use the *Grammar Exercises Answers on Transparencies* for Chapter 17 to facilitate correction by students.

On-Line Exercise Bank Have students complete the exercises on computer. The Auto Check feature will grade their work for you!

Conjunctive Adverbs

1. Remind students that an adverb modifies or describes a verb, an adjective, or another adverb. Conjunctive adverbs function as both adverbs and conjunctions.

2. Write the following sentences on the board. Then ask students how they could use a conjunctive adverb to tie the two thoughts together into one coherent sentence.

   I ate five pieces of pizza for breakfast.

   My stomach feels as if it were going to explode.

   (Example: I ate five pieces of pizza for breakfast; consequently, my stomach feels as if it were going to explode.)

3. Point out that *consequently* is an adverb because it modifies *ate* and a conjunction because it connects the two ideas in the sentence.

Answer Key

▶ **Exercise 34**

1. neither . . . nor; correlative
2. because; subordinating
3. while; subordinating
4. both . . . and; correlative
5. yet; coordinating

Critical Viewing

Analyze Possible answer: He looks as if he is angry or sad.

17.4

Conjunctive Adverbs Conjunctive adverbs are used as conjunctions to connect complete ideas. They are often used as transitions, creating bridges between different ideas by showing comparisons, contrasts, or results.

CONJUNCTIVE ADVERBS		
accordingly	finally	nevertheless
again	furthermore	otherwise
also	however	then
besides	indeed	therefore
consequently	instead	thus
	moreover	

Notice the punctuation that is used before and after the conjunctive adverbs in the following examples. (See Chapter 27 for more about punctuation with conjunctive adverbs.)

EXAMPLES: The film was great; *nevertheless*, I prefer *Show Boat*.
Show Boat starts at 8:00 P.M.; we should, *therefore*, leave soon.

▶ **Exercise 34** **Identifying Conjunctions in Sentences** Write the conjunctions used in the following sentences. Then, identify each as *coordinating*, *correlative*, or *subordinating*.

EXAMPLE: I looked for *The Proud Valley*, but I couldn't find it.
ANSWER: but (coordinating)

1. Paul Robeson became neither a lawyer nor an athlete after his academic career.
2. He did not become a lawyer because there were few opportunities for African Americans at law firms in 1923.
3. He began his celebrated acting career while he was earning his law degree.
4. *The Emperor Jones* was both a critical and a commercial success.
5. Theater audiences hailed Robeson in the title role, yet they knew little of his terrific singing talent.

▼ **Critical Viewing**
Use a subordinating conjunction and a subordinate clause in a sentence that describes the emotions shown on Paul Robeson's face. **[Analyze]**

🖨 **Answers on Transparencies**
Use the *Grammar Exercises Answers on Transparencies* for Chapter 17 to facilitate correction by students.

💻 **On-Line Exercise Bank**
Have students complete the exercises on computer. The Auto Check feature will grade their work for you!

☑ **ONGOING ASSESSMENT: Monitor and Reinforce**

If students have difficulty with Exercise 34, 35, or 36, refer them to the following for additional practice.

In the Textbook	Print Resources	Technology
Section Review Ex. 38, p. 395	*Grammar Exercise Workbook,* pp. 17–18	*Language Lab* CD-ROM, Writing Style *On-Line Exercise Bank,* Section 17.4

Answer Key

▶ Exercise 35

▶ **Exercise 35** **Using Conjunctive Adverbs** Rewrite each pair of sentences, inserting an appropriate conjunctive adverb to connect the related ideas. Punctuate the new sentence correctly.

EXAMPLE: Jackie Robinson faced many difficult challenges in his life. He soldiered on with dignity and grace.

ANSWER: Jackie Robinson faced many difficult challenges in his life; nevertheless, he soldiered on with dignity and grace.

1. Jackie Robinson was a spectacular all-around athlete during college. He is most famous for his baseball career.
2. Robinson next became an officer in the army. He still harbored dreams of playing professional sports.
3. When Robinson started playing professional baseball, there were many talented African American players. African Americans, did not play in the major leagues.
4. Branch Rickey wanted to integrate major league baseball. He was interested in signing Jackie Robinson.
5. Rickey wanted to sign Robinson because Robinson was a talented and fast player. He had courage and dignity.
6. Robinson joined the Brooklyn Dodgers in 1947. He played all ten years of his major league career with the Dodgers.
7. At first, both fans and opposing players taunted and threatened him. Robinson endured this treatment in silence and dignity.
8. In 1947, Robinson was named Rookie of the Year. In 1949, he was named the National League's Most Valuable Player.
9. Robinson was an outstanding fielder and hitter. He was a superior runner and base stealer.
10. Robinson's skills and achievements were many. He was elected to the Baseball Hall of Fame in 1962.

▶ **Exercise 36** **Writing Sentences With Conjunctions and Conjunctive Adverbs** Follow the directions to write sentences. You may need to draw on details and information you've learned in this section.

1. Write two sentences about Branch Rickey's feelings about Jackie Robinson's baseball skills. Use *consequently* in the second sentence.
2. Use *yet* in a sentence about Robinson's behavior when reacting to the opposition he faced.
3. Use *and* in a sentence describing Robinson's personality.
4. Write two or three sentences about Branch Rickey's plan to integrate major league baseball. Use *nevertheless* in one of the sentences.
5. Write three sentences about Robinson's qualifications for the Hall of Fame. Use *furthermore* in one of the sentences.

Language Lab CD-ROM
• Identifying Conjunctions lesson

On-line Exercise Bank
• Section 17.4

Grammar Exercise Workbook
• pp. 17–18

🖥 Internet Tip

Conjunctions are essential in limiting advanced searches. Use AND (as in *Thurgood Marshall* AND *Brown* v. *Board of Education*) to match all of the words in your search string, and use OR to match any of the words.

Answers may vary; samples are given.

1. Jackie Robinson was a spectacular all-around athlete during college; however, he is most famous for his baseball career.
2. Robinson next became an officer in the army; nevertheless, he still harbored dreams of playing professional sports.
3. When Robinson started playing professional baseball, there were many talented African American players; however, African Americans did not play in the major leagues.
4. Branch Rickey wanted to integrate major league baseball; moreover, he was interested in signing Jackie Robinson.
5. Rickey wanted to sign Robinson because he was a talented and fast player; furthermore, he had courage and dignity.
6. Robinson joined the Brooklyn Dodgers in 1947; furthermore, he played all ten years of his major league career with the Dodgers.
7. At first, both fans and opposing players taunted and threatened him; nevertheless, Robinson endured this treatment in silence and dignity.
8. In 1947, Robinson was named Rookie of the Year; moreover, in 1949, he was named the National League's Most Valuable Player.
9. Robinson was an outstanding fielder and hitter; also, he was a superior runner and base stealer.
10. Robinson's skills and achievements were many; consequently, he was elected to the Baseball Hall of Fame in 1962.

▶ Exercise 36

Answers will vary; samples are given.

1. Branch Rickey felt that Jackie Robinson was a fast, talented athlete and a skilled baseball player. Consequently, Rickey chose Robinson to be the first African American in major league baseball.
2. Players and fans taunted Robinson, yet he remained quiet and dignified.
3. Robinson was courageous and dignified.

continued

Prepositions, Conjunctions, and Interjections • 393

Answer Key continued

▶ Exercise 36

4. Prejudice against African Americans had made major league baseball an all-white league. Nevertheless, Branch Rickey decided that it was time to integrate baseball.
5. Jackie Robinson was an excellent athlete. His speed in the field and on the basepaths was legendary. Furthermore, he hit for a good average and with great power.

Interjections

1. Tell students that an interjection is not necessary for a sentence to make sense. It simply emphasizes the emotion expressed in the sentence.

2. Write the following examples on the board. Ask students to find the interjections.

   Wow! Did you see that curve ball? (*Wow* is the interjection.)

   Man, this is taking forever! (*Man* is the interjection.)

3. Ask students to explain how the meaning of each example would change slightly if the interjection were omitted. (The first example would contain less excitement and the second would not convey as much exasperation.)

Answer Key

▶ **Exercise 37**

Answers may vary; samples are given.

1. <u>Hooray!</u> We won the game!
2. <u>Ouch!</u> That paper cut hurt.
3. <u>Well,</u> I'm not sure how to get there.
4. <u>Oh my!</u> We just passed the park.
5. <u>Hey,</u> hurry up and turn around.

Critical Viewing

Deduce Possible answers: Ouch! Hooray! Whew! Rats!

17.4

Interjections

Unlike other parts of speech, interjections never have a grammatical connection to other words in a sentence.

▶ **KEY CONCEPT** An **interjection** is a word that expresses feeling or emotion and functions independently of a sentence. ■

Interjections can express a variety of feelings, such as joy, fear, anger, surprise, exhaustion, dismay, or sorrow.

SOME COMMON INTERJECTIONS				
ah	dear	hey	ouch	well
aha	goodness	hurrah	psst	whew
alas	gracious	oh	tsk	wow

Interjections are set off from the rest of the sentence by either an exclamation mark or a comma.

EXAMPLES: *Whew!* That was a close one.
Hey, wait a minute!

▶ **Exercise 37** **Using Interjections** Write five sentences using an appropriate interjection to express the emotion or feeling indicated. Then, underline each interjection.

1. joy
2. pain
3. hesitation
4. surprise
5. impatience

394 • The Parts of Speech

▶ **More Practice**

Language Lab CD-ROM
• Identifying Interjections lesson

On-line Exercise Bank
• Section 17.4

Grammar Exercise Workbook
• pp. 19–20

◀ Critical Viewing
What interjections might each player use to express his feelings? [**Deduce**]

✓ **ONGOING ASSESSMENT: Assess Mastery**

Use the following resources to assess student mastery of prepositions, conjunctions, and interjections.

In the Textbook	Technology
Chapter Review, Ex. 54, pp. 400–401	*Language Lab* CD-ROM, Writing Style *On-Line Exercise Bank*, Section 17.4

Section Review

GRAMMAR EXERCISES 38–43

Exercise 38   Classifying Conjunctions On your paper, write the conjunction in each sentence. Then, identify each as *coordinating*, *correlative*, or *subordinating*.

1. Charlie Parker and Dizzy Gillespie are two of the founders of bebop.
2. Parker played alto saxophone, and Gillespie played trumpet.
3. Both Parker and Gillespie composed music and led bands.
4. After they played with many bands in the 1930's and 1940's, Gillespie began to jam in Harlem with Parker and others.
5. The recordings they made together are timeless, but many young people have never heard their music.

Exercise 39   Identifying Prepositions, Conjunctions, and Interjections In the following sentences, identify and label the words that are *prepositions*, *conjunctions*, or *interjections*.

1. Duke Ellington played piano, wrote songs, and led one of the greatest big bands ever.
2. In fact, Ellington, with others, founded big-band music, which greatly influenced swing music.
3. Don Redman and Fletcher Henderson were also great, even though they were not as famous.
4. Ellington wrote not only big-band music but also opera!
5. Wow! Did you hear that set?

Exercise 40   Supplying Prepositions Add an appropriate preposition to complete each sentence.

1. Richard Wright was born ___?___ 1908 near a small Mississippi town.
2. He made his way to the North ___?___ working as an unskilled laborer.
3. During the Great Depression, he was the editor ___?___ a newspaper ___?___ New York City.
4. He wrote books that were ahead ___?___ their time.
5. ___?___ many critics, *Native Son* is the best of all his works.

Exercise 41   Find It in Your Reading On your paper, copy the following excerpt from *My Bondage and My Freedom* by Frederick Douglass. Underline prepositional phrases once. Underline prepositions twice. Then, circle conjunctions.

Seized with a determination to learn to read, at any cost, I hit upon many expedients to accomplish the desired end. . . . I used to carry, almost constantly, a copy of Webster's spelling book in my pocket; and, when sent on errands, or when play time was allowed me, I would step, with my young friends, aside, and take a lesson in spelling.

Exercise 42   Find It in Your Writing Review a piece of writing from your portfolio. Identify conjunctions and prepositions you have used. Then, challenge yourself to combine sentences by using conjunctions.

Exercise 43   Writing Application Write an anecdote about a person you admire. Use prepositional phrases to elaborate your points. Use conjunctions to combine thoughts where appropriate.

Section Review • 395

Answer Key continued

Exercise 43

Writing Application
When students finish, have them exchange papers with a partner. Have them underline all prepositional phrases, double underline all prepositions, and circle all conjunctions.

Interest GRABBER Ask students to think of the many roles that they each play. (For example, one student's roles might be all of the following: daughter, sister, musician, athlete, cousin, and friend.) Point out to them that they have many identities, depending on the situation. Parts of speech can have many identities, too, depending on the way they function in a sentence.

Activate Prior Knowledge

Ask students to name the part of speech of the word *part*. When volunteers share their answers, it is likely that some will say *noun*, some will say *verb*, and others will say *adjective*. Write the following sentences on the board to show that all three answers are correct.

Morning is my favorite part *of the day.* (noun)

Don't part *with that ring.* (verb)

Baron is part *spaniel.* (adjective)

Have students think of other words that can act as more than one part of speech.

TEACH

Step-by-Step Teaching Guide

Identifying Parts of Speech

1. Challenge students to think of a word that they think is always a particular part of speech (Example: noun, verb, adjective). Demonstrate to students how most examples can be used another way.

2. Point out to students that they need to examine each word in a sentence to determine its function. It is seldom possible to assign a label to a word without reading the sentence.

Section 17.5

Words as Different Parts of Speech

Many words change from one part of speech to another depending on their function in a sentence.

Identifying Parts of Speech

To *function* means to "serve in a particular capacity." The function of a word may change from one sentence to another.

▶ **KEY CONCEPT** The way a word is used in a sentence determines its part of speech. ■

Look, for example, at the roles played by the word *well* in the following sentences.

AS A NOUN:	Our *well* ran dry.
AS A VERB:	After a scolding, tears *well* in the child's eyes.
AS AN ADJECTIVE:	She does not feel *well* today.

Following is a quick review of the definition of each part of speech. The column of questions in each chart shows you what to ask to determine how a word is being used.

Nouns, Pronouns, and Verbs A **noun** names a person, place, or thing. A **pronoun** stands for a noun. A **verb** shows action, condition, or existence.

Parts of Speech	Questions to Ask Yourself	Examples
Noun	Does the word name a person, place, or thing?	Our *visit* to the *Grand Canyon* delighted *Rosa*.
Pronoun	Does the word stand for a noun?	*They* gave *some* to *him*.
Verb	Does the word tell what someone or something did?	We *played* baseball.
	Does the word link one word with another word that identifies or describes it?	The woman *was* a lawyer. Mother *appeared* happy.
	Does the word merely show that something exists?	The family *is* here.

⏱ TIME AND RESOURCE MANAGER

Resources
Print: *Grammar Exercise Workbook,* pp. 21–22; *Grammar Exercises Answers on Transparencies,* Ch. 17
Technology: *On-Line Exercise Bank,* Section 17.5

In-Depth Coverage	Accelerated Pace
• Work through all key concepts, pp. 396–397. • Assign and review Exercise 44. • Do the Hands-on Grammar activity, p. 398.	• Assign pp. 396–397 for independent student review. • Assign Section Review Exercises 45–47, p. 399.

Theme: Gardening

In this section, you will learn about words as different parts of speech. The exercises and examples are about gardening.

Cross-Curricular Connection: Science

The Other Parts of Speech

An **adjective** modifies a noun or pronoun. An **adverb** modifies a verb, an adjective, or another adverb. A **preposition** relates a noun or pronoun that appears with it to another word. A **conjunction** connects words or groups of words. An **interjection** expresses emotion.

Parts of Speech	Questions to Ask Yourself	Examples
Adjective	Does the word tell *what kind, which one, how many,* or *how much?*	*Those three* apples are an *unusual* color.
Adverb	Does the word tell *where, when, in what way,* or *to what extent?*	Go *home.* Leave *now.* Drive *very slowly.* I am *thoroughly* tired.
Preposition	Is the word part of a phrase that includes a noun or pronoun?	*Near* our house, the carnival was *in* full swing.
Conjunction	Does the word connect other words in the sentence or connect clauses?	*Both* you *and* I will go *because* they need more people; *besides,* it will be fun.
Interjection	Does the word express feeling or emotion and function independently of the sentence?	*Hey,* give me that! *Ouch,* that hurt!

More Practice

On-line Exercise Bank
• Section 17.5

Grammar Exercise Workbook
• pp. 21–22

▶ **Exercise 44** Identifying All Parts of Speech Identify the part of speech of the underlined word in each pair of sentences.

EXAMPLE: (a) The <u>garden</u> hose was left out.
(b) The hose was left out in the <u>garden</u>.

ANSWER: (a) adjective (b) noun

1. (a) Please <u>run</u> the water into the bucket.
   (b) The dog <u>run</u> is next to the garden.
2. (a) I don't like <u>either</u> flower.
   (b) <u>Either</u> is equally fragrant.
3. (a) The stalks tipped <u>over</u>.
   (b) We put a protective cover <u>over</u> the delicate bloom.
4. (a) We worked <u>hard</u> during harvest.
   (b) That was <u>hard</u> work.
5. (a) The harvest took place <u>late</u> in the summer.
   (b) We didn't start until <u>late</u> summer.

▼ **Critical Viewing**
Tulips are common spring flowers. Use the words *spring* and *flowers* as verbs in sentences about tulips. **[Apply]**

Words as Different Parts of Speech • 397

Answer Key

▶ **Exercise 44**

1. verb, noun
2. adjective, pronoun
3. adverb, preposition
4. adverb, adjective
5. adverb, adjective

Critical Viewing

Apply Possible answers: Tulip shoots <u>spring</u> from the frozen soil in late winter. The tulip <u>flowers</u> in early spring.

☑ **ONGOING ASSESSMENT: Monitor and Reinforce**

If students miss more than two items in Exercise 44, refer them to the following for additional practice.

In the Textbook	Print Resources	Technology
Section Review, Ex. 45–47, p. 399	*Grammar Exercise Workbook,* pp. 21–22	*On-Line Exercise Bank,* Section 17.5

⏱ TIME SAVERS!

Answers on Transparencies
Use the *Grammar Exercises Answers on Transparencies* for Chapter 17 to facilitate correction by students.

On-Line Exercise Bank
Have students complete the exercises on computer. The Auto Check feature will grade their work for you!

Hands-on Grammar

Teaching Resources: Hands-on Grammar Activity Book, Ch. 17

1. If you wish to do this activity in class, be prepared with scissors, construction paper, and six-ring binders for the students. Give each student a copy of the Hands-on Grammar activity sheet.

2. Have students follow the directions to prepare their flip books.

3. Possible additional sentences:

   Would you stop at the store on your way home? (verb)
   Would you make a stop at the dry cleaners, too? (noun)
   Did you see the stop light? (adjective)

   She plays volleyball very well. (verb)
   She made a great play on that spike. (noun)
   The children look forward to play time. (adjective)

   Yesterday was a rainy day. (noun)
   Yesterday I stayed home all day. (adverb)

Find It in Your Reading

Encourage students to look for words used in unusual positions in sentences.

Find It in Your Writing

Have students brainstorm for words that can function as different parts of speech.

17.5

Hands-on Grammar

Parts-of-Speech Notch Book

Explore how a single word can function as many parts of speech by creating a notch book. Use four colors of construction paper to make the pages.

Cut the pages as indicated on the drawing, so that each section can turn independently. Label the "notch" of each section as shown.

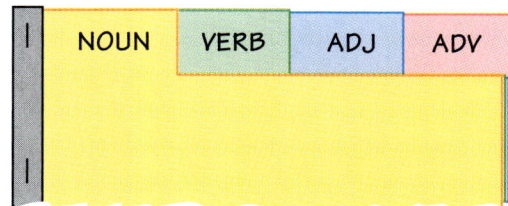

Use the sentences shown in the example as the first ones in your notch book. Add other words that can be used as more than one part of speech, such as *well, opposite, stop,* or *play.* You will not always be able to use a word in every section. Over time, add more sentences to the book.

Find It in Your Reading Choose a simple sentence from a work you are reading. Use two of the words as examples in your parts-of-speech book. Challenge yourself to use two of the words in the sentence as examples of other parts of speech in the other sections of the book.

Find It in Your Writing Choose a simple sentence from a piece of your own writing. Look for a place in the rest of your piece where you have used one of the words in your sentence as a different part of speech. If you cannot find the word used differently elsewhere, challenge yourself to add a sentence that does use it differently.

⏰ TIME SAVERS!

✋ **Hands-on Grammar**
Use the Hands-on Grammar activity sheet for Chapter 17 to facilitate this activity.

✓ ONGOING ASSESSMENT: Assess Mastery

Use the following resources to assess student mastery of parts of speech.

In the Textbook	Print Resources	Technology
Chapter Review, Ex. 55–56, p. 401	*Formal Assessment,* Chapter 17	*On-Line Exercise Bank,* Chapter 17

Section 17.5 Section Review

GRAMMAR EXERCISES 45–50

Exercise 45   Identifying Nouns and Verbs Identify the underlined word as a *noun* or a *verb*.

1. (a) Special <u>lights</u> help the plants grow.
   (b) The sun <u>lights</u> the greenhouse.
2. (a) <u>Show</u> the judge the roses.
   (b) They won first prize in the <u>show</u>.
3. (a) The <u>rain</u> will help the plants.
   (b) It might <u>rain</u> tomorrow.
4. (a) We won't <u>wait</u> long.
   (b) They had a long <u>wait</u> between shows.
5. (a) They had a <u>feeling</u> they would win.
   (b) Still, they were <u>feeling</u> nervous.

Exercise 46   Identifying Adjectives and Adverbs Identify the underlined word as an *adverb* or an *adjective*. Then, tell which word is modified.

1. <u>This</u> is a hard variety to grow.
2. It blooms <u>early</u> in the spring.
3. This bag is <u>light</u>.
4. This daisy grows <u>fast</u>.
5. The garden is reflected in the <u>still</u> water.

Exercise 47   Identifying All the Parts of Speech Identify the parts of speech of the underlined words in each sentence.

1. We have a <u>garden</u> <u>near</u> my house.
2. <u>We</u> go <u>out</u> to relax.
3. <u>In</u> the <u>early</u> morning, it is quiet and peaceful.
4. The flowers <u>turn</u> their <u>blossoms</u> up toward the sun.
5. <u>Gardening</u> does not always <u>cost</u> much.
6. Several plants <u>can be started</u> from <u>cuttings</u>.
7. The <u>place</u> you choose is important.
8. Taller plants can be loosely tied to <u>supporting</u> stakes.

9. The correct amount of <u>water</u> is crucial.
10. You can <u>question</u> experts <u>about</u> problem plants.
11. There is a <u>commercial</u> greenhouse <u>nearby</u>.
12. <u>There</u>, the <u>cost</u> of plants is reasonable.
13. The gardener will tell you <u>where</u> you should <u>place</u> each variety you buy.
14. He will <u>correct</u> gardening errors.
15. He knows the answer to almost any gardening <u>question</u>.

Exercise 48   Find It in Your Reading Read the following excerpt from "The Corn Planting" by Sherwood Anderson. Identify the part of speech of each underlined word.

The farmers who come <u>to</u> our <u>town</u> to trade are a <u>part</u> of the <u>town</u> life. Saturday is the big day. Often the children <u>come</u> to the high school in town. <u>It</u> is so with <u>Hatch</u> Hutchenson. Although his <u>farm</u>, some <u>three</u> miles from town, is small, it is known to be <u>one</u> of the best-kept and best-worked places in all our section.

Exercise 49   Find It in Your Writing Review a piece of writing from your portfolio. Identify at least one example of each part of speech. Find one example of a word that is used as two different parts of speech.

Exercise 50   Writing Application Write an explanation of how to care for a plant. Identify one example of each part of speech. Challenge yourself to use a word, such as *water* or *flower*, for two different functions.

ASSESS and CLOSE

Section Review

Each of these exercises correlates to the instruction on words as different parts of speech, pages 396–397. The exercises may be used for more practice, for reteaching, or for review of the key concepts presented.

Answer Key

Exercise 45

1. noun, verb
2. verb, noun
3. noun, verb
4. verb, noun
5. noun, verb

Exercise 46

1. adjective; variety
2. adverb; blooms
3. adjective; bag
4. adverb; grows
5. adjective; water

Exercise 47

1. noun, preposition
2. pronoun
3. preposition, adjective
4. verb, noun
5. noun, verb
6. verb, noun
7. noun
8. adjective
9. noun
10. verb, preposition
11. adjective, adverb
12. adverb, noun
13. conjunction, verb
14. verb
15. noun

Exercise 48

Find It in Your Reading

1. preposition
2. noun
3. noun
4. adjective
5. verb
6. pronoun
7. noun
8. noun
9. adjective
10. pronoun

continued

Answer Key continued

Exercise 49

Find It in Your Writing
If there is a certain part of speech that students are having trouble identifying, such as an interjection, challenge them to add one in an appropriate place in their writing.

Exercise 50

Writing Application
Remind students to use precise verbs when writing how-to instructions. For example, *water* should be replaced in some cases by a more specific verb such as *sprinkle, spray,* or *soak.*

TIME SAVERS!

Answers on Transparencies
Use the *Grammar Exercises Answers on Transparencies* for Chapter 17 to facilitate correction by students.

On-Line Exercise Bank
Have students complete the exercises on computer. The Auto Check feature will grade their work for you!

400

GRAMMAR EXERCISES 51–57

> **Exercise 51** **Identifying Nouns and Pronouns** On your paper, list and label the common nouns *(CN)*, proper nouns *(PN)*, and pronouns *(PR)* in the following sentences.

1. Highway 61 follows the Mississippi River as it winds its way into the Deep South.
2. Near Clarksdale, Mississippi, you will find the crossroads of Highway 61 and Highway 49.
3. The great bluesmen of yesterday haunt the lands around these mythic highways.
4. In Tutwiler at the turn of the century, W. C. Handy first heard the blues and was instantly fascinated.
5. He went on to write many blues tunes that have become classics, and now many call him the "Father of the Blues."
6. Near Cleveland, Mississippi, you will find the famous Dockery's Plantation.
7. Who lived, worked, and influenced other singers on this farm?
8. Charley Patton himself lived there, where he mentored Tommy Johnson, Willie Brown, Howlin' Wolf, and countless others.
9. Robert Johnson and Son House were also greatly influenced by the music that Patton made in his brief life.
10. Everyone acknowledges the debt that singers of the blues owe him.

> **Exercise 52** **Classifying Nouns** Write whether each noun listed below is (1) *singular* or *plural*, (2) *collective*, (3) *compound*, and (4) *common* or *proper*.

1. bluesmen
2. band
3. Lemon Jefferson
4. folk-blues
5. spirituals
6. Chicago
7. exposure
8. bank account
9. Mississippi
10. state

> **Exercise 53** **Classifying Verbs and Verb Phrases** List the verbs and verb phrases from the following sentences. Then, label each either *AV* for *action verb* or *LV* for *linking verb*. Also, write *T* if it is *transitive* or *I* if it is *intransitive*.

1. Bessie Smith became famous in the 1920's.
2. She had been singing songs since she was a child.
3. For many years, she traveled through the South under the tutelage of Ma Rainey.
4. Ma Rainey may have been the first great blues vocalist.
5. Smith recorded her first songs in 1923.
6. She remained very popular, selling thousands of records.
7. Her voice sounded so deep and expressive.
8. I will listen to *Poor Man's Blues* tonight while I drive home.
9. You can see Bessie Smith in the short film *St. Louis Blues.*
10. She died in a hospital after a terrible car crash.

> **Exercise 54** **Identifying Adjectives, Adverbs, Prepositions, Conjunctions, and Interjections** List and label the *adjectives (ADJ)*, *adverbs (ADV)*, *prepositions (PREP)*, *conjunctions (CONJ)*, and *interjections (INTER)*.

1. Few people sing more sweetly than Mississippi John Hurt
2. Wow! I just love his mellifluous guitar-picking.
3. Hurt seems different from most of the tortured Mississippi bluesmen of lore.
4. People often said his manner was soft-spoken and mild.
5. Beneath this veneer, however, was the soul of a bluesman.
6. When he once briefly toiled as a railroad worker, he learned songs like "Spike Driver Blues."
7. For many decades, Hurt was virtually a forgotten man.
8. He was rediscovered by the folk-blues revivalists of the early 1960's.
9. Oh no! I can't find the song I wanted to hear.
10. Hey, which Hurt song is your favorite?

Exercise 55 Classifying All the Parts of Speech
Identify the part of speech of each underlined word.

Robert Johnson may be the greatest (1) blues musician of all time. He was born (2) in 1911 in Hazelhurst, Mississippi, in the Deep (3) South Delta. He was (4) greatly influenced by the songs of (5) country bluesmen such as Charley Patton, Son House, and Willie Brown. (6) Because they lived (7) nearby on Dockery Plantation, Johnson probably met (8) many of these masters of the (9) blues.

In his (10) early life, Johnson was a (11) sharecropper, but (12 after his wife's death, he left (13) that life (14) behind for the blues. He traveled and played (15) in juke joints, logging camps and farms, as well as on the streets. (16) While he played as far away as New York and Chicago, (17) some say he loved the South best. In the (18) mid-thirties, he made a (19) handful of recordings that continue to have a huge impact on rock and blues musicians. Johnson died in 1938 under (20) mysterious circumstances.

Exercise 56 Revision Practice: Expanding Sentences
Revise each sentence by following the directions indicated in parentheses. Make sure that the word you choose makes sense in the sentence. When you have revised each sentence, make sure it is punctuated correctly and that there are no extra words resulting from the change. When you have finished, read each sentence aloud to a partner.

1. Muddy Waters was born in Mississippi. He is known as one of the greatest Chicago bluesmen. (Add a conjunction to connect the sentences.)
2. Waters was not only a great singer, but also a guitar player. (Add an adjective to modify *guitar player*.)
3. It is generally felt that he was the greatest of the early Chicago electrical blues musicians. (Replace the pronoun *he* with a proper noun.)
4. T-Bone Walker is considered the first bluesman to play the electric guitar. (Add a conjunctive adverb to contrast this sentence with the previous one.)
5. They added the piano, bass, and drums to their electric guitars. (Replace the personal pronoun *they* with an indefinite pronoun.)

Exercise 57 Writing Application
Write about a musician whose work you enjoy. When you have finished, identify proper nouns and proper adjectives, subordinating conjunctions, and adverbs that modify adjectives or other adverbs.

Chapter Review • **401**

Step-by-Step Teaching Guide

Analogies

Teaching Resources: Standardized Test Preparation Workbook, pp. 33–34

1. Tell students that it is important to have a clear understanding of the first word pair. They should think carefully and decide what the relationship of the two words is. Review with students the examples of the six types of word relationships.

2. Have students quickly read through the five possible answers. As they identify the relationship between each pair, they can either eliminate it as an answer or keep it to reconsider.

3. If one of the possible answers seems to fit, students need to return to the original word pair for clarification.

4. Remind students that prefixes and suffixes provide clues to a word's part of speech and can help isolate the root word.

Standardized Test Preparation Workshop

Analogies

Analogy questions test your ability to determine a relationship between a given pair of words and to identify a similar relationship between the words in the second pair. Standardized tests include analogy questions that test the relationships of *Antonyms*, such as fast : slow; *Part-Whole* or *Whole-Part*, such as buttons : sweater; *Definitional/Synonyms*, such as joke : humorous; *Cause-Effect or Effect-Cause*, such as rain : floods; *Functional Relationship*, such as artist : painting; and *Relationship of Degrees*, such as smart : brilliant.

When determining the relationship between words, use the parts of speech as a clue. The words in the correct answer choice will often, but not always, be the same parts of speech combination (nouns, pronouns, verbs, adjectives, or adverbs) as the original pair. Then, find the more specific relationship between the words.

Test Tips

- Make sure that your choice reflects or parallels the structure in the given word pair. If the relationship in the given word pair is cause-effect, then your answer choice should be exactly cause-effect and not effect-cause.

- Sometimes the relationship between two words is multiple. Always probe beneath the first relationship you recognize to see if there is a less obvious but more important secondary relationship.

- Parts of speech may be a clue. Often, but not always, the correct answer choice will be a word with the same part of speech as the given word pair.

Sample Test Item

Directions: Each question below consists of a related pair of words, followed by five pairs of words labeled *A* through *E*. Select the pair that *best* expresses a relationship similar to that expressed in the original pair.

CEASE-FIRE : HOSTILITIES ::

    (A) reckoning : probabilities

    (B) truce : belligerents

    (C) artillery : tanks

    (D) campaign : strategies

    (E) adjournment : proceedings

Answer and Explanation

The correct answer is *(E)*. The noun *adjournment* is caused by the end of *proceedings*, also a noun. In the original pair, the noun *cease-fire* is caused by the end of *hostilities*, also a noun. Answers *(B)* and *(D)* express a similar relationship to the original pair, but neither pair expresses an end to an occurrence. For example, a *truce* is not an end to *belligerents*, and a *campaign* is not an end of *strategies*. Answers *(A)* and *(C)* do not express a cause-effect relationship.

402 • The Parts of Speech

✏ TEST-TAKING TIP

If the relationship of a word pair seems unclear, students need to think about different ways to describe the relationship. Suggest that they try to describe a tone or mood set up between the word pairs, and to match that tone to the original pair.

Remind students that they should not focus on the definitions of the individual words but on

the *relationship* between the words. Use the following as an example:

circus : ringmaster::

clown : entertainer
or
court : judge

Answer: *court : judge*

▶ **Practice**   **Directions:** Each question below consists of a related pair of words or phrases, followed by five pairs of word or phrases labeled *A* through *E.* Select the pair that best expresses a relationship similar to that expressed in the original pair.

1 CRAVEN : COWARDLY ::
(A) liberal : conservative
(B) juvenile : adult
(C) genuine : fake
(D) feeble : fragile
(E) regal : common

2 IMPERVIOUS : ACCESSIBLE ::
(A) impertinent : interfering
(B) articulate : eloquent
(C) parched : dry
(D) priceless : invaluable
(E) obstinate : pliable

3 ISOLATION : LONELINESS ::
(A) gloomy : murky
(B) affliction : comfort
(C) explanation : comprehension
(D) happiness : disaster
(E) impartial : partial

4 SCIENCE : ASTRONOMY ::
(A) geology : physical science
(B) star : planet
(C) notes : music
(D) chemistry : biology
(E) computer language : BASIC

5 PARSIMONY : STINGINESS ::
(A) falsehood : verity
(B) greed : generosity
(C) extraneous : relevant
(D) enthusiasm : passivity
(E) candor : forthrightness

6 INSOLVENT : BANKRUPT ::
(A) rich : poor
(B) lethargic : sluggish
(C) wealthy : fortune
(D) impoverished : poverty
(E) serious : humorous

7 DETERIORATE : CORROSION ::
(A) rain : flood
(B) lecture : lesson
(C) perplex : mystery
(D) musician : orchestra
(E) fatigue : invigoration

8 INNOCUOUS : HARMLESS ::
(A) sensitive : insensitive
(B) habitual : occasional
(C) persuade : conclude
(D) despicable : contemptible
(E) social : antisocial

9 CHALK : CHALKBOARD ::
(A) pen : paper
(B) needle : thread
(C) eraser : mistake
(D) brush : paint
(E) crayon : drawing

10 CANKER : DECAY ::
(A) tense : fear
(B) sun : moon
(C) automobile : driver
(D) tragedy : grief
(E) destruction : earthquake

1. D
2. E
3. C
4. E
5. E
6. B
7. C
8. D
9. A
10. D

Customize for
Less Advanced Students

Have students work in groups to identify the parts of speech of the original word pairs on the practice tests. Then they should exchange ideas about the relationship between each word pair.

Customize for
AP Students

Have students practice identifying the relationship between the original word pairs, using the six possibilities listed in their text. They might benefit by discussing their thought processes in small groups.

Chapter 18 Time and Resource Manager

In-Depth Lesson Plan

	LESSON FOCUS	PRINT AND MEDIA RESOURCES
DAY 1	**Subjects and Predicates** Students learn and apply concepts relating to simple and compound subjects and predicates. (pp. 406–413)	*On-Line Exercise Bank,* Section 18.1 **Teaching Resources** *Grammar Exercise Workbook,* pp. 27–28; *Grammar Exercises Answers on Transparencies,* Ch. 18
DAY 2	**Hard-to-Find Subjects** Students learn and apply concepts relating to hard-to-find subjects and do the Hands-on Grammar activity. (pp. 414–419)	*On-Line Exercise Bank,* Section 18.2 **Teaching Resources** *Grammar Exercise Workbook,* pp. 29–30; *Hands-on Grammar Activity Book,* Ch. 18
DAY 3	**Complements** Students learn and apply concepts relating to direct and indirect objects and objective and subject complements. (pp. 420–427)	*On-Line Exercise Bank,* Section 18.3 **Teaching Resources** *Grammar Exercise Workbook,* pp. 31–38
DAY 4	**Review and Assess** Students review chapter and demonstrate mastery of basic sentence parts. (pp. 428–429)	**Teaching Resources** *Formal Assessment,* Ch. 18

Accelerated Lesson Plan

	LESSON FOCUS	PRINT AND MEDIA RESOURCES
DAY 1	**Subjects and Predicates, Hard-to-Find Subjects** Students cover subjects, predicates, and hard-to-find subjects as determined by the Diagnostic Test. (pp. 406–419)	*On-Line Exercise Bank,* Section 18.1–2 **Teaching Resources** *Grammar Exercise Workbook,* pp. 27–30; *Grammar Exercises Answers on Transparencies,* Ch. 18
DAY 2	**Complements** Students cover complements as determined by the Diagnostic Test. (pp. 420–427)	*On-Line Exercise Bank,* Section 18.3 **Teaching Resources** *Grammar Exercise Workbook,* pp. 31–38
DAY 3	**Review and Assess** Students review chapter and demonstrate mastery of concepts. (pp. 428–429)	**Teaching Resources** *Formal Assessment,* Ch. 18

Options for Adapting Lesson Plans

HOMEWORK

Have students complete any section of the chapter for homework.

FEATURES

Extend coverage with the Grammar in Literature features (pp. 411, 417) and the Standardized Test Preparation Workshop (p. 430).

TECHNOLOGY

Students can use the On-Line Exercise Bank to complete the exercises on computer. The Auto Check feature will grade their work.

INTEGRATED SKILLS COVERAGE

Grammar in Literature SE pp. 411, 417

Writing
Find It in Your Writing SE pp. 413, 418, 419, 427
Writing Application SE pp. 413, 419, 427, 429
Grammar and Style SE p. 408
Integrating Writing Skills ATE p. 416

Spelling SE p. 423

Viewing and Representing
Critical Viewing, SE pp. 404, 407, 409, 410, 412, 414, 417, 420, 422, 424, 426

Real-World Connection ATE p. 412

Technology SE pp. 411, 415

Workplace Skills ATE p. 409

Listening Skills ATE p. 415

ASSESSMENT SUPPORT

Standardized Test Preparation Workshop SE p. 430; ATE pp. 409, 415

Standardized Test Preparation Workbook, pp. 35–36

Formal Assessment, Ch. 18

MEETING INDIVIDUAL NEEDS

Less Advanced Students ATE pp. 420, 421, 431. See also Ongoing Assessments ATE pp. 411, 417, 424, 425.

AP Students ATE p. 426

ESL Students ATE pp. 410, 421

Gifted and Talented Students ATE p. 410

Logical/Mathematical Learners ATE p. 409

Bodily/Kinesthetic Learners ATE p. 412

BLOCK SCHEDULING

Pacing Suggestions
For 90-minute Blocks
• Administer the Diagnostic Test to students to determine instructional coverage.
• Have students complete the necessary exercises in class. Use the Hands-on Grammar activity to provide a change of pace.

Resources for Varying Instruction
• **On-Line Exercise Bank** If your students have access to hardware, a 90-minute block provides an ideal opportunity for students to work on computer.

Professional Development Support
• **How to Manage Instruction in the Block** This Teaching Resource provides management and activity suggestions.

MEDIA AND TECHNOLOGY

For the Student
• **On-Line Exercise Bank,** Sections 18.1–3

For the Teacher
• **Resource Pro** CD-ROM

WRITING AND GRAMMAR WEB SITE

The Interactive Writing and Grammar Web Site provides a wide array of support for students, teachers, and parents. Grammar support includes:

• **On-Line Exercise Bank** with Auto Check scoring
• Diagnostic and assessment support

www.phschool.com

LITERATURE CONNECTIONS

Grammar in Literature selections from *Prentice Hall Literature: Timeless Voices, Timeless Themes,* The American Experience:

from "Pecos Bill Becomes a Coyote," retold by James Cloyd Bowman, SE p. 411

from "Chicago," Carl Sandburg, SE p. 417

Lesson Objectives

1. To recognize complete subjects and predicates and simple subjects and predicates
2. To recognize compound subjects and verbs
3. To identify hard-to-find subjects
4. To understand the function of complements in sentences
5. To demonstrate control over grammatical elements
6. To analyze the characteristics of clearly written texts, including patterns of organization, syntax, and word choice

Critical Viewing

Connect Possible answer: The picture shows a dramatic moment in a Pony Express run.

Chapter 18 Basic Sentence Parts

A Doubtfire Handshake, Charles M. Russell

Throughout history, language has been the tool people use to shape their ideas and communicate with others. During the days of the western frontier, the only way to communicate over long distances was via mail. Pony express riders braved many hardships and dangers to carry messages and packages to the West.

Because today we have many means of communication, the importance of language has not diminished. For communication to be meaningful, a speaker or writer must choose appropriate words and put them in an order that the listener or reader can follow. This chapter will focus on ways in which words are combined to form basic sentence parts.

▲ **Critical Viewing**
What is the subject of this picture ? What verb would you use to complete a sentence about the picture? **[Connect]**

404 • Basic Sentence Parts

☑ **ONGOING ASSESSMENT: Diagnose**

If students miss more than one item in any category, direct them to the relevant pages of the textbook and assign exercises for practice and review.

Basic Sentence Parts	Diagnostic Test Items	Teach	Practice	Section Reviews	Chapter Review
Skill Check A					
Simple and Complete Subjects and Predicates	A 1–10	pp. 406–409	Ex. 1–2	Ex. 5–6	Ex. 28, 31
Compound Subjects and Verbs	A 2, 4, 8–10	p. 411	Ex. 3–4	Ex. 7	
Skill Check B					
Hard-to-Find Subjects	B 11–15	pp. 414–416	Ex. 11	Ex. 12–13	Ex. 29

Diagnostic Test

Each item in the Diagnostic Test corresponds to a specific section in the basic sentence parts chapter. This will enable you to tailor instruction to the particular needs of your students. See "Ongoing Assessment: Diagnose" below for further details.

Diagnostic Test

Directions: Write all answers on a separate sheet of paper.

Skill Check A. Write the sentences, drawing a vertical line between the complete subject and the complete predicate. Then, underline each subject once and each verb twice.

1. Stories of the Wild West tell about many heroes and outlaws.
2. Wild Bill Hickok left home at an early age and tried several careers.
3. He worked as a scout and stagecoach driver.
4. Farm work and law enforcement were also among his jobs.
5. This American frontiersman survived a bear attack.
6. He served as a Union spy in Missouri during the Civil War.
7. This famous figure of the Wild West was appointed Deputy United States Marshal at Fort Riley, Kansas.
8. His courage and his skill as a marksman brought order to this tough town.
9. In Abilene, Kansas, Hickok shot and killed a police officer by accident.
10. Hickok's adventures and escapades made him a legend in his own time.

Skill Check B. Write the subject and verb in each sentence. Underline the subjects once and the verbs twice. Write understood words (those implied, not directly stated) in parentheses.

11. Have you heard of Wild Bill Hickok?
12. In the biography section of the library are several books on this interesting character.
13. There is also a video about him.
14. Did he tour with the Wild West show?
15. See the librarian to find out more information about him.

Skill Check C. Write the complement(s) in each sentence, and label them *DO* (direct object), *IO* (indirect object), *OC* (object complement), *PA* (predicate adjective), or *PN* (predicate nominative). Write *none* if the sentence contains no complements.

16. At a young age, Wyatt Earp drove stagecoaches.
17. He also surveyed land in parts of Kansas.
18. The government named him Chief Deputy Marshal of Dodge City.
19. Within a year, he brought the city peace.
20. Then, he moved to a new town.
21. He had finally received a promotion!
22. Soon, he was named Deputy United States Marshal for the whole Arizona territory.
23. The famous OK Corral gunfight made him a legend.
24. Were the arrested cattle rustlers criminals?
25. He sounds brave!

Basic Sentence Parts • 405

Answer Key

Skill Check A

1. <u>Stories</u> of the Wild West / <u>tell</u> about many heroes and outlaws.
2. <u>Wild Bill Hickok</u> / <u>left</u> home at an early age and <u>tried</u> several careers.
3. <u>He</u> / <u>worked</u> as a scout and stagecoach driver.
4. Farm <u>work</u> and law <u>enforcement</u> / <u>were</u> also among his jobs.
5. This American <u>frontiersman</u> / <u>survived</u> a bear attack.
6. <u>He</u> / <u>served</u> as a Union spy in Missouri during the Civil War.
7. This famous <u>figure</u> of the Wild West / <u>was appointed</u> Deputy United States Marshal at Fort Riley, Kansas.
8. His <u>courage</u> and his <u>skill</u> as a marksman / <u>brought</u> order to this tough town.
9. <u>Hickok</u> / <u>shot</u> and <u>killed</u> a police officer by accident. . . . (In Abilene, Kansas,)
10. Hickok's <u>adventures</u> and <u>escapades</u> / <u>made</u> him a legend in his own time.

Skill Check B

11. <u>you</u> / <u>Have heard</u>
12. <u>books</u> / <u>are</u>
13. <u>video</u> / <u>is</u>
14. <u>he</u> / <u>Did tour</u>
15. <u>(You)</u> / <u>See</u>

Skill Check C

16. stagecoaches (DO)
17. land (DO)
18. him (DO), Chief Deputy Marshal (OC)
19. city (IO), peace (DO)
20. none
21. promotion (DO)
22. Deputy United States Marshal (DO)
23. him (DO), legend (OC)
24. criminals (PN)
25. brave (PA)

✓ ONGOING ASSESSMENT: Diagnose *continued*

Basic Sentence Parts	Diagnostic Test Items	Teach	Practice	Section Reviews	Chapter Review
Skill Check C					
Direct Objects	C 16–19, 21, 23	p. 421	Ex. 17–18	Ex. 23	
Indirect Objects	C 19	p. 423	Ex.19		
Objective Complements	C 18, 23	p. 424	Ex. 20	Ex. 24	Ex. 30, 32–33
Predicate Adjectives and Nominatives	C 22, 24, 25	p. 425	Ex. 21–22		
Cumulative Reviews and Applications				Ex. 8–10, 14–16, 25–27	Ex. 34–35

Show students a photograph from the Old West (several appear in this chapter). Have them describe who or what is featured in the photograph and what action is taking place. Write one or two of their statements on the board and identify the subject and predicate of each.

Activate Prior Knowledge

Ask students to recall events from a book or movie about the Old West. On the board, list nouns and verbs from their statements. Then, have students create sentences utilizing some of these words, pointing out those that are subjects and verbs. (Example: The <u>posse</u> <u>chased</u> the bandits into the hills.) Ask students to expand subjects by adding modifiers, pointing out that these are complete subjects. (Example: The angry posse)

TEACH

Step-by-Step Teaching Guide

Recognizing Complete Subjects and Predicates

1. Have students read the definitions of complete subjects and complete predicates.

2. Ask volunteers to define *action verb, linking verb,* and *verb phrase.* If students are uncertain of these terms, quickly review the related key concepts in Chapter 17.

3. Go over the examples in the chart on page 406. Point out that subjects and predicates may consist of just one word or may be made up of many words.

4. Write the following subject on the board: *The tired, dusty cowboy* Have students supply complete predicates to go with it.

5. Write the following predicate on the board: *. . . wandered across the endless prairie.* Have students supply complete subjects.

6. Have students write a sentence with a split predicate, using the sample sentences at the bottom of page 406 as their model. Ask volunteers to share their sentences.

Subjects and Predicates

In any language, the basic unit of thought that expresses meaning is the sentence. In English, every sentence has two essential parts, a complete subject and a complete predicate. These parts may be either clearly stated or implied.

▶ **KEY CONCEPT** A **sentence** is a group of words with two main parts: a complete subject and a complete predicate. Together, these parts express a complete thought. ■

A *complete subject* is the noun, pronoun, or group of words acting as a noun, plus any modifiers, that tells *who* or *what* the sentence is about. The *complete predicate* is the verb or verb phrase, plus any modifiers and complements, that tells what the complete subject of the sentence does or is. (See Section 18.3 for a definition of complements.) As the following examples show, complete subjects and complete predicates can vary in length.

Complete Subjects	Complete Predicates
Cowboys	roamed.
Buffalo Bill	delivered mail.
Pony express riders	carried packages more than 2,000 miles.
The service	lasted for only eighteen months.

Although the complete subject usually comes first, occasionally part of a complete predicate will be found at the beginning of a sentence with the rest at the end. In the first example below, the adverb *yesterday* modifies *visited.* In the second example, the prepositional phrase *At the exhibit* modifies *saw.* The complete subject is underlined once and the complete predicate, twice.

EXAMPLES: Yesterday <u>my social studies class</u> <u>visited a Wild West exhibit</u>.

<u>At the exhibit</u>, <u>we</u> <u>saw a collection of Wild West memorabilia</u>.

Theme: Wild West

In this section, you will learn about subjects and predicates. The examples and exercises in this section are about the Wild West.

Cross-Curricular Connection: Social Studies

🕐 **TIME AND RESOURCE MANAGER**

Resources
Print: *Grammar Exercise Workbook,* pp. 23–28; *Grammar Exercises Answers on Transparencies,* Ch. 18
Technology: *On-Line Exercise Bank,* Section 18.1

In-Depth Coverage	Accelerated Pace
• Work through all key concepts, pp. 406–411. • Assign and review Exercises 1–4. • Read and discuss Grammar in Literature, p. 411.	• Assign pp. 406–411 for independent student review. • Assign Section Review Exercises 5–6.

Exercise 1 Recognizing Complete Subjects and Predicates

Make two columns as shown in the example. Then, write each complete subject in the first column and each complete predicate in the second column.

EXAMPLE: The tall cowboy tipped his hat politely.

ANSWER:

Complete Subject	Complete Predicate
The tall cowboy	tipped his hat politely.

1. Frederic Sackrider Remington was a famous American artist.
2. He painted scenes of the Wild West.
3. The New York native also sculpted many cowboys and Native Americans.
4. More than 2,700 pieces were created by him.
5. At Yale University, he studied art.
6. Early in his career, he traveled to the West.
7. Later, the artist settled in New Rochelle, New York.
8. Remington's sculptures were influenced by the famous artist Fredrick Ruckstull.
9. Remington's work helped create the myth of the Wild West.
10. The sculpture *Coming Through the Rye* was created in 1902.
11. This famous sculpture is featured in many art books.
12. Remington's action-filled style made him popular.
13. His early works were full of detail.
14. The Metropolitan Museum of Art in New York City contains some of Remington's work.
15. His story is just one of many from the Wild West.

Partners, Charles M. Russell

More Practice

On-line
Exercise Bank
• Section 18.1
Grammar Exercise Workbook
• pp. 23–24

◀ **Critical Viewing**
Suggest a predicate that tells what the man in this photo may be doing.
[Analyze]

Answer Key

▶ **Exercise 1**

1. Frederic Sackrider Remington / was a famous American artist.
2. He / painted scenes of the Wild West.
3. The New York native / also sculpted many cowboys and Native Americans.
4. More than 2,700 pieces / were created by him.
5. he / studied art. (At Yale University)
6. he / traveled to the West. (Early in his career)
7. the artist / settled in New Rochelle, New York. (Later)
8. Remington's sculptures / were influenced by the famous artist Frederick Ruckstull.
9. Remington's work / helped create the myth of the Wild West.
10. The sculpture *Coming Through the Rye* / was created in 1902.
11. This famous sculpture / is featured in many art books.
12. Remington's action-filled style / made him popular.
13. His early works / were full of detail.
14. The Metropolitan Museum of Art in New York City / contains some of Remington's work.
15. His story / is just one of many from the Wild West.

Critical Viewing

Analyze Students may suggest, among other things, that the cowboy *is preparing breakfast or dinner* (complete predicate) or that he *is cooking a meal* (complete predicate). Students might predict that the man and his horse will soon be *roaming across the West* or *riding off into the sunset.* (If they offer these kinds of predicates, have them create sentences using *roaming* and *riding* as verbs)

⏱ **TIME SAVERS!**

🖼 **Answers on Transparencies**
Use the *Grammar Exercises Answers on Transparencies* for Chapter 18 to facilitate correction by students.

💻 **On-Line Exercise Bank**
Have students complete the exercises on computer. The Auto Check feature will grade their work for you!

Simple Subjects and Predicates

1. Ask volunteers to define *noun* and *pronoun*. Have others give examples of each.

2. Explain that sometimes a group of words acts as a noun. For example, in the sentence "Studying diligently will help you succeed," *studying diligently,* though made up of a verb form and adverb, is acting as a noun.

3. Remind students that a sentence, by definition, expresses a complete thought. Though sentences generally include more information, a subject and predicate are the only things that are absolutely necessary. For example, *She walked* is a complete sentence.

4. On the board, write the following sentences (without the underlining, which reveals the answers):

   The tall, dark <u>stranger</u> <u>walked</u> down the dusty street.

   A wild <u>horse</u> <u>ran</u> through the canyon.

   <u>Wyatt Earp</u> quickly <u>captured</u> the outlaw.

   Have students identify the simple subject and the simple predicate of each sentence.

Language Highlight

A *doublet* is one of two or more words in a language that are derived from the same original source but come by different linguistic routes. *Predicate,* which is the doublet of *preach,* is an example of this. Both words come from the Latin *prae-* (pre-) and *dicare* (make known), but *preach* came through Old French on its way to English. However, though the meaning between the two is slightly different, they both relate to "making known"—the predicate makes known what the subject does or is.

18.1

Simple Subjects and Predicates

Each complete subject and complete predicate contains a word or group of words that is essential to the sentence. Without these elements, known as the *simple subject* and *simple predicate,* a sentence is considered incomplete.

▶ **KEY CONCEPTS** The **simple subject** is the essential noun, pronoun, or group of words acting as a noun that cannot be left out of the complete subject. ■

The **simple predicate** is the essential verb or verb phrase that cannot be left out of the complete predicate. ■

In the following chart, the simple subjects are underlined once, and the simple predicates are underlined twice. Notice the other words in the sentences: They either modify the simple subject or the simple predicate of the sentence, or they help the simple predicate complete the meaning of the sentence.

In the last example, notice that the simple subject is *nation,* not *San Marino.* The object of a preposition is never a simple subject. Notice also that the simple predicate is a verb phrase, *has received,* that is interrupted by an adverb.

SIMPLE SUBJECTS AND SIMPLE PREDICATES	
Complete Subjects	**Complete Predicates**
<u>Tickets</u> for the rodeo	<u>sold</u> quickly.
The writer's <u>children</u>	<u>published</u> all of his early poetry in 1868 but none of his sketches.
The tiny <u>nation</u> of San Marino	<u>has</u> always <u>received</u> most of its income from the sale of postage stamps.

Note About *Terminology:* From this point on in this book, the term *subject* will be used to refer to a simple subject and the term *verb* will be used to refer to a simple predicate. Whenever subjects and verbs need to be indicated in examples, subjects will be underlined once and verbs will be underlined twice.

⚙ **Grammar and Style Tip**

Examine complete subjects and complete predicates to evaluate whether groups of words could be replaced with a more precise noun or verb.

Locating Subjects and Verbs Knowing a method for locating subjects and verbs in sentences will help you express complete thoughts in your own writing.

To find the subject, ask, "What word tells what this sentence is about?" Then ask, "What did the subject do?" The answer gives you the verb.

To find the verb, first ask, "What word expresses action or state of being in this sentence?" Then ask, "Who or what?" before the verb. The answer will be the subject of the verb.

Notice how these methods work with the following sentence:

EXAMPLE: The train whistle signaled a warning.

To find the subject, first ask, "What word tells what this sentence is about?"

ANSWER: train whistle (*Train whistle* is the subject.)

Then, to find the verb, ask, "What did the train whistle do?"

ANSWER: signaled (*Signaled* is the verb.)

To find the verb, first ask, "What word expresses action or state of being in this sentence?"

ANSWER: signaled (*Signaled* is the verb.)

Then, to find the subject, ask, "Who or what signaled?"

ANSWER: train whistle (*Train whistle* is the subject.)

▼ **Critical Viewing**
Write a complete sentence describing one difficulty of traveling across the country in a wagon train.
[Draw Conclusions]

Subjects and Predicates • 409

Critical Viewing

Draw Conclusions Possible answer: Wagon trains faced long days on the hot, dusty trail.

Integrating Workplace Skills

Explain to students that most businesses require the use of complete sentences. Name jobs that students might someday consider, and have students suggest sentences that might be used at some point in the job, for example, *firefighter* (You must leave the building.); *astronaut* (What time is the launch?); *doctor* (The cast can come off in two weeks.); *business person* (Next year, we will sell more.); *umpire* (You're out!). Have students identify the subjects and predicates in their statements, then discuss what confusion might arise if one or the other were omitted.

Customize for
Logical/Mathematical Learners

Write the following equation on the board: 73 + 18 = 91. Explain to students that verbs, especially linking verbs, work like the equal sign in the equation. They could erase the symbol and write *is* or *equals,* both of which are verbs, and the equation would still work. Even when the verbs are not linking verbs, they generally relate to what follows in a way that is similar to an equation. For example, *Jenna threw* doesn't tell us anything without having the rest of the "equation"—that is, what she threw—comparable to mathematical concepts like "is a function of." Suggest that students approach sentences logically. Even if they don't always remember specific terms, like *compound predicate,* they should always make sure that their "equations" are complete and make sense.

◆ **STANDARDIZED TEST PREPARATION WORKSHOP**

Grammar and Usage Many standardized tests require students to use their knowledge of subjects and predicates to identify incomplete sentences. Use the following example to demonstrate.

Which of the following is **not** a complete sentence?

A The cattle ranchers agreed to settle their dispute over water rights.

B To settle their dispute, cattle ranchers finally reached an agreement over water rights.

C An agreement among the cattle ranchers about their dispute over water rights.

D Settling their dispute over water rights, cattle ranchers finally reached an agreement.

The correct answer is **C**: The sentence lacks a predicate, and is therefore incomplete.

▶ **Exercise 2**

1. <u>herders</u> / <u>worked</u>
2. <u>They</u> / <u>drove</u>
3. <u>Sources</u> of water / <u>were found</u>
4. <u>predators</u> / <u>hunted</u>
5. <u>stampedes</u> / often <u>occurred</u>
6. <u>Cowboys</u> on the plains / <u>earned</u>
7. <u>era</u> / finally <u>ended</u>
8. <u>farmers</u> / <u>put</u>
9. <u>Transcontinental Railroad</u> / <u>connected</u>
10. <u>need</u> for long cattle drives / <u>was</u>

Critical Viewing

Relate Possible answers: I'd hand over my valuables and hope for the best, I would lie low and hope I wasn't noticed, and so on.

Customize for
Gifted and Talented Students

Have students spin a brief tale about the people depicted in two or three of the photographs in this chapter. Who are these people? What are they like? What do they appear to be doing, and what will happen next? Have students make only one or two separate statements for each photograph. Then have them identify the subjects and the predicates in their tales. If it makes it easier, they can write their statements on paper or on the board and underline the subjects and predicates.

Customize for
ESL Students

Have students write one or two sentences about themselves: where they live, activities they enjoy, and so on. Let them write in their native language, if they are more comfortable. Ask them to underline words that refer to themselves. Explain that, in a sentence about them, they are the subject (probably the pronoun *I* or its equivalent). Explain that in every language, sentences have a subject and predicate, even if they have a different name. Have them underline the action words (verbs). Ask if they know the grammatical terms in their own language for *noun, verb, subject,* or *predicate.* If so, have them write the terms in both languages to reinforce the learning.

George Ives, Road Agent, Olaf Seltzer

▲ **Critical Viewing** Use a compound verb to tell two or more actions you might take if you were a passenger in this stagecoach. **[Relate]**

▶ **Exercise 2** **Identifying Subjects and Verbs** Write the sentences, drawing a vertical line between the complete subject and the complete predicate. Then, underline each subject once and each verb twice.

EXAMPLE: Cattle <u>farmers</u> | <u>sent</u> their herds to market.

1. Cattle herders worked up to twenty hours a day.
2. They drove cattle up and down the Chisholm Trail.
3. Sources of water were sometimes not easily found.
4. Natural predators hunted the cattle.
5. Wild buffalo stampedes often occurred at night.
6. Cowboys on the plains earned only about seven dollars a week.
7. The cowboy era finally ended around 1890.
8. The remaining cattle farmers put fences around their ranges.
9. The famous Transcontinental Railroad connected the two coasts.
10. The need for long cattle drives was over.

▶ **More Practice**

On-line
Exercise Bank
• Section 18.1
Grammar Exercise
Workbook
• pp. 27–28

410 • Basic Sentence Parts

Recognizing More Than One Subject or Verb

Sometimes, a sentence may contain a compound subject or compound verb.

KEY CONCEPT A **compound subject** is two or more subjects that have the same verb and are joined by a conjunction such as *and* or *or.* ■

In the following example, the parts of the compound subject are underlined once. The verb is underlined twice.

EXAMPLE: Neither the horse nor the driver looked tired.

KEY CONCEPT A **compound verb** is two or more verbs that have the same subject and are joined by a conjunction such as *and* or *or.* ■

Notice in the second example that it is not necessary to repeat the same helping verb twice. Some sentence constructions may contain both compound subjects and compound verbs.

EXAMPLES: She sneezed and coughed throughout the trip.
We will load the wagon and leave soon.
The dog and cat eyed each other, circled warily, and then advanced into combat.

GRAMMAR IN LITERATURE

from

Pecos Bill Becomes a Coyote

Retold by James Cloyd Bowman

In this excerpt, you will see that using the two separate compound verbs became *and* believed *and* discovered *and* became *avoids the necessity of having to repeat the subject* he.

Pecos Bill had the strangest and most exciting experience any boy ever had. He *became* a member of a pack of wild Coyotes, and . . . *believed* that his name was Cropear. . . . Later he *discovered* that he was a human being and very shortly thereafter *became* the greatest cowboy of all time.

⊛ Technology Tip

When editing your work, use the copy, cut, and paste functions rather than retyping sentences or paragraphs.

⟳ Learn More

To find additional information about nouns, pronouns, and verbs, see Chapter 17.

Subjects and Predicates • 411

18.1

> **Exercise 3** Locating Compound Subjects and Verbs Write the words that make up the subject and verb in each sentence. Label them *compound subject* and *compound verb.*
> 1. Dogs and wolves are closely related to the coyote.
> 2. A howling coyote and cowboys around a campfire bring to mind a picture of the Wild West.
> 3. Coyotes in desert climates escape the heat and sleep in caves during the daytime.
> 4. Farmers and ranchers sometimes call coyotes prairie wolves.
> 5. Coyotes roam the range and look for food.

> **Exercise 4** Combining Sentences With Compound Subjects and Verbs Combine the two sentences into one sentence with a compound subject or a compound verb.
> 1. Settlers traveled under difficult conditions. Settlers faced many dangers.
> 2. Horses were used to pull covered wagons. Mules were used to pull covered wagons.
> 3. The settlers moved into the unknown. They left the familiar behind.
> 4. The wide open spaces appealed to many. The opportunities for independence also appealed to many.
> 5. The settlers traveled during the day. They camped at night.

▼ **Critical Viewing**
Use a compound subject to describe an advantage of camping for the night in this formation. **[Assess]**

412 • Basic Sentence Parts

☑ **ONGOING ASSESSMENT: Assess Mastery**

Use the following resources to assess student mastery of subjects and predicates.

In the Textbook	Technology
Chapter Review, Ex. 28, 31, pp. 428–429	*On-Line Exercise Bank,* Section 18.1

Section 18.1 Section Review

GRAMMAR EXERCISES 5–10

Exercise 5 **Recognizing Complete Subjects and Predicates** Make two columns. Label one *complete subject* and the other, *complete predicate.* Then, write each complete subject in the first column and each complete predicate in the second column.

1. Jesse James was born in Missouri on September 5, 1847.
2. He was a soldier at the age of seventeen.
3. This infamous outlaw formed a gang with his brother and cousins after the Civil War.
4. They attacked stagecoaches, banks, and railroads.
5. Railroad companies offered rewards for James's capture.
6. In 1876, the gang attempted a robbery of two banks at once in Northfield, Minnesota.
7. All except for Jesse and his brother were captured.
8. The brothers formed another gang.
9. Members of the new gang later turned against the brothers.
10. For Jesse, his brother, and their gangs, crime did not pay.

Exercise 6 **Identifying Subjects and Verbs** Write the sentences, drawing a vertical line between the complete subject and the complete predicate. Underline each subject once and each verb twice.

1. Outlaws of the Wild West often ended their careers badly.
2. Billy the Kid died at the young age of twenty-two.
3. Sheriff Pat Garrett captured the young outlaw.
4. John Wesley Harding, Sam Bass, Black Bart, Butch Cassidy, and others ended their careers in gunfights.

5. Emmett Dalton was badly wounded during a holdup.

Exercise 7 **Revision Practice: Sentence Combining** Revise the following paragraph by combining sentences in places where combining would improve the flow of the writing. Use compound subects or verbs as needed.

A cattle drive was hot, dirty, tiring work. Cowboys learned to live with discomfort. They learned to live with danger. Stampedes were one hazard cowboys faced. Thunder could set off a herd of cattle. A gunshot could, too. Cow towns such as Abilene prospered. Dodge City, a cow town, prospered. After months on the trail, cowboys were ready for a good meal and a soft bed. Dance halls catered to cowboys. Hotels catered to cowboys, too.

Exercise 8 **Find It in Your Reading** Identify the compound verb in this sentence from "Pecos Bill Becomes a Coyote."

The mother and eight or ten of the older children hurried back to the river and hunted everywhere, but they could find no trace of the lost boy.

Exercise 9 **Find It in Your Writing** Look through your portfolio to find at least one example of a compound subject and one example of a compound verb.

Exercise 10 **Writing Application** Write a brief narrative about the travels of an imaginary group of explorers. In each sentence, underline the subject(s) once and the verb(s) twice.

Section Review • 413

Answer Key

Exercise 5

1. Jesse James / was born in Missouri on September 5, 1847.
2. He / was a soldier at the age of seventeen.
3. This infamous outlaw / formed a gang with his brother and cousins after the Civil War.
4. They / attacked stagecoaches, banks, and railroads.
5. Railroad companies / offered rewards for James's capture.
6. the gang / attempted a robbery of two banks at once in Northfield, Minnesota. . . . (In 1876)
7. All except for Jesse and his brother / were captured.
8. The brothers / formed another gang.
9. Members of the new gang / later turned against the brothers.
10. crime / did not pay. . . . (For Jesse, his brother, and their gangs)

Exercise 6

1. <u>Outlaws</u> of the Wild West / often <u>ended</u> their careers badly.
2. <u>Billy the Kid</u> / <u>died</u> at the young age of twenty-two.
3. <u>Sheriff Pat Garrett</u> / <u>captured</u> the young outlaw.
4. <u>John Wesley Harding</u>, <u>Sam Bass</u>, <u>Black Bart</u>, <u>Butch Cassidy</u>, and <u>others</u> / <u>ended</u> their careers in gunfights.
5. <u>Emmett Dalton</u> / <u>was</u> badly <u>wounded</u> during a holdup.

Exercise 7

Answers will vary. Possible combined sentences:
1. Cowboys learned to live with discomfort and danger.
2. Thunder or a gunshot could set off a herd of cattle.
3. Cow towns such as Abilene and Dodge City prospered.
4. Dance halls and hotels catered to cowboys.

continued

Answer Key continued

Exercise 8

Find It in Your Reading
hurried, hunted

Exercise 9

Find It in Your Writing
Answers will vary. If students are unable to find examples, have them rewrite an existing sentence or combine sentences to create a sentence with compound subjects and/or verbs. Have students share their examples with a partner.

Exercise 10

Writing Application
Narratives will vary. Have volunteers share their tales with the class. Pick a sentence in each narrative and have students identify the subject(s) and verb(s).

Interest GRABBER Show students a photograph (perhaps one from this chapter), and have students suggest simple sentences that state what is occurring. (Example: *The man is feeding the horse.*) Then ask a student to repeat his or her statement as a question. (*Is the man feeding a horse?*) Point out that the subject and verb are not in the usual order (part of verb, *is*, precedes subject, *man*).

Activate Prior Knowledge

Ask students to write one simple sentence about something they often do on weekends. Have volunteers share their statements. As they do this, help them determine if their sentences are declarative, interrogative, imperative, or exclamatory. Review the definitions of the four functions of sentences.

TEACH

Step-by-Step Teaching Guide

Subjects in Sentences Beginning With *Here* or *There*

1. Ask students to describe or illustrate the ways in which they use the words *here* and *there*.
2. Define *expletive* for students. (A syllable, word, or phrase used to fill out a sentence but without adding to the meaning. *There is a book on the table* means the same as *A book is on the table. There* adds nothing to the thought.)
3. Write the following sentences on the board: *There is the tallest building in Chicago. Here is the home field of the Chicago Cubs.* Have students reverse the order of each sentence and identify the subject and verb.

Critical Viewing

Relate Possible answer: There are thousands of lights burning in Chicago's downtown buildings. Have students identify subjects and verbs.

Section 18.2

Hard-to-Find Subjects

Most sentences have subjects that can easily be found; some, however, contain subjects that are more elusive. Each of the four sentence functions (declarative, interrogative, imperative, and exclamatory) deserves individual examination.

Subjects in Declarative Sentences Beginning With *Here* or *There*
When *there* or *here* is found at the beginning of a declarative sentence, it is often mistaken for the subject.

▶ **KEY CONCEPT** The subject of a sentence is never *there* or *here*. ■

In normal use, *there* and *here* are usually adverbs that modify the verb by pointing out *where*. Occasionally, *there* may be used merely to start the sentence and will have no adverbial function at all. In this case, *there* is called an *expletive*.

Many sentences beginning with *here* or *there* are inverted: The subject follows the verb. Rearrange such a sentence in subject-verb order to more easily identify the subject.

INVERTED: There <u>are</u> the <u>buses</u>.

REARRANGED: The <u>buses</u> <u>are</u> there.

Sentences Beginning With *There* or *Here*	Sentences Rearranged With Subject Before Verb
There <u>are</u> the downtown <u>buildings</u>.	The downtown <u>buildings</u> <u>are</u> there.
Here <u>is</u> the <u>ticket</u> for your trip.	The <u>ticket</u> for your trip <u>is</u> here.
There <u>is</u> <u>money</u> available.	<u>Money</u> <u>is</u> available.

Occasionally, sentences beginning with *there* or *here* are in normal word order with the subject before the verb.

EXAMPLE: There <u>she</u> <u>is</u>.

414 • Basic Sentence Parts

Theme: Chicago

In this section, you will learn to locate hard-to-find subjects. The examples and exercises in this section are about Chicago.

Cross-Curricular Connection: Social Studies

▼ **Critical Viewing** Comment on the lights of Chicago in a sentence beginning with *There is* or *There are.* **[Relate]**

⏱ **TIME AND RESOURCE MANAGER**

Resources
Print: *Grammar Exercise Workbook,* pp. 29–30; *Grammar Exercises Answers on Transparencies,* Ch. 18
Technology: *On-Line Exercise Bank,* Section 18.2

In-Depth Coverage	Accelerated Pace
• Work through all key concepts, pp. 414–417. • Assign and review Exercise 11. • Read and Discuss Grammar in Literature, p. 417. • Do the Hands-on Grammar activity, p. 418.	• Assign pp. 414–417 for independent student review. • Assign Section Review Exercises 12–13.

Subjects in Declarative Sentences

1. Write on the board: *Among the tallest buildings in the world are Chicago's Sears Tower, the Amoco Building, and the Hancock Building.* Have students identify the subject (*Sears Tower, Amoco Building, Hancock Building*) and the verb (*are*).

2. Have students identify the prepositional phrases in the sentence. (*Among the tallest buildings in the world*). Where would this phrase go in a sentence that was not inverted? (after the verb, *are*)

▶ **KEY CONCEPT** In some declarative sentences, the subject follows the verb in order to receive greater emphasis. ■

By deliberately placing the subject at the end, these sentences put special emphasis on it. Such inverted sentences usually begin with prepositional phrases.

Sentences Inverted for Emphasis	Sentences Rephrased With Subject Before Verb
Toward the elevated train <u>rushed</u> the evening <u>commuters</u>.	The evening <u>commuters</u> <u>rushed</u> toward the elevated train.
Around the corner <u>careened</u> the speeding <u>car</u>.	The speeding <u>car</u> <u>careened</u> around the corner.

Subjects in Interrogative Sentences In some interrogative sentences, the subject comes before the verb in a normal sequence and, thus, is easily identified.

EXAMPLE: Which <u>car</u> <u>gets</u> the best mileage?

Often, however, the sequence is inverted.

▶ **KEY CONCEPT** In interrogative sentences, the subject often follows the verb. ■

An inverted interrogative sentence can begin with a verb, a helping verb, or one of the following words: *how, what, when, where, which, who, whose,* or *why*. To locate the subject, mentally rephrase the sentence in normal order.

Questions	Rephrased as Statements
<u>Is</u> the Chicago <u>Zoo</u> open in the morning?	The Chicago <u>Zoo</u> <u>is</u> open in the morning.
<u>Do</u> <u>they</u> <u>own</u> that house?	They <u>do</u> <u>own</u> that house.
When <u>will</u> the <u>coffee</u> <u>be</u> done?	The <u>coffee</u> <u>will be done</u> when.

🖥 **Internet Tip**

You can sometimes target a search more precisely by using the word *NOT* fully capitalized. For example: "Chicago NOT Fire" would eliminate Chicago listings that include the Great Chicago Fire.

Subjects in Interrogative Sentences

1. Write on the board: *Are you going into town?* Have students identify the subject (*you*) and the verb (*are going*).

2. Remind students that questions are called *interrogative sentences.*

3. Point out that it is generally only linking verbs or helping verbs that can simply be inverted to create a question. (Did you go? Are you Philip?)

4. Explain that, generally, if a question does not begin with a linking verb or helping verb, it will begin with an interrogative word, such as *how, when, where, why* (interrogative adverbs), *which, what, who, whom,* or *whose* (interrogative pronouns).

5. Direct students' attention to the second chart on this page, and show them how rephrasing the question as a statement can help them find the subjects and verbs in questions.

Integrating Listening Skills

Invite several students to the board and ask them a question such as *Is Chicago the largest city in Illinois?* Have them first write the question just as you stated it, then have them rephrase the question as a statement. Ask them to identify the subject and verb.

✏ **STANDARDIZED TEST PREPARATION WORKSHOP**

Grammar and Usage Many standardized tests require students to use their knowledge of hard-to-find subjects to respond correctly. Use the following example to demonstrate:

What is the subject of this sentence?

Far below the ocean's surface cruised the submarine, which was being tested by the Navy.

A ocean
B surface
C submarine
D Navy

The correct answer is **C**. The sentence could be rephrased as follows to make the subject clearer: *The submarine, which was being tested by the Navy, cruised far below the ocean's surface.*

Subjects in Imperative Sentences

1. Explain that imperative sentences give orders or commands.

2. Suggest that students might try restating a statement if they are not certain of the subject. For instance, in the statement *Bill, get the phone,* it might appear that *Bill* is the subject. However, rephrased as a question, the subject (*you*) makes an appearance: *Bill, will you get the phone?*

Integrating Writing Skills

Point out to students that knowing a variety of ways to express ideas is vital to effective writing. Deciding what the writing is supposed to accomplish can help them determine which types of sentences would best convey the message. For instance, a simple declarative statement is short and to the point and useful for business, while a declarative sentence with an inverted verb might be more dramatic and work better in persuasive writing or a novel. Write *imperative, interrogative, declarative, exclamatory* on the board, and then ask students to suggest jobs or types of writing that would make the greatest use of each (police or lawyers, interrogative; managers, imperative). Encourage them to give examples.

Subjects in Exclamatory Sentences

1. Remind students that an exclamatory sentence conveys strong emotion and that it often ends with an exclamation point.

2. Write the following on the board: *This city is huge!; Help!; Avalanche!* Have students identify the subject and verb in each sentence. Where the subject and/or verb are understood, have students supply the understood words. Use these annotations to help students comprehend: *This city is huge!; (You)help (me)!; (You watch out for the) Avalanche!*

18.2

Subjects in Imperative Sentences The subject of an imperative sentence is usually implied rather than specifically stated.

▶ **KEY CONCEPT** In imperative sentences, the subject is understood to be *you*. ■

Notice in the following chart that the subjects of the imperative sentences on the left are not directly expressed. The examples on the right illustrate where the subjects are understood to occur in the sentences.

Imperative Sentences	With Understood *You* Added
First <u>visit</u> the Sears Tower.	First [you] <u>visit</u> the Sears Tower.
After the tour, <u>come</u> home right away.	After the tour, [you] <u>come</u> home right away.
Sue, <u>show</u> me the map.	Sue, [you] <u>show</u> me the map.

In the last example in the chart, notice that *Sue,* the name of the person being addressed, is not the subject of the sentence. The subject is still understood to be *you.*

Subjects in Exclamatory Sentences Some exclamatory sentences have the subject before the verb, but some do not.

▶ **KEY CONCEPT** In an exclamatory sentence, the subject may come after the verb or may be understood. ■

To find the subject in many exclamatory sentences, simply follow the same techniques that you would for finding subjects in interrogative sentences.

EXAMPLES: How <u>could</u> <u>I</u> <u>have known</u>! (<u>I</u> <u>could have known</u> how.)
What <u>does</u> <u>he</u> <u>know</u>! (<u>He</u> <u>does know</u> what.)

Other exclamatory sentences may be so elliptical that both their subject and verb may be understood.

EXAMPLES: Fire! [<u>You</u> <u>put</u> out the) fire!]
Let's go! [<u>We</u> <u>demand</u> to] go!

▶ **More Practice**

On-line Exercise Bank
• Section 18.2
Grammar Exercise Workbook
• pp. 29–30

GRAMMAR IN LITERATURE

from **Chicago**
Carl Sandburg

The first sentence in these lines from the poem is imperative. The subject of Come *and* show *is understood to be* you. *In the inverted second sentence, the subject is* slugger.

Come and *show* me another city with lifted head singing so proud to be alive and coarse and strong and cunning. . . . [H]ere is a tall bold *slugger* set vivid against the little soft cities;

> ◢ **Exercise 11** **Locating Hard-to-Find Subjects** Write the subject and verb in each sentence, underlining subjects once and verbs twice. Put any understood words in parentheses.

EXAMPLE: Where is the meeting?

ANSWER: meeting is

1. On the shores of Lake Michigan sits Chicago.
2. There are few buildings in Chicago taller than the John Hancock building.
3. At its top is an observatory offering a spectacular view of the city.
4. How could you miss it!
5. Go there between 9:00 A.M. and midnight.
6. Listen to the talking telescopes with sound effects.
7. There are four languages offered.
8. Where could you have more fun?
9. Tallest of all Chicago's buildings is the Sears Tower.
10. Did you walk along the lakefront?
11. Also, visit Chicago's famous Navy Pier.
12. What does it offer?
13. Go and see!
14. Does the elevated train go to the zoo?
15. Here is a ticket for the el.

▼ **Critical Viewing** Using question words (*what, which, why, how,* etc.), ask two questions about the modes of transportation depicted in this photograph of a Chicago waterfront area. **[Analyze]**

Hard-to-Find Subjects • **417**

✓ ONGOING ASSESSMENT: Monitor and Reinforce

If students miss more than two items in Exercise 11, refer them to the following for additional practice.

In the Textbook	Print Resources	Technology
Section Review, Ex. 12–13, p. 419	*Grammar Exercise Workbook,* pp. 29–30	*On-Line Exercise Bank,* Section 18.2

Step-by-Step Teaching Guide

Grammar in Literature

1. Read aloud the excerpt from Carl Sandburg's poem "Chicago."

2. Point out that, as the textbook explains, the subject of the first line is the understood *you* and that there is also a compound verb.

3. Ask students to reorder the second sentence so that it begins with the subject. (*A tall bold slugger is set vivid here against the little soft cities*)

4. Explain that poetry, more than any other writing form, is likely to invert subject-verb order and may change the order of other elements in order to concentrate the thoughts and ideas.

More About the Writer

Carl Sandburg spent his youth working numerous odd jobs, studying when he could. He was alternately a laborer, soldier, college student, and hobo. His first break as a writer came in 1914, when some of his poems appeared in *Poetry* magazine and received critical acclaim.

Connections With Literature

Students can find the full poem "Chicago" in *Prentice Hall Literature: Timeless Voices, Timeless Themes,* The American Experience.

Critical Viewing

Analyze Possible answers: Where is the ferryboat going? Who rides the elevated train?

Answer Key

▶ **Exercise 11**

1. <u>Chicago</u> <u>sits</u>
2. <u>buildings</u> <u>are</u>
3. <u>observatory</u> <u>is</u>
4. <u>you</u> <u>could miss</u>
5. (<u>you</u>) <u>Go</u>
6. (<u>you</u>) <u>Listen</u>
7. <u>languages</u> <u>are offered</u>
8. <u>you</u> <u>could have</u>
9. <u>Sears Tower</u> <u>is</u>
10. <u>you</u> <u>Did walk</u>
11. (<u>you</u>) <u>visit</u>
12. <u>it</u> <u>does offer</u>
13. (<u>you</u>) <u>Go, see</u>
14. <u>train</u> <u>Does go</u>
15. <u>ticket</u> <u>is</u>

417

Hands-on Grammar

Teaching Resources: Hands-on Grammar Activity Book, Ch. 18

1. If you wish to do this activity in class, be prepared with construction paper, strips of paper, and scissors. Give each student a copy of the Hands-on Grammar activity sheet, Chapter 18.

2. Have students follow the directions to prepare their projects.

3. Subjects of example sentences:

   1. *You (understood)*

   2. *dog*

   3. *restaurant*

   4. *where you register*

   5. *You (understood)*

Find It in Your Reading

Some students might enjoy using this project to find the subjects in other sentences in "Chicago," by Carl Sandburg.

Find It in Your Writing

Encourage students to revise sentences into a variety of structures using what they have learned in this section.

18.2

Hands-on Grammar

Where's the Subject?

Take a sheet of construction paper and fold a pocket in it as shown in the illustration below. Draw a line down the middle of the pocket, and label the left side *Subject* and the right side *Predicate*. Write the following sentences on strips of paper.

1. Go home!
2. Where is that dog?
3. There is a new restaurant in town.
4. Over there is where you register.
5. Put your name at the top of the page.

Tape a pile of the strips on the paper, as shown, to make a flip book. Write each of the words from the sentences on cards that will fit in the pocket with the words showing.

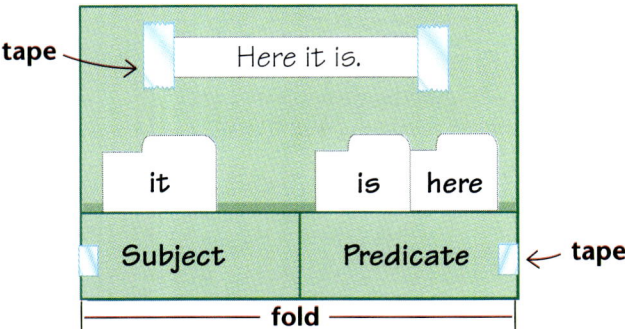

The object of this project is to find the subject of the sentence. As you know from reading the section, the subject is not always easy to find. Put all the words that pertain to the subject on the Subject side of the pocket. Put all the words that pertain to the predicate on the Predicate side of the pocket. Then, when you have correctly identified the subject, flip the sentence over and do the same thing with the next one. Remember that some sentences don't have a written subject, so have a *you* card handy to put into the subject side for those cases.

Find It in Your Reading Do this activity with sentences that you find in your reading. These may be interrogatives, imperatives, exclamations, those beginning with *here* or *there*, or those with inverted word order.

Find It in Your Writing Review some of the writing in your portfolio. Find examples of sentences with hard-to-find subjects. If you can't find any, challenge yourself to write sentences with more variety.

418 • Basic Sentence Parts

Hands-on Grammar
Use the Hands-on Grammar activity sheet for Chapter 18 to facilitate this activity.

✓ ONGOING ASSESSMENT: Assess Mastery

Use the following resources to assess student mastery of hard-to-find subjects.

In the Textbook	Technology
Chapter Review, Ex. 29, p. 428	*On-Line Exercise Bank,* Section 18.2

Section 18.2 Section Review

GRAMMAR EXERCISES 12–16

Exercise 12 Locating Hard-to-Find Subjects Write the subject and verb in each sentence, underlining subjects once and verbs twice. Put any understood words in parentheses.

1. There are so many great sights in Chicago!
2. Have you heard of Frank Lloyd Wright?
3. Was he an architect?
4. Read the travel guide!
5. Here is a section on architecture.
6. There is also a short history of the city.
7. In October 1971, there was a special fireworks display in Chicago.
8. The event commemorated the Great Chicago Fire one hundred years earlier.
9. At the center of the fire was Patrick O'Leary's barn.
10. How did the fire start?
11. There was panic everywhere.
12. Extinguish the fire!
13. Finally helping to douse the fire was a heavy rainstorm.
14. Did you know about the casualties at the zoo?
15. Can you imagine the property damage?

Exercise 13 Writing Questions Rewrite each of the following as a question. Then, locate the subject of each sentence.

1. There was a famous fire in Chicago in 1903.
2. The fire was at the Iroquois Theater.
3. The staff was unprepared for a fire.
4. The lead actor controlled the situation.
5. Many people suffered from smoke inhalation.

Exercise 14 Find It in Your Reading On a separate sheet of paper, copy the following lines from Carl Sandburg's "Grass." Underline the subject of each sentence or clause once. Underline the verb twice. If a subject is understood, write it in parentheses.

Two years, ten years, and passengers ask the conductor:
What place is this?
Where are we now?

I am grass.
Let me work.

Exercise 15 Find It in Your Writing Look through your writing portfolio. Find examples of a declarative sentence with the subject following the verb, an interrogative sentence, an imperative sentence, and an exclamatory sentence. Identify the subject of each sentence. If you cannot find all types of examples, challenge yourself to add those types of sentences for variety.

Exercise 16 Writing Application Prepare the text of a travel brochure for a city in your state. Use inverted sentences, interrogative sentences, and imperative sentences as headings. In each heading you write, identify the subject and the verb.

Section Review • 419

The astronaut checked his (<u>noun</u>).

Have students suggest words to complete the sentence (for example, oxygen, experiment). Ask them to identify the subject. (*astronaut*) Point out that the added noun cannot be used as a subject—the noun completes the predicate.

Activate Prior Knowledge

Have students search through published works to locate sentences with complements. Ask volunteers to read their sentences aloud.

Critical Viewing

Infer Possible answers: The astronaut is wearing a <u>space suit</u>. The suit protects <u>him</u> from extreme temperatures. He feels <u>joyful</u> because he reached the moon.

TEACH

Step-by-Step Teaching Guide

Complements

1. Have students read the definition of a complement. Then, ask why complements are useful. (Possible response: You couldn't tell what was being acted on or how people felt.)

2. Point out that complements may be single words, they may have modifiers, and they may be compound.

Customize for
Less Advanced Students

To help students avoid confusing complements with objects of prepositions, give them pairs of sentences to consider:

They played on the grass.

They played baseball.

Point out that nouns follow verbs in both sentences but that only *baseball* is a complement. *Grass* is part of a prepositional phrase; it completes the preposition, not the verb.

Section 18.3 Complements

The meaning of some sentences is complete when they contain no more than a subject and a verb with perhaps some modifiers, as in *I laughed* or *I laughed wholeheartedly.* In other sentences, however, the verbs need more than modifiers to complete the meaning, as in *The U.S. government established . . .* or *The astronauts are . . .* These sentences require *complements,* such as *NASA* and *courageous,* to finish the meaning of the verbs: *The U.S. government established NASA* and *The astronauts are courageous.*

KEY CONCEPT A **complement** is a word or group of words that completes the meaning of the predicate of a sentence. ■

Five different kinds of complements can be found in English sentences:

- *direct objects*
- *indirect objects*
- *objective complements*
- *predicate nominatives*
- *predicate adjectives*

The last two, which are often grouped together, are called *subject complements.*

This section will explain how each complement works to complete the meaning of a sentence.

◀ Critical Viewing Describe the figure in this photograph by adding complements to these sentences: "The astronaut is wearing . . . " "The suit protects . . ." "He feels . . ." [Infer]

420 • Basic Sentence Parts

⏱ TIME AND RESOURCE MANAGER

Resources
Print: *Grammar Exercise Workbook,* pp. 31–42; *Grammar Exercises Answers on Transparencies,* Ch. 18
Technology: *On-Line Exercise Bank,* Section 18.3

In-Depth Coverage	Accelerated Pace
• Work through all key concepts, pp. 420–425. • Assign and review Exercises 17–22.	• Assign pp. 420–425 for independent student review. • Assign Section Review Exercises 23–24.

Direct Objects

Found only with transitive verbs, direct objects complete the meaning of verbs by receiving action from them.

▶ **KEY CONCEPT** A **direct object** is a noun, pronoun, or group of words acting as a noun that receives the action of a transitive verb. ■

EXAMPLES: We watched the liftoff.

I invited her to our outer-space party.

To find a direct object in a sentence, ask *Whom?* or *What?* after an action verb. If you find no answer, the verb is intransitive and has no direct object. (See Chapter 17 for more about transitive and intransitive verbs.)

EXAMPLES: I was watching the show until midnight. (Was watching *what? Answer:* show)
It taught me about gravity. (taught *whom? Answer:* me)
The meteor crashed into a planet. (Crashed *what? Answer:* none; the verb is intransitive)

In some inverted questions, the direct object will appear near the beginning of the sentence, before the verb. To locate the direct object in this type of question, rephrase the question in normal word order.

INVERTED QUESTION: Which shuttle did you visit?

REWORDED: You did visit which shuttle?

Also, remember that a verb may have more than one direct object, called a *compound direct object.* If a sentence contains a compound direct object, asking *Whom?* or *What?* after the action verb will give you two or more answers.

EXAMPLES: Buzz Aldrin explored the moon and outer space.

He copiloted *Gemini 12* and *Apollo 11* in space.

In the second example, *space* is the object of the preposition *in.* It is not a direct object. You should keep in mind that an object of a preposition can never be a direct object in a sentence.

 Internet Tip

To learn more about space exploration, visit NASA's Web site at **www.NASA.gov**

18.3

▶ **Exercise 17** **Recognizing Direct Objects** Write the direct objects in the following sentences, including all parts of any compound direct objects. If a sentence has no direct object, write *none*.

1. In college, Sally Ride studied physics and English.
2. Then, she applied to the astronaut-training program.
3. Ride earned a pilot's license during training.
4. For her first flight, she rode in the shuttle *Challenger*.
5. On that mission, she launched two satellites.
6. She also launched and retrieved a test satellite.
7. Which shuttle mission did Ride fly for NASA?
8. Sally Ride earned the title First American Woman in Space.
9. While at NASA, she established the Office of Exploration.
10. Later, she produced a report on the future of the space program.

▶ **Exercise 18** **Writing Sentences With Direct Objects** Use each of the following as a direct object in a sentence.

1. her students
2. the movie
3. the space shuttle
4. astronaut
5. NASA

▲ **Critical Viewing**
What missions might these astronauts have accomplished? Use direct objects in your answer.
[Speculate]

▶ **More Practice**

On-line Exercise Bank
• Section 18.3
Grammar Exercise Workbook
• pp. 31–32

Indirect Objects

Indirect objects are found in sentences that already contain direct objects.

KEY CONCEPT An **indirect object** is a noun or pronoun that appears with a direct object and names the person or thing that something is given to or done for. ■

Indirect objects appear only with transitive action verbs. They are usually found after such verbs as *ask, bring, buy, give, lend, make, promise, show, teach, tell,* and *write.* Examples of sentences with indirect objects follow.

EXAMPLES:
    IO   DO
I showed Randy the book.

        IO   DO
They gave the space shuttle a thorough cleaning.

To find the indirect object in a sentence, first make certain that the sentence contains a direct object. Then ask *To or for whom?* or *To or for what?* after the verb and direct object.

EXAMPLES:
          DO
I took her the slides. (Took slides *to or for whom? Answer:* her)

          DO
We sent NASA the letters. (Sent letters *to or for what? Answer:* NASA)

Like direct objects, indirect objects may be compound.

EXAMPLES:
    IO   IO   DO
I lent Richard and Tom my videotape of the launch.

It is important to remember that an indirect object is never the object of the preposition *to* or *for.*

EXAMPLES:
          DO   OBJ OF PREP
She took the NASA souvenir for her sister.

          IO   DO
She took her sister a NASA souvenir.

In the first of the examples you just read, *sister* is not an indirect object. Only when the word *sister* is placed before the direct object and when the preposition *for* is dropped from the sentence does the word *sister* become an indirect object, as you see in the second example.

✦ Spelling Tip

Words like *NASA* are acronyms, or words formed from the first letters of a series of words. They do not require periods after the letters. NASA is an acronym for National Aeronautics and Space Administration.

Step-by-Step Teaching Guide

Indirect Objects

1. Tell students that it can be helpful to identify the subject of the sentence first, because it eliminates one noun or pronoun from consideration. This is particularly important in sentences with hard-to-find subjects. Students should locate the direct object next, since there is no indirect object unless there is a direct object.

2. Write the following sentence on the board; then, using the tips in the textbook, have the class work through the parts of the sentence, writing the terms above words once students have identified them correctly.

   Just give Jana the flowers and get her address for your mother.

   (The subject is an understood *you;* there are two direct objects, *flowers* and *address;* there is one indirect object, *Jana;* and one object of preposition, *mother.*)

3. Remind students that a preposition relates a noun or pronoun to another word in the sentence. Encourage them to review the list of prepositions on page 388. Explain that any time they see a preposition, they should be on the alert because the noun or pronoun that follows will be the object of the preposition. Again, this can help them identify other sentence parts. If they see that a word is the object of a preposition, they know it's not an indirect object.

4. Have students write four sentences of their own, using verbs selected from the list in the textbook followed by indirect and direct objects. Tell them to label each object with *IO* or *DO,* and underline any nouns or pronouns that are the object of a preposition. You can then have them exchange papers with a partner to check sentences and labels.

Answer Key

▶ **Exercise 19**

1. him—indirect object (IO); facts—direct object (DO)
2. NASA—DO
3. shuttles—DO, satellites—DO, probes—DO
4. developments—DO
5. administrator—DO; NASA—object of preposition (OP)
6. government—IO; community—IO; plans—DO
7. programs—DO; countries—OP
8. developments—DO; world—OP
9. success—DO
10. me—IO; guidebook—DO

Critical Viewing

Relate Possible answer: Seeing the rocket take off would give me a thrill.

Step-by-Step Teaching Guide

Objective Complements

1. Explain that in order to identify objective complements, students need to identify the direct object of a sentence. There will never be an objective complement without a direct object.

2. Review the list of verbs that can accept objective complements. Explain that these verbs do not always signal an objective complement. (*I made a cake. Maria called Chan.*) Students should look for a noun or adjective associated with the direct object, and then determine if it is an objective complement. For example, *Maria called Chan clever.* (*Clever* is objective complement.)

3. Write the following sentences on the board, and have students identify the direct objects (DO) and objective complements (OC).

   We elected Leroy president of the student council. (Leroy, DO; president, OC)

   The teacher considered my project the best work in the class. (project, DO; work, OC)

   We named our dogs Jinga and Kahn. (dogs, DO; Jinga, Kahn, OC)

18.3

▶ **Exercise 19** **Recognizing Indirect Objects** Write each underlined item, and identify it as a *direct object*, *indirect object*, or *object of a preposition*.

EXAMPLE: Frank gave his <u>friends</u> <u>gifts</u> from his trip.
ANSWER: friends (indirect object)   gifts (direct object)

1. The tour guide told <u>him</u> <u>facts</u> about NASA.
2. The U.S. government established <u>NASA</u> in 1958.
3. NASA has launched manned <u>space shuttles</u>, <u>satellites</u>, and <u>space probes</u>.
4. NASA does not oversee military <u>developments</u>.
5. The President appoints an <u>administrator</u> for <u>NASA</u>.
6. This person gives the <u>government</u> and the scientific community <u>plans</u> for cooperation.
7. He or she also develops <u>programs</u> with other <u>countries</u>.
8. Space exploration brings new <u>developments</u> to the whole <u>world</u>.
9. The space shuttle program promises continued <u>success</u>.
10. Frank brought <u>me</u> a <u>guidebook</u> for further reading.

Objective Complements

An objective complement completes the meaning of the direct object in a sentence. It occurs, therefore, only in sentences that already contain a direct object.

▶ **KEY CONCEPT** An **objective complement** is an adjective or noun that appears with a direct object and describes or renames it. ■

Objective complements are found only after such verbs as *appoint*, *call*, *consider*, *elect*, *label*, *make*, *name*, or *think*.

EXAMPLES:
          DO   OC
The President named her administrator of NASA.

          DO   OC
I consider her the best candidate for the job.

▼ **Critical Viewing**
What feelings might watching a rocket launch give you? Use an indirect object in your answer. **[Relate]**

☑ **ONGOING ASSESSMENT: Monitor and Reinforce**

If students have difficulty with Exercise 17, 18, or 19, refer them to the following for additional practice.

In the Textbook	Print Resources	Technology
Section Review, Ex. 23, p. 427	*Grammar Exercise Workbook*, pp. 31–34	*On-Line Exercise Bank*, Section 18.3

Exercise 20 **Identifying Objective Complements** Identify the objective complement in each sentence. Then, write the object that is renamed or described.

EXAMPLE: The Soviet Union called the satellite *Sputnik*.
ANSWER: *Sputnik* renames satellite.

1. The scientists thought it wonderful.
2. Critics called the mission unnecessary and wasteful.
3. The officials appointed the dog Laika the passenger.
4. She was the first dog in space, and we consider her a hero.
5. Now, people call *Sputnik* historic and inspiring.

Subject Complements

Direct objects, indirect objects, and objective complements appear with action verbs. Subject complements appear with linking verbs.

KEY CONCEPT A **subject complement** is a noun, pronoun, or adjective that appears with a linking verb and tells something about the subject. ■

There are two kinds of subject complements: *predicate nominatives* and *predicate adjectives*.

KEY CONCEPT A **predicate nominative** is a noun or pronoun that appears with a linking verb and renames, identifies, or explains the subject. ■

EXAMPLES: Neil Armstrong became an astronaut.
          (PN)

John Glenn is a former astronaut and senator.
          (PN)   (PN)

KEY CONCEPT A **predicate adjective** is an adjective that appears with a linking verb and describes the subject of the sentence. ■

Notice that the predicate adjective in the second example is compound.

EXAMPLES: The surface of the planet looked hilly.
          (PA)

Today, space travel seems plausible and exciting.
          (PA)   (PA)

More Practice

On-line Exercise Bank
• Section 18.3
Grammar Exercise Workbook
• pp. 35–36

Learn More

For information about linking verbs, see Chapter 17.

Complements • 425

Exercise 20

1. wonderful; describes *it*
2. unnecessary, wasteful; describe *mission*
3. passenger; renames *dog*
4. hero; renames *her*
5. historic, inspiring; describe *Sputnik*

Step-by-Step Teaching Guide

Subject Complements

1. Remind students that *linking verbs* are verbs that connect the subject to either a noun or an adjective that renames or modifies it; for example, *is, was, will be, appears, tastes, smells, sounds, seems, grows, becomes*, etc.

2. Point out that subject complements are common—linking verbs are almost always followed by a subject complement.

3. Explain that *nominative, noun,* and *pronoun* all share a common root—the Latin word *nomen,* which means "name." Knowing this common root may help students remember that a *predicate nominative* is a noun or pronoun.

4. Write the following on the board:

   Today the sky looks ___.

   The car was a ___ for his birthday.

   The food tastes ___.

   Juana is ___.

   Sean became ___.

   Have students suggest predicate adjectives or predicate nominatives to complete the sentences. Some sentences could take either—*Juana is a girl* (PN) or *Juana is sleepy* (PA), while others can only take an adjective (food tastes *funny, good, spicy*).

ONGOING ASSESSMENT: Monitor and Reinforce

If students have difficulty with Exercise 20, 21, or 22, refer them to the following for additional practice.

In the Textbook	Print Resources	Technology
Section Review, Ex. 24, p. 427	*Grammar Exercise Workbook,* pp. 35–42	*On-Line Exercise Bank,* Section 18.3

18.3

▶ **Exercise 21** **Identifying Subject Complements** Write the subject complement in each sentence, including all parts of any compound subject complements. Then, identify each as a *predicate nominative* or *predicate adjective.*

EXAMPLE: After the mission the crew looked exhausted.

ANSWER: exhausted (predicate adjective)

1. For thousands of years, spaceflight seemed a dream.
2. The desire to fly remained distant and elusive.
3. Nicolaus Copernicus was a Polish astronomer in the sixteenth century.
4. His observations of the universe were quite insightful.
5. Other contributors to the study of astronautics were physicists, mathematicians, and astronomers.
6. The information quickly became very advanced.
7. Poor technology was the obstacle.
8. In the early twentieth century, the study of rocket propulsion was promising.
9. The development of new inventions seemed rapid.
10. The dream of space travel became a reality.

▼ **Critical Viewing**
How dramatic is this photograph? Describe it in several sentences, using subject complements. **[Evaluate]**

▶ **Exercise 22** **Supplying Subject Complements** On your paper, complete each sentence with either a predicate adjective *(PA)* or predicate nominative *(PN),* according to the instructions

EXAMPLE: One of America's greatest achievements is ___?___ . *(PN)*

ANSWER: One of America's greatest achievements is its space program.

1. The organization responsible for our space program is ___?___ . *(PN)*
2. America's investment in the space program seems ___?___ . *(PA)*
3. For astronauts, going into space to repair orbiting equipment becomes ___?___ . *(PN)*
4. Films of astronauts walking in space are ___?___ . *(PA)*
5. From the astronauts' radio reports, space missions sound ___?___ . *(PA)*

▶ **More Practice**

On-line
Exercise Bank
• Section 18.3
Grammar Exercise
Workbook
• pp. 37–38

426 • Basic Sentence Parts

☑ **ONGOING ASSESSMENT: Assess Mastery**

Use the following resources to assess student mastery of basic sentence parts.

In the Textbook	Print Resources	Technology
Chapter Review, pp. 428–429, Ex. 32–33 Standardized Test Preparation Workshop, pp. 430–431	*Formal Assessment,* Chapter 18	*On-Line Exercise Bank,* Chapter 18

Section 18.3 Section Review

GRAMMAR EXERCISES 23–27

Exercise 23 **Recognizing Direct and Indirect Objects** Identify the underlined items as a *direct object, indirect object,* or *object of a preposition.*

1. Satellites carry scientific measuring <u>devices</u> to outer <u>space</u>.
2. They obtain <u>data</u> for scientists and make accurate <u>studies</u> of the planets.
3. Since 1962, Orbiting Solar Observatories have studied solar <u>radiation</u>.
4. Pioneer satellites bring <u>information</u> about space to <u>scientists</u> on Earth.
5. Other types of orbiting observatories send <u>astronomers</u> stellar <u>observations</u>.
6. Scientists expect even greater astronomical <u>discoveries</u> from the Hubble Space Telescope, launched in 1990.
7. Astronauts repaired a <u>flaw</u> in the main mirror of the telescope in 1993.
8. Its observations of a black hole provided much <u>information</u> for <u>study</u>.
9. In 1996, a telescope sent <u>scientists</u> the first <u>images</u> of Pluto's surface.
10. Cameras on many satellites send <u>us</u> <u>photographs</u> of the discoveries.

Exercise 24 **Identifying All Types of Complements** Write all complements in the following sentences. Then label each one *direct object, indirect object, objective complement, predicate nominative,* or *predicate adjective.*

1. Unmanned spacecraft perform many functions.
2. Communications satellites provide companies and the government extensive communication abilities.
3. These satellites transmit television signals, telephone conversations, and digital data.
4. People consider this technology a necessity.
5. Weather satellites observe temperatures and cloud patterns.
6. Other environmental satellites use multispectral optical scanners.
7. Color enhancement makes these images informative and valuable.
8. They show environmentalists soil characteristics and pollution levels.
9. For geologists, images of the Earth's crust become maps of oil deposits.
10. Modern satellite images grow more and more detailed and exact.

Exercise 25 **Find It in Your Reading** Identify the complements in these lines from Archibald MacLeish's "Ars Poetica." Tell what kind of complement each is.

A poem should be palpable and mute
As a globed fruit. . . .

A poem should be wordless
As the flight of birds.

A poem should be motionless in time
As the moon climbs, . . .

Exercise 26 **Find It in Your Writing** Review your portfolio to find examples of at least three kinds of complements. Challenge yourself to add detail to your writing by adding complements to sentences.

Exercise 27 **Writing Application** Write a summary of a science-fiction story, television show, or movie. Identify any complements you use.

ASSESS and CLOSE

Section Review

Each of these exercises correlates to the instruction on complements, pages 420–425. These exercises may be used for more practice, for reteaching, or for review of the key concepts presented.

Answer Key

Exercise 23

1. direct object; object of a preposition
2. direct object; direct object
3. direct object
4. direct object; object of a preposition
5. indirect object; direct object
6. direct object
7. direct object
8. direct object; object of a preposition
9. indirect object; direct object
10. indirect object; direct object

Exercise 24

1. functions—direct object
2. companies, government—indirect objects; abilities—direct object
3. signals, conversations, data—direct objects
4. technology—direct object; necessity—objective complement
5. temperatures, patterns—direct objects
6. scanners—direct object
7. images—direct object; informative, valuable—objective complements
8. environmentalists—indirect object; characteristics, levels—direct objects
9. maps—predicate nominative
10. detailed, exact—predicate adjectives

continued

Answer Key continued

Exercise 25

Find It in Your Reading
line 1: palpable, mute—predicate adjectives
line 3: wordless—predicate adjective
line 5: motionless—predicate adjective

Exercise 26

Find It in Your Writing
Ask volunteers to go to the board and write a sentence from their portfolios. Have the class suggest complements that can be added to make the sentence more descriptive. The sentence could also be rephrased to include more complements, or additional sentences can be created to continue the thought and use more complements.

Exercise 27

Writing Application
Have students share the titles of the stories, TV shows, or movies about which they wrote. Ask them to describe how complements worked in their summaries and which kind of complement was most common.

⏱ TIME SAVERS!

Answers on Transparencies Use the *Grammar Exercises Answers on Transparencies* for Chapter 18 to facilitate correction by students.

On-Line Exercise Bank Have students complete the exercises on computer. The Auto Check feature will grade their work for you!

These exercises correlate to sections of the chapter on basic sentence parts, pages 404–427. The exercises may be used for more practice, for reteaching, or for review of the key concepts presented in the chapter. Answers for all chapter exercises are available in *Grammar Answers Exercises on Transparencies* in your Teaching Resources.

Answer Key

▶ Exercise 28

1. . . . <u>circus</u> / <u>was</u> . . .
2. . . . <u>trick rider</u> . . . Astley / <u>introduced</u> . . .
3. <u>He</u> / <u>was</u> . . .
4. . . . <u>shows</u> / <u>entertained</u> . . . (In addition)
5. The <u>entertainers</u> / <u>held</u> . . .
6. the <u>circus</u> / <u>was introduced</u> . . . (In 1793)
7. <u>John Bill Ricketts</u>, . . . rider, / <u>staged</u> . . .
8. . . . <u>Mount Pitt circus</u> and . . . <u>animal tamer</u> Amburgh / <u>toured</u> and <u>performed</u> . . .
9. <u>Inventor</u> and <u>chemist</u> . . . <u>clown</u> Dan Rice / <u>had</u> . . .
10. the <u>programs</u> and <u>management</u> of circuses / <u>changed</u>. . . . (Then)
11. <u>horses</u> . . . <u>performances</u> / <u>had dominated</u> . . . (Originally)
12. . . . <u>performers</u> / <u>juggled</u>, <u>clowned</u>, and <u>performed</u> . . . (Now)
13. <u>Rope-dancing</u> . . . <u>acts</u> / <u>became</u> . . .
14. . . . <u>trapeze</u> / <u>was invented</u> . . .
15. <u>It</u> / <u>is</u> . . .

▶ Exercise 29

1. <u>Ringling Brothers Circus</u> <u>is</u>
2. <u>Ringling Brothers</u> <u>Did buy</u>
3. <u>productions</u> <u>were</u>
4. <u>they</u> <u>were</u>
5. <u>jugglers</u>, <u>clowns</u> <u>were</u>
6. <u>story</u> <u>is</u>
7. (<u>you</u>) <u>Read</u>
8. <u>they</u> <u>did use</u>
9. <u>tents</u> <u>were</u>
10. <u>plant</u> <u>did do</u>

▶ Exercise 30

1. DO—Circus Maximus
2. PN—enclosure
3. DO—circuses
4. DO—contemporaries
5. PN—holiday
6. PN—events
7. PN—laps

GRAMMAR EXERCISES 28–35

▶ **Exercise 28** **Identifying Subjects and Verbs** Make two columns on your paper; label one *Complete Subject* and the other *Complete Predicate*. Write each complete subject and predicate in the appropriate column. Finally, underline each simple subject once and each verb twice.

1. The first modern circus was in London.
2. A trick rider named Philip Astley introduced the circus throughout Europe.
3. He was responsible for establishing many permanent circuses.
4. In addition, small traveling shows entertained people.
5. The entertainers held their shows in open spaces.
6. In 1793, the circus was introduced to the United States in Philadelphia.
7. John Bill Ricketts, an English trick rider, staged circuses in New York City and Boston.
8. The Mount Pitt circus and animal tamer Isaac Van Amburgh toured and performed in major American cities.
9. Inventor and chemist Gilbert Spaulding and clown Dan Rice had circus troupes.
10. Then, the programs and management of circuses changed.
11. Originally, horses and equestrian performances had dominated.
12. Now, more and more performers juggled, clowned, and performed acrobatics.
13. Rope-dancing and wild-animal acts became very popular.
14. The flying trapeze was invented in 1859.
15. It is now an important part of the modern circus.

▶ **Exercise 29** **Locating Hard-to-Find Subjects** Write the subject and verb in each sentence. Underline each subject once and each verb twice. Put any understood words in parentheses.

1. Famous throughout the country is the Ringling Brothers Circus.
2. Did the five Ringling Brothers buy six other companies?
3. Among them were some very large productions.
4. How enormous they were!
5. There were jugglers and clowns.
6. Here is a story of an exciting life.
7. Read about the early circuses.
8. How many tents did they use?
9. There were usually 300 tents in every show.
10. What did that portable diesel plant do?

▶ **Exercise 30** **Recognizing Complements** Write the complement(s) in these sentences, and label each one *DO* (direct object), *IO* (indirect object), *OC* (objective complement), *PN* (predicate nominative), or *PA* (predicate adjective). Write *none* if the sentence contains no complements.

1. In Roman times, people visited the Circus Maximus.
2. The circus was an enclosure for various events.
3. Political candidates provided circuses for the voting public.
4. Officials impressed contemporaries with games and races.
5. Almost any occasion became a holiday.
6. Chariot races were the main events.
7. Most races comprised seven laps around the track.
8. People also watched athletic contests.
9. Romans promoted riding competitions.
10. Even the emperors considered the circus events exciting and important.

8. DO—contests
9. DO—competitions
10. DO—events; OC—exciting; OC—important

▶ Exercise 31

Answers will vary. Samples are provided.

1. The elephants are the best act.
2. The acrobats and trapeze artists gave the audience a good show.
3. Circus performers work hard.
4. A parade of clowns marched in.
5. The lion tamer performed in the center ring.

Exercise 31 Supplying Subjects and Predicates

Add a subject or a predicate as needed to make each of the following numbered items a complete sentence.

1. The elephants
2. gave the audience a good show.
3. Circus performers
4. A parade of clowns
5. performed in the center ring.

Exercise 32 Writing Sentences With Complements

Use each of the following in a sentence as the kind of complement indicated in parentheses.

1. lion tamer (DO)
2. clowns (IO)
3. foolhardy (OC)
4. ringmaster (PN)
5. brave (PA)
6. exciting (PA)
7. trapeze artist (PN)
8. senator (OC)
9. Sam (DO)
10. Molly (IO)

Exercise 33 Revision Practice: Combining Sentences

Combine the sentences in the paragraph as necessary using compound subjects, compound verbs, and compound complements.

The dedication of the five Ringling Brothers helped build the greatest circus in the world. They also had great organizational skills. Alfred and Charles were born in McGregor, Iowa. John was also born there. Otto was born in Wisconsin, and Albert was born in Chicago. The Ringlings had little money for equipment. They didn't have much money for performers either. The brothers and seventeen other employees sewed and pitched the tent. They played in the band and performed the acts. There were two other Ringling Brothers: Henry, who joined the family business in 1880. Another brother, August, joined the business in 1880, too.

Exercise 34 Writing Application

Write a brief account of a real or an imaginary event that occurs at a circus. When you are finished, underline the subject of each sentence once. Underline the verb of each sentence twice. Circle all the complements. Improve the writing by creating variety with inverted sentences.

Exercise 35 CUMULATIVE REVIEW Parts of Speech and Basic Sentence Parts

Rewrite the following sentences, leaving space between the lines for labels. Then, identify the subject, verbs, and complements, and label all the parts of speech: *N* (nouns), *PRO* (pronouns), *V* (verbs), *ADJ* (adjectives), *ADV* (adverbs), *PREP* (prepositions), *CONJ* (conjunctions), and *INT* (interjections).

1. Circus parades were long and elaborate.
2. They arrived in town by train.
3. Night parades seemed especially exciting.
4. Wow! Those electric lights and torches glowed so brightly!
5. Animals rode in velvet-draped cages.
6. Lions and tigers were among the most popular animals.
7. The threat of danger to trainers made the acts exciting.
8. Workers made the cages strong and sturdy.
9. Artists created special parade wagons for them.
10. Human and animal figures adorned the sides.
11. The wheels featured paint, gilt, and mirrors.
12. People called them "sunbursts."
13. They made the wagons ornate and entertaining.
14. The audience thoroughly enjoyed the show.
15. A steam calliope came last.

Chapter Review • 429

Exercise 32

Answers will vary. Sample answers:

1. Jeff admired the <u>lion tamer</u>.
2. He gave the <u>clowns</u> a tiny car.
3. Some people consider the tightrope walker <u>foolhardy</u>.
4. He was the <u>ringmaster</u>.
5. The lion tamer is <u>brave</u>.
6. The trapeze act is <u>exciting</u>.
7. Bruno is a <u>trapeze artist</u>.
8. The waiters called him <u>senator</u>.
9. Please help <u>Sam</u> with his work.
10. Did you give <u>Molly</u> the tickets?

Exercise 33

Answers may vary. Possible response:

The dedication and organizational skills of the five Ringling Brothers helped build the greatest circus in the world. Alfred, Charles, and John were born in McGregor, Iowa; Otto, in Wisconsin; and Albert, in Chicago. The Ringlings had little money for equipment or performers. The brothers and seventeen other employees sewed and pitched the tent, played in the band, and performed the acts. Two other Ringling Brothers, Henry and August, joined the family business in 1880.

Exercise 34

Writing Application

Have volunteers share their narratives and then ask them to point out any sentences that they think make good use of complements or inverted order.

Exercise 35

Cumulative Review

1. Circus (ADJ) parades (Sub, N) were (V) long (P ADJ) and (CONJ) elaborate (P ADJ).
2. They (Sub, PRO) arrived (V) in (PREP) town (N) by (PREP) train (N).
3. Night (ADJ) parades (Sub, N) seemed (V) especially (ADV) exciting (P ADJ).
4. Wow! (INT) Those (ADJ) electric (ADJ) lights (Sub, N) and (CONJ) torches (Sub, N) glowed (V) so (ADV) brightly (ADV)!
5. Animals (Sub, N) rode (V) in (PREP) velvet-draped (ADJ) cages (N).
6. Lions (Sub, N) and (CONJ) tigers (Sub, N) were (V) among (PREP) the (ADJ) most (ADV) popular (ADJ) animals (N).

continued

Exercise 35

7. The (ADJ) threat (Sub, N) of (PREP) danger (N) to (PREP) trainers (N) made (V) the (ADJ) acts (DO, N) exciting (OC, ADJ).
8. Workers (Sub, N) made (V) the (ADJ) cages (DO, N) strong (OC, ADJ) and (CONJ) sturdy (OC, ADJ).
9. Artists (Sub, N) created (V) special (ADJ) parade (ADJ) wagons (DO, N) for (PREP) them (PRO).
10. Human (ADJ) and (CONJ) animal (ADJ) figures (Sub, N) adorned (V) the (ADJ) sides (DO, N).
11. The (ADJ) wheels (Sub, N) featured (V) paint (DO, N), gilt (DO, N), and (CONJ) mirrors (DO, N).
12. People (Sub, N) called (V) them (DO, PRO) "sunbursts" (OC, N).
13. They (Sub, PRO) made (V) the (ADJ) wagons (DO, N) ornate (OC, ADJ) and (CONJ) entertaining (OC, ADJ).
14. The (ADJ) audience (Sub, N) thoroughly (ADV) enjoyed (V) the (ADJ) show (DO, N).
15. A (ADJ) steam (ADJ) calliope (Subject, N) came (V) last (ADV).

Lesson Objectives

1. To demonstrate control over grammatical elements such as sentence construction
2. To recognize appropriate English usage within a written passage

Step-by-Step Teaching Guide

Recognizing Appropriate Sentence Construction

Teaching Resources: Standardized Test Preparation Workshop, pp. 35–36

1. Review with students what they have learned in this chapter about subjects and predicates, hard-to-find subjects, and the various kinds of complements. Tell them that this workshop gives them an opportunity to apply that knowledge and to practice taking standardized tests.

2. For students who tend to get stuck on questions, suggest that they go quickly on to the next question and return to a difficult question later if time permits.

3. You may wish to provide students with standardized test answer sheets to practice the mechanics of marking in answers.

Standardized Test Preparation Workshop

Recognizing Appropriate Sentence Construction

Knowing how to use the basic parts of a sentence correctly is the foundation for building good writing. Standardized tests measure your ability to identify a complete sentence in a variety of forms and patterns. When answering these test questions, check each group of words for a subject and verb, and then determine whether it expresses a complete thought. Finally, choose the group of words that contains all of the elements of a complete sentence to replace any sentence fragments.

The following question will give you practice with the format used for testing your knowledge of basic sentence parts.

Sample Test Item	Answer and Explanation
Directions: Choose the best way to write the underlined section. If the underlined section needs no change, choose "Correct as is." Alfred Hitchcock, the great director of horror (1) and suspense films. He was inspired at sixteen by the work of Edgar Allan Poe.	The correct answer is *B*. The sentence fragment *Alfred Hitchcock, the great director of horror and suspense films,* does not contain a verb. By combining the two sentences in the underlined passage, the fragment is made into a complete sentence by adding a verb and expressing a complete thought.
1 A The great director of horror and suspense films, Alfred Hitchcock. He was inspired at sixteen by the work of Edgar Allan Poe. **B** Alfred Hitchcock, the great director of horror and suspense films, was inspired at sixteen by the work of Edgar Allan Poe. **C** Alfred Hitchcock, the great director of horror and suspense films and inspired at sixteen by the work of Edgar Allan Poe. **D** Correct as is	

430 • Basic Sentence Parts

Practice 1 **Directions:** Choose the best way to write the underlined section. If the underlined section needs no change, choose "Correct as is."

Thrillers as eerie and frightening as Edgar
(1)
Allan Poe's tales won Alfred Hitchcock

great fame.

First winning acclaim in England. He later
(2)
gained the attention of Hollywood with

such movies as *The Man Who Knew Too*

Much (1934) and *The Thirty-nine Steps*

(1935).

1 A Thrillers as eerie and frightening as Edgar Allan Poe's tales which won Alfred Hitchcock great fame.

B Alfred Hitchcock won with thrillers as eerie and frightening as Poe's.

C Thrillers were written by Alfred Hitchcock.

D Correct as is

2 F First winning acclaim in England, and he later gained the attention of Hollywood with such movies as *The Man Who Knew Too Much* (1934) and *The Thirty-nine Steps* (1935).

G First winning acclaim in England, he later gained the attention of Hollywood with such movies as *The Man Who Knew Too Much* (1934) and *The Thirty-nine Steps* (1935).

H Hitchcock, first winning acclaim in England. He later gained the attention of Hollywood with such movies as *The Man Who Knew Too Much* (1934) and *The Thirty-nine Steps* (1935).

J Correct as is

Practice 2 **Directions:** Choose the best way to write the underlined section. If the underlined section needs no change, choose "Correct as is."

Hitchcock moved to the United States in
(1)
1939. Became a citizen in 1955.

More deeply did these films into the psy-
(2)
chology of the characters. They were also

longer, more complex works than the

English films.

1 A Hitchcock moved to the United States in 1939 and became a citizen in 1955.

B Becoming a citizen in 1955, Hitchcock had moved to the United States in 1939.

C Hitchcock moved to the United States in 1939; became a citizen in 1955.

D Correct as is

2 F More deeply did these films probe into the psychology of the characters and they were also longer, more complex works than the English films.

G Into the psychology of the characters more deeply, they were also longer, more complex works than the English films.

H More deeply did these films probe into the psychology of the characters. They were also longer, more complex works than the English films.

J Correct as is

Answer Key

▶ **Practice 1**
1. D
2. G

▶ **Practice 2**
1. A
2. H

Customize for
Less Advanced Students

If students have difficulty with Practice 1 and 2, go over the items in detail. For Practice 1, identify the problem with each of the incorrect answers. Then ask volunteers to explain the problem with each of the incorrect answers in Practice 2.

Time and Resource Manager

In-Depth Lesson Plan

	LESSON FOCUS	PRINT AND MEDIA RESOURCES
DAY 1	**Prepositional Phrases and Appositive Phrases** Students learn and apply concepts relating to prepositional phrases, appositives, and appositive phrases. (pp. 434–441)	*Language Lab* CD-ROM, Writing Style *On-Line Exercise Bank,* Section 19.1 **Teaching Resources** *Grammar Exercise Workbook,* pp. 43–46; *Grammar Exercises Answers on Transparencies,* Ch. 19
DAY 2	**Verbals and Verbal Phrases** Students learn and apply concepts relating to participles, gerunds, and infinitives and their respective phrases. (pp. 442–453)	*On-Line Exercise Bank,* Section 19.2 **Teaching Resources** *Grammar Exercise Workbook,* pp. 47–52; *Hands-on Grammar Activity Book,* Ch. 19
DAY 3	**Clauses** Students learn and apply concepts relating to independent and subordinate clauses. (pp. 454–465)	*On-Line Exercise Bank,* Section 19.3 **Teaching Resources** *Grammar Exercise Workbook,* pp. 53–58
DAY 4	**Sentences Classified by Structure** Students learn to identify simple, compound, complex, and compound-complex sentences. (pp. 466–469)	*On-Line Exercise Bank,* Section 19.4 **Teaching Resources** *Grammar Exercise Workbook,* pp. 59–60
DAY 5	**Review and Assess** Students review chapter and demonstrate mastery of phrases, clauses, and sentence structure. (pp. 470–471)	**Teaching Resources** *Formal Assessment,* Ch. 19

Accelerated Lesson Plan

	LESSON FOCUS	PRINT AND MEDIA RESOURCES
DAY 1	**Prepositional and Appositive Phrases; Verbals and Verbal Phrases** Students cover concepts relating to phrases as determined by the Diagnostic Test. (pp. 434–453)	*Language Lab* CD-ROM, Writing Style *On-Line Exercise Bank,* Sections 19.1–2 **Teaching Resources** *Grammar Exercise Workbook,* pp. 43–52; *Grammar Exercises Answers on Transparencies,* Ch. 19
DAY 2	**Clauses** Students cover concepts relating to clauses. (pp. 454–465)	*On-Line Exercise Bank,* Section 19.3 **Teaching Resources** *Grammar Exercise Workbook,* pp. 53–58
DAY 3	**Sentence Structure; Review and Assess** Students identify the four sentence structures and review concepts of Chapter 19. (pp. 466–471)	*On-Line Exercise Bank,* Section 19.4 **Teaching Resources** *Grammar Exercise Workbook,* pp. 59–60; *Formal Assessment,* Ch. 19

Options for Adapting Lesson Plans

HOMEWORK
Have students complete any section of the chapter for homework.

FEATURES
Extend coverage with the Grammar in Literature features (pp. 439, 449, 459) and the Standardized Test Preparation Workshop (p. 472).

TECHNOLOGY
Students can use the *On-Line Exercise Bank* to complete the exercises on computer. The Auto Check feature will grade their work.

INTEGRATED SKILLS COVERAGE

Grammar in Literature
SE pp. 439, 449, 459

Writing
Find It in Your Writing, SE pp. 441, 451, 453, 465, 469
Writing Application, SE pp. 441, 453, 465, 469, 471, 475
Grammar and Style, SE pp. 438, 448, 456, 461
Writing Skills, ATE p. 444

Spelling SE pp. 446, 458, 467, 468

Viewing and Representing
Critical Viewing, SE pp. 432, 434, 435, 436, 442, 444, 447, 449, 450, 454, 457, 461, 462, 466

Technology SE pp. 435, 467

Vocabulary ATE pp. 437, 438

Real-World Connection ATE p. 461

ASSESSMENT SUPPORT

Standardized Test Preparation Workshop SE p. 472; ATE pp. 446, 461
Standardized Test Preparation Workbook, pp. 37–38
Formal Assessment, Ch. 19

MEETING INDIVIDUAL NEEDS

Less Advanced Students ATE pp. 446, 455, 473. See also Ongoing Assessments ATE pp. 436, 439, 447, 450, 457, 459, 460, 463, 467.
AP Students ATE pp. 437, 448, 467, 473
ESL Students ATE pp. 443, 458
Verbal/Linguistic Learners ATE p. 438
Visual/Spatial Learners ATE p. 446
Logical/Mathematical Learners ATE p. 467

BLOCK SCHEDULING

Pacing Suggestions
For 90-minute Blocks
• Administer the Diagnostic Test to students to determine instructional coverage.
• Have students complete the necessary exercises in class. Use the Hands-on Grammar activity to provide a change of pace.

Resources for Varying Instruction
• *Language Lab* CD-ROM If your students have access to hardware, a 90-minute block provides an ideal opportunity for students to work on the computer.

Professional Development Support
• *How to Manage Instruction in the Block* This Teaching Resource provides management and activity suggestions.

MEDIA AND TECHNOLOGY

For the Student
• *Language Lab* CD-ROM, Writing Style
• *On-Line Exercise Bank,* Sections 19.1–4

For the Teacher
• *Resource Pro* CD-ROM

WRITING AND GRAMMAR WEB SITE

The Interactive Writing and Grammar Web Site provides a wide array of support for students, teachers, and parents. Grammar support includes:

• *On-Line Exercise Bank* with Auto Check scoring
• Diagnostic and assessment support

www.phschool.com

LITERATURE CONNECTIONS

Grammar in Literature selections from *Prentice Hall Literature: Timeless Voices, Timeless Themes,* The American Experience:

from "The Story of an Hour," Kate Chopin, SE p. 439
from *Crossing the Great Divide,* Meriwether Lewis, SE p. 449
from "To Build a Fire," Jack London, SE p. 459

Lesson Objectives

1. To recognize and use prepositional phrases as adjective and adverb phrases

2. To recognize and use appositives and appositive phrases

3. To distinguish between independent and subordinate clauses and to identify subordinate clauses as adjective, adverb, or noun clauses

4. To recognize essential and nonessential material, to identify elliptical clauses, and to understand the function of introductory words in subordinate clauses

5. To recognize and distinguish among simple, compound, complex, and compound-complex sentences

6. To identify and use participles and participial phrases, gerunds and gerund phrases, and infinitives and infinitive phrases

7. To evaluate writing for both mechanics and content

8. To analyze the characteristics of clearly written texts, including the patterns of organization, syntax, and word choice

Critical Viewing

Deduce Possible answers: The books in the background; the calm, intent expression on the woman's face.

Chapter 19 Phrases and Clauses

▲ Critical Viewing
What clues in this picture suggest that the woman is looking for a work by an author she enjoys reading? [Deduce]

Good writers need to venture beyond the comfortable routine of using only basic sentence patterns when they write. Varying sentence structure with well-placed phrases and clauses adds clarity and style to any good piece of prose. Effective use of phrases and clauses allows writers to personalize their writing, making it distinct from everyone else's. For example, with varied, sophisticated sentences, writers have for centuries given voice to their convictions and offered their unique perspectives on the world.

This chapter describes the various kinds of phrases and clauses that you can use to expand the basic patterns of the sentences you write. Learning to expand the basic patterns of your sentences will help you to express your ideas clearly and to improve the style of your writing.

432 • Phrases and Clauses

☑ ONGOING ASSESSMENT: Diagnose

If students miss more than one item in any category, direct them to the relevant pages of the textbook and assign exercises for practice and review.

Phrases and Clauses	Diagnostic Test Items	Teach	Practice	Section Reviews	Chapter Review
Skill Check A					
Prepositional Phrases	A 1–5	pp. 434–35	Ex. 1–2	Ex. 6, 8	Ex. 50
Appositives	A 1–5	pp. 437–39	Ex. 3–5	Ex. 7–8	Ex. 50
Skill Check B					
Verbals and Verbal Phrases	B 6–10	pp. 442–49	Ex. 12–17	Ex. 18–23	Ex. 51

Diagnostic Test

Directions: Write all answers on a separate sheet of paper.

Skill Check A. Write the prepositional phrases and appositive phrases in the following items. Label each phrase *prep* or *app.*

1. Carol Shields, a Canadian American novelist, writes about simple people and their emotional crises.
2. Her novel *The Stone Diaries* won her the Pulitzer Prize for Fiction.
3. Born in Illinois, Shields moved to Canada with her husband in 1957.
4. Her first novel, *Small Ceremonies*, is about a woman who is writing a biography about a nineteenth-century Canadian author.
5. *The Stone Diaries* is a detailed fictional account of the life of a Canadian woman born in 1905.

Skill Check B. Write the verbal or verbal phrase in the following sentences, and label it *participial, gerund,* or *infinitive.*

6. Having written 270 books in her lifetime, Louisa May Alcott is among America's most prolific authors.
7. She is best remembered for writing the novel *Little Women.*
8. Alcott drew largely on personal experience to write *Little Women.*
9. Writing was the way she supported her poor family.
10. Though her writing fed her family, Alcott's true passion was fighting for women's rights.

Skill Check C. Write the subordinate clause in each item, and identify it as *adjective, adverb,* or *noun.*

11. Maya Angelou, whose powerful writing has inspired a generation of women, has defied social norms all her life.
12. Her literary talents emerged after her grandmother introduced her to literature.
13. Angelou worked as an actor, streetcar conductor, and fund-raiser before she began focusing on her writing in the 1960's.
14. Her autobiographical works and poetry, which offer insight into the experience of black women in the twentieth century, have won numerous awards.
15. Angelou's words will continue to move whoever reads them.

Skill Check D. Label each sentence *simple, compound, complex,* or *compound-complex.*

16. Gwendolyn Brooks was introverted and shy as a child.
17. She grew up reading the classics, and she wrote prolifically.
18. Brooks published her first poem at age thirteen; some thought her a prodigy.
19. Though she worked for a while as a housekeeper and a secretary, Brooks continued writing in her spare time.
20. Eventually, her poems gained recognition, and Brooks, who is considered a very fine writer, has achieved the fame she deserves.

Interest GRABBER Have a student identify and describe one or two objects in the classroom using a common noun and other words that indicate its location (for example, *the book on my desk, the poster over the door*). Write these on the board. Then challenge students to identify the modifier in each. Point out that the prepositional phrases act as modifiers because they describe the nouns. A modifier can consist of more than just one word.

Activate Prior Knowledge

Have a student read aloud one or two sentences from a selection in his or her portfolio. Ask other students to listen for prepositional phrases. As they recognize some of them, write the phrases on the board and ask students to identify the words these phrases modify.

TEACH

Step-by-Step Teaching Guide

Adjective Phrases

1. Students might have difficulty understanding that groups of words, such as prepositional phrases, can act in the same way as single-word modifiers.

2. To help them understand this concept, have them supply a single-word modifier for *dog* in the following sentence: The dog was barking. (The *little* dog was barking; The *friendly* dog was barking.)

3. Then have them supply a prepositional phrase that modifies *dog*. (The dog *in the kitchen* was barking; The dog *on the leash* was barking.)

4. Repeating this exercise will help students understand phrases in the same way they have learned to understand single-word modifiers.

Critical Viewing

Infer Students might suggest responses like *with great sadness* for the first poem and *with bittersweet joy* for the second.

Section 19.1

Appositive Phrases

Phrases can often help the writer overcome the inadequacies of one-word modifiers.

> **KEY CONCEPT** A **phrase** is a group of words without a subject or verb that functions as one part of speech. ■

Two types of phrases frequently used to add detail to sentences are *prepositional phrases* and *appositive phrases*.

Prepositional Phrases

A **prepositional phrase** consists of a preposition accompanied by a noun or pronoun called the object of the preposition. The object may be compound and may have modifiers.

EXAMPLES:
PREP   OBJ   OBJ
near the table and chairs

PREP   OBJ
after a cool, refreshing swim

Prepositional phrases may function as either adjectives or adverbs within sentences.

Adjective Phrases A prepositional phrase that describes a noun or pronoun is an *adjective phrase*.

> **KEY CONCEPT** An **adjective phrase** is a prepositional phrase that modifies a noun or pronoun by telling *what kind* or *which one*. ■

EXAMPLES: The book *on the table* is green. (*Which* book?)
She wrote a novel *about a large family*. (*What kind* of novel?)
I sent my cousin *in Detroit* some books by Isabel Allende. (*Which* cousin?)
She is a writer *with many books to her credit*. (*What kind* of writer? *Which* books?)

More than one adjective phrase may modify the same word.

EXAMPLE: The book by Swanson about women writers is mine.

Theme: Women Writers

In this section, you will learn to identify and use prepositional phrases and appositive phrases. The examples and exercises in this section are about notable women writers.

Cross-Curricular Connection: Social Studies

▲ **Critical Viewing** "My life closed twice before its close—" and "Success is counted sweetest" are two of Emily Dickinson's well-known poems. Use adjective phrases to describe the probable theme of each poem. **[Infer]**

TIME AND RESOURCE MANAGER

Resources
Print: *Grammar Exercise Workbook*, pp. 43–46; *Grammar Exercises Answers on Transparencies*, Ch. 19
Technology: *Language Lab* CD–ROM, Writing Style; *On-Line Exercise Bank*, Section 19.1

In-Depth Coverage	Accelerated Pace
• Work through all key concepts, pp. 434–439. • Assign and review Exercises 1–5. • Read and discuss Grammar in Literature, p. 439.	• Assign pp. 434–439 for independent student review. • Assign Section Review Exercises 6–8.

Adverb Phrases A prepositional phrase that acts as an adverb is an *adverb phrase*.

▷ **KEY CONCEPT** An **adverb phrase** is a prepositional phrase that modifies a verb, an adjective, or an adverb by pointing out *where, when, in what way,* or *to what extent.* ◼

In the following examples, notice how adverb phrases answer any one of the four questions for adverbs.

MODIFYING A VERB:	Elizabeth Bishop was born *in 1911.* (Was born *when*?)
	He talked *with me.* (Talked *in what way*?)
	Except for the conclusion, the book was finished. (Was finished *to what extent*?)
	Beloved is regarded *by many* as Toni Morrison's most successful novel. (Is regarded *to what extent*?)
MODIFYING AN ADJECTIVE:	She is helpful *to everyone.* (Helpful *to what extent*?)
MODIFYING AN ADVERB:	I read early *in the morning.* (Early *to what extent*?)

Sentences can contain more than one adverb phrase, and all of them can modify the same word.

EXAMPLE:	*At Howard University,* Toni Morrison wrote *about compelling characters.* (Wrote *where*? Wrote *in what way*?)

▲ **Critical Viewing**
What adverb phrase would you use to describe the way in which Toni Morrison is smiling? **[Infer]**

◉ **Technology Tip**

Do not rely too heavily on the spell-check feature in your word-processing program. If you type the word *form* instead of the preposition *from,* the spell-check feature will not catch the error. Always proofread your work!

Step-by-Step Teaching Guide

Adverb Phrases

1. Remind students how single-word adverbs function: They modify verbs, adjectives, and other adverbs. Generate examples from the class.

2. Explain that adverb phrases behave the same way: They act as a group of words to modify verbs, adjectives, and other adverbs.

3. Help students differentiate between adverb and adjective phrases by reviewing the questions each type of phrase answers. Write the following information on the board in a chart:

   Adverbs: *Where? When? In what manner? To what extent?*

   Adjectives: *What kind? Which one? How much? How many?*

4. Have students copy this chart into their notebooks and refer to it when they need to distinguish between adjectives and adverbs.

Critical Viewing

Infer Possible answers: With happiness, in great pride, to herself

---

✓ **ONGOING ASSESSMENT: Prerequisite Skills**

If students have difficulty with modifiers, you may find it necessary to review the following to assure coverage of prerequisite knowledge.

In the Textbook	Print Resources	Technology
Adjectives and Adverbs, pp. 380–386	*Grammar Exercise Workbook,* pp. 11–14	*On-Line Exercise Bank,* Section 17.3

1. in 1811—adverb; of a famous Protestant preacher—adjective
2. as a teacher—adverb; with her sister Catherine—adverb
3. about the geography—adjective; of the United States—adjective; in 1833—adverb
4. for children—adverb; under her sister's name—adverb
5. After her brief teaching career—adverb
6. about domestic life—adjective; for local and religious periodicals—adverb
7. in 1850—adverb
8. in serial form—adverb; in the *National Era*—adverb
9. by the story line—adverb
10. in book form—adverb; in 1852—adverb; with an African American hero—adjective

Answers will vary; samples are given.

1. in the morning—adverb
2. about a family crisis—adjective
3. in my story—adjective; with their younger sister—adjective
4. of their great-aunt's affection—adjective
5. by early April—adverb

Critical Viewing

Analyze Possible response: Harriet Beecher Stowe, a middle-aged woman in this picture, has a kindly expression on her face.

19.1

Identifying Adjective and Adverb Phrases

Write the prepositional phrase or phrases in each sentence below. Then, identify each phrase as an *adjective* or *adverb*.

EXAMPLE: The study of writers is fascinating.

ANSWER: of writers (adjective)

1. Harriet Beecher was born in 1811, the seventh child of a famous Protestant preacher.
2. She worked as a teacher with her sister Catherine.
3. Harriet's only book about the geography of the United States was published in 1833.
4. The book, written for children, was published under her sister's name.
5. After her brief teaching career, Harriet married the professor and clergyman Calvin Stowe.
6. To supplement Calvin's teaching salary, she wrote stories about domestic life for local and religious periodicals.
7. When Congress passed the Fugitive Slave Law in 1850, she started a serial novel denouncing slavery.
8. *Uncle Tom's Cabin* was first published in serial form in the *National Era*.
9. The nation quickly became fascinated by the story line.
10. *Uncle Tom's Cabin* was first published in book form in 1852, and it was the first novel with an African American hero.

▲ **Critical Viewing**
Include at least one appositive phrase in a sentence about this picture of Harriet Beecher Stowe. **[Analyze]**

Supplying Adjective and Adverb Phrases

Supply prepositional phrases to complete the following sentences. Then, indicate whether each prepositional phrase is functioning as an *adjective* or an *adverb*.

1. I think I do my best writing ___?___ .
2. These days, I'm working on a story ___?___ .
3. The two main characters ___?___ are in conflict ___?___ .
4. The winner ___?___ will receive an inheritance.
5. I hope to be able to finish the story ___?___ .

436 • Phrases and Clauses

☑ **ONGOING ASSESSMENT: Monitor and Reinforce**

If students miss more than two items in Exercise 1 or 2, refer them to the following for additional practice.

In the Textbook	Print Resources	Technology
Section Review, Ex. 6, 8, p. 441	*Grammar Exercise Workbook*, pp. 43–44	*Language Lab* CD–ROM, Writing Style *On-Line Exercise Bank*, Section 19.1

Appositives and Appositive Phrases

Although they are not modifiers, appositives and appositive phrases are similar to adjective phrases in that they add detail to nouns and pronouns.

Appositives The word *appositive* comes from a Latin verb meaning "to put near or next to."

▶ **KEY CONCEPT** An **appositive** is a noun or pronoun placed next to another noun or pronoun to identify, rename, or explain it. ■

EXAMPLES: Margaret Atwood's specialty, *the historical novel*, can be very entertaining.

His favorite writer, *Annie Dillard*, will read from her work tonight.

Be alert when punctuating appositives. If an appositive contains *nonessential* material (material that can be removed from the sentence without altering its meaning), set the appositive off from the rest of the sentence with commas or other appropriate punctuation, as in the examples above. If, on the other hand, the material is *essential* to the meaning of the sentence, no punctuation is necessary. Below is an example of essential material.

EXAMPLE: The short story *"Fire and Ice"* has a sad ending.

Note also that the terms *restrictive* and *nonrestrictive* are sometimes used instead of *essential* and *nonessential*. (See Chapter 27 for more about punctuating appositives.)

Appositive Phrases An *appositive phrase* is simply an appositive with one or more modifiers.

▶ **KEY CONCEPT** An **appositive phrase** is a noun or pronoun with modifiers that is placed next to a noun or pronoun to add information and details. ■

The modifiers in an appositive phrase can be adjectives, adjective phrases, or other words that function as adjectives.

EXAMPLE: That desk, *the roll-top oak one*, is where I write.

Prepositional Phrases and Appositive Phrases • 437

Appositives and Appositive Phrases

1. Explain that nouns can rename other nouns and, in this way, act as appositives. Use the following sentence as an example: *My teacher Miss Brown is my favorite.* Show that *Miss Brown,* a proper noun, is an appositive since it renames and adds information to the noun *teacher.*

2. Illustrate the difference between essential and nonessential material by writing the following sentences on the board:

   My teacher Miss Brown is my favorite.

   Miss Brown, one of my teachers, is my favorite.

   In the first sentence, *Miss Brown* is essential because the writer must point out which teacher is his favorite. In the second sentence, *one of my teachers* is not essential for the sentence to be clear and to make sense. Therefore, it is set off by commas.

3. Have students determine whether the appositive phrases in the following sentences are essential or nonessential. Have them explain their reasoning.

   The play A Christmas Carol *is a memorable one.* (essential)

   The memorable play, A Christmas Carol, *will be performed this evening.* (nonessential)

Integrating Vocabulary Skills

Synonyms Write the terms *essential* and *restrictive* on the board and have students brainstorm for a list of words with similar meanings. (*necessary, required, mandatory*) Then have them do the same for *nonessential* and *nonrestrictive*. (*unnecessary, superfluous*) Have students keep these terms in a vocabulary list in their notebooks.

Customize for
AP Students

List ten phrases for students to use in sentences of their own. After they write their sentences, have them underline each phrase; label it an adjective, adverb, or appositive phrase; and write down the word it modifies.

⏱ TIME SAVERS!

📃 **Answers on Transparencies** Use the *Grammar Exercises Answers on Transparencies* for Chapter 19 to facilitate correction by students.

💻 **On-Line Exercise Bank** Have students complete the exercises on computer. The Auto Check feature will grade their work for you!

19.1

▶ **KEY CONCEPT** Appositives and appositive phrases can add information to almost any noun or pronoun in a sentence. ■

WITH A SUBJECT:	Beverly Cleary, *winner of many awards for children's fiction,* writes insightfully about the lives of young people.
WITH A DIRECT OBJECT:	E. Annie Proulx won a prestigious commendation, *the Pulitzer Prize for Fiction.*
WITH AN INDIRECT OBJECT:	I gave Dean, *my younger brother,* my old desk.
WITH AN OBJECTIVE COMPLEMENT:	We stained it walnut—*a dark shade.*
WITH A PREDICATE NOMINATIVE:	Her new book is a mystery—*a real page-turner.*
WITH AN OBJECT OF A PREPOSITION:	The stack of books—*all mysteries*—looked inviting.

Appositives and appositive phrases can be compound.

EXAMPLES:	Her writing—*novels and stories*—is acclaimed.
	Elizabeth Bowen, *an Irish novelist and short-story writer,* was a perceptive observer of middle-class life.

Be alert for opportunities to use appositives and appositive phrases to rid your writing of unnecessary words. Often, two sentences can be combined into one by condensing the information from one sentence into an appositive.

TWO SENTENCES:	The professor is a world-renowned expert on medieval history. She lectured on the construction of castles during this period.
SENTENCE WITH APPOSITIVE PHRASE:	The professor, a world-renowned expert on medieval history, lectured on the construction of castles during this period.

⚙ Grammar and Style Tip

A nonrestrictive appositive can be set off with one or two dashes, especially when it is internally punctuated. Dashes give the information in apposition greater emphasis than commas do.

438 • Phrases and Clauses

GRAMMAR IN LITERATURE

from **The Story of an Hour**
Kate Chopin

Notice how the appositive phrase the unsolved mystery *adds information to explain the noun* love *in this paragraph.*

And yet she had loved him—sometimes. Often she had not. What did it matter! What could love, *the unsolved mystery,* count for in face of this possession of self-assertion which she suddenly recognized as the strongest impulse of her being!

▶ **Exercise 3** Identifying Appositives and Appositive Phrases

Write each appositive or appositive phrase. Write *none* if a sentence has no appositives.

EXAMPLE: My friends Jean and Bob are going with me.
ANSWER: Jean and Bob

1. Lillian Hellman, an American dramatist, was born in New Orleans.
2. In New York, Hellman attended two schools—New York and Columbia universities.
3. Her character development, a notable quality of her work, is world renowned.
4. Her subject matter—a condemnation of personal and social evils—is timeless.
5. She adapted two of her plays—*The Lark* and *Candide*—from French works.
6. She received the New York Drama Critic's Circle Award, a prestigious accolade, twice.
7. Most of her plays—thought-provoking dramas—have been made into movies.
8. Hellman, a playwright first, also wrote nonfiction.
9. Her autobiography, *An Unfinished Woman*, won her the National Book Award.
10. The second part of her autobiography, *Pentimento*, is a collection of prose portraits of herself and those whose lives influenced hers.

▶ **More Practice**

Language Lab CD-ROM
• Recognizing and Using Phrases lesson
On-line Exercise Bank
• Section 19.1
Grammar Exercise Workbook
• pp. 45–46

Prepositional Phrases and Appositive Phrases • **439**

Grammar in Literature

1. Have a student read the excerpt from "The Story of an Hour" aloud.
2. Ask students why the phrase italicized in the paragraph is an appositive phrase. (It consists of a noun and a modifier and it renames *love*.)
3. Discuss the way in which the appositive phrase adds to the sentence. What does it tell about the speaker's thoughts on love? (She believes that love is mysterious and impossible to explain.)
4. Ask students to rewrite the appositive phrase, substituting their own thoughts for those of the speaker. Have willing students share their answers.

More About the Writer

Early in her career, Kate Chopin tried to conform to the standards for female writers of her day, which included creating soft, dependent, and unassertive female characters. She was unsatisfied by such work, and her writing began to take a different direction when she read the French writer Guy de Maupassant. He inspired her to write "life, not fiction." Her writings portray women's search for a personal identity. Her novel *The Awakening* was published in 1899 to a controversial and harsh reception. Today that novel is considered to be the first aesthetically successful novel by an American female author.

Answer Key

▶ **Exercise 3**

1. an American dramatist
2. New York and Columbia universities
3. a notable quality of her work
4. a condemnation of personal and social evils
5. *The Lark* and *Candide*
6. a prestigious accolade
7. thought-provoking dramas
8. a playwright first
9. *An Unfinished Woman*
10. *Pentimento*

✓ **ONGOING ASSESSMENT: Monitor and Reinforce**

If students have difficulty with Exercise 3, 4, or 5, refer them to the following for additional practice.

In the Textbook	Print Resources	Technology
Section Review, Ex. 7–8, p. 441	*Grammar Exercise Workbook*, pp. 45–46	*Language Lab CD-ROM,* Writing Style *On-Line Exercise Bank,* Section 19.1

Exercise 4

Answers will vary; samples are given.

1. Margaret Mead, an American anthropologist, is widely known . . .
2. Mead was born in Philadelphia and went to Barnard College, a school in New York City.
3. At Barnard, Mead was introduced to anthropology, a new science devoted to the study of human culture.
4. She conducted studies—notable research—in New Guinea . . .
5. The result of her fieldwork was a tremendously successful book, *Coming of Age in Samoa.*
6. Her other interests—child care and American character and culture—were topics . . .
7. In her analysis of American society, she focused on a particular issue, the problems of young people.
8. Most anthropologists spend their lives studying one primitive society, but Margaret Mead, a brilliant anthropologist, studied half a dozen.
9. In addition to her books—*New Lives for Old, Male and Female,* and others—Mead is known . . .
10. Her clear style of writing and public speaking brought advanced ideas—insights into our culture—to the . . .

Exercise 5

Answers will vary; samples are given.

Diana Chang, an Asian poet, novelist, and translator, was born in 1934. Although not born in China, she spent most of her childhood there. She returned to her birthplace, the United States, after World War II. She attended Barnard College, a college in New York City. Her works include *The Frontiers of Love,* a novel, and *What Matisse Is After,* a collection of poetry. Her poetry, spare and introspective, shows the influence of traditional Asian verse forms. She also translated Asian writings into English.

19.1

▶ **Exercise 4** Using Appositives and Appositive Phrases to Combine Sentences Turn each pair of sentences into a single sentence with an appositive or appositive phrase.

EXAMPLE: I will ask Beth. She is an excellent student.
ANSWER: I will ask Beth, an excellent student.

1. Margaret Mead is widely known for her studies of primitive societies. She was an American anthropologist.
2. Mead was born in Philadelphia and went to Barnard College. It is a school in New York City.
3. At Barnard, Mead was introduced to a new science devoted to the study of human culture. The science was anthropology.
4. She conducted studies in New Guinea, Samoa, and Bali. This was notable research.
5. The result of her field work was a tremendously successful book. It was *Coming of Age in Samoa.*
6. Her other interests were topics of several publications. They included child care and American character and culture.
7. In her analysis of American society, she focused on a particular issue. It was the problems of young people.
8. Most anthropologists spend their lives studying one primitive society, but Margaret Mead studied half a dozen. She was a brilliant anthropologist.
9. In addition to her books, Mead is known for her contributions to various government committees. Her books include *New Lives for Old, Male and Female,* and others.
10. Her clear style of writing and public speaking brought advanced ideas to the general public. The ideas were insights into our culture.

▶ **Exercise 5** Revising a Passage With Appositives Revise the following passage by combining sentences where appropriate, using appositives and appositive phrases.

Diana Chang was born in 1934. She is an Asian poet, novelist, and translator. Although not born in China, she spent most of her childhood there. She returned to her birthplace after World War II. Her birthplace was the United States. She attended Barnard College. Barnard College is a college in New York City. Her works include *The Frontiers of Love* and *What Matisse Is After. The Frontiers of Love* is a novel. *What Matisse Is After* is a collection of poetry. Her poetry is spare and introspective. It shows the influence of traditional Asian verse forms. She also translated Asian writings into English.

440 • Phrases and Clauses

▶ **More Practice**

Language Lab CD-ROM
• Recognizing and Using Phrases lesson
On-line Exercise Bank
• Section 19.1
Grammar Exercise Workbook
• pp. 45–46

☑ **ONGOING ASSESSMENT: Assess Mastery**

Use the following resources to assess student mastery of prepositional and appositive phrases.

In the Textbook	Technology
Chapter Review, Ex. 50, p. 470	*Language Lab* CD-ROM, Writing Style *On-Line Exercise Bank,* Section 19.1

Section 19.1 Section Review

GRAMMAR EXERCISES 6–11

Exercise 6 **Identifying Prepositional Phrases** Identify each prepositional phrase in the following sentences as *adjective* or *adverb*.

1. George Eliot is one of England's finest novelists.
2. Her books give her a place in the top rank of nineteenth-century English writers.
3. George Eliot is the pseudonym of Mary Ann Evans.
4. She was born in Warwickshire in 1819.
5. She went to boarding school in Coventry.

Exercise 7 **Identifying Appositives and Appositive Phrases** Identify each appositive or appositive phrase.

1. George Eliot eventually became assistant editor for the *Westminster Review*, a literary journal.
2. Through her work on the *Westminster Review*, she met many leading literary figures of the period—John Stuart Mill, James Froude, and George Lewes.
3. When she met Lewes—a scientist and critic—she fell in love with him.
4. Eliot's earliest works—*Adam Bede, The Mill on the Floss,* and *Silas Marner*, all set in the Warwickshire countryside—are based on her own life.
5. Many high-school students have read *Silas Marner*, the tale of a friendless weaver redeemed by an orphan girl.

Exercise 8 **Using Prepositional Phrases and Appositives in Sentences** Turn each pair of sentences into one sentence with at least one appositive or appositive phrase and/or prepositional phrase. Underline the phrases you construct.

1. Toni Morrison addresses the black experience in America and celebrates the achievements of the black community. She is an American writer and Nobel laureate.
2. Morrison is a native of Ohio. She grew up during the Great Depression of the 1930's.
3. In 1949, she entered Howard University, where she studied theater and joined a drama group. It was the Howard University Players.
4. After she received her master's degree, Morrison taught. The schools in which she taught were Texas Southern University and Howard University.
5. Morrison then worked as an editor. She worked for a major publishing firm in New York City. New York City is the capital of the publishing world.

Exercise 9 **Find It in Your Reading** Identify three prepositional phrases in the excerpt from "The Story of an Hour" on page 439.

Exercise 10 **Find It in Your Writing** Review a piece of your own writing to find at least one example of a prepositional phrase used as an adjective and one used as an adverb. Challenge yourself to use phrases that add detail to your writing.

Exercise 11 **Writing Application** Write a response to a short story, a poem, or a novel you have enjoyed. Include and identify several adjective and adverb phrases.

Answer Key continued

Exercise 10

Find It in Your Writing
Suggest that students see if the phrases they find can be revised to add more detail to their writing.

Exercise 11

Writing Application
When students finish, have them read their responses aloud to partners. Partners should identify prepositional phrases in each other's writing.

ASSESS

Section Review

Each of these exercises correlates to the instruction on prepositional phrases and appositives, pages 434–440. These exercises may be used for more practice, for reteaching, or for review of the key concepts presented.

Answer Key

Exercise 6

1. of England's finest novelists—adjective
2. in the top rank—adjective; of nineteenth-century English writers—adjective
3. of Mary Ann Evans—adjective
4. in Warwickshire—adverb; in 1819—adverb
5. to boarding school—adverb; in Coventry—adjective

Exercise 7

1. a literary journal
2. John Stuart Mill, James Fronde, and George Lewes
3. a scientist and critic
4. *Adam Bede, The Mill on the Floss,* and *Silas Marner,* all set in the Warwickshire countryside
5. the tale of a friendless weaver redeemed by an orphan girl

Exercise 8

Answers will vary; samples are given.

1. Toni Morrison, <u>an American writer and Nobel laureate</u>, addresses the black experience in America and celebrates the achievements of the black community.
2. Morrison, <u>a native of Ohio</u>, grew up during the Great Depression of the 1930's.
3. In 1949, she entered Howard University, where she studied theater and joined a drama group, <u>the Howard University Players</u>.
4. After she received her master's degree, Morrison taught <u>at Texas Southern University and Howard University</u>.
5. Morrison then worked as an editor <u>for a major publishing firm in New York City</u>, <u>the capital of the publishing world</u>.

Exercise 9

Find It in Your Reading
<u>in</u> face, <u>of</u> this possession, <u>of</u> self-assertion, <u>as</u> the strongest impulse, <u>of</u> her being

continued

441

Tomorrow I am playing soccer.

Playing sports is good exercise.

Playing hard, they collided with each other.

Everyone on the bench wanted to play.

Ask students to identify the use of the word *play* or *playing* in each sentence. (part of verb, gerund as subject, participle or adjective, and infinitive as a direct object) Emphasize that the word acts as a verb only in the first sentence. Tell them that the word *verbal* refers to a verb that is used as something other than a verb.

Activate Prior Knowledge

Have students identify an activity they enjoy, using no more than two words. Write some of these on the board, favoring nouns and verbals. (*playing soccer, singing, hockey, movies*) Then explain how the nouns differ from the verbals. (Nouns are not verb forms.)

TEACH

Step-by-Step Teaching Guide

Forms of Participles

1. Ask students to give you an example of a verb form (*broken, smiling*) used as an adjective (*the broken bat, a smiling baby*).

2. Have them use the following participles in phrases or sentences of their own: *hiking, crying, falling.*

3. Then have them write three more sentences, using *hiking, crying,* and *falling* as verbs. Remind students that not all *–ing* forms are verbals; they are verbals only if they act as nouns or adjectives.

continued

Critical Viewing

Describe Sample response: Reflected in the water, the snowy peaks seemed to shimmer.

Section 19.2 Verbals and Verbal Phrases

Verbals are forms of verbs used as nouns, adjectives, or adverbs. Verbals share two characteristics of verbs: They may be modified by adverbs and adverb phrases, and they can have complements. When a verbal has a modifier or complement, it is called a *verbal phrase.* This section presents the three kinds of verbals—participles, gerunds, and infinitives.

Participles and Participial Phrases

Many adjectives are actually verbals known as *participles.*

> **KEY CONCEPT** A **participle** is a form of a verb that can act as an adjective. ■

EXAMPLES: The *flowing* lava covered the road to Lassen Peak.

The *melting* glacier drained into the Kenai Fjords.

The *frozen* mass is slowly shrinking.

Forms of Participles There are three kinds of participles: *present participles, past participles,* and *perfect participles.* The following chart shows how each participle is formed. (See Chapter 17 for more about the forms of verbs and participles.)

Theme: National Parks

In this section, you will learn how to recognize and use participles, gerunds, and infinitives and their corresponding phrases. The examples and exercises in this section are on the subject of national parks.

Cross-Curricular Connection: Social Studies

◄ **Critical Viewing** Describe this picture, using the participial phrase *reflected in the water* in a sentence that does not include the word *are.* [Describe]

TIME AND RESOURCE MANAGER

Resources
Print: *Grammar Exercise Workbook,* pp. 47–52; *Grammar Exercises Answers on Transparencies,* Ch. 19; *Hands-on Grammar Activity Book,* Ch. 19
Technology: *Language Lab* CD-ROM, Writing Style; *On-Line Exercise Bank,* Section 19.2

In-Depth Coverage	Accelerated Pace
• Work through all key concepts, pp. 442–449. • Assign and review Exercises 12–17. • Read and discuss Grammar in Literature, p. 449. • Hands-on Grammar activity, p. 451.	• Assign pp. 442–449 for independent student review. • Assign Review Exercises 18–23.

KINDS OF PARTICIPLES	FORMS	EXAMPLES
Present Participle	Ends in *-ing*	I took a *fishing* pole. The *winding* trail descended.
Past Participle	Usually ends in *-ed;* sometimes *-en* or another irregular ending	We saw *abandoned* mines. Watch out for that *fallen* branch.
Perfect Participle	Includes *having* or *having been* before a past participle	*Having eaten,* I moved on. *Having been warned,* I did not litter the park.

Participles act like adjectives when they answer the question *Which one?* or *What kind?* about the nouns or pronouns they modify. Do not confuse the verb in a sentence with a participle acting as an adjective. Remember: If the word expresses the action of the sentence, it is a verb; if it describes a noun or pronoun, it is a participle.

Functioning as a Verb	Functioning as a Participle
She pitched the tent.	The *pitched* tent was blown over.
That river is flowing north through the park.	The *flowing* river is deep.

▶ **Exercise 12** **Distinguishing Between Participles and Verbs**
Indicate whether each underlined word acts as an *adjective* or a *verb.*
1. We were <u>hiking</u> along a <u>winding</u> trail.
2. We spotted another <u>hiking</u> party coming toward us.
3. We had <u>raised</u> our hands to wave when we saw the <u>raised</u> hand of the leader waving to us.
4. We asked if they had <u>experienced</u> any <u>camping</u> difficulties.
5. They said <u>experienced</u> hikers like us wouldn't have problems.

▶ **More Practice**
Language Lab CD-ROM
• Recognizing and Using Phrases lesson
On-line Exercise Bank
• Section 19.2
Grammar Exercise Workbook
• pp. 47–48

Verbals and Verbal Phrases • 443

Step-by-Step Teaching Guide continued

4. Read and discuss with students the examples in the right-hand column in the chart on this page. Point out that in each of the examples, the verb acts as an adjective. Verbs that act as adjectives are called *participles.*

5. In their notebooks, have students add a fourth column to the chart and label it *Verbs.* In this column, have them use each participle from the third column as a verb.

6. Remind students that verbs are action words, and give them this sample sentence if they need assistance: *I was fishing with my new pole.*

Customize for
ESL Students

To help students distinguish participles from verbs, give them pairs of sentences such as the following, one using a word as a verb and the other using it as a participle:

I bought a pair of running shoes.

I was running yesterday morning.

Tell them to mentally remove *running* from each sentence. If the sentence still makes sense, the word is probably a participle. (A sentence cannot be complete without a subject and a verb, but it can be complete without an adjective.)

Answer Key

▶ **Exercise 12**

1. hiking—verb
2. hiking—adjective
3. [had] raised—verb; raised [hand]—adjective
4. experienced—verb; camping—adjective
5. experienced—adjective

⏱ **TIME SAVERS!**

🖼 **Answers on Transparencies**
Use the *Grammar Exercises Answers on Transparencies* for Chapter 19 to facilitate correction by students.

💻 **On-Line Exercise Bank**
Have students complete the exercises on computer. The Auto Check feature will grade their work for you!

Participial Phrases

1. Tell students that participles can have their own modifiers or complements to form participial phrases.

2. Then use the first two examples on this page. Have students read each one aloud and answer the following questions about the italicized phrases:

    Which word is the participle? (*swimming, Closing*)

    Which words modify or complement the participle? (*near us now, my backpack*)

    Which word in the sentence does the phrase modify? (*fish, I*)

Integrating Writing Skills

Explain to students that phrases are useful not only for adding information but also for varying the structure of sentences. Show students how to move a phrase to the front of a sentence:

I left my friend's house, saying goodbye as I went.

Saying goodbye as I went, I left my friend's house.

Then ask them to choose a selection from their portfolios and rewrite a series of five sentences so that two or three begin with phrases.

Critical Viewing

Relate Possible answer: Resting peacefully, perhaps dreaming of its next meal, the alligator seems to be feeling content.

19.2

Participial Phrases When participles have complements or modifiers of their own, they become *participial phrases.*

▶ **KEY CONCEPT** A **participial phrase** is a participle that is modified by an adverb or adverb phrase or that has a complement. The entire phrase acts as an adjective in a sentence. ■

Notice that a participial phrase can either follow or precede the word it modifies.

EXAMPLES: The fish *swimming near us now* are lovely.

Closing my backpack, I continued on the trail.

A participial phrase that is nonessential to the basic meaning of a sentence is set off by commas or other forms of punctuation. One that is essential is not enclosed by punctuation.

Nonessential Participial Phrase
Yellowstone's springs, *running with hot water,* spew steam.

Essential Participial Phrase
The springs *running with hot water* spew steam.

Both nonessential and essential participial phrases can be used to combine two short, choppy sentences into one.

TWO SENTENCES: The Everglades are humid. They are teeming with alligators.

COMBINED: The Everglades, teeming with alligators, are humid.

See Chapter 27 for more information about punctuating participial phrases.

▼ **Critical Viewing**
How might this alligator be feeling? How can you tell? Use at least two participial phrases in your answer. [Relate]

Answer Key

▶ **Exercise 13**

Recognizing Participles and Participial Phrases List each participle or participial phrase. Then, indicate whether the participle is *present*, *past*, or *perfect*.

EXAMPLE: The exhausted swimmer finally reached shore.
ANSWER: exhausted (past)

1. Carlsbad Caverns, established as a national park in 1930, is in New Mexico.
2. Nestled in the Guadalupe Mountains, the caverns are open year-round.
3. Water, flowing through limestone, carved out the caverns.
4. First explored scientifically in 1924, the caverns are still not fully mapped.
5. With only 28 miles of known corridors, the area has not been fully explored.
6. The caverns, containing many named chambers, descend to a depth of 1,597 feet below the surface.
7. The Big Room, having enormous dimensions, is the largest underground chamber in North America.
8. Stalactites and stalagmites, ranging in color and size, decorate the cavern's chambers.
9. About 300,000 bats live in the caverns, emerging nightly to hunt for insects.
10. Measuring 46,766 acres, the area comprising Carlsbad Caverns is considered a mid-sized national park.

▶ **Exercise 14**

Punctuating Participial Phrases Write the sentences, underlining each participial phrase. Set off any nonessential participial phrases with commas.

EXAMPLE: The Petrified Forest, <u>first seen by me four years ago</u>, is now my favorite national park.

1. Petrified Forest National Park encompassing part of the Painted Desert is in Arizona.
2. Ancient logs found in the park are now jasper and agate.
3. The park established in 1962 features petrified trunks of coniferous trees.
4. The trees living millions of years ago died naturally.
5. Trunks buried by sediment were penetrated by mineral-rich waters.
6. Wood fibers replaced by minerals were converted to stone.
7. Elements washing away the sediment exposed the trunks.
8. The logs colored brilliantly are very large.
9. Forming a natural bridge, one log has a span of 40 feet.
10. Ancient Native American pueblos built of petrified wood are another feature of the park.

▶ **More Practice**

Language Lab CD-ROM
- Recognizing and Using Phrases lesson

On-line Exercise Bank
- Section 19.2

Grammar Exercise Workbook
- pp. 47–48

Verbals and Verbal Phrases • 445

Answer Key

▶ **Exercise 13**

1. <u>established as a national park in 1930</u>—past
2. <u>Nestled in the Guadalupe mountains</u>—past
3. <u>flowing through limestone</u>—present
4. <u>First explored scientifically in 1924</u>—past; <u>not fully mapped</u>—past
5. <u>known</u>—past
6. <u>containing many named chambers</u>—present; <u>named</u>—past
7. <u>having enormous dimensions</u>—present
8. <u>ranging in color and size</u>—present
9. <u>emerging nightly to hunt for insects</u>—present
10. <u>Measuring 46,766 acres</u>—present; <u>comprising Carlsbad Caverns</u>—present

▶ **Exercise 14**

1. Petrified Forest National Park, <u>encompassing part of the Painted Desert</u>, is in Arizona.
2. Ancient logs <u>found in the park</u> are now jasper and agate.
3. The park, <u>established in 1962</u>, features petrified trunks of coniferous trees.
4. The trees, <u>living millions of years ago</u>, died naturally.
5. Trunks <u>buried by sediment</u> were penetrated by mineral-rich waters.
6. Wood fibers <u>replaced by minerals</u> were converted to stone.
7. Elements <u>washing away the sediment</u> exposed the trunks.
8. The logs, <u>colored brilliantly</u>, are very large.
9. <u>Forming a natural bridge</u>, one log has a span of 40 feet.
10. Ancient Native American pueblos <u>built of petrified wood</u> are another feature of the park.

☑ **ONGOING ASSESSMENT: Prerequisite Skills**

If students miss more than two items in Exercise 13 or 14, refer them to the following for additional practice.

In the Textbook	Print Resources	Technology
Section Review, Ex. 18–19, p. 452	*Grammar Exercise Workbook*, pp. 47–48	*Language Lab* CD-ROM, Writing Style; *On-Line Exercise Bank*, Section 19.2

⏱ **TIME SAVERS!**

Answers on Transparencies Use the *Grammar Exercises Answers on Transparencies* for Chapter 19 to facilitate correction by students.

On-Line Exercise Bank Have students complete the exercises on computer. The Auto Check feature will grade their work for you!

Gerunds

1. Place a short list of present participles on the board. (Examples: *crying, shopping, writing*)

2. Remind students that these can be both participles and verbs, and ask for examples of both. (a *crying* baby, the baby is *crying*)

3. Challenge students to use these words as nouns, not adjectives. (*Crying is something that babies do.*) Here, *Crying* is the subject, a noun. Explain that when a verb form acts as a noun, it is known as a gerund.

4. Have students use some of the gerunds on this page in original sentences. Tell them to label the use of each gerund (subject, direct object, object of a preposition) in their sentences.

Customize for
Less Advanced Students

Students might find it easier to label the use of gerunds if you briefly review the functions of nouns in sentences. Discuss with students the following functions: subjects, direct and indirect objects, objects of prepositions, predicate nominatives, and appositives. Then have them practice identifying each function in sentences such as the ones below.

<u>John</u> walked his <u>dog</u> in the <u>park</u>.
S   DO   OP

Later, <u>John</u> gave his <u>dog</u> a <u>bath</u>.
     S   IO   DO

Customize for
Visual/Spatial Learners

Show students pictures of national parks or recreation sites. Ask them to describe what is going on in the pictures. For example, "A man is climbing a mountain." Write *climbing a mountain* on the board. Explain that *climbing* is a verb here, and then have different students write complete sentences using the phrase as a noun. (*Climbing a mountain is a strenuous activity.*)

19.2

Gerunds and Gerund Phrases

When a verb ending in *-ing* functions as a noun, it is called a *gerund*.

▶ **KEY CONCEPT** A **gerund** is a form of a verb that acts as a noun. ■

EXAMPLES: *Camping* is fun.
                  Some parks allow *fishing*.

The Function of Gerunds in Sentences As nouns, gerunds function in sentences in the same capacity as any other noun. The following chart illustrates some of these roles.

SOME USES OF GERUNDS IN SENTENCES	
As a Subject:	*Hiking* is a pleasant activity.
As a Direct Object:	I mastered *rock-climbing*.
As an Indirect Object:	Agnes gave *rappelling* a try but found it too dangerous.
As an Object of a Preposition:	Eat lunch before *leaving*.
As a Predicate Nominative:	My new hobby is *diving*.
As an Appositive:	My favorite sport, *fishing*, gives me hours of pleasure.

Verbs, participles, and gerunds all can end in *-ing*. To distinguish among them, check the word's use in the sentence.

AS PART OF A VERB PHRASE: The birds are *singing*.

AS A PARTICIPLE: The hikers enjoyed the *singing* birds.

AS A GERUND (subject):   The *singing* filled the park.

Note About *Gerunds and Possessive Pronouns:* Always use the possessive form of a personal pronoun before a gerund.

INCORRECT: We were annoyed by *them littering*.
CORRECT: We were annoyed by *their littering*.

💡 **Spelling Tip**

Do not double the final consonant of a one-syllable word when two vowels or another consonant precede the final consonant: *fear, fearing/park, parking*.

✎ **STANDARDIZED TEST PREPARATION WORKSHOP**

Grammar and Usage Many standardized tests require students to revise errors in compositions. Write the following test question on the board and ask students to identify the correct answer.

The gleeful fans showed him their gratitude by lifting him off the ground, hoisting him onto their shoulders, <u>and to parade him across the field</u>.

How would you correct the structure of the underlined portion?

A and parade him across the field.

B by parading him across the field.

C and parading him across the field.

D correct as is.

The correct answer is **C**. The preposition *by* is completed by three ideas. The first two are gerund phrases (*lifting him off the ground, hoisting him onto their shoulders*); therefore, the third should be a gerund phrase so that all three have parallel construction.

Gerund Phrases Gerunds accompanied by modifiers or complements are called *gerund phrases*.

KEY CONCEPT A **gerund phrase** is a gerund with modifiers or a complement, all acting together as a noun. ■

EXAMPLES: *Low-priced, excellent boating* is available on Yellowstone Lake.

I suggested *lending her my boat.*

Exercise 15 **Identifying Gerunds and Gerund Phrases**
Write each gerund or gerund phrase. Then, identify its function as a *subject, direct object, indirect object, object of a preposition, predicate nominative,* or *appositive.*

1. Preserving Yosemite National Park became a priority in the 1850's.
2. Because of Yosemite's sheer granite cliffs, climbing has become a favorite activity of the park's visitors.
3. Many consider rising before the sun to attack the cliffs.
4. Rock climbers enjoy ascending the monolith El Capitan.
5. Glacier Point is popular for providing spectacular views.
6. Walking along the Mercer River makes one feel at peace.
7. An impressive sight is the cascading of water over cliffs.
8. Giant sequoias invite a favorite tourist activity, taking photographs.
9. The eastern and western parts of the park were connected by rebuilding the Tioga Pass Road.
10. The original road facilitated mining in the area.

More Practice
Language Lab CD-ROM
• Recognizing and Using Phrases lesson
On-line Exercise Bank
• Section 19.2
Grammar Exercise Workbook
• pp. 49–50

◀ **Critical Viewing**
Using at least one gerund phrase, explain why you think so many tourists are drawn to the Petrified Forest. **[Connect]**

Verbals and Verbal Phrases • 447

447

Infinitives

1. Students might have trouble distinguishing infinitives from prepositional phrases beginning with the word *to*. Remind them that infinitives are made up of *to* plus a verb, while prepositional phrases are made up of *to* plus a noun or pronoun.

2. Write the following examples on the board and have students label each an infinitive or a prepositional phrase:

   to the moon (prep. phrase)

   to fly (inf.)

   to ascend (inf.)

   to outer space (prep. phrase)

   to my room (prep. phrase)

3. Have students use each example above in an original sentence. Then have them identify the function of each item in its sentence (subject, direct object, appositive, and so on).

Language Highlight

In Old English, the infinitive form of a verb was identified by its word ending, usually *-an* or *-ian*. For example, the infinitive *to have* was *habban* in Old English. With the influence of Norman French on the language beginning in the eleventh century, such inflectional endings became less common. The word *to* began to be used as an infinitive marker. Previously, this word had been used only as a preposition. Today, *to* is used in both instances.

Customize for
AP Students

Explain that some grammarians caution against splitting an infinitive with an adverb, such as "to *boldly* go" or "to *always* try." Have students hunt for split infinitives in published works and in their portfolios. Have them rewrite the sentence so that the infinitive is not split, and then discuss in small groups which version of the sentence sounds more clear. Example:

Split: I try to always do my homework.

Revised: I try always to do my homework.

Infinitives and Infinitive Phrases

A third type of verbal is the *infinitive*. Infinitives can function as three parts of speech.

▶ **KEY CONCEPT** An **infinitive** is a form of a verb that generally appears with the word *to* and acts as a noun, an adjective, or an adverb. ■

EXAMPLE: *To go* to Yellowstone is my dream. (noun)
I made the decision *to go.* (adjective)
I was excited *to go.* (adverb)

Remember that an infinitive is made up of *to* plus a verb. A prepositional phrase beginning with *to*, on the other hand, is made up of *to* plus a noun or pronoun.

INFINITIVES: to swim, to hike
PREPOSITIONAL PHRASES: to me, to the park

Sometimes, infinitives do not include the word *to*. After the verbs *dare, hear, help, let, make, please, see,* and *watch,* the *to* in an infinitive is usually understood rather than stated.

EXAMPLE: He didn't dare *move.*
I have never seen an eagle *soar.*

The Function of Infinitives in Sentences As the following chart shows, infinitives have many uses in sentences:

INFINITIVES USED AS NOUNS	
As a Subject:	*To move* his arm may cause further injury.
As a Direct Object:	With two weeks off, Nina planned *to relax.*
As a Predicate Nominative:	This summer, Joel's plan was *to travel.*
As an Appositive:	The suggestion, *to return,* was rejected.
INFINITIVES USED AS MODIFIERS	
As an Adjective:	The whole group displayed an ardent desire *to ski.*
As an Adverb:	Everyone thought the reef was beautiful *to see.*

448 • Phrases and Clauses

✿ Grammar and Style Tip

Many infinitive phrases and participial phrases can be moved around within a sentence as long as it is clear which word they modify. Place them in your sentences where you think they create the most desirable effects.

GRAMMAR IN LITERATURE

from **Crossing the Great Divide**

Meriwether Lewis

In the following passage, notice how the use of infinitive phrases (in blue italics) helps the writer express ideas clearly and add variety to his sentences.

At noon the canoes arrived, and we had the satisfaction once more *to find ourselves all together,* with a flattering prospect of being able *to obtain as many horses shortly* as would enable us *to prosecute our voyage by land* should that by water be deemed unadvisable.

Infinitive Phrases Like other verbals, infinitives can be expanded into phrases.

> **KEY CONCEPT** An **infinitive phrase** is an infinitive with modifiers, a complement, or a subject, all acting together as a single part of speech. ■

EXAMPLE: Mr. Wilkins decided *to walk briskly.*
We started *to pack our equipment.*
Dr. Rose left *to buy her son a mountain bike.*

▼ **Critical Viewing**
What would being in this scene inspire you to do? Use at least three infinitive phrases in your answer. **[Relate]**

Critical Viewing

Relate Sample response: This scene might inspire me to climb the mountain to see if I could reach the top or to wade in the clear water.

Exercise 16

1. to conserve natural scenery and wildlife—predicate nominative
2. to provide public recreation areas—adverb
3. To maintain the parks—subject
4. to meet the needs of visitors—adverb
5. to become a national park—adjective
6. To hunt in the park—subject
7. to monitor fishing and mining carefully—direct object
8. to come from the Native Americans who named the area for its yellow cliffs—direct object
9. to see—adjective
10. to cross the valley—adverb

Exercise 17

Answers will vary; samples are given.

1. We decided to picnic near Long Lake. (noun)
2. Jason wanted to climb the cliffs there. (noun)
3. I wanted a safer place to hike. (adj.)
4. We searched the area to find a place we could both agree on. (adv.)
5. Finally, we decided to swim instead. (noun)

Critical Viewing

Evaluate Sample response: The eagle is able to swoop down quickly to capture its prey.

19.2

▲ **Critical Viewing**
Which of the eagle's capabilities make it a fearsome bird of prey? Use infinitive phrases in your answer. **[Evaluate]**

Exercise 16 Identifying Infinitives and Infinitive Phrases

Write each infinitive or infinitive phrase. Then, label each *subject, direct object, predicate nominative, appositive, adjective,* or *adverb.*

EXAMPLE: The bird is ready to fly.
ANSWER: to fly (adverb)

1. The goal of the National Park Service is to conserve natural scenery and wildlife.
2. National parks are designated by Congress to provide public recreation areas.
3. To maintain the parks takes a great deal of money.
4. Guides are happy to meet the needs of visitors.
5. Yellowstone was the first area to become a national park.
6. To hunt in the park is a serious offense.
7. We need to monitor fishing and mining carefully.
8. The name "Yellowstone" is thought to come from the Native Americans who named the area for its yellow cliffs.
9. Mount Washburn is a beautiful sight to see.
10. The Yellowstone River flows north to cross the valley.

Exercise 17 Writing With Infinitives

Write five sentences about a local park or recreation area. Include in each sentence one of the following infinitives. Use at least one as a noun, one as an adjective, and one as an adverb.

1. to picnic
2. to climb
3. to hike
4. to play
5. to swim

More Practice

Language Lab CD-ROM
• Recognizing and Using Phrases lesson

On-line Exercise Bank
• Section 19.2

Grammar Exercise Workbook
• pp. 51–52

⏱ TIME SAVERS!

Answers on Transparencies
Use the *Grammar Exercises Answers on Transparencies* for Chapter 19 to facilitate correction by students.

On-Line Exercise Bank
Have students complete the exercises on computer. The Auto Check feature will grade their work for you!

✔ ONGOING ASSESSMENT: Monitor and Reinforce

If students have difficulty with Exercise 16 or 17, refer them to the following for additional practice.

In the Textbook	Print Resources	Technology
Section Review, Ex. 21–23, p. 453	*Grammar Exercise Workbook,* pp. 51–52	*Language Lab* CD-ROM, Writing Style *On-Line Exercise Bank,* Section 19.2

Hands-on Grammar

Sentence Revision Cube

Practice using verbal phrases to expand and improve sentences by making and using a sentence revision cube. Using construction paper and a ruler, measure equal squares to create the shape below. Cut only the solid lines of the outside shape. Do not cut where the diagram shows dotted lines. Label your cube outline as shown. Fold on the dotted lines to form a cube. Use tape or glue to fasten the tabs to the inside of the cube and hold it together. Begin with a simple sentence, such as *The eagle flies.* Toss the cube. Revise the sentence to include the type of verbal that is shown on the top of the cube. You may need to add other words so that the sentence makes sense.

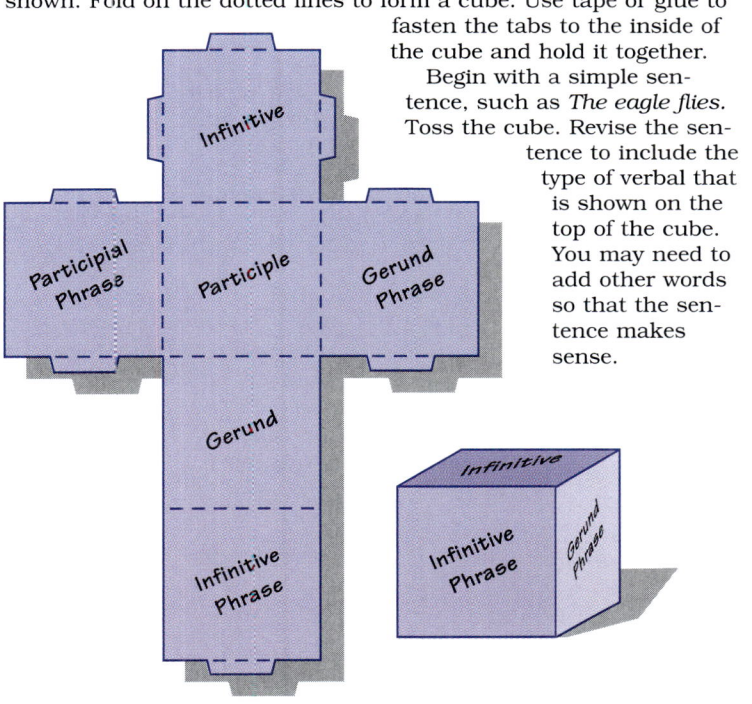

For example, *The eagle flies* might become *The flying eagle soars above the trees.* Toss the cube again, revising the sentences with the type of verbal shown on top. Then, start with a new sentence.

Find It in Your Reading Toss the cube. Look through a short story to find a sentence containing the type of verbal shown. Continue tossing the cube until you have found at least one example of each type of verbal.

Find It in Your Writing Choose several sentences from a piece of writing in your portfolio. Toss the cube, and revise one of the sentences to include the type of verbal shown. Continue until you have used a verbal in each of the sentences.

Verbals and Verbal Phrases • 451

Step-by-Step Teaching Guide

Hands-on Grammar

Teaching Resources: Hands-on Grammar Activity Book, Ch. 19

1. If you wish to do this activity in class, be prepared with scissors, a ruler, and construction paper.

2. Have students follow the directions to prepare and label the cube.

3. Use the following sentences to get students started on the activity, reminding them that they may change the wording as needed. Later, you might ask them to come up with brief sentences of their own.

   The river flows.

   The ancient wood gleamed.

   Nature has many wonders.

Find It in Your Reading

You might have students work with a story you are currently reading in class. Roll the cube; then see who can most quickly come up with the type of construction asked for.

Find It in Your Writing

Do this activity as a class, rolling the cube and having students revise their own writing. When the activity is over, have volunteers read their new sentences aloud.

⊘ **TIME SAVERS!**

✋ **Hands-on Grammar**
Use the Hands-on Grammar activity sheet for Chapter 19 to facilitate this activity.

ASSESS

Section Review

Each of these exercises correlates to the instruction on verbals and verbal phrases, pages 442–451. These exercises may be used for more practice, for reteaching, or for review of key concepts.

Answer Key

▶ **Exercise 18**

1. Operating . . . Interior—present
2. indicating . . . area—present
3. protected for their natural splendor—past
4. preserved for their historic significance—past
5. Having determined . . . activities—perfect

▶ **Exercise 19**

1. Glacier Bay, <u>having been established as a monument in 1925</u>, was . . .
2. The park, <u>located in Alaska</u>, is . . .
3. Glaciers <u>rising 200 feet above sea level</u> form a skyline.
4. <u>Named for the American explorer who first sighted it</u>, Muir . . .
5. . . . of ice <u>flowing down the slopes of Mount Fairweather</u>.
6. <u>Forming a barrier across the head of the bay</u>, Muir Glacier . . .
7. Most of the glacier, <u>extending 760 feet below the water's surface</u>, is not visible.
8. <u>Towering above the glaciers</u>, Mount Fairweather's peak . . .
9. This peak, <u>forming part of St. Elias Range</u>, is also . . .
10 Scientists <u>researching the formation and movement of glaciers</u> consider . . .

▶ **Exercise 20**

1. finding water—predicate nominative
2. crossing the valley's vast desert—object of preposition
3. Searching for gold—subject
4. mining for borax—object of preposition
5. Hiking—subject
6. Disturbing . . . flora and fauna—subject
7. containing . . . Western Hemisphere—object of preposition
8. climbing . . . Fahrenheit—object of preposition
9. hiking . . . sun—direct object
10. resting—subject

Section 19.2 Section Review

GRAMMAR EXERCISES 18–26

▶ **Exercise 18** Identifying Participles and Participial Phrases
Identify each participle or participial phrase. Then, label it *present*, *past*, or *perfect*.

1. Operating as a part of the U.S. Department of the Interior, the National Park Service administers more than twenty types of areas.
2. These areas are divided into three categories, indicating the main purpose of each area.
3. Forests, rivers, and wildlife preserves, protected for their natural splendor, fall under the "natural" category.
4. Areas preserved for their historic significance include battlefields and memorials.
5. Having determined a need to offer opportunities for sports and leisure activities, the National Park Service created several recreation areas.

▶ **Exercise 19** Punctuating Participial Phrases Write the sentences, underlining each participial phrase. Set off any nonessential participial phrases with commas.

1. Glacier Bay having been established as a monument in 1925 was redesignated as a national park in 1980.
2. The park located in Alaska is noted for its tidewater glaciers and mountainous peaks.
3. Glaciers rising 200 feet above sea level form a skyline.
4. Named for the American explorer who first sighted it Muir Glacier is the most famous ice floe in the bay.
5. We learned that the glacier is fed by a stream of ice flowing down the slopes of Mount Fairweather.

452 • Phrases and Clauses

6. Forming a barrier across the head of the bay Muir Glacier ranges from 135 to 210 feet high.
7. Most of the glacier extending 760 feet below the water's surface is not visible.
8. Towering above the glaciers Mount Fairweather's peak reaches an altitude of 15,300 feet.
9. This peak forming part of the St. Elias range is also the highest point in the Canadian province of British Columbia.
10. Scientists researching the formation and movement of glaciers consider Glacier Bay an important resource.

▶ **Exercise 20** Identifying Gerunds and Gerund Phrases Write each gerund or gerund phrase. Then, identify its function as a *subject*, *direct object*, *indirect object*, *object of a preposition*, *predicate nominative*, or *appositive*.

1. A difficult problem in Death Valley is finding water.
2. Many settlers struggled with crossing the valley's vast desert.
3. Searching for gold caused only one miner to perish in Death Valley.
4. The valley later became a center of mining for borax.
5. Hiking is now Death Valley's greatest tourist activity.
6. Disturbing the delicate valley flora and fauna is not allowed under park rules.
7. Death Valley is unique for containing the lowest, driest, and hottest point in the Western Hemisphere.
8. In 1913, the valley's temperature made history by climbing to 134 degrees Fahrenheit.
9. When you visit, avoid hiking in the midday sun.
10. Because of the heat, frequent resting is advised.

✓ ONGOING ASSESSMENT: Assess Mastery

Use the following resources to assess student mastery of verbals and verbal phrases.

In the Textbook	Technology
Chapter Review, Ex. 51, p. 470	*Language Lab* CD-ROM, Writing Style *On-Line Exercise Bank,* Section 19.2

Exercise 21 Identifying Infinitives and Infinitive Phrases
Write each infinitive or infinitive phrase. Then, label it *subject, direct object, predicate nominative, appositive, adjective,* or *adverb.*

1. In 1933, legislation was passed to establish the Civilian Conservation Corps.
2. The corps hired unemployed young men to labor on national lands.
3. Because of the Depression, these men needed to work.
4. Many were sent to Death Valley to prepare the park for the American public.
5. Some 1,200 men worked to finish the Death Valley Monument.
6. Their first task was to build barracks and other permanent structures.
7. Next, they began to install water and telephone lines.
8. These men helped make the park what it is today.
9. Many of the men in the corps were the first to go to war in 1942.
10. To see their work, visit the campgrounds in Death Valley.

Exercise 22 Identifying All Kinds of Verbal Phrases
Identify each participial phrase, gerund phrase, or infinitive phrase in the following sentences.

1. A preserve in South Florida containing marine, terrestrial, and amphibious life is Biscayne National Park.
2. Covering 95 percent of the park's area, water is everywhere.
3. Consequently, many of the area's activities include boating.
4. Most visitors like to engage in these activities before the heat of midday.
5. Embracing 180,000 acres, Biscayne is a protectorate for living coral reefs.
6. The park has the simple beauty of a child's drawing.
7. Biscayne National Park shows America's commitment to protecting rare subtropical environments.
8. The waters, teeming with life, are clear.
9. The coral reef provides a colorful habitat for tropical fish to populate.
10. A snorkler can spend hours drifting lazily in the waters above the reef.

Exercise 23 Using Verbal Phrases to Combine Sentences
Using infinitive, gerund, and participial phrases, combine each pair of sentences into one.

1. Ghost towns were once boom towns. Now they are deserted.
2. There are a number of ghost towns in Death Valley. All were built around the mining industry.
3. When you visit these ghost towns, treat them like museums. Do not disturb anything.
4. Ballarat was named after an Australian gold camp. It was home to 400 people in 1898.
5. Water was carried into the town of Greenwater. Water sold for fifteen dollars a barrel.

Exercise 24 Find It in Your Reading
Find an example of a participle in the excerpt from *Crossing the Great Divide* on page 449.

Exercise 25 Find It in Your Writing
In a piece of writing from your portfolio, find one example of a participle, a gerund, and an infinitive. If you cannot find one, challenge yourself to add at least one of each type of verbal to your writing.

Exercise 26 Writing Application
Write a description of your favorite vacation spot for a travel magazine. Be sure to vary your sentences with at least one participial phrase, one gerund or gerund phrase, and one infinitive or infinitive phrase. Underline and label each.

Section Review • 453

Exercise 21
1. to establish the Civilian Conservation Corps—adverb
2. to labor on national lands—adverb
3. to work—direct object
4. to prepare the park for the American public—adverb
5. to finish the Death Valley Monument—adverb
6. to build barracks and other permanent structures—predicate nominative
7. to install water and telephone lines—direct object
8. (to) make the park what it is today—direct object
9. to go to war in 1942—adjective
10. To see their work—adverb

Exercise 22
1. containing marine, terrestrial, and amphibious life—participial
2. Covering ninety-five percent of the park's area—participial
3. boating—gerund
4. to engage in these activities before the heat of midday—infinitive
5. Embracing 180,000 acres—participial; living—participle
6. drawing—gerund
7. protecting rare subtropical environments—gerund
8. teeming with life—participial
9. to populate—infinitive
10. drifting lazily in the waters above the reef—participial

Exercise 23
Answers will vary; samples are given.
1. Now deserted, ghost towns were once boom towns.
2. A number of ghost towns built around the mining industry are in Death Valley.
3. When you visit these ghost towns, treat them like museums by not disturbing anything.
4. Ballarat, named after an Australian gold camp, was home to 400 people in 1898.
5. Water carried into the town of Greenwater was sold for fifteen dollars a barrel.

Exercise 24
Find It in Your Reading
flattering prospect (lines 2–3)

continued

Exercise 25
Find It in Your Writing
Have students identify the function of each phrase in its sentence. When they finish, have them exchange with partners and make sure each phrase has been correctly identified and labeled.

Exercise 26
Writing Application
Answers will vary; here are sample answers.

Abounding in lush green grass, Ireland is known the world over as the Emerald Isle.—participial

Many people wish to visit the country to research their family trees.—infinitive phrases

Kissing the Blarney Stone is another big tourist attraction.—gerund phrase

453

Write this sentence on the board:

The polar bear blends extremely well with his environment.

Ask students to answer the question, How does the bear blend well (it is white), and then ask how to incorporate this idea into the sentence. Listen for suggestions that sound like adjective clauses, and then insert the clause "which is white" into the sentence. Explain that this type of structure is a clause; it contains its own subject and verb.

Activate Prior Knowledge

Ask students to list things that happen in winter in northern climates. (the water freezes, the weather is cold) Write some of these on the board. Have students try to combine two or more of them into a single sentence. (*The weather is cold, which freezes the water.*) Make sure that the combinations contain subordinate clauses. Ask students to point out the subject and verb in each clause.

TEACH

Step-by-Step Teaching Guide

Clauses

1. Ask students to define this group of words: *We walked into a store.* (sentence or independent clause)

2. Ask students to add an independent clause to the one above, connecting them so that they form a single sentence. (We walked into a store, and *we bought a pair of shoes.*)

3. Return to the independent clause *We walked into a store.* Next to it, write *that sold new shoes.*

4. Ask students to name the subject *(that)* and the verb *(sells)* in this group of words. Point out that this group of words is a subordinate clause because it cannot stand alone as a sentence.

Answer Key

Exercise 27

1. independent   4. subordinate
2. independent   5. independent
3. subordinate

Clauses

Whereas a phrase is a group of words without a subject and a verb, a clause does include a subject and a verb.

> **KEY CONCEPT** A **clause** is a group of words with its own subject and verb. ■

There are two basic kinds of clauses: *independent clauses* and *subordinate clauses.*

Independent and Subordinate Clauses

> **KEY CONCEPTS** An **independent clause** can stand by itself as a complete sentence. A **subordinate clause**, although it has a subject and a verb, cannot stand by itself as a complete sentence; it can only be part of a sentence. ■

Every complete sentence must contain an independent clause. The clause can either stand by itself or be connected to one or more other independent clauses or subordinate clauses.

INDEPENDENT CLAUSE:	Robert E. Peary was an explorer.
TWO INDEPENDENT CLAUSES:	Peary reached the North Pole in 1909, but this claim is still in dispute.
INDEPENDENT CLAUSE:	He reached the pole on a sled
SUBORDINATE CLAUSE:	that was pulled by dogs.

Like phrases, subordinate clauses function in sentences as single parts of speech: as adjectives, as adverbs, or as nouns. This section will describe these three uses of subordinate clauses.

> **Exercise 27** **Distinguishing Clauses** Identify each of the following clauses as *independent* or *subordinate.*
> 1. Icy winds blew.
> 2. He shivered.
> 3. Because night was falling as was the temperature.
> 4. Which caused him to make his way to shelter.
> 5. Please stay warm and dry!

▶ **Critical Viewing** Even an independent person needs to be dependent on someone else when exploring frozen wastelands. Explain this statement, using sentences with more than one clause. [**Make a Judgment**]

In this section, you will learn how to recognize and use adjective, adverb, and noun clauses. The examples and exercises in this section are about Arctic regions.

Cross-Curricular Connection: Social Studies

⏰ TIME AND RESOURCE MANAGER

Resources
Print: *Grammar Exercise Workbook,* pp. 53–58; *Grammar Exercises Answers on Transparencies,* Ch. 19
Technology: *Language Lab* CD-ROM, Writing Style; *On-Line Exercise Bank,* Section 19.3

In-Depth Coverage	Accelerated Pace
• Work through all key concepts, pp. 454–461. • Assign and review Exercises 27–33. • Read and discuss Grammar in Literature, p. 459.	• Assign pp. 454–461 for independent student review. • Assign Section Review Exercises 34–39.

Adjective Clauses

One way to describe, limit, or qualify any noun or pronoun in a sentence is to use an *adjective clause.*

KEY CONCEPT An **adjective clause** is a subordinate clause that modifies a noun or pronoun by telling *what kind* or *which one.* ∎

An adjective clause is usually connected to the word it modifies by one of the relative pronouns (*that, which, who, whom,* or *whose*). Sometimes, it is connected by a relative adverb (such as *after, before, since, when, where,* or *why*).

EXAMPLES: Arctic winters, *which are long and cold,* are severe.

The Arctic is a region *where life is difficult.*

Essential and Nonessential Adjective Clauses

Like participial and appositive phrases, adjective clauses are set off by punctuation only when they are not essential to the meaning of a sentence.

KEY CONCEPTS An adjective clause that is not essential to the basic meaning of a sentence is set off by commas. An essential adjective clause is not set off by commas. ∎

NONESSENTIAL ADJECTIVE CLAUSE:	The ship, *which was a nuclear submarine,* became the first vessel to pass beneath the North Pole.
ESSENTIAL ADJECTIVE CLAUSE:	The first vessel *that passed beneath the North Pole* was a nuclear submarine.

By using either a nonessential or an essential adjective clause, you can often combine the ideas from two sentences into one, thus showing the relationship between the ideas.

TWO SENTENCES:	The *Arktika* was the first surface ship to crack through the Arctic ice pack. It was a Soviet icebreaker.
COMBINED WITH ADJECTIVE CLAUSE:	The *Arktika, which was a Soviet icebreaker,* was the first surface ship to crack the Arctic ice pack.

Clauses • 455

Customize for
Less Advanced Students

It is sometimes difficult to determine whether an adjective clause is essential to a sentence. Discuss with students the examples at the bottom of page 455. Point out that the word *that* often precedes essential information, while the word *which,* preceded by a comma, often introduces nonessential information. Have students write one sentence that uses *that* and one that uses *which.*

Critical Viewing

Make a Judgment Sample response: Even an independent person needs someone around <u>who can help out if an emergency occurs.</u>

Step-by-Step Teaching Guide

Adjective Clauses

1. Use the examples on this page to discuss the function of adjective clauses. Have students read the independent clauses first (*Arctic winters are severe, The Arctic is a region*) and then the adjective clauses (*which are long and cold, where life is difficult*). Ask for the word each adjective clause modifies. (*winters, region*)

2. Ask students to use single-word adjectives in place of the adjective clauses to demonstrate how the clause modifies a word in the independent clause. (Example: *Long, cold* Arctic winters are severe.)

3. Explain that adjective clauses are usually introduced by relative pronouns or relative adverbs. Ask students to identify the part of speech of *which* and *where* in the examples (*which:* relative pronoun; *where:* relative adverb).

Step-by-Step Teaching Guide

Essential and Nonessential Clauses

1. Write the following on the board:
   I studied hard for the history test.
   It was quite difficult.

2. Ask students to combine these sentences (*I studied hard for the history test, which was quite difficult.*) Ask them to label the subordinate clause (*which was quite difficult*) and then to decide whether it is essential or nonessential. Have them explain their reasoning. (It is nonessential because the basic message of the sentence would not change if it were omitted.)

3. Remind them that nonessential clauses such as this one are set off by commas.

4. Have students repeat the exercise with these two clauses:
   Alaska is a state.
   The climate affects the lifestyle in Alaska.

Introductory Words in Adjective Clauses

1. Help students practice using adjective clauses and identifying their functions in sentences. Write these incomplete sentences on the board:

   I mailed the letter that . . .

   There is the man whom . . .

   It is 8:00 P.M., which . . .

   Ask students to complete each sentence (for example, *I mailed the letter* that *was sitting on my desk*). Observe that their completed adjective clauses are linked to the nouns they describe by the italicized introductory words.

2. Point out that relative pronouns also function within their clauses as subjects, direct objects, or other sentence part. Use the chart on this page to illustrate this.

3. Have students isolate the adjective clause in each sentence they formed in Step 1 above. Then, inverting the word order if necessary, have them determine the function of each relative pronoun (for example, *that* is a subject in *that was sitting on my desk*).

19.3

Introductory Words in Adjective Clauses Relative pronouns and relative adverbs not only introduce adjective clauses, but also function within the subordinate clause.

▶ **KEY CONCEPT** A **relative pronoun** or **relative adverb** (1) connects the adjective clause to the modified word and (2) acts within the clause as a subject, direct object, or other sentence part. ■

The following chart shows the various roles of relative pronouns in adjective clauses.

THE USES OF RELATIVE PRONOUNS WITHIN THE CLAUSE

As a Subject
Sentence: The part of Alaska *that is within the Arctic Circle* is cold most of the year.
Clause: that is within the Arctic Circle   S

As a Direct Object
Sentence: The explorer *whom I met last year* has never been to the North Pole.
Reworded clause: I met whom last year   DO

As the Object of a Preposition
Sentence: The climate is one *in which little foliage can grow.*
Reworded clause: little foliage can grow in which   OBJ OF PREP

As an Adjective
Sentence: I saw a dog *whose sled left without him.*
Clause: whose sled left without him   ADJ

Note About *Understood Relative Pronouns:* Sometimes, a relative pronoun is understood rather than expressed. It, nevertheless, still functions in the sentence.

EXAMPLES: The dog sled [*that*] Ted *drove* won the race.

Few Arctic explorers [*whom*] I *know* live in warm climates.

Relative adverbs can act only as adverbs within a clause.

⚙ **Grammar and Style Tip**

The relative pronouns *who, which,* and *that* do not have different singular and plural forms. When one of these pronouns serves as a subject, its verb should agree with the noun or other pronoun to which the relative pronoun refers (its antecedent).

THE USE OF RELATIVE ADVERBS WITHIN THE CLAUSE

Sentence: The temperature will plummet in the hours *after the sun sets.*

Reworded clause: the sun sets after

Exercise 28 **Identifying Adjective Clauses** Write the adjective clause in each sentence, circling the relative pronoun or relative adverb. Then, label the use of the circled word within the clause *subject, direct object, object of a preposition, adjective,* or *adverb.*

EXAMPLE: Arctic winds batter ships that sail the Northwest Passage.

ANSWER: (that) sail the Northwest Passage (subject)

1. The severe cold for which the Arctic is known does not drive away all plant and animal life.
2. Coastal regions, where climate is moderated by warmer ocean waters, have abundant flora and fauna.
3. Spring brings a resurgence of life to the Arctic, which is home to more than 400 species of plants.
4. A multitude of animals, whose names may be familiar to you, also survive in the Arctic region.
5. These animals have extra insulation that keeps them warm in colder months.

More Practice

On-line
Exercise Bank
• Section 19.3
Grammar Exercise
Workbook
• pp. 53–54

◄ **Critical Viewing**
Use a sentence containing an adjective clause to explain for whom or what this dog might be waiting. **[Infer]**

Clauses • 457

Answer Key

Exercise 28

1. for (which) the Arctic is known— object of preposition
2. (where) climate is moderated by warmer ocean waters—adverb
3. (which) is home to more than 400 species of plants—subject
4. (whose) names may be familiar to you—adjective
5. (that) keeps them warm in colder months—subject

Critical Viewing

Infer Sample response: This dog, which is waiting for its master, seems lonely but patient.

☑ **ONGOING ASSESSMENT: Monitor and Reinforce**

If students miss more than one item in Exercise 28, refer them to the following for additional practice.

In the Textbook	Print Resources	Technology
Section Review, Ex. 34, p. 464	*Grammar Exercise Workbook,* pp. 53–54	*Language Lab* CD-ROM, Writing Style; *On-Line Exercise Bank,* Section 19.3

🕐 **TIME SAVERS!**

Answers on Transparencies
Use the *Grammar Exercises Answers on Transparencies* for Chapter 19 to facilitate correction by students.

On-Line Exercise Bank
Have students complete the exercises on computer. The Auto Check feature will grade their work for you!

Adverb Clauses

1. Students might find it easier to identify adverb clauses if you show that they serve the same function as adverbs. Write the following sentences on the board:

   They left _early_.

   They left _before the sun rose_.

   Point out that in both cases, the underlined words answer the question _When?_ about the verb _left_.

2. Tell students that adverb phrases answer other questions as well: _Where? In what manner? To what extent? Under what condition? Why?_

3. Have students choose a verb, such as _leave_, and write five sentences with adverb clauses, one that answers each of the questions listed above.

4. Encourage students to review the list of subordinating conjunctions on page 391 for ideas of ways to introduce their adverb clauses.

Customize for
ESL Students

A more in-depth review of the use of subordinating conjunctions may help students recognize adverb clauses. Give students the list of subordinating conjunctions from page 391. Have them offer a list of short sentences that describe what they did that day. (_I woke up. I got dressed. I ate breakfast. I walked to school._) Then have students combine these sentences in chronological order (_I got dressed after I woke up. I ate breakfast before I walked to school_). Tell them to use words from the list as connecting words.

19.3

Adverb Clauses

Subordinate clauses may also serve as adverbs in sentences.

▶ **KEY CONCEPT** **Adverb clauses** modify verbs, adjectives, adverbs, or verbals by telling _where, when, in what way, to what extent, under what condition,_ or _why._ ■

Each adverb clause contains a subject and a verb and is introduced by a subordinating conjunction, such as _although, because, if, where,_ or _while._ (See Chapter 17 for a more complete list.) An adverb clause can modify any word that an adverb can modify.

ADVERB CLAUSES	
Modified Words	**Examples**
Verb:	The Yukon entered Canada's confederation _after a gold rush brought 100,000 people to the territory._
Adjective:	The miner's children were nervous _whenever he entered a tunnel._
Adverb:	Today's dig lasted longer _than the one yesterday._
Participle:	The miners, cheering _whenever someone made a strike_, were excited.
Gerund:	Digging _wherever miners thought there was gold_ has left the Yukon full of old mines.
Infinitive:	The tired miners wanted to relax _after the workday ended._

Some adverb clauses are _elliptical_, especially those beginning with _as_ or _than_. In an elliptical adverb clause, the verb or both the subject and verb are not stated but are understood. Nevertheless, they still function to make the clause complete.

VERB UNDERSTOOD: I am taller _than he [is]._

SUBJECT AND
VERB UNDERSTOOD: The Yukon has almost as many rural inhabitants _as [it has]_ urban inhabitants.

✐ Spelling Tip

In formal writing, always spell out the word _because_. The shortened form _'cause_ is only used in informal situations.

GRAMMAR IN LITERATURE

from **To Build a Fire**
Jack London

In the following selection, Jack London uses subordinate clauses to add details and to show the relationship between ideas in his sentences. The adverb clause is shown in blue; the adjective clause is shown in red.

Day had broken cold and gray, exceedingly cold and gray, when the man turned aside from the main Yukon trail and climbed the high earth-bank, where a dim and little-traveled trail led eastward through the fat spruce timberland.

Exercise 29 **Identifying Adverb Clauses** Identify the adverb clause in each sentence. Then, indicate whether it modifies a *verb*, an *adjective*, an *adverb*, or a *verbal*.

EXAMPLE: The Yukon was called Rupert's Land until its name was changed to the Northwest Territories in 1868.

ANSWER: until its name was changed to the Northwest Territories in 1868 (verb)

1. The Yukon is located in Canada's northwest corner, where Canada borders Alaska.
2. Before the territory was known as the Yukon, it had two other names.
3. Changing its name again as the nineteenth century ended, the Yukon officially became part of Canada in 1898.
4. Whereas the vast majority of the area is landlocked, its northernmost point borders on the Beaufort Sea.
5. The territory's emblematic stone, blue lazulite, looks bluer than the sky does on a clear summer day.
6. The capital city, Whitehorse, sits near the Yukon River, where the river becomes navigable.
7. Whitehorse replaced Dawson City as the capital after the Gold Rush began.
8. While it is the highest point in Canada, Yukon's Mt. Logan is only the second highest peak in North America.
9. Although we find permafrost in many areas of the Yukon, it appears mostly in its northern regions.
10. To visit the Yukon after winter has set in is a frigid experience.

More Practice

On-line
Exercise Bank
• Section 19.3
Grammar Exercise Workbook
• pp. 55–56

Clauses • 459

✓ **ONGOING ASSESSMENT: Monitor and Reinforce**

If students miss more than one item in Exercise 29, refer them to the following for additional practice.

In the Textbook	Print Resources	Technology
Section Review, Ex. 35, p. 464	*Grammar Exercise Workbook*, pp. 55–56	*Language Lab* CD-ROM, Writing Style; *On-Line Exercise Bank*, Section 19.3

> **Exercise 30**

Answers may vary within reason; samples are given.

1. than most other Canadian provinces (have)
2. as (it has) unforested (areas)
3. than the rest of Canada (has)
4. than (native peoples do) in other provinces
5. than (is) its over-sixty-five population

Step-by-Step Teaching Guide

Noun Clauses

1. Review with students the functions that nouns can perform in sentences—subject, direct object, indirect object, object of a preposition, predicate nominative, and appositive.

2. Divide students into small groups and have each group find the definition for one of the six terms listed above. Have them write down the definition and an example.

3. Have each group share its findings with the rest of the class. This review might make it easier for students to recognize noun clauses that perform these functions.

continued

> **Exercise 30** **Recognizing Elliptical Clauses** Write the elliptical adverb clause in each sentence, adding the understood words, in parentheses, where they belong.

EXAMPLE: The city of Whitehorse has many more people than Dawson City.

ANSWER: than Dawson City (does)

1. The Yukon has a smaller land area than most other Canadian provinces.
2. The territory has as many forested areas as unforested.
3. The Yukon has a lower population density than the rest of Canada.
4. Its native peoples make up a greater percentage of the Yukon's population than in other provinces.
5. Its population under age nineteen is ten times larger than its over-sixty-five population.

Noun Clauses

Noun clauses can perform any function in a sentence that a single-word noun can.

> **KEY CONCEPT** A **noun clause** is a subordinate clause that acts as a noun. ■

The following chart shows the various functions of noun clauses.

USES OF NOUN CLAUSES IN SENTENCES	
Functions in Sentences	**Examples**
Subject:	*Whoever travels the Pelly River* follows in the footsteps of the explorer Robert Campbell.
Direct Object:	You must pack *whatever you will need.*
Indirect Object:	You should give *whoever waits at the camp* a copy of your route.
Object of a Preposition:	Robert Campbell settled trading camps in *whatever regions the Hudson's Bay Company sent him.*
Predicate Nominative:	At 40, Campbell's most notable achievement was *that he established Fort Selkirk.*

460 • Phrases and Clauses

⏱ TIME SAVERS!

Answers on Transparencies
Use the *Grammar Exercises Answers on Transparencies* for Chapter 19 to facilitate correction by students.

On-Line Exercise Bank
Have students complete the exercises on computer. The Auto Check feature will grade their work for you!

✓ ONGOING ASSESSMENT: Monitor and Reinforce

If students miss more than one item in Exercise 30, refer them to the following for additional practice.

In the Textbook	Print Resources	Technology
Section Review, Ex. 36, p. 464	*Grammar Exercise Workbook,* pp. 55–56	*Language Lab* CD-ROM, Writing Style; *On-Line Exercise Bank,* Section 19.3

4. Review with students the items in the chart. In addition to discussing how the introductory word functions in each clause, have them tell you how the clause functions in its sentence.

5. Demonstrate the test at the bottom of the page—substituting words like *it, you,* and *thing* for clauses—by applying it to the noun clauses in the chart.

Critical Viewing

Evaluate Sample response: I think that <u>whoever took this picture</u> has a keen sense of the dramatic.

Real-World Connection

Tell students that most post-secondary institutions (colleges, universities, trade schools) require personal, written statements from applicants. Explain to students that the use of phrases and clauses can enrich sentences in many ways. They can add and connect ideas smoothly, they can vary sentence structure to help make writing more interesting, and they can raise the general level of sophistication of a student's writing.

KEY CONCEPTS Noun clauses frequently begin with *that, which, who, whom,* or *whose.* Other words that can begin noun clauses are *how, if, what, whatever, when, where, whether, whichever, whoever,* or *whomever.* In addition to introducing a noun clause, these words generally serve a function within the clause. ■

SOME USES OF INTRODUCTORY WORDS IN NOUN CLAUSES

Functions in Sentences	Examples
Adjective:	John Bell chose *which tributary to explore.*
Adverb:	We want to know *how we should dress.*
Subject:	I want the recipe from *whoever made that delicious casserole.*
Direct Object:	McGill University's Redpath Museum, *which Sir John William Dawson founded,* specializes in botany and geology.
No Function:	The doctor determined *that she had the measles.*

When *that* has no function in the noun clause other than as an introductory word, it is often omitted.

EXAMPLE: I know [*that*] *you tried your best.*

Because some of the words that introduce noun clauses also introduce adjective and adverb clauses, check the function of the clause in the sentence to determine its type. You can also try substituting the words *it, you, fact,* or *thing* for the clause. If the sentence retains its smoothness, you probably replaced a noun clause.

NOUN CLAUSE: I knew *that this would happen.*

SUBSTITUTION: I knew it.

Grammar and Style Tip

That and *which* are frequently confused. An easy way to know when to use each one properly is to remember this distinction: *That* is not preceded by a comma when it begins a clause; *which* is **always** preceded by a comma when it begins a clause.

▼ **Critical Viewing**
What do you think of the work of the photographer who took this picture? In your answer, use at least one noun clause beginning with *whoever.* **[Evaluate]**

STANDARDIZED TEST PREPARATION WORKSHOP

Grammar and Usage Many standardized tests require students to revise sentences to improve them. Demonstrate with the following.

The museum acquired a priceless painting. The painting had been found in an old trunk.

What is the **best** way to combine the two sentences?

A The museum acquired a priceless painting it was found in an old trunk.

B Found in an old trunk, the museum acquired a priceless painting.

C The museum acquired a priceless painting because it had been found in an old trunk.

D The museum acquired a priceless painting that had been found in an old trunk.

The correct answer is **D**. Because the idea in the second sentence describes the painting, it can be attached as a clause. The adjective clause *that was found in an old trunk* describes the painting. A is a run-on, B contains a misplaced modifier, and C creates an adverb clause that does not logically tell why the painting was acquired.

Answer Key

▶ **Exercise 31**

1. Whoever travels on the Yukon River in winter—subject
2. that they could find gold—direct object
3. whoever found gold in Bonanza Creek—object of preposition
4. whatever claims they could find—direct object
5. Whoever heard of the Klondike gold strike—subject
6. how difficult the Klondike's rugged terrain would be for them—object of preposition
7. Whoever used the Yukon River as the main access route—subject
8. how little gold they found—object of preposition
9. whoever had a good imagination—indirect object
10. whatever they could carry on their backs—predicate nominative

Critical Viewing

Relate Possible answer. The extreme cold of the Arctic winter is what I wouldn't like about the Yukon.

19.3

▶ **Exercise 31** **Identifying Noun Clauses** Write the noun clause in each sentence, indicating whether the clause is functioning as a *subject, direct object, indirect object, object of a preposition, predicate nominative,* or *appositive.*

EXAMPLE: Explorers discovered where the Klondike River flows into the Yukon River.

ANSWER: where the Klondike River flows into the Yukon River (direct object)

1. Whoever travels on the Yukon River in winter must account for the cold temperatures.
2. The miners believed that they could find gold quickly.
3. A frenzy of interest was caused by whoever found gold in Bonanza Creek.
4. Hopeful miners occupied whatever claims they could find.
5. Whoever heard of the Klondike gold strike traveled north, hoping to become rich.
6. Many American miners were unprepared for how difficult the Klondike's rugged terrain would be for them.
7. Whoever used the Yukon River as the main access route in the winter was caught in the ice and had to be rescued.
8. Among the thousands of miners who went to the Klondike, a large percentage were disappointed by how little gold they found.
9. Dreams of gold along the Yukon River gave whoever had a good imagination a reason to travel.
10. Often, their only possessions were whatever they could carry on their backs.

▲ **Critical Viewing**
Use the noun clause *what I wouldn't like* in a sentence about this picture. **[Relate]**

Exercise 32 Classifying Subordinate Clauses

Identify each underlined clause as *adjective, adverb,* or *noun.*

EXAMPLE   Sled dogs love to run, <u>which they have been bred for thousands of years to do.</u> (adverb)

1. The indigenous peoples <u>who live in the far north</u> adapted sled dogs for use as transportation.
2. They used dogs <u>whenever they traveled.</u>
3. Early expeditions <u>that settled colder northern regions</u> would have been impossible without sled dogs.
4. <u>Even though modes of travel have advanced,</u> sled dogs still offer reliable transportation in subzero climes.
5. Sled-dog racing has evolved into a sport <u>that is popular in colder parts of the world.</u>
6. <u>Although small local races were held in the nineteenth century,</u> a major sled-dog race was not staged until 1908.
7. <u>Whoever wants to enter in a sled-dog race today</u> has a choice of more than 3,000 competitions.
8. The number of competitions has increased every year <u>since sled dog-racing was organized.</u>
9. The International Federation of Sled Dog Sports, <u>which governs racing,</u> was formed in 1986 to promote the sport.
10. <u>Because its efforts were effective,</u> sled-dog racing is being considered for inclusion in winter athletic festivals.

Exercise 33 Using Subordinate Clauses to Combine Sentences

Combine each pair of sentences by changing one of the sentences into the type of clause indicated. Underline each subordinate clause.

EXAMPLE: *Combine using an adjective clause*: We saw the landscape. It was breathtaking.

ANSWER: The landscape <u>that we saw</u> was breathtaking.

1. *Combine using an adjective clause*: Whitehorse was a terminal on the White Pass and Yukon Railway. The city is on the Alaska Highway.
2. *Combine using an adverb clause*: Whitehorse was a center of copper mining and fur trapping. Then, it became the capital of the Yukon Territory.
3. *Combine using a noun clause*: Whitehorse was important in the Yukon's history. Many people don't know this.
4. *Combine using an adjective clause*: The city numbers approximately 23,000 people. It is large for the territory.
5. *Combine using an adverb clause*: An economic lull hit Whitehorse in the mid-1980's. The discovery of the world's largest tungsten reserve at Mae Pass revitalized the city.

More Practice

On-line
Exercise Bank
• Section 19.3
Grammar Exercise Workbook
• pp. 57–58

Exercise 32

1. adjective
2. adverb
3. adjective
4. adverb
5. adjective
6. adverb
7. noun
8. adverb
9. adjective
10. adverb

Exercise 33

Answers will vary; samples are given.

1. Whitehorse, <u>which is a city on the Alaska Highway</u>, was a terminal on the White Pass and Yukon Railway.
2. Whitehorse was a center of copper mining and fur trapping <u>before it became the capital of the Yukon Territory</u>.
3. Many people don't know <u>that Whitehorse was important in the Yukon's history</u>.
4. The city, <u>which is large for the territory</u>, numbers approximately 23,000 people.
5. <u>After an economic lull hit Whitehorse in the mid-1980s</u>, the discovery of the world's largest tungsten reserve at Mae Pass revitalized the city.

✓ ONGOING ASSESSMENT: Monitor and Reinforce

If students have difficulty with Exercise 31, 32, or 33, refer them to the following for additional practice.

In the Textbook	Print Resources	Technology
Section Review, Ex. 37–39, pp. 464–465	*Grammar Exercise Workbook,* pp. 53–58	*Language Lab* CD-ROM, Writing Style; *On-Line Exercise Bank,* Section 19.3

⏱ TIME SAVERS!

Answers on Transparencies
Use the *Grammar Exercises Answers on Transparencies* for Chapter 19 to facilitate correction by students.

On-Line Exercise Bank
Have students complete the exercises on computer. The Auto Check feature will grade their work for you!

Section Review

Each of these exercises correlates to the instruction on clauses, pages 454–461. These exercises may be used for more practice, for reteaching, or for review of the key concepts presented.

Answer Key

Exercise 34

1. (who) were interested in mapping new regions—subject
2. after (whom) the Davis Strait is named—object of preposition
3. (whose) explorers were among the most persistent—adjective
4. (where) the Arctic covers the northern part of the country—adverb
5. (whom) explorers sometimes encountered—direct object

Exercise 35

1. Although people live in Arctic—verb
2. than they are in warmer climates—adjective
3. because the animal tolerates cold well—adjective
4. because the climate is not as frigid—verb
5. Wherever the environment will allow it—verb

Exercise 36

Answers may vary; samples are given.
1. than most dogs (do)
2. as that of breeds from warmer climates (is)
3. as the Arctic's (is)
4. than those of most other breeds (do)
5. as a snowshoe hare (does)

Exercise 37

1. how you should train a sled dog—object of preposition
2. Whoever trains a sled dog—subject
3. how one should handle the animal—object of preposition
4. whatever dogs they train—object of preposition
5. that the best time to begin is—direct object; when the dog is still a puppy—predicate nominative

---

Section 19.3 Section Review

GRAMMAR EXERCISES 34–42

▶ **Exercise 34** **Identifying Adjective Clauses** Write the adjective clause in each sentence, and circle the relative pronoun or relative adverb. Then, label the use of the circled word within the clause *subject, direct object, object of a preposition, adjective,* or *adverb.*

1. Europeans who were interested in mapping new regions first explored the Arctic in the sixteenth century.
2. The Englishman John Davis, after whom the Davis Strait is named, trekked to Sanderson's Hope in 1587.
3. Britain, whose explorers were among the most persistent, continued to explore the Arctic for the next 400 years.
4. In Russia, where the Arctic covers the northern part of the country, exploration began in earnest in the 1700's.
5. Much of the Arctic had a scattered, indigenous population, whom explorers sometimes encountered.

▶ **Exercise 35** **Identifying Adverb Clauses** Write the adverb clause in each sentence. Then, indicate whether it modifies a verb, an adjective, an adverb, or a verbal.

1. Although people live in the Arctic, they are still limited by its harsh climate.
2. Food cultivation and animal husbandry are more difficult there than they are in warmer climates.
3. However, reindeer herding is widespread because the animal tolerates cold well.
4. Sheep are raised in southwestern Greenland and in Iceland because the climate is not as frigid.
5. Wherever the environment will allow it, dairy farming supplies milk products to nearby communities.

▶ **Exercise 36** **Recognizing Elliptical Clauses** Write the elliptical adverb clause in each sentence, adding the understood words, in parentheses, where they belong.

1. Sled dogs, such as Alaskan huskies, have much thicker coats than most dogs.
2. In fact, the fur of Alaskan huskies is twice as thick as that of breeds from warmer climates.
3. Their dense fur allows them to endure weather as cold as the Arctic's for long periods.
4. As a breed, sled dogs also tend to have broader feet than those of most other breeds.
5. Their broader feet help them bound through the snow as quickly as a snowshoe hare.

▶ **Exercise 37** **Recognizing and Identifying Noun Clauses** Write the noun clause or clauses in each of the following sentences. Then, indicate whether the clause is functioning as a *subject, direct object, indirect object, object of a preposition, predicate nominative,* or *appositive.*

1. The question of how you should train a sled dog is a difficult one.
2. Whoever trains a sled dog should have experience.
3. Adequate knowledge of how one should handle the animal comes from years of experience.
4. Veteran trainers offer a great deal of love and discipline to whatever dogs they train.
5. These experts say that the best time to begin a sled dog's training is when the dog is still a puppy.

Exercise 38 **Identifying and Classifying Subordinate Clauses** Write the subordinate clause in each sentence, and indicate whether the clause is functioning as an *adjective*, an *adverb*, or a *noun*.

1. White Pass, which is a hazardous mountain trail, was blazed by gold prospectors going to the Klondike in 1897.
2. When news of gold spread, the prospectors sought and established an alternative route to the heavily traveled Chilkoot Pass.
3. To visit White Pass, one must travel to where Alaska and the Canadian province of British Columbia meet.
4. Whoever took the new, treacherous trail had to be prepared for the worst.
5. Many prospectors perished even though they were prepared.
6. Between 1898 and 1900, the White Pass and Yukon Railway was built to traverse the route, which is at an altitude of nearly 3,000 feet.
7. After it was completed, the railway provided safe transportation from the Pacific tidewater to the Yukon Valley.
8. Travel from Skagway to White Horse, the two towns between which the railway ran, was made much more comfortable, too.
9. The railway, which lasted more than eighty years, suspended full-time service in 1982.
10. Even though it no longer runs, the railroad is remembered as an important part of the settlement of the Yukon region.

Exercise 39 **Using Subordinate Clauses to Combine Sentences** Combine each pair of sentences by changing one of the sentences into the type of clause indicated.

1. *Combine using an adjective clause:* Mushers are individuals. They drive and lead sled-dog racing teams.

2. *Combine using an adverb clause:* Some mushers compete using a sled, and others use skis. There are two racing classes.
3. *Combine using an adverb clause:* Mushers have to maintain control of their team. Dogs are swift animals.
4. *Combine using an adjective clause:* The best mushers are excellent dog handlers. These mushers win races often.
5. *Combine using a noun clause:* What is the best way to keep control of a team? This is an important question for mushers.

Exercise 40 **Find It in Your Reading** Identify the word modified by each subordinate clause in the excerpt from "To Build a Fire" on page 459.

Exercise 41 **Find It in Your Writing** Look through your writing portfolio. Find one example of an adjective clause and one of an adverb clause. If you cannot find one, challenge yourself to improve your writing by adding one of each.

Exercise 42 **Writing Application** Write five original sentences about winter weather in your area of the country using the type of clause indicated. Underline all clauses.
1. Write a sentence using a nonessential adjective clause.
2. Write a sentence using an essential adjective clause.
3. Write a sentence using an adverb clause that modifies a verb.
4. Write a sentence using an elliptical adverb clause.
5. Write a sentence using a noun clause that functions in a sentence as the subject.

Section Review • 465

Answer Key

Exercise 38

1. which is a hazardous mountain trail—adjective
2. When news of gold spread—adverb
3. where Alaska and the Canadian province of British Columbia meet—noun
4. Whoever took the new, treacherous trail—noun
5. even though they were prepared—adverb
6. which is at an altitude of nearly 3,000 feet—adjective
7. After it was completed—adverb
8. between which the railway ran—adjective
9. which lasted more than eighty years—adjective
10. Even though it no longer runs—adverb

Exercise 39

Answers will vary; samples are given.

1. Mushers are individuals who drive and lead sled-dog racing teams.
2. Because some mushers . . . skis, there are two racing classes.
3. Mushers have to maintain control of their team because dogs are swift animals.
4. The best mushers, who win races often, are excellent dog handlers.
5. An important question for mushers is what is the best . . .

Exercise 40

Find It in Your Reading
when . . . modifies *had broken*;
where . . . modifies *earth-bank*

Exercise 41

Find It in Your Writing
Have students write down the sentences that contain the clauses. Have them underline the clauses and circle the words they modify.

Exercise 42

Writing Application
Answers will vary; samples are given.

1. In February, which is the time of my birthday, the temperature is sometimes below zero.
2. The season here that seems to last the longest is winter.
3. May usually arrives before it gets warm.
4. Few places have longer winters than we.
5. Whoever loves cold weather should move here.

☑ ONGOING ASSESSMENT: Assess Mastery

Use the following resources to assess student mastery of clauses.

In the Textbook	Technology
Chapter Review, Ex. 52–53, pp. 470–471	*Language Lab* CD-ROM, Writing Style; *On-Line Exercise Bank,* Section 19.3

Sentences Classified by Structure

Sentences are often classified according to the kind and number of clauses they contain.

The Four Structures of Sentences

The structure of a sentence depends on the kind and number of clauses it contains. The following rules define the four different sentence structures:

KEY CONCEPTS A **simple sentence** consists of a single independent clause. ■

A **compound sentence** consists of two or more independent clauses joined by a comma and a coordinating conjunction or by a semicolon. ■

A **complex sentence** consists of one independent—or main—clause and one or more subordinate clauses. ■

A **compound-complex sentence** consists of two or more independent clauses and one or more subordinate clauses. ■

As you study the examples in the chart on the next page, notice that simple sentences can contain compound subjects, compound verbs, or both. Notice also that a subordinate clause may fall between the parts of another clause or even within another clause.

466 • Phrases and Clauses

FOUR STRUCTURES OF SENTENCES

Functions in Sentences	Examples
Simple Sentences:	<u>Ellis Island</u> <u>was</u> the first stop for many immigrants to America. <u>Ed</u> and <u>I</u> <u>checked</u> and <u>rechecked</u> our answer.
Compound Sentences:	My <u>brother</u> <u>bought</u> some stamps yesterday, and <u>he</u> <u>mounted</u> them in his stamp collection. The <u>Statue of Liberty</u> and <u>Ellis Island</u> <u>were</u> the subject of a border dispute between New York and New Jersey; both <u>monuments</u> <u>rest</u> on islands between the two states.
Complex Sentences:	*main clause* The <u>Statue of Liberty–Ellis Island Foundation</u> *subordinate clause* <u>is</u> a nonprofit organization <u>that</u> <u>was founded</u> in 1982. *main* *subordinate clause* *main clause* Our <u>band</u>, <u>which</u> <u>won</u> the trophy, <u>will perform</u> *subordinate clause* after the <u>game</u> <u>is</u> over. *main clause* The largest historic <u>restoration</u> in the United *main clause* *subordinate clause* States <u>was performed</u> by <u>whoever</u> <u>restored</u> *subordinate clause* the main building on Ellis Island.
Compound-Complex Sentences:	*independent clause* <u>I</u> <u>ran</u> down the path to the spot *subordinate clause* *independent clause* where <u>it</u> <u>divides</u>, and then <u>I</u> <u>turned</u> back. *subordinate clause* *independent clause* After <u>it</u> <u>was restored</u>, <u>Ellis Island</u> <u>received</u> *independent clause* a $20 million endowment, but charitable *independent* *subordinate clause* <u>contributions</u>, <u>which</u> <u>come</u> from many *independent clause* sources, <u>are</u> still <u>being accepted</u>.

 Spelling Tip

The adjectives *historic* and *historical* are used differently. *Historic* always modifies something that is important in history. *Historical* always modifies something that occurred in the past, whether or not it was important.

Technology Tip

The grammar checker on most of the word-processing programs may flag perfectly correct compound-complex sentences as run-ons because they are long. Rely on your own sense of grammar to revise and correct your writing.

Customize for
Logical/Mathematical Learners

To help classify a sentence by structure, tell students to underline each phrase that can stand on its own as a complete sentence. Tell them that compound and compound-complex sentences must always contain at least two clauses that can stand on their own as complete sentences.

Customize for
AP Students

Have students examine a paragraph from their portfolios and identify where they have used each of the different sentence structures. Challenge them to rewrite some of their sentences using structures other than the ones they already have used, while still preserving the basic sense of the sentences. Have them discuss the way in which using a variety of sentence structures can make their writing more varied and interesting.

✓ ONGOING ASSESSMENT: Monitor and Reinforce

If students miss more than two items in Exercise 43, refer them to the following for additional practice.

In the Textbook	Print Resources	Technology
Section Review, Ex. 44–46, pp. 469	*Grammar Exercise Workbook,* pp. 59–60	*Language Lab* CD-ROM, Writing Style; *On-Line Exercise Bank,* Section 19.4

19.4

> **KEY CONCEPT** Analyzing the structure of sentences can help you to understand long, involved sentences when you read. It can also help you check the logic and flow of your own ideas when you write. ■

As you could see in the preceding chart, independent clauses in complex sentences are often called *main clauses* to distinguish them from subordinate clauses. The subject and verb of a main clause, in turn, are usually called the *subject of the sentence* and the *main verb* to distinguish them from other subjects and verbs.

> **Exercise 43** **Identifying the Four Structures of Sentences**
> Identify each sentence as *simple, compound, complex,* or *compound-complex.*

EXAMPLE: People have emigrated from their original homelands.

ANSWER: simple

1. Angel Island is the largest island in San Francisco Bay.
2. In 1905, an immigration station was constructed in the China Cove area of the island.
3. Although it was the subject of some public controversy, the station officially opened in 1910.
4. A flood of European immigrants was expected in California when the Panama Canal opened, but the outbreak of World War I curtailed the expected rush of Europeans.
5. Instead, the majority of foreigners who immigrated to America through Angel Island came from Asia.
6. Like many immigrants, the Asians were trying to escape the hardships of their native lands, but they faced further difficulties at Angel Island.
7. The Europeans who arrived in the United States through Ellis Island were processed within a matter of hours or days; on Angel Island, Asian immigrants were detained for weeks or even months.
8. Laws, such as the Chinese Exclusion Act of 1882, restricted Asian immigration to America, and Angel Island effectively became a detention center.
9. Although these laws had an impact on all Asians, those most affected were the Chinese, who comprised more than 70 percent of the immigrants detained on Angel Island.
10. The island was a U.S. Army base from 1863 to 1946, but it became a missile radar site in 1952.

> **More Practice**
>
> On-line
> Exercise Bank
> • Section 19.4
> Grammar Exercise
> Workbook
> • pp. 59–60

> 🖋 **Spelling Tip**
>
> The nouns *emigrant* and *immigrant* are often confused, but they are not interchangeable. An *emigrant* is one who moves *from* a country. An *immigrant* is one who moves *to* a country.

468 • Phrases and Clauses

☑ **ONGOING ASSESSMENT: Assess Mastery**

Use the following resources to assess student mastery of phrases and clauses.

In the Text	Print Resources	Technology
Chapter Review, Ex. 54–56, p. 471	*Formal Assessment,* Chapter 19	*On-Line Exercise Bank,* Chapter 19

Section 19.4 Section Review

GRAMMAR EXERCISES 44–49

Exercise 44 **Identifying the Four Structures of Sentences** Identify each sentence as *simple, compound, complex,* or *compound-complex.*

1. Beginning with the Immigration Act of 1891, the United States federal government assumed the responsibility of immigration.
2. Prior to the Immigration Act, America encouraged open immigration because new immigrants strengthened the young, relatively unpopulated nation.
3. However, certain states began to pass their own immigration laws after the Civil War, and the Supreme Court was forced to step in.
4. In 1875, the Court ruled that the regulation of immigration is the responsibility of the federal government.
5. Enforcing immigration laws, which included processing all immigrants seeking admission to America, was a new legal concept, and it would take the Immigration Service a decade to implement its national policy.

Exercise 45 **Revising Sentences With Subordinate Clauses** Create complex sentences by adding a subordinate clause to the following independent clauses.

1. My friend's grandparents were not born in the United States.
2. They immigrated to America in 1920.
3. They settled in New York.
4. My friend's parents were raised in the United States.
5. Both my friend and I would enjoy visiting Ellis Island.

Exercise 46 **Revising a Passage by Varying Sentence Structure** Revise the following passage to use a variety of sentence structures.

The Immigration and Naturalization Service has altered its focus in recent years. It has also undergone tremendous growth. World migration patterns have changed. Travel has been made easier for business and pleasure by the airplane. Controlling illegal immigration became a primary concern. The Immigration and Naturalization Service (INS) needed more employees. The INS work force numbered approximately 8,000 from World War II through the late 1970's. The INS now includes more than 30,000 employees. There are thirty-six INS districts at home and abroad.

Exercise 47 **Find It in Your Reading** Examine a newspaper or magazine article to find examples of all four sentence structures.

Exercise 48 **Find It in Your Writing** Review one of your own compositions. Revise and improve the work by varying your sentence structure and using subordinate clauses. Be sure that all four types of sentence structure are represented.

Exercise 49 **Writing Application** Write a brief description of a historic landmark in your area. Use each type of sentence structure at least once.

Section Review • **469**

ASSESS and CLOSE

Section Review

Each of these exercises correlates to the instruction on sentences classified by structure, pages 466–468. These exercises may be used for more practice, for reteaching, or for review of the key concepts presented. Answers for all exercises are available in *Grammar Exercises Answers on Transparencies* in your Teaching Resources.

Answer Key

Exercise 44

1. simple
2. complex
3. compound
4. complex
5. compound-complex

Exercise 45

Answers will vary; samples are given.

1. My friend's grandparents, who live in Chicago, were not born in the United States.
2. They immigrated to America in 1920 when they were still very young.
3. They settled in New York though they soon moved west.
4. My friend's parents, who were born in Chicago, were raised in the United States.
5. Both my friend and I would enjoy visiting Ellis Island, which was the first stop for many immigrants.

Exercise 46

Revisions will vary; a sample is given.

(1) In recent years, the Immigration and Naturalization Service has both altered its focus and undergone tremendous growth. (2) World migration patterns have changed because travel for business and pleasure has been made easier by the airplane. (3) Controlling illegal immigration became a primary concern, and the Immigration and Naturalization Service (INS) needed more employees. (4) The INS workforce, which numbered approximately 8,000 from World War II through the late 1970's, now includes more than 30,000 employees in thirty-six INS districts at home and abroad.

continued

Answer Key continued

Exercise 47

Find It in Your Reading
Have students underline the clauses in each sentence and label them either *independent* or *subordinate*. Then have them write down the structure of each sentence.

Exercise 48

Find It in Your Writing
Remind students to avoid writing run-on sentences by using commas, semicolons, and coordinating conjunctions where necessary.

Exercise 49

Writing Application
Students' descriptions will vary. Have volunteers read their completed papers aloud and ask other students to identify the sentence structures they hear.

Each of these exercise correlates with a section of the chapter on phrases and clauses, pages 432–468. These exercises may be used for more practice, for reteaching, or for review of the key concepts presented. Answers for all exercises are available in *Grammar Exercises Answers on Transparencies* in your Teaching Resources.

Answer Key

Exercise 50

1. into two classifications—prepositional phrase, adverb
2. the glockenspiel, kettledrum, tubular bells, and xylophone—appositive
3. of a kettledrum—prepositional phrase, adjective
4. an eighteenth-century invention—appositive; of varying lengths—prepositional phrase, adjective; in a frame—prepositional phrase, adverb
5. bass, snare or tenor drums, castanets, cymbals, gongs, triangles, and tambourines—appositive

Exercise 51

1. Playing the blues—gerund; to express their darkest feelings—infinitive
2. feeling—gerund; performing—gerund
3. expressing their feelings through performance—gerund
4. to employ rasp or growl techniques—infinitive
5. flattened and shaded by the musicians—participial

Exercise 52

1. which is of Spanish origin—adjective
2. that are plucked with the fingers or with a pick—adjective
3. Because it has only four or five strings—adverb
4. which was introduced into the Hawaiian Islands in the late 1870's—adjective
5. which originated in Mesopotamia and Egypt—adjective; than these hand-held stringed instruments (are)—adverb

---

Chapter 19 Chapter Review

GRAMMAR EXERCISES 50–57

Exercise 50 Identifying **Prepositional and Appositive Phrases**
Write the prepositional and appositive phrases in the following items. Identify each prepositional phrase as *adjective* or *adverb*.

1. Percussion instruments are divided into two classifications.
2. Definite pitch instruments—the glockenspiel, kettledrum, tubular bells, and xylophone—can be tuned.
3. The parchment of a kettledrum can be tightened or loosened to change the pitch.
4. The tubular bells, an eighteenth-century invention, are metal tubes of varying lengths hung vertically in a frame.
5. Indefinite pitch instruments—bass, snare or tenor drums, castenets, cymbals, gongs, triangles, and tambourines—cannot be tuned.

Exercise 51 Identifying Verbal **Phrases** Identify each participial phrase, gerund phrase, and infinitive phrase in the following sentences.

1. Playing the blues is one way for some musicians to express their darkest feelings.
2. To these musicians, the blues is as much a way of feeling as it is a way of performing.
3. To many bluesmen, expressing their feelings through performance is the essence of the art.
4. These performers try to employ rasp or growl techniques for this manner of expression.
5. The notes, often flattened and shaded by the musicians, produce sad and mournful sounds.

Exercise 52 Identifying **Subordinate Clauses** Identify the subordinate clause in each sentence, and indicate whether the clause is functioning as an *adjective*, an *adverb*, or a *noun*.

1. The guitar, which is of Spanish origin, is a flat-backed, stringed instrument.
2. It has a long, fretted neck and six strings that are plucked with the fingers or with a pick.
3. Because it has only four or five strings, the banjo is generally played with the fingers.
4. The ukulele, which was introduced into the Hawaiian Islands in the late 1870's, is originally from Portugal.
5. The harp, which also originated in Mesopotamia and Egypt, is much larger than these hand-held stringed instruments.
6. Whoever plays the harp must have strong fingers to pluck the strings.
7. The modern harp has forty-six strings and seven pedals that permit the playing of halftones.
8. Although it has a keyboard, the piano is also a stringed instrument.
9. The piano's steel wire strings sound when they are struck by the covered hammers operated by the keyboard.
10. Upright pianos have strings that are vertical; wing-shaped pianos have strings that are horizontal.

Exercise 53 Writing Sentences **With Clauses** Combine each pair of sentences according to the directions provided.

1. *Combine using an adjective clause:* The clavichord is a predecessor of the piano. It is a stringed instrument with a rectangular keyboard.

---

6. Whoever plays the harp—noun
7. that permit the playing of halftones—adjective
8. Although it has a keyboard—adverb
9. when they are struck by the covered hammers operated by the keyboard—adverb
10. that are vertical; that are horizontal—adjectives

Exercise 53

Answers will vary; samples are given.

1. The clavichord, which is a stringed instrument with a rectangular keyboard, is a predecessor of the piano.
2. When the strings are struck by metal wedges attached directly to the key ends, a vibrato effect is produced.

continued

2. *Combine using an adverb clause*: The strings are struck by metal wedges attached directly to the key ends. A vibrato effect is produced.
3. *Combine using an adjective clause*: The hurdy-gurdy is an instrument of the Middle Ages. It is shaped like a lute.
4. *Combine using an adverb clause*: Turning a crank causes the strings to vibrate. The crank is attached to a wheel.
5. *Combine using a noun clause*: Some people played the hurdy-gurdy. A player was most often a traveling musician of the seventeenth century.

▶ **Exercise 54** **Identifying the Four Structures of Sentences** Identify each sentence as *simple, compound, complex*, or *compound-complex*.

1. The flute is a high-pitched wind instrument.
2. Consisting of a long, slender tube, the flute is played by blowing across a hole at one end.
3. The panpipe is made of a row of reeds or tubes of graduated length that are bound together.
4. The player blows across the open, upper ends to produce sound.
5. The pipe organ is a large wind instrument consisting of various sets of pipes; its keyboard controls the flow of air into the pipes, where sound is produced.
6. Simple organs were widely used in religious services in tenth-century Europe.
7. As the Middle Ages came to a close, portable tabletop organs were introduced.
8. Unlike flutes, which are blown from the side, recorders are blown from the end.
9. The recorder usually has eight finger holes, but it can have as few as three.
10. The bassoon's range is two octaves lower than that of the oboe, and the contrabassoon is an octave lower in pitch.

▶ **Exercise 55** **Writing Sentences With Phrases and Clauses** Use the instructions below to write ten sentences of your own.

1. Write a simple sentence with a prepositional phrase.
2. Write a compound sentence in which the clauses are joined by a comma and a coordinating conjunction.
3. Write a complex sentence with an adverb clause.
4. Write a compound-complex sentence with an adjective clause.
5. Write a compound-complex sentence with an adverb clause.

▶ **Exercise 56** **Revision Practice: Sentence Variety** Revise the following paragraph, combining sentences and using a variety of phrases and clauses.

Jazz has been a popular form of music. The origins of its name are not certain. Originally, its name was not "jazz" but "jass." The first bands to play the style were "jass bands." Jazz has always been primarily brass music because the original New Orleans jazz outfits descended from marching brass bands. Classic jazz bands had between five and seven instruments. Most were wind, but some were string. After World War I, jazz spread rapidly across the nation. It was a dynamic musical form. Originally, the improvisations were not rehearsed. This is not always the case with modern jazz.

▶ **Exercise 57** **Writing Application**
Imagine that you are living one hundred years in the future. Write a description of what you imagine music will be like then. You might point out how the instruments available have evolved from those used today. Use phrases and clauses to be more descriptive and to vary your sentence structure.

Chapter Review • 471

▶ **Exercise 53**

3. The hurdy-gurdy, which is shaped like a lute, is an instrument of the Middle Ages.
4. Because the crank is attached to a wheel, turning it causes the strings to vibrate.
5. Who played the hurdy-gurdy most often in the seventeenth century was a traveling musician.

▶ **Exercise 54**

1. simple
2. simple
3. complex
4. simple
5. compound-complex
6. simple
7. complex
8. complex
9. compound
10. compound

▶ **Exercise 55**

Answers may vary; samples are given.

1. The car was parked near the gate.
2. I found the keys lying in the grass, and I quickly picked them up.
3. Though I waited for two hours, he never showed up.
4. He tried to plan a party, but no one whom he wanted to invite was available.
5. I left the game early; we were losing badly when the fourth quarter began.

▶ **Exercise 56**

Answers will vary; a sample is given.

Jazz, a popular form of music, has a name whose origins are not certain. Originally, its name was not "jazz" but "jass," and the first bands to play the style were "jass bands." Jazz has always been primarily brass music, because the original New Orleans jazz outfits descended from marching brass bands. Classic jazz bands had between five and seven instruments—mostly wind, but some string. After World War I jazz, a dynamic musical form, spread rapidly across the nation. Originally, the improvisations were not rehearsed, which is not always the case with modern jazz.

▶ **Exercise 57**

Writing Application
When students have finished, have volunteers read their descriptions aloud. Have the class listen for appositives, verbals, and subordinate clauses.

1. You may want to review the definitions of clauses and phrases. A clause is a group of words that has a subject and verb. It can stand alone or function as part of a sentence. A phrase is a group of words without both a subject and verb. (*Gesturing wildly,* the driver tried to attract attention.)

2. Emphasize that this practice test measures students' understanding of basic sentence structure.

3. Go over the sample test item and the answer.

4. Explain why A is not a proper rewrite. (The first sentence is a fragment.) Choice C contains a misplaced modifier (Washington was not born at the age of sixteen). Choice D reverses the chronological order of events in the sample item, thus changing the meaning.

5. Assign the two practices, and go over the answers with students.

Standardized Test Preparation Workshop

Recognizing Appropriate Sentence Construction

Knowledge of grammar is tested on standardized tests. Questions that measure your ability to use phrases and clauses also show your understanding of basic sentence construction and style. A phrase is a group of words that acts as a unit without a subject and a verb; a clause is a group of words that contains a subject and verb. When faced with these types of questions, first read the entire passage to get an idea of the author's purpose. Focus on the underlined group of words, and note any similarities or ways they can be combined without changing meaning. Then, choose the rewritten sentence that uses a phrase or clause to combine like ideas without changing the meaning of the author's message.

The following will give you practice with this format.

Test Tips

- Although an answer choice may make sense, it may not be the best way to rewrite the original.
- Read every choice carefully before deciding on your answer.

Sample Test Item	Answer and Explanation
Read the passage, and choose the letter of the best way to rewrite the underlined sentences. Washington Irving was born into a wealthy (1) family. Irving began studying law at the age of sixteen. Though he planned to be a lawyer, he was much more interested in becoming a writer. A. Born into a wealthy family. Washington Irving began studying law at sixteen. B. Born into a wealthy family, Washington Irving began studying law at the age of sixteen. C. Washington Irving began studying law. At the age of sixteen, Washington was born into a wealthy family. D. Washington Irving began studying law at the age of sixteen, and he was born into a wealthy family.	The correct answer is *B*. This is the best rewrite of the two sentences because it combines related ideas without changing the meaning. Changing the first sentence into an introductory phrase illustrates how both ideas describe Irving's background.

472 • Phrases and Clauses

✏ TEST-TAKING TIP

Tell students that on an exam testing appropriate sentence construction, they should keep the following points in mind:

1. Marking an answer that contains a phrase or clause is often a good choice, as in these practice tests.

2. When reading rewritten sentences, avoid selecting a sentence with a dangling or misplaced modifier. (Barking up a tree, he found the beagle.)

3. Though an answer may make sense, it may not be the best way of rewriting the original, as in choice 1C of the sample test item.

4. Avoid marking a sentence that seems wordier than the original sentences, as in choice 1D of the sample test item.

Practice 1

Directions: Read the passage, and choose the letter of the best way to rewrite the underlined sentences.

For a time, Irving lived in Europe. There he
(1)
traveled extensively and learned about

European customs, traditions, and folklore.

Irving was inspired by the European folk
(2)
heritage. He created two of his most

famous stories, "The Legend of Sleepy

Hollow" and "Rip Van Winkle."

1. **A.** While Irving lived in Europe, he traveled extensively and learned about European customs and folklore.
   B. For a time, Irving lived in Europe, and he traveled extensively. He learned about customs and folklore.
   C. Irving traveled extensively and learned about European customs and folklore, after he lived in Europe.
   D. For a time, Irving lived in Europe, there he learned about European customs and folklore.
2. **A.** Irving was inspired. The European folk heritage created two of his most famous stories, "The Legend of Sleepy Hollow" and "Rip Van Winkle."
   B. Two of his most famous stories "The Legend of Sleepy Hollow" and "Rip Van Winkle," were created by the European folk heritage inspiration felt by Irving.
   C. Inspired by the European folk heritage, he created two of his most famous stories, "The Legend of Sleepy Hollow" and "Rip Van Winkle."
   D. He created two of his most famous stories when he was inspired by the European folk heritage, "The Legend of Sleepy Hollow" and "Rip Van Winkle."

Practice 2

Directions: Read the passage, and choose the letter of the best way to rewrite the underlined sentences.

Irving lived in Europe. While he was living
(1)
there, he completed six books.

His patriotism was questioned because of
(2)
his time abroad. When it was questioned,

he responded: "Whatever I have written

. . . has been published as the writing of

an American."

1. **A.** Irving lived in Europe while he completed six books.
   B. When Irving completed six books he lived in Europe.
   C. While Irving lived in Europe, he completed six books.
   D. Completing six books, Irving lived in Europe.
2. **A.** Irving responded: "Whatever I have written . . . has been published as the writing of an American" although his patriotism was questioned because of his time abroad.
   B. When his patriotism was questioned because of his time abroad, Irving responded: "Whatever I have written . . . has been published as the writing of an American."
   C. Irving responded because of his time abroad when his patriotism was questioned: "Whatever I have written . . . has been published as the writing of an American."
   D. Irving's patriotism was questioned although he spent time abroad because he responded: "Whatever I have written . . . has been published as the writing of an American."

Answer Key

▸ Practice 1
1. A
2. C

▸ Practice 2
1. C
2. B

Customize for
Less Advanced Students

Go over the answer choices on the practice tests, and explain why the three "wrong" answers in each case should not have been chosen.

Customize for
AP Students

Urge students to be on the lookout for and avoid choosing run-on sentences as correct answers.

CUMULATIVE REVIEW

Each of these exercises reviews concepts taught in the chapters on the parts of speech, basic sentence parts, and phrases and clauses. The exercises may be used for more practice, for review of the key concepts presented, or for assessment of student mastery of the major concepts.

Answer Key

Exercise A

1. Egypt—proper noun
2. was—linking verb; Greco-Roman—proper adjective
3. during—preposition; who—relative pronoun; Alexander the Great—proper noun
4. several—indefinite adjective; harbor—common noun
5. Sailors—common noun
6. says—action verb
7. lighthouse—common, compound noun; contemporary—adjective
8. These—demonstrative adjective
9. Alas—interjection
10. Not only . . . but also—correlative conjunctions

Exercise B

1. we / will learn
2. King Mausolos / reigned, moved
3. Bryaxis, Leochares, Scopas, and Timotheus / sculpted
4. castle / is
5. (You) Visit

Exercise C

1. Hanging Gardens—direct object
2. hillside—predicate nominative
3. invisible—predicate adjective; water—direct object
4. Hanging Gardens—direct object; paradise—objective complement
5. foundation, locations—compound direct object

Exercise D

1. of Rhodes—prepositional; located at the entrance of the harbor of Rhodes—participial; at the entrance, of the harbor, of Rhodes—prepositional
2. Standing one hundred feet tall—participial; to guard the harbor—infinitive

continued

Cumulative Review

GRAMMAR

Exercise A **Recognizing All the Parts of Speech** Identify the part of speech of the underlined words in the following sentences. Be as specific as possible (e.g., *collective noun, demonstrative pronoun*).

1. The Lighthouse of Alexandria, one of the Seven Wonders of the Ancient World, was located on the island of Pharos in <u>Egypt</u>.
2. Alexandria, founded in 332 B.C., <u>was</u> the capital of <u>Greco-Roman</u> Egypt and a center of culture.
3. The project was commissioned <u>during</u> the reign of Ptolemy, <u>who</u> had assumed power after the death of <u>Alexander the Great</u>.
4. At a height of <u>several</u> hundred feet, it effectively illuminated the <u>harbor</u>.
5. <u>Sailors</u> thirty miles offshore could see the reflection from mirrors in the lighthouse.
6. Legend <u>says</u> that the mirror was also used to detect enemy ships far out in the Mediterranean Sea.
7. The <u>lighthouse</u> was well represented in <u>contemporary</u> writings.
8. <u>These</u> travelers were fascinated by its height and elegance.
9. <u>Alas</u>, it was destroyed in the fourteenth century by two strong earthquakes.
10. <u>Not only</u> was the structure damaged, <u>but also</u> Sultan Qaitbay built a fort using the fallen stones.

Exercise B **Identifying Subjects and Predicates** Write each of the following sentences, underlining each simple subject once and each simple predicate twice.

1. When will we learn more about the Mausoleum at Halicarnassus?
2. King Mausolos of Caria reigned in the far reaches of the Persian Empire and

moved his capital to Halicarnassus.
3. Bryaxis, Leochares, Scopas, and Timotheus sculpted statues of animals and people for decoration.
4. There is now a massive castle containing the stones from the mausoleum.
5. Visit the displays in the British Museum.

Exercise C **Recognizing Complements** List the complements in each of the following sentences and label each *direct object, indirect object, objective complement, predicate nominative,* or *predicate adjective*.

1. King Nebuchadnezzar built the Hanging Gardens of Babylon for his wife.
2. The approach to the gardens was a hillside sculpted into tiers and planted with trees.
3. An irrigation device seemed invisible as it raised water from the river.
4. Historians consider the Hanging Gardens a mysterious paradise that may never have existed.
5. Recent excavations have uncovered the foundation of Nebuchadnezzar's palace and several possible locations for the gardens.

Exercise D **Recognizing Phrases** Write the phrases contained in each of the following sentences. Identify each phrase as a *prepositional phrase*, an *appositive phrase*, a *participial phrase*, a *gerund phrase*, or an *infinitive phrase*.

1. The Colossus of Rhodes was a bronze statue located at the entrance of the harbor of Rhodes.
2. Standing one hundred feet tall, it was erected to guard the harbor.
3. In 305 B.C., the Antigonids, a rival

group from Macedonia, attacked the four cities of Rhodes, Ialysos, Kamiros, and Lindos.
4. A peace agreement, reached one year later, sent the Antigonids away, leaving behind much of their military equipment.
5. After claiming this equipment, the residents of Rhodes sold it.

Exercise E Identifying Clauses

Label the underlined clauses in the following sentences *independent* or *subordinate*. Identify any subordinate clauses as *adjective*, *adverb*, or *noun clauses*, and then label any adjective clauses *essential* or *nonessential*.

1. The Great Pyramid of Giza is the only one of the Seven Wonders of the Ancient World that survives today.
2. The Great Pyramid of Khufu is the only pyramid on the list of wonders, although it is assumed that all three pyramids are included.
3. The tradition of Egyptian pyramid building began around 2560 B.C., when royal tombs became more elaborate.
4. Imhotep, who was a famous Egyptian architect, built the early Step Pyramid of King Zoser.
5. Several other civilizations built elaborate pyramids whenever they wanted to honor their dead.

Exercise F Identifying Sentence Structure

Identify each sentence as *simple*, *compound*, *complex*, or *compound-complex*.

1. The Temple of Artemis at Ephesus and the Statue of Zeus at Olympia are two more of the Seven Wonders of the Ancient World.
2. The Temple of Artemis, which honored the Greek goddess of hunting and nature, was considered the most beautiful structure.

3. The marble temple that was designed by the architect Chersiphron was sponsored by King Croesus, and it was decorated with bronze statues.
4. Zeus, the king of the Greek gods, was represented in a spectacular seated statue of ivory and gold; it was thought that upon standing, he would lift the temple's roof.
5. The throne, decorated with all sorts of mythical figures, was as elaborate as Zeus' body and features.

Exercise G Revision Practice: Varying Sentence Style and Structure

Revise the following passage. Where appropriate and possible, create variety and improve sentence clarity by combining sentences with phrases and clauses or by using compound subjects and predicates.

The statue of Zeus is one of the Seven Wonders of the Ancient World. It was probably the most famous statue in the ancient world. It was located in Olympia, Greece. The statue showed Zeus sitting on his throne. Zeus was the king of all the Greek gods. A Greek sculptor made it. His name was Phidias, and he made it in 435 B.C. He dedicated it to Zeus. The robe was made of gold. The ornaments were made of gold. The body was made of ivory. The statue no longer exists. This is not a surprising fact. Researchers know that when it did exist, Zeus had a wreath. The wreath was on his head. He held a figure of his messenger in his right hand. His messenger's name was Nike. He also held things in his left hand. He held an eagle. He also held a scepter.

Exercise H Writing Application

Write a description of a landmark or "wonder" near your home. Use at least one compound subject, one compound predicate, one appositive phrase, one gerund phrase, one participial phrase, one infinitive phrase, and three subordinate clauses.

Exercise H

Writing Application
Student responses will vary. When students have finished their descriptions, have them exchange papers with a partner and check each other's use of phrases, clauses, and sentence structure.

Exercise D

3. In 305 B.C.—prepositional; a rival group from Macedonia—appositive; from Macedonia—prepositional; of Rhodes, Ialysos, Kamiros, and Lindos—prepositional
4. reached one year later—participial; leaving behind much of their military equipment—participial; of their military equipment—prepositional
5. After claiming this equipment—prepositional; claiming this equipment—gerund; of Rhodes—prepositional

Exercise E

1. that survives today—subordinate, adjective, essential
2. although it is assumed that all three pyramids are included—subordinate, adverb; that all three pyramids are included—subordinate, noun
3. The tradition of Egyptian pyramid building began around 2560 B.C.—independent
4. who was a famous Egyptian architect—subordinate, adjective, nonessential
5. whenever they wanted to honor their dead—subordinate, adverb

Exercise F

1. simple
2. complex
3. compound-complex
4. compound-complex
5. simple

Exercise G

Answers will vary. Possible answer:

The statue of Zeus, one of the Seven Wonders of the Ancient World, was probably the most famous statue of that world. Located in Olympia, Greece, the statue showed Zeus, the king of all the Greek gods, sitting on his throne. A Greek sculptor, Phidias, made the statue in 435 B.C. and dedicated it to Zeus. It is not surprising that the statue, whose robe and ornaments were made of gold and whose body was made of ivory, no longer exists. Researchers know that when it did exist, Zeus had a wreath on his head and a figure of his messenger Nike in his right hand. In his left hand he held an eagle and a scepter.

continued

In-Depth Lesson Plan

	LESSON FOCUS	PRINT AND MEDIA RESOURCES
DAY 1	**Introduction to Effective Sentences; Sentence Combining** Students learn and classify the four functions of a sentence and then combine sentences for sentence variety. (pp. 478–486)	*Language Lab* CD-ROM, Sentence Errors; *On-Line Exercise Bank,* Sections 20.1–2 **Teaching Resources** *Grammar Exercise Workbook,* pp. 61–64; *Grammar Exercises Answers on Transparencies,* Ch. 20; *Hands-on Grammar Activity Book,* Ch. 20
DAY 2	**Varying Sentences** Students learn to vary sentences by adjusting lengths and beginnings. (pp. 487–491)	*On-Line Exercise Bank,* Section 20.3 **Teaching Resources** *Grammar Exercise Workbook,* pp. 65–70
DAY 3	**Avoiding Fragments and Run-ons** Students learn to recognize and correct sentence fragments and run-ons. (pp. 492–499)	*On-Line Exercise Bank,* Section 20.4 **Teaching Resources** *Grammar Exercise Workbook,* pp. 71–74
DAY 4	**Misplaced and Dangling Modifiers; Faulty Parallelism** Students learn to recognize and correct modifier errors and faulty parallelism. (pp. 500–508)	*On-Line Exercise Bank,* Sections 20.5–6 **Teaching Resources** *Grammar Exercise Workbook,* pp. 75–82
DAY 5	**Faulty Coordination** Students learn to recognize and correct faulty coordination in sentences. (pp. 509–513)	*On-Line Exercise Bank,* Section 20.7 **Teaching Resources** *Grammar Exercise Workbook,* pp. 83–86; *Formal Assessment,* Ch. 20

Accelerated Lesson Plan

	LESSON FOCUS	PRINT AND MEDIA RESOURCES
DAY 1	**Combining and Varying Sentences** Students cover four functions of a sentence, sentence combining, and varying sentence beginnings and length. (pp. 478–491)	*Language Lab* CD-ROM, Sentence Errors *On-Line Exercise Bank,* Sections 20.1–3 **Teaching Resources** *Grammar Exercise Workbook,* pp. 61–70; *Grammar Exercises Answers on Transparencies,* Ch. 20
DAY 2	**Fragments and Run-ons; Misplaced and Dangling Modifiers** Students cover sentence fragments, run-ons, and modifier errors. (pp. 492–503)	*On-Line Exercise Bank,* Sections 20.4–5 **Teaching Resources** *Grammar Exercise Workbook,* pp. 71–78
DAY 3	**Faulty Parallelism; Faulty Coordination** Students cover faulty parallelism and faulty coordination in sentences. (pp. 504–513)	*On-Line Exercise Bank,* Sections 20.6–7 **Teaching Resources** *Grammar Exercise Workbook,* pp. 79–86; *Formal Assessment,* Ch. 20

Options for Adapting Lesson Plans

HOMEWORK
Have students complete any stage of the lesson for homework.

FEATURES
Extend coverage with the Grammar in Literature feature (p. 479) and the Standardized Test Preparation Workshop (p. 516).

TECHNOLOGY
Students can use the *On-Line Exercise Bank* to complete the exercises on computer. The Auto Check feature will grade their work.

INTEGRATED SKILLS COVERAGE

Grammar in Literature
SE p. 479

Writing
Find It in Your Writing SE pp. 480, 486, 491, 499, 503, 508, 513
Writing Application SE pp. 480, 486, 491, 499, 503, 508, 513, 515
Grammar and Style SE pp. 493, 506

Viewing and Representing
Critical Viewing, SE pp. 476, 478, 483, 484, 488, 490, 493, 495, 497, 501, 505, 509, 510, 512

Speaking and Listening SE p. 497

Vocabulary
ATE p. 483

Spelling ATE p. 506

Workplace Skills ATE p. 510

ASSESSMENT SUPPORT

Standardized Test Preparation Workshop SE p. 516; ATE pp. 493, 506

Standardized Test Preparation Workbook, pp. 39–40

Formal Assessment, Ch. 20

MEETING INDIVIDUAL NEEDS

Less Advanced Students ATE p. 517. See also Ongoing Assessments, ATE pp. 479, 482, 483, 484, 489, 494, 496, 501, 505, 510, 511.

Gifted and Talented Students ATE p. 484

ESL Students ATE pp. 494, 501

Logical/Mathematical Learners ATE p. 490

BLOCK SCHEDULING

Pacing Suggestions
For 90-minute Blocks
• Administer the Diagnostic Test to students to determine instructional coverage needed.
• Have students complete necessary exercises in class. Use the Hands-on Grammar activity.

Resources for Varying Instruction
• *Language Lab* **CD-ROM** If your students have access to hardware, a 90-minute block provides an ideal opportunity for students to work on computer.

Professional Development Support
• *How to Manage Instruction in the Block* This Teaching Resource provides management and activity suggestions.

MEDIA AND TECHNOLOGY

For the Student
• *Language Lab* **CD-ROM**, Writing Style; Sentence Errors
• *On-Line Exercise Bank,* Sections 20.1–7

For the Teacher
• *Resource Pro* **CD-ROM**

WRITING AND GRAMMAR WEB SITE

The Interactive Writing and Grammar Web Site provides a wide array of support for students, teachers, and parents. Grammar support includes:

• *On-Line Exercise Bank* with Auto Check scoring
• Diagnostic and assessment support

www.phschool.com

LITERATURE CONNECTIONS

Related selection from *Prentice Hall Literature: Timeless Voices, Timeless Themes,* The American Experience:

From *Poor Richard's Almanack,* Benjamin Franklin, SE p. 479

Lesson Objectives

1. To analyze the characteristics of clearly written texts, including the patterns of organization, syntax, and word choice

2. To evaluate writing for both mechanics and content

3. To proofread writing for appropriate style and conventions

4. To recognize appropriate sentence construction of the four types of sentences within the context of a written passage

5. To write and revise written passages by combining sentences and varying sentence length, beginnings, and structures

6. To recognize and correct sentence fragments, run-on sentences, and misplaced and dangling modifiers

7. To recognize correct parallelism in sentences and to correct faulty parallelism

8. To recognize correct coordination in sentences and to correct faulty coordination

Critical Viewing

Connect Possible answer: Conjunctions can connect sentences in a similar way that a bridge connects cities.

Chapter 20 Effective Sentences

When you first begin to write, one of the first things you learn is how to write a complete sentence. As you develop as a writer, it is essential to continue to improve your use of sentences by learning how to vary them and how to avoid sentence errors. This chapter looks at the different types of sentences and provides a variety of strategies to help you use sentences more effectively and avoid problems in your writing.

▲ **Critical Viewing**
What types of words connect sentences in the same way that this bridge connects Philadelphia to towns on the other side of the Delaware River? **[Connect]**

☑ **ONGOING ASSESSMENT: Diagnose**

If students miss more than one item in any category, direct them to the relevant pages of the textbook and assign exercises for practice and review.

Writing Effective Sentences	Diagnostic Test Items	Teach	Practice	Section Reviews	Chapter Review
Skill Check A					
The Four Functions of a Sentence	A 1–5	p. 478	Ex. 1–2	Ex. 3–4	Ex. 64
Skill Check B					
Combining Sentences	B 6–7	pp. 481–484	Ex. 8–12	Ex. 13–15	Ex. 65
Varying Sentences	B 8–10	pp. 487–490	Ex. 19–22	Ex. 23–25	Ex. 65

Diagnostic Test

Directions: Write all answers on a separate sheet of paper.

Skill Check A. Label each sentence *declarative*, *exclamatory*, *interrogative*, or *imperative*, and write the end mark.

1. Have you ever visited Philadelphia
2. It is considered the birthplace of the United States
3. Tell us about the next school trip to Philadelphia
4. The Declaration of Independence and the Constitution were adopted in Philadelphia's Independence Hall
5. Did you know that the city was the colonies' capital during the Revolutionary War

Skill Check B. Revise each of the following sentences according to the directions in parentheses.

6. Philadelphia is located in Pennsylvania. It is located on the Delaware River. (Combine the sentences with a phrase.)
7. Philadelphia ranks among the top ten largest cities in the United States. More than one million people live in Philadelphia. (Combine the sentences with a clause beginning with *because*.)
8. Attracting thousands of Europeans, Philadelphia grew to a population of 4,500 by 1700. (Begin the sentence with a noun.)
9. The largest city in the colonies by 1710 was Philadelphia. (Begin the sentence with a prepositional phrase.)
10. In this city, Benjamin Franklin, along with Thomas Jefferson and other leaders, contributed to forming the new nation and worked together to achieve independence. (Break the long sentence into short sentences.)

Skill Check C. Identify the fragments, run-ons, misplaced or dangling modifiers, problems with parallelism, and problems with faulty coordination in the following sentences. Revise the passage, correcting all sentence errors.

Philadelphia covers 144 square miles. Lying within the boundaries of Philadelphia County and it is a county and a city and the Delaware River separates it from New Jersey running east and south of Philadelphia. When touring the city, a map must be brought along. Philadelphia's city hall more than five acres in the downtown area. On top, which measures 37 feet tall and weighs 53,523 lbs., is a statue of William Penn, it is the world's largest sculpture. Government buildings, a spacious bank, and an office complex that serves many businesses, border the streets around city hall. Moving northwest of the center, four museums can be found. The museums the Academy of Natural Sciences of Philadelphia, the Franklin Institute, the Rodin Museum, and the Philadelphia Museum. Whether you are touring the city for history, learning more about culture, or simply visit the parks, enjoy the city of Philadelphia.

Diagnostic Test

Each item in the Diagnostic Test corresponds to a specific section in the effective sentences chapter. This will enable you to tailor instruction to the particular needs of your students. See "Ongoing Assessment: Diagnose" below for further details.

Skill Check A

1. Philadelphia? (interrogative)
2. States. (declarative)
3. Philadelphia. (imperative)
4. Hall. (declarative)
5. War? (interrogative)

Skill Check B

6. Philadelphia is located on the Delaware River in Pennsylvania.
7. Because more than one million people live there, Philadelphia ranks . . .
8. Philadelphia grew to a population of 4,500 by 1700 by attracting . . .
9. By 1710, Philadelphia was the largest city in the colonies.
10. In this city, Benjamin Franklin, Thomas Jefferson, and other leaders contributed to forming the new nation. They worked together to achieve independence.

Skill Check C

Answers will vary; samples are given.

Philadelphia, *which is both a county and a city*, covers 144 square miles. The Delaware River, *running east and south of Philadelphia*, separates it from New Jersey. When touring the city, *bring a map* along. Philadelphia's city hall *covers* more than five acres in the downtown area. *On top is a statue of William Penn which measures 37 feet tall and weighs 53,523 lbs.; it is the world's largest sculpture.* Government buildings, a spacious bank, and an *office complex* that serves many businesses border the streets around city hall. Northwest of the center *are* four *museums*: the Academy of Natural Sciences of Philadelphia, the Franklin Institute, the Rodin Museum, and the Philadelphia Museum. Whether you are touring the city *to study* history, *to learn* more about culture, or simply *to visit* the parks, enjoy the city of Philadelphia.

✓ ONGOING ASSESSMENT: Diagnose *continued*

Writing Effective Sentences	Diagnostic Test Items	Teach	Practice	Section Reviews	Chapter Review
Skill Check C					
Fragments and Run-ons	C	pp. 492–497	Ex. 29–33	Ex. 34–36	Ex. 66
Misplaced and Dangling Modifiers	C	pp. 500–502	Ex. 40–41	Ex. 42–44	Ex. 67
Faulty Parallelism	C	pp. 504–507	Ex. 48–49	Ex. 50–52	Ex. 68
Faulty Coordination	C	pp. 509–511	Ex. 56–57	Ex. 58–60	Ex. 68
Cumulative Reviews and Applications				Ex. 5–7, 16–18, 26–28, 37–39, 45–47, 53–55, 61–63	Ex. 69–70

Read aloud Emily Dickinson's short poem "I'm Nobody. Who Are You?" Ask students to describe what each line in the poem does:

"I'm Nobody." (states a belief)

"Who are you?" (asks a question)

"Don't tell!" (an order)

"Then there's a pair of us!" (conveys emotion)

Tell students that these lines reflect a different function, and identify each.

Activate Prior Knowledge

Write the sentence "Soldiers march" on the board, and demonstrate how it may be written to perform each of the four sentence functions. Use inflection to read the sentences aloud for declarative (Soldiers march.) then interrogative (Soldiers march?), then exclamatory (Soldiers *march*!), then imperative (Soldiers, march!). Finally, have students compose four original sentences: one for each of the four functions.

TEACH

Step-by-Step Teaching Guide

The Four Functions of a Sentence

1. Emphasize the root word of each function's name, and suggest devices to help students remember them. For instance, point out that a declarative sentence *declares* a fact, an interrogative sentence sounds like "interrogation," and so forth.

2. Point out that while punctuation for the four functions is largely straightforward, use of the exclamation point is discretionary. Because it expresses a high degree of emotion or intensity, it can be used not only in exclamatory sentences but also in some imperative sentences to show special emphasis.

Critical Viewing

Connect Possible answer: When were these houses built? What sort of people live in them now?

Section 20.1

Classifying the Four Functions of a Sentence

Sentences can be classified according to what they do. The four types of sentences in English are *declarative, interrogative, imperative,* and *exclamatory.*

▶ **KEY CONCEPT** A **declarative sentence** states an idea and ends with a period. ■

DECLARATIVE: Elfreth's Alley in Philadelphia is the oldest continuously inhabited street in the country. The street dates back to the 1690's.

▶ **KEY CONCEPT** An **interrogative sentence** asks a question and ends with a question mark. ■

INTERROGATIVE: Do you know how many houses are located on Elfreth's Alley? Are you sure there are thirty-three houses?

▶ **KEY CONCEPT** An **imperative sentence** gives an order or a direction and ends with either a period or an exclamation mark. ■

Most imperative sentences start with a verb. In this type of imperative sentence, the subject is understood to be *you.*

IMPERATIVE: Let's tour Philadelphia. Wait for me!

▶ **KEY CONCEPT** An **exclamatory sentence** conveys strong emotion and ends with an exclamation mark. ■

EXCLAMATORY: All the historic buildings in this city are beautiful!

▶ **Critical Viewing** If you were on a visit to Philadelphia, what interrogative sentences might you use to ask a tour guide about the scene shown here? [Connect]

478 • Effective Sentences

🕐 **TIME AND RESOURCE MANAGER**

Resources
Print: *Grammar Exercise Workbook,* pp. 61–62; *Grammar Exercises Answers on Transparencies,* Ch. 20
Technology: *Language Lab* CD-ROM, Writing Style; *On-Line Exercise Bank,* Section 20.1

In-Depth Coverage	Accelerated Pace
• Work through key concepts, p. 478. • Assign and review Exercises 1–2. • Read and discuss Grammar in Literature, p. 479.	• Assign p. 478 for independent review. • Assign Section Review Exercises 3–4.

Exercise 1 Identifying the Four Functions of Sentences

Identify each sentence as *declarative, interrogative, imperative,* or *exclamatory*. Then, write the end mark for each.

1. I can't believe that Benjamin Franklin was only seventeen years old when he came to Philadelphia
2. He was born in Boston, Massachusetts, in 1706
3. Did you know that Franklin was primarily self-educated
4. Read *The Autobiography* to find out more about his early life
5. Franklin was one of Philadelphia's most influential citizens

Exercise 2 Writing Sentences With Different Functions

Follow the directions to write a sentence for each item below.

1. Write a declarative sentence about a city.
2. Write an exclamatory sentence about a holiday.
3. Write an imperative sentence about a school activity.
4. Write an interrogative sentence about a school subject.
5. Write an interrogative sentence about a current issue.
6. Write an exclamatory sentence about a food.
7. Write a declarative sentence about an animal.
8. Write a declarative sentence about your hometown.
9. Write an imperative sentence about a place you would like to visit.
10. Write an interrogative sentence about an upcoming event.

GRAMMAR IN LITERATURE

from **Poor Richard's Almanack**
Benjamin Franklin

In the following passage from Benjamin Franklin's Poor Richard's Almanack, *you will find interrogative, declarative, and imperative sentences.*

Dost thou love life? Then do not squander time; for that's the stuff life is made of.

Write injuries in dust, benefits in marble.

A slip of the foot you may soon recover, but a slip of the tongue you may never get over.

More Practice

Language Lab
CD-ROM
• Strengthening Sentences lesson
On-line
Exercise Bank
• Section 20.1
Grammar Exercise
Workbook
• pp. 61–62

Classifying the Four Functions of a Sentence • 479

Answer Key

Exercise 1

1. Philadelphia! (exclamatory)
2. 1706. (declarative)
3. self-educated? (interrogative)
4. life. (imperative)
5. citizens. (declarative)

Exercise 2

Samples:

1. Philadelphia is a large city.
2. I love Christmas!
3. Do your homework.
4. Do you like English class?
5. Did you hear about the plane crash?
6. I hate peas!
7. Dogs are friendly.
8. My town is busy on Saturdays.
9. Let's go to Minnesota!
10. Are you ready for the test?

Step-by-Step Teaching Guide

Grammar in Literature

1. Review the definition of a proverb with students (a short statement of a well-known truth) and have them give examples of popular aphorisms.

2. Have student volunteers read the excerpt from *Poor Richard's Almanack.* Ask students to identify the function of each sentence. Point out that good writers vary their sentences—in function as well as structure—for effect.

More About the Writer

Franklin was a printer, writer, diplomat, philosopher, and scientist. He founded the first public library in America, organized the first fire company in Philadelphia, and introduced methods for improving street lighting and paving. He also invented the Franklin stove, valuable because it provided a great deal of heat with efficient consumption of fuel.

Connections With Literature

You can find more from Benjamin Franklin's *Poor Richard's Almanack* in *Prentice Hall Literature: Timeless Voices, Timeless Themes,* The American Experience.

✓ **ONGOING ASSESSMENT: Monitor and Reinforce**

If students miss more than two items in Exercise 1 or 2, refer them to the following for additional practice.

In the Textbook	Print Resources	Technology
Section Review, Ex. 3–4, p. 480	*Grammar Exercise Workbook,* pp. 61–62	*On-Line Exercise Bank,* Section 20.1

Section Review

Each of these exercises correlates to the instruction on the four functions of a sentence, pages 478–479. These exercises may be used for more practice, for reteaching, or for review of the key concepts presented. Answers for all chapter exercises are available in *Grammar Exercises Answers on Transparencies* in your Teaching Resources.

Answer Key

> **Exercise 3**

1. Revolution? (interrogative)
2. protest. (declarative)
3. city. (declarative)
4. back. (imperative)
5. city. (declarative)
6. 1800. or ! (declarative or exclamatory)
7. city? (interrogative)
8. out? (interrogative)
9. city? or ! (interrogative or exclamatory)
10. Philadelphia. (imperative)

> **Exercise 4**

Samples:

1. Trains go faster than buses.
2. Did you see the new comedy?
3. Make a model airplane.
4. We are such good friends!
5. Is the job available?
6. Let's play baseball!
7. I like to travel.
8. Study math carefully.
9. This is my favorite song!
10. Benjamin Franklin was one of the framers of the U.S. Constitution.

> **Exercise 5**

Find It in Your Reading
1. Declarative
2. Interrogative
3. Imperative
4. Imperative
5. Imperative
6. Imperative

> **Exercise 6**

Find It in Your Writing

Do students note patterns in the use of sentence functions in their writing? Challenge students to vary the types of sentences they use.

> **Exercise 7**

Writing Application

Ask students to rewrite sentences, changing the function of each.

480

GRAMMAR EXERCISES 3–7

> **Exercise 3** Identifying the Four Functions of Sentences Label each sentence *declarative*, *interrogative*, *imperative*, or *exclamatory*. Then, write the end mark for each.

1. Have you read about Philadelphia during the time of the American Revolution
2. Yes, it was really a center of colonial protest
3. In 1777, the British captured the city
4. Find out how the city was won back
5. A French fleet was sent to help, and the British withdrew from the city
6. I was surprised to find out that the city was the capital of the United States from 1790 to 1800
7. Is it still a thriving city
8. Why don't you visit and find out
9. Can you believe all the parks, museums, and historical landmarks that can be found in this city
10. Go to Fairmount Park, the chief recreational area in Philadelphia

> **Exercise 4** Writing Sentences With Different Functions Write a sentence for each numbered item using the subject and function indicated. For example, the first sentence should be a declarative sentence about transportation.

1. declarative, transportation
2. interrogative, a movie
3. imperative, a hobby
4. exclamatory, friends
5. interrogative, employment
6. imperative, sports
7. declarative, travel
8. imperative, a school subject
9. exclamatory, music
10. declarative, a historical event

480 • Effective Sentences

> **Exercise 5** Find It in Your Reading
Read the following passage from Benjamin Franklin's *The Autobiography*. Label each sentence *declarative*, *imperative*, *interrogative*, or *exclamatory*.

The precept of *Order* requiring that *every part of my business should have its allotted time*, one page in my little book contained the following scheme of employment for the twenty-four hours of a natural day.

THE MORNING.   *Question.* What good shall I do this day?
5 [AM] Rise, wash, and
6 [AM] address *Powerful Goodness!* Contrive day's business, and take the
7 [AM] resolution of the day; prosecute the present study, and breakfast.
8 [AM]
9 [AM] Work.
10 [AM]
11 [AM]
12 [PM] Read, or overlook my accounts,
1 [PM] and dine.

> **Exercise 6** Find It in Your Writing
Choose a piece of writing from your portfolio. Design a color key for each sentence function. For example, use yellow for interrogative, and so on. Then, identify the function of each sentence in your work by underlining it using the appropriate color.

> **Exercise 7** Writing Application
Write a paragraph about a city in which you are interested or a city you have visited. Use four declarative sentences, one interrogative sentence, one exclamatory sentence, and two imperative sentences.

✓ ONGOING ASSESSMENT: Assess Mastery

Use the following resources to assess student mastery of the four functions of a sentence.

In the Textbook	Technology
Chapter Review, p. 514, Ex. 64	*On-Line Exercise Bank,* Section 20.1

Section 20.2

Sentence Combining

In books written for very young readers, information is presented in short, direct sentences. While this makes the writing easy to read, it doesn't make it enjoyable or interesting to mature readers. Writing for advanced readers should include sentences of varying lengths and complexity to create a flow of ideas. One way to achieve sentence variety is to combine sentences, expressing two or more related ideas or pieces of information in a single sentence.

KEY CONCEPT Sentences can be combined by using a compound subject, a compound verb, or a compound object. ■

EXAMPLE:	Moira enjoyed seeing the Liberty Bell. Tom enjoyed seeing the Liberty Bell.
COMPOUND SUBJECT:	Moira and Tom enjoyed seeing the Liberty Bell.
EXAMPLE:	Lisa paid the driver. Lisa took a seat on the city bus.
COMPOUND VERB:	Lisa paid the driver and took a seat on the city bus.
EXAMPLE:	At Dorney Park, Scott rode the roller coaster. Scott rode the Ferris wheel.
COMPOUND OBJECT:	At Dorney Park, Scott rode the roller coaster and the Ferris wheel.

Exercise 8 **Combining Sentences** Use either a compound subject, a compound verb, or a compound object to combine each pair of sentences. Identify which method you have used to combine them. Sentences should also be revised for clarity.

1. Famous battles of the American Revolution were fought in Pennsylvania.
   Famous battles of the Civil War were fought in Pennsylvania.
2. The Gettysburg National Military Park attracts many tourists.
   The Gettysburg National Military Park provides much information about the Civil War.
3. Parks are one of the state's main tourist attractions.
   The city of Philadelphia is one of the state's main tourist attractions.
4. We visited Gettysburg on our vacation.
   We drove through Lancaster during our vacation.
5. After driving through Lancaster, I wanted to visit the Landis Valley Museum.
   I also wanted to stop at the Susquehanna River.

Theme: Pennsylvania

In this section, you will learn about combining sentences. The examples and exercises are about the history and geography of Pennsylvania.

Cross-Curricular Connection: Social Studies

More Practice

Language Lab CD-ROM
• Varying Sentence Structure
On-line Exercise Bank
• Section 20.2
Grammar Exercise Workbook
• pp. 63–64

Sentence Combining • 481

PREPARE and ENGAGE

 Interest GRABBER Read a page from a children's book and ask students why these books are written this way. (Small children can understand short, simple sentences more easily.) Invite students to suggest revisions to make the text more appropriate for adults. Point out that students have been engaging in sentence combining.

Activate Prior Knowledge

Let students know that adult writers should vary the structures and lengths of their sentences. Have students explain how adult sentences may differ grammatically from children's. (complex sentence structure, uses of phrases as modifiers, and so on).

TEACH

Step-by-Step Teaching Guide

Using a Compound Subject, Verb, or Object

1. Caution students that compounds should be balanced as well as clear; for instance, compound verbs should be written in the same tense.
2. Remind students that compounds do not employ commas unless the compound is a series of three or more items.

Answer Key

Exercise 8

1. Famous battles of the American *Revolution and the Civil War* were . . . (compound object of preposition)
2. The Gettysburg National Military Park *attracts many tourists and provides much information* . . . (compound verb)
3. *Parks and the city of Philadelphia* are *two* of the state's . . . (compound subject)
4. We *visited Gettysburg and drove through Lancaster* during our vacation. (compound verb)
5. After driving through Lancaster, I wanted to visit the *Landis Valley Museum and to stop at the Susquehanna River.* (compound object)

481

Creating a Compound Sentence

1. Emphasize the difference between a clause and a phrase. (The former has a subject and verb.) Point out that a compound sentence contains two or more independent clauses.

2. Make sure students recognize that the combination of a comma and conjunction (*and*) join the independent clauses in the second example. Review other conjunctions: *but, or, nor, for, so, yet.*

3. Remove the word "it" and the comma from the second example and ask if the sentence is still compound. (No, now just the verb is compound.)

Answer Key

▶ **Exercise 9**

1. The flat land of the Erie lowlands was once part of Lake Erie's lake bed, *but it* is now . . .
2. The Appalachian Plateau stretches from New York to Alabama, *but* in Pennsylvania . . .
3. This plateau consists of deep, narrow valleys and land ridges; in these ridges, water . . .
4. Some of the most beautiful waterfalls in the eastern states are found in the Pocono Mountains, *and* there are even more elsewhere . . .
5. Forests cover a large portion of the state; *they* contain . . .

Creating Subordinate Clauses

1. Explain that combining sentences by changing one of them into a subordinate clause clarifies the relationship between ideas. Review various subordinate conjunctions: *although, after, because, while.*

2. Suggest that students ask themselves certain questions about the sentences they wish to combine: Is the relationship cause and effect? Do the sentences contradict one another? Do they present events that occurred at the same time or in a certain sequence?

▶ **KEY CONCEPT** Sentences can be combined by joining two independent clauses to create a compound sentence. ■

Use a compound sentence when combining ideas that are related but independent. Compound sentences are created by joining two independent clauses with a comma and a conjunction or with a semicolon.

EXAMPLE: The ice-cream soda was invented in Philadelphia in 1874. It was an instant success.

COMPOUND SENTENCE: The ice-cream soda was invented in Philadelphia in 1874, and it was an instant success.

▶ **Exercise 9** Revising to Form Compound Sentences
Combine the following pairs of sentences using the directions indicated in parentheses.

1. The flat land of the Erie lowlands was once part of Lake Erie's lake bed. It is now fertile, sandy soil where vegetables and fruits grow. (comma and conjunction)
2. The Appalachian Plateau stretches from New York to Alabama. In Pennsylvania, it is called the Allegheny Plateau. (comma and conjunction)
3. This plateau consists of deep, narrow valleys and land ridges. In these ridges, water from rivers flows in different directions. (semicolon)
4. Some of the most beautiful waterfalls in the eastern states are found in the Pocono Mountains. There are even more waterfalls found elsewhere in the state. (comma and conjunction)
5. Forests cover a large portion of the state. They contain mixtures of hardwood and softwood trees. (semicolon)

▶ **KEY CONCEPT** Sentences can be combined by changing one of them into a subordinate clause. ■

Use a complex sentence when you are combining sentences to show the relationship between ideas. The subordinating conjunction will help readers understand the relationship.

EXAMPLE: Pennsylvania is an important manufacturing state. Service industries make up the largest part of the economy.

COMBINED WITH A SUBORDINATE CLAUSE: Although Pennsylvania is an important manufacturing state, service industries make up the largest part of the economy.

482 • Effective Sentences

▶ **More Practice**

Language Lab CD-ROM
• Varying Sentence Structure
On-line Exercise Bank
• Section 20.2
Grammar Exercise Workbook
• pp. 63–64

☑ **ONGOING ASSESSMENT: Monitor and Reinforce**

If students miss more than one item in Exercise 8 or 9, refer them to the following for additional practice.

In the Textbook	Print Resources	Technology
Section Review, Ex. 13, p. 486	*Grammar Exercise Workbook,* pp. 63–64	*On-Line Exercise Bank,* Section 20.2

Exercise 10 Combining Sentences Using Subordinate Clauses

Using the subordinating conjunction given in parentheses, combine the following pairs of sentences. Sentences should also be revised for clarity.

EXAMPLE: The nation won its independence. Then, it had to establish its own financial system. (after)

ANSWER: After the nation won its independence, it had to establish its own financial system.

1. The establishment of one unified currency and financial system was necessary. The nation was in debt, and some states were even bankrupt. (because)
2. One group of people greatly opposed establishing a federal bank. The First Bank of the United States was established in 1791 in Philadelphia. (although)
3. The bank had a twenty-year charter. It could act as a commercial and central bank during this time. (while)
4. The bank was built as a symbol of democracy. Its neoclassical design recalls the democracy of ancient Greece. (because)
5. The First Bank functioned successfully. The charter was not renewed in 1811. (even though)

Exercise 11 Combining Sentences Using Subordinating Conjunctions

Combine each pair of sentences using a subordinating conjunction. Sentences should also be revised for clarity.

EXAMPLE: Pennsylvania's economy is greatly dependent on service industries. Agriculture also plays a role.

ANSWER: Although Pennsylvania's economy is greatly dependent on service industries, agriculture is also important.

1. Pennsylvania ranks fourth in national coal production. Mining comprises one percent of its gross national product.
2. Pennsylvania is rich in natural resources. It has many mining communities.
3. You are using sand, gravel, limestone, or natural gas. Remember that they may have come from Pennsylvania.
4. Milk is the state's leading agricultural product. Dairy farms flourish in eastern Pennsylvania.
5. The leading crops are corn and hay. Much of it is not sold but used to feed the state's beef and dairy cattle.

▲ Critical Viewing
Write a sentence with a subordinate clause in which you compare the First Bank (shown here) with a bank with which you are familiar. [Compare]

Sentence Combining • 483

ONGOING ASSESSMENT: Monitor and Reinforce

If students miss more than one item in Exercise 10 or 11, refer them to the following for additional practice.

In the Textbook	Print Resources	Technology
Section Review, Ex. 14, p. 486	*Grammar Exercise Workbook,* pp. 63-64	*On-Line Exercise Bank,* Section 20.2

Integrating Vocabulary

Pennsylvania was named for its founder, William Penn, and the Latin word for *woods, sylvania.* Pennsylvania, therefore, means "Penn's woods." Have students choose a state name, research its etymology, and present this research to the class. Make a master list of derivations of state names.

Answer Key

Exercise 10

1. The establishment of one unified currency and financial system was necessary *because* the nation was in debt, and some states were even bankrupt.
2. *Although* one group of people greatly opposed establishing a federal bank, the First Bank of the United States was established in 1791 in Philadelphia.
3. *While* the Bank had a twenty year charter, it could act as a commercial and central bank.
4. *Because* the bank was built as a symbol of democracy, its neoclassical design recalls the democracy of ancient Greece.
5. *Even though* the First Bank functioned successfully, the charter was not renewed in 1811.

Exercise 11

1. Pennsylvania ranks forth in national coal production *even though* mining comprises only one percent of its gross national product.
2. *Because* Pennsylvania is rich in natural resources, it has many mining communities.
3. *When* you are using sand, gravel, limestone, or natural gas, remember that they may have come from Pennsylvania.
4. Milk is the state's leading agricultural product, *while* dairy farms flourish in eastern Pennsylvania.
5. *Even though* the leading crops are corn and hay, much of it is not sold but used to feed the state's beef and dairy cattle.

Critical Viewing

Compare Possible answer: Although the First Bank is more historical, the bank I use is more modern and convenient.

Step-by-Step Teaching Guide

Combining Sentences With Phrases

1. Remind students of the different kinds of phrases: prepositional, participial, gerund, infinitive, and appositive. Ask for examples of each and review their functions.

2. Explain that in the example on this page, it was necessary to add or change words. Point out that the word "against" has been added to create a prepositional phrase. Students should note that certain words may be eliminated from the original pair of sentences.

Customize for
Gifted and Talented Students

Have students rewrite a portion of a children's book using sentence combining. Challenge students to maintain the plot and tone of the story while using more complex sentence structures for a more mature audience.

Answer Key

▶ Exercise 12

1. Native Americans, *such as the Algonquian and Iroquoian tribes,* lived in the Pennsylvania . . .

2. In 1609, *Henry Hudson, an English explorer*, sailed into Delaware Bay.

3. Hudson was trying to find a trade route to the Far East *for the Dutch East India Company.*

4. After Hudson left the area, the Dutch sent *another explorer, Cornelius Hendricksen.*

5. Hendricksen sailed further up the Delaware, *all the way to what is now Philadelphia.*

6. In 1643, the Swedes made the first permanent settlement, *New Sweden,* in the region.

7. In 1655, *the last Dutch governor of New Netherland,* Peter Stuyvesant, leading Dutch troops . . .

8. The English captured the region *in 1664.*

9. *The Duke of York, an English nobleman,* controlled the region until 1681 . . .

10. The region derived its name from two sources: *Penn,* in honor of William Penn's father, and *sylvania,* which means woods.

484

▶ **KEY CONCEPT** Sentences can be combined by changing one of them into a phrase. ■

When you are combining sentences in which one of the sentences just adds detail, change one of the sentences into a phrase.

EXAMPLE: The Pittsburgh Pirates play tomorrow. They play the Philadelphia Phillies.

COMBINED BY USING A PHRASE: The Pittsburgh Pirates play against the Philadelphia Phillies tomorrow.

▶ **Exercise 12** Combining Sentences Using Phrases
Combine the following pairs of sentences by changing one into a phrase. Sentences should also be revised for clarity.

1. Native Americans lived in the Pennsylvania region for hundreds of years before European explorers came. These Native Americans, such as the Algonquian and Iroquoian tribes, lived in the Pennsylvania region.
2. In 1609, Henry Hudson sailed into the Delaware Bay. He was an English explorer.
3. Hudson was trying to find a trade route to the Far East. He was trying to find it for the Dutch East India Company.
4. After Hudson left the area, the Dutch sent someone else. They sent explorer Cornelius Hendricksen.
5. Hendricksen sailed farther up the Delaware River. He sailed all the way to what is now Philadelphia.
6. In 1643, the Swedes made the first permanent settlement in the region. They called it New Sweden.
7. In 1655, Peter Stuyvesant, leading Dutch troops, captured New Sweden. He was the last Dutch governor of New Netherland.
8. The English captured the region. They captured it in 1664.
9. A nobleman controlled the region until 1681, when it was granted to William Penn. The Duke of York controlled it.
10. The region derived its name from two sources. The sources were *Penn*, in honor of William Penn's father, and *sylvania*, which means "woods."

▶ **More Practice**

Language Lab CD-ROM
• Strengthening Sentences lesson
On-line Exercise Bank
• Section 20.2
Grammar Exercise Workbook
• pp. 63–64

▼ **Critical Viewing**
In what time period do you think this artwork of the Delaware River and Philadelphia was created? Why? **[Speculate]**

484 • Effective Sentences

✓ ONGOING ASSESSMENT: Monitor and Reinforce

If students miss more than two items in Exercise 12, refer them to the following for additional practice.

In the Textbook	Print Resources	Technology
Section Review, Ex. 15, p. 486	*Grammar Exercise Workbook,* pp. 63–64	*On-Line Exercise Bank,* Section 20.2

Hands-on Grammar

Clip-on Sentence Combiner

Practice using phrases to combine sentences by using a sentence combining clip-on activity. Write each of the following sentences on a strip of colored paper.

> The trip to Philadelphia was fun.

> The trip was on Saturday.

> Philadelphia is in Pennsylvania.

> Pennsylvania was one of the first states.

In the second sentence of each pair, locate the words that give more information about a word in the first sentence. Cut away the words that are not part of the phrase. Then, use a paper clip to clip the phrase to the first sentence in the pair in the place that it makes the most sense. (Usually, one or more of the words you have cut away will also be part of the first sentence. You will often find that you should clip the phrase near these words from the first sentence.)

Find It in Your Reading Look for phrases in sentences from your science or social studies textbook. Create clip-ons to show how the phrase fits into the sentence.

Find It in Your Writing Choose a piece of writing from your portfolio. Look for sentences that give more information about a word in the preceding or following sentence. Create a clip-on to see whether these sentences could be combined by turning one of them into a phrase. Revise your work where appropriate.

Step-by-Step Teaching Guide

Hands-on Grammar

Teaching Resources: Hands-on Grammar Activity Book, Ch. 20

1. If you wish to do this activity in class, be prepared with scissors, paper clips, and strips of colored paper for the students. Give each student a copy of Hands-on Grammar activity sheet.

2. Have students follow the directions to prepare the strips.

3. You may wish to expand this activity by having students use this method to combine sentences from Exercise 12, page 484, or Section Review Exercise 15, page 486.

Find It in Your Reading

If students have difficulty finding appropriate sentences in textbooks, encourage them to search in popular magazines and newspapers.

Find It in Your Writing

For variety, have students exchange papers from their portfolios and look for sentences to combine in their partners' writing.

Critical Viewing

Speculate Possible answer: The painting must show Philadelphia a long time ago because there are sailing ships and a windmill.

☑ **ONGOING ASSESSMENT: Assess Mastery**

Use the following resources to assess student mastery of sentence combining.

In the Textbook	Technology
Chapter Review, p. 514, Ex. 65	*On-Line Exercise Bank,* Section 20.1

🕐 **TIME SAVERS!**

Hands-on Grammar
Use the Hands-on Grammar activity sheet for Chapter 20 to facilitate this activity.

Section Review

Each of these exercises correlates to the instruction on sentence combining, pages 481–484. These exercises may be used for more practice, for reteaching, or for review of the key concepts presented. Answers for all chapter exercises are available in *Grammar Exercises Answers on Transparencies* in your Teaching Resources.

Answer Key

▶ **Exercise 13**

Sample answers:

1. King Charles II granted Pennsylvania to William Penn, *for the king* believed it would repay a debt to Penn's father.
2. *Penn and other Quakers* wanted a place of religious freedom.
3. He also *desired and supported* religious freedom for all people.
4. Penn gave people personal and property rights *and the right to self-government*.
5. Penn was the governor of Pennsylvania; he wrote a constitution and established a legislative body.

▶ **Exercise 14**

Sample answers:

1. The Amish are also Pennsylvania Dutch, *although* not all Pennsylvania Dutch are Amish.
2. The common background of the Pennsylvania Dutch is German, *while* some also have French backgrounds.
3. The Amish settled in the Pennsylvania region *when* William Penn made it a place of religious tolerance.
4. At home, the Amish speak a dialect of German, *even though* they speak English at school.
5. *Since* the Amish receive their education in a one-room school, *there* are children of many ages in one classroom.

▶ **Exercise 15**

Sample answers:

1. For fun in Lancaster, see the Amazing Maize Maze *made of corn.*
2. The maze, *located in a cornfield,* covers 10 acres.

GRAMMAR EXERCISES 13–18

▶ **Exercise 13 Combining Sentences Using Compound Subjects, Verbs, Objects, and Sentences** Combine each of the following pairs of sentences. Revise as necessary for clarity.

1. King Charles II granted Pennsylvania to William Penn. The king believed it would repay a debt to Penn's father.
2. Penn wanted a place of religious freedom. Other Quakers also wanted to worship freely.
3. Penn also wanted others to have religious freedom. He supported religious freedom for all people.
4. Penn gave people personal and property rights. He gave them the right to self-government.
5. Penn was the governor of Pennsylvania. He wrote a constitution and established a legislative body.

▶ **Exercise 14 Combining Sentences Using Subordinating Conjunctions** Combine each of the following pairs of sentences by making one of the sentences into a subordinate clause. Revise as necessary for clarity.

1. The Amish are also Pennsylvania Dutch. All Pennsylvania Dutch are not Amish.
2. The common background of the Pennsylvania Dutch is German. Some also have French backgrounds.
3. The Amish settled in the Pennsylvania region. William Penn made it a place of religious tolerance.
4. At home, the Amish speak a dialect of German. When they are at school, they speak English.
5. The Amish receive their education in a one-room school. There are children of many ages in one classroom.

▶ **Exercise 15 Combining Sentences Using Phrases** Combine the sentences by making one a phrase. Also, revise the sentences for clarity.

1. For fun in Lancaster, see the Amazing Maize Maze. The maze is made of corn.
2. The maze covers ten acres. The maze is located in a cornfield.
3. I'd like to visit this maze. It is located on a farm called Cherry-Crest Farm.
4. I would like to solve the maze. I want to figure it out without help.
5. I have never solved this type of maze. It is such a large size.

▶ **Exercise 16 Find It in Your Reading** Look through newspapers, magazines, and textbooks to identify at least five pairs of sentences that could be combined into single sentences. Combine each pair. Then, explain whether you think that each combined sentence is or is not more effective than the original pair.

▶ **Exercise 17 Find It in Your Writing** Choose a piece of writing from your portfolio. Identify at least five pairs of sentences that you can combine into single sentences. Then, combine these pairs using at least three different sentence-combining methods.

▶ **Exercise 18 Writing Application** Write an essay about the history of your hometown. After completing the rough draft, review it and mark places where you can combine ideas. Then, revise it, combining at least five pairs of sentences into single sentences. Provide an explanation of why you combined each.

---

3. I'd like to visit this maze *on Cherry-Crest farm.*
4. I would like to solve the maze *without help.*
5. I have never solved *a maze of such a large size.*

▶ **Exercise 16**

Find It in Your Reading
Challenge students to find examples of the same kinds of combined sentences in their assigned reading.

▶ **Exercise 17**

Find It in Your Writing
Have students list the types of combined sentences they find in their portfolios. Do they see a pattern?

▶ **Exercise 18**

Writing Application
Have partners exchange their drafts and check that sentences have been correctly combined.

Section 20.3 *Varying Sentences*

Varying Sentence Length

If you use too many short sentences, your writing will sound choppy. On the other hand, too many long sentences will make your writing dull. Vary your sentence length to create a rhythm and to emphasize key ideas. For example, insert short, direct sentences to interrupt a string of long sentences. Doing so is an excellent way to drive home a main point.

EXAMPLE: In 1787, Pennsylvania became the second state to ratify the Constitution, but important political events took place there before this date. For example, the First and Second Continental Congresses met in Philadelphia, and Congress adopted the Declaration of Independence there. *Pennsylvania played a vital role in the birth of the nation.*

▶ **Exercise 19** **Revising to Improve Variety of Sentence Length** Revise the following passage to establish a greater variety of sentence lengths. Where appropriate, divide long sentences into two or more shorter ones, or rework long sentences to state the ideas more simply and directly.

The women of Pennsylvania contributed greatly to both the American Revolution and the Civil War, providing many different types of support to the soldiers fighting the battles. Female patriots from Pennsylvania include Catherine Smith, who manufactured musket barrels; battle heroine Molly Pitcher; and Sara Franklin Bache and Ester De Berdt Reed, who organized 2,200 women to help soldiers.

Pennsylvanian women also contributed to the abolitionist movement and fought for women's rights. They worked for many reforms, including women's rights, during the 1700's and 1800's; although rights for women changed little during this time, their efforts laid the groundwork for future reforms. Lucretia Mott was one of four women to take part in the formation of the American Anti-Slavery Society in Philadelphia in 1833, and she later became the president of the Female Anti-Slavery Society. Jane Grey Swisshelm, abolitionist and advocate of women's rights, launched an abolitionist paper, *The Saturday Visit[o]r*, which featured arguments against slavery and information on women's rights. Swisshelm's newspapers, essays, and lectures influenced the state legislature to grant married women the right to own property, and in 1848, they also helped to change people's views on women's role in society.

Theme: The History of Pennsylvania

In this section, you will earn about varying your sentences. The examples and exercises are about the history of Pennsylvania.

Cross-Curricular Connection: Social Studies

▶ **More Practice**

Language Lab CD-ROM
• Varying Sentence Structure lesson
On-line Exercise Bank
• Section 20.3
Grammar Exercise Workbook
• pp. 65–70

PREPARE and ENGAGE

Interest GRABBER Ask students to review their portfolios for stories to share with the class. Discuss students' sentence structure. Do students notice a pattern? As the action intensified, did the sentences sound different in some way? How?

Activate Prior Knowledge

Have students scan recent work, looking for passages with varied sentence lengths and structures. Ask volunteers to read such passages aloud. Point out that the length, structure, and word order of sentences should vary to reflect the importance of ideas.

TEACH

Step-by-Step Teaching Guide

Vary Sentence Length

1. Have students read the example to see how a series of long sentences can be broken up by a short sentence to tremendous effect.

2. Note that the last sentence, "Pennsylvania played a vital role in the birth of the nation," stands out because it is so much shorter and simpler than those before it.

Answer Key

▶ **Exercise 19**

Answers will vary; samples are given.

The women of Pennsylvania provided support to the soldiers of both the American Revolution and the Civil War. Catherine Smith manufactured musket barrels. Molly
continued

Answer Key continued

▶ **Exercise 19**

Pitcher fought heroically. Sara Franklin Bache and Ester De Berdt Reed organized 2,200 women to help soldiers.

Pennsylvanian women also fought for abolition and for women's rights. Their work for women's rights during the 1700's and 1800's caused little change during that time. Even so, their efforts laid the groundwork for future reforms. In 1833, Lucretia Mott was one of four women to take part in the formation of the American Anti-Slavery Society in Philadelphia. She later became the president of the Female Anti-Slavery Society. Jane Grey Swisshelm, abolitionist and advocate of women's rights, launched an abolitionist paper, *The Sunday Visit[o]r*. It featured arguments against slavery and information on women's rights. Swisshelm's newspapers, essays, and lectures influenced the state legislature to grant married women the right to own property. In 1848, they also helped to change people's views on women's role in society.

⏱ TIME SAVERS!

🖼 **Answers on Transparencies** Use the *Grammar Exercises Answers on Transparencies* for Chapter 20 to facilitate correction by students.

💻 **On-Line Exercise Bank** Have students complete the exercises on computer. The Auto Check feature will grade their work for you!

Answer Key

Answers will vary; samples are given.

(1) Playing an important role in the Union war effort, Pennsylvania shielded northeastern states during the Civil War when southern forces attempted to move north through the Shenandoah Valley. The valley was a natural highway leading from Virginia to the North. (2) Pennsylvania aided the economic strength of the North with its industrial enterprises, such as the railroads. Pennsylvania also contributed its natural resources, such as steel and iron, which were vital to the war effort. (3) The state governor during the Civil War, Andrew Curtin, was very active in supporting the Union. He created the Pennsylvania Reserve Corps, which consisted of fifteen regiments enlisted for three years of service. (4) After the first Battle of Bull Run, these men joined the Army of the Potomac. Thousands of other Pennsylvanians joined them. In all, 350,000 Pennsylvanians served in the Union Army, including 8,600 African American volunteers. (5) Camp Curtin was one of the main troop concentration centers during the war. The state turned out many important officers, including George B. McClellan.

Critical Viewing

Analyze Possible answer: Battles involved many troops in close combat; artillery was in use; weapons produced heavy smoke.

20.3

▶ **Exercise 20** **Revising to Vary Sentence Lengths** Revise the following paragraph. Break long sentences into two or more sentences or restate the ideas in a simpler way.

(1) During the Civil War, Pennsylvania played an important role in the Union war effort, shielding northeastern states when southern forces attempted to move north through the Shenandoah Valley, a natural highway leading from Virginia to the North. (2) Pennsylvania aided the economic strength of the North with its industrial enterprises, such as the railroads, and with its natural resources, such as steel and iron, which were vital to the war effort. (3) The state governor during the Civil War, Andrew Curtin, was very active in supporting the Union and created the Pennsylvania Reserve Corps, which consisted of fifteen regiments enlisted for three years of service. (4) After the first Battle of Bull Run, these men joined the Army of the Potomac, and thousands of other Pennsylvanians joined them; in all, 350,000 Pennsylvanians served in the Union army, including 8,600 African American volunteers. (5) Camp Curtin was one of the main troop concentration centers during the war, and the state turned out many important officers, including George B. McClellan.

▼ **Critical Viewing**
What does this painting reveal about the nature of combat during the Civil War? **[Analyze]**

Varying Sentence Beginnings

Another way to create sentence variety is to begin your sentences with different parts of speech.

STARTING SENTENCES WITH DIFFERENT PARTS OF SPEECH	
Start with a noun	The natural resources of Pennsylvania were of great use during World War I.
Start with an adverb	Fortunately, Pennsylvania's many natural resources were available to the war effort during World War I.
Start with a participle	Having many important natural resources, Pennsylvania was able to contribute greatly to the war effort.
Start with a prepositional phrase	During World War I, Pennsylvania's natural resources were of great use.

▶ **Exercise 21** Revising to Vary Sentence Beginnings Revise the following sentences so that they begin with the part of speech indicated in parentheses.

1. In 1861, the first school for nurses opened in Pennsylvania. (noun)
2. The state then played an important role in the suffrage movement. (prepositional phrase)
3. Women in Philadelphia boldly organized the Women's Suffrage Association in 1868. (adverb)
4. The General Assembly of Pennsylvania, having seen the need for change, approved the women's suffrage amendment in 1913 and again in 1915. (participial phrase)
5. Both times, unfortunately, the state's male voters rejected the amendment. (adverb)
6. The United States approved the Nineteenth Amendment to the Constitution on June 4, 1919. (prepositional phrase)
7. Pennsylvania, ratifying it just days later, became the seventh state to accept the amendment. (participial phrase)
8. By August 1920, women in Pennsylvania who wanted to vote were protected by the law. (noun)
9. Mary Cassatt, born in Allegheny City, was the only woman whose work was exhibited in a show of the ten greatest American painters. (participial phrase)
10. She received her training at the Pennsylvania Academy of Fine Arts and was awarded a gold Medal of Honor in 1914. (prepositional phrase)

▶ **More Practice**

Language Lab CD-ROM
• Varying Sentence Structure lesson

On-line Exercise Bank
• Section 20.3

Grammar Exercise Workbook
• pp. 65–70

Varying Sentences • **489**

✓ ONGOING ASSESSMENT: Monitor and Reinforce

If students have difficulty with Exercise 20, 21, or 22, refer them to the following for additional practice.

In the Textbook	Print Resources	Technology
Section Review, Ex. 23–25, p. 491	Grammar Exercise Workbook, pp. 65–70	On-Line Exercise Bank, Section 20.3

Use Inverted Word Order

1. Let students know that the word order of subject, verb, and object is so strongly fixed in English that an inverted sentence will usually seem emphatic. Warn students that using inverted order too frequently can seem awkward.

2. Have students practice inverting sentences on their own by rewriting selected sentences from their compositions.

Customize for
Logical/Mathematical Learners

Remind students that sentences are like equations: they must be balanced, they can express multiple functions, and they can be written in a number of ways. Write on the board: $A+B=C$ and $A=C-B$. Point out that these equations simply express the same thing differently.

Answer Key

▶ **Exercise 22**

Answers will vary; samples are given.

1. At one time, Pennsylvania's largest industry was the manufacturing of steel and iron products.
2. From these resources grew the fortunes of men such as . . .
3. Furnished by the steel industry were the rails for the nation's vast rail network . . .
4. A Scotch immigrant, Andrew Carnegie started his career . . .
5. Before he entered railroad management, he also handled messages . . .
6. In 1873 new steel mills began to be built by Carnegie.
7. Great was his success, making him a very rich man.
8. With a pledge to pay the world back through distributing his wealth, Andrew Carnegie . . .
9. To U.S. Steel he sold Carnegie Steel Company in 1901.
10. The rest of his life was spent managing . . .

Critical Viewing

Describe Encourage students to experiment with a variety of sentence lengths, structures, and beginnings.

490

20.3

Using Inverted Word Order

You can also vary sentences by reversing the traditional subject-verb order.

EXAMPLE:

SUBJECT–LINKING VERB–COMPLEMENT: The train is here.
COMPLEMENT–LINKING VERB–SUBJECT: Here is the train.
SUBJECT–VERB–PREPOSITIONAL PHRASE: The ship sailed on the Delaware River.

PREPOSITIONAL PHRASE–VERB–SUBJECT: On the Delaware River sailed the ship.

▶ **Exercise 22** Varying Sentences Using Inverted Word Order Revise the following sentences by inverting them or reversing the traditional order of the words.

1. The manufacturing of steel and iron products was at one time Pennsylvania's largest industry.
2. The fortunes of men such as Andrew Carnegie, Charles M. Schwab, and Eugene Grace were made from these resources.
3. The steel industry furnished the rails for the nation's vast rail network, the steel for rapidly expanding cities, and the arms for national defense.
4. Andrew Carnegie was a Scotch immigrant who started his career as a telegrapher for the Pennsylvania Railroad.
5. He also handled messages for the army during the Civil War before he entered railroad management.
6. Carnegie began to build new steel mills in 1873.
7. His success was great, making him a very rich man.
8. Andrew Carnegie balanced his good fortune with a pledge to pay the world back by distributing his wealth.
9. He sold Carnegie Steel Company to U.S. Steel in 1901.
10. He spent the rest of his life managing his enormous charitable foundation.

490 • Effective Sentences

More Practice

Language Lab CD-ROM
• Varying Sentence Structure lesson
On-line Exercise Bank
• Section 20.3
Grammar Exercise Workbook
• pp. 65–70

▼ **Critical Viewing**
Write a series of sentences describing this picture of steel being manufactured. Vary the length and structure of the sentences. [Describe]

☑ **ONGOING ASSESSMENT: Assess Mastery**

Use the following resources to assess student mastery of sentence variety.

In the Textbook	Technology
Chapter Review, p. 514, Ex. 65	*On-Line Exercise Bank,* Section 20.3

Section Review

GRAMMAR EXERCISES 23–28

> **Exercise 23** **Revising Sentence Length** Revise the paragraph by breaking long sentences into shorter sentences or by making long sentences clearer.

During the 1800's, Pennsylvania was a leader in many science-related fields, including practical inventions, scientific applications in industry and daily life, and precision instruments for astronomy. In medicine, Philadelphia was one of the leading centers for medical advancement in the world, with Hahnemann Medical College, Jefferson Medical College, and the University of Pennsylvania all within its boundaries. Medical colleges were established at the University of Pittsburgh in 1885 and at Temple University in 1901, and these institutions made noteworthy contributions to medicine. Pennsylvanians who made contributions to science included the four Rogers brothers of Philadelphia: James and Robert were noted chemists, William was the state geologist of Virginia and later the president of the Massachusetts Institute of Technology, and Henry directed the first geological survey of Pennsylvania. John A. Roebling, who spent most of his active life in Pennsylvania, led the way in the development of steel-wire rope and bridges, and his son continued his engineering works.

> **Exercise 24** **Revising Sentence Beginnings** Revise the sentences as indicated in the directions in parentheses.

1. Pennsylvania pioneered the development of railroads in the nineteenth century. (prepositional phrase)
2. The Pennsylvania Railroad, chartered in 1846, reached Pittsburgh in 1852. (participial phrase)
3. After 1865, Pennsylvania extended its lines to several major cities. (noun)

4. The Reading and Lehigh Valley systems were to join in the expansion soon. (adverb)
5. Certain trains only transported ore to steel mills. (adverb)

> **Exercise 25** **Inverting Sentences to Vary Beginnings** Revise these sentences, reversing the traditional word order. Also, revise the sentences for clarity.

1. H. J. Heinz, Inc., known as the "good provider," was incorporated in 1905.
2. Food processing at the time had become an important industry.
3. Heinz had a model factory, providing workers a clean, pleasant workplace.
4. Having a job in his factory also provided the opportunity for workers to advance.
5. Heinz was also an activist for consumer rights.

> **Exercise 26** **Find It in Your Reading** Find a news article that demonstrates sentence variety. Make a photocopy. Then, use different-colored highlighters to indicate long and short sentences and varied sentence openers.

> **Exercise 27** **Find It in Your Writing** Rework a piece of writing from your portfolio to improve the variety of your sentences. Where possible, use shorter sentences to emphasize key points.

> **Exercise 28** **Writing Application** Write an article about a recent local or national event. As you write, focus on varying sentence length, structure, and openers. Try to end each paragraph with a short sentence that reinforces the main point.

Section Review • 491

ASSESS

Section Review

Each of these exercises correlates to the instruction on varying sentences, pages 487–490. These exercises may be used for more practice, for reteaching, or for review of the key concepts presented. Answers for all chapter exercises are available in *Grammar Exercises Answers on Transparencies* in your Teaching Resources.

Answer Key

> **Exercise 23**

Sample answer:

During the 1800's, Pennsylvania was a leader in many science-related fields. *These included* practical inventions, scientific applications in industry and daily life, and precision instruments for astronomy. Philadelphia was one of the leading centers for medical advancement in the world. Hahnemann Medical College, Jefferson Medical College, and the University of Pennsylvania *were* all within its boundaries. Medical colleges were established at the University of Pittsburgh in 1885 and at Temple University in 1901. *These* institutions made noteworthy contributions to medicine. Pennsylvanians who made contributions to science included the four Rogers brothers of Philadelphia. *James and Robert Rogers* were noted chemists, William *Rogers* was the state geologist of Virginia and later president of the Massachusetts Institute of Technology, and Henry *Rogers* directed the first geological survey of Pennsylvania. John A. Roebling, who spent most of his active life in Pennsylvania, led the way in the development of steel-wire rope and bridges. *His* son continued his engineering works.

> **Exercise 24**

1. *In the nineteenth century,* Pennsylvania pioneered the development of railroads.
2. *Chartered in 1846,* the Pennsylvania Railroad reached Pittsburgh in 1852.
3. *Pennsylvania* extended its lines to several major cities *after 1865.*
4. *Soon,* the Reading and Lehigh Valley systems were to join in the expansion.
5. *Only* certain trains transported ore to steel mills.

continued

491

Answer Key continued

> **Exercise 25**

1. Incorporated in 1905 was H.J. Heinz, Inc., known as the "good provider."
2. At the time, an important industry had become food processing.
3. Providing workers a clean, pleasant workplace was a model factory operated by Heinz.
4. The opportunity for workers to advance was provided as part of a job in his factory.
5. An activist for consumer rights was a role that was important to Heinz.

> **Exercise 26**

Find It in Your Reading
Students might compile a chart recording the frequency of long sentences, short sentences, and various sentence openers.

> **Exercise 27**

Find It in Your Writing
You might have partners mark one another's writing to get another point of view on where to revise.

> **Exercise 28**

Writing Application
Suggest that students post their articles on-line or explore other means of publishing their work.

Interest GRABBER Write the following fragments on the board:

If I had a million dollars

When I was little

By the time the airplanes land

Have students finish these sentence starters. Discuss what grammatical elements they had to add to make complete sentences.

Activate Prior Knowledge

Ask whether students have answered test questions with fragments (e.g., *because hot air rises, because Southern states seceded from the Union*). Point out that though each contains a subject and a verb, these fragments omit part of the complete idea. Point out that sentences <u>can</u> begin with "because" as long as this word is used as a subordinating conjunction connecting its clause to an independent clause (e.g., *Because hot air rises,* a room will be warmer nearer its ceiling).

TEACH

Step-by-Step Teaching Guide

Recognizing Fragments

1. Help students understand that in order for a word group to be a sentence, it must include at least one independent clause. Remind students that an independent clause has a subject and a verb.

2. Tell students that they can test for sentence completion by asking certain questions: Is there a verb? Is there a subject? Can it stand by itself? If the answer is no to any of these questions, the word group is a fragment.

3. Caution students against certain pitfalls in distinguishing sentences from fragments: The subject of a sentence may be understood (*Wait!*); verbals may be mistaken for verbs.

 Section 20.4

Avoiding Fragments and Run-ons

When you speak to your friends, you don't have to follow rules. You can express incomplete thoughts, or let one thought flow right into another. When you write sentences, on the other hand, you have to follow a set of rules. Sentence errors occur when these rules aren't followed. Two of the most common types of sentence errors are fragments and run-ons.

Recognizing Fragments

A fragment is a group of words with end punctuation that either does not have a subject or a verb or does not express a complete thought. While fragments are considered acceptable in written dialogue and are sometimes used for effect in today's fiction, they are generally not considered acceptable in formal compositions.

▶ **KEY CONCEPT** When you write, avoid fragments by making sure that each of your sentences has a subject and a verb and expresses a complete thought. ■

Most fragments are phrases, subordinate clauses, or words in a series. The following are strategies for correcting each of these types of fragments.

Correcting Phrase Fragments Many phrase fragments can be corrected simply by linking them to words that come before or after them. For example, a noun and its modifiers (a noun phrase) may be meant as an appositive but become detached from the sentence in which it belongs. Similarly, other phrases may be detached from the words they should modify.

FRAGMENT:	*A chair built by my father.*
ADDED TO NEARBY SENTENCE:	Our neighbor asked about a piece of furniture, *a chair built by my father.*
FRAGMENT:	*On top of my dresser.*
ADDED TO NEARBY SENTENCE:	I bought a vase that I keep *on top of my dresser.*

A fragment with a pronoun and a participial phrase can often be added to a nearby sentence if you drop the pronoun.

FRAGMENT:	*One stuffed with down.*
ADDED TO NEARBY SENTENCE:	I bought a pillow *stuffed with down*

492 • Effective Sentences

⏱ TIME AND RESOURCE MANAGER

Resources
Print: *Grammar Exercise Workbook,* pp. 71–74; *Grammar Exercises on Transparencies,* Ch. 20
Technology: *Language Lab* CD-ROM, Sentence Errors; *On-Line Exercise Bank,* Section 20.4

In-Depth Coverage	Accelerated Pace
• Work through all key concepts, pp. 492–497. • Assign and review Exercises 29–33.	• Assign pp. 492–497 for independent student review. • Assign Section Review Exercises 34–36.

Theme: Hobbies and Crafts

In this section, you will learn how to recognize and correct fragments and run-ons. Most of the examples and exercises are about hobbies and crafts.

Cross-Curricular Connection: Art

Step-by-Step Teaching Guide

Correcting Phrase Fragments

1. Begin by explaining that there are two common ways to correct fragments: by attaching the fragment to a nearby sentence or by adding words that turn the fragment into a sentence. Point out that phrases cannot stand alone; prepositional, verbal, and appositive phrases often appear as fragments. These phrases can usually be connected logically to a nearby sentence. If the phrase cannot logically be attached to another sentence, it must be turned into a sentence by adding a subject, a verb, or both.

2. Review the examples on pages 492 and 493, calling attention to reasons why each fragment is not a sentence. The first fragment on page 492, for example, is merely a noun phrase; it can easily be turned into an appositive, or it would need a helping verb to stand alone as a sentence. (A chair was built by my father.) Have students come up with alternate corrections for each example on the pages.

In some situations, you will need to add missing sentence parts to make a phrase fragment into a complete sentence.

A noun fragment will need a verb if the fragment is used as a subject. A noun fragment will need both a subject and a verb if it is used as a complement, an object of a preposition, or an appositive.

FRAGMENT: *The embroidered tapestry.*

COMPLETED
SENTENCES: *The embroidered tapestry* hung on the wall.
We stopped to admire *the embroidered tapestry.* There are unicorns and goats on *the embroidered tapestry.* The museum paid a hefty sum for a family heirloom, *the embroidered tapestry.*

If a noun fragment contains a noun modified by a participial phrase, you may be able to complete the sentence by adding a helping verb to change the participle into a verb.

FRAGMENT: *The weaver making a rug.*

COMPLETED
SENTENCE: *The weaver* is *making a rug.*

▲ **Critical Viewing**
What similarities can you identify between making furniture and writing complete sentences? **[Compare]**

⚙ **Grammar
and Style Tip**

Two main clauses cannot be linked with a comma unless they are joined by a coordinating conjunction such as *and, but, or, nor, for, so,* or *yet.*

Critical Viewing

Compare Possible answer: A sentence, like a piece of furniture, must have all its parts fit closely together.

 STANDARDIZED TEST PREPARATION WORKSHOP

Grammar and Usage Many standardized tests require students to revise errors in compositions. Write the following on the board and ask students to identify the correct answer.

   Benjamin Franklin's Albany Plan, <u>which anticipated the 1787 U.S. Constitution. It provided</u> for local independence within a framework of colonial union. It was too far in advance of public thinking to obtain ratification, however.

How is the underlined portion correctly written?

A Correct as is

B anticipating the 1787 U.S. Constitution. It provided

C which anticipated the 1787 U.S. Constitution, provided

D which anticipated the 1787 U.S. Constitution it provided

The correct answer is **C.** The first part of this passage is a sentence fragment. It can be corrected by combining it with the sentence that follows it by forming a nonessential adjective clause. Note that the subject (*it*) is eliminated.

Correcting Clause and Series Fragments

1. Remind students that subordinate clause fragments must be either attached to a nearby sentence or reworded—usually by eliminating the subordinating conjunction—so that they can stand alone.

2. Suggest that students may find it easiest to eliminate the opening word or words (subordinating conjunction, transitional expression) that make these clauses subordinate.

3. Suggest that while they correct series fragments, students will need to add words such as subjects and verbs or else combine a series fragment with another sentence.

Customize for
ESL Students

Explain to students that though some languages allow writers to omit an explicit subject in sentences or clauses, writers in English must include a subject for all sentences except imperatives, in which the subject *you* may be understood. Model for students how omission of a subject results in a sentence fragment: *Have a large collection of baseball cards. Seems young for his age.* Ask for corrections.

Answer Key

Exercise 29

Sample answers:

1. By displaying and selling their work at crafts fairs, artisans give . . .

2. There are many different types of crafts, including ceramics . . .

3. One of my favorite crafts fairs is held every summer in the . . .

4. There are so many types of works from which you can choose—glassware, rugs, . . .

5. Displaying paintings based on nursery rhymes, one of the artists had . . .

20.4

Correcting Clause Fragments Subordinate clauses cannot stand alone as sentences. Either connect them to nearby independent clauses or add the missing sentence parts.

FRAGMENT: *Because we wanted to avoid crowds.*

COMPLETED SENTENCE: *Because we wanted to avoid crowds, we arrived at the crafts fair early.*

FRAGMENT: *Whatever the artists produce.*

COMPLETED SENTENCE: *People seem to like whatever the artists produce.*

Correcting Series Fragments Always check to see that a series of words has both a subject and a verb.

FRAGMENT: *Tulips bursting out of the ground, daffodils beginning to fade, and violets pushing through the grass.*

COMPLETED SENTENCE: *Tulips bursting out of the ground, daffodils beginning to fade, and violets pushing through the grass* were all captured in the painting.

▶ **Exercise 29** **Identifying and Correcting Fragments**
Rewrite the following groups of words to eliminate fragments.

EXAMPLE: All types of artists are drawn to our town. To attend the crafts fair held every summer.

ANSWER: All types of artists are drawn to our town to attend the crafts fair held every summer.

1. By displaying and selling their work at crafts fairs. Artisans give people across the country a chance to admire and purchase their works.
2. There are many different types of crafts. Ceramics, weaving, knitting, and painting.
3. One of my favorite crafts fairs is held every summer. In the Berkshire Mountains in Massachusetts.
4. Glassware, rugs, tapestries, vases, colorful prints. There are so many types of works from which you can choose.
5. Displaying paintings based on nursery rhymes. One of the artists had the perfect gift for my youngest brother.

☑ ONGOING ASSESSMENT: Monitor and Reinforce

If students have difficulty with Exercise 29 or 30, refer them to the following for additional practice.

In the Textbook	Print Resources	Technology
Section Review, Exercise 34, p. 499	*Grammar Exercise Workbook,* pp. 71–72	*On-Line Exercise Bank,* Section 20.4

Exercise 30 **Proofreading to Correct Fragments** Revise this paragraph, eliminating all fragments.

　　Crafts are decorative or functional objects. Often made by hand. Crafts can come in many forms. For use and enjoyment. Papier-mâché, the craft of fashioning objects from any kind of absorbent paper soaked in water and glue. Bookbinding requires dexterity. It is not difficult to learn. Weaving a method of creating fabric by interlacing two sets of yarn threads. Weaving, plaiting, and coiling techniques to make baskets, mats, and rugs. Wall hangings, bags, and containers made from macramé or ornamental knotting. In embroidery, a needle and thread are used to create designs on fabric. Inserting thin strips of wool through a heavy base fabric with a hand hook. Rug hooking requires patience. In quilting, three layers of fabric are stitched or tied together. A decorative top layer, filler, and a liner.

More Practice

Language Lab
CD-ROM
• Fragments and Run-on Sentences lesson
On-line
Exercise Bank
• Section 20.4
Grammar Exercise
Workbook
• pp. 71–74

◄ **Critical Viewing**
Come up with a fragment that might be used in describing this weaver at work. Explain how you could correct this fragment. **[Connect]**

Answer Key

► **Exercise 30**

1. Crafts are decorative or functional objects, <u>often</u> made by hand.
2. Crafts <u>for use and enjoyment</u> can come in many forms.
3. Papier-mâché <u>is</u> the craft of fashioning objects from any kind of absorbent paper soaked in water and glue.
4. Correct
5. Weaving <u>is</u> a method of creating fabric by interlacing two sets of yarn threads.
6. Weaving, plaiting, and coiling techniques <u>are used</u> to make baskets, mats, and rugs.
7. Wall hangings, bags, and containers <u>can be</u> made from macramé or ornamental knotting.
8. correct
9. Rug hooking, <u>inserting</u> thin strips of wool through a heavy base fabric with a hand <u>hook</u>, requires patience.
10. In quilting, three layers of fabric, <u>a decorative top layer, filler, and a liner</u>, are stitched or tied together.

Critical Viewing

Connect Possible answer: Passing the shuttle back and forth. Correction: Add a subject and verb: The weaver works intently, passing the shuttle back and forth.

Step-by-Step Teaching Guide

Recognizing Run-ons

1. Help students to understand the difference between a fused sentence and a comma splice: A fused sentence is missing punctuation, whereas a comma splice contains punctuation (a comma) used incorrectly. Again, emphasize the importance of reading work aloud to catch sentence errors. Read the example sentences aloud so students can hear where and how run-on sentences should be corrected.

2. Review the seven coordinating conjunctions (*and, but, or, nor, for, so, yet*), and remind students that each of these must be preceded by a comma when joining independent clauses. Point out that certain situations (as illustrated in the chart) will require different methods of correcting run-ons. Suggest that the fourth method, rewriting, may be the most effective option when others don't seem obvious.

Language Highlight

In addition to his skills as an amateur architect, engineer, and inventor, Virginia lawyer Thomas Jefferson was well known for inventing new words, the most famous of which is *belittle* ("reduce in importance, deprecate, disparage"). This word was, in fact, belittled in Great Britain as a corruption of English vocabulary but has since become standard.

Recognizing Run-ons

A *run-on sentence* is two or more complete sentences incorrectly punctuated as if they were one.

KEY CONCEPT Use punctuation, conjunctions, or other methods to join or separate the parts of a run-on sentence. ■

The following chart shows four different ways of correcting run-on sentences.

FOUR WAYS TO CORRECT RUN-ONS	
With End Marks and Capitals	
Run-on	**Sentence**
Elizabeth turned at the sudden noise a bird had crashed into the picture window.	Elizabeth turned at the sudden noise. A bird had crashed into the picture window.
With Commas and Conjunctions	
Run-on	**Sentence**
I baked the cake this morning, I have not frosted it yet.	I baked the cake this morning, but I have not frosted it yet.
With Semicolons	
Run-on	**Sentence**
The novice potter kept trying to make a vase, however he failed each time.	The novice potter kept trying to make a vase; however, he failed each time.
By Rewriting	
Run-on	**Sentence**
My aunt stayed with us for a week, my cousins came too.	My aunt and cousins stayed with us for a week. (Simple sentence with compound subject) When my aunt stayed with us for a week, my cousins came too. (Complex sentence beginning with subordinate clause)

More Practice

Language Lab
CD-ROM
• Fragments and Run-on Sentences lesson
On-line
Exercise Bank
• Section 20.4
Grammar Exercise
Workbook
• pp. 73–74

496 • Effective Sentences

✓ ONGOING ASSESSMENT: Monitor and Reinforce

If students have difficulty with Exercise 31, 32, or 33, refer them to the following for additional practice.

In the Textbook	Print Resources	Technology
Section Review, Ex. 35–36, p. 499	*Grammar Exercise Workbook*, pp. 73–74	*On-Line Exercise Bank*, Section 20.4

Fused Sentences and Comma Splices When you edit your work, be on the lookout for two specific types of run-ons: fused sentences and comma splices. A *fused sentence* consists of two or more sentences not separated or joined by any punctuation. A *comma splice* is two or more sentences separated by a comma instead of by a comma and a conjunction.

FUSED SENTENCE: *The quiltmaker put on a demonstration the crowds came to see her at work.*

COMMA SPLICE: *The potter displayed his vases, the painter showed her portraits.*

▶ **Exercise 31** Identifying and Correcting Run-on Sentences
If a sentence is correct as written, write *correct*. If it is a run-on, rewrite it.

1. My grandmother taught me about quilting I really enjoy this craft.
2. When I was little it was difficult but now it is easier.
3. On Saturdays, I visit her, and we spend time working together.
4. Sometimes we follow a traditional pattern and sometimes we make scenes that tell a story.
5. Last year, my sister started learning to quilt, she enjoys it almost as much as I do.
6. We all sit together for a long time, we have many interesting conversations.
7. My grandmother tells us about her life as a little girl, we are often surprised that it is, in some ways, very similar to our lives.
8. We are making a quilt that shows the generations of our family it has figures representing my grandmother, my mother, and my sister and me as well as our birthdays embroidered on the figures.
9. When it is finished, it will be a work of art we will hang it on the wall in my grandmother's house.
10. I love the time I spend with my grandmother, I love the beautiful quilts we make.

▼ **Critical Viewing**
Why would a craft like quiltmaking be passed on from generation to generation? **[Draw Conclusions]**

Avoiding Fragments and Run-ons • **497**

▶ **Exercise 32**

Both knitted and crocheted fabrics are made from a single strand of thread. <u>The</u> fabric is composed of loops chained together to form a continuous textile. <u>In knitting</u>, the loops of thread are usually formed by means of a pair of rods called needles. Thread of contrasting colors may be introduced to form patterns; the more colors introduced, the more intricate the pattern.

Correct. Each row of stitches is called a course, <u>and</u> each chain of loops hanging vertically from the needles is called a wale.

Knitting developed as a folk craft with traditional regional <u>designs. Ireland</u>, Scandinavia, and the Shetland Islands were distinguished by different patterns.

Knitting and crocheting are <u>similar</u>; however, crocheting is a method of working interlocking loops of thread into a chain by means of a slender rod hooked at one end. A single chain of loops is formed <u>by</u> catching the yarn and drawing it through the previous loop. *Correct.* Little is known about the early history of crocheting. <u>Some</u> ancient cords may have been made by finger crocheting.

▶ **Exercise 33**

Answers will vary. Possible answer:

1. The quilt in progress is a traditional pattern quilt; the quilt on the wall tells a story.
2. You can tell they enjoy quilting because they are smiling.
3. The girl is speaking, but she is looking at her work.
4. The grandmother is pausing. She is listening to the girl speak.
5. The quilt is colorful; it uses many patches of fabric.

20.4

▶ **Exercise 32** **Revising a Passage to Eliminate Run-on Sentences** Copy the following passage on a separate sheet of paper. Revise to eliminate run-on sentences. Use each of the four methods for correcting run-ons at least once.

Both knitted and crocheted fabrics are made from a single strand of thread the fabric is composed of loops chained together to form a continuous textile. Knitting the loops of thread are usually formed by means of a pair of rods called needles. Thread of contrasting colors may be introduced to form patterns the more colors introduced, the more intricate the pattern.

In weft knitting, a hand-knitting process that can also be done by machine, the work progresses back and forth. Each row of stitches is called a course each chain of loops hanging vertically from the needles is called a wale.

Knitting developed as a folk craft with traditional regional designs Ireland, Scandinavia, and the Shetland Islands were distinguished by different patterns.

Knitting and crocheting are similar, however, crocheting is a method of working interlocking loops of thread into a chain by means of a slender rod hooked at one end. A single chain of loops is formed, catching the yarn and drawing it through the previous loop. The chain is made to the planned width of the finished piece, the yarn is turned at the end of the chain, and a second chain is crocheted, each new stitch being looped through a stitch in the previous row. Little is known about the early history of crocheting some ancient cords may have been made by finger crocheting.

▶ **Exercise 33** **Avoiding Run-on Sentences in Writing** Write a description of the picture on the previous page. In your description, include each of the following pairs of features in a single sentence. Be sure you write the sentence without creating a run-on sentence.

EXAMPLE: girl is speaking: grandmother is listening.
ANSWER: The girl is speaking, and the grandmother is listening.

1. quilt in progress is traditional pattern: quilt on wall tells a story
2. they enjoy quilting: they are smiling
3. girl is speaking: girl is looking at her work
4. grandmother is pausing: she is listening to the girl speak
5. quilt is colorful: quilt uses many patches of fabric

✓ **ONGOING ASSESSMENT: Assess Mastery**

Use the following resources to assess student mastery of avoiding fragments and run-ons.

In the Textbook	Technology
Chapter Review, Exercise 66, p. 514	*On-Line Exercise Bank,* Section 20.4

Section Review

GRAMMAR EXERCISES 34–39

> **Exercise 34** **Proofreading to Eliminate Fragments** Revise this paragraph, eliminating all fragments.

Crafts are as old as human history. Most crafts practiced today can be traced back many hundreds of years. Basketry, weaving, and pottery among the earliest basic crafts. Originally fulfilling useful purposes. Crafts are now primarily decorative. Craftwork forming the basis of city economies in Europe up to the Industrial Revolution in the 1800's. Once items could be mass-produced. Artisans were no longer needed.

> **Exercise 35** **Proofreading to Eliminate Run-ons** Revise the following paragraph, correcting all run-ons.

The top layer of a quilt bears a design, generally produced in one of three ways, the fabric may be left plain, so that the quilting stitches form the design. More commonly, the top is made from a process called appliqué pieces are cut from various cloths and stitched onto a background fabric, making pictures and patterns. Tops of quilts may also be pieced or patched in a process known as patchwork units of cloth are sewn together to form geometric patterns. In the final stage of assembly the quilt's three layers are stretched on a frame then, are sewn together. With short running stitches called quilting stitches. This final step is more than mechanical however the design of the top is artfully thrown into relief, allowing the play of light and shadow on the surface.

> **Exercise 36** **Proofreading to Correct Fragments and Run-ons** Revise this passage, eliminating fragments and run-ons.

Gardens come in many different types of designs, styles, and techniques. Including, among others, rock gardens, herb gardens, wildflower gardens, water gardens, and Japanese gardens. A rock garden duplicating the natural environmental conditions in which rock and mountain plants thrive. It is somewhat easier to cultivate than an ordinary garden, the plants are hardier and more resistant to drought and cold and require far less fertilizer than plants that succeed in other types of gardens. Slightly sloping ground is the best location. That is well drained. The most suitable plants for rock gardens are flowering, hardy perennials, in addition, rock gardens are often planted with dwarf trees and shrubs.

> **Exercise 37** **Find It in Your Reading** Choose a passage from a magazine article. Type out the passage, introducing at least two fragments and two run-ons. Exchange papers with a classmate, and correct the errors that your partner has introduced.

> **Exercise 38** **Find It in Your Writing** Choose a piece of writing from your portfolio to review for fragments and run-ons. Mark any instances of these errors. Then, revise your writing to correct these problems.

> **Exercise 39** **Writing Application** Write a brief description of a hobby or craft that you enjoy. Include at least five fragments and five run-ons in your first draft. Then, revise your work, correcting the fragments and run-ons.

ASSESS

Section Review

Each of these exercises correlates to the instruction on fragments and run-ons, pages 492–496. These exercises may be used for more practice, for reteaching, or for review of the key concepts presented.

Answer Key

> **Exercise 34**

1. Correct (two sentences)
2. Basketry, weaving, and pottery are among the earliest basic crafts.
3. Originally fulfilling useful purposes, crafts are now primarily decorative.
4. Craftwork formed the basis of city economies in Europe up to the Industrial Revolution in the 1800's.
5. Once items could be mass-produced, artisans were no longer needed.

> **Exercise 35**

The top layer of a quilt bears a design, generally produced in one of three ways. The fabric may be left plain, so that the quilting stitches form the design. More commonly, the top is made from a process called appliqué; pieces are cut from various cloths and stitched onto a background fabric, making pictures and patterns. Tops of quilts may also be pieced or patched in a process known as patchwork. Units of cloth are sewn together to form geometric patterns. In the final stage of assembly, the quilt's three layers are stretched on a frame and sewn together with short running stitches called quilting stitches. This final step is more than mechanical, however; the design of the top is artfully thrown into relief, allowing the play of light and shadow on the surface.

> **Exercise 36**

Gardens come in many different types of designs, styles, and techniques. These include, among others, rock gardens, herb gardens, wildflower gardens, water gardens, and Japanese gardens.

A rock garden duplicates the natural environmental conditions in which rock and mountain plants thrive. It is somewhat easier to cultivate than an ordinary garden.

continued

Answer Key continued

> **Exercise 36**

continued

The plants are hardier and more resistant to drought and cold and require far less fertilizer than plants that succeed in other types of gardens. Slightly sloping ground that is well drained is the best location. The most suitable plants for rock gardens are flowering, hardy perennials. In addition, rock gardens are often planted with dwarf trees and shrubs.

> **Exercise 37**

Find It in Your Reading
Have students list the strategies they used to avoid fragments and run-ons.

> **Exercise 38**

Find It in Your Writing
Suggest that partners exchange papers and revise one another's sentences.

> **Exercise 39**

Writing Application
Encourage students to expand their descriptions into full-length descriptive essays and submit them to a school publication.

Write the following sentences on the chalkboard:

Hidden in the sock drawer, Maria found her brother's diary.

When he was twelve years old, Steve's father gave him a guitar.

Point out to the class that confusion results from misuse of modifiers. The first example implies that Maria was hidden in the sock drawer. The second example implies that Steve's father was twelve years old. Explain that misplaced modifiers are those placed too far from the elements they modify and that dangling modifiers are meant to modify words that have been omitted mistakenly from their sentences.

Activate Prior Knowledge

Have students review the various kinds of constructions that act as modifiers (adjective phrases and clauses, appositive phrases, verbal phrases). Then, ask students to write a paragraph about their favorite band or performer. Have students underline all of the modifying phrases and clauses and draw arrows to the words they modify.

TEACH

Misplaced Modifiers

1. Remind students that all modifiers must point clearly to the words they modify. Emphasize that, as a rule, related words should be kept as closely together as possible because readers should readily understand what is being modified by any phrase or clause.

2. Point out that misplaced modifiers can interrupt the flow of a sentence. For instance, when a long adverbial element (a lengthy prepositional phrase or adverb clause) separates a subject from its verb or a verb from its object, the result can confound a reader or else force the reader to study the sentence to ascertain its intended meaning.

3. Use the example on this page to show students that in general, misplaced modifiers need only be repositioned closer to the words they are meant to modify.

500

Section 20.5

Misplaced and Dangling Modifiers

As a general rule, a modifier should be placed as close as possible to the word it modifies. If a modifier is misplaced or left dangling in a sentence, it will seem to modify the wrong word or no word at all. This section will examine both of these sentence errors and show you how to correct them.

Misplaced Modifiers

When a modifier is placed too far from the word it should modify, the meaning of the sentence can become unclear.

▶ **KEY CONCEPT** A misplaced modifier seems to modify the wrong word in the sentence. ■

Any phrase or clause that acts as an adjective or adverb can unintentionally be misplaced in a sentence.

MISPLACED MODIFIERS:	George Washington borrowed money to attend his first inauguration *deep in debt.*
	The first inaugural ball was held in the New York State Assembly *attended by many foreign ministers.*

In the first example, the misplaced prepositional phrase seems to modify *inauguration* rather than *George Washington.* In the second example, the misplaced participial phrase seems to modify *New York State Assembly* rather than *ball.*

To correct such sentence errors, simply move the phrase or clause that is misplaced closer to the word that it should logically modify. Some additional rewording may be necessary.

CORRECTED SENTENCES:	*Deep in debt,* George Washington borrowed money to attend his first inauguration.
	Attended by many foreign ministers, the first inaugural ball was held in the New York State Assembly.

500 • Effective Sentences

Exercise 40 Identifying and Correcting Misplaced Modifiers

Rewrite each sentence, correcting the misplaced modifiers.

EXAMPLE: The President receives guests in the Blue Room during state dinners at the White House.

ANSWER: During state dinners, the President receives guests in the Blue Room of the White House.

1. The White House is constructed of Virginia sandstone built in a classical style.
2. Numerous trees grow on the White House property of historical interest.
3. The White House occupies eighteen acres of manicured lawns and gardens constructed before 1800.
4. The architect James Hoban designed the White House who won a public architecture contest.
5. The low-lying terraces were added while Thomas Jefferson was president to the main building.
6. The third floor of the White House is closed to the public consisting primarily of guest rooms.
7. The East Room is the largest room in the White House used mainly for state receptions and balls.
8. The White House has retained its simple character subject to many renovations.
9. Destroying the interior British troops burned the structure during the War of 1812.
10. The White House has been the home of every president except George Washington in American history.

More Practice

Language Lab CD-ROM
• Misplaced Modifiers lesson

On-line Exercise Bank
• Section 20.5

Grammar Exercise Workbook
• pp. 75–78

▼ **Critical Viewing**
Write a sentence with a misplaced modifier describing this view of the White House. How can you correct the misplaced modifier? **[Describe]**

Misplaced and Dangling Modifiers • 501

☑ **ONGOING ASSESSMENT: Monitor and Reinforce**

If students miss more than two items in Exercise 40 or 41, refer them to the following for additional practice.

In the Textbook	Print Resources	Technology
Section Review, Exercise 42–44, p. 503	*Grammar Exercise Workbook,* pp. 75–78	*Language Lab* CD-ROM, Sentence Errors *On-Line Exercise Bank,* Section 20.5

Dangling Modifiers

1. Warn students that while dangling modifiers are fairly easy to repair, these sentence errors are often hard to spot in one's own writing. Remind students regularly to have others read their work to help find any dangling modifiers.

2. Dangling modifiers are often word groups (such as verbal phrases) that suggest but do not name someone or something that performs an action. Dangling modifiers can usually be fixed by rewriting the independent clause to name the missing actor in the subject of the sentence or by naming the missing actor in the modifier. In Exercise 41, for example, sentence 4 can be repaired by naming *Jefferson,* but sentence 6 can only be fixed by adding *the weather* as the subject of the sentence.

Answer Key

▶ **Exercise 41**

1. While rowing George Washington to his inauguration, *the sailors wore white.*
2. On the way to his inauguration, *Washington took a boat* up the Hudson River.
3. After walking to the Capitol, *Thomas Jefferson* was inaugurated.
4. When *Jefferson* was inaugurated, *his predecessor* refused to attend.
5. Stormy early, *the weather cleared by afternoon for Lincoln's inauguration.*
6. *Because it was* snowing heavily, *the weather delayed* Grant's inaugural parade.
7. When *Franklin Roosevelt* was being inaugurated, *his mother* was present.
8. The first of such ceremonies to be televised, *Harry Truman's inauguration* was held on January 20, 1949.
9. After clearing away eight inches of snow, *the plows* enabled John Kennedy's inaugural parade to proceed.
10. Correct

20.5

Dangling Modifiers

▶ **KEY CONCEPT** A dangling modifier seems to modify the wrong word or no word at all because the word it should modify has been omitted from the sentence. ■

DANGLING MODIFIER: *Shortly after his inauguration,* President Kennedy's wife began refurbishing the White House.

CORRECTED SENTENCE: *Shortly after President Kennedy's inauguration,* his wife began refurbishing the White House.

DANGLING MODIFIER: *While touring the White House,* shoes must be worn.

CORRECTED SENTENCE: *While touring the White House,* visitors must wear shoes.

DANGLING MODIFIER: *Importing French furniture,* the White House was decorated.

CORRECTED SENTENCE: *Importing French furniture,* Thomas Jefferson decorated the White House.

▶ **Exercise 41**   **Identifying and Correcting Dangling Modifiers**   If a sentence is correct, write *correct.* If a sentence contains a dangling modifier, rewrite it to make it correct.

1. While the sailors were rowing George Washington to his inauguration, white was worn.
2. On the way to his inauguration, Washington's boat took him up the Hudson River.
3. After walking to the Capitol, Thomas Jefferson's inauguration began.
4. When he was inaugurated, Jefferson's predecessor refused to attend.
5. Stormy early, Lincoln's inauguration cleared by afternoon.
6. Snowing heavily, Grant's inaugural parade was delayed.
7. While being inaugurated, Franklin Roosevelt's mother was present.
8. The first of such ceremonies to be televised, Harry Truman was inaugurated on January 20, 1949.
9. After clearing away eight inches of snow, John Kennedy's inaugural parade proceeded.
10. At his inauguration, Bill Clinton thanked George Bush for his years of service.

502 • Effective Sentences

▶ **More Practice**

Language Lab CD-ROM
• Misplaced Modifiers lesson

On-line Exercise Bank
• Section 20.5

Grammar Exercise Workbook
• pp. 75–78

☑ **ONGOING ASSESSMENT: Assess Mastery**

Use the following resources to assess student mastery of misplaced and dangling modifiers.

In the Textbook	Technology
Chapter Review, Ex. 67, pp. 514–515	*On-Line Exercise Bank,* Section 20.5

Section 20.5 Section Review

GRAMMAR EXERCISES 42–47

Exercise 42 Identifying and Correcting Misplaced Modifiers

Rewrite each sentence, correcting all misplaced modifiers.

1. The Map Room in the White House during World War II was used by Franklin Roosevelt to follow developments.
2. Entertaining guests, the room now serves as a private meeting area for the President or First Lady.
3. The room has been visited by many dignitaries decorated in the Chippendale style.
4. A rare French version of a colonial map hangs on the east wall, covering a case of world maps.
5. The sandstone mantel is simple but large, resting under a map made for Franklin Roosevelt.

Exercise 43 Identifying and Correcting Dangling Modifiers

If a sentence is correct, write *correct*. If a sentence contains a dangling modifier, rewrite it to correct it.

1. After George Washington was elected by a unanimous vote, the trip was made to New York.
2. Having accepted the presidency, precedents would be set by Washington in his administration.
3. To take the oath of office, Article II of the new federal Constitution was followed by Washington.
4. When he was inaugurated, the speech by Washington was short but important.
5. Consulting the members of his newly appointed Cabinet, day-to-day duties were outlined by the President.

Exercise 44 Revising to Correct Misplaced and Dangling Modifiers

Rewrite the following paragraph, correcting any misplaced or dangling modifiers.

(1) To defeat his rivals, the House of Representatives was needed by Thomas Jefferson to vote for him. (2) Listed in Article II, Section 1 of the Constitution, the House has the power to break a tie in the electoral college. (3) After his election, an inauguration with few of the elaborate trappings of the past Federalist administrations was planned. (4) Wanting to appear as an average citizen, Jefferson walked along Pennsylvania Avenue from his boardinghouse for his inauguration. (5) Still under construction, Jefferson was the first President to take the oath of office at the Capitol.

Exercise 45 Find It in Your Reading

Flip through magazines to see whether you can find an example of either a misplaced or a dangling modifier in a print advertisement.

Exercise 46 Find It in Your Writing

Choose a piece of writing from your portfolio to review for misplaced and dangling modifiers. Mark any instances of these errors that you find. Then, revise your writing to correct these problems.

Exercise 47 Writing Application

Imagine that you are running for president of your class at school. Write a speech in which you try to persuade your classmates to vote for you. As you revise, check carefully for misplaced or dangling modifiers. Revise your speech to correct any that you find.

Play a version of the game "One of these things is not like the others" using words and phrases, such as *red, blue, yellow,* and *run* (*run* is the misfit because it is not an adjective, nor is it a color). Do the same with *to swim, to hike,* and *skiing.* Point out that skiing is a present participle; the others are infinitives. Continue this practice with other kinds of phrases in series—as often as necessary—until you are confident that students gain a sense of parallelism. Then turn to the section.

Activate Prior Knowledge

Have students create lists of phrases. Then, call on volunteers to present their lists in complete sentences, each containing at least three phrases in series. Example: *Before school this morning, I ate my breakfast, chose clothes to wear, and walked the dog.* Ask students to identify the grammatical structures in their series and point out that these constitute parallel structures. Continue until volunteers have presented several different kinds of structures—all in series correctly— and be on the lookout for unparallel structures. As you spot these (ask the class to be alert for them, too), have students suggest revisions that will achieve parallelism.

TEACH

Step-by-Step Teaching Guide

Recognizing the Correct Use of Parallelism

1. Help students identify the parallel elements in the Churchill excerpt. Suggest to students that when they draft and revise their work, they get into the habit of underlining parallel items in sentences to check for parallelism.

2. Explain to students that the purpose of parallel structure, like most effective sentence techniques, is to ensure effective communication of ideas. A series of ideas is easier for the reader to understand if each idea is presented in a similar structure; indeed, parallel structure can emphasize and enhance the relationships among parallel ideas.

Section 20.6 *Faulty Parallelism*

Recognizing the Correct Use of Parallelism

Parallel grammatical structures can be two or more words of the same part of speech, two or more phrases of the same type, two or more clauses of the same type, or two or more sentences with the same pattern.

▶ **KEY CONCEPT** **Parallelism** is the placement of equal ideas in words, phrases, clauses, or sentences of similar types. ■

PARALLEL WORDS: Philadelphia is home to many *universities, museums,* and *libraries.*

PARALLEL PHRASES: Philadelphia is famous for *hosting the First Continental Congress, housing the Liberty Bell,* and *publishing the country's first newspaper.*

PARALLEL CLAUSES: *Because we were hot and because we were tired,* we stopped to rest in Fairmount Park.

PARALLEL SENTENCES: *I came. I saw. I conquered.*

Use parallelism to create a rhythm and emphasize key ideas in your writing. The following excerpt is from a speech delivered by Winston Churchill during World War II. Notice how the use of parallel structures creates repetition that builds up to the powerful concluding statement:

EFFECTIVE USE OF PARALLELISM: We shall not flag nor fail. We shall go on to the end. We shall fight in France, we shall fight on the seas and oceans, we shall fight with growing confidence and growing strength in the air, we shall defend our island, whatever the cost may be, we shall fight on the beaches, we shall fight on the landing grounds, we shall fight in the fields and in the streets, we shall fight in the hills; we shall never surrender.

After the first item in a series, sometimes a word is omitted in parallel structures. The word is understood to be part of the phrase or clause because it is in the first item. Churchill, for example, did not repeat *with* in the series *with growing confidence and growing strength in the air.*

504 • Effective Sentences

Theme:
The Birthplace
of Liberty

In this section, you will learn how to use parallelism in your writing and how to avoid faulty parallelism. The examples and exercises provide information about the history of Philadelphia and about its role as the birthplace of liberty.

Cross-Curricular Connection: Social Studies

⏱ TIME AND RESOURCE MANAGER

Resources
Print: *Grammar Exercise Workbook,* pp. 79–82; *Grammar Exercises Answers on Transparencies,* Ch. 20
Technology: *Language Lab* CD-ROM, Writing Style; *On-Line Exercise Bank,* Section 20.6

In-Depth Coverage	Accelerated Pace
• Work through key concepts, pp. 504–507. • Assign and review Exercises 48–49.	• Assign pp. 504–507 for independent review. • Assign Section Review Exercises 50–52.

Exercise 48 Recognizing Parallel Structures Write the parallel structures in each sentence. Then, identify the composition of each as *words*, *phrases*, or *clauses*.

EXAMPLE: Philadelphia is the birthplace of the United States, the home of the Liberty Bell, and the City of Brotherly Love.

the birthplace of the United States, the home of the Liberty Bell, and the City of Brotherly Love (phrases)

1. The Delaware Indians once hunted, farmed, and fished in the area that is now Philadelphia.
2. Dutch sailors visited the area; Swedish families settled there.
3. The Dutch, English, and Swedes fought over the land until the English won control in 1674.
4. In the 1680's, William Penn received a charter, founded the Pennsylvania Colony, and planned the city of Philadelphia.
5. Penn chose Philadelphia as the capital of the colony because of its resources, size, and location.
6. The new colonists who joined Penn were seeking adventure, fleeing poverty, or escaping persecution.
7. Philadelphia grew, the people prospered, and the colony thrived.
8. Benjamin Franklin's newspaper, almanac, and pamphlets helped to establish Philadelphia as a major publishing center.
9. The founding fathers signed the Declaration of Independence and adopted the United States Constitution in Philadelphia.
10. Philadelphia was the capital of Pennsylvania from 1683 to 1799 and was the United States capital from 1790 to 1800.

More Practice

On-line
Exercise Bank
• Section 20.6
Grammar Exercise
Workbook
• pp. 79–82

▼ Critical Viewing
For what effect might the writers of official documents such as the Declaration of Independence have used parallel phrases? [Apply]

IN CONGRESS, JULY 4, 1776.

A DECLARATION

BY THE REPRESENTATIVES OF THE

UNITED STATES OF AMERICA,

IN GENERAL CONGRESS ASSEMBLED.

Answer Key

▶ **Exercise 48**

1. hunted, farmed, fished (words)
2. Dutch sailors visited the area; Swedish families settled there. (clauses)
3. Dutch, English, Swedes (words)
4. received a charter, founded the Pennsylvania Colony, planned the city of Philadelphia (phrases)
5. resources, size, location (words)
6. seeking adventure, fleeing poverty, escaping persecution (phrases)
7. Philadelphia grew, the people prospered, the colony thrived (clauses)
8. newspaper, almanac, pamphlets (words)
9. signed the Declaration of Independence, adopted the United States Constitution (phrases)
10. was the capital of Pennsylvania from 1683 to 1799, was the United States capital from 1790 to 1800 (phrases)

Critical Viewing

Apply Possible answer: to emphasize key ideas; to establish a serious, formal tone

---

✓ ONGOING ASSESSMENT: Monitor and Reinforce

If students miss more than two items in Exercise 48, refer them to the following for additional practice.

In the Textbook	Print Resources	Technology
Section Review, Ex. 50, p. 508	*Grammar Exercise Workbook*, pp. 79–80	*On-Line Exercise Bank*, Section 20.6

Correcting Nonparallel Words, Phrases, and Clauses in Series

1. Emphasize for students that parallel structure is necessary to ensure clarity. Ideas are easier to grasp if they are organized properly, and parallel structure is an effective and important organizational tool. Single words should be balanced with single words of the same part of speech, phrases should be balanced with phrases of the same grammatical type, and so on.

2. On the blackboard, list the correlative conjunctions for students to copy (*either/or, neither/nor, not only/but also, both/and, whether/or*). Stress for students that these conjunctions always appear in pairs and that there are strict rules for the positioning of these elements in a sentence: Specifically, the grammatical structure in the second half of such a structure must be the same as that in the first half.

Integrating Spelling

Gerunds appear very often in parallel structures. Point out that these have special spelling rules. For instance, verbs ending in a consonant sometimes double the consonant when *–ing* is added. Whether to double the final consonant depends on the number of syllables in the word. In general, one-syllable words double the final consonant before an ending and multiple-syllable words do not. Have students practice adding *–ing* to verbs, starting them with examples to highlight this rule: *run* becomes *running, travel* becomes *traveling, swim* becomes *swimming,* and so on. Have students note the exceptions to the rule.

Faulty Parallelism

Faulty parallelism occurs when equal grammatical structures are not used to express equal or related ideas. Faulty parallelism can involve words, phrases, and clauses in series as well as in comparisons.

KEY CONCEPT Correct a sentence containing faulty parallelism by rewriting it so that each parallel idea is expressed in the same grammatical structure. ■

Nonparallel Words, Phrases, and Clauses in Series

When you write, check every series of ideas for parallelism. If you write a description using a series of one-word adjectives, for example, make sure the series does not include a prepositional phrase instead of a suitable one-word adjective.

Notice how nonparallel structures not only interrupt the natural flow of the sentences but also cloud their meanings.

CORRECTING FAULTY PARALLELISM IN SERIES	
Nonparallel Structures	**Corrected Sentences**
NOUN NOUN *Museums, theaters*, and GERUND PHRASE *listening to live music* make Philadelphia an exciting destination.	NOUN NOUN *Museums, theaters*, and NOUN *live music* make Philadelphia an exciting destination.
PREP PHRASE We rowed *past the boathouse*, PREP PHRASE *under the bridge*, and INDEPENDENT CLAUSE *the boat crossed the finish line.*	PREP PHRASE We rowed *past the boathouse*, PREP PHRASE *under the bridge*, and PREP PHRASE *through the finish line.*
My voice teacher says *that I* NOUN CLAUSE *have a very strong voice,* INDEPENDENT CLAUSE but *I sing off key.*	My voice teacher says *that I* NOUN CLAUSE *have a very strong voice* NOUN CLAUSE but *that I sing off key.*

Coordinating conjunctions such as *and, but,* and *or* often connect items in a series. When you proofread your work, use them as a signal to check the items they connect for parallelism.

Grammar and Style Tip

Parallelism not only ensures similarity of form but also enhances coherence by clearly relating paired or opposite units. Effective parallelism will enable you to combine related ideas in a single, well-ordered sentence that you might have otherwise expressed in separate sentences.

STANDARDIZED TEST PREPARATION WORKSHOP

Grammar and Usage Many standardized tests require students to revise errors in compositions. Write the following on the board.

Driving through Pennsylvania, the foliage on the trees was beautiful.

Which of the following items should replace the underlined passage?

A Correct as is

B beautiful was the foliage on the trees.

C the trees looked beautiful with their foliage.

D we enjoyed the beautiful foliage on the trees.

The correct answer is **D**. "Driving through Pennsylvania" is a dangling modifier; logically, foliage cannot drive a car. Because the participial phrase (*Driving through Pennsylvania*) needs to describe something, adding a subject (*we*) to the independent clause completes the logic of the ideas.

Nonparallel Comparisons Do not write a comparison that unnecessarily links different grammatical structures, such as a phrase with a clause, a phrase with another type of phrase, or a phrase with another structure altogether.

CORRECTING FAULTY PARALLELISM IN COMPARISONS

Nonparallel Structures	Correlated Sentences
NOUN I prefer *concerts* to **GERUND PHRASE** *visiting museums.*	**NOUN** I prefer *concerts* to **NOUN** *museums.*
I went to Philadelphia **PREP PHRASE** *because of its baseball team* **ADVERB CLAUSE** rather than *because it is historic.*	I went to Philadelphia **PREP PHRASE** *because of its baseball team* **PREP PHRASE** rather than *for its history.*
GERUND PHRASE AS DO I enjoy *walking in Fairmount Park* **GERUND PHRASE AS SUBJECT** as much as *rowing on the Schuylkill* thrills James.	**GERUND PHRASE AS DO** I enjoy *walking in Fairmount Park* as much as James enjoys **GERUND PHRASE AS DO** *rowing on the Schuylkill.*

> **Exercise 49** **Correcting Faulty Parallelism** Rewrite the sentences, putting each in proper parallel form.
> 1. Philadelphia is considered the birthplace of freedom, and it is the birthplace of our nation.
> 2. The Schuylkill River flows through Philadelphia, through Fairmount Park, and it meets the Delaware River.
> 3. The Delaware River flows into the Atlantic Ocean, and it is a border between Pennsylvania and New Jersey.
> 4. The Delaware River is a border not only for Philadelphia but also divides Pennsylvania and New Jersey.
> 5. The city extends between the two rivers, consists of a regular grid, and it includes four public squares.
> 6. The Benjamin Franklin Parkway cuts diagonally through the city, interrupts the grid layout, and is the connection between City Hall and the Museum of Art.
> 7. City Hall marks the center of Philadelphia, holds a statue of William Penn, and city records are kept there.
> 8. Philadelphia has the deepest freshwater ports, the largest landscaped urban parks, and the statue is the tallest.
> 9. Philadelphia features many historic sites, numerous highly regarded restaurants, and it has excellent museums.
> 10. Philadelphia distinguishes itself by preserving its old buildings and the incorporation of its new structures.

> **More Practice**
> On-line
> Exercise Bank
> • Section 20.6
> **Grammar Exercise Workbook**
> • pp. 79–82

Step-by-Step Teaching Guide

Correcting Nonparallel Comparisons

1. Write the sentence *Giving is as much joy as to receive* on the chalkboard. Help students recognize that *Giving* should be balanced with another gerund, *receiving.* Ask students for another possible solution (*To give is as much joy as to receive*).

2. Use the examples in the chart to further illustrate ways to correct faulty parallelism in comparisons. For practice, have students write alternate versions of each corrected sentence in the chart. Example: *I prefer attending concerts to visiting museums.*

Answer Key

> **Exercise 49**

1. Philadelphia is considered the birthplace of freedom *and* the birthplace of our nation.
2. The Schuylkill River flows *through* Philadelphia, *through* Fairmount Park, and *into* the Delaware River.
3. The Delaware River flows into the Atlantic Ocean *and forms a border* between Pennsylvania and New Jersey.
4. The Delaware River not only *borders* Philadelphia but also *divides* Pennsylvania and New Jersey.
5. The city *extends* between the two rivers, *consists* of a regular grid, *and includes* four public squares.
6. . . . *cuts* diagonally through the city, *interrupts* the grid layout, and *connects* City Hall and the Museum of Art.
7. City Hall marks the center of Philadelphia, holds a statue of William Penn, and *contains* city records.
8. . . . the deepest freshwater ports, the largest landscaped urban parks, and the *tallest statue.*
9. Philadelphia features many historic sites, numerous highly regarded restaurants, and excellent museums.
10. Philadelphia distinguishes itself by preserving its old buildings and *incorporating its new structures.*

✓ **ONGOING ASSESSMENT: Assess Mastery**

Use the following resources to assess student mastery of faulty parallelism.

In the Textbook	Technology
Chapter Review, p. 515, Exercise 68	*On-Line Exercise Bank*, Section 20.6

Section Review

Each of these exercises correlates to the instruction on parallel structures, pages 504–507. These exercises may be used for more practice, for reteaching, or for review of the key concepts presented. Answers for all chapter exercises are available in *Grammar Exercises Answers on Transparencies* in your Teaching Resources.

Answer Key

Exercise 50

1. scientist, statesman, publisher (words)
2. Franklin was born in Boston in 1706; he moved to Philadelphia in 1723. (clauses)
3. excellent in reading, fair in writing, poor in mathematics. (phrases)
4. cut wicks, melt tallow, learn candle making (phrases)
5. Candle making bored Franklin; printing interested him. (clauses)

Exercise 51

1. At age 22, Benjamin Franklin began publishing *The Pennsylvania Gazette* and *writing* most of the articles.
2. Franklin is credited for being the first editor to publish a newspaper cartoon and *to illustrate* a story with a map.
3. Franklin began *Poor Richard's Almanack* to educate, entertain, and *enlighten* Americans.
4. *Poor Richard's Almanack* contains many wise and witty sayings that preach the virtues of industry, frugality, *and honesty*.
5. Franklin introduced many needed reforms to the post office, including a Dead Mail Office, more post riders, and *day and night delivery*.

Exercise 52

Sample answers:

1. My little sister likes to run, to jump, and to skip in our yard.
2. My mother, my father, and my brother sometimes watch her.
3. Whether she goes to the dentist, to the store, or to the library, she will skip part of the way.
4. We tell her that she must stop at corners, look both ways for cars, and listen for any traffic around her.

508

GRAMMAR EXERCISES 50–55

Exercise 50 Recognizing Parallel Structures Write down the parallel structures from each sentence. Then, label each *words*, *phrases*, or *clauses*.

1. As a scientist, statesman, and publisher, Benjamin Franklin is Philadelphia's most famous citizen.
2. Franklin was born in Boston in 1706; he moved to Philadelphia in 1723.
3. At school, Franklin proved himself excellent in reading, fair in writing, and poor in mathematics.
4. After the age of ten, Franklin was kept home to cut wicks, melt tallow, and learn candle making in the family's candle shop.
5. Candle making bored Franklin, but printing interested him.

Exercise 51 Correcting Faulty Parallelism Revise the following sentences as necessary to correct faulty parallelism. If a sentence is already in proper parallel form, write *correct*.

1. At age 22, Benjamin Franklin began publishing *The Pennsylvania Gazette*, and he wrote most of the articles.
2. Franklin is credited with being the first editor to publish a newspaper cartoon and illustrating a story with a map.
3. Franklin began *Poor Richard's Almanack* to educate, entertain, and for the enlightenment of Americans.
4. *Poor Richard's Almanack* contains many wise and witty sayings that preach the virtues of industry, frugality, and being honest.
5. Franklin introduced many needed reforms to the post office, including a Dead Mail Office, more post riders, and had mail delivered night and day.

Exercise 52 Writing Sentences Containing Parallel Structures Use the following items to construct five sentences with parallel structure.

1. to run, to jump, to skip
2. my mother, my father, my brother
3. to the dentist, to the store, to the library
4. stop, look, listen
5. green peppers, cucumbers, beans

Exercise 53 Find It in Your Reading Explain how the use of parallelism contributes to the persuasiveness of this passage from the Declaration of Independence.

We hold these truths to be self-evident: that all men are created equal; that they are endowed by their Creator with certain unalienable rights; that among these are life, liberty and the pursuit of happiness. . . .

Exercise 54 Find It in Your Writing Choose a persuasive essay from your portfolio. Revise your essay to add at least three examples of parallelism. Use the parallel structures to emphasize key ideas and to make your essay more convincing.

Exercise 55 Writing Application Write a short persuasive speech on a current issue about which you feel strongly. Use parallelism at least five times in your speech to emphasize your key points. Present your speech to the class.

---

5. Try incorporating green peppers, cucumbers, and beans into this little story!

Exercise 53

Find It in Your Reading
Have students read the Declaration of Independence in its entirety and look for more parallel structures. It may be found in *Prentice Hall Literature: Timeless Voices, Timeless Themes*, The American Experience, page 140.

Exercise 54

Find It in Your Writing
If students do not find parallel structures in their writing, challenge them to add at least three examples.

Exercise 55

Writing Application
Encourage students to deliver their speeches to the class.

Section 20.7

Faulty Coordination

Faulty coordination occurs when two or more independent clauses that are either unrelated or of unequal importance are joined by *and* or another coordinating conjunction. This section will help you recognize faulty coordination and will show you some methods to correct it.

Recognizing Faulty Coordination

To *coordinate* means to "place side by side in equal rank." Coordination in grammar means that any time you combine two independent clauses with *and* or another coordinating conjunction to form a compound sentence, the clauses should be related and should have equal rank. That is, one idea should not be less important than the other.

▶ **KEY CONCEPT** Use *and* or another coordinating conjunction only to connect related ideas of equal importance. ■

In the following example, the independent clauses on each side of the coordinating conjunction have equal value.

CORRECT
COORDINATION: *I will go, and Mickey will stay.*

Sometimes, however, writers carelessly use *and* to join independent clauses that either should not be joined or should be joined in another way so that the real relationship between the clauses is clear.

FAULTY
COORDINATION: *Philadelphia is both a city and a county, and the Schuylkill River runs through it.*
Downtown Philadelphia is called Center City, and Camden, New Jersey, is across the Delaware River from the city.
The Liberty Bell is in a glass enclosure, and the bell is made of cast iron.

The effect of carelessly stringing together many ideas with *and* is almost always a sentence that sounds awkward.

STRINGY
SENTENCE: The proctor called the roll *and* told us we would be on our honor, *and* then he wrote the examination question on the board, *and* he left the room, *and* he did not return until it was time to collect our papers.

Theme: Philadelphia

In this section, you will learn how to avoid faulty coordination in your writing. The examples and exercises reveal more about the geography and history of Philadelphia.

Cross-Curricular Connection: Social Studies

▼ **Critical Viewing**
What are two ideas of equal importance you might include in a sentence about the Liberty Bell? **[Connect]**

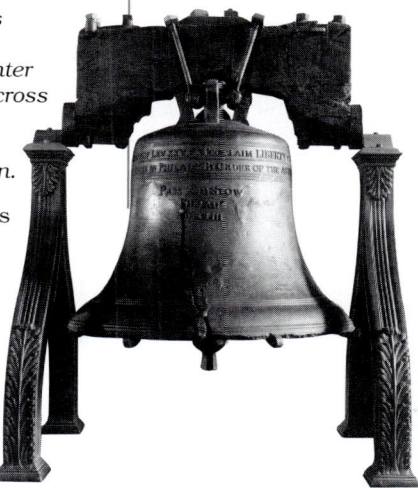

Faulty Coordination • 509

⏱ **TIME AND RESOURCE MANAGER**

Resources
Print: *Grammar Exercise Workbook*, pp. 83–86; *Grammar Exercises Answers on Transparencies*, Ch. 20
Technology: *Language Lab* CD-ROM, Writing Style; *On-Line Exercise Bank*, Section 20.7

In-Depth Coverage	Accelerated Pace
• Work through key concepts, pp. 509–511. • Assign and review Exercises 56–57.	• Assign pp. 509–511 for independent review. • Assign Section Review Exercises 58–60.

PREPARE and ENGAGE

Interest GRABBER Ask students what the logical outcome of a game of tug-of-war between themselves and a fourth-grade class would be. Point out that a sentence with mismatched structures is also unbalanced; figuratively, it will topple logically to one side. Let students know that such an imbalance is called faulty coordination.

Activate Prior Knowledge

Ask students to make lists of the words (coordinating conjunctions) that combine ideas in sentences. Point out that they will need the conjunctions they have listed to ensure that each combined sentence demonstrates a clear relationship among connected ideas in order to avoid faulty coordination.

TEACH

Step-by-Step Teaching Guide

Recognizing Faulty Coordination

1. Help students understand that coordination is used to show an equal emphasis of ideas, while subordination is used to demonstrate unequal emphasis.

2. Point out that coordinated structures draw attention equally to two or more ideas; a coordinating conjunction (*and, but, or, nor, for, so, yet*) and a comma or a semicolon joins ideas of equal weight.

3. In contrast, students should see that subordinate clauses typically begin with subordinating conjunctions (such as *after* or *although*) or relative pronouns (such as *that* or *which*). Understanding this important difference in combining ideas will help students determine whether sentences are properly coordinated.

Critical Viewing

Connect Possible answer: The Liberty Bell cracked when it first arrived in Philadelphia, and it was recast from the same metal.

▶ **Exercise 56** **Identifying Faulty Coordination** Analyze each sentence for problems in coordination. For those sentences in which coordination is used correctly, write *correct*. For the sentences with faulty coordination, write *faulty*.

EXAMPLE: History is an integral part of Philadelphia's character, and the neighborhoods still appear as they did in the past. (faulty)

1. Elfreth's Alley runs between Philadelphia's Arch and Race streets and is America's oldest street of continuously owned homes.
2. Its thirty-five homes were built in the early eighteenth century, and the alley is paved with cobblestones.
3. Society Hill is Philadelphia's chief historic district, and it lies south of Center City.
4. In recent years, Philadelphians have restored hundreds of old homes in Society Hill, and many blocks now look much as they did two hundred years ago.
5. Old churches add to the historic flavor of the streets, and modern apartment buildings stand in contrast.
6. Directly south of Society Hill is Southwark, and it is the oldest section of Philadelphia.
7. William Penn founded Philadelphia in 1682, but Swedish immigrants had settled Southwark decades earlier.
8. Pennsylvania's oldest church is in Southwark, and it was opened in 1640.
9. Germantown is the most widely known neighborhood northwest of Center City, and in 1683 it was founded by Dutch and German settlers.
10. The Germantown settlement was close to the original Philadelphia, but the settlements remained independent of each other for nearly two hundred years.

▲ **Critical Viewing** What details of equal importance might you include in a sentence describing this home in Philadelphia? **[Describe]**

510 • Effective Sentences

☑ ONGOING ASSESSMENT: Monitor and Reinforce

If students miss more than two items in Exercise 56, refer them to the following for additional practice.

In the Textbook	Print Resources	Technology
Section Review, Ex. 58, p. 513	*Grammar Exercise Workbook*, pp. 83–84	*On-Line Exercise Bank*, Section 20.7

Correcting Faulty Coordination

Faulty coordination can easily be corrected.

KEY CONCEPT Revise sentences with faulty coordination by putting unrelated ideas into separate sentences or by putting a less important or subordinate idea into a subordinate clause or a phrase. ■

First, if the independent clauses joined by *and* are not closely related, separate them and drop the coordinating conjunction.

FAULTY COORDINATION:	Philadelphia is both a city and a county, *and* the Schuylkill River runs through it.
CORRECTED SENTENCES:	Philadelphia is both a city and a county. The Schuylkill River runs through it.

A second method of correcting faulty coordination is to change an independent clause that is less important into a subordinate clause.

FAULTY COORDINATION:	Downtown Philadelphia is called Center City, *and* Camden, New Jersey, is across the Delaware River from the city.
CORRECTED SENTENCE:	Downtown Philadelphia, which is across the Delaware River from Camden, New Jersey, is called Center City.

A third method involves reducing an unimportant idea to a phrase—that is, changing the compound sentence into a simple sentence. A clause that can be reduced to a phrase will often begin with a pronoun and a linking verb, such as *he is* or *it was*. In the following example, the second clause has been turned into an appositive phrase.

FAULTY COORDINATION:	The Liberty Bell is in a glass enclosure, *and* it is made of cast iron.
CORRECTED SENTENCE:	The Liberty Bell, a cast-iron bell, is in a glass enclosure.

Stringy sentences should be broken down and revised using any of the three methods just described. Experiment to find the best way to regroup the clauses. Here is one way that the stringy sentence presented earlier can be revised:

REVISION OF STRINGY SENTENCE:	After the proctor called the roll, he told us we would be on our honor. Then, having written the examination question on the board, he left the room. He did not return until it was time to collect our papers.

More Practice

Language Lab CD-ROM
• Strengthening Sentences lesson
On-line Exercise Bank
• Section 20.7
Grammar Exercise Workbook
• pp. 83–86

Faulty Coordination • 511

Step-by-Step Teaching Guide

Correcting Faulty Coordination

1. To practice one method of correcting faulty coordination, write this sentence on the board: "The trees are still green, and we will wash our cars tomorrow." Ask students what is odd about this sentence (these two ideas have no logical connection), and point out that this is an example of faulty coordination. Ask students how to make logical revisions. (The sentence can be separated into two independent ones, perhaps to be used in different paragraphs.)

2. To practice another technique, write another sentence: "The weather will remain warm, and we will wash our cars tomorrow." Point out that this, too, is an example of faulty coordination, but in this case, the relationship between the ideas is not made clear; it is only implied. Ask for suggestions. (Make the first clause a subordinate one: "Because the weather will remain warm, we will wash our cars tomorrow.")

☑ ONGOING ASSESSMENT: Monitor and Reinforce

If students miss more than two items in Exercise 57, refer them to the following for additional practice.

In the Textbook	Print Resources	Technology
Section Review, Ex. 59–60, p. 513	*Grammar Exercise Workbook,* pp. 85–86	*On-Line Grammar Exercises,* Section 20.7

20.7

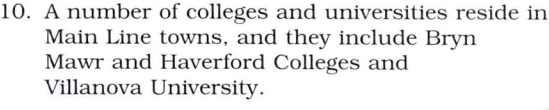 **Exercise 57** **Correcting Faulty Coordination** Write each sentence, correcting the faulty coordination.

EXAMPLE: I made lunch, and it was a Philly cheesesteak sandwich.

ANSWER: I made lunch, a Philly cheesesteak sandwich.

1. The greater metropolitan area of Philadelphia covers more than 3,500 square miles, and it extends north and west into Pennsylvania's Bucks, Chester, Delaware, and Montgomery counties and east across the Delaware River into New Jersey.
2. Nearly five million people live in the Philadelphia metropolitan area, and about one third of Pennsylvania's population is included in that figure.
3. The area encompasses approximately 140 municipalities, and Philadelphia is the largest city in the area.
4. Philadelphia's economy soared after the Civil War, and European emigrants were drawn to the city.
5. Following World War I, many city dwellers looked to move beyond city boundaries, and suburban communities were formed on the outskirts of Philadelphia.
6. Only forty percent of the metropolitan area's population now live within the boundaries of Philadelphia, and thousands of workers commute daily to and from the city by car, bus, or train.
7. The suburbs are now an important part of Philadelphia's fabric, and suburbanites contribute to the city's economy.
8. Philadelphia's best-known suburbs are the Main Line communities, and they are west of the city.
9. These towns get their nickname from their location along the main line of the Penn Central Railroad, but the rail system was once called the Pennsylvania Railroad.
10. A number of colleges and universities reside in Main Line towns, and they include Bryn Mawr and Haverford Colleges and Villanova University.

More Practice

Language Lab CD-ROM
• Strengthening Sentences lesson

On-line Exercise Bank
• Section 20.7

Grammar Exercise Workbook
• pp. 83–86

▼ **Critical Viewing**
How is the purpose served by a coordinating conjunction similar to that served by a bridge? **[Compare]**

512 • Effective Sentences

Section 20.7 Section Review

GRAMMAR EXERCISES 58–63

Exercise 58 **Identifying Faulty Coordination** For the sentences in which coordination is used correctly, write *correct*. For the others, write *faulty*.

1. Philadelphia is a leading center of commerce in the United States and was once one of the world's leading manufacturing cities.
2. Manufacturing has declined in the city since 1950, but it is still an integral part of the city's economy.
3. The service industries have begun to play a greater role in Philadelphia, and the city's economy is more complex.
4. The Port of Philadelphia handles more than 30 million tons of cargo each year and is host to some 5,000 ships.
5. Grain and coal are the city's main exports, and petroleum is imported for processing at the waterfront refineries.

Exercise 59 **Revising to Correct Faulty Coordination** Write each sentence, correcting the faulty coordination.

1. In the early 1800's, coal mines west of Philadelphia provided a huge fuel supply, and industries thrived in the city.
2. Manufacturing industries moved to Philadelphia, and trade was increased by canals, roads, and railroads.
3. Rapid industrialization drew thousands of immigrants to Philadelphia in the mid-1800's, and they competed fiercely for work.
4. The Pennsylvania State Legislature merged the city and Philadelphia County in 1854, and eleven towns became part of Philadelphia.
5. With that act, Philadelphia grew by leaps and bounds, and it had a population of more than 500,000.

Exercise 60 **Avoiding Faulty Coordination in Sentence Combining** Combine each pair of sentences, avoiding faulty coordination.

1. Culture plays a major role in Philadelphia. Theater, music, and the visual arts are all well represented.
2. Philadelphia has a large, active theater district. The Walnut Street Theatre is one of several in the downtown area.
3. The Walnut Street Theatre is the oldest active theater in the United States. It opened in 1809.
4. The Marionette Theater features plays for children. It is located in Fairmount Park.
5. The University of Pennsylvania also has a theater group. The troupe specializes in experimental plays.

Exercise 61 **Find It in Your Reading** Find a travel article about a place that interests you. Then, rework a passage from the article to introduce five examples of faulty coordination. Exchange papers with a partner. Then, identify and correct each instance of faulty coordination your partner has introduced.

Exercise 62 **Find It in Your Writing** Review a piece of writing from your portfolio for faulty coordination. Mark any instances of these errors. Revise your writing to correct these problems.

Exercise 63 **Writing Application** Create a one-page print advertisement to attract visitors to your town. Highlight all the key attractions. Carefully check your advertisement for faulty coordination.

Section Review • 513

ASSESS and CLOSE

Section Review

Each of these exercises correlates to the instruction on faulty coordination, pages 509–511. These exercises may be used for more practice, for reteaching, or for review of the key concepts presented. Answers for all chapter exercises are available in *Grammar Exercises Answers on Transparencies* in your Teaching Resources.

Answer Key

Exercise 58

1. Correct   4. Correct
2. Correct   5. Faulty
3. Faulty

Exercise 59

Sample answers:

1. In the early 1800's, industries thrived in Philadelphia because coal mines west of the city provided a huge fuel supply.
2. Trade was increased when manufacturing industries, attracted by canals, roads, and railroads, moved to Philadelphia.
3. Rapid industrialization drew thousands of immigrants to Philadelphia in the mid-1800's. They competed fiercely for work.
4. Eleven towns became part of Philadelphia when the Pennsylvania State Legislature merged the city and Philadelphia County in 1854.
5. With that act, Philadelphia grew by leaps and bounds to a population of more than 500,000.

Exercise 60

Sample answers:

1. Culture, including theater, music, and the visual arts, plays a major role in Philadelphia.
2. The Walnut Street Theatre is one of several theaters in Philadelphia's large, active theater district.
3. The Walnut Street Theatre, which opened in 1809, is the oldest active theater in the United States.
4. The Marionette Theater, located in Fairmount Park, features plays for children.
5. The University of Pennsylvania also has a theater group that specializes in experimental plays.

continued

Answer Key continued

Exercise 61

Find It in Your Reading
Encourage students to introduce a variety of coordination flaws in their reworked travel articles.

Exercise 62

Find It in Your Writing
Encourage students to consult the examples on page 509 and 511 when reviewing their writing.

Exercise 63

Writing Application
Students might contact local community agencies for examples of such advertisements.

Each of these exercises correlates to a section of the chapter on effective sentences, pages 476–511. The exercises may be used for more practice, for reteaching, or for review of the key concepts presented. Answers for all chapter exercises are available in *Grammar Exercises Answers on Transparencies* in your Teaching Resources.

Answer Key

▶ **Exercise 64**

Answers will vary; samples are given.

1. When did William Penn first journey to Pennsylvania?
2. Penn established the colony for Quakers to escape religious persecution.
3. Did Penn want his colony to be a model of religious freedom?
4. Imagine how the Quakers must have felt when they first arrived!
5. How brave they must have been to leave England for a new home in the wilderness!

▶ **Exercise 65**

Answers will vary; samples are given.

(1–2) Thousands of German and Scotch-Irish settlers arrived in the Middle Colonies in the 1700's. (3–5) Many had read pamphlets written by William Penn urging them to come to Pennsylvania. (6–9) The settlers arrived in Philadelphia and headed west into the backcountry, the area of land along the eastern slopes of the Appalachian Mountains. (10–11) Settlers heading into the backcountry followed an old Iroquois trail that became known as the Great Wagon Road. (12–15) The road was like most roads of the time: rough and rutted with deep mudholes.

▶ **Exercise 66**

Answers will vary; samples are given.

(1–3) The Amish, a North American Protestant group of Mennonite origin, have maintained a conservative, agricultural way of life despite the influences of modern society. (4) The name Amish is derived from Jakob Ammon, a Swiss Mennonite Bishop who insisted that strict discipline be maintained by excommunicating those who broke the rules. (5–6) This entailed the avoidance by the faithful of those

---

GRAMMAR EXERCISES 64–70

▶ **Exercise 64** **Writing the Four Types of Sentences** Rewrite each sentence to fit the function indicated in parentheses. Then, add the appropriate end mark.

1. William Penn first journeyed to Pennsylvania in 1682 (interrogative)
2. Did Penn establish the colony for Quakers to escape religious persecution (declarative)
3. Penn wanted his colony to be a model of religious freedom (interrogative)
4. Can you imagine how the Quakers felt when they first arrived (imperative)
5. Leaving England for a new home in the wilderness demanded bravery (exclamatory)

▶ **Exercise 65** **Combining Sentences and Varying Sentence Length** Rewrite this paragraph, combining some short sentences and leaving others short for emphasis.

(1) Thousands of German settlers arrived in the Middle Colonies. (2) Thousands of Scotch-Irish settlers arrived in the Middle Colonies. (3) They arrived in the 1700's. (4) Many had read pamphlets written by William Penn. (5) The pamphlets urged them to come to Pennsylvania. (6) The settlers arrived in Philadelphia. (7) They headed west. (8) The West was called the backcountry. (9) The backcountry was the area of land along the eastern slopes of the Appalachian Mountains. (10) Settlers heading into the backcountry followed an old Iroquois trail. (11) The trail became known as the Great Wagon Road. (12) The road was like most roads of the time. (13) It was rough. (14) It was rutted. (15) The ruts had deep mudholes.

▶ **Exercise 66** **Proofreading to Correct Fragments and Run-ons** Rewrite this paragraph, correcting any fragments or run-ons.

(1) The Amish have maintained a conservative, agricultural way of life. (2) Despite the influences of modern society. (3) A North American Protestant group of Mennonite origin. (4) The name *Amish* is derived from Jakob Ammon, a Swiss Mennonite Bishop, he insisted that strict discipline be maintained by excommunicating those who broke the rules. (5) This entailed the avoidance by the faithful. (6) Of those excommunicated. (7) Conventional social relationships with the excommunicated, such as making business transactions or eating together. (8) The Amish were subject to persecution in Europe, therefore they migrated in the 1700's to Pennsylvania. (9) Their descendants are called the Pennsylvania Dutch they spread into Ohio, other midwestern states, and Canada. (10) A rural people, their skill in farming is exemplary. (11) The most conservative are known as Old Order Amish. (12) Old Order Amish dress in a plain style. (13) Using hooks and eyes instead of buttons. (14) Instead of automobiles. (15) They ride in horse-drawn buggies.

▶ **Exercise 67** **Proofreading to Eliminate Misplaced and Dangling Modifiers** Rewrite these sentences, correcting any misplaced or dangling modifiers.

1. Other Amish groups are milder in discipline, such as the Conservative Mennonite Conference.
2. Often refusing to vote or to serve in the military, civil affairs are not a part of the Amish way of life.
3. While maintaining their strict way of

---

excommunicated. (7) Conventional social relationships with the excommunicated, such as making business transactions or eating together, were forbidden. (8) The Amish were subject to persecution in Europe; therefore, they migrated in the 1700's to Pennsylvania. (9) Their descendants are called the Pennsylvania Dutch; they spread into Ohio, other midwestern states, and Canada. (10) Correct (11) Correct (12–13) Old Order Amish dress in a plain style, using hooks and eyes instead of buttons. (14–15) They ride in horse-drawn buggies instead of automobiles.

▶ **Exercise 67**

Answers will vary; samples are given.

1. Other Amish groups, such as the Conservative Mennonite Conference, are milder in discipline.
2. Often refusing to vote or to serve in the military, the Amish do not participate in many civil affairs.
3. While maintaining their strict way of life, the Amish often come in conflict with the larger society.

continued

life, conflict with the larger society often happens to the Amish.

4. In particular, they, as a threat to their separate way of life, have resisted compulsory education requirements.

5. The state sought to require Amish children in the case of *Wisconsin* v. *Yoder* to attend school until the age of 16.

Exercise 68 Correcting Sentence Structure

Correct any errors in parallelism or coordination in these sentences.

1. Pennsylvania is a Middle Atlantic State, an original colony, and it played an important role in United States history.
2. The state's nickname is the Keystone State, and it is located east of Ohio.
3. It is called the Keystone State because of its political importance, historical significance, and where it is located.
4. The capital is Harrisburg and the Susquehanna River runs through it.
5. Farming is an important element of Pennsylvania's economy and tourists are attracted to the Amish country.
6. To find good fishing, to see pretty waterfalls, and where three states meet, visit northeastern Pennsylvania.
7. The state boasts an agricultural economy and important industrial areas.
8. Pennsylvania relies on a service-based economy, and several large cities are located there.
9. The state benefits from its location on the eastern seaboard, excellent inland waterways, and there are a lot of natural resources.
10. Factories, coal mines, stone quarries, and farming the land are just some of the many resources in Pennsylvania.

Exercise 69 Proofreading to Eliminate Sentence Errors

Rewrite these paragraphs, correcting sentence errors such as fragments, run-ons, misplaced or dangling modifiers, faulty parallelism, or faulty coordination.

(1) One of Pennsylvania s outstanding characteristics is its great diversity, and there are many scenic attractions, recreational activities, and seasonal festivals to choose from.

(2) The lakes and woodlands of the Pocono Mountains and the Delaware Water Gap, where the Delaware River has cut a spectacular gorge through the mountains of Monroe County, are probably the state's most widely known sights. (3) Other attractions include the many waterfalls of Kitchen Creek, located in Ricket's Glen State Park, the Pine Creek Gorge, known as Pennsylvania's Grand Canyon, and Conneaut Lake in Crawford County is the state's largest natural lake.

(4) Pennsylvania also has many national historical parks. (5) Many of which are open year-round. (6) Independence National Park, which is home to the Liberty Bell, is located in Philadelphia, Independence Hall, also in the park, houses a museum of colonial objects. (7) The Gettysburg National Military Park and Valley Forge National Historical Park, two of the many landmarks that chronicle Pennsylvania's role in historical events and developments.

(8) The range of festivals held annually in the state further demonstrates the diversity of Pennsylvania, from craft fairs to sporting events. (9) The attention of the country is focused on Punxsutawney each February as the emergence of a groundhog from its burrow predicts, according to a legend, the number of weeks remaining in winter. (10) Charter Day, celebrated each March, commemorating the granting of the charter to William Penn to found the Pennsylvania colony.

Exercise 70 Writing Application

Choose an important figure from colonial America. Write an essay explaining why you would like to meet him or her and what you'd expect to learn from that person. Use all of the strategies for improving sentences that you've just learned.

Exercise 67

4. In particular, they have resisted compulsory education requirements as a threat to their separate way of life.
5. In the case of *Wisconsin v. Yoder,* the state sought to require Amish children to attend school until the age of 16.

Exercise 68

Answers will vary; samples are given.

1. Pennsylvania is a Middle Atlantic State and an original colony. It played an important role in United States history.
2. Nicknamed the Keystone State, Pennsylvania is located east of Ohio.
3. It is called the Keystone State because of its political importance, historical significance, and central location.
4. The capital is Harrisburg, through which runs the Susquehanna River.
5. Because farming is an important element of Pennsylvania's economy, tourists are attracted to the Amish country.
6. Tourists visit northeastern Pennsylvania to find good fishing, to see pretty waterfalls, and to see where three states meet.
7. Correct
8. Several large cities are located in Pennsylvania, which relies on a service-based economy.
9. The state benefits from its location on the eastern seaboard, its excellent inland waterways, and its abundance of natural resources.
10. Factories, coal mines, stone quarries, and farmland are just some of the many resources in Pennsylvania.

Exercise 69

Answers will vary; samples are given.

(1) One of Pennsylvania's outstanding characteristics is its great diversity. It has many scenic attractions, recreational activities, and seasonal festivals to choose from.

(2) Correct (3) Other attractions include the many waterfalls of Kitchen Creek, located in Ricket's Glen State Park; the Pine Creek Gorge, known as Pennsylvania's Grand Canyon; and Conneaut Lake in Crawford County, the state's largest natural lake.

continued

Exercise 69

(4-5) Pennsylvania also has many national historical parks, many of which are open year-round. (6) Independence National Park, which is home to the Liberty Bell, is located in Philadelphia. Independence Hall, also in the park, houses a museum of colonial objects. (7) The Gettysburg National Military Park and Valley Forge National Historical Park are two of the many landmarks that chronicle Pennsylvania's role in historical events and developments.

(8) The range of festivals, from craft fairs to sporting events, held annually in the state further demonstrates the diversity of Pennsylvania. (9) Correct (10) Charter Day, celebrated each March, commemorates the granting to William Penn of the charter to found the Pennsylvania colony.

Exercise 70

Writing Application

Assign students to submit a copy of their essays in which they have highlighted each instance of the use of varied sentence openers, correctly-constructed modifying phrases, parallelism, and coordination with a different color of marker.

Lesson Objectives

1. To demonstrate control over grammatical elements such as sentence construction
2. To recognize appropriate English usage within a written passage

Step-by-Step Teaching Guide

Recognizing Appropriate Sentence Construction

Teaching Resources: Standardized Test Preparation Workbook, pp. 39–40

1. Suggest that students treat test-taking as a process and follow the same steps whenever they answer certain types of test questions. Encourage students to keep a test-taking notebook in which they record the format of different kinds of test questions together with tips for approaching them.

2. For example, when test items are written like those on these pages, suggest that students first focus on the bulleted text that lists possible sentence errors. Then, encourage students to read the test sentence and consult each list item in turn until they are able to identify to which category the sentence belongs.

Standardized Test Preparation Workshop

Recognizing Appropriate Sentence Construction

Many standardized tests assess your ability to write effective sentences. In one format used to assess this skill, you are given a passage of writing and asked to identify the best way to rewrite underlined sections. The underlined sections may be one of the following:

- incomplete sentences
- run-on sentences
- correctly written sentences that should be combined
- correctly written sentences that do not need to be rewritten

Test Tip

Try to correct the sample passage on your own without looking at the answers. Then, see whether your correction matches one of the choices.

Sample Test Item	Answer and Explanation
Directions: Read the passage. Some sections are underlined. Choose the best way to rewrite each underlined section. Squirrels have an amazing sense of smell they (1) locate almost all of the nuts they bury by sniffing the ground. **1 A** Squirrels have an amazing sense of smell they locate almost all of the nuts they bury: by sniffing the ground. **B** Squirrels have an amazing sense of smell they locate almost all of the nuts. They bury by sniffing the ground. **C** Squirrels have an amazing sense of smell. They locate almost all of the nuts they bury by sniffing the ground. **D** Squirrels have an amazing sense of smell, they locate almost all of the nuts they bury: by sniffing the ground	The best answer is C. The original sentence is a run-on that should be separated into two sentences.

516 • Effective Sentences

 TEST-TAKING TIP

In a test situation, students may sometimes find it difficult to read sentences or sentence fragments that are numbered, underlined, and set in running text, as here. Encourage students to quickly copy the test question on a separate piece of paper before choosing the correct answer. Students might even rewrite the sentence correctly, and match their rewrite to one of the listed answer options. Let students know that well before the test date they should inquire whether or not they may use scrap paper in the testing site.

Practice 1

Directions: Read the passage. Some sections are underlined. Choose the best way to rewrite each underlined section.

In the minds of many, Robert Frost is inseparable from the New England countryside he so loved. Much of his poetry (1) reflects not only the landscape. But also the characteristic personalities of the region. The New Englanders who (2) populate Frost's poetry are proud, hardworking, and occasionally stubborn. These were drawn from his experience.

1 A Much of his poetry reflects not only the landscape and also the characteristic personalities of the region.

B Much of his poetry reflects not only the landscape, but also the characteristic personalities of the region.

C Much of his poetry. Reflects not only the landscape but also the characteristic personalities of the region.

D Correct as is

2 F The New Englanders who populate Frost's poetry are proud, hardworking, and occasionally stubborn. Drawn from his experience.

G Drawn from his experience, the New Englanders who populate Frost's poetry are proud, hard-working, and occasionally stubborn.

H The New Englanders who populate Frost's poetry are proud, hardworking, and occasionally stubborn. And drawn from his experience.

J Proud, hard-working, and occasionally stubborn, the New Englanders who populate Frost's poetry are drawn from his experience.

Practice 2

Directions: Read the passage. Some sections are underlined. Choose the best way to rewrite each underlined section.

After the Revolution. the Articles of (1) Confederation established a "league of friendship" among the new states. This arrangement did not work well.

The federal Constitution that replaced the (2) Articles required many compromises. It was ratified only after a long fight.

1 A After the Revolution, the Articles of Confederation established a "league of friendship" among the new states, but this arrangement did not work well.

B After the Revolution, the Articles of Confederation established a "league of friendship" in an arrangement that did not work well.

C After the Revolution, the Articles of Confederation, established a "league of friendship" among the new states because this arrangement did not work well.

D Correct as is

2 F The federal Constitution that replaced the Articles required many compromises, but it was ratified only after a long fight.

G The federal Constitution that replaced the Articles required many compromises. So it was ratified only after a long fight.

H Because the federal Constitution that replaced the Articles required many compromises, it was ratified only after a long fight.

J Correct as is

Answer Key

Practice 1
1. B
2. J

Practice 2
1. A
2. H

Customize for
Less Advanced Students

Review the Key Concepts on sentence combining, pages 481 through 484 of the textbook. Alternatively, you can use Grammar Exercise Workbook pages 63 and 64.

In-Depth Lesson Plan

	LESSON FOCUS	PRINT AND MEDIA RESOURCES
DAY 1	**Introduction; Verb Tenses** Students learn and apply concepts relating to the six tenses and four principal parts of verbs. (pp. 518–522)	*Language Lab* CD-ROM, Using Verbs *On-Line Exercise Bank*, Section 21.1 **Teaching Resources** *Grammar Exercise Workbook*, pp. 87–88; *Grammar Exercises Answers on Transparencies*, Ch. 21
DAY 2	**Verb Tenses** *continued* Students learn and apply concepts relating to regular and irregular verbs and verb conjugation. (pp. 523–531)	**Teaching Resources** *Grammar Exercise Workbook*, pp. 89–92
DAY 3	**The Correct Use of Tenses** Students learn to use tenses to express time in the basic, progressive, and emphatic forms. (pp. 532–539)	*On-Line Exercise Bank*, Section 21.2 **Teaching Resources** *Grammar Exercise Workbook*, pp. 93–94
DAY 4	**The Correct Use of Tenses** *continued* Students learn sequence of tenses, time sequence with participles and infinitives, and the use of modifiers to clarify tense, and do the Hands-on Grammar activity. (pp. 539–547)	**Teaching Resources** *Grammar Exercise Workbook*, pp. 95–96; *Hands-on Grammar Activity Book*, Ch. 21
DAY 5	**Subjunctive Mood and Voice** Students learn the use of the subjunctive mood and of active and passive voice. (pp. 548–555)	*On-Line Exercise Bank*, Section 21.3 **Teaching Resources** *Grammar Exercise Workbook*, pp. 97–102; *Formal Assessment*, Ch. 21

Accelerated Lesson Plan

	LESSON FOCUS	PRINT AND MEDIA RESOURCES
DAY 1	**Verb Tenses** Students review verb tenses, with coverage determined by their performance on the Diagnostic Test. (pp. 518–531)	*Language Lab* CD-ROM, Using Verbs *On-Line Exercise Bank*, Sections 21.1 **Teaching Resources** *Grammar Exercise Workbook*, pp. 87–92; *Grammar Exercises Answers on Transparencies*, Ch. 21
DAY 2	**The Correct Use of Tenses** Students cover sequence of tenses, time sequence with participles and infinitives, and modifiers that clarify tense. (pp. 532–547)	*On-Line Exercise Bank*, Section 21.2 **Teaching Resources** *Grammar Exercise Workbook*, pp. 93–96
DAY 3	**Subjunctive Mood and Voice** Students learn the use of the subjunctive mood and of active and passive voice. (pp. 548–555)	*On-Line Exercise Bank*, Section 21.3 **Teaching Resources** *Grammar Exercise Workbook*, pp. 97–102; *Formal Assessment*, Ch. 21

Options for Adapting Lesson Plans

FEATURES

Extend coverage with the Grammar in Literature feature (p.529) and the Standardized Test Preparation Workshop (p. 558)

TECHNOLOGY

Students can use the *On-Line Exercise Bank* to complete the exercises on computer. The Auto Check feature will grade their work.

INTEGRATED SKILLS COVERAGE

Grammar in Literature
SE p. 529

Writing
Find It in Your Writing SE pp. 531, 546, 547, 551, 555
Writing Application SE pp. 531, 547, 551, 555, 557
Grammar and Style SE pp. 523, 533, 549
Writing Skills ATE p. 545

Vocabulary ATE p. 553

Spelling SE p. 537, ATE p. 524

Viewing and Representing
Critical Viewing, SE pp. 518, 522, 525, 527, 529, 530, 538, 549, 550, 553, 554, ATE p. 542

Speaking and Listening SE p. 543

Technology SE p. 526

Real-World Connection ATE pp. 533, 553

Workplace Skills ATE p. 526

ASSESSMENT SUPPORT

Standardized Test Preparation Workshop SE p. 558; ATE pp. 528, 545, 549

Standardized Test Preparation Workbook, pp. 41–42

Formal Assessment, Ch. 21

MEETING INDIVIDUAL NEEDS

Less Advanced Students ATE pp. 524, 528, 550, 559. See also Ongoing Assessments, ATE pp. 521, 525, 527, 530, 538, 544, 554.

AP Students ATE p. 541, 559

Gifted and Talented Students ATE p. 533

ESL Students ATE pp. 528, 553

Verbal/Linguistic Learners ATE p. 526

Logical/Mathematical Learners ATE p. 526

BLOCK SCHEDULING

Pacing Suggestions
For 90-minute Blocks
• Administer the Diagnostic Test to students to determine instructional coverage needed.
• Have students complete necessary exercises in class. Use the Hands-on Grammar activity to provide a change of pace.

Resources for Varying Instruction
• *Language Lab* **CD-ROM** If your students have access to hardware, a 90-minute block provides an ideal opportunity for students to work on computer.

Professional Development Support
• *How to Manage Instruction in the Block* This Teaching Resource provides management and activity suggestions.

MEDIA AND TECHNOLOGY

For the Student
• *Language Lab* **CD-ROM**, Using Verbs
• *On-Line Exercise Bank,* Sections 21.1–3

For the Teacher
• *Resource Pro* **CD-ROM**

WRITING AND GRAMMAR WEB SITE

The Interactive Writing and Grammar Web Site provides a wide array of support for students, teachers, and parents. Grammar support includes:

• *On-Line Exercise Bank* with Auto Check scoring
• Diagnostic and assessment support

www.phschool.com

LITERATURE CONNECTIONS

Related selection from *Prentice Hall Literature: Timeless Voices, Timeless Themes,* The American Experience:

from "A Journey Through Texas" by Alvar Núñez Cabeza de Vaca, SE p. 529

Lesson Objectives

1. To identify and use the four principal parts of verbs
2. To recognize and use correctly the various tenses, forms, and moods of verbs
3. To distinguish between active voice and passive voice and to use voice effectively in sentences
4. To proofread writing for appropriateness of style
5. To demonstrate control over grammatical elements such as verb forms
6. To compose increasingly more involved sentences that contain participles and infinitives in their various functions
7. To evaluate writing for both mechanics and content

Critical Viewing

Speculate Possible answer: Texans withstood a siege by a Mexican army before dying to the last man at the Alamo.

Chapter 21 Verb Usage

Action can happen at any time in the past, the present, or the future. The following sentences, for example, describe actions taking place at different times in Texas.

—Years ago, Texas <u>fought</u> for its independence from Mexico.

—Today, Texans <u>are constructing</u> new homes and other buildings in their growing cities.

The underlined words are verbs, which show both time and action. When you consider the numerous forms and uses of verbs, the many words that can act as verbs, and the likelihood that a sentence will have more than one verb, the chances of misusing verbs are very great. To avoid errors, it is important to know the rules that govern verb usage.

This chapter will show how verbs are formed and the ways in which verbs indicate time. It will also explain how verbs help to express facts, commands, and wishes or possibilities, as well as how verbs can show whether subjects perform or receive action.

▲ **Critical Viewing**
What occurred at this old mission that gave rise to the expression "Remember the Alamo"? Respond with verbs denoting the past. **[Speculate]**

518 • Verb Usage

✓ ONGOING ASSESSMENT: Diagnose

If students miss more than one item in any category, direct them to the relevant pages of the textbook and assign exercises for practice and review.

Verb Usage	Diagnostic Test Items	Teach	Practice	Section Reviews	Chapter Review
Skill Check A					
Six Verb Tenses and Forms	A 1–5	pp. 520–21	Ex. 1–2	Ex. 9	Ex. 45
Skill Check B					
Regular and Irregular Verbs	B 6–10	pp. 522–29	Ex. 3–8	Ex. 10–12	Ex. 44
Skill Check C					
Sequence of Tenses	C 11–15	pp. 532–45	Ex. 16–23	Ex. 24–26	Ex. 46

Diagnostic Test

Directions: Write all answers on a separate sheet of paper.

Skill Check A. Write whether each verb is a *basic form*, a *progressive form*, or an *emphatic form*. Then, identify the verb's tense.

1. My mother drove her car to El Paso.
2. Mike certainly does like Texas sports teams.
3. Near the museum, a performer was singing Mexican songs.
4. Yes, my father did bring me a souvenir from his trip to Dallas.
5. Miguel will be visiting his aunt in Corpus Christi next month.

Skill Check B. Write the appropriate past or past participle for each verb in parentheses.

6. Last summer, my family (drive) to San Antonio.
7. We had never (go) there before.
8. We (see) many interesting sights along the way.
9. Have you ever (eat) Tex-Mex food?
10. My mother has (speak) about a trip to Austin next year.

Skill Check C. Rewrite the sentences, correcting any unnecessary shift in tense. Then write whether the events are *simultaneous* or *sequential*.

11. People know that cowboys and clowns still performed at rodeos.
12. Thousands will be flocking to rodeos because they are so exciting.
13. Cowboys are roping calves when we arrived.
14. I had come to the rodeo because I hope to see the best riders.
15. Often, riders will practice their act until they get it right.

Skill Check D. Where necessary, change the verbs in the following sentences to the subjunctive mood. If the subjunctive is not needed, write *correct*.

16. I wish that I was able to see more of my cousin in Houston.
17. If there was enough room in our house for his snake collection, he would visit us more often.
18. When I told my mother that Frank could keep his snakes in our kitchen, she stared at me as if I was crazy.
19. She prefers that he leaves his snakes at home.
20. However, I noticed that if my mother was home when Frank arrived, she would always invite him in.

Skill Check E. Write whether the following sentences are in the *active* or *passive voice*.

21. Texas has been embraced by musicians.
22. Numerous bluegrass bands have been seen by Texas fans.
23. Many rock-and-roll artists of the 1950's got their start in Texas.
24. A legacy of innovative guitar pickers, piano players, fiddlers, and songwriters is held by West Texas.
25. In fact, a variety of music that the world had never heard was produced by the West Texas Panhandle.

Diagnostic Test

Each item in the Diagnostic Test corresponds to a specific section in the verb usage chapter. This will enable you to tailor instruction to the particular needs of your students. See "Ongoing Assessment: Diagnose" below for further details. Answers for the Diagnostic Test and chapter exercises are available in *Grammar Exercises Answers on Transparencies* in your Teaching Resources.

Answer Key

Skill Check A

1. basic, past
2. emphatic, present
3. progressive, past
4. emphatic, past
5. progressive, future

Skill Check B

6. drove
7. gone
8. saw
9. eaten
10. spoken

Skill Check C

Answers will vary; samples are given.

11. People know that cowboys and clowns still perform at rodeos. (simultaneous)
12. Thousands will flock to rodeos because they are so exciting. (sequential)
13. Cowboys were roping calves when we arrived. (simultaneous)
14. I had come to the rodeo because I hoped to see the best riders. (sequential)
15. Often, riders will practice their act until they get it right. (sequential)

Skill Check D

16. I wish that I **were** able . . .
17. If there **were** enough room . . .
18. . . . as if I **were** crazy.
19. She prefers that he **leave** . . .
20. correct

Skill Check E

21. passive
22. passive
23. active
24. passive
25. passive

✓ ONGOING ASSESSMENT: Diagnose *continued*

Verb Usage	Diagnostic Test Items	Teach	Practice	Section Reviews	Chapter Review
Skill Check D					
Subjunctive Mood	D 16–20	pp. 548–50	Ex. 30	Ex. 31–32	Ex. 47
Skill Check E					
Active and Passive Voices	E 21–25	pp. 552–54	Ex. 36–38	Ex. 39–40	Ex. 48
Cumulative Reviews and Applications				Ex. 13–15, 27–29, 33–35, 41–43	Ex. 49–50

Interest GRABBER Write on the board: *I drive to the store.* Then ask students what one letter can be changed to show that this happened yesterday. (Change *i* to *o* to make *drove*.) Ask them what one word could be added to the original to show that this is going to happen in the future. (*will*) Explain that *tense* is the word that is used to describe the forms of verbs that relate to time.

Activate Prior Knowledge

Ask students to recall an event from the recent past (from their own experience or from a news report) and have them describe the event in a short paragraph, using only verbs that show present time (Example: I want a snack. I go to the store. I find some fruit. I pay the cashier.). Have students share sample sentences. Ask what effect using these verb forms has on the sense of the description. (Sounds odd, can't tell when action took place.) Then have them repeat the exercise using verbs that show past action (I wanted a snack . . .). Ask how this improves understanding of the events described.

TEACH

Step-by-Step Teaching Guide

The Six Verb Tenses: Basic and Progressive

1. Explain to students that, because we live and operate within time, we need ways of describing time. One key way we do this is with verb tense.

2. Write on the board: *yesterday, today, tomorrow.* Then ask students to identify which tenses in each chart go under each heading.

3. Point out that, because some action is ongoing, a form is needed that indicates progress. This is accomplished by the progressive form.

4. Write on the board: *I drive. I am driving.* Then ask students to compose sentences with each that show how each is used in different situations. Have volunteers share their sentences, and emphasize how the progressive form shows action that continues over time.

520

Section 21.1

Verb Tenses

The *tense* of a verb indicates whether something is happening now, was happening at some time in the past, or will be happening at some time in the future.

▶ **KEY CONCEPT** A **tense** is a form of a verb that shows the time of an action or a condition. ■

The Six Verb Tenses

Verbs have six tenses to show the time of an action or condition. Each tense has at least two forms; the present and past tenses have a third form.

▶ **KEY CONCEPT** Each verb tense has a *basic* form and a *progressive* form. The present and past tenses also have the *emphatic*, formed with the helping verb *do, does,* or *did.*

THE BASIC FORMS OF THE SIX TENSES	
Present:	I *learn* more about Texas every day.
Past:	I *learned* something new yesterday.
Future:	I *will learn* more tomorrow.
Present Perfect:	I *have learned* about Texas cities.
Past Perfect:	I *had learned* about the senator before I read her book.
Future Perfect:	I *will have learned* more by year's end.

THE PROGRESSIVE FORMS OF THE SIX TENSES	
Present Progressive:	I *am reading* about Texas's many cities now.
Past Progressive:	I *was reading* about Dallas last night.
Future Progressive:	I *will be reading* about Houston sometime next week.
Present Perfect Progressive:	I *have been reading* about colleges in Texas.
Past Perfect Progressive:	I *had been reading* about Texas cuisine when the lights went out.
Future Perfect Progressive:	I *will have been reading* for an hour when the alarm goes off.

520 • Verb Usage

Theme: Texas

In this section, you will learn about six verb tenses and the progressive and emphatic forms. The examples and exercises in this section are about Texas.

Cross-Curricular Connection: Social Studies

Learn More

For more information about verbs, see Chapter 17.

⏱ TIME AND RESOURCE MANAGER

Resources
Print: *Grammar Exercise Workbook,* pp. 87–92; *Grammar Exercises Answers on Transparencies,* Ch. 21
Technology: *Language Lab* CD-ROM, Using Verbs; *On-Line Exercise Bank,* Section 21.1

In-Depth Coverage	Accelerated Pace
• Work through all key concepts, pp. 520–529. • Assign and review Exercises 1–8. • Read and discuss Grammar in Literature, p. 529.	• Assign pp. 520–529 for independent student review. • Assign Section Review Exercises 9–12.

THE EMPHATIC FORMS OF THE PRESENT AND THE PAST

| Present Emphatic: | I *do talk* to Grandmother quite frequently. |
| Past Emphatic: | I *did talk* to David about his tardiness. |

Exercise 1 Recognizing Basic, Progressive, and Emphatic Forms Identify the tense and form of each verb.

EXAMPLE: Texans have been enjoying chili for years.
ANSWER: present perfect progressive

1. Texas comprises a large part of the western Southcentral region of the United States.
2. Certainly, Texas did derive its name from a Native American word meaning "friends" or "allies."
3. Native Americans had been living in the vast regions of Texas before the arrival of Spaniards and other Europeans.
4. On December 19, 1845, Texas became the twenty-eighth state in the Union.
5. Residents of Texas have been commemorating that occasion for more than 150 years.
6. In the year 2045, Texas will have been a state for 200 years.
7. The state flower is the bluebonnet.
8. Mexico has been influencing Texas culture for centuries.
9. Different cultures and traditions will coexist in Texas for many more years.
10. Texans do cherish their unique culture and history.

Exercise 2 Using the Progressive and Emphatic Forms
Write the progressive or emphatic form of each verb, following the instructions given in parentheses.

EXAMPLE: By 1839, a hill in Austin (past perfect progressive of *choose*) as the site for the capitol.
ANSWER: had been chosen

1. Visitors (present emphatic of *admire*) the Texas capitol.
2. Even before 1888, when it was completed, the capitol (past perfect progressive of *attract*) much attention.
3. The dome (present perfect of *win*) praise for its impressive architectural details.
4. Every day, visitors (present progressive of *climb*) to the galleries around the legislative chambers.
5. Often, from the gallery, spectators (present emphatic of *watch*) the lawmakers at work.

More Practice
Language Lab CD-ROM
• Using Verbs lesson
On-Line Exercise Bank
• Section 21.1
Grammar Exercise Workbook
• pp. 87–88

Verb Tenses • 521

ONGOING ASSESSMENT: Monitor and Reinforce

If students have difficulty with Exercise 1 or 2, refer them to the following for additional practice.

In the Textbook	Print Resources	Technology
Section Review, Ex. 9	*Grammar Exercise Workbook*, pp. 87–88	*Language Lab* CD-ROM, Using Verbs *On-Line Exercise Bank*, Section 21.1

TIME SAVERS!

Answers on Transparencies Use the *Grammar Exercises Answers on Transparencies* for Chapter 21 to facilitate correction by students.

On-Line Exercise Bank Have students complete the exercises on computer. The Auto Check feature will grade their work for you!

521

The Four Principal Parts of Verbs

1. Have students quickly review the verb tense charts. Point out that many of the verb tenses and forms are made up of more than one word. Each group of words includes some version of the verb.

2. Explain that, though it looks as if there are many versions of the verb, there are basically four principal parts that are used to form the various tenses.

3. Ask students to compare the chart of principal parts with the charts of verb tenses and forms and identify how the parts are used. What words do they notice are most commonly used with the parts to "build" tenses (will, have, had, am, was, be, been, do, did).

4. Review how the four principal parts are used:

Present—*used to form the basic present and future tenses and emphatic present and past*

Present participle—*used in progressive forms*

Past—*used to form basic past tense*

Past participle—*used to form the past perfect, future perfect, and present perfect tenses*

(Note: Based on the tense charts, it may not be obvious when a past participle is used rather than past, so you may want to use *took/taken* or another verb in which the past participle differs from the past, as examples.)

5. Have students use *listen* and *speak* (parts shown in chart on this page) to create all the various forms of the tenses.

Answer Key

1. present (comprise)
2. present (derive)
3. present participle (living)
4. past (became)
5. present participle (commemorating)
6. past participle (been)
7. present (is)
8. present participle (influencing)
9. present (coexist)
10. present (cherish)

522

21.1

The Four Principal Parts of Verbs

Every verb has four principal parts. It is from these four principal parts that all of the tenses are formed.

▶ **KEY CONCEPT** A verb has four principal parts: the *present*, the *present participle*, the *past*, and the *past participle*.

THE FOUR PRINCIPAL PARTS			
Present	**Present Participle**	**Past**	**Past Participle**
listen speak	listening speaking	listened spoke	listened spoken

These examples show how each principal part is used.

PRESENT:	The Texas governor *lives* in Austin.
PRESENT PARTICIPLE:	Lawmakers are *debating* in the capitol.
PAST:	The city *wanted* to build a new airport.
PAST PARTICIPLE:	Austin's hills, tall trees, and historic architecture have *delighted* visitors.

▶ **Exercise 3** **Recognizing Principal Parts** Identify the principal part used to form each verb in Exercise 1 on page 521.

EXAMPLE:	People have been admiring the capitol.
ANSWER:	present participle (admiring)

◀ **Critical Viewing**
In what way do you think the Texas capitol building was inspired by the Capitol in Washington, D.C.? Use at least two principal parts of verbs in your response. **[Compare]**

522 • Verb Usage

Critical Viewing

Compare Possible answer: The two wings of the Texas capitol building <u>resemble</u> those of the Capitol in Washington, D.C., and the dome of the Texas capitol may have been <u>inspired</u> by the nation's Capitol dome.

Regular and Irregular Verbs

The changes that occur in the past and past participle forms of a verb determine whether the verb is classified as *regular* or *irregular*.

Regular Verbs The past and past participle of regular verbs are formed according to a predictable pattern.

 KEY CONCEPT A **regular verb** is one in which the past and past participle are formed by adding *-ed* or *-d* to the present form. ■

PRINCIPAL PARTS OF REGULAR VERBS			
Present	**Present Participle**	**Past**	**Past Participle**
laugh	laughing	laughed	(have) laughed
hop	hopping	hopped	(have) hopped
wave	waving	waved	(have) waved

Irregular Verbs The past and past participle of irregular verbs are not formed according to a predictable pattern.

KEY CONCEPT An **irregular verb** is one in which the past and past participle are not formed by adding *-ed* or *-d* to the present form.

You need to know the principal parts of irregular verbs because they often cause usage problems. One common problem is treating an irregular verb as if it were a regular verb (for example, *teached* instead of *taught*). A second problem is confusing the past and past participle when they are different (saying, for example, "I seen" instead of "I saw"). A third problem is spelling. As you read through the charts on the following pages, notice that a final consonant is sometimes doubled to form both the present participle (*getting*) and the past participle (*gotten*). A final *-e* may also be dropped to form the present participle (*arising*).

If you are in doubt about the principal parts of an irregular verb, consult a dictionary. The principal parts are usually listed immediately after the part-of-speech label.

📖 Journal Tip

This section contains a variety of information about Texas. In your journal, take notes on some of the facts that interest you, and review them later to find a topic for an essay or a research report.

⚙ Grammar and Style Tip

Never write *snuck*. The correct past or past participle of *sneak* is *sneaked*.

Step-by-Step Teaching Guide

Regular Verbs

1. Point out to students that, despite what they might think when they see the charts that follow, *most* verbs are regular; that is, the past and past participle of regular verbs are formed by adding *-ed* or *-d* to the present.

2. Have students think of five regular verbs and write down the past and past participle of those verbs. Then ask them to share a few of their examples, writing them on the board. Examples: *create/created, (have) created; divide/divided, (have) divided; trade/traded, (have) traded; hear/heard, (have) heard*

Step-by-Step Teaching Guide

Irregular Verbs

1. Point out to students that they use irregular verbs all the time. They hear them, write them, say them, often without thinking, because they are among our more commonly used verbs.

2. Ask students if they have ever encountered a story in which a character was shown to be uneducated by the improper use of verbs (I done brung, I been teached). Point out that incorrect usage can sound terrible to listeners who know better.

3. Relate that there are some irregular verbs (not shown on the charts) that are odd because the past and past participle are the same as the present—for example, *bid, cost, let, cut, set,* and *shut.* And *read* is almost in this category— it is spelled the same, but is pronounced differently in the past.

4. Have students select five verbs from the first irregular verbs chart and create sentences using the past and past participle. Then ask volunteers to share a few of their sentences.

5. Have students repeat the exercise with five verbs from the second chart (verbs that change in other ways).

6. Optional: State a verb in the present and have students give the past and past participle of the verb.

continued

Step-by-Step Teaching Guide continued

7. Explain that the only way to master irregular verbs is to use them frequently. Eventually, for the more common verbs, the right form will begin to "sound" right.

8. Emphasize to students that the lists that follow do not include all the irregular verbs, so it is important to consult a dictionary whenever they are unsure of the principal parts of a verb.

Customize for
Less Advanced Students

Give students two irregular verbs: *think* and *sneak*. Have them write down their best guesses about the four principal parts of these two verbs. Then, before sharing correct answers, have them check their own by consulting dictionaries. Once everyone agrees on the four principal parts of each, ask students to form two sentences for each verb: one with the past and one with the past participle. Help them respond with correctly worded sentences, either by making suggestions or simply by correcting an initial attempt and having them follow your example. Finally, have students use four verbs of their own choosing, two each from the two charts of irregular verbs, to write pairs of original simple sentences.

Integrating Spelling Skills

Though irregular verbs present a few odd parts, the present participle is formed consistently in all verbs, even the irregular ones: by adding *-ing*. However, in spelling this present participle, there are two things to remember: If a verb ends in a single consonant, that consonant gets doubled (*cut/cutting, run/running, swim/swimming*); if the verb ends in an *-e*, remove it before adding *-ing* (*take/taking, shine/shining*). These are important steps to remember because there are verbs that differ only in that final *-e* (*bid/bide*), and they still need to be different in the present participle (*bidding/biding*).

IRREGULAR VERBS WITH THE SAME PAST AND PAST PARTICIPLE			
Present	**Present Participle**	**Past**	**Past Participle**
bind	binding	bound	(have) bound
bring	bringing	brought	(have) brought
build	building	built	(have) built
buy	buying	bought	(have) bought
catch	catching	caught	(have) caught
creep	creeping	crept	(have) crept
fight	fighting	fought	(have) fought
find	finding	found	(have) found
fling	flinging	flung	(have) flung
get	getting	got	(have) got *or* (have) gotten
grind	grinding	ground	(have) ground
hang	hanging	hung	(have) hung
hold	holding	held	(have) held
keep	keeping	kept	(have) kept
lay	laying	laid	(have) laid
lead	leading	led	(have) led
leave	leaving	left	(have) left
lend	lending	lent	(have) lent
lose	losing	lost	(have) lost
pay	paying	paid	(have) paid
say	saying	said	(have) said
seek	seeking	sought	(have) sought
sell	selling	sold	(have) sold
send	sending	sent	(have) sent
shine	shining	shone *or* shined	(have) shone *or* (have) shined
sit	sitting	sat	(have) sat
sleep	sleeping	slept	(have) slept
spend	spending	spent	(have) spent
spin	spinning	spun	(have) spun
stand	standing	stood	(have) stood
stick	sticking	stuck	(have) stuck
sting	stinging	stung	(have) stung
strike	striking	struck	(have) struck
swing	swinging	swung	(have) swung
teach	teaching	taught	(have) taught
win	winning	won	(have) won
wind	winding	wound	(have) wound
wring	wringing	wrung	(have) wrung

▶ **Exercise 4** Supplying the Correct Forms of Irregular
Verbs Write the appropriate past or past participle for each
verb in parentheses.

EXAMPLE   The Rio Grande has (hold) the imagination of
            Texans.

ANSWER: held

1. Since the early days of Texas's history, the Rio Grande has
   (stand) as a boundary between much of Texas and Mexico.
2. Residents of Texas have often (seek) out the state's many
   lakes and rivers.
3. They may also have (catch) fish in them.
4. Some may even have (build) cabins near Texas's streams.
5. Texas also has numerous state and national parks, where
   people have (seek) to escape the cities.
6. Many Texans have (find) peace of mind near these natural
   resources.
7. Visitors have been (teach) to
   ride horses and ponies on Texas
   ranches.
8. In recent times, urban growth
   (creep) up in Texas, as it did in
   other parts of the country.
9. Modern skyscrapers (bring)
   changes to the look of such places
   as Dallas.
10. Developers have (build) large sub-
    urban communities outside the
    cities.
11. Texas also has thousands of miles
    of highways through areas where
    people once could not have (find)
    a road.
12. The financing of the changes began
    when oil was (strike) in the early
    part of the twentieth century.
13. Texans' ancestors would not have
    (think) that such cities would
    spring up.
14. Giant metropolises now occupy the
    land where small farms once
    (stand).
15. Despite the rapid growth of the
    cities, Texans have not (lose) sight
    of their vast and varied culture.

▶ **More Practice**

**Language Lab
CD-ROM**
• Using Verbs lesson
**On-line
Exercise Bank**
• Section 21.1
**Grammar Exercise
Workbook**
• pp. 89–90

▼ **Critical Viewing**
What verbs tell the
actions of the artist
who created this sculp-
ture? Are they regular
or irregular? [Relate]

Sculpture in Houston by French artist Jean Dubuffet

Verb Tenses • 525

Language Highlight
The word *verb* has a pretty large
family. Derived from the Latin word
verbum, which means "word," *verb*'s
siblings include *proverb, verbal,
verbatim, verbiage,* and *verbose*. All of
these uses are related to the root idea
of "word," from words of wisdom to
lots of words. However, the plural of
verbum, verba, gave rise to the word
verve, which means "enthusiasm,
energy, vigor, spirit, liveliness."

Answer Key

▶ **Exercise 4**

1. stood
2. sought
3. caught
4. built
5. sought
6. found
7. taught
8. crept
9. brought
10. built
11. found
12. struck
13. thought
14. stood
15. lost

Critical Viewing

Relate Possible answers: Regular
verbs: *carved, formed, shaped, created;*
irregular verbs: *built, laid, sought, sent.*

☑ **ONGOING ASSESSMENT: Monitor and Reinforce**

If students miss more than two items in Exercise 4, refer them to the following for additional practice.

In the Textbook	Print Resources	Technology
Section Review, Ex. 10	*Grammar Exercise Workbook,* pp. 89–90	*Language Lab* CD-ROM, Using Verbs *On-Line Exercise Bank,* Section 21.1

⏱ **TIME SAVERS!**

🖼 **Answers on Transparency**
Use the *Grammar Exercises
Answers on Transparencies* for
Chapter 21 to facilitate
correction by students.

💻 **On-Line Exercise Bank**
Have students complete the
exercises on computer. The Auto
Check feature will grade their
work for you!

Customize for
Linguistic Learners

Have students work in pairs to drill each other on the four principal parts of irregular verbs. Have one student supply a present participle (for example, *flying*) from the charts on this page and on page 524. Then, have the other student supply the present *(fly)*, past *(flew)*, and past participle using *have (have flown)* without looking at the chart. Next, have partners switch roles. For extra rigor, suggest that the first partner alternate the forms supplied to the partner so that the partner has to say the other three parts.

Integrating Workplace Skills

Explain to students that the four principal parts of verbs are essential parts in business and other communication, such as business letters, e-mail messages, résumés, and memoranda. Give students practice using verbs to write résumés. First, show them models of verb phrases often used to identify experience or qualifications:

Walked pets for neighbors.

Participated in after-school sports.

Then, have students each write a portion of a résumé, such as *Description of Experience* or *Accomplishments*, using past and past participle forms of verbs.

Customize for
Logical/Mathematical Learners

Point out that, though these verbs are irregular, there are definite patterns to the parts for many of these verbs. Suggest that students go through the charts of irregular verbs (and add others that they know) to find the patterns. Then have them create a list or chart that demonstrates these patterns. (For example: *say*, *pay*, and *lay* all have the same endings and all have similar pasts and past participles: *said*, *paid*, *laid*; *tear* and *wear* have the same endings, and have similar past and past participles: *tore/torn*, *wore/worn*.) Students may work together to create one "master chart," and then present their findings to the class.

IRREGULAR VERBS THAT CHANGE IN OTHER WAYS

Present	Present Participle	Past	Past Participle
become	becoming	became	(have) become
begin	beginning	began	(have) begun
break	breaking	broke	(have) broken
choose	choosing	chose	(have) chosen
come	coming	came	(have) come
do	doing	did	(have) done
draw	drawing	drew	(have) drawn
drink	drinking	drank	(have) drunk
drive	driving	drove	(have) driven
eat	eating	ate	(have) eaten
fall	falling	fell	(have) fallen
fly	flying	flew	(have) flown
forget	forgetting	forgot	(have) forgotten or forgot
freeze	freezing	froze	(have) frozen
give	giving	gave	(have) given
go	going	went	(have) gone
grow	growing	grew	(have) grown
know	knowing	knew	(have) known
lie	lying	lay	(have) lain
ride	riding	rode	(have) ridden
ring	ringing	rang	(have) rung
rise	rising	rose	(have) risen
run	running	ran	(have) run
see	seeing	saw	(have) seen
shake	shaking	shook	(have) shaken
shrink	shrinking	shrank	(have) shrunk
sing	singing	sang	(have) sung
sink	sinking	sank	(have) sunk
speak	speaking	spoke	(have) spoken
spring	springing	sprang	(have) sprung
strive	striving	strove	(have) striven
swear	swearing	swore	(have) sworn
swim	swimming	swam	(have) swum
take	taking	took	(have) taken
tear	tearing	tore	(have) torn
throw	throwing	threw	(have) thrown
wear	wearing	wore	(have) worn
weave	weaving	wove	(have) woven or (have) wove
write	writing	wrote	(have) written

Internet Tip

You can use an online dictionary not only to access definitions of words, but also to find the principal parts of irregular verbs. Simply type "on-line dictionaries" in the query field of your search engine. The first or second result should be a convenient dictionary that you can bookmark for easy use.

Exercise 5 Learning the Principal Parts of Irregular Verbs

Write the *present participle*, the *past*, and the *past participle* of each verb.

EXAMPLE   swim

ANSWER: swimming, swam, swum

1. win	6. stand	11. sing	16. drive
2. shake	7. keep	12. go	17. get
3. become	8. draw	13. steal	18. sit
4. build	9. break	14. rise	19. pay
5. fight	10. drink	15. swing	20. weave

Exercise 6 Revising to Correct Forms of Irregular Verbs

Revise these sentences, correcting irregular verb forms.

EXAMPLE: Which armies fighted at the Alamo?

ANSWER: fought

1. Because Texas and Mexico share a border, many Texans have went to Mexico.
2. Also, numerous Texans have came from Mexico.
3. These immigrants have choosed to work for better wages in the United States.
4. Many Texans who live near the border of Mexico have grew up speaking both English and Spanish.
5. By the early 1500's, Alonso Alvarez de Pineda, a Spanish explorer, had drawed maps of the Texas coast.
6. He reported to Spain on what he seen.
7. He sung the praises of a beautiful country.
8. His exploration begun the Spanish settlement of Texas.
9. In 1528, a Spanish ship sunk off the Texas coast.
10. Members of the expedition had striked out to explore the area.

More Practice

Language Lab CD-ROM
• Using Verbs lesson

On-line Exercise Bank
• Section 21.1

Grammar Exercise Workbook
• pp. 89–90

◄ Critical Viewing
Using past tense forms of irregular verbs, explain the ways in which this ancient mission in San Antonio reflects Spanish influence in Texas. **[Analyze]**

Verb Tenses • 527

Answer Key

► **Exercise 5**

1. winning, won, won
2. shaking, shook, shaken
3. becoming, became, become
4. building, built, built
5. fighting, fought, fought
6. standing, stood, stood
7. keeping, kept, kept
8. drawing, drew, drawn
9. breaking, broke, broken
10. drinking, drank, drunk
11. singing, sang, sung
12. going, went, gone
13. stealing, stole, stolen
14. rising, rose, risen
15. swinging, swung, swung
16. driving, drove, driven
17. getting, got, got (or gotten)
18. sitting, sat, sat
19. paying, paid, paid
20. weaving, wove, woven

► **Exercise 6**

1. gone
2. come
3. chosen
4. grown
5. drawn
6. saw *or* had seen
7. sang
8. began
9. sank
10. struck

Critical Viewing

Analyze Possible Answer: The arches and thick walls *were* Spanish features; the Catholic Church *built* missions and *brought* Spanish culture to Texas.

☑ **ONGOING ASSESSMENT: Monitor and Reinforce**

If students miss more than two items in Exercise 5 or 6, refer them to the following for additional practice.

In the Textbook	Print Resources	Technology
Section Review, Ex. 11–12	*Grammar Exercise Workbook,* pp. 89–90	*Language Lab* CD-ROM, Using Verbs *On-Line Exercise Bank,* Section 21.1

⏱ **TIME SAVERS!**

Answers on Transparencies Use the *Grammar Exercises Answers on Transparencies* for Chapter 21 to facilitate correction by students.

On-Line Exercise Bank Have students complete the exercises on computer. The Auto Check feature will grade their work for you!

Verb Conjugation

1. Ask a volunteer to explain briefly what is meant by the terms first person, second person, and third person.

2. Point out how the various phrases in the conjugation of *run* build on the principal parts of the verb.

3. Ask students to conjugate the verb *write* using the chart on this page as a model.

Customize for
ESL Students

Students may be concerned that they are not getting conjugations right because there are not "enough" forms. Point out to students that in English, there are actually fewer changes to verbs within a conjugation than there are in most other languages. In the present tense, only the third-person singular differs with the addition of an *-s* or *-es*. Even the plural forms don't change. In the other tenses, once students select the correct part (present, past, past participle), the verb doesn't change at all throughout the conjugation of that tense. Only the verb *to be* comes close to varying as much as all verbs do in most other languages.

Customize for
Less Advanced Students

Have students play the following verb-conjugation board game. Use an existing board from a commercial board game or have students draw a simple board along the edges of a sheet of paper. Have students write the names of the six verb tenses—present, past, future, present perfect, past perfect, future perfect—on six index cards. On other index cards, have students write the infinitive forms of roughly forty regular and irregular verbs. Then have students place the two sets of cards face down on the table. At every turn, students draw a verb card. This card contains a verb to be conjugated in the tense that is specified by the tense card. Players who conjugate a verb correctly can move three spaces; if not, they only move one space. The goal of the game is to make one complete turn around the board.

21.1

Verb Conjugation

One way to learn the forms of a verb is through *conjugation*.

▶ **KEY CONCEPT** A **conjugation** is a complete list of the singular and plural forms of a verb in a particular tense. ■

The singular forms of a verb correspond to the singular personal pronouns (*I, you, he, she, it*), and the plural forms correspond to the plural personal pronouns (*we, you, they*).

The chart that follows conjugates the irregular verb *run*. To conjugate a verb, you need to use the principal parts: the present (*run*), the past (*ran*), and the past participle (*run*). You also need to use various helping verbs, such as *has, have, had*, and *will*.

Note that if you were to add the progressive and emphatic tenses to this conjugation, you would also need to use the present participle *running* and forms of *be* and *do* as helping verbs.

CONJUGATION OF THE BASIC FORMS OF *RUN*		
Present	**Singular**	**Plural**
First Person Second Person Third Person	I run you run he, she, it runs	we run you run they run
Past	**Singular**	**Plural**
First Person Second Person Third Person	I ran you ran he, she, it ran	we ran you ran they ran
Future	**Singular**	**Plural**
First Person Second Person Third Person	I will run you will run he, she, it will run	we will run you will run they will run
Present Perfect	**Singular**	**Plural**
First Person Second Person Third Person	I have run you have run he, she, it has run	we have run you have run they have run
Past Perfect	**Singular**	**Plural**
First Person Second Person Third Person	I had run you had run he, she, it had run	we had run you had run they had run
Future Perfect	**Singular**	**Plural**
First Person Second Person Third Person	I will have run you will have run he, she, it will have run	we will have run you will have run they will have run

---

✎ STANDARDIZED TEST PREPARATION WORKSHOP

Grammar and Usage Many standardized tests require students to draw upon their knowledge of verb tenses and forms. Write the following on the board and ask students to identify the correct answer.

Jackson has seeked to find the answer to the riddle.

What revision, if any, is needed in the sentence?

A Delete "has"

B Replace "has seeked" with "has sought"

C Replace "to the riddle" with "of the riddle"

D Correct as is

The correct answer is **B**. Because *seek* is an irregular verb, it does not form its past and participle forms by adding an *-ed* or *-d* to the present. The past and past participle of *seek* is *sought*.

Note About Be: *Be* is one of the most irregular verbs in its principal parts. The present participle is *being*. The past participle is *been*. The present and the past, however, vary depending on the subject.

PRESENT:	I am	we are
	you are	you are
	he, she, it is	they are
PAST:	I was	we were
	you were	you were
	he, she, it was	they were
FUTURE:	I will be	we will be
	you will be	you will be
	he, she, it will be	they will be

GRAMMAR IN LITERATURE

from **A Journey Through Texas**
Alvar Núñez Cabeza de Vaca

The highlighted verbs in this excerpt are all past forms. Which verbs are regular, and which are irregular?

The same Indians *led* us to a plain beyond the chain of mountains, where people *came* to meet us from a long distance. By those we were treated in the same manner as before, and they *made* so many presents to the Indians who *came* with us that, unable to carry all, they *left* half of it. . . . We *told* these people our route *was* towards sunset, and they *replied* that in that direction people *lived* very far away. So we *ordered* them to send there and inform the inhabitants that we were coming and how. From this they *begged* to be excused, because the others *were* their enemies, and they did not want us to go to them.

▼ **Critical Viewing**
Besides the obvious inconveniences of traveling long distances with only horses or donkeys and wagons, what might have been some of the advantages? Respond using past tense verbs. **[Infer]**

Verb Tenses • 529

More About the Writer

In 1528, Alvar Núñez Cabeza de Vaca was treasurer on a Spanish expedition to North America. After a disastrous landing in Florida, Núñez tried to sail to Mexico but landed instead near present-day Galveston, Texas. Captured by Indians, Núñez suffered much hardship during the following years. However, when he was reunited with other Spaniards in 1536, he spoke mainly of the wonders he had seen. Núñez recounted his adventures in *Naufragios* ("Shipwrecks"). His accounts of the legendary Seven Golden Cities of Cibola inspired further exploration. He was appointed governor

of Río de la Plata, but by 1541 he was exploring again, this time in South America.

Critical Viewing

Infer Possible answers: Travel was less expensive; travelers needed no fuel or paved roads; they saw the grandeur of the West.

Answer Key

21.1

▶ **Exercise 7** **Conjugating Verbs** Conjugate the verbs below in the form specified.
1. become (basic)
2. go (progressive)
3. bring (emphatic)
4. give (basic)
5. know (progressive)

▶ **Exercise 8** **Practicing Verb Tenses** Write short sentences, using the form indicated for each verb.

EXAMPLE: spend—past perfect, first-person plural
ANSWER: We had spent.

1. *stand*—past perfect, second-person singular
2. *build*—past, third-person singular
3. *forget*—past progressive, second-person plural
4. *eat*—present perfect, second-person singular
5. *speak*—present perfect progressive, third-person plural
6. *swear*—present emphatic, second-person plural
7. *shrink*—past perfect, first-person singular
8. *drive*—future progressive, third-person singular
9. *give*—past perfect progressive, first-person plural
10. *pay*—future perfect, second-person singular
11. *know*—past emphatic, third-person plural
12. *sleep*—future perfect progressive, second-person plural
13. *seen*—present perfect, third-person singular
14. *grow*—past progressive, first-person singular
15. *shake*—present perfect progressive, second-person plural
16. *do*—future progressive, third-person plural
17. *choose*—past perfect, first-person plural
18. *swim*—past perfect progressive, first-person singular
19. *rise*—past emphatic, third-person singular
20. *write*—future perfect progressive, first-person plural

530 • Verb Usage

▲ **Critical Viewing**
Using "The lights of Dallas" as a subject, conjugate the verb *shine* in the third-person plural. [Relate

▶ **More Practice**

Language Lab CD-ROM
• Using Verbs lesson
On-line Exercise Bank
• Section 21.1
Grammar Exercise Workbook
• pp. 91–92

☑ **ONGOING ASSESSMENT: Monitor and Reinforce**

If students have difficulty with Exercise 7 or 8, refer them to the following for additional practice.

In the Textbook	Print Resources	Technology
Section Review, Ex. 11–12	*Grammar Exercise Workbook,* pp. 91–92	*Language Lab* CD-ROM, Using Verbs *On-Line Exercise Bank,* Section 21.1

Section Review

GRAMMAR EXERCISES 9–15

> **Exercise 9** **Identifying Verb Forms**
Identify the form of each verb as *basic*, *progressive*, or *emphatic*.

1. Texas has been growing rapidly.
2. Now, it ranks as one of the most populous states in the United States.
3. Thousands of Texans will be moving into urban centers
4. Twenty percent do live in rural areas.
5. Texans will remain near cities.
6. My grandmother really enjoys art.
7. Texas does boast numerous museums.
8. I have been planning a trip to the Dallas Museum of Fine Arts.
9. We will see many famous paintings.
10. I do hope to visit her again soon.

> **Exercise 10** **Writing Sentences With Irregular Verbs** Write two sentences for each verb, one in the present perfect tense, and the other in the present progressive.

1. strive
2. fight
3. fall
4. ring
5. shake

> **Exercise 11** **Revising to Correct Verb Forms** Revise these sentences, correcting the form of the verb as necessary. If no change is needed, write *correct*.

1. In 1924, Texans choosed Miriam A. Ferguson as their governor.
2. Texas had become the second state to elect a female governor.
3. She was knowed as "Ma Ferguson."
4. Then, in 1990, Ann Richards begun a term as governor.
5. It had took nearly seventy years for another woman to hold the office.
6. Many other women have led the way in Texas.

7. Barbara Bush, President Bush's wife, has builded her literacy campaign.
8. Barbara Jordan rised as the first African American congresswoman from the South.
9. She also teached politics and ethics at the University of Texas.
10. Lady Bird Johnson, wife of President Lyndon Johnson, done much to beautify the state.

> **Exercise 12** **Revising to Change Verb Tenses** Change the verb in each of these sentences to either the present perfect, past perfect, or future perfect tense.

1. Texas shows great diversity.
2. Its rich soil produces many crops.
3. Many people, however, associate Texas with its oil industry.
4. By 1866, drillers discovered oil.
5. We will learn about the state by next week.

> **Exercise 13** **Find It in Your Reading** Go back to the excerpt from "A Journey Through Texas" on page 529, and identify one progressive and one emphatic verb form.

> **Exercise 14** **Find It in Your Writing** Choose a paper from your portfolio containing verbs written in the perfect tenses. Review it to make sure all the past participles are formed correctly.

> **Exercise 15** **Writing Application** Briefly describe a historical event that took place in your state. Include verbs in the past, present perfect, and past perfect tenses.

Section Review • 531

ASSESS

Section Review

Each of these exercises correlates to the instruction on verb tenses, pages 520–529. The exercises may be used for more practice, for reteaching, or for review of the key concepts presented.

Answer Key

> **Exercise 9**

1. progressive
2. basic
3. progressive
4. emphatic
5. basic
6. basic
7. emphatic
8. progressive
9. basic
10. emphatic

> **Exercise 10**

1. I have striven. I am striving.
2. She has fought. She is fighting.
3. They have fallen. They are falling.
4. You have rung. You are ringing.
5. We have shaken. We are shaking.

> **Exercise 11**

1. In 1924, Texans <u>chose</u>
2. correct
3. She was <u>known</u>
4. Then, in 1990, Ann Richards <u>began</u>
5. It had <u>taken</u> nearly seventy years
6. correct
7. Barbara Bush . . . has <u>built</u>
8. Barbara Jordan <u>rose</u>
9. She also <u>taught</u>
10. Lady Bird Johnson . . . <u>did</u>

> **Exercise 12**

Answers will vary. Possible answers:

1. Texas <u>has shown</u>
2. Its rich soil <u>has produced</u>
3. Many people, . . . <u>have associated</u>
4. By 1866, drillers <u>had discovered</u>
5. We <u>will have learned</u>

continued

Answer Key continued

> **Exercise 13**

Find It in Your Reading
Progressive: we were coming
Emphatic: they did not want

> **Exercise 14**

Find It in Your Writing
Point out that problems are more likely to arise in the perfect basic than in the perfect

progressive. Encourage students to write out the four principal parts of any verbs they had to correct.

> **Exercise 15**

Writing Application
Have volunteers share their paragraphs. Ask them to identify the past, present perfect, and past perfect verbs they used.

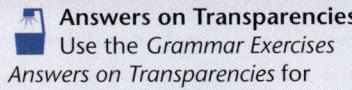

⏱ **TIME SAVERS!**

📰 **Answers on Transparencies** Use the *Grammar Exercises Answers on Transparencies* for Chapter 21 to facilitate correction by students.

💻 **On-Line Exercise Bank** Have students complete the exercises on computer. The Auto Check feature will grade their work for you!

Ask students to identify a period of history that they have studied. Have them tell you a few details about how people lived during that time (encourage the use of past-tense verbs). Then ask students to pretend that they could travel back to that time. Have them share what they would tell those people about the future. (For example: *People will live differently. They will have cars instead of horses. People will be working with "thinking machines" called computers.*) Explain to students that they have been demonstrating the different expressions of time that require the use of different verb tenses.

Activate Prior Knowledge

Have students recall events in their lives that were particularly memorable. Then have each student write briefly about that episode using only verbs in the past tense. (Example: *My parents took me to the roller rink to celebrate my twelfth birthday.*) Have volunteers read their passages. Ask why past tense sounds appropriate. (The events happened in the past.)

TEACH

Step-by-Step Teaching Guide

Uses of Tense in Present Time

1. Explain to students that all the tenses and forms of verbs that they have just covered exist because they are useful for establishing either time or effects. In the case of the present tense, the time is now, the present.

2. Ask students to write their own examples for each of the six uses of the present given. Have volunteers share examples.

3. Point out that the first, third, and fifth examples illustrate action and that the second, fourth, and sixth use a linking verb (forms of the verb *be*) to express conditions.

The Correct Use of Tenses

The tenses of verbs allow you to express time within one of three main categories: the present, the past, and the future. Within each of these main categories, the time of an action or a condition can be expressed in slightly different ways.

As you will learn in this section, each verb form has particular uses that make it different from the other forms.

Present, Past, and Future Time

A clear understanding of the way verbs are used within the three categories of time is important for correct usage.

Uses of Tense in Present Time Present time can be expressed with a basic, a progressive, and an emphatic form.

KEY CONCEPT The three forms of the present tense show present actions or conditions, as well as various continuing actions or conditions. ■

The chart below gives an example of each of the three forms.

FORMS EXPRESSING PRESENT TIME	
Present:	I surf.
Present Progressive:	I am surfing.
Present Emphatic:	I do surf.

The next chart shows the main uses of the present tense.

USES OF THE PRESENT	
Present action:	I *paddle* a raft down the river.
Present condition:	Barbara *is* very upset that the beach is closed.
Regularly occurring action:	Tourists *travel* to Hawaii in the summer.
Regularly occurring condition:	I *am* usually punctual.
Constant action:	The earth *rotates* on its axis.
Constant condition:	People *are* not infallible.

532 • Verb Usage

Theme: Water Sports
In this section, you will learn how to use verb tenses and forms. The examples and exercises in this section are about water sports.

Cross-Curricular Connection: Physical Education

⏱ TIME AND RESOURCE MANAGER

Resources
Print: *Grammar Exercise Workbook*, pp. 93–96; *Grammar Exercises Answers on Transparencies*, Ch. 21
Technology: *Language Lab* CD-ROM, Using Verbs; *On-Line Exercise Bank*, Section 21.2

In-Depth Coverage	Accelerated Pace
• Work through all key concepts, pp. 532–545. • Assign and review Exercises 16–23. • Do the Hands-on Grammar activity, p. 546.	• Assign pp. 532–545 for independent student review. • Assign Section Review Exercises 24–26, p. 547.

When the present tense is used to relate historical events, it is called the *historical present*. Writers sometimes use the historical present to bring to life past actions or conditions.

THE HISTORICAL PRESENT	
Past action expressed in the historical present:	A confident soldier *marches* through France during World War II.
Past condition expressed in the historical present:	For the surfers of the 1940's, Hawaii's gigantic waves *are* very intimidating.

Another use of the present is called the *critical present*. It is frequently used in discussions of deceased authors and their literary works.

THE CRITICAL PRESENT	
Action expressed in the critical present:	Ernest Hemingway *shows* his genius even in his early novels.
Condition expressed in the critical present	Emily Dickinson *is* a famous nineteenth-century poet.

The uses of the present progressive are shown in the next chart. Notice that the continuing actions can be of a long or short duration.

USES OF THE PRESENT PROGRESSIVE	
Long continuing action:	She *is writing* a novel.
Short continuing action:	Samantha *is fixing* the sail.
Continuing condition:	The weather *is being* very unpredictable.

The four main uses of the present emphatic are shown in the chart on the next page.

Grammar and Style Tip

If you begin using the critical present to relate the events of a story, it is important to stay with the present tense and not shift back and forth between the present and the past.

Step-by-Step Teaching Guide

Uses of the Historical Present and the Critical Present

1. Explain to students that the present tense is sometimes used to create an effect rather than to establish the true time of events. Events or conditions from the past are described as if they were happening in the present.

2. Point out that events do not need to be in the distant past. Sports announcers use the historical present all the time. ("He throws to second"—the action is over, but it is still expressed in the present.)

3. Ask students to explain why a writer might choose to use the historical present. (Example: to make events seem more immediate or exciting; to take the reader into the story, as if it were happening now.)

4. Ask why it is appropriate to write about Hemingway and Dickinson in the present. (Possible answers: They are still well known. Their works are still being read.)

5. Have students write two sentences that demonstrate the difference between the historical present and the critical present. (Historical: *Lee's soldiers awake at the trumpet's sound.* Critical: *In this novel, Dickens takes us into the streets of London.*)

Step-by-Step Teaching Guide

Uses of the Present Progressive

1. Point out to students that much of the action in our lives has some duration. It takes some time to do things. The progressive form shows this.

2. Ask students to relate situations in which they have used the present progressive. (*I'm studying. They're playing ball.*)

Customize for
Gifted and Talented Students

Have students use the historical present to write a brief passage about an event from the past. Ask students if using the historical present made them relate differently to their subjects. Have volunteers read their passages aloud. Ask what effect the use of the historical present has. (It brings the people or events to life. It makes history seem more vivid and actual.)

Real-World Connection

Explain that the critical present is not used just for dead authors. It is used in situations where a work is finished but the fame continues or readers or viewers can "relive" the action by enjoying the finished work. For example, a movie critic might say, "Here the director uses tight camera work to get us close to the characters." The action is in the past—the director used the camera—but the critic is "reliving" the moment as he watches that part of the movie. Ask students to look and listen for the critical present in movie previews, book reviews, book jackets, and elsewhere.

Uses of the Present Emphatic

1. Ask students to rephrase the first sentence in the chart by removing the emphatic *do* from the sentence and adding an *-s* to the verb *require*. *(Windsurfing requires much practice.)* Ask students to explain the difference. (The present emphatic makes a stronger, more assertive statement.)

2. Have students think of questions or statements that could prompt each example. (Example: "Do you like raw oysters?")

3. Point out that "Do you play water polo?" can be rephrased as "You do play water polo" to clarify the emphatic form.

Answer Key

Exercise 16

1. Alexi <u>swims</u> (regularly occurring action)
2. She <u>does</u> not want (making a sentence negative)
3. She <u>is</u> thinking (short continuing action)
4. Esther Williams <u>is</u> (present condition)
5. she <u>describes</u> (action expressed in critical present)

Uses of Tense in Past Time

1. Explain to students that, while critics, sportscasters, and writers of historical tales may use present forms to describe past events, most statements about the past use a form of the past tense.

2. Have students look at the list of past forms and then describe how the forms are created. (Helping verbs *have, had, was,* and *did* and present participle *paddling* or past participle *paddled.*)

3. Ask students why they think there are more forms for expressing past time than there are for expressing present time. If no one has any ideas, prompt with suggestions, or simply explain. (Possible answer: The present is only today, while the past has taken place over a long period or time, so more events could have happened at different points in the past.)

USES OF THE PRESENT EMPHATIC	
Emphasizing a statement:	Windsurfing *does require* much practice.
Denying a contrary assertion:	No, I *do* not *like* raw oysters.
Asking a question:	Do you *play* water polo?
Making a sentence negative:	She *does* not *own* a boat.

Exercise 16 Revising Sentences to Change From Past Tense to Present Tense Verbs Revise these sentences, changing the verbs to the present tense. Then, indicate the present tense use of each verb.

1. To prepare for the competition, Alexi swam every day.
2. She did not want to miss her chance to stand out.
3. She was thinking of a famous swimmer-turned-movie star.
4. Esther Williams was a swimmer-actress of the 1940's and 1950's.
5. In her autobiography, *The Million Dollar Mermaid,* she described her glamourous life.

Uses of Tense in Past Time Seven verb forms express actions and conditions that took place some time before the present.

KEY CONCEPT The seven forms that express past time show actions and conditions beginning in the past. ■

FORMS EXPRESSING PAST TIME	
Past:	I paddled.
Present Perfect:	I have paddled.
Past Perfect:	I had paddled.
Past Progressive:	I was paddling.
Present Perfect Progressive:	I have been paddling.
Past Perfect Progressive:	I had been paddling.
Past Emphatic:	I did paddle.

534 • Verb Usage

More Practice

Language Lab CD-ROM
• Using Verbs lesson
On-line Exercise Bank
• Section 21.2
Grammar Exercise Workbook
• pp. 93–94

USES OF THE PAST	
Completed action:	The new recreation center *opened*.
Completed condition:	There *was* a flood in Yosemite Park.

If such words as *yesterday* or *last summer* were added to the sentences in the chart above, the time of the action or condition could be changed from *indefinite* to *definite*.

The present perfect differs from the past in that the time expressed by the present perfect cannot be made definite by adding such words as *yesterday* or *last summer*. The time expressed by the present perfect is always indefinite. The present perfect also differs from the past in that it can show actions and conditions continuing from the past to the present.

USES OF THE PRESENT PERFECT	
Completed action (indefinite time):	I *have seen* an improvement in Grandfather's health.
Completed condition (indefinite time):	I *have been* happy here.
Action continuing to the present:	The baby *has slept* all afternoon.
Condition continuing to the present:	The beach *has been* crowded this week.

The following chart shows the uses of the past perfect. Notice that the past perfect shows a connection between two past events.

USES OF THE PAST PERFECT	
Action completed before another past action:	He *had worked* as a lifeguard before he began his book.
Condition completed before another past condition:	She *had been* an accomplished synchronized swimmer until she became a doctor.

The chart on the next page shows that the three progressive forms express continuous actions or conditions that begin and sometimes end in the past.

Step-by-Step Teaching Guide continued

students to identify these verb pairs in the two examples. *(had worked, began; had been, became)*

6. Then ask students to identify the order of actions in each sentence. (*Working as a lifeguard* came before *beginning his book. Being a synchronized swimmer* came before *becoming a doctor.*)

Step-by-Step Teaching Guide

Uses of the Past

1. Ask students why they think the past tense is the most commonly used form. (Possible answers: It's the easiest; most actions either happened or they didn't, so a simple verb form is all that is needed.)

2. Point out that, in these two examples, the time of the action or condition is unspecified. Therefore, these statements are indefinite; however, they lead us to ask the question "when." Adding phrases that answer that question turns the sentences from indefinite to definite—that is, there is a specific, or definite, time that the past actions or conditions occurred.

3. Have students create two sentences that are past indefinite, and then have them add a phrase that makes them past definite.

Step-by-Step Teaching Guide

Uses of the Present Perfect and Past Perfect

1. Explain to students that, in grammar, the term *perfect* reflects its Latin root, *perfectum,* which means "completed." Actions, events, or conditions expressed in the perfect form were completed by the time of the speaking.

2. Point out to students that, even in the two "continuing action" examples given for the present perfect, all the action described is in the past. If the baby is going to sleep longer, that will need the future tense.

3. Ask students to add a conjunction and clause to the end of each of the two "continuing action" sentences that make it more obvious that the action is completed. For example, "but now, the baby is crying" or "but today, the beach is empty."

4. Point out that, in the past perfect, the completeness of the action or condition is even more obvious, because it happened before another past action.

5. Explain that the past perfect usually works in combination with another verb in past tense. Ask

continued

535

Uses of the Progressive Forms That Express Past Time

1. Write the words *past, present, progressive,* and *perfect* on the board, and ask students to define each separately. (*past*: the time before now; *present*: now; *progressive*: continuing; *perfect*: completed) Then ask them to explain how combining the words would affect their meaning. (*past progressive*: continuing, but in the time before now; *present perfect progressive*: continuing but completed now; *past perfect progressive*: continuing but completed in the past)

2. Have students write two sentences for each progressive form, demonstrating how each would be correctly used.

3. Ask volunteers to share their sentences. Then have students describe the action in the sentence.

Uses of the Past Emphatic

1. Explain to students that the past emphatic behaves just like the present emphatic except that it reflects past actions.

2. Point out that the past emphatic is probably a form with which students are familiar.

3. Ask students to think of conversations in which they have used the past emphatic (*Did you see that? I did do my homework.*) and share examples with the class.

21.2

USES OF THE PROGRESSIVE FORMS THAT EXPRESS PAST TIME	
Past Progressive:	*Long continuing action in the past:* We *were traveling* in Australia last summer. *Short continuing action in the past:* I *was helping* my mother this morning. *Continuous condition in the past:* She *was being* unusually agreeable last night.
Present Perfect Progressive:	*Action continuing to the present:* They *have been building* a canoe.
Past Perfect Progressive:	*Continuing action interrupted by another action:* I *had been resting* until he came.

The uses of the past emphatic are shown in the next chart.

USES OF THE PAST EMPHATIC	
Emphasizing a statement:	Rose *did apologize* for her rudeness.
Denying a contrary assertion:	But I *did swim* across the English Channel!
Asking a question:	*Did* you *buy* a new bathing suit?
Making a sentence negative:	I *did* not *see* the dolphins.

Uses of Tense in Future Time There are four forms used to express future time.

▶ **KEY CONCEPT** The four forms that express future time show future actions or conditions. ■

The chart that follows gives examples.

FORMS EXPRESSING FUTURE TIME	
Future:	I will row.
Future Perfect:	I will have rowed.
Future Progressive:	I will be rowing.
Future Perfect Progressive:	I will have been rowing.

The uses of the future and the future perfect are shown below.

USES OF THE FUTURE AND THE FUTURE PERFECT
Future
Future action: Ed *will dive* into the lake tomorrow.
Future condition: I *will be* at the marina Friday night.
Future Perfect
Future action completed before another: I *will have sailed* around the world by the end of next year.
Future condition completed before another: The survivors *will have been* without food for days by the time help arrives.

Notice that the forms in the next chart are used only to express future actions, not conditions.

USES OF THE PROGRESSIVE FORMS THAT EXPRESS FUTURE TIME
Future Progressive
Continuing future action: John *will be working* in his garden this summer.
Future Perfect Progressive
Continuing future action completed before another: Jennifer *will have been driving* for eight hours by the time she reaches Venice Beach.

💡 **Spelling Tip**

For verbs that end in *oe,* as in *canoe,* keep the last *e* when adding the suffix *-ing.* Hence, *canoe* becomes *canoeing, hoe* becomes *hoeing,* and *shoe* becomes *shoeing.*

The Correct Use of Tenses • 537

Step-by-Step Teaching Guide

Uses of Tense in Future Time

1. Remind students that they are already familiar with the terms *future, progressive,* and *perfect progressive.* Explain that these terms are used similarly to the way they are used in other tenses, but are placed in the future.

2. Point out that, as with other tenses, both action and condition can be expressed in the future. The examples use forms of *be* for condition. Ask students what other verbs can express condition. *(look, feel, seem, appear, taste)*

3. Name one of the six uses of the future (for example, *future condition completed before another*) illustrated in the textbook and have students suggest a sentence that demonstrates that use. Continue naming the uses until all six have been illustrated at least once. You may wish to write some sentences on the board if students are not catching on, modifying them as necessary to make them correct for each use.

4. Referring to the note at the top of page 538, point out that the basic form of the present and the present progressive can be used in certain instances in sentences that express future time. In these instances, the expression of future action relies entirely on another word or phrase in the sentence, not on the verb.

5. Demonstrate how the phrases illustrated no longer express future time when the additional word or phrase is removed. Then have students rephrase the two examples using future forms (*She will leave; I will be kayaking*).

6. Remind students that not all verbs that end in *-ing* are progressive forms. Some verbs that end in *-ing* are gerunds; that is, they are verbs that act as nouns. Also, verb forms that include *to* are infinitives, which are used as nouns, adjectives, or adverbs.

21.2

Note About *Expressing Future Time With the Present Tense:* The basic forms of the present and the present progressive are often used with other words to express future time.

EXAMPLES: She leaves for Yosemite tomorrow.
I am kayaking down the river next Thursday.

▶ **Exercise 17** **Identifying the Uses of Tense in Present Time** On your paper, write the use of the verb in each sentence, using the categories in the charts on pages 532–537.

EXAMPLE: The girls are playing in the lake this morning.
ANSWER: short continuing action

1. Without preparation, a long swim is difficult, especially in rough water.
2. Not surprisingly, people generally prefer a swim in a pool to a swim in the ocean.
3. In 1912, many passengers of the sinking *Titanic* find that ability to swim is of little help.
4. Ernest Hemingway writes about the perils of the ocean.
5. Do you and your friends know lifesaving techniques?

▶ **Exercise 18** **Using Tense in Past Time** Write the indicated form of each verb in parentheses.

EXAMPLE: I (clean—*past progressive*) my surfboard when he called.
ANSWER: was cleaning

1. Surfing (be—*present perfect*) a part of Hawaiian culture for many years.
2. The people of Hawaii (surf—*present perfect progressive*) at its pristine beaches for hundreds of years.
3. According to island legend, the sport (be—*past perfect*) an activity restricted to royalty until the late 1700's.
4. Surfing (win—*past*) fans outside Hawaii after World War II.
5. Since then, the sport (spread—*present perfect*) to many parts of the world.
6. Today, people (surf—*present*) in very remote regions.
7. Surfers (attempt—*present perfect progressive*) to improve the surfboard for many years.
8. In the 1940's, most surfboards (measure—*past*) about 12 feet in length and were made of wood.
9. In the 1950's, many surfers (make—*past emphatic*) their own surfboards out of balsa wood or plywood.
10. Many of these early wooden surfboards (become—*present perfect)* valuable collectibles.

538 • Verb Usage

▲ **Critical Viewing** Use verbs in the present perfect and future tenses to give an account of the surfer's actions. **[Draw Conclusions]**

Answer Key

▶ **Exercise 19**
1. will be
2. will be canoeing
3. will have traveled
4. will have ridden
5. will be
6. will be reducing
7. will have created
8. will make
9. will have occurred
10. will have been carrying

▶ **Exercise 19** **Using Tense in Future Time** Use the form of the verb indicated in parentheses to complete each sentence.

EXAMPLE: If the construction continues at Long Beach, we (go—*future*) to a different beach.

ANSWER: will go

1. Many people believe that canoeing (be—*future*) one of the most popular recreational activities in the future.
2. As long as there are clean rivers and lakes, countless people (canoe—*future progressive*) for fun and exercise.
3. By the end of the summer, they (travel—*future perfect*) through many of the rivers and lakes in the United States.
4. By the end of the trip, these canoers (ride—*future perfect*) in one of the most efficient water vessels ever made.
5. There is little doubt that canoes (be—*future*) even more efficient in the future.
6. Although most aluminum canoes today weigh only around 120 pounds, manufacturers (reduce—*future progressive*) the weight further through advances in technology.
7. By the end of the next decade, it is highly conceivable that manufacturers (create—*future perfect*) a canoe that weighs a fraction of what canoes weigh today.
8. Such a reduction in weight (make—*future*) canoes even easier to transport over land.
9. In the near future, advances in the design and manufacture of canoes (occur—*future perfect*) through the innovations of manufacturers and independent canoeing enthusiasts.
10. Soon, canoes (carry—*future perfect progressive*) people on remote lakes and rivers in North America for more than 400 years.

Sequence of Tenses

When you use sentences that contain more than one verb, it is important to keep the time of the sequence consistent.

▶ **KEY CONCEPT** When showing a sequence of events, do not shift tenses unnecessarily. ■

Verbs in Subordinate Clauses Check the tense of the main verb in a sentence before deciding the tense of the verb in a subordinate clause.

Sometimes, it is necessary to shift tenses when a sentence is complex or compound-complex. The tense of the verb in the main clause determines the tense of the verb in the subordinate clause.

More Practice

Language Lab CD-ROM
• Using Verbs lesson
On-line Exercise Bank
• Section 21.2
Grammar Exercise Workbook
• pp. 93–94

The Correct Use of Tenses • 539

Step-by-Step Teaching Guide

Sequence of Tenses

1. Ask students to define *sequence* (a series, one thing coming after another). Point out that, when showing a sequence of events, it is important that the time expressed by the verbs in a sentence makes sense.

2. Remind students that several of the verb forms that they have just studied help establish sequential activities. Have students review the uses of forms and identify forms that help establish sequence. (*past perfect, past perfect progressive, future perfect, future perfect progressive*)

3. Write on the board: *I had thought I was right until I read that book.* Explain that one often needs to change forms to show sequence, but one can still keep verbs in the same tense. The verbs above are in the past tense.

4. Write on the board: *John has worked all afternoon, but now he is relaxing.* Point out that, despite a then-now sequence, *has worked* is past action expressed with the present perfect—so both verbs are still in the present tense. More importantly, the time sequence remains logical.

continued

Step-by-Step Teaching Guide continued

5. Write on the board: *She will go to the store if he was there on time.* Ask students what is wrong with the sentence. (Time sequence is wrong; the switch in tenses makes the future come before the past.)

6. Tell students that an illogical sequence of verb tenses can happen either within a sentence or between sentences.

7. Point out that there are times when a shift in tense is necessary. For example: *Yesterday I shopped in town; today I'm going to the mall.* The tense shifts but is still logical for the time sequence.

⏱ **TIME SAVERS!**

🖼 **Answers on Transparencies** Use the *Grammar Exercises Answers on Transparencies* for Chapter 21 to facilitate correction by students.

🖥 **On-Line Exercise Bank** Have students complete the exercises on computer. The Auto Check feature will grade their work for you!

Step-by-Step Teaching Guide

Verbs in Subordinate Clauses

1. Ask a volunteer to define "complex sentence." (A complex sentence consists of one independent clause and one or more subordinate clauses.)

2. Explain that the actions or conditions of a verb in one clause can occur simultaneously (at the same time) or sequentially in relation to the verb in the other clause or clauses.

3. Point out that the tense of the verb in the main (independent) clause is the one that establishes the time logic of the sentence.

4. Remind students that, when dealing with time and verb tenses, the thing that is of greatest importance is logic—one tense must relate logically to another, whether events are simultaneous or sequential.

Step-by-Step Teaching Guide

Verbs in Subordinate Clauses: Main Verb in Present, Past, or Future Tense

1. Explain to students that the logical relationship of verbs is not just a matter of trying to "figure it out." Point out that the charts on this and the following page go into greater detail on how to make certain the verbs in subordinate clauses follow logically from the main verb.

2. Tell students that the first thing that is needed is to determine which verb is the main verb. This is done by identifying the sentence's independent clause. (You may wish to ask a student to define *independent clause*—a phrase with a verb and subject that expresses a complete thought and can stand alone as a sentence.)

3. Explain that, once the main verb is identified, the next things students must do is determine the tense of the main verb and determine whether events within the sentence are simultaneous or sequential.

continued

▶ **KEY CONCEPT** The tense of a verb in a subordinate clause should follow logically from the tense of the main verb. ■

In the chart that follows, the main verbs are in the present tense. Notice that the choice of tense in the subordinate clauses affects the logical relationship between the events being described. Some combinations show that the events are simultaneous—that they happened at the same time. Other combinations show that the events are sequential—that one event preceded or followed another.

SEQUENCE OF EVENTS		
Main Verb	**Subordinate Verb**	**Meaning**
Main Verb in Present		
I *know...*	PRESENT that you *work* hard. PRESENT PROGRESSIVE that you *are working* hard. PRESENT EMPHATIC that you *do work* hard.	Simultaneous events: All events take place in the present time.
I *know...*	PAST that you *worked* hard. PRESENT PERFECT that you *have worked* hard. PAST PERFECT that you *had worked* hard. PAST PROGRESSIVE that you *were working* hard. PRESENT PERFECT PROGRESSIVE that you *have been working* hard. PAST EMPHATIC that you *did work* hard.	Sequential events: The working comes before the knowing.
I *know...*	FUTURE that you *will work* hard. FUTURE PERFECT that you *will have worked* hard. FUTURE PROGRESSIVE that you *will be working* hard. FUTURE PERFECT PROGRESSIVE that you *will have been working* hard.	Sequential events: The knowing comes before the working.

In the charts on the next page, the main verbs are in the past and future tenses. Again, note that the choice of tense in the subordinate clauses affects the logical relationship between the events.

540 • Verb Usage

Main Verb in Past		
I *knew...*	PAST that you *worked* hard. PAST PROGRESSIVE that you *were working* hard. PAST EMPHATIC that you *did work* hard.	Simultaneous events: All events take place in past time.
I *knew...*	PAST PERFECT that you *had worked* hard. PAST PERFECT PROGRESSIVE that you *had been working* hard.	Sequential events: The working comes before the knowing.

Main Verb in Future		
I *will know...*	PRESENT if you *work* hard. PRESENT PROGRESSIVE if you *are working* hard. PRESENT EMPHATIC if you *do work* hard.	Simultaneous events: All events take place in the future.
I *will know...*	PAST that you *worked* hard. PRESENT PERFECT that you *have worked* hard. PRESENT PERFECT PROGRESSIVE that you *have been working* hard. PAST EMPHATIC that you *did work* hard.	Sequential events: The working comes before the knowing.

▶ **Exercise 20** **Writing Sentences With Correct Verb Sequences** Complete each sentence with a subordinate clause that relates logically to the main clause.

1. The swimming instructor said that . . .
2. We go over the drills until . . .
3. Our skills will improve if . . .
4. We won our first meet, which . . .
5. I know we will succeed because . . .

When the main verb in a sentence is in one of the perfect or progressive forms, the verb in the subordinate clause will usually be in the present or past. The chart on the following page indicates which forms of a main verb usually require a subordinate verb in the present or in the past. Because there are exceptions to this generalization, you must rely on the meaning of the sentence to determine the tense of the subordinate verb.

▶ **More Practice**

Language Lab CD-ROM
• Using Verbs lesson
On-line Exercise Bank
• Section 21.2
Grammar Exercise Workbook
• pp. 95–96

The Correct Use of Tenses • 541

Step-by-Step Teaching Guide continued

4. To help them articulate simultaneity or sequence, have students mentally insert modifiers into each of the clauses in the examples in the charts. For example: *I know today that you are working hard today.* Point out to students that in this particular example, the knowing and the working are both occurring today and that the events are simultaneous. Alternatively: *I know today that you worked hard yesterday.*

5. Have them repeat this exercise for past and future verbs.

6. Ask students to suggest their own sentences to illustrate the various tenses and show simultaneous or sequential events.

Customize for
AP Students

Review the concept of simultaneous and sequential events and how this is demonstrated in present, past, and future time. Then ask students to locate a passage they consider well written from any source (newspaper, novel, letter). Have them copy a paragraph or two and complete the following: (1) Label the time of the passage, (2) underline the verbs in the clauses of any five sentences, and (3) identify if events are simultaneous or sequential in each sentence.

Answer Key

▶ **Exercise 20**

Sample answers:

1. The swimming instructor said that we had improved since last season.
2. We go over the drills until we are exhausted.
3. Our skills will improve if we practice hard.
4. We won our first meet, which made us feel good.
5. I know we will succeed because we keep improving our times.

Verbs in Subordinate Clauses: Main Verb in Progressive or Perfect

21.2

1. Ask students to determine whether the events described in each example beneath the chart are simultaneous or sequential. If the relationship is sequential, have students identify which came before the other. (*She has forgotten how he suffered*—sequential. The *suffering* came before the *forgetting*.)

2. Have students write a sample sentence for each form listed in the chart under "If the Main Verb Is . . ."

3. Ask volunteers to share some of their examples. If any are incorrect, help students revise the examples so that the tense change flows logically.

4. Explain that the example at the bottom of the page uses the *subjunctive mood,* which will be covered in more detail in the next section. This sentence relates events that did *not* happen. At this point, it is important only that students remember to not repeat the *would have* in the clause that begins with *If.*

5. Have students rephrase the sentence so that it reflects sequential events and uses the guidelines in the chart at the top of the page. You may wish to point out that the main clause follows the subordinate clause in this case. (*Before you arrived, my brother had left.*)

Integrating Representing Skills

Have students create a way of representing sequential and simultaneous events. Suggest math symbols, numbering, positioning (vertical or horizontal), arrows, or other elements that might be used to express time visually. Ask volunteers to share their representations with the class.

If the Main Verb Is . . .	Then the Subordinate Verb Should Usually Be . . .
Present Progressive Present Perfect Progressive Future Perfect Future Progressive Future Perfect Progressive	Present
Present Perfect Past Progressive Past Perfect Past Perfect Progressive	Past

The examples below illustrate the tense changes that occur when the main verb is in one of the perfect or progressive forms.

EXAMPLES: He *is practicing* (present prog) until he *gets* (present) it right.

I *have been swimming* (present perf prog) because I *want* (present) to stay fit.

The boat *will have left* (future perf) by the time we *get* (present) there.

I *will be working* (future prog) at a bank after I *finish* (present) school.

He *will have been waiting* (future perf prog) a year before it *is* (present) ready.

She *has forgotten* (present perf) how he *suffered* (past).

We *were snorkeling* (past prog) when the rain *started* (past).

I *had been* (past perf) a member of the team before she *was* (past).

The sea gulls *had been dying* (past perf prog) until we *found* (past) a cure.

Note About *Would Have:* Do not repeat the helping verbs *would have* in a subordinate clause beginning with *if* when the main verb also contains *would have.* Instead, use the past perfect for the subordinate verb.

INCORRECT: If you *would have arrived* sooner, you *would have met* my older brother.

CORRECT: If you *had arrived* sooner, you *would have met* my older brother.

Time Sequence With Participles and Infinitives The form of a participle or an infinitive often determines whether the events are simultaneous or sequential. The participles can be present (*hearing*), past (*heard*), or perfect (*having heard*). Infinitives can be present (*to hear*) or perfect (*to have heard*).

▶ **KEY CONCEPT** The form of a participle or an infinitive should set up a logical time sequence in relation to a verb in the same clause or sentence. ■

To show simultaneous events, you will generally use the present participle and the present infinitive, even when the main verb is past or future. To show sequential events, you will generally use the perfect participle and the perfect infinitive.

SIMULTANEOUS EVENTS
In Present Time
PRESENT   PRESENT *Hearing* the warning, we *swim* for safety.
PRESENT PRESENT I *want to know* the answer.
In Past Time
PRESENT   PAST *Hearing* the warning, we *swam* for safety.
PAST PRESENT I *wanted to know* the answer.
In Future Time
PRESENT   FUTURE *Hearing* the warning, we *will swim* for safety.
FUTURE PRESENT I *will want to know* the answer.

SEQUENTIAL EVENTS
In Present Time
PERFECT   PRESENT PROG *Having heard* the warning, we *are swimming* for safety. (The hearing comes before the swimming.)
PRESENT PERFECT I *am* glad to *have met* you. (The meeting comes before the being glad.)

Speaking and Listening Tip

Accustom yourself to hearing the correct sequence of verb tenses. With one or two of your classmates, practice reading aloud the examples on these two pages and in Exercises 21 and 22 on the two pages that follow.

Time Sequence With Participles and Infinitives

1. Have volunteers state (or read from the text— pages 442, 444, 448, and 449) the definitions of verbals, participles, participial phrases, infinitives, and infinitive phrases. (Verbal: *word derived from a verb but used as a noun, adjective, or adverb*; Participle: *form of a verb that can act as an adjective*; Participial phrase: *a phrase with participle and modifiers that acts as an adjective in a sentence*; Infinitive: *form of a verb that generally appears with the word* to *and acts as a noun, adjective, or adverb*; Infinitive phrase: *an infinitive with modifiers, a complement, or a subject, all acting together as a single part of speech*.)

2. Explain that it is important to identify participles and infinitives when trying to determine the time within sentences. These verbals should not be confused with the verb that acts as the main verb of the clause.

3. Point out that the participle phrase in the first example on the Simultaneous Events chart, *Hearing the warning*, functions as an adjective to modify the pronoun *we*. This simple sentence contains just one independent clause. Explain to students that the sentence relates events— swimming and hearing—that are simultaneous.

4. Explain that in the second example, the infinitive phrase *to know the answer* functions as the direct object of the sentence. Ask how the sentence shows that these events are simultaneous. (The main verb, *want*, and its direct object, the infinitive *to know*, are both in the present.)

5. Review the next two sets of examples, pointing out how the present participle and present infinitive show simultaneous events even in past and future time.

continued

Step-by-Step Teaching Guide continued

6. Have students write three sentences, one each for present, past, and future simultaneous events, using the present participle *knowing*, the present infinitive *to learn*, or two verbs of your choice. (Examples: *Knowing that there would be a test, I studied all last week. I wanted to learn more about Korean history.*)

Time Sequences With Participles and Infinitives: Sequential Events

1. Point out that, in the first example, the perfect participle, *having heard*, relates an action that was completed in the past, while the progressive *are swimming* in the main clause refers to an ongoing action in the present. Have students suggest another sentence that uses a similar sequence of actions.

2. Ask students how *I am glad to meet you* differs from the next example in the chart. (The present infinitive means the action is happening at the same time as the *I am*—the switch to the perfect infinitive in the example shows that the meeting occurred before the speaker's expression of gladness.)

3. Ask students to explain the time logic of the rest of the examples.

4. Have students suggest sentences that demonstrate sequential events using perfect participles and perfect infinitives. Write some of their examples on the board, making sure that you list at least one successful sentence for each of the three tenses.

Answer Key

▶ **Exercise 21**

Answers will vary; samples are given.

1. Donna is reading about platform diving because she <u>wants</u>
2. It is a sport that <u>requires</u> great balance, strength, and courage.
3. She had been swimming laps because she <u>hoped</u>
4. Divers have been diving off rigid platforms since the sport <u>originated</u>.
5. Platform divers perform acrobatic maneuvers before they <u>fall</u> into the water below them.
6. Many will have had gymnastic training before they <u>begin</u>
7. The diver tucked his body tightly before he <u>executed</u> a somersault.
8. The coach will be showing a film after we <u>finish</u> practice.
9. The team will have beaten all its competitors if it <u>wins</u> this meet.
10. The judges conferred because there <u>had been</u> a discrepancy.

544

21.2

In Past Time

PERFECT   PAST
Having heard the warning, we *swam* for safety.
(The hearing comes before the swimming.)

PAST   PERFECT
He *was* later glad *to have met* you.
(The meeting comes before the being glad.)

Spanning Past and Future Time

PERFECT   FUTURE
Having heard this news, we *will swim* for safety.
(The hearing comes before the swimming.)

FUTURE PERFECT   PERFECT
Years from now, she *will be* glad *to have met* you.
(The meeting comes before the being glad.)

▶ **Exercise 21**   **Revising to Correct Errors in Tense Sequence**
Revise the following sentences, correcting unnecessary shifts in tense. Make any other alterations that improve meaning.

EXAMPLE: After platform diving competitions were first televised, they have become popular.

ANSWER: After platform diving competitions were first televised, they became popular.

1. Donna is reading about platform diving because she wanted to try it herself someday.
2. It is a sport that has required great balance, strength, and courage.
3. She had been swimming laps because she hopes to increase her stamina.
4. Divers have been diving off rigid platforms since the sport originates.
5. Platform divers perform acrobatic maneuvers before they fell into the water below them.
6. Many will have had gymnastic training before they began diving.
7. The diver tucked his body tightly before he executes a somersault.
8. The coach will be showing a film after we finished practice.
9. The team will have beaten all its competitors if it won this meet.
10. The judges conferred because there has been a discrepancy in the scoring.

544 • Verb Usage

▶ **More Practice**

Language Lab CD-ROM
• Using Verbs lesson
On-line Exercise Bank
• Section 21.2
Grammar Exercise Workbook
• pp. 95–96

☑ **ONGOING ASSESSMENT: Monitor and Reinforce**

If students have difficulty with Exercise 21, 22, or 23, refer them to the following for additional practice.

In the Textbook	Print Resources	Technology
Section Review, Ex. 25–26	*Grammar Exercise Workbook*, pp. 95–96	*Language Lab* CD-ROM, Using Verbs *On-Line Exercise Bank*, Section 21.2

▶ Exercise 22

Exercise 22 **Revising to Add the Correct Forms of Participles and Infinitives** Revise each sentence, following the instructions in parentheses.

EXAMPLE: I'm sure you played very well. (Add a phrase with the perfect participle of *watch*.)

ANSWER: Having watched your games before, I'm sure you played very well.

1. Have you ever tried playing water polo? (Change *playing* to a present infinitive.)
2. People seemed to play it in the late 1800's. (Change *to play* to a perfect infinitive.)
3. These early swimmers were reputed to model their game after soccer. (Change *to model* to a perfect infinitive.)
4. We tried the game ourselves last summer. (Add a phrase using the perfect participle of *study*.)
5. We were glad to learn the rules of the game ahead of time. (Change *to learn* to a perfect infinitive.)

Modifiers That Help Clarify Tense

Adverbs such as *often* or *sometimes* and phrases such as *once in a while* or *within a week* are often used to help clarify the time expressed by a verb.

KEY CONCEPT Use modifiers when they can help clarify the tense of a verb. ■

EXAMPLES: *Occasionally*, I enjoy playing volleyball at the beach.
Susan *always* swam with her goggles on.
By next year, Walter will have fished in every river in Colorado.
I swim laps *once a week*.

Exercise 23 **Adding Modifiers to Improve Meaning** Revise each sentence by adding a modifier that indicates time.

1. Water-skiing is one of the most popular water sports in the world.
2. It was considered a sport for daredevils.
3. It is considered a recreational activity that can be enjoyed by almost everyone.
4. Thousands of water-skiers rush to lakes and oceans with their equipment in tow.
5. These places became the site of one of the world's most thrilling pastimes.

⟳ Learn More

To review adverbs and adverb phrases, see Chapter 17 and Chapter 19.

Exercise 22

Some answers will vary; examples are given.

1. Have you ever tried <u>to play</u>
2. People seem <u>to have played</u>
3. These early swimmers were reputed <u>to have modeled</u>
4. <u>Having studied its history</u>, we tried the game ourselves
5. We were glad <u>to have learned</u>

Step-by-Step Teaching Guide

Modifiers That Help Clarify Tense

1. Explain that time is often expressed or clarified by the use of something other than verb tense. Adverbs (*yesterday*), adverbial phrases (*now and then*), and prepositional phrases used as adverbs (*in the spring*) can help clarify time within a sentence.

2. Point out that sometimes it is only the modifiers that indicate time. In sentences like *I leave next week* or *Next year I'm going to college*, the verb gives no indication of time; only the modifiers let you know that these are future events.

Integrating Writing Skills

Explain to students that a key skill of clear writing is precision. Vague or inexact references will confuse and annoy readers, and the message is often lost. Point out that precise modifiers that identify when actions or conditions occurred or existed, even if only within the context of a story, are vital to making certain that readers know what is happening, either to the writer or to the characters in the tale.

Answer Key

Exercise 23

Answers will vary; samples are given.

1. Today, water-skiing is . . .
2. Once, it was considered . . .
3. Now, it is considered . . .
4. Every year, thousands of water-skiers . . .
5. Each summer, these places become . . .

✎ STANDARDIZED TEST PREPARATION WORKSHOP

Grammar and Usage Many standardized tests require students to recognize the form and tense of verbs within the context of a passage. Write the following on the board and ask students to identify the correct answer.

Dexter is raising pigs before he decided to raise pigeons.

How should the underlined verb be written?

A Correct as is
B will be raising
C had been raising
D has been raising

The correct answer is **C**. It is necessary to show that one past action occurred before another past action began. The past perfect progressive (had been raising) expresses an action that occurred both before and during the time Dexter decided to raise pigeons.

Hands-on Grammar

Teaching Resources: Hands-on Grammar Activity Book, Ch. 21

1. If you wish to do this activity in class, be prepared with scissors and two colors of 8-1/2 x 11 paper for the students. Give each student a copy of the Hands-on Grammar activity sheet.

2. Have students follow the directions to prepare the booklets.

3. Encourage students to choose both regular and irregular verbs for their booklets.

Find It in Your Reading

Remind students that the perfect tenses deal with completed actions and review the charts dealing with perfect tenses on page 535 (present and past perfect) and page 537 (future perfect).

Find It in Your Writing

Encourage students to experiment with verb tenses to clarify time relationships in their writing. You might begin with a discussion of what the present progressive does (expresses long continuing action, short continuing action, or continuing condition) and what role it plays in verb sequences. (With present, past, or future main verbs, it describes a simultaneous action.)

21.2

Hands-on Grammar

The Perfect Booklet!

Use a "perfect" two-way booklet to keep track of the perfect tenses.

Begin with a 6" × 8-1/2" sheet of paper. Fold it in half the short way and in half again; then, unfold it. The paper will have three parallel creases. Then, fold the paper in half on the middle crease. With a pair of scissors, cut three slits through the folded edge of the paper at 1-1/2" intervals. Cut *only* as far as the next crease. (See illustration.) Then, unfold and flatten the paper.

3 Slits

Next, cut two 6" × 1-3/4" strips of paper in a color different from that of the full sheet of paper. Weave each strip through the slits in the full sheet, forming a checkerboard pattern. Now, refold the paper on the creases, making a narrow booklet. Notice that opening the booklet on the middle fold on one side gives you two checkered pages; opening the middle fold on the other side gives you four checkered pages—for a total of six.

Now, in the top "square" of each checkered page, print a different perfect tense: Present Perfect, Past Perfect, Future Perfect, Present Perfect Progressive, Past Perfect Progressive, Future Perfect Progressive. Then, choose six verbs, and with two per square, write their perfect tenses on the appropriate pages. When you have finished, you will have a booklet with which to review the perfect tenses.

Find It in Your Reading Look through several pages of a history book, and identify the perfect tenses. Note how many you find in the progressive form.

Find It in Your Writing Review a piece of writing from your portfolio. Identify three verbs in a perfect tense. See if there are any places where you might use a perfect progressive.

546 • Verb Usage

✓ **ONGOING ASSESSMENT: Assess Mastery**

Use the following resources to assess student mastery of the correct use of tenses.

In the Textbook	Technology
Chapter Review, Ex. 45–46, pp. 556–557	*Language Lab* CD-ROM, Using Verbs; *On-Line Exercise Bank,* Section 21.2

Section Review

GRAMMAR EXERCISES 24–29

▶ **Exercise 24   Using Tenses and Forms Correctly** Write the indicated form of each verb in parentheses.

1. Synchronized swimming (be—*present perfect*) a part of American culture for many years.
2. Although skilled swimmers (attempt—*present perfect progressive*) elaborate stunts in the water for centuries, synchronized swimming is thought to have begun in the early 1900's.
3. In 1907, Annette Kellerman (awe—*past*) spectators in New York by performing stunts while floating inside a glass tank.
4. In Chicago in the 1920's, Katherine Curtis (put—*past progressive*) on larger water shows with nearly sixty swimmers.
5. Many skilled swimmers (perform—*past emphatic*) at these shows.
6. It (take—*past*) the efforts of many people before synchronized swimming was recognized as a serious sport.
7. Another sport that (attract— *present emphatic*) swimmers is snorkeling.
8. Many people believe that snorkeling (be—*future*) one of the most popular water activities in the near future.
9. Promoters of the sport (flood—*future progressive*) the media with advertisements to win new fans.
10. By the end of such a media campaign, thousands of people (purchase—*future perfect*) equipment to try the sport.

▶ **Exercise 25   Revising to Correct Shifts in Tenses** Revise these sentences to correct unnecessary shifts in tense.

1. I am reading about how many different swimming strokes there had been.
2. Most people learn the crawl first because it was the easiest.

3. The backstroke will offer an option for those who didn't like water in their faces.
4. The swimmer propels himself with his arms and legs while he was lying on his back.
5. After Jim mastered the backstroke, he goes on to learn the butterfly stroke.

▶ **Exercise 26   Revising by Adding Modifiers to Clarify Tense** Rewrite each of the following sentences by adding a modifier that indicates time.

1. People attempt to swim across large bodies of water.
2. Swimming the English Channel has been a popular goal of endurance swimmers.
3. To train for such a feat, a swimmer must swim many miles.
4. Endurance swimmers attempt to swim even longer distances.
5. These attempts seem daring, but surely more daring attempts will be made.

▶ **Exercise 27   Find It in Your Reading** In the excerpt from *A Journey Through Texas* on page 529, identify one verb in the past progressive tense and one in the past emphatic.

▶ **Exercise 28   Find It in Your Writing** Scan a news story to find verbs that show sequential events. Identify the tense of each verb, and note which event precedes another.

▶ **Exercise 29   Writing Application** Write an account of a time when you participated in or watched a water sport. Include sentences that have more than one verb and that show a sequence of events.

ASSESS

Section Review

Each of these exercises correlates to the instruction on the correct use of tenses, pages 532–545. The exercises may be used for more practice, for reteaching, or for review of the key concepts presented.

Answer Key

▶ **Exercise 24**

1. has been
2. have been attempting
3. awed
4. was putting
5. did perform
6. took
7. does attract
8. will be
9. will be flooding
10. will have purchased

▶ **Exercise 25**

Answers will vary; samples are given.

1. I am reading about how many different swimming strokes there <u>are</u>.
2. Most people learn the crawl first because it <u>is</u> the easiest.
3. The backstroke <u>offers</u> an option for those who don't like water in their faces.
4. The swimmer propels himself with his arms and legs while he <u>is</u> lying on his back.
5. After Jim mastered the backstroke, he <u>went</u> on to learn the butterfly stroke.

▶ **Exercise 26**

Answers will vary; samples are given.

1. Every year, people attempt to swim . . .
2. For decades, swimming . . .
3. . . . must swim many miles every day.

continued

Answer Key continued

▶ **Exercise 26**

4. Sometimes, endurance swimmers attempt . . .
5. . . . will be made in the future.

▶ **Exercise 27**

Find It in Your Reading
Past progressive: we were coming
Past emphatic: they did not want us

▶ **Exercise 28**

Find It in Your Writing
Suggest that, if students do not find any sentences that include sequences of events, they

could rewrite a sentence or combine two shorter sentences so that a sequence is established within one sentence.

▶ **Exercise 29**

Writing Application
Have students trade accounts and check each other's work for correct verb tense sequence. Ask each student to select one sentence in the account they are checking and write in the margin the tense of each verb and, if there is a sequence, which action or condition comes first.

On the board, write, *If I were an explorer, I . . .* Tell students not to copy these words but simply to complete the statement. Have volunteers read their sentence completions to the class. After you have heard several, ask the class what one word occurred in most sentence completions. (*would*) Ask why *would* was appropriate. (It expresses the idea that something else must happen first for what follows to be true.)

Activate Prior Knowledge

Have students recall *If I were . . .* statements that they have heard. Point out that clauses that begin with *if* often indicate that the statement that follows does not reflect a current fact. The statements may be ones that can become true (for example, *If I were to study harder, I would do better on the next test*) and some may never become true (*If I were living in a different time, I would be happier*).

TEACH

Step-by-Step Teaching Guide

The Correct Use of the Subjunctive Mood

1. Have students give one or two examples of the indicative and imperative moods.

2. Explain that the third "mood," the subjunctive mood, refers to a verb form that expresses something—a state of being, an action, or an event—as possible, conditional, or dependent, rather than as actual.

3. Point out that the *If I were* sentences in the Interest Grabber are examples of conditional statements: There is a condition that must be met; that is, something must happen for something else to be true.

4. Tell students that in English there are only a few rules about the subjunctive mood to remember: The verb *to be* appears only in the forms *be* and *were*, and other verbs are affected only in the third person singular, losing their final *-s* or *-es*.

The Subjunctive Mood

Modern English has three *moods*, or ways in which a verb can express an action or condition: indicative, imperative, and subjunctive. The first two are familiar moods found in most of the sentences that you write or speak. The *indicative* mood, the most common, is used to make factual statements (Gail *drives* safely.) and to ask questions (*Does* Gail drive safely?). The *imperative* mood is used to give orders or directions (*Drive* safely.).

Although the *subjunctive* mood has limited use in modern English, it is important to know the instances that it should be used.

The Correct Use of the Subjunctive Mood

You will notice that verbs in the subjunctive mood differ from verbs in the indicative mood in two significant ways. First, in the present tense, a third-person singular verb in the subjunctive mood does not have the usual *-s* or *-es* ending. Second, in the present tense, the subjunctive mood of *be* is *be*, and in the past tense, it is *were*, regardless of the subject.

Indicative Mood	Subjunctive Mood
I want to be sure that he *drives* slowly.	I prefer that he *drive* slowly.
They *are* not punctual.	I demand that they *be* punctual.
I *was* sad.	If I *were* sad, I would tell you.

The subjunctive mood has two general uses:

▶ **KEY CONCEPTS** Use the subjunctive mood (1) in clauses beginning with *if* or *that* to express an idea contrary to fact or (2) in clauses beginning with *that* to express a request, a demand, or a proposal. ■

By checking the *if* and *that* clauses in your own writing, you will be able to use the subjunctive mood correctly.

Theme: Cars and Drivers

In this section, you will learn how to use the subjunctive mood of verbs. The examples and exercises in this section are about cars and drivers.

Cross-Curricular Connection: Social Studies

⏱ TIME AND RESOURCE MANAGER

Resources
Print: *Grammar Exercise Workbook*, pp. 97–98; *Grammar Exercises Answers on Transparencies*, Ch. 21
Technology: *Language Lab* CD-ROM, Using Verbs; *On-Line Exercise Bank*, Section 21.3

In-Depth Coverage	Accelerated Pace
• Work through all key concepts, pp. 548–549. • Assign and review Exercise 30.	• Assign pp. 548–549 for independent student review. • Assign Section Review Exercises 31–32, p. 551.

Expressing Ideas Contrary to Fact

Expressing Ideas Contrary to Fact Ideas that are contrary to fact are usually expressed as wishes or conditions. The subjunctive mood helps to indicate that what is being expressed is not now and may never be true.

EXAMPLES: Alex wished that he *were* a better driver.
If she *were* driving to the beach now, she'd be happy.

Note that when *if* clauses express ideas that may be factual, they do not use verbs in the subjunctive mood.

EXAMPLE: If I want to drive to the lake, I know I'll have to get up early, so I will set the alarm.

Expressing Requests, Demands, and Proposals

The second use of the subjunctive mood implies that the ideas being expressed could or should be true soon. A verb that expresses a request, a demand, or a proposal is often followed by a *that* clause, which will generally call for a verb in the subjunctive mood.

VERBS OFTEN FOLLOWED BY *THAT* CLAUSES WITH SUBJUNCTIVE VERBS

ask	insist	prefer	require
demand	move	propose	suggest
determine	order	request	

REQUEST: We ask that everyone *be* silent during the show.
DEMAND: The driving instructor insists that every student *drive* carefully.
PROPOSAL: I move that the results of the survey *be* published.

🌸 Grammar and Style Tip

Overuse of the subjunctive mood in *that* clauses can give your writing a stilted tone. Sometimes, consider using an infinitive:
I asked *that he drive* safely.
I asked *him to drive* safely.

◄ **Critical Viewing**
Imagine the feelings of this student on getting her driver's license. Putting yourself in her position, how would you react? Answer using the subjunctive mood. **[Relate]**

The Subjunctive Mood • 549

⬧ STANDARDIZED TEST PREPARATION WORKSHOP

Grammar and Usage Many standardized tests require students to draw upon their knowledge and understanding of the subjunctive mood to write correct sentences. Write the following on the board and ask students to identify the correct answer.

If the fog <u>was less thick</u>, our plane would be able to land.

How is <u>was less thick</u> correctly written?

A Correct as is

B wasn't less thick

C is less thick

D were less thick

The correct answer is **D**. Because the sentence presents a condition contrary to fact (the fog is *not* less thick), the use of the subjunctive mood is necessary.

Answer Key

▶ **Exercise 30**

1. Most countries require that a driver **pass** a driving test before operating a motor vehicle.
2. In the United States, the law in most states requires that a driver **be** at least sixteen years old.
3. The law also demands that a person wishing to drive first **prove** his or her ability.
4. States usually insist that the test **be** made up of a written part and a practical part.
5. A person who fails the test may wish that he or she **were** free to drive without a license.
6. The person may prefer that all licensing regulations **be** eliminated.
7. Such a person may feel that the government is treating her as if she **were** a child.
8. However, most citizens prefer that a driver **meet** the requirements mandated by law.
9. If a driver **were** free to drive without meeting requirements, he or she might prove to be a danger to others.
10. A careful driver who has to share the road with incompetent and reckless drivers will soon wish that he or she **were** driving somewhere else.

Critical Viewing

Make a Judgment Possible answer: When a car enters a highway or changes lanes, the law requires that it use a turn signal.

21.3

▶ **Exercise 30** **Revise for the Subjunctive Mood** Revise each sentence, changing the verb to the subjunctive mood wherever necessary.

EXAMPLE: She suggests that Paula drives her own car.
ANSWER: She suggests that Paula drive her own car.

1. Most countries require that a driver passes a driving test before operating a motor vehicle.
2. In the United States, the law in most states requires that a driver is at least sixteen years old.
3. The law also demands that a person wishing to drive first proves his or her ability.
4. States usually insist that the test is made up of a written part and a practical part.
5. A person who fails the test may wish that he or she was free to drive without a license.
6. The person may prefer that all licensing regulations are eliminated.
7. Such a person may feel that the government is treating her as if she was a child.
8. However, most citizens prefer that a driver meets the requirements mandated by law.
9. If a driver was free to drive without meeting any requirements, he or she might prove to be a danger to others.
10. A careful driver who has to share the road with incompetent and reckless drivers will soon wish that he or she was driving somewhere else.

▲ **Critical Viewing**
What does motor-vehicle law require of a driver when he or she is entering a highway or changing lanes? Respond using the subjunctive mood. **[Make a Judgment]**

▶ **More Practice**
Language Lab CD-ROM
• Using Verbs lesson
On-line Exercise Bank
• Section 21.3
Grammar Exercise Workbook
• pp. 97–98

☑ **ONGOING ASSESSMENT: Assess Mastery**

Use the following resources to assess student mastery of the subjunctive mood.

In the Textbook	Technology
Chapter Review, Ex. 47, p.557	*Language Lab* CD-ROM, Using Verbs *On-Line Exercise Bank*, Section 21.3

Section 21.3 Section Review

GRAMMAR EXERCISES 31–35

Exercise 31 **Identifying Mood**
Identify the mood of each underlined verb in the following sentences as indicative, imperative, or subjunctive.

1. The modern automobile <u>is</u> fueled by gasoline.
2. People have also developed cars that <u>are</u> powered by natural gas and electricity.
3. If the world <u>were</u> to run out of gasoline, these alternative vehicles could become very popular.
4. Many people insist that a vehicle <u>do</u> as little harm to the environment as possible.
5. <u>Think</u> of new ways to power the automobile.

Exercise 32 **Revise for Correct Use of the Subjunctive Mood** Revise each sentence, changing the verb to the subjunctive mood as necessary.

1. The automobile industry of the early 1900's may appear to people today as if it was an alien entity.
2. An automobile from this era was often made as if it was a custom-tailored pair of pants.
3. A customer ordered a car and then insisted that the company makes custom parts for that car.
4. While a car was being assembled, its future owner often demanded that the manufacturer follows his suggestions for design changes.
5. A mechanic often wished that he was free to build cars a different way.
6. One manufacturer knew that if he was to produce affordable cars, he would have to be able to build them quickly and uniformly.
7. Likewise, if the manufacturer was able to produce massive quantities of identical parts, he would save much time and money.
8. Such a development required that the building of parts are mechanized.
9. Car builders soon insisted that mechanized procedures are used to manufacture most car parts.
10. In spite of the highly mechanized methods available today, custom car enthusiasts still prefer that a skilled mechanic crafts a car by hand.

Exercise 33 **Find It in Your Reading** Look through some advice columns and editorials in recent newspapers or magazines. See if you can locate any verbs in the subjunctive mood. Then, select a short passage from one of the articles, and identify the mood of each verb.

Exercise 34 **Find It in Your Writing** Look through your writing portfolio. Challenge yourself to find a place where you might include a verb in the subjunctive mood. Revise or add a sentence as necessary. A piece of persuasive writing or a short story might be a good place to look first.

Exercise 35 **Writing Application** Write a short essay stating your opinion about an issue such as the current voting or driving age, TV violence, or gun control. Include at least two sentences with a verb in the subjunctive mood.

ASSESS

Section Review

Each of these exercises correlates to the instruction on the subjunctive mood, pages 548–549. The exercises may be used for more practice, for reteaching, or for review of the key concepts presented.

Answer Key

Exercise 31

1. indicative
2. indicative
3. subjunctive
4. subjunctive
5. imperative

Exercise 32

1. The automobile industry of the early 1900's may appear to people today as if it **were** an alien entity.
2. An automobile from this era was often made as if it **were** a custom-tailored pair of pants.
3. A customer ordered a car and then insisted that the company **make** custom parts for that car.
4. While a car was being assembled, its future owner often demanded that the manufacturer **follow** his suggestions for design changes.
5. A mechanic often wished that he **were** free to build cars a different way.
6. One manufacturer knew that if he **were** to produce affordable cars, he would have to be able to build them quickly and uniformly.
7. Likewise, if the manufacturer **were** able to produce massive quantities of identical parts, he would save much time and money.
8. Such a development required that the building of parts **be** mechanized.
9. Car builders soon insisted that mechanized procedures **be** used to manufacture most car parts.
10. In spite of the highly mechanized methods available today, many custom car enthusiasts still prefer that a skilled mechanic **craft** a car by hand.

continued

Answer Key continued

Exercise 33

Find It in Your Reading
Have students share any usage errors they find as they scan the newspapers. Ask students why they think some people get the use of the subjunctive wrong (don't know about it, don't understand it).

Exercise 34

Find It in Your Writing
Tell students to correct any sentences they find where the subjunctive should have been used but wasn't.

Exercise 35

Writing Application
Have students trade essays with a partner, and have each student check his or her partner's work for correct use of the subjunctive mood, noting any incorrect usage. The partners should discuss the usage being questioned and come to an agreement on correct usage. Remind students that they are checking only for correct usage, not for strength of argument or agreement with opinions.

PREPARE and ENGAGE

 Interest GRABBER Write these sentences on the board.

The cat ate the cake.

The cake was eaten by the cat.

Ask students to explain the difference between the two. (Possible answers: In the first, the cat seems more important; the verb *ate* seems more dynamic.) Point out that the first sentence tells what the subject does; the second, what is done to the subject.

Activate Prior Knowledge

Ask students to recall titles that express action ("We Wear the Mask"). Help students recognize that the verb describes an action done by the subject: It is in active voice. Ask them to rearrange the title so the action is done to the subject. ("The Mask Is Worn by Us") Tell students that this construction is called passive voice.

TEACH

Step-by-Step Teaching Guide

Active and Passive Voice

1. Have a student read the definition of voice, and then point out that linking verbs can never indicate voice because they don't express action.

2. In the first example of active voice, point out that the subject (*Carver*) performs the action of developing. Explain that the verb (*developed*) is transitive because it has a direct object (*products*) that receives the action.

3. Have students compare this example with the parallel example in passive voice. Ask them to identify the grammatical function of *Carver* in this sentence (object of the preposition *by*). Point out that the products are now the focus, and Carver is of secondary importance in the sentence.

4. Review the chart that shows *choose* in the passive voice. Note that the transitive verb is the past participle in all tenses, while the helping verb *be* changes to show tense.

5. Explain that, while the passive voice has its uses, it is less dynamic than the active voice. In most writing, the active voice is preferable.

552

Voice

The form of a verb can be changed to show the relationship between the subject and the verb in a sentence. The form of the verb determines whether the subject is performing the action or having the action performed on it.

▶ **KEY CONCEPT** **Voice** is the form of a verb that indicates whether the subject is performing the action. ■

In English, there are two voices: *active* and *passive*. Only action verbs can indicate voice; linking verbs cannot.

Active and Passive Voice

A verb is active when the subject performs the action and passive when the subject receives the action.

Active Voice Any action verb, regardless of whether it is transitive or intransitive (that is, with or without a direct object), can be in the active voice.

▶ **KEY CONCEPT** A verb is active if the subject performs the action. ■

In both examples below, the subjects perform the action. The first example contains a *transitive* verb and, therefore, has a direct object that receives the action of the verb. The second example has no direct object; its verb is *intransitive*.

ACTIVE VOICE: Carver *developed* seventy-five products from pecans.
Carver *worked* with conviction.

Passive Voice Most action verbs can also be passive.

▶ **KEY CONCEPT** A verb is passive if the action is performed upon the subject. ■

In the examples below, the subjects receive the action. The first example names the performer, *Carver*, although *Carver* is no longer the subject but the object of the preposition *by*. In the second example, the performer of the action is not named.

PASSIVE VOICE: Seventy-five products *were developed* by Carver from pecans.
The work *was done* with conviction.

A passive verb is always a verb phrase made from a form of *be* plus the past participle of a transitive verb. The tense of the helping verb *be* determines the tense of the passive verb.

552 • Verb Usage

Theme: Notable African Americans

In this section, you will learn about active voice and passive voice and their proper use. The examples and exercises in this section are about two notable figures in African American history.

Cross-Curricular Connection: Social Studies

⏱ TIME AND RESOURCE MANAGER

Resources
Print: *Grammar Exercise Workbook*, pp. 99–102; *Grammar Exercises Answers on Transparencies*, Ch. 21
Technology: *Language Lab* CD-ROM, Using Verbs; *On-Line Exercise Bank*, Section 21.4

In-Depth Coverage	Accelerated Pace
• Work through all key concepts, pp. 552–554. • Assign and review Exercise 36–38.	• Assign pp. 552–554 for independent student review. • Assign Section Review Exercises 39–40, p. 555.

THE VERB *CHOOSE* IN THE PASSIVE VOICE

Present:	she is chosen
Past:	she was chosen
Future:	she will be chosen
Present Perfect:	she has been chosen
Past Perfect:	she had been chosen
Future Perfect:	she will have been chosen
Present Progressive:	she is being chosen
Past Progressive:	she was chosen

▶ **Exercise 36** **Identifying and Revising Active and Passive Voice** Identify each verb as *active* or *passive*. Then, revise those that are passive to active, adding or changing words as needed.

EXAMPLE: Peanut butter was invented by G. W. Carver.

ANSWER: (passive) G. W. Carver invented peanut butter.

1. George Washington Carver earned his bachelor's degree in science from Iowa State College in 1894.
2. Following his graduation, he was hired by Iowa State College as a faculty member to teach agriculture.
3. Later, an idle field at a school in Tuskegee, Alabama, was transformed by Carver into a prosperous farm.
4. Peanuts were championed by Carver as a good crop for Alabama soil, and he developed more than three hundred different products—including oil, paint, ink, and butter—from the simple peanut.
5. By the time of his death in 1943, Carver had been recognized by numerous organizations and scientists.

▶ **Exercise 37** **Forming the Tenses of Passive Verbs** Conjugate each verb in the passive voice, using the chart above.
1. drive   2. invent   3. write   4. grow   5. own

▼ **Critical Viewing** What do the pictures in this montage say about the activities of an inventor? Answer with one sentence in the active voice and one in the passive voice. [Draw Conclusions]

George Washington Carver, agriculturist and inventor

▶ **More Practice**
Language Lab CD-ROM
• Using Verbs lesson
On-line Exercise Bank
• Section 21.4
Grammar Exercise Workbook
• pp. 99–102

Voice • 553

Answer Key

▶ **Exercise 36**
1. Active
2. Passive. Iowa State College hired him . . .
3. Passive. Carver transformed an idle field . . .
4. Passive. Carver championed peanuts . . .
5. Passive. Numerous organizations and scientists had recognized Carver . . .

continued

Answer Key continued

▶ **Exercise 37**
Suggest that students use "it" to conjugate each item.
1. it is driven, was driven, will be driven, has been driven, had been driven, will have been driven, is being driven, was being driven
2. it is known, etc.
3. it is written, etc.
4. it is grown, etc.
5. it is frozen, etc.

Critical Viewing

Draw Conclusions Possible answer: An agriculturalist spends time experimenting with plants. Much of Carver's time was spent in the laboratory.

553

Step-by-Step Teaching Guide

Using Active and Passive Voice

1. On the board, write: *I raised two kittens* and *Two kittens were raised by me.* Point out that, although the same information is given in both sentences, the one in the active voice sounds more direct and concise.

2. Explain that there are times when the passive voice is appropriate. The passive voice can be used to emphasize the receiver of the action. In the first example below the second key concept, the sentence emphasizes *wood* more than it emphasizes *Harriet Tubman.*

3. Have students rewrite the sentence in the active voice. *(Harriet Tubman carried wood.)* Point out that the emphasis shifts to Harriet Tubman, who is now the subject.

4. Encourage students to use the active voice whenever possible to make their writing clear, concise, and more dynamic.

Critical Viewing

Analyze Possible answer: Tubman's stern expression shows her strength.

Answer Key

▶ **Exercise 38**

1. Harriet Tubman had a hard life
2. Correct; performer not emphasized
3. Plantation owners forced her
4. In 1849, her masters sold Tubman
5. Correct; passive emphasizes receiver, but could be rewritten "the desire to escape overcame her"
6. Correct; performer unimportant
7. Correct; passive emphasizes receiver, but could be rewritten "People sympathetic to runaway slaves helped Tubman"
8. Active
9. Later Tubman played a significant role
10. Correct; performer unimportant

Using Active and Passive Voice

Once you are able to distinguish between the active and passive voice, you can apply this knowledge to your own writing. The active voice is generally more forceful than the passive voice.

▶ **KEY CONCEPT** Use the active voice whenever possible because it is usually more direct and economical. ■

ACTIVE VOICE: Carver *invented* many products.
PASSIVE VOICE: Many products *were* invented by Carver.

The passive voice has two important uses in English.

▶ **KEY CONCEPTS** Use the passive voice to emphasize the receiver of an action, rather than the performer of an action. Use the passive voice to point out the receiver of an action when the performer is not important or not easily identified. ■

RECEIVER EMPHASIZED: Wood *was carried* by Harriet Tubman.

PERFORMER UNKNOWN: A child *was helped* across the river.

PERFORMER UNIMPORTANT: The runaways *were saved.*

▶ **Exercise 38** **Revising to Correct Unnecessary Use of the Passive Voice** Revise the following passage, changing unnecessary uses of the passive voice to the active voice. Not every use of the passive voice will need to change.

A hard life was had by Harriet Tubman because of the prejudices and injustices of the early 1800's. She was born into slavery in Dorchester County, Maryland, around 1819. She was forced by plantation owners to labor in the fields. In 1849, Tubman was sold by her masters to a distant plantation. Traveling to the new plantation, she was overcome by a desire to escape. She slipped into the woods and stealthily made her way north toward states where slavery had been outlawed. Tubman was helped during her trip by people sympathetic to runaway slaves. She traveled more than one hundred miles and eventually reached Philadelphia, a free city. Later, a significant role was played by Tubman in the Underground Railroad. She was called the "Moses" of her people.

▼ **Critical Viewing** One could say that Harriet Tubman lived her life "in the active voice." What aspect of this photograph suggests Tubman's strength? Answer in the active voice. **[Analyze]**

554 • Verb Usage

☑ **ONGOING ASSESSMENT: Monitor and Reinforce**

If students have difficulty with Exercise 36, 37, or 38, refer them to the following for additional practice.

In the Textbook	Print Resources	Technology
Section Review, Ex. 39–40, p. 555	*Grammar Exercise Workbook,* pp. 99–102	*Language Lab* CD-ROM, Using Verbs *On-Line Exercise Bank,* Section 21.4

Section 21.4 Section Review

GRAMMAR EXERCISES 39–43

Exercise 39 Identifying Active and Passive Voice Identify each verb as *active* or *passive*.

1. In addition to his skills as a scientist, George Washington Carver enjoyed music.
2. While working in Winterset, Iowa, Carver was given piano lessons by Mrs. Millholland, a gifted musician.
3. His skills as a musician helped him later in life.
4. In his early days at Tuskegee, Carver played a series of recitals to raise money for the school's agriculture program.
5. Enough money was raised from those concerts for the purchase of much-needed farm equipment.
6. Carver also enjoyed the visual arts.
7. While at Simpson College, he was coached in painting by Etta Budd.
8. Carver's creativity was nurtured by Budd.
9. Fueled by her encouragement, Carver painted numerous pictures while at Simpson College.
10. Some of Carver's paintings were exhibited by art experts at an exposition in 1893.

Exercise 40 Revising to Change Verbs to the Active Voice Rewrite the following sentences using the active voice. Change or add words as necessary in order to put each verb into the active voice.

1. George Washington Carver is remembered by historians as a pioneer African American scientist.
2. Great sacrifices were made by Carver throughout his professional life.
3. Forty-five years were spent by Carver at Tuskegee.
4. During that time, his services were sought by numerous prestigious institutions.
5. Carver was invited by Thomas A. Edison to join the staff of the famous Edison Laboratories in New Jersey.
6. A large salary was offered to Carver by Edison.
7. That offer, and many other similar offers, were turned down by Carver.
8. Carver was driven by a love of research and the desire to help African Americans.
9. In 1923, an honorary doctor of science degree was given to him by the University of Rochester.
10. A second honorary doctor of science degree was awarded to him by Simpson College.

Exercise 41 Find It in Your Reading Look through a social studies textbook to find examples of the passive voice being used because the performer of an action is unknown or not specific.

Exercise 42 Find It in Your Writing In your own writing, find at least three examples of verbs in the passive voice. If any example contains an unnecessary use of the passive voice, rewrite it in the active voice.

Exercise 43 Writing Application Write an account of an incident you experienced that illustrates the positive value of friendship. Include two appropriate sentences using the passive voice correctly.

Section Review • 555

ASSESS and CLOSE

Section Review

Each of these exercises correlates to the instruction on voice, pages 552–554. The exercises may be used for more practice, for reteaching, or for review of the key concepts presented. Answers for all chapter exercises are available in *Grammar Exercises Answers on Transparencies* in your Teaching Resources.

Answer Key

▶ **Exercise 39**

1. active
2. passive
3. active
4. active
5. passive
6. active
7. passive
8. passive
9. active
10. passive

▶ **Exercise 40**

1. Historians remember George Washington Carver
2. Carver made great sacrifices
3. Carver spent forty-five years
4. Numerous prestigious institutions sought his services
5. Thomas A. Edison invited Carver to join the staff
6. Edison offered Carver
7. Carver turned down that offer
8. A love of research and the desire to help African Americans drove Carver.
9. In 1923, the University of Rochester gave him
10. Simpson College awarded him

▶ **Exercise 41**

Find It in Your Reading
Answers will vary. Examples might include enslaving African Americans, moving into Native American territory, and other events in which the people causing them are less important than the events themselves.

▶ **Exercise 42**

Find It in Your Writing
If students feel that sentences use passive voice appropriately, have them explain why.

▶ **Exercise 43**

Writing Application
Ask volunteers to share the sentences that they wrote in passive voice and explain what is being emphasized in the sentences (or what is unknown) that makes the passive voice appropriate.

✅ ONGOING ASSESSMENT: Assess Mastery

Use the following resources to assess student mastery of phrases and clauses.

In the Textbook	Print Resources	Technology
Chapter Review, Ex. 44–48 Standardized Test Preparation Workshop, pp. 558–559	*Formal Assessment*, Chapter 21	*Language Lab* CD-ROM, Using Verbs *On-Line Exercise Bank*, Chapter 21

Each of these exercises correlates to a section of the chapter on verb usage, pages 518–555. These exercises may be used for more practice, for reteaching, or for review of the key concepts presented.

Answer Key

▶ **Exercise 44**

1. was
2. began
3. chosen
4. studied
5. become
6. toured
7. kept
8. sang
9. won
10. given

▶ **Exercise 45**

1. have been inspiring
2. composed
3. had studied
4. was heading
5. was named
6. have praised
7. will remember
8. will have been enjoying
9. are
10. awakened

▶ **Exercise 46**

1. sequential: electronic instruments came before synthesizer concept
2. simultaneous
3. sequential: technology improved before electronic instruments were treated seriously
4. simultaneous
5. simultaneous
6. simultaneous
7. sequential: need came before synthesizers coming into their own
8. sequential: advances came before synthesizers began providing variety
9. simultaneous
10. sequential: current use comes before future use

▶ **Exercise 47**

1. If there **were** a list . . .
2. After college, Robeson played football professionally and studied law at Columbia Law School until his wife proposed that he **act** in plays.

▶ **Exercise 44** **Supplying the Past Tense or the Past Participle** On your paper, write the appropriate past or past participle of each verb in parentheses in the following sentences.

1. One of the first African Americans to distinguish herself as a classical vocalist (is) Marian Anderson.
2. Born on February 27, 1903, in Philadelphia, Pennsylvania, Anderson (begin) her singing career at Philadelphia's Union Baptist Church.
3. By the time she was a teenager, she had already (choose) to pursue a career as a professional singer.
4. Toward that goal, she (study) with Giuseppe Boghetti, a famous voice teacher.
5. By the age of twenty, she had (become) a successful singer.
6. She (tour) widely in Europe and the United States.
7. These engagements (keep) her busy for much of the 1930's.
8. In 1939, Marian Anderson (sing) before a large crowd outside the Lincoln Memorial in Washington, D.C.
9. By that time, she had (win) recognition as one of the best singers in the world.
10. Anderson's accomplishments have (give) inspiration to numerous African American musicians.

▶ **Exercise 45** **Using Tense in Past, Present, and Future Time** On your paper, write the indicated form of each verb in parentheses.

1. The works of Leonard Bernstein (inspire—present perfect progressive) musicians since the late 1940's.
2. Bernstein (compose—past) incidental music for the movie *The Birds* long before his famous Broadway musicals.

556 • Verb Usage

3. Before he was appointed assistant conductor of the New York Philharmonic in 1943, he (study—past perfect) at the Boston Symphony's summer institute.
4. By 1959, he (head—past progressive) the orchestral and conducting departments at Tanglewood.
5. In 1958, he (name—past, passive voice) music director of the New York Philharmonic.
6. Critics (praise—present perfect) Bernstein's memorable recordings of the works of both Beethoven and the American composer Aaron Copeland.
7. Most people probably (remember—future) him best for his collaboration on the 1957 musical *West Side Story*.
8. By the year 2007, music fans (enjoy—future perfect progressive) its engaging tunes for fifty years.
9. Less known (be—present) Bernstein's operas and ballets.
10. However, Bernstein's televised *Young People's Concerts* certainly (awaken—past) music appreciation in children.

▶ **Exercise 46** **Using Subordinate Verbs, Participles, and Infinitives** Write whether the events described by the verbs in the main and subordinate clauses are *simultaneous* or *sequential*. If they are sequential, list which event came before the other.

1. Athough the synthesizer concept is relatively new, electronic instruments have been around for a long time.
2. While there were some exceptions, most other electronic instruments produced from the 1920's through the 1940's were of the electric organ variety.
3. Because the technology improved in the 1950's, electronic instruments have been treated more seriously.

3. Robeson embraced acting and mastered roles as if he **were** a veteran actor.
4. Not content with only acting, he preferred that his immense talents **be** utilized in other ways.
5. correct

4. People in the industry were predicting that it was only natural for synthesizers to make headway.
5. Electronic synthesizer builders were mostly hobbyists who were searching for new ways to create sound.
6. By the time the late 1960's arrived, musicians and filmmakers were also looking for ways to make unique sounds.
7. Once the need arose, commercial synthesizers came into their own.
8. Because there have been great advances in the technology, synthesizers are now providing musicians with a wide variety of techniques and methods for creating sound.
9. Although the techniques have changed, the basic concept remains the same.
10. Synthesizers—which are now used in almost all musical forms—will continue to provide the backbone of today's most popular music.

▶ Exercise 47   Revising to Supply the Subjunctive Mood
Revise the following sentences, changing the verbs to the subjunctive mood as necessary.

1. If there was a list of people who excelled in music, sports, and theater, Paul Robeson's name would be on it.
2. After college, Robeson played football professionally and studied law at Columbia Law School until his wife proposed that he acts in plays.
3. Robeson embraced acting and mastered roles as if he was a veteran actor.
4. Not content with only acting, he preferred that his immense talents were utilized in other ways.
5. People knew that if Robeson was invited to sing spirituals in concert, he would often be likely to accept.

▶ Exercise 48   Revising for Passive Voice and Active Voice
Revise the following sentences, changing the passive voice to active and the active to passive.

1. In the early 1950's, *Captain Video and the Video Ranger* was watched by children all across the country.
2. The role of Captain Video was played by an actor named Al Hodge.
3. During the show's run, Captain Video battled more than 300 fiendish villains.
4. Captain Video often used reason instead of ray-gun blasts to resolve situations.
5. Freedom, truth, and justice were championed by this hero.

▶ Exercise 49   Writing Application
Imagine that you are a fiction author writing to your editor about the plot of your new novel. Be sure to relate the highlights of the action that will take place. Use action verbs and modifiers that indicate time.

▶ Exercise 50   CUMULATIVE REVIEW
Sentence Revision and Verb Usage
Revise the following paragraph, correcting sentence errors (fragments, run-ons, misplaced and dangling modifers, and faulty parallelism or coordination) and errors in verb usage. Also, combine sentences and change verbs to the active voice as necessary.

In the event that you are not familiar with them. The Katzenjammer Kids were the central characters in what has been the first true color comic strip. Appearing in the Sunday comic pages in December 1897, readers were immediately amused by the antics of Hans and Fritz Katzenjammer. The characters in the comic strip had been the twins, Hans and Fritz, and Mamma Katzenjammer. Another character was the Captain. The long-suffering Captain was targeted by the twins as the victim of their mischief. In the early decades, the Katzenjammer family has adventures all over the world, later they settled on a tropical island. Many fans liked "The Katzenjammer Kids" better than any other comic strip.

▶ Exercise 48
Answers may vary; samples are given.

1. In the early 1950s, children all across the country watched *Captain Video and the Video Ranger.*
2. An actor named Al Hodge played the role of Captain Video.
3. During the show's run, more than 300 fiendish villains were battled by Captain Video.
4. Often, reason instead of ray-gun blasts was used by Captain Video to resolve situations.
5. This hero championed freedom, truth, and justice.

▶ Exercise 49
Writing Application
Have students trade papers with a partner. Ask them to first identify whether the story being proposed is set in the past, present, or future. Have students check their partners' papers for appropriate verb usage and use of modifiers and verbs to indicate time.

▶ Exercise 50
Cumulative Review
Answers may vary. Possible answer:

Perhaps you are familiar with the Katzenjammer Kids, who were the central characters in what was the first true color comic strip. When the strip appeared in the Sunday comic pages in December 1897, readers were immediately amused by the antics of Hans and Fritz Katzenjammer. The characters in the comic strip were the twins, Hans and Fritz; Mamma Katzenjammer; and the Captain. The twins targeted the long-suffering Captain as the victim of their mischief. In the early decades, the Katzenjammer family had adventures all over the world; later they settled on a tropical island. Many fans liked *The Katzenjammer Kids* better than any other comic strip.

Verb Usage

Teaching Resources: Standardized Test Preparation Workbook, pp. 41–42

1. Remind students to read the sentences in the selection for meaning. Grasping the meaning will help them determine when the event is taking place.

2. Point out that listening to each possibility in the context of the sentence will provide clues as to what "sounds right."

3. Suggest that students quickly reread the passage as a whole, inserting the verbs chosen, to make sure the verb tenses are consistent.

Standardized Test Preparation Workshop

Verb Usage

Your knowledge of verb usage is frequently measured on standardized tests. Your ability to determine the correct tense of a verb—present, present perfect, past, past perfect, future, and future perfect and their progressive forms—is tested when you must choose a verb or verb phrase to complete a sentence. When choosing a verb, first read the sentence silently to yourself and determine when it is taking place. Then, choose a verb that indicates the same point in time or tense of the sentence.

The following test items will give you practice with the format of questions that test verb usage.

Test Tip

Read the sentence silently to yourself several times. Each time, substitute one of the answer choices in place of the blank. Eliminate those choices that sound awkward or that change the meaning of the sentence.

Sample Test Items	**Answers and Explanations**
Directions: Read the sentence, and choose the letter of the word or group of words that belongs in each space.	
When I ___(1)___ the road test for my driver's license, the first thing I ___(2)___ after getting in the car was to put on my seat belt.	The correct answer is *D*. The sentence suggests a continuing action in the past that took place at the same time as another past event. Therefore, the past progressive form *was taking* is the correct choice for completing the sentence.

1 A have taken
    B will have been taking
    C had taken
    D was taking	

2 F did
    G done
    H was doing
    J had done
	The correct answer is *F*. The second part of the sentence describes a single action that began and ended in the past. Therefore, the past tense verb *did* is the correct choice for completing the sentence.

558 • Verb Usage

✦ TEST-TAKING TIP

If students clearly comprehend the meaning of the entire text passage, they will be able to recognize more quickly the appropriate verb or verb phrase. They might quickly and silently read the whole passage in order to get a sense of what is going on. When they return to the first sentence, they should be able to choose the correct answer more easily.

Also tell students to pay attention to the first word of each sentence. These are often clues to the time frame.

Practice 1 Directions: Read the passage, and choose the letter of the word or group of words that belongs in each space.

When you ___(1)___ to take your road test, you ___(2)___ proof of your vehicle's registration and insurance coverage. When it is time to start the test, you put on your seat belt first. Next, you ___(3)___ your rearview and side mirrors. In many states, if you forget to do so, your test will be over and you ___(4)___. Once you ___(5)___ out on the road, remember to follow the examiner's instructions.

1 A go
   B have gone
   C will go
   D went

2 F have needed
   G are needing
   H will need
   J will have needed

3 A adjust
   B are adjusting
   C will be adjusting
   D have adjusted

4 F failed
   G fail
   H will have failed
   J have failed

5 A are setting
   B had set
   C will set
   D have set

Practice 2 Directions: Read the passage, and choose the letter of the word or group of words that belongs in each space.

When on the road, check to see that you ___(1)___ the correct driving posture. This means that you ___(2)___ both hands on the steering wheel and ___(3)___ your elbow on an open window. It ___(4)___ important to stay in the correct lane and maintain an appropriate distance from the car in front of you. If you pass, you probably ___(5)___ with excitement at the prospect of taking out the car on your own.

1 A assume
   B have assumed
   C were assuming
   D have been assuming

2 F place
   G have been placing
   H have placed
   J will have placed

3 A are not resting
   B do not rest
   C will not rest
   D had not rested

4 F was
   G is
   H will have been
   J has been

5 A burst
   B will be bursting
   C were bursting
   D have burst

In-Depth Lesson Plan

	LESSON FOCUS	PRINT AND MEDIA RESOURCES
DAY 1	**Pronoun Case: Nominative and Objective** Students learn and apply concepts relating to the nominative and objective cases of pronouns. (pp. 562–567)	*Language Lab* **CD-ROM,** Nouns and Pronouns *On-Line Exercise Bank,* Section 22.1 **Teaching Resources** *Grammar Exercise Workbook,* pp. 103–106; *Grammar Exercises Answers on Transparencies,* Ch. 22
DAY 2	**Pronoun Case: Errors with Possessive Pronouns** Students learn and apply pronoun usage concepts relating to the possessive case and do the Hands-on Grammar activity. (pp. 568–569)	**Teaching Resources** *Grammar Exercise Workbook,* pp. 107–108; *Hands-on Grammar Activity Book,* Ch. 22
DAY 3	**Special Problems with Pronouns** Students learn and apply concepts relating to the use of *who* and *whom* and pronouns in elliptical clauses. (pp. 572–577)	*On-Line Exercise Bank,* Section 22.2 **Teaching Resources** *Grammar Exercise Workbook,* pp. 109–110
DAY 4	**Review and Assess** Students review chapter and demonstrate mastery of pronoun usage. (pp. 578–579)	**Teaching Resources** *Formal Assessment,* Ch. 22

Accelerated Lesson Plan

	LESSON FOCUS	PRINT AND MEDIA RESOURCES
DAY 1	**Pronoun Case: Nominative, Objective, and Possessive** Students cover concepts of pronoun usage as determined by the Diagnostic Test. (pp. 562–569)	*Language Lab* **CD-ROM,** Nouns and Pronouns *On-Line Exercise Bank,* Section 22.1 **Teaching Resources** *Grammar Exercise Workbook,* pp. 103–108; *Grammar Exercises Answers on Transparencies,* Ch. 22
DAY 2	**Special Problems with Pronouns** Students cover special problems with pronouns as determined by the Diagnostic Test. (pp. 572–577)	*On-Line Exercise Bank,* Section 22.2 **Teaching Resources** *Grammar Exercise Workbook,* pp. 109–110
DAY 3	**Review and Assess** Students review chapter and demonstrate mastery of concepts. (pp. 578–579)	**Teaching Resources** *Formal Assessment,* Ch. 22

Options for Adapting Lesson Plans

HOMEWORK

Have students complete any section of the chapter for homework.

FEATURES

Extend coverage with the Grammar in Literature feature (p. 576) and the Standardized Test Preparation Workshop (p. 580).

TECHNOLOGY

Students can use the On-Line Exercise Bank to complete the exercises on computer. The Auto Check feature will grade their work.

INTEGRATED SKILLS COVERAGE

Grammar in Literature
SE p. 576

Writing
Find It in Your Writing SE pp. 569, 571, 577
Writing Application SE pp. 571, 577, 579
Grammar and Style SE p. 566

Viewing and Representing
Critical Viewing SE pp. 560, 563, 567, 573, 574

Speaking and Listening
SE p. 564; ATE pp. 564, 573

Real-World Connection ATE p. 564

Spelling SE pp. 562, 568, 572

Technology SE pp. 573

Vocabulary ATE p. 575

Workplace Skills ATE p. 573

ASSESSMENT SUPPORT

Standardized Test Preparation Workshop SE p. 580;
ATE p. 569, 574

Standardized Test Preparation Workbook, pp. 43–44

Formal Assessment, Ch. 22

MEETING INDIVIDUAL NEEDS

Less Advanced Students ATE pp. 565, 568. See also Ongoing
Assessments ATE pp. 563, 565, 568, 575, 576.

AP Students ATE pp. 564, 566

ESL Students ATE p. 563

Gifted and Talented Students ATE p. 563

Verbal/Linguistic Learners ATE pp. 566, 573

BLOCK SCHEDULING

Pacing Suggestions
For 90-minute Blocks
• Administer the Diagnostic Test to students to determine instructional coverage.
• Have students complete the necessary exercises in class. Use the Hands-on Grammar activity to provide a change of pace.

Resources for Varying Instruction
• **Language Lab CD-ROM** If your students have access to hardware, a 90-minute block provides an ideal opportunity for students to work on computer.

Professional Development Support
• **How to Manage Instruction in the Block** This Teaching Resource provides management and activity suggestions.

MEDIA AND TECHNOLOGY

For the Student
• **Language Lab CD-ROM**, Nouns and Pronouns
• **On-Line Exercise Bank**, Sections 22.1–2

For the Teacher
• **Resource Pro CD-ROM**

WRITING AND GRAMMAR WEB SITE

The Interactive Writing and Grammar Web Site provides a wide array of support for students, teachers, and parents. Grammar support includes:

• **On-Line Exercise Bank** with Auto Check scoring
• Diagnostic and assessment support

www.phschool.com

LITERATURE CONNECTIONS

Grammar in Literature selection from *Prentice Hall Literature: Timeless Voices, Timeless Themes,* The American Experience:

from "The First Seven Years," Bernard Malamud, SE p. 576

Lesson Objectives

1. To recognize pronouns in the nominative, objective, and possessive cases and to use the cases correctly

2. To use *who* and *whom* correctly

3. To use pronouns correctly in elliptical clauses

4. To demonstrate control over grammatical elements such as pronoun usage

5. To evaluate writing for both mechanics and content

Critical Viewing

Analyze Answers will vary. Encourage students to describe what their subjects are wearing and where they are in the room. Sample answer: A man stands at the left rear of the picture. He is wearing a tall hat on his head. His clothing is old fashioned.

Chapter 22 Pronoun Usage

Benjamin Franklin opening the first subscription library in Philadelphia, Charles E. Mills

In the English language, some words may change form according to the way they are used in sentences. This occurs frequently with pronouns. For instance, the form of a pronoun used as a subject may be different from its form as a direct object.

This quality of pronouns helps writers to express simple and complicated ideas effectively. Indeed, writers, editors, and printers all pay special attention to the way pronouns are used in sentences.

In this chapter, you will study the various forms of pronouns and their uses.

▲ **Critical Viewing**
Choose two people in this picture, and describe their actions using such pronouns as *he, she, him, her, his, hers, they, them,* and *their.* [**Analyze**]

✓ ONGOING ASSESSMENT: Diagnose

If students miss more than one item in any category, direct them to the relevant pages of the textbook and assign exercises for practice and review.

Pronoun Usage	Diagnostic Test Items	Teach	Practice	Section Reviews	Chapter Review
Skill Check A					
Identify Pronouns	A 1–5	p. 562	Ex. 1–2	Ex. 8	Ex. 26
Skill Check B					
Identify the Case and Use of Pronouns	B6–15	pp. 564–568	Ex. 3–7	Ex. 9–12	Ex. 27–30

Diagnostic Test

Directions: Write all answers on a separate sheet of paper.

Skill Check A. Identify the pronoun, and tell whether its case is *nominative, objective,* or *possessive.*

1. her biography
2. dedicated the book to him
3. found it in nonfiction
4. they published
5. my favorite author

Skill Check B. Identify the case of each underlined pronoun, and tell how it is used in the sentence.

6. <u>Our</u> eleventh-grade English class used the library extensively to study American authors.
7. <u>I</u>, for one, read a biography of Samuel L. Clemens, who wrote under the pen name Mark Twain.
8. *"The Notorious Jumping Frog of Calaveras County" and Other Sketches* was <u>his</u> first work, and it was considered a financial failure.
9. It was not until one hundred years later that <u>it</u> was reprinted.
10. *The Adventures of Tom Sawyer,* one of Twain's works, was read to <u>me</u> by my grandfather.
11. I read <u>it</u> again myself to relive Tom's adventures.
12. My friend, on the other hand, researched the life of Louisa May Alcott and <u>her</u> literary career.
13. It was <u>she</u> who wrote the *Little Women* series.
14. Abe's and Peter's friend introduced <u>them</u> to many of the works of Jack London, including his boxing stories and his war correspondence.
15. London's interest in the Yukon, California, and the South Pacific inspired <u>him</u> to write extensively about those places.

Skill Check C. Choose the correct pronoun in each sentence.

16. (Who, Whom) wrote *The Sea-Wolf*?
17. From (whom, who) did we receive such works as *Flower Fables* and *Hospital Sketches*?
18. Was it Huck Finn (who, whom) grew up along the Mississippi River?
19. I'm curious about (whoever, whomever) published her first work under the pseudonym Flora Fairfield.
20. I will read (whoever, whomever) the librarian recommends.

Skill Check D. Choose the correct pronoun to complete the elliptical clause.

21. Jack London was as prolific as (he, him).
22. Louisa May Alcott is known to my friends as well as (I, me).
23. They like Twain's works more than (me, I).
24. No authors are more widely known than (them, they).
25. This book is dearer to me than (he, him).

Answer Key

Skill Check A

1. her, possessive
2. him, objective
3. it, objective
4. they, nominative
5. my, possessive

Skill Check B

6. possessive, to show ownership
7. nominative, subject of a verb
8. possessive, to show ownership
9. nominative, subject of a verb
10. objective, object of a preposition
11. objective, direct object
12. possessive, to show ownership
13. nominative, predicate nominative
14. objective, direct object
15. objective, direct object

Skill Check C

16. Who
17. whom
18. who
19. whoever
20. whomever

Skill Check D

21. he
22. me
23. I
24. they
25. him

ONGOING ASSESSMENT: Diagnose *continued*					
Pronoun Usage	**Diagnostic Test Items**	**Teach**	**Practice**	**Section Reviews**	**Chapter Review**
Skill Check C					
Pronouns *Who* and *Whom*	C16–20	pp. 572–574	Ex. 16–17	Ex. 20–21	Ex. 31
Skill Check D					
Pronouns in Elliptical Clauses	D21–25	p. 575	Ex. 18–19	Ex. 22	Ex. 32
Cumulative Reviews and Applications				Ex. 13–15, 23–25	Ex. 33–34

TIME SAVERS!

Answers on Transparencies
Use the *Grammar Exercises Answers on Transparencies* for Chapter 22 to facilitate correction by students.

On-Line Exercise Bank
Have students complete the Diagnostic Test on computer. The Auto Check feature will grade their work for you!

Interest GRABBER Find out (if you do not already know) what the sign-language movements are for *I, me, my/mine, you,* and *yours*. Demonstrate these signs to students without explaining them. Ask what students think they mean. Identify each sign, and then ask how effectively the signs indicate the usage of the pronouns they represent.

Activate Prior Knowledge

Ask students if they have seen any of the *Tarzan* movies. What famous line associated with Tarzan uses a pronoun incorrectly? ("Me Tarzan.") Ask students what using the incorrect case conveys about the character. (lack of education, unfamiliarity with English, primitiveness)

TEACH

Step-by-Step Teaching Guide

The Three Cases of Pronouns

1. Point out the chart to focus students' attention on the three cases and the forms of pronouns within each case.
2. Explain that each case refers to the different uses that pronouns will fill in a sentence.
3. Explain to students that they use different forms of a pronoun depending on its function (subject, direct object, and so on) in a sentence. *It* and *you* are the exceptions.

Answer Key

Exercise 1

Answers will vary. Sample answers:

1. The librarian spent <u>his</u> morning helping people find information, and then <u>he</u> reshelved books.
2. <u>I</u> want you to believe <u>me</u>; this library book is <u>mine</u>.
3. The two students had trouble doing <u>their</u> homework, so <u>they</u> asked the teacher to help <u>them</u>.
4. <u>We</u> will give <u>our</u> presentation tomorrow; <u>ours</u> is third on the schedule.
5. After getting a URL for <u>your</u> Web site, <u>you</u> can design it to be uniquely <u>yours</u>.

Section 22.1 *Case*

Case is characteristic of only two parts of speech: nouns and pronouns.

> **KEY CONCEPT** **Case** is the form of a noun or a pronoun that indicates its use in a sentence. ■

The Three Cases

Both nouns and pronouns have three cases—*nominative, objective,* and *possessive*. Nouns, however, usually present no problem because their form changes only in the possessive case.

NOMINATIVE: The *library* opens in one hour.
OBJECTIVE: There are many resources available in the *library*.
POSSESSIVE: The *library's* collection of periodicals is extensive.

In the first example, *library* is nominative because it is the subject of the verb *opens*; in the second, *library* is objective because it is the object of the preposition *in*. The form changes only in the possessive case. An apostrophe and *s* are added for the singular possessive, and just an apostrophe is added for the plural possessive.

In contrast to nouns, personal pronouns have different forms for all three cases.

> **KEY CONCEPT** The three cases of personal pronouns are nominative, objective, and possessive. The pronoun forms are different in each case. ■

Nominative	Objective	Possessive
I	me	my, mine
you	you	your, yours
he, she, it	him, her, it	his, her, hers, its
we	us	our, ours
they	them	their, theirs

> **Exercise 1** **Writing Sentences With Pronouns** Write sentences using pronouns according to the instructions below.
> 1. Use *he* or *she* and *his* or *hers* in a sentence about a librarian.
> 2. Use *I, me,* and *mine* in a sentence about a library book.
> 3. Use *they, them,* and *their* in a sentence about two students.
> 4. Use *we, our,* and *ours* in a sentence about a presentation.
> 5. Use *you, your,* and *yours* in a sentence about a Web site.

Theme: Books and Libraries

In this chapter, you will learn about pronoun usage. The examples and exercises in this section are about books and libraries.

Spelling Tip

Notice that the possessive pronouns *yours, his, hers, its, ours,* and *theirs* end in *s* but never take an apostrophe.

⏱ TIME AND RESOURCE MANAGER

Resources
Print: *Grammar Exercise Workbook,* pp. 103–108; *Grammar Exercises Answers on Transparencies,* Chapter 22
Technology: *Language Lab* CD-ROM, Nouns and Pronouns; *On-Line Exercise Bank,* Section 22.1

In-Depth Coverage	Accelerated Pace
• Work through all key concepts, pp. 562–568. • Assign and review Exercises 1–7. • Do the Hands-on Grammar activity, p. 569.	• Assign pp. 562–568, for independent student review. • Assign Section Review Exercises 8–12.

▶ **Exercise 2** **Identifying Case** On a separate sheet of paper, write the case of each underlined pronoun.

EXAMPLE: Sheila gave him two books for the report.
ANSWER: objective

1. Our libraries provide <u>us</u> with a wealth of information and literary enjoyment.
2. It is important that you know how to use a library in order to make the most of <u>your</u> visit.
3. Librarians are very knowledgeable and can guide <u>us</u> in our search for material.
4. Card and computer catalogs allow you and <u>me</u> to access information about subjects, titles, and authors.
5. <u>They</u> also provide call numbers that will enable you to find the book in the library.
6. The Dewey Decimal System is used by many libraries to allow <u>them</u> to divide and catalog nonfiction books into ten main categories.
7. <u>They</u> are general topics, philosophy, religion, social science, language, pure science, technology, the arts, language and rhetoric, and geography and history.
8. Fiction books are shelved by the first three letters of <u>their</u> authors' last names.
9. Biographies and autobiographies are assigned the call number 921 and are arranged by <u>their</u> subjects' last names.
10. You will find many reference resources to help <u>you</u> with information about a specific topic.

▶ **More Practice**

Language Lab
CD-ROM
• Pronoun Case lesson
On-line
Exercise Bank
• Section 22.1
Grammar Exercise
Workbook
• pp. 103–104

▶ **Critical Viewing**
To what degree do you think these readers are enjoying the book? Answer this question using at least three pronouns—one in each case. [Analyze]

Case • 563

☑ **ONGOING ASSESSMENT: Monitor and Reinforce**

If students have difficulty with Exercise 1 or 2, refer them to the following for additional practice.

In the Textbook	Print Resources	Technology
Section Review, Ex. 8, p. 570	*Grammar Exercise Workbook,* pp. 103–104	*Language Lab* CD-ROM, Nouns and Pronouns; *On-Line Exercise Bank,* Section 22.1

The Nominative Case

1. Review the three examples in the chart that illustrate use of nominative pronouns. Have students suggest their own sentences to demonstrate that they understand how the nominative case is used when a pronoun is the subject of a verb, a predicate nominative, or in a nominative absolute.

2. Explain to students that pronouns remain nominative even in compound subjects or compound predicate nominatives. Using the examples of compounds, ask students to read each compound subject aloud. Point out that the subject contains a proper noun and a nominative pronoun. Then have students read the sentence *without* the proper noun, noting that this is a good way to test their pronoun choices when they write.

3. Repeat this exercise with appositives. Have students read the example sentences with and without the nouns associated with the pronouns in apposition.

Integrating Speaking and Listening Skills

Have students write sentences that use the predicate nominative in an informal manner, or use the following examples:

It was her who left her shoe at the party. (Correct: she)

It was him who ran from the scene of the crime. (Correct: he)

Have your students rewrite the sentences to reflect correct (formal) usage of the predicate nominative. Then have them say both versions of the sentences out loud. Explain that, while they might hear the objective case used in casual speaking, it is incorrect. While correct usage of nominative pronouns is always preferred, even in informal speaking, in formal speaking and all writing correct usage is required.

22.1

The Nominative Case

The nominative case is used when a personal pronoun acts in one of three ways:

▶ **KEY CONCEPT** Use the nominative case for the *subject* of a verb, for a *predicate nominative*, and for the pronoun in a *nominative absolute*. ■

These uses are illustrated in the following chart:

NOMINATIVE PRONOUNS	
As the subject of a verb:	*They* are going to the library.
As a predicate nominative:	The only one left is *he*.
In a nominative absolute:	*She* having finished her lecture, the students left quietly.

Informal Use of the Predicate Nominative Although formal usage requires a nominative pronoun after a linking verb, people often use the objective case in informal situations. For essays and other formal writing, however, you should make a point to use the nominative case.

INFORMAL: It was me who answered the telephone.
FORMAL: It was I who answered the telephone.

Nominative Pronouns in Compounds When you use a pronoun in a compound subject or predicate nominative, check the case by mentally removing the other part of the compound or by mentally inverting the sentence.

COMPOUND SUBJECT: Joanne and *I* prepared the report.
(*I* prepared the report.)
Doug and *she* solved the problem.
(*She* solved the problem.)

COMPOUND PREDICATE NOMINATIVE: The contestants are Fran and *I*.
(Fran and *I* are the contestants.)
The guilty ones are Ethel and *he*.
(Ethel and *he* are the guilty ones.)

Nominative Pronouns With Appositives When an appositive follows a pronoun used as a subject or predicate nominative, the pronoun should stay in the nominative case.

SUBJECT: *We* New Yorkers are proud of our city's library system.

PREDICATE NOMINATIVE: The only ones invited are *we* juniors.

Speaking an Listening Ti

Together with one or two of your classmates, take turns reading aloud Exercises 3 and 4 on the next page in order to accustom yourselves to using nominative pronouns correctly.

Customize for
AP Students

Point out that many sentences contain more than one clause, each containing its own subject and verb. Then, ask students to locate three compound and three complex sentences in their writing or in any other source in which personal pronouns are used in nominative and objective forms. Have students underline the subject and verb of each clause in each sentence and identify the case of each pronoun (making corrections, if necessary).

Real-World Connection

Nominative pronouns with appositives have long been used to make formal (and sometimes famous) declarations. For instance, the Constitution of the United States of America begins, "We the people of the United States, in order to form a more perfect union . . . " Point out that "We the people" is a nominative pronoun with an appositive. Add that politicians today often use this construction to emphasize their connections with voters. Have you ever heard a politician say, "We citizens" or "We Americans"? When? Where?

> **Exercise 3** Identifying Pronouns in the Nominative Case

Choose the pronoun in the nominative case to complete each sentence. Then, identify the use of the pronoun.

EXAMPLE: Amy and (he, him) collaborated on that book.
ANSWER: he (subject)

1. Paul and (me, I) decided to compose a mystery novel.
2. Charlene and (he, him) deserve credit for the initial idea.
3. The ones who decided the plot structure were (we, us) authors.
4. (I, Me) having finished the outline, Paul began to write.
5. (He, Him) and Amy collaborated on the illustrations.
6. Harold and (they, them) helped the effort by gathering further reference materials.
7. However, it was Carla and (I, me) who carefully edited the finished manuscript.
8. I could not find Paul, (he, him) having left for the publisher's office.
9. The very first readers of the manuscript were (we, us) friends.
10. Both Marc and (her, she) are excellent at handling all aspects of publicity.

> **Exercise 4** Using Pronouns in the Nominative Case Write a nominative pronoun to complete each sentence. Then, identify the use of the pronoun.

1. You and __?__ will study the role of illustration in comic books.
2. It is __?__ who is most talented at drawing cartoons for these types of books.
3. The model for our new cartoon character will be __?__.
4. The new representatives at the cartoon convention will be Jack and __?__.
5. Esther and __?__ will teach us how to create an interesting sketch that matches the character description in the book.
6. The eager participants and __?__ plan to listen carefully to Esther's instructions.
7. __?__ having given the instructions, the participants began their sketches.
8. Karl and __?__ used their thumb prints on a stamp pad as outlines for their sketches.
9. As a result, __?__ learned unusual techniques for illustrating characters.
10. "The winner of the prize for the cartoon with the best personality is __?__!" cried Karl's mother.

> **More Practice**

**Language Lab
CD-ROM**
• Pronoun Case lesson
**On-line
Exercise Bank**
• Section 22.1
**Grammar Exercise
Workbook**
• pp. 105–106

Case • 565

Answer Key

> **Exercise 3**

1. I, subject of a verb
2. he, subject of a verb
3. we, predicate nominative
4. I, nominative absolute
5. He, subject of a verb
6. they, subject of a verb
7. I, predicate nominative
8. he, nominative absolute
9. we, predicate nominative
10. she, subject of a verb

Customize for
Less Advanced Students

Have students rewrite sentences 1, 2, 5, 6, and 10 in Exercise 3, using only the correct pronoun in parentheses as the subject of the sentence, thereby changing compound subjects to simple subjects.

Answer Key

> **Exercise 4**

Nominative pronouns will vary, but the use of the pronouns will not.

1. I, subject of a verb
2. she, predicate nominative
3. he, predicate nominative
4. he, predicate nominative
5. she, subject of a verb
6. I, subject of a verb
7. She, nominative absolute
8. he, subject of a verb
9. they, subject of a verb
10. you, predicate nominative

✓ ONGOING ASSESSMENT: Monitor and Reinforce

If students miss more than two items in Exercise 3 or 4, refer them to the following for additional practice.

In the Textbook	Print Resources	Technology
Section Review, Ex. 9, p. 570	*Grammar Exercise Workbook,* pp. 105–106	*Language Lab* CD-ROM, Nouns and Pronouns; *On-Line Exercise Bank,* Section 22.1

⏱ TIME SAVERS!

Answers on Transparencies
Use the *Grammar Exercises Answers on Transparencies* for Chapter 22 to facilitate correction by students.

On-Line Exercise Bank
Have students complete the exercises on computer. The Auto Check feature will grade their work for you!

The Objective Case

1. Review verbals with students. (A *verbal* is a word derived from a verb but used as a noun, adjective, or adverb. Verbals include participles, gerunds, and infinitives.) If you think it's necessary, review direct objects, indirect objects, and prepositions.

2. Read the examples from the chart. Then read the following sentences aloud and have students identify how the objective pronoun is used in each.

   Jenna offered to drive them *to the library.* (object of infinitive)

   The books awaiting us *were a source of excitement.* (object of participle)

   At the library, there was a library card waiting for me. (object of preposition)

3. Focusing on the examples of compounds, point out that this is where most usage problems in the objective case occur. Encourage students to read the sentence without the noun to see if the pronoun is correct.

4. Compare the use of the objective pronoun with appositives to the use of nominative pronouns with appositives. (Nominative: *We students are studying.* Objective: *The teacher spoke to us students.*)

Customize for
AP Students

Explain that using an objective case pronoun as the subject of an infinitive seems to defy the rules of case (subjects normally are nominative) but that this is the exception. Give students some infinitive phrases (*to fly a kite, to buy me a ticket*) and ask them to make infinitive clauses with objective case pronouns as their subjects (*I told him to fly a kite, I asked her to buy me a ticket*). Then note that each infinitive clause is, in fact, the direct object of the verb in the independent clause. Ask students to write similar sentence structures.

22.1

The Objective Case

Objective pronouns are used for any kind of object in a sentence as well as for subjects of infinitives.

▶ **KEY CONCEPT** Use the objective case for the object of any verb, verbal, or preposition, as well as for the object or subject of an infinitive. ■

The chart below illustrates the uses of objective pronouns.

OBJECTIVE PRONOUNS	
Direct Object	The ending of the novel greatly surprised *me*.
Indirect Object	Reading the tiny print gave *her* a headache.
Object of Participle	The problems bothering *him* remained a secret.
Object of Gerund	Solving *them* will not be easy.
Object of Infinitive	Graham wanted to show *us* his new book club membership.
Object of Preposition	The mail carrier said that the package was for *her*.
Subject of Infinitive	Carol wants Harry and *me* to help organize the author's study group.

Objective Pronouns in Compounds As with the nominative case, most usage problems in the objective case occur with pronouns in compounds. To check your usage, mentally remove the other part of the compound.

EXAMPLES: Al sent Carol and *me* tickets to the dramatic reading.
(Al sent *me* tickets to the dramatic reading.)
The hero rescued Bill and *her* in the second act.
(The hero rescued *her* in the second act.)

You should take special care to use the objective case after the preposition *between*.

INCORRECT: The intermission snacks will be split between you and *I*.

CORRECT: The intermission snacks will be split between you and *me*.

Learn More

For more information about pronouns, see Chapter 17.

Grammar and Style Tip

In some situations where the nominative case is correct, it may sound too formal for your purpose. Consider revising the sentence so that you may correctly use the objective case.

Customize for
Verbal/Linguistic Learners

To practice recognizing and using case forms, read aloud only parts of sentences, omitting nominative and objective case pronouns. Tell students to listen carefully and to volunteer the correct forms of personal pronouns to complete your sentences. Here are some to begin with:

Sheila and ___ saw shoes on sale. (nominative)

The clerk brought Sheila and ___ some to try on. (objective—but point out that the nominative is a common incorrect usage)

Finally, it was Sheila, not ___, who bought a pair. (nominative)

Objective Pronouns With Appositives

When a pronoun used as an object or as the subject of an infinitive has an appositive, make sure you use the objective case.

EXAMPLES: The professor encouraged *us* budding playwrights.

The professor gave *us* students some scenes to rewrite.

Our classmates asked *us* stragglers to hurry up.

 Exercise 5   Identifying Pronouns in the Objective Case

Choose the pronoun in the objective case to complete each sentence. Then, write the use of the pronoun.

1. My father took (I, me) to the Library of Congress on our recent trip to Washington, D.C.
2. The Library of Congress is the largest research library available to (us, we) in the United States.
3. The Library of Congress is the center of all libraries in our nation and provides (them, they) with catalogs of all new publications.
4. One of the library's goals is to make its extensive collections easily accessible to the government and (you, your), the general public.
5. The Library of Congress will allow (we, us) use of its facilities if we are over the appropriate age.
6. A guide was happy to show (they, them) how to obtain special permission to use the library.
7. All researchers intending to use the public reading rooms are required to have reader identification cards issued to (them, they) by the library.
8. A reader identification card is valid for two years, and one must renew (it, its) when it expires.
9. The Office of the Librarian of Congress is solely responsible for making the institution's rules and regulations, enforcing (they, them), and appointing its staff.
10. The reader registration system was initiated by (they, them) to protect the library's collection.

▲ **Critical Viewing**
Describe the effect of this imposing structure on a boy, a girl, and you. Use objective pronouns to refer to each person. **[Analyze]**

▶ **More Practice**

Language Lab CD-ROM
• Pronoun Case lesson

On-line Exercise Bank
• Section 22.1

Grammar Exercise Workbook
• pp. 105–106

Critical Viewing

Analyze Answers will vary. Possible response: The building seemed very formal to <u>me</u>. The pillars gave <u>her</u> an impression of classic Roman buildings. The size of the building made <u>him</u> feel insignificant.

Answer Key

▶ **Exercise 5**

1. me, direct object
2. us, object of preposition
3. them, direct object
4. you, object of preposition
5. us, indirect object
6. them, object of an infinitive
7. them, object of a preposition
8. it, direct object
9. them, object of gerund
10. them, object of preposition

🕐 **TIME SAVERS!**

📖 **Answers on Transparencies** Use the *Grammar Exercises Answers on Transparencies* for Chapter 22 to facilitate correction by students.

💻 **On-Line Exercise Bank** Have students complete the exercises on computer. The Auto Check feature will grade their work for you!

568

22.1

> **Exercise 6** Using Pronouns in the Objective Case Write an objective pronoun that will complete each sentence.
>
> 1. Our cousins were coming, so we decided to assemble a family photo album for ___?___.
> 2. Between my sister and ___?___, we came up with some great photo choices.
> 3. We considered ___?___, and then made our selections.
> 4. Because Grandmother was looking on, we asked ___?___ for suggestions.
> 5. Because our brother is artistic, we decided to ask ___?___ to monogram the album.

Errors to Avoid With Possessive Pronouns

Although errors are less common with the possessive case than with the two other cases, mistakes are sometimes made when pronouns are used before gerunds.

> **KEY CONCEPT** Use the possessive case before gerunds. ■

EXAMPLES: *His* objecting to the research caused an uproar.
I respect *your* maintaining an optimistic outlook.
Tad resents *my* using his writing desk.

Another error to avoid is using an apostrophe with possessive pronouns, which already indicate ownership. Spellings such as *our's*, *their's*, and *your's* are incorrect. In addition, do not confuse a possessive pronoun with a contraction.

POSSESSIVE PRONOUN: The vivid print had retained *its* clarity.
CONTRACTION: *It's* wise to proofread your report.

> **Exercise 7** Using Pronouns in the Possessive Case Choose the correct word in each set of parentheses.
>
> An event that happened 500 years ago has been discussed ever since. (1) (Its, It's) the origin of printing as we know it today. (2) (It's, Its) inventor is thought to have been Johann Gutenberg. (3) (He's, He) responsible for the art of printing with movable type. Of course, the work was done much more slowly than (4) (it's, its) done today. Ink was rolled over the raised surfaces of handset letters within a frame and pressed against a sheet of paper. (5) (Us, Our) learning about Gutenberg has led me to explore further the history of printing.

568 • Pronoun Usage

✓ **ONGOING ASSESSMENT: Monitor and Reinforce**

If students have difficulty with Exercise 5, 6, or 7, refer them to the following for additional practice.

In the Textbook	Print Resources	Technology
Section Review, Ex. 10–12, p. 570	*Grammar Exercise Workbook*, pp. 105–108	*Language Lab* CD-ROM, Nouns and Pronouns; *On-Line Exercise Bank*, Section 22.1

Hands-on Grammar

Pronoun Case Triangle

Create a pronoun case triangle to help you remember the uses of the three cases of pronouns. First, cut out a large triangle with three equal sides from colored paper. Next, fold one point of the triangle so that it touches the opposite side. Then, unfold it, leaving the crease. Fold the other two points of the triangle as well. After folding each point, your triangle should look like the diagram at right. (The dotted lines indicate creases.)

Write the name of each pronoun case on a crease. In the point (shown as a shaded small triangle in the diagram), write the uses of the case.

Turn the triangle over, and write the pronouns of the case on the back of the point that contains the uses.

Reverse side
me, you, him, her, it, us, them

Paper-clip your triangle to a sheet of notebook paper, and keep it in your folder to record examples as you find them.

Find It in Your Reading As you encounter uses of each pronoun case in your reading, record on your notebook paper the sentence in which the pronoun is used.

Find It in Your Writing Look through your portfolio to find examples of each pronoun case. On the paper, write the sentences in which you use the pronouns.

Case • 569

STANDARDIZED TEST PREPARATION WORKSHOP

Grammar and Usage Many standardized tests require students to recognize the cases of pronouns within the context of a passage. Use the following example to demonstrate.

Their hard work paid off in the end. The many hours of preparation helped them as they climbed the steep mountain in record time.

Which word in the above passage is a pronoun in the objective case?

A Their
B they
C them
D many

The correct answer is **C**. The pronoun *them* is objective because it is the direct object of *helped. Their* is a possessive pronoun that shows ownership of *work; they* is a nominative pronoun used as the subject of the verb *climbed*; and *many* is usually an indefinite pronoun but here is used as an indefinite adjective.

Section Review

Each of these exercises correlates to the instruction on case, pages 562–569. The exercises may be used for more practice, for reteaching, or for review of the key concepts presented.

Answer Key

▶ Exercise 8

1. you, nominative; you, objective
2. them, objective
3. He, nominative; she, nominative; you, objective
4. your, possessive
5. them, objective
6. your, possessive
7. your, possessive; it, objective
8. them, objective; their, possessive
9. They, nominative; it, objective; you, objective
10. it, objective

▶ Exercise 9

1. I, subject of a verb
2. We, subject of a verb
3. She, nominative absolute
4. he, predicate nominative
5. he, predicate nominative
6. He, nominative absolute
7. she, subject of a verb
8. they, predicate nominative
9. I, subject of a verb
10. We, nominative absolute

▶ Exercise 10

1. me, object of preposition
2. him, object of preposition
3. us, indirect object
4. us, direct object
5. her, object of preposition
6. her, subject of infinitive
7. us, object of a gerund
8. them, direct object
9. us, object of a participle
10. them, direct object

🕐 **TIME SAVERS!**

📖 **Answers on Transparencies**
Use the *Grammar Exercises Answers on Transparencies* for Chapter 22 to facilitate correction by students.

💻 **On-Line Exercise Bank**
Have students complete the exercises on computer. The Auto Check feature will grade their work for you!

Section 22.1 *Section Review*

GRAMMAR EXERCISES 8–15

▶ **Exercise 8** **Identifying Cases of Pronouns** On a separate sheet of paper, write the personal pronouns you find in each sentence. Identify the case of each personal pronoun.

1. To write a research report, you must first list topics of interest to you.
2. Talk about them with a friend.
3. He or she can help you choose a topic.
4. Write three questions about your topic.
5. Find facts that answer them.
6. Use your notes as supporting details.
7. When your report is ready, read it to friends.
8. Ask them for their reactions.
9. They can edit it with you.
10. Proofread the final result, and check it for capitalization and punctuation.

▶ **Exercise 9** **Choosing Pronouns in the Nominative Case** Choose the pronoun in the nominative case to complete each sentence. Then, identify the use of the pronoun.

1. My friends and (me, I) went to a book-signing event at our local bookstore.
2. (We, Us) waited for more than an hour to meet our favorite author.
3. (Her, She) being a prolific author, millions have read her novels.
4. A press agent was on hand, and it was (he, him) who directed us to the author.
5. "The illustrator is (him, he)!" cried the exultant author.
6. (He, Him) having been highly recommended, we turned to him for help.
7. Billy and (her, she) discovered that a copyright page tells when the copyright of the book was issued.
8. It was (they, them), who reminded us about the copyright laws.

9. Kristin and (me, I) blushed when the author said she would acknowledge our help in the introduction to her book.
10. (We, Us) having praised her work, the author smiled and signed our copies of her book.

▶ **Exercise 10** **Choosing Pronouns in the Objective Case** Choose the pronoun in the objective case to complete each sentence. Then, identify the use of the pronoun.

1. The graphic charts displayed in the book's appendix were drawn by Julie and (I, me).
2. The additional maps were photocopied and delivered to Caroline and (he, him).
3. Give (us, we) students a chance to figure out the definition of the difficult word by looking at the glossary.
4. A kind of miniature dictionary, a glossary supplies (us, we) with meanings of words.
5. The definition of *millennium* was found by (her, she).
6. The bibliography will help Suzie and (her, she) locate additional information on their research topic.
7. Exciting (us, we) most was the variety of information about new computer technology.
8. This list of related books will benefit (they, them) also.
9. The man helping (us, we) with the alphabetized index was the reference librarian.
10. He also reminded (they, them) about the important parts of a book.

✓ **ONGOING ASSESSMENT: Assess Mastery**

Use the following resources to assess student mastery of pronoun case.

In the Textbook	Technology
Chapter Review, Ex. 26–30, pp. 578–579	*Language Lab* CD-ROM, Nouns and Pronouns; *On-Line Exercise Bank*, Section 22.1

Exercise 11 Classifying Pronouns and Their Uses

On a separate sheet of paper, write the case of each personal pronoun and its use.

1. The printing press and its development depended on the refinement of paper in China over several centuries.
2. Did you know Chinese "rag" paper was a cheap cloth and plant-fiber substitute for precious silk paper?
3. Chinese prisoners passed the technology on to their Arab captors in the eighth century.
4. The secrets of the craft were revealed by them to Europeans.
5. They were the same techniques the Chinese had given to the Arabs.
6. Long before Gutenberg and his invention of the printing press, Chinese block printing and movable clay type fed the push toward expanding the range of written material.
7. Although the European innovations came much later, they certainly reached a wider audience.
8. Because their alphabet employs ideograms, the use of movable type was much harder for the Chinese.
9. Consequently, movable type did not change production for the Chinese as dramatically as it did for Europeans.
10. Some historians also assert that the sequential, linear, and standardized character of the printed word especially suited us in the Western world.

Exercise 12 Correcting Errors in Pronoun Usage

Rewrite each sentence, correcting any mistakes in pronoun usage. Write *correct* if the sentence contains no errors.

1. Lee and me attended a poetry reading at the community library.
2. The poets read they're poetry.
3. Bentley sent them and I to the meeting room to inspect the seating plan.
4. Lee informed Philip and she that formal reservations were not necessary.
5. The special events coordinator signaled to Lee and I from behind the podium.
6. Please give her and me a chance before you begin the program.
7. The man seating we students in the front row was Bentley's father.
8. Jules decided to sit between Cynthia and I.
9. After hearing Ben's reading, we thought his' interpretation was best.
10. The entire gathering applauded the authors and there poetic genius.

Exercise 13 Find It in Your Reading

In the following sentence from "The First Seven Years," identify at least one pronoun in each of the three cases and tell how each is used.

He had begged her to go, pointing out how many fathers could not afford to send their children to college. But she said she wanted to be independent.

Exercise 14 Find It in Your Writing

In your portfolio, find two examples of pronouns in each of the three cases. Check to make sure that each is used correctly. Then, write down each pronoun, its case, and its use in the sentence.

Exercise 15 Writing Application

Write a paragraph on the subject of books or libraries. Use at least five of the nouns listed below. For each noun, include a pronoun that refers to it. Try to include pronouns in all three cases. Then, circle each pronoun.

1. author	6. idea
2. book	7. Gutenberg
3. print	8. libraries
4. publisher	9. readers
5. librarian	10. pages

Section Review • 571

Answer Key continued

Exercise 14
Find It in Your Writing
When students finish, have them exchange papers with a partner and check for any errors in pronoun usage.

Exercise 15
Writing Application
Paragraphs should include nouns and corresponding pronouns, as directed. Ask students which nouns they picked. How did using the different types of pronouns help them say what they wanted to say? Were any cases easier to use than others?

Exercise 11
1. its, possessive, to show ownership
2. you, nominative, subject of a verb
3. their, possessive, to show ownership
4. them, objective, object of preposition
5. They, nominative, subject of a verb
6. his, possessive, to show ownership
7. they, nominative, subject of a verb
8. their, possessive, to show ownership
9. it, nominative, subject of a verb
10. us, objective, direct object

Exercise 12
1. Lee and I attended a poetry reading at the community library.
2. The poets read their poetry.
3. Bentley sent them and me to the meeting room to inspect the seating plan.
4. Lee informed Philip and her that formal reservations were not necessary.
5. The special events coordinator signaled to Lee and me from behind the podium.
6. correct
7. The man seating us students in the front row was Bentley's father.
8. Jules decided to sit between Cynthia and me.
9. After hearing Ben's reading, we thought his interpretation was best.
10. The entire gathering applauded the authors and their poetic genius.

Exercise 13
Find It in Your Reading
Possible answers:
1. *He* had begged, nominative, subject of a verb
2. *her* to go, objective, subject of infinitive
3. *their* children, possessive, to show ownership
4. *she* said, nominative, subject of a verb
5. *she* wanted, nominative, subject of a verb

continued

Have students work in pairs. Student A will assume the identity of a famous figure without revealing that identity to his or her partner. Student B will attempt to discover Student A's identity by asking no more than ten questions using *who* or *whom*. When they are done, ask volunteers to repeat their *who* and *whom* questions. For each one, ask why they used *who* or *whom*. Then ask if the class can guess the character. If they can't, reveal the answer.

Activate Prior Knowledge

Ask students if they have ever seen a book, television show, or movie with the words *who* or *whom* in the title. (*For Whom the Bell Tolls, Who Framed Roger Rabbit?*) Then ask students how *who* and *whom* are used in these titles. Finally, ask students to invent titles that use the words *who* or *whom*.

TEACH

Step-by-Step Teaching Guide

Special Problems with Pronouns

1. Review the differences among nominative, objective, and possessive pronoun forms and their functions in sentences.

2. Use the chart to demonstrate the three cases of *who*. Ask students to suggest sentences, using *who* and *whom* correctly, for each pronoun use listed.

3. Encourage students to pay particular attention to the possessive (*whose*) so that they will not confuse it with *who's*.

4. Urge students to pay attention to the use of *who* and its various forms in complex sentences. Use the following sentence, asking students to identify the subordinate clause:

   Agnes is my cousin whom you met on Sunday.

   Then ask students to restate the clause in simple sentence order (*you met whom on Sunday*) and explain why *whom* (direct object), not *who*, is correct.

Section 22.2

Special Problems With Pronouns

The incorrect form of a pronoun may sometimes sound correct. For example, would it be correct to say, "Darlene is more qualified than *me*"? Though the sentence may sound correct to you, it is incorrect because an objective pronoun has been used when a nominative pronoun is needed. This section discusses the proper uses of *who* and *whom* and the use of pronouns in clauses where some of the words are omitted but understood.

Using *Who* and *Whom* Correctly

Deciding which form of *who* and *whom* to use is often a problem. In order to use the correct form, you must understand how the pronoun is used and what case is appropriate.

KEY CONCEPT Learn to recognize the cases of *who* and *whom* and to use them correctly in sentences. ■

The following chart shows the forms of these pronouns and their uses in sentences.

Case	Pronoun	Use in Sentence
Nominative	who, whoever	Subject of a verb Predicate nominative
Objective	whom, whomever	Direct object Object of a preposition
Possessive	whose, whosever	To show ownership

Note about *whose*: The possessive case rarely causes problems, but you should be careful not to confuse the contraction *who's*, meaning "who is," with the pronoun *whose*.

POSSESSIVE PRONOUN: *Whose* car will we take to the job interview?

CONTRACTION: *Who's* going to drive us to the job interview?

Theme: Careers

In this section, you will learn about *who* and *whom* and the correct use of pronouns in elliptical clauses. The examples and exercises in this section are about careers.

Cross-Curricular Connection: Social Studies

Spelling Tip

Remember that *whoever* and *whomever* are compound words.

⏱ TIME AND RESOURCE MANAGER

Resources
Print: *Grammar Exercise Workbook*, pp. 109–110; *Grammar Exercises Answers on Transparencies*, Chapter 22
Technology: *Language Lab* CD-ROM, Nouns and Pronouns; *On-Line Exercise Bank*, Section 22.2

In-Depth Coverage	Accelerated Pace
• Work through all key concepts, pp. 572–576. • Assign and review Exercises 16–19. • Read and discuss Grammar in Literature, p. 576.	• Assign pp. 572–576 for independent student review. • Assign Section Review Exercises 20–22, p. 577.

The nominative pronouns *who* and *whoever* often serve as the subject in questions. They can also serve as predicate nominatives, but this use of *whoever* is rare.

SUBJECT: *Who* wrote the career guide?
                  Whoever undertakes such a
                  challenging job will work hard.

PREDICATE NOMINATIVE: The news commentator was *who*?

The main usage problems with *who* and *whoever* occur when they are used in complex sentences to begin a subordinate clause. It is important to remember that the pronoun's role within the subordinate clause determines the proper case.

┌─── subord. clause ───┐
      S
EXAMPLE: Assign this task to *whoever* will accept it.

In this example, the pronoun seems to be the object of the preposition *to*, but *whoever* is the subject of the clause. The entire subordinate clause acts as the object of the preposition.

The objective pronouns *whom* and *whomever* are also used in questions as either direct objects or objects of prepositions. If you are in doubt about the use of the pronoun, reword the question as a statement with a pronoun. Use the case of the pronoun as a clue to whether you should use *who* or *whom*.

DIRECT OBJECT: *Whom* did you consult?
                        You did consult *her*. [not *she*]

OBJECT OF PREPOSITION: To *whom* are you writing?
                        You are writing to *him*. [not *he*]

It is especially important to examine the pronoun's use in a complex sentence. Begin by isolating the subordinate clause. If necessary, reword the clause (a clause correctly beginning with *whom* or *whomever* will always be inverted). Finally, determine the use of the pronoun and the appropriate case.

EXAMPLES: This waiter is an unpleasant fellow *whom* I dislike.
              Subordinate clause: whom I dislike
              Reworded clause: I dislike *him*. [not *he*]
              Use of pronoun: direct object of *dislike*
              Case for direct object: objective

              John charmed *whomever* he spoke with.
              Subordinate clause: whomever he spoke with
              Reworded clause: he spoke with *them* [not *they*]
              Use of pronoun: object of preposition *with*
              Case for object of preposition: objective

⊙ Technology Tip

Sometimes your spell-check feature will try to separate *who* and *ever* or *whom* and *ever*. Put them back together.

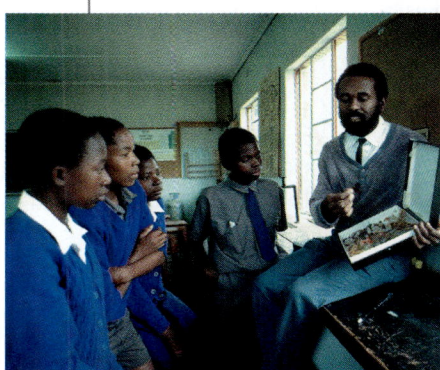

▲ **Critical Viewing**
Explain this scene, using *who* to describe the teacher and *whom* to describe the students. **[Connect]**

Special Problems With Pronouns • **573**

Critical Viewing

Connect The teacher, <u>who</u> holds a display, is explaining an idea to his students, for <u>whom</u> the conversation is interesting.

Integrating Speaking and Listening Skills

Have students work in pairs to write a brief script of a telephone call to arrange a job interview at a company. Tell them specifically to use the pronouns *who* and *whom* in their scripts. (For example, A: This is CD&I. Who is calling please? B: My name is Rosario. May I speak to whoever is in charge of hiring?) Then, have the students read or perform their scripts. Ask classmates to be alert to correct and incorrect uses of pronouns.

Customize for *Verbal/Linguistic Learners*

Have each student write three sentences with *who* and three sentences with *whom*, leaving a blank space where *who* or *whom* should go. Then have each student read his or her sentences—with blanks—to a partner. The responder must supply the correct pronoun form.

Integrating Workplace Skills

Explain to students that in business writing they will frequently use the pronouns *who* and *whom*. They will also encounter situations in which they must use pronouns in elliptical sentences. Ask students to suggest phrases and sentences that they might write in business letters or use in other business situations. Examples may include the following:

To whom it may concern:

To whom shall I fax my résumé?

Who is the person I should contact?

I will send samples to whomever you suggest.

Step-by-Step Teaching Guide

Determining Case in Subordinate Clauses With Parenthetical Expressions

1. Review the concept of parenthetical expressions. Remind students that these are usually phrases that are not basic parts of sentences—subject, verb, complement—and that do not affect the basic grammar of the sentence.

2. Explain to students that parenthetical expressions in subordinate clauses do not affect the case of a pronoun, including *who*. Suggest that they mentally eliminate a parenthetical expression to choose a pronoun.

3. Ask students to offer typical parenthetical expressions (on the other hand, frankly, I'm sure, in fact) and then to use one or two in sentences with *who* or *whom*.

Critical Viewing

Draw Conclusions Answers will vary. Sample answer: The woman <u>who</u> is using the mouse is demonstrating how to use a feature of the computer program. The woman with the pencil, <u>whom</u> the computer operator is teaching, will learn the skill quickly.

Answer Key

▶ **Exercise 16**

1. Who	4. whose
2. Who	5. Who
3. whom	

▶ **Exercise 17**

1. who creates the illusion of life by generating computer images, drawings, or models.
2. who has experience in drawing, cartooning, or graphic design.
3. who use traditional animation, computer graphics animation, or claymation.
4. whoever commissions his or her work.
5. Whoever chooses a career as an animator

Determining Case in Subordinate Clauses With Parenthetical Expressions Ignore expressions such as *they say* or *I suppose* when choosing between *who* and *whom*, because they do not affect the rest of the clause.

EXAMPLES: He is the one *who*, I think, will get the job.
He is the one *whom*, I think, the board will hire.

▶ **Exercise 16** Using Forms of *Who* Correctly in Questions Choose the correct pronoun in each sentence:

1. (Who, Whom) would like to learn about career opportunities in the world of business?
2. (Who, Whom) has the skills to apply for this job?
3. From (who, whom) did you receive this excellent résumé?
4. This report will be (who's, whose) responsibility?
5. (Who, Whom) is most adept at balancing the budget?

▶ **Exercise 17** Using Forms of *Who* Correctly in Clauses Choose the correct form of *who* and *whom*. Then, on a separate sheet of paper, write the subordinate clause.

EXAMPLE: I want to know (who, whom) wrote this.
ANSWER: *who* wrote this

1. An animator is a person (who, whom) creates the illusion of life by generating computer images, drawings, or models.
2. An animator should be someone (who, whom) has experience in drawing, cartooning, or graphic design.
3. Animators are graphic artists (who, whom) use traditional animation, computer graphics animation, or claymation.
4. Part of an animator's job may be to design animation, hand draw or paint characters, and meet with (whoever, whomever) commissions his or her work.
5. (Whoever, Whomever) chooses a career as an animator needs to keep him- or herself up to date with new techniques and computer programs.

▲ **Critical Viewing**
Use *who* in a sentence about the woman using the mouse. Use *whom* in a sentence about the woman with the pencil. [**Draw Conclusions**]

▶ **More Practice**

Language Lab CD-ROM
• Pronoun Case lesson
On-line Exercise Bank
• Section 22.2
Grammar Exercise Workbook
• pp. 109–110

✎ STANDARDIZED TEST PREPARATION WORKSHOP

Grammar and Usage Many standardized tests require students to select the correct case of a pronoun in an elliptical clause within the context of a passage. Use the following example to demonstrate.

Shawna and I took ballet together, but she liked it better than ___.

Choose the correct pronoun to complete the sentence.

A me	C we
B I	D us

The correct answer is **B**. *I* is correct. The elliptical clause is understood to mean "she liked it better than I liked it" or "better than I did." The nominative case is needed because this pronoun is the subject of a verb. *We* and *us* are wrong because, though there is a compound subject at the beginning of the sentence, reference here is to only one person.

Pronouns in Elliptical Clauses

Another problem with pronoun usage occurs in complex sentences containing an *elliptical clause*—that is, a clause in which some words are understood rather than stated. Such clauses generally make a comparison and begin with *than* or *as*.

▶ **KEY CONCEPT** In elliptical clauses beginning with *than* or *as*, use the form of the pronoun that you would use if the clause were fully stated. ■

The case of the pronoun depends on whether the omitted words belong after or before the pronoun. In the examples below, the omitted words are supplied in brackets.

WORDS LEFT OUT AFTER PRONOUN:	Amanda is as capable as *he* [is].
WORDS LEFT OUT BEFORE PRONOUN:	Betty sent Karen more applicants than [she sent] *me*.

When you choose a pronoun for an elliptical clause, mentally complete the clause. If the understood words come *after* the pronoun, use a nominative pronoun. If the understood words come *before* the pronoun, use an objective pronoun.

In some sentences, the case of the pronoun completely changes the meaning of the sentence.

NOMINATIVE PRONOUN:	I liked his career counselor more than *he*.
	I liked his career counselor more than *he* [did].
OBJECTIVE PRONOUN:	I liked his career counselor more than *him*.
	I liked his career counselor more than [I liked] *him*.

In choosing a pronoun for an elliptical clause, follow the steps outlined below:

STEPS FOR CHOOSING A PRONOUN IN ELLIPTICAL CLAUSES

1. Consider the choices of pronouns: nominative or objective.

2. Mentally complete the elliptical clause.

3. Base your choice on what you find.

✓ ONGOING ASSESSMENT: Monitor and Reinforce

If students miss more than one item in Exercise 16 or 17, refer them to the following for additional practice.

In the Textbook	Print Resources	Technology
Section Review, Ex. 20–21, p. 577	*Grammar Exercise Workbook*, pp. 109–110	*Language Lab* CD-ROM, Nouns and Pronouns; *On-Line Exercise Bank*, Section 22.1

Step-by-Step Teaching Guide

Pronouns in Elliptical Clauses

1. Observe that elliptical clauses often make comparisons: Something is taller than something else, for instance, or someone likes something more than he or she likes something else. These are special clauses in which some words have been left out for efficiency of expression.

2. Point out that elliptical clauses, because they omit certain words, can present a writer or speaker with a challenge when choosing the correct pronoun form. The writer must mentally consider the missing words to understand how the pronoun is to be used.

3. Using the example in the textbook, follow the steps required to choose a pronoun for an elliptical clause. Explain to students that they must first complete the clause by supplying the words that have been omitted in order to choose the correct form of the pronoun.

4. Have students practice using pronouns in elliptical clauses by writing and supplying the understood words for the following sentences:

   My cousin likes pizza with extra cheese more than (me, I). (The correct answer is *I*, but choosing *me* creates a sentence with a different meaning. Ask students to explain the meaning of each version.)

   Her brother enjoys talking to baseball players more than (us, we). (Again, ask students to explain the differences in meaning between this sentence with *us* and with *we*.)

Integrating Vocabulary Skills

Elliptical, Ellipsis. Have students find a definition of *elliptical* or *ellipsis* in the dictionary. Ask them to define the phrase *elliptical clause* in their own words ("a subordinate clause with an important element missing, such as a subject or verb"). Then point out that ellipsis points (. . .) form a kind of punctuation used to show that something has been omitted in a sentence for clarity or brevity.

22.2

GRAMMAR IN LITERATURE

from **The First Seven Years**
Bernard Malamud

In the following passage, the objective case whom *is used.*

Neither the shifting white blur outside, nor the sudden deep remembrance of the snowy Polish village where he had wasted his youth could turn his thoughts from Max the college boy, (a constant visitor in the mind since early that morning when Feld saw him trudging through the snowdrifts on his way to school) *whom* he so much respected because of the sacrifices he had made. . . .

▶ **Exercise 18** **Identifying the Correct Pronoun in Elliptical Clauses** Rewrite each sentence, choosing the correct pronoun in parentheses and completing the elliptical clause.

EXAMPLE: She has as many years of experience as (he, him).
ANSWER: She has as many years of experience as *he* does.

1. Your guidance counselor can help you learn more about a career in music therapy than (I, me).
2. In some ways, music therapists are like doctors and can spend as much time with patients as (they, them).
3. The challenge of helping others is more difficult for him than (she, her).
4. Music often has a deeper effect on patients than (we, us).
5. Our therapist can develop John's coordination as well as (she, her).

▶ **Exercise 19** **Using the Correct Pronoun in Elliptical Clauses** Use a pronoun to complete each elliptical clause correctly. Write the word(s) that complete each elliptical clause.

EXAMPLE: Joy is taller than ___?___ .
ANSWER: he (is)

1. The meteorologist knows more about weather than ___?___ .
2. A meteorologist knows the atmosphere better than ___?___ .
3. No other meteorologist is as accurate as ___?___ .
4. His weather forecaster is more knowledgeable than ___?___ .
5. Clouds are more interesting to Joe than ___?___ .

▶ **More Practice**
Language Lab CD-ROM
• Pronoun Case lesson
On-line Exercise Bank
• Section 22.2
Grammar Exercise Workbook
• pp. 109–110

576 • Pronoun Usage

Section 22.2 Section Review

GRAMMAR EXERCISES 20–25

Exercise 20 Using *Who* and *Whom* in Questions On a separate sheet of paper, write the pronoun that completes each question.

1. (Who, Whom) would like to help people learn by working in a museum?
2. From (who, whom) did you acquire your interest in museum employment?
3. (Who, Whom) would be interested in volunteering at a museum to gain work experience?
4. Would a tour guide be a good entry-level position for (whoever, whomever) is interested in a museum career?
5. (Who, Whom) can I contact at the Smithsonian Institution regarding possible internships?

Exercise 21 Recognizing Uses of *Who* and *Whom* On a separate sheet of paper, write the subordinate clause found in each sentence. Then, indicate how the form of *who* or *whom* is used.

1. We applauded the woman who conducted the magnificent symphony orchestra.
2. Coincidentally, she is the same person whom I once saw in a rock band.
3. Whoever aims for a performing career in classical music may aspire to be an orchestral player.
4. That orchestral player is the one to whom she gave lessons.
5. It is wise to give a position in the symphony to whoever has technical expertise in music.

Exercise 22 Using Pronouns in Elliptical Structures Add a pronoun to each sentence that completes the elliptical structure. Then, write out the full elliptical structure.

1. Because she was extremely well prepared and organized, Vivian interviewed better than ___?___.
2. She dressed as professionally as ___?___ for her interview.
3. Vivian had more experience and better job skills than ___?___.
4. No one else in the waiting room was as confident as ___?___.
5. The interview was more important to Vivian than ___?___.

Exercise 23 Find It in Your Reading Determine the use and the case of the pronoun *whom* in the passage from "The First Seven Years" on the previous page. Begin by isolating the subordinate clause to determine how the pronoun is used.

Exercise 24 Find It in Your Writing Deciding when to use *who* or *whom* is often a problem. Look through your portfolio for examples of the pronouns *who* and *whom* in your writing. Using this section as a guide, make sure each example is used correctly.

Exercise 25 Writing Application Think of a family member or friend whose career you admire. Write ten interview questions to learn more about this person's career or place of business. Use each of the following words at least once.

Who	Whoever
Whom	Whomever

Section Review • 577

☑ **ONGOING ASSESSMENT: Assess Mastery**

Use the following resources to assess student mastery of pronoun usage.

In the Textbook	Print Resources	Technology
Chapter Review, p. 579, Ex. 31–32 Standardized Test Preparation Workshop, pp. 580–581	*Formal Assessment*, Chapter 22	*Language Lab* CD-ROM, Nouns and Pronouns; *On-Line Exercise Bank*, Chapter 22

CHAPTER REVIEW

These exercises correlate to sections of the chapter on pronoun usage, pages 560–577. The exercises may be used for more practice, for reteaching, or for review of the key concepts presented in the chapter.

Answer Key

Exercise 26

1. you, objective
2. your, possessive
3. you, nominative
4. It, nominative
5. they, nominative
6. them, objective
7. they, nominative
8. them, objective
9. It, nominative
10. your, possessive

Exercise 27

Some pronouns may vary; their uses will not.

1. she, subject of a verb
2. They, nominative absolute
3. you, subject of a verb
4. us, subject of a verb
5. he (*or* he or she), subject of a verb

Exercise 28

Some pronouns may vary; their uses will not.

1. him, her, object of preposition
2. us, indirect object
3. them, direct object
4. us, subject of infinitive
5. them, direct object

Exercise 29

Pronouns may vary.

1. her
2. mine
3. her
4. their
5. hers

⏱ TIME SAVERS!

🖥 **Answers on Transparencies**
Use the *Grammar Exercises Answers on Transparencies* for Chapter 22 to facilitate correction by students.

🖥 **On-Line Exercise Bank**
Have students complete the exercises on computer. The Auto Check feature will grade their work for you!

Chapter 22 Chapter Review

GRAMMAR EXERCISES 26–34

Exercise 26 Identifying Pronouns
On a separate sheet of paper, write each pronoun you find in this paragraph. Then, tell whether it is *nominative*, *objective*, or *possessive*.

(1) The Internet and the World Wide Web can help you in (2) your search for the perfect career. (3) If you have never used the Internet before, now is the time to begin. (4) It can be an extremely useful tool in any job hunt. (5) Many newspapers have columns in which they publish new Web addresses, called URLs. (6) Some Internet users collect them (7) as though they were baseball cards. (8) Job hunters soon realize that the Internet is a place for them to find information, contacts, counseling, and job vacancies. (9) It may even be used to post (10) your résumé.

Exercise 27 Adding Nominative Pronouns to Sentences On a separate sheet of paper, write a nominative pronoun to complete each sentence. Then, tell its use.

1. The career counselor and __?__ came to our class to discuss résumé writing.
2. __?__ having explained how important a correctly written résumé can be, the class walked away with useful tips.
3. Make sure that __?__ include a cover letter when sending a résumé.
4. When my boss writes a cover letter, __?__ always addresses it to a specific person.
5. If you call a specific person in the company, __?__ will usually help you.

Exercise 28 Adding Objective Pronouns to Sentences On a separate sheet of paper, write an objective pronoun to complete each sentence. Then, tell its use.

1. In the course of our school year, the computer acted as a powerful resource for __?__ and __?__.
2. Our art teacher gave __?__ a computer program detailing twentieth-century Impressionist painters.
3. Claude Monet impressed __?__ as one of the greatest artists profiled in the program overview.
4. The beauty of his gardens at Giverney, outside Paris, inspired __?__ to see his admired paintings of waterlilies.
5. Monet's homogenized use of color and space highlighted __?__ as one of nature's most beautiful flowers.

Exercise 29 Adding Possessive Pronouns to Sentences Use a correct possessive pronoun to complete each sentence.

1. She is using __?__ computer to write a list of references.
2. Her computer's electronic address is similar to __?__.
3. You can bring up __?__ Web page by typing this URL, or Universal Resource Locator.
4. In case you're curious about the arrows, __?__ function is to move you back and forth from screen to screen.
5. The job application that is filled in on the Web page is __?__.

Exercise 30 Revising Sentences by Adding Pronouns
Replace the underlined words with an appropriate pronoun.

1. For job hunters, the Internet is a place to receive counseling. <u>The Internet</u> has some interesting career centers.
2. Some of <u>the career centers</u> can be used at no cost to job hunters.
3. Most people who access career centers are satisfied with <u>career centers</u>.
4. A person can obtain phone numbers of potential employers, whom <u>the person</u> could call for interviews.
5. There are many job vacancies, and the Internet is an excellent place for you to search for <u>job vacancies</u>.
6. If you have a résumé, the Web is an excellent place to post <u>your résumé</u>.
7. Many of <u>the résumés</u> do get seen on the Internet by potential employers.
8. The Internet is a good source, but many jobs are not posted on <u>the Internet</u>.
9. The job seeker can look elsewhere for positions that interest <u>the job seeker</u>.
10. <u>The job seeker</u> could find an exciting new career by networking with friends, family members, and acquaintances.

Exercise 31 Revision Practice
On a separate sheet of paper, rewrite the following paragraph, correcting any errors.

(1) It is said that Tim Berners-Lee was the man who developed the World Wide Web. (2) He was the individual whom experimented at the European Particle Physics Laboratory in Switzerland. (3) Tim used technology to help transmit information to whoever he contacted. (4) Yesterday, we found a great Web page. (5) My classmates and me were very impressed. (6) We didn't know who had created the new Web page. (7) No one was more impressed than me. (8) Once I accessed the page, I wanted to hear from whoever had designed the graphics.

Exercise 32 Using Pronouns in Elliptical Clauses
Complete these similes about a computer programmer, using pronouns in elliptical clauses. Then, using them as a model, create your own similes about an interesting career.

1. As prolific as ___?___
2. As meticulous as ___?___
3. As efficient as ___?___
4. As analytical as ___?___
5. As informative as ___?___

Exercise 33 Writing Application
Using each group of words below, write an original sentence about a career that interests you. Use only one of the words in parentheses in each of your sentences.

1. as imaginative as (I, me)
2. was the person (who, whom)
3. as much as (he, him)
4. as well as (I, me)
5. more than (she, her)

Exercise 34 CUMULATIVE REVIEW Effective Sentences, Verb Usage, and Pronoun Usage
Rewrite the following paragraph, correcting the errors.

(1) Yesterday Linda and Gregg had gone to the lake to do some skating. (2) They took heavy wool socks and they took warm mittens and they took blankets because the temperature was below zero. (3) As they approached the lake. (4) They seen a rabbit scamper across the ice. (5) "If I was that rabbit," Gregg thought, "I would be extremely cold." (6) They arrived at the lake, sat down, and were eating lunch. (7) An icy wind blowed across the shore as they laced up their skates. (8) When Linda had her's on, she advanced to the edge of the lake. (9) Where she waited until Gregg caught up with her. (10) Despite the cold, they feel great.

Lesson Objectives

1. To demonstrate control over grammatical elements such as pronoun case
2. To recognize appropriate sentence construction within the context of a written passage

Step-by-Step Teaching Guide

Using Pronouns

Teaching Resources: Standardized Test Preparation Workbook, pp. 43–44

1. Briefly review with students the rules of pronoun usage they have studied in this chapter. Tell them that standardized tests often include questions that require knowledge of pronoun usage. This lesson will give students a chance to apply the knowledge from this chapter.

2. Encourage students to read test instructions carefully. Not all standardized tests are graded in the same way. Some tests do not penalize students for incorrect answers so that students might increase their scores with a judicious guess.

3. You may wish to provide students with standardized test answer sheets to practice the mechanics of marking in answers.

Standardized Test Preparation Workshop

Using Pronouns

Standardized tests measure your knowledge of the rules of standard grammar, such as correct pronoun usage. Questions test your ability to use the three cases of personal pronouns correctly. When answering these questions, determine what type of pronoun is needed in the sentence—nominative, objective, or possessive. Also, consider the rules for special problems with pronouns—such as, use in compound structures, appositives, elliptical clauses, and the use of *who* and *whom*—before choosing a pronoun. The following test item will give you practice with the format of questions that test your knowledge of pronoun usage.

Test Tips

- Before choosing a pronoun for an elliptical clause beginning with *than* or *as,* mentally complete the clause using an objective or nominative pronoun.
- Base your choice on the pronoun that does not change the meaning of the sentence.

Sample Test Items	Answers and Explanations

Directions: Read the passage, and choose the letter of the word that belongs in each space.
 	
The winners of the science fair were Joy and ___(1)___. The principal gave her and ___(2)___ first-prize medals.
 	
1 **A** me
   B I
   C we
   D us
	The correct answer is *B.* Because the sentence requires a word that renames the subject, or a predicate noun, a nominative case pronoun is the correct choice. Therefore, the pronoun *I* best completes the compound predicate noun.

2 **F** me
   G I
   H we
   J us
	The correct answer is *F.* Because the sentence requires an indirect object, an objective case pronoun is the correct choice. Therefore, the pronoun *me* best completes the compound indirect object.

580 • Pronoun Usage

✏ TEST-TAKING TIP

Effective time management can boost students' confidence when they are taking standardized tests. Encourage students to skim quickly over the passages and answers before they begin a timed section of a test. They can form an impression of which passages look easy and which look more difficult. All the answers count the same, so students should answer the easy questions first and leave time to concentrate on the more difficult items later.

Answer Key

▶ Practice 1 Directions Read the passage, and choose the letter of the word that correctly completes each sentence.

Sam and ____(1)____ worked very hard to complete our project on Kate Chopin. ____(2)____ part was to complete all the research; his job was to write up the report and collect visuals. ____(3)____, the class experts on Chopin, received a very high grade. No one in our class can boast that he or she worked harder than Sam and ____(4)____. In fact, our class was so impressed with our presentation that they gave ____(5)____ a standing ovation.

1 A me
   B I
   C him
   D her

2 F My
   G Her
   H She
   J They

3 A Our
   B Us
   C We
   D Its

4 F her
   G his
   H me
   J I

5 A me
   B we
   C her
   D us

▶ Practice 2 Directions Read the passage, and choose the letter of the word that belongs in each space.

Kate Chopin is my favorite writer. ____(1)____ writings, often controversial, were ignored for many decades. ____(2)____ often depicted women's search for independence. I often group ____(3)____ and Virginia Woolf in the same category. I'm not sure to ____(4)____ I would give the title of best women's rights advocate. However, as a fan of Chopin, I will say that no one writes better than ____(5)____.

1 A His
   B I
   C Her
   D She

2 F Them
   G They
   H Him
   J Her

3 A her
   B she
   C him
   D me

4 F who
   G whose
   H whom
   J theirs

5 A her
   B their
   C us
   D she

▶ Practice 1
1. B
2. F
3. C
4. J
5. D

▶ Practice 2
1. C
2. G
3. A
4. H
5. D

In-Depth Lesson Plan

	LESSON FOCUS	PRINT AND MEDIA RESOURCES
DAY 1	**Subject and Verb Agreement** Students learn and apply agreement concepts covering singular and plural subjects and compound subjects. (pp. 584–588)	*Language Lab* **CD-ROM**, Subject-Verb Agreement *On-Line Exercise Bank*, Section 23.1 **Teaching Resources** *Grammar Exercise Workbook*, pp. 111–114; *Grammar Exercises Answers on Transparencies*, Ch. 23
DAY 2	**Subject and Verb Agreement** *continued* Students learn and apply concepts covering confusing subjects, subjects of linking verbs, collective nouns, indefinite pronouns, and amounts and measurements. (pp. 589–595)	**Teaching Resources** *Grammar Exercise Workbook*, pp. 115–116
DAY 3	**Pronoun and Antecedent Agreement** Students learn and apply agreement concepts covering personal pronouns and antecedents, agreement in number, indefinite pronouns, and reflexive pronouns. (pp. 596–603)	*On-Line Exercise Bank*, Section 23.2 **Teaching Resources** *Grammar Exercise Workbook*, pp. 117–120
DAY 4	**Special Problems With Pronoun Agreement** Students learn and apply concepts covering problems with pronoun agreement. (pp. 604–612)	*On-Line Exercise Bank*, Section 23.3 **Teaching Resources** *Grammar Exercise Workbook*, pp. 121–124; *Hands-on Grammar Activity Book*, Ch. 23
DAY 5	**Review and Assess** Students review chapter and demonstrate mastery of agreement concepts. (pp. 613–617)	**Teaching Resources** *Formal Assessment*, Ch. 23

Accelerated Lesson Plan

	LESSON FOCUS	PRINT AND MEDIA RESOURCES
DAY 1	**Subject and Verb Agreement** Students cover subject and verb agreement concepts as determined by the Diagnostic Test. (pp. 584–595)	*Language Lab* **CD-ROM**, Subject-Verb Agreement *On-Line Exercise Bank*, Ch. 23.1 **Teaching Resources** *Grammar Exercise Workbook*, pp. 111–116; *Grammar Exercises Answers on Transparencies*, Ch. 23
DAY 2	**Pronoun and Antecedent Agreement; Special Problems With Pronoun Agreement** Students cover pronoun and antecedent agreement and special problems with pronoun agreement. (pp. 596–612)	*On-Line Exercise Bank*, Ch. 23.2–23.3 **Teaching Resources** *Grammar Exercise Workbook*, pp. 117–124
DAY 3	**Review and Assess** Students review chapter and demonstrate mastery of concepts. (pp. 613–617)	**Teaching Resources** *Formal Assessment*, Ch. 23

Options for Adapting Lesson Plans

FEATURES

Extend coverage with the Grammar in Literature features (pp. 585, 597, 609) and the Standardized Test Preparation Workshop (p. 616).

TECHNOLOGY

Students can use the On-Line Exercise Bank to complete the exercises on computer. The Auto Check feature will grade their work.

INTEGRATED SKILLS COVERAGE

Grammar in Literature
SE pp. 585, 597, 609

Writing
Find It in Your Writing SE pp. 595, 603, 611, 612
Writing Application SE pp. 595, 603, 612, 615
Grammar and Style SE p. 587

Viewing and Representing
Critical Viewing SE pp. 582, 584, 589, 590, 592, 596, 598, 601, 604, 607, 608, 610

Technology
SE pp. 592, 609

Speaking ATE p. 589

Life Skills ATE p. 593

Workplace Skills ATE p. 605

Real-World Connection ATE p. 600

ASSESSMENT SUPPORT

Standardized Test Preparation Workshop, SE p. 616; ATE pp. 591, 607

Standardized Test Preparation Workbook, pp. 45–46

Formal Assessment, Ch. 23

MEETING INDIVIDUAL NEEDS

Less Advanced Students ATE pp. 586, 607. See also Ongoing Assessments ATE pp. 586, 588, 592, 599, 601, 602, 608, 610.

AP Students ATE p. 588

ESL Students ATE pp. 588, 598

Bodily/Kinesthetic Learners ATE p. 587

Verbal/Linguistic Learners ATE p. 585

BLOCK SCHEDULING

Pacing Suggestions
For 90-minute Blocks
• Administer the Diagnostic Test to students to determine instructional coverage.
• Have students complete the necessary exercises in class. Use the Hands-on Grammar activity to provide a change of pace.

Resources for Varying Instruction
• **Language Lab CD-ROM** If your students have access to hardware, a 90-minute block provides an ideal opportunity for students to work on computer.

Professional Development Support
• **How to Manage Instruction in the Block** This Teaching Resource provides management and activity suggestions.

MEDIA AND TECHNOLOGY

For the Student
• **Language Lab CD-ROM**, Subject-Verb Agreement, Pronouns and Antecedents, Nouns and Pronouns
• **On-Line Exercise Bank,** Sections 23.1–3

For the Teacher
• **Resource Pro CD-ROM**

WRITING AND GRAMMAR WEB SITE

The Interactive Writing and Grammar Web Site provides a wide array of support for students, teachers, and parents. Grammar support includes:

• **On-Line Exercise Bank** with Auto Check scoring
• Diagnostic and assessment support

www.phschool.com

LITERATURE CONNECTIONS

Grammar in Literature selections from *Prentice Hall Literature: Timeless Voices, Timeless Themes,* The American Experience:

from *To His Excellency, General Washington,* Phillis Wheatley, SE p. 585

from "I Hear America Singing," Walt Whitman, SE p. 597

from *Moby-Dick,* Herman Melville, SE p. 609

Lesson Objectives

1. To make verbs agree with their subjects, including singular and plural subjects, compound subjects, confusing subjects, collective nouns, and indefinite pronouns

2. To make pronouns agree with their antecedents

3. To recognize and correct vague, ambiguous, and distant pronoun references

4. To demonstrate control over grammatical elements such as subject-verb agreement and pronoun-antecedent agreement

5. To evaluate writing for both mechanics and content

6. To analyze the characteristics of clearly written texts, including patterns of organization, syntax, and word choice

Critical Viewing

Classify, Distinguish Sample answers: The sun rises each morning. The sun appears to get smaller as it rises (*sun* and *rises* agree, *sun* and *appears* agree—they are all singular).

Chapter 23 Agreement

The bodies in our solar system maintain special relationships. Planets revolve around the sun, and moons revolve around planets. The laws of the universe keep the stars and planets in harmony with each other.

Similarly, subjects and verbs as well as pronouns and their antecedents form special relationships within sentences. For instance, subjects and verbs must always agree in number. Pronouns and their antecedents must also agree in number.

The laws of grammar keep subjects and verbs as well as pronouns and their antecedents in harmony with each other also. For instance, when a subject and its verb work together properly, they are said to agree with each other. In this chapter, you will study the grammatical agreement of subjects and verbs as well as that of pronouns and their antecedents.

▲ **Critical Viewing**
Think of a sentence that tells two things the sun appears to do. How does the subject agree with the verb? [Classify, Distinguish]

582 • Agreement

☑ ONGOING ASSESSMENT: Diagnose

If students miss more than one item in any category, direct them to the relevant pages of the textbook and assign exercises for practice and review.

Agreement	Diagnostic Test Items	Teach	Exercises	Section Reviews	Chapter Review
Skill Check A					
Subject and Verb Agreement	A 1–15	pp. 584–593	Ex. 1–8	Ex. 9–14	Ex. 39–41
Skill Check B					
Pronoun and Antecedent Agreement	B 16–20	pp. 596–602	Ex. 18–24	Ex. 25–27	Ex. 42–43

Diagnostic Test

Directions: Write all answers on a separate sheet of paper.

Skill Check A. Choose the verb in parentheses that agrees with the subject in each sentence.

1. The planets (has, have) always captured people's imaginations.
2. There (is, are) nine planets in our solar system.
3. Astronomers (has, have) studied the planets for centuries.
4. A beautiful sight in the night sky (is, are) the stars.
5. The sun, which is surrounded by the planets, (shines, shine) brightly in the sky.
6. The sun and the moon (is, are) heavenly bodies that observers easily (sees, see).
7. During a solar eclipse, the moon (blocks, block) the sun.
8. Lunar eclipses, which (occurs, occur) from time to time, (is, are) not as dramatic as solar eclipses.
9. The class (is, are) making their own special viewers.
10. (There's, There are) times when observation is more valuable than traditional research.
11. Following the solar eclipse (is, are) discussion groups on planetary motion.
12. Interplanetary physics (is, are) one of my favorite subjects.
13. Each of the planets (has, have) its own orbit around the sun.
14. Some of the planets (is, are) visible without a telescope.
15. Neither my brother nor my friends (has, have) a good telescope.

Skill Check B. Choose the correct pronoun in each sentence.

16. Neither my friend John nor my brother lets me use (his, their) telescope.
17. Sam is going to a store where (you, he) can buy a good telescope.
18. Sam's telescope may need (its, their) magnification adjusted.
19. Both of the models he looked at had (its, their) appealing features.
20. Sam and (myself, I) will study the planets.

Skill Check C. Rewrite the following sentences, correcting the vague, ambiguous, or distant pronoun references.

21. You can see many planets and moons, and it starts with a good telescope.
22. On the news, it talked about a comet coming close to Earth.
23. Marion showed Janet that her telescope was pointed toward the portion of the sky that the comet will cross.
24. My parents were going to give me some books about comets, but they haven't arrived yet.
25. Many stars have disappeared by the time we see them, which not many people realize.

Diagnostic Test

Each item in the Diagnostic Test corresponds to a specific section in the chapter on agreement. This will enable you to tailor instruction to the particular needs of your students. See "Ongoing Assessment: Diagnose" below for further details.

Answer Key

Skill Check A

1. have	9. are
2. are	10. There are
3. have	11. are
4. is	12. is
5. shines	13. has
6. are; see	14. are
7. blocks	15. have
8. occur; are	

Skill Check B

16. his	19. their
17. he	20. I
18. its	

Skill Check C

Answers may vary. Sample answers:

21. An observer can see many planets and moons with a good telescope.
22. On the news, commentators talked about a comet coming close to Earth.
23. Marion showed Janet that Marion's telescope was pointed toward the portion of the sky that the comet will cross.
24. My parents were going to give me some books about comets, but the books haven't arrived yet.
25. Not many people realize that many stars have disappeared by the time we see them.

✓ ONGOING ASSESSMENT: Diagnose *continued*

Agreement	Diagnostic Test Items	Teach	Exercises	Section Reviews	Chapter Review
Skill Check C					
Special Problems with Pronoun Agreement	C 21–25	pp. 604–609	Ex. 31–33	Ex. 34–35	Ex. 44
Cumulative Reviews and Applications				Ex. 15–17, 28–30, 36–38	Ex. 45–47

⏱ TIME SAVERS!

Answers on Transparencies Use the *Grammar Exercises Answers on Transparencies* for Chapter 23 to facilitate correction by students.

On-Line Exercise Bank Have students complete the exercises on computer. The Auto Check feature will grade their work for you!

Interest GRABBER Ask students whether they think the word *everybody* is singular or plural. Write the following sentences on the board:

Everybody is going to the prom.

Everybody are going to the prom.

Explain that *everybody* means "every single body" and that it is always singular. Because *everybody* is singular, the first sentence is correct because the verb *is* is also singular.

Activate Prior Knowledge

Have students give examples of incorrect subject-verb agreement they have heard on television or radio. For example, "Weather and traffic *is* coming up next." (The verb should be the plural *are*.)

TEACH

Step-by-Step Teaching Guide

Singular and Plural Subjects

1. Explain that, in English, only three parts of speech indicate number: nouns, pronouns, and verbs.

2. Point out that, while most plural forms are easily identified by *-s* or *-es*, some nouns have irregular plurals (*ox, oxen; tooth, teeth; mouse, mice*).

3. Write the following sentences on the board. Ask students whether the subjects are singular or plural, and then have them select the correct verbs:

   The planets (travel, travels) through space. (travel)

   The planet Jupiter (has, have) sixteen known moons. (has)

Critical Viewing

Connect, Draw Conclusions Sample answer: The sun is covered by the moon during an eclipse. (singular)

Answer Key

▶ Exercise 1

1. is
2. are
3. travels
4. revolve
5. moves

Section 23.1

Subject and Verb Agreement

Singular and Plural Subjects

There are two basic rules of subject and verb agreement that govern all of the other rules:

▶ KEY CONCEPT A singular subject must have a singular verb. A plural subject must have a plural verb. ■

In the examples below and on the next page, the subjects are underlined once and the verbs, twice.

SINGULAR SUBJECT AND VERB:	He looks through the telescope. This large telescope is powerful. Elizabeth has been studying the solar system.
PLURAL SUBJECT AND VERB:	They look through the telescope. These large telescopes are powerful. We have been studying the solar system.

▶ Exercise 1 **Making Verbs Agree With Their Subjects**

Choose the verb in parentheses that agrees with the subject of each sentence.

1. The Milky Way (is, are) the Earth's home galaxy.
2. Our sun's nine planets (is, are) located in the Milky Way.
3. The sun (travels, travel) through space.
4. The planets (revolves, revolve) around the sun.
5. The solar system constantly (moves, move) through space toward the constellation Hercules.

◀ Critical Viewing Use *sun* and *moon* in a sentence about an eclipse. Is the verb singular or plural? **[Connect, Draw Conclusions]**

Theme: Space

In this section, you will learn how to make subjects and verbs agree. The examples and exercises are about space.

Cross-Curricular Connection: Science

⏰ TIME AND RESOURCE MANAGER

Resources
Print: *Grammar Exercise Workbook*, pp. 111–116; *Grammar Exercises Answers on Transparency*, Ch. 23
Technology: *Language Lab* CD-ROM, Subject-Verb Agreement; *On-line Exercise Bank*, 23.1

In-Depth Coverage	Accelerated Pace
• Work through all key concepts, pp. 584–592.	• Assign pp. 584–592 for independent student
• Assign and review Exercises 1–8.	review.
• Read and discuss Grammar in Literature, p. 585.	• Assign Review Exercises 9–12.

GRAMMAR IN LITERATURE

from To His Excellency, General Washington

Phillis Wheatley

Notice that the singular subject she *agrees with the singular verb* flashes. *The plural subject* nations *agrees with the plural verb* gaze. *The subjects are shown in red, and the verbs are shown in blue. The subject* you *is understood in the second-to-last line.*

Celestial choir! enthron'd in realms of light,
   Columbia's scenes of glorious toils I write.
While freedom's cause her anxious breast alarms,
She flashes dreadful in refulgent arms.
See mother earth her offspring's fate bemoan,
And nations gaze at scenes before unknown!

More Practice

Language Lab CD-ROM
• Subject-Verb Agreement lesson
On-line Exercise Bank
• Section 23.1
Grammar Exercise Workbook
• pp. 111–112

Intervening Phrases and Clauses

A verb must agree with its subject even if a phrase or clause comes between them.

KEY CONCEPT A phrase or clause that comes between a subject and its verb does not affect subject-verb agreement. ■

In the first example below, a prepositional phrase separates a singular subject and its singular verb. In the second example, a clause interrupts a plural subject and its plural verb.

EXAMPLES: Sam, with several of his friends, observes the sky.
The astronomers, who have a large chart, observe the sky.

Pay particular attention to parenthetical expressions interrupting a subject and its verb. These expressions are usually set off by commas and begin with such words as *along with, as well as,* or *including.* They do not affect the agreement of the subject and its verb.

EXAMPLES: Your theory, as well as his ideas, lacks support.
The nine planets, along with their moons, revolve around our sun.

Step-by-Step Teaching Guide

Grammar in Literature

1. Have a volunteer read the excerpt from the poem aloud.

2. Point out the highlighted examples of subject-verb agreement, and then ask students to find other examples of subject-verb agreement in the poem. (*I write; cause alarms*)

More About the Writer

Phillis Wheatley was born in 1753 in Senegal, Africa. When she was eight years old, she was captured, sold into slavery, and brought to Boston. Against all odds, Wheatley learned to read and write in English, Greek, and Latin. She became America's first African American poet. In 1773, a collection of her poems was published in London—the first book published by an African American.

Step-by-Step Teaching Guide

Intervening Phrases and Clauses

1. Review with students the function of phrases and subordinate clauses (*to add information or modify an idea elsewhere in the sentence*) and the difference between them (*clauses contain their own subjects and verbs*).

2. Point out that, although subject-verb agreement can be more difficult when a phrase or clause intervenes, identifying the subject of the sentence first simplifies the task.

3. Examine with students examples on this page. Point out how intervening phrases or clauses modify subjects. With the third example, note that the word in the intervening phrase (*ideas*) is not the same number as the subject and verb. While *ideas* is plural, the subject and verb (*theory, lacks*) are singular.

Customize for
Verbal/Linguistic Learners

Students might benefit from listening to examples where agreement is obvious. Tell students to use the singular subject *my friend* with the following verbs, asking students to speak each answer. (*My friend talks, My friend swims.*) Then provide the plural subject *both boys* and repeat the activity.

My friend . . .	Both boys . . .
1. talks,	1. talk
2. swims,	2. swim
3. laughs	3. laugh
4. works	4. work
5. is singing	5. are singing

1. has
2. have
3. rotates
4. contain
5. has

Customize for
Less Advanced Students

Students may think that verbs ending in –s are plural. Point out that only nouns become plural by adding –s; verbs ending in –s are often singular, though not always. Give students practice recognizing singular verbs ending in –s: *gives, takes, runs, walks.*

Relative Pronouns as Subjects

1. Write on the board:

   These are the stories that are in English.

   Ask students to distinguish the independent and adjective clauses. Once they recognize *that are in English* is the adjective clause, point out that the relative pronoun *that* serves two functions: It renames a word in the independent clause (*stories*, a plural noun), and it is the subject of its clause.

2. Review the five relative pronouns (*that, which, who, whom, whose*) and use the examples on this page to demonstrate the importance of recognizing the antecedent in determining number.

3. Have students write two or three original complex sentences with adjective clauses. Have them circle the relative pronouns, underline antecedents, and write what their number is.

4. As part of their response to Exercise 3, have students indicate both the subject and the number of each verb they select.

Answer Key

1. supports
2. erupt
3. contains
4. make
5. knows

23.1

▶ **Exercise 2** **Making Separated Subjects and Verbs Agree** Choose the verb in parentheses that agrees with the subject of each sentence.

1. Saturn, along with Jupiter and Uranus, (has, have) rings that encircle the planet.
2. Scientists who study the universe (has, have) several theories about the rings around planets.
3. Saturn, which is the sixth planet from the sun, (rotates, rotate) every 10 hours and 14 minutes.
4. The rings of Saturn, unlike those of Jupiter, (contains, contain) mostly ice and rock.
5. One of Jupiter's moons (has, have) a great deal of volcanic activity.

Relative Pronouns as Subjects

When *who, which,* or *that* acts as a subject of a subordinate clause, its verb is singular or plural, depending on the number of its antecedent.

▶ **KEY CONCEPT** The antecedent of a relative pronoun determines its agreement with a verb. ■

In the first example, the antecedent of *who* is *one;* therefore, a singular verb is required. In the next example, the antecedent of *who* is *trainees;* therefore, a plural verb is needed.

EXAMPLES: Sam is the only one of the trainees <u>who</u> <u>has</u> applied.
Sam is the only qualified person among the

astronaut trainees <u>who</u> <u>have applied</u>.

▶ **Exercise 3** **Making Relative Pronouns Agree With Their Verbs** Choose the verb in parentheses that agrees with the subject of each subordinate clause.

1. The sun, which (supports, support) life on Earth, is not a very big star in the Milky Way.
2. Stars are glowing balls of gas that (erupts, erupt) at times.
3. The sun has a gigantic atmosphere that (contains, contain) winds of electrically charged particles.
4. Hydrogen is one of the main gases that (makes, make) up the sun.
5. Our science teacher is someone who (knows, know) many facts about the sun and the solar system.

586 • Agreement

▶ **More Practice**

Language Lab CD-ROM
• Subject-Verb Agreement lesson
On-line Exercise Bank
• Section 23.1
Grammar Exercise Workbook
• pp. 111–112

✓ ONGOING ASSESSMENT: Monitor and Reinforce

If students miss more than one item in Exercise 1, 2 or 3, refer them to the following for additional practice.

In the Textbook	Print Resources	Technology
Section Review, Ex. 9, p. 594	*Grammar Exercise Workbook,* pp. 111–112	*On-Line Exercise Bank,* Section 23.1

Compound Subjects

Four different rules of agreement apply to compound subjects joined by *or, nor,* or *and:*

▶ **KEY CONCEPT** A compound subject joined by *and* is generally plural and must have a plural verb. ■

The conjunction *and* acts as a plus sign. Whether the parts of the compound are all singular, all plural, or mixed in number, they add up to a plural compound subject and therefore require a plural verb.

EXAMPLES: <u>Wind</u> and <u>rain</u> <u>exist</u> on Earth.
<u>Winds</u> and <u>rainstorms</u> <u>exist</u> on Earth.
<u>Winds</u> and <u>rain</u> <u>exist</u> on Earth.

Exceptions to this rule occur when the parts of the compound subject equal one thing and when the word *each* or *every* is used before a compound subject. Each of these situations requires a singular verb.

EXAMPLES: <u>Macaroni</u> and <u>cheese</u> <u>is</u> an easy dish to make.
Each <u>man</u> and <u>woman</u> <u>was waving</u> a flag.

▶ **KEY CONCEPT** Two or more singular subjects joined by *or* or *nor* must have a singular verb. ■

EXAMPLE: Either <u>Jupiter</u> or <u>Saturn</u> <u>makes</u> a fascinating topic of study.

▶ **KEY CONCEPT** Two or more plural subjects joined by *or* or *nor* must have a plural verb. ■

EXAMPLE: <u>Space probes</u> or <u>space shuttles</u> <u>provide</u> information about space.

▶ **KEY CONCEPT** If one or more singular subjects are joined to one or more plural subjects by *or* or *nor,* the subject closest to the verb determines agreement. ■

EXAMPLES: Neither <u>atmosphere</u> nor <u>clouds</u> <u>exist</u> on Mercury.
Neither <u>clouds</u> nor <u>atmosphere</u> <u>exists</u> on Mercury.

🔩 Grammar and Style Tip

Use compound subjects to combine sentences and streamline your writing.

Step-by-Step Teaching Guide

Compound Subjects

1. On the board, write the conjunctions *and, or,* and *nor.* Tell students that compound subjects are subjects joined by one of these three conjunctions.

2. Explain that, while *and* combines things, *or* and *nor* present alternatives; a choice is involved, either one or the other.

3. Ask students for more examples of compound subjects joined by *and* that may be singular (Example: *Jones and Smith* is a local law firm.)

4. Demonstrate that, in examples with *each* and *every,* students can confirm agreement by using just *each* or *everyone* as the subject. For example, the sentence "Each man and woman was waving a flag" could be rephrased "Each was waving a flag."

5. Write the following sentences on the board:

   Neither the stars nor the moon provides as much light as the sun.

   Neither the moon nor the stars provide as much light as the sun.

   Either Venus or Mars appears in the sky as a bright star.

   Ask students to explain why each is correct. Pay special attention to *or* and *neither/nor.*

Customize for
Bodily/Kinesthetic Learners

Place two objects on a flat surface. Ask a student to pick up one object *or* the other. Point out that the student is holding one object and has left behind one object. Ask another student to pick up one object *and* the other. Point out that this student is holding two objects. Explain that this is how the words *and* and *or* function in sentences.

Answer Key

Exercise 4

1. are	6. revolve
2. appears	7. are
3. live	8. was
4. seem	9. are
5. have	10. know

Exercise 5

Answers will vary. Sample answers:
1. The Earth and the moon are close neighbors.
2. Mars and Venus are the planets closest to Earth.
3. A telescope or binoculars make it possible to see several moons of Jupiter.
4. Neither the sun nor the moon has living creatures.
5. The stars and planets are interesting to look at through a telescope.

Exercise 6

1. makes	6. correct
2. correct	7. teach
3. are	8. are
4. are	9. correct
5. learns	10. is

► **Exercise 4** Making Compound Subjects Agree With Their Verbs Choose the verb in parentheses that agrees with the subject in each sentence.
1. Mercury and Venus (is, are) closer to the sun than Earth is.
2. Neither Venus nor Mars (appears, appear) to support life.
3. Neither plants nor animals (lives, live) on these planets.
4. Earth and Venus (seems, seem) nearly the same size.
5. Saturn and Jupiter (has, have) many moons.
6. Titan and several other moons (revolves, revolve) around Saturn.
7. The planet's moons, or its three rings, (is, are) visible through a telescope.
8. Either Jupiter's moons or its single ring (was, were) the subject of a recent study.
9. Phobos and Deimos (is, are) the two moons of Mars.
10. Neither Rick nor his classmates (knows, know) much about Mars.

► **Exercise 5** Writing Sentences With Compound Subjects Use each of these compound subjects in a sentence.
1. The Earth and the moon
2. Mars and Venus
3. A telescope or binoculars
4. Neither the sun nor the moon
5. The stars and planets

► **Exercise 6** Revising to Correct Errors in Subject-Verb Agreement Revise these sentences where necessary to correct errors in agreement. If the sentence has no agreement error, write *correct.*
1. Either Neptune or Pluto make a good topic for a report.
2. Every planet and satellite rotates constantly.
3. Mars and Jupiter is visible to the unaided eye.
4. Neither Uranus nor the other two outer planets is visible without a telescope.
5. Every boy and girl learn about the solar system in school.
6. Either Kim or Barry is creating a model of the solar system for the science fair.
7. Mr. Thomas and Ms. Jassey teaches earth science.
8. Neither Marcia nor her sisters is ready for the science test.
9. Every tenth grader and eleventh grader knows that Earth is the third planet from the sun.
10. Freeze-dried spaghetti and meatballs are a meal available to astronauts.

☑ ONGOING ASSESSMENT: Monitor and Reinforce

If students have difficulty with Exercise 4, 5, or 6, refer them to the following for additional practice.

In the Textbook	Print Resources	Technology
Section Review, Ex. 10–11, p. 594	*Grammar Exercise Workbook,* pp. 113–114	*On-Line Exercise Bank,* Section 23.1

Confusing Subjects

Some subjects—hard-to-find subjects, subjects of linking verbs, collective nouns, nouns that look like plurals, indefinite pronouns, titles, amounts, and measurements—require special attention.

Hard-to-Find Subjects If a subject comes after its verb, you must still make sure the subject and verb agree in number.

▶ **KEY CONCEPT** When a subject comes after its verb, the verb must still agree with the subject in number. ■

A sentence in which the subject comes after its verb is said to be inverted. You can check the subject-verb agreement by mentally putting the sentence in the normal subject-verb order.

EXAMPLES: Beyond our galaxy's stars <u>is</u> another galaxy.
(Another <u>galaxy</u> <u>is</u> beyond our galaxy's stars.)
Which of the science reports <u>has</u> <u>she</u> <u>read</u>?
(<u>She</u> <u>has read</u> which of the science reports?)

The words *here* and *there* at the beginning of a sentence often signal an inverted sentence. When putting the sentence in normal subject-verb order, the word *here* or *there* is no longer necessary.

INVERTED: There <u>is</u> a <u>model</u> of the solar system on the table.
S-V ORDER: A <u>model</u> of the solar system <u>is</u> on the table.

There's and *here's*, contractions for *there is* and *here is*, contain the singular verb *is* and therefore cannot be used with plural subjects.

INCORRECT: Among scientists, there's some <u>believers</u> in life on other planets.

CORRECT: Among scientists, there <u>are</u> some <u>believers</u> in life on other planets.

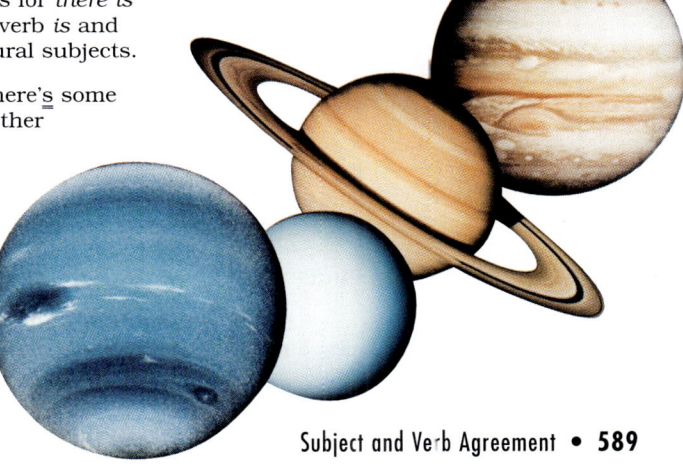

▶ **Critical Viewing** What action verb could you use in a sentence with the subject *planets?* Is it plural or singular in form? **[Analyze]**

Subject and Verb Agreement • 589

Step-by-Step Teaching Guide

Hard-to-Find Subjects

1. Ask students what they remember about hard-to-find subjects. (*Here* and *there* are never subjects; in inverted-order sentences, the subject follows the verb; sometimes subjects are not stated.)

2. Write the following sentences on the board, and then have students use the strategy suggested in the textbook of mentally rewording sentences in normal order to check subject-verb agreement.

    Out of the woods ran two white rabbits. (<u>rabbits</u> <u>ran</u>)

    Here are some books to read. (<u>books</u> <u>are</u>)

    Where did you see my gloves? (<u>you</u> <u>did see</u>)

3. Focus on the contractions *here's* and *there's*. Point out that situations where there is an inversion with a compound subject are tricky. For example:

    Incorrect: *Here's Bill and Roberta.*

    Correct: *Here are Bill and Roberta.*

4. Ask students to create hard-to-find subjects of their own to identify the number of the subject and verb, and to make certain the subject and verb agree.

Critical Viewing

Analyze Sample answer: *Planets orbit the sun at varying speeds.* (plural)

Integrating Speaking Skills

Explain that subject and verb agreement is also important in speaking, especially public speaking. Incorrect agreement can be jarring for listeners and can undercut the speaker's credibility. Have students compose several sentences and recite them out loud, both speaking and listening for correct agreement.

Subjects of Linking Verbs

Collective Nouns

Critical Viewing

Apply Answers might include *rotates, appears.* Point out to students that although *Mars* ends in *s,* it is singular and always takes a singular verb.

Language Highlight

There are several words in English that are the same in the singular and the plural: *deer, fish, sheep, fowl, elk, trout.* The context tells you if you are speaking of one or more (the deer is; the deer are). These words have a common origin—they all come from Old English (dēor, fisc, scēap, fugol, eolh, trūht).

Subjects of Linking Verbs

Another problem with agreement involves linking verbs and predicate nominatives.

▶ **KEY CONCEPT** A linking verb must agree with its subject, regardless of the number of its predicate nominative—the noun or pronoun that renames, identifies, or explains the subject. ■

In the first example below, the subject *craters* agrees with the plural verb *are* in spite of the singular predicate nominative *sign.* In the second example, the nouns are reversed. The subject *sign* agrees with the singular verb *is,* and *craters* is the predicate nominative.

EXAMPLES: Moon <u>craters</u> <u>are</u> one sign of meteor storms.
One <u>sign</u> of meteor storms <u>is</u> moon craters.

Collective Nouns

Collective nouns—such as *audience, team, class,* and *crowd*—name groups of people or things and may be either singular or plural, depending on how they are used.

▶ **KEY CONCEPT** A collective noun takes a singular verb when the group it names acts as a single unit. ■

EXAMPLES: The <u>class</u> <u>is</u> excited to be learning about the solar system.
NASA's <u>committee</u> <u>has decided</u> to launch the shuttle.

▶ **KEY CONCEPT** A collective noun takes a plural verb when the group it names act as individuals with different points of view. ■

EXAMPLES: The <u>class</u> <u>are</u> unable to decide which planets to discuss in their reports.
NASA's <u>committee</u> <u>have been</u> unable to come to an agreement on whether to launch the shuttle.

Nouns That Look Like Plurals Other confusing subjects are nouns that look plural but are singular in meaning.

▲ **Critical Viewing**
Name a verb you can use with the subject *Mars.* **[Apply]**

 Learn More

For a review of linking verbs, see Section 18.2.

KEY CONCEPT Nouns that are plural in form but singular in meaning take singular verbs. ■

Some of these nouns are singular names for branches of knowledge: *acoustics, civics, economics, ethics, mathematics, physics, politics, social studies.* Others have singular meanings because they name single units: *confetti* (one mass of paper bits), *measles* (one disease), *news* (one set of information).

SINGULAR: Physics is a challenging subject.
                 The news was not very interesting yesterday.

Some of these words can be difficult to use correctly. When words such as *acoustics* and *ethics* do not name branches of knowledge but rather indicate characteristics, their meanings are plural. Similarly, words such as *eyeglasses, pliers,* and *scissors*, though they name single items, take plural verbs.

PLURAL   The acoustics in the theater are excellent.
                 My lost eyeglasses were behind the sofa.

Indefinite Pronouns

Some indefinite pronouns are always singular *(anybody, everyone, each,* and so on). Others are always plural *(both, many,* and so on). Two simple rules apply to these indefinite pronouns:

KEY CONCEPT Singular indefinite pronouns take singular verbs. ■

Notice in the examples below that an interrupting phrase does not affect the subject-verb agreement.

EXAMPLES: Each of the planets is rotating at all times.
               Everyone in the class wants to travel in space someday.

KEY CONCEPT Plural indefinite pronouns take plural verbs. ■

EXAMPLES: Both of these planets were formed at about the same time.
               Several of these space probes require further investigation.

For those indefinite pronouns that can be either singular or plural, agreement depends on the number of the antecedent.

Subject and Verb Agreement • 591

Plural-Looking Nouns

1. Explain to students that even a noun that names a branch of knowledge names only one thing—one science, subject, or branch of knowledge.

2. Point out that, while many of the branches of knowledge don't act as nouns without the *s* (*acoustic* and *economic,* for example, are adjectives), *ethics,* when not a branch of knowledge, is a plural of *ethic.*

3. To help students pick the plural verb form, remind students that nouns such as *eyeglasses, scissors,* and *pants* exist only as pairs.

4. Point out that the name of an organization usually takes a singular verb even though the name is in the plural form: *The United Nations is in New York.*

Indefinite Pronouns

1. Remind students that indefinite pronouns require no specific antecedent and, as a result, they can act like nouns.

2. Suggest that students rephrase the examples in the textbook so that the indefinite pronoun has no modifiers. This may require the creation of another sentence for statements to make sense. For example, *Each of the planets is rotating at all times* could be rewritten as *There are nine planets in the system. Each is rotating at all times* or *Each rotates at all times.*

3. Point out that, though most of the examples in the text use linking verbs, rules of agreement apply to all verbs used with indefinite pronouns.

STANDARDIZED TEST PREPARATION WORKSHOP

Grammar and Usage Many standardized tests require students to revise errors in compositions. Write the following on the board and ask students to identify the correct answer.

At any one time, either the scientists or their assistant were paying close attention to the telescope.

How should were paying close attention be rewritten?

A were paid close attention

B was paid close attention

C was paying close attention

D correct as is

The correct answer is **C**. When the correlative conjunction *either . . . or* joins a compound subject, correct agreement is with the closer subject, *assistant,* which is singular. Therefore, the verb (*was paying*) must be singular.

Step-by-Step Teaching Guide

Titles

1. Point out to students that titles of books, plays, television programs, films, musical compositions, and works of art are singular when used as individual subjects.

2. Point out that, although one title uses a singular verb, if more than one title is given, the rules of compound subjects apply when multiple titles act as the subject of a sentence. For example, *"Birches" and "Mending Wall" are poems by Robert Frost.*

Critical Viewing

Distinguish Students should respond that three thousand *is* a large number.

Step-by-Step Teaching Guide

Amounts and Measurements

1. Review the explanations in the text of why and when agreement is singular (amounts express single units, such as one sum of money or one part of a whole).

2. Have students compare this definition to other situations where, despite being plural in form, a subject is really just one unit. (*Measles* is a disease, *ethics* is a branch of knowledge.)

3. Point out that *half* can, in some situations, take a singular verb. For example:

   Half of my sandwich has been eaten!

   Ask students why *Half* is singular. (It is part of a single whole.)

▶ KEY CONCEPT The pronouns *all, any, more, most, none,* and *some* usually take a singular verb if the antecedent is singular and a plural verb if the antecedent is plural. ■

In the first example below, the antecedent of *most* is *planet,* a singular noun. In the second example, the antecedent of *most* is *planets,* a plural noun.

SINGULAR: <u>Most</u> of our planet <u>is</u> water.

PLURAL: <u>Most</u> of the planets <u>are</u> large.

Titles The titles of books or works of art may be misleading if they sound plural or consist of many words.

▶ KEY CONCEPT A title is singular and therefore takes a singular verb. ■

EXAMPLES: <u>Space</u> <u>is</u> a novel by James A. Michener.

<u>The Merry Wives of Windsor</u> <u>is</u> a Shakespearean play.

Amounts and Measurements

Most amounts and measurements, although appearing plural, express single units.

▶ KEY CONCEPT A noun expressing an amount or measurement is usually singular and requires a singular verb. ■

In the first three examples, the subjects agree with singular verbs. *Twelve dollars* equals one sum of money; *thirty miles* equals one measurement; and *two thirds* is one part of a whole. In the last example, *half* refers to individual items and is plural.

EXAMPLES: <u>Twelve dollars</u> <u>is</u> the price of the ticket.

<u>Thirty miles</u> <u>was</u> a long distance to travel.

<u>Two thirds</u> of the produce <u>has spoiled.</u>

<u>Half</u> of the invitations <u>were mailed</u> today.

✺ Technology Tip

If your computer's grammar-check tool highlights a large part of a sentence, check to see whether the subject and verb agree.

▼ Critical Viewing
On a clear, dark night, approximately 3,000 stars can be seen. Would you say 3,000 *is* a large number or 3,000 *are* a large number? **[Distinguish]**

✔ ONGOING ASSESSMENT: Monitor and Reinforce

If students miss more than two items in Exercise 7 or 8 refer them to the following for additional practice.

In the Textbook	Print Resources	Technology
Section Review, Ex. 12–14, p. 595	*Grammar Exercise Workbook,* pp. 115–116	*On-Line Exercise Bank,* Section 23.1

Exercise 7 Making Verbs Agree With Confusing Subjects

Choose the verb in parentheses that agrees with the subject of each sentence.

1. *2001: A Space Odyssey* (is, are) a novel written by Arthur C. Clarke.
2. Physics (is, are) a subject that Clarke studied when he attended the University of London.
3. *Fountains of Paradise* (was, were) also written by Clarke.
4. (Was, Were) both Clarke and director Stanley Kubrick involved with producing the movie version of *2001*?
5. The subject of the movie (is, are) human ventures into space.
6. Our class (has, have) their favorite characters.
7. (There's, There are) many themes in this story.
8. Some (believes, believe) that the book is better than the movie.
9. Some of Clarke's fans (thinks, think) that the movie is the best ever made.
10. Most of the fans also (enjoys, enjoy) other science-fiction movies, such as *Aliens* and *Star Wars*.
11. *Star Wars* (is, are) my all-time favorite science-fiction movie.
12. Following the first movie (was, were) several sequels.
13. NASA's team (is, are) planning a mission to Mars.
14. Many in the agency (hopes, hope) that NASA will send astronauts to Mars.
15. There (is, are) a model of Mars on the cabinet.

Exercise 8 Revising to Correct Errors in Agreement With Confusing Subjects

Revise these sentences where necessary to correct errors in agreement. If there are no errors in agreement, write *correct*.

1. Some in the scientific community believes that conditions on Mars could support life.
2. Do the presence of water in the form of ice indicate that life could have existed on Mars?
3. Everyone sees that the planet's polar icecaps grows and shrinks in a predictable way.
4. Higher than Earth's mountains are Mars' 17-mile-high Olympus Mons.
5. Where was the information about Mars and its moons?
6. About $265 million was the cost of the Mars *Pathfinder* mission.
7. Many in the government considers that cost to be low relative to the cost of other space missions.
8. A billion dollars have been spent on some missions!
9. Everyone were interested in what *Sojourner*, *Pathfinder's* roving component, would find.
10. A group of students plans to follow the flight of the *Mars Polar Lander*, launched in January 1999.

Subject and Verb Agreement • 593

Integrating Life Skills

Using amounts and measures correctly can be useful throughout life. Whether you're trying to explain or write a recipe for a friend, reporting the amount of money you earned, or simply relating the news in your life, numbers will often be involved and need to be communicated. Handled correctly, your "audience" will have a better chance of understanding.

Answer Key

Exercise 7

1. is	9. think
2. is	10. enjoy
3. was	11. is
4. Were	12. were
5. is	13. is
6. have	14. hope
7. There are	15. is
8. believe	

Exercise 8

1. believe
2. Does
3. grow; shrink
4. is
5. correct
6. correct
7. consider
8. has
9. was
10. correct (Could be *plan*, also, if the student believes that members of group were operating as individuals. Student should be able to explain his or her choice.)

✓ **ONGOING ASSESSMENT: Assess Mastery**

Use the following resources to assess mastery of subject and verb agreement.

In The Textbook	Technology
Chapter Review, Ex 39–41, p. 613	*On-Line Exercise Bank,* Section 23.1

Section Review

Each of these exercises correlates to the instruction on subject and verb agreement, pages 584–593. The exercises may be used for more practice, for reteaching, or for review of the key concepts presented.

Answer Key

Exercise 9

1. rotate
2. has
3. have
4. show
5. has
6. derives
7. appears
8. are
9. is
10. observe
11. lasts
12. is
13. agree
14. does
15. is

Exercise 10

1. have
2. provide
3. appears
4. orbit
5. promote
6. hopes
7. were
8. studies
9. is
10. enable

Exercise 11

1. Our nine planets and our sun rotate constantly.
2. Mercury and Venus are closest to the sun.
3. Neither Mercury nor Venus has moons.
4. Either Saturn or Uranus has the greatest number of moons.
5. Ganymede and Europa are two moons of Jupiter that may contain water.

⏰ TIME SAVERS!

📄 **Answers on Transparencies**
Use the *Grammar Exercises Answers on Transparencies* for Chapter 23 to facilitate correction by students.

💻 **On-Line Exercise Bank**
Have students complete the exercises on computer. The Auto Check feature will grade their work for you!

Section 23.1 Section Review

Grammar Exercises 9–17

Exercise 9 **Making Verbs Agree With Their Subjects** Choose the verb in parentheses that agrees with the subject of each sentence.

1. Nine known planets (rotates, rotate) around the sun.
2. Percival Lowell, along with many other scientists, (has, have) studied the skies.
3. Space probes that travel the solar system (has, have) taken photographs of the sun, moon, and planets.
4. Photographs from space probes (shows, show) a planet with many craters.
5. Every age (has, have) had scientists who studied planetary motion.
6. The word *planet*, which (derives, derive) from the Greek word for *wanderer*, describes the nine large bodies rotating around the sun.
7. A planet with worn-down craters (appears, appear) to be older than one with sharp craters.
8. The planets (is, are) named for mythical Roman and Greek gods.
9. Mercury (is, are) the planet closest to the sun.
10. We (observes, observe) Mercury through our telescope just before sunrise or just after sunset.
11. A year on Mercury (lasts, last) 88 Earth days.
12. Mercury, which is one of the hottest planets, (is, are) named for the Roman god of commerce and quick wit.
13. Scientists who study Mercury (agrees, agree) that the side of the planet facing the sun becomes extremely hot.
14. Mercury, because of its low gravitational forces, (does, do) not have an atmosphere.
15. One of the reasons that Mercury's atmosphere escapes (is, are) lack of gravity.

Exercise 10 **Making Verbs Agree With Compound Subjects** Choose the verb in parentheses that agrees with the subject of the sentence.

1. Carl Sagan and other scientists (has, have) studied these bodies.
2. Either the moons or the planets (provides, provide) fascinating topics of study for most scientists.
3. Either asteroids or a comet (appears, appear) in this photograph.
4. The comet Halley and the comet Hale-Bopp (orbits, orbit) the sun in regular and predictable cycles.
5. NASA and the United States government (promotes, promote) public support for the space program.
6. Every man and woman in the space program (hopes, hope) to become an astronaut.
7. Neil Armstrong and Buzz Aldrin (was, were) the first astronauts to walk on the moon.
8. Each astronaut and astronomer (studies, study) gravitational forces in space.
9. Bacon and eggs (is, are) a dish too high in cholesterol for astronauts to eat on a regular basis.
10. A camera and other instruments (enables, enable) further exploration of planets that future astronauts may visit.

Exercise 11 **Revising to Correct Errors in Agreement With Compound Subjects** Revise these sentences, correcting errors in agreement.

1. Our nine planets and our sun rotates constantly.
2. Mercury and Venus is closest to the sun.
3. Neither Mercury nor Venus have moons.

4. Either Saturn or Uranus have the greatest number of moons.
5. Ganymede and Europa is two moons of Jupiter that may contain water.

Exercise 12 · Making Verbs Agree With Confusing Subjects
Choose the verb in parentheses that agrees with the subject of the sentence

1. (There's, There are) only one moon orbiting the Earth.
2. One of NASA's plans to map the moon (includes, include) the *Lunar Prospector.*
3. Various investigations of the moon's gravity and composition (was, were) the mission of *Prospector.*
4. About $70 million (has, have) been spent on the *Lunar Prospector.*
5. Everyone of those involved in the program (believes, believe) that the money was well spent.
6. Some of the scientists (has, have) the idea that the *Prospector* could determine if water exists on the moon.
7. The committee of scientists (agrees, agree) on how to use *Prospector* to such an end.
8. (There's, There are) plans to crash-land the *Prospector* on the moon.
9. Many of the observers (looks, look) forward to studying the dust cloud that will result from the crash landing.
10. Our science class (has, have) been unable to decide which moon to study.

Exercise 13 · Supplying Verbs That Agree With Confusing Subjects
Copy each sentence onto a separate sheet of paper. Then, write *is* or *are* in the blank to complete each sentence

1. There __?__ many reasons to send spacecraft into orbit.
2. Here __?__ one rationale for spending money on the space program.
3. Now __?__ the time to find out whether life exists on other planets.

4. Why __?__ these questions hard to answer?
5. Beyond our galaxy __?__ mysteries that may astound us.

Exercise 14 · Revising for Subject-Verb Agreement
On a separate sheet of paper, revise the following paragraph. Be sure to correct all errors in subject and verb agreement.

(1) Many of today's scientists believes that some moons in our solar system contains water. (2) Does any of these moons hold the answers to a researcher's perplexing questions? (3) There's several questions researchers might ask. (4) Could moons that have water give scientists hints about Earth's resources? (5) Perhaps, the answers to these questions lies in the near future.

Exercise 15 · Find It in Your Reading
Identify two subjects and verbs in the excerpt from "To His Excellency, General Washington" on page 585. Tell whether each verb is singular or plural.

Exercise 16 · Find It in Your Writing
Choose a paragraph from a recent piece of writing. Underline each subject once and each verb twice. Check to make sure that each subject and verb agree.

Exercise 17 · Writing Application
Write a brief factual account of one of the nine planets or a moon in our solar system. After you have completed the paragraph, draw a single line under the subject of each sentence. Draw a double line under each verb. Then, tell whether each verb is singular or plural.

Pronoun and Antecedent Agreement

Have students write a few sentences about two friends sharing a conversation or activity. Tell students that they must write *without using pronouns*. Then, ask them to edit their passages, replacing nouns with appropriate pronouns. Have volunteers read their before and after sentences aloud. Point out the connections between pronouns and their antecedents, and explain that using the wrong pronoun can cause confusion.

Activate Prior Knowledge

Explain to students that they already make pronouns and antecedents agree most of the time. Have students identify the antecedents for each pronoun in the sentences they just wrote. Ask the class if it is clear which nouns are being replaced and how they can tell. (Sometimes it will be proximity; often it will be agreement.)

TEACH

Step-by-Step Teaching Guide

Agreement Between Personal Pronouns and Antecedents

1. Review the importance of making certain that a pronoun-antecedent relationship is obvious. Explain that two ways of doing this are having the pronoun close to the noun it replaces and making certain that no other nouns between the antecedent and the pronoun might confuse the reader.

2. Point out that, in addition to position, agreement is another aid in making certain the reader can recognize the antecedent of the pronoun. Pronouns must agree with antecedents in number, person, and gender.

3. Have volunteers give examples of "person"—first, second, third—to make certain the concept is clear for students.

Critical Viewing

Connect Sample answer: *She* is playing *her* flute.

Antecedents are the nouns (or the words that take the place of nouns) for which pronouns stand. This section will show that just as a subject and verb must agree, so must a pronoun and its antecedent agree.

Agreement Between Personal Pronouns and Antecedents

One rule of pronoun and antecedent agreement governs almost all of the other rules:

▶ **KEY CONCEPT** A personal pronoun must agree with its antecedent in number, person, and gender. ■

You have already learned that the *number* of a pronoun indicates whether it is singular or plural. *Person* indicates whether the pronoun is first person, second person, or third person—that is, if the pronoun refers to the one speaking, the one spoken to, or the one spoken about.

Some nouns and pronouns can also indicate one of three *genders*: *masculine*, for words referring to males; *feminine*, for words referring to females; and *neuter*, for words referring to neither males nor females.

The only pronouns that indicate gender are third-person singular personal pronouns.

GENDER OF THIRD-PERSON SINGULAR PRONOUNS		
Masculine	**Feminine**	**Neuter**
he, him, his	she, her, hers	it, its

In the following example, the pronoun *her* agrees with its antecedent, *Claire*, in number (both are singular), in person (both are third person), and in gender (both are feminine):

EXAMPLE: *Claire* expressed *her* doubts about joining the band.

Theme: Music

In this section, you will learn how to make pronouns agree with their antecedents. The examples are about music.

Cross-Curricular Connection: Music

▲ **Critical Viewing** Using two feminine pronouns, describe what this musician is doing. **[Connect]**

⏱ TIME AND RESOURCE MANAGER

Resources
Print: *Grammar Exercise Workbook*, pp. 117–120; *Grammar Exercises Answers on Transparencies*, Ch. 23
Technology: *Language Lab* CD-ROM, Nouns and Pronouns; *On-Line Exercise Bank*, Section 23.2

In-Depth Coverage	Accelerated Pace
• Work through all key concepts, pp. 596–602. • Assign and review Exercises 18–24. • Read and discuss *Grammar in Literature*, p. 597.	• Assign pp. 596–602 for independent student review. • Assign Section Review Exercises 25–27.

GRAMMAR IN LITERATURE

from **I Hear America Singing**
Walt Whitman

Notice that the pronouns his *and* he *agree with the antecedents* carpenter *and* mason *in number, person, and gender in the following lines:*

The carpenter singing his as he measures his plank or beam.
The mason singing his as he makes ready for work, or leaves off work,

Agreement in Number

Pronoun-antecedent agreement is sometimes a problem when the antecedent is a compound.

> **KEY CONCEPT** Use a singular personal pronoun with two or more singular antecedents joined by *or* or *nor.* ■

EXAMPLE: Neither *Tom* nor *Ken* brought *his* equipment.

> **KEY CONCEPT** Use a plural personal pronoun with two or more antecedents joined by *and.* ■

EXAMPLE: *Sue* and *Stan* have chosen *their* instruments.

An exception to these two rules occurs when it is necessary to distinguish between individual and joint ownership. In the examples below, changing from a singular pronoun to a plural pronoun changes the ownership from individual to joint.

SINGULAR: Neither *Linda* nor *Maria* let me play *her* guitar. (Linda and Maria each own a guitar.)

PLURAL: Neither *Linda* nor *Maria* let me play *their* guitar. (Linda and Maria own the guitar together.)

SINGULAR: My *mother* and *father* discovered that *his* old violin is a valuable antique. (Father owns the violin.)

PLURAL: My *mother* and *father* discovered that *their* old violin is a valuable antique. (Both parents own the violin.)

Step-by-Step Teaching Guide

Grammar in Literature

1. Have students read the excerpt from the poem, and then ask if they can figure out, from the title, what the *his* refers to in each line (song, tune). Read the first line of the poem: "I hear America singing, the varied carols I hear." *Carols* confirms the guess of *song* or *tune.*

2. Ask students what pronouns Whitman would use if he were describing a woman singing (*her, hers, she*) or a group (*their, theirs, they*).

More About the Writer

Before Walt Whitman died, the insight and sensitivity of his poetry was recognized, but when he first published his poems, some critics considered them crude and formless. His first collection of poems, *Leaves of Grass,* printed at Whitman's own expense, appeared in 1855.

Step-by-Step Teaching Guide

Agreement in Number

1. Explain that pronoun number for compound antecedents is governed by three relatively simple rules.

2. Have students read the first two rules, in the key concepts on this page, and then ask them to explain how these first two rules compare with the rules they learned for subject-verb agreement. (They are basically the same: *and* creates a plural, *or* creates a singular.)

3. Point out that the third rule, presented at the top of page 598, differs from the rule for subject-verb agreement. Explain that a pronoun must be plural when *any* part of a compound antecedent is plural, even though a singular verb may be required for subject-verb agreement.

Agreement in Person and Gender

1. Point out that, while the shifts in the examples still seem fairly understandable, these examples are unrelated sentences. Within a paragraph or whole story, these shifts can be very confusing, especially if there are other nouns that might be antecedents.

2. Explain to students that they will likely see boats or ships in literature (or among boating enthusiasts) referred to as *she*. If this common convention were used, the second pronoun in the second example would be *her*, not *its*. The key is consistency within the adopted convention.

3. Note that it is acceptable to use *his or her* when referring to a singular antecedent whose gender is unknown.

Language Highlight

Gender-Neutral Pronouns
Increasingly, writers use *they* as a non-gender-specific, singular pronoun to avoid the use of either a masculine pronoun or the combination of *he or she* whenever gender is not specified. Some who argue in favor of *they* in these cases point out that, in longer passages, having to repeat *he or she* several times is awkward, and *s/he* (another option suggested) is unpronounceable. While this usage is becoming more common, it is still considered substandard, and a careful writer is better off avoiding its use.

Customize for
ESL Students

Remind students that gender refers only to the gender of the antecedent. If we speak of Sally's uncle, it is *her* uncle, with the pronoun agreeing with Sally, not with uncle. Also, in English, gender exists in only third-person singular, not in third-person plural.

Critical Viewing

Relate, Distinguish Sample answer: The band members are wearing their finest uniforms. (*their, band members*)

23.2

▶ **KEY CONCEPT** Use a plural personal pronoun if any part of a compound antecedent joined by *or* or *nor* is plural. ■

EXAMPLE: If my *sisters* or *Carol* arrives, ask *them* to wait.

Agreement in Person and Gender Other errors in agreement with personal pronouns occur when there is an unnecessary shift in person or gender.

▶ **KEY CONCEPT** When dealing with pronoun-antecedent agreement, take care not to shift either person or gender. ■

SHIFT IN PERSON:	*Kris* is going to New York City, where *you* can attend a fine music school.
CORRECT:	*Kris* is going to New York City, where *he* can attend a fine music school.
SHIFT IN GENDER:	The *ship* came loose from *her* moorings, and *it* gently drifted out to sea.
CORRECT:	The *ship* came loose from *its* moorings, and *it* gently drifted out to sea.

Traditionally, a masculine pronoun has been used in reference to a singular antecedent whose gender is unknown. Such use of the masculine pronoun is said to be *generic*, meaning it covers both masculine and feminine genders. Although use of the generic pronoun is still accepted, it is preferable to use *his* or *her* or to rewrite the sentence.

▶ **KEY CONCEPT** When gender is not specified, use *his or her* or rewrite the sentence. ■

EXAMPLES:	Each *member* of the band must practice *his or her* music daily.
	Each *member* of the band must practice daily.
	All *members* of the band must practice *their* music daily.

▼ **Critical Viewing**
Write a sentence about these band members containing at least one pronoun and its antecedent. Identify the pronouns and antecedents you have used. [Relate, Distinguish]

Exercise 18 Avoiding Shifts in Person and Gender

Choose the correct pronoun in parentheses to complete each sentence.

1. Many people are discovering that (you, they) can enjoy different forms of music, such as the blues.
2. New York City attracts many blues musicians because of its large number of nightclubs and (her, its) concert halls.
3. Men and women who have worked hard all day are finding that (you, they) can unwind by listening to Bessie Smith sing the blues.
4. Sue likes to listen to Bessie Smith because (you, she) can relate to the feelings expressed.
5. This club has become very popular since it introduced the blues to (her, its) customers.

Exercise 19 Making Personal Pronouns Agree With Their Antecedents

Choose an appropriate personal pronoun to complete each sentence.

1. Neither my sisters nor Sue bought ___?___ tickets.
2. My aunt and uncle expressed ___?___ gratitude for the concert tickets.
3. Zubin Mehta and ___?___ orchestra gave an outstanding performance.
4. Every orchestra has ___?___ own unique sound.
5. If Luciano Pavarotti or Placido Domingo decides to give concerts this year, tickets for ___?___ shows will sell out.
6. We purchased the piano even though ___?___ keys were stained.
7. Piano students should take ___?___ lessons seriously.
8. Laura and Alyssa are working hard to prepare for ___?___ recital.
9. David and ___?___ brothers are thinking of starting a band.
10. Did the girls or their brother practice before ___?___ performed?

Exercise 20 Revising to Eliminate Shifts in Person and Gender

Revise these sentences where necessary to correct errors in pronoun-antecedent agreement.

1. Many blues fans are finding that you enjoy the music of Ethel Waters.
2. We know that we will need to arrive early to get a good seat at the concert.
3. Henry wants to study music because it will broaden your background.
4. Typical of my friends and me is their interest in music.
5. After jazz musicians have performed in a concert, you need to rest.

More Practice

Language Lab CD-ROM
- Pronouns and Antecedents lesson

On-line Exercise Bank
- Section 23.2

Grammar Exercise Workbook
- pp. 117–118

Pronoun and Antecedent Agreement • 599

Answer Key

▶ **Exercise 18**
1. they
2. its
3. they
4. she
5. its

▶ **Exercise 19**
1. their
2. their
3. his
4. its
5. his
6. its
7. their
8. their
9. his
10. they

▶ **Exercise 20**
1. they
2. correct
3. his
4. our
5. they

☑ **ONGOING ASSESSMENT: Monitor and Reinforce**

If students have trouble with Exercise 18, 19, or 20, refer them to the following for additional practice.

In the Textbook	Print Resources	Technology
Section Review, Ex. 25, p. 603	Grammar Exercise Workbook, pp. 117–118	Language Lab CD-ROM, Nouns and Pronouns On-Line Exercise Bank, Section 23.2

⏱ **TIME SAVERS!**

Answers on Transparencies
Use the Grammar Exercises Answers on Transparencies for Chapter 23 to facilitate correction by students.

On-Line Exercise Bank
Have students complete the exercises on computer. The Auto Check feature will grade their work for you!

Agreement With Indefinite Pronouns

1. Ask students to compare the rules on this page with the rules for subject-verb agreement found on page 584. (Basically the same considerations determine whether the pronoun is singular or plural.)

2. Point out to students that this parallel in rules can make choosing the correct pronouns easier. For example, if the verb is plural, students are safe in using a plural pronoun.

3. Note that, as with compounds, there is one exception to the subject-verb agreement rule, though ocurrences of it will probably be rare. Remind students that they have two options when a sentence sounds as odd as the final example. Go with the logical agreement or rewrite the sentence. (*All* the phones rang at once . . .)

Real-World Connection

Any job that requires written communication—from a police officer filing a report to a businessperson writing a memo to a novelist creating an epic story—requires clarity. If a writer is not careful with pronoun-antecedent agreement, the work he or she produces can be annoying and even misleading. If a police officer, for example, writes, "Three men broke into the store and he pulled a gun," does the officer mean that one man of the three pulled a gun or that all three pulled guns and the writer just failed to make the pronoun agree—or was someone else pulling a gun, such as the shop owner?

23.2

Agreement With Indefinite Pronouns

When an indefinite pronoun (such as *each*, *all*, or *most*) is used with a personal pronoun, both pronouns must agree. Usage problems are rare when both pronouns are plural.

▶ **KEY CONCEPT** Use a plural personal pronoun when the antecedent is a plural indefinite pronoun. ■

EXAMPLE: *Many* of the children were excited about *their* music lessons.

When both pronouns are singular, a similar rule applies:

▶ **KEY CONCEPT** Use a singular personal pronoun when the antecedent is a singular indefinite pronoun. ■

In the following example, the personal pronoun *his* agrees in number with the singular indefinite pronoun *one*. The gender (masculine) is determined by the word *boys*.

EXAMPLE: Only *one* of the boys practiced *his* trumpet.

If other words in the sentence do not indicate a gender, you may use *him or her*, *he or she*, *his or hers*, or rephrase the sentence.

EXAMPLES: *Each* of the musicians wore *his or her* uniform.

The musicians wore *their* uniforms.

For indefinite pronouns that can be either singular or plural (*all*, *any*, *more*, *most*, *none*, and *some*), agreement depends on the antecedent of the indefinite pronoun. In the first example below, *its* is used because the antecedent of *most* is the singular noun *music*. In the second example, *their* is used because the antecedent of *most* is the plural noun *listeners*.

EXAMPLES: *Most* of the music had lost *its* appeal.

Most of the listeners wanted *their* money back.

In some situations, strict grammatical agreement may be illogical. In these situations, you should let the meaning of the sentence determine the number of the personal pronoun.

ILLOGICAL: When *each* of the telephones rang simultaneously, I answered *it* as quickly as possible.

CORRECT: When *each* of the telephones rang simultaneously, I answered *them* as quickly as possible.

Answer Key

Exercise 21 Making Personal Pronouns Agree With
Indefinite Pronouns Choose the correct pronoun to complete each sentence.

1. Most of my friends rent (his, their) instruments for music lessons.
2. Each of us band members has (his or her, our) own favorite kind of music.
3. Not all see (his or her, their) future in music.
4. However, each enjoys (his or her, their) time in the band.
5. One of my friends has in (her, their) collection a book about musical careers.

Exercise 22 Revising to Correct Agreement Errors
Revise these sentences where necessary to correct errrors in pronoun-antecedent agreement. If there are no errors in agreement, write *correct*.

1. Most of the careers have special training associated with it.
2. None guarantees that a person will be successful in them.
3. Some are interesting; I will investigate them further.
4. Each of the band members has their favorite musical group.
5. When anyone in my band goes to a concert, they shares stories with the rest of us.

More Practice

Language Lab CD-ROM
• Pronouns and Antecedents lesson

On-line Exercise Bank
• Section 23.2

Grammar Exercise Workbook
• pp. 119–120

▼ **Critical Viewing**
What indefinite pronouns and personal pronouns could you use in a sentence describing this rock band? **[Analyze, Identify]**

Answer Key

▶ **Exercise 21**
1. their
2. his or her
3. their
4. his or her
5. her

▶ **Exercise 22**
1. them
2. it
3. correct
4. his or her
5. he or she

Critical Viewing

Analyze, Identify Sample answer: Each member of the band seems to take his music very seriously. (indefinite pronoun: *each;* personal pronoun: *his*)

Pronoun and Antecedent Agreement • **601**

✓ ONGOING ASSESSMENT: Monitor and Reinforce

If students miss more than one item in Exercise 21 or 22, refer them to the following for additional practice.

In the Textbook	Print Resources	Technology
Section Review, Ex. 26, p. 603	*Grammar Exercise Workbook,* pp. 119–120	*Language Lab* CD-ROM, Nouns and Pronouns *On-Line Exercise Bank,* Section 23.2

⏱ TIME SAVERS!

Answers on Transparencies
Use the *Grammar Exercises Answers on Transparencies* for Chapter 23 to facilitate correction by students.

On-Line Exercise Bank
Have students complete the exercises on computer. The Auto Check feature will grade their work for you!

Agreement With Reflexive Pronouns

1. Emphasize that reflexive pronouns must refer to another word in the same sentence. They add information about that word, and removing them would change the meaning of the sentence. For example, *The children are now old enough to feed themselves.*

2. Ask students if they remember the other types of pronouns that end in self/selves *(intensive)*. Point out that intensive pronouns also require that the word to which they refer be in the same sentence, but they can be removed without changing the meaning of the sentence. For example, *I wanted to do it myself* is not really different from *I wanted to do it*—the subject is simply intensified.

3. Have the students suggest one or two examples of reflexive pronouns used correctly; then point out how the sentences differ from the incorrect example on the page.

Answer Key

▶ **Exercise 23**

1. I
2. us
3. you
4. me
5. him
6. us
7. them
8. us
9. I
10. us

▶ **Exercise 24**

1. I
2. us
3. me
4. ourselves
5. yourself

Agreement With Reflexive Pronouns

Reflexive pronouns end in *-self* or *-selves* and are used correctly only when they refer to a word earlier in the same sentence, as in "*Frank* made dinner for *himself.*"

▶ **KEY CONCEPT** A reflexive pronoun must agree with an antecedent that is clearly stated. ■

INCORRECT: Our parents listen to my sister and *myself.*
CORRECT: Our parents listen to my sister and *me.*

▶ **Exercise 23** **Using Reflexive Pronouns Correctly** Rewrite each sentence, correcting the misused reflexive pronoun.
1. Rachel and <u>myself</u> enjoy listening to country music.
2. All of the country music CDs in our collection were paid for by <u>ourselves</u>.
3. I said to my mother, "Who but <u>yourself</u> would have bought us tickets to a Garth Brooks concert?"
4. My father said that he will drive <u>myself</u> to the concert.
5. When you pick up the tickets for the concert, ask for Rachel or <u>himself</u>.
6. You'll find the tickets for yourself and <u>ourselves</u> in the envelope.
7. They said that country music did not interest <u>themselves</u>.
8. Who besides <u>ourselves</u> enjoys listening to the music of Loretta Lynn and Tammy Wynette?
9. On television last night, my brother and <u>myself</u> watched the country music special.
10. All of our favorite performers entertained <u>ourselves</u>.

▶ **Exercise 24** **Supplying Correct Pronouns** On your paper, write the reflexive or personal pronoun that correctly completes each sentence.
1. Even on short drives, my friend and ___?___ like listening to the car radio.
2. However, there's occasionally an argument between ___?___ concerning which station to tune in.
3. She prefers country music, but as for ___?___, I like the latest popular music.
4. Often, both of us enjoy ___?___ singing along to oldies from the sixties and seventies.
5. Did you say that you sing along with the radio to keep ___?___ from getting bored on long car trips?

▶ **More Practice**

Language Lab CD-ROM
• Pronouns and Antecedents lesson

On-line Exercise Bank
• Section 23.2

Grammar Exercise Workbook
• pp. 119–120

☑ **ONGOING ASSESSMENT: Monitor and Reinforce**

If students have trouble with Exercise 23 or 24, refer them to the following for additional practice.

In the Textbook	Print Resources	Technology
Section Review, Ex. 27, p. 603	*Grammar Exercise Workbook*, pp. 119–120	*Language Lab* CD-ROM, Nouns and Pronouns *On-Line Exercise Bank*, Section 23.2

Section 23.2 Section Review

GRAMMAR EXERCISES 25–30

Exercise 25 **Making Personal Pronouns Agree With Their Antecedents**
Write an appropriate personal pronoun to complete each sentence.

1. Latin music has ___?___ roots in African, Spanish, and Latin American music.
2. Celia Cruz is a compelling performer. ___?___ is also known by ___?___ title the "Queen of Salsa."
3. Cruz's fans enjoy seeing ___?___ favorite performer put on a show.
4. Carlos Santana and ___?___ band pioneered "Latin rock" when ___?___ added a Caribbean beat to rock-and-roll music.
5. Neither Santana nor ___?___ band could have imagined the fame that would come to ___?___ .

Exercise 26 **Choosing Correct Personal Pronouns** Write the correct pronoun to complete each sentence.

1. My brother and two other students are studying music because of (his, their) vocal talent.
2. Rikki believes that it is important to study Italian to improve (your, her) chances of becoming an opera singer.
3. Many female opera singers are finding out that (they, you) can compete in salary with male singers.
4. After a person has been to the opera, (he or she, they) may feel inspired.
5. *The Magic Flute* is a masterpiece because of (its, their) brilliant score.
6. Both of my teachers brought (his, their) classical music CDs to class.
7. Each of the students reacted to the music in (his or her, their) own way.
8. Some of the music we heard gained (its, their) popularity in the 1800's.

9. Neither of the classical pieces he wrote has (its, their) melody completed.
10. Both of these other pieces have (its, their) merits.

Exercise 27 **Revising to Correct Errors in Reflexive Pronouns** Revise the sentences below to correct any misuse of reflexive pronouns. If the reflexive pronoun is used correctly, write *correct*.

1. My brother bought himself a guitar.
2. My mother and myself encouraged him to practice.
3. Who but himself could make such a racket?
4. Our mother told me to keep my opinions to myself.
5. Still, Mom bought earplugs for myself.

Exercise 28 **Find It in Your Reading** Identify the indefinite and personal pronouns in this line from Walt Whitman's "I Hear America Singing," and tell why they agree.

"Each singing what belongs to him or her
        and to none else, . . ."

Exercise 29 **Find It in Your Writing** Go through your portfolio to find examples of pronouns, especially indefinite pronouns. Make sure that you have used the correct personal pronoun to agree with each indefinite pronoun.

Exercise 30 **Writing Application** Write a paragraph about your favorite musical group. Use at least four personal pronouns and two indefinite pronouns. Check your pronoun agreement.

Section Review • 603

ASSESS

Section Review

Each of these exercises correlates to the instruction on pronoun and antecedent agreement, pages 596–602. The exercises may be used for more practice, for reteaching, or for review of the key concepts presented. Answers for all chapter exercises are available in *Grammar Exercises Answers on Transparencies* in your Teaching Resources.

Answer Key

Exercise 25
1. its
2. She, her
3. their
4. his, they
5. his, them

Exercise 26

1. their	6. their
2. her	7. his or her
3. they	8. its
4. he or she	9. its
5. its	10. their

Exercise 27
1. correct
2. My mother and **I** . . .
3. Who but **he** . . .
4. correct
5. Still, Mom bought earplugs for **me.**

Exercise 28

Find It in Your Reading
Indefinite: Each, none; personal: him or her—*him or her* agree with *Each* because they are singular.

Exercise 29

Find It in Your Writing
Ask students which indefinite pronouns they find most often in their writing. Ask in what situations they find indefinite pronouns to be most useful. (when information is inexact or missing)

Exercise 30

Writing Application
Have students trade paragraphs with a partner. Ask the partner to check the paragraph for pronoun agreement. If agreement is not found, have partners discuss needed changes.

☑ **ONGOING ASSESSMENT: Assess Mastery**

Use the following resources to assess student mastery of pronoun and antecedent agreement.

In the Textbook	Technology
Chapter Review, Ex. 42–43, p. 614	*Language Lab* CD-ROM, Nouns and Pronouns; *On-Line Exercise Bank,* Section 23.2

PREPARE and ENGAGE

Interest GRABBER Write the following sentences on the board:

The seals performed with balls and hoops. They charmed the audience with their antics. They train them to do so many tricks. This is why I love to go to the zoo.

Ask students if they can detect two problems in this passage. (*They* in the third sentence has no antecedent; *This* in the fourth sentence has no clear antecedent, but probably refers to the performance.) Have students suggest replacements for the vague pronouns. (Possible answers: replace *They* with *The trainers* and *This* with *The seals' performance.*)

Activate Prior Knowledge

Ask students to relate times when vague information has created confusion for them or for someone they know. Examples could include vague assembly or operating instructions, vague rumors or announcements, or anything else that gave them less information than they needed. After several examples are shared, point out that precision is important in using pronouns, since vague usage is a common cause of confusion.

Critical Viewing

Compare and Contrast Possible answers: The man is gesturing toward the whale with his arm. It is much bigger than he is. (Or students may simply suggest *he* for the man, *it* for the whale, and *they* for the man and the whale.)

TEACH

Step-by-Step Teaching Guide

Vague Pronoun References

1. Tell students that *vague* means "hazy, lacking precision or clarity, indefinite." Applied to writing, these terms are not flattering. Communication does not occur when words are vague.

continued

Section 23.3

Special Problems With Pronoun Agreement

Once you are familiar with the basic rules of pronoun and antecedent agreement, you can refine your skills in this area. This section will show you how to avoid some common errors that can obscure the meaning of your sentences.

Theme: Marine Life

In this section, you will learn about special problems with pronoun and antecedent agreement. The examples and exercises are about marine life.

Cross-Curricular Connection: Science

◄ **Critical Viewing** What pronoun would you use to refer to the man? What pronoun would you use to refer to the man and the whale? **[Compare and Contrast]**

Vague Pronoun References

One basic rule governs the other, more specific rules of clear pronoun reference:

▶ **KEY CONCEPT** A pronoun requires an antecedent that is either stated or clearly understood to avoid confusion. ■

The pronouns *which, this, that,* and *these* should not be used to refer to a vague or overly general idea.

In the following example, it is impossible to determine exactly what the pronoun *these* stands for because it refers to three different groups of words.

| VAGUE REFERENCE: | Jay was carsick, the dog was restless, and the air conditioner was broken. *These* made our trip to the aquarium unpleasant. |

⏱ TIME AND RESOURCE MANAGER

Resources
Print: *Grammar Exercise Workbook,* pp. 121–124
Technology: *Language Lab* CD-ROM, Nouns and Pronouns; *On-Line Exercise Bank,* Section 23.3

In-Depth Coverage	Accelerated Pace
• Work through all key concepts, pp. 604–609. • Assign and review Exercises 31–33. • Read and discuss Grammar in Literature, p. 609, and Hands-on Grammar activity, p. 611.	• Assign pp. 604–609 for independent student review. • Assign Review Exercises 34–35.

The vague reference can be corrected in two ways. One way is to change the pronoun to an adjective that modifies a specific noun. The second way is to revise the sentence so that the pronoun *these* is eliminated.

CORRECT: Jay was carsick, the dog was restless, and the air conditioner was broken. *These misfortunes* made our trip to the aquarium unpleasant.

                Jay's carsickness, the dog's restlessness, and the air conditioner's breakdown made our trip to the aquarium unpleasant.

▶**KEY CONCEPT**   The personal pronouns *it*, *they*, and *you* should always have a clear antecedent. ■

In the next example, the pronoun *it* has no clearly stated antecedent.

VAGUE   Marge is studying marine mammals next
REFERENCE: year. *It* should be very educational.

Again, there are two methods of correction. The first method is to replace the personal pronoun with a specific noun. The second method is to revise the sentence entirely in order to make the whole idea clear.

CORRECT: Marge is studying marine mammals next year. *The experience* should be very educational.

                Marge's study of marine mammals next year should be very educational.

In the next example, the pronoun *they* is used without an accurate antecedent.

VAGUE   I enjoyed reading *Moby-Dick,* but
REFERENCE: *they* never explained what the whale symbolized.

CORRECT: I enjoyed reading *Moby-Dick,* but *the author* never explained what the whale symbolized.

                I enjoyed reading *Moby-Dick* by Melville, but *he* never explained what the whale symbolized.

VAGUE   When we arrived at the aquarium, they told
REFERENCE: us that the whale show was about to start.

CORRECT: When we arrived at the aquarium, the ticket-taker told us that the whale show was about to start.

                When we arrived at the aquarium, we were told that the whale show was about to start.

2. Point out that these problems are very common, because writers tend to forget that readers don't know what the writer knows. Suggest that students stop whenever they see the potentially vague pronouns and ask "What is this pronoun replacing?" and "Is the reader given enough information to know what this pronoun refers to?"

3. Explain that there are two ways in which pronoun references can be vague: They can refer to vague ideas and generalities or replace vague antecedents.

4. Point out that often a replacement for a vague reference is not a single word. Sometimes a phrase or clause is needed. Suggest this solution:

    What she learns should be very educational.

Point out that this solution utilizes a noun clause in place of *it.*

Integrating Workplace Skills

Have students imagine that they are teachers. Ask them how they would explain the topic of vague pronouns to students who had never considered the topic. Have them write at least one example each of vague and correct usage. Ask volunteers to share their examples.

▶ **Exercise 31**

Answers will vary; below are sample answers.

1. Not everyone knows that whales are warmblooded mammals that breathe with lungs.
2. Our teacher explained that there are two kinds of whales, toothed whales and baleen whales.
3. I learned in science class that baleen whales eat krill.
4. Learning about the eating habits of whales was very interesting.
5. I wasn't surprised to learn that giant baleen whales need many pounds of food to fill their bellies.
6. Baleen whales have baleen plates that hang down from their upper jaw. From the outside, these plates look like half-closed vertical blinds.
7. Baleen plates, which help the whale filter water out and keep food in, look from the inside like thick, white hair.
8. The fact that the bottlenose has teeth means that it has a different diet.
9. Because they hunt with each other, orcas are communal animals.
10. A television documentary showed that the orca's diet consists of sea birds, fish, turtles, and seals.

23.3

▶ **KEY CONCEPT** Use *you* only when the reference is truly to the reader or listener. ■

VAGUE REFERENCE:	*You* couldn't understand a word Jim said.
CORRECT:	*We* couldn't understand a word Jim said.
VAGUE REFERENCE:	In the school my great-aunt attended, *you* were expected to stand up when addressed.
CORRECT:	In the school my great-aunt attended, *students* were expected to stand up when addressed.

Note About *It*: In many idiomatic expressions, the personal pronoun *it* has no specific antecedent. In statements such as "It is late," "It is raining," and "It is true," the idiomatic use of *it* is accepted as standard English.

▶ **Exercise 31** Revising to Correct Vague Pronoun References Rewrite the sentences below, correcting the vague pronouns.

| EXAMPLE: | The whale is a fascinating mammal living in the sea, which has long interested people. |
| CORRECT: | The whale, a fascinating mammal that lives in the sea, has long interested people. |

1. Whales are warmblooded mammals that breathe with lungs, which not everyone knows.
2. There are two kinds of whales—toothed whales and baleen whales. This was explained by our teacher.
3. Baleen whales eat krill, which I learned in science class.
4. We learned about the eating habits of whales. It was very interesting.
5. Giant baleen whales need many pounds of food to fill their bellies, which didn't surprise me.
6. Baleen whales have baleen plates that hang down from their upper jaw. From the outside, these look like half-closed vertical blinds.
7. From the inside, baleen plates look like thick, white hair. This helps the whale filter water out and keep food in.
8. The bottlenose whale has teeth, which means it has a different diet.
9. Orcas hunt with each other. This makes them communal animals.
10. The orca's diet consists of sea birds, fish, turtles, and seals. They showed them in a television documentary.

▶ **More Practice**

Language Lab CD-ROM
• Pronouns and Antecedents lesson
On-line Exercise Bank
• Section 23.3
Grammar Exercise Workbook
• pp. 121–122

606 • Agreement

Ambiguous Pronoun References

A pronoun is *ambiguous* if it can refer to more than one antecedent. When a pronoun has more than one possible antecedent, the sentence is unclear and difficult to understand.

KEY CONCEPTS A pronoun should never refer to more than one antecedent. ■

A personal pronoun should always be tied to a single, obvious antecedent. ■

In the following sentence, *he* is confusing because it can refer to either *Joe* or *Walt*. Revise such a sentence by changing the pronoun to a noun or revising the sentence entirely.

AMBIGUOUS REFERENCE:	Joe told Walt about the whales *he* wanted to observe.
CORRECT:	Joe told Walt about the whales *Walt* wanted to observe.

KEY CONCEPT Do not repeat a personal pronoun in a sentence if it can refer to a different antecedent each time. ■

AMBIGUOUS REPETITION:	When Jon asked his father if *he* could borrow the car, *he* said *he* needed it to go to work.
CLEAR:	Jon asked his father if *he* could borrow the car, because *he* needed it to go to work.
	When Jon asked his father if *he* could borrow the car, his *father* said *he* needed it himself to go to work.

In the example, the second and third uses of *he* are unclear. To eliminate the confusion, one of the repeated pronouns was replaced. Notice in the second correction that the pronoun *himself* helps to clarify the meaning.

▲ Critical Viewing
In what way is this photograph of a whale like a sentence containing an ambiguous pronoun reference?
[Compare]

Special Problems With Pronoun Agreement • 607

Ambiguous Pronoun References

1. Write the following on the board:

   As Luis and Tony watched, the dolphin jumped through the hoop. He said that he had never seen anything like it.

2. Ask students which two pronouns are vague (*He* and *it*).

3. Have students fix the vague sentence so that it reads more clearly. (Possible response: *Tony said that he had never seen a dolphin do that before*).

4. Tell students that common ways for writers to fix their writing are asking questions about each pronoun, putting the work aside for a day and seeing if it still makes sense when they see it with "fresh eyes," and asking someone else to review it for them to make suggestions.

Critical Viewing

Compare Possible answer: Identifying the whale in the photograph is difficult.

Customize for
Less Advanced Students

Work through these examples, showing students how asking questions about a pronoun can help them make certain that all needed information is included.

1. *I was planning to go to the movies, but they say the movie is terrible. (Who is they?)*

2. *Maria and her mother are going to visit her aunt in Boston. (Whose aunt—Maria's or her mother's?)*

3. *We visited Washington, D.C., in the spring and saw the cherry blossoms and the White House. It was really beautiful. (What was beautiful?)*

4. *Mr. O'Neill and his wife are planning to visit his grandparents and their oldest daughter. They are teachers who live in England. (Whose daughter? Who lives in England?)*

✎ STANDARDIZED TEST PREPARATION WORKSHOP

Grammar and Usage Many standardized tests require students to recognize correct usage within the context of a passage. Use the following example to demonstrate.

The passenger peered down from the cargo plane's only window as the pilot eased the engines. Dots of light circled a small lake, and a radio tower rose from the hill behind it. Suddenly, it dove sharply, and he gasped.

How should the underlined sentence be written correctly?

A as is
B Suddenly, the plane dove sharply, and he gasped.
C It dove suddenly, making the passenger gasp.
D Suddenly, the plane dove sharply, and the passenger gasped.

The correct answer is **D**. The passage contains two ambiguous pronoun references (*it* and *he*). The words *the plane* clarify what it was that dove; *the passenger* replaces *he* to avoid confusion with *the pilot*.

Answer Key

23.3

▶ **Exercise 32** **Revising to Correct Ambiguous Pronoun References** Rewrite the following sentences, correcting the ambiguous pronoun references.

1. Marine biologists study undersea animals and plants. They are my favorite topic.
2. Steven hopes to be a marine biologist like his father. He studies the behavior of dolphins.
3. When Steven told his brother Mark about his plans, he said that he would have to go to a school near the ocean to study marine biology.
4. There was an article about dolphins in a magazine, but I couldn't find it.
5. The trainer of a dolphin named Brenda reported that she had invented a new game.
6. Dolphins have been known to befriend humans because they are so playful.
7. Donald, a dolphin who lived off the coast of England, would interact with a local diver. Sometimes, his antics were annoying.
8. Several times, Donald tried to carry off a diver. He was just trying to be friendly, but the experience was frightening.
9. Scientists want to conduct research on the sounds dolphins make. The question is, how do they do it?
10. Because dolphins lack vocal cords, they are not sure how they emit sounds.

▶ **More Practice**

Language Lab CD-ROM
• Pronouns and Antecedents lesson

On-line Exercise Bank
• Section 23.3

Grammar Exercise Workbook
• pp. 123–124

◀ **Critical Viewing**
In two or three sentences, describe the actions of these dolphins. Use the pronouns *it* and *they* at least once, making sure the antecedents are clear. **[Connect]**

608 • Agreement

✔ **ONGOING ASSESSMENT: Monitor and Reinforce**

If students miss more than two items in Exercise 31 or 32, refer them to the following for additional practice.

In the Textbook	Print Resources	Technology
Section Review, Ex. 34, p. 612	*Grammar Exercise Workbook,* pp. 123–124	*Language Lab* CD-ROM, Nouns and Pronouns *On-Line Exercise Bank,* Section 23.3

GRAMMAR IN LITERATURE

from **Moby-Dick**
Herman Melville

Notice that the author repeats the noun Ahab *rather than using the pronoun* he, *which could refer to more than one antecedent.*

. . . Ahab, after rapidly glancing over the bulwarks, and then darting his eyes among the crew, started from his standpoint; and as though not a soul were nigh him resumed his heavy turns upon the deck. With bent head and half-slouched hat he continued to pace, unmindful of the wondering whispering among the men; till Stubb cautiously whispered to Flask, that Ahab must have summoned them there for the purpose of witnessing a pedestrian feat.

Avoiding Distant Pronoun References

A pronoun too far away from its antecedent will cause confusion.

KEY CONCEPT A personal pronoun should always be close enough to its antecedent to prevent confusion. ■

A distant pronoun reference can be corrected by moving the pronoun closer to its antecedent or by changing the pronoun to a noun. In the example below, *it* is too far from the antecedent *leg.*

DISTANT REFERENCE:	Molly shifted her weight from her injured leg. Two days ago, she had fallen, cutting herself on the glass that littered the street. Now *it* was swathed in bandages.
CORRECT:	Molly shifted her weight from her injured leg. Now *it* was swathed in bandages. Two days ago, she had fallen, cutting herself on the glass that littered the street.
	Molly shifted her weight from her injured leg. Two days ago, she had fallen, cutting herself on the glass that littered the street. Now her *leg* was swathed in bandages.

 Internet Tip

Find out more about marine mammals by searching for words such as *whales, dolphins, porpoises, seals, walruses,* and *manatees.*

Step-by-Step Teaching Guide

Grammar in Literature

1. Point out to students the pronoun-antecedent references in this excerpt.

2. Have students try to rewrite the excerpt using only pronouns. Ask them to evaluate both versions of the excerpt and comment on clarity.

More About the Writer

Herman Melville's experience with the sea began when he signed on as a cabin boy aboard a ship bound for Liverpool, England. For years, Melville worked on whalers and frigates, then he returned to the United States during the 1840's and began his writing career. Melville published such works as *Typee, Omoo, Mardi, Redburn, and White-Jacket.* In 1851 he wrote *Moby-Dick*—working so hard on the novel that he was near exhaustion and collapse when it was completed. Melville did not gain recognition for his work during his lifetime. It was after World War I that Melville's works were rediscovered and appreciated.

Step-by-Step Teaching Guide

Avoiding Distant Pronoun References

1. Explain to students that the problem of distant pronoun references is caused by intervening words, phrases, clauses, or sentences.

2. Encourage students to ask themselves to whom or to what a pronoun refers, particularly when they begin a sentence with a pronoun, or if the antecedent is not close.

 TIME SAVERS!

Answers on Transparencies Use the *Grammar Exercises Answers on Transparencies* for Chapter 23 to facilitate correction by students.

On-Line Exercise Bank Have students complete the exercises on computer. The Auto Check feature will grade their work for you!

609

continued

610

23.3

▶ **Exercise 33** **Revising to Correct Distant Pronoun References** Rewrite the following sentences, correcting the distant pronoun references.

1. At the helm of the ship stood the captain, gazing at the horizon. The passengers stood at the edge of the deck. Suddenly, he saw a whale's fluke rising from the water.

2. The waves lapped the sides of the ship. Birds circled overhead. It rose and fell with the swell of the waves.

3. The scientist wanted to see how whales behaved in the deep sea. The ship sailed far out into the ocean. In their natural habitat, their behavior might be quite different from those in captivity.

4. Imagine the problems of studying the lives of whales. A scientist needs to be patient. They spend so little time at the surface and travel far from shore.

5. Researchers can attach a small transmitter to a whale's back. The researchers track the movement and habits of the whale. It uses satellite technology.

6. The U.S. Navy has allowed researchers to use special water microphones, called hydrophones. Whale researchers wish to find out about the sounds made by whales. They allow the researchers to listen to underwater sounds made by whales.

7. A team of whale researchers wanted to find out why humpback whales blow bubbles. The researchers observed the humpbacks off the Alaskan coast. They might be a clue to how the animals hunt.

8. The bubbles emit a special feeding sound. Because fish are trapped by the bubbles, they move toward the surface when they hear it.

9. Barnacles live on the throat, chin, fins, and tail of humpbacks. The barnacles form whitish patterns on the whales. Some researchers recognize them by their "barnacle neckties."

10. On our field trip, we were fortunate to see a pod of humpback whales. In spite of rough seas, we found the trip inspiring. They broke the surface of the water several times.

▲ **Critical Viewing**
In this photograph, how does the closeness of the whale to the ship help to clarify the size relationship between them? **[Analyze]**

☑ **ONGOING ASSESSMENT: Monitor and Reinforce**

If students miss more than two items in Exercise 33, refer them to the following for additional practice.

In the Textbook	Print Resources	Technology
Section Review, Ex. 35, p. 612	*Grammar Exercise Workbook*, pp. 123–124	*Language Lab* CD-ROM, Nouns and Pronouns *On-Line Exercise Bank*, Section 23.3

Hands-on Grammar

Cutting Out Vague Pronoun Reference

Write the following sentence on a strip of paper. Make sure that you begin or end a line with the pronoun *they*.

When we arrived at the aquarium, they told us that the show was starting.

Cut the corner of the paper so that you have a small rectangle with the pronoun *they* written on it. Slide it along the sentence, looking for the noun or pronoun to which *they* refers. (You will not be able to find it!) Correct the vague pronoun reference by turning over the small rectangle and writing a noun that makes sense. Place the noun in the sentence where the pronoun *they* once was. Read the new sentence aloud.

Identify the vague pronoun references in each of the following sentences. Write each sentence on a strip of paper, making sure that the vague pronoun begins or ends a line so that you can easily cut it out. Replace the pronoun with a noun. You might replace some pronouns with more than one word. Read the new sentence or sentences aloud.

Long ago, sailors believed that manatees were mermaids, which not everyone knows.

They say that from a distance, the manatee looks like a human.

The manatee has very big eyes, but this is not enough to convince me.

Find It in Your Reading Find examples of clear pronoun references in a short story.

Find It in Your Writing Choose a piece of narrative writing from your portfolio and check it for vague pronoun references. Revise as needed.

✓ ONGOING ASSESSMENT: Assess Mastery

Use the following resources to assess student mastery of agreement.

In the Textbook	Print Resources	Technology
Chapter Review, Ex. 44, p. 614 Standardized Test Preparation Workshop, pp. 616–617	*Formal Assessment,* Chapter 23	*Language Lab* CD-ROM, Subject-Verb Agreement, Nouns and Pronouns *On-Line Exercise Bank,* Chapter 23

Answer Key continued

▶ **Exercise 33**

10. On our field trip, we were fortunate to see a pod of humpbacks. They broke the surface of the water several times. In spite of rough seas, we found the trip inspiring.

Step-by-Step Teaching Guide

Hands-on Grammar

Teaching Resources: Hands-on Grammar Activity Book, Ch. 23

1. If you wish to do this activity in class, be prepared with scissors for the students. Give each student a copy of the Hands-on Grammar activity sheet.

2. Have students follow the directions to prepare the strips.

3. Possible answers for sentences:

   Sentence 1: Replace *which* with *"and that is a belief that."*

   Sentence 2: Replace *They* with *"People"* or *"Sailors."*

   Sentence 3: Replace *this* with *"eye size."*

4. You may wish to expand this activity by having students use this cut-and-replace method to work with sentences from Exercise 33 that gave them problems.

Find It in Your Reading

Ask students to share some of the examples they found.

Find It in Your Writing

If students find no examples of vague pronoun usage in their writing, suggest that they write a teaching example, showing a vague pronoun and its correction.

⏱ TIME SAVERS!

✋ **Hands-on Grammar**
Use the Hands-on Grammar activity sheet for Chapter 23 to facilitate this activity.

Each of these exercises correlates to an element of special problems with pronoun agreement, pages 604–611. The exercises may be used for more practice, for reteaching, or for review of the key concepts presented.

Answer Key

▶ **Exercise 34**

Answers will vary; samples are given.

1. Grays and humpbacks are both baleen whales. This relationship explains . . .
2. In college, she studied whales and other marine mammals. The course was difficult.
3. Whale researchers sometimes think they cannot be hurt while boating out in the open sea. Their confidence leads them . . .
4. Observers can't always expect . . .
5. Researchers who study the gray whales have found that the whales do not seem . . .
6. The whales seem to migrate during the night. This migration takes a great deal of energy.
7. A person who studies whales must have patience.
8. Sometimes the whales will not come to the surface for long periods, and waiting can be . . .
9. When the whales do surface, they often raise their tail flukes as they dive down again. The raised flukes are a beautiful sight.
10. Many whales use their voices to communicate. Scientists refer to their communications as songs.

▶ **Exercise 35**

Answers will vary; samples are given.

1. A British research team devised a clever way to track the movements of beluga whales: Small transmitters are attached to the whales' backs.
2. Belugas seem to be able to find breathing holes even when traveling under thick arctic ice. They dive deep into the water. Then, they use either eyesight or sonar abilities to find the holes.
3. Other researchers have found that belugas are great imitators of sounds. Belugas can make bird sounds, whistling sounds, and even train sounds. The researchers are trying to find out about other sounds, too.

GRAMMAR EXERCISES 34–38

▶ **Exercise 34** **Revising to Correct Vague and Ambiguous Pronoun References** Rewrite the sentences below to correct the problems with agreement. Make sure that all antecedents are clear.

1. Grays and humpbacks are both baleen whales. This explains why they have so many similarities.
2. In college, she studied whales and other marine mammals. That was difficult.
3. Whale researchers sometimes think that they cannot be hurt while boating out in the open sea. This leads them to take great risks.
4. You can't always expect to see a whale during a whale-watch trip.
5. Researchers who study the gray whales have found that they do not seem to sleep at night.
6. The whales seem to migrate during the night, which takes a great deal of energy.
7. If you study whales, you must have patience.
8. Sometimes the whales will not come to the surface for long periods of time, and this can be frustrating.
9. When the whales do surface, they often raise their tail flukes as they dive down again. That is a beautiful sight.
10. Many whales use their voices to communicate, which we refer to as songs.

▶ **Exercise 35** **Revising to Correct Distant Pronoun References** Rewrite the following sentences, correcting the distant pronoun references.

1. Using small transmitters, a British research team devised a clever way to track beluga whales. The researchers hoped to follow the whales' movements. They are attached to the whales' backs.
2. Belugas seem to be able to find holes

for breathing even when traveling under thick arctic ice. They dive deep into the water. Then, they use either eyesight or sonar abilities to find them.
3. Other researchers have found that belugas are great imitators of sounds. Belugas can make bird sounds, whistling sounds, and even train sounds. They are trying to find out about other sounds, too.
4. One researcher published a paper on whale songs. The researcher had observed whales for several years. It described the different tones that whales emit.
5. The size of belugas is discussed in this article. Belugas are relatively small whales, whose young are only about five feet long. It was published in a scientific journal.

▶ **Exercise 36** **Find It in Your Reading** Identify the pronouns and their antecedents in the following excerpt from *Moby-Dick*. Then, tell whether each is singular or plural.

Soon his steady, ivory stride was heard, as to and fro he paced his old rounds, upon planks so familiar to his tread, that they were all over dented, like geological stones, with the peculiar mark of his walk.

▶ **Exercise 37** **Find It in Your Writing** Look through your writing portfolio. Find three examples of personal pronouns. Revise if necessary to make sure the pronouns agree with their antecedents.

▶ **Exercise 38** **Writing Application** Write a brief description of a body of water you have visited. Check that all your personal pronouns have clear antecedents.

---

4. One researcher published a paper on whale songs. It described the different tones that whales emit. The researcher had observed whales for several years.
5. Belugas are relatively small whales whose young are only about five feet long. The size of belugas is discussed in this article, which was published in a scientific journal.

▶ **Exercise 36**

Find It in Your Reading
pronouns: his, he; antecedent: he; all singular; they; antecedent: planks; plural

▶ **Exercise 37**

Find It in Your Writing
Suggest that students focus on writing they did a few weeks ago, because it will be easier for them to see vague pronoun usage in older writing.

▶ **Exercise 38**

Writing Application
Ask one or two volunteers to read their descriptions out loud. First, have them read straight through. Then, have them stop at each pronoun and ask for its antecedent.

Chapter

23 **Chapter Review**

GRAMMAR EXERCISES 39–47

▶ **Exercise 39** **Making Verbs Agree With Their Subjects** Choose the verb in parentheses that agrees with the subject of each sentence.

1. Killer whales (is, are) carnivores.
2. They (has, have) very large appetites.
3. A killer whale (spends, spend) about half its time hunting for food.
4. Seals, dolphins, sea lions, and other creatures (makes, make) up this whale's diet.
5. The killer whale (hunts, hunt) its prey near shore and in the sea.
6. This mammal, like many others, (excels, excel) at hunting.
7. Sometimes, two or more killer whales (cooperates, cooperate) to hunt.
8. The largest member of a family of whales known as *Delphinidea* (is, are) the killer whale.
9. Killer whales, whose scientific name is *Orcinus orca*, (is, are) also called *orcas*.
10. The orca, compared to the blue whale, (is, are) small.
11. Orcas, which can be found in all the waters of the ocean, (seems, seem) to prefer cold waters.
12. The killer whale's flippers, which (is, are) large rounded fins, can be as long as six feet or more.
13. The dorsal fin on the whale's back contains a gray patch that (helps, help) researchers distinguish one whale from another.
14. The killer whale is an animal that (appears, appear) to be quite intelligent.
15. Each pod has specific calls that only the whales of that pod (makes, make).

▶ **Exercise 40** **Supplying Verbs That Agree With Subjects** Supply a verb to complete each sentence.

1. Dolphins, porpoises, and whales ___?___ to a group of mammals called the cetaceans.
2. Neither a dolphin nor a porpoise ___?___ able to breathe in the water.
3. Every dolphin, porpoise, and whale ___?___ warmblooded.
4. Sea turtles and sharks ___?___ examples of coldblooded animals.
5. Porpoises ___?___ short snouts.
6. A squid or a few fish ___?___ a good meal for a dolphin.
7. The harbor porpoise and the Dall's porpoise ___?___ two of the six kinds of porpoises.
8. Neither the harbor porpoise nor Dall's porpoise ___?___ in the Southern Hemisphere.
9. The Northern Hemisphere and the Southern Hemisphere ___?___ their own porpoises.
10. Both dolphins and porpoises ___?___ able to survive in aquariums.

▶ **Exercise 41** **Revising to Eliminate Agreement Errors** Revise these sentences as necessary to correct agreement errors.

1. Everyone knows that mermaids do not exist.
2. Yet, there's stories that tell of sailors spying creatures that appeared to be half woman, half fish.
3. Some of the leading biologists believes that the sailors were really seeing manatees.
4. Manatees is part of a group of marine mammals called *Sirenia*.
5. Ten thousand dollars was spent on the research project that studied manatees.
6. The news about manatees was very interesting.
7. Some of the manatees' habitats is being destroyed.

CHAPTER REVIEW

Each of these exercises correlates to a section of the chapter on agreement, pages 582–612. The exercises may be used for more practice, for reteaching, or for review of the key concepts presented.

Answer Key

▶ **Exercise 39**

1. are
2. have
3. spends
4. make
5. hunts
6. excels
7. cooperate
8. is
9. are
10. is
11. seem
12. are
13. helps
14. appears
15. make

▶ **Exercise 40**

Answers will vary. Samples are given.

1. belong
2. is
3. is
4. are
5. have
6. make
7. are
8. swims
9. have
10. are

▶ **Exercise 41**

1. correct
2. there are
3. believe
4. are
5. correct
6. correct
7. are
8. correct
9. has
10. correct

🕐 **TIME SAVERS!**

🗔 **Answers on Transparencies** Use the *Grammar Exercises Answers on Transparencies* for Chapter 23 to facilitate correction by students.

🖥 **On-Line Exercise Bank** Have students complete the exercises on computer. The Auto Check feature will grade their work for you!

Answer Key

Exercise 42

1. my	9. his
2. her	10. their
3. its	11. they
4. their	12. their
5. their	13. he or she
6. her	14. their
7. its	15. his or her
8. their	

Exercise 43

1. The debate on whale conservation was won by my team and me.
2. Mary had argued well, so I asked Louise and her to join in the effort.
3. Who besides us is interested in whale conservation?
4. Sam and I may be the only ones who are participating.
5. Jonathan and you might want to draw posters or write letters.
6. correct
7. correct
8. I know that the Luthi twins said that their full schedules made new activities a problem for them.
9. Perhaps you and I can spread the word.
10. The future of whales may depend on people like us.

Exercise 44

Answers will vary; samples are given.

1. The blue whale is the largest animal alive today; it weighs more than the largest land animal that ever lived before.
2. During the feeding season, a blue whale can eat enough food in a day to fill 64,000 cereal bowls, which is an amazing amount.
3. The blue whale travels alone or in pairs, and this fact confounds researchers.
4. A television documentary spoke about blue whales.
5. Using special devices, researchers have identified the four-note songs of blue whales. The whales sing their songs in frequencies too low to be heard naturally by the researchers.
6. As a result of whale studies by researchers and photographers, there is more information than ever about these whales.
7. My mother told my sister that my sister could go on a whale watch.

Chapter Review Exercises cont'd.

8. Some of these manatees need to live in warm water.
9. Our class have agreed to learn more about protecting the habitat of these animals.
10. In Lowry Park in Tampa, Florida, is a statue of a mother manatee and her young.

Exercise 42 Supplying Personal Pronouns That Agree With Antecedents

Write an appropriate personal pronoun to complete each sentence.

1. My brother helped me write ___?___ report on seals.
2. Neither Karen nor Jane brought ___?___ book about seals.
3. When a seal dives, ___?___ pulse rate is reduced.
4. Seals and sea lions can hold ___?___ breath for more than 30 minutes.
5. Seals must return to the land to bear ___?___ young.
6. A mother seal cares for ___?___ young pups.
7. A seal pup knows who ___?___ mother is.
8. Typical of seals, seal lions, and walruses is ___?___ sense of play.
9. Mr. Ortiz, my teacher, enjoys ___?___ visits to a large marine park.
10. Either the dolphins or the seals perform ___?___ tricks for him.
11. Mr. Ortiz's students hope to visit the marine park, where ___?___ can watch the seals.
12. Most of the students raised ___?___ hands when asked if they wanted to go on the trip.
13. Before anyone joins in watching the seals, ___?___ must promise not to disturb the seals' environment.
14. Very few students could not obtain ___?___ permission slips signed by parents.
15. Each of us wants ___?___ chance to observe the seals in action.

Exercise 43 Using Reflexive Pronouns Correctly

Rewrite each sentence, correcting the misused reflexive pronoun. If a sentence does not contain an error, write correct.

1. The debate on whale conservation was won by my team and myself.
2. Mary had argued well, so I asked Louise and herself to join in the effort.
3. Who besides ourselves is interested in whale conservation?
4. Sam and myself may be the only ones who are participating.
5. Jonathan and yourself might want to draw posters or write letters.
6. If we get more supporters, we can be proud of ourselves.
7. Some interested people may find themselves too busy.
8. I know that the Luthi twins said that their full schedules made new activities a problem for themselves.
9. Perhaps you and myself can spread the word.
10. The future of whales may depend on people like ourselves.

Exercise 44 Correcting Pronoun References

Rewrite the sentences below, correcting the vague, ambiguous, or distant pronoun references.

1. The blue whale is the largest animal alive today; it weighs more than the largest one that ever lived before.
2. During the feeding season, a blue whale can eat enough food in a day to fill 64,000 cereal bowls, which is amazing.
3. The blue whale travels alone or in pairs, and this confounds researchers.
4. On a television documentary it spoke about blue whales.
5. Using special devices, researchers have identified the four-note songs of blue whales. They sing them in frequencies too low to be heard naturally by them.
6. As a result of the whale studies by

---

8. My sister bought me a whale poster and a T-shirt, but the T-shirt was not to my taste.
9. My father and my brother are going to take my father's boat out to look for whales.
10. Although they had luck sighting whales the last time, they may not be so lucky this time.
11. We saw two whales on our trip at sea. It had been a long day, but we were glad we went. The trip lasted six hours.
12. Scientists worry about overfishing the waters where whales feed. Scientists wonder if the whales will get enough to eat.
13. There are many ways that a person can learn about whales.
14. Many researchers became interested in studying marine life when they were in high school. They studied biology, chemistry, and other subjects while in college. These courses helped them to find work in a field they love.
15. I told Jake and Sam that I wanted to study whales, and Jake said that studying whales sounded like a good idea.

researchers and photographers, you have more information than ever.

7. My mother told my sister that she could go on a whale watch.
8. My sister bought me a whale poster and a T-shirt, but it was not to my taste.
9. My father and my brother are going to take his boat out to look for whales.
10. Although they had luck sighting whales the last time, it may not go so well this time.
11. We saw two whales on our trip at sea. It had been a long day, but we were glad we went. It lasted six hours.
12. Scientists worry about overfishing in waters where whales feed. They wonder if they will get enough to eat.
13. There are many ways that you can learn about whales.
14. Many researchers became interested in studying marine life when they were in high school. They studied biology, chemistry, and other subjects while in college. This helped them to find work in a field they love.
15. I told Jake and Sam that I wanted to study whales, and he said that sounded like a good idea.

Exercise 45 Using All the Rules of Agreement

Revise the following passage, correcting all errors in agreement.

(1) Seals, sea lions, and walruses belongs to the finfooted pinniped group. (2) It is carnivorous and survives on a diet of meat. (3) Pinnipeds has flippers and torpedo-shaped bodies. (4) Some of the pinnipeds has amazing diving abilities. (5) For example, the Weddell seal of Antarctica have been known to go to depths of nearly 2,000 feet for as long as 25 to 35 minutes. (6) This group of animals continue to surprise you. (7) Pinnipeds is further classified into three families. (8) There's the true seals, which lacks external ears. (9) The second family are the eared seals. (10) Sea lions and fur seals belong to this group. (11) The walrus is in a family by themselves. (12) True

seals and eared seals lives along the coastlines in both polar and temperate regions. (13) Some species makes their homes in tropical areas. (14) Walruses, however, lives only near the North Pole. (15) What animals most interests you?

Exercise 46 Writing Application

Write a brief speech that argues for or against legislation that relates to threatened or endangered species. Write a clear, meaningful argument. Check your pronoun and antecedent agreement, and avoid making unclear pronoun references.

Exercise 47 CUMULATIVE REVIEW
Verb and Pronoun Usage and Agreement

Revise the following sentences, correcting all errors in verb usage, pronoun usage, and agreement. If a sentence has no errors, write *correct*.

1. Jean and her class had went to the aquarium to see dolphins.
2. Jean and her classmates had planned the trip for weeks.
3. Neither Jean nor Laura brung their camera with them.
4. Jean spotted a dolphin that is swimming in a tank.
5. The dolphin swam in circles around it's trainer.
6. The antics and tricks of the dolphin was hilarious.
7. When Jean talked with the trainer about how dolphins communicate, she explained that there is still much to discover.
8. The class learned that dolphins is very social and is usually found in packs.
9. Laura wondered how they learned that dolphins have no sense of smell.
10. After the trip, each of the students have to write a paper on marine mammals.

▶ Exercise 45

Answers will vary; samples are given.

(1) Seals, sea lions, and walruses <u>belong</u> to the fin-footed pinniped group. (2) <u>They are</u> carnivorous and <u>survive</u> on a diet of meat. (3) Pinnipeds <u>have</u> flippers and torpedo-shaped bodies. (4) Some of the pinnipeds <u>have</u> amazing diving abilities. 5) For example, the Weddell seal of Antarctica <u>has</u> been known to go to depths of nearly 2,000 feet for as long as 25 to 35 minutes. (6) This group of animals <u>continues</u> to surprise <u>researchers</u>.

(7) Pinnipeds <u>are</u> further classified into three families. (8) There <u>are</u> the true seals, which <u>lack</u> external ears. (9) The second family <u>is</u> the eared seals. (10) Sea lions and fur seals belong to this group. (11) The walrus is in a family by <u>itself</u>. (12) True seals and eared seals <u>live</u> along the coastlines in both polar and temperate regions. (13) Some species <u>make</u> their homes in tropical areas. (14) Walruses, however, <u>live</u> only near the North Pole. (15) What animals most <u>interest</u> you?

▶ Exercise 46

Writing Application
Have students break up into small groups. Then have one or two volunteers within each group read their speeches to the group. Encourage students in each group to listen for agreement, as well as for a logical argument and solid facts.

▶ Exercise 47

Cumulative Review
1. Jean and her class had <u>gone</u> to the aquarium to see dolphins.
2. correct
3. Neither Jean nor Laura <u>brought</u> <u>her</u> camera.
4. Jean spotted a dolphin that <u>was</u> swimming in a tank.
5. The dolphin swam in circles around <u>its</u> trainer.
6. The antics and tricks of the dolphin <u>were</u> hilarious.
7. When Jean asked the trainer how dolphins communicate, <u>the trainer</u> explained that there is still much to discover.
8. The class learned that dolphins <u>are</u> very social and <u>are</u> usually found in packs.
9. Laura wondered how <u>researchers</u> learned that dolphins have no sense of smell.
10. After the trip, each of the students <u>has</u> to write a paper on marine mammals.

Recognizing Appropriate Sentence Construction

Teaching Resources: Standardized Test Preparation Workbook, pp. 45–46

1. Briefly review the subject-verb agreement key concepts in Section 23.1. This lesson will give students a chance to apply the knowledge they gained from this chapter.

2. For error recognition questions, encourage students to look for the subject and verb first, and then look for errors in the other underlined sections. For revision questions, students should identify errors in the numbered sentence before they look for the correct answer.

3. Encourage students to read test instructions carefully. Not all standardized tests are graded in the same way. Some tests do not penalize students for incorrect answers so that students may increase their scores with a judicious guess.

4. You may wish to provide students with standardized test answer sheets to practice the mechanics of marking in answers.

Standardized Test Preparation Workshop

Recognizing Appropriate Sentence Construction

Standardized tests frequently test your knowledge of the rules of subject and verb agreement. When checking a sentence for errors, first identify the subject. Next, identify the type of subject: *singular, plural,* or *compound.* Then, apply the rules of agreement to make sure that the verb in the sentence agrees with the subject.

The following questions will give you practice with different formats used for items that test your knowledge of subject-verb agreement.

Test Tip

If you are having trouble with a sentence revision, eliminate any answer choices in which the subject and verb clearly do not agree.

Sample Test Items	Answers and Explanations
Directions: Identify which underlined words and phrases in the following sentence contain an error. Neither Julia nor Sean <u>want</u> to miss the (A) (B) (C) <u>lecture</u> <u>on women in the work force</u>. (D) <u>No error</u> (E)	The correct answer is *B.* The subject of the sentence is *Neither Julia nor Sean.* When a compound subject is made up of two singular subjects and joined by *or* or *nor,* the subject takes a singular verb. In this case, the singular form of the verb is *wants.*
Directions: Choose the revised version of the following sentence that eliminates all errors in grammar, usage, and mechanics. Neither Julia nor Sean want to miss the lecture on women in the work force. A Both Julia and Sean don't want to miss the lecture on women in the work force. B Neither Julia nor Sean wants to miss the lecture on women in the work force. C Either Julia or Sean want to miss the lecture on women in the work force. D Julia and Sean don't wants to miss the lecture on women in the work force.	The correct answer is *B.* The subject of the sentence is *Neither Julia nor Sean.* When a compound subject is made up of two singular subjects and joined by *or* or *nor,* the subject takes a singular verb. In this case, the singular form of the verb is *wants.*

616 • Agreement

TEST-TAKING TIP

Remind students that marking the answer sheet incorrectly is an easy mistake to make—and a very costly one. Under the pressure of time, it is easy to skip a number on the grid. If students know the right answers but mark them in the wrong space, they cost themselves points that they deserve.

To avoid the problem, encourage students to mark answers in their test booklets and transfer them to the grid, checking the question numbers carefully. This system also allows students to double check their grids against their test booklets.

Answer Key

▶ **Practice 1**

1. B
2. B
3. D
4. B
5. C

▶ **Practice 2**

1. A
2. H

▶ **Practice 1** Identify which underlined words and phrases in each of the following sentences contain an error.

1. Women <u>has always been</u> <u>a large part</u>
   (A)   (B)   (C)
   <u>of the work force.</u> <u>No error.</u>
       (D)   (E)

2. <u>As the</u> <u>economy expand,</u> <u>more jobs</u>
     (A)   (B)   (C)
   <u>become available.</u> <u>No error</u>
       (D)   (E)

3. <u>Because of an increase</u> <u>in employment</u>
         (A)   (B)
   <u>opportunities,</u> <u>the number of women</u>
              (C)
   <u>working outside the home</u> <u>have grown to</u>
                (D)
   <u>four million.</u> <u>No error.</u>
       (E)

4. <u>At first,</u> <u>they would fills</u> <u>the lowest pay-</u>
      (A)   (B)   (C)
   <u>ing jobs.</u> <u>No error.</u>
      (D)   (E)

5. <u>By 1900,</u> <u>a large number</u> <u>was working</u>
      (A)   (B)   (C)
   <u>as stenographers, typists, secretaries,</u>
               (D)
   <u>and clerks.</u> <u>No error.</u>
       (E)

▶ **Practice 2** Choose the revised version of each numbered sentence that eliminates all errors in grammar, usage, and mechanics.

1 As were done in past centuries, some employers still takes advantage of female employees by paying them less than their male counterparts.

  A As was done in past centuries, some employers still take advantage of female employees by paying them less than their male counterparts.

  B As it was done in past centuries some employers still take advantage of female employees by paying them less than their male counterparts.

  C As it were done in past centuries, some employers still take advantage of female employees by paying them less than their male counterparts.

  D As was done in past centuries, some employers had still taken advantage of female employees by paying them less than their male counterparts.

2 Today, laws mandates that women and all people is treated equally in the workplace.

  F Today, laws mandate that women and all people are treated equally in the workplace.

  G Todays, laws mandate that women and all people are treated equally in the workplace.

  H Today, laws mandate that women and all other people be treated equally in the workplace.

  J Laws today, mandate that women and all other people be treated equally in the workplace.

Time and Resource Manager

In-Depth Lesson Plan

	LESSON FOCUS	PRINT AND MEDIA RESOURCES
DAY 1	**Degrees of Comparison** Students learn and apply the three degrees of comparison using both regular and irregular forms. (pp. 620–627)	*Language Lab* **CD-ROM**, Using Modifiers *On-Line Exercise Bank,* Section 24.1 **Teaching Resources** *Grammar Exercise Workbook,* pp. 125–128; *Grammar Exercises Answers on Transparencies,* Ch. 24
DAY 2	**Making Clear Comparisons** Students learn and make logical comparisons, understand absolute modifiers, and do the Hands-on Grammar activity. (pp. 628–635)	*On-Line Exercise Bank,* Section 24.2 **Teaching Resources** *Grammar Exercise Workbook,* pp. 129–134; *Hands-on Grammar Activity Book,* pp. 47–48
DAY 3	**Review and Assess** Students review the chapter and demonstrate mastery of modifiers indicating comparisons. (pp. 636–637)	**Teaching Resources** *Formal Assessment,* Ch. 24

Accelerated Lesson Plan

	LESSON FOCUS	PRINT AND MEDIA RESOURCES
DAY 1	**Degrees of Comparison** Students learn and apply the three degrees of comparison using both regular and irregular forms. (pp. 620–627)	*Language Lab* **CD-ROM**, Using Modifiers *On-Line Exercise Bank,* Section 24.1 **Teaching Resources** *Grammar Exercise Workbook,* pp. 125–128; *Grammar Exercises Answers on Transparencies,* Ch. 24
DAY 2	**Making Clear Comparisons; Review and Assess** Students learn and make logical comparisons, understand absolute modifiers, and review chapter and demonstrate mastery of concepts. (pp. 628–637)	*On-Line Exercise Bank,* Section 24.2 **Teaching Resources** *Grammar Exercise Workbook,* pp. 129–134; *Formal Assessment,* Ch. 24

Options for Adapting Lesson Plans

HOMEWORK

Have students complete any section of the chapter for homework.

FEATURES

Extend coverage with the Grammar in Literature feature (p. 622) and the Standardized Test Preparation Workshop (p. 638).

TECHNOLOGY

Students can use the *On-Line Exercise Bank* to complete the exercises on computer. The Auto Check feature will grade their work.

INTEGRATED SKILLS COVERAGE

Grammar in Literature
SE p. 622

Writing
Find It in Your Writing SE pp. 627, 635
Writing Application SE pp. 627, 635
Grammar and Style SE pp. 624, 633

Spelling
SE p. 622; ATE p. 621

Viewing and Representing
Critical Viewing, SE pp. 618, 623, 624, 626, 629, 630, 632

Vocabulary ATE p. 622

Writing ATE p. 624

Real-World Connection ATE p. 625

Workplace Skills ATE p. 629

ASSESSMENT SUPPORT

Standardized Test Preparation Workshop SE p. 638; ATE pp. 622, 634
Standardized Test Preparation Workbook, pp. 47–48
Formal Assessment, Ch. 24

MEETING INDIVIDUAL NEEDS

Less Advanced Students ATE pp. 643. See Ongoing Assessments ATE pp. 621, 623, 626, 629, 631, 632, 633.
ESL Students ATE pp. 624, 626
AP Students ATE p. 633
Logical/Mathematical Learners ATE p. 631
Bodily/Kinesthetic Learners ATE p. 621
Verbal/Linguistic Learners ATE p. 630
Visual/Spatial Learners ATE p. 624

BLOCK SCHEDULING

Pacing Suggestions
For 90-minute Blocks
• Administer the Diagnostic Test to students to determine instructional coverage.
• Have students complete the necessary exercises in class. Use the Hands-on Grammar activity to provide a change of pace.

Resources for Varying Instruction
• *Language Lab* **CD-ROM** If your students have access to hardware, a 90-minute block provides an ideal opportunity for students to work on computer.

Professional Development Support
• *How to Manage Instruction in the Block* This Teaching Resource provides management and activity suggestions.

MEDIA AND TECHNOLOGY

For the Student
• *Language Lab* **CD-ROM**, Using Modifiers
• *On-Line Exercise Bank,* Sections 24.1–2

For the Teacher
• *Resource Pro* **CD-ROM**

WRITING AND GRAMMAR WEB SITE

The Interactive Writing and Grammar Web Site provides a wide array of support for students, teachers, and parents. Grammar support includes:

• *On-Line Exercise Bank* with Auto Check scoring
• Diagnostic and assessment support

www.phschool.com

LITERATURE CONNECTIONS

Grammar in Literature selection from *Prentice Hall Literature: Timeless Voices, Timeless Themes,* The American Experience:
from "Sinners in the Hands of an Angry God," Jonathan Edwards, SE p. 622

Lesson Objectives

1. To identify and use the three degrees of comparison: positive, comparative, and superlative

2. To recognize and form comparative and superlative forms of irregular adjectives and adverbs

3. To use the comparative and superlative degrees correctly

4. To make logical, balanced comparisons

5. To recognize appropriate English usage within the context of a written passage

6. To evaluate writing for both mechanics and content

7. To analyze the characteristics of clearly written texts, including the patterns of organization, syntax, and word choice

Critical Viewing

Analyze; Compare Students' responses may include adjectives and adverbs such as *taller/smaller; lightest/heaviest; faster/slower; more quickly/more slowly.*

Chapter 24 Using Modifiers

The Arrival of Winthrop's Ships in Boston Harbor, 1630, W. F. Halsall

Adjectives and **adverbs,** also known as modifiers, are important tools in the effective use of language. Well-chosen modifiers can transform dull sentences into interesting ones. They can provide contrast, emphasis, and shades of meaning.

An important use of modifiers is to make comparisons. For example, when writing about another society, you might use modifiers in this way. If you were studying Puritans of seventeenth-century New England, you would use adjectives and adverbs to highlight the differences between today's society and Puritan life. You would also use modifiers to clearly describe the many elements of Puritan society that were instrumental in shaping our society. This chapter will show you how to use adjectives and adverbs to make comparisons and how to avoid some common usage problems involving comparisons.

▲ **Critical Viewing**
What adjectives and adverbs can you use to compare and contrast the ships in this picture? [**Analyze, Compare**]

618 • Using Modifiers

✓ ONGOING ASSESSMENT: Diagnose

If students miss more than one item in any category, direct them to the relevant pages of the textbook and assign exercises for practice and review.

Using Modifiers	Diagnostic Test Items	Teach	Practice	Section Reviews	Chapter Review
Skill Check A					
Identifying Degrees of Comparison	A 1–5	p. 620	Ex. 1	Ex. 8	Ex. 25
Skill Check B					
Forming Regular Comparatives and Superlatives	B 6–10	pp. 621–622	Ex. 2–4	Ex. 9–10	Ex. 27

Diagnostic Test

Directions: Write all answers on a separate sheet of paper.

Skill Check A. Identify the degree of each underlined modifier as *positive, comparative,* or *superlative.*

1. Puritans in England made the <u>difficult</u> choice to leave their country.
2. They wanted a <u>better</u> life for themselves and their families.
3. They sailed across the Atlantic to establish <u>new</u> colonies in America.
4. Though life was difficult in the new land, Puritans were <u>freer</u> to practice their religion here than they were in England.
5. Their <u>most successful</u> colonies were in New England.

Skill Check B. Write the appropriate comparative or superlative degree of the modifier in parentheses.

6. Which colony was (far) away, New England or Virginia?
7. Of all the factors, which was (important) in the Puritans' decision to come to America?
8. Freedom to practice their religion was their (great) concern.
9. The climate and terrain were (harsh) than the Puritans had anticipated.
10. Their will to succeed was (strong) than the obstacles they had to overcome.

Skill Check C. Write the correct form of the irregular modifier in parentheses.

11. The Puritans often fared (bad) in the new colonies than they had expected.
12. Still, they felt that their choice was the (good) one they could have made.
13. They believed they had (much) opportunity here than in England.
14. There had been (little) religious freedom for the Puritans in England than there was in America.
15. They had to travel (far) than they had expected, but freedom was worth the effort.

Skill Check D. Rewrite the following sentences to make the comparisons logical.

16. Partly because of the Puritans' success in New England, more people in the world speak English than any language.
17. Life was much different for the Puritans than today.
18. The most unique aspect of their immigration was that they came to New England in family groups.
19. Religion was more important to them than anything.
20. The Puritans had more freedom of religion in America than England.

Diagnostic Test

Each item in the Diagnostic Test corresponds to a specific section in the Using Modifiers chapter. This will enable you to tailor instruction to the particular needs of your students. See "Ongoing Assessment: Diagnose" below for further details. Answers for the Diagnostic Test and all chapter exercises are available in *Grammar Exercises Answers on Transparencies* in your Teaching Resources.

Answer Key

Skill Check A

1. positive
2. comparative
3. positive
4. comparative
5. superlative

Skill Check B

6. farther
7. most important
8. greatest
9. harsher
10. stronger

Skill Check C

11. worse
12. best
13. more
14. less
15. farther

Skill Check D

16. than any other language
17. than it is for us today
18. The most admirable aspect
19. than anything else
20. than in England

✓ ONGOING ASSESSMENT: Diagnose *continued*					
Using Modifiers	**Diagnostic Test Items**	**Teach**	**Practice**	**Section Reviews**	**Chapter Review**
Skill Check C					
Forming Irregular Comparatives and Superlatives	C 11–15	pp. 624–625	Ex. 5–7	Ex. 9–10	Ex. 26
Skill Check D					
Forming Logical Comparisons	D 16–20	pp. 628–633	Ex. 14–18	Ex. 19–21	Ex. 28–30
Cumulative Reviews and Applications				Ex. 11–13 Ex. 22–24	Ex. 31–32

🕐 **TIME SAVERS!**

 Answers on Transparencies Use the *Grammar Exercises Answers on Transparencies* for Chapter 24 to facilitate correction by students.

💻 **On-Line Exercise Bank** Have students complete the Diagnostic Test on computer. The Auto Check feature will grade their work for you!

Degrees of Comparison

English has three *degrees*, or forms, of adjectives and adverbs that are used to make comparisons. To recognize the different degrees of comparison, you need to know the name of each degree. They are the positive, the comparative, and the superlative.

KEY CONCEPT The three degrees of comparison are the *positive*, the *comparative*, and the *superlative*. ■

There are three different ways that a word may change form to indicate the comparative and superlative degrees:

(1) *-er* or *-est* may be added at the end of the word.

(2) *more* or *most* may be added before the word.

(3) the word may assume an entirely different form.

DEGREES OF ADJECTIVES		
Positive	**Comparative**	**Superlative**
quick	quicker	quickest
pleasant	more pleasant	most pleasant
bad	worse	worst
DEGREES OF ADVERBS		
slow	slower	slowest
pleasantly	more pleasantly	most pleasantly
badly	worse	worst

Theme: Puritan Life

In this section, you will learn about degrees of comparison. The examples and exercises in this section are about Puritan life.

Cross-Curricular Connection: Social Studies

► Exercise 1 **Recognizing Positive, Comparative, and Superlative Degrees** Identify the degree of each underlined modifier.

EXAMPLE: Life in New England was <u>more difficult</u> than the Puritans had expected.

ANSWER: comparative

1. The Puritans wanted to be <u>free</u> to practice their religion.
2. They sought what they believed to be a <u>purer</u> form of religion than that practiced by the Anglican Church.
3. The Bible was their <u>most important</u> book.
4. They established the Massachusetts Bay Colony in 1629, but other colonies were founded <u>earlier</u> than that.
5. Puritans in New England were <u>more strict</u> than their English counterparts.

More Practice

Language Lab CD-ROM
• Forms of Comparison lesson
On-line Exercise Bank
• Section 24.1
Grammar Exercise Workbook
• pp. 125–126

620 • Using Modifiers

⏱ TIME AND RESOURCE MANAGER

Resources
Print: *Grammar Exercise Workbook*, pp. 125–128; *Grammar Exercises Answers on Transparency*, Ch. 24
Technology: *Language Lab* CD-ROM, Using Modifiers; *On-Line Exercise Bank*, Section 24.1

In-Depth Coverage	Accelerated Pace
• Work through all key concepts, pp. 620–625. • Assign and review Exercises 1–7. • Read and discuss *Grammar in Literature*, p. 622.	• Assign pp. 620–625 for independent student review. • Assign Section Review Exercises 8–10.

Using Regular Forms

Adjectives and adverbs can be either regular or irregular, depending on how their comparative and superlative degrees are formed. The comparative and superlative degrees of most adjectives and adverbs are formed regularly. Two rules govern the formation of regular modifiers. The first concerns modifiers of one or two syllables; the second concerns modifiers of three or more syllables:

KEY CONCEPT Use *-er* or *more* to form the comparative degree and *-est* or *most* to form the superlative degree of most one- and two-syllable modifiers. ■

The more commonly used method of forming the comparative and superlative degrees of one- and two-syllable modifiers is to add *-er* and *-est* rather than *more* and *most*. Though English often allows the use of either method, *more* and *most* should be avoided when the construction sounds awkward. For example, "Life was *more hard* than they thought" sounds much more awkward than "Life was *harder* than they thought."

The examples below show one- and two-syllable modifiers formed regularly with *-er* and *-est*.

EXAMPLES:	bright	brighter	brightest
	crafty	craftier	craftiest
	subtle	subtler	subtlest

More and *most* are used with a number of one- and two-syllable modifiers when *-er* and *-est* would sound awkward. Rely on your ear to determine which words sound awkward with *-er* and *-est*.

EXAMPLES:	just	more just	most just
	pleasing	more pleasing	most pleasing
	devout	more devout	most devout

All adverbs that end in *-ly*, regardless of the number of syllables, form their comparative and superlative degrees with *more* and *most*.

EXAMPLES:	freely	more freely	most freely
	happily	more happily	most happily
	abruptly	more abruptly	most abruptly

 Spelling Tip

When comparing two things, add the word *more* or the suffix *-er*, but never both together!

Degrees of Comparison • 621

Step-by-Step Teaching Guide

Grammar in Literature

1. Have a student read the Jonathan Edwards passage aloud, and then reread the phrase containing *greater*. Ask students for the positive and superlative forms. (*great, greatest*)

2. Repeat this activity with the superlatives (*stoutest, sturdiest*) and ask for the related forms (*stout, stouter/sturdy, sturdier*).

3. Have students discuss what the use of the superlative forms adds to the passage.

More About the Writer

The only son among ten daughters, Jonathan Edwards was a prominent eighteenth-century Puritan preacher who initiated a spiritual renewal in America known as the First Great Awakening. He entered Yale at the age of thirteen, studied theology, and subsequently graduated at the head of his class. As a church pastor, Edwards became famous for his vigorous sermons.

Language Highlight

Explain that in modern English, the word *stout* means "bulky" or "corpulent" and also "fearless." Tell students that *stout*'s Latin derivation, *stultus*, means "foolish."

Integrating Vocabulary Skills

The adjective *omnipotent* derives from the prefix *omni-* meaning "all" and *potent* meaning "powerful." *Omnipotent,* the use of which first appeared in the fourteenth century, means "almighty" and "having virtually unlimited authority." Ask students to list other words with the prefix *omni-*.

Connections With Literature

A longer passage from "Sinners in the Hands of an Angry God" can be found in *Prentice Hall Literature: Timeless Voices, Timeless Themes:* The American Experience.

GRAMMAR IN LITERATURE

from Sinners in the Hands of an Angry God
Jonathan Edwards

The author has used the comparative form greater *and the superlative forms* stoutest *and* sturdiest *to make comparisons in this excerpt. These modifiers are shown in blue italics.*

"If God should only withdraw his hand from the floodgate, it would immediately fly open, and the fiery floods of the fierceness and wrath of God, would rush forth with inconceivable fury, and would come upon you with omnipotent power; and if your strength were ten thousand times *greater* than it is, yea, ten thousand times greater than the strength of the *stoutest, sturdiest* devil in Hell, it would be nothing to withstand or endure it."

When a modifier consists of three or more syllables, the comparative and superlative degrees are easily formed.

▶ **KEY CONCEPT** Use *more* and *most* to form the comparative and superlative degrees of all modifiers with three or more syllables. ■

EXAMPLES:		
delicate	more delicate	most delicate
dependable	more dependable	most dependable
ambitious	more ambitious	most ambitious
generous	more generous	most generous

Note About *Comparisons With Less and* Least: *Less* and *least* mean the opposite of *more* and *most* and can be used to form the comparative and superlative degrees of most modifiers.

EXAMPLES:		
smooth	less smooth	least smooth
acceptable	less acceptable	least acceptable
explicitly	less explicitly	least explicitly

622 • Using Modifiers

💡 Spelling Tip

When comparing three or more things add the word *most* or the suffix *-est,* but never both together.

✎ STANDARDIZED TEST PREPARATION WORKSHOP

Grammar and Usage Many standardized tests require students to form the correct degree of comparison within the context of a passage. Use the following example to demonstrate:

Many people attempt to climb the summit of Mt. Everest, which is the ___ mountain in the world.

A taller

B tallest

C more tall

The correct answer is **B.** The mountain is being compared to all other mountains in the world.

Exercise 2 Forming Comparative and Superlative

Degrees Write the comparative and the superlative form of each modifier.

1. pure
2. simple
3. religious
4. brave
5. important
6. strong
7. democratic
8. smart
9. excited
10. virtuously
11. successfully
12. instrumental
13. early
14. strict
15. restrictive
16. harsh
17. powerful
18. exclusive
19. severe
20. hard

Exercise 3 Supplying Comparative and Superlative

Degrees Write the appropriate comparative or superlative degree of the underlined modifier by following the instructions in parentheses.

EXAMPLE: The Puritans placed <u>strong</u> emphasis on religion than on trade. (comparative)

ANSWER: stronger

1. Many Puritans found their new lives <u>hard</u> than the ones they had left behind. (comparative)
2. The climate was <u>severe</u> than in England. (comparative)
3. The first winter was the <u>difficult</u>. (superlative)
4. Still, they worshiped <u>freely</u> than before. (comparative)
5. Many Puritans found life got <u>easy</u> as more people settled in the colony. (comparative)
6. Not many groups were <u>industrious</u> than the Puritans. (comparative)
7. They were among the <u>rigid</u> thinkers of all. (superlative)
8. Native Americans lived even <u>simply</u> than the Puritans. (comparative)
9. The Puritans formed a government that was <u>democratic</u> than that of England. (comparative)
10. The Massachusetts Bay Colony became the <u>successful</u> of all the New England colonies. (superlative)

Exercise 4 Writing Sentences With Comparative and

Superlative Modifiers Write a sentence correctly using each modifier.

1. more resilient
2. coldest
3. most intelligent
4. more prosperous
5. more devout
6. most sacred
7. more intolerant
8. severest
9. sturdiest
10. bleaker

▶ More Practice

Language Lab CD-ROM
• Forms of Comparison lesson

On-line Exercise Bank
• Section 24.1

Grammar Exercise Workbook
• pp. 125–126

▲ **Critical Viewing**
What does this seal of the Massachusetts Bay Colony suggest about how the Puritans regarded the Native Americans? **[Infer, Interpret, Draw Conclusions]**

Degrees of Comparison • 623

Answer Key

▶ Exercise 2

1. purer, purest
2. simpler, simplest
3. more religious, most religious
4. braver, bravest
5. more important, most important
6. stronger, strongest
7. more democratic, most democratic
8. smarter, smartest
9. more excited, most excited
10. more virtuously, most virtuously
11. more successfully, most successfully
12. more instrumental, most instrumental
13. earlier, earliest
14. stricter, strictest
15. more restrictive, most restrictive
16. harsher, harshest
17. more powerful, most powerful
18. more exclusive, most exclusive
19. more severe, most severe (severer, severest)
20. harder, hardest

▶ Exercise 3

1. harder
2. more severe
3. most difficult
4. more freely
5. easier
6. more industrious
7. most rigid
8. more simply
9. more democratic
10. most successful

▶ Exercise 4

Answers will vary; samples are given.

1. His health is more resilient than hers.
2. It was the coldest day of the week.
3. This is the most intelligent puppy of the litter.
4. Ed is more prosperous than Sue.
5. The minister is more devout than his congregation.
6. The Bible is the most sacred text of the Christian church.
7. That group is more intolerant than this one.
8. It was the severest cold I ever had.
9. This is the sturdiest blanket of all.
10. His news was bleaker than hers.

Critical Viewing

Infer, Interpret, Draw Conclusions
Student answers may vary widely. Possible response: The colonists respected Native Americans' hunting skills; they believed Native Americans needed help.

✓ ONGOING ASSESSMENT: Monitor and Reinforce

If students miss more than two items in Exercise 2, 3, or 4, refer them to the following for additional practice.

In the Textbook	Print Resources	Technology
Section Review, Ex. 9–10, p. 627	*Grammar Exercise Workbook,* pp. 125–126	*Language Lab* CD-ROM, Using Modifiers; *On-Line Exercise Bank,* Section 24.1

Irregular Forms

1. Tell students that certain irregular modifiers may challenge their spelling skills. Use the adjective *hungry* as an example to lead into the discussion. Have students form its comparative and superlative degrees. (*hungrier, hungriest*) Point out that certain adjustments were necessary: dropping the *-y* and adding *-ier* or *-iest*.

2. Next practice using the chart on this page. Ask students first to read the three forms of a modifier, and then to use two forms in original sentences. Do this until you complete the list.

3. Have students recall from memory the comparative and superlative forms you read from the chart.

continued

Customize for
Visual/Spatial Learners

Using the chart on page 624, create a handout that includes only the positive irregular forms. Ask students to fill in the missing forms. As you provide the correct answers, students should circle any incorrect responses they made.

Customize for
ESL Students

Help students speak and write comparisons in sentences by asking them to tell about a shopping trip. Have them identify a store that they know, and then tell about two or three items at a time (*two pairs of shoes, fruit at a fruit stand*) and compare them. (*The blue shoes are more comfortable than the brown ones; the bananas look riper than the pears.*)

Integrating Writing Skills

Good, well, bad, badly Have students think of situations in which all four of these modifiers could be used. Then have them write a short composition using the four modifiers.

Critical Viewing

Compare and Contrast Possible responses: *It has* less property, more chimneys, fewer windows, more angles, fewer stories.

Using Irregular Forms

The comparative and superlative degrees of a few adjectives and adverbs are not formed according to any predictable pattern; they must be memorized.

KEY CONCEPT The irregular comparative and superlative forms of certain adjectives and adverbs must be memorized. ■

The chart below lists the three degrees of these irregular modifiers. Study the chart, and make a mental note of the irregular modifiers that you are likely to misuse. Notice that some modifiers differ only in the positive degree. Both *good* and *well*, for example, have the same comparative and superlative degrees (*better, best*).

DEGREES OF ADJECTIVES		
Positive	**Comparative**	**Superlative**
bad	worse	worst
badly	worse	worst
far (distance)	farther	farthest
far (extent)	further	furthest
good	better	best
late	later	last or latest
little (amount)	less	least
many	more	most
much	more	most
well	better	best

Grammar and Style Tip

Choose vivid, descriptive modifiers to compare people, places, things, and ideas in your writing.

◄ **Critical Viewing** How is this colonial house similar to and different from homes in your neighborhood? **[Compare and Contrast]**

Note About *Bad* and *Badly*: *Bad* is an adjective that can be used after a linking verb. It *cannot* be used as an adverb after an action verb.

INCORRECT: Puritans fared *bad* in English society.

CORRECT: Puritans felt *bad* about English society.

Badly is an adverb that can be used after an action verb. It *cannot* be used as an adjective after a linking verb.

INCORRECT: They felt *badly* about leaving their homes.

CORRECT: The government treated them *badly*.

Note About *Good* and *Well*: Like *bad*, *good* is an adjective that can be used after a linking verb. It cannot be used as an adverb after an action verb.

INCORRECT: They acted *good* in choosing new lives.

CORRECT: They felt *good* about their new lives.

Well is usually an adverb and, like *badly*, can be used after an action verb.

CORRECT: Some Puritans did *well* in the new colony.

Well is an adjective when it is used to mean "healthy." Thus, it can sometimes be used after a linking verb.

CORRECT: After landing, they soon felt *well* again.

▶ **Exercise 5** **Revising to Correct Errors in Irregular Modifiers**
Rewrite each sentence, correcting the underlined irregular modifier by following the instructions in parentheses.
1. The harsh New England winters were <u>more bad</u> than the first Puritan settlers had imagined. (comparative)
2. <u>Much</u> settlers died during the first winter in the new land. (positive)
3. In addition to the cold weather, the settlers were <u>farther</u> challenged by disease and other hardships. (comparative)
4. Despite facing <u>most</u> challenges, the settlers endured and established thriving communities. (positive)
5. Today, the Puritan settlers remain one of the <u>most good</u> examples of the human ability to endure and to overcome obstacles. (superlative)

▶ **More Practice**

Language Lab CD-ROM
• Forms of Comparison lesson

On-line Exercise Bank
• Section 24.1

Grammar Exercise Workbook
• pp. 127–128

Degrees of Comparison • 625

4. First check students' mastery of action and linking verbs. Remind them that linking verbs can include forms like *smells, sounds,* and *looks.*

5. Emphasize that use of the four irregular modifiers—*bad, badly, good,* and *well*—depends on the type of verb. Both *bad* and *good* follow linking verbs; both *badly* and *well* follow action verbs.

6. Note one exception: When *well* means "healthy," it follows a linking verb.

Real-World Connection

Ask students whether they think that precise speech is important during a job interview. Pose this question: When your employer asks about your high school experience, should you say, "I did good" or "I did well"? Often English usage can determine job-interview success.

Answer Key

▶ **Exercise 5**

1. worse
2. Many
3. further
4. many
5. best

Answer Key

▶ **Exercise 6**

1. better
2. farther
3. worse
4. more
5. less
6. most
7. less
8. more
9. better
10. best

▶ **Exercise 7**

1. treated badly
2. did well
3. felt bad
4. little information
5. the further she dug

Critical Viewing

Compare and Contrast Students might use terms like *fussier, more formal, more elaborate.*

24.1

▶ **Exercise 6** **Forming Irregular Comparative and Superlative Degrees** Write the appropriate form of the underlined modifier to complete each sentence.

EXAMPLE: Living conditions may be <u>bad</u> in some ways now, but they were ___?___ for the Puritans.

ANSWER: worse

1. Conditions were not <u>good</u> for the Puritans in England, so they came to New England to find a ___?___ life.
2. They traveled <u>far</u> to get to New England, but those who went south traveled even ___?___ .
3. Some felt <u>bad</u> during the long sea voyage, but many more felt ___?___ during their first winter here.
4. The Puritans were <u>much</u> concerned about government, but they were even ___?___ concerned about religion.
5. They attached <u>little</u> importance to the traditions of the Church of England and ___?___ to those of Roman Catholicism.
6. English Puritans emphasized the literal interpretation of the Bible <u>more</u> than other Protestants did, but American Puritans emphasized it the ___?___ .
7. They had <u>little</u> tolerance for dissenting opinion and still ___?___ for dissenting behavior.
8. They placed <u>much</u> emphasis on public order, but even ___?___ on religious and moral order.
9. Many Puritans who farmed eventually did <u>well</u>, but those who became involved in trade did even ___?___ .
10. Among the <u>good</u> qualities the Puritans passed on to their descendants, their industriousness may have been the ___?___ .

▶ **Exercise 7** **Revising Sentences to Correct Irregular Comparative and Superlative Degrees** Rewrite each sentence with the correct form of the irregular modifier.

1. The Puritans often treated bad anyone with other religious beliefs.
2. While the Puritans eventually did good in New England, it took years after they first arrived for life to get better.
3. She felt badly that she knew so little about her Puritan ancestors.
4. When she asked her parents, they had less information about her heritage, but they encouraged her to learn more.
5. She learned little during her first visit to the library, but the furthest she dug into the material, the more success she had.

626 • Using Modifiers

▶ **More Practice**

Language Lab CD-ROM
• Forms of Comparison lesson

On-line Exercise Bank
• Section 24.1

Grammar Exercise Workbook
• pp. 127–128

▼ **Critical Viewing**
Compare and contrast the attire of John Winthrop (pictured here) with the clothes worn by you and your classmates. **[Compare and Contrast]**

✓ **ONGOING ASSESSMENT: Monitor and Reinforce**

If students have trouble with Exercise 5, 6, or 7, refer them to the following for additional practice.

In the Textbook	Print Resources	Technology
Section Review, Ex. 9–10, p. 627	*Grammar Exercise Workbook,* pp. 127–128	*Language Lab* CD-ROM, Using Modifiers; *On-Line Exercise Bank,* Section 24.1

Section
24.1

Section Review

GRAMMAR EXERCISES 8–13

▶ **Exercise 8** **Recognizing Positive, Comparative, and Superlative Degrees** Identify the degree of each underlined modifier.

1. The Massachusetts Bay Company was granted a <u>small</u> tract of land.
2. Puritans wanted to be one of the <u>most powerful</u> forces in the company.
3. As a result, the Puritans gained <u>greater</u> control of their charter.
4. This development was <u>most unusual</u> in the British Empire at the time.
5. Puritans were <u>wealthier</u> than many other settlers.
6. Their society was <u>more democratic</u> than is usually thought.
7. They believed tax-paying was a duty, and they paid <u>cheerfully</u>.
8. They took <u>better</u> care of the poor than many other societies did.
9. The importance of Bible reading made New England one of the <u>most literate</u> societies in the world.
10. The Puritans founded a college <u>sooner</u> than people in the other colonies did.

▶ **Exercise 9** **Forming Comparative and Superlative Degrees** Write the appropriate comparative or superlative degree of the underlined modifier by following the instructions in parentheses.

1. Puritans were <u>little</u> tolerant of different beliefs than others were. (comparative)
2. The <u>strange</u> punishment for sinners was to shame them. (superlative)
3. The <u>well</u>-known fictional example of shaming is in Nathaniel Hawthorne's novel *The Scarlet Letter*. (superlative)
4. Banishment was often a <u>effective</u> way of dealing with offenders. (comparative)
5. Anne M. Hutchinson was the <u>famous</u> person to be banished. (superlative)

6. The Puritans thought this punishment would cause the <u>little</u> damage. (superlative)
7. She was <u>lucky</u> than other dissenters. (comparative)
8. The Puritans often used <u>violent</u> methods of correction. (comparative)
9. One of the <u>extreme</u> punishments was hanging. (superlative)
10. Roger Williams founded the <u>tolerant</u> colony, Rhode Island. (superlative)

▶ **Exercise 10** **Writing Sentences to Revise Degrees of Comparison** Rewrite ten sentences from Exercises 8 and 9. Change the degree of comparison in each.

▶ **Exercise 11** **Find It in Your Reading** Find two examples of comparative adverbs in this excerpt from "Sinners in the Hands of an Angry God." Identify the degree of comparison of each example.

The wrath of God is like great waters that are dammed for the present; they increase more and more, and rise higher and higher, till an outlet is given. . . .

▶ **Exercise 12** **Find It in Your Writing** Review a piece of your writing, and identify three or more examples of comparative and superlative modifiers. If you cannot find at least three, revise your work to add one example of each form.

▶ **Exercise 13** **Writing Application** Write a brief comparison of two or more people, places, or things. Be sure to use the correct comparative and superlative forms of adjectives and adverbs.

Section Review • 627

ASSESS

Section Review

Each of these exercises correlates to the instruction on regular and irregular comparative forms, pages 620–625. The exercises may be used for more practice, for reteaching, or for review of the key concepts presented. Answers are available in *Grammar Exercises Answers on Transparencies* in your Teaching Resources.

Answer Key

▶ **Exercise 8**

1. positive
2. superlative
3. comparative
4. superlative
5. comparative
6. comparative
7. positive
8. comparative
9. superlative
10. comparative

▶ **Exercise 9**

1. less tolerant
2. strangest
3. best known
4. more effective
5. most famous
6. least
7. luckier
8. more violent
9. most extreme
10. most tolerant

▶ **Exercise 10**

Responses will vary. Have volunteers read their sentences and discuss what other wording changes were needed in them.

▶ **Exercise 11**

Find It in Your Reading
great (positive); more, higher (both comparative)

▶ **Exercise 12**

Find It in Your Writing
Students should correctly identify at least one comparative and one superlative adjective or adverb.

▶ **Exercise 13**

Writing Application
Have volunteers mention the items they compared. Students' comparisons should contain correctly used comparative and superlative forms of adjectives and adverbs.

☑ **ONGOING ASSESSMENT: Assess Mastery**

Use the following resources to assess student mastery of regular and irregular comparative forms.

In the Textbook	Technology
Chapter Review, Ex. 25–27, p. 636	*Language Lab* CD-ROM, Using Modifiers; *On-Line Exercise Bank,* Section 24.1

Write this sentence on the board:

Jason's short story is not as interesting as Mindy.

Ask students to explain precisely what this sentence means. (Mindy is not as interesting as Jason's story.) Ask if this meaning is what the writer probably intended. (Students will probably infer that Mindy must have written a story that was more interesting than Jason's.) Then have students reword the sentence so it make sense. (*as Mindy's,* or *as Mindy's story*)

Activate Prior Knowledge

Write these sentences on the board, and have students explain what, if anything, is wrong with each one.

Her wallet is more newer than mine. (double comparison: *more newer*)

Liz has more money than any girl I know. (illogical comparison: Liz is a girl that I know.)

TEACH

Step-by-Step Teaching Guide

Using Comparative and Superlative Degrees

1. Emphasize to students that simple addition will help them decide whether to use the comparative or superlative degree. For example, use the comparative for two persons, places, or things, and use the superlative for three or more persons, places, or things.

2. Survey possible mistakes in using comparative and superlative degrees. First, remind students to avoid using both *-er* and *more* or both *-est* and *most* to form comparisons. Ask why it would be incorrect to say "He is more faster than I."

Section 24.2

Making Clear Comparisons

Once you have mastered the forms of regular and irregular modifiers, you can learn how to use these forms to make clear comparisons. In this section, you will learn how to use the comparative and superlative degrees correctly, how to make logical comparisons, and how to recognize modifiers that should not be used in comparisons.

Using Comparative and Superlative Degrees

One basic rule covers the correct use of comparative and superlative forms:

▶ **KEY CONCEPT** Use the comparative degree to compare two persons, places, or things. Use the superlative degree to compare three or more persons, places, or things. ■

It is not necessary to mention specific numbers when making a comparison. The context of the sentence should indicate whether two items or more than two items are being compared.

COMPARATIVE: My broker is *more* dependable than Florence's.
My portfolio is *larger* than his.
He requires *less* money than she does.

SUPERLATIVE: That is the *most* dependable broker I know.
This is the *largest* portfolio I have ever had.
He requires the *least* possible number of material things to make him happy.

Occasionally, the superlative degree is used just for emphasis, without any specific comparison. This usage is more acceptable in informal writing than in formal writing.

EXAMPLES: He is the *greatest*!
She was *most treacherously* betrayed.

Note About *Double Comparisons:* A *double comparison* is an error in usage caused by using both *-er* and *more* or both *-est* and *most* to form a regular modifier. A double comparison can also be caused by adding *-er, -est, more,* or *most* to a modifier that is irregular.

INCORRECT: Your workload is *more heavier* than mine.
That stock is performing *worser* than ever.

CORRECT: Your workload is *heavier* than mine.
That stock is performing *worse* than ever.

628 • Using Modifiers

Theme: New York Stock Exchange

In this section, you will learn about using logical comparisons and avoiding absolute modifiers. The examples and exercises in this section are about the New York Stock Exchange.

Cross-Curricular Connection: Social Studies

⏱ TIME AND RESOURCE MANAGER

Resources
Print: *Grammar Exercise Workbook,* pp. 129–134; *Grammar Exercises Answers on Transparency,* Ch. 24
Technology: *Language Lab* CD-ROM, Using Modifiers; *On-Line Exercise Bank,* Section 24.2

In-Depth Coverage	Accelerated Pace
• Work through all key concepts, pp. 628–633. • Assign and review Exercise 14–18. • *Hands-on Grammar* activity, p. 634.	• Assign pp. 628–633 for independent student review. • Assign Section Review Exercises 19–21.

Exercise 14 **Supplying the Comparative and Superlative Degrees** Write the appropriate comparative or superlative degree of the modifier in parentheses.
1. Many people think stocks are (good) than bonds.
2. Some investments are (risky) than others.
3. Stocks often have the (big) financial yield.
4. The (safe) way to invest is to choose low-risk investments.
5. The number of companies selling stocks on the New York Stock Exchange is continually growing (large).
6. Investors who believe stock prices will soar (high) than current levels are called bulls.
7. On the other hand, investors called bears think prices will fall (low).
8. Investors are (confident) during a bull market than a bear market.
9. The (important) feature of any stock exchange is the trading floor.
10. Visitors to the New York Stock Exchange may think the activity on the floor is (confusing) than it actually is.

Exercise 15 **Revising Sentences to Correct Errors in Modifier Usage** Rewrite each sentence, correcting any errors in the usage of comparative modifiers.
1. Each worker on the floor seems to be trying to shout more louder than the others.
2. However, the activity is most organized than it appears.
3. The loud shouting allows more wide participation in trades than one might think.
4. It is the fairer way to determine stock prices competitively.
5. Because of the high volume of trading done, it is essential that the New York Stock Exchange have the advanced technology available.
6. The mostest money ever paid for a seat on the Exchange was almost $1.5 million.
7. The more famous instance of falling stock prices was the Wall Street crash of 1929.
8. The long shutdown in the history of the Exchange was in 1914.
9. Founded in 1792, the New York Stock Exchange is sixteen years youngest than our nation.
10. It is the largest stock market in the world.

More Practice

Language Lab CD-ROM
• Forms of Comparison lesson
On-line Exercise Bank
• Section 24.2
Grammar Exercise Workbook
• pp. 129–130

▲ Critical Viewing
Use comparative modifiers to connect the architecture of the New York Stock Exchange building with the architecture of ancient Greek temples. [Connect]

Clear Comparisons • **629**

Answer Key

▶ **Exercise 14**
1. better
2. riskier, more risky
3. biggest
4. safest
5. larger
6. higher
7. lower
8. more confident
9. most important
10. more confusing

▶ **Exercise 15**
1. louder
2. more organized
3. wider
4. fairest
5. most advanced
6. most
7. most famous
8. longest
9. younger
10. largest

Critical Viewing

Connect Sample comparative words: *older, larger, sturdier, taller*.

Integrating Workplace Skills

Remind students that in many purchasing situations, customers will be comparing two or more items. As a salesperson, it is necessary to understand the comparisons buyers are making to ensure that they receive the proper merchandise. Ask students to create several sentences involving comparisons in a buying situation.

✓ ONGOING ASSESSMENT: Monitor and Reinforce

If students miss more than two items in Exercise 14 or 15, refer them to the following for additional practice.

In the Textbook	Print Resources	Technology
Section Review, Ex. 19, p. 635	*Grammar Exercise Workbook,* pp. 129–130	*Language Lab* CD-ROM, Using Modifiers; *On-Line Exercise Bank,* Section 24.2

⏱ TIME SAVERS!

Answers on Transparencies Use the *Grammar Exercises Answers on Transparencies* for Chapter 24 to facilitate correction by students.

On-Line Exercise Bank Have students complete the exercises on computer. The Auto Check feature will grade their work for you!

Logical Comparisons

1. Explain how an unbalanced comparison occurs: A writer leaves out an important piece of information on one side of a comparison, thereby confusing or misleading the reader.

2. Discuss the example sentences with students. For each sentence, have students tell why the comparison is unbalanced. (Example: In the first, the writer does not intend to compare *Ray* himself with *Jim's portfolio*.) Ask students to identify the missing information. (The writer meant to specify Ray's portfolio, not Ray.) Then ask for solutions. (Add *'s* to Ray or write *Ray's portfolio*.)

continued

Customize for
Verbal/Linguistic Learners

Ask students to listen for balanced and unbalanced comparisons. Create a brief list of seven or eight sentences—some balanced, some unbalanced—or start with these:

Dad's cooking abilities are better than Mom.

Are my eyes greener than Jean?

I like my room more than my sister's.

The legs of a horse are longer than a dog.

Tell students that you are going to read each sentence aloud, sometimes correctly and sometimes incorrectly, and that they should repeat each sentence after you. Tell them to simply repeat it if it is correct, or to revise it and speak the corrected version.

Critical Viewing

Analyze, Draw Conclusions Sample answer: Some workers type more efficiently than others type. His computer is faster than hers.

24.2

Using Logical Comparisons

Two common usage problems involving comparisons are the comparison of unrelated items and the comparison of something with itself.

Balanced Comparisons When you write a comparison, be certain that the two or more things being compared are properly balanced. Otherwise, the comparison may be illogical and even ridiculous.

KEY CONCEPT Make sure that your sentences compare only items of a similar kind. ■

In the following unbalanced sentences, the sentences illogically compare dissimilar things.

UNBALANCED: *Jim's portfolio* is better balanced than *Ray*.
BALANCED: *Jim's portfolio* is better balanced than *Ray's*.

UNBALANCED: The *yield from this stock* is higher than *a bond*.
BALANCED: The *yield from this stock* is higher than the *yield from a bond*.

UNBALANCED: The *damage* from the panic of 1907 was less than the *one* in 1929.
BALANCED: The *damage* from the panic of 1907 was less than *that* from the crash of 1929.

As you can see, *portfolio* cannot be compared to *Ray*, a stock's *yield* cannot be compared to a whole *bond*, and *damage* from a panic cannot be compared to a *panic*. In the last set of examples, note the use of pronouns. The first sentence is incorrect because *one* refers to *panic* rather than to *damage*.

▶ **Critical Viewing**
Use logical comparisons to describe the skills required to perform the tasks shown in this photograph. [**Analyze, Draw Conclusions**]

630 • Using Modifiers

Exercise 16 **Revising Unbalanced Comparisons** Rewrite each sentence, correcting the unbalanced comparison.

EXAMPLE: Emily's stock was more profitable than Luke.
ANSWER: Emily's stock was more profitable than Luke's.

1. The New York Stock Exchange is larger than London.
2. The stock market crash of 1929 was more severe than 1907.
3. The New York Stock Exchange became more important in 1918 than 1914.
4. The number of companies listed on the Exchange now is greater than 1970.
5. We have more advanced technology today than twenty years ago.
6. Information on the stock market is more accessible today than the past.
7. The value of my stock is higher than your stock.
8. The dividends on this stock are lower than that one.
9. Today's investor has greater awareness of the workings of the Exchange than yesterday.
10. Ellen's investments are less risky than Michael.

Other and *Else* in Comparisons

Other and Else in Comparisons Another illogical comparison, which is similar to an unbalanced comparison, results when something is inadvertently compared with itself.

KEY CONCEPT When comparing one of a group with the rest of the group, make sure that your sentence contains the word *other* or the word *else*. ■

Adding *other* or *else* in such situations will make the comparison clear.

ILLOGICAL: John was *busier than any* broker on the floor.
LOGICAL: John was *busier than any other* broker on the floor.

ILLOGICAL: Ruth worked *harder than anyone* in the office.
LOGICAL: Ruth worked *harder than anyone else* in the office.

In the first set of examples, because *John* is one of the brokers on the floor, he cannot logically be compared to all of the brokers, as that group includes himself. The addition of *other* excludes John from the rest of the brokers. In the second set, *Ruth* cannot be compared to all the workers in the office because she herself is one of those workers. The addition of *else* excludes her from the rest of the group.

▶ **More Practice**

Language Lab CD-ROM
• Forms of Comparison lesson
On-line Exercise Bank
• Section 24.2
Grammar Exercise Workbook
• pp. 131–132

🔁 **Learn More**

To review adjectives and adverbs, see Section 17.3, Adjectives and Adverbs.

Clear Comparisons • 631

Step-by-Step Teaching Guide continued

3. Note that the words *other* or *else* are used to help compare one person, place, or thing with the rest of its group.
4. Mention that comparisons within a group are frequently stated incorrectly, especially in informal speech. This error should be avoided in writing.

Answer Key

▶ **Exercise 16**

1. London's
2. that of 1907
3. it had been in 1914
4. it was in 1970
5. than we had twenty years ago
6. in the past (it was in the past)
7. that of your stock (your stock's)
8. on that one (the dividends on that one)
9. yesterday's investor had
10. Michael's

Customize for
Logical/Mathematical Learners

Place the following on the board:

Mary sang louder than anyone in the chorus.

Mary sang louder than anyone else in the chorus.

Next, draw one large square labeled *chorus*. Inside of it insert a smaller circle and label it *M* for *Mary*. Explain that if Mary is a member of the chorus (a subset), she cannot logically be compared to herself.

Then draw one large square labeled *chorus* and adjacent to it a smaller circle labeled *M* for *Mary*. Point out that here Mary is separate from the chorus; she is not a part of it.

Return to the two sentences. Ask which diagram matches the first sentence. (Mary outside the square.) Then ask which diagram matches the second sentence. (Mary inside the square.)

✅ **ONGOING ASSESSMENT: Monitor and Reinforce**

If students miss more than two items in Exercise 16, refer them to the following for additional practice.

In the Textbook	Print Resources	Technology
Section Review, Ex. 20, p. 635	*Grammar Exercise Workbook*, pp. 131–132	*Language Lab* CD-ROM, Using Modifiers; *On-Line Exercise Bank*, Section 24.2

24.2

▶ **Exercise 17** Revising Sentences Using *Other* and *Else* **Correctly in Comparisons** Rewrite each sentence, using *other* or *else* to correct the illogical comparison.

EXAMPLE: The New York Stock Exchange is larger than any exchange.

ANSWER: The New York Stock Exchange is larger than any other exchange.

1. Establishing a stock exchange is fairer than any way to set stock prices.
2. The New York Stock Exchange is more famous than any exchange.
3. There are more stock trades there than anywhere.
4. New York City has a greater impact on the nation's economy than any city has.
5. A secure investment is better than any kind.
6. An industry analyst is often better informed about a certain stock than anyone.
7. There is greater public participation in the market now than at any time.
8. One of the principles of the New York Stock Exchange is to ensure that small investors are treated the same as everyone.
9. The corporate stock of one New York City bank is older than that of any bank.
10. Information on the Exchange travels faster now than at any time.

632 • Using Modifiers

▲ **Critical Viewing** Based on this picture, how do you imagine working on the New York Stock Exchange compares with any jobs you have had? **[Compare and Contrast]**

▶ **More Practice**

Language Lab CD-ROM
• Forms of Comparison lesson
On-line Exercise Bank
• Section 24.2
Grammar Exercise Workbook
• pp. 131–132

Avoiding Comparisons With Absolute Modifiers

Some modifiers cannot be used logically to make comparisons because their meanings are *absolute*—that is, their meanings are entirely contained in the positive degree. For example, if a line is *vertical*, another line cannot be *more* vertical. Either a line is vertical or it is not; there are no degrees of verticality. Some other common absolute modifiers are *dead, entirely, fatal, final, identical, opposite, perfect,* and *unique*.

Often, it is not only the word *more* or *most* that makes an absolute modifier illogical; sometimes an absolute modifier alone is illogical in the context of a sentence. In such cases, it is best to replace the absolute modifier with one that expresses the intended meaning more precisely.

> **KEY CONCEPT** Avoid using absolute modifiers illogically in comparisons. ■

ILLOGICAL: Of all the stock market panics, that one was *the most fatal.*

CORRECT: Of all the stock market panics, that one was the *most severe.*

In the preceding example, *the most fatal* is illogical because something is either fatal or it is not. However, even *fatal* by itself would be an illogical overstatement. *Most severe* better conveys the intended meaning.

> **Exercise 18**   **Revising Sentences to Avoid Comparisons Using Absolute Modifiers**   Correct the illogical comparison in each sentence by replacing the absolute modifier with one or more other words.

1. Some people believe that the stock exchange is the most perfect method of setting prices.
2. It is one of the most unique expressions of capitalism.
3. The most dead time on Wall Street is after the Stock Exchange closes.
4. The American Exchange is identical to the New York Stock Exchange.
5. The Hong Kong Exchange is on the most opposite side of the world from New York City.
6. Specialists are entirely knowledgeable about their particular stocks.
7. They usually have more complete company information than other brokers.
8. Making a profit is the more ultimate desire of investors.
9. One final answer to a robust economy is a strong stock exchange.
10. The crash of 1929 was most fatal to the U.S. economy.

⚙ Grammar and Style Tip

An absolute modifier can never be more or less absolute than it is. Never use the suffix *-er* or *-est* or the words *more* or *most* with an absolute modifier.

> **More Practice**
>
> **Language Lab CD-ROM**
> • Forms of Comparison lesson
> **On-line Exercise Bank**
> • Section 24.2
> **Grammar Exercise Workbook**
> • pp. 133–134

Clear Comparisons • 633

✓ ONGOING ASSESSMENT: Monitor and Reinforce

If students miss more than two items in Exercise 18, refer them to the following for additional practice.

In the Textbook	Print Resources	Technology
Section Review, Ex. 21, p. 635	*Grammar Exercise Workbook,* pp. 133–134	*Language Lab* CD-ROM, Using Modifiers; *On-Line Exercise Bank,* Section 24.2

Hands-on Grammar

Teaching Resources: Hands-on Grammar Activity Book, Ch. 24

1. If you wish to do this activity in class, be prepared with scissors, a ruler, and construction paper.

2. Have students follow the directions to prepare and label the window and shutters.

3. Have students also prepare the strip. Use the words suggested in the activity, or have the class come up with others. Note that this activity works best with modifiers having regular comparative forms.

4. To vary the activity slightly, have students work with modifiers in which a spelling change is required before endings are added. Examples include *flat, red, tidy, noisy.*

Hands-on Grammar

Adjective and Adverb Window Shutters

Practice forming the comparative and superlative forms by doing the following activity:

Cut out a piece of paper approximately 3" x 7". Fold two sides in to form shutters, as shown in the illustration, leaving a space in the middle. Cut two slots about 1" wide, as shown. Under the left shutter, write *more* and *most*. Under the right shutter, write *-er* and *-est*.

On a strip of paper about 1" wide, list adjectives and adverbs, such as *clear, precious, just, incredible, arbitrarily, slow, meaningful, dirty, strict, clever.* Feed the strip of paper through the slots as shown, making sure that a word shows in the window.

Now, decide whether the modifier forms its comparative and superlative degrees with *more* and *most* or with *-er* and *-est.* First, close the right shutter to cover up *-er* and *-est,* and say the word with *more* and with *most.* Then, close the left shutter, and try the word with *-er* and *-est.* By always closing one shutter, you will avoid forming a double comparison. Decide how the comparative and superlative degrees are formed. If you are unsure, consult a dictionary.

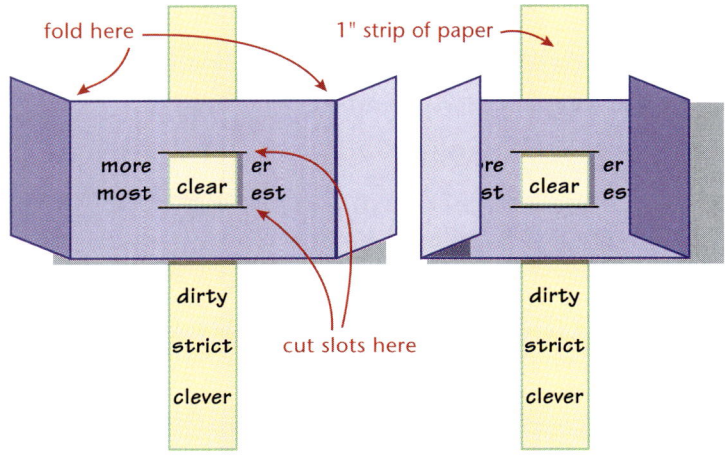

Find It in Your Reading Choose modifiers from a short story you are reading. Create a new strip to use with the window shutters.

Find It in Your Writing Review a piece of writing in your portfolio. Check to see that you have correctly used the comparative and superlative forms of adjectives and adverbs. If you have not used the comparative or superlative of at least two modifiers, challenge yourself to add at least two comparisons to your writing.

634 • Using Modifiers

⏲ TIME SAVERS!

Hands-on Grammar
Use the Hands-on Grammar activity sheet for Chapter 24 to facilitate this activity.

✎ STANDARDIZED TEST PREPARATION WORKSHOP

Grammar and Usage Many standardized tests require students to recognize usage errors within the context of a passage. Use the following example to demonstrate.

Which sentence is correct?

A *John is faster than any runner on his track team.*

B *John is faster than all runners on his track team.*

C *John is faster than any other runner on his track team.*

D *John is faster than any track team member.*

The correct answer is **C.** Because John is part of the group, his track team, he cannot be faster than himself; therefore, he can only be faster than any other member.

Section 24.2 Section Review

GRAMMAR EXERCISES 19–24

Exercise 19 **Using Comparative and Superlative Forms Correctly** Write the appropriate comparative or superlative degree of the modifier in parentheses.

1. The 1929 Wall Street crash was the (devastating) financial crisis ever.
2. The (sad) outcome of the crash was the Great Depression.
3. The New York Stock Exchange is one of the (great) examples of capitalism.
4. Brokers who work there are some of the (busy) people in New York City.
5. Most businesses open at 9:00 A.M., but the Exchange opens (late) than that.
6. The fast pace of trading is (stressful) than some jobs.
7. Nonetheless, many brokers are (happy) in this occupation than they would be in another.
8. At six and a half hours, the trading day is (short) than most working days.
9. The (wise) thing you can do before investing is to consult an expert.
10. It is (easy) to lose money in the stock market than to make it.

Exercise 20 **Revising Illogical Comparisons** Rewrite each sentence, correcting the illogical comparison.

1. Is money in a bank safer than the market?
2. Investing in the market can be riskier than the bank.
3. The profits from that company are larger than last year.
4. Your broker's picks have performed better than my broker.
5. He is more cautious than anyone.
6. As a result, there is less risk with his picks than with any broker.
7. Investing in overseas companies can be riskier than in the United States.
8. Some believe that emerging markets abroad are more risky than anywhere.
9. You can get more return on these companies than on any investments.
10. With care, you can make more money than anyone with this type of trading.

Exercise 21 **Revising to Avoid Absolute Modifiers** Rewrite each sentence, replacing the absolute modifier to correct the illogical comparison.

1. What is the most ultimate price you will pay for that stock?
2. If it does not do well, it will be pretty fatal to your finances.
3. It would be more perfect if the price went up.
4. Do you have absolute complete confidence in your broker?
5. Please confirm that selling those stocks is your most final decision.

Exercise 22 **Find It in Your Reading** Reread the excerpt from "Sinners in the Hands of an Angry God" on page 622. Find one adjective in the comparative and one in the positive degree. Write the other comparative forms for each word.

Exercise 23 **Find It in Your Writing** Look through your writing portfolio for several examples of adjectives in the comparative and in the superlative degrees. Make sure that your comparisons are logical.

Exercise 24 **Writing Application** Write a comparison of two businesses that you patronize. Use modifiers in the comparative degree, and make sure that your comparisons are clear and logical.

Section Review • 635

ASSESS and CLOSE

Section Review

Each of these exercises correlates to a section on clear comparisons, pages 628–634. The exercises may be used for more practice, for reteaching, or for review of the key concepts presented.

Answer Key

Exercise 19

1. most devastating
2. saddest
3. greatest
4. busiest
5. later
6. more stressful
7. happier
8. shorter
9. wisest
10. easier

Exercise 20

Answers will vary; samples are given.

1. than it is in the market
2. than depositing money in the bank
3. than they were last year
4. than my broker's picks
5. than anyone else
6. than with any other broker's
7. than investing in companies in the United States
8. more risky than those anywhere else
9. than on any other investments
10. more money than anyone else with this type of trading

Exercise 21

Answers will vary; samples are given.

1. the highest price
2. will be damaging to your
3. would be beneficial if
4. have the strongest confidence
5. your firm decision

Exercise 22

Find It in Your Reading

Answers will vary; samples are given.

Comparative: greater (great, greatest)
Positive: inconceivable (more inconceivable, most inconceivable)

Exercise 23

Find It in Your Writing

Comparisons should be clear, and modifiers should be in their correct form.

Exercise 24

Writing Application

When students have finished, have them work with partners to identify the comparisons in each other's work.

Answer Key

continued

GRAMMAR EXERCISES 25–32

▶ **Exercise 25** Recognizing Positive, Comparative, and Superlative Degrees
Identify the degree of the underlined modifier.

1. The world of business can be <u>complex</u>.
2. People in business have to think <u>more globally</u> now than ever before.
3. The <u>tiniest</u> fluctuation in a foreign market can have a profound effect on the economy of our country.
4. Companies have to be <u>more aware</u> of what is going on in other parts of the world.
5. Technology is the <u>best</u> way to keep current.

▶ **Exercise 26** Forming Irregular Comparative and Superlative Degrees
Write the correct form of the underlined modifier to complete each sentence.

1. The economy is doing <u>well</u>, but it could be doing ___?___.
2. My broker has <u>little</u> confidence in this stock and even ___?___ in that one.
3. This branch office is <u>far</u> away, but that one is the ___?___ of them all.
4. He has gone <u>far</u> in business, and if he works hard he will go even ___?___.
5. She was <u>late</u> for the meeting, but I arrived the ___?___.
6. This company has <u>many</u> investments, but that company has ___?___.
7. Business is doing <u>badly</u>; it is the ___?___ it has ever been.
8. He felt <u>ill</u> when he read the stock report, and if business doesn't improve, he will only feel ___?___.
9. The London branch is doing <u>well</u>, but the New York branch is doing ___?___ of all.
10. London is <u>far</u> from New York, but Hong Kong is even ___?___ away.

▶ **Exercise 27** Supplying the Correct Comparative and Superlative Degrees Write the appropriate degree of the modifier in parentheses.

1. The (great) desire of business owners is to make a profit.
2. However, an even (noble) goal is to benefit the consumer.
3. The Industrial Revolution caused ways of doing business to change (dramatically) than ever before.
4. The changes came (rapidly) in the twentieth century than they did in the previous one.
5. Generally, change occurred (slow) in the 1800's than it did in the 1900's.
6. Many feel that to own their own business is the (high) goal they can achieve.
7. It may be (difficult) than they imagine.
8. It is often (hard) for an individual to get financing than it is for a large corporation.
9. Because they bear full responsibility for debts, individual owners are (likely) to fail than large corporations are.
10. For some entrepreneurs, the (good) approach of all is to form a partnership or a corporation.

▶ **Exercise 28** Making Logical Comparisons Rewrite each sentence, correcting the illogical comparisons.

1. Business is more complicated now than during the Industrial Revolution.
2. The Industrial Revolution has had a greater impact on the way business is conducted than any event in history.
3. Some believe that James Watt's contribution to the Industrial Revolution is greater than anyone else.
4. There was a greater focus on manufacturing at that time than on anything.

---

5. The Industrial Revolution began earlier in England than the United States.
6. The changes to society caused by the Industrial Revolution were more than the Agricultural Revolution.
7. Prior to the Industrial Revolution, agriculture was more important to the economy than any business.
8. With the shift to manufacturing, there was more unemployment than the Agricultural Revolution.
9. England became more industrialized than anywhere.
10. Today, there are more rules governing the operation of businesses than at any time.

Exercise 29   Revising to Avoid Absolute Modifiers in Comparisons

Rewrite each sentence, correcting the illogical comparisons.

1. The effects of the Depression were very fatal to the United States.
2. Industrial nations were more completely affected than other nations.
3. The Depression seemed pretty endless to most Americans.
4. World War II was most ultimately responsible for ending the Depression.
5. After the war, people looked forward to relatively perfect economic conditions.

Exercise 30   Revising to Use All the Rules of Clear Comparisons

Revise the following sentences, correcting any illogical and unbalanced comparisons.

1. Up-to-date technology is one of the more fundamental business needs.
2. Technology allows the most fastest transfer of information.
3. Today, speedy communication is far important than even a decade ago.
4. The most successful companies often have the more current technology.
5. They usually treat their employees more better than less successful companies do.

6. Sometimes, business activity is slower than others.
7. This slowing down often occurs when there are more products for sale than people.
8. Prices may be lower than a thriving economy.
9. More people were unemployed during the Great Depression than the 1920's.
10. The effects of the Depression were worse in the United States than the rest of the world.

Exercise 31   Writing Application

Write a paper comparing two jobs or careers that you might like to pursue one day. Be sure to use correct comparative and superlative forms of adjectives and adverbs and to avoid any illogical or absolute comparisons.

Exercise 32   CUMULATIVE REVIEW

Sentence Errors; Agreement Errors; Adjective and Adverb Usage Errors Revise the following paragraph.

Among the most important inventions of the twentieth century were the assembly line. Originated in the early 1900's by Henry Ford. This means of production made it possible to manufacture goods more faster than before. Machinery or other articles was produced in large numbers. Replacement parts would now fit most perfectly. On an assembly line, each worker does their special task. You must work quickly and exactly. Workers are often more skilled at one task than any. The assembly of a car is similar to a truck. As a result of mass production, jobs became most plentiful and the economy expanded.

5. than it did in the United States
6. than those caused by the Agricultural Revolution
7. than any other business
8. than there was during the Agricultural Revolution
9. than anywhere else
10. than at any other time

Exercise 29

Answers will vary; samples are given.

1. were devastating to
2. more greatly affected
3. seemed very long
4. most responsible
5. to better economic

Exercise 30

Answers will vary; samples are given.

1. most fundamental business needs
2. fastest transfer of information
3. far more important
4. most current technology
5. better
6. than at other times
7. than people who want to buy them
8. than they are during a thriving economy
9. than in the 1920s
10. than in the rest of the world

Exercise 31

Writing Application
Papers should demonstrate correct use and form of comparatives and superlatives, and all comparisons should be logical.

Exercise 32

Cumulative Review
Answers will vary. Sample answer:

Among the most important inventions of the twentieth century <u>was</u> the assembly line. Originated in the early 1900s by Henry Ford, <u>this</u> means of production made it possible to manufacture goods <u>faster</u> than before. Machinery or other articles <u>were</u> produced in large numbers. Replacement parts would now fit <u>very well</u>. On an assembly line, each worker does <u>his or her</u> special task. <u>He or she</u> must work quickly and exactly. Workers are often more skilled at one task than <u>at any other</u>. The assembly of a car is similar to <u>that of</u> a truck. As a result of mass production, jobs became <u>more</u> plentiful and the economy expanded.

Step-by-Step Teaching Guide

Standard English Usage: Using Modifiers

Teaching Resources: Standardized Test Preparation Workbook, pp. 47–48

1. Remind students how to decide whether to form comparatives and superlatives with *more* or *most* or by adding *–er* or *–est* to the root modifier: For words of three or more syllables, use *more* or *most*. For most one- or two-syllable words, add *–er* or *–est*.

2. Briefly review the comparative and superlative forms of irregular modifiers such as *good, well, bad, badly, much, many, far,* and *little*.

3. Encourage students to read test instructions carefully. Not all standardized tests are graded in the same way. Some tests do not penalize students for incorrect answers so that students may increase their scores with a judicious guess.

4. You may wish to provide students with standardized test answer sheets to practice the mechanics of marking in answers.

Standardized Test Preparation Workshop

Standard English Usage: Using Modifiers

Standardized test questions often measure your ability to use modifiers correctly. One way this is done is to test your ability to choose the correct form of comparison to complete a sentence. Use the following strategies to help you determine which form to use in a sentence:

- If no comparison is being made, use the **positive form** of the modifier.

- If one thing or action is compared to another thing or action, use the **comparative form** of the modifier— ending in *-er* or preceded by *more*.

- If one thing or action is being compared to more than one other thing or action, use the **superlative form** of the modifier—ending in *-est* or preceded by *most*.

- Be aware that some modifiers have **special forms,** such as *good, bad, much,* and *many*.

Test Tip

Be careful not to choose a double comparison, such as *more easier,* to complete a sentence. The correct forms are *more easy* or *easier*.

Sample Test Items	Answers and Explanations

Directions: Read the passage, and choose the word or group of words that belongs in each space.
 	
Baseball has always been considered the ___(1)___ of all sports. It is often called the national pastime, a name that implies that it is ___(2)___ than basketball.
 	
1   A   Americanest
      B   more American
      C   most American
      D   mostest American
	The correct answer for item 1 is *C, most American.* The comparison is being made between baseball and all other sports, so the superlative form should be used.

2   F   more popular
      G   most popular
      H   popularer
      J   popularest
	The correct answer for item 2 is *F, more popular.* The comparison is being made between baseball and basketball, so the comparative form should be used.

638 • Using Modifiers

⬦ TEST-TAKING TIP

Suggest that students use this approach to questions that contain a written passage with blanks to fill: As students read the passage, they should be alert for clues that indicate how the blanks should be filled. Are the blanks in positions where a verb should appear or where a modifier would fit? Does the blank modify a noun, a verb, or an adjective? Are there words that signal the need for a comparative form rather than a superlative form? Encourage students to jot notes in the test booklet. If students decide what they are looking for before they look at the answer set, they will be less vulnerable to distractors that are designed to lead them astray.

Practice 1 **Directions:** Read the passage, and choose the word or group of words that belongs in each space.

Baseball depends ____(1)____ on working as a team than sports that are performed individually, such as tennis or swimming. Although some players may perform ____(2)____ than others, the game can only be won if everyone works together. Even after playing his or her ____(3)____ game, a player still can take comfort in the success of the team. Everyone can have a ____(4)____ game, but the day can be a little ____(5)____ painful with the support of teammates and the success of the team.

1 **A** many
  B more
  C much
  D most

2 **F** good
  G better
  H best
  J more better

3 **A** bad
  B badly
  C worst
  D worse

4 **F** bad
  G badly
  H worse
  J worst

5 **A** less
  B little
  C least
  D littler

Practice 2 **Directions:** Read the passage, and choose the word or group of words that belongs in each space.

One player on the team may be able to hit the ball ____(1)____ than any other player. Another player may be a ____(2)____ pitcher than the rest, and someone else may perform ____(3)____ at first base than at any other position. No matter what his or her role is, each member contributes to the overall effort of the team. The ____(4)____ contributions of a player are to be dependable and supportive. If each member tries his or her ____(5)____, then the team will be a success.

1 **A** far
  B farther
  C further
  D most far

2 **F** good
  G better
  H best
  J more better

3 **A** well
  B better
  C best
  D good

4 **F** important
  G more important
  H most important
  J importantest

5 **A** hard
  B harder
  C hardest
  D more hard

Practice 1
1. B
2. G
3. C
4. F
5. A

Practice 2
1. B
2. G
3. B
4. H
5. C

In-Depth Lesson Plan

	LESSON FOCUS	PRINT AND MEDIA RESOURCES
DAY 1	**Negative Sentences** Students learn to recognize double negatives, to properly form negatives, to achieve understatement, and do a Hands-on Grammar activity. (pp. 642–647)	*On-Line Exercise Bank,* Section 25.1 *Language Lab* **CD-ROM,** Using Modifiers **Teaching Resources** *Grammar Exercise Workbook,* pp. 135–138; *Grammar Exercises Answers on Transparencies,* Ch. 25; *Hands-on Grammar Activity Book,* Ch. 25
DAY 2	**Common Usage Problems** Students learn to avoid common mistakes, such as nonstandard usage (e.g., *irregardless*) and easily-confused words (e.g., *accept/except*) and practice correct usage. (pp. 648–655)	*On-Line Exercise Bank,* Section 25.2 **Teaching Resources** *Grammar Exercise Workbook,* p. 139
DAY 3	**Common Usage Problems** Students learn to avoid common mistakes, such as nonstandard usage (e.g., *like/as*) and easily-confused words (e.g., *then/than*), and practice correct usage. (pp. 656–661)	**Teaching Resources** *Grammar Exercise Workbook,* p. 140
DAY 4	**Review and Assess** Students review chapter and demonstrate mastery of common usage problems. (pp. 662–665)	**Teaching Resources** *Formal Assessment,* Ch. 25

Accelerated Lesson Plan

	LESSON FOCUS	PRINT AND MEDIA RESOURCES
DAY 1	**Negative Sentences; Common Usage Problems** Students cover double negatives, properly formed negative sentences, understatement, and common usage problems. (pp. 642–655)	*On-Line Exercise Bank,* Sections 25.1–25.2 *Language Lab* **CD-ROM,** Using Modifiers **Teaching Resources** *Grammar Exercise Workbook,* pp. 135–138; *Grammar Exercises Answers on Transparencies,* Ch. 25
DAY 2	**Common Usage Problems; Review and Assess** Students complete study of common usage problems, then review entire chapter and demonstrate mastery of concepts. (pp. 656–665)	*On-Line Exercise Bank,* Section 25.2 **Teaching Resources** *Grammar Exercise Workbook,* pp. 139–140; *Formal Assessment,* Ch. 25

Options for Adapting Lesson Plans

HOMEWORK

Have students complete any section of the chapter for homework.

FEATURES

Extend coverage with the Standardized Test Preparation Workshop (p. 664).

TECHNOLOGY

Students can use the *On-Line Exercise Bank* to complete the exercises on computer. The Auto Check feature will grade their work.

INTEGRATED SKILLS COVERAGE

Writing
Find It in Your Writing SE pp. 646, 647, 661
Writing Application SE pp. 647, 661, 663
Grammar and Style SE pp. 644, 652

Spelling
SE pp. 657, 659, ATE p. 658

Viewing and Representing
Critical Viewing, SE pp. 640, 645, 649, 651, 654, 657, 660

Speaking and Listening SE p. 655

Technology
SE pp. 643, 645

Vocabulary ATE p. 659

Language Highlight ATE p. 655

Workplace Skills
ATE p. 656

ASSESSMENT SUPPORT

Standardized Test Preparation Workshop SE p. 664; ATE pp. 643, 658

Standardized Test Preparation Workbook, pp. 49–50

Formal Assessment, Ch. 25

MEETING INDIVIDUAL NEEDS

Less Advanced Students ATE p.643. See also Ongoing Assessments ATE pp. 644, 645, 649, 660.

AP Students ATE p. 649

ESL Students ATE pp. 645, 654, 659

Logical/Mathematical Learners ATE p. 642

Verbal/Linguistic Learners ATE p. 652

Visual/Spatial Learners ATE p. 652

BLOCK SCHEDULING

Pacing Suggestions
For 90-minute Blocks
- Administer the Diagnostic Test to students to determine instructional coverage.
- Have students complete the necessary exercises in class. Use the Hands-on Grammar activity to provide a change of pace.

Resources for Varying Instruction
- On-Line Exercise Bank If your students have access to hardware, a 90-minute block provides an ideal opportunity for students to work on computer.

Professional Development Support
- How to Manage Instruction in the Block This Teaching Resource provides management and activity suggestions.

MEDIA AND TECHNOLOGY

For the Student
- On-Line Exercise Bank, Sections 25.1–2

For the Teacher
- Resource Pro CD-ROM

WRITING AND GRAMMAR WEB SITE

The Interactive Writing and Grammar Web Site provides a wide array of support for students, teachers, and parents. Grammar support includes:

- On-Line Exercise Bank with Auto Check scoring
- Diagnostic and assessment support

www.phschool.com

Lesson Objectives

1. To recognize double negatives and to form negative sentences correctly

2. To identify and use negatives for expressing understatement

3. To recognize and avoid common usage problems with troublesome words and expressions

4. To proofread writing for appropriateness of organization, content, style, and conventions

5. To demonstrate control over grammatical elements

6. To evaluate writing for both mechanics and content

Critical Viewing

Describe Possible answer: This picture does not show a quiet day in the country.

Chapter 25 Miscellaneous Problems in Usage

The bright lights and cacophony of sounds at a carnival can easily distract a visitor, just as usage problems can distract a reader and spoil the clarity of one's writing. Many of these problems do not fall into any of the broad categories of usage covered in preceding chapters. Some problems arise from a conflict between standard and nonstandard usage. Some words can cause problems merely because they have similar meanings or spellings. In this chapter, you will learn how to form negative sentences correctly, and you will study a list of troublesome words and expressions.

▲ **Critical Viewing**
Use a negative sentence to indicate what this scene is *not*. [**Describe**]

☑ **ONGOING ASSESSMENT: Diagnose**

If students miss more than one item in any category, direct them to the relevant pages of the textbook and assign exercises for practice and review.

Miscellaneous Problems in Usage	Diagnostic Test Items	Teach	Practice	Section Reviews	Chapter Review
Skill Check A					
Recognizing Double Negatives	A1–5	pp. 642–643	Ex. 1–3	Ex. 5–6, 8	Ex. 26–28
Skill Check B					
Using Negatives to Achieve Understatement	B6–10	p. 645	Ex. 4	Ex. 7	Ex. 29

Diagnostic Test

Directions: Write all answers on a separate sheet of paper.

Skill Check A. Choose the word in parentheses that best completes each sentence.

1. There isn't (anything, nothing) new about festivals.
2. In very ancient times, people gave thanks for harvests so that they wouldn't anger (no, any) gods.
3. The early Pilgrims (were, weren't) here but one year when they held the first Thanksgiving.
4. Today, people (can, can't) hardly wait for their Thanksgiving feasts.
5. We enjoy many other festivals now because of the many immigrants who didn't like to leave (none, any) of their cultural celebrations behind.

Skill Check B. Identify whether each of these sentences does or does not use understatement.

6. Street fairs are not uncommon in the summer months.
7. They are popular in my town.
8. Frequently, I find something of interest.
9. My friends are happy when I invite them.
10. We do not dislike street fairs.

Skill Check C. Choose the word in parentheses that best completes each sentence.

11. The first celebrations took place more (than, then) two thousand years ago.
12. The first float to (proceed, precede) down a parade route was made in Athens in the sixth century.
13. When people immigrate to a new country, they often underestimate the (affect, effect) of the move.
14. They (adopted, adapted) some old customs to a new culture.
15. For example, because cities don't have much open space, they don't have (nowhere, anywhere) to put large outdoor carnivals.
16. Nevertheless, (a lot, alot) of people do go to them.
17. Street fairs are (different from, different than) carnivals.
18. However, at both you can choose (among, between) a wide variety of food and entertainment.
19. On Independence Day, thousands turn out to celebrate the (principals, principles) on which this country was founded.
20. The parades and music have an emotional (affect, effect).
21. You can often see fireworks, (too, to).
22. My brother likes everything (accept, except) the noise.
23. (Regardless, Irregardless) of their tastes, most people enjoy these community festivities.
24. The celebrations for these holidays (teach, learn) us lessons about our cultural history.
25. We are always (anxious, eager) to attend.

✓ ONGOING ASSESSMENT: Diagnose *continued*

Miscellaneous Problems in Usage	Diagnostic Test Items	Teach	Practice	Section Review	Chapter Review
Skill Check C					
Recognizing and Avoiding Common Usage Problems	C11–25	pp. 648–659	Ex. 12–19	Ex. 20–22	Ex. 30–33
Cumulative Reviews and Applications				Ex. 9–11 Ex. 23–25	Ex. 34

Interest GRABBER On the board, write *I don't know nothing about double negatives.* Ask students to identify the two words causing trouble in the sentence (*don't, nothing*). Circle these words and ask what is wrong with the two circled words. (They are both negative, creating a double negative in the sentence.)

Activate Prior Knowledge

Ask students if they have ever heard people using double negatives. Ask for examples of sentences with double negatives. Write some examples on the board, and ask students to suggest corrections to each faulty sentence construction.

TEACH

Step-by-Step Teaching Guide

Recognizing Double Negatives

1. Have student volunteers read aloud each example in the chart.
2. Explain to students that they usually can correct any double negative by making either of the words positive.
3. Practice changing negative words to positives: *never* (ever), *didn't* (did), *none* (any), *nobody* (anybody).

Customize for
Logical/Mathematical Learners

Have students analyze the logic of some of the examples in the chart at the top of the page. For example, *Carol couldn't do no work* actually means that Carol was unable to do no work or that Carol was able to do work. Because these interpretations are the opposite of the intended meaning of the sentence, they must be incorrect.

Answer Key

Exercise 1

1. ever	6. anywhere
2. didn't	7. anyone
3. anything	8. anywhere
4. didn't	9. never
5. any	10. anything

Section 25.1 *Negative Sentences*

Recognizing Double Negatives

The use of two negative words when one is sufficient is called a *double negative.*

KEY CONCEPT Do not write sentences with double negatives. ■

Notice in the examples in the chart below that double negatives can be corrected in two ways.

CORRECTING DOUBLE NEGATIVES	
Double Negatives	**Corrections**
Tom *doesn't* like *no* carnival rides.	Tom *doesn't* like any carnival rides. Tom likes *no* carnival rides.
Nobody can't march in the parade.	*Nobody* can march in the parade. They *can't* march in the parade.
The band *never* played *none.*	The band played *none.* The band *never* played any marches.

Some sentences can correctly contain more than one negative word. Notice in the example below, however, that each clause contains only one negative word.

EXAMPLE: The girls *didn't* go to the fair because they had *no* money.

Exercise 1 **Avoiding Double Negatives** Choose the word that correctly makes each sentence negative.
1. Don't (ever, never) go to a county fair without a lot of energy.
2. I almost (did, didn't) last the whole day.
3. There wasn't (anything, nothing) I couldn't do there.
4. Without a map, I (did, didn't) know where to start.
5. At first, I couldn't find (any, no) carnival rides.
6. They weren't (anywhere, nowhere) near the food tents.
7. I didn't ask (no one, anyone) for directions.
8. My family couldn't find me (nowhere, anywhere).
9. I was (never, ever) more lost in my life.
10. Still, I didn't leave without winning (nothing, anything).

642 • Miscellaneous Problems in Usage

Theme: Festivals
In this section, you will learn how to form negatives correctly, including how to avoid using double negatives. The examples and exercises in this section are about carnivals and festivals.

Cross-Curricular Connection: Social Studies

More Practice
Language Lab CD-ROM
• Problems With Modifiers lesson
On-line Exercise Bank
• Section 25.1
Grammar Exercise Workbook
• pp. 135–136

🕐 **TIME AND RESOURCE MANAGER**

Resources
Print: *Grammar Exercise Workbook,* pp. 135–138; *Grammar Exercises Answers on Transparencies,* Ch. 25
Technology: *Language Lab* CD-ROM, Using Modifiers; *On-Line Exercise Bank,* Section 25.1

In-Depth Coverage	Accelerated Pace
• Work through all key concepts, pp. 642–645. • Assign and review Exercises 1–4. • Do the Hands-on Grammar activity, p. 646.	• Assign pp. 642–645 for independent student review. • Assign Section Review Exercises 5–8.

Forming Negative Sentences Correctly

There are three ways of making a sentence negative.

Using One Negative Word The most common method of writing negative sentences is to use a single negative word, such as *never, no, nobody, nothing, nowhere, not,* or the contraction *-n't* added to a helping verb.

▶ **KEY CONCEPT** Do not use two negative words in the same clause. ■

DOUBLE NEGATIVE:	The cotton candy <u>wasn't no</u> good.
CORRECT:	The cotton candy <u>wasn't</u> any good.
	The cotton candy was <u>bad</u>.

Using *But* in a Negative Sense *But* used negatively means *only* and should not be used with another negative word.

▶ **KEY CONCEPT** Do not use *but* in its negative sense with another negative. ■

DOUBLE NEGATIVE:	The circus <u>doesn't</u> have <u>but</u> one big top.
CORRECT:	The circus has <u>but</u> one big top.
	The circus has <u>only</u> one big top.

Using *Barely, Hardly,* and *Scarcely* Do not use these words with another negative word.

▶ **KEY CONCEPT** Do not use *barely, hardly,* or *scarcely* with another negative. ■

DOUBLE NEGATIVE:	We <u>didn't barely</u> make the minimum height requirement for the ride.
CORRECT:	We <u>barely</u> made the minimum height requirement for the ride.
DOUBLE NEGATIVE:	My family <u>doesn't hardly</u> celebrate New Year's Eve.
CORRECT:	My family <u>hardly</u> celebrates New Year's Eve.
DOUBLE NEGATIVE:	They <u>hadn't scarcely</u> seen everything before they went home.
CORRECT:	They had <u>scarcely</u> seen everything before they went home.

💻 Internet Tip

The word *not* can be used to help narrow a search on the Internet. For example, on many search engines, the search phrase "sports NOT basketball" will return only those entries that do not pertain to basketball.

Negative Sentences • 643

---

1. comes	6. Nobody
2. had	7. was
3. no	8. is
4. never	9. ever
5. was	10. anyone

▶ **Exercise 3**

Answers may vary; samples are given.

1. Many festivals and celebrations don't have rides and games.
2. Some cultural festivals celebrate but a single art form.
3. Is there anybody who hasn't heard of festivals for music, art, or literature?
4. There is no classical music enthusiast who doesn't know anything about the Salzburg festival in Austria.
5. In Copenhagen, one can scarcely be ignorant of the jazz festival held there each summer.
6. No art lover wants to miss the big art show held in Venice, Italy, every other year.
7. I saw it but once.
8. I could hardly take in all the beautiful works by international artists.
9. The yearly art show on the streets of New York City features only local artists.
10. If you have nothing to do on Saturday, let's go down to Greenwich Village and take a look at the arts and crafts.

25.1

▶ **Exercise 2**   **Avoiding Problems With Negatives**   Choose the word in parentheses that makes each sentence negative without creating a double negative.

1. Thanksgiving (doesn't come, comes) but once a year.
2. The first settlers in Jamestown, Virginia, (had, hadn't) barely survived to celebrate Thanksgiving that first year.
3. They had (no, any) feasts to celebrate.
4. Without a good harvest, which gave hope to the Plymouth colonists, there may (never, ever) have been a feast for Thanksgiving.
5. There (wasn't, was) but one crop that survived that first year: corn.
6. (Nobody, Anybody) failed to rejoice at surviving the harsh New England winter.
7. Abraham Lincoln (wasn't, was) hardly the first American after the colonists to give thanks, but he named Thanksgiving a national holiday.
8. The United States (isn't, is) hardly the only country to celebrate a day of thanks.
9. Canadians don't (never, ever) observe the Thanksgiving Day of the United States because they have their own Thanksgiving Day.
10. Hardly (no one, anyone) in the Virgin Islands fails to celebrate their Thanksgiving Day in honor of the end of the hurricane season.

▶ **Exercise 3**   **Proofreading to Correct Double Negatives**
Proofread each sentence. Then, rewrite each sentence, correcting the double negative.

1. Many festivals and celebrations don't have no rides and games.
2. Some cultural festivals don't celebrate but a single art form.
3. Is there nobody who hasn't heard of festivals for music, art, or literature?
4. There is no classical music enthusiast who doesn't know nothing about the Salzburg festival in Austria.
5. In Copenhagen, one can't scarcely be ignorant of the jazz festival held there each summer.
6. No art lover doesn't want to miss the big art show held in Venice, Italy, every other year.
7. I didn't never see it but once.
8. I couldn't hardly take in all the beautiful works by international artists.
9. The yearly art show on the streets of New York City doesn't feature but local artists.
10. If you don't have nothing to do on Saturday, let's go down to Greenwich Village and take a look at the arts and crafts.

✿ **Grammar and Style Tip**

Although double negatives are used by writers for characterization in dialogue, double negatives are nonstandard and should never be used in formal writing.

▶ **More Practice**

Language Lab CD-ROM
• Problems With Modifiers lesson
On-line Exercise Bank
• Section 25.1
Grammar Exercise Workbook
• pp. 135–136

🕐 **TIME SAVERS!**

📖 **Answers on Transparencies**
Use the *Grammar Exercises Answers on Transparencies* for Chapter 25 to facilitate correction by students.

💻 **On-Line Exercise Bank**
Have students complete the exercises on computer. The Auto Check feature will grade their work for you!

☑ **ONGOING ASSESSMENT: Monitor and Reinforce**

If students miss more than two items in Exercise 1, 2, or 3, refer them to the following for additional practice.

In the Textbook	Print Resources	Technology
Section Review, Ex. 5–6 and 8, p. 647	*Grammar Exercise Workbook*, pp. 135–138	*Language Lab* CD-ROM Using Modifiers; *On-Line Exercise Bank*, Section 25.1

Using Negatives to Achieve Understatement

Sometimes a writer wishes to express an idea indirectly, either to minimize the importance of the idea or to draw attention to it. One such technique is called *understatement*.

KEY CONCEPT Understatement can be achieved by using a negative word and a word with a negative prefix, such as *un-, in-, im-, dis-,* and *under-* ■

EXAMPLES: She was <u>hardly</u> <u>inexperienced</u> at judging contests.
Maria does <u>not</u> <u>dislike</u> the Ferris wheel.

Exercise 4   **Writing Sentences With Understatement**
Rewrite each sentence, using understatement.

EXAMPLE: The boys estimated they would have a lot of fun at the parade.
The boys <u>did not underestimate</u> the fun they would have at the parade.

1. Street fairs are a common sight in most major U.S. cities in the summer.
2. Raoul appreciated the time he had at the fair last weekend.
3. The band stationed at the east end was talented.
4. The goods for sale were expensive.
5. Raoul attends street fairs frequently.

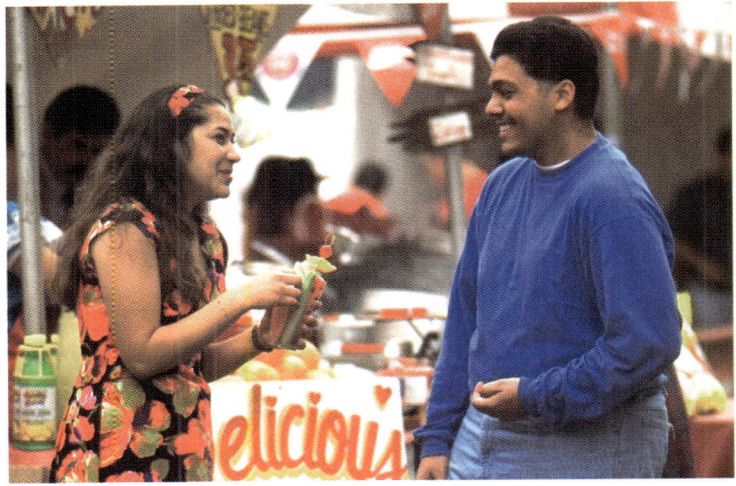

Technology Tip

In formal writing, it is better to write out the negative than to use a contraction. Use the search feature to find -n't, and change it to *not*. Be careful with the words *can't* and *won't*.

◀ **Critical Viewing**
Use understatement to describe how these two people are probably feeling. **[Describe]**

Negative Sentences • 645

Step-by-Step Teaching Guide

Using Negatives to Achieve Understatement

1. Remind students that understatement relies on *irony*—expressing the intended meaning in words that are opposite to their usual meaning.
2. On the blackboard, write, *Paul wasn't exactly unhappy that his teacher had forgotten to assign homework.* Remind students that this sentence logically means that Paul was rather pleased.
3. Explain that this demonstrates irony because it uses negative terms to describe happiness, which is a positive emotion.

Answer Key

▶ **Exercise 4**

Answers may vary; samples are given.

1. Street fairs are hardly an uncommon sight in most major U.S. cities in the summer.
2. Raoul was not unappreciative of the time he had at the fair last weekend.
3. The band stationed at the east end was not untalented.
4. The goods for sale were not inexpensive.
5. Raoul does not attend street fairs infrequently.

Customize for
ESL Students

English-language learners might need some practice in understanding the subtle irony of understatement. Give them some examples that use straightforward terms:

She was not unhappy *that she passed the difficult test.*

He was not unkind *to the adorable lost puppy.*

Read and discuss these examples before moving on to sentences with more difficult structures.

Critical Viewing

Describe Possible answer: They seem not to be having a bad time.

Hands-on Grammar

Teaching Resources: Hands-on Grammar Activity Book, Ch. 25

1. If you wish to do this activity in class, be prepared with long, narrow strips of paper for the students. Be sure students have a copy of Hands-on Grammar activity sheet.

2. Have students follow the directions to prepare the strips.

3. Students' lists may include *never, no, nobody, none, nothing, nowhere, not, -n't, scarcely, hardly, barely,* and (with a reminder that it is not always negative) *but.*

Find It in Your Reading

Encourage students to compare lists so that all lists are as complete as possible.

Find It in Your Writing

Remind students that double negatives used for understatement are appropriate in much writing; such uses of double negatives need not be corrected.

25.1

Hands-on Grammar

Strip Out Double Negatives

Fan-fold a long, narrow strip of paper to create at least fifteen sections. Leave the first, or top, section blank. In each following section of the strip, write a negative word. (See the example on this page.) You may choose to use *-n't* on the "not" section to remind you that contractions formed with *not* are negative words, or you may list each negative contraction on its own section. When you are finished listing negative words, fold the strip and label the front "Negative Words." Use the strip to help you check for double negatives when you proofread.

One strategy you can use when proofreading is to put an *x* on each negative word you find in your writing. If you see two words with an *x* in any sentence, evaluate whether both negative words are needed.

There is ha̶r̶dly ̶n̶o time left to finish the project.

There is hardly *any* time left to finish the project.

Notice that two words on the list are crossed out of the sentence. To restore the intended meaning of the sentence, *no* is replaced with *any.*

Find It in Your Reading Read a short story or a nonfiction article or essay. List all the negative words you find. Compare the list from your reading to the original list you made. If you have missed any negative words, add them to your list. (You do not need to start over; you can tape an additional strip of paper to the first one.)

Find It in Your Writing Use your Negative Words list to proofread a piece of writing from your portfolio.

barely
but (only)
hardly
neither
never
no
nobody
none
no one
not (n't)
nothing
nowhere
only
scarcely

646 • Miscellaneous Problems in Usage

⏱ **TIME SAVERS!**

Hands-on Grammar
Use the Hands-on Grammar activity sheet for Chapter 25 to facilitate this activity.

✓ **ONGOING ASSESSMENT: Assess Mastery**

Use the following resources to assess student mastery of negative sentences.

In the Textbook	Technology
Chapter Review, Ex. 26–29, p. 662	*On-Line Exercise Bank,* Section 25.1

Section 25.1 Section Review

GRAMMAR EXERCISES 5–11

Exercise 5 **Avoiding Double Negatives** Choose the word in parentheses that best completes each sentence.

(1) Carnivals today don't look (nothing, anything) like they did hundreds of years ago. (2) There (were, weren't) no flashing lights or mechanized rides. (3) That doesn't mean people long ago (did, didn't) have fun. (4) Because they didn't have (any, no) electricity for fancy equipment, they played games and music and sold their wares. (5) That's not to say that modern carnivals and their ancient counterparts don't have (no, any) similarities.

Exercise 6 **Identifying and Correcting Double Negatives** Rewrite the following sentences to eliminate double negatives. If the sentence contains no double negative, write *correct*.

(1) You shouldn't hardly be surprised to see costumed people in parades at modern carnivals. (2) Some masquerade costumes are so good, you will not be able to tell who is inside. (3) Some modern carnivals don't never stop traveling. (4) Permanent amusement parks don't have none of the travel problems that carnivals face. (5) We don't live nowhere near an amusement park, so we wait for the carnivals.

Exercise 7 **Writing Sentences With Understatement** Rewrite the following sentences to achieve understatement.

1. We were pleased with the carnival.
2. It was like the one we went to last year.
3. The weather was pleasant.
4. My friends and I were happy.
5. The fireworks were expected.

Exercise 8 **Proofreading Practice: Negative Sentences** Revise the following paragraph. Correct any errors in double negatives that you find.

Mardi Gras didn't begin nowhere near the United States. For hundreds of years, people in Europe celebrated feast days with games and food because they weren't permitted to eat nothing during the fast days that followed. Mardi Gras isn't but one of many feast days they celebrated. French colonists introduced Mardi Gras to America in the 1700's.

Exercise 9 **Find It in Your Reading** Read the following excerpt from Patrick Henry's speech before the Virginia Convention. Identify the words in each sentence that make it a negative sentence.

I have but one lamp by which my feet are guided, and that is the lamp of experience. I know of no way of judging of the future but by the past.

Exercise 10 **Find It in Your Writing** Choose a piece of persuasive writing from your portfolio. Identify the negative sentences you have used. If you have not used any, add one to elaborate on your position.

Exercise 11 **Writing Application** Write a brief description of a celebration, street fair, or carnival you have attended or heard about. Use at least two examples of understatement in your description.

Section Review • 647

ASSESS

Section Review

Each of these exercises correlates to the instruction on negative sentences, pages 642–645. The exercises may be used for more practice, for reteaching, or for review of the key concepts presented. Answers for all chapter exercises are available in *Grammar Exercises Answers on Transparencies* in your Teaching Resources.

Answer Key

Exercise 5

1. anything	4. any
2. were	5. any
3. didn't	

Exercise 6

Answers may vary; samples are given.

1. replace *shouldn't* with *should*
2. correct
3. replace *never* with *ever*
4. replace *don't have* with *have*
5. replace *nowhere* with *anywhere*

Exercise 7

Answers may vary; samples are given.

1. We were not displeased with the carnival.
2. It was not unlike the one we went to last year.
3. The weather was not unpleasant.
4. My friends and I were not unhappy.
5. The fireworks were hardly unexpected.

Exercise 8

Answers may vary; samples are given.

Mardi Gras didn't begin <u>anywhere</u> near the United States. For hundreds of years, people in Europe celebrated feast days with games and food because they weren't permitted to eat <u>anything</u> during the following fast days. Mardi Gras <u>is</u> but one of many feast days they celebrated. French colonists introduced Mardi Gras to America in the 1700's.

Exercise 9

Find It in Your Reading
"I have but one lamp": *but* is negative, so Henry does not say, "I don't have but one lamp."

"No way of judging" is negative, so Henry does not say, "I don't have no way. . . ."

continued

Answer Key continued

Exercise 10

Find It in Your Writing
Students should correct any double negatives they find. In addition, encourage them to look for sentences in which understatement would be appropriate.

Exercise 11

Writing Application
When they finish, have students exchange papers with a partner to make sure they used understatement correctly and did not use any double negatives.

Common Usage Problems

(1) _a, an_ The article _a_ is used before consonant sounds; _an_ is used before vowel sounds. Words beginning with _ho, o,_ or _u_ may have either a vowel sound or a consonant sound.

EXAMPLES: Rain forests are <u>a</u> universal concern.
They have become <u>an</u> issue of international importance.
The rain forest is <u>a</u> habitat for many species of animals and plants.
We need <u>an</u> honest appraisal of the situation.

(2) _accept, except_ _Accept,_ a verb, means "to receive." _Except,_ a preposition, means "leaving out" or "other than."

VERB: We must _accept_ responsibility for preserving the rain forest.

PREPOSITION: If we don't, nothing will be left _except_ scrub.

(3) _adapt, adopt_ _Adapt,_ a verb, means "to change." _Adopt,_ also a verb, means "to take as one's own."

EXAMPLES: Companies must _adapt_ to conform to environmental regulations.
More and more companies are _adopting_ policies geared toward preservation.

(4) _affect, effect_ _Affect_ is almost always a verb meaning "to influence." _Effect_ is usually a noun meaning "result." Occasionally, _effect_ is a verb meaning "to bring about" or "to cause."

VERB: It is not clear how much the destruction of the rain forests _affects_ the world's climate.

NOUN: One _effect_ may be global warming.

VERB: Concern over this situation has _effected_ some change in attitudes toward rain forests.

(5) _aggravate_ _Aggravate_ means "to make worse." Avoid using this word to mean "to annoy."

LESS ACCEPTABLE: Some people are _aggravated_ by disregard for the environment.

PREFERRED: Continued deforestation will _aggravate_ climatic changes.

(6) _ain't_ _Ain't,_ originally a contraction of _am not,_ is not considered acceptable standard English. Avoid using it in all writing and speaking.

(7) _all ready, already_ _All ready_ is an expression meaning

---

"ready." The expression functions as an adjective. *Already* is an adverb meaning "by or before this time" or "even now."

ADJECTIVE: Are people all ready to help preserve the rain forest?

ADVERB: Much destruction has already been done.

(8) all right, alright *Alright* is a nonstandard spelling. Always use the two-word form in your writing.

NONSTANDARD: With help, the rain forest may still be *alright*.

CORRECT: With help, the rain forest may still be *all right*.

(9) all together, altogether These two adverbs have different meanings. *All together* means "all at once." *Altogether* means "completely" or "in all."

EXAMPLES: The monkeys sat in the trees *all together.*
A rain forest is not *altogether* the same as a jungle.

(10) among, between *Among* and *between* are both prepositions. *Among* always implies three or more. *Between* is usually properly used with just two items.

EXAMPLES: Orchids may be found *among* the many different plants of the rain forest.
Vines called *lianas* are found in the layers *between* the upper canopy and the forest floor.

▶ **Exercise 12** **Avoiding Usage Problems** Choose the correct expression to complete each sentence.
1. Our class has (adapted, adopted) a new research project policy.
2. The way we find our information (affects, effects) our grade.
3. He is (annoyed, aggravated) by the lack of information on his topic.
4. He cannot find (a, an) useful Internet site related to his topic.
5. Our group divided the research tasks (among, between) the group members.
6. The rain forest topic was (already, all ready) taken.
7. (Ain't, Aren't) you going to choose another topic?
8. Is this outline (all right, alright) with the group?
9. Some think it is (all together, altogether) too difficult.
10. By now, most of the group has (accepted, excepted) it.

▲ **Critical Viewing**
In one sentence, tell what factors affect the growth of plants. In another sentence, tell the effect of rain and sunshine on plant growth. [Distinguish]

Common Usage Problems • 649

☑ **ONGOING ASSESSMENT: Monitor and Reinforce**

If students have difficulty with any of the Exercises 12 through 19, refer them to the following for additional practice.

In the Textbook	Print Resources	Technology
Section Review, Ex. 20–22, p. 661	*Grammar Exercise Workbook,* pp. 139–140	*On-Line Exercise Bank,* Sect on 25.2

Common Usage Problems: 8–10

1. Read and discuss usage problems 8–10, and use the following ideas to illustrate some of the main points.

2. Have a student volunteer read the definitions of *all together* and *altogether* and explain when it is correct to use each. Then, present students with these examples, and ask them to supply the missing words:

   The conductor said, "___ now," as he led the choir in its weekly practice. (All together)

   The genetic clone was ___ the same as the original. (altogether)

3. Explain to students that a good way to remember the definitions of *among* and *between* is to recognize that the word *between* has the first two letters of the word *two* in it. Hence, *between* is used with two items and *among* is used with more than two items.

Customize for
AP Students

Have students write a series of sentences, each using a pair of words that are often confused; for example, "There is little agreement *among* scientists about the rivalry *between* twins." Challenge them to build these sentences into a cohesive paragraph.

Critical Viewing

Distinguish Possible answer: Water, sunlight, and soil quality affect the growth of plants. Rain and sunshine have a positive effect on plant growth.

Answer Key

▶ **Exercise 12**
1. adopted
2. affects
3. annoyed
4. a
5. among
6. already
7. Aren't
8. all right
9. altogether
10. accepted

Step-by-Step Teaching Guide

Common Usage Problems: 11–17

1. Read and discuss usage problems 11–17 with the students. Use the ideas below to illustrate and expand upon some of the main points.

2. Explain to students that *anxious* has a negative connotation and *eager* has a positive one. Use examples like these:

   People tend to be anxious about receiving bad news.

   We are usually eager to go on vacation.

   On the board, write a short list of activities like canoeing, buying presents, or making a presentation in front of the class. Then, have students write whether they would be anxious or eager to do these things. Have them explain their reasons.

3. Explain to students that a good way to determine the correct use of *anyone, any one, everyone,* and *every one* is to insert the word *single* before the word *one*. When students mean to say any person or every person, the word *single* will not fit. When they mean to say any single person (or thing) or every single person (or thing), the word *single* will fit smoothly. Have them try this method on the example in the textbook.

4. Ask students to name two main reasons for adding an *-s* to the end of a word (to make it plural or possessive). Remind them to avoid adding an *-s* haphazardly, especially to the words *anyway, anywhere, everywhere, nowhere,* and *somewhere.*

---

(11) anxious *Anxious* means "worried," "uneasy," or "fearful." Do not use it as a substitute for *eager.*

AMBIGUOUS: Environmentalists are *anxious* for change.

CLEAR: Environmentalists are *anxious* about the results of deforestation and *eager* for change.

(12) anyone, any one, everyone, every one *Anyone* and *everyone* mean "any person" and "every person," respectively. *Any one* means "any single person (or thing)," and *every one* means "every single person (or thing)."

EXAMPLES: *Anyone* may take an interest in preservation.
Any one of the rain forest plants could provide a life-saving drug.
Everyone should be concerned about the environment.
Every one of the rain forests' plants and animals plays a role in maintaining the ecosystem.

(13) anyway, anywhere, everywhere, nowhere, somewhere These adverbs should never end in *-s.*

NONSTANDARD: There are unknown species *somewheres* in the rain forest.

CORRECT: There are unknown species *somewhere* in the rain forest.

(14) as Do not use the conjunction *as* to mean "because."

LESS ACCEPTABLE: There are few plants on the forest floor *as there* is very little sunlight.

PREFERRED: There are few plants on the forest floor *because* there is very little sunlight.

(15) as to *As to* is awkward. Replace it with *about.*

NONSTANDARD: There is some doubt *as to* whether the rain forests will survive.

CORRECT: There is some doubt *about* the rain forests' survival.

(16) at Do not use *at* after *where.* Simply eliminate it.

NONSTANDARD: Where in the world are rain forests *at?*

CORRECT: Where in the world *are* rain forests?

(17) at about Avoid using *at about.* Use *at, around,* or *near.*

LESS ACCEPTABLE: Many rain forests are found *at about* the equator.

PREFERRED: Many rain forests are found *near* the equator.

▶ **More Practice**

On-line
Exercise Bank
• Section 25.2
Grammar Exercise
Workbook
• pp. 139–140

650 • Miscellaneous Problems in Usage

(18) awful, awfully *Awful* is used informally to mean "extremely bad." *Awfully* is used informally to mean "very." Better writers replace both with more descriptive words. In formal writing, use *awful* only to mean "inspiring fear."

INFORMAL:	The heat is *awful*.
BETTER:	The heat is *debilitating*.
INFORMAL:	It can get *awfully* hot in the rain forest.
BETTER:	It can get *extremely* hot in the rain forest.
FORMAL:	There may be *awful* viruses as yet undiscovered in the rain forests.

(19) awhile, a while *Awhile* is an adverb, which in itself means "for a while." *A while* is an article and a noun usually used after the preposition *for*.

ADVERB:	Vines live off trees *awhile*, but they eventually strangle them.
NOUN:	Concern about the rain forest has been growing for *a while*.

(20) beat, win *Beat* means "to overcome (an opponent)." *Win* means "to achieve victory in."

NONSTANDARD:	A successful plant has *won* the others in competition for resources.
CORRECT:	A successful plant has *beaten* the others in competition for resources.

▶ **Exercise 13** **Avoiding Usage Problems** Choose the correct expression to complete each sentence.
1. There are rain forests (somewhere, somewheres) in Brazil.
2. Gliding is a useful adaptation of animals (as, because) it allows them to move about freely.
3. Countries are concerned (as to, about) how to balance industrial growth and the preservation of rain forests.
4. Where do ants (live, live at) in the rain forest?
5. Pharmaceutical companies are (anxious, eager) to find new medicines.
6. We saw a frog sitting (near, at about) the edge of the stream.
7. We got (awfully, very) wet.
8. A snake could be hiding under (anyone, any one) of these leaves.
9. The detrimental effects of a venomous snakebite last for (awhile, a while).
10. Pharmaceutical companies are trying to (beat, win) one another to develop valuable medicines.

▲ **Critical Viewing**
Revise this sentence about the frog in the picture: "The frog is awfully small." [Describe]

Common Usage Problems: 18–20

1. Read and discuss with students the usage problems 18–20. Use the suggestions below to illustrate some of the main ideas.

2. Write these sentences on the blackboard:

   These pancakes taste awful.

   My dog is awfully good at fetching sticks.

   Explain to students that although we often use *awful* to mean "very bad" and *awfully* to mean "very," the correct definition of *awful* is "inspiring fear" or "filling with awe." Have them recognize that it does not make sense to say that pancakes are inspiring fear or that a dog is good at fetching sticks in a manner that inspires fear. Then, have students suggest revisions to the sentences using more appropriate adjectives and adverbs like *dry* or *spongy* and *extremely* or *surprisingly*.

3. Explain to students that *awhile* is an adverb and means "for a while" and is distinct from *a while*, which is an article and a noun and usually follows the preposition *for*. Then, have students write sentences with *awhile* and *a while*, following the model provided on this page.

Answer Key

▶ **Exercise 13**

1. somewhere
2. because
3. about
4. live
5. eager
6. near
7. very
8. any one
9. a while
10. beat

Critical Viewing

Describe Possible answer: The frog is extremely small.

651

Common Usage Problems: 21–26

1. Read and discuss usage problems 21–26 with students. Use the ideas that follow to further illustrate some of the main points.

2. Explain to students that one way to remember the difference between *beside* and *besides* is to recognize that the word *beside*, which means "next to" or "at the side of," has the word *side* in it. The word *besides,* which means "in addition to," has an *s* in addition to the word *beside.*

3. On the board, write the following sentences and ask students to supply *bring* and *take* correctly:

   ___ this present from me to her. (Take)

   ___ this package from her to me. (Bring)

   Suggest that students note the word *in* in *bring* and remember "move to a nearer place," or "bring in." Note the *a* in *take* and remember "take away."

4. Have students list as many clipped words as they can in two minutes. Have them share their words with the class, and remind them to avoid using these and other clipped terms in formal writing.

Customize for
Visual/Spatial Learners

Visually represent the difference between *bring* and *take* by having pairs of students demonstrate the acts of bringing and taking before the class. For instance, tell Student A to carry a pencil to Student B and to describe the act: *I am taking this pencil to Harry.* Then have Student B describe the action: *Carla is bringing me the pencil.* Repeat this as necessary with additional pairs of students.

Customize for
Verbal/Linguistic Learners

Some clipped words, such as *phone* and *gym,* are used so frequently that students might not realize that they have been clipped. Give them a list of clipped words and have them supply the complete word from which each was taken. Remind them to avoid clipped words in formal writing.

25.2

(21) because Do not use *because* after *the reason.* Say "The reason is . . . that" or reword the sentence.

NONSTANDARD: *One reason* to preserve the environment is because it will benefit humans.

CORRECT: We try to preserve the environment *because* it will benefit humans.

(22) being as, being that Avoid using either expression. Use *because* instead.

NONSTANDARD: *Being as* (or *that*) the ecosystem is so fragile, competition among plants and animals is fierce.

CORRECT: *Because* the ecosystem is so fragile, competition among plants and animals is fierce.

(23) beside, besides *Beside* means "at the side of" or "close to." *Besides* means "in addition to."

EXAMPLES: Mangrove forests are often found *beside* rain forests near the coastline.
There are other kinds of rain forests *besides* the equatorial kind.

(24) bring, take *Bring* means "to carry from a distant place to a nearer one." *Take* means the opposite: "to carry from a near place to a more distant place."

EXAMPLES: I saw a movie about a man who *brings* a diseased monkey to the United States.
Birds and bats *take* seeds from plants and disperse them throughout the forest.

(25) can, may *Can* means "has the ability to." *May* means "has permission to" or "possible or likely to."

ABILITY: Some rain forest animals *can* climb trees.

PERMISSION: Everyone *may* join our effort to preserve the environment.

POSSIBILITY: There *may* be a solution that pleases everyone.

(26) clipped words Avoid using clipped or shortened words—such as *gym, phone,* or *photo* in formal writing.

INFORMAL: There are no *phones* deep in the rain forest.

FORMAL: There are no *telephones* deep in the rain forest.

✿ Grammar and Style Tip

Avoid using wordy expressions such as "being as" to sound formal or academic. Choose the most direct way of expressing your point.

(27) different from, different than Use *from*.

LESS ACCEPTABLE:	The rain forest of the Amazon Basin is *different than* that of the northwestern United States.
PREFERRED:	The rain forest of the Amazon Basin is *different from* that of the northwestern United States.

(28) doesn't, don't Do not use *don't* with third-person singular subjects. Use *doesn't* instead.

NONSTANDARD:	A rain forest *don't* have a dry season.
CORRECT:	A rain forest *doesn't* have a dry season.

(29) done *Done*, the past participle of *do*, should always follow a helping verb.

NONSTANDARD:	We *done* what we could to help.
CORRECT:	We *have done* what we could to help.

(30) due to *Due to* means "caused by" and should be used only when the words "caused by" can logically be substituted.

NONSTANDARD:	Few plants live on the forest floor *due to* lack of sunlight.
CORRECT:	The scarcity of plants on the forest floor is *due to* lack of sunlight.

▶ **Exercise 14** Proofreading to Correct Usage Problems
Proofread each of the following sentences. On a separate sheet of paper, correctly write any sentences that contain errors or nonstandard usage. If a sentence contains no errors, write "correct as is."

1. A successful cure will take a great deal of money to the company that discovers it.
2. They may even discover a drug to cure cancer.
3. Many magazines feature photos of the rain forest.
4. Some species are found no place on Earth beside the rain forest.
5. Being as there is little change in temperature, there is great biological diversity.
6. Another reason for this diversity is that there is little distinction among the seasons.
7. The vine done much damage to the trees.
8. The tree will soon die due to the fact that the vine is strangling it.
9. She says that she don't know much about the rain forest.
10. Nocturnal animals are different than those that come out during the day.

▶ **More Practice**

On-line Exercise Bank
• Section 25.2
Grammar Exercise Workbook
• pp. 139–140

Common Usage Problems • **653**

Common Usage Problems: 31–40

1. Read and discuss usage problems 31–40 with students. Use the suggestions that follow to further illustrate some of the main ideas.

2. Explain to students that *farther*, which has the word *far* in it, refers to distance, and *further* means "additional." Have them offer examples relating to distance (I walked farther today than yesterday) and examples relating to degree or extent (I thought further about my problem).

3. Explain to students that the verb *get* is not always the best choice for a sentence. On the board, write Sentence 1 below and ask what is weak about it (*got* can be replaced with a more specific verb choice). Then ask for substitutions, such as Sentence 2:

   Sentence 1: *My cousin* got *taller in just a few months.*

   Sentence 2: *My cousin* grew *taller in just a few months.*

4. On the board, write:

   good car

   lovely dress

   nice tie

   Explain to students that although *good, lovely,* and *nice* are acceptable adjectives, they are overused and not very expressive. Have students list three more-specific adjectives to describe each of the nouns in the above example.

5. Explain that both *in* and *into* are prepositions, but one indicates location (in) and the other direction or motion (into). Offer a few more examples for students to complete:

   There are many gases ___ the air. (in)

   Our lungs help us pull oxygen from the air ___ our bloodstream. (into)

6. Encourage students to become familiar with the words *rather* and *somewhat*. If they feel that these two words sound stuffy or stilted, explain that the alternatives (*kind of, sort of*) will sound unsophisticated or childish to many. Remind them to be aware of their audience when choosing words.

continued

25.2

(31) each other, one another *Each other* and *one another* are usually interchangeable. At times, however, *each other* is more logically used in reference to only two; *one another,* in reference to more than two.

EXAMPLES: Animals and plants in the rain forest often benefit *each other* (or *one another*).
In a symbiotic relationship, both organisms involved benefit *each other.*
Ideally, we should care for the rain forest as we care for *one another.*

(32) farther, further *Farther* refers to distance. *Further* means "additional" or "to a greater degree or extent."

EXAMPLES: The African rain forests are *farther* from here than those of South America.
Further study is being done to ascertain the effects of humans on the rain forest.

(33) fewer, less Use *fewer* with objects that can be counted. Use *less* with quantities and qualities that cannot be counted.

EXAMPLES: *fewer* animals, *fewer* resources, *fewer* acres
less rainfall, *less* diversity, *less* acreage

(34) get, got, gotten These forms of the verb *to get* are acceptable in standard usage, but, whenever possible, it is best to use a more specific word.

INFORMAL: *get* water, *got* more fragile, have *gotten* encouragement

BETTER: *obtain* water, *became* more fragile, have *received* encouragement

(35) gone, went *Gone* is the past participle of *go* and should be used as a verb only with a helping verb. *Went* is the past tense of *go* and is never used with a helping verb.

NONSTANDARD: The bird *gone* away, but the monkeys remain.
The bird *should never have went* near the snake.

CORRECT: The bird went away, but the monkeys remain.
The bird *should never have gone* near the snake.

(36) good, lovely, nice These three adjectives are weak and overused. Try to use a more specific adjective.

WEAK: *good* example, *lovely* green leaves, *nice* aroma

BETTER: *useful* example, *lush* green leaves, *pleasing* aroma

654 • Miscellaneous Problems in Usage

▼ **Critical Viewing**
Revise the following sentence about the parrot in the picture: "The parrot has nice colors." **[Describe]**

Customize for
ESL Students

Have students use the verbs *gone, went, get, got,* and *gotten* to write sentences about places that they have visited. Allow them to practice the forms of *go* and *get* in simple sentences before they begin writing about places. Afterward, have them share their sentences with their classmates.

Critical Viewing

Describe Possible answer: The parrot has vibrant colors.

(37) in, into *In* refers to position. *Into* suggests motion.

EXAMPLES: Many insect species live *in* the rain forest.
Plants take nutrients from the soil *into* their roots.

(38) irregardless Avoid this word. Use *regardless*.

(39) kind of, sort of Do not use *kind of* or *sort of* to mean "rather" or "somewhat."

(40) lay, lie *Lay* means "to put or set (something) down." Its principal parts—*lay, laying, laid,* and *laid*—are usually followed by a direct object. *Lie* means "to recline." Its principal parts—*lie, lying, lay,* and *lain*—are never followed by a direct object.

LAY: That fungus is poisonous; *lay* it down at once.
New legislation *is laying* the foundation for the future.
He *laid* the camera aside after he took the picture.
The ant queen *has laid* her eggs in that hollow branch.

LIE: *Lie* on the grass, and watch the clouds drift by.
The root of that tree *is lying* above ground.
The snake *lay* on the branch.
These seeds *have lain* on the ground a long time.

▶ **Exercise 15** **Avoiding Usage Problems** Choose the correct expression to complete each sentence.

1. He had (got, gotten) a thorough medical examination when he returned from the tropics.
2. She gave a(n) (good, effective) speech.
3. Scientists travel (in, into) the rain forest to look for new species.
4. We enjoyed the speech, (irregardless, regardless).
5. Rain forest trees and the fungi that grow in their roots help (each other, one another) to obtain nourishment.
6. The tree will not die because it has (fewer, less) vines than it did before.
7. Scientists are (kind of, somewhat) concerned about global warming.
8. Scientists will explore the issue (farther, further).
9. Some of these logs have (laid, lain) here for years.
10. The scientists (gone, went) home when they finished their research.
11. Global warming is partly (due to, because of) increased levels of carbon dioxide in the Earth's atmosphere.
12. He took many (photos, photographs) while he was in Brazil.
13. Nocturnal animals are different (from, than) those that come out during the day.
14. That animal (don't, doesn't) look too friendly.
15. She is going to the equator (irregardless, regardless) of the hot weather.

▶ **More Practice**

On-line Exercise Bank
• Section 25.2
Grammar Exercise Workbook
• pp. 139–140

 Speaking and Listening Tip

Read the correct version of each sentence out loud to a partner to develop the habits of standard usage in speaking as well as in writing.

Step-by-Step Teaching Guide continued

7. Have students practice using the principal parts of *lay* and *lie*. With *lay,* for instance, ask them to verbalize statements as they put a book down on another's desk; for example: *I lay the book on Jerry's desk. I laid it there yesterday, too.* Do the same with *lie*. Then have students use both *lie* and *lay* in the same sentence:

> *The goose that lays golden eggs likes to lie under the shade of a tall tree.*

Language Highlight

Point out to students that some of the usage problems studied in this chapter are characteristic of colloquial English and American dialect. Nonstandard words and expressions like *ain't, anyways, have ought to,* and negative sentences remain part of the rich tradition of American speech and literature. The writings of Mark Twain, for instance, reflect many of the colloquialisms of eighteenth- and nineteenth-century America. Point out to students that such expressions are to be used in their milieu but should only become parts of students' writing when used for a specific purpose, such as dialogue or descriptive writing.

Answer Key

▶ **Exercise 15**

1. gotten
2. effective
3. into
4. regardless
5. each other
6. fewer
7. somewhat
8. further
9. lain
10. went
11. due to
12. photographs
13. from
14. doesn't
15. regardless

⏱ **TIME SAVERS!**

Answers on Transparencies Use the *Grammar Exercises Answers on Transparencies* for Chapter 25 to facilitate correction by students.

On-Line Exercise Bank Have students complete the exercises on computer. The Auto Check feature will grade their work for you!

Step-by-Step Teaching Guide

Common Usage Problems: 41–46

1. Read and discuss usage problems 41–46 with students. Use the suggestions that follow to help clarify some of the main points.

2. Point out that when *like* is used as a preposition, it is part of a prepositional phrase, such as *like a politician*, and is followed closely by an object of the preposition. *As* and *as if*, on the other hand, are subordinating conjunctions that begin adverb clauses; they are closely followed by the subject and verb of the clause, such as *as a politician should speak*. Have students complete this sentence:

   Our mayor thinks ___ all other politicians do. (as)

3. Demonstrate that *loose* and *lose* are different parts of speech. *Loose* is an adjective: *His tie is loose* (*loose* describes *tie*). *Lose* is a verb (*I lose, I lost, we have lost*).

4. Place *maybe* and *may be* on the board, and ask students to identify their differences: (*Maybe* is an adverb and will modify a verb: *Maybe I will go. May be* is a verb phrase; *may* is the helper, and *be* is the main verb.) Have students complete each statement with the correct form:

   The bandleader thinks that ___ the musicians forgot their music. (maybe)

   He realizes that their poor playing ___ due to their nervousness. (may be)

Integrating Workplace Skills

Explain to students that a proofreader or editor is a person who reads documents and corrects grammatical errors and common usage problems. Then ask students to look for documents that have been checked by an editor (suggest that they look at newspapers, magazines, and brochures) to find examples of some of the words and expressions studied in this chapter. Have them copy five of these statements and explain why each usage is correct. Offer extra credit if they find and correct errors in edited material.

---

(41) learn, teach *Learn* means "to acquire knowledge." *Teach* means "to give knowledge to."

EXAMPLES: You can *learn* much about the rain forest from that documentary.
Experience has *taught* us that the rain forest is beneficial to us.

(42) leave, let *Leave* means "to allow to remain." *Let* means "to permit."

NONSTANDARD: *Let* the snake alone, and it won't trouble you.

CORRECT: *Leave* the snake alone, and it won't trouble you.

(43) like *Like* is a preposition and should not be used in place of the subordinating conjunction *as*.

NONSTANDARD: That exhibit looks *like* a rain forest should look.

CORRECT: That exhibit looks as a rain forest should look.
That exhibit looks *like* a rain forest.

(44) loose, lose *Loose* is usually an adjective or a part of such idioms as *cut loose, turn loose,* or *break loose. Lose* is always a verb, generally meaning "to miss from one's possession."

EXAMPLES: The branch is *loose,* and it may fall.
Without our help, these animals will *lose* their habitat.

(45) maybe, may be *Maybe* is an adverb meaning "perhaps." *May be* is a helping verb and a verb.

ADVERB: *Maybe* we can preserve the rain forest if we all work together.

VERB: It *may be* too late to save it.

(46) of Do not use the preposition *of* in place of the verb *have.* Moreover, do not use *of* after *outside, inside, off,* and *atop.* Simply eliminate it.

NONSTANDARD: We *should of* tried to stop the damage <u>inside of</u> the rain forest.

CORRECT: We *should have* tried to stop the damage <u>inside</u> the rain forest.

More Practice

On-line
Exercise Bank
• Section 25.2
Grammar Exercise
Workbook
• pp. 139–140

656 • Miscellaneous Problems in Usage

(47) OK, O.K., okay In informal writing, *OK*, *O.K.*, and *okay* are acceptably used to mean "all right." In formal writing, however, do not use either the abbreviations or *okay*.

(48) only *Only* should be placed in front of the word it logically modifies.

EXAMPLES:
> *Only* people can protect the environment.
> (No one else can protect it.)
> People can protect *only* the environment.
> (They can protect nothing else.)

(49) ought Never use *ought* with *have* or *had*. Simply eliminate *have* or *had*.

NONSTANDARD:
> We hadn't *ought* to have cut down so many trees.

CORRECT:
> We *ought* not to have cut down so many trees.

(50) outside of Do not use this expression to mean "besides" or "except."

NONSTANDARD:
> Many species are found nowhere else *outside of* the rain forest.

CORRECT:
> Many species are found nowhere else *except* the rain forest.

▲ **Critical Viewing**
Use "only" in a sentence about this wildcat called a margay. **[Describe]**

Exercise 16 **Avoiding Usage Problems** Choose the correct expression to complete each sentence.

1. Scientists hope to (teach, learn) other people about exotic animals.
2. That animal (maybe, may be) looking for food.
3. The soil is not very (loose, lose) where it is mostly clay.
4. Gorillas are not playful (as, like) the chimps are.
5. The roots are not very deep (inside, inside of) the ground.
6. Some insect species are (found only, only found) in the rain forest.
7. It is best to (let, leave) animals alone while they are eating.
8. (Outside of, Except for) seedlings, little grows there.
9. Rain forest plants and animals have adapted (okay, well) to the hot, humid environment.
10. You (had ought, ought) to read more about it.

Exercise 17 **Writing Sentences With Correct Usage**
Write a sentence correctly using each word.

1. loose   2. learn   3. like   4. lose   5. teach

Common Usage Problems • **657**

🖋 Spelling Tip

To distinguish between the spelling of *loose* and *lose*, remember that *lose* has *"lost"* an o.

Step-by-Step Teaching Guide

Common Usage Problems: 47–50

1. Read and discuss usage problems 47–50 with students. Use the following suggestions to elaborate on the instruction of some of the main concepts.

2. Explain to students that when writing formally, they should not use *okay, OK,* or *O.K.* None of these is standard usage. Help them to brainstorm for a list of alternative expressions, such as *all right, correct,* and *appropriate.*

3. On the board, write the sentence *Cotton candy costs only one dollar.* Then, move the word *only* to a different place in the sentence so that it modifies a different word. For instance, *Only cotton candy costs one dollar.* Ask students to analyze the change in the sentence's meaning. (In the first, it describes the amount; in the second, the candy.) Have them repeat the exercise with their own sentences.

Answer Key

▶ **Exercise 16**

1. teach
2. may be
3. loose
4. as
5. inside
6. found only
7. leave
8. Except for
9. well
10. ought

▶ **Exercise 17**

Answers will vary. Possible answers:

1. I have some <u>loose</u> change.
2. Let's <u>learn</u> to snowboard.
3. The clouds look <u>like</u> rain clouds.
4. Did you <u>lose</u> your coat?
5. Please <u>teach</u> me how to make those cookies.

Critical Viewing

Describe Possible answer: The margay is found only in the rain forest.

Common Usage Problems: 51–56

1. Read and discuss usage problems 51–56 with students. Use the suggestions that follow to further illustrate some of the main points.

2. Make note that the popular usage of *media* today is both singular and plural, although the plural is more accurate. Then, on the board, write these singular words:

   radius

   podium

   stadium

   Ask students for the plurals of these words. If they are unsure, have them consult a dictionary. Plurals are *radii, podia,* and *stadia* or *stadiums*. Explain to students that they must be careful not to confuse the singular and plurals of special nouns that form their plurals in uncommon ways.

3. Explain to students that *precede* means "to go or appear before" and *proceed* means "to move or go forward." Also, point out that even though the words have similar pronunciations, they are spelled differently. The spelling might help them remember the difference between the two: The *pre-* in *precede* means "before."

4. Explain to students that *said* and *say* are different principal parts of the same verb. Review these if necessary: *say* (present), *saying* (present participle), and *said* (past). Remind them that *said* is a verb in the past tense; *says* is in the present tense.

Integrating Spelling Skills

Mnemonic Devices Explain to students that some spellers use mnemonic devices to remember difficult words. Have a student look up *mnemonic* in a dictionary ("related to improving the memory"). Point out some generally known methods of remembering certain words; for instance, the difference between *principal* and *principle*. Tell them that *principle* (the law) ends in "le" just like "rule." Encourage students to suggest other mnemonic devices to help them avoid common usage problems.

25.2

(51) plurals that do not end in -s The plurals of certain nouns from Greek and Latin are formed as they were in their original language. Words such as *criteria, media,* and *phenomena* are plural and should not be treated as if they were singular (*criterion, medium, phenomenon*).

INCORRECT:	The *media is* instrumental in raising environmental awareness.
CORRECT:	The *media are* instrumental in raising environmental awareness.

(52) precede, proceed *Precede* means "to go before." *Proceed* means "to move or go forward."

EXAMPLES: Dr. Scott's research *preceded* Dr. Fagle's. Will you *proceed* with your research?

(53) principal, principle As an adjective, *principal* means "most important" or "chief." As a noun, it means "a person who has controlling authority." *Principle*, always a noun, means "a fundamental law."

ADJECTIVE:	Broadleaf evergreens are the *principal* trees of the equatorial rain forests.
NOUN:	The school's *principal* encourages environmental awareness.
NOUN:	Life in the rain forest operates according to fundamental biological *principles*.

(54) real *Real* means "authentic." The use of *real* to mean "very" or "really" should be avoided in formal writing.

INFORMAL:	Lianas are *real* tight around the trees.
FORMAL:	Lianas are *very* tight around the trees.

(55) says *Says* should not be used as a substitute for *said*.

NONSTANDARD:	Yesterday an environmentalist *says* that less than two percent of the original coastal rain forest of Brazil is left.
CORRECT:	Yesterday an environmentalist *said* that less than two percent of the original coastal rain forest of Brazil was left.

(56) than, then *Than* is used in comparisons. Do not confuse it with the adverb *then*, which usually refers to time.

EXAMPLES: Temperate rain forests have a greater temperature range *than* equatorial rain forests. Read this book, and *then* decide whether you want to help the rain forest.

658 • Miscellaneous Problems in Usage

✏ STANDARDIZED TEST PREPARATION WORKSHOP

Grammar and Usage Many standardized tests require students to recognize and solve common usage problems. Use the following example to demonstrate.

   (1) *The principal laid down numerous regulations at school.*

   (2) *The person who created the rules did not abide by his own principles.*

   (3) *He listened to his own advice less frequently than other people did.*

   (4) *He hadn't ought to leave early if he doesn't want to.*

Which sentence above contains a common usage error?

A 1	**C** 3
B 2	**D** 4

The correct answer is **D**. You should not use *ought* with *had* or *have*. The correct way to express D is *He shouldn't have to leave early if he doesn't want to.*

(57) that, which, who *That* refers to people or things; *which* refers only to things; *who* refers only to people.

EXAMPLES: Plants have several ways to capture the nutrients *that* they need.
He is a man *that* (or *who*) cares about the environment.

(58) their, there, they're *Their*, a possessive pronoun, always modifies a noun. *There* can be used either as an expletive at the beginning of a sentence or as an adverb. *They're* is a contraction for *they are*.

PRONOUN: Many trees get *their* nutrients with the help of fungi that live among the roots.

EXPLETIVE: *There* is little we can do to repair the damage already done.

ADVERB: I've never been to Africa, but I'd like to go *there* someday.

CONTRACTION: From what I've heard of the rain forests, *they're* very hot.

(59) to, too, two *To*, a preposition, begins a prepositional phrase or an infinitive. *Too*, an adverb, modifies adjectives and other adverbs. *Two* is a number.

PREPOSITION: *to* the tropics, *to* Brazil
INFINITIVE: *to* grow, *to* survive
ADVERB: *too* hot, *too* densely populated
NUMBER: *two* species, *two* types

(60) when, where Do not use *when* or *where* directly after a linking verb. Also, do not use *where* in place of *that*.

NONSTANDARD: The annual flood is *when* fish enter the rain forest in large numbers.
The rain forest is *where* the greatest biological diversity on Earth is found.
I heard the other day *where* destruction is proceeding at an alarming rate.

CORRECT: During the annual flood, fish enter the rain forest in large numbers.
The greatest biological diversity on Earth is found in the rain forest.
I heard the other day that destruction is proceeding at an alarming rate.

💡 **Spelling Tip**

Remember that spell checkers on word-processing programs will accept *their*, *there*, and *they're* as correctly spelled. Proofread to check correct spellings of homophones such as these.

Common Usage Problems: 57–60

1. Read and discuss usage problems 57–60 with students. Use the following suggestions to further illustrate some of the main ideas.

2. Ask students to supply the correct word (*than* or *then*) in each sentence:

   I am older___ my younger sister. (than)

   We'll exercise first and ___ rest. (then)

   When a student offers a correct answer to the first sentence, ask the student to explain it. (*Than* helps to make a comparison.) Explain that *than* is a subordinating conjunction that starts an elliptical adverb clause: *than my sister* (is).

3. Ask students to complete this sentence:

   Mrs. Robinson is the person ___ fixes things ___ need repair. (who, that)

   If they offer *who*, remind them that *who* is a pronoun and ask for its antecedent (*Mrs. Robinson*). Briefly review relative pronouns and antecedents. Ask which relative pronoun can complete the second blank (*that*). Make sure students understand that *that* can be used for both people and things but that *who* must refer only to people.

4. On the board, write <u>They're</u> all <u>there</u>, but <u>their</u> luggage is in Brazil and circle the three underlined words. Review the definitions of *there*, *they're*, and *their*. Then, have students write sentences using each word. If they have trouble grasping the meaning of *they're*, have them undo the contraction and write it out as *they are*.

5. Dictate three brief phrases to students, each phrase containing *to*, *too*, or *two*. Have students write the spelling that they believe is correct in each phrase. Here are three: *to the store; two bags of groceries; I'll go, too*. Review the answers.

Customize for
ESL Students

Have students write sentences with the homophones *to*, *two*, and *too* and *their*, *there*, and *they're*. Then give them six index cards each, and have them write one word on the front of each card and a correct sentence for the word on the back. Students can then practice with each other by holding up the word for a partner to see and answering with a sentence that uses the word properly.

Integrating Vocabulary Skills

Greek and Latin Roots Have students research common prefixes, suffixes, and roots that derive from Greek and Latin words. A short list may be culled from the examples on the previous pages: *pre-, pro-, med-, phenom-, -ceed* or *-cede*. Then, have them list other words that have the same prefixes, suffixes, or roots to see whether they have similar definitions. Examples: *precede* ("to go before") and *predict* ("to say in advance").

25.2

▶ **Exercise 18** **Avoiding Usage Problems** Choose the correct expression to complete each sentence.

1. Some of the timber from the temperate forests is (really, extremely) valuable.
2. The valuable timber is the (principle, principal) reason for industry to enter the area.
3. Many people believe that protection of the rain forests should be a guiding (principle, principal).
4. They think it's wiser to prevent damage (then, than) to observe the results.
5. Studies are (preceding, proceeding) with the help of research teams.
6. Yesterday, he (says, said) that he had watched a program about the rain forest.
7. Some criteria for judging a rain forest (includes, include) latitude, temperature, and rainfall.
8. The temperature never falls (to, too, two) low in the rain forest.
9. The summer is (when, the season when) the temperature is hottest.
10. Very heavy rainfall is a striking (phenomenon, phenomena) of a rain forest.

▶ **Exercise 19** **Proofreading to Correct Usage Problems**

On a separate sheet of paper, revise the following paragraph to eliminate awkward or problematic usage. You may need to reorder words.

The trees are generally taller in the temperate forests then they are in the tropical ones. The floor of a rain forest is a place of very little light. Most animals have special abilities that help them survive in there habitat. Some animals who are common to rain forests include monkeys, parrots, hummingbirds, bats, tree frogs, snakes, and beetles. Scientists which study these species of animals find the variety of species astounding.

▶ Critical Viewing
Compare these flowers with flowers in your area. Use the word *than* in your comparison. [Compare]

▶ **More Practice**

On-line Exercise Bank
• Section 25.2
Grammar Exercise Workbook
• pp. 139–140

☑ **ONGOING ASSESSMENT: Monitor and Reinforce**

If students have difficulty with any of the Exercises 12 through 19, refer them to the following for additional practice.

In the Textbook	Print Resources	Technology
Section Review, Ex. 20–22, p. 661	*Grammar Exercise Workbook,* pp. 139–140	*On-Line Exercise Bank,* Section 25.2

Section Review

GRAMMAR EXERCISES 20–25

Exercise 20 **Using *a* and *an***
Complete each expression with *a* or *an*.

1. ___?___ unusual amount of rain
2. ___?___ unique environment
3. ___?___ arboreal species
4. ___?___ excellent source
5. ___?___ uniform layer
6. ___?___ honest living
7. ___?___ hot climate
8. ___?___ one-sided relationship
9. ___?___ herbivorous mammal
10. ___?___ insectivore

Exercise 21 **Avoiding Usage Problems** Choose the correct expression to complete each sentence.

1. If we (accept, except) the idea that rain forests are essential to the environment, we must search for alternatives to deforestation.
2. Ants have (adapted, adopted) all the layers of the forest in which to make their homes.
3. Some diseases (affect, effect) the nervous system.
4. Others are less serious; they are simply (aggravating, annoying).
5. Whatever the time of year, the rain forests (ain't, aren't) going to be dry.
6. Many new species have (already, all ready) been discovered.
7. It is never (alright, all right) to do nothing.
8. If nobody does anything, there will be no (farther, further) progress.
9. There are (fewer, less) insect species in the temperate forests than in other types of forests.
10. The rain forest has (gotten to be, become) a major concern since the 1970's.

Exercise 22 **Proofreading to Correct Usage Problems** Rewrite each sentence, correcting the error in usage.

(1) The rain forest of the Amazon Basin may contain more than ten million species of plants and animals all together. (2) Between these millions of species are found large numbers of insects. (3) Are you anxious to see the rain forest? (4) Everyone of the millions of species is necessary. (5) Ants live everywheres in the rain forest. (6) Anacondas constrict their prey, which makes these snakes awfully dangerous. (7) As to length, they can grow to more than thirty feet. (8) It is a good thing those snakes live at the rain forest and not here. (9) The tree is still laying where it fell. (10) Some mammals are learned survival techniques by their parents.

Exercise 23 **Find It in Your Reading** Review a newspaper or magazine article to find examples of correct usage for at least four of the usage issues identified in this chapter.

Exercise 24 **Find It in Your Writing** Choose one piece of writing in your portfolio. Check it carefully for the usage problems discussed in this chapter. Identify examples of correct usage. Correct any usage errors that you find.

Exercise 25 **Writing Application** Write a brief description of the climate in your area. Check your work for the usage errors discussed in this chapter.

ASSESS and CLOSE

Section Review

Each of these exercises correlates to the instruction on common usage problems, pages 648–660. The exercises may be used for more practice, for reteaching, or for review of the key concepts presented.

Answer Key

Exercise 20
1. an
2. a
3. an
4. an
5. a
6. an
7. a
8. a
9. a
10. an

Exercise 21
1. accept
2. adopted
3. affect
4. annoying
5. aren't
6. already
7. all right
8. further
9. fewer
10. become

Exercise 22
1. altogether
2. Among
3. eager
4. Every one
5. everywhere
6. very
7. About
8. in
9. lying
10. taught

Exercise 23

Find It in Your Reading
If students find errors in usage, have them correct each error and explain the reasoning behind each correction.

Exercise 24

Find It in Your Writing
After students finish, have them exchange papers with a partner and check that all usage problems have been identified and corrected.

Exercise 25

Writing Application
If students notice certain errors that they make repeatedly, have them reread the relevant instruction in their textbooks.

✓ ONGOING ASSESSMENT: Assess Mastery

Use the following resources to assess student mastery of miscellaneous problems in usage.

In the Textbook	Print Resources	Technology
Chapter Review, pp. 662–663, Exercises 26–33	*Formal Assessment,* Chapter 25	*On-Line Exercise Bank,* Chapter 25

⏱ TIME SAVERS!

Answers on Transparencies
Use the *Grammar Exercises Answers on Transparencies* for Chapter 25 to facilitate correction by students.

On-Line Exercise Bank
Have students complete the exercises on computer. The Auto Check feature will grade their work for you!

CHAPTER REVIEW

Each of these exercises correlates with a section in the chapter on miscellaneous problems in usage, pages 642–660. The exercises may be used for more practice, for reteaching, or for review of the key concepts presented.

Answer Key

Exercise 26

1. anything
2. anywhere
3. ever
4. any
5. can't
6. ever
7. anything
8. anywhere
9. anything
10. any

Exercise 27

Answers may vary; samples are given.

1. Other primates <u>are</u> hardly as intelligent as the chimpanzee.
2. correct
3. Research shows that primates can't <u>ever</u> learn to speak as humans do.
4. correct
5. Their communication system <u>is</u> nothing like ours.

Exercise 28

Answers may vary; samples are given.

Anacondas don't have <u>any</u> venom. They <u>have</u> but one way to kill their prey: They squeeze the life out of it. Hardly <u>anyone</u> could survive an anaconda attack. Fortunately, anacondas scarcely <u>ever</u> attack humans. Anacondas are the only species that squeeze their prey. Boa constrictors and pythons also use constriction, not venom.

Exercise 29

Answers may vary; samples are given.

1. Insects account for not a little of the rain forests' animal diversity.
2. They are not unresponsible for spreading many diseases.
3. Mosquitoes carry the not undebilitating disease malaria.
4. It is not impossible to see which mosquitoes are carrying the disease.
5. If properly treated, malaria is not incurable.

662

Exercise 26   Avoiding Double Negatives   Choose the word in parentheses that makes each sentence negative without forming a double negative.

1. An anaconda isn't (anything, nothing) like a rattlesnake.
2. Rattlesnakes don't live (anywhere, nowhere) near the rain forest.
3. They don't (ever, never) grow as long as anacondas do.
4. Anacondas don't have (any, no) rattles at the end of their tails.
5. Without the massive bulk of the anaconda, the rattlesnake (can, can't) squeeze the life from its prey.
6. Rattlesnake prey isn't (ever, never) as big as that of the anaconda.
7. After a large meal, an anaconda doesn't have to eat (anything, nothing) for nearly a month.
8. You don't want to be (anywhere, nowhere) near a hungry anaconda.
9. To most people, there is hardly (anything, nothing) more frightening than the sight of a snake.
10. Research has shown that most people have a strong reaction even to a picture of a snake, although scientists don't yet know (no, any) definite reason why that would be.

Exercise 27   Proofreading Sentences to Correct Double Negatives   Proofread the following sentences. Then, rewrite each sentence, correcting any double negatives. If a sentence contains no errors, write *correct*.

1. Other primates aren't hardly as intelligent as the chimpanzee.
2. There aren't any mammals but humans that can speak.

3. Research shows that primates can't never learn to speak as humans do.
4. Because we aren't able to communicate with their system, researchers have tried using sign language.
5. Their communication system isn't nothing like ours.

Exercise 28   Proofreading a Paragraph to Correct Double Negatives   Proofread the following paragraph. Copy it on a separate sheet of paper, correcting any double negatives.

Anacondas don't have no venom. They don't have but one way to kill their prey: They squeeze the life out of it. Hardly no one could survive an anaconda attack. Fortunately, anacondas scarcely never attack humans. Anacondas are scarcely the only species that squeeze their prey. Boa constrictors and pythons also use constriction, not venom.

Exercise 29   Using Understatement   Rewrite each sentence using understatement.

1. Insects account for most of the rain forests' animal diversity.
2. They are responsible for spreading many diseases.
3. Mosquitoes carry the debilitating disease malaria.
4. It is possible to see which mosquitoes are carrying the disease.
5. If properly treated, malaria is curable.

Exercise 30 Avoiding Usage Problems

Choose the correct expression to complete each sentence.

1. Trees make up a (good, large) proportion of all plant species in the rain forest.
2. They need to (get, receive) great quantities of water.
3. Evergreen shrubs like holly (can, may) be found in the more temperate climates.
4. Some evergreens (loose, lose) all their leaves for a brief period.
5. Others are continually shedding (they're, their) leaves and growing new ones.

Exercise 31 Proofreading Sentences to Correct Usage Problems

Rewrite each sentence, correcting the error in usage.

1. Extinctions of which we are unaware may all ready have taken place.
2. Every one has probably heard about the extinction of the dodo bird.
3. Most dodo species became extinct at about the sixteenth century.
4. Artists done paintings of dodos, but no complete specimens were ever preserved.
5. Ornithology is a wide field of study as there are many types of birds throughout the world.

Exercise 32 Proofreading Paragraphs to Correct Usage Problems

Rewrite the following passage, correcting all the errors in usage.

Their are several types of rain forests altogether. They are classified in various ways. Two lose classifications are tropical and temperate. Tropical rain forests maybe farther classified into equatorial, subtropical, monsoon, and montane. These labels depend primarily on where the forest is at. The latitude of a forest is a key factor in its climate. However, latitude is not only the determining factor. Altitude is kind of important, to. Both latitude and altitude effect the biodiversity of the rain forest. The higher latitudes and altitudes are where there is less diversity.

There are more species of plants in the equatorial forests then in other forests but less individuals of each species. Most of the plant and animal species depend on each other for survival. Due to there great natural diversity, the rain forests are a good potential source of food and medicines. A small percentage of rain forest plants has only been tested for chemical value so far. Outside of diosgenin, other drugs found in the rain forest include reserpine and curare. Natural phenomena, such as fire and landslides, also has an impact on the rain forests They're impact is minimal compared to that of human activity. One reason to preserve the rain forest is because we can't gauge the benefits that remain hidden in them.

Exercise 33 Writing Sentences With Correct Usage

Write sentences, following the directions given below.

1. Use *effect* and *affect* in a sentence about a snowstorm.
2. Use *ought* in a negative sentence about missing athletic practice.
3. Use *loose* and *lose* in a sentence about a puppy.
4. Use *precede* in a sentence about a meal course.
5. Use *one another* in a question about a discussion.

Exercise 34 Writing Application

Write a brief description of a habitat. Include information about animals that can be found in that habitat and the ways in which the animals are suited for living in the habitat.

Exercise 30

1. large
2. receive
3. may
4. lose
5. their

Exercise 31

1. already
2. Everyone
3. during
4. have done
5. since

Exercise 32

Answers may vary; a sample is given.

There are several types of rain forests all together. They are classified in various ways. Two loose classifications are tropical and temperate. Tropical rain forests may be further classified into equatorial, subtropical, monsoon, and montane. These labels depend primarily on where the forest is. The latitude of a forest is a key factor in its climate. However, latitude is not the only determining factor. Altitude is somewhat important, too. Both latitude and altitude affect the biodiversity of the rain forest. The higher latitudes and altitudes contain less diversity.

There are more species of plants in the equatorial forests than in other forests but fewer individuals of each species. Most of the plant and animal species depend on one another for survival. Because of their great natural diversity, the rain forests are a good potential source of food and medicines. Only a small percentage of rain forest plants has been tested for chemical value so far. Besides diosgenin, other drugs found in the rain forest include reserpine and curare. Natural phenomena, such as fire and landslides, also have an impact on the rain forests. Their impact is minimal compared to that of human activity. One reason to preserve the rain forest is that we can't yet gauge the benefits that remain hidden in it.

continued

Exercise 33

Answers will vary; samples are given.

1. The snowstorm affected the roads and airports, but the worst effect was the broken power lines.
2. We ought not to miss practice.
3. We didn't know the puppy had gotten loose from its pen, so we nearly lost him.
4. The salad usually precedes the main course.
5. Did the three students discuss trigonometry with one another?

Exercise 34

Writing Application
Encourage students to consult with partners if they need help correcting any problems in usage. When they finish, have them share their work in small groups.

Step-by-Step Teaching Guide

Standard English Usage

Teaching Resources: Standardized Test Preparation Workbook, pp. 49–50

1. Remind students of the many particular usage rules they have studied in this chapter. Tell them that standardized tests often focus on those particular fine points of English usage. This lesson will give students a chance to apply the knowledge from this chapter.

2. Encourage students to read test instructions carefully. Not all standardized tests are graded in the same way. Some tests do not penalize students for incorrect answers so that students may increase their scores with a judicious guess.

3. You may wish to provide students with standardized test answer sheets to practice the mechanics of marking in answers.

Standardized Test Preparation Workshop

Standard English Usage

Standardized tests frequently test your mastery of standard English usage. Some items focus on choosing the correct word to fill in a blank; others may test your ability to avoid or correct double negatives.

The following questions will give you practice with a format that is used to assess your understanding of standard English usage.

Test Tip

When looking for the best word or group of words to complete a sentence, read the whole sentence as if the words were in the sentence. Do this for each of the choices.

Sample Test Items

Directions: Read the passage, and choose the word or group of words that belongs in each space. Mark the letter of your answer.

The Drama Club is holding auditions next Wednesday. Hardly __(1)__ in the club will miss the auditions __(2)__ everyone wants to be in the play.

1 A everyone
   B no one
   C anyone
   D nobody

2 A being as
   B being that
   C although
   D because

Answers and Explanations

1 The correct answer is *C*. The word *anyone* completes the sentence according to the conventions of standard English usage and makes sense in the space. This choice also avoids double negatives, which would be created by *no one* or *nobody*.

2 The correct answer is *D*. *Being as* and *being that* are not standard English usage. The word *because* is preferred for the intended meaning. The word *although* would not make sense in the space.

✏ TEST-TAKING TIP

Suggest that students use this approach when they are not certain of the correct answer. Look for answers that you can be certain are wrong. Cross them out in the test booklet. Eliminating some wrong answers increases the likelihood of choosing the correct answer— even if a student has to guess which of two alternatives is the correct one.

Practice 1 Read the passage, and choose the word or group of words that belongs in each space.

Many English words come to us from other languages. The __(1)__ of other languages on English is extensive. Over time, many words have been __(2)__ from other languages to fit new needs. In the same way, English __(3)__ other languages. Almost __(4)__ in the world is there a place that English words are not used to some degree. __(5)__ English is spoken so widely in businesses around the world, many call it the language of commerce. As people from different countries travel and interact, new words are __(6)__ into languages. The increased mobility of people __(7)__ much to create greater understanding between people who speak different languages. There are scarcely __(8)__ remaining that create fragmentation. Nonetheless, cultures continue to maintain some of their unique qualities and remain __(9)__ one another. It wouldn't be __(10)__ advantage if everyone were exactly the same.

1   **A** affectation
    B affect
    C effect
    D effectiveness

2   **F** adopted
    G adapted
    H adoption
    J adaptation

3   **A** affectations
    B affects
    C effects
    D effectiveness

4   **F** nowheres
    G nowhere
    H everywheres
    J everywhere

5   **A** Being as
    B Being that
    C Because
    D Because of

6   **F** excepting
    G excepted
    H accepting
    J accepted

7   **A** done
    B has done
    C do
    D doing

8   **F** any barriers
    G no barriers
    H none
    J any

9   **A** different
    B different than
    C differing
    D different from

10   **F** an
    G no
    H a
    J none

Answer Key

▶ **Practice 1**

1. C
2. G
3. B
4. G
5. C
6. J
7. B
8. F
9. D
10. F

CUMULATIVE REVIEW

Each of these exercises reviews concepts taught in the chapters on usage, Ch. 20–25. The exercises may be used for more practice, for review of the key concepts presented, or for assessment of student mastery of the major concepts.

Answer Key

▶ **Exercise A**

Answers may vary; samples are given.

1. Only <u>people</u> who can appreciate a wide variety of artistic styles will enjoy their visit to a modern art museum.
2. correct
3. In the 1930's, American artists, although they studied in Europe, <u>chose</u> a distinctly American style.
4. Paintings and graphics depicting the Great Depression <u>are</u> the focus of the exhibit.
5. Either Grant Wood or Thomas Hart Benton, known as Regionalist <u>painters</u>, found <u>his</u> inspiration in rural life.
6. correct
7. Hopper's works, which use light in a unique way, also <u>examine</u> loneliness and isolation.
8. My two favorite artists, Andrew Wyeth and Edward Hopper, both painted realistically. However, <u>Wyeth's</u> work had a dreamlike quality as well.
9. The drip paintings of Jackson Pollock <u>were</u> part of a movement <u>that</u> was called abstract expressionism.
10. Symbolism, myth, and the subconscious <u>were</u> expressed in <u>this</u> new style of spontaneous painting.

▶ **Exercise B**

1. most
2. more, anything else
3. interesting
4. precisely
5. more, minimalism's

▶ **Exercise C**

Art is my <u>favorite</u> class of the week. Although I sometimes think I am the least talented in my class, I get more enjoyment from the creative process <u>than</u> all my classmates. Last month, we did the most <u>unusual</u> project we have ever done. We had to do three paintings of the same subject, each one with <u>fewer</u> colors than the one before. The techniques

---

Cumulative Review

USAGE

▶ **Exercise A** **Revision Practice: Pronoun and Verb Usage** Revise the following sentences to eliminate problems in pronoun and verb usage. You may need to reorder, add, or eliminate words in a sentence.

1. Only someone who can appreciate a wide variety of artistic styles will enjoy their visit to a modern art museum.
2. Who do you think is the most interesting artist?
3. In the 1930's, American artists, although they had studied in Europe, choosed a distinctly American style.
4. Paintings and graphics depicting the Great Depression is the focus of the exhibit.
5. Either Grant Wood or Thomas Hart Benton, known as Regionalist painters, found their inspiration in rural life.
6. Urban settings or small-town environments are the subjects of many Edward Hopper works.
7. Hopper's works, which use light in a unique way, also examines loneliness and isolation.
8. My two favorite artists, Andrew Wyeth and Edward Hopper, both painted realistically. However, his work had a dreamlike quality as well.
9. The drip paintings of Jackson Pollock was part of a movement who was called abstract expressionism.
10. Symbolism, myth, and the subconscious was expressed in their new style of spontaneous painting.

▶ **Exercise B** **Using Adjectives and Adverbs** Choose the word or group of words in parentheses that form a correct comparison in the following sentences.

1. Abstract expressionism was established as the (more, most) dominant of

all American styles, but some artists rebelled against it.
2. Pop artists drew their inspiration (more, most) from advertisements and everyday objects than from (anything, anything else).
3. Using the influence of Pop Art, photorealism became more (perfect, interesting).
4. With the help of photography, images such as neon signs were (precisely, most precisely) detailed.
5. Conceptual art's expression was even (more, most) abstract than (minimalism, minimalism's).

▶ **Exercise C** **Revision Practice: Modifiers** Revise the following paragraph to eliminate problems with adjective and adverb usage.

Art is my most favorite class of the week. Although I sometimes think I am the least talented in my class, I get more enjoyment from the creative process of all my classmates. Last month, we did the most unique project we have ever done. We had to do three paintings of the same subject, each one with less colors than the one before. The techniques we used were difficulter than ones we had used previously. Nonetheless, the experience taught me to depict form without relying solely on color. In some ways, it was more easy to paint the one with less colors of all than it was to do the one with the most colors. Next week, we will be experimenting with Pop Art. Our teacher told us that Pop artists drew their inspiration most from advertisements and everyday objects than from anything. By studying some of the work of Pop artists, we hope to make our own work more perfect.

---

we used were <u>more difficult</u> than ones we had used previously. Nonetheless, the experience taught me to depict form without relying solely on color. In some ways, it was <u>easier</u> to paint the <u>picture</u> with <u>the fewest</u> colors of all than it was to do the one with the most colors. Next week, we will be experimenting with Pop art. Our teacher told us that Pop artists drew their inspiration <u>more</u> from advertisements and everyday objects than from anything <u>else</u>. By studying some of the work of Pop artists, we hope to make our own work more <u>nearly</u> perfect.

▶ **Exercise D** **Revision Practice: Active and Passive Voice** Revise each of the following sentences to be in the active voice. You will need to reorder words. You may also add words to some sentences.

1. Art from non-European cultures was examined by artists in France and Germany.
2. African sculpture had been studied by Maurice de Vlaminck.
3. The direction of abstract painting was chosen by other groups who had been inspired by indigenous and folk arts.
4. The credit for developing Cubism is given to Pablo Picasso and Georges Braque.
5. In Cubism, an abstract and analytical approach to the subject that involves determining the basic geometric shapes is taken.

▶ **Exercise E** **Combining and Varying Sentences** Rewrite the following sentences according to the instructions in parentheses.

1. Science changed in the late nineteenth and early twentieth centuries. Art styles also changed. (Create a compound subject, and start with a phrase.)
2. Expressionism, Cubism, and Futurism emerged. (Invert the subject-verb order.)
3. Édouard Manet became increasingly concerned with how he painted forms. Impressionists like Camille Pissarro and Claude Monet were concerned with the effects of light on their subjects. (Create a compound sentence, and start with an adverb.)
4. Georges Seurat modified the Impressionist technique into a series of dots called Pointillism. His style involved juxtaposing colors. (Combine by turning one sentence into a subordinate clause, and start with a participial phrase.)

5. Paul Gaugin exaggerated forms. He also exaggerated color to create decorative shapes. (Create a compound direct object, and start with an infinitive.)

▶ **Exercise F** **Revision Practice: Effective Sentences** Rewrite the following paragraph, revising to correct fragments, run-on sentences, misplaced or dangling modifiers, faulty parallelism, or faulty coordination.

A new generation of painters used distortions of line, their spacing in pictures, and color. Gave form to objects yet remained abstract. These painters which only lasted from 1898 to 1908 were involved in a movement called Fauvism. The name comes from the French *les fauves*, "the wild beasts," which was a negative label originally applied to the artists' first exhibition it was never accepted by the painters themselves. They used complementary colors, and they applied them with flat strokes.

▶ **Exercise G** **Proofreading for Common Usage Problems.** Proofread and rewrite the following sentences, correcting all usage problems.

Artists in the 1980's didn't have but one reaction to Minimalism and other abstract styles. They had all ready experimented with impersonal styles when artists adapted a type of narrative painting. Irregardless of history, this Neo-Expressionism wasn't hardly very revolutionary. It hadn't known nothing of the principals of German Expressionists from earlier in the twentieth century. They're style was a very unique combination of distorted forms and strong colors.

Answer Key continued

▶ **Exercise D**

Answers may vary; samples are given.

1. Artists in France and Germany examined art from non-European cultures.
2. Maurice de Vlaminck studied African sculpture.
3. Indigenous and folk arts inspired other groups, who chose the direction of abstract painting.
4. Critics credit Pablo Picasso and Georges Braque with developing cubism.
5. Cubism takes an abstract and analytical approach to the subject that involves determining the basic geometric shapes.

▶ **Exercise E**

Answers may vary; samples are given.

1. In the late nineteenth and early twentieth centuries, art styles and science changed.
2. There emerged Expressionism, Cubism, and Futurism.
3. Increasingly, Édouard Manet became concerned with how he painted forms, and impressionists like Camille Pissarro and Claude Monet were concerned with the effects of light on their subjects.
4. Modifying the Impressionist technique into a series of dots, Georges Seurat developed a style called Pointillism, which involved juxtaposing colors.
5. To create decorative shapes, Paul Gauguin exaggerated forms and color.

▶ **Exercise F**

Answers may vary; samples are given.

A new generation of painters used distortions of line, the spacing of lines, and color. Their work gave form to objects yet remained abstract. These painters were involved in a movement called Fauvism, which lasted only from 1898 to 1908. The name, which comes from the French *les fauves,* "the wild beasts," was a negative label orginally applied to the artists' first exhibition; it was never accepted by the painters themselves. They used complementary colors, applying the paint with flat strokes.

continued

Answer Key continued

▶ **Exercise G**

Answers may vary; samples are given.

Artists in the 1980's <u>had</u> but one reaction to Minimalism and other abstract styles. They had <u>already</u> experimented with impersonal styles when artists <u>adopted</u> a type of narrative painting. <u>Regardless</u> of history, this Neo-Expressionism <u>was</u> hardly revolutionary. It <u>had</u> known nothing of the <u>principles</u> of German Expressionists from earlier in the twentieth century. <u>Their</u> style was <u>an unusual</u> combination of distorted forms and strong colors.

In-Depth Lesson Plan

	LESSON FOCUS	PRINT AND MEDIA RESOURCES
DAY 1	**Using Capitals to Begin a Sentence and for Proper Nouns** Students learn and apply capitalization concepts covering capitals for first words, proper nouns, and geographical and place names. (pp. 670–674)	*Language Lab* CD-ROM, Capitalization and Punctuation *On-Line Exercise Bank,* Section 26.1 **Teaching Resources** *Grammar Exercise Workbook,* pp. 141–142; *Grammar Exercises Answers on Transparencies,* Ch. 26
DAY 2	**Using Capitals for Proper Nouns** *continued* Students learn and apply concepts covering capitals for events, times, and various groups. (pp. 675–678)	*Language Lab* CD-ROM, Capitalization and Punctuation *On-Line Exercise Bank,* Section 26.1 **Teaching Resources** *Grammar Exercise Workbook,* pp. 141–142
DAY 3	**Using Capitals for Proper Adjectives and for Titles** Students learn and apply capitalization concepts covering proper adjectives and titles, and do the Hands-on Grammar activity. (pp. 679–685)	*Language Lab* CD-ROM, Capitalization and Punctuation *On-Line Exercise Bank,* Section 26.1 **Teaching Resources** *Grammar Exercise Workbook,* pp. 143–144; *Hands-on Grammar Activity Book,* Ch. 26
DAY 4	**Review and Assess** Students review the chapter and demonstrate mastery of capitalization concepts. (pp. 686–689)	**Teaching Resources** *Formal Assessment,* Ch. 26

Accelerated Lesson Plan

	LESSON FOCUS	PRINT AND MEDIA RESOURCES
DAY 1	**Using Capitals to Begin a Sentence and for Proper Nouns** Students cover capitalization concepts as determined by the Diagnostic Test. (pp. 670–678)	*Language Lab* CD-ROM, Capitalization and Punctuation *On-Line Exercise Bank,* Section 26.1 **Teaching Resources** *Grammar Exercise Workbook,* pp. 141–142; *Grammar Exercises Answers on Transparencies,* Ch. 26
DAY 2	**Using Capitals for Proper Adjectives and for Titles** Students cover capitalization concepts as determined by the Diagnostic Test. (pp. 679–685)	*Language Lab* CD-ROM, Capitalization and Punctuation *On-Line Exercise Bank,* Section 26.1 **Teaching Resources** *Grammar Exercise Workbook,* pp. 143–144
DAY 3	**Review and Assess** Students review the chapter and demonstrate mastery of concepts. (pp. 686–689)	**Teaching Resources** *Formal Assessment,* Ch. 26

Options for Adapting Lesson Plans

HOMEWORK

Have students complete any section of the chapter for homework.

FEATURES

Extend coverage with the Grammar in Literature feature (p. 682) and the Standardized Test Preparation Workshop (p. 688).

TECHNOLOGY

Students can use the *On-Line Exercise Bank* to complete the exercises on computer. The Auto Check feature will grade their work.

INTEGRATED SKILLS COVERAGE

Grammar in Literature
SE p. 682

Writing
Grammar and Style SE p. 683
Find It in Your Writing SE p. 685
Writing Application SE p. 687

Spelling
SE p. 679; ATE p. 677

Viewing and Representing
Critical Viewing SE pp. 671, 674, 678, 680, 684

Technology
SE pp. 673, 675

Vocabulary ATE p. 675

Workplace Skills ATE p. 675

Real-World Connection ATE p. 672

ASSESSMENT SUPPORT

Standardized Test Preparation Workshop SE p. 688;
ATE pp. 680, 683
Standardized Test Preparation Workbook, pp. 51–52
Formal Assessment, Ch. 26

MEETING INDIVIDUAL NEEDS

Less Advanced Students ATE p. 684. See also Ongoing
Assessments ATE pp. 681, 684.
ESL Students ATE pp. 672, 673
Gifted and Talented Students ATE pp. 675, 681
Verbal/Linguistic Learners ATE p. 676
Visual/Spatial Learners ATE p. 673

BLOCK SCHEDULING

Pacing Suggestions
For 90-minute Blocks
• Administer the Diagnostic Test to students to determine instructional coverage.
• Have students complete the necessary exercises in class. Use the Hands-on Grammar activity to provide a change of pace.

Resources for Varying Instruction
• *Language Lab* **CD-ROM** If your students have access to hardware, a 90-minute block provides an ideal opportunity for students to work on computer.

Professional Development Support
• *How to Manage Instruction in the Block* This Teaching Resource provides management and activity suggestions.

MEDIA AND TECHNOLOGY

For the Student
• *On-Line Exercise Bank,* Section 26

For the Teacher
• *Resource Pro* **CD-ROM**

WRITING AND GRAMMAR WEB SITE

The Interactive Writing and Grammar Web Site provides a wide array of support for students, teachers, and parents. Grammar support includes:

• *On-Line Exercise Bank* with Auto Check scoring
• Diagnostic and assessment support

www.phschool.com

LITERATURE CONNECTIONS

Grammar in Literature selection from *Prentice Hall Literature: Timeless Voices, Timeless Themes,* The American Experience:
from "A Confederate Account of the Battle of Gettysburg," Randolph McKim, SE p. 682

Lesson Objectives

1. To place capitals correctly at the beginnings of sentences, quotations, and lines of poetry
2. To identify and capitalize all proper nouns, proper adjectives, and titles
3. To use capitalization correctly in the titles of individuals and of works
4. To produce legible work that shows accurate spelling and correct use of conventions of capitalization
5. To evaluate writing for both mechanics and content

Critical Viewing

Draw Conclusions Students may conclude that Civil War violence caused severe damage to cities and private property. Sentences will reflect students' conclusions; words that should begin with a capital letter would include the first word in the sentence, the Civil War, and any proper nouns students use, such as the South, the North, or names of generals, battles, or places.

26 Capitalization

The process of writing existed long before capital letters; the first examples of capital letters are seen in writing from around the fifth century B.C. At that time, capital letters were straight, sharp-cornered letters used for inscriptions in stone or metal. Although the straight lines were easier to carve, rounded lowercase letters were preferred for most handwriting. Capital letters were saved for important things, such as a person's name or the beginning of a new thought. Today, the conventions of written English call for capitals to be used in similar ways.

▲ **Critical Viewing**
Looking at the remains of this town, what sentence would you write about the intensity of the Civil War? Which words in your sentence should begin with a capital letter? **[Draw Conclusions]**

668 • Capitalization

☑ ONGOING ASSESSMENT: Diagnose

If students miss more than one item in any category, direct them to the relevant pages of the text and assign exercises for practice and review.

Capitalization	Diagnostic Test Items	Teach	Practice	Section Review	Chapter Review
Skill Check A and B					
Identify proper nouns and adjectives	A 1–5	pp. 672–677 679–680	Ex. 2–5		Ex. 8–9
Capitals for first words	B 6–10 C 11, 13,15–16, 18	pp. 670–671	Ex. 1		Ex. 7 Ex. 10–11

Diagnostic Test

Directions: Write all answers on a separate sheet of paper.

Skill Check A. Copy each of the underlined items, and tell whether it is a proper noun or proper adjective.

1. Stephen Douglas
2. Confederate cavalry
3. Veterans Day
4. American soldier
5. Lincoln Memorial

Skill Check B. Write the words that should be capitalized in the following sentences.

6. at the outset of the civil war, most northerners thought that the south would be defeated within a few months.
7. after the battle of bull run in april 1861, however, it became clear that the war would last much longer.
8. during the coming years, tens of thousands of men would participate in hundreds of battles all across america.
9. the confederacy, which consisted of eleven states—including south carolina, alabama, georgia, and louisiana—was led by president jefferson davis.
10. the northern states, known as the union, were led by men such as abraham lincoln and secretary of state william seward.

Skill Check C. Copy the following paragraph, using capital letters as needed.

(11) most of the fighting took place in southern states, (12) but battles were also fought in the west and along the atlantic coast. (13) for instance, the first ironclad ships, the *monitor* and the *merrimack*, (14) battled each other near the mouth of the james river off the coast of virginia. (15) small towns—such as murfreesboro, tennessee, and perryville, kentucky, (16) became the sites of ferocious battles. after more than four years (17) of bitter fighting, the war ended with the surrender of general robert e. lee to general ulysses s. grant. (18) today, the civil war era is kept alive (19) by books, such as *the red badge of courage*, and (20) historic landmarks, such as kennesaw mountain battlefield.

Skill Check D. Correct the capitalization in each underlined group of words. If no correction is needed, write *correct*.

21. We enjoyed the Shakespearean Play that we saw at the theater.
22. The theater is located on the corner of Saddle and West streets.
23. The british actors stayed after the performance to answer questions.
24. My grandmother knew one of the actors.
25. He signed grandma's program with a flourish.

Each item in the Diagnostic Test corresponds to a specific concept in the capitalization chapter. This will enable you to tailor instruction to the particular needs of your students. See "Ongoing Assessment: Diagnose" below for further details.

Skill Check A

1. PN, PN
2. PA
3. PN, PN
4. PA
5. PN, PN

Skill Check B

6. At, Civil War, Northerners, South
7. After, Battle of Bull Run, April
8. During, America
9. The Confederacy, South Carolina, Alabama, Georgia, Louisiana, President Jefferson Davis
10. The Northern, Union, Abraham Lincoln, Secretary of State William Seward

Skill Check C

11. Most, Southern
12. West, Atlantic Coast
13. For, *Monitor, Merrimack*
14. James River, Virginia.
15. Small, Murfreesboro, Tennessee, Perryville, Kentucky
16. After
17. General Robert E. Lee, General Ulysses S. Grant
18. Today, Civil War
19. *The Red Badge of Courage*
20. Kennesaw Mountain Battlefield

Skill Check D

21. Shakespearean play
22. Correct
23. British actors
24. Correct
25. Grandma's program

☑ ONGOING ASSESSMENT: Diagnose *continued*

If students miss more than one item in any category, direct them to the relevant pages of the text and assign exercises for practice and review.

Capitalization	Diagnostic Test Items	Teach	Practice	Section Review	Chapter Review
Skill Checks C and D					
Capitals for proper nouns and adjectives	B 6–10 C 11–15, 17–18, 20 D 21–23	pp. 672–677 679–680	Ex. 2–4		Ex. 7,
Capitals for titles	B 9–10 C 17, 19 D 24–25	pp. 681–684	Ex. 6		Ex. 10, 11
Cumulative Reviews and Applications					Ex. 12–14

Answers on Transparencies Use the *Grammar Exercises Answers on Transparencies* for Chapter 26 to facilitate correction by students.

On-Line Exercise Bank Have students complete the Diagnostic Test on computer. The Auto Check feature will grade their work for you!

PREPARE and ENGAGE

Interest GRABBER Write the following sentence on the board: *if the statue of liberty could move, would she decide to face new york or new jersey or the atlantic ocean?* Then, ask what is wrong with the sentence (no capitals) and how they know when capitals are needed. Point out that *If* should be capitalized because it begins the sentence, *Statue of Liberty* is capitalized because it is a proper noun (the name of a landmark), and that *New York, New Jersey,* and *Atlantic Ocean* are capitalized because they are proper names for places.

Activate Prior Knowledge

Have students offer the names of places they have visited, the titles of books or movies they have enjoyed, and the names and titles of famous people about whom they have heard. As these are offered, write some of each type on the board. Ask what all of these words have in common. (They all require capital letters.) Discuss with students what they think capital letters accomplish.

TEACH

Step-by-Step Teaching Guide

Using Capitals to Begin a Sentence

1. Point out that capitalization at the beginning of a sentence helps make the meaning clear when sentences follow each other.

2. Spend time on the concept of "first words." While students may have little trouble recognizing first words of ordinary sentences, they may not readily think of other kinds of first words. Ask what these first words are. (first word of a quotation, first word of a sentence following a colon, first word of a line of poetry)

3. Clarify some exceptions: first word of an independent clause following a semicolon, first word of a phrase or list following a colon.

4. Have students identify the examples that illustrate each type of first word on this and the following page. Then have them suggest examples of their own.

Just as road signs help to guide people through a town, capital letters help to guide readers through their reading. Capitalization signals the start of a new sentence or points out certain words within a sentence to give readers visual clues that aid in their understanding.

▶ **KEY CONCEPT** To **capitalize** means to begin a word with a capital letter. ■

Using Capitals to Begin a Sentence

Always signal the start of a new idea by capitalizing the first word in a sentence.

▶ **KEY CONCEPT** Capitalize the first word in declarative, interrogative, imperative, and exclamatory sentences. ■

DECLARATIVE:	The war was long and costly.
INTERROGATIVE:	Where was the battle fought?
IMPERATIVE:	Watch for enemy soldiers.
EXCLAMATORY:	What an astounding turn of events!

▶ **KEY CONCEPT** Capitalize the first word in interjections and incomplete questions. ■

INTERJECTIONS:	Oh! Wonderful!
INCOMPLETE QUESTIONS:	What? How many?

▶ **KEY CONCEPT** Capitalize the first word of a quotation. Do not capitalize the first word of a continuing quotation interrupted by identifying words or a quotation that is the continuation of the writer's thought. ■

EXAMPLES:	Joe exclaimed, "The enemy is in the field!" (speaker's words follow the introductory words)
	"As the ship came plowing through the water," he said, "she cut the waves like a sword cutting through silk." (speaker's words interrupted by identifying words)
	At the end of the battle, Grant remarked that it was "the saddest affair I have witnessed in war." (speaker's words are a continuation of the writer's thought)

670 • Capitalization

Theme: The Civil War

In this chapter, you will learn about capitalizing proper nouns, adjectives, titles, and the first words of sentences. The examples and exercises in this chapter are about the Civil War.

Cross-Curricular Connection: Social Studies

🕐 **TIME AND RESOURCE MANAGER**

Resources
Print: *Grammar Exercise Workbook*, pp. 141–144
Technology: *On-Line Exercise Bank*, Section 26.1

In-Depth Coverage	Accelerated Pace
• Work through all key concepts, pp. 670–684.	• Assign pp. 670–684 for independent student review.
• Assign and review Exercises 1–6.	
• Read and discuss *Grammar in Literature*, p. 682.	• Assign Review Exercises 7–11.

▶ **KEY CONCEPT** Capitalize the first word after a colon only if the word begins a complete sentence. Do not capitalize the word if it begins a list of words or phrases. ■

SENTENCE FOLLOWING A COLON:	He repeated his statement emphatically: He was unable to continue marching.
LIST FOLLOWING A COLON:	The soldiers were issued the following equipment: backpacks, uniforms, canteens, and blankets.

▶ **KEY CONCEPT** Capitalize the first word in each line of traditional poetry, even if the line does not start a new sentence. ■

EXAMPLE: I think that I shall never see
A poem lovely as a tree. — Joyce Kilmer

▶ **Exercise 1** **Capitalizing First Words** Copy the following items, adding capitals where necessary.

EXAMPLE: patriots lined up at recruitment centers.
ANSWER: Patriots lined up at recruitment centers.

1. the American Civil War was fought from 1861 until 1865.
2. despite the terrible consequences that he knew war would bring, President Lincoln made his decision: the Union would be preserved.
3. one senator from Kansas said that he would be willing to do battle for his principles.
4. "it is well that war is so terrible," said Robert E. Lee, "lest we grow too fond of it."
5. in his inaugural address, President Lincoln said that peace would be achieved "with malice toward none, with charity for all."
6. both armies consisted of three main elements: infantry, cavalry, and artillery.
7. how many families would lose fathers, sons, and brothers in the fighting to come?
8. more Americans perished in the Civil War than in all other wars in which Americans fought.
9. "exult, O shores, and ring, O bells!
but I with mournful tread,
walk the deck my captain lies,
fallen cold and dead."—Walt Whitman
10. hurrah! the war is finally over!

▼ **Critical Viewing**
General Robert E. Lee was commander of the Confederate forces. What details in this photo reveal something of his character? Begin your answer with "These details represent Lee's character:" and capitalize the words following the colon correctly. [Analyze]

▶ **More Practice**

On-line
Exercise Bank
• Chapter 26
Grammar Exercise Workbook
• pp. 141–142

Critical Viewing

Analyze Students may note Lee's well-fitting uniform and neat beard and hair and may infer that he was clean in habits, well organized, and perhaps well-to-do. The portrait is a formal one, which might indicate a serious nature. Notice that the proper adjective *Confederate* is capitalized in the caption. Students' responses should use capitalization following the colon if the word begins a complete sentence.

Answer Key

▶ **Exercise 1**

1. **The** American Civil War was fought from 1861 until 1865.
2. **Despite** the terrible consequences he knew a war would bring, President Lincoln made his decision: **The** Union would be preserved.
3. **One** senator from Kansas said that he would be willing to do battle for his principles.
4. "**It** is well that war is so terrible," said Robert E. Lee, "lest we would grow too fond of it."
5. **In** his inaugural address, President Lincoln said peace would be achieved "with malice toward none, with charity for all."
6. **Both** armies consisted of three main elements: infantry, cavalry, and artillery.
7. **How** many families would lose fathers, sons, and brothers in the fighting to come?
8. **More** Americans perished in the Civil War than in all other wars in which Americans fought.
9. "**Exult**, O shores, and ring, O bells!
But I with mournful tread,
Walk the deck my captain lies,
Fallen cold and dead."
— Walt Whitman
10. **Hurrah! The** war is finally over!

🕐 **TIME SAVERS!**

📄 **Answers on Transparencies** Use the *Grammar Exercises Answers on Transparencies* for Chapter 26 to facilitate correction by students.

💻 **On-Line Exercise Bank** Have students complete the exercises on computer. The Auto Check feature will grade their work for you!

Step-by-Step Teaching Guide

Capitals for Proper Nouns: Names

1. Explain that most nouns are common nouns that identify *nonspecific* people, places, or things. Each proper noun names a *particular* person, place, or thing. Have students identify the classification of the following words: student (CN), Henry Smyth (PN), city (CN), car (CN), Boston (PN), Evans High School (PN), and team (CN).

2. Remind students that names given to people and animals are proper nouns and must be capitalized. The entire name, including initials and nicknames, must be capitalized. Have students write or suggest the entire name of one person in each of the following categories:
   - Historical figure
   - Sports personality
   - Entertainment personality, recording star
   - Person who uses a nickname
   - Pet animal

Customize for
ESL Students

Ask students to give examples of words that are capitalized in other languages they know or speak and to offer reasons that these words are capitalized. Encourage students to identify similarities and differences between requirements of capitalization in English and requirements in other languages.

Real-World Connection

Almost all writing that students will do for official, business, and social purposes will require the correct use of capital letters. (Examples: application forms, memos, addresses on envelopes, invitations, to name just a few.) Point out to students that the improper use of capital letters signals to readers that the writer might not understand the conventions of English. Ask students for examples of official documents they have seen or used that required the user to use capital letters correctly.

Using Capitals for Proper Nouns

Nouns, as you may remember, are either common or proper. Common nouns identify classes of people, places, or things.

EXAMPLES: sailor, brother, leader
street, city, country
cannon, ship, magazine

Proper nouns, on the other hand, name specific examples of each class and should be capitalized.

> **KEY CONCEPT** Capitalize all proper nouns. ■

EXAMPLES: Jennifer, Professor Wilkens, Governor Percy, Main Street, Halloran House, Chicago, *The Red Badge of Courage*, U.S.S. *Monitor*, *The Cliffside News*

Names Each part of a person's name—the given name, the middle name, and the surname—should be capitalized.

> **KEY CONCEPT** Capitalize each part of a person's name even when the full name is not used—Bill, John, Sarah. ■

EXAMPLES: Jean Grogan, R. R. Brighton, Ernesto H. Sanchez

Capitalize the proper names that are given to animals.

EXAMPLES: Flipper, Traveler, Rin Tin Tin

> **Exercise 2** **Writing Sentences With Capital Letters** On your paper, write a sentence for each numbered item. Supply capital letters wherever necessary.

EXAMPLE: civil war battlefield
ANSWER: We visited a Civil War battlefield.

1. jefferson davis
2. confederate soldiers
3. *north & south* magazine
4. president abraham lincoln
5. troops stationed in north carolina

> **More Practice**
>
> On-line Exercise Bank
> • Chapter 27
> **Grammar Exercise Workbook**
> • pp. 141–142

672 • Capitalization

Answer Key

> **Exercise 2**

Answers will vary. Sample answers:

1. The first president of the Confederacy was Jefferson Davis.
2. Confederate soldiers often suffered from poor food and inadequate shelter.
3. I read about a Civil War battle reenactment in *North & South* magazine.
4. President Abraham Lincoln was determined to preserve the union.
5. Union troops stationed in North Carolina faced difficult battles in the swamps and marshes along the coast.

Geographical and Place Names Although there is a wide variety of categories of geographical and place names, a single general rule for capitalization applies:

▶ **KEY CONCEPT** Capitalize geographical and place names. ■

Examples of different kinds of geographical and place names are listed in the following chart. Each item should serve as a model for similar names.

GEOGRAPHICAL AND PLACE NAMES	
Streets	Madison Avenue, First Street, Chicken Valley Road
Boroughs, Towns, and Cities	Brooklyn, Oakdale, Michigan City
Counties, States, and Provinces	Champlain County, New Mexico, Quebec
Nations and Continents	Austria, Kenya, the United States of America, the Union, Asia, the Confederate States of America
Mountains	the Adirondacks, Mount Washington
Valleys and Deserts	the San Fernando Valley, the Mojave Desert, the Gobi Desert
Islands and Peninsulas	Aruba, the Faroe Islands, Cape York Peninsula
Sections of a Country	the Northeast, Siberia, the Great Plains
Scenic Spots	Gateway National Park, Carlsbad Caverns
Rivers and Falls	the Missouri River, Victoria Falls
Lakes and Bays	Lake Cayuga, Green Bay, the Bay of Biscayne
Seas and Oceans	the Sargasso Sea, the Indian Ocean
Celestial Bodies	the Milky Way, Mars, the Big Dipper
Monuments and Memorials	the Tomb of the Unknown Soldier, Kennedy Memorial Library, the Soldiers and Sailors Monument
Buildings	Madison Square Garden, the Cleveland Museum of Art, Fort Hood, the Astrodome, the White House
School and Meeting Rooms	Room 6, Laboratory 3B, the Red Room, Conference Room C

🖥 **Internet Tip**

It is important to use proper capitalization in your writing; however, when you are conducting an Internet search, it is not necessary to capitalize proper nouns. Search engines will look for all instances of a word or phrase whether or not it is capitalized.

Customize for
ESL Students

Have students choose any three of the headings from the chart on page 673 (Geographical and Place Names) and write these on their papers, making three columns. Then, ask students to list one or more examples under each of the headings. Encourage students whose English is most limited to list examples in their first languages, and then help them identify (spell and capitalize) corresponding examples in English.

Capitals for Proper Nouns: Geographical and Place Names

1. Remind students that geographical and place names are capitalized when they refer to a specific place but not to a general location. For example, *Hawaiian Islands* is capitalized, but *islands* by itself is not.

2. Emphasize that words that merely indicate direction are not capitalized—for example, "six miles *southwest* of Albany." Words used to denote a specific section in a larger area are capitalized—for example, "the *Southwest*." (a region of the country)

3. Point out that words like *park, stadium, theater,* and *university* are capitalized only if they refer to a specific place and are part of a proper noun: "We will go to the *stadium*"; "Yankee *Stadium*." Have students offer additional examples, stating or writing both the common and proper nouns.

4. Explain that the exceptions to the capitalization rule for celestial bodies are *sun* and *moon. Earth* should be capitalized only when referred to as a planet.

Customize for
Visual/Spatial Learners

Focus students' attention on the chart on page 673 (Geographical and Place Names). Have them draw their own charts placing the headings (Streets, Nations and Continents, Rivers and Falls) in styles and patterns of organization that make sense to them. For example, they might want to organize their charts by places nearby versus places far away; by natural places (lakes, mountains) versus human-made (streets, cities); or simply in a different format than the chart in the textbook. Then have students supply examples of their own to complete their charts.

Language Highlight

Sometimes capital letters are called upper case letters. This idiom is based on an early printing practice. In the days of typesetting by hand, the more commonly used letters were in a type box or case that a typesetter could easily reach—the lower case. Letters that were used less frequently, such as capital letters, were kept in a case that was placed a little farther away, usually above the lower case—that is, the letters were stored in the upper case.

Critical Viewing

Analyze Possible answers: the names of the town, county, and state; the name of the section of the country; if this is the scene of a battle, the name of the battle.

Note About *Capitalizing Directions:* Words indicating direction can be used in two ways: (1) to name a section of a larger geographical area or (2) simply to give or indicate direction. Words indicating direction are capitalized only when they refer to a section of a larger geographical area.

EXAMPLES: The courier made his way through the *South.*
The train stops two miles *east* of the city.

Note About *Capitalizing Names of Celestial Bodies:* Two celestial bodies whose names are not capitalized are *moon* and *sun.* They are exceptions to the rule.

EXAMPLE: When the *moon* passes between the *sun* and the *Earth,* a solar eclipse occurs.

Note About *Capitalizing* **theater, hotel, university,** *and* **similar words:** Do not capitalize words such as *theater, hotel, university, park,* and so forth unless the word is part of a proper name.

EXAMPLES: We visited Stone Mountain Park.
I will meet you at the park.

▼ **Critical Viewing**
If you had background information about this picture, what details might be capitalized? For example, you would capitalize the names of the people who live in the houses. Give at least three other examples of words that would be capitalized. **[Analyze]**

674 • Capitalization

Events and Times Capitalize references to historic events, periods, and documents as well as dates and holidays.

▶ **KEY CONCEPT** Capitalize the names of specific events and periods in history. ■

SPECIAL EVENTS AND TIMES	
Historic Events	the Siege of Vicksburg, the Black Plague, the Battle of Chickamauga, World War I, Strategic Arms Limitations Talks (SALT)
Historical Periods	the Manchu Dynasty, the Age of Napoleon, Reconstruction, the Great Depression
Documents	the Bill of Rights, the Gettysburg Address, the Constitution of the United States
Days and Months Holidays Religious Holidays	Monday, June 22, the third week in May Labor Day, Memorial Day, Veterans Day Rosh Hashanah, Christmas, Easter
Special Events	the Riverhead High School Clambake, the World Series, the Civil War Antiques Show, Tanglewood Music Festival

Most college dictionaries and general encyclopedias include extensive listings of historic events and periods that can be consulted if you are unsure about their capitalization.

Note About *Capitalizing Seasons* Although days and months are capitalized, you should not capitalize seasons unless the name of the season is being used as a proper noun or adjective.

EXAMPLES: The soldiers were particularly uncomfortable during the *summer* because of their wool uniforms.

The *Autumn* Harvest Dance is next week.

🖥 **Internet Tip**

Use the Internet to learn more about the Civil War. Search key words, such as *Civil War, Confederacy,* or *secession.* For narrowly defined topics, try more specific words, such as *Fort Sumter* or *Abraham Lincoln.*

Capitals for Proper Nouns: Events and Times

1. Refer to the chart on page 675, Special Events and Times. Have students add at least one example to each category. For example, they might add the *Declaration of Independence* to the "Documents" category. If they need ideas, suggest that students look at calendars, history books, or the events section of a local paper.

2. Encourage students to consult a dictionary whenever they are unsure about capitalization.

3. Remind students that the names of seasons are not capitalized, but that days and months are.

Integrating Workplace Skills

In class, brainstorm for ideas about writing that students might do someday in the workplace that requires a knowledge of how to use capital letters. Examples might include titles on reports, titles of source documents, names of customers or competing organizations, titles and proper names on interoffice correspondence, business letters, special events, and corporate identity.

Integrating Vocabulary Skills

Remind students that many proper adjectives are forms of names of countries and regions of the world. For instance, *Polish* is a form of *Poland; Sudanese* is a form of *Sudan.* Ask students to identify countries and regions and then to supply the proper adjective forms. Have a volunteer make a master list of these proper nouns and proper adjectives for you to use later (see Integrating Spelling on page 677).

Customize for
Gifted and Talented Students

Quickly review the common way of creating an adjective from a country's name (adding *-ish, -an,* or *-ese*) and then explain that for many places, the adjective describing things related to the place is not so obvious. Give examples such as these: someone from *Kosovo* is a *Kosovar* and someone from *Naples* is *Neopolitan.* Have students use an encyclopedia, geography book, travel literature, or the Internet to discover other places that have related proper adjectives that are not obvious. (Possibilities might include *Liverpool/Liverpuddlian, Hungary/Magyar, Moscow/Muscovite, Glasgow/Glaswegian, Israel/Israeli.*)

Capitals for Proper Nouns: Various Groups

1. Point out that just as we capitalize proper names of people, so, too, we capitalize the proper names of groups.

2. Ask students to review the chart on various groups. What is accomplished by using capitalization with names of groups like those listed? (Possible answers: shows respect, helps identify them as specific organizations, many contain proper names.)

3. Have students name at least one additional example in each category.

4. Review the notes on capitalization that refer to deities. Point out that the word *god* is not capitalized when referring to characters from ancient mythology, nor are the pronouns associated with them. However, the proper names of the mythological deities, such as Apollo and Zeus, are capitalized. You may want to note that similar respect is shown to deities in other religions by pointing out that Brahma and Allah are capitalized.

Customize for
Verbal/Linguistic Learners

Select a passage containing proper nouns (possibilities would be Skill Check B or C from the Diagnostic Test at the beginning of the chapter or one of the Civil War tales from *Prentice Hall Literature: Timeless Voices, Timeless Themes,* The American Experience) and read one sentence at a time to the class. Ask students to listen carefully and to stop you whenever you speak a word that should be capitalized (other than first words of sentences).

Alternatively, you could have students work in pairs, with one student reading a passage aloud while the other listens carefully and stops the reader every time he or she reaches a word that should be capitalized.

26

▶ **KEY CONCEPT** Capitalize the names of organizations, government bodies, political parties, races, nationalities, languages, and religions. ■

VARIOUS GROUPS	
Clubs	Rotary, Knights of Columbus, San Francisco Athletic Club
Organizations	the Red Cross, American Association of University Women, the Urban League
Institutions	the Metropolitan Museum of Art, the Chicago Symphony, the Mayo Clinic
Schools	John F. Kennedy High School, Exeter Academy, Michigan State University, Colby College, United States Naval Academy
Businesses	General Motors, R.J. Whipple and Sons, Prentice Hall
Government Bodies and Organizations	Department of State, Federal Trade Commission, House of Representatives, Parliament (United Kingdom), North Atlantic Treaty Organization (NATO), the United States Army
Political Parties	Republicans, the Democratic party
Nationalities	American, Mexican, Chinese, Israeli, Canadian, Swiss
Languages	English, Italian, Polish, Swahili
Religions and Religious References	*Christianity:* God, the Lord, the Father, the Holy Spirit, the Bible, the New Testament, the Holy Father *Judaism:* God, the Lord, the Prophets, the Torah, the Talmud *Islam:* Allah, the Prophets, the Koran, Mohammed, Muslims *Hinduism:* Brahma, the Bhagavad Gita, the Vedas *Buddhism:* the Buddha, Mahayana, Hinayana

Note About *Capitalizing References to Mythological Gods:*
When referring to ancient mythology, do not capitalize the word *god.*

EXAMPLES: the *gods* of Olympus
the Greek *goddess* Athena

▶ **KEY CONCEPT** Capitalize the names of awards; the names of specific types of air, sea, space, and land craft; and brand names. ■

OTHER IMPORTANT PROPER NOUNS	
Awards	the Pulitzer Prize, Phi Beta Kappa, the Medal of Honor
Specific Air, Sea, Space, and Land Craft	Condorjet 898, the U.S.S. *Kearsarge*, *Apollo V*, Road Ranger 4x4
Brand Names	Biska Treats, Dento-White

▶ **Exercise 3** **Capitalizing Proper Nouns** On a separate sheet of paper, rewrite the words in the following sentences that should be capitalized.

EXAMPLE: Jefferson davis was president of the confederacy.
ANSWER: Davis, Confederacy

1. Ulysses s. grant, who would become a general in the union army, began his career inauspiciously.
2. He was born the son of a farmer in point pleasant, ohio, in a small cabin near the ohio river.
3. When he was old enough, grant studied such subjects as latin and english at both the maysville seminary and the presbyterian academy in ripley, ohio.
4. He continued his education at the united states military academy, which is located on the hudson river in west point, new york.
5. Upon his graduation, grant was sent to the west, where he fought in the mexican war.

▶ **More Practice**

On-line
Exercise Bank
• Chapter 26
Grammar Exercise Workbook
• pp 141–142

Capitals for Other Important Proper Nouns

1. Direct students' attention to the chart for "Other Important Proper Nouns." Ask them what general rule of capitalizing proper nouns would make it seem obvious that these names would be capitalized. (These names identify specific things, rather than general categories.)

2. Ask students if there are any items on this list they don't recognize. Then point out that one advantage of capitalization is that even without knowing what the item is, they already know something about it because it begins with a capital letter. Capitalization can draw attention to important items.

3. Have students share the names of specific craft, including fictional spacecraft (such as the *Enterprise* in *Star Trek*). Explain that capitalization rules make it possible to know how to handle even fictional items. You may also wish to point out that in addition to being capitalized, the names of specific ships are also italicized— for example, U.S.S. *Ohio,* H.M.S. *Bounty.*

Integrating Spelling Skills

Use the lists of proper nouns and proper adjectives that students created during the Integrating Vocabulary activity on page 675. Now read randomly from this list, asking students to write the words on a piece of paper. After having read five or ten words, ask volunteers to spell the words aloud. Ask students to check their answers as you proceed.

Answer Key

▶ **Exercise 3**

1. S. Grant, Union
2. Point Pleasant, Ohio; Ohio River
3. Grant; Latin, English; Maysville Seminary; Presbyterian Academy; Ripley, Ohio
4. United States Military Academy; Hudson River; West Point, New York
5. Grant, West, Mexican War

Answer Key

Exercise 4

1. Fought near **Washington, D.C.**, the **First Battle of Manassas** was the first pitched battle between the **North** and **South**.
2. The **North** hoped to capture the **Confederate** capital at **Richmond, Virginia**, and bring an early end to the war.
3. Union forces attacked **Confederate** positions along a small creek called **Bull Run** on **July** 18, 1861.
4. Early in the morning, **Yankee** troops charged toward a dusty road known as the **Warrenton Turnpike**.
5. Confederate forces retreated toward **Henry House Hill**.
6. More than 11,000 **Confederate** reinforcements were brought in from the **Shenandoah Valley**.
7. Men and women from **Washington, D.C.**, crossed the **Potomac River** into **Virginia** so they could watch the battle.
8. Albert **Ely**, a member of **Congress**, was captured by **Southern** troops during the fighting.
9. After losing the battle, the weary **Union** soldiers staggered down **Pennsylvania Avenue**, past the unfinished **Washington Monument**, and on toward the **White House**.
10. Educated at **West Point**, **General George McClellan** took command of the **Union** forces following the battle.

Critical Viewing

Speculate Possible answers: the soldiers might talk about their families back home, or the last or next battle. Proper nouns might be names of family members or friends, names of home towns and home states, names of officers and other soldiers.

TIME SAVERS!

Answers on Transparencies Use the *Grammar Exercises Answers on Transparencies* for Chapter 26 to facilitate correction by students.

On-Line Exercise Bank Have students complete the exercises on computer. The Auto Check feature will grade their work for you!

678

26

◄ **Critical Viewing** Imagine what these two Civil War soldiers would have to say to each other. What proper nouns might enter their conversation? **[Speculate]**

Exercise 4 **Proofreading for Capitalization of Proper Nouns** On a separate sheet of paper, write the following paragraph, adding the missing capitals.

EXAMPLE: For his bravery during the battle of shiloh, the young lieutenant was awarded the medal of honor.

ANSWER: For his bravery during the Battle of Shiloh, the young lieutenant was awarded the Medal of Honor.

Fought near washington, d.c., the first battle of manassas was the first pitched battle between the north and south. The north hoped to capture the confederate capital at richmond, virginia, and bring an early end to the war. Union forces attacked confederate positions along a small creek called bull run on july 18, 1861. Early in the morning, yankee troops charged toward a dusty road known as the warrenton turnpike. Confederate forces retreated toward henry house hill. More than 11,000 confederate reinforcements were brought in from the shenandoah valley. Men and women from washington, d.c., crossed the potomac river into virginia so they could watch the battle. Albert ely, a member of congress, was captured by southern troops during the fighting. After losing the battle, the weary union soldiers staggered down pennsylvania avenue, past the unfinished washington monument, and on toward the white house. Educated at west point, general george mcclellan took command of the union forces following the battle.

678 • Capitalization

More Practice

On-line Exercise Bank
• Chapter 26
Grammar Exercise Workbook
• pp. 141–142

Learn More

For more information on proper nouns, see Chapter 17.

Using Capitals for Proper Adjectives

A proper adjective is either an adjective formed from a proper noun or a proper noun used as an adjective.

 KEY CONCEPT Capitalize most proper adjectives. ■

PROPER ADJECTIVES FORMED FROM PROPER NOUNS:	Australian kangaroo, Shakespearean play, Afghan hound, European settlers, Spanish ambassador
PROPER NOUNS USED AS ADJECTIVES:	the Senate floor, the Stevenson speeches, Shakespeare festival, a Bible class

Care must be taken in a number of cases to use proper adjectives correctly. Some proper adjectives have become so commonly used that they are no longer capitalized.

EXAMPLES: herculean effort, french fries, pasteurized milk, quixotic hope, venetian blinds

Brand names are often used as proper adjectives.

KEY CONCEPT Capitalize a brand name when it is used as an adjective, but do not capitalize the common noun it modifies. ■

EXAMPLES: Timo watches, Switzles chocolate

KEY CONCEPT Do not capitalize a common noun used with two proper adjectives. ■

One Proper Adjective	Two Proper Adjectives
Mississippi River	Ohio and Mississippi rivers
Washington Street	Washington and Madison streets
Suez Canal	Suez and Panama canals

✦ Spelling Tip

Sometimes a brand name used as an adjective will also show ownership and will need an apostrophe: *Mr. Nutty's* peanuts, *Pico's* spices.

Step-by-Step Teaching Guide

Capitals for Proper Adjectives With Hyphens

1. Review the two key concepts regarding hyphenation.

2. Ask students in what contexts they most often see hyphenated adjectives. (in sports, or in discussing language or nationality, and so on) What are some examples of hyphenated adjectives that do not involve any capitalization? (*all-pro, league-wide,* or any hyphenated adjective that does not include a proper noun)

3. Ask students to list common hyphenated adjectives that do include capitalization. (Spanish-speaking, pro-Albanian, Sino-Russian)

4. Remind students that including the hyphen is important because it is what turns two separate words into one adjective.

Critical Viewing

Connect Sample sentence: President Lincoln sometimes visited Union troops and officers in the field.

Answer Key

Exercise 5

1. Pennsylvania Avenue
2. pro-Union states
3. soldiers of the Confederacy
4. Mississippi River valley
5. Chesapeake Bay
6. Northwest Tennessee
7. European influences
8. the Bill of Rights
9. British diplomats
10. Ulysses S. Grant
11. Native American
12. Blue Ridge Mountains
13. Santa Fe, New Mexico
14. Irish accent
15. French-speaking advisors

Prefixes used with proper adjectives should be capitalized only if they refer to a nationality.

> **KEY CONCEPT** Do not capitalize prefixes attached to proper adjectives unless the prefix refers to a nationality. ■

EXAMPLES: all-American   Anglo-American

> **KEY CONCEPT** In a hyphenated adjective, capitalize only the proper adjective. ■

EXAMPLE: Chinese-speaking American

> **Exercise 5** **Capitalizing Proper Nouns and Proper Adjectives** Copy each of the following items onto a separate sheet of paper, making the necessary corrections.

EXAMPLE: Missouri and Savannah Rivers
ANSWER: Missouri and Savannah rivers

1. pennsylvania avenue
2. pro-union states
3. soldiers of the confederacy
4. mississippi river valley
5. Chesapeake bay
6. northwest tennessee
7. European Influences
8. the bill of rights
9. british diplomats
10. ulysses s. grant
11. native american
12. blue ridge mountains
13. santa fe, new mexico
14. irish accent
15. French-Speaking advisors

 Learn More

For more information on using hyphens to clarify the meaning of words, see Chapter 27.

> **More Practice**
>
> On-line Exercise Bank
> • Chapter 26
> Grammar Exercise Workbook
> • pp. 141–142

▶ **Critical Viewing** Which letters would be capitalized in a sentence about this picture? **[Connect]**

680 • Capitalization

✎ STANDARDIZED TEST PREPARATION WORKSHOP

Mechanics Many standardized tests require students to recognize and use capital letters correctly. Use the following example to demonstrate.

In the Spring, the Russian troops began moving Westward toward the Center of Europe. The late March snows had melted and left only mud to delay the troops' progress.

Which of the following words should remain capitalized in the passage?

A Spring   **C** Center

B Westward   **D** Europe

The correct answer is **D**. *Europe* is the name of a continent. Seasons are never capitalized. *Westward* is a direction, not the name of a region. *Center* is a common noun.

Using Capitals for Titles

Capitals are used for titles of people and titles of literary and artistic works. The charts and rules on the following pages will guide you in capitalizing titles correctly.

▶ **KEY CONCEPT** Capitalize a person's title only when it is used with the person's name or when it is used as a proper name. ■

WITH A PROPER NAME:	At dusk, Sergeant Mason gave the order to attack.
AS A PROPER NAME:	Here is your sword, General.
IN A GENERAL REFERENCE:	The senator followed the progress of the debate.

The following chart illustrates the correct form for a variety of titles. Study the chart, paying particular attention to compound titles and titles with prefixes or suffixes.

SOCIAL, BUSINESS, RELIGIOUS, MILITARY, AND GOVERNMENT TITLES	
Commonly Used Titles	Sir, Madam, Miss, Professor, Doctor, Reverend, Bishop, Sister, Father, Rabbi, Corporal, Major, Admiral, Mayor, Governor, Ambassador
Abbreviated Titles	*Before names:* Mr., Mrs., Ms., Dr., Hon. *After names:* Jr., Sr., Ph.D., M.D., D.D.S., Esq.
Compound Titles	Vice President, Secretary of State, Lieutenant Governor, Commander in Chief
Titles With Prefixes or Suffixes	ex-Congressman Randolph, Governor-elect Loughman

Using Capitals for Titles

1. Explain that a title that includes a person's name makes the identification of that person even more specific—not just any John Smith, but *Dr. John Smith.*

2. Point out that as with other nouns, it is the specific that is capitalized, not the general. For example: Is there a doctor in the house? Yes, this is Dr. Cortez.

3. Refer to the chart on this page. Discuss which of these titles students have seen before and where they've seen them.

4. Emphasize that capitals are not needed for all words in titles, just the important words. Prefixes and suffixes added to titles are not capitalized. For example: ex-Lieutenant Governor.

5. Point out that the titles of certain officials are capitalized even when they are not followed by a proper name. Again, this applies only when the use is specific. There is only one President of the United States, for instance. However, you would still write, "The presidents of several countries . . ." because you would not be referring to a specific person.

Customize for
Gifted and Talented Students

Ask students to create an original paragraph relating an event they experienced, reviewing a movie, or reporting something they learned on the news. Tell them to use as many words that require capitalization as possible. Suggest that they start by reviewing the charts in this chapter to get ideas. When students have finished writing, have them comment on the reason for the capitalization of each word and which rules they found applied most often in their own writing.

☑ **ONGOING ASSESSMENT: Monitor and Reinforce**

If students miss more than two items in any of the Exercises 1–5, refer them to the following for additional practice.

In the Textbook	Print Resources	Technology
Chapter Review, Ex. 7–9, p. 686	*Grammar Exercise Workbook,* pp. 141–142	*On-Line Exercise Bank,* Section 26.1

Step-by-Step Teaching Guide

Grammar in Literature

1. Ask one student to read the passage aloud.

2. Have students divide a piece of paper into two columns, writing *Common Nouns* over one column and *Proper Nouns* over the other. Then ask them to list all the nouns in the story in one column or the other.

3. Ask volunteers to explain the specific reason that each of the nouns in the *Proper Noun* column is capitalized. (title/General, name/Ewell, organization/each of the military regiments, geographical location/Culp's Hill, Virginia)

More About the Writer

Born in Virginia, Reverend Dr. Randolph McKim was a Confederate soldier before he entered the ministry. His tales of the Civil War battles in which he fought give us an eyewitness account of the actions of his Virginia regiment. After the war, Dr. McKim became a minister and served as rector of Epiphany Church in Washington, D.C., for 32 years. In addition to stories, he wrote the inscription for the Confederate Memorial in Arlington National Cemetery.

Connections With Literature

A longer excerpt from "A Confederate Account of the Battle of Gettysburg" can be found in *Prentice Hall Literature: Timeless Voices, Timeless Themes,* The American Experience.

GRAMMAR IN LITERATURE

from A Confederate Account of the Battle of Gettysburg

Randolph McKim

In the following passage, names of people, places, and battalions are capitalized.

Then came General Ewell's order to assume the offensive and assail the crest of Culp's Hill, on our right. . . .

On swept the gallant little brigade, the Third North Carolina on the right of the line, next the Second Maryland, then the three Virginia regiments (10th, 23d, and 37th), with the First North Carolina on the extreme left.

Titles for heads of state, high-ranking officials, and some members of royalty are capitalized. For example, the incumbent President, Vice President, and Chief Justice of the United States Supreme Court, the Queen of England, the Prince of Wales, or the Sultan of Brunei.

▶ **KEY CONCEPT** Capitalize the titles of certain high government officials even when the titles are not followed by a proper name. ■

EXAMPLE: The Senate approved the *President's* choice for *Chief Justice.*

Occasionally, the titles of other government officials may be capitalized as a sign of respect when referring to a specific person whose name is not given.

EXAMPLE: The *Governor* dedicated the monument to the fallen soldiers.

▶ **KEY CONCEPT** Relatives are often referred to by titles. These references should be capitalized when used with or as the person's name. ■

WITH THE PERSON'S NAME: In the summer, Uncle Ted enjoys gardening.

AS A NAME: He says that Grandmother enjoys gardening, too.

682 • Capitalization

Step-by-Step Teaching Guide

Capitals for Titles

1. Ask students to identify the rules they have already covered that might give them an idea of why titles of things are capitalized. (Specific things capitalized are a book title, for example.)

2. Have them look at the chart of titles and identify what, besides capitalization, is used to identify different works (italics, quotation marks). Tell them that they will learn the different applications of these elements in the next chapter; however it is good to be aware of the fact that italics and quotation marks are often associated with the titles of works.

3. Point out that the articles (*a, an, the*) and shorter prepositions (*of, in, to*) are not capitalized unless they are used as the first word of the title. Ask students to name titles that include articles and/or shorter prepositions within the title ("Battle Hymn of the Republic") and titles that begin with an article (*The New York Times*).

KEY CONCEPT Do not capitalize titles showing family relationships when they are preceded by a possessive noun or pronoun. ■

EXAMPLES: my aunt, her father, Jeff's mother

KEY CONCEPT Capitalize the first word and all other key words in the titles of books, periodicals, poems, stories, plays, paintings, and other works of art. ■

The following chart lists examples to guide you in capitalizing titles and subtitles of various works. Note that the articles (*a, an,* and *the*) are not capitalized unless they are used as the first word of a title or subtitle. Conjunctions and prepositions are also left uncapitalized unless they are the first or last word in a title or subtitle or contain four letters or more. Note also that verbs, no matter how short, are always capitalized.

TITLES OF WORKS	
Books	*The Red Badge of Courage* *Battle Cry of Freedom: The Civil War Era*
Periodicals	*International Wildlife* *The Saturday Review of Literature*
Poems	"The Raven" "The Rime of the Ancient Mariner"
Stories and Articles	"Editha" "The Fall of the House of Usher" "Here Is New York"
Plays	*Our American Cousin* *Our Town*
Paintings	*Starry Night* *The Mona Lisa*
Music	*The Unfinished Symphony* "Heartbreak Hotel"

⚙ **Grammar and Style Tip**

When you title your own written works, consider using a short, interest-catching title followed by a colon and a longer explanatory subtitle. Remember to follow the rules for capitalizing words in titles.

✎ STANDARDIZED TEST PREPARATION WORKSHOP

Mechanics Many standardized tests require students to recognize and use capital letters correctly. Use the following example to demonstrate.

My Grandmother cooked Thanksgiving dinner for Uncle Bob, Bishop Green, Assistant Principal Brown, and all the rest of her relatives.

Which word in the passage should not be capitalized?

A Grandmother   **C** Uncle

B Thanksgiving   **D** Assistant

The correct answer is **A**. *Grandmother* is a title showing a family relationship, but it is preceded by a possessive pronoun. Grandmother is not addressed directly nor is the word *grandmother* followed by a proper noun in this sentence. *Thanksgiving* is a holiday, *Uncle* is part of a compound proper noun, and *Assistant* is part of a title that includes a proper noun.

Step-by-Step Teaching Guide

Capitals for Titles: Courses

1. Point out that the simple, general rules of capitalization work for specific applications. Courses that are specific (*Science 101*) are capitalized; courses that are general are not (*Are you taking math this semester?*). Also, as always, proper nouns (*Latin, French*) are capitalized, whether they are courses or not.

2. Ask students if they can give examples of course titles other than what the examples show.

Answer Key

▶ **Exercise 6**

1. President Lincoln's Gettysburg Address, Civil War
2. *Harper's Weekly,* Vice President Johnson, Chief Justice Taney
3. *The New York Times, Boston Herald*
4. *The Liberator,* Mr.
5. *The New York Tribune's,* Brigadier General, Virginia
6. *Leslie's Weekly, Augusta Chronicle*
7. *The Sharpshooter*
8. Confederate, "Dixie," Northern, "The Battle Hymn, Republic"
9. Civil War, "When Johnny Comes Marching Home Again," "Yankee Doodle"
10. *When Will This Cruel War Be Over?*

Critical Viewing

Connect Possible answers: the title President applies to Lincoln. Works might include *Gone with the Wind,* "O Captain, My Captain," or *Gettysburg.*

Customize for
Less Advanced Students

Give students additional practice using the following list of words, some of which need to be capitalized. Ask students to write a sentence for each word, capitalizing as necessary:
1. science
2. thanksgiving
3. spring
4. american history textbook
5. crane's *the red badge of courage*

▶ **KEY CONCEPT** Capitalize titles of educational courses when they are language courses or when they are followed by a number or preceded by a proper noun or adjective. ■

WITH CAPITALS: Latin, Honors Biology, History 105
WITHOUT CAPITALS: geology, psychology, woodworking

▶ **Exercise 6** **Capitalizing Titles of People and Things** Copy each of the following sentences, adding any necessary capitals. Underline words that are printed in italics.

EXAMPLE: After operating on the man for several hours, dr. Roberts was able to save his life.

ANSWER: After operating on the man for several hours, Dr. Roberts was able to save his life.

1. Many people recognize president lincoln's gettysburg address from the civil war era, but many other great works derive from this period.
2. For example, *harper's weekly* was an immensely popular periodical that was probably read by such notables as vice president johnson and chief justice taney.
3. Also widely read were *the new york times,* the *boston herald,* and a host of other newspapers that also reported the progress of the war.
4. A newspaper called *the liberator,* published by mr. William Lloyd Garrison, helped to propel the cause of abolition.
5. Perhaps inspired by *the new york tribune*'s cry of "Forward to Richmond!" brigadier general McDowell marched his troops into virginia.
6. Other newspapers, such as *leslie's weekly* and the *augusta chronicle,* relied on battlefield artists to illustrate their articles.
7. Battlefield artist Winslow Homer published many works during the war, but he is best known for his painting *the sharpshooter.*
8. During the war, Confederate soldiers adopted the song "dixie" as their anthem, while northern soldiers preferred "the battle hymn of the republic."
9. Many songs were popular during the civil war, including "when johnny comes marching home again" and "yankee doodle," which are still known today.
10. Even some diaries of the period, such as Emma Simpson's *when will this cruel war be over?,* remain available.

684 • Capitalization

▼ **Critical Viewing**
What titles apply to Abraham Lincoln himself? What book, poem, or movie titles do you know that pertain to Lincoln or the Civil War era? How are they capitalized? [**Connect**]

▶ **More Practice**

On-line Exercise Bank
• Chapter 26
Grammar Exercise Workbook
• pp. 143–144

✓ **ONGOING ASSESSMENT: Monitor and Reinforce**

If students miss more than two items in Exercise 6, refer them to the following for additional practice.

In the Textbook	Print Resources	Technology
Chapter Review, Ex. 10, p. 686	*Grammar Exercise Workbook,* pp. 143–144	*On-Line Exercise Bank,* Section 26.1

Hands-on Grammar

Capitalization Rules Reference

Create a capitalization reference tool to keep in your notebook. Choose four different colors of notebook-size paper. Divide the top one inch of each page into four equal sections. From the first page, cut away the three sections closest to the right side of the page. From the second page, cut away two sections. From the third page, cut away only one section. Do not cut any sections from the last page. Stack the pages in order, with the first cut page on top. Staple them, or fasten the pages with clips. Then, label the top strips as shown. The notches and colors will make it easy for you to select the category you need. On each page, write abbreviated versions of the rules. (See the example page for proper nouns below.) Make a cover for your reference pages, and keep the booklet in your folder.

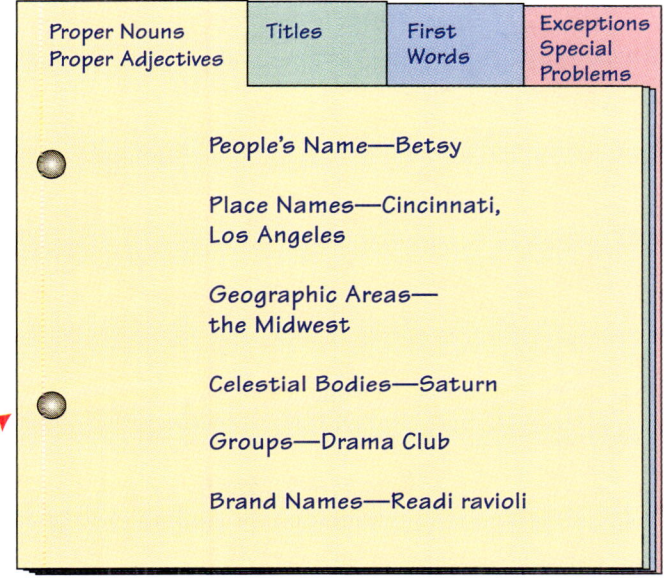

After attaching the cover, use paper fasteners to bind the pages together.

Find It in Your Reading As you read for pleasure or for school assignments, look for words that illustrate each of the capitalization rules. Add them to your reference pages as examples.

Find It in Your Writing Look through selected pieces of writing from your portfolio for words you have capitalized. Add them to the appropriate page in your reference. (Do not add numerous words that illustrate the same rule. Look for a range of words that illustrate a variety of rules.)

Step-by-Step Teaching Guide

Hands-on Grammar

Teaching Resources: Hands-on Grammar Activity Book, Ch. 26

1. If you wish to do this activity in class, be prepared with scissors and four colors of 8-1/2-by-11-inch paper for the students. Give each student a copy of Hands-on Grammar activity sheet.

2. Have students follow the directions to prepare their reference tools.

3. Encourage students to write extremely short versions of the rules—keyword reminders if possible—to keep the reference tool from becoming too cluttered.

Find It in Your Reading

Suggest that students be very selective about adding examples so that every rule has an example but none has similar examples.

Find It in Your Writing

Students can survey their portfolios to see which capitalization rules give them the most difficulty. Encourage students to highlight their most troublesome rules or position them high in the column.

 TIME SAVERS!

Answers on Transparencies Use the Hands-on Grammar activity sheet for Chapter 26 to facilitate this activity.

685

Chapter Review

Each of these exercises correlates to the concepts taught on capitalization. The exercises may be used for more practice, for reteaching, or for review of the key concepts presented. Answers for all chapter exercises are available in *Grammar Exercises Answers on Transparencies* in your Teaching Resources.

Answer Key

1. On
2. After
3. "Would
4. Opposed, "If
5. However; (following the colon) He

1. Mexican War; Ulysses S. Grant; Fort Vancouver; Pacific Ocean
2. April
3. Missouri; Rocky Mountains; Great Plains
4. Grant; Christmas
5. Civil War

1. pro-American
2. Shenandoah Valley
3. the U.S. Navy
4. West Point student
5. Potomac and Hudson rivers
6. the Missouri Compromise
7. Monday morning
8. *Morningside News*
9. Democratic candidate
10. Confederate currency
11. African American
12. Peachtree Street
13. Stephen Crane's stories
14. Virginia soldiers
15. the magazine *Harper's Weekly*

Answers will vary. Sample answers:

1. Elisa is a visitor from Germany.
2. Have you ever been to San Antonio, Texas?
3. Do you think Michael Collins was a good leader?
4. Timber wolves hunt caribou on the tundra.
5. *National Geographic* had an article about African wild dogs.
6. I think *The Old Man and the Sea* is Hemingway's best book.
7. Reggae music has strongly influenced American popular music.
8. The Red River floods destroyed many homes.
9. I visited Monticello two summers ago.
10. The United Kingdom is governed by Parliament.

GRAMMAR EXERCISES 7–14

Exercise 7 Capitalizing First Words

On a separate sheet of paper, write the words in the following sentences that should be capitalized.

1. on June 3, 1808, Jefferson Davis was born in Todd County, Kentucky.
2. after attending both Transylvania University and the United States Military Academy at West Point, he held a number of government positions: soldier, congressman, and senator.
3. "would you believe it," Varina Davis wrote of her future husband, "he is refined and cultivated and yet . . . a Democrat."
4. opposed to the idea of dissolving the Union, Davis stated in 1857, "if the issues are boldly and properly met, my hope is that the Constitution will prevail."
5. however, when his home state of Mississippi seceded, he made a decision that would impact the course of history: he would join the Confederacy.

Exercise 8 Capitalizing Proper Nouns

On a separate sheet of paper, write the words in the following sentences that should be capitalized.

1. After the mexican war ended, ulysses s. grant was transferred to fort vancouver on the coast of the pacific ocean.
2. Grant's military service came to an abrupt end in april 1854, and he made the long journey home.
3. As he traveled back to his family in missouri, he passed over the rocky mountains and crossed the great plains.
4. Once he was home, a number of failed business ventures left grant so

destitute that he sold his pocket watch in order to buy christmas presents.
5. It was not until his success during the civil war that he became an important figure in history.

Exercise 9 Capitalizing Proper Nouns and Adjectives

Copy each of the following items onto a separate sheet of paper, making the necessary corrections. Underline words printed in italics.

1. Pro-American
2. shenandoah valley
3. the U.S. navy
4. west point student
5. Potomac and Hudson Rivers
6. the missouri compromise
7. Monday Morning
8. *morningside news*
9. Democratic Candidate
10. confederate currency
11. african american
12. peachtree street
13. Steven Crane's Stories
14. Virginia Soldiers
15. the magazine *harper's weekly*

Exercise 10 Writing Sentences With Correct Capitalization

Write a sentence with each of the following items. Capitalize as needed.

1. friend's name
2. place you'd like to visit
3. person from Ireland
4. wolf from Alaska
5. magazine you have read
6. book you have read
7. music from another country
8. river near your home
9. home of a historic figure
10. government of another country

Exercise 11 Using All of the Rules of Capitalization

On a separate sheet of paper, copy each of the following sentences, inserting capitals where necessary.

1. in the tumultuous election of november 1860, the republican candidate, mr. abraham lincoln, was elected president of the united states.
2. it was he who would face the arduous task of guiding america through the difficult years of the civil war.
3. lincoln left springfield, illinois, and traveled to the white house in washington. d.c., in the winter of 1861.
4. he told supporters, "i go to assume a task more difficult than that which devolved upon general washington. unless the great god who assisted him shall be with and aid me, i must fail."
5. in his inaugural address, president lincoln told the south that he wished to avoid war, but he would not allow any state to secede from the union.

Exercise 12 Proofreading Practice

Revise the following passage, correcting errors in capitalization. Underline words that should be printed in italics.

(1) By the time lincoln had taken office, the states of south carolina, mississippi, alabama, and georgia had already formed a separate government, the confederate states of america. (2) On april 12, 1861, the confederacy opened fire on union troops stationed at fort sumter, a small outpost in charleston harbor: the civil war had begun. (3) Newspapers in the south, such as the *montgomery advertiser* and the *charleston mercury*, reported the attack. (4) Confederates sang songs, including "the bonnie blue flag." (5) In the north, more than 100,000 new yorkers gathered in union square to express their outrage and to call for retaliation. (6) Lincoln reacted swiftly to the south's act of war by meeting with congress to request more soldiers for the army. (7) The war finally ended when general lee surrendered to the northern army at a small virginia town on the appomattox river. (8) angered by the north's victory, a pro-southern sympathizer named john wilkes booth resolved to assassinate president lincoln on good friday, april 14,1865. (9) President and mrs. lincoln were at ford's theater watching a play called *our american cousin* when booth fatally shot lincoln. (10) The president's body lay in state in the east room of the white house until it was taken to his home in illinois. (11) Lincoln was buried in oak ridge cemetery.

Exercise 13 Explaining Reasons for Capitalization

Identify each example of capitalization in these excerpts from a letter Robert E. Lee wrote to his son. Give the reason for each capitalization.

January 23, 1861

I received Everett's *Life of Washington* which you sent me, and enjoyed its perusal. How his spirit would be grieved could he see the wreck of his mighty labors! . . . It is idle to talk of secession. Anarchy would have been established, and not a government, by Washington, Hamilton, Jefferson, Madison, and the other patriots of the Revolution. . . .

Exercise 14 Writing Application

Write a summary of an event or a situation in American history. Include important names, dates, and places. When you have finished, underline each capitalized word. Give the reason for each capitalization.

Standardized Test Preparation Workshop

Proofreading for Spelling, Capitalization, and Punctuation Errors

Many standardized tests measure your ability to proofread a passage and identify the type of error contained in a given section. The following sample items will allow you to practice this skill.

Sample Test Item	Answers and Explanations

Directions: Read the passage and decide which type of error, if any, appears in each underlined section.
 	
The River Edge School held its assembly (1)
 	
on Monday at 3:00. The Principal spoke
 	
before the entire group. My Grandmother, (2)
my aunt, and my brother attended.
 	
1 A Spelling error
    B Capitalization error
    C Punctuation error
    D No error
	The correct answer for item 1 is *B.* The title *principal* is not capitalized when it is not used with a proper noun.

2 A Spelling error
    B Capitalization error
    C Punctuation error
    D No error
	The correct answer for item 2 is *B.* Titles showing family relationships, such as *grandmother*, are not capitalized when they are preceded by a possessive pronoun, such as *my.*

688 • Capitalization

Practice 1
1. A
2. G
3. B
4. F
5. C

Practice 2
1. D
2. G
3. A
4. G
5. D

▶ **Practice 1** **Directions:** Read the passage and decide which type of error, if any, appears in each underlined section.

One of my favorite short storys is "The
(1)   (2)
Minister's black Veil" by Nathaniel

Hawthorne. I read it for my American liter-

ature class—english 11-2. I have this
(3)
class with Proffesor Quinn at 1:00 p.m
(4)   (5)
 Mon.–Fri.

1 A Spelling error
   B Capitalization error
   C Punctuation error
   D No error

2 F Spelling error
   G Capitalization error
   H Punctuation error
   J No error

3 A Spelling error
   B Capitalization error
   C Punctuation error
   D No error

4 F Spelling error
   G Capitalization error
   H Punctuation error
   J No error

5 A Spelling error
   B Capitalization error
   C Punctuation error
   D No error

▶ **Practice 2** **Directions:** Read the passage and decide which type of error, if any, appears in each underlined section.

Did you know Professor Quinn belongs to
(1)
the Hawthorne association of teachers.
(2)
He is considered an expert on writing.

He mets with other members in Salem,
(3)
MA, every Summer. He visits the
(4)
Northeast at this time of year.
(5)

1 A Spelling error
   B Capitalization error
   C Punctuation error
   D No error

2 F Spelling error
   G Capitalization error
   H Punctuation error
   J No error

3 A Spelling error
   B Capitalization error
   C Punctuation error
   D No error

4 F Spelling error
   G Capitalization error
   H Punctuation error
   J No error

5 A Spelling error
   B Capitalization error
   C Punctuation error
   D No error

Time and Resource Manager

In-Depth Lesson Plan

	LESSON FOCUS	PRINT AND MEDIA RESOURCES
DAY 1	**End Marks and Commas** Students learn and apply concepts relating to periods, question marks, exclamation marks, and commas. (pp. 692–715)	*Language Lab* **CD-ROM**, Punctuation *On-Line Exercise Bank*, Sections 27.1–2 **Teaching Resources** *Grammar Exercise Workbook*, pp. 145–152; *Grammar Exercises Answers on Transparencies*, Ch. 27
DAY 2	**Semicolons and Colons** Students learn and apply concepts relating to semicolons and colons. (pp. 716–723)	*On-Line Exercise Bank*, Section 27.3 **Teaching Resources** *Grammar Exercise Workbook*, pp. 153–154
DAY 3	**Quotation Marks and Underlining** Students learn and apply concepts relating to quotation marks, underlining, and italics. (pp. 724–741)	*On-Line Exercise Bank*, Section 27.4 **Teaching Resources** *Grammar Exercise Workbook*, pp. 155–160
DAY 4	**Dashes to Apostrophes** Students learn and apply concepts relating to dashes, parentheses, brackets, hyphens, and apostrophes. (pp. 742–763)	*On-Line Exercise Bank*, Sections 27.5–6 **Teaching Resources** *Grammar Exercise Workbook*, pp. 161–172; *Hands-on Grammar Activity Book*, Ch. 27
DAY 5	**Review and Assess** Students review chapter and demonstrate mastery of punctuation concepts. (pp. 764–767)	**Teaching Resources** *Formal Assessment*, Ch. 27

Accelerated Lesson Plan

	LESSON FOCUS	PRINT AND MEDIA RESOURCES
DAY 1	**End Marks and Commas** Students cover concepts relating to periods, question marks, exclamation marks, and commas as determined by the Diagnostic Test. (pp. 692–715)	*Language Lab* **CD-ROM**, Punctuation *On-Line Exercise Bank*, Sections 27.1–2 **Teaching Resources** *Grammar Exercise Workbook*, pp. 145–152; *Grammar Exercises Answers on Transparencies*, Ch. 27
DAY 2	**Semicolons to Underlining** Students cover concepts relating to semicolons, colons, quotation marks, underlining, and italics. (pp. 716–741)	*On-Line Exercise Bank*, Sections 27.3–4 **Teaching Resources** *Grammar Exercise Workbook*, pp. 153–160
DAY 3	**Dashes to Apostrophes** Students cover concepts relating to dashes, parentheses, brackets, hyphens, and apostrophes. (pp. 742–767)	*On-Line Exercise Bank*, Sections 27.5–6 **Teaching Resources** *Grammar Exercise Workbook*, pp. 161–172; *Formal Assessment*, Ch. 27

Options for Adapting Lesson Plans

FEATURES

Extend coverage with the Grammar in Literature features (pp. 710, 730, 744) and the Standardized Test Preparation Workshop (p. 768).

TECHNOLOGY

Students can use the *On-Line Exercise Bank* to complete the exercises on computer. The Auto Check feature will grade their work.

INTEGRATED SKILLS COVERAGE

Grammar in Literature SE pp. 710, 730, 744

Writing
Find It in Your Writing SE pp. 695, 715, 723, 741, 755, 763
Writing Application SE pp. 695, 715, 723, 741, 755, 763, 767, 771
Grammar and Style SE pp. 696, 729, 742, 747, 749, 752, 761

Spelling SE pp. 730, 757; ATE pp. 731, 757

Viewing and Representing
Critical Viewing, SE pp. 690, 693, 697, 700, 703, 705, 706, 711, 713, 716, 718, 721, 722, 725, 727, 728, 733, 737, 743, 745, 746, 748, 751, 757, 759

Vocabulary ATE p. 694

Workplace ATE pp. 709, 746

Technology SE pp. 694, 708, 717, 735, 739, 745, 752

Speaking and Listening ATE pp. 693, 760

Real-World Connection ATE pp. 725, 737

ASSESSMENT SUPPORT

Standardized Test Preparation Workshop SE p. 768; ATE pp. 703, 728, 753, 760

Standardized Test Preparation Workbook, pp. 53–54

Formal Assessment, Ch. 27

MEETING INDIVIDUAL NEEDS

Less Advanced Students ATE p. 769. See Ongoing Assessments ATE pp. 693, 697, 699, 700, 702, 706, 712, 722, 727, 729, 733, 738, 744, 748, 749, 752, 761.

AP Students ATE pp. 710, 769

Gifted and Talented Students ATE p. 719

ESL Students ATE pp. 720, 757

Musical/Rhythmic Learners ATE p. 726

Visual/Spatial Learners ATE p. 699

Verbal/Linguistic Learners ATE p. 761

BLOCK SCHEDULING

Pacing Suggestions
For 90-minute Blocks
• Administer the Diagnostic Test to students to determine instructional coverage.
• Have students complete the necessary exercises in class. Use the Hands-on Grammar activity to provide a change of pace.

Resources for Varying Instruction
• *Language Lab* **CD-ROM** If your students have access to hardware, a 90-minute block provides an ideal opportunity for students to work on computer.

Professional Development Support
• *How to Manage Instruction in the Block* This Teaching Resource provides management and activity suggestions.

MEDIA AND TECHNOLOGY

For the Student
• *Language Lab* **CD-ROM**, Punctuation
• *On-Line Exercise Bank,* Sections 27.1–6

For the Teacher
• *Resource Pro* **CD-ROM**

WRITING AND GRAMMAR WEB SITE

The Interactive Writing and Grammar Web Site provides a wide array of support for students, teachers, and parents. Grammar support includes:

• *On-Line Exercise Bank* with Auto Check scoring
• Diagnostic and assessment support

www.phschool.com

LITERATURE CONNECTIONS

Grammar in Literature selections from *Prentice Hall Literature: Timeless Voices, Timeless Themes,* The American Experience:

from "Here is New York," E. B. White, SE p. 710
from "The Writer in the Family," E. L. Doctorow, SE p. 730
from *Hiroshima,* John Hersey, SE p. 744

Lesson Objectives

1. To use periods, question marks, and exclamation marks correctly

2. To use commas correctly

3. To use semicolons and colons correctly

4. To use quotation marks, single quotation marks, and italics correctly

5. To identify situations requiring dashes, parentheses, brackets, and hyphens and to use them correctly

6. To use apostrophes correctly

7. To produce legible work that shows correct use of the conventions of punctuation such as italics and ellipses

8. To evaluate writing for both mechanics and content and to respond productively to peer review of his or her own work

9. To demonstrate proficiency in each aspect of the listening process

Critical Viewing

Analyze Possible answer: The tern's wingspan is more than twice the length of its body.

Chapter 27 Punctuation

▲ **Critical Viewing** Make an observation about the breadth of the tern's wingspan. Can you then change the statement to a question simply by raising your voice at the end? **[Analyze]**

To punctuate correctly requires a knowledge of the parts of a sentence and their relationships to each other. It also requires an understanding of different types of sentences and the punctuation marks used either to separate or to join them.

Punctuation marks are so important that sentence meaning is easily affected by them. Observe how a simple change in punctuation results in very different meanings:

The Arctic tern's head is black. (statement of fact)
The Arctic tern's head is black? (question)
Did you see Ann? (Did someone see Ann?)
Did you see, Ann? (Did Ann see something?)

An effort to master the rules in this chapter will help you greatly in your writing. Study the rules carefully, and refer to this chapter whenever you are uncertain about a particular problem in punctuation.

✓ **ONGOING ASSESSMENT: Diagnose**

If students miss more than one item in any category, direct them to the relevant pages of the text and assign exercises for practice and review.

Punctuation	Diagnostic Test Items	Teach	Practice	Section Review	Chapter Review
Skill Check A					
Using End Marks	A 1–5	pp. 692–694	Ex. 1–2	Ex. 3–6	Ex. 69
Skill Check B					
Using Commas	B 6–10	pp. 698–704	Ex. 12–17	Ex. 22–26	Ex. 80
Skill Check C					
Using Semicolons and Colons	C 11–15	pp. 716–20	Ex. 30–32	Ex. 33–34	Ex. 81

Diagnostic Test

Directions: Write all answers on a separate sheet of paper.

Skill Check A. Write the following sentences, using proper end marks to punctuate them.

1. Most species of penguins live in the frigid Antarctic
2. Have you ever seen one
3. Wow Temperatures in the Antarctic can reach 62° below zero
4. Really That is absolutely remarkable
5. There are penguins at the zoo Do you want to go see them

Skill Check B. Write the following sentences, inserting commas where necessary.

6. Aside from living in Antarctica penguins live in other places.
7. Penguins inhabit Australia South Africa and South America.
8. The largest species is the emperor penguin which can reach a height of four feet.
9. Incidentally the little blue penguin is the smallest.
10. Both have blue-gray patches on their soft warm feathers.

Skill Check C. Write the following sentences, inserting colons and semicolons where necessary.

11. The emperor penguin has another distinguishing feature a bright red patch on the side of its face.
12. Not all penguins look alike for example, the yellow-eyed penguin has two crests of feathers on its face.
13. The six other species that have crests live in a variety of places New Zealand, Tasmania, and Argentina.
14. Two species of penguins even live in the tropics a current of icy water makes this possible.
15. Penguins cannot fly however, they are excellent swimmers.

Skill Check D. Write the following sentences, inserting quotation marks where necessary.

16. Do you know how penguin feathers are shaped? he asked.
17. I replied, No, I don't.
18. Most birds have a variety of long and short feathers, he said.
19. If you look at the feathers on a penguin, he explained, you will see that they are short.
20. Most birds shed their feathers gradually, he said.

Skill Check E. Write the following sentences, inserting apostrophes and dashes where necessary.

21. The penguins body is designed to withstand extreme cold.
22. The penguins small features help to conserve body heat.
23. Its true that a penguin has a thick layer of fat under its skin.
24. The feathers waterproofing effect helps keep the penguin warm.
25. Small features, a layer of fat, and a waterproof coat of feathers all of these things help the penguin survive in the cold.

Diagnostic Test

Each item in the Diagnostic Test corresponds to a specific section in the punctuation chapter. This will enable you to tailor instruction to the particular needs of your students. See "Ongoing Assessment: Diagnose" below for further details.

Skill Check A

1. Antarctic**.**
2. one**?**
3. Wow**!** . . . below zero**!**
4. Really**?** . . . remarkable**!**
5. zoo**.** . . . them**?**

Skill Check B

6. Antarctica,
7. Australia, South Africa,
8. penguin,
9. Incidentally,
10. soft,

Skill Check C

11. feature**:**
12. alike**;**
13. places**:**
14. tropics**;**
15. fly**;**

Skill Check D

16. "Do . . . shaped?"
17. "No, . . . don't."
18. "Most . . . feathers,"
19. "If . . . penguin,"; "you . . . short."
20. "Most . . . gradually,"

Skill Check E

21. penguin's
22. penguin's
23. It's (true)
24. feathers'
25. feathers—all

✓ ONGOING ASSESSMENT: Diagnose *continued*

Punctuation	Diagnostic Test Items	Teach	Practice	Section Review	Chapter Review
Skill Check D					
Using Quotation Marks	D 16–20	pp. 724–736	Ex. 38–47	Ex. 48–52	Ex. 82–83
Skill Check E					
Using Apostrophes	E 21–24	pp. 756–762	Ex. 71–73	Ex. 74–75	Ex. 85
Using Dashes	E 25	pp. 742–753	Ex. 56–61	Ex. 62–67	Ex. 84
Cumulative Reviews and Applications				Ex. 7–9, 27–29, 35–37, 53–55, 68–70, 76–78	Ex. 86–89

⏱ TIME SAVERS!

Answers on Transparencies Use the *Grammar Exercises Answers on Transparencies* for Chapter 27 to facilitate correction by students.

On-Line Exercise Bank Have students complete the Diagnostic Test on computer. The Auto Check feature will grade their work for you.

Interest GRABBER Place these words on the board:

Wow is that a dragon I like your costume

Ask students to read this aloud and to determine how many different ideas they see (three). Then, ask how these ideas and emotions can be represented for readers (end marks). Ask students to suggest ways to rewrite these words. Point out the appropriate uses of end marks and capitalization:

Wow! Is that a dragon? I like your costume.

Activate Prior Knowledge

Ask students to write down one comment made during a recent conversation that would end with either a period, a question mark, or an exclamation mark. Have volunteers read their sentences aloud.

TEACH

Step-by-Step Teaching Guide

The Period

1. Emphasize to students that a period can end any sentence that is not exclamatory or interrogative.
2. Read the key concept and have students read the examples of declarative statements.
3. To check their grasp of indirect questions, have them make the example interrogative. (Did you see the bald eagle?)

Answer Key

▶ **Exercise 1**

Answers will vary; samples are given.

1. A goldfinch likes thistle seed.
2. Look under "Pets" in the Yellow Pages.
3. Herman asked what kinds of birds make good pets.
4. Sherri believes that pet birds are too sensitive to cold.
5. Review the chapter about birds.

Section 27.1

End Marks

The three end marks are the period (.), the question mark (?), and the exclamation mark (!). They have a number of basic uses as well as a few more specialized uses.

Basic Uses of End Marks

Most of the basic uses of end marks are for full sentences. A few, as you will see, are for words and phrases.

The Period The period is the most common end mark.

▶ **KEY CONCEPT** Use a period to end a declarative sentence, a mild imperative, and an indirect question. ■

A **declarative statement** is a statement of fact or opinion.

STATEMENT OF FACT:	There are more than 10,000 species of birds.
STATEMENT OF OPINION:	The veterinarian believes my parrot will recover from its illness.

Some declarative sentences include an indirect question.

INDIRECT QUESTION:	My father asked whether we saw the bald eagle.

An **imperative sentence** gives a direction or a command. Often, the first word of an imperative sentence is a verb.

DIRECTION:	Fill the birdfeeder first, and then, hang it in the tree.
COMMAND:	Clean the bird cage.

▶ **Exercise 1** **Writing Declarative and Imperative Sentences**
Write declarative and imperative sentences with end punctuation, following the instructions below.

EXAMPLE:	command about pigeons
ANSWER:	Feed these breadcrumbs to the pigeons.

1. statement of fact about a bird
2. direction for finding pet store listings in the Yellow Pages
3. indirect question about a bird
4. statement of opinion about pet birds
5. command about studying for a science test

Theme: Birds

In this section, you will learn when to use periods, question marks, and exclamation marks. The examples and exercises in this section are about birds.

Cross-Curricular Connection: Science

▶ **More Practice**

On-line Exercise Bank
• Section 27.1
Grammar Exercise Workbook
• pp. 145–146

⏱ **TIME AND RESOURCE MANAGER**

Resources
Print: *Grammar Exercise Workbook,* pp. 145–146; *Grammar Exercises Answers on Transparencies,* Ch. 27
Technology: *On-Line Exercise Bank,* Section 27.1

In-Depth Coverage	Accelerated Pace
• Work through all key concepts, pp. 692–694. • Assign and review Exercises 1–2.	• Assign pp. 692–694 for independent student review. • Assign Section Review Exercises 3–6, p. 695.

The Question Mark Use a question mark with a direct question.

▶ **KEY CONCEPT** Use a question mark to end an interrogative sentence, an incomplete question, or a statement intended as a question. ■

Often, the word order as well as the punctuation of an interrogative sentence is different from that of a declarative sentence.

EXAMPLES: Why are there so many birds in our yard**?**
            Are bats considered birds or mammals**?**

A question mark is also used with one or more interrogative words when a complete sentence is not necessary.

EXAMPLE: Penguins have lost the ability to fly. Why**?**

Occasionally, a question mark is used at the end of a statement that asks a question.

EXAMPLE: Birds eat grasshoppers**?**

Use care, however, in ending statements with question marks. It is better to rephrase the statement as a direct question.

STATEMENT WITH A
QUESTION MARK: The geese haven't migrated yet**?**

REVISED INTO A
DIRECT QUESTION: Haven't the geese migrated yet**?**

The Exclamation Mark An exclamation mark signals an exclamatory sentence, an imperative sentence, or an interjection. It indicates strong emotion and should be used sparingly.

▶ **KEY CONCEPT** Use an exclamation mark to end an exclamatory sentence, a forceful imperative sentence, or an interjection expressing strong emotion. ■

EXCLAMATORY
SENTENCES: This new information changes nothing!
                 That vulture is frightening!

IMPERATIVE
SENTENCES: Don't let the bird out of the cage this time!
                 Remember to feed my parrot!

Depending on emphasis, an exclamation mark or a comma can be used with an interjection.

WITH AN
EXCLAMATION MARK: Oh! What an enormous bird!

WITH A COMMA: Oh, it is only an owl.

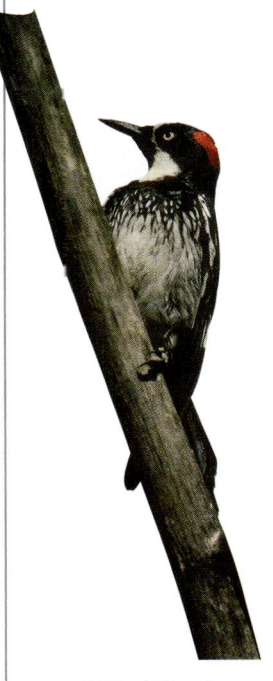

▲ **Critical Viewing**
Write three questions you would try to answer in a research project about this bird. Make sure to punctuate each one correctly. **[Question]**

End Marks • 693

✓ ONGOING ASSESSMENT: Monitor and Reinforce

If students miss more than one item in Exercise 1 or 2, refer them to the following for additional practice.

In the Textbook	Print Resources	Technology
Section Review, Ex. 3–6, p. 695	*Grammar Exercise Workbook,* pp. 145–146	*On-Line Exercise Bank,* Section 27.1

The Question Mark

1. Emphasize to students that question marks are used to end any sentence that requires an answer.

2. Have students read each pair of examples and tell you why question marks have been used.

3. Finally, have students offer original statements requiring question marks.

The Exclamation Mark

1. Explain that exclamation marks denote forceful comments, commands, or emotions. Tell students that overuse of exclamation marks can weaken the effect of one's writing.

2. Have students read the key concept and review the definitions of *imperative sentence* and *interjection*.

3. Give students additional examples of imperative and exclamatory sentences and ask students to identify them by type:

    Don't ever feed the wild bears! (imperative)

    It's dangerous to feed the wild bears! (exclamatory)

Critical Viewing

Question Possible answers: Why does it have such a long bill? Where does it live? What does it eat?

Integrating Speaking and Listening Skills

Intonation Explain to students that a speaker's emphasis on certain words (intonation) signals whether an idea is a question, a statement, or a command. Have students ask each other for the right time and then observe the words they emphasized. (Probably a noun: What <u>time</u> is it?) Then, have students say aloud the sentences in Exercise 1 on page 692 to experiment with intonation and word emphasis.

Other Uses of End Marks

1. Explain that the typical abbreviation ends with a period. Add that no space follows a period within an abbreviation. Example: *Ph.D.*

2. Tell students that most companies don't abbreviate their names, but they might abbreviate the word *Incorporated* as *Inc.* or *Company* as *Co.*

3. Point out that unless an exclamation mark or question mark is required, the period in the abbreviation serves as the end mark for the sentence.

4. Write the following examples on the board, asking a student to provide the proper end mark:

   Will we travel to Vancouver, B.C. (?)

   Let's hire Nancy Maltin, Esq. (no additional period required)

5. Have students follow the outline on this page, pointing out how end marks are used in outline format. For example, Roman numerals do not require a period.

Integrating Vocabulary Skills

Acronyms Ask students whether they know the definition of *acronym* (a word formed from the initials of a name or phrase). Ask which word in the examples on this page is a well-known acronym (NASA), and ask them to think of others (scuba, NATO, AWOL). Point out that acronyms generally do not need periods.

Answer Key

▶ **Exercise 2**

1. sanctuary**?**
2. month**.**
3. fun**!** or **.**
4. facts**.**
5. feathers**?**

27.1

Other Uses of End Marks

▶ **KEY CONCEPT** Most abbreviations end with a period. ■

ABBREVIATIONS WITH PERIODS:	in., Dr., etc., Sr., A.M. D.D.S., Ave., Mrs., Tex., Co., B.C.
ABBREVIATIONS WITHOUT PERIODS:	FBI, NASA, TX, COD

When an abbreviation ending with a period is found at the end of a sentence, do not add another period as an end mark.

INCORRECT:	The speaker will be Adam Martin, Jr..
CORRECT:	The speaker will be Adam Martin, Jr.

If an end mark other than a period is required, however, you must add the end mark.

EXAMPLE:	Is the speaker Adam Martin, Jr.?

▶ **KEY CONCEPT** Use a period after numbers and letters in outlines. ■

EXAMPLE:
    I. Maintaining your pet's health
        A. Diet
            1. For a puppy
            2. For a mature dog
        B. Exercise
        C. Cleanliness
        D. Preventing accidents

▶ **Exercise 2** **Using End Marks** Copy the following items, punctuating each of them correctly.

EXAMPLE:	The hawk flew high above the rocks
ANSWER:	The hawk flew high above the rocks**.**

1. Have you ever visited the bird sanctuary
2. I went there with my class last month
3. It was so much fun
4. We had a very knowledgeable tour guide who told us many interesting facts
5. For instance, did you know that birds are the only animals that have feathers

694 • Punctuation

🖥️ **Internet Tip**

When entering World Wide Web addresses, be sure to include the proper end marks. For example, in the address **www.chess.com**, you must always place a period after **www** and before **com**. This same rule applies to the suffixes **edu**, **net**, **org**, and **gov**.

▶ **More Practice**

On-line Exercise Bank
• Section 27.1
Grammar Exercise Workbook
• pp. 145–146

✓ **ONGOING ASSESSMENT: Assess Mastery**

Use the following resources to assess student mastery of end marks.

In the Textbook	Technology
Chapter Review, p. 764, Ex. 79	*On-Line Exercise Bank*, Section 27.1

Section 27.1 Section Review

GRAMMAR EXERCISES 3–9

Exercise 3 Using End Marks
Rewrite the following sentences, adding the proper end marks.

1. I asked if all birds had the ability to fly
2. No, not all of them
3. Is the ostrich a flightless bird
4. Did you know that the ostrich is the largest bird in the world
5. Wow Ostriches can run as fast as 40 miles per hour

Exercise 4 Using Periods in Special Situations
Copy the following items, adding any necessary periods. Not every item will need punctuation.

1. 9:37 PM
2. Stephanie Davis, MS
3. Blue Ridge Canoe Co
4. Flagstaff, Ariz
5. http://www xyxco edu
6. Dear Mr Jackson:
7. 3 tsp cinnamon
8. ASPCA
9. 125 BC to AD 560
10. 1423 21st St

Exercise 5 Using All Kinds of End Marks
Rewrite the following items, adding periods, question marks, and exclamation points as needed.

1. He asked what kind of hawk was soaring above us
2. Dr Smith began the program to reestablish the owl population
3. This label is on the carton: 1 doz Grade A eggs
4. Astounding Did you see that eagle grab the fish out of the lake
5. Mom reminded us to be sure to set up the birdbath before Apr 18

Exercise 6 Proofreading for End Marks
Revise the following paragraph, adding or correcting end marks as needed.

Yesterday, we heard a lecture on exotic birds by Dr Alan Lee, Jr.. The lecture was scheduled for 10 AM, but it was delayed an hour! Dr. Lee was coming from Fresno, Calif, and his flight was late. He began by asking if anyone in the audience had an exotic bird as a pet? Several had finches or cockatoos Dr Lee then talked about toucans, macaws, and the speckled mousebird. How stunning his slides were.

Exercise 7 Find It in Your Reading
Read this excerpt from E. B. White's "Here Is New York." Explain why the author used a period rather than an exclamation mark after the word "anymore."

When she turned up, the day after the move, at the same grocer's that she had patronized for years, the proprietor was in ecstasy—almost in tears—at seeing her. "I was afraid," he said, "now that you've moved away I wouldn't be seeing you anymore."

Exercise 8 Find It in Your Writing
Look through your portfolio for at least three examples of an abbreviation. Write these down, and then exchange lists with a partner to make sure the abbreviations are properly punctuated.

Exercise 9 Writing Application
Write a short anecdote about an animal—either imaginary or real. In it, use at least one period, one question mark, and one exclamation mark. Also, use at least one abbreviation that contains a period.

Place this sentence on the board:

Have you eaten Grandpa?

Ask students for its meaning and expect a diverse opinion. (The speaker is asking Grandpa whether he has dined, or the speaker is interviewing a cannibal.) Then, ask which punctuation mark might save Grandpa from a horrible fate. (a comma) Show students that placing a comma after *eaten* sets off *Grandpa* as a parenthetical, a noun in direct address.

Activate Prior Knowledge

Have students write a sentence about an important event. Write some of the sentences on the board. (*My birthday party was last week.*) Then, ask students to suggest additional phrases or words that would make these sentences more specific or interesting. (Example: *My birthday party last week was noisy, colorful, and fun.*) For each expanded sentence, incorporate elements that require commas, such as a series of adjectives or introductory elements.

TEACH

Step-by-Step Teaching Guide

Commas With Compound Sentences

1. Ask a student to read aloud the first example on this page. Ask whether each clause could stand by itself as a complete sentence. (It can.) Then, ask how the two clauses are connected. (comma and conjunction)

2. Write an example on the board. (*Max ate all of the tuna salad, and he drank all of the soda.*) Ask students to identify the conjunction and comma that join the clauses.

3. Remove *he* and ask whether the sentence is still compound. (It isn't.) Ask students if the comma is still necessary and why.

Section 27.2 Commas

The comma is used to separate a number of basic elements and to set off many different kinds of added elements within sentences. As you learn the rules for the correct use of the comma, you will at the same time reinforce your understanding of sentence structure. Study the rules, making certain you understand each relationship described within them.

Commas With Compound Sentences

A single independent clause expresses a complete thought and often stands alone as a simple sentence. Two independent clauses, correctly joined and punctuated, form a compound sentence. The conjunctions used to connect independent clauses are called *coordinating conjunctions.* The seven coordinating conjunctions are *and, but, for, nor, or, so,* and *yet.*

▶ **KEY CONCEPT** Use a comma before the conjunction to separate two independent clauses in a compound sentence. ■

EXAMPLES: I had a meeting with my guidance counselor, and then I applied to several schools in New York.
My mother loves the country, but my father prefers the city.
She might go to a museum, or she might go to the opera.

As you can see, the ideas in the independent clauses in a compound sentence are clearly related to each other. Compound sentences should not be formed unless there exists some type of relationship between the independent clauses.

Although a comma and a coordinating conjunction are used to separate two independent clauses in a compound sentence, a comma is not used to separate a compound verb in a simple sentence. Compare the following two examples.

COMPOUND
SENTENCE: Leslie went to Broadway, and she saw a play.
SIMPLE
SENTENCE: Leslie went to Broadway and saw a play.

The second sentence has only one subject, *Leslie.* Before placing a comma before a conjunction, you should always make sure that you have a complete sentence on both sides of the conjunction, not just a compound verb.

Theme: New York City

In this section, you will learn about the many uses of commas. The examples and exercises in this section are about New York City.
············
Cross-Curricular Connection: Social Studies

✸ Grammar and Style Tip

Do not join two sentences with only a comma. Place a comma between two sentences when they are linked by the coordinating conjunctions *for, and, nor, but, or, yet,* or *so.*

⏱ TIME AND RESOURCE MANAGER

Resources
Print: *Grammar Exercise Workbook,* pp. 147–152; *Grammar Exercises Answers on Transparencies,* Chapter 27
Technology: *Language Lab* CD-ROM, Punctuation; *On-Line Exercise Bank,* Section 27.2

In-Depth Coverage	Accelerated Pace
• Work through all key concepts, pp. 696–710. • Assign and review Exercises 10–20. • Read and discuss *Grammar in Literature,* p. 710.	• Assign pp. 696–710 for independent student review. • Assign Section Review Exercises 21–26, pp. 714–715.

Exercise 10 Using Commas to Separate Independent Clauses
Copy each of the following sentences, adding commas as needed.

EXAMPLE: I wanted to go to the concert in Central Park but it was sold out.

ANSWER: I wanted to go to the concert in Central Park, but it was sold out.

1. New York City was founded by the Dutch in 1626 but it was called New Amsterdam.
2. The British seized the city in 1664 and renamed it New York City.
3. A fleet of British ships was sent to capture the city but the ships did not attack.
4. The governor of New Amsterdam was told to surrender peacefully or the city would be attacked.
5. The city was surrendered so no one was injured.
6. The Dutch did not want to lose control of the city yet they could not defend it against the British fleet.
7. It quickly expanded for many people chose to settle there.
8. In 1700, the first library was opened and construction on the city hall was completed.
9. Henry Hudson was not the first explorer to discover what would become New York City nor was he the first to view the river that bears his name.
10. In New York City, many people became dissatisfied with British rule and rebelled.

Exercise 11 Proofreading for Comma Usage in Compounds
Rewrite the following sentences, adding or deleting commas as necessary.

EXAMPLE: I want to see the Statue of Liberty and I will!
ANSWER: I want to see the Statue of Liberty, and I will!

1. The Statue of Liberty was built in France, and then shipped to New York.
2. Frédéric-Auguste Bartholdi designed the statue and Alexandre Gustave Eiffel devised the interior framework.
3. It was originally named Liberty Enlightening the World but is now known as the Statue of Liberty.
4. The French people paid for the construction of the statue and Americans donated the money to build the pedestal.
5. It was completed in 1886 and dedicated on October 28.

More Practice

On-line
Exercise Bank
• Section 27.2
Grammar Exercise Workbook
• pp. 147–148

▲ Critical Viewing
Using a compound sentence, compare the relative positions of New York City and Liberty Island as shown in this photograph. Where in your sentence would you use a comma? [Compare]

Answer Key

Exercise 10

1. in 1626,
2. (no commas needed)
3. the city,
4. peacefully,
5. surrendered,
6. the city,
7. expanded,
8. opened,
9. New York City,
10. (no commas needed)

Exercise 11

1. (no commas needed)
2. designed the statue,
3. (no commas needed)
4. of the statue,
5. (no commas needed)

Critical Viewing

Compare Possible answer: New York City is in the distance, but Liberty Island is in the foreground. A comma separates the two independent clauses.

✓ **ONGOING ASSESSMENT: Monitor and Reinforce**

If students miss more than two items in Exercise 10 or 11, refer them to the following for additional practice.

In the Textbook	Print Resources	Technology
Section Review, Ex. 21, p. 714	*Grammar Exercise Workbook,* pp. 147–148	*Language Lab* CD-ROM, Punctuation *On-Line Exercise Bank,* Section 27.2

⏱ **TIME SAVERS!**

🖥 **Answers on Transparencies**
Use the *Grammar Exercises Answers on Transparencies* for Chapter 27 to facilitate correction by students.

🖥 **On-Line Exercise Bank**
Have students complete the exercises on computer. The Auto Check feature will grade their work for you!

1. Review the differences among words, phrases, and clauses. Use these examples: *in the attic* (phrase), *what I wanted* (clause), *bananas* (word).

2. Explain that commas separate items in a series of three or more words, phrases, or clauses.

3. Have a student read the examples aloud. Ask students to identify the words that make up each series.

4. Point out that a comma and a conjunction are used to join the last two items in the series.

5. Finally, point out the two examples at the bottom of the page and explain that these are special situations in which commas are not used in series.

27.2

Commas With Series and Adjectives

Like independent clauses, items in a series and certain kinds of adjectives should be separated by commas.

Series A series consists of three or more words, phrases, or subordinate clauses of a similar kind. A series can occur in any part of a sentence.

▶ **KEY CONCEPT** Use commas to separate three or more words, phrases, or clauses in a series. ■

WORDS:	The subway car was crowded, noisy, and fast. I like to put ham, pepperoni, turkey, and cheese on my deli sandwiches.
PHRASES:	We explored the city by bus, by train, and by car.
CLAUSES:	The survey revealed that many New Yorkers were satisfied with the mayor, that they supported the new laws, and that they wanted the fiscal policy to continue.

As you may know, in a variant style for using commas in a series, the last comma before the conjunction is dropped. You are likely to find the full use of commas easier to follow, however. This is especially true when the omission of the final comma leads to confusion, as it does in the following example. By always using a comma after all but the final item in a series, you can avoid this problem.

| CONFUSING: | The crowds, the aromas from the hot dog carts and the talkative taxi drivers made the trip memorable. |
| ALWAYS CLEAR: | The crowds, the aromas from the hotdog carts, and the talkative taxi drivers made the trip memorable. |

When conjunctions are used to separate all of the items in a series, no commas are needed.

| EXAMPLE: | We wanted to watch the game and eat hot dogs and then see the fireworks. |

Do not use commas between items that are paired so often that they are thought of as one item. In the following example, *peanut butter and jelly* are considered a single item.

| EXAMPLE: | We ate grilled cheese sandwiches, baloney sandwiches, and peanut butter and jelly sandwiches. |

Learn More

To learn more about phrases and clauses, see Chapter 19.

🖥 **Answers on Transparencies**
Use the *Grammar Exercises Answers on Transparencies* for Chapter 27 to facilitate correction by students.

💻 **On-Line Exercise Bank**
Have students complete the exercises on computer. The Auto Check feature will grade their work for you!

☑ **ONGOING ASSESSMENT: Prerequisite Skills**

If students have difficulty with phrases and clauses in a series, you may find it necessary to review the following to ensure coverage of prerequisite knowledge.

In the Textbook	Print Resources	Technology
Phrases and Clauses, p. 432	*Grammar Exercise Workbook*, pp. 43–44, 53–58	*On-Line Exercise Bank*, Sections 19.1 and 19.3

Adjectives When two or more adjectives precede a noun, they sometimes will need to be separated with commas.

KEY CONCEPT Use commas to separate adjectives of equal rank. ■

Adjectives are equal in rank if you can insert the word *and* between them without changing the meaning of the sentence. Another way to determine whether adjectives are of equal rank is to reverse the order in which they appear. If the sentence still sounds correct, the adjectives are of equal rank. Adjectives of equal rank are called *coordinate adjectives.*

EXAMPLES: A tall, majestic building rose above the skyline.
            The bright, bold sign was posted above the door.

If you cannot place the word *and* between the adjectives or reverse their order without changing the meaning of the sentence, do not use commas between them. Adjectives that must remain in a specific order are called *cumulative adjectives.*

KEY CONCEPT Do not use commas to separate adjectives that must stay in a specific order. ■

EXAMPLES: The second-oldest building in the city was renovated.
            The long ticket line is moving faster than the shorter reservations line.

Exercise 12 **Supplying Commas to Separate Items in a Series** Copy each of the following sentences, inserting commas to separate items as needed.

EXAMPLE: Buses cars and trucks crowded the city streets.
ANSWER: Buses, cars, and trucks crowded the city streets.

1. New York City is an enormous place with many things to do much to see and lots of places to go.
2. The city is divided into five boroughs: Manhattan the Bronx Queens Brooklyn and Staten Island.
3. Some of the famous buildings that dominate the city skyline are the Empire State Building the Chrysler Building and Trump Tower.
4. You can go to the top of the Empire State Building walk onto the observation deck and look out across the entire city.
5. The Metropolitan Museum of Art exhibits paintings by famous artists such as Gauguin Monet Van Gogh and Cézanne.

▶ **More Practice**

On-line
Exercise Bank
• Section 27.2
Grammar Exercise
Workbook
• pp. 147–148

Commas • 699

Step-by-Step Teaching Guide

Commas With Adjectives

1. Have a student read the first key concept and ask what "equal rank" means. (The adjectives are equal in importance in modifying the same word.)
2. Tell students that adjectives are of equal rank if the word *and* can be inserted without changing the meaning of the sentence.
3. Have students read the second key concept and the examples beneath it.
4. Give additional examples and ask students where commas should be placed:

   long narrow dark hallway (after *long* and *narrow*)

   extremely long hallway (none— *extremely,* adverb, modifies *long*)

   The tree had a huge red fragrant blossom. (after *huge* and *red*)

   The dark narrow staircase was very steep. (after *dark*)

   The door had a big green sticker. (none—adjectives must stay in specific order)

Customize for
Visual/Spatial Learners

Attach four pictures—each of a single object—to the board. Have the students write sentences that contain this series of items. Ask a student to insert commas and conjunctions into their proper places. Then, write descriptive words under the photos and ask another student where the commas and conjunctions would go. Again, have the class write sentences that include the modifiers (phrases in series).

Answer Key

▶ **Exercise 12**

1. things to do, much to see, and lots of places to go.
2. Manhattan, the Bronx, Queens, Brooklyn, and Staten Island.
3. Empire State Building, the Chrysler Building, and Trump Tower.
4. Empire State Building, observation deck,
5. such as Gauguin, Monet, Van Gogh, and Cézanne.

☑ **ONGOING ASSESSMENT: Monitor and Reinforce**

If students miss more than one item in Exercise 12, refer them to the following for additional practice.

In the Textbook	Print Resources	Technology
Section Review, Ex. 22, p. 714	*Grammar Exercise Workbook,* pp. 147–148	*Language Lab* CD-Rom Punctuation *On-Line Exercise Bank,* Section 27.2

27.2

Exercise 13 Distinguishing Between Coordinate and Cumulative Adjectives
Copy each sentence with coordinate adjectives, inserting a comma between them. For sentences with cumulative adjectives, just write *cumulative*.

EXAMPLE: The large European ship entered the harbor. (cumulative)

1. I visited New York City during the hot humid month of August.
2. My grandfather took me to see some of the many fascinating sites.
3. We traveled on the noisy crowded subway.
4. It took us right into the heart of the city in just forty short minutes.
5. We walked up the long steep stairway to the street.
6. The city was bustling with throngs of busy impatient people.
7. My grandfather hailed a bright yellow taxi.
8. We drove past the tall impressive skyscrapers.
9. Rockefeller Center was the first of many interesting stops.
10. Our long exciting day finally ended after we stopped at Central Park.

Exercise 14 Revising to Correct Commas in a Series and With Adjectives
Revise this paragraph, inserting or deleting commas as necessary.

New York is a city of festivals conventions and parades. Every year, on a blustery, mid-March afternoon, you can see a long steady stream of colorful, marching bands and floats moving up Fifth Avenue. The green white, and orange flags and the bright, green stripe painted on the avenue tell you it's Saint Patrick's day. The Easter Parade also takes place on Fifth Avenue; however, instead of formal organized marchers, masses of ordinary New Yorkers promenade in their finery. The splendor of the day is the great array of extraordinary eye-catching "Easter bonnets." Some of the most exciting, New York parades take place on lower Broadway in the Canyon of Heroes. Here is where astronauts champion ball teams, and war heroes have been honored by admiring crowds politicians and blizzards of paper thrown from skyscraper windows.

More Practice

On-line
Exercise Bank
• Section 27.2
Grammar Exercise
Workbook
• pp. 147–148

▲ Critical Viewing
How are words in an unpunctuated sentence like people in a crowd? [Relate]

✓ ONGOING ASSESSMENT: Monitor and Reinforce

If students miss more than two items in Exercise 13 or 14, refer them to the following for additional practice.

In the Textbook	Print Resources	Technology
Section Review, Ex. 23, p. 714	*Grammar Exercise Workbook*, pp. 147–148	*Language Lab* CD-Rom, Punctuation *On-Line Exercise Bank*, Section 27.2

Commas After Introductory Material

Most introductory material is set off with a comma.

KEY CONCEPT Use a comma after an introductory word, phrase, or clause. ■

Study the following examples to see what types of introductory material should be set off with commas.

INTRODUCTORY WORDS:	Well, I find it difficult to decide.
	Yes, Charles agrees with our plan to visit Central Park.
	Oh, did he really say that?
COMMON EXPRESSIONS:	Of course, I'll do it for you.
INTRODUCTORY ADVERBS:	Certainly, you may borrow the book about New York.
	Frantically, they searched for a parking spot.
PREPOSITIONAL PHRASES:	At the very top, my father paused to enjoy the view.
	In the heart of the city, you will find many skyscrapers.
PARTICIPIAL PHRASES:	Walking slowly, she reached the subway in about ten minutes.
	Written carefully, the speech was a masterpiece.
INFINITIVE PHRASES:	To get to the train before it left, she ran all the way.
	To get to Broadway, they rode in a taxi.
ADVERB CLAUSES:	When the team got off the plane, hundreds of onlookers began to cheer.
	If you intend to travel to New York this summer, you should make your plans now.

It is not absolutely necessary to set off short prepositional phrases. However, you may find that a comma is needed with a two- or three-word phrase in order to avoid confusion.

CLEAR:	At Times Square we met our friends.
CONFUSING:	Inside the house walls began to crumble.
CLEAR:	Inside the house, walls began to crumble.

Step-by-Step Teaching Guide

Commas After Introductory Material

1. Tell students that an introductory word, phrase, or clause must be set off from the rest of the sentence by a comma.

2. Have students read the sentences beneath the key concept and identify the introductory material (word, phrase, or clause) in each.

3. Point out to students that short prepositional phrases of two or three words are not always set off by a comma.

4. Focus on the examples at the very bottom of the page to remind students that commas should be used to avoid confusion.

⏱ TIME SAVERS!

Answers on Transparencies
Use the *Grammar Exercises Answers on Transparencies* for Chapter 27 to facilitate correction by students.

On-Line Exercise Bank
Have students complete the exercises on computer. The Auto Check feature will grade their work for you!

701

1. Born in December, 1882,
2. The son of a military man,
3. After his father left the army,
4. While living overseas,
5. Initially serving as a clerk,
6. correct
7. Attending New York University Law School at night,
8. Already fluent in German, Croatian, and Italian,
9. Upon his graduation from law school,
10. Within a few years,
11. When the United States entered World War I,
12. Courageously serving the country,
13. Following the war,
14. A Republican,
15. The following year,
16. A fiercely honest and determined man,
17. Of course,
18. From the very beginning of his administration,
19. To eliminate the influence of organized crime,
20. Although La Guardia's term as mayor ended in 1945,

27.2

▶ **Exercise 15** Using Commas After Introductory Material

Copy each sentence that needs a comma, inserting the comma where it is needed. If a sentence does not require a comma, write *correct*.

EXAMPLE: Chris have you visited Grand Central Station yet?
ANSWER: Chris, have you visited Grand Central Station yet?

1. Born in December, 1882 Fiorello La Guardia would become one of New York City's best-known mayors.
2. The son of a military man La Guardia was born in New York, but he grew up at an army base in Arizona.
3. After his father left the army the family moved to Trieste, Italy.
4. While living overseas the young La Guardia joined the U.S. consular service.
5. Initially serving as a clerk he would eventually become the consular agent in the city of Fiume.
6. In 1906 La Guardia returned to New York.
7. Attending New York University Law School at night he worked as an interpreter at Ellis Island during the day.
8. Already fluent in German, Croatian, and Italian La Guardia soon mastered Spanish, French, and Yiddish.
9. Upon his graduation from law school he quit his job at Ellis Island and opened a small law practice.
10. Within a few years La Guardia was elected to the U.S. House of Representatives.
11. When the United States entered World War I he left Congress and enlisted in the Army Air Service.
12. Courageously serving the country La Guardia worked as a pilot on the Italian front.
13. Following the war he returned to Congress and served for seven consecutive terms.
14. A Republican La Guardia was eventually swept from office when Democrat Franklin Roosevelt became president in 1932.
15. The following year he was elected New York City's mayor.
16. A fiercely honest and determined man La Guardia reformed the city's government.
17. Of course his policies met with much resistance.
18. From the very beginning of his administration La Guardia appointed highly qualified, nonpartisan people to the city government.
19. To eliminate the influence of organized crime he initiated a campaign against all forms of gambling.
20. Although La Guardia's term as mayor ended in 1945 many of his contributions to New York City are still evident today.

▶ **More Practice**

On-line Exercise Bank
• Section 27.2
Grammar Exercise Workbook
• pp. 149–150

✓ **ONGOING ASSESSMENT: Monitor and Reinforce**

If students miss more than two items in Exercise 15, refer them to the following for additional practice.

In the Textbook	Print Resources	Technology
Section Review, Ex. 24, p. 714	*Grammar Exercise Workbook,* pp. 149–150	*Language Lab* CD-ROM, Commas *On-Line Exercise Bank,* Section 27.2

Commas With Parenthetical and Nonessential Expressions

Commas are also used to set off two types of expressions that often fall in the middle or at the end of a sentence:

Parenthetical Expressions Parenthetical expressions consist of one or more words that, in a sense, interrupt the flow of a sentence. Such expressions are set off by one or more commas, regardless of where they occur in a sentence.

▶ **KEY CONCEPT** Use commas to set off parenthetical expressions. ■

Below are some common types of parenthetical expressions. Notice that a parenthetical expression may fall in the middle or at the end of a sentence. Notice also that each sentence is complete without the parenthetical expression.

NOUNS OF DIRECT ADDRESS:	Please, Ben, could you help me? I'll do it right away, Mother.
CONJUNCTIVE ADVERBS:	The tennis match, therefore, was held after the rain shower. They did their best, however.
COMMON EXPRESSIONS:	I am explaining his theory, I believe, as clearly as I can. You know, of course, that she is ill.
CONTRASTING EXPRESSIONS:	We took the subway, not the bus, to work. New York City, not Chicago, has the Twin Towers.

▼ **Critical Viewing**
How do you think it feels to live and work in a "vertical city"? Respond, using at least one parenthetical expression. **[Evaluate]**

Commas • 703

Step-by-Step Teaching Guide

Commas With Parenthetical Expressions

1. Once students read the definition of *parenthetical expressions,* ask volunteers to supply definitions in their own words. Ask whether a parenthetical is essential to the meaning of a sentence. (It isn't.)

2. Tell students that parenthetical expressions are set off from their sentences because they are not basic parts of the sentence.

3. Have students read the four example sentences aloud and identify which word or phrase is parenthetical.

4. Point out that parenthetical phrases can be in the middle of a sentence or at the end of a sentence and that the sentence is complete without the parenthetical expression.

5. Ask students to add commas and identify the types of parenthetical expressions in additional examples:

   *Moreover the article made us think. (*after *Moreover,* conjunctive adverb*)*

   *After receiving the call I think he decided to leave. (*after *call* and *think,* common expression*)*

   *The whale not the tuna is a mammal. (*after *whale* and *tuna,* contrasting expression*)*

Critical Viewing

Evaluate Possible answer: Working in a vertical city would, I believe, be exciting, but living there might be, in a way, claustrophobic.

STANDARDIZED TEST PREPARATION WORKSHOP

Grammar and Usage Many standardized tests require students to use their understanding of punctuation to respond correctly. Read the sentence below and answer the question.

Which is the right way to write the following sentence?

The writer Judith Guest believes, in rising early working hard, and following a guiding principle.

A Correct as is.

B The writer, Judith Guest, believes in rising early working hard, and following a guiding principle.

C The writer Judith Guest believes in rising early, working hard, and following a guiding principle.

D The writer Judith Guest, believes in rising early, working hard and following a guiding principle.

The correct answer is **C.** The sentence contains a series of three phrases that must be separated by commas. No commas are needed to set off *Judith Guest,* however, because this appositive is essential.

⏱ **TIME SAVERS!**

📄 **Answers on Transparencies** Use the *Grammar Exercises Answers on Transparencies* for Chapter 27 to facilitate correction by students.

💻 **On-Line Exercise Bank** Have students complete the exercises on computer. The Auto Check feature will grade their work for you!

Commas With Nonessential Expressions

1. Once students read the first paragraph, ask them to summarize it with an original key concept. (Example: Do not set off expressions that are essential to understanding the meaning of the sentence.)

2. Read the examples of essential elements together and ask students to reread each sentence, leaving out the italicized expression. Ask whether the remaining sentence is perfectly clear. (It isn't.)

3. Then, read the second key concept together, and ask students to compare the first example with the similar sentence in the examples at the top of the page. Ask why this expression is nonessential. (It is not necessary to identify Henry Fonda.)

4. For additional practice, have students identify the underlined words as essential or nonessential expressions:

    The race was won by champion runner <u>Jackie Joyner Kersee</u>. (essential)

    The Ferris wheel, <u>which is closed at night</u>, is my favorite ride. (nonessential)

    The boat dock, <u>where seagulls circle overhead</u>, burned yesterday. (nonessential)

    The woman <u>running the convention</u> was my aunt. (essential)

27.2

Essential and Nonessential Expressions Depending on their importance in a sentence, appositives, participial phrases, and adjective clauses can be either essential or nonessential. (The terms *restrictive* and *nonrestrictive* may also be used.) An essential phrase or clause is necessary to the meaning of the sentence. It helps to describe or identify the person or object the sentence is about.

▶ **KEY CONCEPT** Do not use commas to set off essential expressions. ■

ESSENTIAL APPOSITIVE:	The part was played by the famous actor *Henry Fonda.*
ESSENTIAL PARTICIPIAL PHRASE:	The man *wearing the white cap* is my uncle.
ESSENTIAL ADJECTIVE CLAUSE:	The paragraph *that we propose to add* changes the entire bill.

The preceding examples illustrate three kinds of essential elements. In the first example, the appositive *Henry Fonda* identifies a specific actor. In the next example, the participial phrase *wearing the white cap* identifies a specific man. In the last example, the adjective clause *that we propose to add* indicates which paragraph. The items are all essential because they limit or restrict identification to the person or thing described in the appositive, phrase, or clause. Because they cannot be removed without changing the meaning of the sentence, they require no commas.

Nonessential elements also provide information, but that information is not necessary to the meaning of the rest of the sentence. Because nonessential elements do not alter the meaning, they do require commas.

▶ **KEY CONCEPT** Use commas to set off nonessential expressions. ■

NONESSENTIAL APPOSITIVE:	The part was played by Henry Fonda, *the famous actor.*
NONESSENTIAL PARTICIPIAL PHRASE:	This graceful bridge, *built in the 1800's,* spans a lake in Central Park.
NONESSENTIAL ADJECTIVE CLAUSE:	The lake, *which sometimes freezes in winter,* is lovely for summer boating.

In the first clause, Henry Fonda is clearly identified. The appositive *the famous actor* is not needed to identify a particular person. The same thing is true of the other examples. Although the nonessential material may be interesting, the sentences can be read without them and still make sense.

A comma signals a pause in a sentence. With a partner, take turns reading Exercises 16 and 17 aloud. Accustom yourself to hearing where commas belong to set off parenthetical and other nonessential expressions.

Exercise 16 Using Commas to Set off Parenthetical Expressions

Copy the following sentences, inserting commas to set off parenthetical expressions.

EXAMPLE: His reasoning therefore was faulty.

ANSWER: His reasoning, therefore, was faulty.

1. The bitter rivalry between Alexander Hamilton and Aaron Burr is in my opinion one of the most interesting events in New York City's history.
2. Burr was a Republican not a Federalist like Hamilton.
3. Hamilton in fact thwarted Burr's political activities at every turn.
4. It was Hamilton most likely who prevented Burr from becoming president in 1800.
5. He also checked Burr's bid to be governor of New York in 1804 I believe.
6. Burr therefore challenged the reluctant Hamilton to a duel.
7. The duel as you may know took place on July 11, 1804.
8. It was Burr not Hamilton who won the duel.
9. Hamilton was killed; Burr however was discredited, and his political career was finished.
10. If Hamilton had survived, the history of New York would have been much different I suppose.

More Practice

On-line
Exercise Bank
• Section 27.2
Grammar Exercise
Workbook
• pp. 149–150

▼ Critical Viewing
Contrast this peaceful Central Park scene with what you know or believe about the city that surrounds it. Include a parenthetical expression in your response. [Contrast]

Commas • 705

Answer Key

▶ Exercise 16

1. The bitter rivalry between Alexander Hamilton and Aaron Burr is, in my opinion, one of the most interesting events in New York City's history.
2. Burr was a Republican, not a Federalist like Hamilton.
3. Hamilton, in fact, thwarted Burr's political activities at every turn.
4. It was Hamilton, most likely, who prevented Burr from becoming president in 1800.
5. He also checked Burr's bid to be governor of New York in 1804, I believe.
6. Burr, therefore, challenged the reluctant Hamilton to a duel.
7. The duel, as you may know, took place on July 11, 1804.
8. It was Burr, not Hamilton, who won the duel.
9. Hamilton was killed; Burr, however, was discredited, and his political career was finished.
10. If Hamilton had survived, the history of New York would have been much different, I suppose.

Critical Viewing

Contrast Possible answer: This picture shows a part of New York City that is peaceful, not bustling.

27.2

▶ **Exercise 17** **Supplying Commas to Set Off Nonessential Expressions** Copy the sentences that contain nonessential expressions, inserting one or more commas as needed. If a sentence does not require any commas, write *correct*.

1. Grand Central Terminal which was renovated recently is one of New York City's most famous landmarks.
2. Its history stretches back to 1831 when the first rail line into New York City was established.
3. Between 1831 and 1836, a station that was built for the New York and Harlem lines was located in the heart of the city.
4. Several lines including the New York and New Haven line and the Hudson River line began serving the city shortly thereafter.
5. The shipping magnate Cornelius Vanderbilt eventually purchased both lines and consolidated them.
6. In 1869 he purchased property for a new centralized train depot that would be located at the corner of Madison Avenue and 42nd Street.
7. The renowned architect James B. Snook designed the building.
8. Grand Central Depot as it was called cost Vanderbilt roughly $6.4 million.
9. The new building which would service all of the railroad lines operating in the city was opened in October 1871.
10. The improvements and expansions that led to the rebirth of the depot as Grand Central Terminal were completed by the turn of the century.

▶ **More Practice**

On-line Exercise Bank
• Section 27.2
Grammar Exercise Workbook
• pp. 149–150

◀ Critical Viewing
Why do you think so few commas appear in signs? What does this tell you about the uses of the comma? **[Deduce]**

✓ **ONGOING ASSESSMENT: Monitor and Reinforce**

If students miss more than two items in Exercise 16 or 17, refer them to the following for additional practice.

In the Textbook	Print Resources	Technology
Section Review, Ex. 25, p. 715	*Grammar Exercise Workbook*, pp. 149–150	*Language Lab* CD-Rom, Commas *On-Line Exercise Bank*, Section 27.2

Other Uses of the Comma

Many other situations also require the use of commas.

Geographical Names   Geographical names are often made up of several parts.

KEY CONCEPT   When a geographical name is made up of two or more parts, use a comma after each item. ■

EXAMPLES: My uncle in New York, New York, is a lawyer.
We traveled to Niagara Falls, Ontario, Canada, by car.

Dates   Commas are also used with dates made up of several parts, such as month, day, and year.

KEY CONCEPT   When a date is made up of two or more parts, use a comma after each item except in the case of a month followed by a day. ■

EXAMPLES: Thursday, September 26, is my birthday.
I saw a Broadway play on October 6, 2000.
On April 8, 1999, my brother was born.

If dates contain only months and years, commas are not necessary.

EXAMPLE: November 1989 was the month David Dinkins was elected mayor of New York City.

Titles After a Name   Some titles require commas.

KEY CONCEPT   When a name is followed by one or more titles, use a comma after the name and after each title. ■

EXAMPLES: Theresa Kelly, M.D., is my doctor.
John Roe, Sr., Ph.D., lectured on Greek drama.
Did Prentice-Hall, Inc., publish this book?

Step-by-Step Teaching Guide

Addresses, Salutations, and Closings

1. Explain to students that an address used in a sentence is punctuated with commas after each element with the exception of a ZIP code.

2. Have students compare the two examples of address formats. In the first, emphasize placement of the commas; in the second, point out that each element is on a separate line and that the commas are placed only between the city and state.

3. Have students read the second key concept and review definitions of *salutation* and *closing*. Explain to students that salutations and closings in personal letters are always followed by commas. Ask why commas are used in these instances. (to separate these elements from the body of the letter and from the signature)

Step-by-Step Teaching Guide

Large Numbers

1. Have a student read the key concept and then read the example numbers aloud.

2. Review the placement of commas in numbers: at the thousands position, at the millions position, and so on.

3. Note the examples at the bottom of the page and explain that sometimes commas are not used in long numbers because the numbers are for reference and identification. (driver's license number, social security number)

4. For additional practice, write these phrases on the board and have students add commas:

   125894 cars for sale (125,894)

   2235648 people at the fair (2,235,648)

   6527 entries in the contest (6,527)

708

Addresses Commas are used to separate the items in addresses.

> **KEY CONCEPT** Use a comma after each item in an address made up of two or more parts. ■

EXAMPLE: We sent the package to Emma Chandee, 1237 Oakland Parkway, Anytown, New York 10583.

In the preceding example, commas are placed after the name, street, and city. Do not use a comma between the state and the ZIP Code.

In an address in a letter or on an envelope, a comma between the city and the state only is needed.

EXAMPLE: Emma Chandee
1237 Oakland Parkway
Anytown, NY 10583

Salutations and Closings Commas are used after the salutation and closing in letters.

> **KEY CONCEPT** Use a comma after the salutation in a personal letter and after the closing in all letters. ■

SALUTATIONS: Dear Jimmy, Dear Aunt Harriet, My dear friend,

CLOSINGS: Your friend, Sincerely, Yours truly,

Large Numbers Commas make large numbers easier to read.

> **KEY CONCEPT** When writing numbers of more than three digits, place a comma before every third digit counting from the right. ■

EXAMPLES: 186,000 miles per second
2,527 people
3,625,353 peanuts

Do not, however, use commas in ZIP Codes, telephone numbers, page numbers, serial numbers, years, or house numbers.

ZIP CODE:	07624
TELEPHONE NUMBER:	(207) 555-2457
PAGE NUMBER:	Page 1127
SERIAL NUMBER:	081 32 5334
YEAR:	A.D. 2002
HOUSE NUMBER:	2787

708 • Punctuation

 Internet Ti

You can use the Internet to find addresses and phone numbers. Go to a search engine, and click once on the ho▮ link to White Pages c Yellow Pages. You ca also look up ZIP Codes through the U.S. Postal Service site: **http://www. usps.gov**

Elliptical Sentences In an elliptical sentence, even though words are left out, the meaning is clearly understood. Inserting a comma in an elliptical sentence makes it easier to read.

▶ **KEY CONCEPT** Use a comma to indicate the words left out of an elliptical sentence. ■

EXAMPLE: Tom read the paper quickly; Rachel, more slowly.

Even though the words *read the paper* have been omitted from the second clause in the preceding elliptical sentence, the meaning is not lost. The comma inserted in place of the missing words helps to make the meaning clear.

Direct Quotations Commas also set off direct quotations.

▶ **KEY CONCEPT** Use commas to set off a direct quotation from the rest of the sentence. ■

EXAMPLES: "I finished my report on the Empire State Building," Linda stated happily.
Kevin sighed, "I wish mine were done."
"Perhaps," Linda replied, "yours will be better than mine because you've spent more time on it."

For Clarity You may also need to use a comma to prevent readers from misunderstanding a sentence.

▶ **KEY CONCEPT** Use a comma to prevent a sentence from being misunderstood. ■

UNCLEAR: For New York police horses have been a mode of transportation.
CLEAR: For New York police, horses have been a mode of transportation.

Learn the rules about the use of commas, and apply them in your writing. Take care not to use commas where none are required.

▶ **KEY CONCEPT** Make certain that you know why you are inserting a comma in a sentence. In this way, you will not overuse them. ■

Because the comma is one of the most frequently used punctuation marks, some people sprinkle commas carelessly throughout their writing.

Commas • 709

Step-by-Step Teaching Guide

Elliptical Sentences and Direct Quotations

1. Have a student read the first key concept aloud and ask what it means when a sentence is *elliptical*. (A word or words are omitted or implied.)

2. Ask a student to read the example by inserting the implied words. (Example: Rachel *read the paper* more slowly.) Point out that this sentence would <u>not</u> require a comma.

3. Read the second key concept and explain that commas that set off direct quotations help to distinguish the speaker from the quotation.

4. Have two students read the examples as though they were Linda and Kevin—by reading only the quotations. Point out the function of the quotation marks, and then have students tell you why commas appear where they do. (to separate speaker from quotation)

Step-by-Step Teaching Guide

Using Commas for Clarity

1. Remind students of the principle reason for using commas: to avoid confusion.

2. After examining the example, offer additional examples, and ask students to explain the possible confusion caused by a lack of a comma in each.

   While the dog was eating the burglar escaped. (comma after *eating*)

   With no towels drying off at the beach is difficult. (comma after *towels*)

3. Point out that too many commas can make a sentence confusing. Have students read the note at the bottom of the page.

Integrating Workplace Skills

Numbers Punctuation is very important in a work environment. A misplaced comma in an order for one thousand items could mean the difference between a huge profit and a loss. Ask students to think of places on order forms and other documents where misuse of commas might cause problems. (Examples: checks, bank statements, purchase orders)

Step-by-Step Teaching Guide

Grammar in Literature

1. Ask students what punctuation other than end marks is used in this excerpt. (semicolons, commas, and parentheses)

2. Ask students what purpose the semicolons and commas serve. (They separate items in series.)

3. Next, have students discuss the examples of misused commas. Have students identify the comma rule that each violates.

More About the Writer

E. B. White co-authored *The Elements of Style,* a book about grammar and writing that many writers use and appreciate. Beginning in 1929, E. B. White wrote for the weekly magazine *The New Yorker* and remained there for the rest of his career. White's literary renown was enhanced further by his children's classics *Stuart Little* and *Charlotte's Web.* In *Charlotte's Web,* a clever spider befriends and saves a young pig. Curious fans of the book would frequently track White down at home in Maine. To his amusement, the fans' most common request was to see the site of *Charlotte's Web.*

Connections With Literature

The full text of "Here Is New York" by E.B. White may be found in *Prentice Hall Literature:Timeless Voices, Timeless Themes,* The American Experience. Encourage students to observe closely how White combines many ideas into a single sentence.

Customize for
AP Students

After students have read "Here Is New York," have them analyze the grammatical structures of the sentence within parentheses. (The semicolons separate three independent clauses, and the commas separate a series of three verb phrases within the third independent clause.) Then, have students hunt among their own or professional writing to find uses of commas within complex structures.

These examples illustrate some of the ways in which commas are often misused. Avoid these misuses when using prepositional phrases or compound elements in sentences.

MISUSED WITH PREP-OSITIONAL PHRASES:	Yesterday, I saw a fluffy, aristocratic-looking poodle, on Park Avenue.
CORRECT:	Yesterday, I saw a fluffy, aristocratic-looking poodle on Park Avenue.
MISUSED WITH COMPOUND SUBJECTS:	I thought the four pizzas, and the two hoagies, would never arrive.
CORRECT:	I thought the four pizzas and the two hoagies would never arrive.
MISUSED WITH COMPOUND VERBS:	I looked at her, and asked her to leave.
CORRECT:	I looked at her and asked her to leave.
MISUSED WITH COMPOUND OBJECTS:	I love the house, and the garden.
CORRECT:	I love the house and the garden.
MISUSED WITH CLAUSES:	She asked what you wanted, and where you were going.
CORRECT:	She asked what you wanted and where you were going.

GRAMMAR IN
LITERATURE

from Here Is New York
E. B. White

Notice that in the third clause of the sentence in parentheses, E. B. White uses commas to separate the three parts of a compound predicate.

. . . The Empire State Building shot 1250 feet into the air when it was madness to put out as much as six inches of new growth. (The building has a mooring mast that no dirigible has ever tied to; it employs a man to flush toilets in slack times; it has been hit by an airplane in a fog, struck countless times by lightning, and been jumped off of by so many unhappy people that pedestrians instinctively quicken step when passing Fifth Avenue and Thirty-fourth Street.)

Exercise 18 Using Commas in Other Situations Copy the following sentences, inserting commas where necessary.

EXAMPLE: The speed of light is 186000 miles per second.
ANSWER: The speed of light is 186,000 miles per second.

1. Theodore Roosevelt Jr. was born in New York City in 1858.
2. On May 24 1883 the Brooklyn Bridge was first opened to the public.
3. Grand Central Terminal officially opened at 12:01 A.M. on Sunday February 2 1913.
4. New York New York is a densely populated city in the northeastern United States.
5. The plane took off from John F. Kennedy Airport, bound for Paris France.

Exercise 19 Proofreading a Letter for Comma Errors
Rewrite the following letter, inserting and deleting commas where necessary.

2672 Highland Avenue
Somewhere, Maryland, 33056
May 4 2000

Dear Austin

Your last letter indicated that you have lined up your summer intern position with Rush Green and Stipe Inc. in New York City. I see your plans are concrete; mine not so.

With high hopes I applied to all the companies you did. I even wrote to Harris Johnson, Jr. for a position at HiTek Corp., but got no response.

I'm very eager to work in a city with more than 8000000 people, and with so many great things to see and do. Although I still haven't heard from any of the companies. I'm not going to give up hope. As my mom said to me last night "Just hang in there." She added if I don't hear something by next week, she will call my Uncle Phil, who has a business in Ridgewood, New Jersey across the Hudson River from New York. He is sure to have a spot for his ambitious talented nephew!

Wish me luck, and write soon.

Your friend
Pete

More Practice

On-line
Exercise Bank
• Section 27.2
Grammar Exercise Workbook
• pp. 151–152

▼ **Critical Viewing**
In a postcard to a friend, how would you describe this view of New York at night? How would you punctuate your salutation and closing? **[Analyze]**

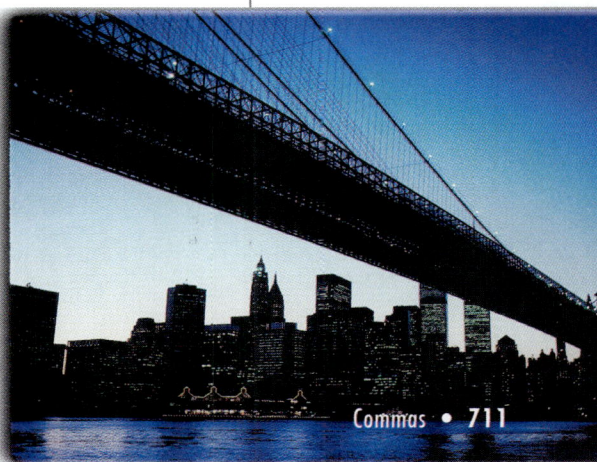

Commas • 711

Answer Key

▶ **Exercise 18**

1. Theodore Roosevelt, Jr., was born in New York City in 1858.
2. On May 24, 1883, the Brooklyn Bridge was first opened to the public.
3. Grand Central Terminal officially opened at 12:01 A.M. on Sunday, February 2, 1913.
4. New York, New York, is a densely populated city in the northeastern United States.
5. The plane took off from John F. Kennedy Airport bound for Paris, France.

▶ **Exercise 19**

2672 Highland Avenue
Somewhere, Maryland 33056
May 4, 2000
Dear Austin,

Your last letter indicated that you have lined up your summer intern position with Rush, Green, and Stipe, Inc., in New York City. I see your plans are concrete; mine, not so.

With high hopes I applied to all the companies you did. I even wrote to Harris Johnson, Jr., for a position at HiTek Corp. but got no response.

I'm very eager to work in a city with more than 8,000,000 people and with so many great things to see and do. Although I haven't heard from any of the companies, I'm not going to give up hope. As my mom said to me last night, "Just hang in there." She added, if I don't hear something by next week, she will call my Uncle Phil, who has a business in Ridgewood, New Jersey, across the Hudson River from New York. He is sure to have a spot for his ambitious, talented nephew!

Wish me luck and write soon.
Your friend,
Pete

Critical Viewing

Analyze Possible answer: Dear Max, The skyline here sparkles beautifully after sunset. Yours, Scott

▶ **Exercise 20**

1. Theodore Roosevelt, Jr.,
2. His family roots in New York can be traced back to Klaes Martensen van Roosevelt,
3. Roosevelt was born in the city on October 27, 1858.
4. His parents lived in Gramercy Park,
5. correct
6. Roosevelt's father, Theodore Roosevelt, Sr., was
7. As a young boy, Roosevelt suffered from asthma, and
8. His father, hoping to improve Teddy's health, installed
9. Roosevelt became active in boxing, wrestling, swimming, riding, and hunting.
10. In the years that followed, Roosevelt's health did, in fact, improve dramatically.
11. By 1872, he had left New York to travel to such places as Cairo, Egypt, and Vienna, Austria.
12. He lived at the home of a kind, generous family
13. At the age of eighteen, Roosevelt
14. During these years he met Alice Hathaway Lee, whom
15. He returned to New York with his wife, and they settled
16. correct
17. He decided that his future was in politics, not law.
18. In November of 1881, Roosevelt was elected to the state assembly in Albany, New York.
19. He soon won the respect of his colleagues by exposing corruption, by resolving tough issues, and by working for reform.
20. He would serve one-year terms in the legislature in 1882, 1883, and 1884.

continued

27.2

▶ **Exercise 20** **Using Commas Correctly** Copy each of the following sentences, inserting commas where necessary.

EXAMPLE: A trip to the city I think is a good idea.
ANSWER: A trip to the city, I think, is a good idea.

1. Theodore Roosevelt Jr. was one of the most famous people ever to live in New York City.
2. His family roots in New York can be traced back to Klaes Martensen van Roosevelt who came to New Amsterdam in 1649.
3. Roosevelt was born in the city on October 27 1858.
4. His parents lived in Gramercy Park one of the more exclusive neighborhoods in the city.
5. An elegant brownstone building located on East 20th Street was where he grew up.
6. Roosevelt's father Theodore Roosevelt Sr. was a successful businessman in the city.
7. As a young boy Roosevelt suffered from asthma and he was always very sickly.
8. His father hoping to improve Teddy's health installed a gymnasium in the family home.
9. Roosevelt became active in boxing wrestling swimming riding and hunting.
10. In the years that followed Roosevelt's health did in fact improve dramatically.
11. By 1872 he had left New York to travel to such places as Cairo Egypt and Vienna Austria.
12. He lived at the home of a kind generous family in Germany for almost two years.
13. At the age of eighteen Roosevelt enrolled at Harvard University and became an excellent student.
14. During these years he met Alice Hathaway Lee whom he would eventually marry after his graduation.
15. He returned to New York with his wife and they settled into a home in the heart of the city.
16. Roosevelt began taking courses at Columbia University Law School but soon dropped out.
17. He decided that his future was in politics not law.
18. In November of 1881 Roosevelt was elected to the state assembly in Albany New York.
19. He soon won the respect of his colleagues by exposing corruption by resolving tough issues and by working for reform.
20. He would serve one-year terms in the legislature in 1882 1883 and 1884.

▶ **More Practice**

On-line Exercise Bank
• Section 27.2
Grammar Exercise Workbook
• pp. 151–152

✓ **ONGOING ASSESSMENT: Monitor and Reinforce**

If students have difficulty with Exercises 18, 19, or 20, refer them to the following for additional practice.

In the Textbook	Print Resources	Technology
Section Review, Ex. 26, p. 715	*Grammar Exercise Workbook,* pp. 151–152	*Language Lab* CD-ROM, Punctuation *On-Line Exercise Bank,* Section 27.2

◀ **Critical Viewing**
Why might this street in New York City sometimes be referred to as a "canyon"? Answer in a sentence with compound elements that would require at least two commas. **[Draw Conclusions]**

21. Two of the worst tragedies in Roosevelt's life occurred on February 14 1884 when both his wife and his mother died.
22. However after spending time in the West and in Washington D.C. Roosevelt returned to public service in New York.
23. He was elected police commissioner in 1895 and he immediately began reforming the city's police department.
24. He would become the governor of New York just a few short years later yet that was merely the start of his dramatic career.
25. Roosevelt who would go on to become the Vice President President and the recipient of the Nobel Peace Prize eventually died at his home on Sagamore Hill in Oyster Bay Long Island in 1919.

Commas • **713**

Answer Key continued

▶ **Exercise 20**

21. Two of the worst tragedies in Roosevelt's life occurred on February 14, 1884, when both his wife and his mother died.
22. However, after spending time in the West and in Washington, D.C., Roosevelt returned to public service in New York.
23. He was elected police commissioner in 1895, and he immediately began reforming the city's police department.
24. He would become the governor of New York just a few short years later, yet that was merely the start of his dramatic career.
25. Roosevelt, who would go on to become the Vice President, President, and the recipient of the Nobel Peace Prize, eventually died at his home on Sagamore Hill in Oyster Bay, Long Island, in 1919.

Critical Viewing

Draw Conclusions Possible answer: The high, looming walls and towering buildings close in the narrow, crowded street, much like canyon walls tower high above the river that formed them.

Language Highlight

Prior to the mid-seventeenth century, there was no specific system of punctuation marks until British academics called for a system of pauses to aid in understanding spoken, printed, and handwritten texts. Until the eighteenth century, this discipline was known as *pointing*. (The word *punctuation* comes from the Latin root *punctus,* meaning "pricking" or "point.") Sometime before 1750, the word *punctuation* replaced *pointing*.

☑ **ONGOING ASSESSMENT: Assess Mastery**

Use the following resources to assess student mastery of comma usage.

In the Textbook	Technology
Chapter Review, p. 764, Ex. 80	*Language Lab* CD-ROM, Punctuation *On-Line Exercise Bank,* Section 27.2

Section Review

Each of these exercises correlates to the instruction on commas, pages 696–713. The exercises may be used for more practice, for reteaching, or for review of the key concepts presented.

Answer Key

Exercise 21

1. demolished,
2. ornate,
3. specifications,
4. higher,
5. architecture, yet

Exercise 22

1. Woolworth Building, the Bank of Manhattan, and the Chrysler Building.
2. ahead of schedule, under budget, and to the complete satisfaction of its owners.
3. 200,000 cubic feet of limestone and granite, ten million bricks, and 730 tons of aluminum and steel.
4. patient, clever, and meticulous.
5. A glass, steel, and aluminum tower

Exercise 23

1. cold, hard steel
2. cumulative
3. long, difficult hours
4. remarkable, often-discussed ten-day period.
5. A noisy, excited crowd

Exercise 24

1. Built at the end of the eighteenth century,
2. When the Revolutionary War ended,
3. As the city expanded,
4. Unfortunately,
5. correct

Section 27.2 Section Review

GRAMMAR EXERCISES 21–29

Exercise 21 **Punctuating Simple and Compound Sentences** Copy each sentence that requires punctuation, adding commas where necessary. If no comma is required, write *correct*.

1. In 1928 the Waldorf–Astoria Hotel was demolished and construction of the Empire State Building began in 1930.
2. The architecture of many buildings at that time was ornate but designer William F. Lamb chose a simple design.
3. Lamb had to design the building according to certain specifications or the city would not allow it to be built.
4. Zoning laws in the city required that tall buildings become narrower as they got higher so Lamb incorporated into his design several tiers that were set back from the building's base.
5. Lamb's final design is one of the most striking in modern architecture yet it is said that he based it upon the shape of a pencil.

Exercise 22 **Using Commas to Separate Items in a Series** Copy each of the following sentences, inserting commas to separate items as needed.

1. The Empire State Building would rise higher than the Woolworth Building the Bank of Manhattan and the Chrysler Building.
2. The structure was finished ahead of schedule under budget and to the complete satisfaction of its owners.
3. The exterior of the building contains 200,000 cubic feet of limestone and granite 10 million bricks and 730 tons of aluminum and steel.
4. Architect William Lamb was patient clever and meticulous.
5. A glass steel and aluminum tower was mounted on the top of the building.

714 • Punctuation

Exercise 23 **Distinguishing Between Coordinate and Cumulative Adjectives** Copy each sentence with coordinate adjectives, inserting a comma where necessary. For sentences with cumulative adjectives, write *cumulative*.

1. More than 60,000 tons of cold hard steel was required to complete the Empire State Building.
2. Marble was quarried from all over Europe for the lavish front entrance.
3. Construction crews worked long difficult hours high above the city.
4. The workers added fourteen floors during one remarkable often-discussed ten-day period.
5. A noisy excited crowd turned out for the grand opening of the building on May 1, 1931.

Exercise 24 **Using Commas After Introductory Material** Copy each sentence that needs a comma, inserting the comma where it is needed. If a sentence does not require a comma, write *correct*.

1. Built at the end of the eighteenth century Gracie Mansion is the official residence of the mayor of New York City.
2. When the Revolutionary War ended a Scottish immigrant named Archibald Gracie purchased the land and built a large home on it.
3. As the city expanded it appropriated the mansion and its surrounding land in 1896, turning the area into a park.
4. Unfortunately the building was neglected, and it fell into disrepair.
5. By 1923 preservationists had restored the mansion, and it briefly served as the Museum of New York City.

▶ **Exercise 25   Using Commas to Set Off Parenthetical and Nonessential Expressions** Copy the following sentences, inserting commas where necessary to set off parenthetical expressions.

1. Central Park which was one of New York's largest public works projects first opened in 1859.
2. The wealthy citizens who admired the public parks of London and Paris pushed for the development of a large park in New York City.
3. Three years of debate over price and location of the park finally came to an end in 1853 when the state legislature authorized the park's construction.
4. The city therefore acquired more than 700 acres in the center of Manhattan.
5. The land was for the most part undesirable for homes and other private development.

▶ **Exercise 26   Proofreading to Correct Comma Errors** Revise each of the following sentences, inserting or deleting commas as necessary.

1. Since the founding of New York City Brooklyn and Manhattan have been important parts of the city.
2. Until the late 1800's people, who wished to travel from one borough to the other, had to rely on ferryboats which would shuttle them back and forth across the East River.
3. In 1867 New York legislators finally agreed to fund a bridge, and chartered the New York Bridge Company to do the job.
4. The company soon chose John A. Roebling a wire manufacturer and engineer to design the bridge, and oversee its construction.
5. His design called for a rail line a walkway for pedestrians and a roadway for horse-drawn carriages.
6. Unfortunately in July, 1869 John A.

Roebling died in an accident.
7. His son Washington Roebling succeeded him.
8. Work on the bridge began in January, 1870, but by 1871 Washington Roebling was crippled by disease.
9. His wife took over the job of instructing the engineers while Roebling supervised the work from his Brooklyn bedroom window.
10. The Brooklyn Bridge eventually opened on May 24 1883.
11. During its construction twenty-seven men had died, including its designer John A. Roebling.

▶ **Exercise 27   Find It in Your Reading** Read the following excerpt from E. B. White's "Here Is New York." Then, explain the rules governing his use of commas.

. . . The subterranean system of telephone cables, power lines, steam pipes, gas mains, and sewer pipes is reason enough to abandon the island to the gods and the weevils. Every time an incision is made in the pavement, the noisy surgeons expose ganglia that are tangled beyond belief.

▶ **Exercise 28   Find It in Your Writing** In your portfolio, look for examples of coordinate and cumulative adjectives. If you can't find any examples, challenge yourself to add one or two. Make sure you have used commas correctly in each example.

▶ **Exercise 29   Writing Application** Write a paragraph about the history of an interesting home, building, or other architectural structure near your school. When you finish, review all of the rules for commas, and make sure you have used commas correctly in your paragraph.

Section Review • 715

▶ **Exercise 25**

1. Central Park, which was one of New York's largest public works projects,
2. correct
3. finally came to an end in 1853,
4. The city, therefore,
5. The land was, for the most part,

▶ **Exercise 26**

1. Since the founding of New York City,
2. Up until the late 1800s, people who . . . to the other had to rely on ferryboats, which
3. In 1867, . . . bridge and chartered
4. John A. Roebling, a wire manufacturer and engineer, to design the bridge and
5. a rail line, a walkway for pedestrians, and a roadway
6. Unfortunately, in July 1869,
7. son, Washington Roebling,
8. in January 1870, but, by 1871,
9. engineers, while Roebling
10. on May 24, 1883.
11. construction, twenty-seven men had died, including its designer, John A. Roebling.

▶ **Exercise 27**

Find It in Your Reading
lines 1–3—commas to separate items in a series, in this case multiple objects of the preposition *of*
line 6—comma after an introductory adverb clause

▶ **Exercise 28**

Find It in Your Writing
For a variation, have students exchange a piece from their portfolios and mark any errors in the use of commas with coordinate and cumulative adjectives.

continued

Answer Key continued

▶ **Exercise 29**

Writing Application
Have students double-check their use of commas by exchanging papers with a partner, marking any errors, and then returning the papers to their owners to be corrected.

🕐 **TIME SAVERS!**

📄 **Answers on Transparencies**
Use the *Grammar Exercises Answers on Transparencies* for Chapter 27 to facilitate correction by students.

🖥 **On-Line Exercise Bank**
Have students complete the exercises on computer. The Auto Check feature will grade their work for you!

Interest GRABBER Make a puzzle for students to assemble from these words and punctuation marks:

Words: *went, we, therefore, we, needed, store, to, the, and groceries*

Marks: **. ; ,**

Have each student construct one complete sentence from these pieces.

Correct answer: *We needed groceries; therefore, we went to the store.*

Activate Prior Knowledge

Have students write two sentences describing their favorite childhood toy. Then, have them read their sentences out loud and write some of them on the board. (Example: *My teddy bear is brown. He has a ribbon around his neck.*) Ask students how a punctuation mark can join these two related sentences. *(My teddy bear is brown; he has a ribbon around his neck.)* Explain the main purpose of the semicolon (to join independent clauses that contain closely related ideas).

TEACH

Step-by-Step Teaching Guide

The Semicolon

1. Once students read the Key Concept, explain that writers sometimes choose a semicolon over a comma and coordinating conjunction to create a close connection between two related independent clauses.

2. Then, have students read the two examples aloud and explain the difference between them. (In the second, the two ideas are very closely connected.)

3. Remind students not to capitalize the first word of the independent clause following a semicolon.

Critical Viewing

Compare Possible answers: Like a marriage, each independent clause has specific duties and information to convey that is related to the other independent clause.

716

Semicolons and Colons

The semicolon (;) and the colon (:) are similar-looking punctuation marks with very different uses. A semicolon can be used to establish a relationship between two or more independent clauses and also to prevent confusion in sentences containing other internal punctuation marks. A colon can be used as an introductory device to point ahead to additional information, for clarification, and in other special situations.

The Semicolon

Semicolons are used to connect two independent clauses containing similar or contrasting ideas. Often, the independent clauses connected by a semicolon are similar to each other in structure as well as in meaning.

▶ **KEY CONCEPT** Use a semicolon to join independent clauses that are not already joined by the conjunction *and, but, for, not, or, so,* or *yet.* ■

A semicolon is not the most common way to separate independent clauses. In most cases, they are joined with a comma and coordinating conjunction.

EXAMPLE: The First Lady is married to the President, but her role is also very important.

When you write a sentence containing two or more independent clauses and no coordinating conjunction, however, use a semicolon instead of a comma to join them.

The semicolon is a stronger punctuation mark than a comma. It replaces both the comma and the conjunction. Do not capitalize the word following the semicolon unless the word is a proper noun or a proper adjective.

EXAMPLE: Martha Washington was the first First Lady; she was married to George Washington.

Sometimes, the first word of a second independent clause is a conjunctive adverb or a transitional expression.

716 • Punctuation

Theme: American First Ladies

In this section, you will learn about the uses of semicolons and colons. The examples and exercises in this section are about American First Ladies.

Cross-Curricular Connection: Social Studies

▼ **Critical Viewing**
A President and a First Lady have many separate and independent roles. In what way are they like a sentence containing a semicolon? **[Compare]**

⏱ **TIME AND RESOURCE MANAGER**

Resources
Print: *Grammar Exercise Workbook,* pp. 153–154; *Grammar Exercises Answers on Transparencies,* Chapter 27
Technology: *Language Lab* CD-ROM, Semicolons, Colons, and Quotation Marks; *On-Line Exercise Bank,* Section 27.3

In-Depth Coverage	Accelerated Pace
• Work through all key concepts, pp. 716–720. • Assign and review Exercises 30–32.	• Assign pp. 716–720 for independent student review. • Assign Section Review Exercises 33–34, p. 723.

Semicolons With Conjunctive Adverbs and Transitional Expressions

▶ **KEY CONCEPT** Use a semicolon to join independent clauses separated by either a conjunctive adverb or a transitional expression. ■

Conjunctive adverbs are adverbs used as conjunctions to connect independent clauses. Common conjunctive adverbs are *accordingly, also, besides, consequently, furthermore, however, indeed, instead, namely, nevertheless, otherwise, similarly, therefore,* and *thus. Transitional expressions* are expressions that connect one independent clause with another. Transitional expressions include *as a result, at this time, first, for instance, in fact, on the other hand, second,* and *that is.*

CONJUNCTIVE ADVERBS:	We think of Washington, D.C., as the nation's capital; *however,* the capital used to be in New York City. Then, the capital moved to Philadelphia; *therefore,* the First Family moved as well.
TRANSITIONAL EXPRESSIONS:	Martha Washington entertained graciously; *in fact,* she set a precedent for First Ladies. She enjoyed her role as hostess; *on the other hand,* there was a great deal of pressure to set a good example.

Another use of the semicolon is with independent clauses or series that already contain a number of commas. The use of a semicolon can help prevent confusion in these sentences.

▶ **KEY CONCEPT** Use a semicolon to avoid confusion when independent clauses or items in a series already contain commas. ■

INDEPENDENT CLAUSES:	Abigail Adams, who was descended from a prestigious colonial family, had little formal education; still she was an eager reader.
ITEMS IN A SERIES:	She read inspirational works, like the Bible, and philosophy; religious sermons and essays; nonfiction, including historical accounts; and she turned to her husband, John, for further instruction.

In the preceding example, semicolons are used to separate the three major parts of the series. Commas are used within the major parts to set off the modifying participial phrases. When items in a series contain appositives or adjective clauses, semicolons should also be used to separate the major parts of the series.

🖥 Internet Tip

To locate more information about First Ladies of the United States, type "First Ladies" in the query field of your search engine or go directly to "The First Ladies" Web site from **www.whitehouse.gov**

Step-by-Step Teaching Guide

Semicolons With Conjunctive Adverbs and Transitional Expressions

1. Have a student read the first key concept aloud.
2. Ask students to recall conjunctive adverbs and to explain the function they serve in sentences. (They are adverbs acting as conjunctions to link two independent clauses.)
3. Ask a student to read the first example aloud. Have him or her name the conjunctive adverbs used (*however, therefore*).
4. Point out that the semicolon comes before, and a comma comes after the conjunctive adverb.
5. Ask students to identify the transitional expressions in the second group of examples. (*in fact, on the other hand*)
6. Remind them that the transitional expressions are punctuated the same way as the conjunctive adverbs. (semicolon and then comma if joining independent clauses)
7. Ask students to think of additional transitions. (examples: *first, next, soon*)

Step-by-Step Teaching Guide

Semicolons to Avoid Confusion

1. Read aloud the second key concept on this page.
2. Ask a student to list the independent clauses in the first example.
3. Ask why the semicolon is placed before the conjunction. (to avoid confusion)
4. Have a student list the items in a series in the second example.
5. Tell students that the semicolons separate items in series that require internal commas. Point out that, in this case, the second semicolon joins independent clauses.

✓ ONGOING ASSESSMENT: Prerequisite Skills

If students have difficulty with semicolons with conjunctive adverbs, you may find it necessary to review the following to ensure coverage of prerequisite knowledge.

In the Textbook	Print Resources	Technology
Conjunctive Adverbs, pp. 388–395	*Grammar Exercise Workbook,* pp. 17–18	*On-Line Exercise Bank,* Section 17.4

Exercise 30

1. Reading was a common interest of Abigail and her husband; therefore, it acted as a strong bond between them.
2. John Adams went to Harvard, and there he studied for a career in law.
3. They were married in 1764; at this time, Abigail was only nineteen years old.
4. They lived on a small farm outside Boston; however, John Adams's law practice was in town.
5. Later, Abigail looked after the children, and John traveled as a circuit judge.
6. The couple were frequently apart; as a result, Abigail wrote hundreds of letters.
7. Abigail, ahead of her time with many of her ideas, became a trusted and influential advisor to her husband, and he discussed all of the politics of the day with her.
8. Living in France was a new experience for the Adamses: John Adams served at his diplomatic post, which was in Paris; Abigail lived there with him, observing the manners of the French; both of them met social discourtesies bravely.
9. John Adams was the first president to live in Washington, D.C.; indeed, the city was still a wilderness.
10. Abigail's letters have left a legacy of a loving marriage; furthermore, they help us better understand the history of our nation.

Critical Viewing

Connect Possible answer: Adams sits straight up; her expression is serious, and her eyes are alert.

▶ **Exercise 30** Understanding the Use of the Semicolon

Copy the following sentences. Insert semicolons where necessary. Some of the sentences may require only a comma to separate independent clauses.

EXAMPLE: Abigail Adams had great curiosity in fact, she was to become one of the most well-read women in America.

ANSWER: Abigail Adams had great curiosity; in fact, she was to become one of the most well-read women in America.

1. Reading was a common interest of Abigail and her husband therefore, it acted as a strong bond between them.
2. John Adams went to Harvard and there he studied for a career in law.
3. They were married in 1764 at this time, Abigail was only nineteen years old.
4. They lived on a small farm outside Boston however, John Adams's law practice was in town.
5. Later, Abigail looked after the children and John traveled as a circuit judge.
6. The couple were frequently apart as a result, Abigail wrote hundreds of letters.
7. Abigail, ahead of her time with many of her ideas, became a trusted and influential political advisor to her husband and he discussed all the politics of the day with her.
8. Living in France was a new experience for the Adamses: John Adams served at his diplomatic post, which was in Paris Abigail lived in Paris with him, observing the manners of the French both of them met social discourtesies bravely.
9. John Adams was the first President to live in Washington, D.C. indeed, the city was still a wilderness.
10. Abigail's letters have left a legacy of a loving marriage furthermore, they help us better understand the history of our nation.

▶ **More Practice**

On-line
Exercise Bank
• Section 27.3
Grammar Exercise
Workbook
• pp. 153–154

▼ **Critical Viewing**
Describe Abigail Adams's posture and the expression on her face using two closely related independent clauses that could be joined by a semicolon. [**Connect**]

The Colon

The colon (:) is a distinctive punctuation mark with a number of important uses. One important use of the colon is to introduce a list following an independent clause.

KEY CONCEPT Use a colon before a list of items following an independent clause. ■

EXAMPLES:	Dolley Madison entertained all kinds of people: politicians, diplomats, and the general public.
	Her husband, James Madison, was many things: congressman, President, and writer of the Federalist papers.
	The United States government has three branches: the executive, the legislative, and the judicial.

Details may be listed without using a colon. Compare the following examples with the preceding ones.

ALSO CORRECT:	Dolley Madison entertained all kinds of people, including politicians, diplomats, and the general public.
	The United States government consists of the executive branch, the legislative branch, and the judicial branch.

In each of the examples above, the list is not preceded by an independent clause, so no colon is used. Always make sure that an independent clause precedes the list before you insert a colon. The independent clause before a list often begins or ends in a phrase such as *the following* or *the following items*, signaling the need for a colon.

KEY CONCEPT Use a colon to introduce a quotation that is formal or lengthy or a quotation that does not contain a "he said/she said" expression. ■

EXAMPLES:	In *The Living White House,* Rosalynn Carter writes about the history of the White House: "I also have found real pleasure in learning the details about the furniture of the Federal period."
	Helen Taft said about her husband: "It has always been my ambition to see Mr. Taft President of the United States."

A casual quoted remark or dialogue should be introduced by a comma even if lengthy. Use a colon only for more formal quotations and for those without "he said/she said" expressions.

Other Uses of Colons

1. Have students read aloud the key concepts on this page.

2. Explain the relationship between the two sentences in the first example. (The second sentence is capitalized and explains the first sentence.) Remind students that a list following an independent clause does not ordinarily begin with a capital except in lists containing proper nouns or proper adjectives.

3. Have a student read the second example aloud. Explain that the colon indicates a slight pause, which helps emphasize the appositive that follows it.

4. As students examine the chart, ask them to think of additional examples of these special writing situations.

Customize for
ESL Students

Help students learn to write numbers numerically by writing these phrases on the board: *twelve o'clock, six twenty* A.M., *two o'clock* A.M., *three fifty* P.M., *one forty-five* P.M. Ask the students to read each one aloud and then to write each as a numerical time. Tell them to pay special attention to uses of colons.

27.3

▶ **KEY CONCEPT** Use a colon to introduce a sentence that summarizes or explains the sentence before it. ■

EXAMPLE: Mary Todd Lincoln was very active during the Civil War: She visited hospitals, read to the soldiers, wrote them letters, and raised money.

As you see in the preceding example, the colon serves as an introductory device for the sentence that amplifies the preceding sentence. Notice that a capital letter follows the colon because the words following make a complete sentence.

▶ **KEY CONCEPT** Use a colon to introduce a formal appositive that follows an independent clause. ■

A colon is a stronger mark than a comma, so using a colon gives more emphasis to the appositive it introduces.

EXAMPLE: Mrs. Lincoln strongly supported the main Union policy: antislavery.

The colon has a number of other uses as well.

SPECIAL SITUATIONS REQUIRING COLONS	
Time expressed in numerals	7:10 P.M. 12:01 A.M.
References to periodicals (volume number: page number)	*Psychology Today;* 24:189 *Science* 169:611–612
Biblical references (chapter number: verse number)	Deuteronomy 4:11
Subtitles of books and magazines	*The Causes of World War I: A Chronology of Events*
Salutations in business letters	Gentlemen: Dear Ms. Wills:
Labels used to signal important ideas	**Warning:** Trespassers will be prosecuted.

☑ **ONGOING ASSESSMENT: Prerequisite Skills**

If students have difficulty with colons introducing formal appositives, you may find it necessary to review the following to ensure coverage of prerequisite knowledge.

In the Textbook	Print Resources	Technology
Prepositional Phrases and Appositives, p. 434	*Grammar Exercise Workbook,* pp. 43–46	*On-Line Exercise Bank,* Section 19.1

Answer Key

▶ **Exercise 31**

Exercise 31 **Understanding the Use of the Colon** Copy the following items, inserting colons where necessary.

EXAMPLE: Eleanor Roosevelt was sent to boarding school in England when she was young fifteen years old.

ANSWER: Eleanor Roosevelt was sent to boarding school in England when she was young: fifteen years old.

1. Eleanor Roosevelt was the first of the modern First Ladies for one major reason She resolved to have a career of her own.
2. Upon returning home to New York, she married her distant relative Franklin Roosevelt.
3. She became involved in various women's groups the League of Women Voters and the Women's Trade Union League.
4. Dear Mrs. Roosevelt
5. In 1921, Franklin Roosevelt was stricken with a debilitating illness polio.
6. Eleanor Roosevelt championed a wide range of social causes youth employment, civil rights, and women's rights.
7. She believed in the activity of women "Women should not be afraid to soil their hands. Those who are not afraid make the best politicians."
8. Many recent First Ladies have continued to support important causes mental health (Rosalynn Carter); foster grandparents (Nancy Reagan); beautification of the land (Lady Bird Johnson); and literacy (Barbara Bush).
9. Barbara Bush established The Foundation for Family Literacy; this is part of its mission to establish literacy as a value in every family in America.
10. Many of Bush's experiences are chronicled in her book *Barbara Bush A Memoir.*

▶ **More Practice**

On-line
Exercise Bank
• Section 27.3
Grammar Exercise Workbook
• pp. 153–154

▶ **Critical Viewing**
What is the response of these children to hearing Barbara Bush, former President George Bush's wife, read to them? If the book had a subtitle, what punctuation mark would separate it from the main title? **[Infer]**

▶ **Exercise 31**

1. Eleanor Roosevelt was the first of the modern First Ladies for one major reason: She resolved to have a career of her own.
2. Upon returning home to New York, she married her distant relative: Franklin Roosevelt.
3. She became involved in various women's groups: the League of Women Voters and the Women's Trade Union League.
4. Dear Mrs. Roosevelt:
5. In 1921, Franklin Roosevelt was stricken with a debilitating illness: polio.
6. Eleanor Roosevelt championed a wide range of social causes: youth employment, civil rights, and women's rights.
7. She believed in the activity of women: "Women should not be afraid to soil their hands. Those who are not afraid make the best politicians."
8. Many recent First Ladies have continued to support important causes: mental health (Rosalynn Carter); foster grandparents (Nancy Reagan); beautification of the land (Lady Bird Johnson); and literacy (Barbara Bush).
9. Barbara Bush established The Foundation for Family Literacy; this is part of its mission: to establish literacy as a value in every family in America.
10. Many of Bush's experiences are chronicled in her book *Barbara Bush: A Memoir.*

Critical Viewing

Infer Possible answers: The children seem to enjoy having Barbara Bush read to them. A colon would separate a subtitle from a title.

⏱ **TIME SAVERS!**

Answers on Transparencies
Use the *Grammar Exercises Answers on Transparencies* for Chapter 27 to facilitate correction by students.

On-Line Exercise Bank
Have students complete the exercises on computer. The Auto Check feature will grade their work for you!

▶ **Exercise 32**

1. While Mrs. Kennedy lived in the White House, she had it restored and redecorated**;** as a result, it was declared a national museum.
2. She wrote a book to raise funds for this project**:** *The White House: An Historic Guide.*
3. She searched old government buildings for antiques and worked with antique experts**;** in fact, she even asked citizens to send back White House furnishings or other items that had been sold.
4. Mrs. Kennedy was a patron of the arts**;** it was her clothing that made her an international trendsetter.
5. She helped convince the French government to lend the United States a famous painting**:** the *Mona Lisa.*
6. With her husband, Mrs. Kennedy shared many dreams**:** American space exploration, civil rights, and better education for all citizens.
7. She was riding with President Kennedy when he was assassinated at approximately 12**:**30 P.M. on November 22, 1963.
8. After this sad event, she made a decision**:** She would move to New York City and live more privately.
9. Books had always been her greatest love**;** therefore, she became an editor.
10. Jackie Kennedy describes her proudest work as First Lady**:** "To call attention to what was finest in America, what should be esteemed and honored."

Critical Viewing

Classify Possible answer: As an editor, she had to decide where to add and delete punctuation marks to eliminate confusion and make ideas clearer.

⏱ TIME SAVERS!

📘 **Answers on Transparencies**
Use the *Grammar Exercises Answers on Transparencies* for Chapter 27 to facilitate correction by students.

💻 **On-Line Exercise Bank**
Have students complete the exercises on computer. The Auto Check feature will grade their work for you!

27.3

▶ **Exercise 32** **Using Semicolons and Colons Correctly** Copy each of the following items, adding semicolons and colons where appropriate.

EXAMPLE: Jacqueline Kennedy was First Lady during the administration of her husband John F. Kennedy.

ANSWER: Jacqueline Kennedy was First Lady during the administration of her husband: John F. Kennedy.

1. While Mrs. Kennedy lived in the White House, she had it restored and redecorated as a result, it was declared a national museum.
2. She wrote a book to raise funds for this project *The White House An Historic Guide.*
3. She searched old government buildings for antiques and worked with antique experts in fact, she even asked citizens to send back White House furnishings or other items that had been sold.
4. Mrs. Kennedy was a patron of the arts it was her clothing that made her an international trendsetter.
5. She helped convince the French government to lend the United States a famous painting the *Mona Lisa.*
6. With her husband, Mrs. Kennedy shared many dreams American space exploration, civil rights, and better education for all citizens.
7. She was riding with President Kennedy when he was assassinated at approximately 12 30 P.M. on November 22, 1963.
8. After this sad event, she made a decision she would move to New York City and live more privately.
9. Books had always been her greatest love therefore, she became an editor.
10. Jackie Kennedy describes her proudest work as First Lady "To call attention to what was finest in America, what should be esteemed and honored."

▶ **More Practice**

On-line
Exercise Bank
• Section 27.3
Grammar Exercise Workbook
• pp. 153–154

▲ **Critical Viewing**
Jacqueline Kennedy worked as an editor after leaving public life. What kind of decisions about punctuation would she have had to make while on the job? **[Classify]**

☑ ONGOING ASSESSMENT: Monitor and Reinforce

If students miss more than two items in Exercise 31 or 32, refer them to the following for additional practice.

In the Textbook	Print Resources	Technology
Section Review, Ex. 33–34, p. 723	*Grammar Exercise Workbook,* pp. 153–154	*Language Lab* CD-ROM, Semicolons, Colons, and Quotation Marks *On-Line Exercise Bank,* Section 27.3

Section 27.3 Section Review

GRAMMAR EXERCISES 33–37

Exercise 33 **Proofreading for Semicolons and Colons** Revise the following sentences, adding, deleting, or changing semicolons and colons.

1. While she was just a girl, Betty Ford admired Eleanor Roosevelt "I really liked the idea that a woman was speaking out and expressing herself; rather than just expressing the views of her husband."
2. Ford lived in New York City, where she studied dance with Martha Graham: she also worked as a model.
3. When she moved back to her home in Grand Rapids, Michigan, she made a career decision She would teach modern dance to poor children in the city.
4. She met Gerald Ford when he was a busy young lawyer, in fact, at the time he was running for Congress.
5. The Equal Rights Amendment was an issue while Ford was in Congress it was a bill that Betty Ford strongly supported.
6. In 1973, President Richard Nixon selected her husband to fill an important position Vice President.
7. President Nixon resigned suddenly: Gerald Ford then became president of the United States.
8. Ford, in his inaugural address, acknowledged his wife "I am indebted to no man and only to one woman, my dear wife, Betty."
9. Betty Ford spoke openly about the traditional roles of women wife, mother, and homemaker.
10. In 1976, Jimmy Carter defeated Gerald Ford Carter's wife, Rosalyn, became the new First Lady.

Exercise 34 **Proofreading a Letter** Read the following letter. Rewrite it, inserting the proper semicolons and colons.

September 1, 1962

Dear Mrs. Kennedy
   I am writing about our visit to the White House at 1 30 P.M. last Tuesday. My daughter and I were greatly looking forward to an interesting visit indeed, all of our expectations were met. My daughter would have liked to see more of the private quarters the kitchen, the bathroom, and the bedrooms. Of course, we saw the sign No visitors beyond this point. We understood that these areas were off limits nevertheless, we were very happy with the visit. The tour guide was friendly and entertaining furthermore, he was extremely knowledgeable about American history. You have a splendid residence we were glad to be able to see it.
                    Sincerely yours,
                    Maggie Geiger

Exercise 35 **Find It in Your Reading** Reread the passage from "Here Is New York" on page 710. Explain in writing why the author used semicolons after the words "to" and "times."

Exercise 36 **Find It in Your Writing** In a piece of your writing, find two related independent clauses that are linked by a comma and coordinating conjunction. Rewrite the sentence so that the clauses are joined by a semicolon instead.

Exercise 37 **Writing Application** Write a paragraph about packing for a trip. Use a colon to introduce a list of "must haves."

Section Review • 723

✓ ONGOING ASSESSMENT: Assess Mastery

Use the following resources to assess student mastery of semicolons and colons.

In the Textbook	Technology
Chapter Review, p. 765, Ex. 81	*Language Lab* CD-ROM, Punctuation *On-Line Exercise Bank,* Section 27.3

Interest GRABBER Ask two students to perform a brief skit in front of the room in which they talk about a show or sport they both enjoy. Then, have student volunteers come to the board to write full sentences about what they heard, using as many of the speakers' words as they can remember. (Example: Jane said, "I play soccer every weekend.") Have the class help each student use punctuation marks correctly to show what words are the speakers'.

Activate Prior Knowledge

Ask students to recall the name of a favorite book or song and then write a direct quotation telling what someone else has said about it. (Example: Sue told me, "I read *Old Yeller* and thought it was very sad.") Have some students read their sentences aloud. Place one on the board without punctuation and ask for the punctuation marks needed (quotation marks and commas) and where they should be placed.

TEACH

Step-by-Step Teaching Guide

Quotation Marks for Direct Quotations

1. Once students read the key concepts, tell them that an indirect quotation doesn't use the person's exact words but instead paraphrases the meaning.

2. Use the example of directly and indirectly quoted versions. Have students read both aloud and explain the difference.

3. Point out that in direct quotations, periods and commas always go inside the final quotation marks.

4. Have students read the final example on this page, and ask where this style of quotation might be used. (Examples: as a headnote to a chapter in a book, as a final idea in an article)

Section 27.4

Quotation Marks and Underlining

Direct quotations from other people can support the ideas or arguments of a writer. Direct quotations also enliven short stories, novels, and other works of fiction. When the characters themselves speak, the writing becomes more exciting.

Study the many rules and examples in this section carefully to master the use of quotation marks. This section will also discuss the use of underlining as well as quotation marks to indicate different types of titles, names, and words.

Quotation Marks for Direct Quotations

Before direct quotations can be discussed, it is important to distinguish between *direct* and *indirect quotations.*

▶ **KEY CONCEPTS** A **direct quotation** represents a person's exact speech or thoughts and is enclosed in quotation marks (" "). ■

An **indirect quotation** reports only the general meaning of what a person said or thought and does not require quotation marks. ■

DIRECT QUOTATION:	The journalist said, "I expect to be finished with the article before the deadline."
INDIRECT QUOTATION:	The journalist said that he expected to be finished with the article before the deadline.

An indirect quotation rephrases someone else's words. It does not use the exact words of the speaker. In a direct quotation, the words of the speaker are quoted exactly.

Sometimes, the exact words of the speaker are not available, and the only way to express the speaker's sentiments is to rephrase them in an indirect quotation. If the actual words of the speaker are available, however, they should usually be used in order to achieve dynamic, strong writing.

A sentence that is an uninterrupted direct quotation requires quotation marks around it.

EXAMPLE: "To be a journalist is to have a ringside seat to the unfolding of history." —Wes Gallagher

Notice that the preceding quotation begins with a capital letter and is a complete sentence. Each sentence of quoted material should always begin with a capital letter.

724 • Punctuation

Theme: Journalism

In this section, you will learn about the many uses of quotation marks and underlining. The examples and exercises in this section are about journalism.

Cross-Curricular Connection: Social Studies

⏱ TIME AND RESOURCE MANAGER

Resources
Print: *Grammar Exercise Workbook,* pp. 155–160; *Grammar Exercises Answers on Transparencies,* Chapter 27
Technology: *Language Lab* CD-ROM, Punctuation; *On-Line Exercise Bank,* Section 27.4

In-Depth Coverage	Accelerated Pace
• Work through all key concepts, pp. 724–736. • Assign and review Exercises 38–47. • Read and discuss *Grammar in Literature,* p. 730.	• Assign pp. 724–736 for independent student review. • Assign Section Review Exercises 48–52.

Quotations of Phrases

1. Tell students that when only a part of a direct quotation is used, it is enclosed in quotation marks.

2. Read the examples aloud. Explain that the first word in each quotation is capitalized only if it is the beginning of a sentence.

3. Point out that titles are capitalized regardless of their positions in a sentence.

4. Give students another example: *In Fitzgerald's* The Great Gatsby, *"West Egg is the less fashionable" town.* Ask students why West Egg is capitalized. (proper name)

▶ **KEY CONCEPT** The first word of a quoted phrase or fragment is capitalized only when it falls at the beginning of a sentence or when it would be capitalized regardless of its position in a sentence. ■

Notice in the following examples that quotation marks are still placed around the quoted words, but the need for capitalization changes.

EXAMPLES: In "Memories of Christmas," Dylan Thomas mentions that one Christmas "was so much like another."

"The song of the people, transformed by the experiences of each generation" is what holds people together, according to Alice Walker.

Many direct quotations contain two parts: the actual words of the speaker (the direct quotation) and a group of words identifying the speaker. The words identifying the speaker are called conversational tags or "he said/she said" expressions. They include such common expressions as *she said, he replied, the professor explained,* and *Gary asked.* The possibilities are almost endless, but they all have one feature in common: Conversational tags are not enclosed in quotation marks.

There are three ways of using a conversational tag in a sentence: as an introductory expression, as a concluding expression, or as an interrupting expression.

▶ **KEY CONCEPT** Use a comma or colon after an introductory expression. ■

EXAMPLE: The tour guide explained, "*The New York Times* was founded in 1851 by Henry J. Raymond."

In the preceding example, the conversational tag comes first and is set off from the direct quotation with a comma. If the introductory expression is more formal in tone or if it contains no conversational tag, use a colon instead of a comma.

EXAMPLE: She gazed at the assembled crowd: "Thank you for the honor you have awarded me."

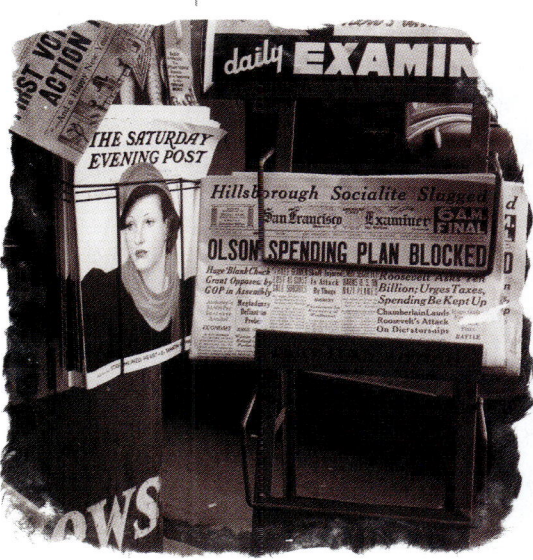

▲ **Critical Viewing**
Why do journalists make extensive use of quotation marks? Why don't they just describe the statements of newsmakers? **[Infer]**

Conversational Tags

1. Have a student read the second key concept on this page. Point out that words identifying a speaker of a direct quotation (he said/she said expressions) are called conversational tags.

2. Explain that conversational tags can come at the beginning, middle, or end of a quotation.

3. Then, point out that less formal introductory expressions are set off with commas, while more formal ones can be set off with colons.

Critical Viewing

Infer Possible answers: A direct quotation from a newsmaker may sometimes be a stronger statement than the same idea paraphrased by a journalist.

Real-World Connection

Every news story contains important facts that must be reported correctly. Point out that direct quotations help bring facts to light because they report the exact words of witnesses. Ask students why the public depends on direct quotations to respond to important issues in the news and to form opinions. (Examples: to make informed choices of political candidates, to decide to support important causes)

Quotation Marks and Underlining • 725

Punctuation With Concluding and Interrupting Expressions

1. Start with the first key concept and have students identify the conversational tag in the example.

2. Have a volunteer explain each of the punctuation marks used. (a pair of quotations around the speaker's words, a comma inside the final quotation mark, and a period at the end of the tag)

3. Read the second key concept and again have students identify the conversational tag.

4. Point out that this tag interrupts a speaker's words. Have a volunteer read only those words.

5. Ask why the tag is set off by commas. (The quoted statement has not ended; the tag interrupts it.)

6. Read the third key concept and have students identify the conversational tag. Ask how many complete quoted sentences precede the tag (two) and how many follow it (three).

7. Finally, ask why the tag is followed by a period. (The period precedes the beginning of a new quoted sentence.)

Customize for
Musical/Rhythmic Learners

Give students practice hearing and spotting the difference between quoted words and conversational tags. Tell them to clap twice every time you reach a spot where a quotation begins or ends—a spot where a quotation mark should be placed. To begin, read a passage without claps and then re-read it, asking students to respond with claps where appropriate. Use these and then add more from the models in this section:

"To be or not to be," wrote Shakespeare, "that is the question."

It was Emerson who wrote, "If a man owns land, the land owns him."

Sometimes, a direct quotation comes before a conversational tag.

KEY CONCEPT Use a comma, question mark, or exclamation mark after a quotation followed by a concluding expression. ■

EXAMPLE: "*The New York Times* was founded in 1851 by Henry J. Raymond," the tour guide explained.

In the preceding example, a comma follows the direct quotation, and a period is used after the conversational tag because it ends the sentence. Notice also that the comma comes before the quotation mark.

In addition to preceding or following a quotation, there is a third way of using a conversational tag: The conversational tag can interrupt the direct quotation.

KEY CONCEPT Use a comma after the part of a quoted sentence that is followed by an interrupting expression. Use another comma after the expression. ■

EXAMPLE: "*The New York Times*," the tour guide explained, "was founded in 1851 by Henry J. Raymond."

In this example, the quotation has been interrupted by a conversational tag. Both parts are enclosed in quotation marks, and there are commas before and after the conversational tag. Once again, the first comma comes before the quotation mark.

A final rule must be followed whenever a conversational tag interrupts a quotation that is several sentences long:

KEY CONCEPT Use a comma, question mark, or exclamation mark after a quoted sentence that comes before an interrupting expression. Use a period after the expression. ■

EXAMPLE: "I want to have time to look for my children and see how many I can find. Maybe I shall find them among the dead," said Chief Joseph of the Nez Percé. "Hear me, my chiefs. I am tired; my heart is sick and sad. From where the sun now stands I will fight no more forever."

Writers vary their use of conversational tags in the ways shown in the preceding examples to achieve variety.

▶ **Exercise 38** Using Quotation Marks With Direct
Quotations Copy each sentence that needs punctuation,
adding whatever punctuation is needed. In one instance, a
quoted fragment has been underlined so that you can tell
where it begins and ends. If a sentence is not a direct quotation and requires no quotation marks, write *indirect*.

EXAMPLE: His editor explained why he did not agree
with him.

ANSWER: indirect

EXAMPLE: We have different ethical standards, he said.

ANSWER: "We have different ethical standards," he said.

1. You're scheduled to cover the city council meeting tonight
my editor told me.
2. I'm looking forward to it! I replied, and I was.
3. I went on to tell him that I had a tantalizing lead about a
scandal that was about to break.
4. What is it? he wanted to know.
5. I had heard that the mayor might resign this evening, but
I didn't completely trust my source. I told my editor this.
6. Interesting, he mused. I think you should take Joe with you.
7. Joe is our best photographer, and I told my editor that I
liked his idea.
8. Just last week, our paper had
written that the mayor is <u>one of
the most honest men in politics
today</u>, but in tomorrow's paper,
who knows what we'll write?
9. Make sure Joe gets shots of both
the council and the audience, he
instructed me. We may have a big
story here!
10. I told him that I'd catch Joe on
my way out of the building.

▶ **Critical Viewing**
Why might a person speaking
with a journalist insist upon being
quoted directly, with quotation
marks around any statements,
rather than having the remarks
paraphrased by a writer?
[Speculate]

▶ **More Practice**

**On-line
Exercise Bank**
• Section 27.4
**Grammar Exercise
Workbook**
• pp. 155–156

▶ **Exercise 38**

1. "You're scheduled to cover the
city council meeting tonight,"
my editor told me.
2. "I'm looking forward to it!" I
replied, and I was.
3. I went on to tell him that I had a
tantalizing lead about a scandal
that was about to break. (indirect)
4. "What is it?" he wanted to know.
5. I had heard that the mayor
might resign this evening, but
I didn't completely trust my
source. I told my editor this.
(indirect)
6. "Interesting," he mused. "I think
you should take Joe with you."
7. Joe is our best photographer,
and I told my editor that I liked
his idea. (indirect)
8. Just last week, our paper had
written that the mayor is "one of
the most honest men in politics
today," but in tomorrow's paper,
who knows what we'll write?
9. "Make sure Joe gets shots
of both the council and the
audience," he instructed me.
"We may have a big story here!"
10. I told him that I'd catch Joe on
my way out of the building.
(indirect)

Critical Viewing

Speculate Possible answer:
A speaker can avoid being
misunderstood—or misrepresented—
if a journalist reports exactly what is
said and places the words inside
quotation marks.

Quotation Marks and Underlining • **727**

✓ **ONGOING ASSESSMENT: Monitor and Reinforce**

If students miss more than two items in Exercise 38, refer them to the following for additional
practice.

In the Textbook	Print Resources	Technology
Section Review, Ex. 48, p. 740	*Grammar Exercise Workbook,* pp. 155–156	*Language Lab* CD-ROM, Punctuation *On-Line Exercise Bank,* Section 27.4

⏱ **TIME SAVERS!**

Answers on Transparencies
Use the *Grammar Exercises
Answers on Transparencies* for
Chapter 27 to facilitate
correction by students.

On-Line Exercise Bank
Have students complete the
exercises on computer. The Auto
Check feature will grade their
work for you!

Other Punctuation Marks With Quotation Marks

1. Tell students that they will encounter unusual situations that require careful placement of punctuation marks.

2. Read the first key concept and explain that periods and commas always are placed inside final quotation marks. Use the examples to demonstrate.

3. Then, read the second key concept and point out that semicolons and colons do not behave exactly as commas do; instead, they fall outside the final quotation mark because they connect or set off items from the quotations.

4. Point out also that the independent clause following the colon is capitalized.

5. Finally, read the third key concept aloud and emphasize that these marks may also appear outside the final quotation mark if these are not part of the meaning of the quotation.

6. Again, have students read the examples at the bottom of this page and at the top of the next page. Ask a student to explain why the question and exclamation marks appear outside the quotation marks in the latter examples. (They are logically parts of the tags, not the quotations.)

Critical Viewing

Evaluate Possible answer: Readers and viewers might consider direct quotations to be more reliable sources of information.

27.4

Other Punctuation Marks With Quotation Marks

Quotation marks are used in conjunction with many other punctuation marks. Unfortunately, the location of the quotation marks in relation to the other punctuation marks is not always the same. It varies depending on the other punctuation marks and, in some cases, on the meaning of the sentence.

The rule for commas and periods is always the same.

▶ **KEY CONCEPT** Always place a comma or a period inside the final quotation mark. ■

EXAMPLES: The reporter said, "I'm ready if you are**.**"

"I took several pictures of the candidate**,**" the photographer said.

The rule is the reverse when quotation marks are used with semicolons and colons.

▶ **KEY CONCEPT** Always place a semicolon or colon outside the final quotation mark. ■

EXAMPLES: I fully understand what she means by a "call for drastic action"**;** the situation becomes more pressing each day.

We emphatically deny these "nasty accusations"**:** They are ill-founded and not based on fact.

The rules for the use of quotation marks with question marks and exclamation marks are more complicated.

▶ **KEY CONCEPT** Place a question mark or an exclamation mark inside the final quotation mark if the end mark is part of the quotation. ■

The question mark in the first of the following examples is placed inside the quotation mark because it belongs to the quotation itself. The same is true of the exclamation mark in the second example. It belongs inside the quotation mark because it is part of the quotation itself.

EXAMPLES: Marie asked, "Have the reporters phoned yet**?**" The spokesman exclaimed, "We demand our rights**!**"

Notice the difference when the exclamation mark or question mark refers to the entire sentence.

728 • Punctuation

▲ **Critical Viewing**
What makes a reader or viewer choose one newspaper or newscast over another? Does the inclusion of direct quotes have any effect on this decision? **[Evaluate]**

✎ STANDARDIZED TEST PREPARATION WORKSHOP

Grammar and Usage Many standardized tests require students to revise errors in compositions. Use the following example.

Which of these sentences is written and punctuated correctly?

A "Well," asked Mona, "are you going to finish the painting today"?

B "Well, asked Mona, are you going to finish the painting today"?

C "Well," asked Mona, "are you going to finish the painting today?"

D "Well," asked Mona, "Are you going to finish the painting today?"

The correct answer is **C**. In A, the question mark should have been placed inside the end quotation mark. In B, the quotation should not have included the conversational tag. In D, the continuation of the quotation should not have been capitalized.

EXAMPLES: Did the editor state, "This is an equal opportunity organization"**?**

Run from anyone who whispers, "I have a deal you can't refuse"**!**

In each example, the end mark goes outside of the puncuation mark because it belongs to the entire sentence, not to the quote. You should also place the end mark outside if both the quote and the entire sentence require a question mark or an exclamation mark.

Exercise 39 Using Other Punctuation Marks With Direct Quotations

Copy each of the following sentences, adding quotation marks as needed. Quoted fragments are underlined.

EXAMPLE: The magazine staff looked up when Jennifer shouted, We must leave *now*!

ANSWER: The magazine staff looked up when Jennifer shouted, "We must leave *now*!"

1. Our journalism professor stated: This business is all about hard-hitting questions, honest answers, and a bit of wisdom.
2. The city editor asked, Do we have any witnesses who will talk to us about the fire?
3. This article is well written, he said. The reporter was fair and accurate.
4. Are you certain? he asked his source. These are explosive allegations you are making.
5. Did your article state: The defendant refused to comment?
6. Quick! I yelled to our photojournalist. Take the picture, and let's get out of here!
7. If that article isn't on my desk by 6 P.M., my editor warned, you better start looking for another job.
8. Moved to the front page, the editorial called for the senator's immediate resignation; other papers expressed similar demands.
9. There is the central and very serious mission of *communicating*—gathering facts, yes; understanding them, yes; but then going that essential step further. —Conrad Fink
10. The world does not want to wait for the assessment of history; it wants the information at the time history is being made. —M. L. Stein

More Practice

On-line Exercise Bank
• Section 27.4
Grammar Exercise Workbook
• pp. 157–158

Grammar and Style Tip

Don't combine commas with other end marks when writing quotations. An exclamation mark, for example, will supersede a comma. For example: *"Look out!" he yelled.*

Answer Key

Exercise 39

1. Our journalism professor stated: "This business is all about hard-hitting questions, honest answers, and a bit of wisdom."
2. The city editor asked, "Do we have any witnesses who will talk to us about the fire?"
3. "This article is well written," he said. "The reporter was fair and accurate."
4. "Are you certain?" he asked his source. "These are explosive allegations you are making."
5. Did your article state: "The defendant refused to comment"?
6. "Quick!" I yelled to our photojournalist. "Take the picture and let's get out of here!"
7. "If that article isn't on my desk by 6 P.M.," my editor warned, "you better start looking for another job."
8. Moved to the front page, the editorial called for the "senator's immediate resignation"; other papers expressed similar demands.
9. "There is the central and very serious mission of *communicating*—gathering facts, yes; understanding them, yes; but then going that essential step further."—Conrad Fink
10. "The world does not want to wait for the assessment of history; it wants the information at the time history is being made."—M. L. Stein

---

✓ ONGOING ASSESSMENT: Monitor and Reinforce

If students miss more than two items in Exercise 39, refer them to the following for additional practice.

In the Textbook	Print Resources	Technology
Section Review, Ex. 49, p. 740	*Grammar Exercise Workbook,* pp. 157–158	*Language Lab* CD-ROM, Punctuation *On-Line Exercise Bank,* Section 27.4

🕐 TIME SAVERS!

Answers on Transparencies
Use the *Grammar Exercises Answers on Transparencies* for Chapter 27 to facilitate correction by students.

On-Line Exercise Bank
Have students complete the exercises on computer. The Auto Check feature will grade their work for you!

Quotation Marks in Special Situations

You also need to know how to use quotation marks in dialogues and in quotations of more than one paragraph. In addition, you may want to leave out part of a person's words in a quotation or to include one quotation within another. The following rules will guide you in these special situations.

Dialogue and Long Quotations In many stories and novels, the use of dialogue, or direct conversation between two or more people, plays an important role. Much of what is happening is indicated through the words of the characters.

Each writer develops his or her own style in writing dialogue. The writer must follow the rules for writing quotations, however, so that the reader will know who is speaking.

▶ **KEY CONCEPT** When writing dialogue, begin a new paragraph with each change of speaker. ■

GRAMMAR IN LITERATURE

from **The Writer in the Family**
E. L. Doctorow

The structure of this dialogue makes it easy to tell that Aunt Frances is speaking in the first and third paragraphs; Jonathan is speaking in the second; and Jonathan's mother is speaking in the fourth.

"Jonathan? This is your Aunt Frances. How is everyone?"

"Fine, thank you."

"I want to ask one last favor of you. I need a letter from Jack. Your grandma's very ill. Do you think you can?"

"Who is it?" my mother called from the living room.

"OK, Aunt Frances," I said quickly. "I have to go now. We're eating dinner."

Another type of quotation consists of several paragraphs in a row. For this type of quotation, quotation marks are placed at the beginning of each paragraph and at the end of the final paragraph.

▶ **KEY CONCEPT** For quotations longer than a paragraph, put quotation marks at the beginning of each paragraph and at the end of the final paragraph. ■

EXAMPLE:

> "When messages are misunderstood, it is easy to blame the speaker. The listener, however, must share the responsibility for effective communication. It takes a lot of concentration and effort to be a good listener. Statistics show, in fact, that most people are poor listeners. The average person misses about 75 percent of what he or she hears.
>
> "The encouraging fact is that no one has to remain a poor listener. Listening, like speaking, reading, or writing, is a skill that can be learned. Learning to listen does, however, take a lot of self-motivation and practice."
>
> —J. Regis O'Connor

When you are quoting several paragraphs, make certain that you remember to include the final quotation mark.

Ellipsis Marks and Single Quotation Marks There are two other special problems involving the use of quotation marks. The first concerns the use of ellipsis marks (. . .) in a shortened quotation. Frequently, a writer wishes to include only a portion of a long quotation in a piece of writing. In such a situation, ellipsis marks can be used to show that some words have been omitted.

▶ **KEY CONCEPT** Use three ellipsis marks in a quotation to indicate that words have been omitted. ■

Ellipsis marks can be used at the beginning, in the middle, or at the end of a quotation.

AN ENTIRE QUOTATION:
"Whenever I prepare for a journey I prepare as though for death. Should I never return, all is in order. This is what life has taught me."
—Katherine Mansfield

ELLIPSES AT THE BEGINNING:
Katherine Mansfield speaks of preparing for a trip ". . . as though for death."

ELLIPSES IN THE MIDDLE:
Katherine Mansfield once wrote, "Whenever I prepare for a journey I prepare . . . for death."

ELLIPSES AT THE END:
Walt Whitman once wrote, "I hear America singing. . . ."

Quotations Longer Than a Paragraph

1. Explain to students that, for quotations longer than one paragraph, the quotation marks are placed at the beginning of each paragraph and at the end of the final paragraph.

2. Have students read the example. Point out that the final sentence in the first paragraph has no closing quotation mark.

3. Ask students why this style of punctuating long quotations is helpful to readers. (The lack of closing quotation marks signals that the quotation continues.)

Ellipsis Marks in Quotations

1. Place ellipsis marks on the board (. . .) and ask students whether they know the meaning of these punctuation marks. (They replace omitted words.)

2. Ask why a writer might use ellipses (to include only the relevant parts of a quotation) and in what kinds of situations. (reports, articles, interviews)

3. Have a student read each example and point out the position of each ellipsis. Ask why ellipses might appear at the beginning, middle, or end. (The unnecessary words might precede or follow the desired portions.)

Integrating Spelling Skills

Ellipsis Marks As students study ellipsis marks, explain that the word derives from the Greek *eleipsis* meaning "to fall short." Point out that the plural form is *ellipses*, spelled by changing the *i* to *e*. Ask students for other words that end in *-is* (Examples: *hypothesis, axis*) and ask students to form their plurals (*hypotheses, axes*).

Step-by-Step Teaching Guide

Single Quotations Marks

1. Ask students when using single quotations may make sense (when quoting a statement that already includes a quotation).

2. Have a student read the example. Ask the class whose speech is identified by the regular marks (the teacher's) and whose by the single quotes (the raven's).

Answer Key

▶ **Exercise 40**

Answers will vary. Possible answers:

1. When Einstein said, "Not everything that can be counted counts . . . ," I think he meant that we keep number records of a lot of unimportant things.
2. "I think," said Cynthia, "that Zola made a good point about producing artistic work when he said, 'The artist is nothing without the gift, but the gift is nothing without work.'"
3. "What do you think Jefferson meant," asked Mr. Vittori, "when he said, 'I find that the harder I work, the more luck I seem to have'?"
4. Martin Luther King, Jr., must have felt betrayed when he said, "In the end, we will remember . . . the silence of our friends."
5. "Collette seemed to see writing as its own reward when she said, 'Writing only leads to more writing,'" commented the student.

Notice that when a period is part of the quotation, as in the last two examples, it is added to the ellipsis marks to conclude the sentence.

The second special problem involving quotation marks concerns a quotation within a quotation. A quotation within a quotation is set off with single quotation marks (' ') instead of the regular double marks (" "). The larger quotation is still set off with double quotation marks.

▶ **KEY CONCEPT** Use single quotation marks for a quotation within a quotation. ■

EXAMPLE: I can still hear our tenth-grade English teacher reciting the line from Poe: "Quoth the Raven, 'Nevermore.'"

Notice that the single quotation mark goes outside the period, just as a double quotation mark does.

If a quotation within a quotation causes confusion, rephrase the material to eliminate the quotation within a quotation.

▶ **Exercise 40** **Writing Sentences With Ellipsis Marks and Single Quotation Marks** Write five original sentences, each incorporating either part of one of the quotations below (using ellipsis marks) or the whole quotation inside another quotation (using single quotation marks).

EXAMPLE: "We have just begun to fight."
ANSWER: The teacher asked us, "Do you know who said, 'We have just begun to fight'?"

EXAMPLE: "From what we get, we can make a living; what we give, however, makes a life." —Arthur Ashe
ANSWER: I'm going to volunteer because, as Arthur Ashe said, ". . . what we give . . . makes a life."

1. "Not everything that can be counted counts, and not everything that counts can be counted." —*Albert Einstein*
2. "The artist is nothing without the gift, but the gift is nothing without work." —*Emile Zola*
3. "I find that the harder I work, the more luck I seem to have." —*Thomas Jefferson*
4. "In the end, we will remember not the words of our enemies, but the silence of our friends." —*Martin Luther King, Jr.*
5. "Writing only leads to more writing." —*Collette*

732 • Punctuation

Exercise 41 Using Ellipsis Marks and Single Quotation

Marks Copy each of the following sentences, inserting double quotation marks (" ") and single quotation marks (' ') as needed. Underline any words that are printed in italics. The quoted fragments are underlined.

EXAMPLE: I asked, Were you serious when you said, I won't?

ANSWER: I asked, "Were you serious when you said, 'I won't'?"

1. "In his triumphant speech, the lawyer for the newspaper said, We have won a victory for freedom of the press, and then he smiled broadly."
2. "I refer you to the First Amendment, which states, Congress shall make no law . . . abridging the freedom of speech, or of the press."
3. "The so called <u>Yellow Press</u> is any newspaper which glows with the color of sunshine and throws light into dark places." —Ella Wheeler Wilcox
4. The author of the editorial wrote, Our senator has done . . . an adequate job representing the district.
5. The court reporter overheard the defendant tell the judge, Stone walls do not a prison make. . . .
6. "As a journalist, I was able to get into the locker room, where I heard one player grumbling about what he called <u>the worst playing field in the history of the game</u>."
7. "He kept saying, Would you at least consider me for the foreign correspondent position? but the editor always refused."
8. The title of Hemingway's book *For Whom the Bell Tolls* refers to a line in one of John Donne's meditations, which states, . . . never send to know for whom the bell tolls; it tolls for thee.
9. The speaker observed: My statement was interrupted by a reporter who asked me, Do you think you will run for office?
10. When it comes to freedom of the press, most journalists agree with Patrick Henry, who said, . . . but as for me, give me liberty or give me death.

Exercise 42 Writing Original Dialogue

Write approximately one page of original dialogue about two characters attempting to solve a problem or resolve a dispute. Include a few lines of description. Enclose the lines of dialogue in quotation marks. Include enough conversational tags so that there is no confusion about who is speaking.

More Practice

On-line
Exercise Bank
• Section 27.4
Grammar Exercise
Workbook
• pp. 157–158

▲ **Critical Viewing**
Why might a journalist choose to shorten a direct quotation? What should a reader be aware of when he or she sees ellipsis marks in a quotation? **[Interpret]**

Answer Key

Exercise 41

1. 'We have won a victory for freedom of the press,'
2. 'Congress shall make no law . . . abridging the freedom of speech, or of the press.'"
3. "The so called 'Yellow Press' is
4. "Our senator has done . . . an adequate job representing the district."
5. "Stone walls do not a prison make. . . ."
6. 'the worst playing field in the history of the game.'"
7. 'Would you at least consider me for the foreign correspondent position?'
8. ". . . never send to know for whom the bell tolls; it tolls for thee."
9. "My statement was interrupted by a reporter who asked me, 'Do you think you will run for office?'"
10. ". . . but as for me, give me liberty or give me death."

Critical Viewing

Interpret Possible answer: A journalist might need only a portion of a quotation to make a point. Readers should realize that the journalist has not used the entire statement, and that the speaker's full intent might not be revealed.

Answer Key

Exercise 42

When students finish writing, have them exchange papers and mark any errors in the use of quotation marks. Then have them return the papers to their owners to be corrected. Encourage students to refer to their books for reminders about the rules for using quotation marks.

✓ ONGOING ASSESSMENT: Monitor and Reinforce

If students have difficulty with Exercise 40, 41, or 42, refer them to the following for additional practice.

In the Textbook	Print Resources	Technology
Section Review, Ex. 50, p. 740	*Grammar Exercise Workbook,* pp. 157–158	*Language Lab* CD-ROM, Punctuation *On-Line Exercise Bank,* Section 27.4

⏱ TIME SAVERS!

📄 **Answers on Transparencies** Use the *Grammar Exercises Answers on Transparencies* for Chapter 27 to facilitate correction by students.

💻 **On-Line Exercise Bank** Have students complete the exercises on computer. The Auto Check feature will grade their work for you!

Underlining for Long Works

1. Ask students how the titles of books normally are written in print (in italics) and then explain that in handwritten material, a writer cannot easily simulate italics; hence, writers underline to achieve the same purpose.

2. Have a student read the key concept aloud. Then, have students scan the kinds of works that should be underlined.

3. For each type of work, ask students to supply additional examples.

27.4

Underlining, Italics, and Quotation Marks

There are various ways of indicating titles in writing. In books, periodicals, and other printed publications, italics are used to indicate many types of titles. In handwritten material, the writer underlines items that in print would be italicized. When using a word processor, you may choose to underline or use italic type. Other types of titles require the use of quotation marks. Quotation marks are used in both printed and hand-written materials.

The following rules will help you use underlining and quotation marks correctly in titles and in other situations.

Underlining and Italic The titles of long works are generally indicated by underlining or italic type.

▶ **KEY CONCEPT** Underline or italicize the titles of books and other long written works, of publications that are published as a single work, of plays, and of other works of art. ■

BOOKS:	I want to read Nancy Wolcott's <u>Women and the American Experience</u>.
MAGAZINES:	The <u>Atlantic Monthly</u> is a very good magazine.
NEWSPAPERS:	I subscribe to <u>The New York Times</u>.
PAMPHLETS:	Distributed at the start of the Revolutionary War, Thomas Paine's <u>Common Sense</u> helped to turn the tide of public opinion.
LONG POEMS:	<u>The Rime of the Ancient Mariner</u> is one of my favorite poems.
MOVIES:	At the time of its release, <u>Titanic</u> was the most expensive movie ever made.
MUSICALS:	Critics called <u>Oklahoma!</u> a work of genius.
PLAYS (two acts or longer):	<u>The Glass Menagerie</u> is a sad play about the fragile nature of humanity.
WORKS OF ART:	<u>Mona Lisa</u> is a masterful example of Da Vinci's talent.
ALBUMS:	I bought a copy of The Beatles' <u>Abbey Road</u>.
TV PROGRAMS:	Did you watch <u>60 Minutes</u> last night?
OPERAS AND SYMPHONIES:	Mozart's <u>Figaro</u> is my favorite opera.

▶ **KEY CONCEPT** Underline or italicize the names of individual air, sea, space, and land craft.

EXAMPLE: The President arrived on <u>Air Force One</u>.

▶ **KEY CONCEPT** Underline or italicize foreign words or phrases not yet accepted into English. ■

EXAMPLES: The famous star signed the letter <u>con amore</u>, "with love."
The French expression <u>mère de famille</u> means "mother of a family."
The composer's notation read <u>con spirito</u>, "with spirit."

Some foreign words and phrases retain their foreign pronunciation but are no longer underlined or italicized because they are now considered part of our language.

NOT UNDERLINED: amour, caveat emptor, cliché, blitzkrieg, gourmet, milieu, siesta, staccato, chauffeur, pizza, dilettante

Individual numbers, letters, and words used to name themselves are underlined or italicized to make them stand out.

▶ **KEY CONCEPT** Underline or italicize numbers, symbols, letters, and words used as names for themselves. ■

NUMBERS: Is that a <u>3</u> or an <u>8</u>?
SYMBOLS: Use a <u>?</u> after a direct question.
LETTERS: He has a strange way of writing his <u>f</u>'s and <u>t</u>'s.
WORDS: She often uses <u>nevertheless</u> to connect her ideas.

Underlining or italics may also be used to emphasize a particular word or phrase.

▶ **KEY CONCEPT** Underline or italicize words that you wish to stress. ■

EXAMPLE: Be sure to study the rules <u>carefully</u>.

Do not overuse underlining to emphasize your meaning. Rely instead on a precise choice and arrangement of words.

💿 **Technology Tip**

When using a word processor, you can italicize titles rather than underlining them. An icon for italics—as well as for underlining and boldface—appears on the toolbar of most word processors.

Underlining and Quotation Marks

1. Read aloud the first key concept and then the examples. Ask students to identify the type of work in each example.

2. Then, ask students to suggest original sentences using a title that would be enclosed in quotation marks.

3. Explain to students that some titles are never written with underlining or quotation marks. Read the second key concept aloud.

4. Read the final key concept, and have students read the examples aloud. Ask students to identify the documents that are not underlined and to identify their part of speech. (proper nouns)

Answer Key

Exercise 43

Answers will vary. Possible answers:

1. I'm looking forward to receiving my first issue of <u>National Geographic</u> magazine.
2. Do you want to see the re-release of <u>Sixteen Candles</u>?
3. The Gettysburg Address gave a strong view about the importance of preserving the Union.
4. I like old songs like "All You Need Is Love."
5. I just finished George Orwell's <u>Animal Farm</u>, and I thought it was a really funny commentary on politics.

27.4

Quotation Marks Like underlining, quotation marks are used to indicate certain titles.

> **KEY CONCEPT** Use quotation marks around the titles of short written works (including one-act plays and short poems), chapters in a book, episodes in a series (including individual episodes of television programs), songs, and parts of long musical compositions or collections. ■

EXAMPLES: I admire the poem "I Hear America Singing."

"Charles" is one of my favorite short stories.

His favorite song by The Beatles is "Something."

Read Chapter 1, "Dynamic Democracy," in <u>Freedom's Ferment</u>.

Titles Without Underlining or Quotation Marks Two types of titles should not be underlined or enclosed in quotation marks. The first type is made up of religious works.

> **KEY CONCEPT** Do not underline, italicize, or place in quotation marks the name of the Bible, its books and divisions or versions or other holy scriptures, such as the Torah and the Koran. ■

EXAMPLE: Will you read from Genesis in the Old Testament?

Other titles that should not be underlined or enclosed in quotation marks are government documents.

> **KEY CONCEPT** Do not underline, italicize, or place in quotation marks the titles of government charters, alliances, treaties, acts, statutes, speeches, or reports. ■

EXAMPLES: The Taft-Hartley Labor Act was passed in 1947.

We memorized the Preamble to the Constitution.

Exercise 43 **Writing Sentences Containing Titles** Write sentences, following the instructions given below. Be sure to use underlining and quotation marks correctly.

1. Write a sentence about subscribing to a new magazine.
2. Write a question inviting someone to a new movie.
3. Write a sentence about President Lincoln's famous speech at Gettysburg.
4. Write a sentence about a favorite song.
5. Write a sentence recommending a book you like.

Exercise 44 **Revising to Supply Underlining** Revise each of the following sentences, underlining where necessary.

EXAMPLE: The movie Gone With the Wind was made in 1939.
ANSWER: The movie <u>Gone With the Wind</u> was made in 1939.

1. A favorite bon mot among journalists is, "Write the things that you have seen."
2. The city's great newspapers sent photographers to take pictures of the Queen Elizabeth 2 as it first docked in New York Harbor.
3. The theater critic for the local paper reviewed the recent performance of Death of a Salesman.
4. It's hard to read that reporter's notes because he never crosses his t's or dots his i's, and he writes a 7 with a line through it.
5. On the news was a photo essay about Vincent van Gogh and his painting Sunflowers.
6. Have you read the book The American Journalist by David Weaver and G. Cleveland Wilhoit?
7. My editor told me never to say the word can't when talking about a story.
8. As they say in Germany, it is verboten to enter the building without a press pass.
9. Woodward and Bernstein were reporters for the Washington Post when they broke the Watergate story.
10. Never use the @ in place of the word at in formal writing.

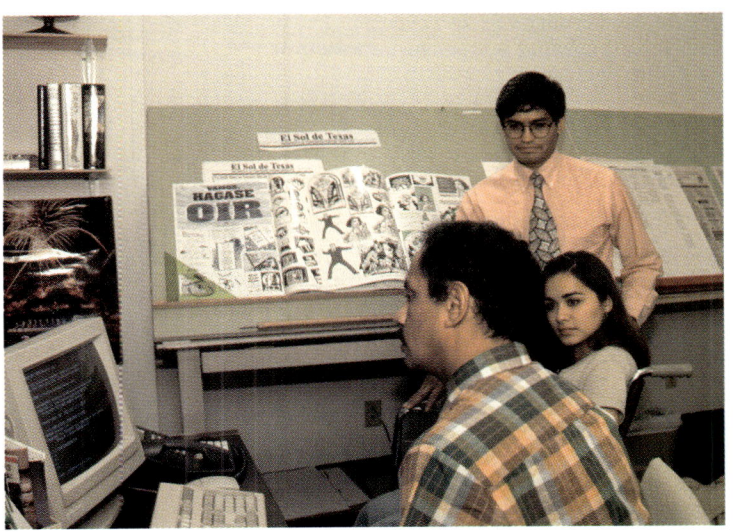

> ### ◀ Critical Viewing
> Why is it helpful to use quotation marks around story titles such as "The Birds" when conducting a search on the Internet? [Relate]

Answer Key

▶ Exercise 44

1. A favorite <u>bon mot</u> (French: witty saying)
2. The city's great newspapers sent photographers to take pictures of the <u>Queen Elizabeth 2</u>
3. recent performance of <u>Death of a Salesman</u>.
4. never crosses his <u>t</u>'s or dots his <u>i</u>'s, and he writes a <u>7</u> with a line through it.
5. Vincent van Gogh and his painting <u>Sunflowers</u>.
6. Have you read the book <u>The American Journalist</u>
7. the word <u>can't</u> when talking about a story.
8. As they say in Germany, it is <u>verboten</u> (German: forbidden)
9. Woodward and Bernstein were reporters for the <u>Washington Post</u>
10. Never use the @ in place of the word <u>at</u> in formal writing.

Critical Viewing

Relate Possible answer: Quotation marks around titles will specify that the words must be grouped together and thereby narrow the search.

Real-World Connection

Discuss with students the importance of punctuation in social and business communication on the Internet. Ask students to speculate about how much sentence structure matters when someone cannot hear the tone of your voice. Are quotation marks important in casual on-line conversations? (Punctuation clarifies meanings in every type of written communication.)

Answer Key

Exercise 45

1. Novelist John Steinbeck worked as a war correspondent for <u>Newsday</u> in the 1960's.
2. Ernie Pyle, a famous correspondent during World War II, wrote the book <u>Brave Men</u>.
3. <u>USA Today</u> has become one of the most widely read newspapers in the country.
4. When President Lincoln delivered the Gettysburg Address in 1864, newspapers of the day criticized the speech because it was uncharacteristically short. (correct)
5. I found that Chapter 4, "Public Affairs Reporting," was particularly helpful for this assignment.
6. In 1735, a court case involving John Peter Zenger's newspaper, the <u>New York Weekly Journal</u>, helped establish freedom of the press in this country.
7. My journalism professor handed out a pamphlet called <u>How to Become a Better Writer in Three Easy Steps</u>.
8. Walt Whitman was an occasional journalist who gained fame after he published his book of poems <u>Leaves of Grass</u>, which included his poem "Song of Myself."
9. The young journalist was constantly referring to his copy of <u>Webster's New World™ Dictionary</u>.
10. The reporter for <u>The Record</u> covered a story in Uzbekistan.

Exercise 46

1. "The little fellow felt that he never had a chance. . . ."
2. in the movie <u>A River Runs Through It</u>.
3. Never use the word <u>ain't</u> in formal writing.
4. "At home the newspaper costs only a quarter," she said. "How much does it cost here?"
5. are all <u>9</u>'s and <u>7</u>'s.

27.4

27.4

Exercise 45 **Using Underlining and Quotation Marks for Titles** Copy each sentence that needs underlining or quotation marks, making the needed change. If neither is required, write *correct*.

EXAMPLE: Amendment XVI of the Constitution of the United States permits the taxing of income.

ANSWER: correct

1. Novelist John Steinbeck worked as a war correspondent for Newsday in the 1960's.
2. Ernie Pyle, a famous correspondent during World War II, wrote the book Brave Men.
3. USA Today has become one of the most widely read newspapers in the country.
4. When President Lincoln delivered the Gettysburg Address in 1864, newspapers of the day criticized the speech because it was uncharacteristically short.
5. I found that Chapter 4, Public Affairs Reporting, was particularly helpful for this assignment.
6. In 1735, a court case involving John Peter Zenger's newspaper, the New York Weekly Journal, helped establish freedom of the press in this country.
7. My journalism professor handed out a pamphlet called How to Become a Better Writer in Three Easy Steps.
8. Walt Whitman was an occasional journalist who gained fame after he published his book of poems Leaves of Grass, which included his poem Song of Myself.
9. The young journalist was constantly referring to his copy of Webster's New World™ Dictionary.
10. The reporter for The Record covered a story in Uzbekistan.

Exercise 46 **Proofreading for Quotation Marks and Underlining** Revise each of the following sentences, adding quotation marks and underlining as needed.

EXAMPLE: Read the poem Barbara Frietchie today, Tim said.
ANSWER: "Read the poem 'Barbara Frietchie' today," Tim said.

1. Syndicated columnist Will Rogers summed up Hoover's defeat by Roosevelt by stating, The little fellow felt that he never had a chance. . . .
2. Brad Pitt's character is a reporter for a small Montana newspaper in the movie A River Runs Through It.
3. Never use the word ain't in formal writing.
4. At home, the newspaper costs only a quarter, she said. How much does it cost here?
5. The digits in the phone number are all 9's and 7's.

More Practice

On-line
Exercise Bank
• Section 27.4
Grammar Exercise
Workbook
• pp. 159–160

Learn More

To learn more about properly punctuating titles, refer to Chapter 26, Capitalization.

✓ **ONGOING ASSESSMENT: Monitor and Reinforce**

If students have difficulty with Exercise 43, 44, 45, 46, or 47, refer them to the following for additional practice.

In the Textbook	Print Resources	Technology
Section Review, Ex. 51–52, pp. 740–741	*Grammar Exercise Workbook*, pp. 159–160	*Language Lab* CD-ROM, Punctuation *On-Line Exercise Bank*, Section 27.4

▶ **Exercise 47** **More Proofreading for Quotation Marks and Underlining** Revise each of the following sentences, adding quotation marks and underlining as needed.

EXAMPLE: When Roberto leaves, he always says, Adios, amigo.

ANSWER: When Roberto leaves, he always says, "Adios, amigo."

1. I recommend that all journalists keep a copy of The World Almanac on their desks.
2. The new version of Our Town received a terrible review in last night's newspaper.
3. Chapter 8, Dateline—The World, explores the international impact of journalism.
4. No, the editor told him, we can't stop the presses.
5. The correspondent recorded the words of the general, who stated, The war will be over by Christmas.
6. We were served coq au vin at the Press Club dinner.
7. The movie All the President's Men tells the true story of two reporters working in Washington, D.C.
8. Ambrose Bierce was a cynical journalist who wrote a mock-dictionary called The Devil's Dictionary.
9. When writing for the magazine, always spell out the number four.
10. Janice heard an announcement on the news today that said Van Gogh's Starry Night sold for more than ten million dollars.
11. Reporters for the Los Angeles Times have won numerous awards for journalistic excellence.
12. Do not, I repeat, do not forget to edit the article before it goes to the printer!
13. What will you write about? my professor asked me.
14. National Public Radio played Beethoven's Fifth Symphony in its entirety.
15. The editor hit the ? key on the keyboard and inserted the necessary end mark into the paragraph.
16. Author and journalist Steven Crane wrote his short story The Open Boat after having been shipwrecked in 1896.
17. Crane's first novel, Maggie: A Girl of the Streets, was published in 1893.
18. She overuses the transition however in her magazine articles.
19. Did you know that one of my favorite columnists writes for Rolling Stone?
20. She said, I always read a chapter or two of a novel before I go to sleep.

🖥 **Internet Tip**

To find out more about careers in journalism, try searching the Internet with key words such as *journalism, photojournalism, newspapers,* or *the press.* You can also try a more specific search using the names of particular newspapers or magazines.

Answer Key

▶ **Exercise 47**

1. a copy of The World Almanac on their desks.
2. The new version of Our Town
3. Chapter Eight, "Dateline—The World,"
4. "No," the editor told him, "we can't stop the presses."
5. "The war will be over by Christmas."
6. We were served coq au vin (French—chicken cooked in wine)
7. The movie All the President's Men
8. mock-dictionary called The Devil's Dictionary.
9. spell out the number four.
10. Van Gogh's Starry Night sold for more than ten million dollars.
11. Reporters for the Los Angeles Times
12. Do not, I repeat, do not forget
13. "What will you write about?"
14. Beethoven's Fifth Symphony
15. The editor hit the ? key
16. short story "The Open Boat"
17. novel Maggie: A Girl of the Streets
18. the transition however
19. one of my favorite columnists writes for Rolling Stone?
20. She said, "I always read a chapter or two of a novel before I go to sleep."

Section Review

Each of these exercises correlates to the instruction on quotation marks and underlining, pages 724–736. These exercises may be used for more practice, for reteaching, or for review of the key concepts presented.

Answer Key

▶ **Exercise 48**

1. "When a dog . . . not news," editor John B. Bogart once said. "When a man . . . is news."
2. "both aggressive and honest"
3. (correct)
4. said, "The press . . . our society."
5. himself, "That's how . . . story."

▶ **Exercise 49**

1. asked himself, "Am I telling . . . putting a spin on it?"
2. "I know what he expects," he sighed. "If only . . . lofty goals."
3. who the "good guys" are.
4. "Get in there and get the story!"
5. "developing as we speak";

▶ **Exercise 50**

1. 'I think that . . . pass the bill'?"
2. 'I have . . . your ability.'"
3. 'The plaintiff . . . the journalist.'
4. 'We will not . . . from a source.'
5. 'I think . . . the Senate.'"

▶ **Exercise 51**

1. novel: Crime and Punishment
2. song: "And I Love Her"
3. movie: Remains of the Day
4. musical: Phantom of the Opera
5. chapter: "Using Nouns and Verbs"
6. painting: Guernica
7. radio series: All Things Considered
8. television series: Happy Days

Answers may vary; samples are given.

9. Aesop taught that people shouldn't always try to win, saying, "Be content . . . one cannot be first in everything."
10. Warning of the danger of small wastes of money, Ben Franklin said, "Beware . . . a small leak will sink a great ship."

GRAMMAR EXERCISES 48–55

▶ **Exercise 48** **Proofreading for Quotation Marks With Direct Quotations** Revise each sentence that requires punctuation, adding whatever punctuation is needed. A quoted fragment is underlined so that you can tell where it begins and ends. If no additional punctuation is needed, write *correct*.

1. When a dog bites a man, that is not news editor John B. Bogart once said. When a man bites a dog, that is news.
2. The editor told the new writers that he expected them to be both aggressive and honest in their reporting.
3. A spokesman told reporters that the military base was being shut down because it was no longer needed.
4. In class today, Professor Wilkens said The press plays a crucial watchdog role in our society.
5. As he walked back to his desk, the reporter thought to himself That's how I'll write the lead for this story.

▶ **Exercise 49** **Using Other Punctuation Marks With Quotation Marks** Copy each of the following sentences, adding quotation marks. Quoted fragments are underlined.

1. Before he submitted his article, the writer asked himself, Am I telling this story honestly, or am I putting a spin on it?
2. I know what he expects, he sighed. If only I can reach those lofty goals.
3. It's hard to write a neutral story when it's obvious who the good guys are.
4. Get in there and get the story! he shouted above the noise.
5. The story is developing as we speak; reporters are on their way to the scene right now.

▶ **Exercise 50** **Proofreading for Single Quotation Marks** Revise each of the following sentences, inserting single quotation marks (' ') as needed.

1. "Did you read about the president who said, I think that if we can eliminate the bickering, . . . then we will be able to pass the bill?"
2. "His editor constantly encouraged the young writer, telling him I have complete confidence in your ability."
3. "In that case, the court declared: The plaintiff must show actual malice on the part of the journalist. This decision changed the face of journalism."
4. "Make sure you read the first section of our code of ethics, which states: We will not accept any gifts or preferential treatment from a source. Memorize it before you start writing."
5. "In the interview, she told me, I think he is a good candidate for the Senate."

▶ **Exercise 51** **Using Underlining, Quotation Marks, and Ellipsis Marks** Underline or enclose in quotation marks the titles below. Use part of each quotation (items 9 and 10) in a sentence, with ellipsis marks to indicate missing words.

1. novel: Crime and Punishment
2. song: And I Love Her
3. movie: Remains of the Day
4. musical: Phantom of the Opera
5. chapter: Using Nouns and Verbs
6. painting: Guernica
7. radio series: All Things Considered
8. television series: Happy Days
9. "Be content with your lot; one cannot be first in everything." —Aesop
10. "Beware of small expenses; a small leak will sink a great ship." —Benjamin Franklin

---

✓ ONGOING ASSESSMENT: Assess Mastery

Use the following resources to assess student mastery of quotation marks and underlining.

In the Textbook	Technology
Chapter Review, p. 765, Ex. 82–83	*Language Lab* CD-ROM, Punctuation *On-Line Exercise Bank,* Section 27.4

Exercise 52 Proofreading for Quotation Marks and Underlinings

Revise each of the following sentences, adding quotation marks and underlining as needed. Quoted fragments are underlined. If no additional punctuation is required, write *correct*.

1. I always keep a copy of Bartlett's Familiar Quotations on my desk, and I looked up entries under Journalism.
2. Historian Geoffrey C. Ward once said Journalism is merely history's first draft.
3. I get up in the morning with an idea for a three-volume novel, said humorist Don Marquis, and by nightfall, it's a paragraph in my [newspaper] column.
4. An anonymous journalist once wrote, Doctors bury their mistakes. Lawyers hang them. But journalists put theirs on the front page.
5. Reporter Carl Bernstein wrote that journalism is the lowest form of popular culture.
6. "I think many journalists agree with Alexander Smith, who said, To be quoted is the only fame I care for."
7. That's the nice thing about this job, former President Reagan said. You get to quote yourself shamelessly.
8. A writer who uses quotations to show that he is learned and well read . . . will only gain the contempt of his reader, according to Henry Fowler.
9. British playwright Tom Stoppard stated, . . . I still believe that if you wish to change the world, journalism is a more short-term weapon.
10. The newspaper's lawyer said that the reporter was within his rights according to the Constitution.
11. When writing a formal article, you should never use the & in place of the word and.
12. Cape Canaveral was packed with reporters waiting for the launch of the space shuttle Atlantis.
13. The movie critic said that The Wizard of Oz was great for all ages.
14. How many times during his speech did he say, I am clearly the best man for the job?
15. As they say in France, it is time to put stylo à feuille.

Exercise 53 Find It in Your Reading

Find a short magazine or newspaper article that illustrates at least three of the different rules for quotations, ellipsis marks, and underlining. Remember that most words that would be underlined in handwritten material will appear in italics in a printed article. Copy the sentences and write out the rules that are being illustrated.

Exercise 54 Find It in Your Writing

Look in your portfolio for a selection that might be made more vivid or interesting by including a direct quotation. For example, if you wrote a piece about your student government, you might include a quotation from your student body president. Obtain a relevant quotation, and add it to your work, making sure to punctuate it correctly.

Exercise 55 Writing Application

Choose one of the categories listed in Exercise 51 (novel, song, movie, etc.), and write a paragraph reviewing an item in that category. For example you might review the movie *Titanic* or the novel *Things Fall Apart*. In your review, use at least two direct quotations. Make sure to follow all the rules for quotations and underlining. If you use only part of a quotation, remember to use ellipsis marks.

Exercise 52

1. <u>Bartlett's Familiar Quotations</u> . . . under "Journalism."
2. "Journalism . . . first draft."
3. "I get up . . . novel," said humorist Don Marquis, "and by nightfall . . . column."
4. "Doctors . . . front page."
5. journalism is the "lowest form of popular culture."
6. 'To be quoted is the only fame I care for.'"
7. "That's . . . this job," former . . . said. "You get . . . shamelessly."
8. to "show that he is learned and well read . . . " will only gain . . .
9. Tom Stoppard stated, ". . . I still believe . . . short-term weapon."
10. (correct)
11. . . . never use the <u>&</u> in place of the word <u>and</u>.
12. . . . space shuttle <u>Atlantis</u>.
13. . . . <u>The Wizard of Oz</u> was . . . .
14. say, "I am clearly the best man for the job"?
15. . . . to put <u>stylo à feuille</u>. (French: pen to paper)

Exercise 53

Find It in Your Reading
Ask students to share some of their examples with the class. Did any of them find instances in which the rules of quotations or underlining were used incorrectly? If so, encourage them to correct these errors.

Exercise 54

Find It in Your Writing
If students are having trouble obtaining a quotation from a person, encourage them to find one from a book or a magazine article on the topic. If possible, give them time to do research in your school library.
continued

Answer Key continued

Exercise 55

Writing Application
When they finish, have students exchange papers and mark any errors in the use of quotation marks or underlining. After students correct their work, compile the reviews into a packet to keep as reference material in your classroom.

⏱ TIME SAVERS!

Answers on Transparencies
Use the *Grammar Exercises Answers on Transparencies* for Chapter 27 to facilitate correction by students.

On-Line Exercise Bank
Have students complete the exercises on computer. The Auto Check feature will grade their work for you!

Ask students to write a simple sentence about a historical figure. *(George Washington was the first U.S. President.)* Then, have them write a second sentence stating another fact about that person. *(He could not tell a lie.)* Ask how the second sentence could be inserted into the first sentence. *(with dashes or parentheses)* Have students write their sentences using dashes. *(George Washington—he could never lie—was the first U.S. President.)*

Activate Prior Knowledge

Ask students to list in a single sentence three things they would like to own. As some offer these things to the class, write one or two on the board, being careful to use the numbers 1, 2, and 3. Example:

At the top of my list are 1 a new car, 2 leather driving gloves, and 3 a driver's license.

Explaining that this section includes parentheses, ask students where these marks might help clarify information in the sentence. (to set off numbers)

TEACH

Step-by-Step Teaching Guide

Dashes

1. Explain that a dash is a powerful punctuation tool used to indicate a change in thought, an interrupting idea, or a summarizing statement.

2. Have a student read each example in the chart and then identify the words that have been set off by dashes.

3. Offer another example, and ask students where to place a dash:

   To see his old home and his old school that was all he wished for. (dash after *school*)

Dashes, Parentheses, Brackets, and Hyphens

This section will present some of the less frequently used punctuation marks: dashes (—), parentheses (( )), brackets ([ ]), and hyphens (-). These punctuation marks should not be used indiscriminately. There are special rules for the use of each. Even though you may not be called upon to use them often, it is important to learn the rules that govern their use.

Dashes

The dash, a much stronger mark than a comma, signals a sudden break in the structure or thought of a sentence. A simple, dramatic punctuation mark, the dash should not be used haphazardly in place of the comma and other separators. Overuse of the dash reduces its dramatic effect and indicates a lazy writer, one who has not mastered the rules of punctuation.

There are several rules governing use of the dash, the first of which is the broadest.

▶ **KEY CONCEPT** Use dashes to indicate an abrupt change of thought, a dramatic interrupting idea, or a summary statement. ■

The following chart shows the three basic uses of the dash.

USES OF THE DASH	
To indicate an abrupt change of thought	The article doesn't provide enough information on Japan—by the way, did you find it in the school library?
To set off interrupting ideas dramatically	The pagoda was built—you may find this hard to believe—in one month. The pagoda was built—where did they get the money?—in one month.
To set off a summary statement	A good scholastic record and good political connections—if you have these, you may be able to get a job in a congressional office.

Words such as *all*, *these*, *those*, *this*, and *that* will often be found at or near the beginning of a summary sentence preceded by a dash.

Theme: Japan

In this section, you will learn about the many uses of dashes, parentheses, brackets, and hyphens. The examples and exercises in this section are about Japan.

Cross-Curricular Connection: Social Studies

Grammar and Style Tip

Avoid the frequent use of dashes simply to replace commas and periods. Even in informal writing, overuse of dashes will look haphazard and may even confuse your meaning.

⏱ TIME AND RESOURCE MANAGER

Resources
Print: *Grammar Exercise Workbook*, pp. 161–168; *Grammar Exercises Answers on Transparencies*, Chapter 27
Technology: *On-Line Exercise Bank*, Section 27.5

In-Depth Coverage	Accelerated Pace
• Work through all key concepts, pp. 742–753. • Assign and review Exercises 56–61. • Read and discuss *Grammar in Literature*, p. 744.	• Assign pp. 742–753 for independent student review. • Assign Section Review Exercises 62–67.

▶ **KEY CONCEPT** Use dashes to set off a nonessential appositive or modifier when it is long, when it is already punctuated, or when you want to be dramatic. ■

Although they are usually set off with commas, nonessential appositives and modifiers may also be set off with dashes.

APPOSITIVES: Two Japanese islands—Honshu and Hokkaido—were the group's destinations.

Yesterday, I met three old neighbors from Osaka—Kenji Oe, his brother Nobuo, and their friend Shizuo Akiyama—and learned about all the changes in the old neighborhood. Some students—for example, Mitsuye, Fran, and Kevin—always do well on tests.

MODIFIERS: Mount Fuji—which is called *Fujiyama* in Japanese—can be seen from many places in Tokyo. Matsushika Hokusai (1760–1849)—who was a master Japanese painter and wood engraver—produced numerous works featuring Mount Fuji.

Dashes may be used to set off one other special type of sentence interrupter—the parenthetical expression.

▶ **KEY CONCEPT** Use dashes to set off a parenthetical expression when it is long, already punctuated, or especially dramatic. ■

EXAMPLES: The searing heat—it was ninety all last week, and on Monday and Tuesday of this week it was over one hundred—has forced many of the citizens of Tokyo to stay indoors.
The sushi—have you ever seen such an elaborate presentation of food?—was an unusual taste experience.

▲ **Critical Viewing**
Mt. Fuji's last volcanic eruption was in 1708. What might happen to Tokyo if the volcano were to become active again? Answer in a sentence, using dashes to set off a dramatic parenthetical expression. **[Speculate]**

Step-by-Step Teaching Guide

More Uses of Dashes

1. Read the two key concepts aloud.

2. Then have students read each example aloud, beginning with the first set, and ask them to identify the nonessential appositives and modifiers in each.

3. Explain this to students: Parenthetical expressions that are long, punctuated, or dramatic can be set off with dashes for clarity or for effect, but commas often are also correct. In many instances, choosing dashes over commas is a stylistic preference.

4. Have students identify all example sentences on this page in which they think the dashes added clarity. (the ones with nonessential and parenthetical elements that are already punctuated)

Critical Viewing

Speculate Possible answer: If Fujiyama erupted after all these years—can you imagine such a thing happening?—Tokyo would probably be terribly damaged and many lives could be in danger.

743

Grammar in Literature

1. Have a student read the excerpt from *Hiroshima* aloud.

2. Have students isolate the nonessential appositive that has been set off.

3. Ask why the author might have chosen dashes, not commas, to set off this appositive. (to avoid confusion, since the appositive already contained commas)

More About the Writer

John Hersey worked as a foreign correspondent for *Time* and *Life* magazines during World War II. After the war, the Secretary of the Navy awarded Hersey a commendation for his bravery in moving wounded soldiers to safety during the battle for Guadalcanal. His nonfiction work *Hiroshima* chronicled the effects of the atomic bomb; it is considered by many to be his finest work.

Connections With Literature

A more extensive passage from *Hiroshima* by John Hersey may be found in *Prentice Hall Literature: Timeless Voices, Timeless Themes,* The American Experience. As students read it, encourage them to watch for ways Hershey packs his sentences with detailed information.

Answer Key

▶ **Exercise 56**

1. Japan—**I could study it for days!**—is
2. *Dai Nippon*—**Great Land of the Sun.**
3. founded—**according to legend**—in
4. islands—**Honshu, Kyushu, Shikoku, and Hokkaido**—and
5. Honshu—**thought of as the mainland**—is
6. Fujiyama—**what a sight!**—is
7. its majesty—**it is the cultural heart of Japan.**
8. disasters—**especially earthquakes and tsunamis**—have plagued
9. earthquake—**which originated north of the cities of Nagasaki and Minamata**—struck
10. populated—**more than 126 million people live . . . Texas.**

27.5

GRAMMAR IN LITERATURE

from **Hiroshima**
John Hersey

Notice in this excerpt that John Hersey uses dashes to set off nonessential appositives.

At nearly midnight, the night before the bomb was dropped, an announcer on the city's radio station said that about two hundred B-29s were approaching southern Honshu and advised the population of Hiroshima to evacuate to their designated "safe areas." Mrs. Hatsuyo Nakamura, the tailor's widow, who lived in the section called Nobori-cho and who had long had a habit of doing as she was told, got her three children—a ten-year-old boy, Toshio, an eight-year-old girl, Yaeko, and a five-year-old girl, Myeko—out of bed and dressed them and walked with them to the military area known as the East Parade Ground, on the northeast edge of the city.

▶ **Exercise 56** **Revising to Supply Dashes** Revise the following sentences, inserting dashes where appropriate.

EXAMPLE: Tokyo is Japan's most populous city more than eighteen million people inhabit it.

ANSWER: Tokyo is Japan's most populous city—more than eighteen million people inhabit it.

1. The history and culture of Japan I could study it for days! is unique and interesting.
2. The Japanese call their country *Dai Nippon* Great Land of the Sun.
3. Japan was founded according to legend in 660 B.C.
4. The country consists of four main islands Honshu, Kyushu, Shikoku, and Hokkaido and hundreds of smaller islands.
5. Of these, Honshu thought of as the mainland is the largest.
6. Fujiyama what a sight! is the tallest mountain in Japan.
7. Tens of thousands of people are drawn to the mountain every year to witness its majesty it is the cultural heart of Japan.
8. Natural disasters especially earthquakes and tsunamis have plagued Japan throughout its history.
9. In 1995, an earthquake which originated north of the cities of Nagasaki and Minamata struck the city of Kobe.
10. Japan is densely populated more than 126 million people live in an area smaller than the state of Texas.

744 • Punctuation

▶ **More Practice**

On-line
Exercise Bank
• Section 27.5
Grammar Exercise
Workbook
• pp. 161–162

☑ **ONGOING ASSESSMENT: Monitor and Reinforce**

If students miss more than two items in Exercise 56 or 57, refer them to the following for additional practice.

In the Textbook	Print Resources	Technology
Section Review, Ex. 62, p. 754	*Grammar Exercise Workbook,* pp. 161–162	*On-Line Exercise Bank,* Section 27.5

Exercise 57 **More Revising to Supply Dashes** Revise the following sentences, inserting dashes where appropriate.

1. Several cities in Japan Yokohama is one example have populations of well over two million people.
2. Kyoto an ancient, culturally significant city that dates back to the eighth century was the capital of Japan until the 1860's.
3. Today, Tokyo located on the island of Honshu is the country's capital.
4. Tokyo an enormous modern city rivals New York and London.
5. Ethnic Japanese make up the bulk of the country's population more than 99 percent but a small number of other cultures are represented as well.
6. Most Japanese practice the religions of Shinto or Buddhism less than one percent of the population is Christian.
7. Theater in Japan Kabuki, Noh, and Bunraku are the three main types is an important part of Japanese culture.
8. The Japanese are also avid sports fans more than fifteen million people attend baseball games each year.
9. Rice is an essential food in Japan most people eat at least two servings every day.
10. The Japanese are steeped in culture and tradition, yet they are leading the way into the twenty-first century they are on the cutting edge of technology.

◉ Technology Tip

To form a dash when using a word processor, place two hyphens between the words that will be set apart by the dash. Do not include any spacing. Many programs will draw the two hyphens together to form a dash.

You can also go to the Help feature in your word processor to learn how to make dashes by using the keyboard.

◀ Critical Viewing

A dash may be used to set off an abrupt change in thought. How might the sights and sounds in a busy city like Tokyo cause many abrupt changes in the thoughts of a person walking down this street? **[Connect]**

Answer Key

▶ **Exercise 57**

1. Japan—**Yokohama is one example**—have
2. Kyoto—**an ancient, culturally significant city that dates back to the eighth century**—was
3. Today, Tokyo—**located on the island of Honshu**—is
4. Tokyo—**an enormous modern city**—rivals
5. country's population—**more than 99 percent**—but
6. Buddhism—**less than one percent . . . Christian.**
7. Japan—**Kabuki, Noh, and Bunraku are the three main types**—is
8. sports fans—**more than fifteen million people attend . . . each year.**
9. food in Japan—**most people eat at least two servings every day.**
10. century—**they are on the cutting edge of technology**.

Critical Viewing

Connect Possible answer: Changes in visual stimuli introduce new ideas; dashes help to show relationships between interrupting ideas and a writer's train of thought.

Dashes, Parentheses, Brackets, and Hyphens • **745**

⏱ TIME SAVERS!

Answers on Transparencies Use the *Grammar Exercises Answers on Transparencies* for Chapter 27 to facilitate correction by students.

On-Line Exercise Bank Have students complete the exercises on computer. The Auto Check feature will grade their work for you!

Parentheses

Parentheses are used to enclose material in a sentence or a paragraph. Although commas are generally used for this purpose, parentheses are preferred in certain cases. Parentheses are the strongest separators a writer can use. Because of their strength, they should be used infrequently.

Basic Uses of Parentheses

Parentheses are most often used to set off asides or explanatory information. Even here, caution must be used.

▶ **KEY CONCEPT** Use parentheses to set off asides and explanations only when the material consists of one or more sentences, or when the material is not essential. ■

EXAMPLES: There are many three- and five-story wooden pagodas in the Kansai area of Japan. (In the distant past, there were even seven- and nine-story pagodas.)

Despite many powerful earthquakes (including the disastrous earthquake of 1995), there are almost no records reporting the collapse of these ancient high-rises.

▶ **KEY CONCEPT** Use parentheses to set off numerical explanations such as dates of a person's birth and death and around numbers and letters marking a series. ■

EXAMPLES: Akira Kurosawa (1910–1998) was an internationally celebrated Japanese filmmaker.
The committee can be reached at (607) 555-3001.
My teacher ranks our great presidents in this way: (1) Abraham Lincoln, (2) George Washington, (3) Theodore Roosevelt, (4) Thomas Jefferson, and (5) Franklin D. Roosevelt.
Her report on energy will deal with the use of (a) wood, (b) coal, (c) oil, and (d) solar power.

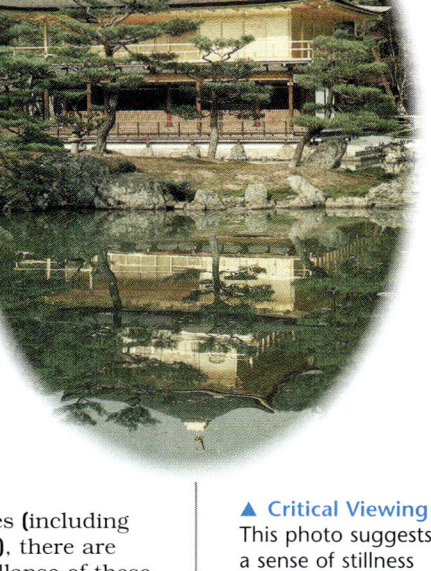

▲ Critical Viewing
This photo suggests a sense of stillness and reflection. Write an example of how parentheses can be used to include an aside or a reflection within a sentence. [Relate]

Other Punctuation Marks Used With Parentheses

Sometimes parentheses and other punctuation marks are used together. Several rules govern these uses.

KEY CONCEPT When a phrase or declarative sentence interrupts another sentence, do not use an initial capital or end mark inside the parentheses. ■

EXAMPLE: Sarah (she has always loved animals) took in the stray kitten and fed it.

KEY CONCEPT When a question or exclamation interrupts another sentence, use both an initial capital and an end mark inside the parentheses. ■

EXAMPLES: The car (Do you think we could be out of gas?) won't start.
On Sunday (What a beautiful day it was!) we climbed to the top of Bald Mountain and had a picnic.

When a sentence in parentheses falls between two other sentences, use the following rule:

KEY CONCEPT With any sentence that falls between two complete sentences, use both an initial capital and an end mark inside the parentheses. ■

EXAMPLE: I started working on Saturday morning for a florist. (It was difficult to get up so early.) My duties include arranging flowers and delivering them all over town.

KEY CONCEPT In a sentence with a set-off phrase, place any punctuation belonging to the main sentence after the parentheses. ■

EXAMPLES: When I arrived (about two o'clock), he was waiting.

The artist had finally accepted the invitation to exhibit his works (after having been invited twice before); therefore, he spent the summer preparing the material for display.

🌸 Grammar and Style Tip

Parentheses should be used sparingly because they interrupt the flow of your writing. In most instances, the information should be worked into the body of your writing.

Other Punctuation Marks Used With Parentheses

1. Read the first key concept and example. Point out that the declarative statement does not begin with a capital. Ask students whether it is a complete sentence (it is) and how they might remember not to capitalize it. (It has no end mark.)

2. Read the second key concept aloud and have students read the examples. Ask what type of item is in parentheses in the first example (a question) and in the second (an exclamatory sentence). Ask how they might remember to capitalize these. (They have their own end marks.)

3. Summarize for students: If a sentence in parentheses requires an end mark other than a period, then the first letter of the first word should be capitalized.

4. Have students read the third key concept and the example. Ask why parentheses are appropriate here. (The second sentence interrupts the logical progression between the first and third sentences with an additional idea.)

5. Read the final key concept aloud, and then examine each example. In the first, point out that the phrase in parentheses is part of an introductory adverb clause, so the comma will follow the entire clause. In the second example, the semicolon follows the first independent clause, which includes the final parenthesis.

▶ **Exercise 58**

1. The Japanese flag (**called** *Hinomaru*) depicts the rising sun.
2. General Douglas MacArthur **(1880–1964)** supervised the occupation of Japan at the end of World War II.
3. The three main types of traditional Japanese theater are **(a)** Kabuki, **(b)** Noh, and **(c)** Bunraku.
4. The worst natural disaster to strike modern Japan was the Great Kanto Earthquake **(more than 100,000 people were killed)** in 1923.
5. I believe the phone number for the Japanese consulate is **(800)** 555-5309.
6. The *Kojiki* **(which means Record of Ancient Matters)** is the oldest collection of writings in Japan.
7. Learning to read and write Japanese is difficult **(There are more than three thousand characters to learn!)**, but learning to speak Japanese is even harder.
8. The emperor of Japan **(Akihito is the emperor I read about)** is largely a symbolic position today.
9. Japan's enormous population **(126 million people)** lives in an area that is significantly smaller than the state of Texas.
10. Tokyo **(Will it ever stop growing?)** is one of the most densely populated cities in the world.

Critical Viewing

Infer Possible answer: Material in parentheses can explain what happened before or what will happen later.

748

27.5

▶ **Exercise 58** **Revising to Supply Parentheses** Revise the following items, adding parentheses, any other punctuation marks, and capitals where necessary. Underline the words that are in italics.

EXAMPLE: Tickets for the play are hard to get it is a play I have wanted to see for a long time! we finally were able to get some for next week.

ANSWER: Tickets for the play are hard to get. (It is a play I have wanted to see for a long time!) We finally were able to get some for next week.

1. The Japanese flag called *Hinomaru* depicts the rising sun.
2. General Douglas MacArthur 1880–1964 supervised the occupation of Japan at the end of World War II.
3. The three main types of traditional Japanese theater are a Kabuki, b Noh, and c Bunraku.
4. The worst natural disaster to strike modern Japan was the Great Kanto Earthquake more than 100,000 people were killed in 1923.
5. I believe the phone number for the Japanese consulate is 800 555-5309.
6. The *Kojiki* which means Record of Ancient Matters is the oldest collection of writings in Japan.
7. Learning to read and write Japanese is difficult there are more than three thousand characters to learn!, but learning to speak Japanese is even more difficult.
8. The emperor of Japan Akihito is the emperor I read about is largely a symbolic position today.
9. Japan's enormous population 126 million people lives in an area that is significantly smaller than the state of Texas.
10. Tokyo will it ever stop growing? is one of the most densely populated cities in the world.

▲ Critical Viewing The traditional clothing shown here suggests a different time. How can text within parentheses evoke a different time from the rest of the sentence? [Infer

---

✓ **ONGOING ASSESSMENT: Monitor and Reinforce**

If students miss more than two items in Exercise 58, refer them to the following for additional practice.

In the Textbook	Print Resources	Technology
Section Review, Ex. 63, p. 754	*Grammar Exercise Workbook,* pp. 163–164	*On-Line Exercise Bank,* Section 27.5

Brackets

Brackets have one major use: to enclose a word or words inserted by a writer into a quotation from someone else.

▶ **KEY CONCEPT** Use brackets to enclose a word or words you insert in a quotation when you are quoting someone else. ■

EXAMPLE: Edmund Morris describes an attempt by Theodore Roosevelt to feed his hungry regiment during the Spanish-American War. "On the morning of June 26 [1898], Roosevelt got wind of a stockpile of beans on the beach [in Cuba] and marched a squad of men hastily down to investigate."

Brackets are sometimes also used with the Latin expression *sic* (meaning "thus") in a quotation to show that the original writer misspelled or misused a word or phrase. The expression *sic* calls attention to the original form used by the author.

EXAMPLE: As a recommendation, he wrote, "He don't [sic] lie."

▶ **Exercise 59** **Using Brackets** Copy the following items, adding brackets where you find them most appropriate.

EXAMPLE: "The results of this vote 98–2 indicate overwhelming support for our proposal," he stated.

ANSWER: "The results of this vote [98–2] indicate overwhelming support for our proposal," he stated.

1. The misprinted guide book read, "Tokeo is a fast-paced, ultra-modern city with much to see and do."
2. At a monument in Hiroshima, Japan, the words, "Rest in peace. The mistake nuclear war shall not be made again," are inscribed on a small plaque.
3. "We the Japanese people have resolved to endure the unendurable and suffer what is insufferable." —Emperor Hirohito
4. "People with high ideals don't necessarily make good politicians. If it noble politics is so important, we should leave the job to the scientists and the clergy." —Michio Watanabe
5. "You will find the same label Made in Japan on the back of many computers, stereos, televisions, and cameras."

Grammar and Style Tip

Do not misuse brackets in place of parentheses. Brackets should be used only to insert new words into material that has been directly quoted. They inform the reader that you have added words that will clarify information taken from other sources.

More Practice

On-line
Exercise Bank
• Section 27.5
Grammar Exercise Workbook
• pp. 165–166

Brackets

1. Draw brackets on the board [ ] to show how they differ from parentheses.
2. Explain that the main use of brackets is to enclose a word or words that a writer inserts in a quotation by someone else.
3. Then have students read the Key Concept and example aloud. Ask why *1898* is in brackets. (It was not included in the original quotation.)
4. Explain to students that the Latin expression *sic* means "thus" and is used in brackets in a quotation to indicate the original writer's misspelling or misuse of a word or phrase.
5. Ask a student to read the last example aloud. Ask what *[sic]* tells us. (The word *don't* is incorrect; it should read *doesn't*.)

Answer Key

▶ **Exercise 59**

1. The misprinted guide book read, "Tokeo **[sic]** is a fast-paced, ultra-modern city with much to see and do."
2. At a monument in Hiroshima, Japan, the words, "Rest in peace. The mistake **[nuclear war]** shall not be made again," are inscribed on a small plaque.
3. "We **[the Japanese people]** have resolved to endure the unendurable and suffer what is insufferable."—Emperor Hirohito
4. "People with high ideals don't necessarily make good politicians. If it **[noble politics]** is so important, we should leave the job to the scientists and the clergy."—Michio Watanabe
5. "You will find the same label **[Made in Japan]** on the back of many computers, stereos, televisions, and cameras."

✓ ONGOING ASSESSMENT: Monitor and Reinforce

If students miss more than one item in Exercise 59, refer them to the following for additional practice.

In the Textbook	Print Resources	Technology
Section Review, Ex. 64, pp. 754–755	*Grammar Exercise Workbook,* pp. 165–166	*On-Line Exercise Bank,* Section 27.5

Hyphens

Hyphens are used to join certain numbers and parts of words, to join some compound words, and to divide words at the ends of lines. Although it resembles the dash, the hyphen is distinctly shorter. In handwritten material, be sure to make your hyphens half as long as your dashes. In typewritten material, use one hyphen mark for a hyphen (-) and two hyphen marks for a dash (--).

Hyphens are used with numbers, word parts, and compound words.

Numbers Hyphens help to make the meaning of compound numbers clear.

> **KEY CONCEPT** Use a hyphen when writing out the numbers *twenty-one* through *ninety-nine*. ■

EXAMPLES: thirty-three inches   forty-seven acres

> **KEY CONCEPT** Use a hyphen with fractions used as adjectives. ■

EXAMPLES: one-half inch   three-fifths majority

If a fraction is used as a noun instead of an adjective, the hyphen is not used.

EXAMPLE: *Three quarters* of the report on Japan is completed.

Word Parts Certain word parts are also joined by hyphens.

Use a hyphen after a prefix that is followed by a proper noun or adjective.

EXAMPLES: pro-Japanese   all-American   mid-October

Certain prefixes are often found before proper nouns and proper adjectives. They include the following: *ante-, anti-, mid-, post-, pre-, pro-,* and *un-.*

Three other prefixes and one suffix are always used with a hyphen.

> **KEY CONCEPT** Use a hyphen in words with the prefixes *all-, ex-,* and *self-* and words with the suffix *-elect.* ■

EXAMPLES: all-powerful   ex-football player
          self-adjusting brakes   president-elect

Compound Words Hyphens are also used to join some compound words.

▶ **KEY CONCEPT** Use a hyphen to connect two or more words that are used as one word unless the dictionary gives a contrary spelling. ■

Some compound nouns are written as one word, others are written as separate words, and still others are joined by a hyphen. If you are uncertain as to how a compound word should be spelled, consult a dictionary.

EXAMPLES: brother-in-law
two-year-olds
secretary-treasurer
jack-of-all-trades

Compound modifiers, as well as compound nouns, sometimes require hyphens.

▶ **KEY CONCEPT** Use a hyphen to connect a compound modifier that comes *before* a noun unless it includes a word ending in -*ly* or is a compound proper adjective or compound proper noun acting as an adjective. ■

EXAMPLES
WITH HYPHENS:
a strong-willed businessman
an up-to-date design
well-attended Japanese festival

EXAMPLES
WITHOUT HYPHENS:
a highly unlikely suspect
the North American continent

Although compound adjectives in front of a noun are usually hyphenated, a hyphen is generally not needed when compound adjectives follow a noun.

EXAMPLE: The Japanese festival is *well attended*.

If your dictionary spells a word with hyphens, however, that word always should be hyphenated.

EXAMPLE: That design is *up-to-date*.

▲ **Critical Viewing**
Hyphens are used to join certain numbers and words. What common elements—such as history, culture, or interests—join many of the people pictured here? **[Connect]**

Hyphens With Compound Words

1. Explain to students that hyphens join certain compound words and that dictionaries are always useful in checking such spellings.

2. Read the first key concept aloud and then have students note the number of words in each example. Point out that these hyphenated words act as nouns even though they sometimes contain other words such as prepositions.

3. Explain that these nouns can be made plural or singular. Ask how the first example is made plural (brothers-in-law) and then note that two-year-old is made plural by adding an -*s* at the end. Remind students to check dictionaries when writing the plurals of these words.

4. Read aloud the second key concept, as well as the two sets of examples, and point out that these hyphenated words are adjectives. Ask why each of the examples contains hyphens. (They are used as single-word modifiers of nouns.)

5. Explain to students that compound adjectives are not hyphenated when they follow the nouns they describe. Use the examples at the bottom of the page to demonstrate.

Critical Viewing

Connect Possible answer: People appear to be participating in a celebration, possibly in recognition of common religious beliefs or in commemoration of a historical event that is important to their culture.

Step-by-Step Teaching Guide

Using Hyphens for Clarity

1. Explain to students that a hyphen is sometimes used in a word when a certain combination of letters might confuse the reader.

2. Use the examples under the first key concept to demonstrate. Write each example without the hyphen on the board. Point out that the meanings of the words would be unclear without the hyphens.

3. Read aloud the second key concept, and then have a student read both examples aloud. Have the class explain the difference in meaning between the two. (In the first, the car is clearly a new one; in the second, it is the person who is described as new.)

Answer Key

▶ **Exercise 60**

1. high-scoring player
2. pre-Cambrian
3. ex-governor
4. little-known fact
5. correct
6. correct
7. pro-American
8. correct
9. mother-in-law
10. post-war

Step-by-Step Teaching Guide

Using Hyphens at the Ends of Lines

1. Explain to students that, if it is necessary to divide a word at the end of a line, they should apply the five rules on these pages.

2. Read aloud the first key concept. Remind students that one-syllable words are never divided. Tell students that, when dividing a word with more than one syllable, the hyphen is placed at the end of a line.

continued

For Clarity Another use of hyphens is to prevent the misreading of a word or group of words.

▶ **KEY CONCEPT** Use a hyphen within a word when a combination of letters might otherwise be confusing. ■

EXAMPLES: a bell-like sound   a semi-invalid
           a re-served ball   an expensive co-op

▶ **KEY CONCEPT** Use a hyphen between words when necessary for clarity. ■

EXAMPLES: The *new-car owner* worried about potholes.
           The *new car-owner* was proud of her acquisition.

▶ **Exercise 60** **Using Hyphens to Combine Words** Copy each item that needs hyphenation, adding hyphens where necessary. If an item does not require a hyphen, write *correct*.

EXAMPLE: Japanese speaking guest
ANSWER: Japanese-speaking guest

1. high scoring player
2. pre Cambrian
3. ex governor
4. little known fact
5. South American continent
6. one tenth of a mile
7. pro American
8. unusually warm summer
9. mother in law
10. post war

Using Hyphens at the Ends of Lines

Although you should try not to divide a word at the end of a line, sometimes it is necessary. Certain rules can help you divide words correctly when you must divide them.

The most important rule involves dividing words between syllables.

▶ **KEY CONCEPT** If a word must be divided, always divide it between syllables. ■

Never divide one-syllable words. When you divide a word of more than one syllable, place the hyphen at the end of the first line. Also, take care never to use a hyphen at the end of the last line on a page. If you are unsure of how to divide a word into syllables, consult a dictionary.

EXAMPLE: Did you finish the difficult American history assignment that was due today?

⚙ **Grammar and Style Tip**

Although they look similar, do not confuse hyphens with dashes. Hyphens are used to join words together, and dashes are used to separate different thoughts.

💻 **Internet Tip**

If you cannot reach a Web site that contains a hyphen in its address, check to make sure that you have not added unnecessary spacing. Even one space within a hyphenated word will make the address incorrect.

✓ **ONGOING ASSESSMENT: Monitor and Reinforce**

If students miss more than two items in Exercise 60 or 61, refer them to the following for additional practice.

In the Textbook	Print Resources	Technology
Section Review, Ex. 65–67, p. 755	*Grammar Exercise Workbook,* pp. 167–168	*On-Line Exercise Bank,* Section 27.5

Step-by Step Teaching Guide
continued

KEY CONCEPT Prefixes and suffixes provide natural places for division. If a word contains word parts, it can almost always be divided between the prefix and the root or the root and the suffix. ■

PREFIX:	ex-tract	in-dent
SUFFIX:	care-less	play-ful

KEY CONCEPT Do not divide a word so that a single letter or the letters -ed stand alone. ■

INCORRECT:	hast-y	a-round	i-dentity	chas-ed
CORRECT:	hasty	around	iden-tity	chased

KEY CONCEPT Avoid dividing proper nouns and proper adjectives. ■

INCORRECT:	Jeff-rey	Euro-pean
CORRECT:	Jeffrey	European

KEY CONCEPT Divide a hyphenated word only after the hyphen. ■

INCORRECT:	I would like to introduce you to our new ed-itor-in-chief.
CORRECT:	I would like to introduce you to our new editor-in-chief.

Exercise 61 **Using Hyphens to Divide Words at the Ends of Lines** If a word has been divided as it should be if it appeared at the end of a line, write *correct.* If it has been divided incorrectly, write the word as it should appear.

EXAMPLE:	dre-am
ANSWER:	dream

1. Japan-ese
2. dolph-in
3. employ-ed
4. in-tellect
5. yel-low
6. mou-se
7. Geor-gia
8. ex-cruciating
9. gre-en
10. com-puter

Learn More

Refer to Chapter 26 on capitalization to learn more about using the hyphen with proper nouns.

More Practice
On-line
Exercise Bank
• Section 27.5
Grammar Exercise
Workbook
• pp. 167–168

3. Have students read aloud the second and third key concepts and then give them additional words for practice. Place these on the board and ask students to divide each word, if possible:

   ready (can't be divided)

   alternate (alter-nate or al-ternate)

   supposed (sup-posed)

   receipt (re-ceipt)

   fighter (fight-er)

   gracious (gra-cious)

4. Read the fourth key concept and explain to students that proper nouns and proper adjectives are never divided.

5. Have students read the examples and offer additional proper nouns and adjectives. (*British, Catherine, Himalayan, Illinois, San Francisco*)

6. Read the last key concept and use the examples to demonstrate. Ask students for another correct way to hyphenate this word (after *in-*).

Answer Key

Exercise 61

1. Japanese [no division]
2. dol-phin
3. em-ployed
4. correct
5. correct
6. mouse
7. correct
8. correct
9. green
10. correct

STANDARDIZED TEST PREPARATION WORKSHOP

Grammar and Usage Many standardized tests require students to revise errors in compositions. Use the following example:

The speaker at the banquet was not well known to the audience.

What is the error in the above sentence?

A Spelling error   **C** Grammar error

B Punctuation error   **D** No error

The correct answer is **D**, no error. No hyphen is required when a compound adjective follows the noun it describes. Had the sentence been written *The well-known speaker,* a hyphen would have been correct because the compound adjective is followed by the noun it modifies.

Section Review

Each of these exercises correlates to the instruction on dashes, parentheses, brackets, and hyphens, pages 742–753. These exercises may be used for more practice, for reteaching, or for review of the key concepts presented.

Answer Key

▶ **Exercise 62**

1. Tokyo—**do you know much about it?**—is the largest city
2. city of Tokyo—**how can that be?**—because
3. changed in the 1800's—**it used to be called Edo.**
4. capital of Japan—**Kyoto had been the capital**—in 1868.
5. The Imperial Palace—**where the emperor of Japan lives**—is
6. National Diet Building—**Japan's legislature.**
7. The Kanda Shrine—**one of the oldest and most highly attended in Tokyo**—is known
8. countries—**the United States, France, and Great Britain are just a few**—Tokyo is
9. The city's economy—**it supports more than eight million workers**—gains
10. corporations—**all these things make Tokyo a vital city.**

▶ **Exercise 63**

1. Edo (**which means "Gate of the Inlet"**) was
2. shogun (**he was Minamoto Yoritomo**).
3. centuries (**700 years**) of shogun rule.
4. General Ota Dokan (**he was also a shogun**) built a fortress
5. The Tokugawa clan ruled over Edo for 250 years (**1603–1854**).
6. much of the city (**Edo Castle was destroyed**).
7. population (**more than one million people**).
8. fire (**the tragic event occurred in 1872**), which
9. Meiji Restoration (**1868–1913**),
10. Tokyo (**which also became the nation's capital**) has been

▶ **Exercise 64**

1. war with Japan [**World War II**]."
2. speak the language [**Japanese**], I
3. wars with "the Spaniards and the Portugals [**sic**]."

continued

754

GRAMMAR EXERCISES 62–70

▶ **Exercise 62**   Revising to Supply

Dashes Revise the following sentences, adding dashes where appropriate.

1. Tokyo do you know much about it? is the largest city in Japan.
2. In actuality, there is no such place as the city of Tokyo how can that be? because the government has designated it a special administrative unit and not a city.
3. The city's name was changed in the 1800's it used to be called Edo.
4. It became the capital of Japan Kyoto had been the capital in 1868.
5. The Imperial Palace where the emperor of Japan lives is located in the center of the city.
6. Located nearby are many government buildings, including the National Diet Building Japan's legislature.
7. The Kanda Shrine one of the oldest and most highly attended in Tokyo is known for festivals that celebrate the traditions of the city.
8. An important business center for many countries the United States, France, and Great Britain are just a few Tokyo is at the heart of international trade.
9. The city's economy it supports more than eight million workers gains its strength from more than 800,000 businesses.
10. Government buildings, religious sanctuaries, and large corporations all these things make Tokyo a vital city.

▶ **Exercise 63**   Revising to Supply

Parentheses Revise the following sentences, adding parentheses where appropriate.

1. Edo which means "Gate of the Inlet" was the original name of Tokyo.

754 • Punctuation

2. The history of Tokyo dates back to the twelfth century and the rise of the first shogun he was Minamoto Yoritomo.
3. Minamoto Yoritomo won a civil war, which gave rise to centuries 700 years of shogun rule.
4. In 1457, General Ota Dokan he was also a shogun built a fortress known as Edo Castle.
5. The Tokugawa clan ruled over Edo for 250 years 1603–1854.
6. In 1657, a major fire ravaged much of the city Edo Castle was destroyed.
7. By the middle of the eighteenth century, Edo was a great city with a large poulation more than one million people.
8. The city was plagued by yet another fire the tragic event occurred in 1872, which devastated the portion of the city known as Ginza.
9. During the period called the Meiji Restoration 1868–1913, Edo was renamed Tokyo, and it became the nation's capital.
10. Since then, Tokyo which also became the nation's capital has been at the forefront of modernization in Japan.

▶ **Exercise 64**   Revising to Supply

Brackets Revise the following sentences, adding brackets where appropriate.

1. Their history teacher told them, "For tonight's homework, read the section about America's war with Japan World War II."
2. "Because so few of you speak the language Japanese, I will act as a translator," the tour guide said.
3. Will Adams, an Englishman who came to Japan in 1600, told the great shogun Ieyasu of England's wars with "the Spaniards and the Portugals."

✓ ONGOING ASSESSMENT: Assess Mastery

Use the following resources to assess student mastery of dashes, parentheses, brackets, and hyphens.

In the Textbook	Technology
Chapter Review, p. 766, Ex. 84	*On-Line Exercise Bank*, Section 27.5

4. At the news conference, the President said, "When he the Japanese Foreign Trade Minister arrives later this week, I hope to discuss the trade imbalance between our two countries."

5. Describing the arrival of Matthew Perry's squadron in Japan, author Noel Busch wrote, "On July 8, his four ships, bristling with bigger guns than any Japanese had seen before, swung . . . into Edo Bay." (using brackets, insert the date 1853)

Exercise 65   Using Hyphens to Combine Words
Copy each of the following items, adding hyphens where necessary. If an item does not require a hyphen, write *correct*.

1. twenty seven
2. self made millionaire
3. happily married couple
4. pre Revolutionary War
5. post modern art
6. multi colored flag
7. two family house
8. one fourth cup
9. North Carolina mountains
10. much needed assistance
11. three hundred forty three
12. one half of the class
13. self cleaning oven
14. South China Sea
15. well done assignment

Exercise 66   Using Hyphens to Divide Words at the Ends of Lines
Assume that the following words fall at the end of a line. If they are properly divided with a hyphen, write *correct*. If the hyphen has been used incorrectly, write the word as it should appear at the end of a line.

1. excit-ed
2. help-ful
3. ha-mmer
4. Ger-man
5. win-ner

6. lo-ose
7. nine-teen
8. Mich-ael
9. si-mple
10. blu-ish

Exercise 67   Writing Sentences With Parentheses, Dashes, Brackets, and Hyphens
Write sentences according to the following instructions.

1. Use parentheses in a sentence about your elementary school.
2. Use dashes in a sentence about two movies you'd like to see.
3. In a sentence describing a person, use a hyphen in a compound adjective preceding a noun.
4. Quote a friend or a family member, adding some clarifying information in brackets.

Exercise 68   Find It in Your Reading
Look through the excerpt from *Hiroshima* in your literature book, and find three examples of the use of dashes, parentheses, brackets, or hyphens. Write down each one, and explain which rule it illustrates.

Exercise 69   Find It in Your Writing
Look through your portfolio for examples of the use of dashes, parentheses, brackets, or hyphens. Determine whether or not these punctuation marks are necessary and, if so, whether they are used correctly. Make all necessary corrections.

Exercise 70   Writing Application
Reread the excerpt from *Hiroshima* on page 744, and write a one-paragraph summary of it. In your paragraph, correctly use dashes, parentheses, brackets, or hyphens at least three times.

Section Review • **755**

Exercise 69
Find It in Your Writing
If students are having trouble deciding whether a particular punctuation mark is necessary or correct, have them consult a classmate.

Exercise 70
Writing Application
You may want to review the concept of a summary before students begin to write. Remind them that a summary should include only the details that readers would need in order to understand the key features of the excerpt. It should include only factual details, not statements of opinion.

Exercise 64
4. "When he [the Japanese Foreign Trade Minister] arrives later this week
5. "On July 8, [1853], his four ships, bristling with bigger guns

Exercise 65
1. twenty-seven
2. self-made millionaire
3. correct
4. pre-Revolutionary War
5. post-modern art
6. multi-colored flag
7. two-family
8. one-fourth cup
9. correct
10. much-needed assistance
11. three hundred forty-three
12. correct
13. self-cleaning oven
14. correct
15. well-done assignment

Exercise 66
1. ex-cited
2. correct
3. ham-mer
4. German
5. correct
6. loose
7. correct
8. Michael
9. sim-ple
10. correct

Exercise 67
Answers will vary. Possible answers:

1. My elementary school (it was named for Alexander Graham Bell) had about 800 students.
2. I'd like to rent some old Bogart movies—*Casablanca* and *The Maltese Falcon*, for example—and spend the evening at home.
3. Adelle is a bright, well-rounded person.
4. Mark asked, "Shouldn't one [he often said *one* when he meant *you*] cook with a lower flame?"

Exercise 68
Find It in Your Reading
For more practice, have students repeat the exercise in another selection in their literature book. Have them share some of their findings in small groups when they finish.

continued

Interest GRABBER Ask several students to volunteer small items for a demonstration. Collect three or four pens, rulers, or backpacks. Then, hold up each item and ask students to complete this phrase to indicate to whom each item belongs: *This is ___.* (Examples: *Kims ruler, Erics and Jons pens*). Then, ask students to add correct punctuation:

> *Kim's ruler*
>
> *Eric's and Jon's pens*

Activate Prior Knowledge

Ask students for nouns (people, places, things, and ideas) that they associate with friends and relatives. Place some of their suggestions on the board. Examples:

pecan pie	*my Aunt Dolly*
surfboard	*my brother Angel*
love of music	*Mom and Dad*

Then, ask students to create phrases that show ownership: *Aunt Dolly's pecan pie, my brother Angel's surfboard, Mom and Dad's love of music.*

TEACH

Step-by-Step Teaching Guide

Forming Possessives of Singular and Plural Nouns

1. Explain to students that apostrophes are used with nouns (but not with personal pronouns) to show ownership.

2. For the first key concept, point out that most singular nouns require an 's even if they already end in -s. Use the examples of Moses and Hercules to illustrate the exception.

3. Read aloud the second key concept, and then have a student explain how each example is changed to show ownership.

4. Then, explain that plural nouns not ending in -s or -es add an apostrophe and an -s to show possession.

Section 27.6 # Apostrophes

Pay close attention to the meaning of each of the following rules for using apostrophes. Then, study the examples illustrating each rule carefully.

Forming Possessives of Nouns

An apostrophe is used to show possession or ownership. The location of the apostrophe depends upon the characteristics of the noun.

Singular Nouns The first rule involves the use of the apostrophe with singular nouns.

▶ **KEY CONCEPT** Add an apostrophe and -s to show the possessive case of most singular nouns. ■

EXAMPLES:		
	the book of the girl	the girl's book
	the leaf of the shrub	the shrub's leaf
	the crib of the baby	the baby's crib
	the check of the waitress	the waitress's check

Notice that a singular noun ending in -s usually uses an apostrophe and an -s to form the possessive. The only exceptions are classical and biblical names, which add only an apostrophe to form the possessive.

EXAMPLES:	
	Moses' brother
	Hercules' strength

Plural Nouns Two rules are necessary to form the possessive case of plural nouns. First, there is a rule for forming the possessive case of plural nouns ending in -s or -es. Second, there is a rule for plurals that do not end in an -s or -es.

▶ **KEY CONCEPT** Add an apostrophe to show the possessive case of plural nouns ending in -s or -es. ■

EXAMPLES:		
	the shirts of the boys	the boys' shirts
	the figures in the charts	the charts' figures
	the groups in the classes	the classes' groups

▶ **KEY CONCEPT** Add an apostrophe and an -s to show the possessive case of plural nouns that do not end in -s or -es. ■

EXAMPLES:		
	the suits of the men	the men's suits
	the toys of the children	the children's toys

756 • Punctuation

Theme: Japan

In this section, you will learn about the many uses of apostrophes. The exercises in this section contain more information about Japan.

Cross-Curricular Connection: Social Studies

⏱ TIME AND RESOURCE MANAGER

Resources
Print: *Grammar Exercise Workbook,* pp. 169–172; *Grammar Exercises Answers on Transparencies,* Chapter 27
Technology: *On-Line Exercise Bank,* Section 27.6

In-Depth Coverage	Accelerated Pace
• Work through all key concepts, pp. 756–761.	• Assign pp. 756–761 for independent student
• Assign and review Exercises 71–73.	review.
• *Hands-on Grammar* activity, p. 762.	• Assign Section Review Exercises 74–75.

Compound Nouns A compound noun contains two or more words. To form a possessive of a compound noun, use the following rule.

KEY CONCEPT Add an apostrophe and an -s (or just an apostrophe if the word is a plural ending in -s) to the last word of a compound noun to form the possessive. ■

The following examples illustrate some of the different kinds of compound nouns commonly used to form possessives.

NAMES OF BUSINESSES AND ORGANIZATIONS:	Major and Marker's baby powder the Red Cross's volunteers Ozu and Sons' Electronics
TITLES OF RULERS AND LEADERS:	King George III's army the Chief Justice's decision Shogun Yoritomo's decree
HYPHENATED COMPOUND NOUNS:	my father-in-law's ranch the secretary-treasurer's report

Expressions Involving Time and Amounts These expressions also require the use of apostrophes.

KEY CONCEPT To form possessives involving time and amounts, use an apostrophe and -s or just an apostrophe if the possessive is plural. ■

TIME:	a month's vacation three months' work
AMOUNT:	a dime's worth three dimes' worth

💡 **Spelling Tip**

To form the plural possessive of most nouns ending in *ife*, such as *knife* and *wife*, the *ife* is dropped and *ives* is added. An apostrophe follows the *s* to form *knives'* and *wives'*.

▶ **Critical Viewing** Yoritomo was the first shogun—or military ruler. The title then was passed down from generation to generation. Using possessive nouns, describe a possible order of descent. [**Speculate**]

Apostrophes • 757

Step-by-Step Teaching Guide

Joint and Individual Ownership

1. Read the key concept and ask students to explain the difference between something that is *joint* (it is combined with someone or something else) and something that is *individual* (it is considered by itself).

2. Then, have students read the examples and decide which shows joint ownership and why (Will and Martin own the same dog) and which shows individual ownership and why (each girl owns her own paper).

3. Ask students to create other examples of joint and individual ownership. Write some of these on the board and have students provide apostrophes. Examples:

   Martin and Day Department Store (*'s* after *Day*—joint)

   Sue and Marie hands (*'s* after *Sue* and after *Marie*—individual)

Answer Key

Exercise 71

1. nature's
2. Japan's
3. country's
4. correct
5. plates'
6. Island's
7. earthquake's
8. People's
9. Tokyo's and Yokohama's
10. government's
11. Wright's
12. Kobe's
13. dollars'
14. children's
15. area's

Joint and Individual Ownership Sometimes people share ownership, and sometimes several people claim individual ownership. The difference affects the use of the apostrophe.

▶ **KEY CONCEPT** To show joint ownership, make the final noun possessive. To show individual ownership, make each noun possessive. ■

JOINT OWNERSHIP: Will and Martin's dog, a greyhound, has won a number of prizes.

INDIVIDUAL OWNERSHIP: Susan's, Marie's, and Alice's papers were graded by the teacher.

▶ **Exercise 71** **Proofreading to Correct Apostrophes in Possessive Nouns** Revise the following sentences, correcting the possessive form wherever necessary. If a sentence contains no error, write *correct*.

EXAMPLE: I bought five dollar's worth of stamps.
ANSWER: I bought five dollars' worth of stamps.

1. One of natures most destructive forces is the earthquake.
2. Japans' people have been plagued by earthquakes throughout their history.
3. The countries' islands are situated on top of fault lines.
4. Fault lines are areas where the massive portions of Earth's crust, called tectonic plates, bump against each other.
5. The plate's bumping causes shock waves to ripple through the ground, thus creating an earthquake.
6. In 1923, an earthquake ravaged huge parts of Tokyo, Honshu Islands largest city, and the port of Yokohama.
7. The earthquakes' force leveled much of both cities.
8. Peoples' homes were destroyed, and buildings were toppled.
9. Tokyo and Yokohama's casualties numbered more than 100,000.
10. The governments' response was to rebuild the city, engineering most buildings to withstand future earthquakes.
11. The architect Frank Lloyd Wrights Imperial Hotel survived the quake and won praise for its construction technology.
12. Kobes' earthquake in 1995 killed 3,600 people and destroyed 55,000 homes.
13. The earthquake caused more than 100 billion dollar's worth of damage.
14. Businesses, hospitals, and childrens' schools were caught in the devastation.
15. The areas geologic history shows that a powerful earthquake had hit at almost the same spot in 1916.

▶ **More Practice**

On-line Exercise Bank
• Section 27.6
Grammar Exercise Workbook
• pp. 169–170

Forming Possessives of Pronouns

Two additional rules are needed to show possession with indefinite pronouns and personal pronouns. Indefinite pronouns require the use of an apostrophe and an -s to show possession.

KEY CONCEPT Use an apostrophe and an -s with indefinite pronouns to show possession. ■

EXAMPLES:
nobody's turn	somebody's house key
one's homework	each other's handkerchiefs
everybody's friend	one another's bathing caps

Notice in the last two examples that an apostrophe and an -s are added only to the last word of a two-word pronoun.

A different rule applies when the possessives of personal pronouns are formed.

KEY CONCEPT Do not use an apostrophe with the possessive forms of personal pronouns. ■

The possessive forms of personal pronouns (*his, hers, its, ours, yours, theirs*, and so on) already show possession. Thus, they do not need apostrophes.

EXAMPLES:
his old car
that hobby of *hers*
its tail
that house of *ours*
that paper of *yours*
that responsibility of *theirs*

Do not confuse the contractions *who's, it's,* and *they're* with possessive pronouns. *Who's, it's,* and *they're* are contractions for *who is* or *who has, it is* or *it has,* and *they are.* Remember that *whose, its,* and *their* show possession.

PRONOUNS:
Whose homes were damaged?
Its tremors were felt many miles away.

CONTRACTIONS:
Who's aware of the extent of the devastation in Kobe?
It's the site of a terrible earthquake.

▼ **Critical Viewing**
This expressway was toppled by the Kobe earthquake. What do you think were some of the immediate effects on people living and working nearby? Include possessive indefinite pronouns in your answer. **[Draw Conclusions]**

Apostrophes • **759**

1. its
2. their
3. anyone's
4. his
5. whose

Step-by-Step Teaching Guide

Forming Contractions With Verbs

1. Review the definition of *contraction*.

2. Use the chart to demonstrate the difference between a contraction and its spelling before it is contracted. For each example, have students tell you which letters are omitted to form the contraction.

3. Ask students to volunteer additional contractions. (*we'd, I'd, he's*) Write these on the board.

Integrating Speaking and Listening Skills

Contractions Explain to students that the use or lack of use of contractions helps denote a certain level of language. For instance, frequent and regular use of contractions in a speech or composition creates an informal tone; conversely, avoiding contractions creates a more formal impression. Have students choose a written or oral presentation they have recently delivered and tell them to present it two ways to the class: one on a formal level without contractions, and the other on an informal level.

27.6

▶ **Exercise 72** Using Apostrophes Correctly With Pronouns

Copy each of the following sentences, choosing the correct possessive form from the choices in parentheses.

EXAMPLE: I need (somebody else's, somebody elses') opinion.

ANSWER: I need somebody else's opinion.

1. While touring the country of Japan, we visited some of (its, it's) cultural and historical sites.
2. We went to see the Buddhist temple in Nara, where monks practice (they're, their) religion.
3. We tried not to disturb (anyone's, anyones') activities.
4. It is hard to believe that a monk might spend (his, he's) entire life there.
5. We also went to see Edo Castle, built by a warlord (who's whose) name I can't remember.

Forming Contractions

A contraction is formed by removing a letter or letters from a word or phrase and replacing the missing letter(s) with an apostrophe.

Contractions With Verbs The most common type of contraction involves verbs.

COMMON CONTRACTIONS WITH VERBS		
Verbs with *not*	cannot should not were not will not	can't shouldn't weren't won't
Pronouns with *will* or *shall*	she will we shall	she'll we'll
Pronouns with *would*	he would they would	he'd they'd
Pronouns with *have*	we have they have	we've they've
Pronouns or Nouns With the Verb *be*	I am you are she is Michael is	I'm you're she's Michael's

Notice that *will not* in the preceding chart becomes *won't*, changing letters as well as replacing letters with an apostrophe.

760 • Punctuation

▶ **More Practice**

**On-line
Exercise Bank**
• Section 27.6
**Grammar Exercise
Workbook**
• pp. 169–170

🔵 **Learn More**

For additional information about using possessive pronouns, see Chapter 22.

✏️ STANDARDIZED TEST PREPARATION WORKSHOP

Grammar and Usage Many standardized tests require students to recognize errors in sentences. Use the following example.

The captain has asked whose going to board the boat.

What is the error in this sentence?

A Spelling   **C** Grammar

B Punctuation   **D** No error

The answer is **A**, spelling. The word *whose* should be written *who's* or *who is*. This is a spelling error because the writer has chosen the spelling of a pronoun in place of words that sound the same. Although one correct solution (*who's*) would contain an apostrophe, the other (*who is*) does not, so the error is not in punctuation.

KEY CONCEPT Contractions should be used sparingly in formal writing. Reserve them to add flavor to dialogue. In other cases, write out the words. ■

Contractions With Numbers and Poetry Contractions are sometimes used in informal writing to replace the century portion of a year.

EXAMPLES: the class of '03   the blizzard of '98

Contractions are sometimes used in poetry to achieve a poetic effect.

EXAMPLES: e'en (for *even*)   o'er (for *over*)

Contractions With *o', d',* and *l'* The letter *o* followed by an apostrophe makes up the abbreviated form of the words *of the.* The letters *d* and *l* mean *of* or *of the* when used as a contraction with a proper name, often from a language such as French, Italian, or Spanish.

EXAMPLES: o'clock   O'Sullivan   d'Angelo   *l'Abbe*

These contractions are used most often with surnames.

Contractions in Dialogue When writing dialogue, use any contractions the speaker might use to give the flavor of the speaker's style. You may also want to include a regional dialect or a foreign accent. Because these often include unusual pronunciations involving omitted letters, you may have to insert apostrophes to indicate omitted letters.

EXAMPLES: 'Tis a long way you'll have to be goin'.
Don' you be afoolin' me.

Overuse of the apostrophe reduces its effectiveness. Thus, you should not overuse it—even in dialogue.

Exercise 73 **Using Apostrophes in Contractions** Write the contraction for each of the following items.

EXAMPLE: should not
ANSWER: shouldn't

1. should have
2. I am
3. we will
4. he is
5. we are
6. they have
7. would not
8. it is
9. 1957
10. Maggie is

Grammar and Style Tip

When proper nouns contain contractions, always check to make sure they are correctly punctuated and capitalized. Sometimes, a name will contain a capital on both sides of an apostrophe, as in *O'Mara.*

Forming Other Contractions

1. Explain to students that apostrophes can replace missing numbers in years and missing letters in poetry to form contractions.

2. Have students read the two examples at the top of this page.

3. Write *o', d',* and *l'* on the board and ask students to read the examples on this page. Ask for additional examples of surnames that use apostrophes.

4. Read aloud the explanation of contractions in dialogue. Explain that this device is typically used in narratives to create realism.

5. Ask students to think of unusual dialogue they have read. (The writing of Mark Twain is a good example.)

Customize for
Linguistic Learners

Onomatopoeia Have students think of words that sound like their meanings and point out that this device is called *onomatopoeia.* (Examples might include *plush, hush, plop, whoosh.*) Compare this device to contractions used in some dialogues, asking why writers use such devices (to make events and descriptions come to life). Finally, have students say these words out loud and then use them in original sentences.

Answer Key

Exercise 73

1. should've
2. I'm
3. we'll
4. he's
5. we're
6. they've
7. wouldn't
8. it's
9. '57
10. Maggie's

✓ ONGOING ASSESSMENT: Monitor and Reinforce

If students miss more than two items in Exercise 71, 72, or 73, refer them to the following for additional practice.

In the Textbook	Print Resources	Technology
Section Review, Ex. 74–75, p. 763	*Grammar Exercise Workbook,* pp. 169–172	*On-Line Exercise Bank,* Section 27.6

Hands-on Grammar

Teaching Resources: Hands-on Grammar Activity Book, Ch. 27

1. If you wish to do this activity in class, be prepared with scissors, paper strips, and extra sheets of paper for the students. Make sure students have a copy of the *Hands-on Grammar* activity sheet for Chapter 27.

2. Have students follow the directions to prepare their slides.

3. Suggest other words that can form contractions (such as *we have, they have, I am, you are, she is,* and *Jim is*) for students to put on the slide strips.

4. You may wish to expand this activity by having students add to their slide strips words from Exercise 73 that gave them problems.

27.6

Hands-on Grammar

Contractions Slide

Use a Contractions Slide to review which letters are dropped and where apostrophes belong in common contractions. Start by cutting out three strips of paper, 1" wide and about 14" long; number them *1, 2, 3.* On each strip, print several of the words from the following lists. Make all the letters the same size and equally spaced.

STRIP 1	STRIP 2	STRIP 3
ISNOT	IHAVE	IWOULD
ARENOT	SHEWILL	YOUWOULD
DIDNOT	WEHAVE	HEWOULD
WERENOT	YOUARE	WEWOULD
COULDNOT	YOUWILL	THEYWOULD

Next, take a piece of 6-1/2" x 8-1/2" paper, and cut three narrow pairs of 1" slits in it about 3" from the right-hand edge. The width of the space between the first pair of slits should be that of one printed letter; the second pair, the width of two letters; and the third pair, the width of four letters. (You should be able to weave the strips of paper through the slits.) Then, in the middle of each pair of slits, draw a large apostrophe. (See the illustration.)

Finally, slide strip *1* through the top pair of slits, stopping each time the apostrophe covers the *o* in *not.* Repeat with strip *2,* stopping where the apostrophe covers the third and fourth letters from the end; and with strip *3,* stopping when the apostrophe covers the letters *woul.* Each time, what will remain is the proper form of a contraction. Write other words on the backs of the strips, and continue reviewing contractions on your Contractions Slide.

Find It in Your Reading Review a magazine article or short story, and note the frequency and types of contractions used.

Find It in Your Writing Review a piece of your writing, making sure you have used and formed contractions correctly.

🕐 **TIME SAVERS!**

Hands-on Grammar
Use the *Hands-on Grammar* activity sheet for Chapter 27 to facilitate this activity.

Section Review

GRAMMAR EXERCISES 74–78

Exercise 74 **Proofreading for All the Rules for Apostrophes** Revise the following sentences, using apostrophes to form contractions, possessive nouns, and possessive pronouns where appropriate. In addition, revise any incorrect use of apostrophes.

1. Ive had fun in my film class, but now that were studying director Akira Kurosawas movies, Im enjoying it even more.
2. He didnt plan to become one of Japans most important directors.
3. Hed produce fifty years worth of movies before his death in 1998.
4. Its said that his ancestry can be traced back to ancient Japans samurai warriors.
5. However, nobodys certain about this information.
6. Kurosawas best known for the movies *Rashomon, The Seven Samurai,* and *Ran.*
7. Theyll be considered classics long after weve seen them.
8. Kurosawa turned two of Shakespeares plays into movies, and hes also adapted one of Russian author Fyodor Dostoyevskys novels.
9. Weve watched all three of them, and theyve become favorites of ours'.
10. Its obvious that in the film business, everyones always borrowing from somebody elses work.

Exercise 75 **Writing Sentences With Possessives and Contractions** Following the instructions in each item, write sentences that use possessives or contractions. Use apostrophes as needed.

1. Describe the singing voice of a friend, using his or her name.
2. Write a sentence about something you will or would do.
3. Ask a question in an attempt to find out the owner of a lost item. Use the possessive of an indefinite pronoun.
4. Write a sentence announcing that you will arrive somewhere at noon. Spell out the time.
5. Write a sentence describing identical jackets belonging to two friends. Name both friends.

Exercise 76 **Find It in Your Reading** Look around your hometown or school for signs, posters, and other printed materials that might contain apostrophes. Write down five examples and the rules they illustrate. If an apostrophe is used incorrectly, explain why, and then correct the error.

Exercise 77 **Find It in Your Writing** Look through your portfolio for five examples of apostrophes. Write down the sentence in which each word appears, and then trade papers with a partner. Refer to the rules explained in this section, and mark any apostrophes that are used incorrectly.

Exercise 78 **Writing Application** Choose a part of Japanese culture or history mentioned in this chapter that you find interesting. Read more about it in the library or on the Internet, and then write a one-paragraph summary of the information you found. Use at least three apostrophes in your paragraph.

ASSESS and CLOSE

Section Review

Each of these exercises correlates to the instruction on apostrophes, pages 756–761.

Answer Key

Exercise 74

1. **I've** had . . . **we're** studying . . . **Kurosawa's** . . . **I'm** enjoying
2. He **didn't** . . . one of **Japan's**
3. **He'd** produce fifty **years'** worth
4. **It's** said . . . ancient **Japan's**
5. However, **nobody's**
6. **Kurosawa's** best known
7. **They'll** be . . . **we've** seen them.
8. **Shakespeare's** plays . . . **he's** also . . . **Dostoyevsky's** novels.
9. **We've** watched . . . **they've** become . . . of **ours.**
10. **It's** obvious . . . **everyone's** always . . . **else's**

Exercise 75

Answers will vary. Possible answers:

1. Sebastian's singing voice is squeaky.
2. I would be reluctant to borrow money I couldn't repay.
3. Is this someone's notebook?
4. I'll arrive at the stadium at twelve o'clock.
5. Terry's and Jeremy's jackets look just alike.

Exercise 76

Find It in Your Reading
If students encountered errors in the use of apostrophes, have them determine which rule was most often misused.

Exercise 77

Find It in Your Writing
Have students make a one-page list of rules governing apostrophes to keep in the back of their portfolios. Encourage them to refer to this list when proofreading their work.

Exercise 78

Writing Application
When students finish, have them exchange paragraphs with a partner. Have each student write down the three examples of apostrophes and the rule which governs each example. Have them mark any errors and return the papers to their partners to be corrected.

ONGOING ASSESSMENT: Assess Mastery

Use the following resources to assess student mastery of punctuation.

In the Textbook	Print Resources	Technology
Chapter Review, pp. 764–767 Ex. 85–88 Standardized Test Preparation Workshop, pp. 768–769	*Formal Assessment,* Chapter 27	*Language Lab* CD-ROM, Punctuation *On-Line Exercise Bank,* Chapter 27

Each of these exercises correlates to a section of the chapter on punctuation, pages 690–763. The exercises may be used for more practice, for reteaching, or for review of the key concepts presented.

Answer Key

▶ **Exercise 79**

1. 1.7 million years**?**
2. remarkable**!** Don't you agree**?**
3. the Asian continent**.**
4. people began farming**.**
5. by 5,000 B.C. and began . . . settlements and farms**.**

▶ **Exercise 80**

1. The Shang dynasty, which lasted from c.1600 B.C. to 1027 B.C., is the first of many distinct historical
2. such as wheat, barley, and rice.
3. such as pigs, sheep, and oxen and
4. As the archaeological record shows, the Chinese
5. more than five hundred years, the last
6. During the Zhou dynasty, Chinese culture
7. size of the country prevented . . . far from the capital, so they divided
8. Each state was, in turn, ruled
9. By the year 770 B.C., several
10. Eventually, with no central control, states
11. This era, known as the Period of the Warring States, lasted for nearly two hundred years, but, oddly enough, it had a beneficial effect.
12. existence, only qualified people rose to positions of power, and
13. taxing their citizens, so they could employ honest, effective
14. By the end of the Zhou dynasty, . . . Confucianism, Taoism, and Legalism.
15. warring states, and in 221 B.C., it unified China. [second comma is optional]

GRAMMAR EXERCISES 79–89

▶ **Exercise 79** Proofreading to **Supply and Correct End Marks** Revise each of the following items, adding or correcting punctuation as necessary.

1. Did you know that humans have occupied China for more than 1.7 million years.
2. I think that is absolutely remarkable Don't you agree.
3. Chinese civilization initially developed along the Yellow River and then slowly spread into the interior of the Asian continent
4. I asked the reference librarian if she could tell me when the indigenous people began farming?
5. Most early Chinese gave up their nomadic way of life by 5,000 BC and began establishing primitive settlements and farms!

▶ **Exercise 80** Proofreading to **Supply Commas or Correct Comma Usage** Revise the following sentences, adding or correcting commas as necessary.

1. The Shang dynasty which lasted from c.1600 B.C. to 1027 B.C. is the first of many distinct, historical periods in China.
2. The people of this period were mainly farmers who grew crops such as wheat barley and rice.
3. They also domesticated animals such as pigs sheep and oxen, and began to cultivate silkworms.
4. As the archaeological record shows the Chinese mastered the ability to create bronze tools and weapons at this time.

5. After maintaining power for more than five hundred years the last of the Shang rulers was overthrown by the kingdom of Zhou.
6. During the Zhou dynasty Chinese culture spread throughout most of what is considered modern-day China.
7. The immense size of the country, prevented the Zhou rulers from exercising direct control over areas that were far from the capital so they divided the country into small states.
8. Each state was in turn ruled by lords, who were family members or influential friends of the king.
9. By the year 770 B.C. several of these states had allied themselves with barbarian people from outside China; together they forced the Zhou government to relinquish much of its power.
10. Eventually, with no central control states soon began fighting among themselves.
11. This era known as the Period of the Warring States lasted for nearly two hundred years, but oddly enough it had a beneficial effect.
12. Because each state was fighting for its very existence only qualified people rose to positions of power and the practice of hiring friends and relatives was abolished.
13. Most states began taxing their citizens so they could employ honest effective bureaucrats to run the government.
14. By the end of the Zhou dynasty a period of enlightenment gave rise to the philosophies of Confucianism Taoism and Legalism.
15. The state of Qin eventually managed to subdue all of the warring states and in 221 B.C. it unified China.

Exercise 81 Supplying Colons and Semicolons

Supply colons and semicolons as necessary in the following sentences.

1. During the thirteenth century, Western civilization was essentially ignorant of China and its people until the advent of one man Marco Polo.
2. When Polo was only six years old, his father and uncle went to China they would not return for nine years.
3. Polo might have pursued any number of career paths as a young man nevertheless, he chose to follow in the footsteps of his father.
4. In 1271, he joined his father and uncle on a trip to China it would take them three years to reach that distant country.
5. On their journey, they passed through many countries present-day Turkey, Israel, Jordan, Iran, Iraq, Afghanistan, and Russia.
6. Many of the cultures that the Polos came in contact with were unknown to the West They were the first Europeans to encounter them.
7. Once they reached China, Marco Polo became a good friend of the emperor Kublai Khan consequently, he was sent on diplomatic missions throughout the Chinese Empire on Khan's behalf.
8. Khan valued the three Europeans' political and military advice in fact, he trusted the younger Polo's judgment so much that he made him a governor.
9. When the Polos wished to return home, Kublai Khan did not want to let them leave however, he finally relented in 1292.
10. Polo's account of his travels to China was written in Italy in 1299 it was the only source of information on China for nearly two hundred years.

Exercise 82 Using Quotation Marks

Use quotation marks to properly punctuate the following sentences. Any quoted fragments are underlined.

1. The Chinese philosopher Confucius said, Good government has been obtained when those who are near are made happy and those who are far off are attracted. . . .
2. Confucius also said that the relationship between a government and its people is like that between the wind and the grass; in other words, he was saying that the people must be flexible to the ideas of government.
3. The superior man is modest in his speech, Confucius said, but exceeds in his actions.
4. Confucius wrote, Learning without thought is labor lost: He meant that you must consider the things you have learned if you wish to fully understand them.
5. Confucius also said that a man should have no friends not equal to himself.

Exercise 83 Supplying Underlining and Quotation Marks in Titles

Properly underline or enclose in quotation marks each of the following items.

1. book: The Great Gatsby
2. movie: The Joy Luck Club
3. article in a magazine: How to Remodel Your Kitchen
4. album: James Taylor's Greatest Hits
5. painting: The Night Watch
6. chapter in a book: The Early Years
7. newspaper: The Augusta Tribune
8. short poem: Refugee in America
9. individual aircraft: The Spirit of St. Louis
10. short story: An Occurrence at Owl Creek Bridge

Exercise 81
1. advent of one man: Marco Polo.
2. to China; they would not return for nine years.
3. as a young man; nevertheless,
4. a trip to China; it would take
5. countries: present-day
6. unknown to the West: They
7. emperor Kublai Khan; consequently,
8. military advice; in fact, he trusted
9. want to let them leave; however,
10. written in Italy in 1299; it was

Exercise 82
1. The Chinese philosopher Confucius said, "Good government . . . far off are attracted. . . ."
2. its people "is like that between the wind and the grass"; in other words,
3. "The superior man is modest in his speech," Confucius said, "but exceeds in his actions."
4. Confucius wrote, "Learning without thought is labor lost": He meant
5. Confucius also said a man should "have no friends not equal to himself."

Exercise 83
1. book: The Great Gatsby
2. movie: The Joy Luck Club
3. article in a magazine: "How to Remodel Your Kitchen"
4. album: James Taylor's Greatest Hits
5. painting: The Night Watch
6. chapter in a book: "The Early Years"
7. newspaper: The Augusta Tribune
8. short poem: "Refugee in America"

continued

Answer Key continued

Exercise 83
9. an individual aircraft: The Spirit of St. Louis
10. short story: "An Occurrence at Owl Creek Bridge"

TIME SAVERS!

Answers on Transparencies Use the *Grammar Exercises Answers on Transparencies* for Chapter 27 to facilitate correction by students.

On-Line Exercise Bank Have students complete the exercises on computer. The Auto Check feature will grade their work for you!

Answer Key

Exercise 84

1. in the mid-nineteenth century (1841–1898) gave the British
2. World War II (1939–1945),
3. On July 1, 1997—according to the Sino-British Joint Declaration signed in 1984—the British
4. The city—now a modern hub of banking, trading, and shipping—
5. Cultural attractions—like the much-anticipated . . . Festival—draw . . . (Note: Parentheses may be used rather than dashes.)

Exercise 85

Answers may vary. Possible answers:

1. **Everybody's** been talking about
2. two **weeks'** worth
3. Beijing, which is **China's** capital
4. **I've** never had
5. There **isn't** anyone in our class **who's** going to forget about it.

Exercise 86

1. Through the course of history, Chinese . . . periods: the classical age, the medieval age, and the modern age.
2. at the end of the Zhou dynasty (500 B.C.–A.D. 200).
3. of the three periods, and it produced . . . theories, including Taoism, Naturalism, Mohism, and Legalism.
4. of this era, however, is Confucius (Have you heard of him?), a . . . from Lu, China, an area in present-day Shandong Province.
5. As a young man, he served . . . a variety of low-level positions . . . minister of justice; however, he devoted . . . to teaching.
6. morally, ethically, and spiritually virtuous man.
7. classic literature of ancient China.
8. virtue; as a result, peace . . . family, the society, and the government.
9. One of his most widely-known sayings . . . civilization's Golden Rule: "Do not do to others what you would not like yourself."
10. in a virtuous way, then . . . embraced by the people.

continued

Chapter Review Exercises cont'd.

Exercise 84 Revising for Dashes, Parentheses, Hyphens, and Brackets

Use dashes, parentheses, hyphens, and brackets to punctuate the following sentences.

1. A series of treaties in the mid nineteenth century 1841–1898 gave the British firm control over Hong Kong until 1997.
2. During World War II 1939 1945, Japanese forces invaded and occupied Hong Kong for almost four years.
3. On July 1, 1997, according to the Sino British Joint Declaration signed in 1984 the British government peacefully returned Hong Kong to Chinese sovereignty.
4. The city now a modern hub of banking, trading, and shipping is a popular destination for Western tourists.
5. Cultural attractions like the much anticipated Hong Kong Arts Festival and the Hong Kong International Film Festival draw visitors annually.

Exercise 85 Forming Contractions and Possessives

Where possible, combine pronouns with verbs to form common contractions. Also, add apostrophes where needed to form possessive nouns.

1. Everybody has been talking about what a great time we had on our class trip to Beijing.
2. We were there for two weeks worth of fun and excitement.
3. Beijing, which is Chinas capital city, was heavily populated.
4. I have never had such an interesting vacation.
5. There is not anyone in our class who is going to forget it.

Exercise 86 Proofreading for All the Rules of Punctuation

Revise the following sentences, correcting or adding punctuation as necessary.

1. Through the course of history Chinese scholars have originated a number of doctrines that can be classified into three distinct periods the classical age the medieval age and the modern age
2. The classical age of Chinese philosophy emerged during a period of political instability at the end of the Zhou dynasty 500 BC AD 200
3. It is regarded as the most enlightened of the three periods and it produced a wide variety of theories including Taoism Naturalism Mohism and Legalism
4. The most famous philosopher of this era however is Confucius Have you heard of him a traveling sage from Lu China an area in present day Shandong Province
5. As a young man he served the regional government in a variety of low level positions and eventually attained the post of minister of justice however he devoted most of his life to teaching
6. Confucius advocated the concept of a morally ethically and spiritually virtuous man
7. He believed that a person could achieve such virtues by observing the principles set forth in the classic literature of ancient China
8. Confucius argued that individuals should work to achieve personal virtue as a result peace and prosperity would extend to the family the society and the government
9. One of his most widely known sayings communicates the same idea as the Western civilizations Golden Rule Do not do to others what you would not like yourself
10. He felt that if those in power conducted their personal and professional lives in

766 • Punctuation

766

a virtuous way then their example would be embraced by the people

11. Confucius also promoted the idea of returning to the strong centralized authority of the old imperial government whose rule would bring unity and order to the political disorder of his time

12. In carrying on your government he said why should you use killing at all

13. He continued by saying Let your [political] desires be for what is good and the people will be for good

14. Confucius collection of sayings was compiled by his students into a book called the Analects shortly after his death he died in 479 BC

15. Hes also believed to be the author of the Spring and Autumn Annals a book that chronicles a two hundred year period of Lu history from 771 to 579 BC

Exercise 87 **Proofreading Paragraphs for All Rules of Punctuation**

Revise the following paragraph, correcting or adding punctuation as needed. A numbered section might contain more than one error or no errors.

(1) Over the past few decades the campaign against smoking has intensified (2) Research has linked smoking to cancer heart disease and emphysema. (3) Many committed concerned individuals and groups have worked to raise Americans awareness of the dangers of smoking. (4) Cigarette packaging contains the following warning The Surgeon General has determined that cigarette smoking is dangerous to your health. (5) Some studies even show that nonsmokers are at risk from the smoke of others. (6) Nevertheless some people continue to (7) smoke in fact the number of cigarettes consumed daily has actually increased. (8) Are there any signs of hope (9) As a result of pressure from nonsmokers, changes are occurring. (10) Areas in public places for example restaurants have been set aside for nonsmokers. (11) Ads for tobacco products have been banned from TV. (12) New ads educate people about smoking, and speak out against it. (13) Many people have been able to stop smoking but the best solution is (14) not to start (15) What can you do to help asked our school nurse.

Exercise 88 **Writing and Punctuating Original Sentences** Choose a subject with which you are familiar. It might be a person you know, a sport you play, a restaurant you like, or a topic you're studying in one of your classes. Then, write sentences, following the directions below.

1. Describe three features of your subject, using commas in a series.
2. Write something you like about your subject, using your subject as a possessive noun.
3. Quote something that someone else has said about your subject, inserting a remark or clarification of your own inside the quotation.
4. Complete a sentence that begins, "These two things are good (or bad) about [your subject]."
5. Describe one thing that may affect your subject in the future; add a contrary or explanatory comment in the middle or at the end of the sentence.

Exercise 89 **Writing Application**

Choose a well-known person of Chinese descent—an athlete, a politician, a musician, a writer, and so on—and write a paragraph about his or her life. You can find biographical information about your subject in the library or on the Internet. Correctly use at least five of the key concepts you learned in this chapter.

Exercise 86

11. strong, centralized . . . imperial government, whose rule . . . his time.
12. "In carrying on your government," he said, "why should you use killing at all?"
13. He continued by saying, "Let your . . . what is good, and the people will be for good."
14. Confucius's collection . . . called the Analects shortly after his death (**He** died in 479 B.C.).
15. He's . . . the Spring and Autumn Annals, a book . . . two-hundred-year period . . . (from 771 to 579 B.C.)

Exercise 87

[1] decades, . . . intensified.
[2] cancer, heart disease, and
[3] committed, concerned Americans'
[4] warning: "The . . . health."
[5] correct [6] Nevertheless,
[7] smoke; in fact, [8] hope?
[9] non-smokers, [10] places—for example, restaurants and airplanes—have [11] correct [12] smoking and [13] smoking, [14] start. [15] "What can you do to help?" asked

Exercise 88

Answers will vary. Possible answers:

1. Arnulfo is a good student, a talented athlete, and a skilled musician.
2. I particularly like Arnulfo's piano playing.
3. Coach Lolino said, "If he works hard, he could play in D-1 [Division 1 of the NCAA—the biggest colleges with the most competitive basketball programs]."

continued

Exercise 88

4. These two things are especially good about Arnulfo: He doesn't take himself too seriously, and he really cares about other people.
5. His talent can take him a long way—unless he lets his casual attitude distract him.

Exercise 89

Writing Application

When students finish, have them exchange papers with a classmate, mark all punctuation errors, and return the papers to their partners to be corrected. Then, have students share their work with the class.

TIME SAVERS!

Answers on Transparencies Use the *Grammar Exercises Answers on Transparencies* for Chapter 27 to facilitate correction by students.

On-Line Exercise Bank Have students complete the exercises on computer. The Auto Check feature will grade their work for you!

Lesson Objectives

1. To apply standard punctuation rules, including commas, colons, semicolons, quotation marks, and end marks

2. To demonstrate correct use of the conventions of punctuation

3. To proofread for punctuation within the context of a written passage

Step-by-Step Teaching Guide

Proofreading

Teaching Resources: Standardized Test Preparation Workbook, pp. 53–54

1. Remind students that an independent clause contains a subject and a verb and is a complete thought on its own, or "independent." A dependent clause also has a subject and verb, but it "depends" on more information to be a complete thought. Point out that dependent clauses often begin with words such as *before, after, when, since,* and *until.*

2. Give students several examples of different titled items, such as books, articles, television shows, poems, etc. Review which are underlined (italicized) and which are within quotation marks.

3. Review with students what constitutes a series, and demonstrate comma and semicolon usage.

Standardized Test Preparation Workshop

Proofreading

Some standardized tests include items that test your knowledge of punctuation rules. Most often, these test items involve identifying errors in punctuation. Remember these basic rules to help you identify such errors:

- End marks denote the end of a sentence and will identify the type of sentence.

- Commas separate items in a series; set off introductory words, phrases, or clauses at the beginning of a sentence; and set off elements from the rest of the sentence.

- Colons introduce a list of items, whereas semicolons connect independent clauses.

- Quotation marks are used for direct quotations and for some titles; underlining or italics are used for some titles and to call attention to some words.

- Abbreviations and titles end with a period.

The following sample items will give you practice with identifying punctuation errors.

Test Tip

Don't choose the first rewrite that appears to be error free. Read each choice carefully, and then choose your answer.

Sample Test Items	**Answers and Explanations**

Directions: Choose the best way to write each underlined section. If the underlined section needs no change, mark the choice "Correct as is."
 	
 "Wow"!, I exclaimed. "I can't believe it
 (1)   (2)
 we are finally here.
 	
 1 A "Wow!" I exclaimed.
   B "Wow," I exclaimed,
   C "Wow"! I exclaimed.
   D Correct as is
	
	 The correct answer for item 1 is **A.** The exclamation point belongs inside of the closing quotation marks because it is part of the direct quotation.

2 A "I can't believe it, we are finally here."
   B I can't believe it; we are finally here.
   C "I can't believe it; we are finally here."
   D Correct as is
	The correct answer for item 2 is **C.** The direct quotation needs to be enclosed in quotation marks, and the semicolon is needed to join the two independent clauses.

✏ TEST-TAKING TIP

Tell students that if they are fairly certain that a specific punctuation mark belongs in a sentence, they should look carefully at only those choices that include that mark. By immediately eliminating the options that contain mistakes, students can concentrate on the other options, one of which is correct.

Practice 1 **Directions:** Choose the best way to write each underlined section. If the underlined section needs no change, mark the choice "Correct as is."

After the school year ended I took a liter-
(1)
ary tour of New England. The tour includ-
(2)
ed visits to historic sites that were signifi-

cant to the following writers Longfellow,

Hawthorne Frost Thoreau and Dickinson.

We left our high school at 6 pm on Friday,
(3)
and arrived in Concord Massachusetts at

10 pm. We were greeted, by a writer, for
(4)
the Atlantic Monthly magazine. She had
(5)
just published an article Literary Stops in

New England the article that had mapped

out our trip. "Let's go!" I shouted after she
(6)
had finished her speech, and off we went.

1 A After the school year ended—I took a literary tour of New England.
B After the school year ended: I took a literary tour of New England!
C After the school year ended, I took a literary tour of New England.
D Correct as is

2 F The tour included: visits to historic sites that were significant to the following writers, Longfellow, Hawthorne, Frost, Thoreau, and Dickinson.
G The tour included: visits to historic sites; that were significant to the following writers, Longfellow, Hawthorne, Frost, Thoreau, and Dickinson.

H The tour included visits to historic sites that were significant to the following writers: Longfellow, Hawthorne, Frost, Thoreau, and Dickinson.
J Correct as is

3 A We left our high school at 6 P.M. on Friday and arrived in Concord, Massachusetts, at 10 P.M.
B We left our high school at 6 p.m. on Friday, and arrived in Concord, Massachusetts at 10 p.m.
C We left our high school at 6 PM Friday, and arrived in Concord Massachusetts at 10 PM.
D Correct as is

4 F We were greeted, by a writer, for the *Atlantic Monthly* magazine.
G We were greeted by a writer for the *Atlantic Monthly* magazine.
H We were greeted by a writer, for the Atlantic Monthly magazine.
J Correct as is

5 A She had just published an article Literary Stops in New England, the article that had mapped out our trip.
B She had just published an article *Literary Stops in New England,*—the article that had mapped out our trip.
C She had just published an article, "Literary Stops in New England"—the article that had mapped out our trip.
D Correct as is

6 F "Let's go!" I shouted after she had finished her speech and off we went.
G Let's go, I shouted after she had finished her speech, and off we went.
H "Let's go" I shouted, after she had finished her speech, and off we went.
J Correct as is

Answer Key

Practice 1

1. C
2. H
3. A
4. G
5. C
6. J

Customize for
Less Advanced Students

Tell students to practice eliminating possible answer choices by locating punctuation marks that they recognize immediately as incorrect. They should read their final choice silently to clarify accuracy.

Customize for
AP Students

Students should pay close attention to the errors in each underlined sentence before moving to the answer choices. In this way, they can immediately eliminate those answers that do not include the correction.

Each of these exercises reviews concepts taught in the chapters on capitalization and punctuation. The exercises may be used for more practice, for review of the key concepts presented, or for assessment of student mastery of the major concepts.

Answer Key

Exercise A

1. In, African Americans, New York, Chicago, Detroit
2. Northern, African Americans, South
3. Harlem, New York City
4. Alain Locke, Harlem, Manhattan, Mecca, Negro
5. Between World War, Great Depression, Harlem Renaissance
6. The, Jean Toomer's, *Cane*
7. It, African American, United States
8. Langston Hughes, Missouri, Lincoln University, Pennsylvania, Harlem Renaissance
9. During, Poet Laureate, Harlem
10. Hughes, Broadway
11. He, Spanish Civil War, *Chicago Defender, New York Post*
12. Another, Zora Neale Hurston, Columbia University, German American, Franz Boas
13. Hurston, Eatonville, Florida, United States
14. Hurston, Jamaica, Haiti, Bermuda
15. Her, *Their Eyes Were Watching God, Jonah's Gourd Vine*, Harlem Renaissance, Ralph Ellison, Toni Morrison

Exercise B

1. writers, poetry, and literature**?**
2. Wow**!** . . . Ellington**;** . . . music**.**
3. Ellington, . . . D.C., . . . school, . . . band**:** . . . Serenaders**.**
4. ideas, . . . music**;** . . . creative**.** (or . . . music. Most . . .)
5. musicians**;** . . . Miley, . . . trumpeter, . . . group**.**
6. later, in 1927, . . . Club, . . . Harlem**.**
7. Indigo"**?**
8. orchestra, . . . pieces**;** subsequently, . . . radio**.**
9. Wow**!** . . . U.S. . . . 1931**.**

continued

Cumulative Review

MECHANICS

▶ **Exercise A** Proofreading for Missing Capitalization Revise the following sentences, adding capital letters as necessary.

1. in the 1920's and 1930's, many african americans moved to urban centers like new york, chicago, and detroit.
2. northern factories offered jobs that african americans in the south needed.
3. harlem, part of new york city, emerged as the center of social and cultural life.
4. alain locke called the harlem region of manhattan the "mecca of the new negro."
5. between world war I and the great depression, the harlem renaissance was a time of renewed creativity.
6. the beginning of this movement is unofficially marked by the publication of jean toomer's novel *cane* in 1923.
7. it was one of the first novels to realistically tell the story of african american life in the united states.
8. The writer langston hughes, born in missouri and educated at lincoln university in pennsylvania, is frequently associated with the harlem renaissance.
9. during that time, he was referred to as the poet laureate of harlem.
10. hughes, although known for his poetry, also wrote a broadway play and many books.
11. he was a newspaper correspondent during the spanish civil war and later a columnist for the *chicago defender* and the *new york post*.
12. another writer, zora neale hurston, studied at columbia university under the german american anthropologist franz boas.
13. hurston was born in eatonville, florida, the first incorporated all-black town in the united states and the subject of her first anthropological field study.

14. hurston also traveled to jamaica, haiti, and bermuda, where she collected folklore and studied customs.
15. her novels, including *their eyes were watching god* and *jonah's gourd vine*, influenced other harlem renaissance writers and later authors such as ralph ellison and toni morrison.

▶ **Exercise B** Proofreading for End Marks, Commas, Semicolons, and Colons Revise the following sentences, inserting end marks, commas, semicolons, and colons where necessary.

1. Was the Harlem Renaissance only about writers poetry and literature
2. Wow I have heard the music of Duke Ellington he was one of the greats in the history of jazz music
3. Duke Ellington born Edward Kennedy Ellington in Washington DC played piano in high school and he formed a small band The Duke's Serenaders
4. Searching for new musical forms and ways of arranging his musical ideas Ellington created original music most of his writing was very personal and creative
5. In 1923 he moved to New York City and sought out other talented musicians James "Bubber" Miley a talented trumpeter helped transform Ellington's band into a respected jazz group
6. Several years later in 1927 Ellington began performing at The Cotton Club which was the most prominent nightclub in Harlem
7. Is that where he performed some of his compositions from "Mood Indigo"
8. With his twelve-member orchestra Duke Ellington recorded numerous pieces subsequently they were played nationally on the radio
9. Wow What a hit he made on his first US tour in 1931

10. Is it true that he was awarded the US Medal of Freedom and the French Legion of Honor

Exercise C Using All the Rules of Punctuation

Write the following sentences, inserting end marks, commas, semicolons, colons, quotation marks, underlining, dashes, brackets, parentheses, hyphens, and apostrophes where necessary.

1. WEB Du Bois wrote that African American theater should be 1 "about us 2 by us 3 for us and 4 near us
2. This goal was not achieved during the Harlem Renaissance however art and poetry flourished at that time
3. The painter William H Johnson came to New York in 1918 and enrolled at the National Academy of Design He studied under George Luks and Charles Hawthorne
4. Reflecting the poetry of that time Langston Hughes 1902 1967 wrote in his poem The Weary Blues I got the Weary Blues sic
5. Didnt Hughes after traveling to Russia Haiti and Japan use his poetry for the social and political causes that he championed

Exercise D Proofreading for Capitalization and Punctuation

Write the following dialogue, inserting the proper capitalization, quotation marks, and other punctuation and indenting paragraphs where appropriate for dialogue.

(1) I didn't know that the harlem renaissance included art and music I said. I was excited to learn about bessie smith and josephine baker

(2) its true martin said that most classes concentrate on the literature everyone knows about the poetry of langston hughes and countee cullen

(3) early on i replied i loved the poem the negro speaks of rivers which was published in crisis magazine in 1921 wasnt that magazine edited by WEB du bois

(4) martin replied it was du bois also wrote the book the souls of black folk which is included in my collection called three negro classics.

(5) oh yes I added that collection also includes james weldon johnsons autobiography what else did you read in that class you took at dartmouth college

(6) i remember it very well we met in room 2 of wentworth hall every tuesday and thursday afternoon i enjoyed jessie redmon fausets novel there is confusion and wallace thurmans novel infants of the spring martin told me

(7) did you read any women authors i know you read one book by zora neale hurston

(8) thats true martin answered we also read nella larsens novel passing and hurstons autobiography called dust tracks on the road

(9) wait a second wasnt that book published in 1942 isnt that after the harlem renaissance took place in new york i asked confused

(10) thats true said martin but the harlem renaissance was more than a specific time period it was a cultural revolution that continues even today

Exercise E Writing Application

Write a short dialogue between two people discussing a historical time or an event in history that interests you. Be sure to follow all the rules of capitalization and punctuation.

Exercise B

10. U.S. . . . Honor?

Exercise C

1. W.E.B. . . . [1] about us, [2] by us, [3] for us, and [4] near us."
2. Renaissance; however, . . . time.
3. William H. Johnson . . . Design. . . . Hawthorne.
4. time, . . . Hughes (1902–1967) . . . "The Weary Blues," "I . . . Blues [sic]."
5. Didn't Hughes, . . . Russia, Haiti, and Japan, . . . championed?

Exercise D

(1) "I . . . Harlem Renaissance . . . music," I said. "I . . . Bessie Smith and Josephine Baker."

(2) "It's true," Martin said, "that . . . literature. Everyone . . . Langston Hughes and Countee Cullen."

(3) "Early on," I replied, "I . . . 'The Negro Speaks of Rivers,' . . . *Crisis* . . . 1921. Wasn't . . . W.E.B. Du Bois?"

(4) Martin replied, "It was. Du Bois . . . *The Souls of Black Folk*, . . . *Three Negro Classics*."

(5) "Oh, yes," I added, "that . . . James Weldon Johnson's autobiography. What . . . Dartmouth College?"

(6) "I . . . well. We . . . Room 2 of Wentworth Hall every Tuesday and Thursday afternoon. I enjoyed Jessie Redmon Fauset's novel *There Is Confusion* and Wallace Thurman's novel *Infants of the Spring*," Martin told me.

(7) "Did . . . authors? I . . . Zora Neale Hurston."

(8) "That's true," Martin answered. "We also read Nella Larsen's novel *Passing* and Hurston's . . . *Dust Tracks on the Road*."

(9) "Wait a second! Wasn't . . . 1942? Isn't . . . Harlem Renaissance . . . New York?" I asked, confused.

(10) "That's true," said Martin, "but the Harlem Renaissance . . . period. It . . . today."

Exercise E

Writing Application

Remind students to begin a new paragraph each time the speaker changes. When students finish, have them exchange dialogues with a partner. Have them mark any errors and return the papers to their partners to be corrected.

Sentence Diagraming Workshop

Subjects and Verbs

To diagram the most basic subject-verb sentence pattern, draw a horizontal line and place the simple subject on the left and the simple verb on the right. Separate the two with a vertical line.

EXAMPLE:
$\overset{S}{\text{Jerome Martin}}$ $\overset{V}{\text{would have frowned.}}$

| Jerome Martin | would have frowned |

Adjectives and adverbs are placed on slanted lines below the words they modify.

EXAMPLE:
$\overset{ADJ}{\text{The}}$ $\overset{ADV}{\text{very}}$ $\overset{ADJ}{\text{tasty}}$ $\overset{S}{\text{dessert}}$ $\overset{V}{\text{had been prepared}}$ $\overset{ADV}{\text{quite}}$
$\overset{ADV}{\text{easily.}}$

When *you* is understood to be the subject of an imperative sentence, write it in parentheses. Inverted sentences are also diagramed in the usual subject-verb order. The capital letter shows you the word that begins the sentence.

EXAMPLES:
IMPERATIVE   INVERTED
Go home.   Will Steve play today?

When *there* or *here* functions as an adverb, put the word on a slanted line beneath the verb. If *there* is an expletive used merely to begin the sentence, however, write it on a horizontal line over the subject. The placement of the expletive is also used for interjections and nouns of direct address.

EXAMPLES:

EXP
There is a park nearby.

INT N of DA
Well, Jan, are you going?

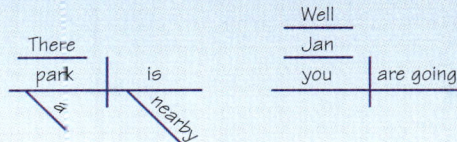

Exercise 1 **Diagraming Subjects, Verbs, and Modifiers**

Correctly diagram each sentence.

1. Harry skates well.
2. The tiny dancer fell down.
3. There was an extremely severe thunderstorm today.
4. Alice, begin immediately.
5. Did the crowd clap loudly?

Adding Conjunctions

In a diagram, a conjunction is written on a dotted line drawn between the words that are connected by the conjunction. The following example shows how conjunctions are diagramed to indicate the connection between compound adjectives and compound adverbs.

EXAMPLE:

CONJ   CONJ
The tan and white moth fluttered back and forth.

Conjunctions that connect compound subjects and verbs are also written on dotted lines. Notice in the following example how the horizontal line has been split to allow each part of the compound subject and the compound verb to be on a separate line. Also, note how the correlative conjunctions *both* and *and* are placed.

EXAMPLE:

CONJ   CONJ
Both the corn and the tomatoes were planted

CONJ
last spring and have been weeded regularly.

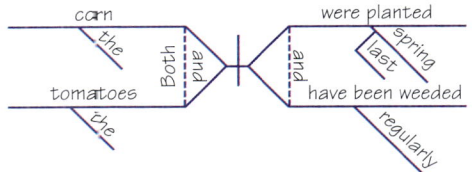

Sentence Diagraming Workshop • 773

1.

2.

3.

4.

5.

1.

2.

3.

4.

5.
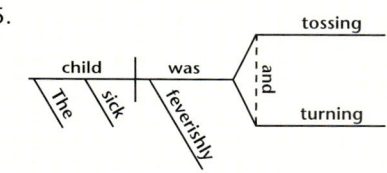

Notice in the last example that modifiers are placed as always under the words they modify. If a word modifies both parts of a compound subject or verb, it is placed under the main line of the diagram. Likewise, if parts of a compound verb share the same helping verb, the helping verb is written on the main line of the diagram.

EXAMPLE: Anxiously, we have been watching and waiting.

Exercise 2 **Diagraming Conjunctions** Correctly diagram each sentence.
1. My teacher and her husband live here.
2. The burglar entered quickly but silently.
3. The bright and witty entertainer will perform tonight.
4. The nervous squirrels ran away and hid.
5. The sick child was feverishly tossing and turning.

Complements

Because complements complete verbs, they are placed on the predicate side of the diagram. Place the direct object on the main horizontal line following the verb. Separate the direct object from the verb with a short vertical line. Indirect objects are located directly under the verb on a short horizontal line extended from a slanted line.

EXAMPLES: I stapled the papers.   He lent me a pen.

Objective complements sit on the main line after the direct object. A short slanted line pointing toward the direct object separates them.

EXAMPLE: The club elected her president.

774 • Sentence Diagraming Workshop

Both subject complements—predicate nominatives and predicate adjectives—are diagramed in the same way. Place them on the same line following the verb. Separate them from the verb with a line slanting toward the subject.

EXAMPLES: The puppy felt soft.   That tree is an elm.

Diagram compound complements by splitting the line on which they appear and adding any conjunctions that connect them.

EXAMPLE: She gave Vic and Mary their coats and hats.

▶ **Exercise 3**   **Diagraming Complements**   Correctly diagram each sentence.
1. Henry and Mike are practicing their tournament speeches.
2. Carlos intently watched the butterflies and the moths.
3. My dear aunt left me a huge, old desk.
4. The old bridge appears both too narrow and too unsafe.
5. My manager thinks me very efficient and quite reliable.

Prepositional Phrases

A prepositional phrase is diagramed directly beneath the word it modifies. The preposition is placed on a slanted line, and the object sits on a horizontal line. Place any modifiers of the object of the preposition on slanted lines below the horizontal line. If the object of the preposition is compound, diagram it in the same way other compound parts are diagramed.

EXAMPLE: The cup *of hot soup* is sitting *on the table or the stove.*

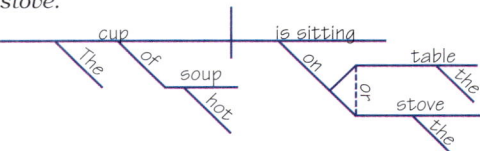

Sentence Diagraming Workshop • **775**

1.

2.

3.

4.

5.

1.

2.

3.

4.

5.
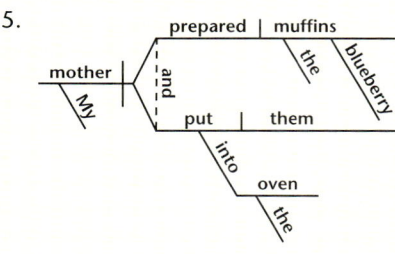

If a prepositional phrase modifies the object of another prepositional phrase, diagram it below the other phrase as shown in the first example. If a prepositional phrase modifies an adjective or adverb, an extra line is added as in the second example.

EXAMPLES: I ate cereal *with strawberries on it.*

He left early *in the morning.*

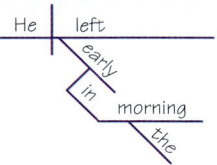

When two or more prepositional phrases modify the same word, place them side by side under the word they modify.

EXAMPLE: Go *down the hall* and *to the left.*

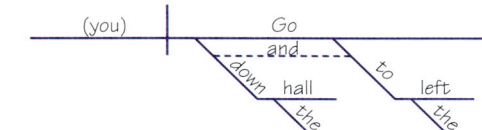

Exercise 4 **Diagraming Prepositional Phrases** Correctly diagram each sentence.
1. The magazine on that chair has an article about birds.
2. Yesterday, George sent his winter coat to the cleaners.
3. A crowd gathered at the foot of the hill.
4. The detective descended into the basement and disappeared into the great darkness.
5. My mother prepared the blueberry muffins and put them into the oven.

Appositive Phrases

Place an appositive in parentheses beside the noun or pronoun it renames. Position any modifiers of the appositive in the usual way beneath the appositive.

APPOSITIVE PHRASE

EXAMPLE: My friend, *the one with the suitcase,* is leaving for Greece.

> **Exercise 5** **Diagraming Appositive Phrases** Correctly diagram each sentence.

1. Our dessert, strawberry crepes with cream, pleased our guests immensely.
2. At her party, she received some placemats, orange ones with yellow borders.
3. My friend Linda plays a good game of charades.
4. They gave the babysitter, a neighborhood girl, a generous bonus.
5. With great delight, the audience watched the movie, a farce about airplane disasters.

Verbal Phrases

As you study the following explanations and examples, remember that a verbal is never diagramed on a single straight line and that any verbal can have a complement.

Participles and Participial Phrases Because a participle functions as an adjective, place it directly beneath the noun or pronoun it modifies. Write it partly on a slanted line and partly on a horizontal line with any modifiers beneath it. When a participle has a complement, such as a direct object, place it after the participle on the horizontal line. Separate the complement from the participle with the usual line.

PARTICIPLE PHRASE

EXAMPLE: The cars *loudly honking their horns* disrupted my sleep.

> **Exercise 5**

1.

2.

3.

4.

5.

A nominative absolute, formed from a noun and participle that are grammatically separate from the rest of the sentence, is positioned above the rest of the sentence.

NOMINATIVE ABSOLUTE

EXAMPLE: *His work finished for the day,* he left.

Gerunds and Gerund Phrases

Gerunds used as subjects, direct objects, or predicate nominatives are placed on a stepped line atop a pedestal. If a gerund functions as an appositive, parentheses are placed around the base of the pedestal. Any modifiers or complements are diagramed in the usual way. The example below shows a gerund phrase used as a subject.

EXAMPLE: GERUND PHRASE
Catching a big fish was a great thrill.

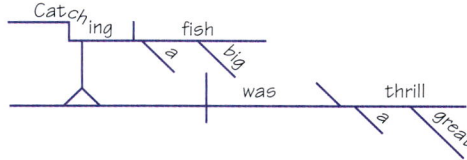

When a gerund or gerund phrase functions as an indirect object or as the object of a preposition, the stepped line extends from a slanted line.

EXAMPLE: GERUND PHRASE
We helped *by carrying the packages to the car.*

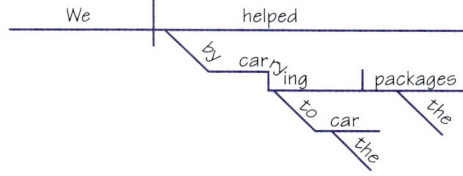

Infinitives and Infinitive Phrases Because infinitives can act as nouns, adjectives, or adverbs, they are diagramed in several different ways. Like gerunds, an infinitive used as a noun is diagramed on a pedestal, but the line on which the infinitive sits is different. The following infinitive phrase is acting as the direct object. Notice that the modifiers and complements are diagramed in the usual way.

EXAMPLE: Howard wanted *to get Debbie a record album.*

When an infinitive acts as an adverb, its diagram is similar to that of a prepositional phrase. Once again, any modifiers or complements are placed in their usual positions.

EXAMPLE: Today is the day *to begin our work.*

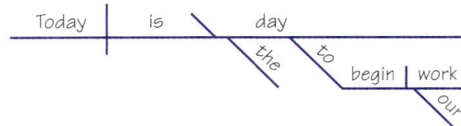

If an infinitive has an understood *to,* add it to the diagram but place it in parentheses. In addition, when an infinitive has a subject, place it on a horizontal line stretching out from the left side of the infinitive.

EXAMPLE: We saw Bob run *into the grocery store.*

1.

2.

3.

4.

5.
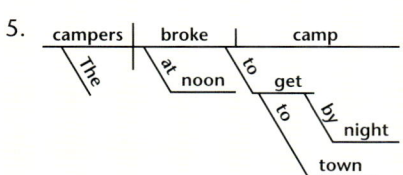

▶ **Exercise 6** **Diagraming Verbal Phrases** Correctly diagram each sentence.
1. Seeing the Picasso exhibit was a wonderful experience.
2. Leaping from the underbrush, a timid doe began to cross in front of us.
3. Tatum wished to buy a horse to ride in shows.
4. We tricked them into revealing the winners.
5. The campers broke camp at noon to get to town by night.

Compound, Complex, and Compound-Complex Sentences

Compound Sentences Diagram each independent clause of a compound sentence as you would a separate sentence. Then, join the verbs of the clauses with a dotted step line. On the step line, write either the coordinating conjunction or the semicolon that joins the two clauses.

INDEPENDENT CLAUSE   INDEPENDENT CLAUSE
EXAMPLE: *The curtain fell; the audience applauded*

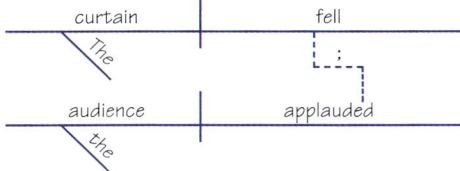

Complex Sentences To diagram complex sentences, you need to know how to diagram the three kinds of subordinate clauses: adjective, adverb, and noun.

Diagram an adjective clause below the main clause as if it were a separate sentence. Then, join the adjective clause to the word it modifies with a slanted, dotted line stretching from the relative pronoun or relative adverb. In the following example, the relative pronoun is a direct object in the subordinate clause, which modifies the subject of the main clause.

ADJECTIVE CLAUSE
EXAMPLE: The man *whom I telephoned* was busy.

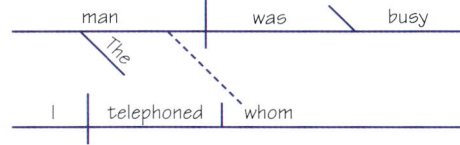

When a relative pronoun functions as an object of a preposition or as an adjective, you must bend the dotted line to connect the clauses properly. You must also bend the dotted line when a relative verb introduces an adjective clause. A relative adverb that introduces an adjective clause always modifies the verb in the subordinate clause.

EXAMPLE: I remember the time *that I visited Frankfurt.*

Occasionally, a relative pronoun in an adjective clause may be understood but not directly stated. Include the understood relative pronoun in the diagram, and enclose it in parentheses.

EXAMPLE: The turkey *I am stuffing* weighs ten pounds.

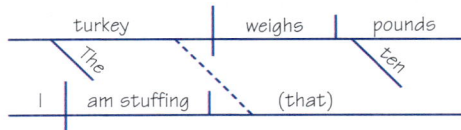

Diagram an adverb clause as you would an adjective clause; however, write the subordinating conjunction on the dotted line connecting the two clauses. This dotted line should extend from the verb in the adverb clause to the modified verb, adjective, adverb, or verbal in the main clause.

EXAMPLE: *Since she left,* I have had more time.

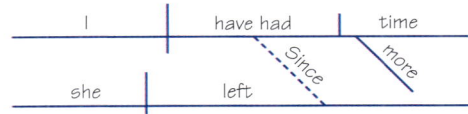

Add any words left out of an elliptical adverb clause to the diagram and enclose them in parentheses.

EXAMPLE: Marge is *taller than I.*

1.

2.

3.

4.

5.

6.

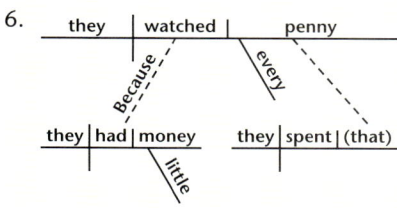

You may bend the dotted line connecting an adverb clause to an independent clause. In the example below, the adverb clause modifies an infinitive phrase that is the subject of the independent clause.

EXAMPLE: To ask permission *before you leave early* is a rule.

ADVERB CLAUSE

To diagram a noun clause, place the entire clause on a pedestal in the place the noun clause occupies within the main clause. In the following example, the noun clause functions as the subject of the main clause.

NOUN CLAUSE

EXAMPLE: *Who will win the game* remains the question.

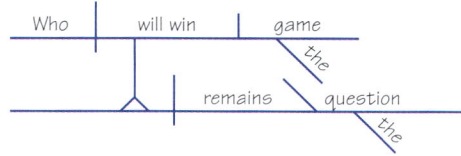

When a noun clause's introductory word has no other function than to introduce its clause, it is diagramed on the pedestal.

NOUN CLAUSE

EXAMPLE: I heard *that you were ill*.

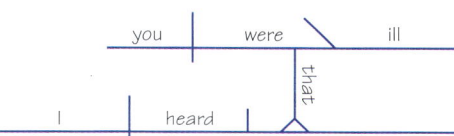

782 • Sentence Diagraming Workshop

Compound-Complex Sentences Because you now know how to diagram both compound and complex sentences, compound-complex sentences should pose few problems. First, diagram the independent clauses. Then, diagram and connect each subordinate clause as you would if you were diagraming a complex sentence.

EXAMPLE: ADVERB CLAUSE
When I arrived at work, I had many

disrupting telephone calls, but I still finished
everything *that I had to do.*   ADJECTIVE CLAUSE

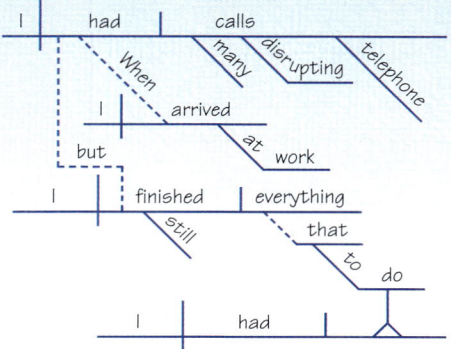

> **Exercise 7** **Diagraming Compound, Complex, and Compound-Complex Sentences** Correctly diagram each sentence. The first three sentences are compound, the next four are complex, and the last three are compound-complex.
>
> 1. My arms ached, but I continued to swim more laps.
> 2. The wind dispersed the smog, yet by dusk it had returned.
> 3. Did Helen attend the concert, or did she get a refund for her ticket?
> 4. Ursula LeGuin, who writes fantasy stories, will speak to us on Friday.
> 5. I must get whatever is necessary to repair this lock.
> 6. Because they had little money, they watched every penny they spent.
> 7. When you buy a house, look for any railroad tracks in the vicinity.
> 8. While I watched with interest, the workers measured the carpet, but they miscalculated on the amount needed.
> 9. She mailed the letter before the sun was up, but by noon she began to regret her decision.
> 10. If we go to Washington, I want to see the White House, and my sister plans to visit the Smithsonian.

Sentence Diagraming Workshop • **783**

7.

8.

9.

10.

783

Objectives

1. To develop critical listening and effective speaking skills and apply them to various types of presentations

2. To understand and evaluate visual images and messages in a variety of media

3. To produce visual images, messages, and meanings that communicate with others

4. To expand vocabulary through reading and listening and by developing skills in using context, word structure, word origins, and reference tools to determine word meanings

5. To develop and apply reading strategies for a variety of purposes and texts

6. To develop study and research skills and become familiar with reference tools and the resources of libraries and the Internet

7. To develop skills in taking tests in various formats

8. To learn and apply specific communication and procedural skills of the workplace, including problem-solving and managing time and money

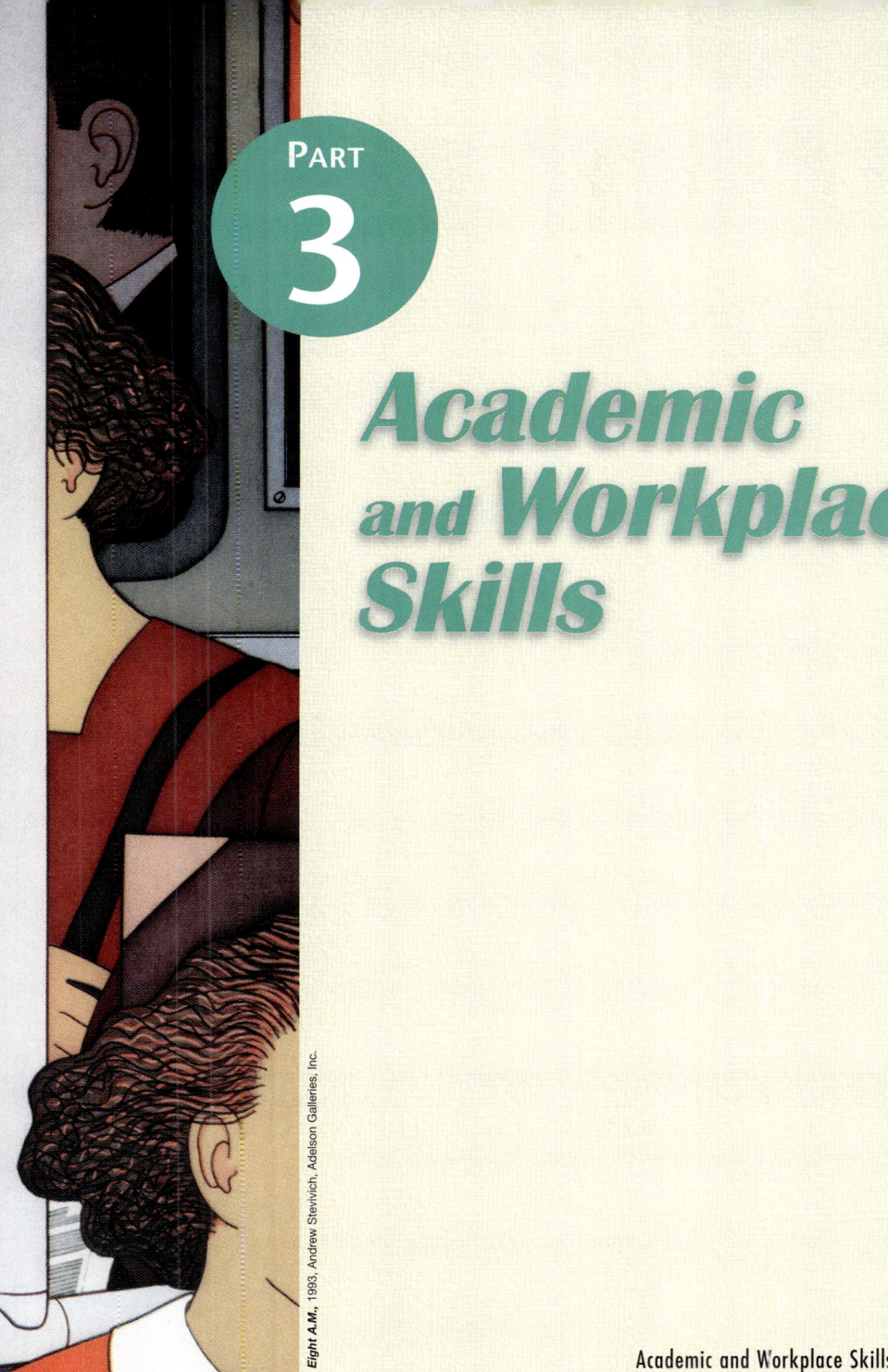

Eight A.M., 1993, Andrew Stevovich, Adelson Galleries, Inc.

PART 3

Academic and *Workplace* Skills

Academic and Workplace Skills • **785**

Responding to Fine Art

Eight A.M. (1993) by Andrew Stevovich

Use this work of art to start a discussion about the definition of academic and workplace skills.

1. Have students examine the painting on pages 784–785. You might use the following questions to prompt discussion:

   Is the train standing still or moving? Where are the passengers heading? Which details suggest answers to these questions? What might the passengers be thinking or reading about?

2. Students might suggest that the characters are heading to work. Ask them to explain how writing is important in the workplace. What are some other skills that are necessary for success in almost every workplace? Which skills do students hope to improve?

About the Artist

Andrew Stevovich (b. 1948) is a Boston-area artist known for producing "narratives" of common people, along with "the mysteries and struggles of modern life, and the sometimes simple, sometimes complex relationships between men and women." Stevovich's perfectly manicured people are painted "curvilinear" and are usually found in contrasting horizontal and vertical settings, as in his 1993 colored etching *Eight A.M.* Art critic Leon Nigrosh wrote in 1999 that Stevovich claims that he is "an abstract artist, simply concerned with placement, pattern, line, and color—and that his paintings just happen to look like people."

Time and Resource Manager

In-Depth Lesson Plan

	LESSON FOCUS	PRINT AND MEDIA RESOURCES
DAY 1	**Speaking and Listening Skills** Students learn key elements of speaking in a group discussion, speaking in public, and preparing, presenting, and evaluating a speech. (pp. 786–790)	*Teaching Resources* *Academic and Workplace Skills Activity Book,* pp. 1–2
DAY 2	**Speaking and Listening Skills** *continued* Students learn to listen critically and ask different types of questions. (pp. 791–793)	**Teaching Resources** *Academic and Workplace Skills Activity Book,* p. 3
DAY 3	**Viewing Skills** Students interpret maps and graphs and view media and fine art critically. (pp. 794–799)	**Teaching Resources** *Academic and Workplace Skills Activity Book,* pp. 4–7
DAY 4	**Representing Skills** Students create graphic organizers, use formatting, work with multimedia, create a video, and learn about performing and interpreting. (pp. 800–805)	**Teaching Resources** *Academic and Workplace Skills Activity Book,* pp. 8–12
DAY 5	**Review and Assess** Students review chapter and demonstrate mastery of concepts. (pp. 805–807)	**Teaching Resources** *Formal Assessment,* Ch. 28

Accelerated Lesson Plan

	LESSON FOCUS	PRINT AND MEDIA RESOURCES
DAY 1	**Speaking and Listening Skills** Students learn key elements of effective speaking and listening skills. (pp. 786–793)	**Teaching Resources** *Academic and Workplace Skills Activity Book,* pp. 1–3
DAY 2	**Viewing and Representing Skills** Students cover use of graphic organizers, work with multimedia, and learn about performing and interpreting. (pp. 794–805)	**Teaching Resources** *Academic and Workplace Skills Activity Book,* pp. 4–12
DAY 3	**Review and Assess** Students review chapter and demonstrate mastery of concepts. (pp. 805–807)	**Teaching Resources** *Formal Assessment,* Ch. 28

Options for Adapting Lesson Plans

HOMEWORK

Have students complete any stage of the lesson for homework.

FEATURES

Extend coverage with the Standardized Test Preparation Workshop (p. 806).

INTEGRATED SKILLS COVERAGE

Viewing and Representing
Critical Viewing SE pp. 786, 788, 791, 794, 799, 803
Representing ATE p. 789

Real-World Connection
ATE p. 802

Research
SE p. 788; ATE p. 796

Technology
SE pp. 797, 803

Vocabulary
ATE p. 791

ASSESSMENT SUPPORT

Standardized Test Preparation Workshop SE p. 806; ATE p. 798
Standardized Test Preparation Workbook, pp. 55–56
Formal Assessment, Ch. 28

MEETING INDIVIDUAL NEEDS

Less Advanced Students ATE pp. 800, 807. See also Ongoing Assessments ATE pp. 790, 793, 796, 803.

AP Students ATE pp. 797, 803, 807

ESL Students ATE pp. 788, 793, 801

Logical/Mathematical Learners ATE p. 795

Visual/Spatial Learners ATE p. 790, 799

BLOCK SCHEDULING

Pacing Suggestions
For 90-minute Blocks
• Have students complete the Speaking and Listening Skills sections in a single period.
• Focus one class period on Viewing Skills and Representing Skills. Allow an additional period for student presentations.

Resources for Varying Instruction
• *Academic and Workplace Skills Activity Book,* pp. 1–12

Professional Development Support
• *How to Manage Instruction in the Block* This Teaching Resource provides management and activity suggestions.

MEDIA AND TECHNOLOGY

For the Teacher
• *Resource Pro* **CD-ROM**

WRITING AND GRAMMAR WEB SITE

The Interactive Writing and Grammar Web Site provides a wide array of support for students, teachers, and parents.

www.phschool.com

Lesson Objectives

1. To communicate effectively in conversations and group discussions

2. To use informal, standard, and technical language effectively to meet the needs of purpose, audience, occasion, and task

3. To use language and rhetorical strategies skillfully in informative and persuasive messages

4. To make informed, accurate, truthful, and ethical presentations

5. To demonstrate proficiency in critical, empathic, appreciative, and reflective listening

6. To use effective strategies to evaluate one's own listening

7. To respond to informational elements in texts, such as graphic displays

8. To investigate the source of a media presentation such as who made it and why it was made

9. To present interpretations such as telling stories, performing original works, and interpreting poems and stories for a variety of audiences

Critical Viewing

Interpret Students might notice a speaker reaching out to her audience and the audience listening intently to the speaker.

Chapter
28 Speaking, Listening, Viewing, and Representing

Speaker, 1996, Diana Ong

Written work is only one avenue for sending and receiving information. Much of what you need to comprehend comes to you aurally or through visual representation. To understand and remember effectively, you must learn to listen and view accurately and critically. It is also important that you learn to give information orally and visually. By developing your skills in speaking, listening, viewing, and representing, this chapter will help increase your effectiveness as a communicator.

▲ **Critical Viewing**
What communication skills do you see represented in this painting? **[Interpret]**

🕐 TIME AND RESOURCE MANAGER

Resources
Print: *Academic and Workplace Skills Activity Book*, pp. 1–3

In-Depth Coverage	Accelerated Pace
• Read and discuss public speaking and critical listening strategies in class. • Have students practice these strategies by preparing and presenting speeches in class.	• Assign students to review pp. 786–793 independently. • Have students prepare speeches independently and then present them in class.

Section 28.1
Speaking and Listening Skills

Speaking and listening are forms of communication you use every day. In certain situations, however, special skills and strategies can increase the effectiveness of your communication. The concepts and strategies offered in this section will help you improve both your speaking and listening skills.

Speaking in a Group Discussion

A **group discussion** is an informal meeting of people that is used to openly discuss ideas and topics. The group discussions you participate in will, for the most part, involve your classmates and focus on the subjects you are studying. To benefit the most from a group discussion, you need to learn to participate in it.

▶ **KEY CONCEPT** A group discussion is a good way to express your opinions, as well as to hear the opinions of others, in an informal setting. ■

Communicate Effectively Before you speak, think about the points you want to make and which words will best express them. Organize these points in logical order. Recall examples or supporting facts to illustrate your points as you speak. Also, remember to speak clearly, pronouncing words slowly and carefully.

Ask Questions Asking questions is valuable for two reasons. The first reason is to enhance your understanding of another speaker's ideas. The second reason is to ask questions to call attention to possible errors in other speakers' points.

Make Relevant Contributions Stay focused on the topic being discussed. Relate discussion points to your own experience and knowledge. When you contribute information or ideas, make clear how your contributions are connected to the topic.

▶ **Exercise 1** Holding a Group Discussion With three to five other students, hold a 15-minute group discussion about a topic you are studying in class. Review some relevant material from your textbooks to generate ideas and supporting information for your statements.

▶ **More Practice**

Academic and Workplace Skills Activity Book
• p. 1

✓ ONGOING ASSESSMENT: Diagnose

Use one of the following options to diagnose students' current level of proficiency in speaking, listening, viewing, and representing.

Option 1 Have students make a list of critical listening strategies. If they having trouble thinking of strategies other than taking notes, they will need extra support in this area.	**Option 2** Show students a print ad from a magazine and ask them to list at least two persuasive techniques t uses. If students have difficulty with this exercise, they will need extra support in critical viewing skills and evaluating persuasive techniques.

PREPARE and ENGAGE

Interest GRABBER Have students brainstorm for a list of things to do and not to do when speaking in public. Have them copy the lists into their notebooks and refer to them as they prepare their speeches later in the chapter.

Activate Prior Knowledge

Ask students to form small groups and discuss public speaking experiences they have had. What did they do well? What did they find difficult? Have each group compile a list of things they'd like to learn about public speaking.

TEACH

Step-by-Step Teaching Guide

Speaking in a Group Discussion

Teaching Resources: Academic and Workplace Skills Activity Book, p. 1

1. Point out to students that they have spent their entire lives communicating in group discussions (lunchroom conversations, slumber parties, bus rides, and so on).

2. Brainstorm with the class for a list of rules to abide by in a group discussion. Their lists might include the following ideas: do not interrupt another group member, try not to needlessly repeat ideas, phrase questions and criticisms in a polite manner, and give all group members a chance to speak.

Answer Key

▶ **Exercise 1**

Before they begin this activity, have groups create posters entitled "Rules for Group Discussions" that include the rules generated in Step 2 above. Hang them in the classroom for students to refer to during small-group and whole-class discussions.

Speaking in Public

Teaching Resources: Academic and Workplace Skills Activity Book, p. 2

1. Give students examples of speeches they may have heard recently, and ask them to classify them according to type (examples: the principal's commencement address, a monologue by a comedian, a televised celebrity urging young people to stay in school).

2. Point out to students that some speeches may contain elements of more than one category. For example, the State of the Union Address is informative about many domestic and foreign issues. However, it may also be persuasive. The president often uses the speech to appeal for support for new programs.

Customize for
ESL Students

Public speaking can be frightening for students. One strategy to help them to overcome their natural fears is to encourage them to choose a topic related to their culture. Choosing a subject they know a lot about will give them extra confidence.

Critical Viewing

Draw Conclusions The speaker is communicating in a lively way with his audience; he is not relying too much on his notes. The listeners are paying attention and taking notes.

Answer Key

Exercise 2

Answers will vary. Have students support their answers with at least two pieces of evidence from the speech.

Exercise 3

Answers will vary. Remind students to consider speeches they've studied in history class.

Speaking in Public

Public speaking usually refers to the presentation of a speech before an audience. Getting a speech ready requires more preparation than is needed for a group discussion. The more time you invest in preparing and practicing your speech, the better your audience will receive it.

Recognize Different Kinds of Speeches

The kind of speech you give will depend upon your topic, your purpose, and the audience to whom it will be delivered.

> **KEY CONCEPT** Choose an appropriate kind of speech by considering the topic and purpose of the speech, as well as the intended audience. ■

- An **informative speech** explains an idea, a process, or an object. Descriptions and explanations may include technical language or terms.
- A **persuasive speech** attempts to convince the audience to agree with the speaker's position or to take some action. In a persuasive speech, the speaker generally follows the conventions of standard English usage.
- An **entertaining speech** offers the audience something to enjoy. It may be included in other kinds of speeches for variety or emphasis. The language of an entertaining speech is usually standard or informal.
- An **extemporaneous speech** is an informal speech given to suit an occasion, event, or audience. It is presented without the aid of a prepared manuscript.

> **Exercise 2** **Listening to Examples** Listen to a famous speech on CD or audiotape. Identify the type of speech it is by analyzing its characteristics.

> **Exercise 3** **Listing Kinds of Speeches** Give two examples of topics for each type of speech described above. Then, identify appropriate audiences for each.

🗐 Research Tip

Look in encyclopedias or biographical references to learn about great speakers of the twentieth century.

▲ **Critical Viewing**
What speaking and listening skills are being demonstrated in this photograph? **[Draw Conclusions]**

Prepare and Present a Speech

Once you know what kind of speech to give and have chosen a topic, you will need to gather information, outline your speech, prepare note cards, and practice your speech.

KEY CONCEPT Follow a series of steps to plan, prepare, practice, and present your speech. ■

Prepare Your Speech

- **Research your topic.** Use the library or other sources to find reliable information to support your claims.
- **Evaluate your material.** Do you think that your material is biased in any way? Make sure that you are giving an accurate, truthful, and ethical presentation.
- **Make an outline.** Include introductory and background material, a logical sequence of major points and supporting details, and an effective summary and conclusion.
- **Prepare numbered note cards.** Use key words and phrases, exact quotations, indentations, capital letters, and other means of highlighting important information.

Present Your Speech

- **Read over your outline and note cards.** Become very familiar with the material.
- **Utilize rhetorical strategies.** Repeat key words and use parallel structure; for example, "We cannot wait; we must take action."
- **Use verbal strategies.** Vary the pitch and tone of your voice. Speak clearly, and project your voice so you can be heard. Slow down or pause to emphasize key points.
- **Take advantage of nonverbal strategies.** Make eye contact with your listeners. Use your posture and gestures to reflect or emphasize your message.

> **The Baseball Team**
>
> A. Why more training is needed
>   1. to improve hitting and fielding
>   2. to increase endurance
>
> B. What training involves
>   1. weight training
>   2. cardiovascular exercises
>   a. running
>   b. biking
>
> C. What training leads to
>   1. better win-loss percentage
>   2. possible trip to playoffs

Exercise 4 **Preparing and Giving a Speech** Write a brief persuasive or informative speech on a topic of interest to you. Practice your speech, and present it to the class.

Exercise 5 **Receiving and Using Feedback** After you present your speech to the class, meet with a small group of your classmates. Ask them to critique your speech. Did it hold their interest? Were there factual errors? Rewrite your speech based on their critiques.

> **More Practice**
> Academic and Workplace Skills Activity Book
> • p. 2

Speaking and Listening Skills • **789**

Step-by-Step Teaching Guide

Prepare and Present a Speech

1. Emphasize to students the importance of choosing a topic that interests them. If they come across as apathetic or bored about their topic, they are likely to bore their audience as well.

2. Encourage students to avoid writing out their entire speech word for word. Key points and phrases will allow them to interact more with the audience. Encourage students to use note cards.

3. Students might want to make a speech that teaches a simple skill (examples: cutting out a paper snowflake or French-braiding hair). Have students "teach" at least three other students their skill before making the demonstration to the class. The experience of public speaking will be much easier the first time if they have a peer with them as they address the class.

Integrating Representing Skills

Encourage students to create visual aids such as graphs and charts to support their topics. This kind of evidence will strengthen their argument while adding visual appeal to their speech.

Answer Key

Exercise 4

Encourage students to make their speeches relevant and interesting by choosing a current community issue. They might try to persuade the class to vote for a certain candidate for mayor or explain the recent debate about the town curfew.

Exercise 5

Encourage students to be specific in their criticism and praise. In other words, they should explain exactly what held their interest or at what point the speech seemed to digress from the main idea.

789

Evaluate a Speech

1. Point out to students that a speech is only effective if the audience understands the point the speaker is making.

2. Emphasize to students the importance of posture, physical control (for example, avoiding distracting mannerisms), and voice projection.

3. Show students a few short clips from televised speeches by different speakers. Have the class work together to evaluate these speeches according to the checklist on this page. They can use this discussion as a model when they begin to evaluate one another's speeches.

Customize for
Visual/Spatial Learners

If a video camera is available, taping the speeches is an excellent way to allow students to evaluate themselves. This will make clear to them the specific skills they need to improve. Allow students to view the videos privately and complete an evaluation form for their own speeches.

Answer Key

▶ **Exercise 6**

Encourage speakers to present their speeches again after they've had time to read and incorporate their classmates' advice.

28.1

Evaluate a Speech

When you evaluate a speech, you judge its strengths (which public-speaking skills were successful) and weaknesses (which skills need more work). Work with peers to evaluate one another's speeches. Use the suggestions of your peer reviewers to improve your delivery and content.

▶ **KEY CONCEPT** Evaluate a speech in a way that benefits the speaker and you. ■

The checklist below gives suggestions for evaluating another person's speech:

CHECKLIST
FOR EVALUATING A SPEECH

☐ Did the speaker introduce the topic clearly, develop it well, and conclude it effectively?

☐ Did the speaker support each main idea with appropriate details?

☐ Did the speaker approach the platform confidently and establish eye contact with the audience?

☐ Did the speaker's facial expressions, gestures, and movements appropriately reinforce the words spoken?

☐ Did the speaker vary the pitch of his or her voice and the rate of his or her speaking?

☐ Did the speaker enunciate all words clearly?

▶ **Exercise 6** **Evaluating a Speech** Using the checklist in this section, make a detailed evaluation of a speech given in class. List two or more skills used effectively by the speaker, and consider using them in a future speech you will give.

Learn More

To learn more about persuasive techniques in advertising, review Chapter 8.

☑ ONGOING ASSESSMENT: Monitor and Reinforce

If students feel they need more feedback than the checklist provides, try one of these strategies.

Option 1 Instead of using a checkmark, have students rate each category on a scale of 1–5. Then, have the speaker discuss his or her score with the listener.	**Option 2** Have speakers add three specific questions to the checklist. This way, they will receive feedback about the issues they feel are most important or troubling.

Listening Critically

Speaking is one half of the communication process. The other half of the process is listening. Learning how to become a critical listener is an important step toward comprehension and successful communication.

KEY CONCEPT Improve your critical listening skills through the use of listening strategies and self-evaluation. ■

Learn the Listening Process You are probably already aware that listening means more than hearing sounds. Like all communication, listening is interactive. It requires participation on the part of the listener.

Focus Your Attention The most important step in listening is to focus your attention on the speaker and his or her words. Ignore all people, objects, noises, and thoughts that can distract you from listening. Increase your interest in the subject by acquiring information about it and by finding a connection between the subject and your life.

Interpret the Information When you listen to a speaker and interpret his or her message successfully, you identify and understand important information. Use the following suggestions to guide you:

- Listen for words and phrases that are emphasized or repeated.
- Visualize important statements, and test your understanding by rephrasing them in your own words.
- Write down important sentences, and summarize ideas.
- Watch for nonverbal signals—tone of voice, gestures, and facial expressions—that may alert you to important ideas.
- Link the information currently being given to previous information to form a meaningful pattern.

Respond to the Speaker's Message When you have finished listening, respond to the information you heard. Decide whether you agree or disagree with persuasive messages. Identify which elements of informative messages you find most interesting or useful. If possible, ask questions to clarify your understanding.

Exercise 7 **Using the Listening Process** Apply the strategies on this page as you listen to a speech, a classroom lecture, or a presentation by a classmate. In writing or in group discussions, summarize the speaker's main points and share your response.

▼ **Critical Viewing**
What listening strategies do you see being used in this photograph? **[Analyze]**

More Practice

Academic and Workplace Skills Activity Book
- p. 3

Speaking and Listening Skills • **791**

Step-by-Step Teaching Guide

Listening Critically

Teaching Resources: Academic and Workplace Skills Activity Book, p. 3

1. Explain to students that an important aspect of effective listening is knowing one's own weaknesses. For example, some students may be easily distracted when they sit toward the back of the room. Encourage students to make an effort to avoid the things that distract them.

2. Students might find it helpful to take notes on the important ideas of a speech. Students cannot reread a speech as they can an essay. Taking notes will give them a way to refresh their memory.

Integrating Vocabulary Skills

Encourage students to jot down unfamiliar words as they listen to the speeches. Not only will they benefit from asking about these words at the end of the speech, but the speaker will benefit from realizing that certain terminology may be appropriate only for certain audiences.

Critical Viewing

Analyze The listener is focusing her attention on the speaker. Her facial expression acknowledges that she understands what he is saying.

Answer Key

Exercise 7

Have students compare and contrast their summaries to make sure they did not miss any important information.

Use Different Types of Listening

1. Point out to students that they already use the various types of listening skills in each of the circumstances listed in the chart. Have students meet in small groups and share examples of occasions on which they've used each type of listening.

2. Can students think of an instance in which they've had to use more than one type of listening? (For example, students might mention a speech by a recruiter from a local college. They might use critical listening to form an opinion about the school's athletic programs, reflective listening to ask questions and obtain information about academic requirements, and empathic listening to identify with the recruiter and try to imagine what daily life is like at that school.)

Ask Different Types of Questions

1. Give a short speech on a topic of your choice. Have each student write an open-ended, a closed, and a factual question about the speech.

2. Have students share some of their questions. Point out that the audience often learns by listening to the questions of fellow audience members. They might obtain information they did not even realize they missed when they were listening to the speech.

Use Different Types of Listening Different situations call for different types of listening, and part of being a critical listener involves knowing what type of listening is the most appropriate for a given situation. There are four main types of listening: *critical, empathic, appreciative,* and *reflective.*

Types of Listening

Type	How to Listen	Situations
Critical	Listen for facts and supporting details to understand and evaluate the speaker's message.	Informative or persuasive essays, class discussions, announcements
Empathic	Imagine yourself in the other person's position, and try to understand what he or she is thinking.	Conversations with friends or family
Appreciative	Identify and analyze aesthetic or artistic elements, such as character development, rhyme, imagery, and descriptive language.	Oral presentations of a poem, dramatic performances
Reflective	Ask questions to obtain information, and use the speaker's responses to form new questions.	Class or group discussions

Ask Different Types of Questions A good listener always clarifies his or her understanding of a speaker's message. The best way to do this is by asking questions, but different questions have different purposes. If you understand the purposes of the following types of questions, you will be able to obtain the information you want to know:

- An **open-ended** question does not lead to a specific response. Use this question to open up discussion. *(Why do you think the school newspaper needs more funding?)*

- A **closed** question leads to a specific response and must be answered yes or no. *(Do you read the newspaper?)*

- A **fact** question is aimed at obtaining a particular piece of information and must be answered with facts. *(How many newspapers did the school print last year?)*

Answers will vary. Have students meet in small groups and share their examples. Remind them to use effective listening skills during their group discussions.

Exercise 8 Using the Different Types of Listening and Questions Identify at least one example of each type of listening and each type of question. Use examples from life, from television, from movies, or from descriptions in stories.

Evaluate Your Listening One way to improve your listening skills is to evaluate them to find out which listening skills work for you and which skills need improvement. Use the following strategies to evaluate your listening skills:

Rephrase and Repeat Statements You can test your understanding of a speaker's statements by rephrasing and then repeating them to the speaker. If the speaker agrees with your paraphrase, you know that you have understood him or her. If, however, the speaker disagrees with your paraphrase, ask the speaker to correct it or to clarify it.

Compare and Contrast Interpretations Write your interpretation of a speaker's message, and compare and contrast it with another student's interpretation. Use a Venn diagram to list the points on which you agree and disagree. Resolve these points of disagreement through discussion and, if necessary, by appealing to the speaker.

Research Points of Interest or Contention Use the library or other reference tools to acquire more information about the speaker's topic or to check questionable facts of the presentation.

Interpretation A   Interpretation B

Step-by-Step Teaching Guide

Evaluate Your Listening

1. After evaluating their listening skills, have students make a list of skills they still need to work on.

2. Remind students that they don't have to wait for in-class speeches to work on their listening skills. They can practice by concentrating on listening in other classes, in conversations with family members, and even at get-togethers with friends.

Customize for
ESL Students

Rephrasing and repeating statements will be especially beneficial for some students. It can be difficult to understand information after hearing it just once. Encourage students to record any rephrased and repeated statements in their notes.

Answer Key

▶ **Exercise 9**

As they read, students might notice errors in their writing, such as too many run-on sentences or fragments. Hearing work read aloud is a good way to notice errors. Remind students to use this strategy when proofreading written assignments.

Exercise 9 Evaluating Your Listening Skills Working with two other classmates, have one classmate read a speech or paper that he or she has recently written.

1. Tell the speaker to pause every paragraph or every few sentences, and take turns with your other classmate rephrasing and repeating the speaker's statements.
2. Ask the speaker to read the entire speech or paper while you and your other classmate take notes. Then, compare and contrast your interpretation.
3. Write an evaluation of your listening skills. Identify areas of strength and areas for improvement.

▶ **More Practice**

Academic and Workplace Skills Activity Book
• p. 3

☑ **ONGOING ASSESSMENT: Monitor and Reinforce**

To help familiarize students with the different types of questions, try one of the following options.

Option 1 Have students look through their literature or social studies textbook and write down ten to fifteen chapter review questions. Then, have them label each one *open-ended*, *closed*, or *factual*. Discuss their answers.

Option 2 When a student asks a question in class, pause for a moment to identify which type of question it is. Students will begin to see which types of questions to use for eliciting certain kinds of information.

Interpreting Maps and Graphs

Teaching Resources: Academic and Workplace Skills Activity Book, p. 4

1. Challenge students to make a map of their neighborhood or their school. Have them give their map a purpose. For example, they may want to make a map of the school designating specific areas where freshmen, sophomores, juniors, and seniors have locker assignments. Another example is "unofficial territories for student groups." They can make a map of the cafeteria tables, color-coded to show where each grade level usually sits.

2. Charting "unofficial territories" is an exercise that leads to a deeper understanding of maps: boundaries are not permanent. This exercise will help students realize that a printed map in a book is not always up to date; boundaries change frequently in the school and around the world.

Critical Viewing

Evaluate The student is using a world map. It shows the location, size, and boundaries of the world's countries.

Section 28.2 Viewing Skills

In today's highly visual world, an understanding of visual representations enhances your ability to receive information.

Interpreting Maps and Graphs

Textbooks, newspapers, magazines, and other written works utilize maps, graphs, and photographs to help convey information. Accurate interpretation of such visual representations increases your ability to understand important information.

> **KEY CONCEPT** Analyze and interpret maps, graphs, and photographs in order to become a more knowledgeable consumer of information. ■

To analyze and fully understand visual representations such as those discussed in this section, determine your purpose for viewing them; study the title, caption, and labels; examine symbols and details; and make connections with the text.

Maps

Maps serve a great variety of purposes. They can give the layout of a small neighborhood or chart the skies, indicate changing political boundaries or reveal early human knowledge of geography.

Consider these tips as you interpret maps:
1. Determine the type and purpose of the map.
2. Examine the symbols, scale, orientation, and other pertinent data.
3. Relate the information on the map to any written information accompanying it.

▼ **Critical Viewing**
What kind of a map is the student in this picture using? What kind of information can be obtained from this kind of map? **[Evaluate]**

794 • Speaking, Listening, Viewing, and Representing

⏱ TIME AND RESOURCE MANAGER

Resources
Print: *Academic and Workplace Skills Activity Book,* pp. 4–7

In-Depth Coverage	Accelerated Pace
• Read and discuss pp. 794–799. • Give students time to complete Exercises 10–14. • Discuss their answers.	• Have students read pp. 794–799 independently. • Have students choose one exercise on these pages to complete in class. • Discuss their answers.

Graphs

Examine the three types of graphs:

Line Graph A line graph shows the relationships between two sets of information; in this case, temperature and time.

1. Read the title. The title summarizes the purpose of the graph and the type of information you will find.
2. Identify the type of information that is shown on the horizontal and vertical data lines.
3. Identify patterns of change, and search the text for possible reasons for the changes.

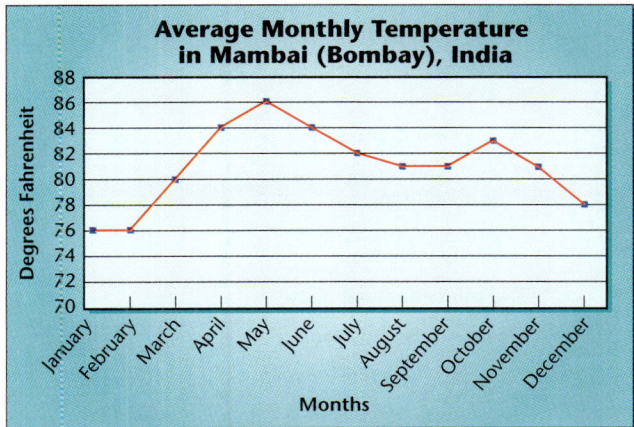

Bar Graph A bar graph compares and contrasts amounts by showing different heights or lengths of the bars.

1. Look across the bottom or at the title to determine the kinds of information being compared.
2. Determine similarities and differences in the data, and search the text for possible causes of the similarities and differences.

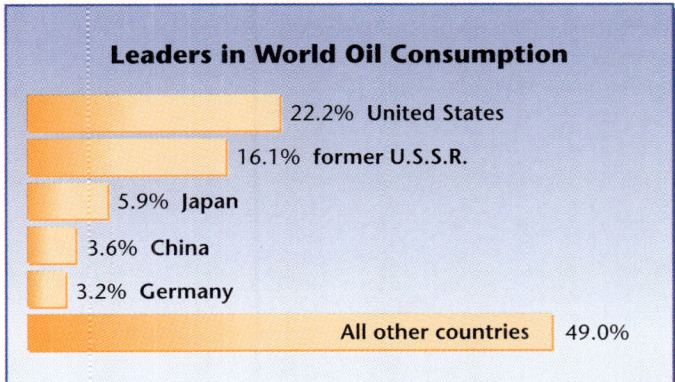

Step-by-Step Teaching Guide

Graphs

Teaching Resources: Academic and Workplace Skills Activity Book, p. 5

1. Have students study the line graph depicting the average monthly temperature in Mambai. Ask them to consider the differences between their local weather and that of Mambai. (They should note that the range of temperatures in Mambai is very slight, with only a ten-degree difference between extremes.)

2. Point out that although at first glance the graph appears to show a wide variation in temperatures, reading the chart carefully reveals otherwise. Emphasize the importance of reading a graph carefully before drawing conclusions.

Customize for
Logical/Mathematical Learners

Students can see from the bar graph that the United States accounts for twenty-two percent of world consumption. Have students find out what percent of the world's population lives in the United States and then compare these two figures.

Integrating Research Skills

Challenge students to make pie graphs that offer information about the class. They might survey class members on the careers they want to pursue, the after-school activities in which they participate, or something else that interests them. Have them tally their results and represent them in a pie graph that they can share with the class.

Answer Key

▶ **Exercise 10**

Answers will vary. For each graph students examine, have them answer this question: Why did the writer choose to make this type of graph as opposed to another type?

▶ **Exercise 11**

After students make their graphs, have them write one paragraph that summarizes the data and one paragraph that analyzes it.

Pie Graph A pie graph illustrates the relationship of parts to each other and to a whole.
1. Read the title to determine what kind of information is being represented and what the whole (100%) stands for.
2. Determine what each wedge represents, and relate the wedges to one another and to the whole.
3. Relate the pie graph information to the text to determine the significance of and possible reasons for the size of each wedge.

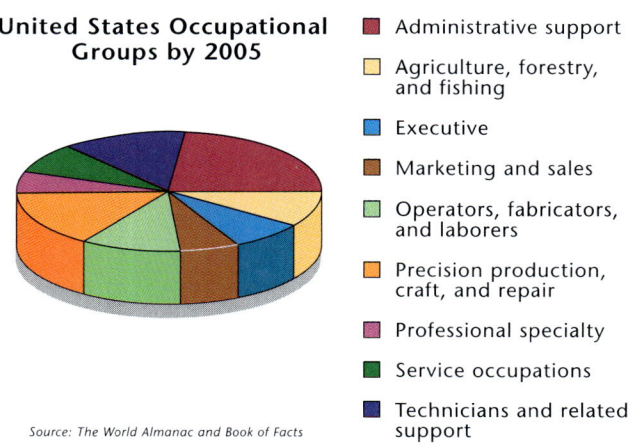

United States Occupational Groups by 2005

- ■ Administrative support
- □ Agriculture, forestry, and fishing
- ■ Executive
- ■ Marketing and sales
- ■ Operators, fabricators, and laborers
- ■ Precision production, craft, and repair
- ■ Professional specialty
- ■ Service occupations
- ■ Technicians and related support

Source: The World Almanac and Book of Facts

▶ **Exercise 10** **Interpreting Maps and Graphs** Using your science and/or social studies text, find two examples of a map, line graph, bar graph, or pie graph. Compare and contrast the types of data represented in each.

▶ **Exercise 11** **Creating a Graph** Using information from a textbook, an encyclopedia, the sports statistics in the newspaper, or an almanac, create a graph. First, decide which type of graph would present your material most effectively. Then, create your graph.

▶ **More Practice**

Academic and Workplace Skills Activity Book
• pp. 4–5

☑ ONGOING ASSESSMENT: Monitor and Reinforce

If students need more pactice reading and interpreting graphs, try the following strategy.

Have each student write three questions that relate to the pie graph. Have them trade with a partner and answer the questions. Both writing and answering questions will prompt them to read and make sense of the data. If necessary, have students repeat this exercise with graphs from their science, social studies, or math textbooks.

Viewing Information Media Critically

Each day, the media send out enormous amounts of information, much of it in visual representations. You must learn to differentiate the various media and critique the information you receive. It is important to distinguish between fact and opinion, accuracy and error, truth and propaganda. Critical observers become alert and responsible consumers of information.

KEY CONCEPT To become a knowledgeable consumer of information, identify and evaluate the different kinds of information and images presented in all media. ■

Recognize Kinds of Information Media Television, documentary films, and the Internet are just a few of the visual media through which information is communicated.

The following chart illustrates several kinds of programs and information found in nonprint information media:

NONPRINT INFORMATION MEDIA			
Form of Medium	Topic(s)	Coverage and Content	Point of View
Television News Program	Current events or news	Brief summaries illustrated by video footage	Gives objective information
Documentary	One topic of social interest	Story shown through narration and video footage	Expresses controversial opinions
Interview	Topics of social interest	Conversations of questions and answers	Presents opinions of interviewer
Editorial	Current or controversial topics	Commentary by a single person supported by statistics or facts	Presents the opinions of a single individual
Commercial	Products, people, and ideas	Short message of images and slogans	Presents information to sell something

 Technology Tip

Many television and radio programs have Internet sites where you can get background on a topic. Use the program's title in a key-word search.

Step-by-Step Teaching Guide

Evaluate Persuasive Techniques

1. Have students choose one television commercial or print ad and apply the strategies for evaluating persuasive techniques.

2. Ask them to provide specific examples of at least two of the persuasive techniques that are being used. The examples might be quotations, images, or a description of the ad's overall tone.

3. Have students meet in small groups and share their results.

Step-by-Step Teaching Guide

Evaluate Information From the Media

1. Ask students to brainstorm for a list of strategies they can use to check the accuracy of questionable information from the media. For example, a good way to obtain information about a new type of vitamin might be to consult a doctor or nutritionist, or to talk to people who have used it. A good way to obtain information about a political candidate is to read various newspaper accounts and Web sites about him or her.

2. Remind students that not everything they see on television, even on a respected news program, is completely accurate and free of bias. They should always use critical listening and viewing skills.

Answer Key

▶ Exercise 12

Students might choose to turn this assignment into a multimedia presentation, supplementing their analyses with actual clips of the newscasts.

▶ Exercise 13

When they finish, have students create their own ad for this product. They can combine some of the effective strategies from the existing ads with new ideas of their own.

Evaluate Persuasive Techniques The media use certain persuasive techniques to influence your understanding of information. Knowledge of these persuasive techniques, as well as other concepts, will help you become a more critical viewer:

Facts and opinions are two very different types of information. Watch for opinions that are stated as if they were facts.

Bias is a leaning, or partiality, toward a particular viewpoint. Consider whether information is one-sided or allows for several perspectives.

Loaded language and images are emotional words and visuals that make you feel strongly about something—either positive or negative. They are used to persuade you to think and act in certain ways.

Music, slogans, and repetition are often employed to intensify the impact of images and messages you receive. Watch for examples in ads as well as political speeches and campaigns.

Evaluate Information From the Media Wise consumers must go beyond recognition and carefully evaluate information received through the media. Use the following strategies when evaluating information from the media:

- Be aware of the kind of program you are watching and the kind of information you are receiving. Be alert to the content, purposes, and limitations of the information.
- Be careful to identify facts, opinions, biases, and loaded language and images.
- Check the accuracy of questionable information.
- Use knowledgeable observation to develop your own views about issues, people, and information.

▶ **Exercise 12** Analyzing News Coverage Choose a current news event, and observe its coverage on three major newscasts. Take notes regarding the placement and length of each report and the presence of any of the concepts and techniques discussed in this section. Your analysis should compare and contrast the three newscasts, indicating which gave the most objective coverage.

▶ **Exercise 13** Analyzing Television Commercials Select a type of product and observe commercials for it presented by three competing companies. Record examples of the techniques discussed in this section, and compare and contrast the techniques used by the different companies. Decide which one presented the most persuasive advertisement, and explain the reasons for your choice.

▶ **More Practice**

Academic and Workplace Skills Activity Book
• p. 6

798 • Speaking, Listening, Viewing, and Representing

✎ STANDARDIZED TEST PREPARATION WORKSHOP

Critical Thinking Standardized tests may require students to differentiate between facts and opinions.

Read the following statements and decide which one is a fact.

1. Standardized tests play a major role in the admissions process at many schools.

2. Standardized tests are not a good measure of a student's ability to learn.

3. Standardized tests are a better way to measure a student's intelligence than his or her grades.

4. Students should start preparing for standardized tests exactly nine months before taking them.

A 1   C 3

B 2   D 4

Students should recognize that **A** is the correct answer. None of the other statements can be proven.

Viewing Fine Art Critically

Paintings, drawings, photographs, and other forms of the visual arts present a subjective view of the world. Through line and shape, color and technique, artists capture a vast array of moments and moods. Learning to analyze various elements in a work of art can lead you to a meaningful and personal response.

KEY CONCEPT Analyze and interpret the elements of visual art that lead to a meaningful and enjoyable response. ■

The Reaper, c.1881, Louis C. Tiffany, National Academy of Design, New York City

---

INTERPRETING ELEMENTS OF VISUAL ART

1. **What kind of work are you viewing (painting, drawing, photograph, and so on)?**

2. **What are the subject and central focus of the piece?**

3. **What mood, theme, or message does the work convey?**

4. **What techniques does the artist use (color versus black-and-white photography, bold versus impressionistic lines and shapes, vivid versus muted colors, and so on)?**

5. **Is your overall response to the work more positive or more negative? Why?**

▲ **Critical Viewing** What are the subject and central focus of this painting? [**Analyze**]

Exercise 14 **Interpreting Visual Art** Consider the questions in the chart Interpreting Elements of Visual Art, and react to the artwork *The Reaper.* Describe your reactions in an essay.

▶ **More Practice**

Academic and Workplace Skills Activity Book
• p. 7

Viewing Skills • **799**

Step-by-Step Teaching Guide

Viewing Fine Art Critically

Teaching Resources: Academic and Workplace Skills Activity Book, p. 7

1. Explain to students that the term *subjective* means "open to interpretation." There is no one way to view or analyze a work of visual art. However, students must be able to defend their opinions with specific details.

2. To demonstrate that every work of visual art is open to interpretation, show students pictures that are seemingly unbiased or objective (examples: pictures of a school, an apple, a dog).

3. Ask students to write one sentence about how each picture makes them feel. Then share the responses with the class. Students will be amazed to realize how differently they think. Even the simplest image can evoke a wide range of responses.

Critical Viewing

Analyze The reaper is the central focus of the painting. The eye is immediately drawn to the reaper because of his size and his central location.

Answer Key

▶ **Exercise 14**

Answers will vary. Make sure students defend their interpretations with details from the painting.

Customize for *Visual/Spatial Learners*

Rather than asking students to write responses for Exercise 14, allow them to draw a response to the work of art. Have them assign a title that serves as a sequel or answer to the work. Then ask them to share their work and interpretation with the class.

Creating Graphic Organizers

Teaching Resources: Academic and Workplace Skills Activity Book, p. 8

1. Have students read a newspaper article and then create a graphic organizer that represents the article's main idea. They should choose the type of organizer that best suits the material.

2. Remind students that the headlines, subheads, and section heads of articles should provide hints as to how they might organize the information.

3. Ask students to share their results with the class, explaining why they chose the organizer they did. Discuss the choices they made, and offer feedback for more effective organizational strategies.

Customize for
Less Advanced Students

Students will be more likely to understand the uses of outlines, flow charts, webs, and Venn diagrams if you show examples of them. As you share these examples, have students list one or two school assignments for which each graphic organizer might be useful.

Section 28.3

Representing Skills

In this section, you will learn how to represent information using graphic organizers, multimedia presentations, and performances.

Creating Graphic Organizers

Organization skills are crucial when attempting to comprehend or present a great amount of information. Using graphic organizers and other aids to put information in visual format helps make the information easier to understand and remember.

▶ **KEY CONCEPT** To help you comprehend or present great amounts of information, put it into visual formats such as graphic organizers. ■

There are many kinds of graphic organizers, including outlines, flowcharts, webs, Venn diagrams, and timelines. Use the following strategies to create graphic organizers as you read, study, and present information:

- **Identify your purpose.** Determine what information or parts of the text you need to comprehend. This process will help you narrow your focus, eliminate extraneous information, and choose the most appropriate graphic organizer.

- **Utilize text features.** Make use of organizational features in textbooks (titles, headings, subheadings, boldfaced words and phrases) to design a graphic organizer for note taking. Use a web, for example, by placing a section heading in the central circle, subheadings in the radiating circles, and details around each subheading.

- **Examine the kind of information being organized.** This step will help you determine the most appropriate graphic organizer to use. Are you examining chronological events? Use a timeline. Comparing and contrasting? A Venn diagram is a good choice. Analyzing cause-and-effect relationships? Try a flowchart. Looking for the main idea and supporting details? Outlines and webs are helpful.

You can enhance both oral and written presentations by including visual representations like those that follow.

Charts, Graphs, and Tables When you are presenting numbers, statistics, or other complex data, charts, graphs, and tables can help you organize, simplify, and clarify your material.

800 • Speaking, Listening, Viewing, and Representing

⏱ TIME AND RESOURCE MANAGER

Resources
Print: *Academic and Workplace Skills Activity Book,* pp. 8–12

In-Depth Coverage	Accelerated Pace
• Read and discuss pp. 800–805 in class. • Have students work on Exercise 15 and then share their graphic organizers. • Divide students into small groups to work on Exercises 16–19.	• Assign students to read pp. 800–805 independently. • Divide students into small groups to work on Exercises 15–19.

Maps For many formal and informal uses, maps can provide beneficial visual support. They can be used to depict numerous types of information—from storm tracks to troop movements.

Diagrams, Illustrations, and Pictures Simple line drawings, diagrams, and hand-drawn pictures can visually represent a process or specific features of a topic. A graphic organizer, like the web (or cluster chart) below, can be useful in presenting information.

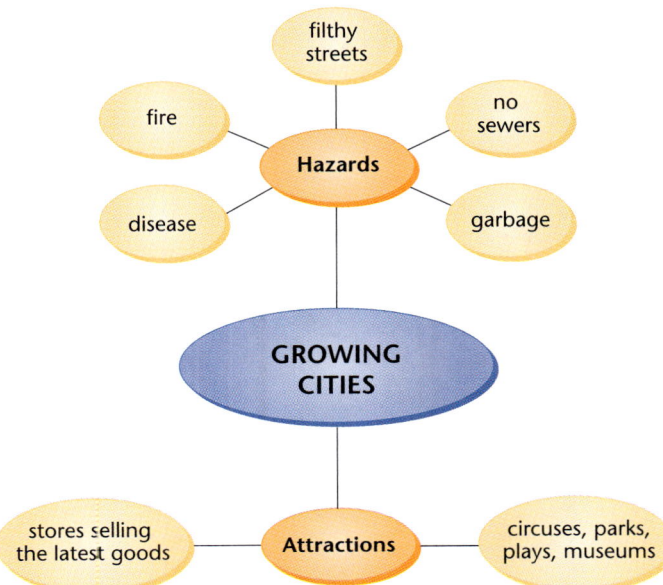

> **Exercise 15** **Creating Graphic Organizers and Visual Aids for Science and Social Studies** Select a chapter from your social studies or science textbook, and complete the following activities:
> 1. Examine the chapter content and determine what types of graphic organizers or other visual aids would best represent the information visually.
> 2. Create one graphic organizer or aid to illustrate a portion of the chapter, and present this information to your class.

> **More Practice**
> Academic and Workplace Skills Activity Book
> • p 8

Using Formatting

Teaching Resources: Academic and Workplace Skills Activity Book, p. 9

1. After students use formatting to create a visual product, have the rest of the class use the critical viewing techniques taught in this chapter to analyze it.

2. Students should examine the visual product for facts and opinions, bias, loaded language or images, slogans, repetition, and general clarity.

Real-World Connection

Provide samples of formatted information for the students to analyze (examples: flyers, posters, and brochures from various companies). Students should be able to recognize the producer, purpose, and audience for each one. Encourage students to brainstorm for a list of skills and attributes required to create these products.

Answer Key

▶ **Exercise 16**

Answers will vary. Be sure to emphasize to students the importance of accurately providing the necessary information (phone numbers, e-mail addresses, times and dates of meetings) on a flyer.

28.3

Using Formatting

With computer technology comes access to a wide choice of creative formats. From boldface to bullets, columns to clip art, word processing offers an abundance of possibilities to design clever, eye-catching visual products. To capture a reader's interest or call attention to key concepts, try some of the following features:

- Capitals or boldfaced type to call attention to headings and key words or ideas

- Italics or underlining to emphasize a line or word

- Numbered lists to indicate steps to be followed in a sequence

- Bulleted lists to highlight items that can be presented in any order

- Creative fonts to make headings or special titles stand out

- Multicolumn format, graphics, borders, clip art, and colored type to enliven any or all parts of the material

Drama Club

Get in on the Action!

Join the Drama Club
- Perform
- Direct
- Build sets
- Design costumes
- Make new friends

Come to our organizational meeting.

WHEN: Wednesday Feb. 12
3:30 P.M.
WHERE: Auditorium

Bring a friend!

▶ **Exercise 16** Using Formatting to Design a Brochure
Select a feature of your school (athletics, student council, or fine arts), a club of which you are a member, or a community group of special interest. Using the technology tips from this section and your own creative ideas, design a brochure to attract and encourage others to become involved.

Working With Multimedia

Enhance an oral report with music, artwork, charts, or a slide show or video, and you have created a multimedia presentation. In this era of advanced technology, the possibilities are limitless. Through careful planning and skillful execution, you can produce a dramatic, dynamic, and distinguished multimedia presentation.

Tips for Preparing a Multimedia Presentation

- Plan and write your presentation.
- Determine what parts of your report you wish to illustrate through the use of media.
- Select one or several media that will enhance your topic and complement each other.
- Make certain that each medium can be seen and heard clearly by all members of the audience. Use large type and images, for example, on an overhead projector, and place charts and posters within sight of everyone.
- Plan how and when you will incorporate the media into your report. Be sure to spread them throughout the presentation. If needed, ask an assistant to run the equipment.
- Write a highlighted outline of the text on note cards indicating the use of each medium.
- Carefully stage and practice the entire presentation several times. To ensure a smooth flow to the presentation, position yourself and all media items so that you can move easily among them.
- Set up in advance, making certain that all equipment is in good working condition, that volume and focus are appropriately adjusted, and that all items are positioned within sight of the entire audience.
- Create a backup plan in case the equipment malfunctions.

> **Technology Tip**
>
> Conduct a technology survey among students and adults. Interview them about the kind of word processor or desktop publisher they use and the features they enjoy most.

▲ **Critical Viewing**
What kind of medium is this student using in her report? What are some advantages of this medium? **[Analyze]**

> **Exercise 17** Preparing a Multimedia Presentation
>
> Working with two or three classmates, choose a topic of interest from science, social studies, literature, or another school subject. Following the suggestions in this section, prepare, practice, and present a dynamic multimedia report.

> **More Practice**
>
> Academic and Workplace Skills Activity Book
> • p. 10

Representing Skills • **803**

Step-by-Step Teaching Guide

Working with Multimedia

Teaching Resources: Academic and Workplace Skills Activity Book, p. 10

1. Point out to students that multimedia presentations, such as slide shows and videos, take place almost every day in school. Multimedia presentations are tools that engage the visual and auditory senses to enhance learning.
2. Remind students that visual aids should contribute to the main point, not distract from it.
3. Write the following topics on the board: *baseball, ballet, country music, Mexican food, designer clothes.* Ask students to brainstorm for the types of multimedia they could use in a presentation about each of the topics. Discuss how and why some aids may be more or less useful than others.

Customize for
AP students

Challenge students to learn something new by working with a form of media with which they are not very familiar. They might consult classmates or the school's audio-visual specialist for instruction and ideas.

Answer Key

> **Exercise 17**

Students might arrange to show their presentations to a group of interested community members after school. They can use formatting techniques to create flyers to hang around town to advertise the event.

Critical Viewing

Analyze The student is showing a transparency on an overhead projector. Using a transparency is less laborious than writing on the chalkboard and less costly than making photocopies.

☑ ONGOING ASSESSMENT: Monitor and Reinforce

If students are having trouble planning their multimedia presentations, try one of the following options.

Option 1 Have students perform simple oral presentations first. Then, the audience can suggest ways of making their presentations more interesting and dynamic by adding visual aids.	**Option 2** Have students make an approximate imitation of a multimedia presentation they have already seen. For example, they might have seen a slide show on why students should stay in school. They can use the same format, but a slightly different topic, such as why it's important to make good grades.

Creating a Video

Teaching Resources: Academic and Workplace Skills Activity Book, p. 11

1. Once students have formed groups and decided on a purpose for their video, have them narrow the focus of their project. A common problem with videos is the attempt to do too much. A narrow focus will allow them to fully explore the possibilities of the project without losing control of it. (Example: attempting to film a half-hour sitcom will most likely be an overwhelming task given the time and resource constraints. A thirty-second commercial may be a more viable project.)

2. Encourage students to divide the tasks according to the talents and interests of the group members. Some students might prefer to work on writing the script, while others might want to edit, act, videotape, or direct.

Answer Key

▶ **Exercise 18**

Challenge students to choose an issue that they feel needs some type of reform, such as welfare policy or the need for more funding for public schools. A well-done documentary may serve a positive purpose beyond the classroom. Have students share their documentaries with an audience who can make a difference. (For example, they might send the documentary about school funding to a state senator.)

28.3

Creating a Video

Whether to inform or entertain, videos are powerful communication vehicles. They may vary greatly in length and serve a wide variety of purposes, but whatever their lengths and purposes, effective videos require detailed planning and preparation.

▶ **KEY CONCEPT** Create an effective video to inform, entertain, or do both. ■

Developing a video of any length involves this basic process:

Tips for Creating a Video

1. Write a shooting script that contains not only the dialogue of the characters but also directions for camera angles, settings, costumes, and props.
2. Create a storyboard. Much like a cartoon strip, a storyboard illustrates the sequence of camera shots.
3. Select and get permission to use specific shooting sites.
4. Obtain costumes, props, music, sound effects, and any other necessities. Line up a crew to assist with any special effects.
5. Cast the roles, and hold rehearsals.
6. Plan a shooting schedule, and distribute it to the cast and crew.
7. Film the scenes. Remember to hold the camera steady, pan and zoom slowly and smoothly, and shoot more than you need. It is easier to cut than to film again.
8. Edit the video.

Storyboard

Production: Portrait of a Winner
Location: High-School Tennis Court
Scene: 2

Wide view of Tom on court practicing serves.
① Voice-over narrates.

Move in to close-up on Tom.
② Tom explains his practice.

Close-up on coach.
③ Coach's comments.

▶ **Exercise 18** **Creating a Storyboard and Documentary**

Prepare to shoot a 7- to 10-minute documentary. Create a storyboard to illustrate the sequence of events you wish to film. Follow the basic tips discussed in this section, including careful planning and rehearsing, to create a quality documentary.

▶ **More Practice**

Academic and Workplace Skills Activity Book
• p. 11

Performing and Interpreting

From ancient times to the present, the performing arts have been a dynamic and moving medium. To be an effective performer requires skill and practice.

KEY CONCEPT Plan and present an interpretive performance. ■

Tips for Preparing an Interpretive Performance Use the following strategies when preparing for a performance:

1. Study the text to understand its tone, mood, and meaning. Jot down notes, and highlight the parts you consider especially important.
2. Read the text aloud several times, experimenting with the tone, pitch, and volume of your voice. Vary these elements to achieve the desired moods and effects.
3. Memorize the text.
4. Practice the memorized text, using appropriate postures, gestures, and movements.
5. Incorporate costumes, props, sets, and music to enhance the meaning of the text.
6. Rehearse repeatedly to revise and polish. Ask another person to view your performance and offer suggestions, or make a video and critique yourself.

Exercise 19 **Preparing an Interpretive Performance** Use the steps discussed in this section to prepare a 3- to 4-minute interpretive performance of a poem or an excerpt from another work of literature.

More Practice

Academic and Workplace Skills Activity Book
• p. 12

Reflecting on Your Speaking, Listening, Viewing, and Representing

Review the concepts discussed in this chapter. Write a one-page reflection on your experiences, responding to the following questions:

- How have I increased my knowledge of the importance of good speaking and listening skills?
- What helped me to become more critical in my viewing practices?
- What kinds of visual representations have I found most beneficial in presenting information?
- What activities in this section did I find most enjoyable? Most challenging? Why?

Representing Skills • 805

Performing and Interpreting

Teaching Resources: Academic and Workplace Skills Activity Book, p. 12

1. Encourage students to choose a poem or monologue that appeals to them. Their enthusiasm will make their performance more enjoyable for them and for the audience.

2. Make sure students seek answers to questions about words with unclear meanings or pronunciations. Performers might lose credibility if they do not understand the words they are using.

Answer Key

> **Exercise 19**

Encourage students to perform an excerpt from a story or poem they read in class this year. It will be interesting to compare and contrast the interpretations of several different students.

ASSESS and CLOSE

Step-by-Step Teaching Guide

Assessment

Teaching Resources: Formal Assessment, Ch. 28

1. Use one of the Assess Mastery options provided in the Ongoing Assessment chart.

2. You may wish to use the following options
   - review the Standardized Test Preparation Workshop on pages 806–807 and have students complete the practice item.
   - administer the Chapter 28 assessment to measure students' grasp of concepts presented.

☑ **ONGOING ASSESSMENT: Assess Mastery**

Use one of the following strategies to assess mastery of speaking, listening, viewing, and representing skills.

Self-Assessment Ask students to reflect on what they've learned in this chapter. Have them write down the most useful strategy they learned for each of the four major skills.	**Teacher Assessment** You may wish to assign one of the exercises in the chapter as a "final exam" for the chapter. Assess students' presentations and their skills as critical viewers of their classmates' presentations.

Step-by-Step Teaching Guide

Interpreting Graphic Aids

Teaching Resources: Standardized Test Preparation Workbook, pp. 55–56

1. Tell students to examine a graphic aid before reading the questions that relate to it. This will make the questions more clear, because students will know exactly what they are referring to.

2. Have students examine the chart on page 807. Ask them to predict one question that might be asked about it.

3. Have students complete the practice test. Remind them to refer to the chart as often as necessary.

4. When they finish, check to see which items, if any, gave students difficulty. Discuss the answers.

Standardized Test Preparation Workshop

Interpreting Graphic Aids

Some standardized tests contain questions testing your ability to gather details, draw conclusions, and interpret from the information provided in maps, charts, graphs, and other graphic aids. The following sample items will help you become familiar with these types of questions.

Test Tip

As you examine each graphic aid, ask yourself what each part of the graphic means or represents in relation to the whole.

Sample Test Items

Directions: Read the passage and review the chart. Then, answer the questions that follow.

After the Civil War, the United States began to evolve into a new country. One area of impressive growth was the increasing number of inventions.

United States Patents Issued 1861–1900

Five-Year Periods	Number of Patents
1861–1865	20,725
1866–1870	58,734
1871–1875	60,976
1876–1880	64,462
1881–1885	97,156
1886–1890	110,358
1891–1895	108,420
1896–1900	112,188

1 During which time period shown on the chart did the number of patents issued decrease?

   A 1876–1880

   B 1886–1890

   C 1891–1895

   D 1866–1870

2 What logical conclusion could you draw about the relationship between the growth of the country and the number of patents issued?

   F As the patents increased, the population decreased.

   G As the population of the country grew, so did the number of patents.

   H People immigrated to the country from Ireland and Germany.

   J The population remained the same while a handful of inventors became more successful.

Answers and Explanations

The correct answer for item 1 is *C,* 1891–1895. During those years, 108,420 patents were issued, which were fewer than the 110,358 patents issued in the preceding five years.

The correct answer for item 2 is *G,* As the population of the country grew, so did the number of patents. This is the most logical conclusion to draw based on the information provided in the passage and the chart.

TEST-TAKING TIP

Tell students that when a test requires them to interpret a chart or graph, they should note its title, read all headings and footnotes, and pay attention to the way it is organized. They should then refer to it as they read the test items.

Students might feel intimidated by charts and graphs because they often contain highly specialized information. However, remind them that the purpose of a chart or graph is to show complicated or detailed information in a form that is easy to understand and remember.

▶ **Practice 1** **Directions:** Read the passage, and answer the questions that follow:

During the late 1800's, the country grew in size. The growing number of immigrants varied during different periods of time. Each group added a unique stitch to the American tapestry.

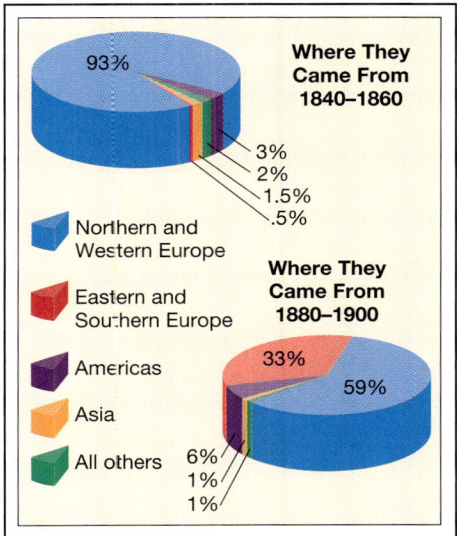

Where They Came From 1840–1860

- 93%
- 3%
- 2%
- 1.5%
- .5%

Northern and Western Europe
Eastern and Southern Europe
Americas
Asia
All others

Where They Came From 1880–1900

- 33%
- 59%
- 6%
- 1%
- 1%

1 Between 1880 and 1900, immigration most significantly increased from

  A Northern and Western Europe

  B Eastern and Southern Europe

  C Americas

  D Asia

2 Between 1840 and 1860, most immigrants came from

  F Northern and Western Europe

  G Eastern and Southern Europe

  H Americas

  J Asia

3 Which of the following would be the best interpretation of the information provided?

  A The late 1800's were a difficult time in Europe.

  B While immigration had primarily been from Northern and Western Europe from the 1840's to the 1860's, it decreased during the 1880's to 1900, and it increased from Eastern and Southern Europe and the Americas.

  C Immigration increased during the 1880's to 1900's from Asia, the Americas, and Eastern and Southern Europe while decreasing from all other areas.

  D Immigration in all areas increased in the last twenty years of the century.

4 Which of the following would be the best interpretation of the information provided?

  F More people came to the United States from Northern and Western Europe than from all other areas combined.

  G Fewer people came to the United States from Asia between 1840 and 1860 than between 1880 and 1900.

  H Immigration from the Americas had tripled by the year 1900.

  J Immigration from Northern and Western Europe was twice as high as from Eastern and Southern Europe between the years 1880 and 1900.

Answer Key

▶ **Practice 1**

1. B
2. F
3. B
4. F

Customize for
Less Advanced Students

Students sometimes feel that all of the answer choices in a multiple choice question look reasonable. To avoid this problem, encourage them to answer the question before looking at the answer choices. If their own answer matches one of the answer choices on the test, it is probably correct. Also, they can usually confirm their answer by referring to the graphic.

Customize for
AP Students

To give students practice with a graphic that uses horizontal and vertical axes, ask them to make a line or bar graph using the information in the table on page 806.

Time and Resource Manager

In-Depth Lesson Plan

	LESSON FOCUS	PRINT AND MEDIA RESOURCES
DAY 1	**Developing Vocabulary** Students learn strategies for developing vocabulary, such as wide reading, context clues, connotation and denotation, and analogies. (pp. 809–813)	*Teaching Resources* *Academic and Workplace Skills Activity Book,* pp. 13–16
DAY 2	**Studying Words Systematically; Studying Word Parts and Origins** Students learn and apply strategies for studying vocabulary words. (pp. 814–819)	*Teaching Resources* *Academic and Workplace Skills Activity Book,* pp. 17–22
DAY 3	**Improving Your Spelling** Students learn strategies for improving spelling, such as studying problem words, keeping a spelling notebook, and applying spelling rules. (pp. 820–823)	*Teaching Resources* *Academic and Workplace Skills Activity Book,* pp. 23–25
DAY 4	**Improving Your Spelling** *continued* Students learn strategies for improving spelling words with confusing endings and for proofreading carefully. (pp. 824–829)	*Teaching Resources* *Academic and Workplace Skills Activity Book,* pp. 26–29; *Formal Assessment,* Ch. 29

Accelerated Lesson Plan

	LESSON FOCUS	PRINT AND MEDIA RESOURCES
DAY 1	**Developing Vocabulary** Students learn and apply strategies for developing vocabulary. (pp. 809–813)	*Teaching Resources* *Academic and Workplace Skills Activity Book,* pp. 13–16
DAY 2	**Studying Words Systematically; Studying Word Parts and Origins** Students learn and apply strategies for studying vocabulary words. (pp. 814–819)	*Teaching Resources* *Academic and Workplace Skills Activity Book,* pp. 17–22
DAY 3	**Improving Your Spelling** Students learn and apply strategies for improving spelling and for proofreading carefully. (pp. 820–829)	*Teaching Resources* *Academic and Workplace Skills Activity Book,* pp. 23–29; *Formal Assessment,* Ch. 29

Options for Adapting Lesson Plans

HOMEWORK

Have students complete any section of the chapter for homework.

FEATURES

Extend coverage with the Standardized Test Preparation Workshop (p. 830).

TECHNOLOGY

Students may use the Internet to conduct independent research. Have them print out their completed work.

INTEGRATED SKILLS COVERAGE

Integrating Research Skills
SE pp. 810, 814
ATE p. 825

Viewing and Representing
Critical Viewing, SE pp. 808, 810, 814, 821

Technology
SE pp. 815, 821
ATE p. 822

Speaking
ATE p. 822

Study Skills
ATE p. 828

Real-World Connection
ATE p. 829

ASSESSMENT SUPPORT

Standardized Test Preparation Workshop SE p. 830;
ATE p. 823

Standardized Test Preparation Workbook, Ch. 29

Formal Assessment, Ch. 29

MEETING INDIVIDUAL NEEDS

Less Advanced Students ATE pp. 816, 826, 828, 831. See also
Ongoing Assessments ATE pp. 813, 815, 819.

ESL Students pp. 815, 819, 825, 831

AP Students ATE pp. 812, 817, 823

Gifted and Talented Students ATE p. 826

Visual/Spatial Learners ATE p. 820

BLOCK SCHEDULING

Pacing Suggestions
For 90-minute Blocks
- Have students complete the strategies for developing vocabulary and studying words in a single period.
- Focus one class period on spelling strategies and proofreading carefully.

Professional Development Support
- **How to Manage Instruction in the Block** This Teaching Resource provides management and activity suggestions.

MEDIA AND TECHNOLOGY

For the Teacher
- **Resource Pro** CD-ROM

WRITING AND GRAMMAR WEB SITE

The Interactive Writing and Grammar Web Site provides a wide array of support for students, teachers, and parents.

www.phschool.com

▶ *Lesson Objectives*

1. To expand vocabulary through wide reading, listening, and discussing

2. To rely on context to determine meanings of words and phrases and to discriminate between connotative and denotative meanings

3. To recognize synonyms, antonyms, and homophones

4. To read and understand analogies

5. To use reference material, such as a dictionary or thesaurus, to determine precise meaning and usage

6. To learn techniques for remembering the meanings of new words

7. To apply meanings of prefixes, roots, and suffixes in order to comprehend

8. To research word origins as an aid to understanding meanings, derivations, and spellings as well as influences on the English language

9. To recognize problem words

10. To learn techniques to improve spelling and proofreading

Critical Viewing

Deduce By reading a variety of texts, students will encounter many unfamiliar words, including special words related to specific subjects (such as biology, mathematics, and history).

Vocabulary and Spelling

▲ **Critical Viewing**
In what ways does reading a variety of texts increase your vocabulary? **[Deduce]**

If you compared the vocabulary and spelling abilities you possess today with those of your middle-school years, you would see a significant difference. As your reading has increased, the number of words you understand and are able to spell has substantially increased as well.

Your reading vocabulary—the words you are able to understand from your reading—will almost always be greater than the vocabulary you use in conversation. Working to increase your vocabulary is useful in three ways: You can get information from the textbooks you read, you can use words to communicate effectively in your writing, and you can speak precisely and persuasively. By improving your spelling, you can give your reader a better understanding of your ideas and the message you want to convey.

808 • Vocabulary and Spelling

⏱ TIME AND RESOURCE MANAGER

Resources
Print: *Academic and Workplace Skills Activity Book*, pp. 13–16

In-Depth Coverage	Accelerated Pace
• Cover pp. 808–813 in class. • Discuss types of context and do Exercise 1 in class. • Assign Exercises 2–3 for homework. • Do Exercise 4 in class, creating a test sentence for each pair of capitalized words.	• Discuss pp. 808–813 with the class. • Assign Exercises 1–4 for students to complete independently.

Developing Vocabulary

Section 29.1

One of the most valuable tools you can ever hope to own is a well-developed vocabulary. Words are for communication, written and spoken. Developing techniques for building your vocabulary is a worthwhile occupation.

Listening, Discussing, and Wide Reading

Whether you know it or not, you have been accumulating words since the day you were born. A child just beginning school has a vocabulary of about 13,000 words. A literate adult speaker of English has a vocabulary of approximately 60,000 words. Most of the new words a person learns are learned through listening, discussing, and reading.

▶ **KEY CONCEPT** The most common ways to increase your vocabulary are listening, reading, and taking part in conversations. ■

Listen for and Use New Words When you were a toddler, you didn't know very many words. Your vocabulary increased, however, at a rapid pace as you learned words for the things and people around you. First, you heard the words spoken. Then, you learned to repeat them. Eventually, you were able to put the words into sentences and hold conversations.

Listening and discussing are good ways to expand your vocabulary even now. Listening in class, chatting with other people, watching television, listening to the radio, and listening to recorded works of literature and speeches are all ways to expose yourself to new words. When you hear an unfamiliar word, jot it down and look it up in a dictionary. Try to use the word in conversation. This will put it into your vocabulary.

Wide Reading Another excellent way to build your vocabulary is by reading. Try to read a wide variety of books and magazines. When you encounter unfamiliar words or familiar words used in new ways, jot them down and look them up in a dictionary.

Textbooks, newspapers, magazines, novels, and articles on the Internet can all be good resources for extending your vocabulary.

Recognizing Context Clues

Teaching Resources: Academic and Workplace Skills Activity Book, p. 13

1. Point out that, while the term *context* is defined as the words surrounding a word, students can often take advantage of an even larger context than that. Often, thinking about the subject being read (for example, science or literature) contributes to the process of determining a word's meaning.

2. Explain that one way to infer meaning when definitions are not given is to *find, substitute,* and *confirm.* First, *find* other words in the sentence that give clues, then *substitute* familiar words in the sentence to *confirm* that the inference works in context.

3. Write these sentences on the board and have the class find context clues and infer meanings for the words *astute* and *trepidation.*

   Although young, the boy was an astute buyer. He noted the price, considered the value of the product, then calculated how much he had already spent. (shrewd, wise)

   The children watched with trepidation as firemen attempted to rescue their mother from the burning building. (concern; fear)

4. Point out that, while context clues are helpful, it is always wise to check a dictionary to confirm meaning.

Critical Viewing

Infer Answers will vary, but might include reading the word in context, considering the subject, or even checking to see if there is a glossary.

Answer Key

> **Exercise 1**

Wording will vary, but should reflect something of the following ideas:

- discourse: *communication*
- expository: *explanatory*
- critique: *analysis*
- résumé: *summary of qualifications*
- peripheral: *outside the bounds of what is needed*

810

29.1

Recognizing Context Clues

The **context** of a word refers to the group of words surrounding it. When you encounter an unfamiliar word in your reading, you can make inferences about its meaning by looking for context clues in the surrounding words.

> **KEY CONCEPT** Use context clues to determine the meaning of unfamiliar words in your reading. ■

Types of Context Clues The following is a list of several types of context clues. Study them, so you can later recognize the ways in which surrounding words can give you clues to the meaning of unfamiliar words.

Formal Definition: Gives the actual meaning of the word.

Familiar Words: Words a reader may know help provide a word's meaning.

Compare and Contrast: Presents an idea or concept that is either clearly similar or clearly opposite to the unfamiliar word's meaning.

Synonyms and Antonyms: Use words with similar meanings (synonyms) or opposite meanings (antonyms) to give the meanings of unfamiliar words.

EXAMPLE: Because the patient was *debilitated* by both the illness and the medication, his doctor recommended physical therapy to strengthen him.

Familiar words in the sentence give clues: *Medication* and *illness* suggest a weakened condition; *therapy* and *strengthen* confirm this idea.

> **Exercise 1** **Using Context Clues in General Reading**

Use context clues to determine the meaning of each underlined word. Check your answers in a dictionary.

Within the range of written <u>discourse</u>, there are several kinds of writing. One type of writing is called <u>expository</u> because it explains ideas in a sequence. Another kind, a <u>critique</u>, examines the strengths and weaknesses of a specific work.

Another form of writing that is useful in job seeking is called a <u>résumé</u>, which includes information about a job applicant's education and previous employment. Information other than these details is considered <u>peripheral</u> and should not be listed.

810 • Vocabulary and Spelling

Research Tip

Find a book about art history in the library. Locate three sentences in the book that provide context clues that help to determine the meaning of a word. Add the new words to your notebook.

▼ **Critical Viewing**
How might a student such as this one figure out the meaning of unfamiliar words in his textbook? **[Infer]**

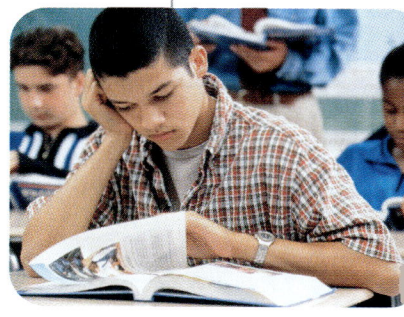

Denotation and Connotation

Context can help you determine a word's exact meaning. Knowing the denotations and connotations of a word can help you discriminate between shades of meaning.

KEY CONCEPT The denotation of a word is its literal definition. Its connotations include the ideas, images, and feelings that are associated with the word in people's minds. ■

The dictionary defines a patriot as "one who loves and loyally or zealously supports one's own country." That is just the definition of the word. But what comes to mind when you hear the word *patriot*? You may think of words such as *soldier, pride,* and *self-sacrifice.* You may picture a minuteman in a tricorn hat. You may think of Nathan Hale who regreted that he had but one life to give for his country. You may think of Betsy Ross sewing a flag for a new nation. All of these are connotations associated with the word *patriot.* As you strengthen your vocabulary, be aware of both positive and negative connotations of the words you use.

Exercise 2 **Discriminating Between Denotation and Connotation** Read each pair of sentences below. For each pair, write a sentence explaining the different connotations of the underlined words. Use a dictionary to help you.

1. George Washington <u>implored</u> the American people to accept the new Constitution.
   George Washington <u>begged</u> the American people to accept the new Constitution.
2. Patriotic leaders began a <u>campaign</u> to ensure ratification.
   Patriotic leaders began a <u>crusade</u> to ensure ratification.
3. On foot, on horseback, and by coach, these <u>indomitable</u> men traveled to farms, villages, and cities.
   On foot, on horseback, and by coach, these <u>stubborn</u> men traveled to farms, villages, and cities.
4. They went from town to town to explain the <u>gist</u> of the Constitution.
   They went from town to town to explain the <u>significance</u> of the Constitution.
5. They spread their message with enthusiasm and <u>fervor</u>.
   They spread their message with enthusiasm and <u>eagerness</u>.

More Practice

Academic and Workplace Skills Activity Book
• p. 14

Denotation and Connotation

Teaching Resources: Academic and Workplace Skills Activity Book, p.14

1. Point out that, not only can context help a reader determine a word's meaning, the connotation of a word, once determined, can help the reader determine the writer's tone and understand the meaning of the whole passage.
2. Tell students that in many cases, experience and context are the only ways to determine subtle differences between words with similar meanings (such as *profuseness* and *prodigality*), but generally the dictionary will be their greatest ally, giving both definitions and, in many cases, synonym studies.

Answer Key

Exercise 2

Answers will vary, but should reflect the following ideas:

1. Both words mean to ask earnestly for, but *begged* is more informal, while *implored* is more formal and adds to the idea warm feeling and great humility.
2. Both are series of activities aimed at achieving a goal, but a *crusade* has the added dimension of implying a goal of overcoming some evil.
3. While *indomitable* has the positive connotation of standing firm, *stubborn* has a more negative connotation of standing firm because one is obstinate, rather than brave and spirited.
4. *Gist* is more vague—one gets the general idea—while *significance* means one gets the meaning and understands the importance.
5. *Eagerness* implies being impatient or excited, while *fervor* means intensely emotional, showing great warmth; *fervor* is more passionate than *eagerness*.

Recognizing Related Words

Teaching Resources: Academic and Workplace Skills Activity Book, p. 15

1. Ask students to define *synonym*, *antonym*, and *homophone*.

2. Point out that synonyms and antonyms, besides helping students remember meanings, can also enliven their writing. For example, instead of repeating that someone is smart, they could use synonyms such as *intelligent*, *learned*, *erudite*, *bright*, or *gifted*. Or if a character had negative traits, knowing that the opposite of *merciful* is *ruthless* could add depth to the writing.

3. Put a word such as *pretty* on the board and give students one minute to brainstorm for as many synonyms as they can. Repeat for antonyms. Write their answers on the board.

4. Explain to students that homophones are not related words and will not help them discover meaning, but they can confuse readers. Homophones are important to recognize because they are a common trap for writers, who might use a word that sounds right but use the wrong form (*they're, their, there*; *steak, stake*; *sheer, shear*).

Customize for
AP Students

Relate to students that, like homophones, homonyms also sound alike. Sometimes they are spelled differently, but homonyms are often spelled exactly alike. The key is the different origins and meanings. Have students look up the different definitions and origins of *curry, compound, lap, mail, pen, shore, pound*.

Answer Key

Exercise 3

1. antonyms	6. antonyms
2. homophones	7. synonyms
3. synonyms	8. synonyms
4. antonyms	9. synonyms
5. homophones	10. synonyms

Recognizing Related Words

Discovering how words can relate to other words is a good way to increase your vocabulary. For example, many words have *synonyms*, *antonyms*, and *homophones*.

> **KEY CONCEPT** **Synonyms** are words that are similar in meaning. **Antonyms** are words that are opposite in meaning. **Homophones** are words that sound alike but have different meanings and spellings. ■

Synonyms Synonyms can help you remember the meaning of a word, for it is often easier to remember a one-word synonym than to remember a long dictionary definition. For example, you may be able to remember the word *countenance* by remembering its synonym, *face*.

Antonyms Knowing an antonym for a word—its opposite meaning—can give you a clue about the word's meaning. To remember that the word *fervent* means "impassioned," for example, try to recall that its antonym is *indifferent*.

Homophones It is important to recognize words that are homophones—words that sound alike but have different meanings and spellings—so you can use their correct forms in your writing. You would, for example, want to make sure that you did not confuse the words *waste* ("discarded material") and *waist* (a part of the body). Although the words have the same pronunciation, they have different meanings and spellings.

> **Exercise 3** Recognizing Synonyms, Antonyms, and Homophones Identify each pair of words below as *synonyms*, *antonyms*, or *homophones*.
> 1. garrulous/taciturn
> 2. capitol/capital
> 3. malign/vilify
> 4. rash/calculating
> 5. whole/hole
> 6. frugal/wasteful
> 7. garish/gaudy
> 8. sardonic/cynical
> 9. avid/eager
> 10. relinquish/abandon

Using Related Words in Analogies

Working with *analogies*, a type of word problem often found on standardized tests, strengthens your vocabulary by increasing your understanding of connections between word meanings. It will also benefit you to practice analogies because they are typical items found in aptitude and achievement tests.

KEY CONCEPT **Analogies** present a pair of words that have some relationship to each other. ■

Look at the following analogy, and see whether you can find the pair of words whose relationship is the most similar to the capitalized pair:

EXAMPLE: MYTH : STORY ::
             a. flower : redness
             b. literature : poetry
             c. bonnet : hat

The answer is **C**.

The way to solve analogies is to form a clear idea of the relationship between the capitalized words. In this example, the relationship between the words is *type*—a *myth* is a type of *story*. A *flower* is not a type of *redness*. *Literature* is not a type of *poetry*; although poetry is a type of literature, that is not what the analogy states. A *bonnet*, however, is a type of *hat*. Other common analogy relationships include *part to whole*, *defining characteristic*, *instrument*, *degree*, and *sequence*.

Exercise 4 **Working With Analogies** First, identify the analogy relationship expressed in the capitalized pair. Then, choose the lettered pair that best expresses this relationship.
1. PEACH : FRUIT ::
   a. vegetable : apple   b. peas : beans
   c. turnip : vegetable
2. BOUQUET : FLOWER ::
   a. key : door   b. chain : link
   c. skin : body
3. JOY : ECSTASY ::
   a. admiration : love   b. life : hope
   c. happiness : sorrow
4. CARPENTER : HAMMER ::
   a. doctor : surgeon   b. woodsman : axe
   c. attorney : judge
5. MARMALADE : ORANGE ::
   a. lemons : fruit   b. ketchup : tomato
   c. jelly : jam

⟳ Learn More

For more practice with analogies, see the Standardized Test Preparation Workshop on page 362.

▶ More Practice

Academic and Workplace Skills Activity Book
• p. 16

Developing Your Vocabulary • **813**

Step-by-Step Teaching Guide

Using Related Words in Analogies

Teaching Resources: Academic and Workplace Skills Activity Book, p. 16

1. Point out to students that they have probably encountered the term *analogy* before. Speakers and writers often say or write, "Let me give you an analogy," and then make a comparison that illustrates their point.

2. *Analogy* indicates that "one thing is similar to another." On *analogy tests*, students are asked to recognize a relationship between two words; they must then select another pair of words that have a similar relationship.

3. Suggest that students ask themselves the following questions when faced with an analogy test:

   How are the two words different?

   How are they similar?

   What is the relationship of one to the other—part-to-whole, type, defining characteristic, instrument, degree, or sequence?

4. Emphasize that analogies should be as precise as possible. For example, *wing* is a part of a *bird* and *head* is a part of a *human*, so it seems like a part-to-whole analogy, but *wing* is not analogous to *head*—it would be more analogous to *arm*.

Answer Key

▶ **Exercise 4**

1. A *peach* is a type of fruit. C is correct; a *turnip* is a type of vegetable.
2. A *bouquet* is made up of flowers. B is correct; a *chain* is made up of links.
3. *Ecstasy* is a form of joy. A is correct; *love* is a form of admiration.
4. A *hammer* is a tool used by a carpenter. B is correct; an *axe* is a tool used by a woodsman.
5. *Marmalade* can be made from oranges. B is correct; *ketchup* can be made from tomatoes.

✓ ONGOING ASSESSMENT: Monitor and Reinforce

If you observe that students are having difficulty with Exercise 3 or 4, try the following strategies.

| **Option 1** Have students work in pairs on Exercise 3, using a dictionary to define the words and a thesaurus to find synonyms. | **Option 2** Ask students to suggest pairs of words in the following format: "X is to Y . . ." and have volunteers complete the phrase by suggesting an appropriate analogy: ". . . as A is to B." Then have them explain why the two pairs are analogous. |

Step-by-Step Teaching Guide

Using Resource Materials

Teaching Resources: Academic and Workplace Skills Activity Book, p. 17

1. Stress that, for effective communication, it is important to be precise in selecting words. Dictionaries make this possible.

2. Point out the four types of information found in most dictionary entries: pronunciation, part of speech, meaning, and etymology.

3. Explain that a thesaurus supplies words that are similar in meaning to the word that is looked up.

Answer Key

> **Exercise 5**

Wording will differ but should reflect the following ideas:

1. *trajectory*—the curved path of a projectile, comet, or planet
2. *repudiate*—1) refuse to accept; reject 2) refuse to acknowledge or pay
3. *salubrious*—favorable or conducive to good health; healthful
4. *impart*—1) give or share part of; give 2) communicate; tell
5. *quiescent*—quiet and motionless

> **Exercise 6**

Responses will vary; examples are given.

1. *censor*—The <u>examiner</u> perused the letters for signs of hidden messages.
2. *harmony*—The twin brothers shared a quiet <u>compatibility</u>.
3. *benign*—The doctor removed the <u>harmless</u>, but unsightly, growth.
4. *foment*—The rabble-rousers tried to <u>evoke</u> violence from the crowd.
5. *audacity*—The <u>boldness</u> of the sales pitch made me fear dishonesty.

Critical Viewing

Infer Students may suggest that the student is using a dictionary or thesaurus.

Section 29.2

Studying Words Systematically

Using Resource Materials

There are many useful materials you can use, either in print or on-line. In either form, two of the most valuable tools are a dictionary and a thesaurus.

> **KEY CONCEPT** Use a **dictionary** to find the meaning, spelling, pronunciation, and origin of words. Use a **thesaurus** to find words that most precisely express your meaning. ■

Use a Dictionary You should make it a habit to consult a dictionary every time you come across an unfamiliar word. It is a good idea to keep a dictionary nearby, where you can easily access it. When you look up a word in a dictionary, make use of the information that appears with the definition:

- Study the pronunciation given in parentheses after the word. If you can pronounce a word, you are more likely to use it.
- Note the word's part of speech, which appears as an abbreviation (*n.*, *v.*, *adj.*). A word can change its meaning, depending upon its usage.
- Note the origin of the word (its etymology), which usually appears after the part of speech.
- Read all the many meanings given for a word.

Use a Thesaurus A thesaurus helps increase your vocabulary. If you have used the same word several times, you can use a thesaurus to find a new word that is, perhaps, more interesting and more expressive. Be sure to check the meaning of the new word to see whether it fulfills your purpose in writing.

Research Tip

Choose five words, and use a thesaurus to find a synonym for each of them. Then, use a dictionary to see whether there are any subtle differences between each word and its synonym.

▲ **Critical Viewing** What study tools might this student be using? [**Infer**]

> **Exercise 5** **Using a Dictionary to Increase Your Vocabulary** Look up each word below in a dictionary, and write its definition or definitions.
> 1. trajectory   3. salubrious   5. quiescent
> 2. repudiate   4. impart

> **Exercise 6** **Using a Thesaurus to Increase Your Vocabulary** In a thesaurus, find a word similar to each word below. Use each new word in a sentence.
> 1. censor   3. benign   5. audacity
> 2. harmony   4. foment

814 • Vocabulary and Spelling

⏱ TIME AND RESOURCE MANAGER

Resources
Print: *Academic and Workplace Skills Activity Book*, pp. 17–18

In-Depth Coverage	Accelerated Pace
• Cover pp. 814–815 in class. • Have students do Exercises 5–6 in class. Share results. • Assign Exercise 7 for homework.	• Discuss pp. 814–815 with the class. • Assign Exercises 5–7 for students to complete independently.

Remembering Vocabulary Words

In addition to a dictionary and a thesaurus, there are other study aids that you can use to add words to your vocabulary.

KEY CONCEPT Use a variety of techniques to remember the meanings of new words. ■

Use a Vocabulary Notebook Divide your page into three columns with the following headings: the *word* you want to learn; a *bridge* word, or hint to help you remember the word's meaning; and the word's *definition*.

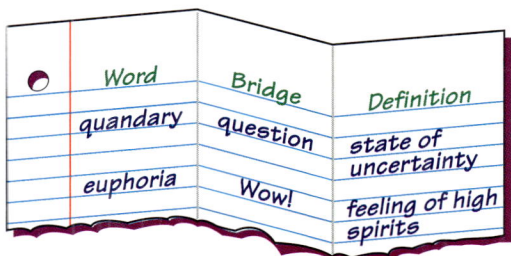

Word	Bridge	Definition
quandary	question	state of uncertainty
euphoria	Wow!	feeling of high spirits

Use Flashcards and a Tape Recorder On the front of an index card, write a word you want to remember and a bridge word. On the back, write the definition. Then, flip through the cards, supplying the definitions for the words. Use the bridge word to assist you. Continue in this method until you can correctly define all the words.

Record a vocabulary word into a tape recorder. Leave a space of about five seconds, and then give the definition. Continue in this way with all your words. Then, replay the tape, filling in each blank space with the word's definition. Keep replaying the tape until you can give all the definitions easily.

Work With a Partner Using flashcards and vocabulary notebooks, take turns quizzing each other on vocabulary. In the first round, read the words and have your partner define them. If your partner is slow to respond, provide the bridge word. Repeat the words until your partner can correctly define all of them. In the second round, exchange roles.

Exercise 7 Adding New Words to Your Vocabulary
Identify five unfamiliar words from each of your major subjects. Enter the words and their definitions in your vocabulary notebook. Study the words using one of the above methods. Then, test yourself by using each word in a sentence.

Technology Tip

Find a short entry about an unfamiliar technical subject in an on-line encyclopedia. Find an unfamiliar word, look it up in a dictionary, and add it to your notebook.

More Practice

Academic and Workplace Skills Activity Book
• p. 18

Studying Words Systematically • **815**

Step-by-Step Teaching Guide

Remembering Vocabulary Words

Teaching Resources: Academic and Workplace Skills Activity Book, p. 18

1. Explain that writing things down has been shown to be one of the most effective ways of learning and remembering something.

2. Another effective tool for remembering things is a *mnemonic aid*, a clue or trigger idea that helps you remember things.

3. Point out that this idea for a vocabulary notebook combines two effective memory techniques: writing down and creating a mnemonic aid.

4. Encourage students to keep a notebook of words they particularly like but might not be able to use every day.

5. Ask students if they have ever used flash cards or a tape recorder as a memory aid. Why would these be helpful? (Repetition is very important in processing information into long-term memory.)

6. Supply cards or ask students to bring them to class. Have students select words they want to remember (they might start with the ones in Exercises 1–3, or you might suggest or assign a list based on literature or other topics being covered in class). Suggest they try the flashcard or tape recorder ideas in the text with these words.

7. Give students some class time during the week to practice with a partner, quizzing each other on the words they have selected.

Customize for ESL Students

Instead of assigning Exercise 7, ask students to create a vocabulary notebook by collecting a list of ten to fifteen new words they hear or see during one week. Suggest that the bridge word could be a word in their native language.

Answer Key

Exercise 7

Answers will vary, depending on the words students choose.

ONGOING ASSESSMENT: Monitor and Reinforce

If you observe that students are having difficulty with Exercises 5, 6, or 7, try the following strategy.

Have students work in pairs. Students take turns suggesting a word (if necessary, the word can be picked at random from the dictionary), and the partner has the option of looking it up and giving a definition or finding it in the thesaurus to select a synonym. Then each student should use the word in a sentence.

Using Prefixes

Teaching Resources: Academic and Workplace Skills Activity Book, p. 19

1. Point out that even the word "prefix" has a prefix—*pre-,* which means "before in rank or time." It indicates that a prefix is fixed (attached) to the front of a word. Suggest that students add *pre-* to their lists of prefixes, along with the opposite of *pre-,* which is *post-,* as in *postscript.*

2. Explain that knowing prefixes helps, but context must be considered, too. Some words look as if they have these prefixes, but have different origins (e.g., *opaque* comes from a Greek word, *opacus,* and doesn't use the Latin *op-)* or are close but unrelated (Latin *ante-* means "before," but may be confused with Greek *anti-).*

3. Suggest that students make flash cards or other memory aids for prefixes, and use them to practice.

4. Urge students to add prefixes to the list as they find them.

Customize for
Less Advanced Students

Ask students to use a dictionary to find each of the ten common prefixes and any others you wish them to learn. Have students copy the dictionary entry for each word, and then find one or two words to illustrate the prefix's use.

Answer Key

Exercise 8

1. *monoplane*—an airplane with one pair of wings
2. *interpose*—to place something in between
3. *addendum*—a part added to the original
4. *obtrude*—thrust forward
5. *expunge*—blot out
6. *misanthrope*—one who hates or distrusts all people
7. *inexpert*—not expert
8. *overextend*—to extend beyond reasonable capabilities
9. *interchangeable*—able to be switched between two situations
10. *confabulate*—talk together

Studying Word Parts and Origins

You can improve your vocabulary by learning about word structure, or the parts that make up a word. The three word parts that can combine to form a word are a root (such as *-duc-* in pro*duc*tion), a prefix (such as *pro-* in *pro*duction), and a suffix (such as *-tion* in produc*tion*). Many of these word parts come from the Latin, Greek, and Anglo-Saxon languages.

Learning Prefixes

A prefix is one or more syllables at the beginning of a word.

▶ **KEY CONCEPT** The prefix adds to the meaning of the root. ■

Prefixes Learn the meanings and origins of the prefixes below. The abbreviations *L., Gr.,* and *A.S.* mean Latin, Greek, and Anglo-Saxon, the languages from which the prefixes have come.

TEN COMMON PREFIXES

Prefix and Origin	Meaning	Examples
ad- (ac-, af-, al-, ap-, as-, at-) [L.]	to, toward	*ad*join, *af*fix, *al*lure, *ap*point
anti- [Gr.]	against	*anti*pathy
com- (co-, col-, con-, cor-) [L.]	with, together	*com*press, *con*tribute
ex- (e-, ec-, ef-) [L.]	forth, from, out	*ex*press, *e*migrate
in- (il-, im-, ir-) [L.]	not	*in*human, *il*legal
inter- [L.]	between	*inter*national
mis- [A.S.]	wrong	*mis*place
mono- [Gr.]	alone, one	*mono*poly
ob- (o-, oc-, of-, op-) [L.]	toward, against	*ob*ject, *o*mit, *oc*casion, *of*fer
over- [A.S.]	above, in excess	*over*flow

▶ **Exercise 8** **Defining Words With Prefixes** Using your knowledge of prefixes, figure out the meaning of each word below. Then, check your answers in a dictionary.

1. *mono*plane
2. *inter*pose
3. *ad*dendum
4. *ob*trude
5. *ex*punge
6. *mis*anthrope
7. *in*expert
8. *over*extend
9. *inter*changeable
10. *con*fabulate

816 • Vocabulary and Spelling

⏱ TIME AND RESOURCE MANAGER

Resources
Print: *Academic and Workplace Skills Activity Book,* pp. 19–22

In-Depth Coverage	Accelerated Pace
• Cover pages 816–819. • Do Exercises 8–14 in class. • Find a book on interesting word origins and bring it to class. Share some of the more unusual stories.	• Assign reading of pp. 816–819 for homework. Discuss in class. • Assign exercises for students to complete independently.

Learning Roots

Teaching Resources: Academic and Workplace Skills Activity Book, p. 20

1. Point out that several examples of free roots are listed in the prefix chart (*join* of adjoin, *lure* of allure, *migrate* of emigrate, etc.).

2. If the dictionaries you use in class do not spell out the derivations of words (*Old English* vs. *OE*), show students where they can find a list of the abbreviations used.

3. Demonstrate to students how knowing both the root and the prefix can help them determine meaning. For example, using -*ject* from the list, ask what *project* and *interject* might mean (throw forward, throw between). Have them compare these guesses with the real meanings.

4. Have students look up the elements of sympathy and antipathy to further illustrate how this works.

Customize for
AP Students

Ask students to think of words that include the following roots, then look up the words and find the meaning and origin of the roots (e.g., for *morph, morphology* or *amorphous*). Have them then use the word in a sentence.

vert   pan   tract   junct   morph

Answer Key

▶ **Exercise 9**

Examples will vary.

1. *ab-,* Latin, meaning *away, from,* or *down,* as in abdicate.
2. *dis-,* Old French or Latin, meaning *away* or *apart,* as in dismiss.
3. *epi-,* Greek, meaning *on, over, beside,* or *among,* as in epidemic.
4. *sub-,* Latin, meaning *under, beneath,* or *below,* as in submarine.
5. *pro-,* Latin, meaning *moving forward* or *ahead of,* as in progress.

▶ **Exercise 10**

1. to go
2. to lead
3. to drive or beat
4. to stretch
5. to bring or carry

Exercise 9 Defining Prefixes and Prefix Origins Using a dictionary, write the definition of each prefix and its origin. Then, provide an example for each prefix.

1. ab- (a-, abs-)   3. epi-   5. pro-
2. dis- (di-, dif-)   4. sub- (sic-, suf-, sup-)

Learning Roots

The root of a word contains its basic meaning. Learning roots is the foundation for developing your vocabulary.

KEY CONCEPT The **root** carries the word's basic meaning. ■

Roots Roots that stand alone are *free* roots. Roots that need a prefix or suffix are *bound* roots, like most of the roots in the following chart. The abbreviations *L.* and *Gr.* mean Latin and Greek.

TEN COMMON ROOTS

Root and Origin	Meaning	Examples
-cap- (-capt-, -cept-, -ceipt-, -ceive-, -cip-) [L.]	to take, seize	capable, captivate, accept, receipt, receive, recipient
-fac- (-fact-, -fec-, -fect-, -fic-) [L.]	to do, make	facsimile, manufacture, infection, defect, fiction
-ject- [L.]	to throw	reject
-leg- (-log-) [Gr.]	to say, speak	legal, logic
-plic- (-pli-, -ploy-, -ply-) [L.]	to fold	duplicate, pliable, employ, reply
-pon- (-pos-) [L.]	to put, place	postpone, deposit
-quir- (-ques-, -quis-) [L.]	to ask, say	inquire, question, inquisitive
-sist- [L.]	to stand	insist
-string- (-strict-) [L.]	to bind, tighten	stringent, constrict
-vad- (-vas-) [L.]	to go	invade, evasive

Exercise 10 Finding Common Roots Look up each set of words in the dictionary, paying close attention to the word's root, shown in italics. Then, write the basic meaning shared by each pair of words.

1. procedure, proceed   4. extension, extent
2. produce, reduce   5. transfer, inference
3. pulsate, propel

Studying Word Parts and Origins • 817

Using Suffixes

Teaching Resources: Academic and Workplace Skills Activity Book, p. 21

1. Review the definition of *suffix* and emphasize that suffixes change both the word form and the part of speech.

2. Have students look at the examples in the chart and identify the original form of the word to which the suffix was added (e.g., *maniac/mania; scenic/scene; defiant/defy*; etc.). Have them name the part of speech of the original words (will always be different than the part of speech identified on the chart).

Answer Key

Exercise 11

1. e
2. a
3. b
4. c
5. d

Exercise 12

1. *-ance,* Latin, used to form nouns, meaning an act or fact of ___ing, e.g., an *utterance* is an act of uttering, or quality or state of being ___ed, e.g., *annoyance* is a state of being annoyed.
2. *-ate,* Latin, used to form adjectives, verbs, and nouns, several meanings, including to become, as in *evaporate.*
3. *-ist,* Greek, used to form nouns, meaning a person who does or practices, such as *moralist* or *botanist.*
4. *-ive,* Latin, used to form adjectives, meaning of or relating to, such as *inductive* or *creative.*
5. *-or,* Latin, used to form nouns, meaning a person or thing that ___s, such as *inventor,* a person who invents.

Exercise 13

1. defective
2. attendance
3. inducement
4. defensive
5. minimize

> **Exercise 11** **Using Roots to Define Words** Write down each word, paying close attention to the word's root, shown in italics. Then, write the letter of the word's meaning next to each word.

1. pro*fic*ient   a. to move something to a different place
2. trans*pose*   b. an introduction to a written work
3. pro*logue*   c. to capture the attention or affection of
4. *capt*ivate   d. to take in or admit
5. re*cept*ive   e. highly competent

Using Suffixes

When a suffix is added to a root, the word's part of speech usually changes.

> **KEY CONCEPT** The **suffix,** which is added to the end of the root, can change the word's meaning or part of speech. ■

Suffixes Suffixes are unique in that they change both word forms and parts of speech. In the chart, the abbreviations *L., Gr.,* and *A.S.* mean Latin, Greek, and Anglo-Saxon.

TEN COMMON SUFFIXES		
Suffix and Origin	**Meaning and Examples**	**Part of Speech**
-ac (-ic) [Gr.]	characteristic of: mani*ac*, scen*ic*	noun or adjective
-ant (-ent) [L.]	that shows, has, or does: defi*ant*, depend*ent*	noun or adjective
-ful [A.S.]	full of: scorn*ful*	adjective
-fy [L.]	to cause to become: clari*fy*	verb
-ish [A.S.]	of, tending to: fool*ish*	adjective
-ism [Gr.]	act, practice, or result of: tru*ism*	noun
-ity [L.]	state of being: advers*ity*	noun
-ize (-ise) [Gr.]	to make: idol*ize*	verb
-ous (-ious) [L.]	marked by, given to: pomp*ous*	adjective
-tion (-ion, -sion, -ation, -ition) [L.]	state of being: ac*tion*, mis*sion*	noun

More Practice

Academic and Workplace Skills Activity Book
• pp. 19–21

818 • Vocabulary and Spelling

Exercise 12 Defining Suffixes For each suffix, write its definition, origin, and part of speech. Use a dictionary to assist you.

1. -ance (-ence)   3. -ist   5. -or
2. -ate   4. -ive

Exercise 13 Using Suffixes to Define Words Add a suffix to each word that will change it to match the part of speech in the third column. Check spellings in a dictionary.

Word	Part of Speech	New Part of Speech
1. defect	noun	adjective
2. attend	verb	noun
3. induce	verb	noun
4. defense	noun	adjective
5. minimum	noun	verb

Exploring Etymologies (Word Origins)

The **etymology** of a word is the history of its origin and development.

KEY CONCEPT Knowing the etymology of a word can help you understand its meaning, as well as how it might be related to other words. ■

Listed below are several ways in which words evolve:
• Words are borrowed from other languages.
• Words change meaning over time and through usage.
• Words are invented, or coined, to serve new purposes.
• Words are combined or shortened.
• Words can be formed from acronyms, or the use of initials.

Exercise 14 Using a Dictionary to Learn About Etymologies Find the word origins of each word below. Write the word origin, and then write a sentence using the word.

1. quirt   6. gazpacho   11. algebra
2. vendetta   7. travelogue 12. werewolf
3. rubberneck 8. sonar   13. ship
4. percent   9. bamboo   14. sandwich
5. tawdry   10. radio   15. scuba

> **More Practice**
> Academic and Workplace Skills Activity Book
> • p. 22

Exploring Etymologies

Teaching Resources: Academic and Workplace Skills Activity Book, p. 22

1. Tell students that people often confuse the term <u>et</u>ymology, the study of words, with <u>ent</u>omology, the study of insects.

2. Have students use a dictionary to learn how these words evolved.
   khaki (borrowed from Hindi)
   laser (acronym: <u>l</u>ight <u>a</u>mplification by <u>s</u>timulated <u>e</u>mission of <u>r</u>adiation)
   fax (shorten form of *facsimile*)
   safari (borrowed from Swahili)

3. Explain that English has more words than any other language because it borrows so many.

Customize for
ESL Students

Have students create a list of words or roots that they have noted in English that are either derived from or related to words in their native languages. Have them share these words in class.

Answer Key

> **Exercise 14**

Sentences will vary; origin and general meaning, if needed, are given.

1. Mexican Spanish; riding whip
2. Italian; blood feud
3. slang; person who stares, a sightseer; to stare or gape.
4. Medieval Latin; parts in a hundred
5. English, shortened from Sain<u>t</u> <u>Audrey</u>'s lace; showy and cheap
6. Spanish; a cold soup
7. French and Middle English; a lecture describing travels
8. <u>so</u>und <u>na</u>vigation <u>r</u>anging; device that finds water depth or objects in water
9. Dutch, from Malay; tree-like grass
10. shortened from radiotelegraphy
11. Arabic; branch of mathematics
12. Old English; person who changes into a wolf
13. Old English; large boat or plane
14. Earl of Sandwich
15. <u>s</u>elf-<u>c</u>ontained <u>u</u>nderwater <u>b</u>reathing <u>a</u>pparatus

---

✓ ONGOING ASSESSMENT: Monitor and Reinforce

If you observe that students are having difficulty with Exercises 8–14, try one of the following strategies.

Option 1 Give students classroom time to work on dictionary skills. You may want to review how words are alphabetized (check the first letter, then move to the second letter of the word, and so on). Then suggest words and have students look them up, offering assistance to any who appear to be having difficulty.

Option 2 Divide the class into pairs and have partners work through a difficult exercise together.

Studying Problem Words

Teaching Resources: Academic and Workplace Skills Activity Book, p. 23

1. Use the Steps for Reviewing Problem Words to analyze one word. For example, *sherbet* is commonly misspelled because it is commonly mispronounced (many say "sherbert").

2. Point out that, for *sherbet*, the appearance of the word and the correct pronunciation of the word contribute to making it easier to remember the correct spelling.

3. Explain that definitions and word origins may also assist in remembering how a word is spelled. For example, *complement* means "complete," and both have two *e's*; or *Wednesday* comes from the Old English for "Woden's day," which helps one remember that the *d* needs to be included.

4. Explain that it is important to spell words correctly, both to make writing credible, and so that the reader understands what is being said.

5. Refer students to the item on homophones (page 812) to demonstrate an additional reason why it is necessary to be careful with spelling.

Customize for
Visual/Spatial Learners

After they complete Exercise 17, encourage students to create visual symbols for their five words and draw them in their notebooks. These can later be displayed (on posters or on the board) for class memory aids.

Answer Key

▶ **Exercise 15**

1. counterfeit
2. controversial
3. acquaintance
4. preferable
5. admittance

▶ **Exercise 16**

Answers will vary. Ask students to share some of their hints for remembering the difficult words.

820

Section 29.4 *Improving Your Spelling*

The best way to improve your spelling is to use editing and study techniques to reduce the number of misspelled words in your writing and to learn the spelling patterns that govern most of the words in the English language.

Studying Problem Words

Whether you have trouble spelling everyday words or words you seldom use, review sessions and spelling techniques—such as memory aids—can help you master problem words.

▶ **KEY CONCEPT** Use review sessions and spelling techniques to help you learn problem words. ■

Study Problem Words Use the steps in the chart below to help you analyze your personal list of problem words.

STEPS FOR REVIEWING PROBLEM WORDS

1. *Look* at each word carefully to notice the arrangement or pattern of the letters. Try to see the word in your mind.
2. *Pronounce* each syllable of the word to yourself.
3. *Write* the word, and check its spelling in a dictionary.
4. *Review* your list until you can write each word correctly.

▶ **Exercise 15** **Working With Problem Words** Choose the correct word. Check your answers in a dictionary.
1. The cashier noticed the (counterfit, counterfeit) bill.
2. People thought the idea was (controversial, controversal).
3. She was an (aquaintance, acquaintance), not a friend.
4. The new plan was (preferible, preferable) to the old one.
5. He was refused (admittance, admittence) to the restaurant.

Develop Memory Aids Some words may be easier to learn through the development and use of special memory aids. There are several methods for remembering how to spell difficult words. One idea is to look for a short, familiar word within a longer one and create a sentence you will remember:

EXAMPLE: friend
In the *end*, you can depend on a *friend*.

▶ **Exercise 16** **Developing Memory Aids** Choose five words that you have trouble spelling, and create a memory aid for each one. Write the hints in your notebook to help you remember the correct spelling.

820 • Vocabulary and Spelling

▶ **More Practice**

Academic and Workplace Skills Activity Book
• p. 23

⏱ TIME AND RESOURCE MANAGER

Resources
Print: *Academic and Workplace Skills Activity Book*, pp. 23–29

In-Depth Coverage	Accelerated Pace
• Cover pages 820–829 in class. • Focus on steps for reviewing problem words and ask students to create a personal spelling list in their notebooks. • Assign Exercises 15–19 as homework. • Discuss using prefixes and suffixes, *ie* and *ei* words, and confusing endings. Complete Exercises 20–25 in class.	• Read pp. 820–829 independently. • Review concepts in class. • Have students do Exercises 15–25 independently, in class, or as homework.

Keeping a Spelling Notebook

You can reduce spelling errors if you keep track of and study words that are difficult for you. The best place to do this is in a special section of your notebook.

KEY CONCEPT Make a personal spelling list of difficult words, enter it in your notebook, and keep it up to date. ■

Setting Up Your Spelling Notebook Create a page with four columns. In the first column, record the misspelled words as you wrote them incorrectly. In the second column, record the correct spelling of the word. In the third column, enter the dates that you practice the words. In the fourth column, write hints that help you remember the correct spelling.

PERSONAL SPELLING LIST

Misspelled Words	Correct Spelling	Practice Dates	Memory Aids
hankerchif	handkerchief	4/11	*hand, chief*
guaranty	guarantee	4/11, 4/18	*tee* off (golf)
nucular	nuclear	4/18, 4/25	a *clear* day
exaust	exhaust	4/18, 4/25	silent *H*
milage	mileage	4/25	*mile + age*

Exercise 17 **Finding Examples in Everyday Life for Your Spelling Notebook** Choose five words you frequently misspell. Find examples in magazines, newspapers, school announcements, and on grocery containers. Copy or paste the words in your spelling notebook.

Exercise 18 **Spelling Difficult Words**
Decide if each of the following words is spelled correctly. If it isn't, look it up in a dictionary to find the correct spelling. Then, record it in your spelling notebook, and practice it.

1. decieve
2. Wednesday
3. seperate
4. licence
5. arosol

6. distinguish
7. vaccum
8. labratory
9. neccessary
10. grammer

Technology Tip

When you use the spell-check feature of a word-processing program, make a note of the words the program finds. Add words that are not typos to your notebook.

▼ **Critical Viewing**
How will writing vocabulary words in a notebook and with a keyboard help this student to learn them? **[Analyze]**

Improving Your Spelling • 821

Step-by-Step Teaching Guide

Keeping a Spelling Notebook

Teaching Resources: Academic and Workplace Skills Activity Book, p. 24

1. Remind students that writing things down is one of the keys to remembering those things.

2. Show students how they can keep a record of difficult words they discover, as well as aids for remembering the word.

3. Suggest that students start the list with words in this lesson that give them difficulty, but keep it up with words they find misspelled in future work. They can use either a sheet of paper or the form in the activity book.

4. Point out that the spelling rules in this lesson can be used in the memory aid column of this chart.

Answer Key

Exercise 17

Answers will vary. Have students share some of the words they have selected. Encourage others to consider adding these words to their own notebooks, if they recognize them as words that might be misspelled.

Exercise 18

1. deceive
2. correct
3. separate
4. license (though *licence* is correct in Britain and appears in most U.S. dictionaries, with "license" as the definition. Point out that *license* is preferred U.S. spelling)
5. aerosol (you may need to help students with this one, since the misspelling is so early in the word)
6. correct
7. vacuum
8. laboratory
9. necessary
10. grammar

Critical Viewing

Analyze Students may note that the act of writing or typing the word may help fix the words in memory.

Regular Plurals

Teaching Resources: Academic and Workplace Skills Activity Book, p. 25

1. Discuss the four points for forming regular plurals in class.

2. Ask volunteers for examples of words in each of the four categories along with the rule that governs forming the plural. Write the singular and plural of the word on the board.

Integrating Technology Skills

Ask students to perform an on-line search to see if they can find the twenty most commonly misspelled words in America. Suggest key words to enter so students can begin their search. (Examples: *spelling errors, spelling mistakes*.)

Integrating Speaking Skills

Point out to students that an understanding of how to create plurals can translate into improved speaking skills, as well. As jarring as incorrect usage is in print, it is even more noticeable in speaking—for example, if they used *wifes* instead of *wives*. Point out that using the dictionary for pronunciation as well as definitions will also help them improve their speaking. If words are not pronounced correctly, the speaker faces the twin dangers of being misunderstood or being dismissed as not reliable.

29.4

Applying Spelling Rules

Master the spelling rules in this section, and you will be able to spell many words without having to memorize them or stop and think about their spelling. By learning rules for writing plurals, writing words with prefixes and suffixes, and choosing between *ie* and *ei*, you will not only improve your spelling but also save time.

Forming Plurals

The plural form of a noun is the form that means "more than one." Plural forms can be either *regular* or *irregular*.

> **KEY CONCEPT** The regular plural form of most nouns is formed by adding *-s* or *-es* to the singular. ■

Regular Plurals As a general rule, you can just add *-s* to form a regular plural. With certain regular plurals, however, you may have to choose whether to add *-s* or *-es*. Occasionally, you may also have to change a letter or two in the word.

1. Words ending in *s, ss, x, z, sh,* or *ch* form their plurals by adding *-es* to the base word:

   circus + -es = circuses   dress + -es = dresses
   tax + -es = taxes   waltz + -es = waltzes
   wish + -es = wishes   bench + -es = benches

2. Words ending in *y* or *o* preceded by a vowel form their plurals by adding *-s* to the base word:

   key + -s = keys   buoy + -s = buoys
   rodeo + -s = rodeos   patio + -s = patios

3. To form the plurals of words ending in *y* preceded by a consonant, change the *y* to *i* and add *-es*. For most words ending in *o* preceded by a consonant, add *-es*. For musical terms ending in *o*, simply add *-s*:

   city + -ies = cities   enemy + -ies = enemies
   echo + -es = echoes   tomato + -es = tomatoes
   piano + -s = pianos   solo + -s = solos

4. To form the plurals of some words ending in *f* or *fe*, change the *f* or *fe* to *v* and add *-es*. For words ending in *ff*, always add *-s*:

   leaf + -es = leaves   loaf + -es = loaves
   wife + -es = wives   life + -es = lives
   chief + -s = chiefs   proof + -s = proofs
   staff + -s = staffs   cliff + -s = cliffs

822 • Vocabulary and Spelling

Irregular Plurals Irregular plurals are not formed according to the rules on the previous page. If you are unsure how to form a plural, check a dictionary. Irregular plurals are usually listed right after the pronunciation of the word. If no plural form is given in the dictionary, simply add -s or -es to the singular form. Below is a list of common irregular plurals:

IRREGULAR PLURALS		
Singular Forms	**Ways of Forming Plurals**	**Plural Forms**
ox	add *-en*	oxen
child	add *-ren*	children
tooth, mouse, woman	change one or more letters	teeth, mice, women
radius, focus, alumnus	change *-us* to *-i*	radii, foci, alumni
alumna	change *-a* to *-ae*	alumnae
crisis, emphasis	change *-is* to *-es*	crises, emphases
medium, datum, curriculum	change *-um* to *-a*	media, data, curricula
phenomenon, criterion	change *-on* to *-a*	phenomena, criteria
deer, sheep	plural form same as singular	deer, sheep
	plural form only	scissors, slacks

Note About *Plurals of Compound Words*: To form the plural of a compound word—that is, a word made up of two or more separate or hyphenated words—add -s or -es to the main noun in the compound word. For example, *rule of thumb* becomes *rules of thumb*, and *editor-in-chief* becomes *editors-in-chief*.

▶ **Exercise 19** **Forming Plurals** Write the plural for each word. Consult a dictionary if necessary.

1. radio
2. soprano
3. wife
4. fox
5. supply
6. lynx
7. chief
8. son-in-law
9. crisis
10. X-ray
11. tomato
12. waltz
13. rodeo
14. mouse
15. criterion
16. alumnus
17. gratuity
18. fantasy
19. ballerina
20. memorandum

▶ **More Practice**

Academic and Workplace Skills Activity Book
• p. 25

STANDARDIZED TEST PREPARATION WORKSHOP

Plurals Standardized test questions may require students to demonstrate their knowledge of plurals and agreement. Use the following sample to give students practice.

Which word does not agree with the other elements in this sentence?

Dogs chew their bone.

A dogs
B their
C bone
D chew

Students should recognize that **C**, *bone*, is the word that does not agree with other elements in this sentence. The correct answer is *bones* as it is plural and is in agreement with *dogs, chew,* and *their,* which are all plural.

Irregular Plurals

1. Have students study the chart of irregular plurals. Discuss what makes these words irregular plurals.

2. Ask students if they can think of other irregular plurals. Have them give both the plural and singular (*goose/geese; fish/fish*).

3. Make certain students understand the way to make plurals of compound words. Write the following on the board and have students suggest where the -s goes: passer-by (*passers-by*); aide-de-camp (*aides-de-camp*); sergeant at arms (*sergeants at arms*). Note that students may not recognize the word *sergeant*. Ask if students are familiar with the word, and if not, pronounce it for them.

4. Point out that it is not always true that the first word of a compound noun gets the -s. It is the word that is being modified that gets the -s. Hence, for coffee tables and jack-'o-lanterns, the -s goes at the end.

Customize for
AP Students

Tell students that adding -s to the end of a word to make it plural comes into English through its French heritage. Have students look up the words in the Irregular Plurals chart to discover the origins of these words and organize them by similar origins. (For example, *child* and *sheep* are both derived from Old English; *crisis* and *criterion* come from Greek.)

Answer Key

▶ **Exercise 19**

1. radios
2. sopranos
3. wives
4. foxes
5. supplies
6. lynxes
7. chiefs
8. sons-in-law
9. crises
10. X-rays
11. tomatoes
12. waltzes
13. rodeos
14. mice
15. criteria
16. alumni
17. gratuities
18. fantasies
19. ballerinas
20. memoranda

Adding Prefixes and Suffixes

Teaching Resources: Academic and Workplace Skills Activity Book, p. 26

1. Remind students of what they have already learned about prefixes and suffixes earlier in the chapter on pages 816–818.

2. Emphasize that although adding a prefix does not affect the spelling of the original word or root, many prefixes change their own spelling when joined to roots. Refer students to the chart on page 816 for examples.

3. After Exercise 20 is completed, have students share some of the words they have formed. Write their words on the board. Add any combinations they overlooked (see answer key below).

4. Ask students to study carefully the three types of spelling changes that occur when adding suffixes.

5. Work through some examples of spelling changes with the class. Write the examples on the board.

6. Point out that the suffix *-ed* shown in example 2 of words ending in *-y* makes the word past tense. Remind students that *pay* is an irregular verb, and that most irregular verbs either do not take the *-ed* suffix at all, or change like *pay*. Ask students to think of the verbs that change like *pay* (*lay/laid, say/said*) as well as a few samples of verbs that don't use *-ed* at all to from the past (*sing/sang, ride/rode*).

Answer Key

▶ **Exercise 20**

Answers will vary; examples are given.

1. advent, invent, prevent, circumvent
2. complex, perplex
3. improve
4. misspell
5. invert, convert
6. profound
7. compact, impact
8. permissive, admissive
9. circumscribe, inscribe
10. inspire, perspire, conspire

29.4

Adding Prefixes and Suffixes

A **prefix** is one or more syllables added at the beginning of a word to form a new word. A **suffix** is one or more syllables added to the end of a word.

▶ **KEY CONCEPT** Adding a prefix to a word does not affect the spelling of the original word. Adding a suffix often changes the spelling of the word. ■

Prefixes When a prefix is added to the word, the spelling of the root remains the same (*in-* + *sincere* = *insincere*; *un-* + *necessary* = *unnecessary*). With certain prefixes, however, the spelling is changed when joined to the root to make the pronunciation easier (*in-* becomes *im-* before *mortal* to form *immortal*).

▶ **Exercise 20** **Spelling Words With Prefixes** Form new words by combining roots with these seven prefixes. Remember that you may have to change the form of some prefixes. Use a dictionary to check your answers.

ad-, circum-, com-, in-, mis-, per-, pro-

1. -vent	4. -spell	7. -pact	10. -spire
2. -plex	5. -vert	8. -missive	
3. -prove	6. -found	9. -scribe	

Suffixes Some words require spelling changes when suffixes are added.

Spelling changes in words ending in *y*: Use the following rules for spelling changes of words ending in *y*, paying careful attention to the rule's exceptions.

1. When adding a suffix to words ending in *y* preceded by a consonant, change *y* to *i*. Most suffixes beginning with *i* are the exception to the rule:

ply + -able = pliable   happy + -ness = happiness
defy + -ing = defying   cry + -ing = crying

2. For words ending in a *y* preceded by a vowel, make no change when adding most suffixes. A few short words are the exceptions:

annoy + -ance = annoyance   enjoy + -ment = enjoyment
day + -ly = daily   pay + -ed = paid

Spelling changes in words ending in *e:* Use the following rules for spelling changes for words ending in *e*, paying careful attention to the rule's exceptions:

1. For words ending in *e*, drop the *e* when adding a suffix beginning with a vowel. The exceptions to the rule are (1) words ending in *ce* or *ge* with suffixes beginning with *a* or *o*, (2) words ending in *ee*, and (3) a few special words:

   move + -able = movable   drive + -ing = driving
   trace + -able = traceable   courage + -ous = courageous
   see + -ing = seeing   agree + -able = agreeable
   dye + -ing = dyeing   be + -ing = being

2. For words ending in *e*, make no change when adding a suffix beginning with a consonant. A few special words are the exceptions:

   peace + -ful = peaceful   brave + -ly = bravely
   argue + -ment = argument   judge + -ment = judgment

Doubling the final consonant before suffixes: Use the following rules for cases in which a final consonant may or may not change, paying careful attention to the rule's exceptions:

1. For words ending with a consonant + vowel + consonant in a stressed syllable, double the final consonant when adding a suffix beginning with a vowel. The exceptions to the rules are (1) words ending in *x* or *w* and (2) words in which the stress changes after the suffix is added:

   mud + -y = mud dy   submit + -ed = submit ted
   mix + -ing = mixing   row + -ing = rowing
   refer + -ence = ref erence   confer + -ence = con ference

2. For words ending with a consonant + vowel + consonant in an unstressed syllable, make no change when adding a suffix beginning with a vowel. There are no major exceptions to the rule:

   an gel + -ic = angel ic   fi nal + -ize = fi nalize

Exercise 21 **Spelling Words With Suffixes** Write the correct spelling for the words below. Check a dictionary.

1. retire + -ment
2. loyal + -ist
3. confer + -ence
4. hurry + -ing
5. rebel + -ion
6. comply + -ance
7. appear + -ance
8. convey + -or
9. abbreviate + -ion
10. imagine + -ary

► **More Practice**
Academic and Workplace Skills Activity Book
• p. 26

Spelling *ie* and *ei* Words and Words ending in *-cede*, *-ceed*, and *-sede*

Teaching Resources: Academic and Workplace Skills Activity Book, p. 27

1. Before students refer to this section, write the rule on the board:

   Place i before e except after c or when sounded like a, as in neighbor or weigh.

2. Ask how many students are familiar with the rule and use it regularly.

3. Explain that, though there are many rules that can help with spelling, for the exceptions to the *ie/ei* rule, along with words ending in *-cede*, *-ceed*, and *-sede*, the only way to learn them is by memorizing them.

4. Encourage students to list these tricky words in their spelling notebooks.

5. Allow class time for students to practice these spellings, perhaps with partners, before assigning the exercises.

Customize for
Less Advanced Students

You may want to allow these students to do the exercises with partners. Alternatively, you could allow them to use a dictionary, to reinforce correct spellings, and to get them in the habit of checking.

Customize for
Gifted and Talented Students

After they have completed Exercise 23, challenge these students to create a short narrative or paragraph containing several words that use *-cede*, *-ceed,* and *-sede* as suffixes.

29.4

Spelling *ie* and *ei* Words and Words Ending in *-cede*, *-ceed*, and *-sede*

Words containing *ie* and *ei* and words with the endings *-cede*, *-ceed*, and *-sede* often prove troublesome to spellers.

For most words containing *ie* or *ei*, you can use the traditional rule: "Place *i* before *e* except after *c* or when sounded like *a* as in *neighbor* or *weigh*." For exceptions, as well as for words ending in *-cede*, *-ceed*, and *-sede*, it is often best to memorize the correct spellings.

> **KEY CONCEPT** For *ie* and *ei* words, use the traditional rule after memorizing the exceptions. Words that end in *-cede*, *-ceed*, and *-sede* should also be memorized. ■

ie and ei Words The *ie* and *ei* rule applies to many words, but like most rules, it has exceptions.

Exceptions for ie words: counterfeit, either, foreign, forfeit, heifer, height, heir, leisure, neither, seismology, seize, sheik, sleight, sovereign, their, weird

Exceptions for ei words: ancient, conscience, efficient, financier, sufficient

> **Exercise 22** Spelling *ie* and *ei* Words Use *ie* or *ei* to complete each numbered word below.

Even at the (1) h _ _ ght of (2) th _ _ r (3) ach _ _ vement, the (4) _ _ ght athletes (5) consc _ _ ntiously practiced every day. All (6) bel _ _ ved that (7) th_ _ r (8) r _ _ gn as champions would be (9) br _ _ f if they became so (10) conc _ _ ted that they thought they could succeed without hard work.

Words Ending in *-cede*, *-ceed*, and *-sede* The best way to handle words that end with these suffixes is to memorize the correct spelling. The words ending in **-cede** are *accede, concede, intercede, precede, recede, secede*. The three words endings in **-ceed** are *exceed, proceed, succeed*, and the only word ending in **-sede** is *supersede*.

> **Exercise 23** Working With Words Ending in *-cede, -ceed, or -sede* Write the incomplete word for each sentence, filling in the blanks with *-cede, -ceed,* or *-sede*.
> 1. The new regulations super _ _ _ _ the old ones.
> 2. The candidate will not con _ _ _ _ defeat.
> 3. The wedding ceremony will pre _ _ _ _ the reception.
> 4. They probably will suc _ _ _ _ in their new business.
> 5. It is time to pro _ _ _ _ with the meeting.

More Practice

Academic and Workplace Skills Activity Book
• p. 27

Answer Key

> **Exercise 22**
> 1. height
> 2. their
> 3. achievement
> 4. eight
> 5. conscientiously
> 6. believed
> 7. their
> 8. reign
> 9. brief
> 10. conceited

> **Exercise 23**
> 1. supersede
> 2. concede
> 3. precede
> 4. succeed
> 5. proceed

Other Confusing Endings

There are a few groups of suffixes that sound very similar but are spelled differently. For this reason, you should learn to distinguish confusing suffixes and to identify common words that each suffix forms.

KEY CONCEPT Learn to distinguish between confusing groups of suffixes. ■

Learn Confusing Endings There are certain endings that are similar and easy to confuse. Study the following lists, and consult a dictionary.

-able, -ible The suffixes *-able* and *-ible* are often confusing, and it is probably best to check a dictionary if you are in doubt about a spelling. Following is a list of some of the words with these endings.

COMMON WORDS ENDING IN *-able* AND *-ible*

acceptable	imaginable	accessible	possible
believable	probable	flexible	responsible
capable	reasonable	horrible	sensible

-ance (-ant) and -ence (-ent) The most helpful guideline for remembering which spelling to use is that words containing a "hard" *c* or *g* sound usually end with the *a* spelling. Those with a "soft" *c* or *g* sound will usually have the *e* spelling. There are, however, many *-ance* and *-ence* words that do not contain soft or hard *c* or *g* sounds.

COMMON WORDS ENDING IN *-ance* AND *-ence*

abundance	defiance	absence	excellence
acquaintance	importance	convenience	independence
appearance	radiance	patience	correspondence

-ary, -ery There are not many words ending in *-ery* that have the sound *(-airy)*. Most words with that sound are spelled *-ary*.

COMMON WORDS ENDING IN *-ery* AND *-ary*

cemetery	stationery (paper)	dictionary	culinary
millinery	monastery	imaginary	lectionary

Most words with endings that sound similar will have the *-ary* spelling. If you have any doubt whether a word ends in *-ary* or *-ery*, check the spelling of the word in a dictionary.

-cy and -sy Only a handful of English words end with *-sy*. Memorize the words that end with *-sy*, and you will be reasonably safe in using *-cy* for the others.

COMMON WORDS ENDING IN *-sy*

courtesy	ecstasy	fantasy	hypocrisy
curtsy	embassy	heresy	idiosyncrasy

1. courteous
2. cautious
3. sensible
4. dictionary
5. liquefy
6. incredible
7. hypocrisy
8. correspondence
9. strenuous
10. gorgeous
11. dependable
12. flexible
13. cemetery
14. radiance
15. independence
16. stationery
17. stationary
18. conscious
19. ecstasy
20. brilliance

Customize for
Less Advanced Students

Ask students to work in pairs to complete Exercise 24. As homework, ask them to use each word in a simple sentence. Student pairs can then discuss their sentences during the next lesson.

Integrating Study Skills

Remind students of the importance of regularly checking the spelling of unfamiliar words and becoming familiar with those that are difficult but common. Points are deducted for poor spelling on standardized tests, as well as on essays and reports.

29.4

-efy and **-ify** As with many of the other pairs of suffixes, one of these suffixes is much more common than the other. In this case, the ending *-efy* is rarely used except for the four words in the following chart.

COMMON WORDS ENDING IN *-efy*

liquefy	putrefy	rarefy	stupefy

-eous, -ious, -uous Confusion sometimes arises over the spelling of words ending in *-eous*, *-ious*, and *-uous*. Some of this confusion can be resolved by carefully noticing the pronunciation of the word. Words ending in *-uous*, for example, can be distinguished from the others if they are pronounced carefully. Deciding whether to use *-eous* or *-ious* is more difficult because pronunciation does not help you. It is probably best to memorize these words or check their spellings in a dictionary.

COMMON WORDS ENDING IN *-uous, -eous,* AND *-ious*

ambiguous	courageous	righteous	laborious
conspicuous	courteous	anxious	precious
continuous	erroneous	cautious	rebellious
ingenuous	gorgeous	conscious	religious
strenuous	outrageous	delicious	superstitious

▶ **Exercise 24** Writing Words With Confusing Endings Fill in the blanks below. Consult a dictionary if necessary.

1. court _ _ _ s
2. caut _ _ _ s
3. sens _ ble
4. diction _ _ y
5. liqu _ fy
6. incred _ ble
7. hypocri _ y
8. correspond _ nce
9. stren _ _ _ s
10. gorg _ _ _ s
11. depend _ ble
12. flex _ ble
13. cemet _ ry
14. radi _ nce
15. independ _ nce
16. station _ ry (paper)
17. station _ ry (unmoving)
18. consc _ _ _ s
19. ecst _ _ y
20. brill _ _ nce

Proofreading Carefully

When you are writing, you are often thinking about the content—the ideas you want to express. However, when you have finished writing, you should proofread for spelling errors.

KEY CONCEPT When you proofread your work, focus on each individual word. ■

To discover the proofreading methods that work best for you, use a variety of strategies. Following are some common proofreading strategies:

- Read your work, aloud or silently, to yourself.
- Proofread only one line at a time. Use a ruler or other device to focus on the line you are proofreading and to cover up the lines you are not proofreading.
- Read backwards, from the last word to the first. This forces you to focus only on the words themselves.
- Consult a dictionary when you come across a word that you suspect is spelled incorrectly.
- Check the spelling of proper nouns.

Exercise 25 **Proofreading Carefully** Write down the correct spelling of all misspelled words in each sentence below (proper nouns are correct). Use a dictionary if necessary.

(1) Within one hundred miles of Washington, D.C., there was a rurual hamlet knoun as Colvin Hollows. (2) It could be reached only by a trial that cut threw the Appalachian canyons. (3) The townspeople were desendants of settlers from a century ago. (4) At one time, the town was completly isalated from the outside world. (5) Families lived in huts and took care of there psycical needs by farming and hunting.

Reflecting on Your Spelling and Vocabulary

Review your personal spelling list, the spelling rules in your notebook, and the methods you use to increase your vocabulary. See whether the spelling lists contain a pattern of the types of words with which you have difficulty. In a journal entry, ask yourself:

- Which words are easiest for me, and which words are most difficult?
- What kinds of spelling errors do I typically make?
- Which method helped me to learn the greatest number of words?

Proofreading Carefully

Teaching Resources: Academic and Workplace Skills Activity Book, p. 29

1. Assure students that even successful professional writers make mistakes on early drafts of their work. However, they always proofread their work, often several times.

2. Ask students if they have used any of the five proofreading strategies listed here.

3. Discuss with students the skills they have used before, how the skills worked for them, and the techniques they might try in the future.

Answer Key

▶ **Exercise 25**

1. rural, known
2. trail, through
3. descendants
4. isolated
5. their, physical

ASSESS and CLOSE

Assessment

Teaching Resources: Formal Assessment, Chapter 29

1. Give students time in class to answer the "Reflecting" questions. Encourage them to make any additional notes about what they learned in this chapter.

2. Check to make certain that students have begun their spelling and vocabulary lists. Encourage them to continue adding to these lists.

3. Review the chapter by asking students to state the key points of the chapter.

4. You may also wish to administer the Chapter 29 assessment from *Formal Assessment* in Teaching Resources to gauge students' grasp of concepts presented.

Real-World Connection

Explain to students that there is no area of life where careful proofreading will not improve their communication. The difference between *not* and *now* is a good example. There is only one letter difference between the two, but a mix-up would make a great difference in a response to an invitation, for example. In business, proofreading is even more important, because one's income may depend on it.

Lesson Objectives

1. To rely on context to determine meanings of words and phrases
2. To apply word structure in order to comprehend
3. To recognize appropriate sentence construction within the context of a written passage

Step-by-Step Teaching Guide

Using Vocabulary in Sentence Completion and Reading Comprehension Items

Teaching Resources: Standardized Test Preparation Workbook pp. 57–58

1. Tell students that some tests may measure both their understanding of the vocabulary in a passage and their ability to determine from context the correct word to complete a sentence, and that they will practice some typical test items that do so.

2. Go through the sample test items and answers with students, emphasizing that choosing the correct answers utilizes skills covered in Chapter 29.

3. Assign Practices 1 and 2 and go over the answers with students.

Standardized Test Preparation Workshop

Using Vocabulary in Sentence Completion and Reading Comprehension Items

On standardized tests, sentence completion items and reading comprehension questions can test your vocabulary. Use the skills you have studied in this chapter, including the use of word structure and context, to help you answer such questions successfully. Following are examples of questions in a variety of formats.

Test Tips

- When reading sentence completion items, pay close attention to transitional or connecting words and phrases, such as *and*, *but*, *because*, and *although*.
- In the reading comprehension sections, you may find it helpful to read the questions before reading the passage.

Sample Test Item	Answers and Explanations
Directions: The sentence below has one blank indicating that something has been omitted. Beneath the sentence are five words or sets of words labeled *A* through *E*. Choose the word or set of words that, when inserted in the sentence, best fits the meaning of the sentence as a whole. Write the letter of that word on your paper. Though he is ___?__ , his nephew still invites him to dinner every year. (A) cheerful (D) agile (B) entertaining (E) healthy (C) misanthropic	The correct answer is *C*. The uncle is *misanthropic*. You can use the context clues "though" and "invites him" to infer that the uncle has some negative quality. Next, you can apply your knowledge of the prefix *mis-* to determine that *misanthropic*, like *mistake* and *misfortune*, is a word indicating something negative. Eliminate the other answer choices, which indicate positive or neutral qualities in this context.
Read the question that follows the sentence. Decide which is the best answer. Mark the letter for that answer. Frederic, who routinely ignored the <u>prognostications</u> of meteorologists, left the house wearing only a short-sleeved shirt. The word *prognostications* as used in this sentence most likely means— (A) predictions (C) threats (B) storms (D) preferences	The correct answer is *A*. *Prognostications* means "predictions." Use the context clues "routinely ignored" and "left . . . a short-sleeved shirt" to determine that, in this context, ignoring "prognostications" includes dressing for pleasant weather. You can conclude that Frederic is ignoring the meteorologist's idea of what the weather will be like and that *prognostications* means "predictions."

830 • Vocabulary and Spelling

TEST-TAKING TIP

Tell students that transition words and phrases are often helpful context clues in a sentence completion item. Phrases and words such as *instead of*, *in addition to*, *however*, *though*, *nevertheless*, and *also* may be good clues.

You might give them extra practice with these items, asking them to fill in the best words.

1. *Because* I was ___ for dinner at home, I had to eat by myself. (late)

2. *Although* the bus was early, I was ___ to arrive on time. (able)

Remind students that reading the questions before reading through the passage to which the questions refer will help them know what to look for as they read.

Practice 1 **Directions:** Each sentence below has one or two blanks, each blank indicating that something has been omitted. Beneath the sentence are five words or sets of words labeled **A** through **E**. Choose the word or set of words that, when inserted in the sentence, best fits the meaning of the sentence as a whole. Write the letter of that word on your paper.

1. "I wish I had a longer _____ between performances," complained the pianist. "My fingers need a rest."
   (A) post-mortem
   (B) circumlocution
   (C) prelude
   (D) interval
   (E) solo

2. Instead of revolving around the sun in a circle, this asteroid has a(n) _____ orbit.
   (A) rapid
   (B) eccentric
   (C) interplanetary
   (D) circular
   (E) regular

3. He was the first historian to translate the _____ on the stone.
   (A) impulsion
   (B) aversion
   (C) excavation
   (D) circumspection
   (E) inscription

4. To correct your spelling error, simply _____ the *i* and the *e*.
   (A) translate
   (B) transpose
   (C) transcend
   (D) interpolate
   (E) integrate

5. Spilling soda all over myself just when the movie got to the good part was a(n) _____ event.
   (A) fortunate
   (B) premature
   (C) tenacious
   (D) infelicitous
   (E) constructive

Practice 2 **Directions:** Read the passage. Then, read each question that follows the passage. Decide which is the best answer to each question. Mark the letter for that answer.

In his famous poem "Fire and Ice," Robert Frost asks whether the world will end in fire or in ice—in a great, furious fireball or in the sudden cessation of all warmth and activity. "Fire," he answers at first. He is thinking of the destruction caused by greed, ambition, and other forms of human desire, which seem to "burn" powerfully enough to end all things. Yet if the world "had to perish twice" (line 5), he reflects, ice would also be powerful enough for the job. He writes, ". . . for destruction ice / Is also great / And would suffice" (lines 7–9). Here, Frost reminds us of the destructive power of cold hatred.

1. In this passage, the word *cessation* means —
   (A) beginning
   (B) end
   (C) hissing
   (D) explosion

2. In this passage, the word *perish* means —
   (A) come to an end
   (B) turn in a circle
   (C) start over again
   (D) burn up

3. In this passage, the word *suffice* means —
   (A) be frozen
   (B) be great
   (C) be enough
   (D) be hot

Answer Key

Practice 1
1. D
2. C
3. E
4. B
5. D

Practice 2
1. B
2. F
3. C

Customize for
Less Advanced Students

You may need to point out the context clues in the first practice, items 1 and 2 (*between* and *instead of*) and reteach certain common prefixes and roots (such as *circum-, inter-, in-, pre-, trans-,* and *-script*).

Customize for
ESL Students

Be sure that students understand these common words in test directions: *indicating* = showing; *inserted* = added, put in; *omitted* = left out; and *beneath* = under.

In-Depth Lesson Plan

	LESSON FOCUS	PRINT AND MEDIA RESOURCES
DAY 1	**Reading Methods and Tools** Students study textbook features and learn strategies for reading textbooks. (pp. 832–839)	**Teaching Resources** *Academic and Workplace Skills Activity Book,* pp. 30–34
DAY 2	**Reading Nonfiction Critically** Students learn strategies for reading, analyzing, and evaluating nonfiction. (pp. 840–845)	**Teaching Resources** *Academic and Workplace Skills Activity Book,* pp. 35–38
DAY 3	**Reading Literary Writing** Students learn strategies for reading and analyzing fiction, drama, and poetry. (pp. 846–849)	**Teaching Resources** *Academic and Workplace Skills Activity Book,* pp. 39–42
DAY 4	**Reading from Varied Sources; Chapter Review** Students learn strategies for reading various sources such as journals, newspapers, speeches, and electronic texts. Students review the concepts presented in the chapter. (pp. 850–851)	**Teaching Resources** *Academic and Workplace Skills Activity Book,* p. 43; *Formal Assessment,* Ch. 30

Accelerated Lesson Plan

	LESSON FOCUS	PRINT AND MEDIA RESOURCES
DAY 1	**Reading Methods and Tools; Reading Nonfiction Critically** Students learn strategies for reading and analyzing textbooks and other nonfiction materials. (pp. 832–845)	**Teaching Resources** *Academic and Workplace Skills Activity Book,* pp. 30–38
DAY 2	**Reading Literary Writing; Reading from Varied Sources** Students learn strategies for reading literary writing and other print and electronic texts. (pp. 846–851)	**Teaching Resources** *Academic and Workplace Skills Activity Book,* pp. 39–43; *Formal Assessment,* Ch. 30

Options for Adapting Lesson Plans

HOMEWORK

Have students complete any of the exercises for homework.

FEATURES

Extend coverage with the Standardized Test Preparation Workshop (p. 852).

INTEGRATED SKILLS COVERAGE

Viewing and Representing
Critical Viewing SE pp. 832, 841, 844, 847, 848, 851

Research
SE pp. 835, 842, 845; ATE p. 839

Technology
SE p. 836

Vocabulary
ATE pp. 846, 853

Listening Skills
ATE pp. 840, 845

Real-World Connection
ATE p. 845

Workplace Skills
ATE p. 835

ASSESSMENT SUPPORT

Standardized Test Preparation Workshop SE p. 852; ATE p. 842

Standardized Test Preparation Workbook, pp. 59–60

Formal Assessment, Ch. 30

MEETING INDIVIDUAL NEEDS

Less Advanced Students ATE p. 853; See also Ongoing Assessments ATE pp. 835, 837, 845, 849.

AP Students ATE p. 836

ESL Students ATE p. 834, 851

Logical/Mathematical Learners ATE p. 837

Visual/Spatial Learners ATE p. 836

Interpersonal Learners ATE p. 841

Verbal/Linguistic Learners ATE p. 843

Gifted and Talented Learners ATE p. 847

Bodily/Kinesthetic Learners ATE p. 848

Musical/Rhythmic Learners ATE p. 849

BLOCK SCHEDULING

Pacing Suggestions
For 90-minute Blocks
- Have students review the Reading Methods and Tools section and complete Exercises 1–5 in a single period.
- Focus one class period on Reading Nonfiction Critically. Allow an additional period for Reading Literary Writing and Reading from Varied Sources.

Resources for Varying Instruction
- *Academic and Workplace Skills Activity Book,* pp. 30–43

Professional Development Support
- *How to Manage Instruction in the Block* This Teaching Resource provides management and activity suggestions.

MEDIA AND TECHNOLOGY

For the Teacher
- *Resource Pro* **CD-ROM**

WRITING AND GRAMMAR WEB SITE

The Interactive Writing and Grammar Web Site provides a wide array of support for students, teachers, and parents.

www.phschool.com

Lesson Objectives

1. To use text organizers to locate and categorize information

2. To establish and adjust purpose for reading

3. To monitor reading strategies and make modifications when understanding breaks down

4. To use study strategies such as note taking, outlining, and using study-guide questions to better understand texts

5. To produce summaries of texts by identifying main ideas and their supporting details

6. To analyze text structures for how they influence understanding

7. To draw inferences and support them with text evidence and experience

8. To evaluate the credibility of information sources

9. To recognize logical, deceptive, and/or faulty modes of persuasion in texts

10. To expand vocabulary and determine meaning of words through wide reading in varied sources

Critical Viewing

Speculate Students may feel that the girl likes the solitude, the light, or the "feeling" she gets from reading in an environment that is away from her home and responsibilities.

Chapter 30 Reading Skills

Reading, 1973, Bill Morrow Jackson, Wichita Art Museum

Reading is a visual means of acquiring and retaining information. It is the method by which the majority of students learn best. Reading involves mastering skills in a number of reading-related areas and learning to apply those skills properly. Two of these areas are textbook reading and reading style. By gaining and applying skills in these two important areas, you will become a more efficient and effective reader.

▲ **Critical Viewing**
Why might the girl in this picture have chosen this place in which to read? **[Speculate]**

🕐 TIME AND RESOURCE MANAGER

Resources
Print: *Academic and Workplace Skills Activity Book*, pages 30–34

In-Depth Coverage	Accelerated Pace
• Read and discuss pp. 832–834. • Have students work in groups on Exercise 1. • Read and discuss pp. 835–839. • Assign Exercises 2–4 to be done in class.	• Assign pp. 832–839 for reading. • Have students work on Exercises 1–4 in class.

Reading Methods and Tools

Section 30.1

As you proceed in life and in school, the material you read increases in quantity and difficulty. Improving your reading skills can improve your performance in your classes. These same reading skills will also increase your enjoyment and appreciation of material that you read on your own.

Reading Textbooks

KEY CONCEPT Use textbook reading and study aids to help you understand and remember what you read. ■

Observing Textbook Sections A textbook is structured for comprehension. It contains a variety of reading aids that can help you understand the material with the least difficulty.

TEXTBOOK SECTIONS

Table of Contents This section lists units and chapters with their page numbers. Use it for a quick overview of the book.

Front of the Book

Preface or Introduction This section states the author's purpose in writing the book and may give suggestions for using the book.

Front of the Book

Index This section lists alphabetically all topics covered in the book and the pages on which they can be found. Use it to quickly locate specific topics.

Back of the Book

Glossary This section gives an alphabetical list of all the specialized terms used in the book and defines them. Use it to find definitions.
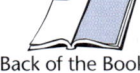
Back of the Book

Appendix This section includes charts, lists, documents, or other material related to the subject of the book. Use it as a reference source.

Back of the Book

Bibliography This section includes lists of books and articles that the author has used or referred to in writing the book. Use it for follow-up study or for research projects.

Back of the Book

Reading Skills • 833

✓ ONGOING ASSESSMENT: Diagnose

Use one of the following options to diagnose students' current level of proficiency with reading skills.

Option 1 Ask students to explain what they do to increase comprehension when they encounter a difficult text. If students do not know any strategies to use on such occasions, they will need extra support in the section on reading strategies.

Option 2 Give students a paragraph from a textbook. Have them read it and write down the main idea. Read their answers. Students who have trouble with this exercise will need extra support in note-taking and outlining skills.

PREPARE and ENGAGE

Interest GRABBER Ask students to write down the career they plan to pursue. Explain that every job requires a certain amount of reading. Challenge them to make a list of the types of materials they will have to read at their particular job. What reading skills will they need to improve in order to excel at this job?

Activate Prior Knowledge

Have students make a four-column chart, labeling the columns *English, Math, Social Studies,* and *Science.* Have them explain the reading skills they use for each subject. Do they use the same reading strategies in all of their classes? If not, how do the strategies differ? Why do they use different strategies in certain classes?

TEACH

Step-by-Step Teaching Guide

Reading Textbooks

Teaching Resources: Academic and Workplace Skills Activity Book, p. 30

1. Before students scan the chart, have them close their books. Write on the board all six terms from the chart and challenge students to define them. Have them share their definitions.

2. Have students open their books and compare their definitions to those in the chart. Are they familiar with all six terms? Which textbook reading aids do they find most useful?

3. Point out that not every book has all six items. Also, an appendix might be called a "reference section," "resources," or "handbook." Give students time to locate as many of these sections as there are in this textbook (all are present except preface and bibliography; the appendix is called "resources"). Ask them why it is helpful to be familiar with the locations of these text aids. (Students should note that these features can help them find information quickly and easily.)

Identifying Textbook Features

Textbooks have special features designed to help you find, organize, and review material:

▶ **KEY CONCEPT** Use the special features of your textbook to aid your reading and studying of the material. ■

Titles, Headings, and Subheadings Printed in large, heavy type and in different sizes and colors, headings give you an idea of what the material is about. They also divide the material into sections so that you can learn it more easily. Main topics usually have larger and more prominent headings; subtopics have smaller headings.

Overviews Often, a chapter or unit will begin with an overview, outline, or summary of what is to be covered. Use the overview to preview and review the chapter or unit.

Questions and Exercises These are often located at the end of a chapter. Review questions and exercises before you read the chapter to give you an idea of the main points to look for as you read. Afterward, answer the questions and exercises to retain the information you have read.

Pictures, Captions, and Graphics A picture can make a confusing idea clearer. Usually, next to a picture there is a caption—information describing the picture. Graphics such as maps, graphs, and diagrams present complex information in a clear format.

▶ **Exercise 1** **Examining Two Textbooks** Select two textbooks in different subjects, and examine them by answering these questions:
1. How is the table of contents in each text organized (by theme, chronologically, or by some other method)?
2. If the texts contain prefaces, do they explain the books' purposes and give suggestions for using the books? Which preface is more helpful?
3. Which text's chapter headings can you more easily turn into questions?
4. Are the end-of-chapter questions in each text useful for study? Are the questions in one text more helpful?
5. Does each text contain an index, a glossary, an appendix, and a bibliography? How do the elements help you to use the book's material?

Using Reading Strategies

You probably do not have one specific reading style, nor should you. In order to read effectively, you need to know how to pair your reading style with your purpose in reading.

> **KEY CONCEPT** Change your reading style whenever your purpose in reading changes. ■

Vary Your Reading Style

Skimming When you skim a text, you look it over quickly to get a sense of its contents. Look for highlighted or bold type, headings, and topic sentences. Skimming allows you to take in just enough information to get a general idea of the material.

Scanning When you scan a text, you look it over to find specific information. Look for words related to your topic or purpose for reading.

Close Reading When you closely read a text, you read it carefully to understand and remember its ideas. This process involves identifying main ideas, finding relationships between ideas, and drawing conclusions about what you read.

Using Question-Answer Relationships (QARs) You can master answering questions by understanding how they are written. There are four general types of questions. Once you learn these types, you will be able to answer questions more easily.

QUESTION-ANSWER RELATIONSHIPS

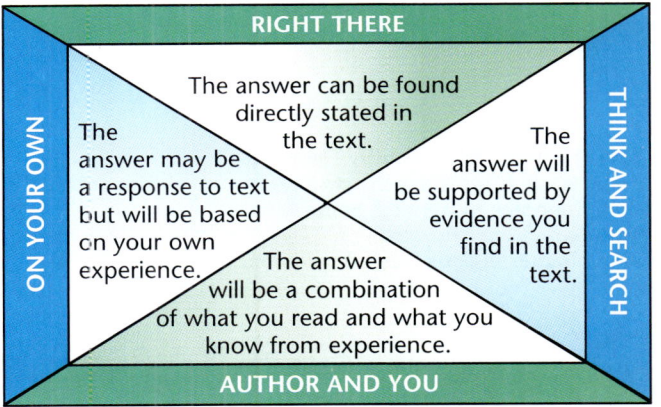

RIGHT THERE
The answer can be found directly stated in the text.

ON YOUR OWN
The answer may be a response to text but will be based on your own experience.

THINK AND SEARCH
The answer will be supported by evidence you find in the text.

The answer will be a combination of what you read and what you know from experience.

AUTHOR AND YOU

🔲 **Research Tip**

Keep a log of your reading-style use. During a period of a week or two, note which style(s) you use for different reading materials. Then, determine which style is most useful for each type of material.

Step-by-Step Teaching Guide

Using Reading Strategies

Teaching Resources: Academic and Workplace Skills Activity Book, p. 32

1. Read and discuss the four techniques. Remind students that names can be deceiving—many people think that because skimming is about getting a quick overview, it can be done without effort or thought. That is not true. Skimming requires attention and memory skills.

2. Choose a brief text, such as a magazine or newspaper article, and give each student a copy of it. Have them use each of the four reading strategies to retrieve specific information (statistics, quotations, names of people, places, or organizations involved).

3. Then, give them a copy of a set of chapter review questions from their literature or social studies textbook. Have them read each question and label the type of each (Right There, Think and Search, Author and You, or On Your Own). What clues and signal words helped them to label each question?

Integrating Workplace Skills

A doctor often uses each of these reading strategies within a short time. A physician at a large hospital may have to scan a patient's chart, skim a ward log, closely read an article in a medical journal, and use QARs when examining a case file. Can students think of other workers that frequently use all four strategies?

✅ **ONGOING ASSESSMENT: Monitor and Reinforce**

If students have difficulty differentiating among the various reading styles, try one of the following options.

Option 1 Have students read the questions in the Standardized Test Preparation Workshop on pages 852–853. Ask them to decide which reading style best fits each question, and then have them explain their choices.

Option 2 Give each student a short newspaper article and have them write three questions about it: one that requires skimming, one scanning, and one close reading. Have them trade questions with partners and use the various reading styles to answer them.

Step-by-Step Teaching Guide

Study Aids

1. Ask students whether they have ever read something for a test and then quickly forgotten the material. Have students share their experiences.

2. Explain that the SQ4R method can help them to retain information.

3. Read and discuss the steps in SQ4R. Use the following questions to prompt discussion: Why is it helpful to preview a text before reading it? How can questioning help me read more actively? Why is it helpful to review material on a regular basis, as opposed to just on the night or two before a test?

Answer Key

▶ **Exercise 2**

1. close reading
2. scanning
3. close reading

▶ **Exercise 3**

Ask students to discuss how these new strategies affected their ability to comprehend and remember what they read.

Customize for
AP Students

Challenge students to do some research on a story or author they enjoyed reading this year. Ask them to write one paragraph that summarizes what they learn. Then, have them write another paragraph explaining which reading strategies they found most useful for this assignment, and why.

Customize for
Visual/Spatial Learners

Encourage these students to use self-sticking notes to mark places in the text where they used a specific reading strategy. This will not only remind them to use the strategy in that place, but it will also help them to visually associate certain types of text with certain reading skills.

Study Aids You can study your textbooks more efficiently by mastering the following six skills: **S**urvey, **Q**uestion, **R**ead, **R**ecite, **R**ecord, and **R**eview. These six skills, abbreviated as SQ4R, will prepare and guide your reading and later help you recall important information.

THE SQ4R METHOD

 Survey — Preview the material you are going to read for these features: chapter title, headings, subheadings, introduction, summary, and questions or exercises.

 Question — Turn each heading into a question about what will be covered under that heading. Ask the questions *who, what, when, where,* and *why* about it.

 Read — Search for the answers to the questions that have been posed in the step above.

 Recite — Orally or mentally recall questions and their related answers.

 Record — Take notes to further reinforce the information. List the main ideas and the major details.

Review — Review the material on a regular basis, using some or all of the steps above.

▶ **Exercise 2** Varying Your Reading Style Identify the reading style you would use first in each of the following situations.
1. You are assigned a history chapter to read for homework.
2. You are looking for the date of a specific event.
3. You are taking notes on a chapter of your science textbook.

▶ **Exercise 3** Using the SQ4R Method Use the SQ4R method to study a chapter or section of a textbook that has been assigned to you. Write a brief explanation of how you used the method and the questions you asked.

💿 **Technology Tip**

Use a graphics or word-processing program on your computer to prepare an SQ4R form to use as you read. Prepare sections for each of the method's skills, and use the forms as you read critically.

Outlining What You Read

A **formal outline** is a method of organizing the information you read according to main ideas, major details, and supporting details.

▶ **KEY CONCEPT** Use a formal outline to arrange important information and ideas. ■

When you make a formal outline, you should do the following:

- Use Roman numerals for main ideas. Use capital letters for major details. Use Arabic numerals for supporting details.
- Use indentation to indicate importance. Main ideas begin at the left. Items begin farther to the right as they become less important.
- Never place a single item under any main idea. Always place two or more items or no item at all.

The example below illustrates a formal outline on graphology.

Graphology ———————— Topic

Main Ideas

I. Definition of graphology
   A. Study of handwriting
   B. Source of information about people
      1. Health
      2. Character
      3. Personality
   C. Based on natural occurrences
      1. Uniqueness of each person's handwriting
      2. Changes in life affect handwriting

Major Details

Supporting Details

II. Items studied by graphologists
   A. Pressure
      1. Fine lines = shyness
      2. Heavy lines = strength and power
   B. Slant
      1. Upward slant = ambition
      2. Downward slant = pride

▶ **Exercise 4** **Making a Formal Outline** Using an assigned chapter of a textbook, make a formal outline of one section. Give your outline at least two main ideas.

☑ **ONGOING ASSESSMENT: Monitor and Reinforce**

If students are having trouble making a formal outline, try one of the following strategies.

Option 1 Review with students the concept of topic sentences. Explain that they can often find the main idea of a paragraph in its first or last sentence. The other sentences should contain elaboration or supporting details.

Option 2 Students might feel more comfortable with a web diagram, which, like an outline, also shows the way details in a selection are organized around a few main ideas. Point out that the center of the web is the most important idea, and the ideas lessen in importance as they branch farther away from the center.

Step-by-Step Teaching Guide

Outlining What You Read

Teaching Resources: Academic and Workplace Skills Activity Book, p. 33

1. Ask students to define the term *outline* as it relates to drawing. Students will most likely mention a line bounding the limits of an object, showing its shape. Explain that a written outline shows the shape or form of a piece of writing.

2. Read the page aloud. Ask students to identify the following features in the sample outline:

   the main idea/topic (Graphology)

   the two supporting ideas (I and II)

   the five subtopics of these two ideas (A, B, C, etc.)

   at least one detail for each subtopic (1, 2, 3, etc.)

3. Have students choose a topic, such as learning a foreign language, planning a day trip, or running for class office. Work with the class to write an outline about the topic. Have one student record the outline on the board.

Answer Key

▶ **Exercise 4**

Make sure students use standard outline style and numbering, and that they include at least two items under each main idea.

Customize for

Logical/Mathematical Learners

These students will find outlining easy and natural because it is a logical way of imposing order on a text. Have them work with students who are struggling at this task. It might be helpful for them to explain outlining to their partners in their own words.

837

Using Graphic Organizers

Teaching Resources: Academic and Workplace Skills Activity Book, p. 34

1. Help students understand the function of graphic organizers by showing them a calendar. This is a visual way of organizing time and the way we spend it. It offers a simple, visual way of organizing information. Have students think of other examples of everyday graphic organizers.

2. Have students give examples of types of writing that would be sensible to organize on a timeline. Have them create a timeline based on a chapter in their social studies books or on highlights from their own lives.

3. Name an event that occurred recently in your school or community, such as the building of a new playground. Ask students to brainstorm for a list of things that caused this event. Then, have them think about how this event/effect might itself be a cause, and have them predict the effects it might have.

30.1

Using Graphic Organizers

A graphic organizer is a tool to use for organizing, summarizing, and reviewing information that you find in your reading. With a graphic organizer, you arrange and combine ideas in an order that allows you to make sense of the information.

▶ **KEY CONCEPT** Use graphic organizers to help you understand text ideas and the relationships among them. ■

Analyze Chronological Order

Using a Timeline Use a timeline to represent events in chronological order. Use the top of the timeline to name the event and the bottom of the timeline to indicate time elapsed or to jot down details about the event.

Analyze Cause and Effect

Using Cause and Effect Most events have more than one cause and more than one effect. Look for the range of contributing and resulting factors when analyzing cause-and-effect relationships.

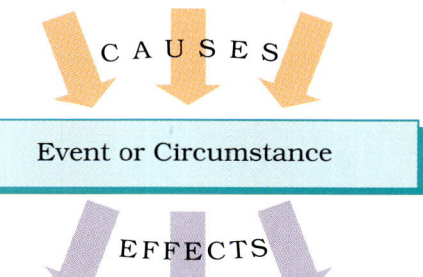

You can use the graphics function of your word-processing program to design your basic graphic organizers. You may want to design and print out several graphic organizers that you use frequently, and refer to them as you read.

Analyze Comparison and Contrast

Making a Venn Diagram The simplest way to visually represent similarities and differences is with a Venn diagram. In a Venn diagram, the overlapping sections of circles are used to show what the two subjects have in common. The portions that do not overlap are used to list distinct features or qualities of that subject. You can also analyze comparisons and contrasts point by point or subject by subject.

Point by Point When analyzing similarities and differences point by point, first identify the points being compared and contrasted. Then, take notes using an outline like the one shown here.

Subject by Subject When analyzing similarities and differences subject by subject, look at all the features of Subject A that will also be considered for Subject B. Take notes using an outline like the one shown here.

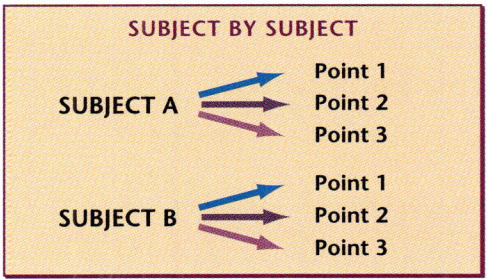

Reading Methods and Tools • 839

Step-by-Step Teaching Guide

Analyze Comparison and Contrast

1. Students will probably be familiar with Venn diagrams. Ask students for a description of how these diagrams are used. If necessary, review how they visually represent comparison and contrast. You may want to draw a Venn diagram on the board and ask students to use it to compare and contrast two things.

2. Explain that point by point and subject by subject are not only graphic organizers, but are also good ways to organize material in a written piece. Effective use of these organizers can work as an outline for a comparison-and-contrast essay.

3. Demonstrate these two organizational strategies using either subjects suggested by students or the following example comparing two cars:

   point 1: mileage—car A
                     —car B

   point 2: price—car A
                 —car B

   point 3: features—car A
                     —car B

   OR

   subject: car A—mileage
                     —price
                     —features

   subject: car B—mileage
                     —price
                     —features

Integrating Research Skills

Explain to students that we all rely on research, whether we do it ourselves or rely on the results of someone else's study. For example, when a coach gives a scouting report on an opposing team or when someone buys a new car after reading reports on various brands and styles, it is obvious how productive good research can be. Graphic organizers help people keep track of what they learn when they do research.

Analyzing and Evaluating

Teaching Resources: Academic and Workplace Skills Activity Book, p. 35

1. Ask students to define the term *nonfiction*. (Nonfiction is writing that is not fiction—prose writing that deals with real people, things, and events. Biographies, histories, science reports, and cookbooks are examples of nonfiction.) Explain that even though nonfiction deals with facts, it is still subject to the individual viewpoint of the author. Readers must be aware of the factors affecting nonfiction.

2. Give students a copy of a magazine or newspaper article. Have them work in pairs and use as many of the strategies explained on this page as possible. For example, when reading an article about protecting whales, you can infer that the author values whales. You could generalize that whales are somehow threatened or endangered. If the writer's bias is toward the whales, he or she might make no comments about who would be affected by the recommended changes. In evaluating the writer's points and credibility, you may find that every fact is true, but you may feel you need more facts to get the whole story.

3. Explain to students that they should be especially wary of information they come across on the Internet. Almost anyone can post information on a Web site, and it is easy to disguise fiction as fact. They should use the strategies on this page to examine it and, if possible, they should always double-check it.

Section 30.2

Reading Nonfiction Critically

A work of nonfiction presents a writer's perspective or ideas on a subject. It should be read critically to analyze and evaluate the writer's ideas and the validity of his or her work.

Analyzing and Evaluating

▶ **KEY CONCEPT** Use general reading strategies in order to examine, evaluate, and form judgments about what you read. ■

Make Inferences Writers don't always say everything they mean. Often they suggest, or imply, ideas. You need to infer the author's larger point or message by looking beyond the details and information provided.

Make Generalizations Put facts and details together to make valid generalizations. For example, if the author writes about people who have difficulty training their dogs, you can make the generalization that some dogs are difficult to train. Avoid using words like *all*, *always*, and *never* in generalizations. These absolute words often make a generalization invalid because few statements are *always* true.

Recognize the Author's Purpose or Bias Be aware that the writer's purpose can influence what he or she includes and how he or she chooses to present the material. Writers often, deliberately or not, present an issue through their own bias—their point of view on a subject. Look for factors that might bias a writer's opinion.

Evaluate the Writer's Points or Statements Weigh the evidence a writer brings to bear on a subject. Consider whether the examples, reasons, or illustrations used to support points are sound and effective.

Evaluate Credibility Question the writer's assertions, points, portrayals, and presentation. Find out whether the writer has the experience or expertise to write with authority on the topic.

Recognize Persuasive Techniques Be on the lookout for faulty logic in persuasive messages. Evaluate whether the support offered is sound. Consider also whether it is relevant. Be wary of emotional appeals.

Judge the Writer's Work Apply your critical judgment to the work as a whole. As you look at the work in its totality, consider questions like these: Do the statements or points follow logically? Is the material clearly organized? Are the writer's points interesting and well supported?

⏱ TIME AND RESOURCE MANAGER

Resources
Print: *Academic and Workplace Skills Activity Book*, pages 35–38

In-Depth Coverage	Accelerated Pace
• Read and discuss pages 840–843. • Have students complete Exercises 6 and 7 in class. • Read pages 844–845 and have students work independently on Exercise 8.	• Assign pages 840–845 for independent reading. • Assign Exercises 6–8 for homework. • Respond to difficulties with the exercises as needed.

Distinguishing Between Fact and Opinion

In order to decide whether the material you are reading is reliable, you must be able to distinguish between fact and opinion.

KEY CONCEPT Analyze material to decide whether the information presented is reliable. ■

A *fact* is a statement that can be verified, or proved true by objective means. Use records, experimentation, or observation to verify the statement. An *opinion* is a statement that cannot be verified by objective means. An opinion is subjective and must be supported with related facts before it can be accepted as valid. An opinion can express a person's feelings about an idea or a situation. It can also express a judgment or make a prediction based on facts. However, an opinion is valid only if sufficient facts are stated to support it.

FACT:	The actress has appeared in five movies.
OPINION:	The actress is very talented.
SUPPORTING FACT:	The actress has won two Academy Awards.
PREDICTION:	The actress will win an Academy Award for this movie.

Exercise 5 Analyzing Fact and Opinion Statements Identify the first sentence of each numbered item as *fact* or *opinion*. Tell whether or not the opinions are supported.

1. Camping is a fun way to vacation. Campers can enjoy the outdoors and relax.
2. The word *apnea* means the "suspension of breathing."
3. Many people keep dogs as pets.
4. Everyone should learn to play a musical instrument.
5. Cats are better pets than dogs. Cats are prettier than dogs.

▶ Critical Viewing Many people have strong opinions about pets and endangered animals. Why do you think this is so? **[Speculate]**

Reading Nonfiction Critically • 841

Step-by-Step Teaching Guide

Distinguishing Fact From Opinion

Teaching Resources: Academic and Workplace Skills Activity Book, p. 36

1. Explain that newspaper editorials express opinions that are usually based on facts. Have students read and discuss an editorial from a recent edition of a school or local newspaper. Allow them to discuss the editorial, explaining whether they agree or disagree with it, and why.

2. Explain that opinion pieces often serve as the basis for thought and discussion. People react to these opinions and, through this process, develop their own opinions and ideas.

3. Stress to students that both facts and opinions are valuable. It is just important not to mistake one for the other.

Answer Key

Exercise 5

1. opinion; supported
2. fact
3. fact
4. opinion; unsupported
5. opinion; unsupported

Customize for
Interpersonal Learners

Have students choose a newspaper editorial they find interesting. Organize a formal debate about the subject of the editorial. Make sure students have prepared their arguments ahead of time. Remind them that in this forum, they will be forced to defend their opinions with facts.

Critical Viewing

Speculate Students may suggest that animals mostly are trusting, comforting beings and deserve the best treatment from humans.

Step-by-Step Teaching Guide

Inductive Reasoning

Teaching Resources: Academic and Workplace Skills Activity Book, p. 37

1. Write the following example on the board to use as a model of inductive reasoning.

   Fact 1: *You read carefully.*

   Fact 2: *Your homework is neat and on time.*

   Fact 3: *You listen in class.*

   Valid generalization: *You're a good student.*

2. Have students think of times they have used inductive reasoning. Did they use it to draw conclusions about something they read? A conversation they had?

Step-by-Step Teaching Guide

Deductive Reasoning

1. Explain that deductive reasoning is sometimes used in solving mysteries or crimes. A detective offers a reasonable theory about what might have happened. He or she then examines the facts, and, if they all fit the theory, it is assumed to be correct.

2. Ask students to consider some of the dangers of using deductive reasoning. (People might be likely to examine only the facts that will confirm their original theories.)

Step-by-Step Teaching Guide

Analogies

1. Tell students that people often use analogies to explain or illustrate ideas. Have students complete the following analogies:

   The human body is like a machine because. . .

   The moon is like a face because. . .

   A dog is like a best friend because. . .

2. Have students share and discuss their answers. Then, challenge them to make false analogies for the human body, the moon, and a dog. Make sure they understand the definition of a false analogy.

Applying Modes of Reasoning

Once you have verified facts and determined that opinions are valid, your next step in critical reading is to analyze the presentation of information. You need to think logically and reasonably about your material in order to draw valid conclusions about it.

KEY CONCEPT Think logically to draw valid conclusions. ■

When you think logically, you use *reasoning* to lead to or support a conclusion. In addition to other forms of reasoning, there are two kinds of formal reasoning: inductive and deductive.

Inductive Reasoning

Moving from specific facts to a conclusion or generalization based on those facts is *inductive reasoning.* A valid generalization is a statement that is supported by evidence and is true in a large number of cases. All generalizations may be open to questioning because there is usually some doubt in reliability—either stated or implied. However, the more evidence you have, the more reliable your generalization will be. If the rules for logical reasoning are not followed, the result is a logical fallacy, or an error in logic.

Deductive Reasoning

Moving from general to specific is *deductive reasoning.* Deduction starts from a general statement that is assumed to be true and applies that statement to specific cases. All of the supporting facts and evidence must be verified before you can consider the conclusion valid.

Analogies

An analogy is a comparison between two things that are similar in some ways but essentially unlike. A *true analogy* compares two different objects or events that are similar in some important way. The comparison relates something unfamiliar to something more familiar. A *false analogy* is one that overlooks essential dissimilarities between the two things being compared. Often, there is some logic in the comparison, but important evidence is omitted. To detect a false analogy, look for provable relationships in a comparison.

🔲 Research Tip

Legal arguments are based on logic. Notice court cases that are summarized in the news or portrayed in movies, books, and television programs. Examine the logic for fallacies and effectiveness.

✏️ STANDARDIZED TEST PREPARATION WORKSHOP

Syllogisms Standardized tests may require students to identify whether a syllogism (or example of deductive reasoning) is true or false.

Choose the valid syllogism from the following list.

A The flu epidemic is sweeping our town. Keesha wasn't in school today. Keesha must have the flu.

B Every child I babysit for is a two-year-old. Many two-year-olds have short attention spans. All the children I babysit have short attention spans.

C All the basketball players have to maintain at least a B average. Colin is on the basketball team. Colin has a B average or better.

D I left the car lights on. Now the car won't start. It must be the starter.

Students should recognize that the only valid syllogism is **C.** The others sound sensible, but they cannot be proven.

Logical Fallacies to Avoid

A logical fallacy is a proposition or argument that does not stand up under scrutiny because it is

- not a truthful representation of the facts.
- not a valid interpretation of the facts.

Identifying Hasty Generalizations One example of a logical fallacy is a *hasty generalization*—a statement that is made about a large number of cases or a whole group on the basis of a few examples, without taking into account exceptions or qualifying factors.

EXAMPLE OF A HASTY GENERALIZATION:	Many of my friends are allergic to cats. None are allergic to dogs. Cats cause more allergies than dogs do.

To avoid being fooled by a hasty generalization, ask yourself the following questions:

- How many illustrations or examples are being offered?
- Is it probable that there are many exceptions?
- Does my own experience contradict what is stated?

Recognizing Circular Reasoning Circular reasoning occurs when the supporting facts for an argument are weak or nonexistent. In this case, the original idea is often restated as if it were evidence.

EXAMPLE OF CIRCULAR REASONING:	We have too much homework. I can never get all my homework done at night. Therefore, teachers should give less homework.

To avoid being fooled by circular reasoning, ask yourself the following questions:

- Does the supporting statement add new information?
- Is the support offered strong enough?

▶ **Exercise 6** **Identifying Forms of Reasoning** Identify the form of reasoning or the logical fallacy that applies to each of the following statements.
1. When I sleep fewer than eight hours I wake up tired. Therefore, I probably need eight hours of sleep a night.
2. The new stove must be defective somehow; it either burns the food or leaves it raw.
3. Both passengers are going to Rome; they must be together.
4. The highways of a country are like a circulatory system for goods and materials.
5. Half of the people in my class like spinach, so half of the population probably likes spinach.

Step-by-Step Teaching Guide

Logical Fallacies to Avoid

1. Read and discuss the section on logical fallacies.
2. Challenge students to think of examples of each type of fallacy. Here are some examples:

   Hasty Generalization: *Teenagers and adults do not understand one another.*

   Circular Reasoning: *I'm really out of shape. People who exercise are in good shape. I can't exercise because I'm not in good shape.*

Customize for
Verbal/Linguistic Learners

Students might find it easier to detect logical fallacies by talking through them with a classmate or with you. They can then write down the steps that they took to examine the chain of logical thinking.

Answer Key

▶ **Exercise 6**

1. inductive; valid
2. inductive; valid
3. deductive; invalid
4. analogy; valid
5. hasty generalization; invalid

Evaluate Word Choice and Language Use

Teaching Resources: Academic and Workplace Skills Activity Book, p. 38

1. Give students a simple statement. (Example: Claudia did not pass the test.) Then, challenge them to rewrite this statement six times, once for each of the six uses of language explained on these pages. Examples:

   Denotation: *Claudia received a mark of sixty percent on the test.*

   Connotation: *Claudia flunked.*

   Irony: *Claudia did her usual brilliant job on the test.*

   Understatement: *Claudia could have done better on the test.*

   Jargon: *Claudia's aggregate score was below established academic minimums.*

   Euphemism: *Claudia did not realize her full potential on the test.*

2. Ask students to discuss how language changes the way facts are interpreted. Have they ever thought carefully about how to say something so that their audience responds in a certain way?

3. Have students look through magazines to find examples of each type of language use. Have them share and discuss their examples.

Critical Viewing

Support Students should realize that newspapers rely on both denotations and connotations. However, reporters often use connotation to express subtly an opinion they do not feel free to express openly.

Evaluating Word Choice and Language Usage

Language is a tool we use to make sense of the world. Until we can express a thought in words, we usually do not understand the thought and cannot explain it to someone else. In addition to thoughts, we express feelings by means of words.

▶ **KEY CONCEPT** Learn to identify different uses of language. ■

In your reading, you will find language used in various ways. Recognizing when language is being used to communicate honestly and when it is being used to distort information is an important skill. When you think critically, you need to distinguish between language that presents material clearly and honestly and language that misrepresents ideas and manipulates emotions.

Denotation The denotation of a word is found in a dictionary. It is a word's literal meaning and conveys a neutral tone. Factual or technical information contains denotation—material that is not necessarily meant to pass judgment.

Connotation Words acquire connotative meanings through their usage over time. A word's connotation is its implied meaning; it can take on a positive or negative tone. Certain connotations are emotionally charged and may be used to distort meaning or suggest different interpretations. Generally, the connotation of a word emphasizes certain characteristics or specific information, or it reveals implied or hidden attitudes.

◀ **Critical Viewing** Do newspaper articles depend more on the denotations or the connotations of words? Explain. **[Support]**

844 • Reading Skills

Irony Irony is the general term for literary techniques that portray differences between appearance and reality, expectation and result, or meaning and intention.

Understatement When an important idea is played down or treated casually, it is considered to be an understatement.

Inflated Language and Jargon When a writer uses scholarly, technical, or scientific words and overly long phrases, it is considered inflated language. Sometimes, inflated language is used to impress the reader or listener. It can be used to conceal the meaning behind the words.

One type of inflated language spoken by people in a specialized profession or hobby is called jargon. Although jargon appears to be scientific or technical, it often obscures otherwise simple ideas. Jargon can end up making language vague and meaningless.

Euphemism Words and phrases that are considered unpleasant or offensive are sometimes replaced with euphemisms. A euphemism is used to soften the meaning that a more direct word would convey.

▶ **Exercise 7** Analyzing and Evaluating Uses of Language

Match each numbered item to the description of language use. Use each letter only once.

1. Reckless spending is the roct of the problem.
2. We may downsize to reduce costs.
3. The ratio of personnel to workstations is unbalanced in light of the current space requirements.
4. The change will not be easy.
5. So few people appreciate the benefits of an enforced resignation.

a. Irony
b. Understatement
c. Euphemism
d. Negative connotations
e. Inflated language

📀 Research Tip

Advertising campaigns often capitalize on language use. Observe advertisements in all forms of media, and analyze the language used. Note when language use is effective and when it is misleading.

Real-World Connection

Explain that each use of language is useful in some situations and misleading or inappropriate in others. For example, in some careers irony would make communication difficult. (Example: For doctors to rely on irony might be inappropriate because they are people whose words we are accustomed to take seriously.) Other careers rely on irony to communicate. (Example: A comedian uses ironic comments to make people laugh or look at things in a different way.)

Integrating Listening Skills

Students might benefit from completing this exercise aurally. Read the statements aloud with a lot of drama. Students might find it easier to detect irony and other language uses from listening closely to your tone of voice.

Answer Key

▶ **Exercise 7**

1. d
2. c
3. e
4. b
5. a

✓ **ONGOING ASSESSMENT: Monitor and Reinforce**

If students are having difficulty understanding the difference between connotation and denotation, use the following strategy.

Have students choose a simple word, such as *sad*. Ask them to look in the thesaurus and write down a list of as many synonyms as possible for the word (examples: unhappy, forlorn, miserable, shattered). Ask students whether describing someone as *sad* is the same as describing him or her as *miserable* or *forlorn*. They should note that although the words have the same basic meaning, they vary in degree and tone. They have the same denotation, but very different connotations.

Analyzing and Evaluating

Teaching Resources: Academic and Workplace Skills Activity Book, p. 39

1. Explain to students that using a variety of strategies is one of the keys to successful reading. Some strategies may seem natural, but all can be learned and practiced.

2. Point out that, in establishing a purpose for reading, students may have more than one purpose. This step refers to a primary purpose. For example, if they are studying for a test, their primary purpose might be to find out. However, in order to do this, they may need to interpret, and it is possible that they will enjoy the reading, too.

3. Go over each of the six additional strategies, asking students to share examples of when they have used the strategies and how they worked.

4. Remind students that more than one strategy can be used at a time. In fact, using more than one strategy makes it more likely that they will understand and enjoy a work.

5. Point out that the purpose will often help determine the strategies they use. For example, *analyze* would be more likely to go along with *to understand* than *to enjoy*. However, no purpose limits the strategies that can be used. A reader can read to enjoy and still use all the strategies if they add to the enjoyment.

Integrating Vocabulary Skills

As students progress through high school English, they will begin to learn more literary terms. If they are not yet familiar with terms such as *protagonist*, *denouement*, and *diction*, suggest reference books in which they can look up definitions of literary terms. Encourage students to use these terms as they discuss literary writing.

Section 30.3

Reading Literary Writing

To understand and appreciate works of fiction, you must use your judgment and your imagination. It is just as important for you to respond personally to what you are reading. General reading strategies presented here can be applied to all types of fiction. You will also find specific strategies for reading short stories and novels, drama, and poetry.

Analyzing and Evaluating

▶ **KEY CONCEPT** Use a variety of reading strategies to increase your understanding of fictional works. ■

Establish a Purpose for Reading Before you begin to read a piece, decide why you are reading. Establish a purpose for reading, such as to find out, to understand, to interpret, to enjoy, or to solve a problem.

Ask Questions As you read, question what's going on in the text. For example: *Who* is speaking? *When* and *where* does an event take place? *What* caused it to happen? *Why* does a character say what he or she does? Read to find answers to your questions.

Reread or Read Ahead Reread a sentence, paragraph, stanza, or scene to find the connections among words and ideas. Read ahead to find more information about words and ideas.

Make Personal Connections Use your own experiences to better understand characters, events, and ideas. Think about the ways in which people and events in your own life connect to characters and events in the text.

Read Aloud Use this technique with poetry to hear the sound and rhythm of the lines; use it with drama to appreciate dialogue. Read other works of fiction aloud to gain a better sense of the author's voice.

Analyze You analyze nonfiction for reliability, but you can use the same strategy to analyze fiction to discover the effect of and reason for an author's choices. In addition to understanding specifics, this strategy will give you an overall sense of the piece.

Respond As you read, think about characters, events, conflicts, images, and other literary elements and how you respond to them. When you finish reading, think about what the work means to you, what the theme of the piece is, and how the work has affected your perspective on life.

846 • Reading Skills

⏱ TIME AND RESOURCE MANAGER

Resources
Print: *Academic and Workplace Skills Activity Book*, pages 39–43

In-Depth Coverage	Accelerated Pace
• Read and discuss pp. 846–851. • Assign Exercises 8–9 to be done in class. • Assign Exercise 10 as homework. • Take the class to the school library to complete Exercise 11.	• Assign pp. 846–851 for independent reading. • Have students complete Exercises 8–11 on their own. Discuss their answers in class.

Reading Fiction

In a great work of fiction—a novel or short story—every word has been chosen carefully to express a precise meaning. A plot has been structured, characters delineated, clues dropped, and themes deliberately implied to create a unique yet believable world. By applying the following strategies, you can more fully appreciate the fictional world a writer has so carefully constructed:

Envision the Action in Your Mind
A skilled writer describes action clearly and vividly to help you picture the scenes of a story in your mind. Allow yourself to be carried away by the pictures painted by the author's words.

Connect the Literature to Your Own Experiences
If you empathize, or feel as another does, you'll be able to put yourself in a character's shoes. Imagine yourself in the story's setting and in the character's situations.

Question and Predict
In life, you ask yourself questions about people's actions and motivations. What was he *really* doing? Why did she say that? Relate to a work of literature in the same way. Ask yourself why the characters behave as they do. When you find yourself wondering how a series of events will unfold, pause and predict what will happen. When you are trying to predict outcomes, look back, recall, and carefully weigh what you have experienced so far.

Draw Inferences and Conclusions
Fictional characters and situations don't come neatly labeled "Villain" or "Disaster" —you have to infer information from the clues you're given. Use a character's attitudes and actions to read "between the lines." When you've finished reading a piece of fiction, reflect on its overall meaning. What general ideas does the writer want you to carry away?

Connect to Historical Context
Consider the events and customs of the time in which the work was written. These factors will influence the way an author portrays characters.

▶ **Exercise 8** **Reading Short Stories and Novels** Read a short story from your textbook or another source. Write a brief explanation of how you applied each of the strategies on this page.

▲ **Critical Viewing**
What clues indicate that this girl is actively involved in what she is reading? **[Analyze]**

Step-by-Step Teaching Guide

Reading Fiction

Teaching Resources: Academic and Workplace Skills Activity Book, p. 40

1. Read aloud the strategies for reading fiction on page 847.

2. To practice these strategies, distribute copies of a well-known fairy tale, such as "Cinderella."

3. Have volunteers read the fairy tale aloud. Ask students how they envision the story. What does the setting look like? What do the characters look like?

4. Next, ask them to connect the story to their own experiences. Have they ever been treated unfairly the way Cinderella was? Have they ever had to search for someone or something the way the prince searches for Cinderella?

5. Encourage students to question the story. Why do the stepsisters act as they do? Why does Cinderella react the way she does?

6. Ask students to draw conclusions about the story. Why do people tell this story to children? What is its message?

Answer Key

▶ **Exercise 8**

Encourage students to cite specific examples of passages to which they applied each strategy.

Customize for
Gifted and Talented Students

Have students choose a short story or novel they've read in class this year. Challenge them to do research on the historical context of the selection. Also, have them research the author's views on the events of the day. Have them write a one-page report on how they believe the events and customs of the time affect the way the piece is written.

Critical Viewing

Analyze Students may observe that she looks intent, her eyes and thoughts appear to be focused on the book.

Reading Drama

Teaching Resources: Academic and Workplace Skills Activity Book, p. 41

1. Help students become familiar with reading an author's stage directions. Give them copies of a short excerpt from a play. Discuss elements the author mentions, such as scenery, lighting, and the movement of the actors.

2. Discuss the importance of these elements. For example, how does the lighting affect the overall mood of the play? How can a change in position (e.g., sitting as opposed to standing) affect the way the audience interprets a character? How might it affect the way characters relate to one another?

3. Students might find it helpful to sketch storyboards to help them envision each scene as they read a play.

Answer Key

▶ **Exercise 9**

For a variation, have students read the first acts of two plays by different authors. Have them compare and contrast the stage directions.

Customize for
Bodily/Kinesthetic Learners

Challenge students to act out a scene from the excerpt you studied in the step-by-step teaching guide above. Remind students to follow the author's stage directions. Students might want to assign roles, such as director, costume director, and lighting director, to help them approach the material in an organized manner.

Critical Viewing

Analyze Students may say that an air of seriousness must be maintained, per directions, and that costuming must be correct for the time period.

30.3

Reading Drama

While plays share many elements with prose, fiction, and poetry, the greatest difference is that a drama is designed to be acted out on a stage before an audience. The story unfolds through dialogue and action and is integrated with the setting that the audience observes—largely from scenery and props. Stage directions indicate when and how the actors move and sometimes suggest sound and lighting effects. When you read a play, you are reading a script; you must always keep in mind that it was written to be performed.

Envision the Action Reading a play without envisioning the action is like watching a movie with your eyes shut. Use scenery and prop descriptions, stage directions, and other details to create the scene in your mind. Where and when does the action take place? How and where do the actors move? What do they sound like? What goes on between the characters, and what do they say to one another?

Connect the Play to Its Historical Context Explore the play's setting. When does the action of the drama occur? What conditions existed during that time period? If the drama takes place in a historical or foreign setting, consider that customs and accepted conduct may differ from those with which you are familiar.

Summarize Dramas are often broken into acts or scenes. These breaks give you an opportunity to review the action. What is the conflict? What happens to move it toward its resolution? Put the characters' actions and words together as you summarize.

▶ **Exercise 9** **Reading Drama** Read the first act or the first few scenes of a play. List three details describing the play's setting, and elaborate briefly on its historical context; describe the main character(s) in the act or scenes you read; identify two events and the stage directions that indicate them; and describe the action that takes place.

▲ **Critical Viewing**
What stage directions would you expect to find in the written version of this scene from *The Crucible*? What historical details would the playwright have to provide? [**Analyze**]

848 • Reading Skills

Reading Poetry

Because a poem generally comes at the truth sideways rather than head on, you must use a number of strategies to help you unravel the meaning the poet has hidden within the lines.

Identify the Poem's Speaker Identifying the speaker of a poem is an important first step in gaining insight into a poem. The speaker may be the poet or a fictional character created by the poet.

Engage Your Senses Poems use images—words or phrases that appeal to the five senses—to convey meaning. As you read, picture the visual images in all their detail. Hear the sounds described, and imagine the textures and scents. When you engage your senses, you will find greater enjoyment and meaning in the poem. To help you engage poetry on the sensory level, you may want to use a sensory chart, to which you can add words or images from a poem.

Relate Structure to Meaning Notice where sentences begin and end and how ideas are grouped into stanzas; the start of a new stanza often signals the introduction of a new thought or idea.

Paraphrase Pause occasionally to restate passages in your own words.

Connect to a Historical Context Understanding the social, political, economic, and literary environment in which a poem was written will help you grasp its meaning.

Listen to the Poem To fully appreciate a poem, you must listen to it. Try reading the poem aloud. Analyze the melodies of literary language, paying attention to rhythms and to the repetition of certain sounds. Consider how they contribute to the mood and meaning of the work.

> **Exercise 10** **Reading Poetry** Select a poem from your textbook or personal reading. Read the poem aloud, and listen to its sound. Then, write an analysis of the poem in which you identify the speaker; characterize three images; describe the poem's rhythms and repetition; explain what you think is the poem's meaning; and conclude with a description of the poem's overall effect.

Reading Literary Writing • 849

Reading from Varied Sources

Teaching Resources: Academic and Workplace Skills Activity Book, p. 43

1. Explain to students the advantages to reading from varied sources: They are more likely to get the whole story. They are more likely to have a deeper and richer appreciation of a subject. They can often connect with one form more easily than another.

2. Point out that diaries, letters, and journals offer first-hand experience and observations. The information is what the writer actually saw and experienced. Even if the writer's point of view is different from the reader's, the reactions are genuine. And first-hand accounts, while sometimes biased, just as often offer observations of events that are more reliable than later interpretations.

3. To demonstrate how varied reading can add depth to a subject, share this example with students: For World War II, *The Diary of Anne Frank* would relate the actual experiences and emotions of a young girl during the war; newspapers from the time would relate statistics and developments; and transcripts of speeches, such as those of Winston Churchill, would underscore attitudes and strategies.

4. Point out that electronic texts are not really a different type of information, but just a different way of obtaining it. Often, the speeches, stories, and newspaper articles that one could read on paper are also available on the Internet. However, one might be able to access organizations or clubs that are interested in a topic, or find articles and resources not available locally. Underscore the importance of being careful on the Internet, to make sure sources are reliable.

Section 30.4

Reading From Varied Sources

Information is made available to you in a wide variety of formats. These sources include—but are not limited to—books, magazines, Web pages, advertisements, newspapers, letters, and speeches. By familiarizing yourself with different types of sources, you will widen the range and type of information you can learn and use.

Read Diaries, Letters, and Journals

Diaries, letters, and journals are firsthand accounts of events or circumstances. Although they are not usually written with publication in mind, they are often published after the writer's death with the permission of his or her family. Some may be written by people whose achievements make them interesting subjects. Others are written by people who lived in interesting times. Keep in mind when you read these primary sources that not all the information in them will be strictly factual. Much of what you read will reflect the writer's personal opinions.

Read Newspapers

Newspapers, which are printed on a daily or weekly basis, are an excellent source of information on current events and issues in your community, in the United States, and around the world. When you read a newspaper, take into account whether the coverage is local, national, or global. Each section of a newspaper has its own purpose. For example, editorial pages offer opinions and evaluations of the topics they cover. Other sections give an unbiased, factual account of the topics they cover. As with all sources, read newspapers critically. Keep an eye out for bias or faulty logic.

Read Transcripts of Speeches and Interviews

A transcript is a written record of what was spoken. You can obtain transcripts of most famous speeches in library resources. Books and other references contain the printed record of what a speaker said. Interview transcripts are usually available through the media that produced the interview. For example, for a transcript of an interview on television, you can write to the television station that produced the program. Speeches and interviews offer one person's perspective on an issue, a situation, or a condition. These thoughts, unlike those set down in diaries or letters, are usually intended for publication. Like diaries and letters, speeches and interviews reveal the person's opinions.

Read Electronic Texts

Web pages, electronic advertising, and e-mail—each of these presents text through an electronic medium. Whether you read text on screen or on a page, read critically. When you read a Web page, consider the source when you evaluate the reliability of the information presented. Look for evidence that the creator of the page has background and expertise in the area. Determine whether the page is sponsored by a company or group that wants to promote a particular point of view. The Internet can be an excellent resource, but as is true with all resources, you must use it with a critical awareness.

▲ **Critical Viewing**
For what types of information might these students be searching? **[Infer]**

▶ **Exercise 11** **Reading Varied Sources** Choose an event or time period from American history, such as the Civil War, the Depression, or the bombing of Pearl Harbor. Find an account of the event or the period in at least three different sources described on these pages. Write a summary of the information you find in each. Then, in a brief evaluation, compare and contrast the type of information you found in each, as well as the unique perspective you gained from reading each source.

Reflecting on Your Reading

After a week of applying reading skills and strategies to both nonfiction and fiction works, think about the experience of using them. Use these questions to direct your reflection:

- Which textbook sections and features do I use most often? For what purpose do I use them?

- Which reading strategies will be most useful to me when I am studying? Which will I use when I am doing research?

- In what ways will the questioning strategies help me analyze and evaluate what I read?

- Which strategies for reading fiction do I find most useful? Which do I find most difficult to use? Which strategies do I want to try to use more often? Why?

Jot down your responses and ideas in a journal or notebook. If you like, compare your thoughts and ideas with those of a partner.

Reading From Varied Sources • 851

Step-by-Step Teaching Guide

Making Inferences and Predictions

Teaching Resources: Standardized Test Preparation Workbook, pp. 59–60

1. Remind students that they do not need to memorize the passage they read. They can and should refer to it as often as necessary while answering the related questions.

2. Explain to students that the answers to reading questions can always be found in the passage. In other words, students do not need background knowledge of meteorology to answer questions on a passage about the weather. They just have to read carefully.

3. Explain also that while all answers can be found in the passage, they are not always spelled out. Sometimes they are suggested or implied. The reader must make logical inferences based on information in the text.

Standardized Test Preparation Workshop

Making Inferences and Predictions

The reading sections of standardized tests often measure your ability to make inferences. You can make inferences, or draw logical conclusions, about what you have read, about characters and stories, or you can make them about the author's purpose or point of view. Some questions require you to make a prediction or anticipate future actions or outcomes from the material you have read. Some tests will ask you to read a passage, think about it by responding to a question, and explain your response in writing.

The following sample items will help you prepare for answering these types of questions on standardized tests.

Test Tip

Before answering difficult questions, first mark them. Then, answer all the easy questions. Finally, go back and use the majority of your time to work on those questions that you have marked.

Sample Test Items	Answers and Explanations
Directions: Read each passage. Then, answer the questions that follow the passage. from "To Build a Fire," Jack London Day had broken cold and gray, exceedingly cold and gray, when the man turned aside from the main Yukon trail and climbed the high earth-bank, where a dim and little-traveled trail led eastward through the fat spruce timberland. It was a steep bank, and he paused for breath at the top. . . .	

1 The author opens the story with this description to—
 	
  A establish setting
 	
  B describe weather conditions
 	
  C explain the story's title
 	
  D provide information on the Yukon trail
	The correct answer is *A*. The details and word choice establish the setting of the story as isolated and forbidding. The details do not explain the story's title or provide factual information about the Yukon trail. Although the weather is described, it is described as part of the overall setting.

READ, THINK, and EXPLAIN: Answer the following question. Base your answer on "To Build a Fire." What kind of mood does the author establish in this passage? Support your answer with details from the story.	Your answer should include examples of word choice, such as *cold, gray,* and *dim,* as well as details such as the lonely setting and the steep bank, to show that the mood of the passage is lonely and desolate.

852 • Reading Skills

TEST-TAKING TIP

Students might find it helpful to read the related questions before reading a passage on a standardized test. This will help to focus their reading. It will prevent them from spending valuable time on concepts they don't need to know about.

Another way for students to focus their reading is to underline the main idea and the details that support it. This will help them focus on the most important parts of the passage. They can write in the test booklet itself.

Practice 1 **Directions:** Read each passage. Then answer the questions that follow the passage.

from "An Episode of War," Stephen Crane

. . . His lips pursed as he drew with his sword various crevices in the heap, until brown squares of coffee, astoundingly equal in size, appeared on the blanket. He was on the verge of a great triumph in mathematics, and the corporals were thronging forward, each to reap a little square, when suddenly the lieutenant cried out and looked quickly at a man near him as if he suspected it was a case of personal assault. The others cried out also when they saw blood upon the lieutenant's sleeve.

He had winced like a man stung, swayed dangerously, and then straightened. The sound of his hoarse breathing was plainly audible. He looked sadly, mystically, over the breast-work at the green face of a wood, where now were many little puffs of white smoke.

1 What does the author reveal about the lieutenant in the description of the rationing of coffee?
   A. The lieutenant is a man who is prepared for the unexpected.
   B. The lieutenant is orderly and expects things to happen in an orderly, predictable fashion.
   C. The lieutenant is a serious military official and is fair to all the men.
   D. The lieutenant is a mathematician.

2 The little white puffs of smoke indicate
   F. where the fire for the coffee is being burned
   G. where the shot that wounded the lieutenant came from
   H. the mist and clouds that surround the army camp
   I. where fireworks were lit

3 What effect does the lieutenant's injury during the performance of an everyday task have?
   A. It causes the soldiers to leave the coffee in an attempt to overtake the shooter.
   B. It emphasizes the inability to control things during a war.
   C. It frightens the soldiers.
   D. It annoys the military generals.

4 Which words BEST describe the lieutenant's reaction?
   F. shocked and disoriented
   G. angry
   H. relieved to no longer have to deal with the coffee
   I. happy because he can go home

5 The lieutenant will most likely
   A. finish rationing the coffee
   B. go to the field hospital
   C. write a letter home
   D. go into the woods alone

Practice 2 **Directions:** Answer the following question. Base your answer on "An Episode of War."

READ, THINK, and EXPLAIN: How does the way in which the lieutenant is wounded make him a sympathetic character? Use details and information from the passage to explain your answer.

▶ **Practice 1**

1. B
2. G
3. B
4. F
5. B

▶ **Practice 2**

Answers will vary. Students should note that the lieutenant is a sympathetic character because he is wounded while performing an act of kindness—distributing rations equally among his men.

Customize for
Less Advanced Students

Students might find the first paragraph difficult to understand. Point out that reading the first question gives them a summary of what takes place in that paragraph: The lieutenant is preparing to ration coffee to his men when something unexpected happens.

Integrating Vocabulary Skills

Encourage students to use context clues to determine the meaning of *thronging* and *winced*. They should note that *throng* means "to press forward," which they can infer because they know the soldiers are eager to get their rations. *Wince* means "to shrink back in pain, embarrassment, or alarm." Which clues in the passage might help them arrive at this definition?

In-Depth Lesson Plan

	LESSON FOCUS	PRINT AND MEDIA RESOURCES
DAY 1	**Basic Study Skills** Students develop a study plan and take organized notes on their reading and classroom lectures in outline and summary form. (pp. 854–857)	**Teaching Resources** *Academic and Workplace Skills Activity Book*, pp. 44–45
DAY 2	**Reference Skills** Students gather information using a full complement of library resources, including electronic catalogs and other non-print materials. (pp. 858–863)	**Teaching Resources** *Academic and Workplace Skills Activity Book*, pp. 46–48
DAY 3	**Using Dictionaries** Students survey a dictionary's contents and distinguish an array of types of dictionaries. (pp. 864–867)	**Teaching Resources** *Academic and Workplace Skills Activity Book*, p. 49
DAY 4	**Using Other References** Students consult encyclopedias, atlases, and almanacs as well as electronic and media resources such as videos, CD-ROMs and the Internet. (pp. 868–871)	**Teaching Resources** *Academic and Workplace Skills Activity Book*, 50–52
DAY 5	**Test-Taking Skills** Students learn to budget time to preview, answer questions on, and proofread tests, and how to approach various types of questions on standardized tests such as the SAT and ACT. (pp. 872–877)	**Teaching Resources** *Academic and Workplace Skills Activity Book*, pp. 53–54; *Formal Assessment*, Ch. 31

Accelerated Lesson Plan

	LESSON FOCUS	PRINT AND MEDIA RESOURCES
DAY 1	**Basic Study and Reference Skills** Students review the full array of library resources available to them, as well as strategies for organizing their studies. (pp. 854–867)	**Teaching Resources** *Academic and Workplace Skills Activity Book*, pp. 44–49
DAY 2	**Reference Tools and Test-Taking Skills** Students work independently to review the use of reference tools such as videotape and the Internet, and review test-taking skills and strategies. (pp. 868–877)	**Teaching Resources** *Academic and Workplace Skills Activity Book*, pp. 50–54; *Formal Assessment*, Ch. 31

Options for Adapting Lesson Plans

HOMEWORK
Have students conduct independent library research.

FEATURES
Extend coverage with the Standardized Test Preparation Workshop (p. 878).

TECHNOLOGY
Students may use the Internet to conduct independent research. Have them print out their completed work.

INTEGRATED SKILLS COVERAGE

Research Skills
SE pp. 860, 862, 864, 866, 868, 872; ATE p. 862

Technology Skills SE pp. 855, 856, 858, 869, 870, 871; ATE p. 871

Vocabulary Skills SE p. 867; ATE p. 866

Spelling Skills ATE p. 861

Workplace Skills ATE p. 856

Current Events ATE p. 857

Viewing and Representing
Critical Viewing, SE pp. 854, 857, 859, 861, 863, 869, 871, 876
ATE p. 870

Speaking and Listening SE p. 874

Real-World Connection ATE pp. 870, 875

ASSESSMENT SUPPORT

Standardized Test Preparation Workshop, SE p. 878;
ATE pp. 875, 879
Standardized Test Preparation Workbook, pp. 61–62
Formal Assessment, Ch. 31

MEETING INDIVIDUAL NEEDS

Less Advanced Students ATE pp. 855, 862, 864, 872, 879.
See also Ongoing Assessments ATE pp. 856, 874.
Gifted and Talented Students ATE p. 863
AP Students ATE pp. 859, 879
ESL Students ATE pp. 856, 861
Logical/Mathematical Learners ATE p. 868
Visual/Spatial Learners ATE p. 860

BLOCK SCHEDULING

Pacing Suggestions
For 90-minute Blocks
• Have students review the extensive Reference Skills section in a single period.
• Focus one class period on Test-Taking Skills. Give students a half-hour sample ACT or SAT test.

Resources for Varying Instruction
• *Academic and Workplace Skills Activity Book,* pp. 44–54

Professional Development Support
• *How to Manage Instruction in the Block* This Teaching Resource provides management and activity suggestions.

MEDIA AND TECHNOLOGY

For the Teacher
• *Resource Pro* CD-ROM

WRITING AND GRAMMAR WEB SITE

The Interactive Writing and Grammar Web Site provides a wide array of support for students, teachers, and parents.

www.phschool.com

Lesson Objectives

1. To use study strategies such as note taking, outlining, and using study-guide questions to better understand texts

2. To compile information from primary and secondary sources in systematic ways using available technology

3. To use writing as a study tool to clarify and remember information

4. To read in varied sources such as diaries, journals, textbooks, maps, newspapers, letters, speeches, memoranda, electronic texts, and other media

5. To use reference material such as glossary, dictionary, thesaurus, and available technology to determine precise meaning and usage

6. To investigate the source of a media presentation or production such as who made it and why it was made

7. To locate appropriate print and non-print information using text and technical resources, including databases and the Internet

8. To produce summaries of texts by identifying main ideas and their supporting details

9. To construct images such as graphic organizers based on text descriptions and text structures

Chapter 31 Study, Reference, and Test-Taking Skills

▲ Critical Viewing
On what type of project do you think this student is currently working? On what do you base your answer? **[Speculate]**

The more skillful you become at studying, the more you will be able to concentrate your efforts on doing your best work. Good study skills can be the key to success in school—you will find that you will need to study less, you will improve your grades, and you will increase your performance on college entrance exams. Overall, your attitude toward school and test-taking will be more positive.

In this chapter, you will learn more about making the most of your study time. You will also learn more about finding information in printed and electronic sources. In addition, you will receive valuable tips that can help you improve your test scores.

854 • Study, Reference, and Test-Taking Skills

Critical Viewing

Speculate Students may suggest that the student is working on a research project.

⏱ TIME AND RESOURCE MANAGER

Resources
Print: *Academic and Workplace Skills Activity Book,* pp. 44–45

In-Depth Coverage	Accelerated Pace
• Cover pp. 854–857 in class. • Give students time to complete Exercises 1–3 in class.	• Discuss study planning and note taking with the class. • Assign Exercises 1–3 for students to complete independently.

Basic Study Skills

Developing a Study Plan

Time management is essential to your success in school. A study plan can help you to use time to your best advantage.

> **KEY CONCEPT** Develop a study plan in order to manage and use your time most efficiently. ■

Study Area Working in an area that you associate only with studying will enable you to concentrate so that you can do your work better. Set up a study area that is free of distractions, quiet, well lit, and contains all the necessary materials.

Study Schedule Establishing a study schedule will help you fit in all of your assignments and activities. Make a study schedule that will fit your personal needs.

MAKING A STUDY SCHEDULE

1. Block out time periods in which you have activities, such as the regular school day, after-school clubs or sports, dinner, etc.
2. Block out study periods of no longer than forty-five minutes each. Take a ten-minute break between each period.
3. Schedule study periods for those times when you are most alert.
4. Plan to study your most difficult subject first.
5. Use study hall and free time at school to complete some assignments.

Assignment Book Keeping track of your assignments in an assignment book will enable you to organize your time to complete both short-term and long-term assignments efficiently. A long-term assignment, such as a research paper, can be divided into short-term goals that you must meet in order to complete the assignment.

> **Exercise 1** **Evaluating Your Study Plan** Identify the study skill you need to improve most: setting up a study area, making a study schedule, or keeping an assignment book. Work to improve that skill for one week, and then evaluate your progress.

🖳 Technology Tip

Create computer forms for your study schedule and assignment book using software such as a word-processing, spreadsheet, or time-management program. You can update and change your forms as your needs change.

Customize for
Less Advanced Students

To help students complete Exercise 1, have them create a chart that includes the study skill they have chosen to work on, their goal, and the steps they will take each day to reach it. Ask students to record their progress on the chart every day.

PREPARE and ENGAGE

Interest GRABBER Ask students what they enjoy, if anything, about studying, finding information in reference sources, and taking tests (learning new things, being rewarded with good grades, etc.). Then, ask what they do not like about these activities. Tell the class that the guidelines in this chapter will help them to study, use reference sources, and take tests more easily and effectively.

Activate Prior Knowledge

Ask students to share specific questions they have about studying, using reference materials, and taking tests. What do they hope to learn about these subjects? List their questions on the board, and remind students to look for answers to them as they progress through the chapter.

TEACH

> **Step-by-Step Teaching Guide**

Developing a Study Plan

Teaching Resources: Academic and Workplace Skills Activity Book, p. 44

1. After students read "Developing a Study Plan," use questions such as these to prompt discussion:

   How do you keep track of your assignments?

   What do you consider to be your main obstacle in studying effectively?

2. Discuss each of the elements of the study schedule shown on this page. Do students think this study schedule is viable? Why or why not? How might they alter it to make it work?

Answer Key

> **Exercise 1**

After students have identified skills that need improvement, meet with them individually to go over their plans.

Taking Notes

Teaching Resources: Academic and Workplace Skills Activity Book, p. 45

1. After students read "Taking Notes," ask whether their notes should be clear enough for everyone to read. Why? (The notes should be clear enough for the notetaker to read. Unreadable notes are useless. Notetakers can make up their own abbreviations and shortcuts, as long as they remember what they mean.)

2. Have students identify the main ideas and supporting details in the outline on this page. Discuss how they can distinguish between these two groups in an outline. (Example: with Roman numerals, letters, or numbers)

Answer Key

▶ **Exercise 2**

After students have completed their notes, have students share results in class.

Integrating Workplace Skills

Outlining Tasks Have students imagine they are supervisors in a workplace of their choosing. Ask them to outline a typical project in that workplace so their employees can carry it out.

Customize for ESL Students

For Exercise 2, suggest that students listen to a taped version of a newscast. That way, they can slow it down when necessary in order to focus on words or phrases they did not understand the first time.

31.1

Taking Notes

Taking notes is an active way to organize and condense material you need to learn. To take useful notes on classroom lectures and activities, as well as on what you read in textbooks, make sure that you have an organized notebook or binder.

- Notes for each subject should be separated by a labeled divider.
- Notes should be neat, with the date and topic on each page.

▶ **KEY CONCEPT** Use outlines or summaries to take notes while listening or reading. ■

Modified Outline A *formal outline* is a method for taking notes that shows the relationship between main ideas and other ideas that support them (see Section 13.2 for an example). A *modified outline* is a skeleton of the subject—it allows you to organize information quickly. Use a modified outline to record information from lectures, films, discussions, and books. You can also use it to organize ideas before answering questions on an essay test.

In the modified outline below, main ideas are underlined and supporting details are numbered. Notice the short phrases and occasional abbreviations or symbols that are used.

MODIFIED OUTLINE:

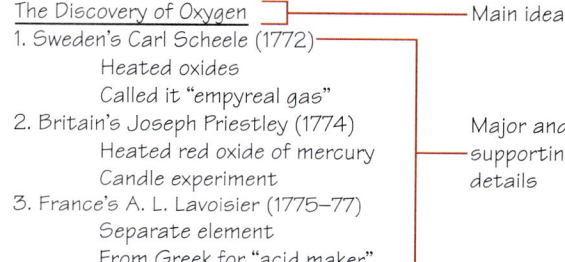

▶ **Exercise 2 Making a Modified Outline** Listen to a television newscast and take notes in modified outline form, using your own words. After the newscast, read your notes, and fill in any information that is needed to make them more clear.

⊙ Technology Tip

Word-processing programs often have an outlining feature. You may find it helpful to use this feature as you outline material you are studying.

✓ **ONGOING ASSESSMENT: Monitor and Reinforce**

Use one of the following strategies to help students determine what information to include when making an outline or taking notes.

Option 1 Have students choose a class to take notes in for a week. At the end of the week, meet with students and review their notes. If they are not including enough detail, encourage them to write enough so that each main point is supported by at least one detail.

Option 2 Show students the class notes of a student who is a comfortable and efficient notetaker. Discuss the qualities that make these notes so useful.

Summary Another useful way to record information is to write a summary of it. In a *summary*, you state the main ideas of a lecture or printed material in your own words, using a few complete sentences. You may take notes in a modified outline and then summarize them, or you may take notes in summary form directly from listening or reading.

Exercise 3 **Writing a Summary** Write a summary of the notes you took in your modified outline of a television newscast. You may repeat the exercise with another newscast, using summary writing to take notes directly from listening.

Learn More

Graphic organizers are another excellent tool for taking notes. To learn about using graphic organizers to take notes and present your ideas, see Chapter 28.

◀ **Critical Viewing**
Do you think that this looks like an effective study space? Why or why not? **[Analyze]**

Basic Study Skills • 857

Step-by-Step Teaching Guide

Using the Library

Teaching Resources: Academic and Workplace Skills Activity Book, p. 46

1. Invite students to name some types of materials they have accessed in the school or community library during the past six months (encyclopedia entries, magazine and newspaper articles, bibliographical information, etc.). What type of catalog did they use? Did they have any difficulties?

2. Ask students to discuss whether people should be permitted to use library computers to send and receive personal e-mail. Should libraries offer this service?

Step-by-Step Teaching Guide

The Card Catalog

1. Review with students the three kinds of cards, or databases, in a catalog: author, title, and subject. Discuss how they are similar and different. (They all have the same information, presented in a different order.)

2. Ask which kind of card students would look for in the following situations:

   to find more books by a certain writer (author card)

   to find information about eating disorders (subject)

   to find out when a certain book was published (title)

   to find out what a certain book is about (title)

   to find a certain writer's newest book (author)

   to find two different opinions about the causes of the Civil War (subject)

Section 31.2 Reference Skills

A tremendous amount of information is available through libraries and media centers, as well as through your own computer. This section explores how and where to access the information and how to use the reference sources most effectively.

Using the Library

Libraries, or media centers, are organized carefully to help you find what you need. You will find some, or all, of these resources offered: fiction and nonfiction books, audio- and videocassettes, periodicals (newspapers, magazines, and scholarly journals), microfilm, vertical files, pamphlets and other small printed materials, reference works in printed and electronic form, and access to the Internet and on-line databases.

Using the Library Catalog A *library catalog* is an alphabetically arranged record of books and audiovisual materials that are in the library.

In the past, a library catalog was a system of cards that were filed alphabetically in drawers. You may still find a library catalog that is organized this way, but you are just as likely to find a library catalog organized in printed booklets or in an electronic format.

▶ **KEY CONCEPT** Use the library catalog to find information about a library's books and other materials. ■

Card Catalog A card catalog lists books, tapes, and CDs on index cards, with each item having a separate *author card* and *title card*; if the book is nonfiction, it will also have at least one *subject card*. Cards are filed alphabetically in cabinets of small drawers.

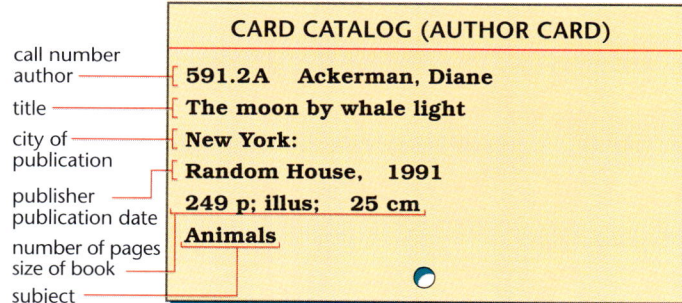

CARD CATALOG (AUTHOR CARD)

call number
author — 591.2A   Ackerman, Diane
title — The moon by whale light
city of publication — New York:
publisher — Random House,   1991
publication date — 249 p; illus;   25 cm
number of pages
size of book — Animals
subject

858 • Study, Reference, and Test-Taking Skills

Technology Tip

Ask a librarian whether you can access the library's electronic catalog from a computer outside the library. If so, find out whether you need to download software (usually at no cost) to connect to the on-line catalog.

⏱ TIME AND RESOURCE MANAGER

Resources
Print: *Academic and Workplace Skills Activity Book*, p. 46–52

In-Depth Coverage	Accelerated Pace
• Cover pp. 858–871 in class. • Arrange for the class to visit the school library. One trip might focus on the card catalog and the location of different types of materials. A second trip might focus solely on print reference materials.	• In class, answer students' questions about card catalogs, locating information on the library shelves, using dictionaries and other reference sources, and accessing the Internet. If possible, have the school librarian visit the class. • Assign Exercises 4–11 for students to complete independently.

Printed Catalog A printed catalog lists books on printed pages, with each book listed alphabetically by author, by title, and—if nonfiction—by subject. Often, there are separate booklets for author, title, and subject listings.

Electronic Catalog An electronic catalog lists books in a database that you can access from computers in the library or by using special software on your home computer. Search by typing in the author, title, or subject—often key words or just an author's last name will locate the information you want. Copy status may also be included—whether the book is checked in or available at a branch library or through an interlibrary loan system.

▲ **Critical Viewing**
How does this library compare with the one in your school? **[Compare and Contrast]**

ELECTRONIC CATALOG

Author: Ackerman, Diane.
Title: The moon by whale light.
Published: New York: Random House, 1991.
Description: 249 p.; ill.; 25 cm.
Subject: Animals.
Call No.:   591.2A.
Status: On shelf.

▶ **Exercise 4** **Using the Library Catalog** Visit your school or local library, and use the catalog to answer these questions.
1. What kind of catalog does the library use—card, printed, or electronic? Where is it located?
2. Who wrote *The Sun Also Rises*? Is it fiction or nonfiction?
3. What are the titles, subjects, and call numbers of the books in your library by the author Italo Calvino?
4. What are the titles, authors, and call numbers of three books about space exploration published since 1990?
5. What are the titles, authors, and call numbers of two nonfiction books about architecture that are more than one hundred pages long?

Customize for
AP Students

After completing Exercise 4, challenge pairs of students to write five of their own questions similar to the ones listed. Stress that another student must be able to answer the questions by accessing the library's card catalog. Then, have pairs exchange questions and answer those on each other's lists.

Step-by-Step Teaching Guide

The Printed Catalog

1. Ask students to name some advantages to having a printed catalog. (It is not affected by a loss of power or technical glitches; it is easy to use.)

2. Discuss with students the need to list each book three different ways in the catalog. Would one listing per book be adequate? (No. If books were listed only by their authors or titles, how could one find other books on the same topic? If books were listed only by their subjects, how would one find books by a favorite author?)

Step-by-Step Teaching Guide

The Electronic Catalog

1. Write on the chalkboard these tips for searching an electronic catalog.

   • *If you are searching by subject, type in a specific word or phrase.*

   • *If you are searching by author, type in the last name first, followed by a comma and the first name. Spell carefully.*

   • *If you are searching by title, do not type in the articles (The, A, An) in the beginning of the title.*

2. Assign Exercise 4.

Answer Key

▶ **Exercise 4**

After students complete their library visit, collect their written answers or discuss their findings in class.

Critical Viewing

Compare and Contrast Answers will vary. Ask students to find at least two points of comparison between the libraries.

Going From Catalog to Shelf

Teaching Resources: Academic and Workplace Skills Activity Book, p. 47

1. Have students make a quick-reference list of the location symbols used in your library's card catalog. (Example: Are fiction books marked with an *F* or *Fic*? Does the identification in the card catalog include all or part of the author's last name?) Have students keep these lists in their notebooks.

2. Help students understand the example of how nonfiction topics are organized in the Dewey Decimal System. (*Engineering* is a type of *Technology*; *Applied Physics* is a type of *Engineering*; *Steam Engineering* is a type of *Applied Physics*, and so on.)

3. Ask students to name other categories of *Engineering* that might be in the 620 division (*Chemical, Civil, Electrical, Nuclear*).

4. Ask students where they would look for a book about Benjamin Franklin by Robert Middlekauff (in the biography section under *F* for *Franklin*).

5. Point out that books in the reference section must be used in the library and cannot be borrowed. Ask students to explain the reason for this rule (to make sure the books are always available for all students).

Customize for
Visual/Spatial Learners

Ask students, working in pairs, to draw a diagram of the school library or media center. Have them mark the location of each section described on pages 860–861, plus any other resources their library offers. You might hang this diagram in your classroom for students' reference.

31.2

Going From Catalog to Shelf

Besides the title and the author, the most important piece of information in a library catalog entry is the *location symbol*. In order to locate an item on the shelf, match the symbols and numbers found in a catalog entry with the symbols and numbers found on the item itself.

Libraries classify books into two main groups: *fiction* (stories created by an author) and *nonfiction* (factual material). Nonfiction includes two smaller groups—*biographies* and *reference books*—that are usually shelved separately.

KEY CONCEPT Use catalog entry location symbols to find materials on library shelves. ■

Fiction Books Catalog entries for fiction will usually have the location symbol *F* or *Fic*, indicating that the books are located in the fiction section of the library. Some libraries include either all or just the first few letters of the author's last name below the location symbol.

Nonfiction Books Most high-school and public libraries arrange nonfiction books by the *Dewey Decimal System* of classification. This classification system divides knowledge into ten main classes, numbered from 000 to 999. Each of the classes is divided into ten divisions, and each of the divisions is divided into ten subdivisions. When necessary, the subdivisions can be divided even further.

EXAMPLES OF THE WAY NONFICTION BOOKS ARE CLASSIFIED

MAIN CLASS:	600–699	Technology
DIVISIONS:	620	Engineering
SUBDIVISIONS:	621	Applied Physics
FURTHER DIVISIONS:	621.1	Steam Engineering
	621.15	Engines
	621.16	Stationary Engines
	621.165	Turbine Engines

Catalog entries for nonfiction include a *call number* in the location symbol. In a library that uses the Dewey Decimal System, the call number is a Dewey Decimal number. The numbers of the call number are generally followed by the first letter or letters of the author's last name. A library designed for research usually does not contain shelves of books (stacks) for users to browse and locate their own books. In a research library, you submit a call slip to the librarian and get "called" when the book has been retrieved.

Research Tip

Some college and university libraries will allow you access for your research. They may have materials that are not available to you at your school or public libraries.

Locating Biographies and Special Materials

Although biographies can be shelved in the library's history section (the 920's of the Dewey Decimal System) and reference books may be shelved in the specific section that corresponds to their subject, these materials are often found in separate sections.

Biographies The life stories of individual people are marked with the location symbol *B* or *BIO* (for biography) or *92* (short for 920). Biographies are shelved alphabetically by the subject of the book—Franklin D. Roosevelt, instead of by the author of the book (biographer), Doris Kearns Goodwin.

Collective biographies, or books that contain chapter-length biographies about a number of people, will usually be shelved with the library's history section. Their location symbols include 920 through 929 as their call numbers.

Reference Materials Most libraries have an area for reference materials that is separate from the other books. These materials may include booklets as well as books. Any library reference material almost always will carry the letter *R* or *Ref* above the call number. Usually, items that are classified as *Reference* cannot be removed from the library.

Nonprint Materials A variety of symbols may mark nonprint materials—matching the special format of the items. For example, *VC* might be used above a call number to indicate a videocassette. Since most nonprint materials will be kept separately and are often unavailable for direct access, you should ask the librarian for help in finding and using these materials.

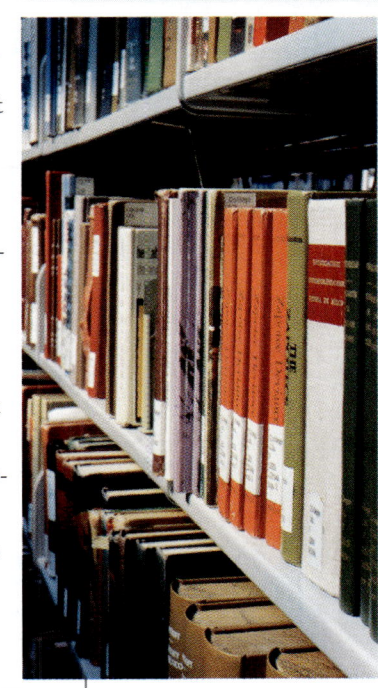

▲ **Critical Viewing**
Where on these books would you find their Dewey Decimal System identification codes? **[Identify]**

> **Exercise 5** **Using Your Library Skills** Follow the steps listed below to prepare a list of materials on a topic of your choice. Then, write a brief paragraph stating how you would like to develop these materials into a research paper.
> 1. Select a topic for research. It may be a topic that you are researching for one of your other classes.
> 2. Find ten items in the library catalog related to your topic. Choose a variety of materials, including at least three non-print materials.
> 3. Copy the essential information from the catalog entry: title, author, and location symbol or call number.
> 4. Find the materials in the library.
> 5. Revise your list if any materials cannot be located or do not seem appropriate and useful for your topic.

Use Periodicals and Periodical Indexes

Teaching Resources: Academic and Workplace Skills Activity Book, p. 48

1. Show students the kinds of periodical indexes that are available in the school library or media center, including electronic indexes. Encourage students to browse through the indexes and become familiar with their content and organization.

2. Explain that, after students use printed indexes to identify the magazine or newspaper articles they want to review, they must locate the periodicals that contain those articles. The current year's issues might be on the library shelf, while older issues might be stored in another location in the library or on microfiche. *Microfiche* is a kind of microfilm that can store images of printed material. If the article is from a past year, encourage students to ask the librarian for assistance in locating it.

3. Tell students that some electronic indexes will display entire articles on the screen. They can print these articles out, sometimes for a small fee per page.

Customize for
Less Advanced Students

You may wish to have students work in groups focusing on library and reference skills. Students will be more comfortable and library staff workers can assist and explain more efficiently.

31.2

Using Periodicals, Periodical Indexes, and the Vertical File

Periodical is a term applied to anything published regularly during the year. Periodicals include magazines and journals, but they can include newspapers as well. A *periodical file* lists articles that appear in periodicals by subject and date. In the *vertical file*, you can find the information contained in booklets or pamphlets.

▶ **KEY CONCEPT** Use periodicals to supplement research with specialized or current information; periodical indexes to find articles in periodicals, and the vertical file to find small printed materials. ■

Periodicals Some periodicals are of general interest, while others are devoted to specialized topics. Because of their current nature, periodicals can be a valuable research aid for information that is not available in books.

Periodical Indexes Periodical indexes, which may be published in print or electronic form, are updated regularly and cite articles that appeared during a specified period of time. Many indexes make it possible for you to look up information in periodicals by either subject or author.

SOME COMMON PERIODICAL INDEXES

- *Readers' Guide to Periodical Literature*, often referred to as the *Readers' Guide*, which covers all types of periodicals
- *Art Index, Humanities Index*
- *Business and Technology Index*

Below is a sample entry from the *Readers' Guide*:

```
            SAMPLE READERS' GUIDE ENTRY

subject heading ─────────[ TRACK AND FIELD ATHLETICS
                   See also
cross-references ─────────[ Mile running
                           Pole vaulting
subheading─┘  Women          topic clarified in brackets
title of article─┘ For the record [Joyner-Kersee and F Griffith Joyner].
             illustrated with portraits
author─┘      K. Casey. il pors Ladies Home Journal v116 no 4
name of periodical ─────────        volume and number│
pages ─────────[ p. 148-51+ Ap  1999     ┌─date
                      └─continued at rear of magazine
```

Research Tip

It is part of a librarian's job to assist the library's users. Do not expect him or her to do your research for you, but take advantage of the librarian's extensive knowledge of the materials that are available. Often, they can guide you to the best sources to meet your needs.

Integrating Research Skills

Caution students to evaluate the credibility and biases of research sources before they take information from them. Students should ask themselves questions such as these when evaluating their sources:

Does this source present a balanced description or argument, or it is biased in one direction?

Does this source have a reputation for providing accurate, factual information?

Does the author of this book or article have the expertise and experience to back up his or her statements?

Does this source offer the most current information on this topic? (Example: The date of sources for historical topics may not be important, but sources for scientific and health issues should be up-to-date.)

How to Use Periodical Indexes In *printed indexes*, citations are listed alphabetically by subject and sometimes by author. Sometimes, the citations contain abstracts, or brief summaries, of the articles. In *electronic indexes*, citations are part of a database and come up on your screen after you search by typing in specific information, such as the subject, the author's name, or the date; you can also search with key words that will lead you to specific articles. Electronic indexes may also provide full text—an electronic version of the complete articles cited for some or all articles.

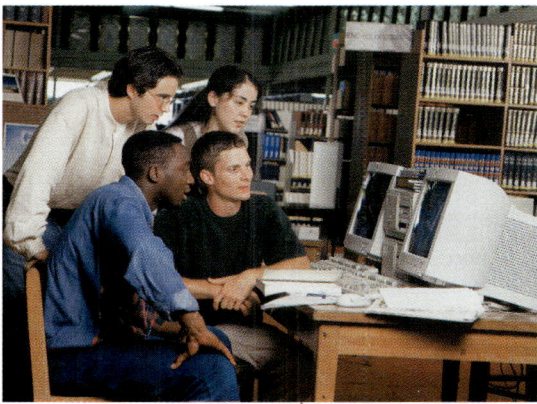

Vertical Files Pamphlets are similar to magazines and newspapers in that they often contain current information. Libraries usually store pamphlets in a vertical file—a file cabinet with large drawers. Pamphlets can be found on such topics as welfare, state parks, child abuse, and education. In addition, there may be booklets, folded maps, original newspaper and magazine clippings, and photos. Do not hesitate to ask the librarian whether information on the topic of your research might be found in the vertical file.

▲ **Critical Viewing**
In what types of activities might these students be involved? On what do you base your answer? **[Speculate]**

▶ **Exercise 6** **Using Periodicals and Periodical Indexes** Visit your school or local library to find answers to these questions about periodicals and periodical indexes.
1. Which printed indexes does the library have? Which electronic indexes are available?
2. Which newspapers does the library carry? Is microfilm or microfiche available for back issues of the newspapers?
3. Give the titles of three news magazines that the library has. In what format are they available?
4. Using the most current issue of the *Readers' Guide*, find an article citation and read the article in a copy of the magazine in the library. (Many libraries will store copies of the most current magazines and newspapers for reference use until they are bound or transferred onto microfilm.)
5. Use an electronic index to locate and find an article for which full text is provided in electronic form. Would you have found that article in the hard-copy material that the library provides?

Using Dictionaries

Teaching Resources: Academic and Workplace Skills Activity Book, p. 49

1. Have a volunteer read aloud the descriptions of types of dictionaries to the class. Discuss the differences among unabridged, abridged, and specialized dictionaries.

2. Show students the kinds of dictionaries available in your classroom and in the school library.

3. Organize groups of students and ask each group to study the content and uses of a different kind of dictionary and report on it to the class.

Customize for
Less Advanced Students

Provide a different kind of dictionary to each student, pair of students, or small group. Read one of the tasks listed in Exercise 7. Then, ask each student or group to look in their dictionaries and report on what they find. Compare the results for each dictionary.

Answer Key

▶ Exercise 7

1. unabridged
2. specialized
3. abridged
4. unabridged
5. specialized

31.2

Using Dictionaries

Of all general reference materials, you probably use a dictionary most often. A *dictionary* is a collection of words and their meanings, along with other information, such as a word's pronunciation, usage, and history. If you refer to a dictionary merely to check the meaning or spelling of words, however, you are not getting all you can out of this valuable resource.

KEY CONCEPT Dictionaries contain a wealth of information about words. Use the dictionary that best suits your needs. ■

Distinguishing Types of Dictionaries There are dictionaries published for almost every audience: for students to use in their studies, for adults to use at home or at work, and for scholars to use in their research. Many dictionaries are available in both printed and electronic form. The following chart describes the three main types of dictionaries.

THREE TYPES OF DICTIONARIES

Unabridged	Exhaustive study of the English language containing more than 250,000 words
Abridged	Compact edition containing listings of 55,000 to 160,000 words
Specialized	Edition limited to words of a particular field, such as foreign languages or mathematics

Exercise 7 **Choosing a Dictionary** For each situation, answer which kind of dictionary (*unabridged*, *abridged*, or *specialized*) would be the most appropriate.
1. finding special detailed information about a word
2. finding a comprehensive definition of a legal or medical term
3. finding a word's basic meaning
4. finding the origin of a word
5. finding the translation of a foreign word

🔎 Research Tip

Unabridged dictionaries are often found on stands in various places in library reading rooms. When you want to look up a word, take a notebook with you because this large dictionary is too bulky to be moved.

Finding Words in Printed Dictionaries A word listed in the dictionary, with all the information about it, is called an *entry*. In printed dictionaries, entry words are arranged alphabetically. To speed your search for a word, some dictionaries provide the following aids:

- **thumb index**—a series of right-hand notches, labeled alphabetically, which indicate the section of entries for words that start with that particular letter or letters

- **guide words**—the two words printed in large type at the top of a dictionary page showing the first and last words covered on the page

To speed your search for a word, use these features:

The Four-Section Approach The four-section approach is a search strategy for finding words quickly. To use this strategy, follow these two steps:

1. Mentally divide the dictionary into the four sections:

ABCD	MNOPQR
EFGHIJKL	STUVWXYZ

2. When you go to look up a word, decide into which section the word falls. For example, if you want to look up *homage*, you know that the word falls near the middle of the second section. If, on the other hand, you want to look up *scabbard*, you know that the word falls near the beginning of the last section.

Finding Words in Electronic Dictionaries In electronic dictionaries, you usually find a word's entry simply by typing the word and having the computer search the dictionary database. If you are unsure of a word's spelling, you can usually type in the first few letters and see a list of words that are similar in spelling.

▶ **Exercise 8** **Working With a Dictionary** Use a dictionary to answer the following questions.
1. In what order would these entry words appear?
   protein—parallel—mortar—cultivate—network
2. Which of the following entry words would appear on a page with the guide words *introduction* and *invention*?
   intrude—introduce—intuitive—invent—inventive
3. What two guide words appear on the page with *midyear*?
4. Which word is not spelled correctly?
   existence—resistance—priviledge—judgment—tranquillity
5. Which word is spelled correctly?
   advisir—accomodate—lightening—fullfill—nickel

Finding Words in Dictionaries

1. Remind students that guide words are organized alphabetically in all dictionaries.
2. To help students practice using guide words, write these two words on the board.

   reprise   *repute*

3. Then, read aloud the list of words below, or write them on the board so students can check the spelling. Ask students which of these words would appear on a page with the guide words above.

   reproduction (yes)

   resemblance (no)

   republican (yes)

   repurchase (yes)

   reprint (no)

Four-Section Approach

1. To have students practice finding words quickly, write the groups of letters shown on page 865 on the board. Number them as shown.

1. ABCD	3. MNOPQR
2. EFGHIJKL	4. STUVWXYXZ

2. Read aloud each word below and have students quickly identify the section where they would look for it.

fraud (2)	*tertiary* (4)
biodegrade (1)	*mire* (3)
peculiar (3)	*eligible* (2)
cirrus (1)	

Answer Key

▶ **Exercise 8**

1. cultivate, mortar, network parallel, protein
2. intrude, intuitive, invent
3. Answer will depend on dictionary used.
4. priviledge (privilege)
5. nickel

Step-by-Step Teaching Guide

Dictionary Entries

1. Organize students into five groups and give each group at least one dictionary. If possible, give all groups the same kind of dictionary. Assign each group two of the ten components listed on pages 866–867.

2. Give groups time to read their assigned sections and find examples in their dictionaries. Point out that they might find information quickly by using the table of contents and the preliminary matter in the front of the dictionary.

3. Have groups take turns making short presentations about their components. As they give examples, ask other groups to turn to that page in their own dictionaries.

4. As the groups make their presentations, ask the following questions.

> **Spelling:** *How can you tell which spelling is preferred?* (If both are equal, they are joined by *or*. Secondary variants follow the word *also*.)
>
> **Syllabification**: *How can you tell when a word has a hyphen in it?* (The hyphen is indicated by a long dash, not a short dash or dot.)
>
> **Pronunciation:** *How can you tell how to interpret the pronunciation symbols?* (Each page includes a pronunciation key.)
>
> **Part of speech:** *Why would the same word be labeled as a noun and as an adjective?* (Many words can be used as more than one part of speech. Have students list some examples.)

continued

Integrating Vocabulary Skills

Synonyms Point out that many dictionary entries include synonyms, much like a thesaurus. Before deciding to use a synonym for a particular word, urge students to look it up and make sure it has the connotation they are looking for.

Looking at the Parts of a Dictionary Entry In a dictionary, a *main entry* consists of a word and all the information about it. The word (a single word, a compound word, an abbreviation, a prefix or suffix, or the name of a person or place) is called an *entry word*.

Preferred and Variant Spellings English words usually have only one correct spelling, as shown by the entry word. Some words, however, can be spelled in more than one way. The spelling most commonly used is called the *preferred spelling*. A less commonly used spelling is called a *variant spelling*. Most dictionaries provide both preferred and variant spellings.

Syllabification Dots, spaces, or slashes in an entry word indicate where that word may be divided into syllables. When breaking words at the end of a line, remember that you cannot leave a syllable of just one letter on a line by itself. Words with one syllable and contractions are never divided.

Pronunciation Usually appearing right after the entry word, the pronunciation uses symbols to show how to say the word. The syllable that gets the most emphasis has a *primary stress*, usually shown by a heavy mark after the syllable [']. Words of more than one syllable may also have a *secondary stress*, usually shown by a shorter, lighter mark ['].

Part-of-Speech Label The dictionary also tells you how a word can be used in a sentence—whether it functions as a noun, verb, or some other part of speech. This information is given as an abbreviation, usually after the pronunciation.

SAMPLE DICTIONARY ENTRY

① **liv·ery** (liv′ər ē) *n.*, pl. **-er·ies** [ME, allowance of food, gift of clothes to a servant, thing delivered <OFr *livree*, pp. of *livrer*, to deliver < L *liberare*, to LIBERATE] **1** an identifying uniform such as was formerly worn by feudal retainers or is now worn by servants or those in some particular group, trade, etc. **2** the people wearing such uniforms **3** characteristic dress or appearance **4** a) the keeping and feeding of horses for a fixed charge b) the keeping of horses, vehicles, or both, for hire ☆c) LIVERY STABLE ☆**5** a place where boats can be rented **6** [Historical] *Eng. Law* the legal delivery of property, esp. landed property, into the hands of the new owner.

②③④⑤⑥⑦

1. Entry Word
2. Pronunciation
3. Part-of-Speech Label
4. Plural Form
5. Etymology
6. Definitions
7. Usage Labels

🔲 Research Tip

Unabridged dictionaries frequently include sentences and phrases that show words in context. This feature will help you understand the correct and precise usage of a word.

✓ ONGOING ASSESSMENT: Prerequisite Skills

If students have difficulty interpreting the part-of-speech labels in dictionary entries, you may find it helpful to refer them to the following materials to review prerequisite knowledge.

In the Textbook	Print Resources	Technology
Parts of Speech, pp. 364–398	*Grammar Exercise Workbook,* pp. 1–22	*On-Line Exercise Bank,* Sections 17.1–17.5

Plurals and Inflected Forms After the part-of-speech label, the dictionary may also show the plural forms of nouns and inflected forms (past tense and participle forms of verbs) if there is anything irregular about their spelling.

Etymology The origin and history of the word is called its etymology. The etymology usually appears in brackets, parentheses, or slashes near the start or end of the entry. It often uses abbreviations for languages, all of which are explained in the dictionary's key to abbreviations.

Definition The meaning of a word is called its definition. Definitions are numbered if there is more than one. Often, they include an example that illustrates the use of that meaning in a phrase or sentence.

Usage Labels Words labeled *Archaic (Arch.)*, *Obsolete (Obs.)*, *Poetic*, or *Rare* are not widely used today. Those labeled *Informal (Inf.)*, *Colloquial (Colloq.)*, or *Slang* are not considered part of formal English. Those labeled *Brit.* are used mainly in countries associated with Britain, not in the United States.

Field Labels Words used in a special way by people in a certain occupation or activity have field labels, such as *History (Hist.)*, *Mathematics (Math.)*, and *Chemistry (Chem.)*.

Idioms and Derived Words At the end of an entry, idioms—expressions that contain the entry word—may be listed and defined. Derived words, words formed from the entry word (along with their part-of-speech labels) may also be listed.

> **Exercise 9** **Working With a Dictionary** Use a dictionary to follow the directions below.
> 1. Mark the pronunciation for the word *excruciating*.
> 2. What part of speech is the word *concoct*?
> 3. What is the variant spelling of *empanel*?
> 4. Write the plural of the word *parenthesis*. Write the inflected forms of the words *recur* and *control*.
> 5. Describe the etymology of the word *peninsula*.
> 6. Look up *pass* in a dictionary, and write three sentences that use three different meanings for the word.
> 7. Compare and contrast American and British uses of *entrée*.
> 8. Write the definition of *spin* that follows the field label for *flight*.
> 9. Find a dictionary that explains the meaning of the idiom "if worst comes to worst." Describe the meaning of the phrase.
> 10. Look up the word *depressor* in a dictionary. From what word and language is it derived?

⊙ Vocabulary Tip

Etymologies are a valuable aid for extending your vocabulary. Knowing a word's origin can help you remember it and can help you unlock the meaning of related words with a common orgin.

Answer Key continued

> **Exercise 9**

6. Student sentences may resemble the following: *We passed the slow truck. I passed the test. Please pass the peas.*
7. In American usage, *entrée* refers to the main course of a meal. In British usage, *entrée* refers to the dish served before the main course.
8. "a rapid descent, often uncontrolled, of an aircraft in a spiral path"
9. "if the worst happens"
10. from *depress*, ultimately from the Latin

Step-by-Step Teaching Guide continued

5. Ask students the following questions about the components listed on this page.

   Plurals and Inflected Forms: *What are "inflected forms"?* (variations in the tense, gender, number, voice, person, or mood of an entry word)

   Etymology: *What is the meaning of these abbreviations? OE* (old English), *ME* (middle English), *fr.* (from, *not* French), *F* (French), *Gk* (Greek), *and L* (Latin)

   Definition: *Is the first definition given used more frequently than the second or third definitions?* (Not necessarily, they are just different definitions.)

   Usage Labels: *Should writers avoid using words marked* Obs. *or* Colloq.*? Why?* (They should avoid using these words in formal writing. These words are no longer widely used or they are too informal.)

   Field Labels: *Why would an ordinary word be labeled* Chem.*?* (It has a different meaning in the field of chemistry.) Have students find an example of this, such as *element*.

   Idioms and Derived Words: *Why is it necessary to define idioms if the entry word has already been defined?* (The meaning of the entry word often changes in an idiom.) Have students find an example of this.

6. Assign Exercise 9.

Answer Key

> **Exercise 9**

Responses will vary according to the dictionaries students use.

1. ek skrü´shē ā´ting
2. verb
3. *impanel*
4. *parentheses; recurred, recurring; controlled, controlling*
5. *Peninsula* derives from the Latin words *paene* (almost) and *insula* (island).

continued

Using Other Print References

Teaching Resources: Academic and Workplace Skills Activity Book, p. 50

1. Explain that encyclopedias are good places to start a research project because they offer an overview of a topic. After students understand the basic idea, they can focus on specific aspects of the topic.

2. Organize the class into small groups. Assign the topics below, or other topics you choose, to two groups each. One of the groups will check the topic in a print encyclopedia, and the other will check it in an electronic version.

   • *the geography of Southeast Asia*
   • *the status of the International Space Station*
   • *the history of the railroad in the United States*

3. After the groups research their topics, ask each pair of groups to describe the type and clarity of the information they found, including graphics and links to other resources.

4. Invite students to name some facts and information they would expect to find in an almanac. (climate information, weights and measures, mayors of large cities, basic facts about the world's nations, world records)

Answer Key

▶ **Exercise 10**

1. Argentina has the highest mountain, Aconcagua (22,831 feet).
2. Russia
3. Montana, Wyoming, Utah, Nevada, Oregon, Washington
4. T.S. Eliot
5. Hadrian's Wall was built to protect Roman Britain from attackers from the north.

31.2

Using Other Print References

In addition to consulting nonfiction books and periodicals, take advantage of a library's reference section when conducting research. The materials in a reference section include general references, which cover broad areas of knowledge and usually do not go into great detail, and specialized references, which focus on a specific topic. Be aware that both types of references usually cannot be checked out.

▶ **KEY CONCEPT** Use general reference works to check basic facts or to explore the range of a topic; use specialized reference books to gather detailed information about one aspect of a broad topic. ■

Encyclopedias General encyclopedias contain articles on a wide range of subjects. The information usually fills a series of books—twenty or more volumes. The alphabetical order and indexes help users find information quickly. Not all topics have a specific article, but the index—usually in one or two separate volumes—directs you to articles that cover particular topics.

Almanacs Almanacs provide up-to-date statistics and other facts on such topics as government, history, geography, astronomy, population, and sports. Relatively inexpensive, almanacs can be found in bookstores as well as in libraries.

Atlases and Gazetteers Atlases include maps accompanied by informative text, such as facts and charts about population distribution, seasonal temperature and rainfall, agricultural and industrial production, and natural resources. When using an atlas, use the index to determine which map you need for a particular place. Unlike atlases, most gazetteers do not contain maps. Instead, they offer brief descriptions of places, arranged alphabetically like entries in a dictionary. In short, gazetteers are geographical dictionaries.

Specialized Reference Works For more detailed information than general reference works provide, there are specialized reference works. These works include specialized dictionaries and thesauruses (or dictionaries of synonyms), specialized encyclopedias, and biographical reference works.

▶ **Exercise 10** Using Reference Works Use reference works to answer these questions.
1. In what country is South America's highest mountain?
2. What country did Catherine the Great come from?
3. What states border Idaho?
4. Who won the Nobel Prize for Literature in 1948?
5. What was the purpose of Hadrian's Wall?

868 • Study, Reference, and Test-Taking Skills

Research Tip

Check each of your textbooks for suggestions on appropriate reference works for researching topics for the corresponding classes.

Customize for
Logical/Mathematical Learners

Before students begin Exercise 10, invite them to predict the sources that will contain the answer to each question. Have students record their predictions and check later to see whether they were correct.

Using Electronic and Media References

In today's world, you are not limited to using books to conduct research. You can take advantage of a wide range of electronic and media resources, including video collections, CD-ROMs, the Internet, and on-line subscription services.

Video References Often, you can get excellent information on a topic by watching a video. Consult your librarian to find out about videos such as the following:

- **News programs** offer current information and insights into how people reacted to historical events as they happened.
- **Documentaries** give in-depth information on specific topics.
- **Special-interest series** provide extended, detailed coverage of many aspects of a topic—for example, the Bill Moyers series on the history of the English language provides valuable insights into how the language evolved.

CD-ROM References Many types of reference works are available on CD-ROM, as well as in printed form.

- **CD-ROM encyclopedias** can provide as much information on a single disc as a twenty-volume book collection. Many CD-ROM encyclopedias also include video and audio segments. To find information, use the search function.
- **CD-ROM atlases** are set up as a database so you can enter a place name or key word to run a computer search for the appropriate map.

Electronic Databases Electronic databases can be found on CD-ROMs or on the Internet. They provide large collections of data on specific topics, and you can search for the data that helps you. The advantages of storing data electronically are that computer disks and servers do not require the space of file cabinets, and the computer searches quickly and thoroughly to give you complete search results in little time.

Technology Tip

Although electronic reference works are valuable resources for your research, your library probably has a limited number of computer terminals for users. Ask the librarian if there is a time when there may be less demand for the computers.

▼ **Critical Viewing**
What are the key differences between conducting research in books and researching on a computer? **[Compare]**

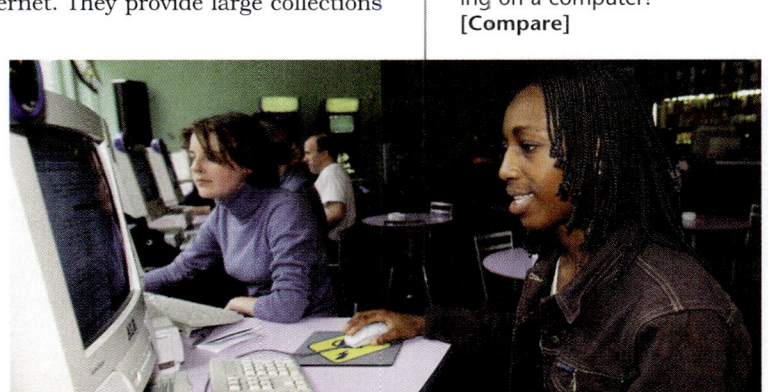

Step-by-Step Teaching Guide

Using Electronic and Media References

Teaching Resources: Academic and Workplace Skills Activity Book, p. 51

1. Ask students to identify topic areas for which video references would be particularly suitable. (Students may cite video recordings that serve as eye-witness accounts of history, such as Elvis Presley's career or the history of television newscasts.)

2. Have students compare the information offered by print and electronic maps. Which type is more complete? Which type is easier to read?

3. The software for many electronic maps will help users find the best route from one location to another. Have students choose two cities, one in your state and one in a neighboring state. Ask one group of students to use a printed map and one to use an electronic map. Have both trace a route from the first city to the second and then compare their results. Did the electronic map indicate the same route, a better one, a more convoluted one?

Critical Viewing

Compare Students may cite differences in speed and quantity. Computers allow researchers to access many more sources in much less time.

Using the Internet

Teaching Resources: Academic and Workplace Skills Activity Book, p. 52

1. Invite students to share the kinds of information they have gathered and the kinds of services they have received from the Internet.

2. Discuss how the Internet is shaping our lives and our lifestyles. Ask students how it is affecting their lives. How would their lives change if there were suddenly no Internet? What would they do without e-mail and chat rooms? How do they expect the Internet and its uses to change by the time they are thirty years old?

3. Determine whether your school's library subscribes to any electronic databases. Arrange for a librarian to demonstrate how to access them and to describe the types of information they offer. Encourage students to use these databases at their earliest opportunity and report to the class on their experiences.

Integrating Viewing and Representing Skills

Comparing Servers A growing number of Internet Service Providers (ISPs) are available. Have students identify two or three and compare them. How do the ISPs use design, color, sound effects, organization, and other techniques to make themselves user friendly? What are the disadvantages or limitations of each ISP? What groups of people do students think are the intended users of each ISP? Which of these ISPs do students prefer? Why?

Real-World Connection

Let students know that many jobs require proficient reference skills. For example, someday they may need to analyze their company's competition. Or, they might need to find a new supplier or determine a fair price for supplies or services. Being able to locate and use the appropriate reference sources, especially those on the Internet, will make them valuable employees.

31.2

Using the Internet

The Internet is a worldwide network, or Web, of computers connected by phone and cable lines. When you go on-line, or hook up to the Internet, you have access to information at a tremendous number and variety of Web sites. Each Web site has its own address, or URL (Universal Resource Locator). The sites usually consist of several Web pages of text, graphics, and sometimes audio or video displays, which you can download or save on your computer.

KEY CONCEPT Use the Internet for all kinds of information, but judge Web sites for reliability. ■

Locating Appropriate Web Sites If you know a reliable Web site and its address (URL), simply type the address into the URL window of your Web browser. If you do not have a specific site in mind, use a search engine, such as *Yahoo* or *Lycos.* Enter key words connected to a topic to find Web sites related to that topic.

- Some search engines are useful for searching broad categories—they allow you to start with broad topics and narrow them down to more specific categories that you might not have considered.
- Some search engines are useful if you already know the specific direction that your search will take.
- Some search engines are "crawlers" that find the top "hits" from other search engines. You may find what you want in the results or determine a particular search engine to use to produce the best results for your search.

Evaluating Web Sites All Internet sources are not created equal. Anyone with a computer and an Internet linkup can transmit data or create a Home Page. As a result, it is essential to critically evaluate any sites you come across. Use the following questions to guide your evaluation.

QUESTIONS FOR EVALUATING WEB SITES
1. What is the source of the information—a respected publisher or organization, a discussion group, or an individual? Are original sources provided?
2. Does the source have credentials—such as experience in the subject or affiliation with a recognized organization?
3. Is the source objective, or is the organization or individual seeking to persuade you to think or act in a certain way?
4. How does the information compare with that presented on other related sites?
5. Is the information up to date?

870 • Study, Reference, and Test-Taking Skills

⊙ Technology Tip

Whenever possible, copy and paste URLs from an electronic source to the location (address) line of your browser. This common editing feature allows you to transfer URLs among word-processing programs, e-mail, and the Internet. It's easier, saves time, and there is no chance that you will type one or two letters or numbers of the URL wrong.

Evaluating Information on Web Sites Once you have determined that a Web site is reliable, it is still necessary to look critically at the information it presents. Check to see that each statement that is presented is backed up by evidence. In addition, verify the information using at least one—and preferably two—additional sources. Keep in mind that these sources can be books as well as electronic sources.

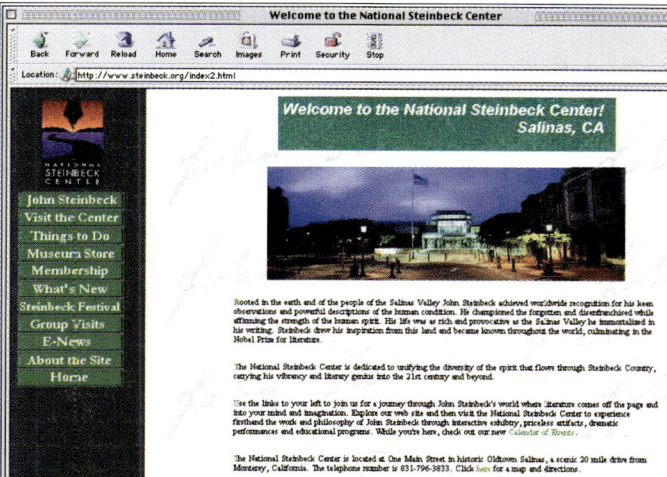

Exercise 11 Using the Internet Using a computer in your library, school computer lab, or at home, go on-line and research information to carry out the following research tasks.

1. Use the Internet to find a mailing address for the San Francisco Opera Association.
2. Use the Internet to find the year that the original production of *Death of a Salesman* opened on Broadway, who directed it, and who the major star of the play was.
3. Choose a topic for a literary analysis. List the names and URLs of four Web sites that you think can help you.
4. Find one of Shakespeare's sonnets on the Internet. Record the name and URL of your source.
5. From a reliable Web site, find out about the history of baseball leagues.

⊙ Technology Tip

You can often print out a Web page or download it onto a diskette. On a home computer, you can also highlight and copy and paste it into a file in your word-processing program.

◄ **Critical Viewing**
What can you tell about this Web site based on its Home Page? **[Analyze]**

Evaluating Information on Web Sites

1. Emphasize for students that the Internet does not necessarily contain more recent and reliable information simply because it is a newer medium for research. A library visit can be an equally valid, or even more rewarding, avenue of inquiry.

2. Suggest that students take economic factors into account when they evaluate a site. How does the site seem to generate revenue?

Integrating Technology Skills

Tell students that combining two key words with AND will locate Web sites or articles that include both words somewhere in the file. For example, if you type in *San Francisco AND opera*, the search engine will list all Web sites that mention San Francisco and opera in general. However, combining key words with the plus sign (+) will generate a list of Web sites or articles in which those words occur as one phrase. Thus, if you type in *San Francisco + opera*, the search engine is more likely to help you locate the address of the San Francisco Opera Association.

Answer Key

▶ **Exercise 11**

You may wish to have students work in small groups on this exercise. Allow time for students to compare results in class.

Critical Viewing

Analyze Students may note that the Home Page focuses on the National Steinbeck Center in Salinas, California, and offers information relating to Center activities and John Steinbeck.

Test-Taking Strategies

1. Discuss ways students can preview a test, such as checking to see how long it is so that they can budget their time. They can also read all headings and subheadings to see what is covered.

2. Ask students to share tips they have found helpful in answering questions. Stress the importance of reading the directions so they can provide the correct answers and put them in the correct places.

3. Suggest that students skim the test and answer the questions they are sure of first. Explain that if they spend too much time struggling with difficult questions, they might not have time to answer the ones they know. They can come back to the difficult questions after they have answered the others.

4. Stress the value of proofreading. Invite volunteers to describe times when they missed a question because of an error they could have easily corrected, if they had noticed it. Discuss ways to avoid such errors.

Customize for
Less Advanced Students

Students might find it helpful to discuss test strategies in reference to a specific test you gave this year, rather than about tests in general. This might give them more concrete examples of how test-taking strategies can be used.

Section 31.3 Test-Taking Skills

Taking Tests

Tests are an important part of school and can play a key role in determining your acceptance into college, graduate school, and certain occupations. By learning what types of questions are included and by following strategies for approaching a test, you can improve your performance.

Strategies for Taking a Test

Regardless of the type of test you are taking, there are strategies you can use to maximize your performance. The chart below lists some of these strategies, dividing them into tasks to be completed before taking the test, strategies to follow while taking the test, and a proofreading process to follow before you turn in the test.

> **KEY CONCEPT** Divide your time among previewing the test, answering the questions, and proofreading. ■

HOW TO TAKE A TEST

LOOK OVER THE TEST

1. Skim the test to get an overview of the types of questions.
2. Decide how much time you must spend on each section.
3. Plan to devote the most time to questions that are hardest or worth the most points.

ANSWER THE QUESTIONS

1. Answer the easy questions first. Put a check next to harder questions, and come back to them later.
2. If permitted, use scratch paper to jot down your ideas.
3. Read each question at least twice before answering it.
4. Supply the single best answer.
5. Answer all questions on the test unless you are told not to guess or that there is a penalty for wrong guesses.
6. Do not change your first answer without a good reason.

PROOFREAD ANSWERS

1. Check that you have followed the directions completely.
2. Reread test questions and answers. Make sure that you have answered all the questions.

872 • Study, Reference, and Test-Taking Skills

Research Tip

There are many books and computer programs to help prepare students for taking tests. Check your library or media center for these materials, and take advantage of the practice exercises you find in them.

⏱ TIME AND RESOURCE MANAGER

Resources
Print: *Academic and Workplace Skills Activity Book*, pp. 53–54

In-Depth Coverage	Accelerated Pace
• Cover pp. 872–875 in class. • Give students time to complete Exercise 12. • Provide sample standardized tests so students can practice answering different kinds of objective questions.	• Discuss test-taking and answering different kinds of objective questions with the class. • Assign Exercise 12 for students to complete independently.

Answering Different Kinds of Questions

Familiarize yourself with the features of each type of question so you can answer questions efficiently and accurately when you encounter them on classroom or standardized tests.

KEY CONCEPT Use specific strategies for handling each type of test question to achieve higher test scores. ■

Multiple-Choice Questions Vocabulary and general comprehension are often tested with a multiple-choice format. Three to five possible answers are provided for each question. Typically, only two will come close to being the correct answer.

EXAMPLE: In the following sentence, circle the letter of the underlined word that is used incorrectly.

Tom and <u>me</u> <u>are</u> going to see the movie with <u>her</u>.
a. me   c. her
b. are   d. none of the above

ANSWER: a. (The sentence should read, "Tom and *I* are going to see the movie with her.")

Follow these steps to answer multiple-choice questions:

ANSWERING MULTIPLE-CHOICE QUESTIONS

1. Try answering the question before looking at the choices. If your answer is one of the choices, select that choice.
2. Eliminate the obviously incorrect answers, crossing them out if you are allowed to write on the test paper.
3. Change a question into a statement by inserting your answer. See if the statement makes sense.

Matching Questions Matching questions require you to connect items in one column with items in a second column. The columns may or may not have an equal number of items.

EXAMPLE: Match the words on the left with the definitions on the right by writing the letter of the correct definition in the blank.

_____1. erosion   a. large body of moving ice and snow
_____2. windbreak   b. wearing away of rock and soil on the Earth's surface
_____3. glacier   c. barrier that causes wind speed to decrease
                         d. ridge deposited by a glacier

ANSWERS: 1: b; 2: c; 3: a

See the chart on the next page for steps for answering matching questions.

Step-by-Step Teaching Guide

Answering Multiple-Choice and Matching Questions

1. Ask students what might happen under the following circumstances.

   They quickly choose the answer to a multiple-choice question without reading all the choices. (They might not realize that a better answer is listed.)

   They do not notice that the question includes the word not. (They choose the wrong answer.)

2. Review the multiple-choice example. Point out key words in the instruction, including *underlined* and *incorrectly*.

3. Work with students to make a list of key words to look for in multiple choice questions. Key words might be defined as words that will change the question if they are missed. (Examples: *incorrect, correct, not, most, least, best,* etc.)

4. Review the matching example. Remind students to make sure they follow instructions carefully, and to read all the items in both columns before starting to answer.

Step-by-Step Teaching Guide

Answering True-False and Fill-in Questions

1. Suggest that as students work on true-or-false questions, they look for absolute words, such as *always, never, all,* and *none.* Emphasize that as most conditions include exceptions, absolute words often appear in false statements.

2. Stress that if any part of the statement is false, the whole statement should be marked false.

3. If the fill-in is a word missing from a sentence, encourage students to read the completed sentence to see whether it makes sense.

4. Stress the importance of good penmanship in filling in answers. Answers may be marked wrong if they are illegible.

ANSWERING MATCHING QUESTIONS

1. Determine immediately if there are an equal number of items in each column and whether the items in the second column may be used more than once.
2. Read all the items in both columns before you try to match.
3. Match easy items first. *Lightly* cross out each used answer.

True-or-False Questions True-or-False questions may appear to be the easiest type of questions. However, it is essential to be aware that just one word can change a true statement into a false one. Read the questions carefully.

Look at the strategies below:

ANSWERING TRUE-OR-FALSE QUESTIONS

1. If a statement seems true, be sure the whole thing is true.
2. Pay special attention to the word *not,* which often changes the whole meaning of a statement.
3. Pay special attention to the words *all, always, never, no, none,* and *only.* They often make a statement false.
4. Pay special attention to the words *generally, much, many, most, often, sometimes,* and *usually.* They often make a statement true.

Fill-in or Short-Answer Questions These questions give you more freedom than other kinds of test questions. There is usually more than one way to state an answer. However, since no answer choices are offered, you must recall the information for the answer.

EXAMPLE: List two ways in which good roads were important to western settlers.

a._____

b._____

> ### Speaking and Listening Tip
>
> In test situations, you may be called on to present oral responses to short-answer questions. Take time to think before you present each answer. Then, try to be as concise as possible, while still providing evidence to back up your points.

☑ ONGOING ASSESSMENT: Monitor and Reinforce

Give students an opportunity to practice answering the type of test questions they find most difficult. Try one of the following strategies.

Option 1 Have students look in library books or on the Internet for sample standardized tests. Have them print out samples of the types of questions they find most difficult and practice answering them. Afterward, they should consult the answer keys in the books or on the Web sites to check their progress.

Option 2 Have students write five test questions on a topic they are studying in history or science class. The questions should be written in the style of the question type they find most difficult. Often, writing test questions can clue them in to the kinds of strategies that test writers sometimes use.

Analogy Questions A *verbal analogy* is an expression of a relationship between two words. Analogy questions test your ability to see the relationship between two given words and to apply that relationship to other words.

EXAMPLE: Choose the pair of words whose relationship is most similar to that expressed by the capitalized pair of words.

1. LETTER : WORD ::
   a. club : people   d. homework : school
   b. page : book   e. product : factory
   c. picture : crayon

ANSWER: B is the correct answer because each letter is a part of a word and each page is a part of a book; both relationships are *part to whole.*

There are many other types of analogy relationships. The following chart shows some of the most common ones.

COMMON ANALOGY RELATIONSHIPS	
Relationship	**Example**
Synonym	joy : elation
Antonym	despair : hope
Quality	library : quiet
Degree (greater or lesser)	shout : speak
Part to whole	page : book
Kind	milk : beverage
Sequence	engagement : marriage
Proximity	shore : water
Device	telescope : astronomer

To answer an analogy question, follow these steps:
1. Define both words in the initial pair. If you cannot define both words, skip the question and go on to the next one.
2. Analyze how the initial words relate to each other.
3. Make certain that you keep each pair of words in the given order. If you reverse the order, you will come up with an incorrect answer.
4. Make certain that the relationship of the parts of speech are the same in the pair you choose as they are in the initial pair.

▶ **Exercise 12** **Analyzing Types of Questions** Review your old tests, and identify the types of questions that they include. Then, answer the following questions.
1. Is there a type of question you have difficulty answering?
2. Do different subject areas use different types of questions?

🖉 STANDARDIZED TEST PREPARATION WORKSHOP

Analogies Standardized test questions may require students to answer analogy questions. Provide students with opportunities to practice analogies.

Choose the pair of words whose relationship is most similar to that expressed by the capitalized pair.

SOCCER : FIELD ::

A court : basketball
B practice : competition
C tennis : court
D book : library

Students should recognize that **C** is the correct answer because tennis is played on a court as soccer is played on a field. A is incorrect because the relationship is reversed. B and D have different relationships altogether.

Answering Analogy Questions

Teaching Resources: Academic and Workplace Skills Activity Book, p. 53

1. Emphasize that the first step in answering an analogy question is figuring out the relationship between the first set of words.

2. Have a volunteer read aloud the common analogy patterns on page 875. Ask students to suggest additional examples for each pattern.

3. Tell students that the correct answers in analogy questions will be the same parts of speech as the original set of words. (Example: if the first set is a noun and a verb, the answer will be a noun and a verb.)

4. Explain how you would answer the example analogy on page 875. First, you would determine the relationship between the first set of words (part to whole). Then, you would figure out the relationship between the sets of words in the possible answers to find the one that matches. (A page is part of a book.) Have students explain why the other choices are incorrect.

5. Stress that **A** is wrong because the relationship is whole to part, rather than part to whole. The answer must show the same relationship as the original words.

Real-World Connection

Let students know that test-taking skills will help them throughout life as they complete applications and other forms at home and at their workplace. In each instance they will need to pay attention to the question, watch for key words, phrase their answers carefully, and proofread.

Answer Key

▶ **Exercise 12**

After students respond to the questions, ask volunteers to share their experiences with different types of test questions.

Performing on Standardized Tests

Teaching Resources: Academic and Workplace Skills Activity Book, p. 54

1. Encourage students to develop strategies to help them relax before, during, and after a test.

2. Remind students that exercise can help them meet challenges. A brisk walk in the morning after breakfast helps clear the mind, and helps work off test-day jitters.

3. Suggest that students practice taking a few deep breaths from time to time during a test to help them focus.

4. Suggest that students not rush from the testing site too quickly. Encourage them to take time to reflect on the experience, and to consult with others who took the same test. Students might ask themselves questions such as these:

   Did this test seem to go well or badly? Why?

   Did I have enough time to answer all the questions, or did I feel rushed?

   What might I do differently next time?

Critical Viewing

Speculate Students may advise that the test-taker follow any of the suggestions on this page, or read test questions with special care.

31.3

Performing on Standardized Tests

In addition to the tests you take in school, there will most likely be many occasions in which you will take standardized tests. These may include state tests, high-school exit exams, and college board tests, such as the SAT and the ACT. The following tips will help you to perform well on standardized tests.

TIPS FOR TAKING STANDARDIZED TESTS

1. **Get plenty of sleep** the night before the test. If you are tired, you will not perform as well.

2. **Eat a healthy meal** before you take the test. It is essential to be well nourished.

3. **Build confidence by preparing thoroughly.** Confidence is one of the keys to success on standardized tests. To build your confidence, prepare thoroughly—if possible, starting weeks—even months—before the test. The more prepared you are, the more confident you will be.

4. **Come prepared** for the test. Find out before you go to the test which supplies—pencils, paper, calculator, and so on—you need or are allowed to bring.

5. **Take care in filling in bubble sheets.** If you skip an item on the test, make sure that you skip the corresponding row on the bubble sheet. Check over your bubble sheet before you turn in your test.

6. **Budget your time.** Know how much time you have for each section; how many questions the section contains; and how much time you can allow for each question. Skip questions you can't answer so that you don't run out of time to complete the test.

◀ **Critical Viewing** What is some advice you might offer to this student to help her on the standardized test she is taking? **[Speculate]**

Types of Standardized Tests

Another key to successful performance on a standardized test is being familiar with the test format. Following are standardized tests you might take:

PSAT The PSAT is the preliminary SAT—see the description below. The PSAT is given nationwide and provides students with the opportunity to practice for the SAT. PSAT results determine which students are eligible for National Merit Scholarships.

The PSAT has the same format as the SAT with the following exceptions: (1) The PSAT contains fewer sections than the SAT. (2) The PSAT contains items that test your knowledge of usage and mechanics; the SAT does not.

SAT The SAT is used by many colleges as one factor in admissions decisions. It is given nationwide, once a month from October through June except in February. If you are dissatisfied with your SAT scores, you may repeat the test; however, all previous scores will be reported to schools as well as the most recent scores. SATs have a math portion and a verbal portion. The verbal portion contains the following sections:

SECTIONS OF THE VERBAL PORTION OF THE SAT

1. **Sentence-completion questions** test your knowledge of vocabulary by asking you to fill in a blank within a sentence or passage with an appropriate word.
2. **Analogy questions** are like the ones on page 875.
3. **Critical-reading questions** are multiple-choice questions that are asked in response to a pair of related reading passages.
4. **Writing sections** will ask you to respond to a prompt.

ACT The ACT is another test used by colleges as one factor in admissions decisions. The questions—all multiple-choice—focus on English, math, reading, and science reasoning. The English portion asks you to identify errors in grammar, usage, mechanics, logic, and organization. The reading portion presents four passages from different content areas, followed by questions that test your reading and reasoning skills.

Learn More

The Standardized Test Preparation Workshops that appear at the end of every chapter throughout this book provide instruction and practice in all of the types of items covered in these tests.

Reflecting on Your Test-Taking Skills

Think about strategies presented in this section and how they apply to you. Use these questions to help you reflect:

- How can I budget my time better while taking tests?
- How can I apply new test-taking strategies when I take tests?

Step-by-Step Teaching Guide

Types of Standardized Tests

1. Assure students that SAT and ACT scores are only one factor that helps to determine whether or not students are admitted into a college or university.

2. Let students know that other admission factors include transcripts of students' grades, their application essays, and the breadth and scope of their extracurricular activities. Most institutions are looking for a well-rounded applicant, not simply a set of high test scores.

ASSESS and CLOSE

Step-by-Step Teaching Guide

Assessment

Teaching Resources: Formal Assessment, Ch. 31

1. After they have answered the questions, encourage students to acquire any of several guides to preparing for the SAT and ACT, such as Barron's or Kaplan's. These contain sample tests in every test area, and detailed explanations of test-taking skills and strategies. Students may use these guides together with the answers to the questions to pinpoint where they may need more practice.

2. For assessment, use the following options:
   - review the Standardized Test Preparation Workshop on pages 878–879 and have students complete the practice questions.
   - administer the Chapter 31 assessment in *Formal Assessment* to measure students' grasp of concepts presented.

Lesson Objectives

1. To establish and adjust purpose for reading
2. To respond to informational and aesthetic elements in texts
3. To identify main ideas and supporting details
4. To draw conclusions from information gathered

Step-by-Step Teaching Guide

Reading: Constructing Meaning From Informational Texts

Teaching Resources: Standardized Test Preparation Workbook, pp. 61–62

1. Go over the bulleted points with students.
2. Have students read the passage and answer the sample question. Then, check to see that students have answered correctly.
3. Have students continue with the four questions about the passage.
4. Go over students' answers, and ask students to explain why each right answer is correct.

Standardized Test Preparation Workshop

Reading: Constructing Meaning From Informational Texts

When you take a standardized test, you often must answer questions about a passage you have read. These questions test your ability to construct meaning from the information provided in the passage. When answering these types of questions, you will be required to do the following:

- Identify the main idea, stated or implied, of a section of the passage.
- Identify the best summary—a concise restating of the key points of the passage.
- Distinguish between facts and nonfacts.
- Recognize the author's point of view and purpose for writing the passage.

The following sample item will give you practice answering these types of questions. To answer the sample question, refer to the passage on the next page.

Test Tip

When answering a main-idea question, make sure your choice is entirely correct and includes as much relevant information as possible.

Sample Test Item	Answer and Explanation
Directions: Read the passage. Then, read each question that follows. Decide which is the best answer to each question. Which of the following is an OPINION expressed in the passage? **A** In 1996, a team of archaeologists located the remains of a fort. . . . **B** Those who believed that it had been washed away must have been shocked at the discovery. **C** Almost half of these objects date to the first years of the English settlement. **D** When archaeologist William Keslo found a shard of pottery . . .	The correct answer is *B*. It does not include information that can be backed up by facts. The other choices are all facts from the passage.

✏️ TEST-TAKING TIP

Tell students that after reading an informational text, they may read a multiple-choice answer that seems correct, but in fact is wrong because it does not contain enough relevant information (see 4A). Or one choice may be a statement about a possible future happening, which is therefore an opinion statement (see 3D). At other times a statement may be correct but is a detail and not the main idea (see 1D).

Explain that if students encounter unfamiliar words in an informational text, they should try to get the meaning from context but not worry if they can't understand every word. Getting the main idea of each paragraph in a passage and of the passage as a whole is the key to success on a test of this type.

▶ **Practice 1** **Directions:** Read the passage. Then, read each question that follows the passage. Decide which is the best answer to each question.

In 1996, a team of archaeologists located the remains of a fort built by John Smith and Jamestown's original inhabitants. Starting in 1994, it took archaeologists two and a half years to positively prove that the fort had not been washed away by the James River. Those who believed that it had been washed away must have been shocked at the discovery. When archaeologist William Keslo found a shard of pottery that he believed dated to 1545, he kept digging, and in four seasons of excavations has found more than 160,000 artifacts from the seventeenth-century colony.

Almost half of these objects date to the first years of the English settlement. The artifacts include a bone whistle, a trumpet mouthpiece, coins, a thimble, and gaming dice the size of a pencil eraser. Soldiers were not allowed to play dice, so they carved them so small that their superior officers could not see them. As the project continues, further discoveries will be made about the town's growth, evolving architectural types, and day-to-day life in early seventeenth-century Jamestown.

1 What is the main idea of the first paragraph of this passage?

A Archaeologists have discovered the Jamestown Fort and disproved the long-held belief that it was washed away by the James River.

B In 1996, a group of archaeologists did some work in the Jamestown area.

C Many were surprised to find out that the James Fort wasn't washed away by the James River.

D It took a team of archaeologists two and a half years to prove that the Jamestown Fort wasn't washed away by the James River.

2 You can tell from the passage that the author views the discovery—

F as a waste of time and money.

G with disbelief about whether it is truly the fort.

H with optimism about all that can be learned.

J with indifference about its impact on how we view history.

3 Which of the following is an OPINION expressed in the passage?

A he kept digging, and in four seasons of excavations has found more than 160,000 artifacts from the seventeenth-century colony.

B The artifacts included a bone whistle, a trumpet mouthpiece, coins, a thimble, and gaming dice.

C Almost half of these objects date to the first years of the English settlement.

D As the project continues, further discoveries will be made about the town's growth, evolving architectural types, and day-to-day life in early seventeenth-century Jamestown.

4 Which of the following is the best summary of this passage?

F William Keslo discovered an artifact that has led to the unearthing of the Jamestown Fort.

G Archaeologists have proved that the Jamestown Fort had not been washed away and have also discovered numerous artifacts that will help us learn about life at the fort.

H In 1996, archaeologists found the Jamestown Fort and disproved the long-held belief that it was washed away by the James River.

J The discoveries made at the Jamestown Fort have helped us learn about life during the early seventeenth century.

Customize for
Less Advanced Students

If students had difficulties with reading the passage, go over any words they may have had trouble with, showing them how context can help them get the meanings of *archaeologists, inhabitants, shard, excavations,* and *artifacts*. Assure them that they can use the same strategy when taking any test.

Customize for
AP Students

Suggest that when reading informational texts independently, students practice writing summaries and statements of main idea.

Answer Key

1. A
2. H
3. D
4. G

In-Depth Lesson Plan

	LESSON FOCUS	PRINT AND MEDIA RESOURCES
DAY 1	**Working With Others** Students develop workplace skills with the interview process and learn how to interact with people in the business world. (pp. 880–882)	**Teaching Resources** *Academic and Workplace Skills Activity Book,* p. 55
DAY 2	**Learning Teamwork** Students learn about working together as a group. (pp. 883–884)	**Teaching Resources** *Academic and Workplace Skills Activity Book,* p. 55
DAY 3	**Moving Toward Your Goals** Students learn about setting goals, internships, and problem solving. (pp. 885–887)	**Teaching Resources** *Academic and Workplace Skills Activity Book,* p. 56
DAY 4	**Managing Time** Students learn about time and money management, and apply math and computer skills to real-life situations. (pp. 888–891)	**Teaching Resources** *Academic and Workplace Skills Activity Book,* pp. 57–60
DAY 5	**Review and Assess** Students review chapter and demonstrate mastery of workplace skills. (pp. 892–893)	**Teaching Resources** *Formal Assessment,* Ch. 32

Accelerated Lesson Plan

	LESSON FOCUS	PRINT AND MEDIA RESOURCES
DAY 1	**Working With Others; Learning Teamwork** Students develop workplace skills with the interview process, learn how to interact with people in the business world, and how to work together as a group. (pp. 880–884)	**Teaching Resources** *Academic and Workplace Skills Activity Book,* p. 55
DAY 2	**Moving Toward Your Goals; Managing Time** Students learn about setting goals, internships, problem solving, time and money management, and apply math and computer skills to real-life situations. (pp. 885–891)	**Teaching Resources** *Academic and Workplace Skills Activity Book,* pp. 56–60
DAY 3	**Review and Assess** Students review chapter and demonstrate mastery of workplace skills. (pp. 892–893)	**Teaching Resources** *Formal Assessment,* Ch. 32

Options for Adapting Lesson Plans

HOMEWORK

Have students conduct independent library research.

FEATURES

Extend coverage with the Standardized Test Preparation Workshop (p. 892).

TECHNOLOGY

Students may use the Internet to conduct independent research. Have them print out their completed work.

INTEGRATED SKILLS COVERAGE

Research Skills
SE pp. 881, 888

Technology Skills SE p. 891

Reading/Writing Skills
Standardized Test Preparation Workshop: Reading Informational Texts, SE p. 892

Job Search Skills ATE p. 886

Problem Solving Skills ATE p. 890

Viewing and Representing
Critical Viewing, SE pp. 880, 884, 886, 888, 889, 891

Speaking and Listening ATE p. 883

Real-World Connection
ATE p. 881

BLOCK SCHEDULING

Pacing Suggestions
For 90-minute Blocks
• Have students go over the Moving Toward Your Goals, Managing Time, and Managing Money sections in a single period.
• Focus one class period on Applying Math Skills and Applying Computer Skills.

Resources for Varying Instruction
• *Academic and Workplace Skills Activity Book,* pp. 55–60

Professional Development Support
• *How to Manage Instruction in the Block* This Teaching Resource provides management and activity suggestions.

ASSESSMENT SUPPORT

Standardized Test Preparation Workshop SE p. 892; ATE p. 886

Standardized Test Preparation Workbook, pp. 63–64

Formal Assessment, Ch. 32

MEDIA AND TECHNOLOGY

For the Teacher
• *Resource Pro* CD-ROM

MEETING INDIVIDUAL NEEDS

Less Advanced Students ATE p. 893. See also Ongoing Assessments ATE pp. 882, 884, 889.

AP Students ATE p. 887

ESL Students ATE pp. 886, 890, 893

Verbal/Linguistic Learners ATE p. 888

Logical/Mathematical Learners ATE p. 889

Visual/Spatial Learners ATE p. 884

WRITING AND GRAMMAR WEB SITE

The Interactive Writing and Grammar Web Site provides a wide array of support for students, teachers, and parents.

www.phschool.com

Lesson Objectives

1. To demonstrate proficiency in each aspect of the listening process such as focusing attention, interpreting, and responding

2. To use effective strategies for listening

3. To use effective strategies to evaluate one's own listening such as asking questions for clarification, comparing and contrasting interpretations with others, and researching points of interest or contention

4. To use effective listening to provide appropriate feedback in a variety of situations such as conversations and discussions and informative or persuasive presentations

5. To communicate effectively in conversations and group discussions while problem solving and planning

6. To learn techniques for managing time and money

7. To better understand the value of acquiring math and computer skills

Critical Viewing

Analyze Students may feel that the people exchange ideas and discuss pros and cons of proposed plans of action.

Chapter

32 Workplace Skills and Competencies

▲ **Critical Viewing**
How do these people use communication skills in their work? **[Analyze]**

In each new experience, you use your communication skills to gather the information needed to function effectively. In the workplace, good communication skills will help you gather and share the information required for your job, whatever that job may be.

This chapter will help you improve your ability to communicate effectively with others, to set and achieve goals, and to solve problems. There will also be suggestions on how to work more efficiently by budgeting your time and, as you grow more independent, on how to manage your money properly. In addition, you will discover how to learn more about the field of your choice through internships and how math and computer skills help you in your everyday life.

880 • Workplace Skills and Competencies

⏱ TIME AND RESOURCE MANAGER

Resources
Print: *Academic and Workplace Skills Activity Book,* p. 55

In-Depth Coverage	Accelerated Pace
• Cover pp. 880–882 in class. • You might assign Exercise 1 a week ahead of time to allow students to set up their interviews. • Provide an opportunity for them to share their experiences in small groups or with the class. • Have students work in small groups to act out the role-plays on p. 882.	• Discuss the basics of interviewing with the class. • Assign Exercise 1 for students to complete independently.

Working With Others

You will be expected to interact effectively with people, whether you are pursuing further study or entering the work force. This section offers tips on enhancing your ability to communicate in one-on-one and group situations.

Learn One-on-One Communication

When you apply for a job or for admission to a college, you can make a good impression by learning good one-on-one communication skills. You will then need to refine those skills to work well with the people you meet at work or on campus.

Interviews Learning how to interview properly can increase your chances of being accepted for an internship, hired for a job, or admitted to the school of your choice.

▶ **KEY CONCEPT** An interview requires careful preparation, professionalism, courtesy, and follow-through. ■

📘 Research Tip

To help plan your career goals, investigate fields of interest at the career center of a local college.

THE INTERVIEW PROCESS

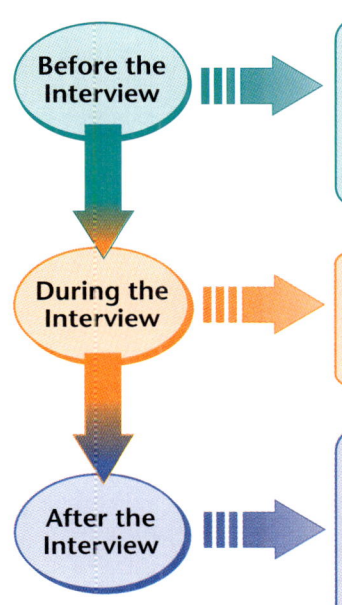

Before the Interview

1. Find out when, where, and with whom the interview is.
2. Gather references, and prepare your résumé.
3. Learn about your potential employer or the college at which you are applying, and prepare questions.
4. Select a neat, appropriate outfit for the interview.

During the Interview

1. Smile and maintain eye contact.
2. Ask and answer questions politely and concisely.
3. Thank the interviewer, and ask when a decision will be made.

After the Interview

1. In a follow-up letter, restate your interest in the internship, job, or college and extend your thanks.
2. When the deadline for a decision arrives, call to check the status.
3. If you are applying for a job and the position has been filled, ask the company to keep your résumé on file.

Workplace Skills and Competencies • **881**

Real-World Connection

Explain to students that interviewers often ask applicants to name their strengths and the areas in which they could improve. Evaluating their skills and competencies can also help students determine which important skills are missing or inadequate. Then, students can take steps to remedy the situation.

PREPARE and ENGAGE

🔆 **Interest GRABBER** Ask students to compare and contrast going to high school with working at a paid job. How are they similar? How are they different? Which is more difficult? In what ways? What kinds of skills are required in both situations? What skills are needed only at a workplace? Which are needed only at school?

Activate Prior Knowledge

Ask students to think about interviews they've had for part-time or summer jobs, for appointed positions at school or in other organizations, or for other reasons. Have volunteers describe their interviews. What skills do they consider most important for a successful interview? After this discussion, compare their ideas with those listed in the chart on page 881.

TEACH

Step-by-Step Teaching Guide

The Interview Process

Teaching Resources: Academic and Workplace Skills Activity Book, p. 55

1. After reading the chart aloud, use questions such as these to prompt discussion:

   How can you find out more about an employer or a college? (Ask other people and use the Internet.)

   What kinds of questions should you ask during a job interview? (Examples: What kind of work would I do? What would my hours be?)

   Is a follow-up letter really necessary if you thank the interviewer at the end of the interview? Why? (Yes, it shows your interest in the job or college, and your maturity.)

2. Have students ask and discuss other questions they have about the steps of the interview process.

Step-by-Step Teaching Guide

Successful Interaction

1. Have students move their chairs into a circle or a U-shape so they can see each other better. Explain that being able to see one another encourages interaction.

2. Have a volunteer read aloud the interaction suggestions on this page.

3. Help students recognize the importance of these tips by asking the following questions:

   What message does someone send by interrupting another person? (My opinion is more important than yours.)

   Does asking questions mean that you were not listening? (No, it can show that you are interested and want more information.)

   How can you determine the appropriate level of formality? (You can do this by considering the age and status of the other person, the setting, and the reason for the discussion.)

   How can you show respect nonverbally? (You can do this by maintaining eye contact, listening intently, and not interrupting.)

4. Have pairs of students role play the situations at the bottom of page 882. Ask students which of the tips above they found the easiest to follow. Which one was the most difficult? Why?

Answer Key

▶ **Exercise 1**

You might serve as the interviewer, pretending to be a human resources director, for example. If possible, videotape the interviews so students can analyze their performances afterward. As they watch the tape, guide them to focus on the interaction tips and determine whether they successfully carried them out.

▶ **Exercise 2**

Role-playing can often lapse into silliness or pontificating. Keep an eye on the development of each scenario to keep it focused and reality based.

Successful Interaction Whether you are working on a project with co-workers, speaking to professors, or dealing with clients, the way you present information and ideas affects how they are heard and received by others. It is important to keep in mind that interaction is a two-way street. Listening is as important as speaking.

▶ **KEY CONCEPT** Successful interaction requires sensitivity to and respect for others, as well as the ability to listen. ■

Follow these suggestions for effective interaction:

Listen without interrupting.

Clarify by asking questions.

Use an appropriate level of formality.

Be respectful of different opinions.

▶ **Exercise 1** **Interviewing at a College or Business** Arrange an interview to learn more about a college or business of your choice. Follow the tips in this section to make a good impression. Afterward, tell the class about the experience.

▶ **Exercise 2** **Interacting With Others in Various Situations** With other students, role-play the following situations, using the tips for effective interaction as a guide.
1. You must handle a customer who returns merchandise and wants a refund despite the store's no-refund policy.
2. An early riser, you must work out an acceptable living arrangement with your college roommate, who stays up studying half the night.
3. Your colleague at work does not agree with you on an important issue and confronts you at a meeting.

▶ **More Practice**

Academic and Workplace Skills Activity Book
• p. 55

882 • Workplace Skills and Competencies

☑ **ONGOING ASSESSMENT: Monitor and Reinforce**

To give students more pointers on successful interviews, try one of the following strategies.

Option 1 Have students talk with an adult who has conducted interviews and ask about the best and worst experiences he or she has had. Which job applicants were the most impressive, and why? Which were the least impressive, and why? If they could offer the students one suggestion, what would it be?

Option 2 Tell students that one of the best ways to sharpen their interview skills is through practice. Remind them that even if they do not get a job offer from an interview, the interview itself was still valuable because it gave them a chance to improve their speaking and listening skills.

Learn Teamwork

You might work as part of a team to organize a campaign, serve on a committee, or prepare a presentation. Teamwork requires good communication skills. To work well together, group members must know and respect each other's roles.

Roles in Group Discussions A group is typically made up of a facilitator, a recorder or note taker, a timekeeper, and several participants, all of whom must be organized, focused on the discussion, and aware of their responsibilities to be able to succeed at their task. In a group that meets regularly, group members take turns handling the functions of facilitator and other responsibilities.

▶ **KEY CONCEPT** Members of a group assume distinct, yet equally important, roles to realize a common goal. ■

The illustration below outlines the roles and responsibilities of individual group members:

Facilitator
Guides discussion from start to finish; mediates disputes

Recorder
Records key points; prepares report of discussion

Timekeeper
Keeps track of time allowed for parts of discussion

Participants
Contribute and debate ideas

▶ **KEY CONCEPT** Effective participation in group discussions requires an exchange of ideas, constructive debate, and courtesy. ■

Use the following tips for successful group discussions:
- Listen respectfully to all points of view.
- Share your perspective, and encourage others to do so.
- Work with an agenda.
- Stick to the topic.

Workplace Skills and Competencies • **883**

TIME AND RESOURCE MANAGER

Resources
Print: *Academic and Workplace Skills Activity Book*, p. 55

In-Depth Coverage	Accelerated Pace
• Cover pp. 883–884 in class. • Give small groups time to complete Exercise 3. If you wish, assign students to groups to make sure each group includes a range of skill levels.	• Discuss team roles in class. • Assign Exercise 3 for students to complete in groups.

Step-by-Step Teaching Guide

Roles in Group Discussions

Teaching Resources: Academic and Workplace Skills Activity Book, p. 55

1. After students individually read this page, invite them to describe times when they have worked in a group that assigned roles. Write the following questions on the board to prompt discussion.

   Which roles did group members carry out?

   Did having roles help the group work together? In what ways?

2. Discuss whether group members should be allowed to refuse to carry out a role. (Example: Should a shy member be required to take a turn as facilitator? Why or why not?) Help students see that everyone should take turns.

Step-by-Step Teaching Guide

Group Discussion

1. Help students explore the dynamics of group discussions by asking how people can show respect in a discussion. (Do not interrupt. Do not insult others or their ideas. Encourage quiet members to share their opinions.)

2. Review the tips for successful group discussions with the class.

3. Discuss the probable results when group members do not show each other respect. (It can cause anger and miscommunication; it can prevent work from being done because members will hesitate to share their ideas.)

4. Ask students to explain why having an agenda is important. (It will keep the group focused.)

Integrating Speaking and Listening Skills

Invite a pair of students to role-play a discussion in which they disagree about an issue while demonstrating respect for each other. If necessary, take one role yourself. Afterward, ask the class to name the ways the volunteers showed respect for each other.

Customize for
Spatial Learners

As groups begin Exercise 3, remind them to create a written agenda that visual learners can refer to as the meeting progresses. Students can use the agenda on page 884 as a model. Groups might also make nametags to identify the role of each group member. Give each group large sheets of paper so the recorder can write the group's decisions, questions, and goals for the next meeting in a form that everyone can see.

Language Highlight

Latin Roots Tell students that the word *agenda* is based on the Latin word *agendum*, which came from the word *agere*, meaning "to drive." Ask students whether they can see the connection between *agenda* and its action. (An agenda drives or directs a meeting.) Other words with the same base include *agency* and *agent*. Both words suggest a driving or directing force.

Critical Viewing

Speculate The woman on the right may be the facilitator; the others seem to be giving her their attention. The woman on the left may be the recorder; she has pencil in hand. The other two people may be participants, either of whom may also be the timekeeper.

Answer Key

Exercise 3

Have students switch assignments within the groups so that they have experience with different roles.

Meetings Some discussions are organized as meetings. When you plan a meeting, list the issues and topics to be covered by outlining on an agenda the points to be discussed. Identify any materials or information that will be needed, and decide who will be responsible for this. Assign (or participate in choosing) a facilitator, a timekeeper, and a recorder, or note taker. At the end of the meeting, list follow-up activities and questions. Choose a time, and identify goals for the next meeting.

> **AGENDA**
> **Planning Meeting**
> **November 3**
>
> **Attendance:** Rebecca, Gregory, Amy, Elaine, Doug, Jeff
>
> **Facilitator:** Rebecca
> **Note Taker:** Gregory
> **Timekeeper:** Amy
>
> 1. Review and amend agenda
>   (All — 5 minutes)
>
> 2. Brainstorming for ideas
>   (All — 10 minutes)
>
> 3. Presentation of sales results
>   (Elaine — 10 minutes)
>
> 4. Discussion of sales results
>   (All — 20 minutes)

▼ **Critical Viewing**
What role do you think each person is playing at this meeting? **[Speculate]**

▶ **Exercise 3 Organizing a Group Fund-raiser** With five classmates, organize a fund-raiser for a class field trip. Make an agenda for the initial meeting, assign roles, hold the meeting, list follow-up questions and activities, and identify goals for the next meeting.

884 • Workplace Skills and Competencies

☑ ONGOING ASSESSMENT: Monitor and Reinforce

To give students more pointers on successful interviews, try one of the following strategies.

Option 1 Before the students arrive, write on the board an agenda for that day's class period. Allow time at the end of the period to discuss the agenda with the students. Did you cover everything on the agenda? Was the proper amount of time alloted out for each task? What events caused the class to stray from or change the agenda? Is it always a bad idea to change an agenda? Was it helpful to have the agenda posted in a visible location?

Option 2 Have students form small groups to work on one of the exercises in this chapter. Have some of the groups create agendas, and let the others start working without making a plan. When they finish, have the groups compare their experiences. Which groups were more organized and efficient? Why?

Moving Toward Your Goals

When you dream about something you would like to achieve and you plan to accomplish that dream in a set time, you have set a goal. Goals may focus on improving your interviewing skills, raising your SAT scores, or traveling to another country. Some goals can be achieved in weeks; others take years. When goals conflict with one another, you must decide what is most important to you.

Set Your Goals

Personal goals, such as improving study habits or becoming more physically fit, focus on your development as a person. Professional goals, such as obtaining an internship, focus on your career. Despite their distinctions, personal and professional goals often affect each other. Therefore, you should know your goals and what it will take to achieve them.

To set and achieve a goal, you must define your objective as specifically as possible and map out a time frame in which to complete it.

▶ **KEY CONCEPT** Setting a goal means identifying a specific objective and a time frame in which to complete it. ■

STEPS FOR PLANNING AND ACCOMPLISHING GOALS

3. As you progress toward the goal, evaluate what is working and what is not. Adjust the steps as needed.

2. Break the goal down into specific steps, each step having a reasonable time frame.

1. Write down the goal as specifically as possible. Consider how your strengths and weaknesses will affect this goal.

Step-by-Step Teaching Guide

Set Your Goals

Teaching Resources: Academic and Workplace Skills Activity Book, p. 56

1. Help the class work through the steps on this page. Use a sample goal suggested by students. (Example: getting a driver's license or earning money to buy something special.)

2. For Step 1: Urge students to set goals that are important to them. Contrast vague and specific goals, such as "getting better grades" versus "earning a B in American history." Remind students to be realistic in choosing goals. Setting a goal that is too low is pointless, while setting one too high will just lead to frustration.

3. For Step 2: Help students break the class's sample goal into reasonable steps and put them in chronological order. Ask a volunteer to write the steps on the board, along with a timeline.

4. For Step 3: Point out that people may proceed more quickly, or slowly, toward their goals than they had expected. Ask students to suggest events that might affect the timelines they have devised. If they encounter obstacles, urge them to adjust their timelines instead of giving up.

5. Further explore setting goals by asking students to consider the following questions. Why don't people always reach their goals? (They may set goals that are too hard to reach or not important enough to work toward, or they may get distracted or discouraged.) What do you think is the biggest challenge for young people in setting and reaching their goals? (finding time, getting started, etc.)

⏱ TIME AND RESOURCE MANAGER

Resources
Print: *Academic and Workplace Skills Activity Book*, p. 56

In-Depth Coverage	Accelerated Pace
• Cover pp. 885–887 in class, discussing student-generated examples. Invite students who have set and reached goals to share them with the class. • Give students time to complete Exercises 4–6.	• Discuss setting goals and solving problems in class. • Assign Exercises 4–6 for students to complete independently.

Integrating Job Search Skills

Tell students that another way to explore careers is through an informational interview. To set up such an interview, they can ask people in fields that interest them for a brief meeting. They might ask questions such as these:

How do you spend a typical day?

What do you like best about this job? What would you like to change about it?

What training and other preparation would you recommend for someone entering this field?

Customize for
ESL Students

As students approach Exercise 5, encourage them to invite or recommend bilingual speakers. They might explore one or more of the following questions: In what ways do interview skills differ in other cultures? What types of jobs require fluency in more than one language? What kinds of opportunities does the future job market hold for bilingual people?

Critical Viewing

Infer The firm handshake and direct eye contact imply that the interview is at least starting out well.

Answer Key

▶ **Exercise 4**

Students will be challenged to find out what is required to attain the goals they have chosen. Be prepared to help them in seeking out career centers, college brochures, travel agencies, and the like.

▶ **Exercise 5**

In communities where representation of certain career fields is narrow, you may again have to urge students to make use of the Internet and Web sites to come up with details on careers and internships.

32

▲ Critical Viewing
How do you think this interview is going to go? Why do you think so? **[Infer]**

Internships One step you can take toward a professional goal is to work as an intern. Internships are positions that employers create for people who want to learn more about a career. The job may entail basic duties, such as running errands and opening mail, or specific skills, such as writing press releases or building theater props. In all cases, the intern, who may be unpaid, learns about a field by working alongside professionals.

▶ **Exercise 4** **Creating an Action Plan** In your notebook, create a detailed plan for accomplishing one of the following goals: begin a career as an electrician or other technically trained professional, gain acceptance to the college of your choice, or take a trip to another country. Find out what is required to attain the goal. Then, include in your plan the steps needed to achieve the goal and the time and resources required for each step.

▶ **Exercise 5** **Learning About Careers and Internships** Select a field in which you are interested. Contact people in that field, and invite them to your class to discuss their occupation. If the organizations they work for offer internships, ask them to explain the responsibilities handled by interns.

886 • Workplace Skills and Competencies

⬥ **STANDARDIZED TEST PREPARATION WORKSHOP**

Critical Thinking Standardized test questions may require students to be familiar with certain workplace skills. Provide students with opportunities to practice critical thinking.

Which of the benefits below does NOT result from creating an action plan?

A a clear goal
B a guarantee of reaching the goal
C specific steps in reaching a goal
D a date by which the goal should be reached

Students should recognize that **B** does not necessarily result from writing an action plan. Sometimes, even the most well-planned goals cannot be achieved for various reasons.

Solve Problems

As you work toward your personal and professional goals, you should know how to solve problems that may arise. Effective problem solving involves identifying the problem and generating and evaluating possible solutions. Solving particularly difficult problems often entails creative thinking. Creative thinking can help you generate a variety of possible solutions with which to work.

Creative Thinking There are often several ways to overcome an obstacle. Think creatively to solve a problem; consider unusual or nonstandard solutions.

▶ **KEY CONCEPT** Solving a problem requires a thorough understanding of what's wrong, a number of ideas for possible solutions, and a careful review of each one. ■

Stimulate your creative problem-solving skills by following these suggestions:

- Pose the problem to others, and listen to their advice.
- Imagine how someone with particular talents might solve the problem. What approach, for example, might an inventor take? An artist? A computer specialist?
- Increase the number of solutions by writing down all ideas—however fanciful or impractical. Sometimes, an impractical idea can be made workable with just a few adjustments.
- Interact with people from different cultures and backgrounds to widen your frame of reference and help you generate a greater variety of ideas.

▶ **Exercise 6** **Solving Problems With Creative Thinking** You want a job as a reporter for a daily newspaper, but you must have published articles to be considered for the position. How do you get published without first having a job? In your notebook, analyze this problem by following the steps to effective problem solving. Come up with three possible solutions by practicing your creative thinking. One idea for getting an article published, for example, could be to volunteer to write press releases for a nonprofit group and to submit them to the local paper.

▶ **More Practice**

Academic and Workplace Skills Activity Book
- page 56

Solve Problems

Teaching Resources: Academic and Workplace Skills Activity Book, p. 56

1. After students read page 887, guide them in creating a list of steps they can use to solve problems. Work with students to create a list like the one below, and write it on the board.

   - *Define/state the problem. Sometimes just clearly stating what is wrong contributes to solving the problem.*
   - *Brainstorm for possible solutions. The more solutions to be considered, the better. Write down every possibility. An impractical idea might be adjusted to become the best solution.*
   - *Evaluate the solutions. This is the time to weed out solutions that really will not work.*
   - *Consider the consequences of the remaining solutions. Nearly every action has positive and negative consequences. The best solution will have more positives than negatives.*
   - *Choose a solution and try it. Monitor the results and change course if the solution is not working.*

2. Discuss with students the benefits and pitfalls of asking others for advice about solving problems.

Customize for
AP Students

After students complete Exercise 6, have them investigate how well-known reporters got started. Did they suddenly become successful or did they struggle for recognition? When choosing a journalist to study, students might review a list of journalists who have won Pulitzer Prizes in reporting or photography. Have students share what they learn with the class.

Answer Key

▶ **Exercise 6**

Allow students to brainstorm with classmates if ideas beyond the one mentioned are not forthcoming.

Teaching Resources: Academic and Workplace Skills Activity Book, p. 57

1. Help the class explore the challenges of managing time by discussing these questions:

   Do you think adults or young people have more trouble managing their time? Why? (The ability to manage time is not an age-related issue. Both adults and young people have trouble managing their time.)

   Do you think it is fair to judge someone as "incapable" if that person cannot manage his or her time wisely? (Whether it is fair or not, people do tend to question why others cannot manage their time.)

2. Explore the need to prioritize tasks, perhaps labeling them as *A* (urgent), *B* (important), or *C* (no time constraints). Have students suggest examples for each level of task. Discuss why a task might move from the *B* list to the *A* or *C* list.

3. Discuss the value of keeping a "to-do" list. Explain that many people have daily, weekly, and "when there is time" lists.

Customize for
Verbal/Linguistic Learners

Spatial learners can create a grid for Exercise 7 on their own, but you might guide verbal learners to do so by using a model. Have students show each day of the week in their grids, with each day broken into hour-long segments.

Critical Viewing

Analyze Students should realize that procrastination and forgetfulness are human traits that are best overcome by the prodding of a time-management scheme.

Answer Key

▶ **Exercise 7**

The ranking of "to-do" list items may be highly subjective. The activities include anything listed that is not assigned a specific time and day of the week.

32

Managing Time

Whether you choose to pursue a bachelor's degree or a plumber's license, you will eventually face a task that must be completed in a set amount of time. Knowing how to use time efficiently can mean the difference between being viewed as a capable person or as one who can't manage the job.

To budget your time, outline appointments and activities and know which are most important. Create "To-Do" lists to remind yourself of important tasks.

SAMPLE PLANNER

To-Do List

1. Call Ms. Zimbler for fund-raising information.

2. Pick up art for posters.

3. Drop off brochures at Nancy's.

Mon	9:30 Planning Meeting
Tues	
Wed	3:00–5:00 Work
Thur	7:00 P.M. Baby-sit
Fri	
Sat	10:00 Bake Sale
Sun	

▶ **KEY CONCEPT** To manage your time, record and prioritize a schedule of appointments, deadlines, and activities. ■

▶ **Exercise 7** **Managing a Schedule** Plan a weekly schedule with the following responsibilities: a job twenty minutes from home from 10 A.M. to 2 P.M., Monday through Friday; college classes ten minutes from home from 6 P.M. to 9 P.M., Monday, Wednesday, and Friday; a daily one-hour workout; and guitar lessons from 1 P.M. to 3 P.M., Saturday. Fit in nine hours of study time, a two-hour dentist visit, a movie with friends, time to write five letters, and a stop at the cleaners. Include a daily to-do list that ranks activities according to importance.

📙 Research Tip

You can find easy-to-understand guides to managing your time and money at your local library.

▲ **Critical Viewing**
Why is managing your time so important? **[Analyze]**

🕐 TIME AND RESOURCE MANAGER

Resources
Print: *Academic and Workplace Skills Activity Book*, pp. 57–58

In-Depth Coverage	Accelerated Pace
• Cover pages 888–889 in class. • If possible, bring in examples of guides for managing time and money from the school or community library. • Give students time to complete Exercises 7 and 8.	• Discuss with the class the basics of managing time and money. • Assign Exercises 7 and 8 for students to complete independently.

Managing Money

Money, like time, is limited. A budget will help you manage money wisely. In the workplace, you may be expected to record and manage expenses for your part of a project.

KEY CONCEPT To manage money, record and prioritize a budget of available funds, regular expenses, and projected (or expected) expenses. ■

In most budgets, incoming money, called *credit*, is shown in black. Outgoing money, called *expenses* or *debits*, is usually written in red. For a budget to work, total expenses should not exceed total credits. If they do, the budgeter needs to prioritize and make decisions to cut spending or to come up with ways to increase income.

SAMPLE BUDGET

Drama Club Budget

	Regular Income	Regular Expenses	Projected Expenses
Club Dues	50.00		
From Sponsors	100.00		
Weekly Bake Sale	125.00		
Bake Sale Supplies		25.00	
Posterboard and Paint			10.00
T-shirts for Members			125.00
Weekly Meeting Snacks		15.00	
Total	275.00	40.00	135.00

▲ **Critical Viewing**
Why is managing money a difficult thing for many people to do? [Speculate]

Exercise 8 **Managing a Budget** Create a budget for a service club. The club has twenty members, each of whom pays $1.00 a week in dues. They hold a weekly car wash, the income from which averages $75.00. The materials for the car wash cost $10.00. The club usually buys pizza for the workers, at a cost of $50.00. The group wants to give $200.00 to a charity. Create a budget for the group, and answer these questions:
1. How long will it take for the group to have the $200.00?
2. What suggestions would you make for reducing expenses?
3. What suggestions would you make for increasing income?

More Practice
Academic and Workplace Skills Activity Book
• pages 57–58

Step-by-Step Teaching Guide

Managing Money

Teaching Resources: Academic and Workplace Skills Activity Book, p. 58

1. Explore this topic by asking students why they think *budget* is a negative term to many people. (Many people think a budget keeps them from buying the things they really want.) Does being on a budget mean that they cannot spend money as they wish? Why or why not? (No, but you have to set priorities so you can buy the things you want after you pay your bills.) What can students do to help themselves stay on a budget? (Set up a realistic budget. Put aside some money for fun.)

2. Invite volunteers to share any experiences they have had in budgeting their money. What tips would they like to pass on to classmates?

Customize for
Logical/Mathematical Learners

As students work on Exercise 8, encourage them to check each other's math. Perhaps students who are more comfortable with math can serve as "financial advisors" for their classmates. After the class completes the exercise, you might ask volunteers to put the service club's budget on the chalkboard to allow other students to check their work.

Critical Viewing

Speculate Students may feel that the "down-the-road" expenses rarely have the impact of "money-in-your-hand" availability for impulse spending.

Answer Key

Exercise 8
1. six weeks
2. Eliminate the pizzas for workers; raise dues.
3. Suggestions: come up with alternate fundraisers for days when rain prohibits car washes.

✓ ONGOING ASSESSMENT: Monitor and Reinforce

Some students may have more experience than others with managing a budget. For students with little or no experience, try one of the following strategies.

Option 1 Have students talk to a willing friend, parent, or other adult about how he or she manages a budget. What types of fixed expenses does he or she have? What other types of expenses tend to arise?

Option 2 Students might have a number of questions about money or budgets that they feel uncomfortable asking in front of the class. Have students write these questions anonymously on slips of paper. Make a list of some of the questions, assign students to research them, and have them share their answers with the class.

Step-by-Step Teaching Guide

Applying Math Skills

Teaching Resources: Academic and Workplace Skills Activity Book, p. 59

1. Discuss the importance of math skills with the class. Ask students to brainstorm for situations in which math skills are necessary (shopping, applying for a job, and so on).

2. Have students complete these exercises to practice their math skills.

   A. Making Purchases
   Gasoline costs $1.18 a gallon at Gas Station A. It costs $1.32 at Gas Station B, but you can get a 15% discount if you use a certain credit card. Which station offers a better deal? (Station B: a 15% discount brings the gas down to $1.12 a gallon.)

   B. Estimating Costs
   Your club is fixing a meal of a salad and a casserole for group of twelve elderly people. You must keep the costs down to $4 a person. You know that salad ingredients will cost $15 and casserole fixings will be about $25. Can you afford to buy brownies for dessert or should you bake them yourself? (You can afford to buy them if they cost no more than $8.)

   C. Determining the Value of Your Time
   A neighbor offers you $35 to watch her two children on a Saturday from 9:00 A.M. until 7:00 P.M. You expect to make at least $4 an hour when you baby-sit. Should you take this job? (It is a tough decision because the job pays $3.50/hour. It would depend on your schedule and on the kids.)

Integrating Problem Solving Skills

After students read this page, ask them to suggest other ways they can use math to help solve problems.

Customize for
ESL Students

As students tackle Exercise 9, make sure they understand what is expected. Ask them to explain the task in their own words. Match them up with a more-fluent English speaker for assistance if necessary.

890

Applying Math Skills

On the job, math skills can help you analyze information to make wise decisions about what to buy and what to charge. Whether you work for yourself or someone else, you will need to make these decisions.

> **KEY CONCEPT** Use math skills to determine the best buy for your needs. ■

In life and in the workplace, your math skills can help you to determine the best buy on anything you purchase. For example, one store may advertise paint at $3.00 per gallon when you buy twenty or more gallons. Another may sell paint at 10 percent off the usual price of $4.00 per gallon no matter how many you buy. To decide between paints, you must calculate 10 percent of $4.00, how many cans you need, and which buy is the best for your needs.

> **KEY CONCEPT** Use math skills to determine costs. ■

Math skills can help you figure out how much a job or project will cost. First, figure out the amount of materials or supplies you will need. Then, use math to figure out the total cost of the materials, based on the price per foot, piece, can, or other unit of measurement.

> **KEY CONCEPT** Use math skills to determine the value of your time. ■

When you are offered a salary or a price for a job, use math skills to figure out how much you are being paid per hour. Figure out how many hours the job will take. Then, divide the total pay by the number of hours you will spend on the job. Use this number to determine if you are being paid fairly. For example, if you are offered $50.00 to do a job that will take you approximately 25 hours, you are being paid $2.00 per hour.

> **Exercise 9** **Using Math Skills to Give an Estimated Price**
> A neighbor has asked you to build a fence around her garden. The garden is 10 feet by 12 feet. Use your math skills to estimate how much you will charge her. Figure out the cost of lumber. Estimate how long the job will take you, and calculate your own hourly rate. Then, ask a partner to act as the neighbor, to role-play a negotiation of the price. Write an explanation of how you arrived at the final price.

> **More Practice**
> Academic and Workplace Skills Activity Book
> • pages 59–60

⏱ TIME AND RESOURCE MANAGER

Resources
Print: *Academic and Workplace Skills Activity Book,* pp. 59–60; *Formal Assessment,* Ch. 32

In-Depth Coverage	Accelerated Pace
• Cover pages 890–891 in class. • Give students time to complete Exercise 10. Have them do some research to obtain the missing information, such as the cost of lumber, or estimate those costs as a class. • Bring in newspapers for Exercise 10.	• Discuss the basics of applying math and computer skills as a class. • Assign Exercises 7 and 8 for students to complete independently.

Applying Computer Skills

Keyboarding skills, knowledge of formatting techniques and other software tools, and the ability to use the Internet to obtain information will benefit you, whether you're working for a grade or a paycheck.

KEY CONCEPT The computer is a tool that can help you work more efficiently. Employers value employees who are familiar with a variety of computer programs and functions. ■

Like all tools, computers can make a job easier to do. What you use the computer for depends on the job you are doing. The illustration below shows some common computer programs you might use on the job:

Spreadsheets
Word Processing
Internet
Databases

💿 Technology Tip

Computer software often has a feature built in that helps you create a résumé. Type in the word *résumé* at the Help command to investigate this feature.

Exercise 10 Investigating Applications of Computer Skills

Look through the classified ads of your newspaper. Make a list of the computer programs and skills mentioned and the types of jobs that require them. Find out what the programs or skills are, and find out what they are used for. Find out where in your area classes or workshops on these topics are offered.

🌐 Learn More

To learn what information to include in an effective résumé and follow-up letter, see Chapter 17, "Workplace Writing."

Reflecting on Your Workplace Skills and Competencies

Think about what you have learned in this chapter. Begin by answering the following questions in your notebook:

- In what areas am I strongest? Why?
- What skills should I improve? Why?

Workplace Skills and Competencies • **891**

Applying Computer Skills

Teaching Resources: Academic and Workplace Skills Activity Book, p. 60

1. Have students share any computer skills they have used at their part-time or summer jobs, or at school. Ask students whether they learned these skills on the job. If not, how did they learn them?

2. Choose a specific workplace, such as a fast-food restaurant, a veterinarian's office, an insurance company, or a bank. Ask students to brainstorm for the ways computers are used at these workplaces.

3. Ask students why learning how to use computers and software is important. (New technology is constantly being developed, and people who are familiar with it are valuable to employers.)

4. Refer students to the technology tip on this page.

ASSESS and CLOSE

Assessment

Teaching Resources: Formal Assessment, Chapter 32

1. Have students answer the Reflecting questions independently and then share their answers in small groups.

2. For assessment, use the following options:

   - review the Standardized Test Preparation Workshop on pages 892–893, and have students complete the practice exercises.

   - administer the Chapter 32 assessment in *Formal Assessment* to measure students' grasp of the concepts presented.

Answer Key

▶ Exercise 9

As an alternative, have students estimate the price of a class or school project that is under consideration. All estimates, of course, will be highly speculative.

▶ Exercise 10

Students can consult in-school computer-lab instructors for suggestions on how to find where classes are held.

Lesson Objectives

1. To analyze text structures such as compare/contrast, cause/effect, and chronological order for how they influence understanding

2. To analyze the characteristics of clearly written texts, including the patterns of organization

Step-by-Step Teaching Guide

Reading Informational Texts

Teaching Resources: Standardized Test Preparation Workbook, pp. 63–64

1. Go over the sample test items with students, including the answers and explanations.

2. Have a student read the Test Tips at the top of the page.

3. Assign the practice test.

Standardized Test Preparation Workshop

Reading Informational Texts

Standardized tests often measure your ability to apply your skills at following directions in the correct sequence. The following sample test item will give you practice in answering these types of questions.

Test Tip

Pay attention to the sequence that directions present. Note why one step must follow the next.

Sample Test Items	Answers and Explanations
Directions: Read the flyer, and then answer the questions that follow. **Ice Skating Lessons** Novice 3:30 Intermediate 4:30 Expert 5:30 Bring your own skates, helmet, and knee, wrist, and elbow pads. Put on your gear. Then, meet outside the double doors to the Eagle rink.	
1 According to the directions what do you need to bring to the lesson? **A** skates **B** a registration form **C** money for the fee **D** skates, helmet, and other protective gear	The correct answer for item 1 is *D*, "skates, helmet, and other protective gear." These are the only items that the directions tell you to bring.
2 According to the directions, which of the following should you do first? **F** meet with your class **G** register for lessons **H** put on your skates and other gear **J** find out what level skater you are	The correct answer for item 2 is *H*, "put on your skates and other gear." Although the other answers may be things that should have been tended to first, they are not addressed in the directions.

892 • Workplace Skills and Competencies

✏ TEST-TAKING TIP

Tell students that when they take a test on following directions, it is important to note transitional words in the test prompt, such as *first, next, before, after, earlier, later, last,* and so on.

A test item on following directions will not necessarily order events chronologically. For example, students may encounter these words and phrases at any place in a passage: *before, she had already, earlier in the day, the night before,* all of which indicate something that happened at an earlier time.

▶ **Practice 1** **Directions:** Read the passage, and then answer the questions that follow.

New Users and Users Wishing to Work on a New Disk or Computer

Type your name here.

Enter the name of your class or your teacher's name here (optional).

Choose a disk where you want the program to store your work.

Click **Cancel** to return to the first sign-in screen.

Click **OK** once you have signed in and selected a drive.

New Student Sign-in

1. Enter your name:
2. Enter your class or teacher (optional):
3. Choose where to store your work.

   Click the name of hard disk or floppy:
   SMITH–HD
   Language-Arts

   Cancel   OK

Joy had study hall this period. Earlier in the day, she had taken a grammar test and did not feel confident about the results. After getting permission from her study hall teacher, she headed for the computer room. She planned on using the grammar program to brush up on her skills. Joy sat down at her computer and opened the manual for the Language Lab. The manual explained how to get started, and off she went. She felt smarter already!

1 Which of these did Joy do first?
   A took a grammar test
   B had study hall
   C went to the computer room
   D opened the manual

2 What does #1 in the computer manual direct you to do?
   F choose a disk to store your work
   G click OK
   H enter your name
   J enter your teacher's name

3 What happens when you press the Cancel button?
   A the program shuts down
   B you are returned to the first sign-in screen
   C you are taken to a menu of lessons
   D you can change the disk to store your work

4 When Joy reached her study hall class, she—
   F took her seat and studied
   G asked her teacher's permission to go to the lab
   H opened the computer manual
   J started working on her grammar skills

5 What important step did Joy take before beginning the grammar lessons?
   A She read the manual and followed the directions for sign-in.
   B She asked the computer-lab assistant to sign her in to the program.
   C She tried to get the grammar program working without any help.
   D Joy arrived at the computer room.

6 The final step Joy is directed to take before beginning is—
   F click Cancel
   G choose a disk to store her work
   H enter her teacher's name
   J click OK

Customize for
ESL Students

Some students may have difficulty with the idioms in this passage. Explain if necessary "*headed for* the computer room" and "*brush up* on her skills."

Customize for
Less Advanced Students

Give students who had difficulty with this test extra practice by scrambling a list of directions, perhaps for a fire drill, and asking them to put the directions in order.

Answer Key
   1. A
   2. H
   3. B
   4. G
   5. A
   6. J

Citing Sources and Preparing Manuscript

Preparing Manuscript

The presentation of your written work is important. Your work should be neat, clean, and easy to read. Follow your teacher's directions for placing your name and class, along with the title and date of your work, on the paper.

For handwritten work:

- Use cursive handwriting or manuscript printing, according to the style your teacher prefers. The penmanship reference below shows the accepted formation of letters in cursive writing.
- Write or print neatly.
- Write on one side of lined 8-1/2" x 11" paper with a clean edge. (Do not use pages torn from a spiral notebook.)
- Indent the first line of each paragraph.

- Leave a margin, as indicated by the guidelines on the lined paper. Write in a size appropriate for the lines provided. Do not write so large that the letters from one line bump into the ones above and below. Do not write so small that the writing is difficult to read.
- Write in blue or black ink.
- Number the pages in the upper right corner.
- You should not cross out words on your final draft. Recopy instead. If your paper is long, your teacher may allow you to make one or two small changes by neatly crossing out the text to be deleted and using a caret [^] to indicate replacement text. Alternatively, you might make one or two corrections neatly with correction fluid. If you find yourself making more than three corrections, consider recopying the work.

PENMANSHIP REFERENCE

For word-processed or typed documents:

- Choose a standard, easy-to-read font.
- Type or print on one side of unlined 8 $\frac{1}{2}$" x 11" paper.
- Set the margins for the side, top, and bottom of your paper at approximately one inch. Most word-processing programs have a default setting that is appropriate.
- Double-space the document.
- Indent the first line of each paragraph.
- Number the pages in the upper right corner. Many word-processing programs have a header feature that will do this for you automatically.

- If you discover one or two errors after you have typed or printed, use correction fluid if your teacher allows such corrections. If you have more than three errors in an electronic file, consider making the corrections to the file and reprinting the document. If you have typed a long document, your teacher may allow you to make a few corrections by hand. If you have several errors, however, consider retyping the document.

For research papers:

Follow your teacher's directions for formatting formal research papers. Most papers will have the following features:

- Title page
- Table of Contents or Outline
- Works-Cited List

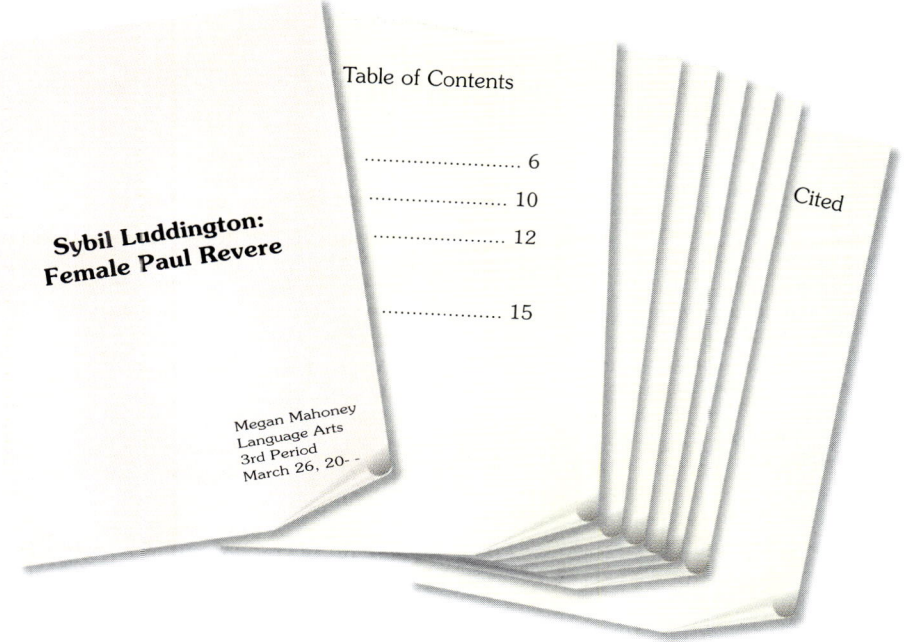

Incorporating Ideas From Research

Below are three common methods of incorporating the ideas of other writers into your work. Choose the most appropriate style by analyzing your needs in each case. In all cases, you must credit your source.

- **Direct Quotation:** Use quotation marks to indicate the exact words.
- **Paraphrase:** To share ideas without a direct quotation, state the ideas in your own words. While you haven't copied word-for-word, you still need to credit your source.
- **Summary:** To provide information about a large body of work—such as a speech, an editorial, or a chapter of a book— identify the writer's main idea.

Avoiding Plagiarism

Whether you are presenting a formal research paper or an opinion paper on a current event, you must be careful to give credit for any ideas or opinions that are not your own. Presenting someone else's ideas, research, or opinion as your own—even if you have rephrased it in different words—is *plagiarism*, the equivalent of academic stealing, or fraud.

You can avoid plagiarism by synthesizing what you learn: Read from several sources and let the ideas of experts help you draw your own conclusions and form your own opinions. Ultimately, however, note your own reactions to the ideas presented.

When you choose to use someone else's ideas or work to support your view, credit the source of the material. Give bibliographic information to cite your sources of the following information:

- Statistics
- Direct quotations
- Indirectly quoted statements of opinions
- Conclusions presented by an expert
- Facts available in only one or two sources

Crediting Sources

When you credit a source, you acknowledge where you found your information and you give your readers the details necessary for locating the source themselves. Within the body of the paper, you provide a short citation, a footnote number linked to a footnote, or an endnote number linked to an endnote reference. These brief references show the page numbers on which you found the information. To make your paper more formal, prepare a reference list at the end of the paper to provide full bibliographic information on your sources. These are two common types of reference lists:

- A **bibliography** provides a listing of all the resources you consulted during your research.
- A **works-cited list** indicates the works you have referenced in your paper.

Choosing a Format for Documentation

The type of information you provide and the format in which you provide it depend on what your teacher prefers. These are the most commonly used styles:

- **Modern Language Association (MLA) Style** This is the style used for most papers at the middle-school and high-school level and for most language arts papers.
- **American Psychological Association (APA) Style** This is used for most papers in the social sciences and for most college-level papers.
- *Chicago Manual of Style* **(CMS) Style** This is preferred by some teachers.

On the following pages, you'll find sample citation formats for the most commonly cited materials. Each format calls for standard bibliographic information. The difference is in the order of the material presented in each entry and the punctuation required.

MLA Style for Listing Sources

Book with one author	Pyles, Thomas. *The Origins and Development of the English Language.* 2nd ed. New York: Harcourt Brace Jovanovich, Inc., 1971.
Book with two or three authors	McCrum, Robert, William Cran, and Robert MacNeil. *The Story of English.* New York: Penguin Books, 1987.
Book with an editor	Truth, Sojourner. *Narrative of Sojourner Truth.* Ed. Margaret Washington. New York: Vintage Books, 1993.
Book with more than three authors or editors	Donald, Robert B., et al. *Writing Clear Essays.* Upper Saddle River, NJ: Prentice-Hall, Inc., 1996.
A single work from an anthology	Hawthorne, Nathaniel. "Young Goodman Brown." *Literature: An Introduction to Reading and Writing.* Ed. Edgar V. Roberts and Henry E. Jacobs. Upper Saddle River, NJ: Prentice-Hall, Inc., 1998. 376–385. [Indicate pages for the entire selection.]
Introduction in a published edition	Washington, Margaret. Introduction. *Narrative of Sojourner Truth.* By Sojourner Truth. New York: Vintage Books. 1993, pp. v–xi.
Signed article in a weekly magazine	Wallace, Charles. "A Vodacious Deal." *Time* 14 Feb. 2000: 63.
Signed article in a monthly magazine	Gustaitis, Joseph. "The Sticky History of Chewing Gum." *American History* Oct. 1998: 30–38.
Unsigned editorial or story	"Selective Silence." Editorial. *Wall Street Journal* 11 Feb. 2000: A14. [If the editorial or story is signed, begin with the author's name.]
Signed pamphlet	[Treat the pamphlet as though it were a book.]
Pamphlet with no author, publisher, or date	*Are You at Risk of Heart Attack?* n.p. n.d. [n.p. n.d. indicates that there is no known publisher or date.]
Filmstrips, slide programs, and videotape	*The Diary of Anne Frank.* Dir. George Stevens. Perf. Millie Perkins, Shelley Winters, Joseph Schildkraut, Lou Jacobi, and Richard Beymer. Twentieth Century Fox, 1959.
Radio or television program transcript	"The First Immortal Generation." *Ockham's Razor.* Host Robyn Williams. Guest Damien Broderick. National Public Radio. 23 May 1999. Transcript.
Internet	*National Association of Chewing Gum Manufacturers.* 19 Dec. 1999 <http://www.nacgm.org/consumer/funfacts.html> [Indicate the date you accessed the information. Content and addresses at Web sites change frequently.]
Newspaper	Thurow, Roger. "South Africans Who Fought for Sanctions Now Scrap for Investors." *Wall Street Journal* 11 Feb. 2000: A1+ [For a multipage article, write only the first page number on which it appears, followed by a plus sign.]
Personal interview	Smith, Jane. Personal interview. 10 Feb. 2000.
CD (with multiple publishers)	Simms, James, ed. *Romeo and Juliet.* By William Shakespeare. CD-ROM. Oxford: Attica Cybernetics Ltd.; London: BBC Education; London: HarperCollins Publishers, 1995.
Article from an encyclopedia	Askeland, Donald R. (1991). "Welding." *World Book Encyclopedia.* 1991 ed.

APA Style for Listing Sources

The list of citations for APA is referred to as a Reference List and not a bibliography.

Book with one author	Pyles, T. (1971). *The Origins and Development of the English Language* (2nd ed.). New York: Harcourt Brace Jovanovich, Inc.
Book with two or three authors	McCrum, R., Cran, W., & MacNeil, R. (1987). *The Story of English.* New York: Penguin Books.
Book with an editor	Truth, S. (1993). *Narrative of Sojourner Truth* (M. Washington, Ed.). New York: Vintage Books.
Book with more than three authors or editors	Donald, R. B., Morrow, B. R., Wargetz, L. G., & Werner, K. (1996). *Writing Clear Essays.* Upper Saddle River, New Jersey: Prentice-Hall, Inc. [With six or more authors, abbreviate second and following authors as "et al."]
A single work from an anthology	Hawthorne, N. (1998) Young Goodman Brown. In E. V. Roberts, & H. E. Jacobs (Eds.), *Literature: An Introduction to Reading and Writing* (pp. 376–385). Upper Saddle River, New Jersey: Prentice-Hall, Inc.
Introduction to a work included in a published edition	[No style is offered under this heading.]
Signed article in a weekly magazine	Wallace, C. (2000, February 14). A vodacious deal. *Time, 155,* 63. [The volume number appears in italics before the page number.]
Signed article in a monthly magazine	Gustaitis, J. (1998, October). The sticky history of chewing gum. *American History, 33,* 30–38.
Unsigned editorial or story	Selective Silence. (2000, February 11). *Wall Street Journal,* p. A14.
Signed pamphlet	Pearson Education. (2000). *LifeCare* (2nd ed.) [Pamphlet]. Smith, John: Author.
Pamphlet with no author, publisher, or date	[No style is offered under this heading.]
Filmstrips, slide programs, and videotape	Stevens, G. (Producer & Director). (1959). *The Diary of Anne Frank.* [Videotape]. (Available from Twentieth Century Fox) [If the producer and the director are two different people, list the producer first and then the director, with an ampersand (&) between them.]
Radio or television program transcript	Broderick, D. (1999, May 23). The First Immortal Generation. (R. Williams, Radio Host). *Ockham's Razor.* New York: National Public Radio.
Internet	National Association of Chewing Gum Manufacturers. Available: http://www.nacgm.org/consumer/funfacts.html [References to Websites should begin with the author's last name, if available. Indicate the site name and the available path or URL address.]
Newspaper	Thurow, R. (2000, February 11). South Africans who fought for sanctions now scrap for investors. *Wall Street Journal,* pp. A1, A4.
Personal interview	[APA states that, since interviews (and other personal communications) do not provide "recoverable data," they should only be cited in text.]
CD (with multiple publishers)	[No style is offered under this heading.]
Article from an encyclopedia	Askeland, D. R. (1991). Welding. In *World Book Encyclopedia.* (Vol. 21 pp. 190–191). Chicago: World Book, Inc.

CMS Style for Listing Sources

The following chart shows the CMS author-date method of documentation.

Book with one author	Pyles, Thomas. *The Origins and Development of the English Language,* 2nd ed. New York: Harcourt Brace Jovanovich, Inc., 1971.
Book with two or three authors	McCrum, Robert, William Cran, and Robert MacNeil. *The Story of English.* New York: Penguin Books, 1987.
Book with an editor	Truth, Sojourner. *Narrative of Sojourner Truth.* Edited by Margaret Washington. New York: Vintage Books, 1993.
Book with more than three authors or editors	Donald, Robert B., et al. *Writing Clear Essays.* Upper Saddle River, New Jersey: Prentice-Hall, Inc., 1996.
A single work from an anthology	Hawthorne, Nathaniel. "Young Goodman Brown." In *Literature: An Introduction to Reading and Writing.* Ed. Edgar V. Roberts and Henry E. Jacobs. 376–385. Upper Saddle River, New Jersey: Prentice-Hall, Inc., 1998.
Introduction to a work included in a published edition	Washington, Margaret. Introduction to *Narrative of Sojourner Truth,* by Sojourner Truth. New York: Vintage Books, 1993. [According to CMS style, you should avoid this type of entry unless the introduction is of special importance to the work.]
Signed article in a weekly magazine	Wallace, Charles. "A Vodacious Deal." *Time,* 14 February 2000, 63.
Signed article in a monthly magazine	Gustaitis, Joseph. "The Sticky History of Chewing Gum." *American History,* October 1998, 30–38.
Unsigned editorial or story	*Wall Street Journal,* 11 February 2000. [CMS states that items from newspapers are seldom listed in a bibliography. Instead, the name of the paper and the relevant dates are listed.]
Signed pamphlet	[No style is offered under this heading.]
Pamphlet with no author, publisher, or date	[No style is offered under this heading.]
Filmstrips, slide programs, and videotape	Stevens, George. (director). *The Diary of Anne Frank.* 170 min. Beverly Hills, California: Twentieth Century Fox, 1994.
Radio or television program transcript	[No style is offered under this heading.]
Internet	[No style is offered under this heading.]
Newspaper	*Wall Street Journal,* 11 February 2000. [CMS states that items from newspapers are seldom listed in a bibliography. Instead, the name of the paper and the relevant dates are listed.]
Personal interview	[CMS states that, since personal conversations are not available to the public, there is no reason to place them in the bibliography. However, the following format should be followed if they are listed.] Jane Smith. Conversation with author. Wooster, Ohio, 10 February 2000.
CD (with multiple publishers)	Shakespeare, William. *Romeo and Juliet.* Oxford: Attica Cybernetics Ltd.; London: BBC Education; London: HarperCollins Publishers, 1995. CD-ROM.
Article from an encyclopedia	[According to CMS style, encyclopedias are not listed in bibliographies.]

Sample Works-Cited List (MLA)

Carwardine, Mark, Erich Hoyt, R. Ewan Fordyce, and Peter Gill. *The Nature Company Guides: Whales, Dolphins, and Porpoises*. New York: Time-Life Books, 1998.

Ellis, Richard. *Men and Whales*. New York: Knopf, 1991.

Whales in Danger. "Discovering Whales." 18 Oct. 1999. <http://whales.magna.com.au/DISCOVER>

Sample Internal Citations (MLA)

It makes sense that baleen whales such as the blue whale, the fin whale, the bowhead whale, the humpback whale, and the sei whale (to name just a few) grow to immense sizes (Carwardine 19–21).

The blue whale has grooves running from under its chin to partway along the length of its underbelly. As in some other whales, these grooves expand and allow even more food and water to be taken in (Ellis 18–21).

Author's last name

page numbers where information can be found

Internet Research Handbook

Introduction to the Internet

The Internet is a series of networks that are interconnected all over the world. The Internet allows users to have almost unlimited access to information stored on the networks. Dr. Berners-Lee, a physicist, created the Internet in the 1980's by writing a small computer program that allowed pages to be linked together using key words. The Internet was mostly text-based until 1992, when a computer program called the NCSA Mosaic (National Center for Supercomputing Applications at the University of Illinois) was created. This program was the first Web browser. The development of Web browsers greatly eased the ability of the user to navigate through all the pages stored on the Web. Very soon, the appearance of the Web was altered as well. More appealing visuals were added, and sound was also implemented. This change made the Web more user-friendly and more appealing to the general public.

Using the Internet for Research

Key Word Search

Before you begin a search, you should identify your specific topic. To make searching easier, narrow your subject to a key word or a group of key words. These are your search terms, and they should be as specific as possible. For example, if you are looking for the latest concert dates for your favorite musical group, you might use the band's name as a key word. However, if you were to enter the name of the group in the query box of the search engine, you might be presented with thousands of links to information about the group that is unrelated to your needs. You might locate such information as band member biographies, the group's history, fan reviews of concerts, and hundreds of sites with related names containing information that is irrelevant to your search. Because you used such a broad key word, you might need to navigate through all that information before you find a link or subheading for concert dates. In contrast, if you were to type in "Duplex Arena and [band name]" you would have a better chance of locating pages that contain this information.

How to Narrow Your Search

If you have a large group of key words and still don't know which ones to use, write out a list of all the words you are considering. Once you have completed the list, scrutinize it. Then, delete the words that are least important to your search, and highlight those that are most important.

These **key search connectors** can help you fine-tune your search:

AND: narrows a search by retrieving documents that include both terms. For example: *baseball AND playoffs*

OR: broadens a search by retrieving documents including any of the terms. For example: *playoffs OR championships*

NOT: narrows a search by excluding documents containing certain words. For example: *baseball NOT history of*

Tips for an Effective Search

1. Keep in mind that search engines can be case-sensitive. If your first attempt at searching fails, check your search terms for misspellings and try again.

2. If you are entering a group of key words, present them in order, from the most important to the least important key word.

3. Avoid opening the link to every single page in your results list. Search engines present pages in descending order of relevancy. The most useful pages will be located at the top of the list. However, read the description of each link before you open the page.

4. When you use some search engines, you can find helpful tips for specializing your search. Take the opportunity to learn more about effective searching.

Internet Research Handbook • 901

Other Ways to Search

Using On-line Reference Sites

How you search should be tailored to *what* you are hoping to find. If you are looking for data and facts, use reference sites before you jump onto a simple search engine. For example, you can find reference sites to provide definitions of words, statistics about almost any subject, biographies, maps, and concise information on many topics. Some useful on-line reference sites:

On-line libraries
On-line periodicals
Almanacs
Encyclopedias

You can find these sources using subject searches.

Conducting Subject Searches

As you prepare to go on-line, consider your subject and the best way to find information to suit your needs. If you are looking for general information on a topic and you want your search results to be extensive, consider the subject search indexes on most search engines. These indexes, in the form of category and subject lists, often appear on the first page of a search engine. When you click on a specific highlighted word, you will be presented with a new screen containing subcategories of the topic you chose. In the screen shots below, the category *Sports & Recreation* provided a second index for users to focus a search even further.

Evaluating the Reliability of Internet Resources

Just as you would evaluate the quality, bias, and validity of any other research material you locate, check the source of information you find on-line. Compare these two sites containing information on the poet and writer Langston Hughes:

Site A is a personal Web site constructed by a college student. It contains no bibliographic information or links to sites that he used. Included on the site are several poems by Langston Hughes and a student essay about the poet's use of symbolism. It has not been updated in more than six months.

Site B is a Web site constructed and maintained by the English Department of a major university. Information on Hughes is presented in a scholarly format, with a bibliography and credits for the writer. The site includes links to other sites and indicates new features that are added weekly.

For your own research, consider the information you find on Site B to be more reliable and accurate than that on Site A. Because it is maintained by experts in their field who are held accountable for their work, the university site will be a better research tool than the student-generated one.

Tips for Evaluating Internet Sources

1. Consider who constructed and who now maintains the Web page. Determine whether this author is a reputable source. Often, the URL endings indicate a source.

   - Sites ending in *.edu* are maintained by educational institutions.
   - Sites ending in *.gov* are maintained by government agencies (federal, state, or local).
   - Sites ending in *.org* are normally maintained by nonprofit organizations and agencies.
   - Sites with a *.com* ending are commercially or personally maintained.

2. Skim the official and trademarked Web pages first. It is safe to assume that the information you draw from Web pages of reputable institutions, on-line encyclopedias, on-line versions of major daily newspapers, or government-owned sites produce information as reliable as the material you would find in print. In contrast, unbranded sites or those generated by individuals tend to borrow information from other sources without providing documentation. As information travels from one source to another, the information has likely been muddled, misinterpreted, edited, or revised.

3. You can still find valuable information in the less "official" sites. Check for the writer's credentials and then consider these factors:

   - Don't let official-looking graphics or presentations fool you.
   - Make sure the information is updated enough to suit your needs. Many Web pages will indicate how recently they have been updated.
   - If the information is borrowed, see whether you can trace it back to its original source.

Respecting Copyrighted Material

Because the Internet is a relatively new and quickly growing medium, issues of copyright and ownership arise almost daily. As laws begin to govern the use and reuse of material posted on-line, they may change the way that people can access or reprint material.

Text, photographs, music, and fine art printed on-line may not be reproduced without acknowledged permission of the copyright owner.

Glossary of Internet Terms

attached file: a file containing information, such as a text document or GIF image, that is attached to an e-mail message; reports, pictures, spreadsheets, and so on transmitted to others by attaching these to messages as files

bandwidth: the amount of information, mainly compressed in bits per second (bps), that can be sent through a connection within a specific amount of time; depending on how fast your modem is, 15,000 bits (roughly one page of text) can be transferred per second

bit: a binary digit of computerized data, represented by a single digit that is either a 1 or a 0; a group of bits constitutes a byte

bookmark: a feature of your Web browser that allows you to place a "bookmark" on a Web page to which you wish to return at a later time

browser: software designed to present material accessed on the Web

bulletin-board system: a computer system that members access in order to join on-line discussion groups or to post announcements

case-sensitivity: the quality of a search engine that causes it to respond to upper- or lowercase letters in different ways

chat room: informal on-line gathering sites where people share conversations, experiences, or information on a specific topic; many chat rooms do not require users to provide their identity, so the reliability or safety of these sites is uncertain

cookie: a digitized piece of information that is sent to a Web browser by a Web server, intended to be saved on a computer; cookies gather information about the user, such as user preferences, or recent on-line purchases; a Web browser can be set to either accept or reject cookies

cyberspace: a term referring to the electronic environment connecting all computer network information with the people who use it

database: a large collection of data that have been formatted to fit a certain user-defined standard

digerati: a slang term to describe Internet experts; an offshoot of the term *literati*

download: to copy files from the Internet onto your computer

e-mail: electronic mail, or the exchange of messages via the Internet; because it is speedier than traditional mail and offers easier global access, e-mail has grown in popularity; e-mail messages can be sent to a single person or in bulk to a group of people

error message: a displayed communication or printout that reports a problem with a program or Web page

FTP site (file transfer protocol): a password-protected server on the Internet that allows the transfer of information from one computer to another

GIF (Graphic Interchange Format): a form of graphics used on the Web

graphics: information displayed as pictures or images instead of text

hits: items retrieved by a key word search; the number tracking the volume of visits to a Web site

home page: the main Web page for an individual or an organization, containing links to subpages within

HTML (HyperText Markup Language): the coding text that is the foundation for creating Web pages

interactivity: a quality of some Web pages that encourages the frequent exchange of information between user and computer

Internet: a worldwide computer network that supports services such as the World Wide Web, e-mail, and file transfer

JPEG (Joint Photo Experts Group, the developers)**:** a file format for graphics especially suited to photographs

K: a measurement of file size or memory; short for "Kilobyte", 1,000 bytes of information (see *bit*)

key word: search term entered into the query box of a search engine to direct the results of the search

link: an icon or word on a Web page that, when clicked, transfers the user to another Web page or to a different document within the same page

login: the procedure by which users gain access to a server or a secure Web site; usually the user must enter a specific user name and password

modem: a device that transfers data to a computer through a phone line. A computer's modem connects to a server, which then sends information in the form of digital signals. The modem converts these signals into waves, for the purpose of information reception. The speed of a modem affects how quickly a computer can receive and download information

newbie: jargon used to describe Internet novices

newsgroup: an on-line discussion group, where users can post and respond to messages; the most prevalent collection of newsgroups is found on USENET

query box: the blank box in a search engine where your search terms are input

relevance ranking: the act of displaying the results of a search in the order of their relevance to the search terms

search engines: tools that help you navigate databases to locate information; search engines respond to a key word search by providing the user with a directory of multiple Web pages about the key word or containing the key word

server: a principal computer that provides services, such as storing files and providing access to the Internet, to another computer

signature: a preprogrammed section of text that is automatically added to an e-mail message

surfing: the process of reading Web pages and of moving from one Web site to another

URL (Uniform Resource Locator)**:** a Web page's address; a URL can look like this:

http://www.phwg.phschool.com or
http://www.senate.gov/~appropriations/ labor/testimony

usenet: a worldwide system of discussion groups, or newsgroups

vanity pages: Web sites placed on-line by people to tell about themselves or their interests; vanity pages do not have any commercial or informational value

virus: a set of instructions, hidden in a computer system or transferred via e-mail or electronic files, that can cause problems with a computer's ability to perform normally

Web page: a set of information, including graphics, text, sound, and video, presented in a browser window; a Web page can be found by its URL once it is posted on the World Wide Web

Web site: a collection of Web pages that are linked together for posting on the World Wide Web

W3: a group of Internet experts, including networking professionals, academics, scientists, and corporate interests, who maintain and develop technologies and standards for the Internet

WWW (World Wide Web)**:** a term referring to the multitude of information systems found on the Internet; this includes FTP, Gopher, telnet, and http sites

zip: the minimizing of files through compression; this function makes for easier transmittal over networks, a receiver can then open the file by "unzipping" it

Commonly Overused Words

When you write, use the most precise word for your meaning, not the word that comes to mind first. Consult this thesaurus to find alternatives for some commonly overused words. Consult a full-length thesaurus to find alternatives to words that do not appear here. Keep in mind that the choices offered in a thesaurus do not all mean exactly the same thing. Review all the options, and choose the one that best expresses your meaning.

about approximately, nearly, almost, approaching, close to

absolutely unconditionally, perfectly, completely, ideally, purely

activity action, movement, operation, labor, exertion, enterprise, project, pursuit, endeavor, job, assignment, pastime, scheme, task

add attach, affix, join, unite, append, increase, amplify

affect adjust, influence, transform, moderate, incline, motivate, prompt

amazing overwhelming, astonishing, startling, unexpected, stunning, dazzling, remarkable

awesome impressive, stupendous, fabulous, astonishing, outstanding

bad defective, inadequate, poor, unsatisfactory, disagreeable, offensive, repulsive, corrupt, wicked, naughty, harmful, injurious, unfavorable

basic essential, necessary, indispensable, vital, fundamental, elementary

beautiful attractive, appealing, alluring, exquisite, gorgeous, handsome, stunning

begin commence, found, initiate, introduce, launch, originate

better preferable, superior, worthier

big enormous, extensive, huge, immense, massive

boring commonplace, monotonous, tedious, tiresome

bring accompany, cause, convey, create, conduct, deliver, produce

cause origin, stimulus, inspiration, motive

certain unquestionable, incontrovertible, unmistakable, indubitable, assured, confident

change alter, transform, vary, replace, diversify

choose select, elect, nominate, prefer, identify

decent respectable, adequate, fair, suitable

definitely unquestionably, clearly, precisely, positively, inescapably

easy effortless, natural, comfortable, undemanding, pleasant, relaxed

effective impressive, striking, powerful, successful

emphasize underscore, feature, accentuate

end limit, boundary, finish, conclusion, finale, resolution

energy vitality, vigor, force, dynamism

enjoy savor, relish, revel, benefit

entire complete, inclusive, unbroken, integral

excellent superior, remarkable, splendid, unsurpassed, superb, magnificent

exciting thrilling, stirring, rousing, dramatic

far distant, remote

fast swift, quick, fleet, hasty, instant, accelerated

fill occupy, suffuse, pervade, saturate, inflate, stock

finish complete, conclude, cease, achieve, exhaust, deplete, consume

funny comical, ludicrous, amusing, droll, entertaining, bizarre, unusual, uncommon

get obtain, receive, acquire, procure, achieve

give bestow, donate, supply, deliver, distribute, impart

go proceed, progress, advance, move

good satisfactory, serviceable, functional, competent, virtuous, striking

great tremendous, superior, remarkable, eminent, proficient, expert

happy pleased, joyous, elated, jubilant, cheerful, delighted

hard arduous, formidable, complex, complicated, rigorous, harsh

help assist, aid, support, sustain, serve

hurt injure, harm, damage, wound, impair

important significant, substantial, weighty, meaningful, critical, vital, notable

interesting absorbing, appealing, entertaining, fascinating, thought-provoking

job task, work, business, undertaking, occupation, vocation, chore, duty, assignment

keep retain, control, possess

kind type, variety, sort, form

know comprehend, understand, realize, perceive, discern

like (adj) similar, equivalent, parallel

like (verb) enjoy, relish, appreciate

main primary, foremost, dominant

make build, construct, produce, assemble, fashion, manufacture

mean plan, intend, suggest, propose, indicate

more supplementary, additional, replenishment

new recent, modern, current, novel

next subsequently, thereafter, successively

nice pleasant, satisfying, gracious, charming

old aged, mature, experienced, used, worn, former, previous

open unobstructed, accessible

part section, portion, segment, detail, element, component

perfect flawless, faultless, ideal, consummate

plan scheme, design, system, plot

pleasant agreeable, gratifying, refreshing, welcome

prove demonstrate, confirm, validate, verify, corroborate

quick brisk, prompt, responsive, rapid, nimble, hasty

really truly, genuinely, extremely, undeniably

regular standard, routine, customary, habitual

see regard, behold, witness, gaze, realize, notice

small diminutive, miniature, minor, insignificant, slight, trivial

sometimes occasionally, intermittently, sporadically, periodically

take grasp, capture, choose, select, tolerate, endure

terrific extraordinary, magnificent, marvelous

think conceive, imagine, ponder, reflect, contemplate

try attempt, endeavor, venture, test

use employ, operate, utilize

very unusually, extremely, deeply, exceedingly, profoundly

want desire, crave, yearn, long

Commonly Misspelled Words

The list on these pages presents words that cause problems for many people. Some of these words are spelled according to set rules, but others follow no specific rules. As you review this list, check to see how many of the words give you trouble in your own writing. Then, read the instruction in the "Vocabulary and Spelling" chapter in the book for strategies and suggestions for improving your own spelling habits.

abbreviate	athletic	catastrophe	curious
absence	attendance	category	cylinder
absolutely	auxiliary	ceiling	deceive
abundance	awkward	cemetery	decision
accelerate	bandage	census	deductible
accidentally	banquet	certain	defendant
accumulate	bargain	changeable	deficient
accurate	barrel	characteristic	definitely
ache	battery	chauffeur	delinquent
achievement	beautiful	chief	dependent
acquaintance	beggar	clothes	descendant
adequate	beginning	coincidence	description
admittance	behavior	colonel	desert
advertisement	believe	column	desirable
aerial	benefit	commercial	dessert
affect	bicycle	commission	deteriorate
aggravate	biscuit	commitment	dining
aggressive	bookkeeper	committee	disappointed
agreeable	bought	competitor	disastrous
aisle	boulevard	concede	discipline
all right	brief	condemn	dissatisfied
allowance	brilliant	congratulate	distinguish
aluminum	bruise	connoisseur	effect
amateur	bulletin	conscience	eighth
analysis	buoyant	conscientious	eligible
analyze	bureau	conscious	embarrass
ancient	bury	contemporary	enthusiastic
anecdote	buses	continuous	entrepreneur
anniversary	business	controversy	envelope
anonymous	cafeteria	convenience	environment
answer	calendar	coolly	equipped
anticipate	campaign	cooperate	equivalent
anxiety	canceled	cordially	especially
apologize	candidate	correspondence	exaggerate
appall	capacity	counterfeit	exceed
appearance	capital	courageous	excellent
appreciate	capitol	courteous	exercise
appropriate	captain	courtesy	exhibition
architecture	career	criticism	existence
argument	carriage	criticize	experience
associate	cashier	curiosity	explanation

extension
extraordinary
familiar
fascinating
February
fiery
financial
fluorescent
foreign
forfeit
fourth
fragile
gauge
generally
genius
genuine
government
grammar
grievance
guarantee
guard
guidance
handkerchief
harass
height
humorous
hygiene
ignorant
illegible
immediately
immigrant
independence
independent
indispensable
individual
inflammable
intelligence
interfere
irrelevant
irritable
jewelry
judgment
knowledge
laboratory
lawyer
legible
legislature
leisure
liable

library
license
lieutenant
lightning
likable
liquefy
literature
loneliness
magnificent
maintenance
marriage
mathematics
maximum
meanness
mediocre
mileage
millionaire
minimum
minuscule
miscellaneous
mischievous
misspell
mortgage
naturally
necessary
negotiate
neighbor
neutral
nickel
niece
ninety
noticeable
nuclear
nuisance
obstacle
occasion
occasionally
occur
occurred
occurrence
omitted
opinion
opportunity
optimistic
outrageous
pamphlet
parallel
paralyze
parentheses

particularly
patience
permanent
permissible
perseverance
persistent
personally
perspiration
persuade
phenomenal
phenomenon
physician
pleasant
pneumonia
possess
possession
possibility
prairie
precede
preferable
prejudice
preparation
prerogative
previous
primitive
privilege
probably
procedure
proceed
prominent
pronunciation
psychology
publicly
pursue
questionnaire
realize
really
recede
receipt
receive
recognize
recommend
reference
referred
rehearse
relevant
reminiscence
renowned
repetition

restaurant
rhythm
ridiculous
sandwich
satellite
schedule
scissors
secretary
siege
solely
sponsor
subtle
subtlety
superintendent
supersede
surveillance
susceptible
tariff
temperamental
theater
threshold
truly
unmanageable
unwieldy
usage
usually
valuable
various
vegetable
voluntary
weight
weird
whale
wield
yield

Abbreviations Guide

Abbreviations, shortened versions of words or phrases, can be valuable tools in writing if you know when and how to use them. They can be very helpful in informal writing situations, such as taking notes or writing lists. However, only a few abbreviations can be used in formal writing. They are: *Mr., Mrs., Miss, Ms., Dr., A.M., P.M., A.D., B.C., M.A, B.A., Ph.D.,* and *M.D.*

The following pages provide the conventional abbreviations for a variety of words.

Abbreviations of Common Titles

Ambassador	Amb.	Lieutenant	Lt.
Attorney	Atty.	Major	Maj.
Brother	Br.	President	Pres.
Brigadier-General	Brig. Gen.	Professor	Prof.
Captain	Capt.	Representative	Rep.
Commander	Cmdr.	Reverend	Rev.
Colonel	Col.	Secretary	Sec.
Commissioner	Com.	Senator	Sen.
Corporal	Cpl.	Sergeant	Sgt.
Doctor	Dr.	Sister	Sr.
Father	Fr.	Superintendent	Supt.
Governor	Gov.	Treasurer	Treas.
Honorable	Hon.	Vice Admiral	Vice Adm.

Abbreviations of Academic Degrees

Bachelor of Arts	B.A. (or A.B.)	Esquire (lawyer)	Esq.
Bachelor of Science	B.S. (or S.B.)	Master of Arts	M.A. (or A.M.)
Doctor of Dental Surgery	D.D.S.	Master of Business Administration	M.B.A.
Doctor of Divinity	D.D.		
Doctor of Education	Ed.D.	Master of Fine Arts	M.F.A.
Doctor of Laws	LL.D.	Master of Science	M.S. (or S.M.)
Doctor of Medicine	M.D.	Registered Nurse	R.N.
Doctor of Philosophy	Ph.D.		

Abbreviations of States

State	Traditional	Postal Service	State	Traditional	Postal Service
Alabama	Ala.	AL	Montana	Mont.	MT
Alaska	Alaska	AK	Nebraska	Nebr.	NE
Arizona	Ariz.	AZ	Nevada	Nev.	NV
Arkansas	Ark.	AR	New Hampshire	N.H.	NH
California	Calif.	CA	New Jersey	N.J.	NJ
Colorado	Colo.	CO	New Mexico	N.M.	NM
Connecticut	Conn.	CT	New York	N.Y.	NY
Delaware	Del.	DE	North Carolina	N.C.	NC
Florida	Fla.	FL	North Dakota	N.Dak.	ND
Georgia	Ga.	GA	Ohio	O.	OH
Hawaii	Hawaii	HI	Oklahoma	Okla.	OK
Idaho	Ida.	ID	Oregon	Ore.	OR
Illinois	Ill.	IL	Pennsylvania	Pa.	PA
Indiana	Ind.	IN	Rhode Island	R.I.	RI
Iowa	Iowa	IA	South Carolina	S.C.	SC
Kansas	Kans.	KS	South Dakota	S.Dak.	SD
Kentucky	Ky.	KY	Tennessee	Tenn.	TN
Louisiana	La.	LA	Texas	Tex.	TX
Maine	Me.	ME	Utah	Utah	UT
Maryland	Md.	MD	Vermont	Vt.	VT
Massachusetts	Mass.	MA	Virginia	Va.	VA
Michigan	Mich.	MI	Washington	Wash.	WA
Minnesota	Minn.	MN	West Virginia	W. Va	WV
Mississippi	Miss.	MS	Wisconsin	Wis.	WI
Missouri	Mo.	MO	Wyoming	Wyo.	WY

Common Geographical Abbreviations

Apartment	Apt.	National	Natl.
Avenue	Ave.	Peninsula	Pen.
Building	Bldg.	Park, Peak	Pk.
Block	Blk.	Province	Prov.
Boulevard .	Blvd.	Point	Pt.
County	Co.	Road	Rd.
District	Dist.	Route	Rte.
Drive	Dr.	Square	Sq.
Fort	Ft.	Street	St.
Island	Is.	Territory	Terr.
Mountain	Mt.		

Abbreviations of Traditional Measurements

inch(es)	in.	ounce(s)	oz.
foot, feet	ft.	pound(s)	lb.
yard(s)	yd.	pint(s)	pt.
mile(s)	mi.	quart(s)	qt.
teaspoon(s)	tsp.	gallon(s)	gal.
tablespoon(s)	tbsp.	Fahrenheit	F.

Abbreviations of Metric Measurements

millimeter(s)	mm	liter(s)	L
centimeter(s)	cm	kiloliter(s)	kL
meter(s)	m	milligram(s)	mg
kilometer(s)	km	centigram(s)	cg
milliliter(s)	mL	gram(s)	g
centiliter(s)	cL	Celsius	C

Other Commonly Used Abbreviations

about (used with dates)	c., ca., circ.	manager	mgr.
and others	et al.	manufacturing	mfg.
anonymous	anon.	market	mkt.
approximately	approx.	measure	meas.
associate, association	assoc., assn.	merchandise	mdse.
auxiliary	aux., auxil.	miles per hour	mph
bibliography	bibliog.	miscellaneous	misc.
boxes	bx(s).	money order	M.O.
bucket	bkt.	note well; take notice	N.B.
bulletin	bull.	number	no.
bushel	bu.	package	pkg.
capital letter	cap.	page	p., pg.
cash on delivery	C.O.D.	pages	pp.
department	dept.	pair(s)	pr(s).
discount	disc.	parenthesis	paren.
dozen(s)	doz.	Patent Office	pat. off.
each	ea.	piece(s)	pc(s).
edition, editor	ed.	poetical, poetry	poet.
equivalent	equiv.	private	pvt.
established	est.	proprietor	prop.
fiction	fict.	pseudonym	pseud.
for example	e.g.	published, publisher	pub.
free of charge	grat., gratis	received	recd.
General Post Office	G.P.O.	reference, referee	ref.
government	gov., govt.	revolutions per minute	rpm
graduate, graduated	grad.	rhetorical, rhetoric	rhet.
Greek, Grecian	Gr.	right	R.
headquarters	hdqrs.	scene	sc.
height	ht.	special, specific	spec.
hospital	hosp.	spelling, species	sp.
illustrated	ill., illus.	that is	i.e.
including, inclusive	incl.	treasury, treasurer	treas.
introduction, introductory	intro.	volume	vol.
italics	ital.	weekly	wkly
karat, carat	k., kt.	weight	wt.
left	L.		

Proofreading Symbols Reference

Proofreading symbols make it easier to show where changes are needed in a paper. When proofreading your own or a classmate's work, use these standard proofreading symbols.

insert	I proofred.
delete	Ip proofread.
close up space	I proof read.
delete and close up space	I proofreade.
begin new paragraph	¶ I proofread.
spell out	I proofread 10 papers.
lowercase	I Proofread.
capitalize	i proofread.
transpose letters	I proofraed.
transpose words	I only proofread her paper.
period	I will proofread
comma	I will proofread and she will help.
colon	We will proofread for the following errors
semicolon	I will proofread she will help.
single quotation marks	She said, "I enjoyed the story The Invalid."
double quotation marks	She said, I enjoyed the story.
apostrophe	Did you borrow Sylvias book?
question mark	Did you borrow Sylvia's book
exclamation point	You're kidding
hyphen	online
parentheses	William Shakespeare 1564–1616

Student Publications

To share your writing with a wider audience, consider submitting it to a local, state, or national publication for student writing. Following are several magazines and Web sites that accept and publish student work.

Periodicals

Creative Kids P.O. Box 8813, Waco, TX 76714

Merlyn's Pen: The National Magazine of Student Writing P.O. Box 1058, East Greenwich, RI 02818

Skipping Stones P.O. Box 3939, Eugene, OR 97403

The McGuffey Writer McGuffey Foundation School, 5128 Westgate Drive, Oxford, OH 45056

Writing! General Learning Corporation, 900 Skokie Boulevard, Northbrook, IL 60062

On-line Publications

MidLink Magazine http://longwood.cs.ucf.edu:80/~MidLink/

Wild Guess Magazine http://members.tripod.com/~WildGuess/

Contests

Annual Poetry Contest National Federation of State Poetry Societies, 3520 State Route 56, Mechanicsburg, OH 43044

National Written & Illustrated By . . . Awards Contest for Students Landmark Editions, Inc., 1402 Kansas Avenue, Kansas City, MO 64127

Paul A. Witty Outstanding Literature Award International Reading Association, Special Interest Group for Reading for Gifted and Creative Students, c/o Texas Christian University, P.O. Box 32925, Fort Worth, TX 76129

Seventeen Magazine Fiction Contest Seventeen Magazine, 850 Third Avenue, New York, NY 10022

The Young Playwrights Festival National Playwriting Competition 321 East 44th Street, Suite 906, New York, NY 10036

Glossary

A

accent: the emphasis on a syllable, usually in poetry

action verb: a word that tells what action someone or something is performing (*See* linking verb.)

active voice: the voice of a verb whose subject performs an action (*See* passive voice.)

adjective: a word that modifies a noun or pronoun by telling *what kind* or *which one*

adjective clause: a subordinate clause that modifies a noun or pronoun

adjective phrase: a prepositional phrase that modifies a noun or pronoun

adverb: a word that modifies a verb, an adjective, or another adverb

adverb clause: a subordinate clause that modifies a verb, an adjective, an adverb, or a verbal by telling *where, when, in what way, to what extent, under what condition,* or *why*

adverb phrase: a prepositional phrase that modifies a verb, an adjective, or an adverb

allegory: a literary work with two or more levels of meaning—a literal level and one or more symbolic levels

alliteration: the repetition of initial consonant sounds in accented syllables

allusion: an indirect reference to a well-known person, place, event, literary work, or work of art

annotated bibliography: a research writing product that provides a list of materials on a given topic, along with publication information, summaries, or evaluations

apostrophe: a punctuation mark used to form possessive nouns and contractions

appositive: a noun or pronoun placed after another noun or pronoun to identify, rename, or explain the preceding word

appositive phrase: a noun or pronoun with its modifiers, placed next to a noun or pronoun to identify, rename, or explain the preceding word

article: one of three commonly used adjectives: *a, an,* and *the*

assonance: the repetition of vowel sounds in stressed syllables containing dissimilar consonant sounds

audience: the reader(s) a writer intends to reach

autobiographical writing: narrative writing that tells a true story about an important period, experience, or relationship in the writer's life

B

ballad: a song that tells a story (often dealing with adventure or romance) or a poem imitating such a song

bias: the attitudes or beliefs that affect a writer's ability to present a subject objectively

bibliography: a list of the sources of a research paper, including full bibliographic references for each source the writer consulted while conducting research (*See* works-cited list.)

biography: narrative writing that tells the story of an important period, experience, or relationship in a person's life, as reported by another

blueprinting: a prewriting technique in which a writer sketches a map of a home, school, neighborhood, or other meaningful place in order to spark memories or associations for further development

body paragraph: a paragraph in an essay that develops, explains, or supports the key ideas of the writing

brainstorming: a prewriting technique in which a group jots down as many ideas as possible about a given topic

C

case: the form of a noun or pronoun that indicates how it functions in a sentence

cause-and-effect writing: expository writing that examines the relationship between events, explaining how one event or situation causes another

character: a person (though not necessarily a human being) who takes part in the action of a literary work

characterization: the act of creating and developing a character through narration, description, and dialogue

citation: in formal research papers, the acknowledgment of ideas found in outside sources

clause: a group of words that has a subject and a verb

classical invention: a prewriting technique in which writers gather details about a topic by analyzing the category and subcategories to which the topic belongs

climax: the high point of interest or suspense in a literary work

coherence: a quality of written work in which all the parts flow logically from one idea to the next

colon: a punctuation mark used before an extended quotation, explanation, example, or series and after the salutation in a formal letter

comma: a punctuation mark used to separate words or groups of words

comparison-and-contrast writing: expository writing that describes the similarities and differences between two or more subjects in order to achieve a specific purpose

complement: a word or group of words that completes the meaning of a verb

compound sentence: a sentence that contains two or more independent clauses with no subordinate clauses

conclusion: the final paragraphs of a work of writing in which the writer may restate a main idea, summarize the points of the writing, or provide a closing remark to end the work effectively (See introduction, body paragraph, topical paragraph, functional paragraph.)

conflict: a struggle between opposing forces

conjugation: a list of the singular and plural forms of a verb in a particular tense

conjunction: a word used to connect other words or groups of words

connotation: the emotional associations that a word calls to mind (See denotation.)

consonance: the repetition of final consonant sounds in stressed syllables containing dissimilar vowel sounds

contraction: a shortened form of a word or phrase that includes an apostrophe to indicate the position of the missing letter(s)

coordinating conjunctions: words such as *and, but, nor,* and *yet* that connect similar words or groups of words

correlative conjunctions: word pairs such as *neither . . . nor, both . . . and,* and *whether . . . or* used to connect similar words or groups of words

couplet: a pair of rhyming lines written in the same meter

cubing: a prewriting technique in which a writer analyzes a subject from six specified angles: description; association; application; analysis; comparison and contrast; and evaluation

D

declarative sentence: a statement punctuated with a period

demonstrative pronouns: words such as *this, that, these,* and *those* used to single out specific people, places, or things

denotation: the objective meaning of a word; its definition independent of other associations the word calls to mind (See connotation.)

depth-charging: a drafting technique in which a writer elaborates on a sentence by developing a key word or idea

description: language or writing that uses sensory details to capture a subject

dialect: the form of a language spoken by people in a particular region or group

dialogue: a direct conversation between characters or people

diary: a personal record of daily events, usually written in prose

diction: a writer's word choice

direct object: a noun or a pronoun that receives the action of a transitive verb

direct quotation: a drafting technique in which writers indicate the exact words of another by enclosing them in quotation marks

documentary: nonfiction film that analyzes news events or another focused subject by combining interviews, film footage, narration, and other audio/visual components

documented essay: research writing that includes a limited number of research sources, providing full documentation parenthetically within the text

drafting: a stage of the writing process that follows prewriting and precedes revising in which a writer gets ideas on paper in a rough format

drama: a story written to be performed by actors and actresses

E

elaboration: a drafting technique in which a writer extends his or her ideas through the use of facts, examples, descriptions, details, or quotations

epic: a long narrative poem about the adventures of a god or a hero

essay: a short nonfiction work about a particular subject

etymology: the history of a word, showing where it came from and how it has evolved into its present spelling and meaning

exclamation mark: a punctuation mark used to indicate strong emotion

exclamatory sentence: a statement that conveys strong emotion and ends with an exclamation mark

exposition: writing to inform, addressing analytic purposes such as problem and solution, comparison and contrast, how-to, and cause and effect

extensive writing: writing products generated for others and from others, meant to be shared with an audience and often done for school assignments (*See* reflexive writing.)

F

fact: a statement that can be proved true (*See* opinion.)

fiction: prose writing about imaginary characters and events

figurative language: writing or speech not meant to be interpreted literally

firsthand biography: narrative writing that tells the story of an important period, experience, or relationship in a person's life, reported by a writer who knows the subject personally

five *W*'s: a prewriting technique in which writers gather details about a topic by generating answers to the following questions: *Who? What? Where? When?* and *Why?*

fragment: an incomplete idea punctuated as a complete sentence

freewriting: a prewriting technique in which a writer quickly jots down as many ideas on a topic as possible

functional paragraph: a paragraph that performs a specific role in composition, such as to arouse or sustain interest, to indicate dialogue, to make a transition (*See* topical paragraph.)

G

generalization: a statement that presents a rule or idea based on particular facts

gerund: a noun formed from the present participle of a verb (ending in *-ing*)

gerund phrase: a group of words containing a gerund and its modifiers or complements that function as a noun

grammar: the study of the forms of words and the way they are arranged in phrases, clauses, and sentences

H

helping verb: a verb added to another verb to make a single verb phrase that indicates the time at which an action takes place or whether it actually happens, could happen, or should happen

hexagonal writing: a technique in which a

writer analyzes a subject from six angles: literal level, personal allusions, theme, literary devices, literary allusions, and evaluation

homophones: pairs of words that sound the same as each other yet have different meanings and different spellings, such as *hear/here*

how-to writing: expository writing that explains a process by providing step-by-step directions

humanities: forms of artistic expression including, but not limited to, fine art, photography, theater, film, music, and dance

hyperbole: a deliberate exaggeration or over-statement

hyphen: a punctuation mark used to combine numbers and word parts, to join certain compound words, and to show that a word has been broken between syllables at the end of a line

I

I-Search report: a research paper in which the writer addresses the research experience in addition to presenting the information gathered

image: a word or phrase that appeals to one or more of the senses—sight, hearing, touch, taste, or smell

imagery: the descriptive language used to re-create sensory experiences, set a tone, suggest emotions, and guide readers' reactions

imperative sentence: a statement that gives an order or a direction and ends with either a period or an exclamation mark

indefinite pronoun: a word such as *anyone*, *each*, or *many* that refers to a person, place, or thing, without specifying which one

independent clause: a group of words that contains both a subject and a verb and that can stand by itself as a complete sentence

indirect quotation: reporting only the general meaning of what a person said or thought; quotation marks are not needed

infinitive: the form of a verb that comes after the word *to* and acts as a noun, adjective, or adverb

infinitive phrase: a phrase introduced by an infinitive that may be used as a noun, an adjective, or an adverb

interjection: a word or phrase that expresses feeling or emotion and functions independently of a sentence

interrogative pronoun: a word such as *which* and *who* that introduces a question

interrogative sentence: a question that is punctuated with a question mark

interview: an information-gathering technique in which one or more people pose questions to one or more other people who provide opinions or facts on a topic

intransitive verb: an action verb that does not take a direct object (*See* transitive verb.)

introduction: the opening paragraphs of a work of writing in which the writer may capture the readers' attention and present a thesis statement to be developed in the writing (*See* body paragraph, topical paragraph, functional paragraph, conclusion.)

invisible writing: a prewriting technique in which a writer freewrites without looking at the product until the exercise is complete; this can be accomplished at a word processor with the monitor turned off or with carbon paper and an empty ballpoint pen

irony: the general name given to literary techniques that involve surprising, interesting, or amusing contradictions

itemizing: a prewriting technique in which a writer creates a second, more focused, set of ideas based on an original listing activity. (*See* listing.)

J

jargon: the specialized words and phrases unique to a specific field

journal: a notebook or other organized writing system in which daily events and personal impressions are recorded

K

key word: the word or phrase that directs an Internet or database search

L

layering: a drafting technique in which a writer elaborates on a statement by identifying and then expanding upon a central idea or word

lead: the opening sentences of a work of writing meant to grab the reader's interest, accomplished through a variety of methods, including providing an intriguing quotation, a surprising or provocative question or fact, an anecdote, or a description

learning log: a record-keeping system in which a student notes information about new ideas

legend: a widely told story about the past that may or may not be based in fact

legibility: the neatness and readability of words

linking verb: a word that expresses its subject's state of being or condition (*See* action verb.)

listing: a prewriting technique in which a writer prepares a list of ideas related to a specific topic. (*See* itemizing.)

looping: a prewriting activity in which a writer generates follow-up freewriting based on the identification of a key word or central idea in an original freewriting exercise

lyric poem: a poem expressing the observations and feelings of a single speaker

M

main clause: a group of words that has a subject and a verb and can stand alone as a complete sentence

memoir: autobiographical writing that provides an account of a writer's relationship with a person, event, or place

metaphor: a figure of speech in which one thing is spoken of as though it were something else

meter: the rhythmic pattern of a poem

monologue: a speech or performance given entirely by one person or by one character

mood: the feeling created in the reader by a literary work or passage

multimedia presentation: a technique for sharing information with an audience by enhancing narration and explanation with media, including video images, slides, audiotape recordings, music, and fine art

N

narration: writing that tells a story

narrative poem: a poem that tells a story in verse

nominative case: the form of a noun or pronoun used as the subject of a verb, as a predicate nominative, or as the pronoun in a nominative absolute (*See* objective case, possessive case.)

noun: a word that names a person, place, or thing

noun clause: a subordinate clause that acts as a noun

novel: an extended work of fiction that often has a complicated plot, many major and minor characters, a unifying theme, and several settings

O

objective case: the form of a noun or pronoun used as the object of any verb, verbal, or preposition, or as the subject of an infinitive (*See* nominative case, possessive case.)

observation: a prewriting technique involving close visual study of an object; a writing product that reports such a study

ode: a long formal lyric poem with a serious theme

onomatopoeia: words such as *buzz* and *plop* that suggest the sounds they name

open-book test: a form of assessment in which students are permitted to use books and class notes to respond to test questions

opinion: beliefs that can be supported but not proved to be true (*See* fact.)

oral tradition: the body of songs, stories, and poems preserved by being passed from generation to generation by word of mouth

outline: a prewriting or study technique that allows writers or readers to organize the presentation and order of information

oxymoron: a figure of speech that fuses two contradictory or opposing ideas, such as "freezing fire" or "happy grief"

P

parable: a short, simple story from which a moral or religious lesson can be drawn

paradox: a statement that seems to be contradictory but that actually presents a truth

paragraph: a group of sentences that share a common topic or purpose and that focus on a single main idea or thought

parallelism: the placement of equal ideas in words, phrases, or clauses of similar types

paraphrase: restating an author's idea in different words, often to share information by making the meaning clear to readers

parentheses: punctuation marks used to set off asides and explanations when the material is not essential

participial phrase: a group of words made up of a participle and its modifiers and complements that acts as an adjective

participle: a form of a verb that can act as an adjective

passive voice: the voice of a verb whose subject receives an action (*See* active voice.)

peer review: a revising technique in which writers meet with other writers to share focused feedback on a draft

pentad: a prewriting technique in which a writer analyzes a subject from five specified points: actors, acts, scenes, agencies, and purposes

period: a punctuation mark used to end a declarative sentence, an indirect question, and most abbreviations

personal pronoun: a word such as *I, me, you, we, us, he, him, she, her, they,* and *them* that refers to the person speaking; the person spoken to; or the person, place, or thing spoken about

personification a figure of speech in which a nonhuman subject is given human characteristics

persuasion: writing or speaking that attempts to convince others to accept a position on an issue of concern to the writer

phrase: a group of words without a subject and verb that functions as one part of speech

plot: the sequence of events in narrative writing

plural: the form of a word that indicates more than one item is being mentioned

poetry: a category of writing in which the final product may make deliberate use of rhythm, rhyme, and figurative language in order to express deeper feelings than those conveyed in ordinary speech (*See* prose, drama.)

point of view: the perspective, or vantage point, from which a story is told

portfolio: an organized collection of writing projects, including writing ideas, works in progress, final drafts, and the writer's reflections on the work

possessive case: the form of a noun or pronoun used to show ownership (*See* objective case, nominative case.)

prefix: one or more syllables added to the beginning of a word root (*See* root, suffix.)

preposition: a word that relates a noun or pronoun that appears with it to another word in the sentence to indicate relations of time, place, causality, responsibility, and motivation

prepositional phrase: a group of words that includes a preposition and a noun or pronoun

presenting: a stage of the writing process in which a writer shares a final draft with an audience through speaking, listening, or representing activities

prewriting: a stage of the writing process in which writers explore, choose, and narrow a topic and then gather necessary details for drafting

problem-and-solution writing: expository writing that examines a problem and provides a realistic solution

pronoun: a word that stands for a noun or for another word that takes the place of a noun

prose: a category of written language in which the end product is developed through sentences and paragraphs (*See* poetry, drama.)

publishing: a stage of the writing process in which a writer shares the written version of a final draft with an audience

punctuation: the set of symbols used to convey specific directions to the reader

purpose: the specific goal or reason a writer chooses for a writing task

Q

question mark: a punctuation mark used to end an interrogative sentence or an incomplete question

quicklist: a prewriting technique in which a writer creates an impromptu, unresearched list of ideas related to a specific topic

quotation mark: a punctuation mark used to indicate the beginning and end of a person's exact speech or thoughts

R

ratiocination: a systematic approach to the revision process that involves color-coding elements of writing for evaluation

reflective essay: autobiographical writing in which a writer shares a personal experience and then provides insight about the event

reflexive pronoun: a word that ends in -*self* or -*selves* and names the person or thing receiving an action when that person or thing is the same as the one performing the action

reflexive writing: writing generated for oneself and from oneself, not necessarily meant to be shared, in which the writer makes all decisions regarding form and purpose (*See* extensive writing.)

refrain: a regularly repeated line or group of lines in a poem or song

relative pronoun: a pronoun such as *that, which, who, whom,* or *whose* that begins a

subordinate clause and connects it to another idea in the sentence

reporter's formula: a prewriting technique in which writers gather details about a topic by generating answers to the following questions: *Who? What? Where? When?* and *Why?*

research: a prewriting technique in which writers gather information from outside sources such as library reference materials, interviews, and the Internet

research writing: expository writing that presents and interprets information gathered through an extensive study of a subject

response to literature writing: persuasive, expository, or narrative writing that presents a writer's analysis of or reactions to a published work

revising: a stage of the writing process in which a writer reworks a rough draft to improve both form and content

rhyme: the repetition of sounds at the ends of words

rhyme scheme: the regular pattern of rhyming words in a poem or stanza

rhythm: the form or pattern of words or music in which accents or beats come at certain fixed intervals

root: the base of a word (*See* prefix, suffix.)

rubric: an assessment tool, generally organized in a grid, to indicate the range of success or failure according to specific criteria

run-on sentence: two or more complete sentences punctuated incorrectly as one

S

salutation: the greeting in a formal letter

satire: writing that ridicules or holds up to contempt the faults of individuals or of groups

SEE method: an elaboration technique in which a writer presents a statement, an extension, and an elaboration to develop an idea

semicolon: a punctuation mark used to join independent clauses that are not already joined by a conjunction

sentence: a group of words with a subject and a predicate that expresses a complete thought

setting: the time and place of the action of a piece of narrative writing

short story: a brief fictional narrative told in prose

simile: a figure of speech in which *like* or *as* is used to make a comparison between two basically unrelated ideas

sonnet: a fourteen-line lyric poem with a single theme

speaker: the imaginary voice assumed by the writer of a poem

stanza: a group of lines in a poem, seen as a unit

statistics: facts presented in numerical form, such as ratios, percentages, or summaries

subject: the word or group of words in a sentence that tells whom or what the sentence is about

subordinate clause: a group of words containing both a subject and a verb that cannot stand by itself as a complete sentence

subordinating conjunction: a word used to join two complete ideas by making one of the ideas dependent on the other

suffix: one or more syllables added to the end of a word root (*See* prefix, root.)

summary: a brief statement of the main ideas and supporting details presented in a piece of writing

symbol: something that is itself and also stands for something else

T

theme: the central idea, concern, or purpose in a piece of narrative writing, poetry, or drama

thesis statement: a statement of an essay's main idea; all information in the essay supports or elaborates this idea

tone: a writer's attitude toward the readers and toward the subject

topic sentence: a sentence that states the main idea of a paragraph

topic web: a prewriting technique in which a writer generates a graphic organizer to identify categories and subcategories of a topic

topical paragraph: a paragraph that develops, explains, and supports the topic sentence related to an essay's thesis statement

transition: words, phrases, or sentences that smooth writing by indicating the relationship among ideas

transitive verb: an action verb that takes a direct object (*See* intransitive verb.)

U

unity: a quality of written work in which all the parts fit together in a complete, self-contained whole

V

verb: a word or group of words that expresses an action, a condition, or the fact that something exists while indicating the time of the action, condition, or fact

verbal: a word derived from the verb but used as a noun, adjective, or adverb (*See* gerund, infinitive, participle.)

vignette: a brief narrative characterized by precise detail

voice: the distinctive qualities of a writer's style, including diction, attitude, sentence style, and ideas

W

works-cited list: a list of the sources of a research paper, including full bibliographic references for each source named in the body of the paper (*See* bibliography.)

Glossary • 923

Index

Note: **Bold numbers** show pages on which basic definitions appear.

The program authors would like to acknowledge the work of the following writers whose ideas have influenced the writing strategies presented in this series.

Brock, Paula. "Help Me, Quick." *R&E Journal 2* (1998): 14–16.

Burke, Kenneth. *A Grammar of Motives.* Berkeley: University of California Press, 1969.

Cooper, Charles R., and Lee Odell. *Evaluating Writing: Describing, Measuring, Judging.* Urbana, IL: National Council of Teachers of English, 1977.

Corbett, Edward P. J., and Robert J. Connors. *Classical Rhetoric for the Modern Student.* New York: Oxford University Press, Inc., 1998.

Cowan, Gregory, and Elizabeth Swan. *Writing.* New York: John Wiley, 1980.

Elbow, Peter. *Writing Without Teachers.* New York: Oxford University Press, 1973.

Emig, Janet. *The Composing Process of Twelfth Graders.* Urbana, IL: National Council of Teachers of English, 1971.

Lane, Barry. *After the End: Teaching and Learning Creative Revision.* Portsmouth, NH: Heinemann Educational Books, Inc., 1993.

Rico, Gabriele Lusser. *Writing the Natural Way.* Los Angeles: J. P. Tarcher, 1983.

Reif, Linda. *Seeking Diversity.* Portsmouth, NH: Heinemann Educational Books, 1992.

Stillman, Peter R. *Families Writing.* Cincinnati, OH: Writer's Digest Books, 1989.

Acknowledgments

Staff Credits

The people who made up the *Prentice Hall Writing and Grammar: Communication in Action* team—representing design services, editorial, editorial services, electronic publishing technology, manufacturing & inventory planning, marketing, marketing services, market research, online services & multimedia development, product planning, production services, project office, and publishing processes—are listed below. Bold type denotes the core team members.

Ellen Backstrom, Betsy Bostwick, Evonne Burgess, **Louise B. Capuano, Sarah Carroll, Megan Chill,** Katherine Clarke, Rhett Conklin, Martha Conway, Harold Crudup, **Harold Delmonte,** Laura Dershewitz, Donna DiCuffa, Amy Fleming, Libby Forsyth, Ellen Goldblatt, Elaine Goldman, Jonathan Goldson, **Rebecca Graziano,** Rick Hickox, Kristan Hoskins, Jim Jeglikowski, Carol Lavis, **George Lychock,** Gregory Lynch, William McAllister, **Frances Medico,** Perrin Moriarty, Loretta Moser, Margaret Plotkin, Maureen Raymond, Shannon Rider, **Steve Sacco,** Gerry Schrenk, **Melissa Shustyk,** Annette Simmons, Robin Sullivan, **Elizabeth Torjussen, Doug Utigard**

Additional Credits

Ernie Albanese, Diane Alimena, Susan Andariese, Michele Angelucci, Penny Baker, Susan Barnes, Louise Casella, Lorena Cerisano, Cynthia Clampitt, Elizabeth Crawford, Ken Dougherty, Vince Esterly, Kathy Gavilanes, Beth Geschwind, Michael Goodman, Diana Hahn, Jennifer Harper, Evan Holstrom, Alex Ivchenko, Leanne Korszoloski, Sue Langan, Rebecca Lauth, Dave Liston, Maria Keogh, Christine Mann, Vicki Menanteaux, Gail Meyer, Artur Mkrtchyan, LaShonda Morris, Karyl Murray, Omni-Photo Communications, Kim Ortell, Patty Rodriguez, Brenda Sanabria, Carolyn Sapontzis, Ken Silver, Slip Jig Image Research Services, Sunnyside, NY, Ron Spezial, Barbara Stufflebeem, Gene Vaughan, Karen Vignola, Linda Westerhoff

Grateful acknowledgment is made to the following for copyrighted material:

California Reading Association

"Our English Language: One From All" by Richard Lederer. Published in *The California Reader.* Volume 29, No. 2, Winter 1996. Reprinted by permission.

Siv Cedering

"Suppose" by Siv Cedering from *Color Poems* published by Calliopea Press. Copyright © 1978 by Siv Cedering.

Harcourt, Inc.

Preface to *Baba: A Return to China Upon My Father's Shoulders* by Amy Tan. Copyright © 1994 by Belle Yang. Used by permission of Harcourt, Inc.

The New York Times

"In the Dark" by Stephen Kuusisto from The New York Times Magazine March 21, 1999. Copyright © 1999 by The New York Times. Used by permission.

Oxford University Press

"Introduction" by Betty Bao Lord, from *The Chinese-American Family Album* by Dorothy & Thomas Hoobler. Copyright © 1994, 1998 by Oxford University Press, Inc. Used by permission of Oxford University Press, Inc.

Pantheon Books a division of Random House

Excerpt from *Through the Ivory Gate* by Rita Dove. Copyright © 1992 by Rita Dove. Published in the United States by Pantheon Books, a division of Random House.

The Post Eagle

"See Ya' at the Subway" by Edwina Armstrong from *The Post Eagle.* Copyright © by The Post Eagle.

Random House, Inc.

Excerpt From *The Glass Menagerie* by Tennessee Williams. Copyright © 1945 by Tennessee Williams and Edwina D. Williams; renewed 1973 by Tennessee Williams. Used by permission of Random House, Inc.

Runner's World Magazine

"Healthy Aging" by Marlene Cimmons from Runner's World. Copyright © 1999 by Runner's World Magazine.

Time, Inc.

"Reunion Rules" by Amy Dickinson from *Time Magazine,* August 23, 1999. Copyright © 1999 by Time Magazine. Used by permission.

United Nations Educational, Scientific and Cultural Organization

"Pedal Power" by Lambert Benoît from *The UNESCO Courier,* January 1998. Copyright © 1998 by The UNESCO Courier. Reprinted by permission of the UNESCO Courier.

W.W. Norton & Company, Inc.

"Crossing Spider Creek" by Dan O'Brien from *Flash Fiction: Very Short Stories.* Copyright © 1992 by James Thomas, Denise Thomas, and Tom Hazuka. Published by W.W. Norton & Company, Inc.

Note: Every effort has been made to locate the copyright owner of material reprinted in this book. Omissions brought to our attention will be corrected in subsequent editions.

Photo Credits

Photo Credits

Art, Springville, Utah; Gift of Lynn Anderson, Salt Lake City, SMA 1992.078; **226:** Mary Kate Denny /Tony Stone Images **232:** ©The Stock Market/John Henley; **235:** image©Copyright 1998 PhotoDisc, Inc.; **237:** Richard T. Nowitz/COR-BIS; **238:** Photofest; **242:** *Miracle of Life,* 1996, Christian Pierre, Private Collection/SuperStock; **244:** ©The Stock Market/Tom & Dee Ann McCarthy; **247:** *Les Coureurs (The Runners),* Robert Delaunay, Museum of Modern Art, Troyes, France/ Lauros-Giraudon, Paris/SuperStock ; **249:** ©The Stock Market/Jose L. Pelaez; **251:** Amy C. Etra/PhotoEdit; **256:** ©1999 Barbara Peacock/FPG International Corp.; **259:** Mark Richards/PhotoEdit; **262:** *Fireside in Virginia,* 1950, (detail), Queena Stovall, New York State Historical Association, Cooperstown, New York. Photo by Richard Walker; **266:** John Martin/The Image Bank; **268:** Royal Library, Copenhagen; **273:** *Tourists,* Woody Gwyn, Courtesy of the artist; **276:** Michael Newman/ PhotoEdit; **285:** Grantpix/Monk-meyer; **286:** ©The Stock Market/T & D McCarthy; **289:** *Gamin,* Augusta Savage, Schomburg Center for Research in Black Culture, Art and Artifacts Division, The New York Public Library, Astor, Lenox and Tilden Foundations; **292:** ©The Stock Market/Jose Palaez; **294:** Photofest; **298:** Courtesy of the artist; **305:** *The White Mantel,* 1927–29, Frank Harmon Myers, National Museum of American Art, Washington DC/Art Resource, NY; **315:** Will Hart; **318:** AP/Wide World Photos; **319:** Vintage Books; **321:** RNT Productions/CORBIS; **322:** Photofest; **326:** Michael Newman/ PhotoEdit; **330:** ©1999 Rob Gage/ FPG International Corp.; **333:** Nick Rains; Cordaiy Photo Library/COR-BIS; **336:** Graham Harris/Tony Stone Images; **338:** M.C. Escher, design drawing for intarsia wood panel with fish. ©1999 Cordon Art B.V. - Baarn-Holland. All Rights Reserved; **340:** Corel Professional Photos CD-ROM™; **344:** ©The Stock Market/ Jose L. Palaez; **354:** Myrleen Cate/ PhotoEdit; **355:** ©1997, VCG/FPG International Corp.; **356–386:** Michael Springer/Liaison Agency; **390:** Courtesy of the Library of Congress; **392:** Courtesy National Archives; **394–412:** Corel Professional Photos CD-ROM™; **414 & 417:** Silver Burdett Ginn; **420–426:** NASA; **432:** image© Copyright 1998 PhotoDisc, Inc.; **434:** Courtesy of the Library of Congress; **435:** AP/Wide World Photos; **436:** Courtesy of the Library of Congress; **442–462:** Corel Professional Photos CD-ROM™; **466:** Courtesy of the Library of Congress; **476–495:** Corel Professional Photos CD-ROM™; **497:** Tom & Pat McCarthy/ PhotoEdit; **501 & 505:** Corel Professional Photos CD-ROM™; **509:** Philadelphia Convention & Visitors Bureau; **510–518:** Corel Professional Photos CD-ROM™; **522:** Texas State Preservation Board; **525:** Corel Professional Photos CD-ROM™; **527:** Pearson Education/PH School; **529 538:** Corel Professional Photos CD-ROM™; **549:** Pearson Education/PH College; **550:** Corel Professional Photos CD-ROM™; **553–560:** Courtesy of the Library of Congress; **563:** Ken Karp Photography; **567–582:** Corel Professional Photos CD-ROM™; **584–592:** NASA; **596 & 598:** Corel Professional Photos CD-ROM™; **601:** Pearson Education/PH School; **604:** Florida Department of Commerce/ Division of Tourism; **607–610:** Corel Professional Photos CD-ROM™; **618 & 623:** Courtesy of the Library of Congress; **624:** Massachusetts Development and Industrial Commission; **626:** Courtesy of the Library of Congress; **629:** New York Convention & Visitors Bureau; **630–640:** Corel Professional Photos CD-ROM™; **645:** Pearson Education/ PH School; **649–660** Corel Profes-sional Photos CD-ROM™; **668–680:** Courtesy of the Library of Congress; **684:** Courtesy of the Library of Congress; **690–713:** Corel Professional Photos CD-ROM™; **716:** Courtesy of the Library of Congress; **721:** The White House Photo Office; **722:** Corel Professional Photos CD-ROM™; **725:** Courtesy of the Library of Congress; **727:** Michael Littlejohn/ Pearson Education/PH College; **728–737:** Pearson Education/PH College; **743–757:** Corel Professional Photos CD-ROM™; **759:** AP/Wide World Photos; **784:** *Eight A.M.,* 1993, Andrew Stevovich, Adelson Galleries, Inc.; **786:** *Speaker,* 1996, Diana Ong/SuperStock ; **788:** Michelle Bridwell/PhotoEdit; **791:** Pearson Education/PH School; **794:** Ken Karp/PH Photo; **799:** *The Reaper,* c.1881, Louis C. Tiffany, oil on can-vas, National Academy of Design, New York City; **803:** Ken Karp/PH Photo; **808:** Mark Lewis/Tony Stone Images; **810:** ©The Stock Market/Mug Shots; **814:** Bill Aron/PhotoEdit; **821:** John Brooks/Tony Stone Images; **832:** *Reading,* 1973, oil on masonite, Billy Morrow Jackson, Wichita Art Museum, purchased with funds donated by Mr. and Mrs. Donald C. Slawson; **841:** Tim Wright/CORBIS; **844:** Esbin/Anderson/Omni-Photo Communications, Inc.; **847:** ©The Stock Market/Charles Gupton; **848:** Photofest; **851:** ©1993, Billy Barnes/ FPG International Corp.; **854:** ©The Stock Market/Jose L. Pelaez; **857:** Kevin Morris/Tony Stone Images; **859:** Jeff Greenberg/Omni-Photo Communications, Inc.; **861:** Gary Conner/PhotoEdit; **863:** ©Navaswan/FPG International Corp.; **869:** Inge Yspeert/CORBIS; **871:** ©Stuart Schwartz/The National Steinbeck Center; **876:** ©The Stock Market/Charles Gupton; **880:** Layne Kennedy/COR-BIS; **884:** Don Miller/Monkmeyer; **886:** Pearson Education/PH School; **888:** image©Copyright 1998 PhotoDisc, Inc.; **889:** ©The Stock Market/Jean Miele